土14
 话 说

HEILUNGKIANG

Aigun

Amur

Ussuri

Sungari

Harbin

Changchun

KIRIN

Tumen

NINGHSIA-HUI
Autonomous Region

Region

Autonomous

Mukden
(Shenyang)

LIAONING

Yalu

Mongolian

Huhehot

Great Wall

WU-T'AI

Peking
Tientsin

HOPEH

Port Arthur-Dairen

Yinchwan

Paoting

T'AI-HANG

Taiyuan

Wu-ch'i

SHANSI

Tsinan

SHANTUNG

Tsingtao

Yenan

Lanchow

Hwang Ho

(Yellow)

Grand Canal

KIANGSU

Hui-ning

Chengchow

HONAN

Shanghai

Sian

Hwai

SHENSI

Hofei

Nanking

La-tzu-t'ou

HUPEH

Wuhan

ANHWEI

Hangchow

Fourth Front
Army

SZECHWAN

Yangtze

TA-PIEH

CHEKIANG

Chengtu

Tung-t'ing

P'o-yang

Chungking

Changsha

Nanchang

CHINGKANGSHAN

Tsun-i

KIANGSI

Foochow

Kweiyang

First Front Army

HUNAN

Juichin

FUKIEN

KWEICHOW

Amy

KWANGSI-CHUANG
Aut Region

KWANGTUNG

Swatow

Canton

TAIWAN

Nanning

Macao

HONG KONG

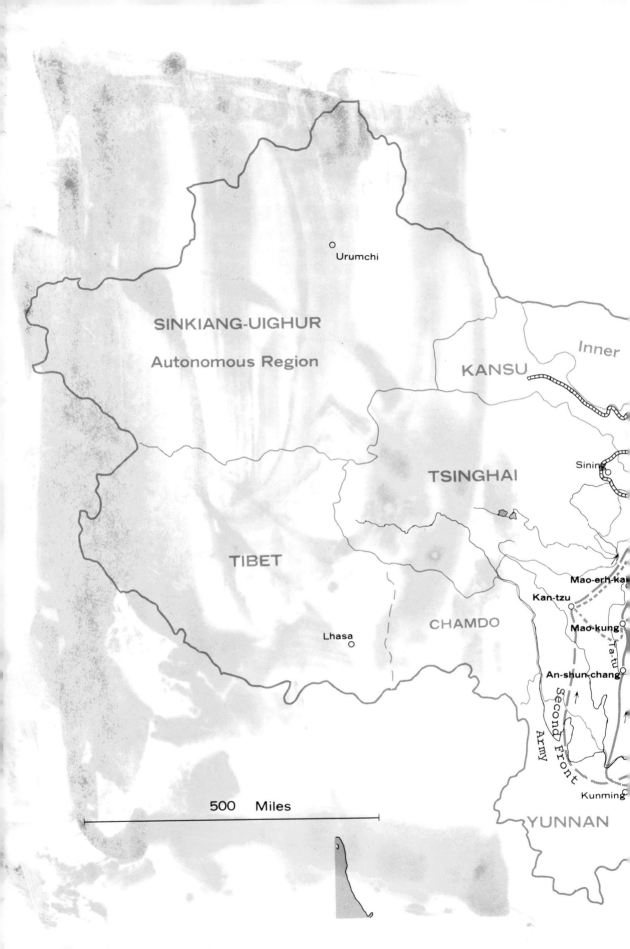

SINKIANG-UIGHUR

Autonomous Region

Urumchi

KANSU

Inner

TSINGHAI

Sining

TIBET

Mao-erh-kai

Kan-tzu

Mao-kung

CHAMDO

Lhasa

An-shun-chang

Second Front

Army

Ta-tu

Kunming

500   Miles

YUNNAN

Biographic Dictionary
of Chinese Communism
1921–1965

VOLUME I: Ai Szu-ch'i–Lo I-nung

Donald W. Klein / *Anne B. Clark*

Harvard University Press   Cambridge, Massachusetts   1971

Contents

Foreword

Donald Klein and Anne Clark are more than the "compilers" of this volume; they are, in fact the authors. They describe in their Introduction how the book has been put together and why. This Foreword gives some information about them, mainly facts that the reader should know but that these collaborating scholars would be too modest to mention.

Anne Bolling Clark (Mrs. Samuel B. Clark), after graduating from the University of Chicago and studying Fine Arts at Radcliffe, became a biographic specialist during World War II. She spent ten years in that capacity in Washington, first in the Office of Strategic Services and then in the State Department's Biographic Information Division, where she became chief of the China–Southeast Asia Branch. She also served two years as a biographic specialist in the American embassy in Tokyo. After leaving government service, she was from 1956 to 1963 a staff member of the Project on Men and Politics in Modern China, headed by Howard L. Boorman and housed at Columbia, which produced the four-volume *Biographic Dictionary of Republican China*. Since career and family each seemed intent on liberating her from the other, Anne Clark became a part-time researcher on the staff of the East Asian Research Center at Harvard in 1963 and continued her work here for several years.

Donald Walker Klein received his B.A. and M.A. from the University of Florida in 1950 and 1951. He became interested in biographic work and the East Asian field during seven years of military and government service. He studied for two years, beginning his Ph.D. in the graduate school at Columbia, then from 1962 to 1964 served as an adviser to the Union Research Institute in Hong Kong, where he made use of the public files of biographic information available at the American Consulate-General. The present volume thus took shape in his mind some dozen years ago and when he came to Harvard for the period 1965–1967 he brought with him his personal files of data on some 5,000 individuals and 300 organizations.

A major project like this requires for its completion the special devotion of one dynamic worker, usually known metaphorically as the anchor man, spark plug, or priceless ingredient. Whatever the metaphor, Don Klein has done the job. The appendix tables, an invaluable contribution in themselves, are his creation, and he has done most of the post-1949 biographic research.

Klein and Clark's professionalism is fully indicated in their introduction, where they describe their solutions to problems, as well as in their Acknowledgments, where it is made plain that they have secured valuable help from many able people but have relied fundamentally on the old adage: if you want it done right, do it yourself. Out of 433 main biographies, they themselves did 422. Unlike the many Who's Who volumes compiled for the current scene, and therefore of only temporary utility, their dictionary begins with the Chinese Communist movement in 1921 and follows it through to 1965. The authors are historians, aware that the record of Chinese history has always been hung on a biographical framework and convinced that in this respect times have not changed. They provide data on some 700 additional persons in the text and 450 more in the appendices to make a total, with variants, of about 1,750 names listed with their Chinese characters in the Glossary-Name Index. Having completed their selection as of 1965, they wisely refused to be stampeded by the subsequent Cultural Revolution. Since this volume also corrects a multitude of errors that have crept into less comprehensive and basic works, it now gives us a primary tool with which to study, over a 45-year period, the greatest revolutionary effort in the annals of mankind.

A Harvard word should be said about Columbia, because this work is much more a joint project than the title page can indicate. Both authors worked at Columbia before their collaboration at Harvard. The sister project, one might dutifully say elder-sister project, on Republican China from 1911 to 1949, headed by Howard L. Boorman, was located at Columbia; and the superb facilities of the East Asian Library there, in addition to the leading specialists mentioned in the Acknowledgments, have been of great assistance at all times. In the China field no center is an island unto itself. We all help each other.

August 1970
John K. Fairbank, Director
East Asian Research Center

Acknowledgments

An acknowledgments page never satisfies the debts which authors owe to their friends and colleagues. To set down a word or two of thanks to so many people seems paltry indeed when we think of the time and talent which others so generously offered. Nonetheless we must make the effort. We happily and even proudly join the long line of those before us who have thanked John K. Fairbank, whose encouragement and advice from beginning to end has been invaluable. John M. H. Lindbeck, who had so much to do with originating this project, is also due a warm note of gratitude.

Of the 433 biographies, eleven were prepared by others. S. T. Leong wrote those for Chang T'ai-lei, Ch'en Kung-po, Ch'en Tu-hsiu, Ch'ü Ch'iu-pai, Li Ta-chao, P'eng P'ai, Su Chao-cheng, Teng Chung-hsia, and Yang Ming-chai. Merle Goldman prepared the biographies of Hu Feng and Chou Yang. We are of course very indebted to them, but in fairness we should note that some changes were made by us, and thus we and not they are responsible for the final versions.

We were assisted in this volume by Lois B. Hager in more ways than we can recall. She undertook many of the tedious tasks in preparing a volume of this length, and did so always with diligence and good humor. Her contributions were especially important in preparing the numerous appendices and glossary, and they are all the more noteworthy in that during her three-year association with us she also produced two children.

We owe another very special debt of gratitude to Howard L. Boorman, the director of the Project on Men and Politics in Modern China at Columbia University. He made available to us the texts of valuable interviews which he conducted in Hong Kong some years ago. We have mentioned many of these in footnotes which, for the sake of brevity, are cited under the short title for Mr. Boorman's project: Modern China Project.

Roy Hofheinz and Sydney Liu were particularly generous in sharing their considerable knowledge. They drew to our attention innumerable sources and helped us avoid errors which we would have otherwise certainly made.

A large number of people read portions of the text, but in this regard we must single out Ellis Joffe, James P. Harrison, and C. Martin Wilbur, each of whom read large sections and each of whom made singularly useful suggestions.

Jane P. Shapiro translated some Russian materials which added useful information not available to us from other sources.

Susan Horsey also played a large role in preparing the appendices and glossary. Without her help in the final stages of preparing this book, we might never have meshed the complex appendices with the other parts.

The following persons, in large or small measure, have also contributed to this volume: George Akita, Phyllis M. Andors, William Ayers, Aryeh Blumberg, Conrad Brandt, Heath Chamberlain, Edward Chung-man Chan, Peter Chen, Ai-li Chin, Chou Shao-tung, O. Edmund Clubb, Richard Diao, Sheriden Dillon, J. Mason Gentzler, L. Carrington Goodrich, Walter Gourlay, René Goldman, Olive Holmes, Julie Lien-ying How, Hsiao Tso-liang, Winston Hsieh, Hu Ch'ang-tu, Chalmers A. Johnson, Hilary Joseph, Yasue Klein, Li Yu-ning, Jane L. Lieberthal, Lin Yü-ho, Ling Nai-min, Linda Marks, A. C. Miller, Harriet C. Mills, Charles Neuhauser, Michel Oksenberg, Robert Parkinson, David Roy, Mark Selden, John S. Service, Anderson Shih, Richard Sorich, Suh Dae-sook, Frederick C. Teiwes, T. K. Tong, Daniel Tretiak, Tang Tsou, Tsuruoka Atsuo,

Lyman P. Van Slyke, Ezra Vogel, Kenneth R. Walker, Derek J. Waller, Holmes H. Welch, Morris Wills, and Eugene Wu. We have surely but inadvertently failed to mention others, and to them we extend our apologies and thanks.

This lengthy manuscript went through many typewriters. We wish to thank in particular Dorothy Blewitt, Kate March, Shari H. Teiwes, and Patricia Poulos.

Finally, we thank and salute Joan Ryan, our able editor at Harvard University Press. Under the best of circumstances, editing a book of this length is a herculean task. In addition, Miss Ryan was plagued by a manuscript which, because of its format, contains a tremendous number of repetitious phrases.

D.W.K.
A.B.C.

Introduction

This volume contains 433 biographies of men and women who contributed to the Chinese Communist movement from the establishment of the Chinese Communist Party in 1921 to 1965. The focus, of course, is on individuals, but we have also tried to give the history of the movement as seen through their careers. Moreover, the 96 appendices are structured to lead the reader to key events and organizations in the Party's history and to bring together information about various groups of men and their activities. The paragraphs below are discussions of technical points involved in preparing this work.

Selection of Entries

Because the CCP was on the threshold of national power at the time of the Seventh Party Congress in 1945, we have used as our first "core" group *all* of the 77 persons elected to the Central Committee. The second core group consists of *all* of the 195 persons elected at the first and second sessions of the Eighth Party Congress (1956–1958). Because of the overlap in these two groups, the combined figure is slightly over 200, or nearly half our total entries.

We used a variety of criteria in the selection of the other half of our entries. First, we made an intensive examination of early Party history, covering the period from its founding to 1927 when so many members lost their lives. This might have led us to include all those who attended the inaugural congress in 1921. Several of them were omitted, however, because they soon left the Party or even went over to the KMT. In selecting a more broadly defined group of "founders," we were guided (but, we trust, not biased) by the entries in the many collections of Communist biographies of "martyrs," the standard term for those who died in the Communist cause. Orthodox or Maoist

histories were also consulted, but these suffer from two flaws: the omission of Mao's enemies, or if not their omission, their dismissal as rascals or worse. For the degree of balance we may have attained, we are indebted to the pioneering studies of early Communist history by C. Martin Wilbur, Julie How, Conrad Brandt, Benjamin I. Schwartz, John K. Fairbank, Hsiao Tso-liang, and others.

A second criterion of selection derives from what might be called the militarization of the Party from 1927 to 1949. It is a truism that CCP membership and positions in the Red Army were virtually one and the same during those years. Consequently, many key military men are included, even if after 1949 their careers dwindled to relative insignificance— which, incidentally, is seldom the case.

Most of the other criteria in the selection of entries were applied to the post-1949 period. We asked which persons held the most important positions for the longest periods. These people included cabinet ministers; provincial Party secretaries, governors, commanders, and political commissars; ambassadors; leaders of mass organizations; members of Party control and discipline organizations; ideologues; and, military service arms' personnel (such as those in the air force). In many instances, there was little information about the man's pre-1949 career, and the pattern of post-1949 activities was so self-evident that it required only a few paragraphs to describe.

Representativeness is another criterion, particularly after 1949 when the nation was unified and relatively stable. We have tried to deal with all phases of Chinese Communism and have not hesitated to include the proverbial doctors, lawyers, and Indian chiefs. We have thus included leaders of non-Communist political parties (Hsu Te-heng), industrialists (Li

Chu-ch'en), religious leaders (Ta P'u-sheng), dissident KMT military commanders (Chao Shou-shan), scientists (Li Szu-kuang), and agricultural specialists (Yang Hsien-tung), to mention only a few. We believe that such wide representation is proper because the Communists themselves stress the involvement of "all strata of society" in the political process.

Some modifications of our broad criteria for selection deserve elaboration. Sometimes one man was selected over another because he was involved in an activity or controversy of importance to the Communist movement, thereby providing us with the opportunity to discuss it. For example, the biography of Fu Lien-chang, the "first doctor of the Red Army," gave us an opportunity to describe the evolution of health services in the Communist movement and that of Lo Ming, a way to describe a vital controversy during the Kiangsi Soviet period.

Still another qualification concerns relatives, by blood or marriage, of major biographees. In certain cases it would have been easy to justify the inclusion of politically active wives of prominent men, but where possible we have chosen to discuss their careers, in abbreviated form, in the biographies of their husbands.

Finally, our selection has been influenced by the entries in Howard L. Boorman, ed., *Biographical Dictionary of Republican China.* On the one hand, both the Boorman dictionary and our own had to take account of certain towering figures—whether defined by an era or a political movement. On the other hand, the inclusion of some individuals by Boorman allowed us to exclude them. (Fu Tso-i and Chu Hsueh-fan, both of whom held PRC ministerial posts for many years after 1949, are cases in point.)

Format of a Typical Biography

At the outset it should be noted that the biographies were written for three types of persons: scholars, journalists, and government officials. With these readers in mind, we have presupposed a rudimentary knowledge of twentieth-century China and international Communism.

Each biography contains a heading which in a word or phrase describes the man's position —government bureaucrat, military man, and so on. In many biographies, usually the longer ones, the initial paragraph summarizes the individual's career. After presenting the vital statistics, such as place of birth and early education, we attempt to define the individual's earliest "revolutionary" experience. Where appropriate we have added vignettes of friends and teachers who, though unimportant themselves, often influenced the subjects of our biographies in their early careers.

Stress on Organizational Ties. The typical biography then moves to specific organizational connections with revolutionary parties —sometimes the KMT, but more frequently of course the CCP. Virtually by definition, none of the individuals in this volume were Communists by avocation. Setting aside those cases where information is lacking, it is clear that the overwhelming majority held specific posts within the Party apparatus or the Red Army early in their careers. As a consequence, this volume tends to stress organizations throughout a man's career. Once again, we feel this is a reflection of the Communist movement, where the supreme achievement is to "serve the Party," not the self. In this regard, the standard obituary of a second echelon leader is instructive. This contains the vital statistics of birth and death, and highly stylized assertions noting that Comrade Li was "influenced by the October Revolution" and was "devoted to the thought of Mao Tse-tung." Beyond these comments, however, the obituary usually lists no more than the various positions a man held, so that we learn nothing of his family, nor of his ability, intelligence, temperament, hobbies, likes, or dislikes.

Another point about organizational affiliations is worth noting. The Chinese Communists have had few "shadow" leaders—men appointed to high office, only to leave the country on an "extended tour of Europe" or to suffer from an "unexpected" illness. There are, of course, some figures who hold political posts only in a nominal sense, but these are usually easy to detect, and where appropriate we have made comments to this effect.

Significant Events. The typical biography also stresses significant events, of which there is an abundance. Indeed, many biographies, particularly of major leaders, seem to move from one traumatic incident to the next. We have already mentioned obituaries of second echelon leaders, but in terms of our own emphasis on key events we might comment on the obituaries of major leaders. In these, after presenting the vital statistics, the stylized comments, and organizational affiliation, the text focuses almost exclusively on the events in which the subject participated—the May 30th Incident, the Nanchang Uprising, the Canton Commune, the Long March. Important events of this kind usually pertain to pre-1949 China. But a broadly analogous counterpart can be found in the post-1949 period in the endless "movements" (*yun-tung*), such as land reform, which are so characteristic of that period. Failure to survive a movement seldom meant death, but it could and often did mean assignment to menial tasks in remote areas. Many of the biographies demonstrate this point.

Locale and Dates. Considerable attention is given to the location of an individual at any given time, particularly in pre-1949 China. Those who have wrestled with this problem will recognize its importance, particularly at moments of historic crises. Chinese Communism has had many "capitals": Shanghai, Canton, Wuhan, Juichin, Yenan, Peking. Nor is it quixotic to maintain that for a brief moment— in 1928—it was in Moscow! It was often quite literally a life-and-death matter whether a man was in Shanghai or Wuhan in 1927, or whether he was in the relative safety of Yenan or behind enemy lines in 1940. Similar considerations have led to our emphasis on dates. To use the Shanghai illustration again, there was a world of difference between work in Shanghai in late March 1927 and mid-April 1927. The problem is less acute in post-1949 China, but even then the difference between a speech at the beginning or the end of the month can be important if a Central Committee plenum changed a policy between these dates.

Speeches and Writings. We often cite the speeches and writings of the Chinese elite. These are frequently woven into the text, but they are sometimes placed at the end of the biography if this form seems more appropriate. To uncover *all* the speeches and articles of *all* the entries in this volume would be an endless task. We do not pretend to have done this, nor to have read thoroughly (or even read at all) many of the works cited in these pages. We have, however, scanned many major publications in both the pre- and post-1949 periods, and we have drawn freely upon secondary works which contain discussions of important articles and speeches. We have not hesitated to cite speeches, articles, and books where we felt they might be of value to others wishing to probe a subject more deeply. Beyond their research value, speeches and writings are an important part of the political process in China. There is no passive political figure in China; one must "participate," and among the more obvious ways to do so is to write an article or deliver a speech. Equally important, though by no means peculiar to China, speeches and articles are a vital means of communication. There are few developments in pre- or post-1949 China for which one cannot find a keynote speech or article. To use a term now in some disrepute, the "party line" is normally communicated in articles or speeches, regardless of whether or not the line was also communicated in internal, official directives.

Cut-off Date and the Cultural Revolution. Of the 433 biographies, 90 percent were alive in 1949 and slightly over 80 percent by 1969. Consequently most of the final paragraphs of the biographies are written in the present tense. The cut-off date is early 1965. This date coincides with the end of the first session of the Third NPC, which at the time seemed to be a convenient breaking point. Since then, of course, the cataclysmic Cultural Revolution has erupted. We were greatly tempted to scrap some of our entries and add scores of emerging figures. The extraordinary unity of the elite for so many decades was shattered, and over-night the heroes of yesterday became today's villains. The temptation to change course was set aside, because it seemed truer to the histori-cal record to maintain our basic list. Within our criteria, these were the men who in our judgment made the greatest impact on the Communist movement over a period of four and a half decades.

We have, however, made two accommoda-tions to events of the late 1960's. First, we have indicated, usually in only a sentence or two, that many of the individuals were victims of the Cultural Revolution. But the reader should be cautioned that this has not been a systematic practice, largely because the facts were often unknown. Second, insofar as the election of a new Central Committee in 1969 represents the "results" of the Cultural Revo-lution, Appendices 50 and 51 are structured to give the reader a quick view of its victors and victims.

Bibliography. At the end of many biogra-phies, a brief paragraph deals with the perti-nent bibliographic sources. Where other au-thors have already performed this task, for ex-ample, Stuart Schram in his biography of Mao, we have referred the reader to their works.

Sources

A work of this sort draws upon a variety of sources which even the most carefully con-structed bibliography can never satisfactorily reveal. In the broadest sense, we have relied upon English, Chinese, and to some extent Japanese language materials for pre-1949 China, and mainly on English language sources for the post-1949 period.

Pre-1949 Sources. The pre-1949 English language sources include many accounts from journalists, contemporary magazine articles, and United States Government diplomatic papers. Added to these are the pioneering monographic works by Conrad Brandt, C. Martin Wilbur, Benjamin I. Schwartz, and others, most of which drew heavily or exclu-sively on Chinese materials. By the 1960's these works were supplemented by a rich flow of books from Chow Tse-tsung, Hsiao Tso-liang, John Israel, Mark Selden, Roy Hof-heinz, James E. Sheridan, Donald Gillin, Jean Chesneaux, Stuart Schram, and many others. These too drew heavily or exclusively on Chi-nese materials. The pre-1949 English language materials published by the Chinese Commu-nists themselves are practically nil. However, they did publish in Chinese an enormous amount about themselves. These publications are divided into two categories. First, there are contemporary journals and newspapers of that era; many of these are available in the original, others in reprints. However, much of this rich material has only recently been released from archives (especially in Taiwan), and most of it has not yet been subjected to rigorous bibli-ographic control. Second, after 1949, the Chi-nese Communists published great quantities of materials which deal with their earlier history. Minor fragments have been translated into English, but most of this material is found only in Chinese language newspaper and magazine articles, pamphlets, and books. These sources are also in need of bibliographic control, al-though some steps have already been taken.

Post-1949 Sources. There is now a rich and growing body of English language publications about post-1949 China by Western scholars. We drew upon these sources in preparing bi-ographies of the most senior leaders. Not sur-prisingly, however, these same works are of minor use in dealing with the second echelon leaders. Thus for well over half of our 433 entries, we have generated the material our-selves directly from primary Chinese Commu-nist materials. In so doing we have been in-debted to the collation by the American Con-sulate General in Hong Kong of the massive output of the New China News Agency. The American, Japanese, and British governments, as well as the Union Research Institute in Hong Kong, have also compiled many useful Who's Whos, governmental directories, check-lists of personnel, and the like. In addition to the English language output of the New China News Agency, the Foreign Language Press in Peking has published hundreds of books and pamphlets in English. For biographic pur-poses, these can be described as valuable during the 1950's and marginal thereafter. The same description applies to such familiar publications as *People's China, China Reconstructs, China Pictorial,* and *Peking Review.*

Notes

The notes to each biography are exclusively bibliographic. In general, we use notes frequently for the pre-1949 period, but only sparingly for the post-1949 period because our sources for the former, whether primary or secondary, are relatively obscure.

Most of the post-1949 sources are readily available, often in both English and Chinese. For example, the proceedings of the Eighth Party Congress in 1956 are covered in many sources, and anyone wishing to do further research would have no problem finding them. Some notes to primary sources, both in the pre- and post-1949 periods, may appear to be footnoting the obvious (such as an appointment date of an official). Frequently, however, we use this means to tell the reader that various secondary sources have been repeating misinformation, of which there is much in the field of Chinese Communist biographic materials.

Appendices

The 96 appendices were prepared with a view to collecting data of use to readers in various disciplines. Some of these appendices are of use only to specialists in the Chinese Communist movement, others to experts in comparative government, and still others to those who wish to study the continuities and discontinuities between traditional China and the People's Republic. Some deal with personal data, such as native province, education, and career specialization. The rest are related to organizations, for example, cumulative listings of every cabinet minister and every provincial governor since 1949.

Viewed in another fashion, the appendices fall into two categories. Some of them, such as those dealing with native province and education, bring together data pertaining exclusively to the 433 biographies. The remainder contain names of the 433 entries *plus* other persons not mentioned in the biographies. For example,

there are only a few ambassadors among the 433 biographies, but Appendix 82 lists every ambassador from 1949 to 1965. All such names, with the appropriate appendix number, are listed in the Glossary–Name Index. The net result is that the appendices add information on some 600 persons beyond the 433 biographees.

Glossary–Name Index

The Glossary–Name Index contains the Chinese characters for approximately 1,750 names, divided into the following categories: (1) the names of the subjects of the 433 biographies; (2) some 700 persons mentioned in the biographies, for example, relatives, friends, and colleagues; (3) approximately 450 names of persons in the appendices who are neither among the 433 biographic entries nor among the 700 persons mentioned in the biographies; (4) finally, some 175 alternate names for persons in any of the above categories.

Integration of the Biographies, Appendices, and Glossary–Name Index

As a general goal, we have attempted to integrate the major events and organizations described in the various parts of this dictionary. The frequent use of "q.v." and "see under" is intended to guide the reader from one biography to another. For example, references in a biography to the Nanchang Uprising ask the reader to "see under" Yeh T'ing for specific details. Yeh's biography mentions several of the key participants, but it would have been impractical and ponderous to mention all of them. Thus Appendix 25 is provided to give the reader a complete list.

Another major effort has been made to link the biographees with the innumerable organizations mentioned throughout the text. For example, the reader will normally be informed that "Minister Wang" assumed his post in the "newly established" (hypothetical) 10th Ministry of Machine Building and continued to hold the post until the ministry was abolished. But if the same ministry was re-created five years later and headed by another man, we have not described this development in "Minister Wang's" biography. However, the reader could find this information in Appendix 59, which describes organization and personnel changes in the ministries. To continue this hypothetical case, the reader could then turn to the Glossary–Name Index to find the characters for the new minister and any further references to him.

Special Problems and Miscellaneous Technical Points

Peking and Peiping. During the period which this volume covers, the present capital of China was known as Peking, then Peiping, and then Peking again. It would have been overly cumbersome to make the constant changes required, and therefore we used Peking throughout the text. For the record, Peking was renamed Peiping in June 1928 when the "new" (that is, KMT) national government was inaugurated with Nanking as its capital. On September 27, 1949, on the eve of the establishment of the PRC, the Communists reverted to the use of Peking.

Geographic Place Names. We have followed the standard practice of using the postal system for provinces and for well-known cities such as Canton. For all other place names we employ the Wade-Giles system, and where appropriate these names are hyphenated. The three familiar exceptions are Chingkangshan, Juichin, and Yenan. Also, because of the annoyance of locating places on inadequate maps and in gazetteers, we have tried to guide the reader by mentioning well-known nearby cities or familiar landmarks.

Personal Names. Many Western works on China contain spellings of Chinese names which vary slightly from the accepted standards. Therefore, even in direct quotations, we have altered these to spare the reader the pedantic use of brackets to indicate slight variations.

"The Party." The word "Party," when capitalized, refers exclusively to the Chinese Communist Party and not, for example, to the Kuomintang or one of the minor political parties.

The Indefinite Article. In almost any Chinese Communist organization there is more than one (and often 10 or 20) vice-chairman, vice-premier, deputy commander, etc. In many instances it can be very misleading to omit the indefinite article, thereby suggesting that the person in question was, for example, the *only* vice-chairman. The text, therefore, contains countless references to "a" vice-chairman, etc.

Biographic Dictionary of Chinese Communism, 1921–1965

ABBREVIATIONS

CB	*Current Background*
CCP	Chinese Communist Party
CPPCC	Chinese People's Political Consultative Conference
ECMM	*Extracts from China Mainland Magazines*
JMJP	*Jen-min Jih-pao* (*The People's Daily*)
KMT	Kuomintang (i.e., the Chinese Nationalists' political party)
NPC	National People's Congress
PLA	People's Liberation Army
PRC	People's Republic of China
SCMM	*Selections from China Mainland Magazines*
SCMP	*Survey of China Mainland Press*

Ai Szu-ch'i

(c. 1910–1966; T'eng-ch'ung, Yunnan). Marxist philosopher; vice-chairman, China Philosophy Association; vice-president, Higher Party School.

Ai Szu-ch'i was among the most important Chinese Communist interpreters and popularizers of Marxist-Leninist thought. His 30-year career with the Party began in Shanghai in the mid-thirties; he was among the leading lecturers, writers, and editors during the Yenan era, and after the PRC was established he continued in these capacities, his principal work being with the Central Committee's Higher Party School in Peking. Though nothing is known of Ai's younger years, it is apparent that he received some higher education, for by the early thirties he was working and writing in Shanghai, then the major center for leftist and Communist intellectuals. In 1934 he published *Ta-chung che-hsueh* (Philosophy of the masses), a popular version of Marxist ideology that went through 32 editions during the next 12 years. One writer on 20th-century Chinese intellectual history claims that this work "spearheaded the movement of the '30s . . . to capture the intelligentsia" and that it was "marked by its effectiveness as propaganda." This same authority continues: "It is a skillful piece of writing to instill in the people a sense (not necessarily a complete understanding) of dialectical materialism, giving the people the terms and directions of thought."[1] This work was one of the earliest of the numerous books, tracts, and articles that were to flow from Ai's prolific pen in the next 30 years.[2] In 1935, just one year after *Ta-chung che-hsueh* was published, Ai was admitted into the CCP, and from that same year until 1937 he was one of the editors of a Marxist review known as *Tu-shu sheng-huo* (Intellectual life), a journal that was ultimately shut down by the KMT authorities.

During his days in Shanghai, Ai was closely associated with such important Communist propagandists as Chou Yang and Chang Han-fu (q.v.). In 1936 he was one of the leading protagonists in a lively battle of slogans among the left-wing intellectuals.[3] One side, led by Chou Yang, argued in favor of the so-called "literature for national defense," which meant that writers had to mute their criticisms of the KMT in order to strengthen the national united front against Japan. The opposition was led by famed writer Lu Hsun who feared that any compromises vis-à-vis the KMT would dilute the revolutionary ardor of China's intellectuals. Lu's group organized a rival organization and promoted their own slogan, "people's literature for the national revolutionary struggle." Ai was on the side of the national defense literature and was thus on the "correct" side in terms of the Communist policy enunciated in 1935 at the Seventh Comintern Congress that called for an international united front against fascism. This important debate is treated more fully in the biography of Chou Yang. In addition to these activities, Ai was chief editor by 1937 of *Wen-hua chan-hsien* (Cultural front),[4] a newspaper published every 10 days; also, together with Chang Han-fu, he was on the editorial board of *Chan-hsien* (War front), still another newspaper that dealt with political and military affairs.[5]

Like so many of the intelligentsia in Shanghai, Ai left for the Communist stronghold at Yenan when war against Japan erupted in mid-1937. He remained in Yenan for the next decade, establishing himself as one of the most important Communist philosopher-propagandists. During these 10 years he taught at the Anti-Japanese Military and Political Academy (K'ang-ta), and he was director of the Cultural Research Office of the Party Central Committee's Central Research Institute, "a higher research organ for the training of the Party's theoretical cadres."[6] He also served as secretary-general of the Central Committee's Cultural Committee and as a deputy editor of the Party's most important newspaper, the *Chieh-fang jih-pao* (Liberation daily). In addition, he engaged in the translation of various Marxian classics,[7] and from 1938 he was president of the "Society of the New Philosophy," which he had helped to establish.[8]

Together with such Party stalwarts as Chou Yang, Ch'en Po-ta, and Fan Wen-lan (qq.v.), Ai was among the most active participants in the Party-sponsored *cheng-feng* ("rectification") movement that began in 1942. A point stressed by Ai and the others that was in keeping with the spirit of the movement was the need to use "literary forms familiar to the Chinese masses rather than literary styles imported from the West." In this connection, he was one of the leading opponents of the important Marxian writer-translator Wang Shih-wei, who opposed these ideas.[9] Wang fell from power at this time, as did popular authoress Ting Ling (although Ting later reemerged, only to be purged again in the 1950's). Following the ouster of Ting, in June 1942 Ai assumed her post as editor of the cultural page of the *Chieh-fang jih-pao*. He was reported to be a member of the Shensi-Kansu-Ninghsia (Shen-Kan-Ning) Border Region Government Council by 1943, and by the following year he was also teaching philosophy at Yenan University, where his colleague Chou Yang was president. Ai was also active in the Shen-Kan-Ning Cultural Association; a visitor to Yenan in the spring of 1944 described him as one of the five persons responsible for the association, a group that included Wu Yü-chang (q.v.) and Chou Yang.[10] Ai was again associated with Wu in 1948 at the North China University (Hua-pei ta-hsueh), located in the Communists' Shansi-Hopeh-Shantung-Honan Border Region. Wu was the president and another colleague of

Ai's, historian Fan Wen-lan, was the vice-president of the university.

By the early part of 1949 Ai was in Peking and at a youth congress held in May of that year he was elected to the First National Committee of the All-China Federation of Democratic Youth; he was then about 39 and he retained the post until the next congress in mid-1953. In July 1949 Ai became a vice-chairman of the Preparatory Committee for the China New Philosophy Research Association, continuing in the post when the organization was formally established in 1951 (under a slightly altered title: China Philosophy Association). Ai's was probably the guiding Party hand in the Philosophy Association, for the chairman, Li Ta, was not a Party member even though he had been among the Party founders in 1921. Li had left the Party in the twenties, and although he held positions of nominal power in the PRC after 1949, he was finally denounced in 1966 during the "great proletarian cultural revolution" shortly after Ai's death. Also in July 1949 Ai had been named to Standing Committee membership for the China Social Sciences Workers' Conference, and in that capacity he attended the inaugural session in September 1949 of the CPPCC, the organization that brought the new government into existence on October 1. During the CPPCC sessions, he served on an *ad hoc* committee chaired by Kuo Mo-jo to issue public statements on the work of the CPPCC. In the new PRC Government Ai became a member, again under Kuo Mo-jo, of the Culture and Education Committee, one of the four major committees under the Government Administration Council (the cabinet). He held this post, as well as Council membership in the Association for the Reform of the Chinese Written Language and membership on the First Executive Board of the Sino-Soviet Friendship Association, until the latter part of 1954.

In September 1949 the Communists began to publish *Hsueh-hsi* (Study), the Party's most important theoretical and political journal until it was superseded by *Hung-ch'i* (Red flag) in 1958. Ai served from the outset as a member of the editorial board and was among its most prolific contributors, particularly in the early numbers of the journal. For example, the first seven issues of *Hsueh-hsi* (then a monthly) carried no less than five articles or speeches by Ai, in addition to advertisements for his previously published books and essays on Marxism-Leninism. Over the ensuing years he was to write several more articles for *Hsueh-hsi,* including a blistering attack on the bourgeoisie for the March 16, 1952, issue during the course of the "five-anti" campaign against businessmen and another article on the need to study Stalin's teachings that appeared in the March 2, 1954, issue.

In July 1950 Ai became a member of the newly formed Southwest Military and Administrative Committee, and although he retained this position until the Committee was reorganized in early 1953, there is no indication that he spent any time in the southwest. In fact, at the very time he was appointed to the post, he was identified as a professor of the Party Central Committee's Marx-Lenin Institute in Peking, the most important CCP school for the training of cadres. Ai remained with the institute, known from the mid-fifties as the Higher Party School, until his death. By the late summer of 1957 he was identified as the director of the School's Philosophy Pedagogic Research Office, and by March 1961 he had become a vice-president, a position he was holding at the time of his death. Though relatively little information has been published about the Higher Party School, Ai worked during his time there under at least three presidents, Yang Hsien-chen, Wang Ts'ung-wu, and Lin Feng (qq.v.).

Like most important Party leaders, Ai was called upon to lend his name to the various "mass" organizations. Thus, from 1950 to 1958 he was a member of the National Committee of the China Peace Committee, and from 1954 to 1959 he was a Standing Committee member of the Chinese People's Association for Cultural Relations with Foreign Countries. An assignment more germane to Ai's field of work was with the CPPCC's Study Committee, whose task was to promote the intensive study (particularly among the non-Communist CPPCC members) of Marxist-Leninist works, the writings of Mao Tse-tung, and various policy statements issued by the central government; he was a member of the Study Committee from February 1952 until the latter part of 1954. Equally germane was Ai's work with the Academy of Sciences. In December 1954, in conjunction with the Union of Chinese Writers, the Academy inaugurated a series of forums to criticize the thought of Hu Shih, an activity that occupied much of Ai's time over that winter, and later in December he was named as one of nine members to establish the Research Institute of Philosophy under the Academy, and then when the Academy formed the Department of Philosophy and Social Sciences in May–June 1955, Ai was appointed as a member, another post he held until his death 11 years later.

Ai was a deputy from Kweichow to the First and Second NPC's (1954–1964), but he represented his native Yunnan in the Third NPC that opened in late 1964. Yet any part that he may have played in the PRC's legislative body was clearly peripheral to his continuing importance as a writer and lecturer on Marxism-Leninism. For example, Ai contributed articles on this subject for *Hung-ch'i* (Red flag, issues of July 16, 1958, and February 16, 1959) and for the January 31, 1959, issue of the *JMJP*. Similarly, he was often called upon to write commemorative articles or to give speeches marking important Communist holidays; for instance, he authored an article on the 80th anniversary of Stalin's birth for the December 21, 1959, issue of the *JMJP* and in April 1961 he spoke at a rally commemorating the 91st anniversary of Lenin's birth. One of Ai's last articles (*JMJP,* November 1, 1964) was a refutation of the views of Yang Hsien-chen, his former superior in the Higher Party School who was the object of a sustained ideological attack in the Party press in 1964. In August 1964 Ai was a member of the Chinese delegation to the Peking Symposium, a meeting attended by 367 delegates from 44 nations, mainly in Asia, Africa, and Latin America (see under Chou P'ei-yuan and Fan Ch'ang-chiang).

Ai died in Peking on March 22, 1966, at the age of 56. He was lauded in death for his contributions to the Party, and a 64-member funeral committee was established to arrange for funeral and memorial services. Ironically, within a few weeks of his death at least 10 funeral committee members had fallen victim to the great proletarian cultural revolution, including his colleague of 30 years, Chou Yang. Writing before Ai's death, the previously quoted authority on Chinese intellectual history has stated that it was "generally agreed that Ai . . . has been the Communist Party's chief thinker."[11] Though this may be a somewhat exaggerated assessment of his role in the Communist movement, particularly in view of the writings of such persons as Ch'en Po-ta, Liu Shao-ch'i, and Mao Tse-tung himself, there is little doubt that Ai's efforts to popularize Marxian thought were of considerable importance. This was illustrated in an article by Sha Ying (believed to be a pseudonym for a top-ranking Party leader), who paid tribute to Ai's ability to reach a wide audience. Writing for the *JMJP* of October 11, 1962, Sha wrote: "I remember in the early stage of the [Sino-Japanese War], books such as [Ai's *Philosophy of the Masses* were] very popular among the reading public. This book . . . really gave definite enlightenment to those studying theory for the first time. When reminiscing of those days, readers generally had more profound impressions of such books. The broad masses of readers now still are in need of books of this type."[12]

1. D. W. Y. Kwok, *Scientism in Chinese Thought, 1900–1950* (New Haven, Conn., 1965), p. 192.

2. *Ibid.,* p. 205; Union Research Service, Hong Kong, Biographical Service no. 786, June 28, 1963.

3. C. T. Hsia, *A History of Modern Chinese Fiction, 1917–1957* (New Haven, Conn., 1961), p. 296.

4. Union Research Service.

5. Chün-tu Hsüeh, *The Chinese Communist Movement, 1937–49* (Stanford, Calif., 1962), p. 45.

6. Boyd Compton, *Mao's China: Party Reform Documents, 1942–44* (Seattle, Wash., 1952), p. 75.

7. Chang Ching-lu, ed., *Chung-kuo ch'u-pan shih-liao pu-pien* (Supplementary historical materials on Chinese publishing; Peking, 1957), pp. 448, 449.

8. O. Briere, *Fifty Years of Chinese Philosophy, 1898–1948* (New York, 1965), p. 35.

9. Merle Goldman, "Writers' Criticisms of the Party in 1942," *The China Quarterly,* no. 17:205-228 (January–March 1964).

10. Chao Ch'ao-kou, *Yen-an i-yueh* (One month in Yenan; Shanghai, 1946), p. 118.

11. Kwok, p. 192.

12. *SCMP* 2848, p. 2.

An Tzu-wen

(c.1904–   ; Shensi?). Director, CCP Organization Department; member, CCP Central Committee.

An Tzu-wen is one of the Party's top organizational specialists. He worked in north China during the Sino-Japanese War and since the PRC was established in 1949 he has devoted most of his time to the CCP Organization Department, becoming the director in 1957. He headed the Ministry of Personnel from 1950 to 1954 and was elected a Party Central Committee member in 1956. An is one of the major spokesmen for Party policies and is the author of numerous articles, most of them dealing with Party organizational questions and problems.

There is conflicting evidence about An's place of birth; it was probably in Sui-te in north Shensi, but Japanese sources use Hunan. He is said to have graduated from the Sui-te Normal School in Shensi and then to have studied at Peking Normal College, presumably in the 1920's. An is reported to have joined the CCP while a student in Peking. He subsequently went to the USSR for further study. He was imprisoned in Peking in the mid-1930's, but when the war broke out in mid-1937, he was working as a Party organizer in an area some 50 miles northeast of Lin-fen in Shansi Province.[1] He was then working with Chang Yu-ch'ing, a Party leader captured and killed by the Japanese in 1942 in Taiyuan, the Shansi capital. The area where Chang and An worked was known as the T'ai-yueh region; by 1942 An was a member of the T'ai-yueh Party Committee. This region was a part of the territory controlled by the Eighth Route Army's 129th Division (commanded by Liu Po-ch'eng), and together with the T'ai-hang mountain area to the northeast, it made up one of the major divisions of the Communist Shansi-Hopeh-Shantung-Honan (Chin-Chi-Lu-Yü) Border Region (see under Yang Hsiu-feng). Among his colleagues during this period were such important political and military figures as Po I-po and Ch'en Keng (qq.v.).

An's activities in the latter years of the war and during the early postwar years are not documented. However, he was apparently assigned to Manchuria after the war ended in 1945; in any event, he was identified in 1949 as a deputy director of the Industry Department under the Northeast Administrative Committee (NEAC), the name of the principal administrative unit for the Communist government in Manchuria from 1946 to mid-1949. An was in Peking in September 1949 to attend the first session of the CPPCC, the organization that inaugurated the new central government (October 1). He attended the CPPCC as one of 16 CCP delegates, a group that included such prominent Communists as Mao Tse-tung, Liu Shao-ch'i, and Chou En-lai. An was not elected to the CPPCC National Committee in 1949, but when the Second National Committee was formed in December 1954, he was named as a member representing the CCP. He has also served as a CCP representative on the Third and Fourth National Committees, which first met in April 1959 and December 1964–January 1965, respectively. In addition, he has been a member of the governing CPPCC Standing Committee in the Second, Third, and Fourth CPPCC's.

An's work with the CPPCC has been minor in contrast to his duties within the Party. As early as 1946 he was reported as director of the important CCP Organization Department. P'eng Chen (q.v.), a far more senior leader, became the director that same year, and as a consequence An was made a deputy director. P'eng returned to the directorship in about 1949 and held it until 1952 when Central Committee member Jao Shu-shih (q.v.) assumed the post. An, in the meantime, continued as the deputy director. In 1954–55 Jao was charged with plotting against the top Party leadership. Jao and his major accomplice Kao Kang were dismissed (see under Kao Kang). Subsequent to these events, the Organization Department apparently lost some of its power, with a number of its functions being transferred to two other Central Committee organs: the Committee for Organs Directly under the Central Committee and the Committee for Organs Directly under the Central People's Government (see under Kung Tzu-jung). An was apparently unaffected by the dismissal of Jao Shu-shih, but the Organization Department remained without a director until An assumed the post sometime in 1957. In September of the previous year he had been elected a full member of the Central Committee, at the Eighth National Congress. While the Congress was in session An served as a member of its Credentials Committee.

Though An's primary responsibilities have been in Party organizational work, in the period from 1949 to 1954 he was also assigned to other tasks ostensibly outside the purview of the CCP. From October 1949 to December 1954 he was a member of the First Executive Board of the Sino-Soviet Friendship Association, then one of the most active of the "mass" organizations. When the PRC Government was established in October 1949 An was appointed a member of the People's Supervision Committee (PSC), one of the four major committees subordinate to the Government Administration Council (the cabinet). This position placed him in the governmental counterpart to the Party Organization Department, but it is evident that it was a far less authoritative body. The PSC was headed by T'an P'ing-shan, one of the Party founders, who had left the CCP in 1927 but who returned to Peking in 1949 to work with the new Communist government. In a position of more power, An served as head of the Ministry of Personnel, created in September 1950. He held the post until September 1954 when the ministry was abolished with the inauguration of the constitutional government. In this capacity, he gave a number of reports before the Government Administration Council, as in November 1951 when he spoke on regulations relating to the appointment and dismissal of government functionaries. In addition, in 1951–52 he was a member of the Central Austerity Examination Committee, headed by An's colleague from the war years, Po I-po. He was also a vice-chairman of Li Wei-han's Labor Employment Committee (1952–1954), formed to deal with unemployment problems. Finally, in 1953 he was a member of the Committee for Drafting the Election Law; headed by Chou En-lai, this committee drafted the law for the elections to the First NPC. The First NPC was initially convened in September 1954 at which time the constitutional government was inaugurated.

When the new government was created in 1954, An relinquished most of his responsibilities with the government bureaucracy. As already described, he has continued to sit in the CPPCC, but after the formation of the NPC in 1954 the CPPCC became an advisory body and now exercises little power. Although a member of the elite, An does not appear to be a policy maker, but he frequently serves as the Party's spokesman at important meetings, particularly during important ideological campaigns. One of the most prolific writers for the press, some of An's more important speeches and articles are listed below:

"Strengthen the Work of Party Reform and Party Expansion on the Foundations of the Victory in the Three-anti and Five-anti Movements," *JMJP,* July 1, 1952 (CB 191).

"Achievements in Work Connected with Cadres during the Past Three Years," NCNA, September 30, 1952 (*CB* 218).

"Training the People's Civil Servants," *People's China*, no. 1 (January 1, 1953).

"The Consolidation of Party Organizations," *People's China*, no. 13 (July 1, 1953).

"Collective Leadership Ensures the Victory of the CCP," *For a Lasting Peace, for a People's Democracy!*," Chinese edition, no. 33 (September 1954).

"The Door of the Party Is Always Wide Open to Youths," *Chung-kuo ch'ing-nien* (China youth), no. 20 (October 16, 1956).

"Basic Methods to Perform Cadres' Work in the Future," *Cheng-chih hsueh-hsi* (Political study), no. 4 (April 13, 1957).

"The Communist Party Can Lead Scientific, Cultural, and Educational Work," *Chung-kuo ch'ing-nien*, no. 13 (July 1957).

"Learn the Lesson, Strengthen Party Character," *JMJP*, September 11, 1957.

"Refutation of the Rightists over the Question of Cadres' Policy," *Chung-kuo ch'ing-nien pao* (China youth newspaper), September 20, 1957.

"Carry Out Resolutely and Thoroughly the Cadre Work Line of the Party," *JMJP*, December 5, 1957.

"A Correct Approach to the Problems of Retirement of Women Cadres," *Chung-kuo fu-nü* (Women of China), no. 2 (February 1, 1958).

"How to Understand Correctly the Question of Enforcing the Supply System among Cadres," *Kuang-ming jih-pao*, December 2, 1958.

"Further Strengthen the Directing Role of Party Organs in People's Communes," *Hung-ch'i* (Red flag), no. 24 (December 16, 1959).

"Strengthen Party-building to Meet the Development of the Situation," *Hung-ch'i*, no. 24 (December 16, 1960; translated in *SCMM* 243).

"The Cultivation of Successors to the Revolutionary Cause Is a Strategic Task of the Party," *Hung-ch'i*, nos. 17–18 (September 23, 1964; translated in *SCMM* 438).

Although most of An's work has been oriented toward domestic Party organizational work, he has also been involved in international relations. For example, he is often on hand when important foreign visitors come to Peking, especially those from foreign Communist parties. An's only visit abroad since 1949 took place from May to August 1958 when he accompanied Party veteran Tung Pi-wu to Bulgaria, Czechoslovakia, and East Germany to attend Party congresses in those nations.

An has served on the funeral committees of several important Communists who have died in the post-1949 period. Protocol undoubtedly accounted for his membership on some of these committees, but it is of interest that three of the deceased men had been leaders in the Peking student movement of 1935–36, a time when An was in north China. All three of the deceased, Huang Ching, P'eng T'ao (qq.v.), and Chu Ming (political commissar of the PLA Signal Corps

at the time of his death in 1964), belonged to the National Liberation Vanguard of China (see under Li Ch'ang), a militant student organization established in 1936, which soon came under CCP control. Many of its members joined the Communists in north China after the Sino-Japanese War began in mid-1937. The fact that An was on the funeral committee for these three men suggests he may have had earlier connections with them.

During the "Hundred Flowers" period, when a certain amount of free speech was tolerated, An was subjected to some harsh criticism delivered during a public forum held in Peking in May 1957. He was accused of occupying a 10-room house while other cadres were forced to live in overcrowded quarters. It was further asserted that his daughter had two rooms in this house, even though she boarded at school during most of the week. An was one of the very few important Party leaders criticized in public during the "Hundred Flowers" campaign, but there was nothing to indicate that it has hindered his career during the next decade. However, in 1966, during the early phases of the Great Proletarian Cultural Revolution, he was sharply attacked in the press and presumably stripped of his authority.

1. Ch'i Wu, *I-ko ko-ming ken-chü te ch'eng-chang; k'ang-Jih chan-cheng ho chieh-fang chan-cheng shih-ch'i te Chin-Chi-Lu-Yü pien-ch'ü kai-k'uang* (The establishment and growth of a revolutionary base: A general account of the Shansi-Hopeh-Shantung-Honan Border Region during the anti-Japanese war and the war of liberation; Peking, 1958), p. 19.

Burhan Shahidi

(c. 1896–   ; Aksu, Sinkiang?). Prominent National minorities leader; former Sinkiang governor; chairman, China Islamic Association.

Burhan Shahidi was the Nationalist governor of Sinkiang when he defected to the Communists on the eve of the establishment of the PRC. He remained in Sinkiang in the early years of the PRC, but since the mid-fifties he has devoted much of his time to cultivating relations with nations having large Muslim populations, an activity that has taken him to Asia and the Middle East on a number of occasions.

Burhan is also known by the Sinicized form of this name, Pao Erh-han. There is some dispute about his national origins; a contemporary source who knew Burhan describes him as a Tatar,[1] but Chinese Communist publications always refer to him as a Uighur. (Tatars and Uighurs are both Turkic minorities.) The Communists would naturally prefer a Uighur identification because this is the largest minority group in Sinkiang and the one given official recognition in 1955 with the formation of the Sinkiang-Uighur Autonomous Region. Sources also conflict in regard to Burhan's place of birth. It appears that he was born in Aksu (Aqsu), an oasis trading center in Sinkiang's Tarim Basin that has the largest concentration of Uighurs in the province. But according to other sources he was born in Kazan, the Volga homeland of the Tatar race, and presently the capital of the Tatar Autonomous S.S.R. in the Soviet Union. Burhan's Turkic origins are evidenced by his Caucasian features and complexion. He was reared as a Muslim and is said to speak Chinese, Russian, and German, in addition to his native Turkic language. If he was born in Sinkiang, his parents took him at an early age to Kazan, where he received the equivalent of a high school education. After graduating in 1912 he went to Germany, where he enrolled in the Department of Politics and Economics at the University of Berlin. He received a degree in 1916 and returned with his parents to Sinkiang. By 1918 he was in Tihwa working for a trading firm. The following year, as a clerk, he entered the provincial government of Yang Tseng-hsin, then governor of Sinkiang. He rose rapidly in the provincial bureaucracy, first becoming an interpreter for the finance department, then a member of the Sinkiang customs department, later a member of the provincial mint, and finally, about 1925, director of the highway administration.

In 1928, when Chin Shu-jen, who had previously brought about Governor Yang's assassination, became governor of Sinkiang himself, he made Burhan responsible for foreign affairs in the provincial government. However, he did not long remain in Chin's government, for the latter was an old-fashioned bureaucrat who preferred to give the important posts to relatives or friends from his native Kansu. Therefore, Burhan spent the years 1928 to 1932 in Germany, where he acted as a purchasing agent for his government in Sinkiang. The job presumably did not keep him entirely occupied, for it is also reported that he returned to his studies at the University of Berlin. He went back to Sinkiang in 1933, the year that Chin Shu-jen was forced to flee to the U.S.S.R. Burhan's return probably followed Sheng Shih-ts'ai's coup, making Sheng the successor to Yang in April 1933.

Burhan was in Sinkiang or nearby sections of the Soviet Union during the early years that Sheng controlled Sinkiang, spending most of the time from 1933 to 1937 in the Soviet Union working in the trade centers where the population was related to the peoples of Sinkiang. Immediately after his return from Europe to Sinkiang in 1933, he served briefly as pacification commissioner in the Altai region of Sinkiang but was soon transferred to work for which he was better qualified, becoming consul (chosen from

Sinkiang) in the Chinese mission at Andizhan, Uzbekistan, and later at Zaisan, Kazakhstan. About 1937 he returned from Zaisan and became manager of the Sinkiang Local Products Company, the official trade monopoly that managed trade between the provincial administration and the Soviet purchasing agency, Sovsintorg (Soviet-Sinkiang Trading Company). The year was a difficult one as regards relations between Sheng and the Russians, for the effects of the Moscow trials were beginning to influence politics in Sinkiang. Garegin Apresoff, the Russian consul general in Tihwa, was subsequently recalled to Russia to be tried and executed for a "Trotskyite conspiracy," and Sheng, as he reports in his brief autobiography, sided with the Stalin group. With rather slender evidence to support his charges, Sheng claims that he uncovered a "Trotskyite plot" that was being organized in Sinkiang and was to begin with an uprising in April 1937. The fantastic charges involved possible connections with Germans and Japanese supposedly trying to establish a central Asian base in the name of anti-fascism, with hopes of putting Trotsky back in power. Though the evidence for Sheng's supposed "plot" was slender, the effects of his suspicions were serious, and Burhan and 400 others spent the next seven years (1938–1944) in prison because they had come under surveillance by his agents.[2]

In the summer of 1942 Sheng made an abrupt about-face from Russia to China, but by 1944 the Nationalist Government, to whom he had transferred his support, had Sinkiang affairs sufficiently under control to dispense with him. In October 1944 Wu Chung-hsin, Sheng's successor, released Burhan and many others from prison. Burhan was made a deputy commissioner of Civil Affairs, and in 1945 he was commander of the Peace Preservation Corps in Sinkiang, the force with which the Nationalists planned to hold the area. Events did not go smoothly in Sinkiang, where the non-Chinese population resented the control of Nanking as much as they had resented Sheng Shih-ts'ai. In July 1946 Chang Chih-chung, who had headed the Generalissimo's headquarters for the northwest, replaced Wu Chung-hsin as provincial governor and made Burhan one of his two vice-governors, the other being the Uighur leader Akmedjan Kasimov (Kasimi). As a Nationalist official Burhan now became a member of the Executive Headquarters of the KMT (1947) and served for nearly two years as a member of the Nationalist State Council. Also in 1947 he was made director of the Urumchi chapter of the Sino-Soviet Cultural Association (a leftist organization) and chancellor of Sinkiang University.

Over the next two years Sinkiang continued to be in a state of turmoil. In 1947 there was open rebellion between Nationalist authorities and the Turki group led by Akmedjan Kasimov, whose headquarters were in Kuldja in western Sinkiang. In December 1948, as a last desperate measure to pacify the rebels, the Nationalists replaced the elderly KMT Uighur, Masud Sabri (by then the governor of Sinkiang), with Burhan. The latter, a recently recruited member of the KMT, had not left Tihwa when Akmedjan's followers did, but as Burhan was not strongly entrenched in the KMT, he was acceptable both to Kuldja and to Nanking. Earlier he had suggested replacing Sung Hsi-lien, commander of the Nationalist forces in Sinkiang, by T'ao Chih-yueh, a native of Hunan who had arrived in Sinkiang in the summer of 1948. In the next year the Nationalists lost the China mainland. The turnover in Sinkiang came in late September 1949, while the First CPPCC was in session and on the eve of the inauguration of the PRC that the CPPCC had met to establish. The change was effected when Burhan went over to the Communists, bringing with him T'ao Chih-yueh and his 60,000 troops.[3] Within a few weeks elements of the Communists' First Field Army arrived in Tihua (later Urumchi), the Sinkiang capital, under the command of Wang Chen (q.v.). Wang became the ranking CCP official in Sinkiang and the dominant figure there, and Burhan was rewarded with the governorship of Sinkiang (December 1949), assuming in addition the post of president of the Sinkiang People's Court. He is said to have joined the CCP at the time of the Communist takeover, but he has not held any office in the Party organization in Sinkiang, nor, in later years, in Peking.

Early in 1950 the Communists established the multi-provincial Northwest Military and Administrative Committee (NWMAC) to govern Shensi, Kansu, Ninghsia, Tsinghai, and Sinkiang. Burhan was a member of the NWMAC and retained his membership when the NWMAC was reorganized into the Northwest Administrative Committee in early 1953. He continued as a member until the regional administrations were abolished in 1954, serving also during these four years as a member of the regional Nationalities Affairs Committee. In addition, he was the chairman of the Sinkiang branch of the Sino-Soviet Friendship Association (SSFA) from 1950 to an uncertain date. Burhan was reportedly in Moscow for medical treatment in 1950–1951, but he was back in China in time to deliver a report on Sinkiang affairs before a session of the First CPPCC held in October–November 1951 in Peking. At the close of this session he was elected to the First National Committee of the CPPCC and has since been affiliated with this organization, advancing to Standing Committee membership in February 1953. Then, as a representative of the national minorities, he served during the term of the Second and Third CPPCC's (1954–1964) as a vice-chairman of the National Committee. He was dropped as a vice-chairman when

the Fourth CPPCC was organized in January 1965, but he continues to represent the national minorities as a member of the National Committee. Burhan has also worked on two subordinate committees under the CPPCC, having been a member of both the Study Committee (1956–1959) and the Local Work Committee (1957–1959); the former is concerned with the promotion of the study of Marxist works, particularly among the many non-Party members of the CPPCC, and the latter with fostering the activities of the CPPCC in the provinces. Burhan's primary duties in the early years of the PRC were in Sinkiang, but other responsibilities took him to Peking from time to time. In addition to his affiliation with the CPPCC in Peking, he was named to membership on two public service bodies headquartered in Peking; since April 1950 he has been on the Executive Committee of the Chinese People's Relief Administration and since November 1951 he has served on the National Committee of a child-care organization known as the Chinese People's Committee in Defense of Children.

When the Communists came to power in 1949, their only provincial-level "autonomous" government was in Inner Mongolia (see under Ulanfu). In mid-1952 the first steps were taken to create a parallel administration in Sinkiang as a gesture to the large Uighur population living there. Thus, Burhan was named to chair the preparatory committee that ultimately brought into existence the Sinkiang-Uighur Autonomous Region (SUAR). However, two men on this committee, Wang En-mao and Saifudin (qq.v.), nominally subordinate to Burhan, were in fact his political superiors. Wang En-mao had replaced Wang Chen as the top CCP official in Sinkiang in 1952, and Saifudin was the fourth Party secretary. When the SUAR was finally established in October 1955, Burhan, the governor for nearly six years, was replaced by Saifudin. Burhan, in turn, only received a post as a member of the SUAR Council. A few weeks later he replaced Saifudin as chairman of the Sinkiang chapter of the CPPCC, a position of far less importance. The net effect of these changes was that Burhan was eased out of positions of authority in Sinkiang, where in fact he has spent very little time since the mid-fifties. By the early sixties his position had further declined and he ranked only as one of several vice-chairmen of the Sinkiang CPPCC.

In the interim, Burhan was elected as a deputy from Sinkiang to the First NPC, the legislative body that inaugurated the constitutional government at its initial session in September 1954. He was reelected to the Second NPC (1959–1964) and to the Third NPC that opened in late 1964. Burhan was one of the more active legislators during the term of the First and Second NPC's (1954–1964); he was a member of both the

Budget Committee and the Nationalities Committee (advancing to a vice-chairmanship on the latter in 1956). He additionally served on the *ad hoc* Motions Examination Committee for the NPC sessions held in September 1954 and July 1955.

At approximately the same time as the Communists were initiating the processes to establish the SUAR, the Preparatory Committee of the China Islamic Association was formed (July 1952). Burhan became the chairman, remaining so after the organization was formally inaugurated in May 1953. Although Saifudin is patently the most important Uighur in China, Burhan's chairmanship of the Islamic Association presents him to the outside world as the most important representative of China's millions of Muslims. In this respect his career is similar to that of Ta P'u-sheng (q.v.), a vice-chairman of the Islamic Association. There is little to suggest that the Islamic Association is important domestically, but it has frequently been used as an instrument in Peking's semi-official relations with other Muslim nations (e.g., Indonesia), particularly since the mid-1950's when the Chinese began to exert great efforts to expand their international ties in Asia and the Middle East. As a direct consequence Burhan has frequently represented the PRC abroad and holds posts in several organizations involved in foreign relations, an early example occurring in May–June 1955 when the Communists established the China-Indonesia Friendship Association with Burhan as chairman. This took place during the state visit to Peking by Indonesian Prime Minister Ali Sastroamidjojo, when the Chinese were attempting to capitalize on the good will they had generated a few weeks earlier at the famous Bandung Conference. Later in June he was a member of the Chinese delegation to the World Peace Congress in Helsinki; he was elected there to membership on the World Peace Council (WPC), a position he presumably still retains. And in July 1955 he became a Board member of the important Chinese People's Institute of Foreign Affairs (see under Chang Hsi-jo).

Burhan's trip to Helsinki in 1955 was only the first of a score of journeys he was to make in the next seven years. Perhaps the most important of these was a seven-month 10-nation tour of the Middle East in 1956; Burhan's 71-member cultural delegation was one of the first significant groups sent by the PRC to the Middle East, a visit that took place at a time when Peking did not have diplomatic relations with a single nation in that area. Between February and June his delegation visited Egypt, the Sudan, Ethiopia, Syria, and Lebanon. Burhan met a number of leading cultural and political figures in each nation, and in Cairo (April) and Damascus (June) he signed cultural cooperation agreements. In early July most of the delegation left for Peking,

but Burhan remained behind to lead Peking's 1956 mission to Mecca, and while in Saudi Arabia he saw the king, the prime minister, and the finance minister. He then made brief visits to Egypt, Syria, Lebanon, Jordan, Libya, Tunisia, and Afghanistan before returning to Peking in September. Immediately after returning home he reported on his extended journey before the Party's Eighth National Congress.

Most of Burhan's later trips abroad were in connection with either the Communist-sponsored "peace" movement or the closely related Afro-Asian "solidarity" movement. He has attended WPC meetings in East Germany, March 1957; Ceylon, June 1957; India, March 1958; Sweden, July 1958, May 1959, July 1960, December 1961; and, the U.S.S.R., February 1959. In June 1958 he led a China Peace Committee delegation to Poland, and in March–April 1959 he was in Iraq to attend the Second Congress of the Iraqi Peace Partisans. While in Baghdad he also signed the first Sino-Iraqi cultural cooperation agreement. Burhan was also in New Delhi in March 1960 to attend the Indian Conference for Peace and Disarmament. He has been among the most active participants in the meetings of the Afro-Asian People's Solidarity Organization (see under Chu Tzu-ch'i), attending congresses or executive committee meetings in Cairo (December 1957–January 1958, January 1961, and December 1961) and Conakry, Guinea (April 1960). In addition to these trips, he has made still others. In January 1958 he was an official PRC delegate to the funeral of Rumanian Presidium President Groza, and in November of the same year he was deputy leader of the Chinese delegation to Moscow for ceremonies marking the 41st anniversary of the Russian Revolution. Finally, in August–September 1961 Burhan was a member of Kuo Mo-jo's NPC delegation to Indonesia and Burma.

Concomitant with the PRC's expanding foreign relations in the fifties and sixties, a number of "mass" or "people's" organizations were established in Peking to handle various facets of Peking's foreign affairs. Burhan has been connected with an exceptionally large number of these organizations. From its establishment in February 1956 to mid-1965 he was a member of the Asian Solidarity Committee of China, and from 1958 (when it was renamed the Afro-Asian Solidarity Committee) he served as a vice-chairman. In November 1956, during the Suez crisis, the China-Egypt Friendship Association (FA) was formed; Burhan was named as chairman and a year later he was also named to the Council of the China-Syria FA. Then, immediately following the merger of Syria and Egypt into the United Arab Republic, Peking merged its two organizations into the China-United Arab Republic FA (February 1958), naming Burhan as the chairman, a post he still holds. In December

1956 he was appointed as a Standing Committee member of the Chinese People's Association for Cultural Relations with Foreign Countries. A little over a year later (February 1958), shortly after the government counterpart "Commission for Cultural Relations with Foreign Countries" was established under the State Council, Burhan was appointed as a member. In the period from 1958 to 1962 he received still other assignments in organizations concerned with international relations. In July 1958 he was elected a vice-chairman of the reorganized China Peace Committee, and in April 1960 he became a vice-chairman of the China-Africa People's Friendship Association. He was also named as a vice-chairman in April 1962 to the newly established Asia-Africa Society of China, an organization formed to promote scholarly studies on these two continents. Burhan relinquished the Peace Committee post in mid-1965, but he retains the other two.

Burhan's work for the Communists since the mid-1950's has been oriented toward international relations, particularly in connection with nations where his religious background, and the fact that he belongs to a national minority, could be expected to give him a special entree. When not abroad on one of his many missions, he is most often mentioned in the press in connection with visitors to Peking. Yet he has also continued to play a role of some significance in domestic affairs. Upon the formation in May–June 1955 of the Academy of Sciences' Department of Philosophy and Social Sciences, Burhan became a departmental member, and in December of the following year he was appointed to head the Academy's newly established Institute of National Minority Languages (a post he probably still holds). Since March 1956 he has been a vice-chairman of the Political Science and Law Association of China, and from May 1957 to November 1958 he was a member of the State Council's Scientific Planning Commission. In mid-1961 he was also identified as a member of the Nationalities History Research Advisory Committee, established to promote the compilation of a series of books on China's national minority groups.

Most of Burhan's writings since 1949 have been concerned with either religious or national minority policy questions, a number of which have appeared in *Min-tsu t'uan-chieh* (Nationalities unity), the leading journal on minority affairs. In the spring of 1953 the Communists reported that they had just published China's first Uighur-Chinese-Russian dictionary, a work that Burhan had compiled in 1942 while in jail.[4] In 1962 the Chinese press further reported the staging of a drama based on a trilogy by Burhan entitled *Undying Sparks*. The trilogy covers the period from 1911 to the "completion of land reform" in Sinkiang in 1953; the second book,

said to have been written in 1942 (also in prison), deals with the lives of two Uighur heroes who "fought shoulder to shoulder" with Han Chinese against "feudal oppression."[5] This theme, of course, reflects the CCP policy of the cooperation between Han Chinese and minority nationality groups. Still another work translated by Burhan when in prison was Sun Yat-sen's *San-min chu-i*, which he rendered into Uighur.

Burhan's most active period seems to have ended in the early 1960's, as suggested by the fact that his last trip abroad was in 1961. Moreover, he was not re-elected a vice-chairman of the CPPCC in early 1965 and a few months later he was also dropped as a vice-chairman of both the Afro-Asian Solidarity Committee and the China Peace Committee. However, there is no indication that his inactivity resulted from political difficulties; rather, it appears to be the result of his advancing years (he reached the age of 70 in 1966). Burhan is reported to have had two wives and at least eight children, five daughters and three sons; the eldest son once studied in Moscow. His present wife, Rashida (sinicized La-hsi-ta), is a Tatar. In the early fifties she was a vice-chairman of the Northwest Women's Working Committee of the All-China Federation of Democratic Women, and since 1953 she has served on the Federation's Executive Committee. She has also represented the Women's Federation in the CPPCC since 1959 and, like her husband, has been active in the Political Science and Law Association, where she has held a seat on the National Council since 1958. La-hsi-ta has been abroad on at least four occasions, the first of which was in June 1953, when she attended the Communist-sponsored World Women's Congress in Copenhagen. Later that month she attended a World Peace Council meeting in Budapest, and she was a member of women's delegations that visited Pakistan in November 1955 and India in December 1956.

1. Allen S. Whiting and Sheng Shih-ts'ai *Sinkiang: Pawn or Pivot?* (East Lansing, Mich., 1958), p. 179.

2. *Ibid.,* pp. 170–181.

3. *Hsin-hua yueh-pao* (New China monthly), 1.4:873 (February 15, 1950).

4. *SCMP* 550, p. 15.

5. *SCMP* 2734, pp. 18–19.

Chang Ai-p'ing

(c.1908–   ; Szechwan). Deputy chief-of-staff, PLA; alternate member, CCP Central Committee.

Chang Ai-p'ing has worked in the Communist movement since his days in the Shanghai underground in the mid-twenties. A veteran of the Red Army from its earliest days, he made the Long March and served in the New Fourth Army during the Sino-Japanese War. After spending the early years of the PRC in east China, he was transferred to Peking and has been a deputy chief-of-staff of the PLA since 1955. He was elected an alternate member of the Party Central Committee in 1956.

Chang was born about 1908 in Szechwan and attended a middle school in Shanghai in the mid-twenties. He left the city for a time, but after Chiang Kai-shek's anti-Communist coup there in April 1927 he returned and engaged in under-ground work. During the course of this work he was arrested on "several occasions."[1] By 1927 he was working among the peasants in Hunan, where dissatisfaction with the local authorities was described by Mao Tse-tung in his famous "Report on an Investigation of the Peasant Movement in Hunan" in 1927. In that year Chang was a Red guerrilla fighter in the vicinity of Tung-t'ing Lake, and after the KMT-CCP split in mid-1927 he joined the forces of P'eng Te-huai (q.v.). In July 1928 Chang took part in P'eng's successful coup at P'ing-chiang, northeast Hunan, by which time he had become acting commander of a regiment in P'eng's Army. Chang left P'eng's forces about 1929 and went to eastern Kiangsu (in the vicinity of the city of Ju-kao), where he was in the short-lived 14th Red Army's First Division. The 14th Army, consisting of 2,000 troops, was established in the latter part of 1929 but was decimated in September 1930 as it attempted to carry out Li Li-san's (q.v.) policies of capturing major ur-ban centers. After this defeat Chang fled to south Kiangsi to join the Communists at Juichin where Chu Te and Mao Tse-tung had their headquarters.

Chang had arrived in Kiangsi area by the end of 1930 at the time of the Fu-t'ien Incident (see under P'eng Te-huai and Li Li-san). The Inci-dent resulted from a power struggle between Mao's forces and a group generally regarded as followers of the Li Li-san. Chang was charged with assisting the latter group, known in Maoist histories as the A-B (Anti-Bolshevik) Corps. Jen Pi-shih (q.v.), a key political figure close to Mao, was assigned in 1931 the task of conducting a thorough investigation of Chang's past career and of his alleged involvement with the A-B Corps.[2] Chang was eventually exonerated and, to judge from his later career, did not suffer from the apparently erroneous charges.

In the early thirties before the Long March, Chang was engaged in youth work that included connections with the Youth Vanguards (teen-agers who performed quasi-military tasks for the Red Army).[3] He was also one of the founders in 1932 of the Workers' and Peasants' Dramatic Society.[4] Among the other founders was Miss Li Po-chao, the wife of Yang Shang-k'un (q.v.), a top Party official in Kiangsi. According to some reports Chang also attended the Red Army

Academy that opened near Juichin in 1933. Dur-ing the Long March (1934–1935) he com-manded the 11th Regiment of P'eng Te-huai's Third Army Corps. After his arrival in north Shensi Chang was an instructor at the Anti-Japanese Military and Political Academy (K'ang-ta).[5]

By 1939 Chang had returned to east-central China, where he worked with guerrilla units in Communist-held areas of eastern Anhwei, then under the control of the New Fourth Army. In early 1940 he was commanding a column of guerrillas in the Huai-pei area along the Huai River. In the summer his units were attacked by Nationalist troops commanded by Wang Kuang-hsia, but they escaped without serious losses. After portions of the New Fourth Army were wiped out in southern Anhwei in January 1941 (the New Fourth Army Incident—see under Yeh T'ing), they reorganized the army, transferring certain leaders from northwest China. Huang K'o-ch'eng (q.v.) came from Yenan to assume command of the Third Division and was con-currently put in charge of military affairs in north Kiangsu, where the Communists had previously infiltrated and were now rapidly expanding. Under him Chang became commander of the Eighth Brigade of the Third Division (early 1941) and deputy commander of the North Kiangsu (Su-pei) Military District. He held this position until sometime in 1944 when he became commander of the Fourth Division and moved southward into Chekiang. Chang took over com-mand of the Fourth Division from P'eng Hsueh-feng (q.v.), who was killed in battle in Septem-ber 1944.

In 1947 Chang's Fourth Division became part of the East China People's Liberation Army, the force with which the Communists conquered the coastal provinces and which two years later was renamed the Third Field Army. From 1948 to 1954 Chang was chief-of-staff of both this army and the East China Military Region (ECMR). He was made commander of the Third Field Army Naval Headquarters in Shanghai in 1949, and from 1949 to sometime in 1951 was political commissar of the ECMR Naval Headquarters (which included Shanghai). Transferred to the Chekiang Military District in 1951, he was in charge there for about two years. In September 1952 Chang was placed on the Communists' over-all administrative committee for the govern-ment of East China, the East China Military and Administrative Committee, which was reorgan-ized into the East China Administrative Commit-tee in 1953, with Chang continuing to serve as a member. He returned from Chekiang to Shang-hai in late 1952 or early 1953 and remained there until 1954. On occasion he was also re-ported in Nanking, where the PLA has several military academies.

When the constitutional government was established in September 1954 and the regional governments abolished, Chang's previous posts were eliminated but he soon received other important military positions. In September 1954 he was appointed a member of the newly created military advisory body, the National Defense Council; he was reappointed in April 1959 and January 1965. In June 1955 Chang was identified as a deputy chief-of-staff of the PLA, a position he still retains. Three months later he was among the many military leaders awarded the newly created decorations for service in the Red armies from 1927 to 1950, the Orders of August First, Independence and Freedom, and Liberation. At this same time he was made a colonel-general (the equivalent of a three-star general in the U.S. Army).

Chang has made at least two trips abroad. In January 1958 he was a member of the military delegation that Marshal Yeh Chien-ying led to India. In December 1960 he headed the military group of a "goodwill" delegation Chou En-lai took to Rangoon to celebrate the 13th anniversary of Burma's independence. Chang's long career was rewarded in May 1958, when he was elected an alternate member of the Central Committee at the Second Session of the Eighth Party Congress.

Since the late fifties Chang has been present at many of the official functions in Peking, often as a representative of the General Staff when foreign dignitaries visit China. His appearances were especially frequent in 1960 and 1961 in connection with visiting Burmese leaders.

Chang's publications include articles for the *JMJP* (June 10, 11, 1959, and August 6, 1964), as well as a collection of articles and essays entitled *Ts'ung Tsun-i tao Ta-tu Ho* (From the Tsun-i [Conference] to the Ta-tu River). The latter, published in Hong Kong in 1960, contains five pieces about his military career in the thirties and forties, including one of the few articles ever written on the 14th Red Army.

1. *Chung-kuo ch'ing-nien* (Chinese youth), no. 59:8 (February 24, 1951).
2. *Ibid.*
3. *Ibid.; Hung-se Chung-hua* (Red China; Juichin [?]), September 27, 1932.
4. Nym Wales, *Red Dust* (Stanford, Calif., 1952), p. 183.
5. *Ibid.*

Chang Chi-ch'un

(1905–   ; Li-ling hsien, Hunan). Director, Culture and Education Office, State Council; deputy director, Propaganda Department, CCP; member CCP Central Committee.

A veteran Red Army political officer from the 1920's, Chang Chi-ch'un is today one of the most important Party officials in the fields of propaganda and education. He was elected an alternate member of the Party Central Committee in 1945 and was promoted to full membership in 1956. Chang was born in Li-ling hsien, the native hsien of such other prominent Communists as Li Li-san and Tso Ch'üan. Chang has also been known by the alias of Yü Tai-ch'un.

After completing middle school Chang, then in his 20th year, enrolled in the first class of the Whampoa Military Academy (June 1924–February 1925), where he was given infantry training.[1] Japanese sources assert that he also received training in the USSR, presumably in the mid-twenties. In any case, by the late summer of 1927 he was in China, where in his native Hunan he participated in the Autumn Harvest Uprisings led by Mao Tse-tung and others. When these failed he apparently joined Mao's retreating forces, because by the end of 1927 he had joined the Workers' and Peasants' Red Army as a political officer, and in the next year he joined the CCP.

Chang was transferred by 1929 to Shanghai, where for a brief time he engaged in trade union work for the outlawed Shanghai General Labor Union. In August of that year, together with top Party leaders P'eng P'ai and Yang Yin (qq.v.), Chang was arrested by the International Settlement police. They had been betrayed by a fellow Communist. Chang was identified at that time as a deputy director of a special unit (subordinate to the General Labor Union), which was responsible for controlling picket lines during strikes.[2] He and his colleagues were turned over to Nationalist military authorities and taken to Lung-hua, the well-known prison outside Shanghai. P'eng and Yang were executed a few days later, but Chang somehow managed to escape this fate and subsequently made his way to the hinterlands of Kiangsi where Chu Te and Mao Tse-tung were leading Red Army units. By 1930 he was director of the Propaganda Department of the Fourth Army, one of the major components of the Chu-Mao First Army Corps. In the following year he was transferred to the same post in the Fifth Army Corps, and in this capacity he made the Long March.[3] Many elements of the Fifth Corps did not reach north Shensi until late 1936, but it is not known if Chang was with these men or with forces led by Mao, which arrived a year earlier.

After completing the Long March Chang was assigned as an instructor in 1937 to the Anti-Japanese Political and Military Academy (K'ang-ta), and by 1939 he was director of the Academy's Political Department. His record during the war years is poorly documented, but he probably remained at K'ang-ta. In any case, his long Party career was given recognition when at the Seventh Party Congress (April–June 1945) he was elected one of the 33 alternate members of the CCP Central Committee. By the same year he was serving as director of the Political Department of the Shansi-Hopeh-Shantung-Honan (Chin-Chi-Lu-Yü) Military Region. This highly important region was under the command of Liu Po-ch'eng, with Teng Hsiao-p'ing (qq.v.) as the political commissar. By September 1946 Chang was further identified as a deputy political commissar of the Region; his fellow deputy commissar was the important leader Po I-po.[4] Thus, from the end of the Sino-Japanese War to the defeat of the Nationalists in 1949–50, Chang was a key figure in Liu Po-ch'eng's forces, known as the Central Plains Field Army by 1947. Continuing in his dual political role, Chang was with Liu's forces when they crossed the Yellow River in mid-1947 and thrust southward into the Ta-pieh Mountains on the Hupeh-Honan-Anhwei borders.[5] Returning to the north, he also took part in the fighting along the Lunghai Railway, which led to the fall of Kaifeng and Chengchow, Honan. When the latter city was finally captured in October 1948, Chang was named chairman of the Chengchow Military Control Commission. By the following spring he had left this post to continue with Liu Po-ch'eng's units (now known as the Second Field Army) as they crossed the Yangtze. Still serving as deputy political commissar, Chang was in Nanking from the early summer to the fall of 1949, after which he moved with Liu's forces into southwest China. Chungking fell to the Communists on November 30, and a few days later Chang was appointed chairman of the city's Military Control Commission.

Although Chang was of Central Committee rank, he was politically overshadowed in his first years in the southwest by such top Party leaders as Teng Hsiao-p'ing, Liu Po-ch'eng, Ho Lung, and Sung Jen-ch'iung. Nonetheless, as the military, government, and Party organs were established for the southwest in 1949–50, Chang received significant appointments. By the latter part of 1950 he had become both a deputy political commissar and head of the Political Department of the Southwest Military Region, positions that continued to place him directly under the jurisdiction of Political Commissar Teng Hsiao-p'ing. In July 1950 the Communists established their governmental administration for the provinces of Szechwan, Kweichow, Yunnan, and Sikang; known as the Southwest Military and Administrative Committee (SWMAC), it was headquartered in Chungking where Chang was working. He was named to membership on the SWMAC and in March 1951 he was appointed to head at the same time the Land Reform Committee of the SWMAC, one of its most important subordinate organizations. Chang continued in both posts when the SWMAC was reorganized into the Southwest Administrative Committee in February 1953. Within the Party apparatus for

the southwest he became the second deputy secretary of the Southwest CCP Bureau by October 1952, placing him below Secretary Ho Lung, Second Secretary Liu Po-ch'eng, and First Deputy Secretary Sung Jen-ch'iung. In fact, however, both Ho and Liu were frequently called to Peking in the 1952–1954 period, and thus Sung and Chang's significance in Southwest Party affairs was enhanced.

In 1954 Chang relinquished all his positions in the southwest and was transferred to Peking. His first national assignment was as a deputy from Szechwan to the First NPC (1954–1959); he was re-elected from Szechwan to the Second NPC (1959–1964) as well as the Third NPC, which opened in December 1964. More important, however, by October 1954 he was identified as a deputy director of the Party Propaganda Department, a position he still retains under Director Lu Ting-i, an alternate member of the Party Politburo. Among his colleagues in this important department are fellow Deputy Directors Ch'en Po-ta, Hsu T'e-li, and Chou Yang, all of Central Committee rank. He advanced further in the Party hierarchy at the Eighth National Congress in September 1956. While the Congress was in session Chang served on the *ad hoc* Secretariat (headed by his former superior Teng Hsiao-p'ing), and at the close of the meetings he was promoted from alternate to full membership on the Party Central Committee.

In the meantime, Chang was named to represent the CCP on the Second National Committee of the CPPCC when it was established in December 1954. He was also appointed at this time as a member of the Standing Committee, the governing organ of the quasi-legislative CPPCC when the National Committee is not in session. Chang also served on both the National and Standing Committees of the Third CPPCC (1959–1964). In June 1957 he received a new post in the central government, which is closely related to his assignment in the Propaganda Department; the new position was as a deputy director of the State Council's Second Staff Office, an organization responsible for coordinating the activities of the State Council ministries dealing with culture, education, and science. Chang worked in the Second Staff Office under Lin Feng (q.v.), one of the Party's top specialists in educational affairs; on occasions Chang served as the acting director. Then, during a partial government reorganization in September 1959, the Second Office was renamed the Culture and Education Office, with Chang succeeding Lin Feng as the director. Since that time most of Chang's public appearances have been in this capacity.

Chang received another post directly subordinate to Lin Feng in January 1960 when he was appointed vice-chairman of the State Council's Spare-time Education Committee. However, he is probably less active in this position than another vice-chairman, Li Chieh-po (q.v.). In the following month he was named as a vice-chairman of the preparatory committee for a national conference of "advanced workers" in the fields of cultural and educational work. The conference, convened in June 1960, was one of the largest ever held in the history of the PRC (see under Lin Feng); during the conference Chang served on the presidium (steering committee). His involvement in cultural and educational affairs has also been illustrated by inspection trips he has taken around China, by his participation in major cultural festivals, and by articles he has written for the Chinese press. In 1958, for example, Chang went to Canton to issue instructions to personnel at the newly founded Chi-nan University (for training returned overseas Chinese); in June 1964 he was one of the "responsible personnel" attending a festival of Peking operas devoted to contemporary (as opposed to classical) themes, and in the same month he spoke before a national conference of pediatricians. His writings, dealing mainly with education, include an article for the Party's leading journal, *Hung-ch'i* (Red flag, issue of February 1, 1960). Chang has also lent his name to various *ad hoc* bodies established to commemorate major historic events, as in November 1956 when he was on the presidium for a rally marking the 90th anniversary of the birth of Sun Yat-sen, and in September 1961 when he was a member of the preparatory committee set up to commemorate the 50th anniversary of the 1911 Revolution.

While the major portion of Chang's activity has been devoted to domestic affairs, he has played a limited role in international affairs, having made three trips abroad between 1961 and 1964. In January 1961 he was the chief CCP representative at the 19th Congress of the Swedish Communist Party. He led a "friendship" delegation to North Korea in September 1963 to attend celebrations commemorating the 15th anniversary of the founding of the Korean Democratic People's Republic, and in September–October 1964 he was in North Vietnam for festivities marking the 15th anniversary of the PRC.

---

1. *Huang-p'u t'ung-hsueh tsung ming-ts'e* (Whampoa student directory; n.p., 1933), p. 655.

2. *Hung-ch'i p'iao-p'iao* (Red flag fluttering; Peking, 1957), V, 45.

3. *Hsing-huo liao-yuan* (A single spark can start a prairie fire; Hong Kong, 1960), p. 50.

4. *Jen-min te chün-tui* (The people's military forces [a newspaper published by the Political Department of the Chin-Chi-Lu-Yü Military Region], September 15, 1946).

5. *The Great Turning Point* (Peking, 1962), p. 131.

Chang Ch'i-lung

(1900–   ; Liu-yang Hsien, Hunan). Specialist in supply and marketing cooperatives; alternate member, CCP Central Committee.

Chang Ch'i-lung, a Communist Party member since the 1920's, served as a political officer and Party-government official in Manchuria in the late forties and early fifties. He was a key figure in the All-China Federation of Supply and Marketing Cooperatives throughout the 1950's, and in the latter part of the decade was the *de facto* head of this organization. He has been an alternate member of the Party Central Committee since 1956.

Chang was born in 1900 in Liu-yang hsien, Hunan, some 50 miles east of Changsha near the Kiangsi border. Liu-yang is also the home of such prominent Communists as Sung Jen-ch'iung, Wang Shou-tao, Wang Chen, and Lo Chang-lung. Nothing is known of Chang's early life except that he is reported to have studied for a year at a normal school in Changsha, after which he became a teacher. In 1924 he joined the CCP.

Chang was presumably in Changsha on May 21, 1927, a time of rapidly deteriorating relations between the Communists and the KMT, when Hsu K'o-hsiang, a regimental commander of T'ang Sheng-chih's Nationalist Army, launched a sudden attack on labor and leftist organizations there. These groups had been sympathetic to the CCP, which had hoped to organize them to cooperate with peasant associations that had been formed in the surrounding countryside in preparation for further revolutionary work. However, Hsu's attack decimated the Party in Changsha and forced it underground. Afterwards, in the winter of 1927, Chang and two fellow Party workers, Wang Shou-tao and Wang Chen (qq.v.), escaped to Liu-yang, which was the native hsien of all three, to carry on their underground work. There had been a peasant insurrection in Liu-yang in September 1927 during the Autumn Harvest Uprisings, and as early as 1928 a small Communist soviet was established there, which Chang is reputed to have founded in association with Wang Shou-tao and Huang Kung-lueh (q.v.). While in Liu-yang, Chang was briefly imprisoned by the Nationalists. After his release he served as secretary and chairman of the Liu-yang hsien soviet. By 1933 Chang was identified as a vice-chairman and head of the Justice Department of the Hunan-Hupeh-Kiangsi Soviet Government. The Hunan-Hupeh-Kiangsi base, which included the Liu-yang area, was part of the Chinese Soviet Republic established in November 1931 and was one of 14 guerrilla bases evacuated by the main Communist armies when they left for the northwest on the Long March in 1934.

Between 1933 and 1937 Chang's activity remains undocumented. However, there are two reports that, in view of other events, may indicate his political affiliations at the time. According to an account from a Communist newspaper of the period, he was sentenced to 14 months imprisonment in September 1933 for accepting a bribe to free captive Nationalist General Chang Ch'ao.[1] A 1951 article commemorating Jen Pi-shih (q.v.) also states that Jen, who was assigned to the Hunan-Hupeh-Kiangsi Soviet in May 1933, "saved" Chang from "leftist dogmatism"[2] (see under Wang Shou-tao). The term "leftist dogmatism," with reference to the 1930's, is ordinarily associated with the so-called Russian-returned student clique (see under Ch'en Shao-yü) that had won control of the CCP Central Committee at the Fourth Plenum held in Shanghai in January 1931. Because of Nationalist harassments the "returned students" were subsequently forced to seek refuge in the rural Communist base in southeast Kiangsi, where Mao Tse-tung, Chu Te, and other Communist military and political leaders had made their headquarters. A political struggle ensued between the local and newly arrived leaders, in which each side tried to discredit the other. The reports about Chang's "dogmatism" suggest that he may have been censured by the Mao group, but there is no further clarification of his alleged imprisonment. He was not identified again until 1937 when he was reported in Yenan.

By 1947 Chang was identified as a deputy political commissar in Lin Piao's Northeast Democratic Allied Army. This army (renamed the Fourth Field Army in 1949) was responsible for the Communist takeover of Manchuria. Chang's next assignment was in northern Manchuria, where he became the ranking Party secretary of the Heilungkiang Provincial Committee. He only held the post briefly, however, for Chao Te-tsun replaced him by April 1950. Chang was then transferred to southern Manchuria, where by July 1950 he was the ranking Party secretary in Liaotung Province. From August 1951 he also served as chairman of the Economic Planning Committee of the Liaotung People's Government, and from September as a member of the Northeast People's Government (NEPG) established by the Communists in 1949 to govern Manchuria. The NEPG was reorganized into the Northeast Administrative Committee in January 1953, at which time Chang was dropped from membership. It was probably about this time that he also relinquished his post on the Liaotung Planning Committee, as well as the secretaryship of the Liaotung Party Committee, to which Kao Yang succeeded by May 1953.

In 1950, while still in Manchuria, Chang began his work in the cooperative movement, in which he has since become a leading specialist. The Communists organized their chief mass organization for cooperatives at the first conference of the All-China Federation of Cooperatives in July 1950. At the close of the Congress a provisional Board of Directors was elected. Po I-po (q.v.), a leading economic specialist, became chairman, and Chang was named as a Board member. The Federation underwent a minor reorganization in July 1952, the provisional board becoming a permanent one. By 1953 Po I-po, heavily occupied elsewhere, turned over the leadership of the Federation to Ch'eng Tzu-hua (q.v.), who became the acting director. At the same time Chang was promoted to a deputy directorship, ranking immediately after Ch'eng. At a congress held in July 1954, the Federation was again reorganized and renamed the All-China Federation of Supply and Marketing Cooperatives (ACFSMC). Chang was made a member of the First National Committee and the Standing Committee. Immediately after the congress, new officers were elected. Ch'eng Tzu-hua became director, and Chang the senior deputy director. By about 1957 Chang was *de facto* head of the Federation in place of Ch'eng Tzu-hua, who was occupied with other responsibilities. Throughout the 1950's Chang was a frequent speaker at numerous Federation meetings. For example, in February 1957 at the third session of the First National Committee of the ACFSMC, he reported on the Federation's work during 1956 and its tasks for 1957. He has also had many contacts with foreign visitors who come to China to inspect cooperatives, and on two occasions in 1957 he went abroad in connection with work in this field. One trip took him to the U.S.S.R. in the summer of 1957, and in December he attended the Fourth Congress of the Hungarian Consumers Cooperatives in Budapest.

Chang's work with cooperatives has also brought him into the top government legislative councils. In December 1954 he was elected a representative of the ACFSMC to the Second National Committee of the CPPCC. He continued to serve in the CPPCC through the term of the Second National Committee but was not re-elected to the Third Committee, which held its first session in April 1959. However, in 1958 he had been elected as a Hunan deputy to the more important legislative branch, the NPC. When the first session of the Second NPC was held in April 1959, he became a member of the NPC Standing Committee.

At the Eighth National Party Congress in September 1956, Chang was elected an alternate member of the Central Committee. In October 1958 he was identified as a deputy director of the Central Committee's important Organization Department. Although Chang has been mentioned in the latter post only this one time, he may still hold it.

Chang has also given some time to such activities as spare-time education; he was one of 18 members named to the Spare-Time Education Committee, established under the State Council in January 1960. Similarly, in June 1960 he was a member of the presidium of the national conference for "advanced" cultural and educational workers. In April of that year he accompanied the head of the Mongolian Communist Party on a visit to Wuhan and Chengchow, and in November 1962 he attended a banquet given by Politburo members Liu Shao-ch'i, Chou En-lai, and Teng Hsiao-p'ing for a visiting delegation from the Norwegian Communist Party. Since 1962, however, Chang has not often been mentioned in the news. Moreover, his role in the NPC was reduced following the formation of the Third NPC in late 1964. As already described, Chang was a deputy from his native Hunan to the Second NPC (1959–1964) and served on the important Standing Committee. When the elections were held for the Third NPC, he was elected from Heilungkiang (where he had served 15 years earlier) but was not named again to the Standing Committee. He did serve on the NPC Credentials Committee, but this is a much less important body than the permanent Standing Committee. Paralleling his less active role in the NPC has been Chang's relative inactivity in the cooperative movement, the work that occupied so much of his time through the 1950's. He was listed as the senior deputy director of the Federation of Supply and Marketing Cooperatives in the semi-official *Jen-min shou-ts'e* (People's handbook) as late as the 1962 edition. In subsequent editions, however, his name was omitted, thereby confirming the fact that he was removed from this important position. Furthermore, P'an Fu-sheng (q.v.) officially succeeded Ch'eng Tzu-hua as head of the ACFSMC in 1963, ending Chang's tenure as *de facto* head.

1. *Hung-se hsiang-kan* (Red Hunan-Kiangsi), October 19, 1933, Union Research Institute files, Hong Kong.
2. *SCMP* 216, p. 1.

Chang Chia-fu

(c.1900–   ). Deputy-director, Office of Culture and Education, State Council; historian.

Chang Chia-fu was probably born around 1900, for by 1927 he was a researcher in the Institute of Social Sciences of the Academia Sinica. It is probable that he joined the Communist movement by the 1930's, if not earlier. This deduction is made from the fact that Chang was sufficiently familiar with Kuan Hsiang-ying, a prominent Party Central Committee figure who died in 1946, to supply Kuan's biographer with details about his career.[1] Kuan spent the last decade of his life in the northwest in Yenan and the Shansi-Suiyuan border area. Therefore, it may be that Chang was also in this area during the years of the Sino-Japanese War. He was definitely in that area when the Communists won control of the mainland in 1949.

In May 1949 Sian fell to the forces under the command of Ho Lung, another key figure in the Shansi-Suiyuan area during the Sino-Japanese War. The Sian Municipal Military Control Commission was immediately established under the chairmanship of Ho, with Chang as one of its members. By the latter part of the same year he was heading the Propaganda Department for the Party's Northwest Bureau, a position he held until a transfer in early 1953 took him to Peking. Under the civil government structure for the northwest, known as the Northwest Military and Administrative Committee (NWMAC), Chang was named to membership on the Committee (January 1950–January 1953). Also under the NWMAC he was a vice-chairman of the Culture and Education Committee. The ostensible head of this Committee was Yang Ming-hsien, but in view of the fact that Yang is not a CCP member, it is likely that Chang actually directed the affairs of this important body. He also held this post until his transfer in early 1953. Apart from his Party and government positions, Chang's extracurricular activities included a vice-chairmanship of the Northwest Branch of the China Peace Committee by May 1952.

Chang was relieved of his posts in the Northwest and called to Peking, where in January 1953 he was made a vice-president of the Academy of Sciences under Academy President Kuo Mo-jo. In the following month he was a member of the Academy delegation led by Ch'ien San-ch'iang (q.v.) to Moscow. Chang was identified at this time as a historian. This was the first large delegation of Chinese scientists to visit the Soviet Union; it remained there for three months. In April 1954 the Academy took its first major steps toward the establishment of departments governing four major academic fields. Chang was named as the deputy director of the Department of Social Sciences. Ultimately, when these departments were set up in May–June 1955, Chang was dropped to simple membership under Department Director Kuo Mo-jo. In October 1955, Chang was also named to a special Science Scholarship Committee that was established under Academy auspices to stimulate research and scientific writings.

When the First NPC was established in 1954, thus inaugurating the constitutional government, Chang served as a deputy from Shansi. However, in the Second and Third NPCs (which opened their initial sessions in April 1959 and December 1964, respectively), he was transferred to be a deputy from Inner Mongolia.

When Chang was first assigned to the Academy of Sciences in 1953 it was clearly the principal organization concerned with directing Chinese scientific research and development. However, following the announcement of an ambitious 12-Year Scientific Plan in early 1956, the Communists created (March 1956) a Scientific Planning

Commission under the State Council with Vice-Premier Ch'en I as the chairman. At this point, Chang was removed from his vice-presidency in the Academy and transferred to the new Committee, being named as a deputy secretary-general. Two months later, in May 1956, he received an appointment more fitting to his experience, theretofore largely devoted to administration and Party-directed propaganda in the fields of education and culture. This was as a deputy director of the Second Staff Office of the State Council, one of eight offices then directing and coordinating the activities of several ministries and bureaus of the State Council. In May 1957, when the Scientific Planning Commission was reorganized, Chang was dropped from his post on that organization. Then in September 1959 the Second Staff Office was redesignated with a name denoting its function, the Office of Culture and Education; Chang was reappointed as a deputy director at this time and continues to hold the post.

In 1957, when the "Hundred Flowers Campaign" was still encouraging some freedom of speech, Chang was criticized for being "so bureaucratic and sectarian that he forbade non-Party members to enter his office in the Academy." This criticism from non-Party channels, however, obviously did not damage his career. In December 1958 and again in June 1960 he served on the presidium (steering committee) for two nationwide conferences of "advanced" workers, the first in agriculture and the latter in culture and education. A long period then passed before Chang was again in the news. Finally, in late 1962, he was named as an alternate member of the Party's Central Control Commission. This important Commission, charged with discipline and inspection functions within the Party, was expanded in accordance with a decision taken at the 10th Plenum of the Party Central Committee in September 1962. For reasons of internal security, the Control Commission seldom receives press attention, and as a consequence Chang was seldom mentioned in the press after assuming this post. As already noted, however, he was re-elected in 1964 as a deputy from Inner Mongolia to the Third NPC, and when the permanent NPC Bills Committee was named at the close of the first session (January 1965), Chang was selected as a member.

---

1. *Hung-ch'i p'iao-p'iao* (Red flag fluttering; Peking, 1957), V, 234.

Chang Chih-hsiang

(c.1915–   ). Vice-chairman, Commission for Cultural Relations with Foreign Countries, State Council.

Chang Chih-hsiang was born about 1915 according to a former Chinese Communist govern-ment official.[1] Prior to 1949 his experience had been as a political commissar in the Chinese Communist armies. In the period after the Communist takeover he has become one of the most influential and widely traveled of those persons concerned with "cultural" relations and liaison abroad.

From 1949 to 1954 he served as deputy director of the Political Department of the North China Military Region, which included the provinces of Hopeh and Shansi (and, before they were abolished, Chahar, Pingyuan, and Suiyuan), spending these years in Peking, the headquarters of the Military Region. In July 1949 he attended the inaugural congress of the mass organization for culture, literature, and art, the All-China Federation of Literary and Art Circles. Representation at the congress, attended by over 800 delegates, was by geographic area, except for a military delegation, which was led by Chang. He served on the congress presidium (steering committee) as well as on a special committee that considered proposals to be placed before the congress. At the close of the congress he was elected to the Standing Committee of the All-China Federation of Literary and Art Circles (ACFLAC), a position he held until the second congress in September–October 1953. At the same time that the ACFLAC was established, several subordinate organizations were formed. One of them was the All-China Association of Literary Workers, chaired by the well-known author Mao Tun (q.v.). Chang was named to membership on the National Committee of this association, also retaining it until the fall of 1953.

Another organization that Chang helped to establish was the All-China Athletic Federation. When the Preparatory Committee was formed in October 1949 he was named to it as a representative of the North China Military Region, serving on the committee until the Federation was formally inaugurated in June 1952. Other activities of the early 1950's include membership on the Standing Committee of the Peking branch of the China Peace Committee, a position he may still hold. He also served on the presidium for the first All-Army Sports Meet held in August 1952 to mark the 25th anniversary of the founding of the PLA. But Chang's major impact on the Chinese Communist movement did not begin until 1954 when he retired from active army duties and was switched to the cultural field. In October 1954 he was appointed as a vice-minister of the Ministry of Culture, then headed by Mao Tun, with whom Chang had earlier been associated; he retained this post for three and a half years. In the following May he made his first trip abroad, leading a 74-member classical theater group on a nine-nation tour which lasted for eight months (May 1955–January 1956). This was one of the first important cultural forays into the non-Communist world.

The group was well received by audiences in France, the Netherlands, Belgium, Czechoslovakia, Switzerland, Italy, England, Yugoslavia, and Hungary. While in Italy (October 1955) Chang attended the Congress of Mayors of World Capitals, representing Peking Mayor P'eng Chen.

While abroad Chang was identified as a Standing Committee member of the Chinese People's Association for Cultural Relations with Foreign Countries, an important mass organization whose name describes its purpose, established in May 1954. It was not until 1957, however, that he was officially carried on the roster of this association; then, in April 1959, he was elevated to a vice-chairmanship, a post he continues to hold. In March 1958 Chang was removed as a vice-minister in the Ministry of Culture but at the same time was made a vice-chairman of the Commission for Cultural Relations with Foreign Countries, the governmental counterpart of the mass organization of the same name described above. The government Commission was created in February 1958 and has been headed since that time by non-Communist Chang Hsi-jo. A former Commission employee who worked in the organization in 1964 stated that it was common knowledge that Chang Chih-hsiang, in fact, was actually in charge of the work of the Commission.[2] This assertion seems to be borne out by the fact that for brief periods in 1959, 1960, and 1961 he served as acting chairman. (However, his authority was probably lessened late in 1964 when Li Ch'ang, outranking Chang by virtue of his post as an alternate member of the Party Central Committee, was named as an additional vice-chairman.)

In the interim, Chang had traveled abroad again when, in March 1957, he led a cultural delegation to Mongolia and while there signed a cultural cooperation plan for 1957. (Such annual "executive plans" are part of the Chinese Communist pattern of cultural exchanges; broad cultural agreements are normally signed first and are then followed by the signing of more detailed annual executive plans. In this instance Chang signed a plan in pursuance of an economic and cultural agreement signed in 1952.) Apart from his 1955–1956 tour of Europe and this trip to Mongolia, Chang has been abroad on nine other occasions in the period from 1958 to 1964, trips that have taken him to eight different countries: Sweden (July 1958 and March 1959); Bulgaria (November–December 1959); Greece (May–June 1960); Burma (December 1960–January 1961); Mongolia (July 1961); North Korea (April–May 1962); North Vietnam (December 1962); and, Cuba (December 1963–January 1964). The trips to Sweden were for meetings held by the Communist-backed World Peace Council; that to Mongolia was for the 40th anniversary of the Mongolian People's Republic; and

the one to Cuba for the fifth anniversary of the Castro government. But each of the other journeys was as leader of cultural delegations. Chang's visit to Greece is of interest because exceedingly few Chinese Communists have visited that country (which maintains diplomatic ties with Nationalist China).

Between 1957 and 1964, Chang signed no less than 13 annual cultural plans and one major cultural agreement. Aside from the one already mentioned in Mongolia (March 1957), he signed three more abroad; Bulgaria (December 1959); North Vietnam (December 1962), Cuba (January 1964). In Peking he signed another nine plans or agreements: Hungary (January 1959); Poland (February 1960); North Vietnam (February 1960); Mongolia (February 1960); the U.S.S.R. (February 1961); Ghana (August 1961); Mongolia (January 1962); the U.S.S.R. (May 1963); Cuba (July 1963). It should be noted that all these, excepting only that with Ghana, were negotiated with Communist countries.

Chang's involvement in foreign relations is illustrated in various other ways, including his participation in "friendship associations." From 1958 to 1962 he was named to posts within six different associations: China-Mongolia FA (Chairman, September 1958); China-Latin America FA (Standing Committee member, March 1960); China-Africa People's FA (Standing Committee member, April 1960); Sino-Soviet FA (acting secretary-general, by October 1960); China-Ceylon FA (Council member, September 1962); and, China-Cuba FA (vice-chairman, December 1962). Except for the Sino-Soviet Friendship Association, each of these dates represents the date the association was founded; Chang retains all these posts except the chairmanship of the China-Mongolia FA, which he relinquished in August 1961, and the position in the Sino-Soviet FA, which was assumed by another man in late 1964.

Chang has also held or continues to hold a few more posts worthy of brief notation. From 1959 to 1964 he served as a member of the Third National Committee of the CPPCC as a representative of "organizations for peaceful and friendly relations with foreign countries," but he was not re-elected to the Fourth Committee, which first met at the end of 1964. In June 1963, in response to Indonesian President Sukarno's initiative, the Chinese formed a preparatory committee to participate in the "Games of the New Emerging Forces" (GANEFO; see under Jung Kao-t'ang). Chang was selected as a member, and when the preparatory committee was made into a permanent national committee in August 1964 he was again named as one of the members. Finally, in August 1964, he was a delegate to the huge Peking Scientific Symposium, a series of meetings attended by 367 delegates from 44 nations (mainly in Asia, Africa, or Latin America). Apart from all of these positions, Chang has made a large number of appearances in Peking since the mid-1950's in greeting and entertaining groups, such as "friendship" and cultural delegations. He can be regarded as one of the more important of the international cultural liaison officials of the PRC.

1. Interview with a former official in the Commission for Cultural Relations with Foreign Countries, Cambridge, Mass., June 1965.
2. *Ibid.*

Chang Chih-i

(Wuhan, Hupeh). Deputy-director, United Front Work Department, CCP.

Chang Chih-i, a native of Wuhan, has come to be one of the Party's foremost spokesmen in national minorities affairs. He probably gained some familiarity with minority problems in the late 1930's when he was working for the Party in Sinkiang, a province predominantly populated by non-Han Chinese. Chang was known to have been in Sinkiang in about 1939 when a number of important Party leaders such as Ch'en T'an-ch'iu, Mao Tse-min (Mao Tse-tung's brother), and Ma Ming-fang (qq.v.) were working there.[1] These men were in Sinkiang with the sufferance of Sheng Shih-ts'ai, the provincial governor, who from the outbreak of the Sino-Japanese War to about 1942 was on friendly terms with the Soviet government in Moscow and the Chinese Communists. After Sheng's 1942 break with the Communists, he imprisoned and executed some important Communists (including Ch'en T'an-ch'iu and Mao Tse-min), but Chang had already left the area, because by 1941 he was working with Ch'en I's New Fourth Army in east China where he was director of the Political Department of the 15th Brigade of the Fifth Division. The Fifth Division was created after the Nationalists routed a large part of the Communist Army in central China in the military coup known as the New Fourth Army Incident (January 1941). The Division, composed of guerrilla forces from the "Honan-Hupeh Volunteers," which had been brought together in the area north of Hankow by Li Hsien-nien (q.v.), established a headquarters in the Hupeh-Honan-Anhwei Military Area in the spring of 1941. Here Chang was director of the Political Department of the Third Military Sub-district.

Chang presumably remained in east-central China with Li Hsien-nien throughout the 1940's, for he was with Li's forces in the spring of 1949 when the Communists captured Hupeh and its leading city, Wuhan. Chang was assigned to his native Wuhan as a vice-mayor serving under Mayor Wu Te-feng (q.v.), another native of Hupeh. At this same time he was also director of the United Front Work Department of the CCP's Central China Bureau. When this Bureau was enlarged into the Central-South Bureau in the latter part of 1949 (reflecting the expansion of the area of control as the Communist armies pushed southward), Chang retained the directorship, a position he held until the Bureau was abolished in the fall of 1954. The directorship of the United Front Work Department placed him in control of Party relations with both the non-Communist intellectuals and the national minority groups in central-south China.

Hupeh Province was one of the six provinces that, for administrative purposes within the government structure, was subordinate to the Central-South Military and Administrative Committee (CSMAC), brought into existence under the chairmanship of Lin Piao in February 1950. It was to the CSMAC (known as the Central-South Administrative Committee after January 1953) that Chang devoted the major portion of his time until 1954. Within a month of its creation he was named as the CSMAC secretary-general, and in November 1951 he was appointed to head the Nationalities Affairs Committee, his field of special competence. In December 1951 he became a vice-chairman of the Political and Legal Affairs Committee under Li Hsueh-feng, later to become a Central Committee member. Then in May 1953 Chang replaced Li as the chairman. He also served as a vice-chairman of an *ad hoc* committee for the region established in November 1951 to promote the Party drive against corruption and waste. The committee was headed by Teng Tzu-hui, the top economic specialist of the CSMAC in the early 1950's.

During this same period Chang's extracurricular activities brought him onto several committees concerned with different phases of Party work in the central-south region. Thus he was secretary-general of the central-south branch of the China Peace Committee in 1950, and in 1952 he was vice-chairman of the Wuhan Anti-Corruption Committee and a member of committees concerned with flood control and the prevention of epidemics. In January 1953 he led a delegation to visit the national minorities in Honan.

Chang was first appointed to a post in the national government in November 1952, when he became a vice-chairman of the Nationalities Affairs Commission, the principal government organization handling minority affairs (then under the Government Administration Council). However, he continued to work in central-south China until 1954, when regional governments were abolished with the inauguration of a constitutional government. In that year Chang was elected to represent his native Hupeh in the First NPC. At the close of the initial NPC session in September 1954, he was named to the Nationalities Committee, the body concentrating on minority questions as they concern the Congress, and one of two NPC Committees that are active between the national congresses. Chang became a vice-chairman of the Nationalities Committee in mid-1955, and continued to serve there throughout the term of the First NPC (1954–1959). He was not, however, re-elected to the Second NPC that opened in April 1959, but he was elected as a Honan deputy to the Third NPC that held its initial session in December 1964–January 1965.

By April 1955 Chang also received an important promotion in the CCP, becoming a deputy director of the national CCP United Front Work Department, a position he still holds. The Department was headed by Li Wei-han until 1965 and thereafter by Hsu Ping (qq.v.). In May 1955 Chang was made a deputy director of the Eighth Staff Office of the State Council. Also headed by Li Wei-han, the Eighth Office was in charge of coordinating the work of the State Council's ministries, commissions, and bureaus concerned with united front work, overseas Chinese, and national minority affairs. Chang remained in the Eighth Office until it was abolished in September 1959 when the State Council underwent a partial reorganization. In March 1957 Chang was named as a CCP representative on the Second National Committee of the CPPCC to fill a vacancy. In October of the same year he was appointed as a deputy secretary-general of the CPPCC National Committee, serving under Secretary-general Hsu Ping. He was again named to membership on the Third National Committee of the CPPCC, formed in April 1959, and at the close of the National Committee's initial session he was elevated to Standing Committee membership. In addition to continuing under the Third Committee as a deputy secretary-general, he was also a vice-chairman of its Local Work Committee, posts he held until the Fourth Committee of the CPPCC was established in December 1964–January 1965. Chang was named to the Fourth Committee as a "specially invited personage" (rather than from the CCP); however, he was not re-elected to the Standing Committee. Both these facts suggest a somewhat lessened role within this organization.

Since coming to Peking in late 1954, Chang has made a tremendous number of public appearances at events related to work with national minority groups, non-Communist intellectuals, and religious groups. To cite two random but typical examples, he spoke at a national conference of Christians held late in 1960 and early 1961, and in July 1962 he was a speaker at the graduation ceremony of the Central Institute of Socialism, a special school for training non-Communist intellectuals. He has also been a steady contributor to a number of newspapers and journals, most frequently writing about national minority or religious questions. He has written most of his articles for such publications as *Min-tsu t'uan-chieh* (Nationalities unity), the chief organ dealing with minority questions, or for the *Kuang-ming jih-pao,* the newspaper ostensibly edited by the eight non-Communist political parties. Among his more important writings are two articles on Party policies toward religion; one was entitled "Atheists and Theists Can Cooperate Politically and Travel the Road of Socialism" (1958) and the other "Correctly Understand and Implement the Party's Policy on Freedom of Religious Belief" (1962).[2] But his most important work is a major historical and ideological treatment of the minorities question, a book entitled *Chung-kuo ko-ming te min-tsu wen-t'i ho min-tsu cheng-ts'e chiang-hua* (A discussion of nationalities questions and policies in the Chinese revolution; Peking, 1956). George Moseley has translated and annotated Chang's book, publishing it under the title *The Party and the National Question in China* (Cambridge, Mass., 1966).

1. *Hung-ch'i p'iao-p'iao* (Red flag fluttering; Peking, 1957), V, 150.
2. Translated in *CB* 510, pp. 11–20, and *SCMM* 318, pp. 1–6, respectively.

Chang Chih-jang

(1893–   ; Kiangsu). Vice-president, Supreme People's Court.

Chang Chih-jang, a non-Communist, is one of Communist China's outstanding legal experts. Educated in both China and the United States, Chang is representative of a number of well-trained specialists utilized by the Communists since the establishment of the PRC in 1949.

Chang was born on December 28, 1893. Semi-official Communist directories list his place of birth as Wu-chin (Ch'ang-chou), a city on the Grand Canal in Kiangsu Province. Other sources, however, claim that he was born in Chefoo (Yen-t'ai) in Shantung. According to Japanese reports, Chang has also been known by the name Chang Chi-lung. He graduated from Futan University in Shanghai in 1915 and then proceeded to the United States for further education. He studied at the University of California (1916–1917) and spent two semesters in 1919 at Columbia University studying law.

Following his return to China, Chang embarked on a legal career of considerable distinction as a practicing lawyer, a professor of law, and as an editor of journals dealing with international problems. For many years he taught law at Futan University, ultimately serving as Dean of the Futan Law School from 1945 to 1947. He was also a lecturer at National Central University in Nanking and at a branch of Tung-wu University in Shanghai. During the thirties and forties, in both Shanghai and Chungking (during the war years), he participated in editing *Wen-t'i*

(Problems), *Kuo-min chou-k'an* (National weekly), *Wen-chai* (Digest), and *Hsien-cheng yueh-k'an* (Constitution monthly), all magazines dealing with national and international problems. His work with these magazines brought him into contact with such prominent Chinese political leaders as Chin Chung-hua, Sha Ch'ien-li, and Miss Shih Liang (qq.v.), each of whom cooperated with the Communist regime after 1949 (though not necessarily as members of the CCP). Chang gained national fame in 1936–1937 when he served as a legal counselor for several persons arrested and imprisoned for their persistent demands that the Nationalist Government exert greater efforts to resist the steady encroachments of the Japanese in the mid-thirties. Those imprisoned came to be known as the "seven gentlemen," and their imprisonment remained a *cause célèbre* until their release in July 1937 shortly after the outbreak of the Sino-Japanese War (see under Shih Liang).

Like so many other intellectuals from the coastal cities, Chang fled to the wartime capital at Chungking during the war against Japan. There he became associated with the China Democratic League, a political party that continues to exist under the Communist government as one of the eight ostensibly democratic (non-Communist) political parties. After the war Chang returned to Shanghai where, as already noted, he was again associated with his alma mater, Futan University. Fearing arrest in early 1949 for his leftist tendencies, he went to Hong Kong, but after only a brief time there he went by sea to north China. He was in Peking in time (June 1949) to serve as a member of the Preparatory Committee of the CPPCC. This Committee, chaired by Mao Tse-tung, had several subcommittees that worked throughout the summer of 1949 on special questions that were to be discussed when the CPPCC met in plenary session in September 1949 to establish the central government. As a person with legal training, Chang was logically assigned to serve on the committee charged with the task of drafting the Organic Law of the soon-to-be-established central government, one of the key documents that was eventually ratified in September 1949. Chang attended the inaugural session of the CPPCC as a representative of China's social scientists. And, when the central government was staffed in October 1949, he received three appointments, each related to the legal field. Under the Government Administration Council (the cabinet), he was named to membership on the Law Commission and the Political and Legal Affairs Committee. He was also named as a vice-president of the Supreme People's Court. When the constitutional government was inaugurated in 1954 at the First NPC, both the Law Commission and the Political and Legal Affairs Committee were abolished. However, he was reappointed to the Supreme

Court and, as of the mid-1960's, is the only man at the presidential or vice-presidential level who has served on China's highest court continuously from 1949. He served on the First NPC (1954–1959) as a deputy from Kiangsu; he was reelected for the term of the Second NPC (1959–1964) and again for the Third NPC that opened in December 1964.

As a Supreme Court vice-president, Chang has on occasions made official reports before government bodies. He gave a report, for example, in September 1951 before a meeting of the Government Administration Council and was one of the speakers at the government-sponsored Second National Judicial Conference in April 1953. He has also been a participant in several of the many professional and "mass" organizations established by the Communists. The most prominent of these in Chang's field is the Political Science and Law Association of China (PSLAC). From 1951 to 1953 he served as a member of the PSLAC Preparatory Committee, and he has been a vice-chairman since the organization was permanently established in April 1953. He was also a member of the PSLAC's Secretariat from August 1958 until October 1964.

As a Western-trained lawyer, Chang has also been utilized by the Communists as an appropriate person to deal with the many non-Communist parliamentarians and lawyers who have visited China; similarly, he has served as the leader of delegations sent abroad to attend legal meetings. In January 1955 he led a group of Chinese lawyers to Calcutta for the Conference of Asian Lawyers, and in May of the next year he led another jurists' delegation to Brussels to attend the sixth congress of the Communist-dominated International Association of Democratic Lawyers. Also, in March–April 1961, Chang was in Japan as head of a delegation of lawyers attending the preparatory meeting of the Afro-Asian Lawyers' Conference.

Like many Chinese personalities having regular contact with foreigners, Chang belongs to organizations related to one or another aspect of international relations. He has been a National Committee member of the China Peace Committee since 1950, a member of the Asian Solidarity Committee from its formation in February 1956 (known as the Afro-Asian Solidarity Committee since May 1958), a Council member of the China-Egypt Friendship Association from November 1956 (known as the China-United Arab Republic Friendship Association following the merger in early 1958 of Egypt and Syria), and the president of the China-Ceylon Friendship Association since its formation in September 1962. Chang has also been a Council member of the Asia-Africa Society of China since April 1962 when the society was established with the avowed purpose of advancing the level of Chinese research on both Asia and Africa.

As a vice-president of the Supreme Court, Chang has obviously been in close contact with some of China's top leaders, particularly those who have specialized in legal affairs—most notably Tung Pi-wu, Hsieh Chueh-tsai (both former presidents of the Supreme Court), and Wu Te-feng, the most prominent figure in the Political Science and Law Association of China since the mid-fifties. However, because he is not a Party member, it is most unlikely that Chang exerts any significant political authority. It should also be noted that the field of law in China suffered a sharp setback in the wake of the 1957–1958 "rectification" campaign; until that time the legal profession was making slow but discernible progress, but since then it appears to have had low priority. Nonetheless, Chang serves as a living example of the Party's continuing policy of maintaining the united front in the legal field.

Chang Ch'in-ch'iu

(c. 1902–   ; Chekiang). Early CCP leader in Oyüwan Soviet; vice-minister, Ministry of Textile Industry.

Miss Chang Ch'in-ch'iu is one of the more important women in the history of the Chinese Communist Movement. She was trained in the Soviet Union, where she belonged to the "28 Bolsheviks" group. In the early thirties Chang held important posts in Chang Kuo-t'ao's Oyüwan Soviet, and after making the Long March she worked during the war years in Yenan. Chang has been a vice-minister of the Ministry of Textile Industry since the PRC was established in 1949.

Miss Chang was born in Chekiang about 1902. In 1924–25 she was a student at radical Shanghai University, which included on its faculty a number of important Communists (see under Ch'ü Ch'iu-pai). While there she came under the influence of Hsiang Ching-yü (q.v.), the wife of Ts'ai Ho-sen and the most important woman Communist of that period. Many of the students were very active in the Shanghai labor movement. Chang, for example, was assigned in 1924 to work in a part-time night school in an industrial district of the city, and she also participated in numerous strikes of 1924–25 that were in part led by the Communists. The most important of these was the one resulting from the May 30th Incident.[1] She was sent to Moscow about 1928 to attend Sun Yat-sen University, where she became one of the protégés of Pavel Mif, the University chancellor and a Comintern official. The group has been known both as the "28 Bolsheviks" and the "Russian-returned" students. With Mif and his other protégés, she returned to China in the spring of 1930 and in the summer of 1931 was sent with some of them to the Oyüwan area. Chang Kuo-t'ao (q.v.) was also sent there in 1931 to take charge of reorganizing political

work. Although he was not one of Mif's students, he had known them well in Moscow and consequently used some of them in Oyüwan. Shen Tse-min (q.v.), the brother of the well-known writer Mao Tun, headed the local Party committee and Ch'en Ch'ang-hao (q.v.) was in charge of youth work. Chang was made responsible for work among women. It was probably during their time in Oyüwan that she married the first of her three husbands, Shen Tse-min.

In 1932, pressured by Nationalist attempts to eradicate Communism in central China, most of the Oyüwan group sought refuge in a remote area of northwest Szechwan, where they established another small soviet in the winter of 1932. The group was led by Chang Kuo-t'ao and Hsu Hsiang-ch'ien (q.v.), head of the Oyüwan Fourth Front Army. Chang accompanied them and served from 1933 to 1935 as director of the Army's Women's Work Department and as chairman of a hospital under its control.[2] Because of poor health, Shen Tse-min remained in Oyüwan, where he died or was in killed in 1934. At the Second All-China Congress of Soviets held in January–February 1934 at the Soviet capital in southeast Kiangsi, where Mao had his headquarters, Chang was elected (probably *in absentia*) as a member of the Central Executive Committee of the Chinese Soviet Republic. The following year, the Fourth Front Army moved west to Mao-kung, west Szechwan, where it joined Mao Tse-tung's Long Marchers in the summer. The biography of Chang Kuo-t'ao describes the army's arrival in north Shensi in the fall of 1936. Miss Chang was probably still with the army at that time.

In 1937 Chang taught at the Yenan Chinese Women's University and at the Shen-pei (North Shensi) Public School. She apparently remained in Yenan, the capital of the Shensi-Kansu-Ninghsia Border Region Government, throughout the Sino-Japanese War, for in November 1941 she was a deputy to the Second Assembly of the Border Region, which was held in that city. She also attended the Assembly's second session when it met in December 1944.

After the war Chang devoted much of her time to the field of women's work. In December 1948 she was one of 11 women in a delegation led by the senior woman Communist, Ts'ai Ch'ang (q.v.), to the Second Congress of the Women's International Democratic Federation in Budapest. In the following spring she was secretary-general of the Preparatory Committee for the All-China Federation of Democratic Women (ACFDW), the mass women's organization. At the Federation's inaugural congress in March–April 1949, Chang was elected to its Executive and Standing Committees. She was also made director of the ACFDW's Production Department but was replaced toward the end of 1950. In June 1949, representing the ACFDW, Chang was elected as a member of the Preparatory Committee for the CPPCC. When the First CPPCC met in September to establish the central government, Miss Chang was made a member of the First National Committee of the CPPCC. Immediately following the inauguration of the PRC on October 1, 1949, she was appointed a vice-minister of the Ministry of Textile Industry, a position she still retains. The appointment of a woman to this post was particularly appropriate for, as Chang herself has noted in a 1953 article, 60 per cent of the workers and staff members in the cotton textile industry are women.[3] She held a closely related post in the early PRC years, when she served on the Preparatory Committee of the All-China Textile Workers' Trade Union.

Like most of the higher-echelon government administrators, Chang also received posts in the many "mass" organizations. In October 1949 she was made a member of the National Committee of the China Peace Committee, and in the same month she was elected to the Sino-Soviet Friendship Association's Executive Board. She was removed from the Peace Committee in 1950 but retained her post in the Friendship Association until late 1954 when it was reorganized. From 1950 to 1954 she was also active in the All-China Federation of Cooperatives, serving until 1952 on its Provisional Board of Directors and thereafter on the permanent board. In 1953 and again in 1957 she was re-elected to the Executive Committee of the Women's Federation, and she still retains the post.

Since the mid-fifties Miss Chang's work (which has not received much attention in the national press) has been increasingly centered around her position in the Textile Ministry and her commitments to other organizations have correspondingly decreased. In September 1953 she accompanied government administrator Li Jen-chün to Bucharest for the inaugural session of the Joint Committee for Sino-Rumanian Scientific and Technical Cooperation, and 13 months later she attended the second session, which was convened in Peking. Chang was abroad again in December 1953, when she led an 11-member delegation from her ministry to Moscow to inspect the Soviet textile industry.

Miss Chang has represented her native Chekiang Province in the First, Second, and Third NPC's, which opened their inaugural sessions in September 1954, April 1959, and December 1964, respectively. In April 1956 she delivered the opening speech at a national conference of "outstanding workers" in the textile industry. Addressing a conference of superintendents of textile mills in Shanghai in January 1957, she stressed the necessity of raising the quality and quantity of textile products, and in July of that year she emphasized the same theme in a report to the fourth session of the First NPC. Since the last-mentioned occasion, most of her public appearances have been ceremonial in nature. In the fall of 1962, for example, she attended a banquet for the wife of the Indonesian president, and in April 1964 she was present at a banquet for a delegation of women from Albania.

Chang divorced her second husband, Ch'en Ch'ang-hao (q.v.), and in the late 1950's married Su Ching-kuan. Su was a vice-minister of Public Health from 1949 until his death in May 1964. Chang wrote a brief article commemorating him, which appeared in the JMJP of June 23, 1964.

1. *Lieh-shih Hsiang Ching-yü* (Martyr Hsiang Ching-yü; Peking, 1958), pp. 24–25; Wang Yi-chih, "A Great Woman Revolutionary," *China Reconstructs,* 14.3:26 (March 1965).
2. Norman Hanwell, "The Chinese Red Army," *Asia,* 36.5:319 (May 1936).
3. Chang Ch'in-ch'iu, "Women in the Textile Industry," *People's China,* no. 9 (May 1, 1953).

Chang Chin-fu

(Chang Ching-fu). (Chekiang). Science administrator; alternate member, CCP Central Committee.

Chang Chin-fu first came into prominence when Communist troops in east-central China were reorganized immediately after the New Fourth Army Incident in January 1941 (see under Yeh T'ing). Under the reorganization, Ch'en I became the acting commander of the New Fourth Army and veteran military leader Chang Yun-i was named as the deputy commander. Concurrently, Chang Yun-i was placed in command of the Second Division, a unit that operated in the South Huai [River] Military Area, a region that lay in the border districts in southeastern Anhwei and southwestern Kiangsu. Chang Chin-fu served in this division as the deputy director of the Political Department.[1] He probably remained in this region throughout the wars with both the Japanese and the Chinese Nationalists, because when next identified (1949) he was in Hangchow, a city not far from the operational area of the former Second Division.

Hangchow, the capital of Chang's native Chekiang, was captured by the Communists in May 1949. After its capture, he served briefly as a vice-mayor of the city, but by the latter part of the year he had transferred to work under the Chekiang Provincial People's Government. By late 1949 he was heading this government's Staff Office as well as its Industry Office, and early in 1950 he also became a vice-chairman of the Finance and Economics Committee for the province. He relinquished the first two positions in 1951, but in February of that year he was promoted to the chairmanship of the Chekiang Finance and Economics Committee. In the same month he was also elevated to membership on the Chekiang Provincial People's Government Council and appointed as a member of the Finance and Economics Committee of the East China Military and Administrative Committee (ECMAC), the larger regional government for east China. He was promoted to a vice-chairmanship of the regional financial committee in October 1952, after which he relinquished his posts in the Chekiang Government. The vice-chairmanship of the Finance and Economics Committee of the East China Administrative Committee (as the ECMAC was known after December 1952) was apparently Chang's only position from late 1952 until mid-1954 when the ECAC was abolished.

In 1954 Chang was transferred to Peking, where he assumed two new posts. In the national legislative branch, he was elected as a deputy from Anhwei to the First NPC, which brought the constitutional government into existence at its first session in September 1954. Under the reorganized central government, Chang was assigned to a vice-ministership under the new Ministry of Local Industry. Inasmuch as Minister Sha Ch'ien-li (q.v.) is a non-Communist, it is likely that Chang was head of Party affairs during his term with the Ministry. He remained with the Ministry until May 1956, when it was abolished, with part of its activities taken over by the Ministry of Food Industry. Although he relinquished the ministerial portfolio in 1956, he has continued to serve in the NPC. He was re-elected from Anhwei to the Second NPC (1959–1964) and again to the Third NPC, which opened its initial session in December 1964.

Chang's entrance upon a new career as a science administrator in early 1956 was coincidental with the announcement of an ambitious 12-Year Scientific Plan in March 1956. At the same time, the Scientific Planning Commission was established as an organ of the State Council, with Chang as a member and secretary-general. When the Commission was reorganized in May 1957, he relinquished his post as secretary-general to Fan Ch'ang-chiang, another science administrator, but retained his membership in the Commission. In November 1958, during still another reorganization, the Commission was merged with the State Technological Commission to form the Scientific and Technological Commission, headed by veteran Communist Nieh Jung-chen. Temporarily, Chang was dropped from membership on the new organization. Early in 1956, approximately at the same time that he had assumed his new position with the Scientific Planning Commission, he was also made one of the vice-presidents of the Academy of Sciences. Two years later (February 1958), he was further identified as the secretary of the Party Committee within the Academy. He continues to hold the vice-presidency of the Academy and probably also the secretaryship. Two other Party

science administrators in the Academy, P'ei Li-sheng and Tu Jun-sheng (qq.v.), probably share the burdens of Party work within the Academy, although as an alternate member of the Party Central Committee, Chang clearly outranks both P'ei and Tu. Chang Chin-fu gained his seat on the Central Committee in May 1958, when the second session of the Eighth National Party Congress was held in Peking.

Since 1958 Chang has been carrying many responsibilities both in the Academy and in the Party-directed program for scientific development throughout China. He was among a group of government leaders who, in June 1958, presided over and spoke before meetings held in Wuhan to discuss technical problems involved in launching a multi-purpose engineering project on the Yangtze River. Early in June 1958, at a meeting of the second congress of the CCP organization within the Academy of Sciences, principles were approved that had been raised by Chang on the role of the Party in a further "leap forward" in scientific work. Early in September he spoke at meetings of technical institutes in Changchun, Kirin, which were sponsored by the Academy, and on September 27, 1958, he presided over a ceremony in the suburbs of Peking to inaugurate China's first research atomic reactor and cyclotron. In the spring of 1959 he sat on the preparatory committee for a national conference of "advanced workers" to carry out the policy of the Great Leap Forward in the fields of industry, communications, finance, and trade. When the conference was held in October 1959, Chang was among the large group serving on its presidium.

Since April 1959, Chang has represented the China Scientific and Technical Association in the CPPCC. He served as a member of the Third National Committee (1959–1964), as well as on the more influential Standing Committee, and was named to the Fourth National Committee, which held its first session in December 1964–January 1965. At the close of this session, he was once again named to the Standing Committee. In January 1960 he was appointed to the State Council's newly formed Spare-Time Education Committee, and in June of that year served on the presidium (steering committee) of a national conference of "advanced workers" in culture and education. In October 1962 Chang returned to the State Council's Scientific and Technological Commission as a vice-chairman under Chairman Nieh Jung-chen. His position stands out because he is the only one of several vice-chairmen (as of 1965) who is also a senior official in the Academy of Sciences. Prior to 1963, Chang had not played a significant role in international scientific liaison. However, in May–June 1963 he led an Academy of Sciences delegation to North Korea where he signed a plan for the implementation of the Sino-Korean Scientific

Cooperation Agreement during the year 1963. He was again involved with foreign scientists in August 1964 when the Chinese Communists staged the large Peking Scientific Symposium, meetings attended by 367 delegates from 44 countries, the overwhelming majority from Asia, Africa, or Latin America. Chang was the only one of the six deputy heads of the Chinese delegation who is of Party Central Committee stature. (The nominal head of the Chinese delegation, American-trained Chou P'ei-yuan, is not a Communist.) Subsequently, the task of delivering an official report on the symposium before the NPC Standing Committee (September 19, 1964) fell to Chang.

The evidence available on Chang's career as a science administrator suggests that his role centers largely on the management of Party affairs within scientific organizations. There is no evidence that he has any specialized scientific knowledge nor that he participates in any scientific work. These assertions seem to be borne out by the fact that his available writings are almost completely polemical in nature. A revealing example is found in the June 7, 1958, issue of the *JMJP* under the title "Liberate Yourself in Thinking and Implement with Firmness the Party's General Line for Socialist Construction in the Field of Science."

---

1. Koain, *Sohoku kyōsan chiku jitsujō chōsa hōkokusho* (Investigation report on the current situation in the North Kiangsu Communist region; Shanghai, 1941), chart following page 142.

Chang Ching-wu

(1905–   ; Lin-li hsien, Hunan). Former Party official in Tibet; alternate member, CCP Central Committee.

A veteran of the Red Army from the late twenties, Chang Ching-wu was the leading official in Tibet from the 1951 conquest of the region until 1965. Chang was born in 1905, probably in Lin-li hsien in northern Hunan (although some sources use Honan). Little is known of his early background aside from the fact that in 1929 he was a guerrilla fighter in Anhwei.[1] At this time there was a certain amount of Communist direction among bands of peasant guerrillas in Anhwei, one such band in southwest Anhwei having been the focus of CCP activity since 1926. By about 1929 these guerrilla units began to cooperate with similar bands across the borders of Hupeh and Honan. Subsequently, Communist activity in the three provinces was united under the direction of the Oyüwan Soviet. It seems likely that Chang was a participant in this important soviet (see under Chang Kuo-t'ao), in part because he was later closely associated with Hsu Hsiang-ch'ien, the top Oyüwan

military leader. Like most of these men, Chang Ching-wu probably made the Long March, but if in fact he was with the forces of Chang Kuo-t'ao and Hsu Hsiang-ch'ien, then he reached north Shensi in late 1936, almost a year after Mao Tse-tung and his forces had arrived. By 1939 Chang was commander of the PLA's Shantung Column, and two years later he was serving under Hsu Hsiang-ch'ien in Shantung as commander of one of the columns in Hsu's forces. Hsu, the deputy commander of Liu Po-ch'eng's 129th Division, had been sent to Shantung in the spring of 1939 to strengthen the local resistance there.

Chang was called back to Yenan by the late summer of 1942, and from approximately 1943 to early 1946 he was chief-of-staff of the Joint Defense Headquarters. This military command had been formed about 1940 by a merger of Ho Lung's forces in the Shansi-Suiyuan area with those stationed in the Shensi-Kansu-Ninghsia Border Region. Chang was also reported in 1945 as a brigade commander in Ho Lung's 120th Division.

In early 1946 the Peking Executive Headquarters was established in accordance with the agreement worked out by U.S. Special Envoy George C. Marshall between the Nationalists and Communists. Its task was to implement a cease-fire, and in order to bring about a cessation of hostilities in local areas, a number of mobile truce teams were established. Holding the simulated rank of major general, Chang served on one of these teams in Manchuria. But later in 1946 he was assigned to the Peking Headquarters as chief-of-staff to Yeh Chien-ying (q.v.), the chief Communist representative.

Chang was with the forces that captured Sian, capital of Shensi, in late May 1949. He became a member of the Sian Military Control Commission under Ho Lung, as well as commander of the Sian Garrison Headquarters. Later that year he followed Ho Lung to the southwest, serving under him there as deputy chief-of-staff of the Southwest Military Region. Chang was transferred to PLA Headquarters in Peking about mid-1950; he was on the presidium for a national conference of "fighting heroes" in the PLA in September–October 1950 and assumed (by October 1950) the directorship of the People's Armed Forces Department, the department in charge of the militia under the People's Revolutionary Military Council (PRMC). At an October 1950 conference of "people's armed forces" attended by senior military leaders Chu Te and Lo Jung-huan, Chang gave the major report, stressing the importance of the militia, its past history as an integral part of the CCP movement, and the future tasks it faced. Interest in the militia at this time was probably heightened by the Korean War, which had begun in June 1950.

Concurrently with his post as head of the militia, Chang was also identified in January 1951 as director of the Staff Office of the PRMC. But both positions were soon relinquished in favor of a new assignment, one that would occupy virtually his entire time for the next 15 years. In his new task Chang served as one of three delegates under Chief Delegate Li Wei-han (q.v.) to negotiate an agreement for the "peaceful liberation" of Tibet. A delegation from the so-called Tibetan Local Government had arrived in Peking for talks with the Chinese in the spring of 1951 in the wake of the Chinese invasion of Tibet begun in the previous fall. The negotiations lasted from April 29 to May 21, and on May 23, 1951, Chang and the others signed the "Agreement of the Central People's Government and the Local Government of Tibet on Measures for the Peaceful Liberation of Tibet." Chang was subsequently named as the "Representative of the Central People's Government in Tibet"; he set out from Peking on June 30 and two weeks later (traveling via Calcutta) arrived in southern Tibet where he first met the 16-year-old Dalai Lama, the spiritual ruler of the Tibetans. A few weeks later Chang proceeded to Lhasa, the Tibetan capital, arriving there on August 8, a historic date in modern Sino-Tibetan relations. Chang's arrival and his early days in Tibet have been described by the Dalai Lama following his self-exile in India in March 1959.[2] Chang's earliest days in Tibet placed him in the highly uncomfortable position of being the new viceroy without access to immediate military force—his arrival in Lhasa having proceeded by about two months the arrival of PLA forces commanded by Chang Kuo-hua (q.v.), who had been fighting his way westward from China across the incredibly rugged Tibetan terrain. However, by the end of 1951 Chang Ching-wu had approximately 6,000 troops to call upon.[3] With this backing, the Communists immediately set about organizing Tibet with a view to ultimate integration into the mainstream of Communist life. Chang was a major figure in these activities and was thus frequently mentioned in the press in connection with his appearances at meetings with local Tibetan leaders, holidays of various sorts (including both Chinese Communist anniversaries and local Tibetan religious holidays), and the inauguration of institutions brought to Tibet by the conquerors (such as the opening of a branch of the People's Bank of China in Lhasa in February 1952).

The frequency of Chang's appearances in Tibet suggests that he remained there from his arrival in mid-1951 until 1954. He summarized these years in an article for the *JMJP* of May 23, 1954, to mark the third anniversary of the "liberation of Tibet." In 1954 Chang was elected as a deputy from Szechwan to the First NPC. (He was subsequently elected from Szechwan to the Second and Third NPC's, which held their initial sessions in April 1959 and December 1964–January 1965, respectively.) In the late summer of 1954 he accompanied the Dalai Lama (still a teenager) from Lhasa to Peking for the first session of the NPC; this was the first visit a Dalai Lama had made to Peking in nearly half a century.

For reasons that are not clear, Chang did not return to Tibet until a year and a half after the NPC session in September 1954. In the meantime he received new appointments and new honors. As a representative of the CCP, Chang was named to the Second National Committee of the CPPCC in December 1954 and was also elected to the permanent body of the CPPCC, the Standing Committee. (He was re-elected to both committees in April 1959 when the Third CPPCC was formed, but not to the Fourth CPPCC, which opened its first session in late 1964.) Also in December 1954, Chang attended the second national conference of the Sino-Soviet Friendship Association as a PLA representative. In March 1955 he presented before the State Council the most complete report yet available on Tibet,[4] and at the same meeting the decision was taken to set up the Preparatory Committee of the Tibet Autonomous Region, an organization formally established 13 months later (see below).

In July 1955 Chang was appointed chief of the Staff Office of the PRC Chairman (chu-hsi pan-kung-t'ing), that is, head of an administrative office directly under Chairman Mao Tse-tung (and, after April 1959, Chairman Liu Shao-ch'i). Such a post would seem to require Chang's presence in Peking, but in fact he spent most of the next decade in far-off Tibet. Nonetheless, he continues to hold this position. Soon after, in September 1955, he received the three standard military awards, the Orders of August First, Independence and Freedom, and Liberation, which indicates that Chang must have held significant military positions from the late 1920's or early 1930's.

In the spring of 1956 the Communists made a major effort to consolidate their rule in Tibet. This received organizational expression with the formal establishment of the Preparatory Committee of the Tibet Autonomous Region in April 1956. For the inauguration the central government in Peking sent a huge delegation led by Vice-Premier Ch'en I, with Chang serving as one of his eight deputy leaders. Apart from the formal meetings, there was a long series of banquets and other festive gatherings, most of which were attended by Ch'en and Chang. After six weeks in Tibet, Chang accompanied Ch'en back to Peking in June. He was apparently in attendance at the Eighth Party Congress in September 1956, when he was elected the sixth-ranking alternate member of the Central Committee.

Soon after the Congress, Chang was back in Tibet. The Dalai Lama was then preparing to visit India; he described Chang's concern about this visit, coming as it did so soon after the Hungarian Rebellion. "He talked about this so long," the Dalai Lama has written, "that I realized it was the hint of a warning that no other country would be allowed to interfere in Tibet."[5] It was at this time (November 1956) that he was first identified as secretary of the Tibet Work Committee of the CCP (although there is little doubt that he had been the senior Party official in Tibet from his arrival there in 1951). Although Chang's next two years in Tibet appeared to be uneventful, seen in retrospect they were obviously a time of ferment. He was in Peking in March 1959 when armed rebellion against Han Chinese rule broke out among the Tibetans, with their leader, the youthful Dalai Lama, fleeing to India. Chang hurried back to Tibet and remained there until the next spring, when he returned to Peking for a NPC session. Obviously, his assignment was to bring order back to revolt-ridden Tibet. Chang described the Chinese "victory" in Tibet in a *Hung-ch'i* (Red flag) article of March 1, 1960.

Chang's pattern of activity from 1960 to early 1965 was not notably different from that of his previous years. He appears to have spent most of his time in Tibet, but he returned occasionally to Peking for such important affairs as meetings of the NPC. As already noted, he has served from 1954 as a deputy from Szechwan to the NPC; at the first session of the Third NPC (held in December 1964–January 1965) he was named for the first time to membership on the NPC Standing Committee, the organization in charge of NPC affairs when the annual congress meetings are not in session. Chang apparently did not return to Tibet after the NPC meetings, and by the middle of 1965 he had been replaced by Chang Kuo-hua as the ranking secretary there. Chang Ching-wu's new assignment was not immediately revealed, but by May 1966 he was identified as a deputy director of the Party's United Front Work Department. Because one of the major responsibilities of this department is to deal with non-Han minority groups, the selection of Chang was evidently based on his long experience with the Tibetans.

----

1. *Kung-ch'ing-t'uan, wo-te mu-ch'in* (The Communist Youth League, my mother; Peking, 1958), p. 28.
2. The Dalai Lama, *My Land and My People* (New York, 1962), pp. 89–97.
3. *Ibid.,* p. 91.
4. *CB* 332.
5. *My Land and My People,* p. 142.

Chang Chung-liang

(1912–   ; Fu-p'ing hsien, Shensi). Former Party leader in northwest China; alternate member, CCP Central Committee.

Chang Chung-liang has spent most of his career in northwest China where, in the first decade of the PRC, he was the top Party official in Tsinghai and then Kansu. He was born in 1912 in Fu-p'ing hsien, about 30 miles north of Sian, the Shensi capital. (Other sources suggest he was native to Yao-hsien, a few miles northwest of Fu-p'ing.) In 1928, when still in his teens, Chang was active in the peasant movement in his native Shensi, probably in association with Liu Chih-tan (q.v.), the leading Communist in Shensi. Chang reportedly spent a few years in jail in the early thirties, but he was back with the Communists in north Shensi in the mid-1930's when he attended the Anti-Japanese Military and Political Academy (K'ang-ta) in Yenan. During the Sino-Japanese War he was an Eighth Route Army officer in Shensi, and by 1946 he was a deputy commander of the Third Garrison Brigade, a unit subordinate to the Shensi-Kansu-Ninghsia-Shansi-Suiyuan Joint Defense Army. Chang was a military representative in the Third Assembly of the Shensi-Kansu-Ninghsia Border Region Government, which first met in Yenan in April 1946. He remained in the northwest during the civil war and by 1948 was identified as a political commissar in P'eng Te-huai's forces.

In the early years of the PRC, Chang was the top official in Tsinghai Province. Soon after P'eng Te-huai's First Field Army captured Sining in September 1949, Chang became the ranking secretary of the Tsinghai Party Committee. In January 1950, upon the establishment of the Tsinghai Provincial People's Government, he was appointed a vice-governor, and later in the year he added to his roster of key posts in Tsinghai when he became political commissar of the provincial military district. His dominance in the province was further illustrated when he was appointed to head two of the Tsinghai Government's most important organs: the Finance and Economics Committee (August 1950) and the Land Reform Committee (July 1951). From 1950 to 1953 Chang was a member of the Northwest Military and Administrative Committee (NWMAC), the over-all administration for the northwest region. He retained his membership when the Committee was reorganized into the Northwest Administrative Committee in January 1953. Moreover, from March 1950 he also served as a member of the NWMAC's Finance and Economics Committee.

In July 1952 Chang was selected to head a study group organized by Tsinghai cadres to study the *Selected Works of Mao Tse-tung*. Four months later, in November, he became the Tsinghai governor, replacing Chao Shou-shan (q.v.), who was transferred to Shensi. Chang remained in Tsinghai as the top official for two more years.

In mid-1954 Chang was transferred to Kansu. It was just at this time that Ninghsia Province was being incorporated into neighboring Kansu. Chang was present at a Party meeting in Lanchow in early August 1954 that was attended by delegates from Kansu and Ninghsia. At the close of the conference he was named as one of 41 men (being listed first) to form a "new" Kansu Party Committee. He thus replaced Chang Te-sheng (q.v.) as the ranking Party secretary in Kansu, a position that was redesignated as first secretary by November 1956. Chang Chung-liang's new responsibilities placed him in charge of an enlarged province of some 13,000,000 people, of whom one tenth were non-Han Chinese. Also in August 1954, he was elected a deputy from Kansu to the First NPC, and when the Congress held its first session in September 1954 he was appointed a member of the permanent Nationalities Committee of the NPC, presumably because of his experience in the northwest where so many non-Han Chinese live. He was not, however, re-elected to the Second NPC that first met in April 1959. In addition to his role as the senior Party leader in Kansu, Chang was also elected as the chairman of the First and Second Kansu Provincial Committees of the quasi-legislative CPPCC (in February 1955 and December 1959, respectively).

In May 1958, presumably in recognition for his work in the northwest, Chang was elected an alternate member of the Party Central Committee at the Second Session of the Eighth Party Congress. In the same month he took part with Mao Tse-tung and other important leaders in the building of a reservoir near Peking, a demonstration given nationwide press coverage to illustrate the Party's respect for physical labor. In November 1958 he attended the CCP's important Sixth Plenum in Wuhan, the meeting that sharply cut back the more extreme measures connected with the Great Leap Forward. These appearances outside Kansu were rather exceptional for Chang; almost all his time in the middle and late 1950's was spent in Kansu, where he was the top Party official. During these years his activities in Kansu received rather regular coverage in the national press. Chang, in fact, was a contributor to the *JMJP* on at least three occasions during the Great Leap Forward years, writing articles on this subject for the issues of May 17, 1958, October 6, 1958, and September 20, 1960.

Chang made regular appearances in Kansu through November 1960 and then quite suddenly fell from political favor. Within two months a new Kansu first secretary was identified (Wang Feng, q.v.), after which nothing further was heard of Chang for five years. He reappeared in late 1965 in Nanking, identified only as a "responsible" official.

Chang Han-fu

(c.1905–   ; Ch'ang-chou, Kiangsu). Vice-minister of Foreign Affairs; alternate member, CCP Central Committee.

Chang Han-fu is one of Peking's most important diplomats and has served in the Foreign Ministry since the Communist takeover in 1949. He spent most of the war years in Chungking, where he worked as a journalist and aide to Chou En-lai. He has been an alternate member of the Party Central Committee since 1956.

Chang was born about 1905. Since he became known as a writer in the early thirties he has used the name Chang Han-fu, although his original name was Hsieh Chi-tai. He comes from Ch'ang-chou (Wu-chin), which lies on the Grand Canal in Kiangsu between Nanking and Shanghai. Chang studied at Tsinghua University in Peking but apparently did not graduate. According to some reports he went to the United States for graduate work in political science and economics. He is alleged to have been deported from the United States about 1929 for leftist activities, but these accounts conflict with reports that he did not return to China until 1933, after which he served a jail term in the mid-thirties. Still other reports assert that Chang studied in England. Whatever the certainties of his early career, his knowledge of English suggests that he spent some time in either the United States or England.

Upon his return to China, Chang went to Shanghai, where he was associated with a group of leftist intellectuals that included Liu Shih, a member of the National Salvation Association, Li Kung-p'u, who also belonged to the Association, and Ai Szu-ch'i (q.v.), who later became famous as a Communist polemicist and theoretician. All four men wrote for *Tu-shu sheng-huo* (Study life), a magazine that was popular among the younger generation. The dates of Chang's association with this journal are uncertain, but it was probably in the mid-thirties. In 1937 Chang became an editorial committee member of *Chan-hsien* (War front), a Shanghai publication that appeared at five-day intervals and dealt with wartime political and military affairs.[1] Serving on the editorial committee with Chang were Ai Szu-ch'i and Chang Nai-ch'i, the latter then a financial expert and a key member of the National Salvation Association. In addition to Chang Han-fu's editorial work with *Chan-hsien,* he is known to have contributed articles to issues published in 1937.

Chang became a CCP member in 1938. The following year he was in the wartime capital, Chungking, where he was on the staff of the important Communist daily, *Hsin-hua jih-pao* (New China daily). He became editor-in-chief in 1942, remaining so for the next four years. During the early war years he frequently contributed articles on international affairs to the Communist weekly,

Ch'ün-chung (The masses),[2] and in 1939 he and Hsu Ti-hsin (q.v.), an economic expert, published a translation of Engels' writings on capitalism.[3] In the Chungking period Chang began an association that was to serve him well after 1949, when Chou En-lai, the first Communist foreign minister, brought a number of his associates into the Foreign Ministry. It was about 1939 that Chang began working for Chou as a secretary. Chou was in Chungking during the war as the principal Communist representative in the Nationalist capital.

In 1945 Chang went to the United States to attend the founding conference of the United Nations. He was one of two Communist aides to veteran CCP member Tung Pi-wu (q.v.), the only Communist member of the Chinese delegation. Tung and his two aides, Chang and Ch'en Chia-k'ang (q.v.), arrived in New York from Chungking on April 21 and reached San Francisco in time for the conference that opened on April 25. Tung took no active part in the proceedings, although his presence there caused considerable interest, especially on the part of left-wing groups. His press and public relations were handled by his English-speaking secretaries, Chang and Ch'en, and while in San Francisco, Chang himself addressed meetings sponsored by Chinese members of the American Communist Party. At the close of the U.N. meeting Tung and his group toured the United States in the latter half of 1945, visiting New York and its City Council in July.[4] In December 1945 they returned to Chungking, where presumably Chang continued work for a short while with the *Hsin-hua jih-pao*. The paper was closed down by the Nationalists in February 1947, but Chang had left Chungking for Shanghai before that date. On January 15, 1946, after a silence of six years, he contributed an article to *Ch'ün-chung,* then being published in Shanghai.[5] In 1946 he was an editor of the magazine, and after the Nationalists closed down its Shanghai office, he moved to Hong Kong and resumed publishing from there, serving as editor from January 1947 through the year 1948. Other contributors to *Ch'ün-chung* at this time were such well-known Communist publicists as Ch'en Po-ta, Lu Ting-i, and Li Wei-han. At the end of 1948 Chang left Hong Kong for Communist-controlled territory.

After returning to the mainland, Chang left journalism for the field of foreign affairs, a change in which his wartime association with Chou En-lai is likely to have played a part. His first assignments were with the municipal administrations established in Tientsin and Shanghai as the Red armies began to take over the mainland. From January to May 1949 he directed the Alien Affairs Office of the Municipal People's Government in Tientsin, and from the late summer to the fall he was in charge of a similar office in

Shanghai. Then, with the establishment of the central government in Peking in October, Chang was transferred to the capital to serve as a vice-minister in the Foreign Ministry, then presided over by Premier Chou En-lai. When first appointed, Chang was outranked in Party stature by Wang Chia-hsiang and Li K'o-nung (qq.v.), and in the subsequent years other appointments to a vice-ministership were given to men of higher political rank. However, Chang is the only one of the many vice-ministers (as of the mid-1960's) who has served continuously since 1949. In December 1949 he was given the additional assignment of heading the Foreign Ministry's Committee on Foreign Treaties (although this committee was apparently abolished in the early fifties).

Chang's duties within the Ministry of Foreign Affairs (MFA) have been wide ranging, involving him in relations with both Communist and non-Communist nations. He appears to be the administrative head of the MFA, as suggested, for example, in August 1952, when he reported to the Government Administration Council (the cabinet) on "unified measures for entering into treaties, agreements, protocols, and contracts with foreign countries." Similarly, he has frequently spoken before government organizations on treaties signed by the PRC, as in November 1956, when he presented a report on agreements signed with the Nepalese Government. On numerous occasions he has participated in, or led, negotiations with foreign governments, both at home and abroad. One of his more important assignments was in heading the Chinese side in talks with the Indian Government over the status of Tibet, negotiations held in Peking from December 31, 1953, to April 29, 1954. The resulting agreement provided for the withdrawal of all Indian troops in Tibet, in addition to other terms that had the effect of dissolving Indian activities in Tibet. For almost two months in late 1954 Chang led the Chinese side in preliminary talks with Indonesian officials on the difficult problem of settling the dual nationality status of Chinese living in Indonesia. These negotiations were later continued by Peking's ambassador to Indonesia, Huang Chen (q.v.).

As a senior figure in the MFA, Chang has been abroad on several occasions since the Communists came to power in 1949. In April 1955 he was a member of Chou En-lai's delegation to the famous Afro-Asian ("Bandung") Conference in Indonesia. In the period from February to April 1959 he visited India, Iraq, and the United Arab Republic, although the nature of his visit was not disclosed. In April of the following year he accompanied Chou En-lai and Ch'en I (who had by then replaced Chou as foreign minister) to Burma, India, and Nepal to hold discussions concerning border questions. After returning briefly to south China, the group then made brief visits to Cambodia and North Vietnam. Chang's most difficult assignment abroad took place in 1961–1962 when he was the ranking deputy under Ch'en I at the Conference on Laos held in Geneva. The Chinese group arrived in Geneva in May 1961. Ch'en I was present for the early stages of the negotiations, but he left for home in early July, leaving Chang in charge. Chang spent most of the next year in Geneva, during which time he made a number of speeches before the Conference. Twice, during periods of adjournment, he returned to Peking. Still serving as acting head of the Chinese delegation, Chang was present in Geneva for the final negotiations in July 1962, although delegation leader Ch'en I arrived in time to sign the agreement for the PRC on July 21. Chang's work in Geneva brought him into regular contact with the large American delegation led by Averell Harriman.

Chang was abroad twice in 1964, the first time in October–November, when he accompanied Ch'en I to Algeria to attend celebrations marking the 10th anniversary of the Algerian Revolution. While in Algiers he took part in talks with Algerian President Ben Bella. En route to Algeria Ch'en and Chang stopped over briefly in Karachi, where they conferred with Pakistani Foreign Minister Bhutto on questions of common interest —talks held at a time when Sino-Pakistani relations were growing increasingly close. A few days after returning to China, Ch'en and Chang were sent abroad again, this time to Cambodia to take part in celebrations commemorating the 11th anniversary of Cambodian independence. In April 1965 Chang accompanied Chou En-lai to Indonesia for the 10th anniversary celebrations of the Bandung Conference, and in June 1965 he was again with Chou when the latter led a Chinese delegation to Pakistan and Tanzania, where talks were held concerning the convocation of a second Afro-Asian conference.

Chang has devoted most of his time to the Foreign Ministry, but he has also held other posts of varying importance. He received the first of these in December 1949 when the Chinese People's Institute of Foreign Affairs (CPIFA) was established. The CPIFA was formed to deal with nations not having diplomatic relations with the PRC, and since it was set up Chang has served as a member of its Board of Directors. He has also served since March 1950 on the Board of the Bank of China, the financial institution in charge of overseas banking. He was a deputy from Kiangsu to the First NPC (1954–1959), and although he did not serve in the Second Congress, he was elected from Honan to the Third NPC that opened in December 1964. Chang was also named to membership on the State Council's Commission for Cultural Relations with Foreign Countries soon

after the Commission was established in February 1958. Most important, however, was his election to alternate membership on the Party Central Committee at the Eighth National Congress held in September 1956.

Chang married Kung P'u-sheng in July 1949, and through his wife is related to Ch'iao Kuanhua (q.v.) the husband of his wife's sister, Kung P'eng, an assistant minister in the Foreign Ministry since 1964. The Kung sisters were well known in Christian and Y.W.C.A. circles in Shanghai during the 1930's, and Kung P'u-sheng was also known to Western diplomats and journalists in Chungking during World War II. She was born to a Christian family in Shanghai in September 1913. Her father was a former officer in the Nationalist army. Educated at St. Mary's Episcopal School in Shanghai, Kung received her B.A. in English from Yenching University in 1936 and an M.A. in religion from Columbia University in 1942. In the late 1930's she was a Y.W.C.A. student secretary in Shanghai. She returned to the U.S. in 1945, working in a research section of the U.N. Human Rights Commission from 1946 to 1948. When she went back to China, she immediately became active in the Communist mass organization, the All-China Federation of Democratic Women. As soon as the Foreign Ministry was created in 1949, she became deputy director of the International Organization and Conference Department and remained deputy director until 1958 when she became the director. She has made a number of trips abroad, the most notable being in 1950 when she went to the U.N. with the Communist Chinese group led by Wu Hsiu-ch'üan that was in New York from November to December to bring the Formosa question before the Security Council. In 1961 she accompanied her husband to Geneva for the Conference on Laos as an adviser to the Chinese delegation. The Changs are unusual among the Chinese Communist elite: a husband-and-wife team, both of them prominent and both prominent in the same field. In combination with Kung's sister and her husband, another husband-and-wife team in the foreign office, the families are unique, all four being of considerable prominence and all four in the same field. The family no doubt owes its position to its connections with Chou En-lai, who has put a number of his close associates in the Foreign Ministry. Chang and his wife both speak fluent English, again a rarity among today's elite. They have at least one son and one daughter. Chang has been described by a diplomat who negotiated with him regularly in the mid-fifties as being intelligent, but not very agreeable.

1. Chün-tu Hsüeh, *The Chinese Communist Movement, 1937–1949* (Stanford, Calif., 1962), p. 45.

2. *Ibid.,* p. 6.

3. Chang Ching-lu, ed., *Chung-kuo ch'u-pan shih liao pu-pien* (Supplementary historical materials on Chinese publishing; Peking, 1957), p. 449.

4. Howard L. Boorman, "Tung Pi-wu: A Political Profile," *The China Quarterly,* no. 19:76 (July–September 1964).

5. Chün-tu Hsüeh, p. 6.

Chang Hao, *see* **Lin Yü-ying.**

Chang Hsi

(1912–1959; P'ing-hsiang, Hopeh). Administrator; alternate member, CCP Central Committee.

The only information concerning Chang's career before 1949 comes from his obituary. He was born in 1912 in P'ing-hsiang, a small town in southern Hopeh about 20 miles east of Hsing-t'ai on the Peking-Hankow Railway. It is claimed that he was influenced by the patriotic activity that was so prevalent among the Chinese youths in the late 1920's. In 1931, when he was 19, he joined the Communist Youth Corps presumably at the Hsing-t'ai Fourth Normal School where "he first participated in revolutionary activity." While a student at this school, he served as secretary of the Youth Corps chapter there. In 1932 he was arrested and imprisoned until 1936. During his imprisonment it was said that he "did not abandon the struggle against the enemy" and "displayed the high standards" of a Communist. As the official obituary gives the year 1934 as the date that Chang joined the CCP, he was apparently admitted while in prison.

Though only a bare outline is available of Chang's post-imprisonment career, it is sufficient to establish the fact that he was one of the more important Communists in the Hopeh-Shantung-Honan area during and after the Sino-Japanese War. His official positions listed in the obituary for this period (but without dates) are as follows: Secretary of the Hopeh-Shantung-Honan Special Party Committee; Secretary of the Hopeh-Honan District Party Committee; Secretary of the T'ai-nan (presumably "south of the T'ai-hang Mountains") District Party Committee; Secretary of the Hopeh-Shantung-Honan District Party Committee; Secretary of the West Honan District Party Committee and concurrently political commissar for the West Honan Military District.

Three of the most important Communists in these areas during the war years were Yang Te-chih, Yang Yung, and Su Chen-hua (qq.v.), each of whom was a member of Chang's funeral committee when he died in 1959. A broad outline of the military and political activities in the Hopeh-Shantung-Honan area can be found in the biographies of these three men, who led forces

of the Eighth Route Army's 115th and 129th Divisions into this strategic area in 1938–1939 and who remained there throughout the war. Chang's obituary states that during these years, under the leadership of the Party center, he "activated the masses" and contributed to the guerrilla warfare effort behind the Japanese lines.

In 1949 Chang became the ranking Party secretary in Honan, a post he retained until mid-1952, presumably being replaced by P'an Fu-sheng (q.v.), who took over in Honan by early 1953. During these same years he also served as a member of the Central Committee's Central-South Bureau, headed by Party and military veteran Lin Piao. The governmental counterpart of the Central-South Bureau was established in February 1950 under the name Central-South Military and Administrative Committee. Chang was named to membership on this Committee; in July of 1950 he was also appointed as a member of the Honan Provincial Government and in December of the same year he was named chairman of that Government's Finance and Economic Committee. Finally, in terms of official positions, he was serving as the political commissar of the Honan Military District in August 1952. One of the few clues to his major work in the early 1950's comes from his obituary, which states that in these years he was engaged in "advancing the land reform and agricultural cooperatives movements."

In November 1952, on the eve of the First Five-Year Plan (1953–1957), the State Planning Commission was created in Peking. It was headed by the ill-fated Kao Kang (q.v.), destined to be purged in 1955, and included some of the most eminent political figures in the regime, men such as Ch'en Yun, Lin Piao, Teng Hsiao-p'ing, and Li Fu-ch'un. Chang was appointed as one of the 15 original members of the Commission and remained with the organization until his death six years later. As a consequence of this transfer, he was removed from his posts in central China. In the fall of 1954, when the central government was undergoing a major reorganization, Chang was elevated to a vice-chairmanship on the Planning Commission, serving now under Chairman Li Fu-ch'un. In December 1954 he was named as a CCP representative to the Second National Committee of the quasi-legislative CPPCC, another post he held until his death. He was mentioned in the national press rather regularly in 1955; in February of that year he gave a major report on the First Five-Year Plan before a meeting of the New Democratic Youth League, and in April 1955 he presented an official report to the State Council on the Second National Provincial and Municipal Planning Conference. He reached the apex of his career in September 1956 when he was elected an alternate member of the Central Committee at the Eighth National Party Congress. From that time, however, he may have been in poor health, for his activities received little attention in the press. He died of cancer at age 47 in Peking on January 8, 1959. His death was prominently featured in the press and his funeral committee, headed by State Planning Commission Chairman Li Fu-ch'un, included most of the top economic officials in the regime. The final tribute in his obituary stated that he had made major contributions to the establishment and development of economic planning in China.

Chang Hsi-jo

(c.1889–   ; Ch'ao-i, Shensi). Non-Party intellectual; president, Chinese People's Institute of Foreign Affairs; chairman, Commission for Cultural Relations with Foreign Countries, State Council.

Chang Hsi-jo is one of the leading non-Party intellectuals in Communist China. Educated as a political scientist in both the United States and England, he has devoted most of his time while serving in the PRC to the fields of education and international cultural liaison.

Chang was born about 1889 in eastern Shensi in the small town of Ch'ao-i, a few miles from the Yellow River. Nothing is known of his early life and education, but when he was 19 (about 1908) he joined Sun Yat-sen's T'ung-meng hui and participated in the 1911 Revolution against the Manchus.[1] When the T'ung-meng hui was reorganized into the KMT in 1912, Chang became a member of the KMT's Shensi branch; however, he dropped his membership a year later when he left for the United States to further his education. He did graduate work at both Columbia University and the London School of Economics. During his days in England he studied under Harold Laski, the famed intellectual of the British left-wing. Chang is said to have studied the writings of Jean Bodin, a French political writer of the 16th century.[2] Japanese sources claim that he also attended universities in Berlin and Paris; in any case, he is known to have toured Europe,[3] presumably in his student days. As a result of his education abroad, Chang is fluent in English and competent in French.[4]

Following his return to China he taught political science at the Peking College of Law and Politics and at China University, also in Peking. These two professorships were a prelude to a long teaching career in the major universities of China that lasted into the early days of the Communist regime. He did most of his teaching at Peking's Tsinghua University. Although Chang was not affiliated with the Nationalist government for long, he did serve in 1927–1928 as head of the Department of Higher Education, and from 1942 to 1947 he was officially a member of the Third and Fourth Nationalist-sponsored Peo-

ple's Political Councils, although he did not attend the sessions after 1942, reportedly because he believed them to be too partisan. Chang's disillusionment with the KMT became apparent during the war years. He spent these years in Kunming, where Tsinghua, Peking, and Nankai Universities had been merged as a wartime measure into the National Southwest Associated University. During these years in Kunming (where he headed the university's Political Science Department), Chang was a leader in liberal circles and, as such, was an outspoken critic of Chiang Kai-shek's government. After the war he returned to Peking where he headed Tsinghua's Political Science Department and also continued his criticism of the KMT as well as the policy of the American government to aid Chiang.

When the Communists took power in Peking in January 1949 Chang was still holding the chairmanship of the Political Science Department at Tsinghua University, although by the fall of that year he was reported to be teaching in the Social Sciences Department at Peking University.[5] His first assignment under the Communists was as a delegate to the Communist-front World Peace Congress held in Prague in April 1949. In the following month he was named as a vice-chairman of the Committee for Higher Education under the North China People's Government (NCPG), an assignment that lasted until the NCPG was absorbed by the central government in the fall of 1949 when the PRC was officially established.

Throughout the summer of 1949, the Communists undertook detailed preparations to form the central government as well as a number of professional and "people's" organizations. Chang played a role in these activities; for example, in July 1949 he attended a large conference of social scientists. One of the results of this conference was the formation (in September) of a preparatory committee for the China New Political Science Research Association, with Chang as one of the vice-chairmen. (However, when the organization was permanently established in 1953, Chang did not receive any post.) It was also in mid-1949 that he took part in the preparatory work for the establishment of the Sino-Soviet Friendship Association (SSFA), and when the association was formally inaugurated in October 1949, he became a member of its executive board, a position he continues to hold.

It was also in the summer of 1949 that Chang took part in the preliminary work of the CPPCC, the organization that formally brought the PRC into existence in the fall. As was befitting his role as a well-known and respected professor, Chang attended the First CPPCC (September 1949) as a representative of "non-partisan democratic personages," a category that included such famed intellectuals as Kuo Mo-jo and economist Ma Yin-ch'u. He served on the Presidium (steering committee) for the September sessions and at the close of the meetings was named to the Standing Committee of the CPPCC; when the Second, Third, and Fourth CPPCC's were formed in 1954, 1959, and 1965, he was reappointed to the Standing Committee, the governing body when the National Committee is not in session. More important, however, was his membership on the Central People's Government Council (CPGC), the supreme organ of governmental authority in the PRC until 1954; the CPGC was headed by Mao Tse-tung and invested with broad legislative, executive, and judicial functions. Utilizing his background as a prominent political scientist, the Communists also appointed Chang to a vice-chairmanship of the Political and Legal Affairs Committee of the Government Administration Council (the cabinet), of which Chou En-lai was the premier. In the same month that the government was formed he was also named to the Standing Committee of the China Peace Committee, another position he continues to hold. Two months later (Decemer 1949), the Chinese People's Institute of Foreign Affairs was established under the presidency of Chang. The purpose of this institute is to promote a wider understanding of foreign affairs and to engage in research. In fact, it has been most frequently used as a semi-official organ of government, through which the PRC has maintained wide contacts abroad. Its status as a semi-official body is well-illustrated by the fact that Chou En-lai serves as the honorary chairman. Of the many posts that Chang holds, this is probably the one to which he devotes most of his time. It has kept him constantly in the news, particularly when foreign visitors are in Peking.

In his capacity as the chairman of the Chinese People's Institute of Foreign Affairs Chang was one of the Chinese leaders who, in the spring of 1952, sent an invitation to "leaders of the peace movement" in Asia proposing the convocation of a conference held in October 1952 under the title of the Asian and Pacific Regions Peace Conference. Chang attended the conference as an official Chinese delegate; the theme of the conference coincided with one of Peking's major propaganda campaigns in 1952, namely, the alleged waging by the United States of bacteriological warfare in the Korean War.

During a governmental reorganization in November 1952, some of the functions of the Ministry of Education were placed under a new Ministry of Higher Education. Chang was named at this time as minister of Education, but when the ministries were merged in February 1958, he relinquished his position. In 1953, in preparation for the elections to the First NPC, he was named to the Committee for Drafting the Election Law. When the elections were held the following year he was elected as a deputy from Peking to the

First NPC and was subsequently re-elected to the Second and Third NPC's, which opened in April 1959 and in December 1964. In May 1954 he was named to the Standing Committee of the Chinese People's Association for Cultural Relations with Foreign Countries, another position that he still retains. Four years later (February 1958), at the same time that he relinquished the ministership of Education, the Communists formed the Commission for Cultural Relations with Foreign Countries under the State Council. In broad terms, the "people's" association deals principally with countries not having diplomatic relations with Communist China, whereas the Commission works mainly with nations that do have diplomatic ties with Peking. Aside from his major post in the Institute of Foreign Affairs, Chang devotes most of his time to work of the Commission. For example, in the period from 1958 through 1964 he negotiated and signed 14 cultural cooperation agreements or protocols with 13 different nations. Although he has been the chairman of the Commission since its establishment in 1958, two former employees of the Commission claim that the real authority is vested in two senior Party members who are nominally subordinate to Chang, Commission Vice-chairmen Chang Chih-hsiang and Ch'en Chung-ching (qq.v.).[6]

Unlike some of his fellow non-CCP intellectuals, Chang seems to have avoided political difficulties, even though he proved to be a sharp critic of the Party during the "hundred flowers" period in the spring of 1957. Speaking on May 13 at a forum called by the Party's United Front Work Department, Chang charged that the CCP had been guilty of subjectivism, bureaucratism, sectarianism, and doctrinairism; he bluntly stated that many Party members had a very "low level" of knowledge and that many of them acted as though they were the "first people on earth" because they had won the revolution. Two days later he continued his criticisms of the Party, maintaining that it had been guilty of four "deviations": (1) a proclivity for bigness and a fondness for achievement; (2) undue haste for results; (3) contempt for the past; and (4) a blind belief in the future. Although many other non-Party personalities lived to regret similar criticisms, Chang was apparently never held to task for these sharp comments.

A fine vignette of Chang has been drawn by Edgar Faure, the former French premier who visited China in 1956. Faure was clearly impressed by Chang, whom he described as a "cultivated and discreet" man with a "fine wit." "His very appearance, his dress and his manners show him to be a statesman in the western sense." Well aware that Chang was not a Party member, Faure described him as "far from being a puppet personality chosen for reasons of window-dressing from the gallery of complaisant fellow-travellers of the old regime." Faure also visited Chang's private residence in Peking, where he found that everything was "discreet luxury and order."[7]

1. Edgar Faure, *The Serpent and the Tortoise* (New York, 1958), p. 4.
2. *Ibid.*
3. *Ibid.*, p. 5.
4. *Ibid.*, p. 4.
5. Maria Yen, *The Umbrella Garden* (Hong Kong, 1957), p. 169.
6. Interview with former Commission staff members, Hong Kong, May 1964, and Cambridge, Mass., June 1965.
7. Edgar Faure, *The Serpent and the Tortoise*, pp. 4–5.

Chang Hsiu-chu

Labor leader; deputy director, Agriculture and Forestry Office, State Council.

Nothing is known of the early career of Chang Hsiu-chu, but by the early 1950's he was a labor official of some prominence. He was first identified in early 1951, as a deputy director of the Education and Culture Department of the All-China Federation of Labor (ACFL). At the important Seventh Trade Union Congress in May 1953, Chang served as a deputy secretary-general of the congress and at the close of the sessions was chosen for membership on the Executive Committee of the All-China Federation of Trade Unions (ACFTU), the new name for the ACFL. Two years later (August 1955), he was elevated to membership on both the ACFTU Presidium and Secretariat, the two organs charged with managing the work of the Federation when the Executive Committee is not in session. Concurrently with these posts, he also served from 1953 to 1956 as the head of the ACFTU Propaganda Department. On the eve of the Eighth Trade Union Congress, Chang wrote an article entitled "Trade unions are an important force in socialist revolution and socialist construction," which appeared in the *JMJP* of November 30, 1957. Two days later the Eighth Congress opened, with Chang serving as a member of the Congress Presidium (steering committee). At the close of the meetings, he was re-elected to membership on the ACFTU Executive Committee, Presidium, and Secretariat.

As Chang advanced in rank within the Trade Union Federation, he was called upon to represent it within other organizations or to attend conferences requiring the presence of labor leaders. For example, he was named as a representative of the ACFTU to the Second National Committee of the CPPCC in December 1954, and when the Third National Committee was formed (1959–1964), he again served as an ACFTU delegate. Also in December 1954 he represented the labor organization at the Second National Conference of the Sino-Soviet Friendship Association.

From March 1956 to April 1959, Chang served as a member of the Study (hsueh-hsi) Committee of the CPPCC National Committee, a committee responsible for stimulating the study of Party doctrines through the holding of special meetings and short-term courses; presumably Chang's assignment was to promote such activities within the trade union organization. Later in 1956 he was given a somewhat similar task in another field when he was named as a vice-chairman of the newly formed preparatory committee charged with "disseminating scientific and technical information" to workers. In addition to these positions, from the mid-1950's Chang was a frequent participant in national conferences of "advanced" workers. To cite two random but typical examples, he served as a deputy secretary-general both for a conference of industrial and communications workers in October 1959 and for another of cultural and educational workers in June 1960. He also lent his name to various special committees as, for example, the Preparatory Committee for Commemorating the 40th Anniversary of the May Fourth Movement, an *ad hoc* group set up in April 1959.

Chang's work, particularly in the labor movement, took him abroad on seven occasions between 1952 and 1961. A brief summary follows:

1952 Member of a delegation to "comfort" Chinese troops in North Korea, October.

1955 Member of an ACFTU delegation led by Liu Ning-i to Yugoslavia, September–October.

1957 Chief of a trade union delegation to East Germany for May Day.

1958 Attended the Fourth Congress of Polish Trade Unions, April.

1959 Member of a delegation led by Liu Ch'ang-sheng to the 12th Congress of the "All-Soviet Union of Trade Unions," March.

1960 Chief of a trade union delegation to Indonesia to attend the Third National Congress of the Indonesian Central Organizations of Trade Unions, August–September.

1961 Chief of an ACFTU delegation to Moscow to attend May Day celebrations, April–May.

Until 1959, Chang's assignments were almost exclusively concerned with labor activities. From that time, however, he began to widen his field of activities. In 1959–1960 he received two assignments in organizations subordinate to the State Council: he was named a member of the Physical Culture and Sports Commission in September 1959 and a member of the Spare-time Education Committee in January 1960. Then in August 1960 he was named a member of the National Committee of the All-China

Federation of Literary and Art Circles at the close of the Third Congress of this organization. In late 1962 Chang's career came to an abrupt turning point. In November 1962 he was named as a deputy director of the State Council's Agriculture and Forestry Office, a highly important office headed by Politburo member T'an Chen-lin and charged with supervising and coordinating the work of several ministries. One month later, because he had been "transferred in his work," Chang was removed as one of the secretaries of the ACFTU Secretariat, the critically important organ that runs the ACFTU on a day-to-day basis. Thus, though he retains his membership on the ACFTU Executive Committee and Presidium, it is clear that Chang's days as a top labor leader are behind him.

As already noted, during the period from 1954 to 1964, Chang served on the National Committee of the CPPCC as a representative of the Federation of Trade Unions. By the time the Fourth Committee was organized in late 1964, however, he had changed to new work and hence was selected for membership on the National Committee as a representative of the "peasants." And, when the committee met for its first session in December 1964–January 1965, Chang served as a member of the presidium (steering committee).

Chang Kuo-chien

(1912–1962; Fukien). Veteran Party official; vice-chairman, State Economic Commission.

Chang Kuo-chien was a Red Army veteran and a senior official in the Communists' security-intelligence apparatus. In the period after the late 1940's he concentrated on the fields of transportation and communications, and at the time of his death in 1962 he was a vice-chairman of the State Economic Commission.

Chang was born in 1912. According to his obituary, the major source of information on Chang's career before 1949, he was a native of Fukien who was reared in a family of overseas Chinese tobacco factory workers in Java. (Considering the Chinese use of the term "native," he may well have been born in Indonesia.) He began his revolutionary career upon returning to China in 1925 when he was 13. Two years later he joined the CCP. At some time in these years he attended a university.

Chang's obituary lists his major posts, and although no dates are given many of them can be surmised from the history of the period. His first known post, presumably in the early thirties, was as secretary of the Shanghai-Woosung District Party Committee. Afterwards, he advanced to the provincial Party apparatus governing Shanghai, becoming executive officer (kan-shih) of the Organization Department of the Kiangsu Provincial Committee. He was then transferred to the Communist rural base area in the Kiangsi-

Fukien borderlands where he became secretary-general of the Fukien CCP Committee. Later he was made director of the National Defense Bureau (Kuo-chia pao-wei chü) in Juichin, Kiangsi. In the latter post it seems probable that he was associated with Teng Fa (q.v.), a key figure in Party intelligence and security operations.

Chang's obituary stated that he had been "captured by the enemy on three occasions." The course of his career suggests that these episodes occurred in the late twenties or early thirties, when large numbers of Communists were arrested by the Nationalist police in Shanghai.

Chang continued in the Defense Bureau post during the Long March that began in 1934 from Kiangsi. During the latter stages of the March, or perhaps after arriving in north Shensi, he was a member of the 30th Red Army, serving as head of the Organization Department's Political Section and concurrently as director of the Defense Department. The 30th Army was part of Hsu Shiang-ch'ien's (q.v.) Fourth Front Army, which separated from Mao Tse-tung's forces during the Long March and did not reach Shensi until the latter part of 1936 or early 1937. After war with Japan began in mid-1937, Chang was less directly involved in military affairs, for during the early war years he was associated with two of the more important cadre training institutes. He served as director of the Political Departments of both the North Shensi (Shen-pei) Public School and the North China Associated (Hua-pei lien-ho) University. The former was established in Yenan in November 1937, and the latter was set up behind enemy lines in the Shansi-Chahar-Hopeh (Chin-Ch'a-Chi) Border Region in 1939, drawing some of its staff from the North Shensi Public School. The duration of Chang's work with the North China Associated University is not known, but by the latter stages of the war and in the postwar period he was in Hopeh. At some time during this period he served successively as head of the Social Affairs Department (intelligence and security) of the Central Hopeh Party Committee, and as deputy secretary and concurrently director of the Social Affairs Department of the Kalgan (Chang-chia-k'ou) Municipal Committee. This important city in north Hopeh (then Chahar) was held by the Communists until October 1946 and retaken in December 1948. He also served as deputy secretary and head of the Social Affairs Department for the Shansi-Chahar-Hopeh Party Bureau. To this point in his career Chang had worked principally in military or security assignments, but his obituary reveals that in the Shansi-Chahar-Hopeh Party Bureau he was also deputy director of the Finance Committee's Staff Office. This was the first of a number of posts in the economic sector that Chang held in the ensuing years.

As the Communists began to consolidate their

position in north China in late 1940's, they established the North China People's Government (NCPG), which, in essence, was a merger of the Shansi-Chahar-Hopeh and the Shansi-Hopeh-Shantung-Honan Border Regions. Under the NCPG, which existed from August 1948 to October 1949, Chang headed the Business Section of the Communications Department. When the national government was established in October 1949, he was named as director of the Communications Section of the Central Financial and Economic Planning Bureau headed by Sung Shao-wen (q.v.), who had probably been a colleague of Chang's from their days in Hopeh. Chang's Communications Section was expanded in June 1950 to become the Communications and Transport Planning Section. During this same period he received two other posts involving communications. In December 1949 he was named to the eight-member Board of Directors of the Central Air Transport Company and in August 1951 he was appointed to a special committee charged with supervising the reconstruction of T'ang-ku, the port city for Tientsin.

With the advent of the constitutional government in the fall of 1954, Chang was made a deputy director of the Sixth Staff Office of the State Council (October), an office that coordinated the work of government organs concerned with transportation and communications. He held this post until the Staff Offices were reorganized in September 1959, at which time he was transferred to a vice-chairmanship in the important State Economic Commission. When the Scientific Planning Commission (also under the State Council) was established in March 1956, Chang was named a deputy secretary-general; he remained in this post until a reorganization of May 1957, after which he was simply a Commission member, retaining this position until still another reorganization in November 1958.

After 35 years as a Communist Party member Chang died from illness in Peking on July 21, 1962, at the age of 50. At the time of his death his principal post was a vice-chairmanship on the State Economic Commission. His few public appearances in the years immediately before his death suggest his health had been failing for some time. Chang's funeral committee was headed by the chairman of the State Economic Commission, Po I-po.

Chang Kuo-hua

(Kiangsi). Commander, Tibet Military Region; first secretary, Tibet Autonomous Region CCP Committee.

A veteran PLA officer, Chang Kuo-hua commanded the Communist troops that conquered Tibet in 1950–1951. He has remained in Tibet since that time, serving as the top military official

there. He was the second most important Communist leader in Tibet until 1965 when he succeeded First Secretary Chang Ching-wu, thus being placed in command of both the military district and the Party committee.

No specific facts are available about Chang's career before the Sino-Japanese War. However, it is possible to deduce some information from the fact that in 1955 (see below) he received a second class Order of August First. This military award was given to Red Army veterans who were active from the birth of the Red Army in 1927 until the outbreak of the Sino-Japanese War a decade later; moreover, the second class order signifies service as an officer at either the regimental or battalion level. It seems probable, therefore, that Chang joined the Red Army in his native Kiangsi and then made the Long March with the forces led by Chu Te and Mao Tse-tung.

The supposition that Chang was a Long Marcher seems all the more probable from the first account of his activities in Sino-Japanese War times when he was serving as the political commissar of the Fourth Training Brigade of the 115th Division of the Communists' Eighth Route Army. The command was a significant one, for a brigade is the major subordinate element of a division. The 115th Division, under the command of Lin Piao, was largely made up from troops that had formerly belonged to the First Front Army, the well-known force that Chu Te and Mao Tse-tung had brought from Kiangsi to northwest China on the Long March. Chang was identified with the training brigade at some time prior to 1944, but by that year he had transferred to the staff of the 129th Division of Liu Po-ch'eng and was serving in the Hopeh-Shantung-Honan Military Region in the dual capacity of secretary of a district Party committee and political commissar of a military district, that was in turn a part of the three-province border area military base. The Hopeh-Shantung-Honan Military Region belonged to the larger Shansi-Hopeh-Shantung-Honan (Chin-Chi-Lu-Yü) Border Region (see under Liu Po-ch'eng and Yang Hsiu-feng), which gave the Red armies the necessary line of communications between the Communist capital at Yenan and the military operations in coastal Shantung Province. Important Party members also operating at Chang's military base area at the same time were Yang Te-chih, Yang Yung, and Su Chen-hua (qq.v.), high-ranking officers on Liu Po-ch'eng's staff. Liu's 129th Division was responsible for military control of the Chin-Chi-Lu-Yü Region.

Two years after hostilities with the Japanese ceased (1947), Chang had risen to be the commander of the Kiangsu-Anhwei-Honan Military Region, which was occupied then by Liu's army as one of the two Communist forces that were capturing the territory from the Nationalists. The Communist victory in January 1949 at Suchow

(Hsu-chou), Kiangsu, was one of the turning points in the civil war with the Nationalists. From January 1949 Liu's army, then named the Second Field Army, played a major role in the conquest of the Mainland, expanding west into Szechwan, and eventually ending its campaigns with the conquest of Tibet. Chang, who spent almost a decade on Liu's staff, was briefly identified at an uncertain date as the commander of the 18th Corps of the Second Field Army, the military unit responsible for the takeover of Ch'eng-tu, the Szechwan capital (December 1949). However, Chang's command of the 18th Corps must have occurred briefly in 1950 sometime after the takeover. Possibly he succeeded Chou Shih-ti (q.v.), who was commander of the corps at the time of the takeover.

Early in 1950, when most of the southwest was already under Communist control, Chang began to participate in the plans for the conquest of Tibet. In what is probably the most extensive account of the invasion of Tibet, Chang has written that the over-all planning was directed by Liu Po-ch'eng, Ho Lung, and Teng Hsiao-p'ing, the Communists' top officials in the southwest in the early days of the PRC.[1] More specifically, he stated that Ho Lung "personally planned and made preparations for the expedition" into Tibet. Thus, in the spring of 1950, Chang marched westward from Szechwan on the difficult route to Lhasa, the Tibetan capital. By October his forces had captured Chamdo (Ch'ang-tu), the capital of the Chamdo area of Sikang Province. Following this defeat of the badly organized and ill-equipped local Tibetan forces, the Tibetans, in effect, sued for peace by agreeing to send a negotiating team to Peking. Chang returned to Peking himself, and on May 23, 1951, he was one of the signers of the "Agreement on Measures for the Peaceful Liberation of Tibet." The other negotiators for the Chinese side were chief delegate Li Wei-han, then head of the Party's United Front Work Department, Chang Ching-wu, who was to become the top Party official in Tibet, and Liao Chih-kao (qq.v.), then the Communists top official in Sikang, the province closest to Tibet.

While Chang had been leading his forces into Chamdo in the summer of 1950 he had been named to membership on the Southwest Military and Administrative Committee (SWMAC), formed in July 1950 under the chairmanship of Liu Po-ch'eng. Although the SWMAC did not officially control Tibet, it is evident that it maintained close links with Tibet and provided the logistic support that was necessary to garrison Communist forces there. When the SWMAC was reorganized into the Southwest Administrative Committee in February 1953, Chang was reappointed to membership, holding the post until the dissolution of the regional governments in 1954. After he had taken part

in the 1951 negotiations described above, Chang returned to the command of his troops in the Chamdo area and, in July 1951, began to move west again. The ensuing difficulties his troops encountered were due more to the extraordinarily difficult terrain than to organized resistance by the Tibetans. Finally, in October, his forces reached Lhasa, only a short time after the arrival of Chang Ching-wu, the official representative of the PRC in Tibet, who had gone to Lhasa via India.

The processes of consolidating Communist rule in Tibet are described in the biography of Chang Ching-wu, the top Communist official there from his arrival in 1951 until his transfer in 1965. Chang Kuo-hua was clearly the number two man until 1965, and his principal duties were in the military establishment—a role of special significance in view of the fact that Communist rule in Tibet has been essentially a military occupation. One of the initial steps taken by the Chinese was the formation of the Tibet Military District in February 1952 under the command of Chang Kuo-hua, who continues to hold the position. By the following year he was also secretary of the Military District's CCP Committee, a post he held to about 1955. Although Chang's prime responsibilities have been in Tibet, from time to time he has returned to Peking and has been given various posts in the national government. He has been a deputy from Tibet to the First, Second, and Third NPC's, which held their initial sessions in September 1954, April 1959, and December 1964–January 1965, respectively, and for the NPC sessions held in 1955 and 1958 he served on the presidium (steering committee). Chang has also been a member of the PRC National Defense Council since its formation in September 1954, and when military awards were first given in 1955, he received first class Orders of Independence and Freedom and of Liberation, and, as already noted, a second class Order of August First. These three awards cover military service from 1927 to 1950. At this same time he was also made a PLA lieutenant-general, the equivalent of a two-star general in the U.S. Army. Since December 1957 he has also been a member of the Eighth Executive Committee of the All-China Federation of Trade Unions, although nothing in his background seems to have been connected with the labor field. Chang's most important trip back to China took place in September 1956, when he spoke before the Party's Eighth National Congress on conditions in Tibet.

In March 1955 the PRC initiated the first steps toward the establishment of a government structure in Tibet when the State Council formed the Preparatory Committee for the Tibet Autonomous Region. To give the appearance of self-rule among the Tibetans, the Dalai Lama and the Panchen Lama were appointed as chairman and first vice-chairman, respectively, of the Preparatory Committee. The Dalai and the Panchen Lamas, Tibet's two most exalted spiritual leaders, both ran into difficulties with their Han Chinese masters in later years, with the former fleeing to India in 1959 and the latter being denounced by the Communists in 1964. Chang was named as second vice-chairman of the Preparatory Committee, although it was obvious that he was the dominant figure. The next step in the process of establishing a government in Tibet occurred in Lhasa in April 1956 when, amidst much fanfare, Vice-Premier Ch'en I arrived with a large delegation from Peking to take part in the formal inauguration of the Preparatory Committee, the body that ostensibly served as the highest organ of government in Tibet until 1965. Not long before the Ch'en I mission to Tibet, Chang had been identified as the deputy secretary of what the Communists then called the Tibet Work Committee of the CCP, a post that placed him below Secretary Chang Ching-wu. It is probable, however, that both Changs had held these Party posts from the time of their arrival in Tibet in 1951. The term deputy secretary was changed to second secretary in 1962, but the post, in effect, was the same.

The period of the greatest amity between the Han Chinese and the Tibetans seems to have been in the mid-fifties. It fell to Chang to articulate some of the more conciliatory policies enunciated by the central government. Thus, in the spring of 1957, Chang revealed the decision to delay various "democratic reforms" (e.g., land reform) for a period of six years, that is, until the end of the Second Five-Year Plan (1962). He even added, "Whether or not reforms will be carried out during the Third Five-Year Plan will depend upon the conditions at that time." In addition, Chang stated that large numbers of Han cadres sent into Tibet would be withdrawn. Within two years, however, Communist policies underwent an about-face in the wake of the Tibetan Rebellion of March 1959, which witnessed the flight of the Dalai Lama to India together with a number of the members of the Tibetan Preparatory Committee. The Communists immediately reorganized the Committee. Because the official line was that the Dalai Lama had been "abducted by imperialists," the Panchen Lama was made the acting chairman — the theory being that the real chairman, the Dalai Lama, would return in due course. Chang was appointed as the ranking vice-chairman, although he obviously continued to be the power behind the scenes on the Preparatory Committee. He received an additional assignment under the Preparatory Committee in November 1959 when he was named to head the newly established Land Reform Committee, a clear indication that the six-year moratorium on "reforms" had been swept aside.

The Tibetan Rebellion of 1959 coincided both with the Great Leap Forward and with the rapid deterioration of Sino-Indian relations. Both these facts have had the effect of sharply curbing the availability of source materials on Tibet, and thus on Chang's activities there. Yet even from the meager materials available, it is evident that he has continued to be a top Communist official in Lhasa, and it is equally evident that the Han Chinese intend to give no quarter to the Tibetans. His importance was made abundantly clear in December 1964 when Chang delivered a report before a session of the Tibetan Autonomous Region. He flayed certain Tibetans for "scheming" to restore the "integration of politics and religion" in Tibet and claimed that the "serf-owner class had not disappeared." "Unreconciled to their defeat," they have tried "by hook and crook to attempt a restoration," and thus the struggle was "still protracted and complicated" and would be "at times even violent." Chang's remarks were, in fact, an indirect attack on the Panchen Lama, who a few days later was denounced by name at a session of the NPC in Peking; speaking before the Congress, Premier Chou En-lai announced that the Panchen Lama had been removed as acting chairman of the Tibet Preparatory Committee, but "in order to give him a last opportunity to turn over a new leaf," he was to be allowed to remain a member of the Preparatory Committee.

Chang Kuo-hua moved to the top position in the Communist hierarchy in Tibet in 1965 with the departure for China Proper of Chang Ching-wu. Thus, by August 1965, Chang Kuo-hua had assumed the Party first secretaryship in Tibet. Then, in the following month, the Preparatory Committee was transformed into the permanent Tibet Autonomous Region Government, being placed on par with other autonomous regions in China (e.g., the Inner Mongolia Autonomous Region). At this time Ngapo Ngawang Jigme (A-p'ei A-wang-chin-mei) became chairman of the Region. Ngapo, whose wife is the sister of the Dalai Lama, is one of Tibet's most important political figures. It was he who had negotiated the above-mentioned 1951 agreement providing for the entry of Chinese troops into Tibet, and after that date he had served the Communists in a variety of posts. He has been, for example, a deputy commander (under Chang) of the Tibet Military District since 1952, and he had also served as secretary-general of the Tibet Preparatory Committee from its inauguration in 1956. The Communists further illustrated their trust in Ngapo by naming him acting chairman of the Preparatory Committee after the denunciation of the Panchen Lama in late 1964. Chang was not given any position in the new Tibet Autonomous Region government structure; however, concurrently with the formation of the Region in September 1965, he was elected chairman of the newly established Second Tibet Committee of the CPPCC, the quasi-legislative organization that is supposed to serve as a link between Communists and non-Communists. Of interest is the fact that the Panchen Lama, by now stripped of all his other posts in both national government and in Tibet, was named as a member of the Standing Committee of the Tibet Committee of the CPPCC. This act symbolized the degree to which Han-Tibetan relations had been eroded over the years — the Dalai Lama had fled the country and the Panchen Lama had been given a humiliatingly low position. Only Ngapo Ngawang Jigme has retained a semblance of power, and it is likely that he is regarded by local Tibetans as a traitor. Chang Kuo-hua faces the difficult task of incorporating Tibet into the mainstream of Chinese life, probably with little hope of cooperation from the two million Tibetans.

As might be expected, most of Chang's writings for the press have been in connection with Tibet. In addition to the article cited earlier, he has written for the English-language journal *People's China,* as well as the two leading Communist publications, *Hung-ch'i* (Red flag) and the *JMJP.*[2] Some of his more important articles and speeches have been published by a research organization in Hong Kong under the title *Tibetan Sourcebook.*[3]

1. *SCMP* 2854, pp. 1–12.
2. *People's China,* no. 10:7–11 (May 16, 1953); *Hung-ch'i,* no. 23:32–36, December 1, 1960; *JMJP,* October 27, 1964.
3. Ling Nai-min, *Tibetan Sourcebook* (Hong Kong, 1964), pp. 159–161, 197–205, 219–221, 235–241.

Chang Kuo-t'ao

(1897– ; Chi-shui, Kiangsi). A founder of the CCP; important early Party leader.

Chang Kuo-t'ao (also known as Chang T'e-li) attended the founding Congress of the CCP in 1921 and was among the most important early Party leaders. In the 1920's he was one of the moving forces behind the CCP-sponsored labor movement and was deeply involved in the continuing intra-Party debate concerning CCP collaboration with the KMT. He was also among the first Chinese to have close ties with the Comintern. Chang was the chief Party leader in the Oyüwan Soviet area after 1931, but when he was driven from this region in 1932 he moved his forces to Szechwan, and from there he began an important leg of the Long March in 1935. From 1935 to 1937 Chang and Mao Tse-tung were engaged in a series of bitter disputes that centered in part on questions of the strategy and

destination of the Long Marchers. The two rivals took their forces on different routes, Chang moving westward toward Tibet while Mao moved north to Shensi. Unfortunately for Chang, his units were disastrously defeated in Kansu, and by the time he reached Yenan he was in no position to challenge the Mao leadership. Chang left the Communist movement in 1938 and has since lived in semi-retirement, one of his occupations being the writing of his autobiography. Published in installments, which began in 1966, this contains valuable information and insights into the early days of the Chinese Communist movement.[1]

Chang's family was originally from commercial Chi-shui, situated on the Kan River in central Kiangsi. However, much of his youth was spent in Shang-lu-shih, a small market center for P'ing-hsiang hsien in western Kiangsi. P'ing-hsiang, the seat of Chang family property, knew many of the conditions affecting neighboring Li-ling hsien in Hunan where Mao Tse-tung found one of his first revolutionary proving grounds for organizing peasant insurgency. P'ing-hsiang had long been a center for local secret societies and experienced several peasant uprisings in the early years of the 20th century. The atmosphere in which he grew up was to have its influence upon young Chang, who attended a private school in Shang-lu-shih before he went to a public primary school at the hsien seat from about 1909 to 1911. He was there at the time of the 1911 Revolution, which overthrew the Ch'ing dynasty. P'ing-hsiang, Chang states, decided to join the revolution by the beginning of November 1911. Thus he was already sympathetic to the cause of revolution when his family of wealthy landowners sent him to Peking National University (Peita) to spend four years acquiring a university education. Chang entered Peita in 1916. He soon became acquainted with a number of the radical young intellectuals at the university and came to know Ch'en Tu-hsiu, dean of the School of Letters at Peita from early 1917, and Li Ta-chao (qq.v.), who joined the staff as chief librarian in February 1918. The latter was only about eight years Chang's senior. All three were interested in the study of Marxism, and under the influence of the two older men Chang soon became one of the most active young Marxists at the university.[2] He demonstrated with other Peita students and faculty members in the incident of 1919, which opened the May Fourth Movement. The Peking Marxists chose Chang and Liu Jen-ching (who also left the CCP later on) as their representatives to the First CCP Congress, held in Shanghai in July 1921. Only a small number of Chinese were then true Marxists. The small group at the Congress undertook to get the Party underway by establishing three posts. The most important of these was given to Ch'en Tu-hsiu, the head of the new

Party (variously called "secretary" and "general secretary"), whereas Chang was made director of Organization. In this capacity he was concerned with such problems as recruitment, appointments to Party offices, and discipline, as well as the controversial question of CCP relations with the KMT. In the same month that the CCP was established, the Secretariat of the Chinese Labor Unions was established. Chang had been active in organizing labor in the Peking area during the previous winter (see under Teng Chung-hsia) and was thus a logical choice to direct the new organization. In the spring of 1922 the Secretariat sponsored the First National Labor Congress, at which time the chairmanship of the labor organization passed to Teng Chung-hsia, whose biography contains further information about the formative period of the CCP-sponsored labor movement.

Chang actually spent much of the interval between the First and Second CCP Congresses in connection with Comintern affairs in the Soviet Union. He left China in October 1921, crossing the border at Manchouli and stopping en route to Moscow at Irkutsk to contact the headquarters of the Comintern's Far Eastern Bureau. There he had an opportunity to become acquainted with Gregory Voitinsky, the Comintern agent who had visited China in 1920 (see under Yang Ming-chai). Chang arrived in Moscow in November or December and met some of the Chinese students from Yang Ming-chai's Foreign Language School who were furthering their studies, among them Liu Shao-ch'i (q.v.). Chang's major purpose in going to the USSR was to attend the Comintern Congress of the Toilers of the East, which opened in Moscow on January 21, 1922 (see under Chang T'ai-lei). He presented a detailed report on the work of the CCP Central Committee to the Congress, which was attended by about 125 delegates from the Far East. Ch'ü Ch'iu-pai (q.v.) acted as the Chinese interpreter for the Congress and also translated some of the Congress documents into Chinese for the benefit of his countrymen. Chang was one of three Chinese delegates elected to the Congress presidium, and while in Moscow he and some of the Chinese delegates had an interview with Lenin. At one point Lenin wanted to give a special message to the Chinese delegate who represented the railway workers union but who knew no Russian; as Lenin knew no Chinese he spoke in English and asked Chang to translate.

Chang returned to China to attend the Second CCP Congress, which was held in July 1922. He cast a negative vote on an important question put before the delegates: whether or not CCP members should also join the KMT. In doing this he took the opposite view from his friends, Teng Chung-hsia and Li Ta-chao. After the Congress Chang returned to work in north China,

and in 1923 he participated in the strikes among workers for the Pinghan (Peking-Hankow) Railway, the important line connecting Peking with the south. The strike was forcefully put down by the northern warlord Wu P'ei-fu in February, and Chang returned to Russia to report on the failure. In his three weeks in Moscow he reported several times to Voitinsky, who was still important in the Comintern's Far Eastern Bureau. By the time the Third CCP Congress met in Canton (June 1923) Chang had returned to China and was present. He still felt strongly that the CCP should preserve its separate identity, but, more important, he led the group which sought to preserve the independence of the labor movement. Chang's group was defeated on the issue regarding the labor movement, but two months later this decision was reversed in accord with Chang's position. In the meantime, shortly after the Third Congress, Mao Tse-tung was named to head the Party Organization Bureau, a position Chang had assumed at the First CCP Congress.

In the fall of 1923 he was again working in Peking where he met both Borodin and Voitinsky as they passed through the city and argued with them over the Comintern view of the CCP joining the KMT. When plans were made for the KMT to hold its First National Congress (January 1924), Chang and Li Ta-chao were chosen as official Party delegates from Peking to attend. After considering the question of admitting Communist Party members into the KMT, the Congress voted in favor of allowing Communists to enter the KMT as individuals, but they were not to be forced to give up membership in the Communist Party. Following this decision Chang himself became an alternate member of the KMT Central Executive Committee, even though he had opposed such dual Party membership when the Communist Party had considered it two years earlier. He returned to Peking in May but was soon arrested along with his wife, and both were held in prison for several months by the northern government (which opposed both the CCP and the KMT). Chang was still in Peking in January 1925 when the CCP held its Fourth National Congress in Shanghai; he was re-elected to the Party Central Committee and was also put in charge of the Committee's special labor committee. In the March following the Congress, Chang and his wife transferred to Shanghai where they found themselves living next door to Liu Shao-ch'i and his new wife. The Chang home now became the headquarters for the special labor committee and its members, Liu Shao-ch'i, Li Li-san, Hsiang Ying, Teng Chung-hsia, and Lin Yü-nan, all of whom were to play important parts in subsequent CCP developments. According to Chang, after the important labor insurrections of May 30, 1925, the CCP formed both a Military Department and a

Peasant Movement Committee, with Chang in charge of the former. In this capacity he directed much of the recruiting of Communist cadets to join the military forces of the Northern Expedition, and after these armies entered Hanyang and Hankow in the fall of 1926, Chang transferred his Military Department headquarters from south China to Hankow to be closer to the new revolutionary center. He was soon joined there by Chou En-lai, who had been training cadets for the expeditionary forces at Whampoa in Canton.

In April–May 1927 Chang was present for the Wuhan meeting of the Fifth CCP Congress (see under Ch'en Tu-hsiu), where he was elected to the newly established Politburo. The question of continuing the alliance with the KMT came up for discussion and Chang voted against it. But Ch'en Tu-hsiu, the CCP general secretary, who had sided with Chang at the Second CCP Congress in opposing his party's joining the KMT, felt in 1927 that the alliance should be continued, and this position won the deciding votes. Despite Ch'en's stand, relations between the two parties rapidly deteriorated, and as they did, tensions increased within the CCP where a faction wanting to sever relations was growing. At this moment Chang found himself caught between the two opposing groups, one in favor of making an immediate break, the other still wanting to hold back. The final KMT-CCP split in mid-1927 involved Chang as it did most of the other top CCP leaders. The break came at Nanchang, the Kiangsi capital, where Communist military leader Chu Te commanded the troops that garrisoned the city. A few weeks earlier Chang Fa-k'uei and his Second Front Army had moved into Kiukiang (Chiu-chiang), the Yangtze riverport above Nanchang. Chang's army included a number of Communist Party members and sympathizers, some fresh from their Whampoa training where they may have come into the Communist force initially recruited by Chang for the Northern Expedition. At the end of July, just before the break occurred on August 1, the Party headquarters at Wuhan had made its plans for insurrection and dispatched Chang to Kiukiang and Nanchang with the instructions for the Party operatives there, preparing them for action and for the revolt to take place within the Nanchang garrison force.[3] Chang was, it seems, only lukewarm about the prospects for an action taken so hastily, but nonetheless he brought the instructions to the key military leaders involved, and the revolt took place on August 1. No sooner were the Communists in control than they established a 25-member Revolutionary Committee to take charge and gave Chang supervision of the section for Peasants and Workers. On August 5 the Communists were driven out of the city and on August 7, at the emergency meeting of the Party at

Kiukiang, Ch'ü Ch'iu-pai took over the leadership of the Party and Ch'en Tu-hsiu was ousted. Chang followed the Communist armies as they fled south to Swatow, but after they suffered a second defeat there in late September, he fled to Hong Kong and prepared to go to Moscow.

Chang was in Moscow for the opening of the Sixth CCP Congress in June–July 1928 when over 80 Chinese delegates assembled there partially to escape the vigilance of the Nationalist police, because the Party had been driven underground in China. The Congress discussed the split in the CCP leadership since the Fifth Congress, but it was even more deeply affected by the political situation in the Soviet Union where Stalin had recently won over Trotsky, and the Kremlin, acting through the Comintern, wished to assure itself that foreign Communist parties were cleansed of heterodoxy.[4] The Sixth CCP Congress was immediately followed, on July 17, by the opening of the Sixth Comintern Congress, at which the China question was heatedly debated. At the Sixth CCP Congress Chang heard himself called to account for his previous "right opportunist" policies, but he was returned to the CCP Central Committee elected by the Congress.

After the CCP and Comintern Congresses, Chang remained in Moscow where he was a member of the five-member CCP delegation to the Comintern, a group headed by Ch'ü Ch'iu-pai and including Chang's friend Teng Chung-hsia. Over the course of the next year or so he came into conflict with Comintern official Pavel Mif; the details are described in the biography of Ch'ü Ch'iu-pai. And, according to his own testimony, after Chou En-lai's arrival in Moscow in 1930, both he and Ch'ü were "kept in the background" because of their "hostility to Mif," a situation which in effect led to Chang's temporary retirement from political life in Moscow.[5] Ch'ü and Chang had apparently stood together in their opposition to Mif, but when Ch'ü returned to China in 1930, he attacked Chang at the important Third Plenum held in September 1930. Ch'ü asserted that the Comintern and the CCP were in agreement in their assessments of the revolutionary situation in China, but that Chang and other "rightists" had distorted the two views.

Chang managed to clear his name with the Comintern by the end of 1930, and then in January 1931 he left for home, having spent three years in the Soviet capital. He arrived in Shanghai to find the CCP in another crisis. In his absence Li Li-san (q.v.), in spite of Comintern planning, had taken control of the Party leadership, but his headstrong maneuvers had neither pleased the Kremlin nor met with success in China. To remedy the situation the Comintern had sent Pavel Mif, the pro-Stalinist head of Sun Yat-sen University in Moscow, to China in the spring of 1930 to attempt to alter Li's policies. The manner in which Mif and his former students, often called the "28 Bolsheviks," managed to oust Li and gain control of the CCP leadership in early 1931 is described in the biography of Ch'in Pang-hsien. When Chang appeared in Shanghai in April 1931 his relationship to the Mif followers was somewhat ambiguous. As already described, he had opposed some of Mif's policies in Moscow, yet several of Mif's "28 Bolshevik" clique were his good friends. About the time of Chang's arrival in Shanghai, the CCP held a high-level conference and decided to send representatives of the Mif group to take charge of political work in the rural bases where the Party had been at work for several years. Chang was chosen to head the political work in Oyüwan, a Red base on the borders of Hupeh, Honan, and Anhwei provinces. He was accompanied by several of the "28 Bolsheviks," among them Shen Tse-min (q.v.), whom he already knew well, and Ch'en Ch'ang-hao (q.v.), who took charge of youth work.[6] In Oyüwan they joined Hsu Hsiang-ch'ien (q.v.), a Whampoa graduate sent by the Party to the area in 1929. Chang headed the Party's Central Sub-bureau in Oyüwan and therefore led the political reorganization that took place there after his arrival.

The Nationalist armies fairly well isolated Oyüwan in 1931, making it difficult for Chang's group to communicate with Mao Tse-tung and the elements of the Party based in southern Kiangsi at Juichin where a strong soviet was being built. On November 7, 1931, the Party called a congress of delegates from all the Red guerrilla areas. The Congress formally initiated a government known as the Chinese Soviet Republic, with Mao Tse-tung as chairman and Chang as one of the two vice-chairmen. Chang was also appointed "People's Commissar of Justice," the equivalent of a cabinet post, and he became a member of the government's top military organ, the Revolutionary Military Council, headed by Chu Te. Chang did not attend the Congress although he did send a representative from Oyüwan.[7] However, there is good evidence that he himself found it convenient to stay away, for on the same day that Mao opened the Congress at Juichin, Chang called one in Oyüwan. This was called the Second Congress of the Oyüwan Soviet Area, but little is known about it. Chang was the acknowledged political chief in Oyüwan, Hsu headed military affairs, Shen took charge of local Party work, and Ch'en was assigned the youth work. An official telegram from the Central Sub-bureau in Oyüwan, signed by these four men in October 1932, suggests that they were the principal leaders there at that date.[8] Chang was not in Juichin at any time after the November 1931 congress, but he continued to serve, however nominally, as a vice-chairman

of the Chinese Soviet Republic. When the Republic held the Second All-China Congress of Soviets in January–February 1934, he was retained as a vice-chairman, but he was dropped as Commissar of Justice, and was possibly also removed from the Military Council.

In the meantime, growing Communist strength had provoked aggressive action from Chiang Kai-shek and other KMT leaders who were unwilling to tolerate strong Red bases in Central China. In early 1932 the Generalissimo began to prepare for the fourth of his "annihilation" campaigns against the Communists. When launched, his forces bore down especially heavily upon Oyüwan, and the leadership there decided to retreat. In the fall of 1932 the Fourth Front Army led by Chang, Hsu, Ch'en, and others, evacuated Oyüwan, retreating westward across Honan and southern Shensi into northern Szechwan where in an area beyond the Ta-pa mountains on the upper reaches of the Ch'u River they set up headquarters in December 1932. In May 1933 they established the small T'ung-Nan-Pa Soviet, named for its three principal hsien, T'ung-chiang, Nan-chiang, and Pa-chung (see under Wang Hung-k'un). Back in Oyüwan a military leader from Hupeh, Hsu Hai-tung (q.v.), together with Shen Tse-min, had been left to guard Chang's retreat, but in 1934 Hsu was also forced to evacuate the area.

While Chang was settling down in T'ung-Nan-Pa, Mao Tse-tung and his forces were making preparations to evacuate Kiangsi in the face of increasing attacks from the Nationalists, and they finally began the Long March in October 1934. During the march some form of communication between the two groups existed. The story of their arrangements to meet in western Szechwan has not been told, but in early 1935 Chang, Hsu, and the Fourth Front Army began to move westward into the northwest corner of Szechwan where they met Mao and his armies in June 1935, rendezvousing near the small town of Mao-kung. In August they held another conference farther north at Mao-erh-kai to discuss political disagreements and for a second time to try to fix the destination of the marchers and the strategy to cover their route. Now the opposition between Mao and Chang that had been present for some time came to a head; the two leaders separated, Chang going west, Mao north, each taking with him sections of his own army and certain units of the other's. Mao and his army went to Shensi; Chang, now joined by Chu Te and Liu Po-ch'eng (qq.v.), turned toward Tibet. With Chang went the Ninth and 31st Armies of the Fourth Front Army, and the Fifth and Ninth Armies from Mao's First Front Army. Mao took his own First and Third Armies, plus the Fourth and 30th Armies from Chang's force. These units are often described as the "right-route" (or "east-route") army taken by Mao and the "left-route" (or "west-route") army led by Chang.[9] Chang wintered his forces near the trade-route town of Kan-tzu in the far western part of Sikang province.

Under circumstances that remain largely unexplained, the Fourth Front Army was met in Kan-tzu in June 1936 by another Red Army. This was the third group of Red marchers to retreat westward from the Nationalists in the middle 1930's. Ho Lung, Jen Pi-shih, and Hsiao K'o's Second Front Army started its march from a small base on the Hunan-Hupeh-Szechwan-Kweichow border about a year later than Mao had started from Kiangsi. Once the two armies had met, Jen and Ho apparently convinced Chang to follow them north to rejoin Mao. The joint force now moved northward, but as they passed through Ninghsia province another dispute broke out about the eventual destination, and Chang and three of the units separated from the rest. Chang led his troops across the Yellow River into the Kansu Corridor where they were attacked by troops under northwest Moslem leader Ma Pu-fang, and the Communists were all but annihilated. The worst of the fighting centered about Ku-lang, not far outside the Great Wall. Chang, having lost his armies, had to escape into Ninghsia, where he joined the remaining troops from the Fourth Front Army; he was with this group when it met forces under Mao's control in Kansu in the fall of 1936. When the two groups met, Chang's military strength was so weakened that he was no longer able to offer the threat to Mao Tse-tung's leadership that he might have had with his full military component, which may at one time have numbered about 50,000 men.[10] When Mao and Chang had met in Szechwan, Chang's army was considerably larger than Mao's.

After Chang arrived in Yenan the Communists established, in September 1937, the Shensi-Kansu-Ninghsia Border Region Government under the chairmanship of Lin Po-ch'ü (q.v.). Chang was made vice-chairman of the government, which, in effect, replaced the "Chinese Soviet Republic," established six years earlier in Kiangsi. As already described, Chang had been a vice-chairman of the Soviet Republic, and thus in a sense he was merely continuing in this same post. But Chang's days as a political leader were numbered. His differences with Mao had not healed, and during the following months the bitter feeling must have deepened. Although Chang appears to lay some of the blame for the Kansu Corridor disaster to the headstrong leadership of Ch'en Ch'ang-hao, who had been his political commissar on the march through Kansu, the disastrous loss of troops did not enhance his military reputation. Chang found it necessary to escape from Communist territory in 1938 and by the time the Sixth CCP Plenum was held in October–November 1938, he had

been read out of the Party. In a major report to the Plenum, Mao described Chang's alleged transgressions against Party discipline. According to Mao (and the annotators of his *Selected Works*), the struggle against Chang had been successfully concluded at a Politburo meeting a year and a half earlier (April 1937). Chang had been condemned at that meeting and had "pretended to acquiesce in the condemnation but actually made preparations for his final betrayal of the Party." Mao, in his 1938 report, stated that the Party had tried to "save" Chang but, because the latter "threw himself into the arms" of the KMT, the CCP "could not but resolutely expel him." Finally, Mao noted that this punitive action had been endorsed by the Comintern.[11] In regard to the Comintern, it is noteworthy that at the Seventh Comintern Congress in mid-1935, Mao, Chang, Ch'en Shao-yü (of the "28 Bolsheviks"), and Chou En-lai were the only Chinese Communists elected full members of the Comintern Executive Committee. This may have been an indication that, as of 1935, Moscow was playing no favorites and wanted the various CCP factions to have equal recognition.

After leaving Yenan, Chang found refuge in Hankow, then the capital of the Nationalist Government, and later moved on to Chungking when the Nationalists made it their capital. From 1939 to 1945, while the Sino-Japanese War continued, Chang took some part in government and KMT affairs. In 1945 he was elected to the KMT Central Executive Committee, and in the next year he became director of the Kiangsi regional office of the Chinese National Relief and Rehabilitation Association. When the Chinese Communists were completing their conquest of the mainland in 1949, Chang moved to Hong Kong where he has continued to live quietly in retirement while working on his autobiography.

Chang is the only high-ranking CCP defector still alive and among the most prominent members to leave the Party. His political career ended in his 40th year, but his role in early Communist Party developments was extremely important and certainly rivaled Mao's in the first two decades of the Party's history. He is, of course, regularly excoriated in orthodox Maoist histories.

In February 1924 Chang married Yang Tzu-lieh, who has assisted him with the writing of his autobiography and is living with him in Hong Kong. She comes from Hupeh and joined the CCP in Wuhan during its founding year in 1921.

1. Chang Kuo-t'ao, "Wo-te hui-i" (My recollections), *Ming Pao yueh-k'an* (Ming Pao monthly; Hong Kong), vol. 1, nos. 3–12 (March–December 1966); vol. 2, nos. 13–14 (January–February 1967).

2. Chow Tse-tsung, *The May Fourth Movement* (Cambridge, Mass., 1960), p. 244.

3. C. Martin Wilbur, "The Ashes of Defeat,"

The China Quarterly, no. 18:44–52 (April–June 1964).

4. Benjamin I. Schwartz, *Chinese Communism and the Rise of Mao* (Cambridge, Mass., 1951), p. 116.

5. Tso-liang Hsiao, *Power Relations within the Chinese Communist Movement, 1930–1934* (Seattle, Wash., 1961), pp. 62–63.

6. *Ibid.,* p. 193.

7. Agnes Smedley, *Red Flood over China* (Moscow, 1934), p. 377.

8. Tso-liang Hsiao, p. 195.

9. Liu Po-ch'eng, "Looking Back on the Long March," *The Long March: Eyewitness Accounts* (Peking, 1963), p. 218.

10. Edgar Snow, *Random Notes on Red China* (Cambridge, Mass., 1957), p. 100.

11. *Selected Works of Mao Tse-tung* (London, 1954), II, 244–261, 293.

Chang Lien-hua

Secretary-general, All-China Sports Federation.

Chang Lien-hua, whose antecedents are unknown, emerged in the 1950's as one of the leading administrators of China's large and ever expanding athletic programs. Aside from his colleague Jung Kao-t'ang (q.v.), Chang is probably the most important official in the day-to-day administration of Chinese sports. He first came to national attention in June 1954 when he attended a congress of the International Federation of Football (Soccer) Associations (an affiliate of the International Olympic Organization) in Bern, Switzerland. He was identified at that time merely as being an official in the All-China Athletic Federation (alternately known as the Chinese Olympic Committee and officially renamed the All-China Sports Federation in July 1964). Within the next decade Chang was to make seven more trips abroad, each involving athletics. In June 1955 he went to attend the 50th session of the International Olympic Committee (IOC) in Paris, and in January 1956 he was in Cortina d'Ampezzo, Italy, for the 51st IOC meeting; while there, he was an official "observer" of the Seventh Winter Olympic Games. In June of 1956 Chang was again in Europe, this time in Lisbon for the 30th Congress of the International Federation of Football Associations (IFFA), and when the Federation would not expel the Chinese Nationalist delegation, he walked out of the meeting. (Chang is one of the very few Chinese Communists to have visited Portugal.) Two years later (June 1958), Chang led a group to another IFFA Congress (the 31st) in Stockholm and once more walked out when the Taiwan issue arose. Two days later, on June 7, 1958, he formally announced that Peking had withdrawn from the IFFA. Two months later, in August 1958, Chang was given the task of

making the official announcement that the PRC had withdrawn from the International Olympic Committee. As might be expected, his withdrawal statement was accompanied by a stinging denunciation of the "two Chinas" plot, which he claimed had caused the Chinese action.

In the meantime, Chang received a number of official and semi-official positions with an expected concentration in the field of physical education. By November 1955 he was deputy chief of the International Liaison Department of the State Council's Physical Culture and Sports Commission, a body established in November 1952. By May 1958 Chang was promoted to the directorship of the Liaison Department and still retains this post. In January 1956, while Chang was in Italy (see above), he was elected to the preparatory committee for participation in the 16th Olympic Games held later that year in Melbourne, Australia. The preparation was in vain, however, for at the last minute Peking refused to take part owing to Taiwan's participation. He also had taken an active part in the third congress of the All-China Athletic Federation in October 1956. He made a report before the gathering on a revision in the Federation's regulations, and was then elected a Standing Committee member as well as secretary-general of the organization, positions to which he was re-elected at the fourth congress in January–February 1964. Subsequent to this he has been identified as a leading official in Federation affiliate organizations, such as the China Track and Field Federation, of which he was mentioned as a vice-chairman in February 1957. Between 1958 and 1963 he was also named to four newly established friendship associations. He became a Council member of the Sino-Iraq Friendship Association (FA) in September 1958; the secretary-general of the China-Hungary FA in the same month; a Standing Committee member of the China-Latin America FA in March 1960; and, Council member of the China-Japan FA in October 1963.

In addition to the five trips abroad already mentioned, Chang made three more between 1961 and 1964. In June–July 1961 he led a soccer team to Albania and the U.S.S.R.; he was a deputy leader of a sports delegation to Indonesia in November–December 1962; and in August 1964 he was a member of a delegation to Indonesia to attend a conference of the "Games of the New Emerging Forces" (GANEFO) Federation. The Chinese had taken a very active part in GANEFO (see under Jung Kao-t'ang). When the Chinese set up a preparatory committee in June 1963 to participate in the first games (held later that year in Indonesia), Chang was named as the secretary-general. And in August 1964, immediately prior to his departure for the above-mentioned trip to Indonesia, he was named secretary-general of the permanent National Committee of the PRC for the GANEFO.

Although Chang does not appear to be an official of particular political significance, he does stand as a symbol of the emphasis that the PRC has placed on the development of sports in China. The international political benefits derived from this emphasis are already clear, if only because of the prestige gained from the rather outstanding Chinese record in sports competition, particularly with other Asian nations. The political aspects become more overt when a Chinese official — like Chang, on August 10, 1964 — signs a joint statement with an exiled South African denouncing the International Olympic Committee for racial discrimination.

Chang Lin-chih

(Hopeh). Minister of Coal Industry; alternate member, CCP Central Committee.

An early north China Party organizer, Chang Lin-chih has held important ministerial posts in Peking since the early fifties. He was a Party member in the early thirties working in the southern part of his native Hopeh. By 1932 Chang was engaged in Party organizational work in and around Nan-kung and Wei-hsien in southeastern Hopeh.[1] He apparently remained in this general vicinity for several years, because when the war broke out in 1937 he was the Hopeh-Shantung-Honan Party "representative." In this capacity he was the major Communist figure in establishing the Party's Northwest Shantung and West Shantung "special committees" in and around the city of Liao-ch'eng in western Shantung not far from the Hopeh border.[2] It is probable that Chang was in this area in 1938 when units of Liu Po-ch'eng's 129th Division led by Hsu Hsiang-ch'ien (q.v.) pushed into this region. Nothing more is known of Chang's wartime activities, but in March 1946 he was in Han-tan (southwest Hopeh), where he was a member of the presidium for the second session of the First Shansi-Hopeh-Shantung-Honan Assembly. This was the legislative arm of the important Chin-Chi-Lu-Yü Border Region Government, of which Yang Hsiu-feng (q.v.) was the chairman. Liu Po-ch'eng was the key military figure in the Chin-Chi-Lu-Yü area, and by the late forties Chang Lin-chih was a political commissar in the Third Army Corps of Liu's Second Field Army, the field army that pushed from central China into the southwest in 1949. Chang presumably came under the jurisdiction of Teng Hsiao-p'ing, the political commissar of the Second Field Army. When Nanking was captured in late April 1949, Chang was named to membership on the Municipal Military Control Commission under the chairmanship of Liu Po-ch'eng. A few days later (May 11), when the Nanking Municipal People's Government was established Chang and K'o

Ch'ing-shih (q.v.) were appointed as the two vice-mayors, again serving under Liu Po-ch'eng. However, Chang only remained there a brief time, for by the end of November the Communist forces with which he was associated had moved into the southwest and had captured the key city of Chungking in Szechwan. In early December 1949, as the Communists began to set up their organs of control, Chang received three posts: deputy secretary of the Municipal Party Committee, vice-chairman of the Municipal Military Control Commission, and member of the preparatory committee of the Chungking General Labor Union.

With Chungking as his base, Chang was active in southwest China between 1949 and 1952, a period in which he held important positions on the civil administrations governing the area, as well as in the Party Committee for Chungking. Thus he was made deputy director of the southwest branch office of the All-China Federation of Labor in Chungking (1950), a member of the Southwest Military and Administrative Committee (1950), the regional administration for southwest China that governed Szechwan, Kweichow, Yunnan, Sikang, and Chungking, and also a member of the Committee's important Land Reform Committee. From 1950 he served as a member of the Chungking Municipal People's Government Council, and sometime in 1952 he was promoted to the position of ranking secretary of the Chungking Party Committee.

In mid-1952 there was a partial reorganization of the central government that brought about the transfer from the provinces to Peking of a number of persons to fill newly created positions. Chang was one of these. In August 1952 the Second Ministry of Machine Building was created from sections of the Ministry of Heavy Industry with Chao Erh-lu (q.v.) as the minister and Chang Lin-chih as one of the vice-ministers. In this capacity Chang was a member of the delegation to Prague led by Liu Lan-po in July 1954 to attend the second meeting of the Joint Committee for Sino-Czech Scientific and Technical Cooperation. Liu signed a protocol on scientific cooperation on September 2, and then the delegation left for China.

In 1954 Chang was elected as a deputy from his native Hopeh to the First NPC, which held its initial session in September 1954. However, he was switched to the Yunnan constituency for the Second NPC (1959–1964) and then back to Hopeh for the Third NPC, which held its first session in December 1964–January 1965. In April 1955, as a reflection of the growing complexities of Chinese industry, the central government created the Third Ministry of Machine Building to manage the electrical power engineering industries. Chang was relieved of his vice-ministership and named to head this new industry. Then, in May 1956, during a partial government reorganization, the name was changed to the Ministry of Power Equipment Industry, with Chang continuing as the minister. He received Party recognition for his work in industrial development in September 1956 when he was made an alternate member of the Central Committee at the Eighth National Party Congress.

Since 1955 Chang has held a ministerial post and for a brief period he held two. The government had continued to reorganize its ministries dealing with industrial problems, and thus the Ministry of Power Equipment Industry, established in May 1956, was merged with other industrial ministries in February 1958, at which time Chang lost the Power Equipment portfolio. However, in September 1957 he had succeeded Ch'en Yü (appointed governor of Kwangtung) as the Minister of Coal Industry, and from that time he has been chiefly concerned with China's developing coal industry.

Since 1952, when he was brought into the national government, Chang has been quite active in public affairs. For example, he has served on preparatory committees for national conferences of "advanced workers" in 1956 and 1960; he is occasionally reported away from Peking, as in February 1959 when he attended an industrial conference in Shanghai and in May 1960 when he spoke at a conference in Shantung regarding the utilization of coal. Unlike many figures of national stature, Chang has not been called upon to take part in the activities of the many "people's" organizations, presumably an effort to utilize fully his technical skills in the important ministries with which he has been associated.

Among his writings are: "The Coal Industry Will Catch Up with Britain Next Year," *JMJP,* June 6, 1958; "Continue to Launch Mass Movements in the Coal Industry," *Hung-ch'i* (Red flag), December 1, 1958; "Carry Out a Revolution in the Organization of Production in Coal Mining Enterprises," *Hung-ch'i,* December 1, 1959; "Fight for the Development of the Coal Industry at High Speed," *JMJP,* October 7, 1959.

---

1. Ch'i Wu, *I-ko ko-ming ken-chü te ch'eng-chang; k'ang-Jih chan-cheng ho chieh-fang chan-cheng shih-ch'i te Chin-Chi-Lu-Yü pien-ch'ü kai-k'uang* (The establishment and growth of a revolutionary base; a general account of the Shansi-Hopeh-Shantung-Honan Border Region during the anti-Japanese war and the war of liberation; Peking, 1958), p. 18.
2. *Ibid.,* p. 203.

Chang P'ing-hua

(1903–   ; Hunan). Former first secretary, Hunan CCP Committee; deputy director, CCP Propaganda Department; alternate member, CCP Central Committee.

Chang P'ing-hua was a top Party official in Wuhan in the early years of the PRC and was deeply involved in a serious case of malfeasance. Although temporarily demoted, he soon advanced to more important work and from the mid-fifties to the mid-sixties was one of the top officials in Hupeh and then Hunan. In mid-1966 he was transferred to Peking, where he became a deputy director of the Party's Propaganda Department. Chang has been an alternate member of the Party Central Committee since 1958.

A native of Hunan, where he was born in 1903, Chang was active at the Communist base on the borders of Hunan, Hupeh, and Kiangsi in the early 1930's and was in this area in 1933 when Jen Pi-shih (q.v.) was sent there to take charge of political affairs (see under Wang Shou-tao). During the Sino-Japanese War Chang was a political officer under Ho Lung who commanded the 120th Division of the Communist Eighth Route Army that was stationed in the Shansi-Suiyuan Border Region for most of the war years. To judge from an article that Chang wrote for the *Chung-kuo ch'ing-nien pao* (China youth newspaper) on July 2, 1963, he apparently spent a part of the war years in Yenan.[1] Nothing else is known of his career before the Communist conquest in 1949. When Communist forces captured Wuhan, the important Yangtze River industrial city, in May 1949, Chang became the ranking secretary of the Wuhan Party Committee. In February 1950 the Communists established the Central-South Military and Administrative Committee (CSMAC), the body that administered Honan, Hupeh, Hunan, Kiangsi, Kwangsi, and Kwangtung from 1950 to 1954. Although Chang was not named as one of the original members of the CSMAC, he was added to membership in March 1950, and at the same time he was also appointed as a member of the CSMAC's Finance and Economics Committee. On the day he received these assignments, he was also named as a member of the Wuhan Municipal People's Government, a position that placed him under Mayor Wu Te-feng (q.v.). Four months later he was named to membership on the Wuhan Government's Finance and Economics Committee, and then in September of the same year he succeeded Wu Te-feng as the chairman. In September Chang was also appointed chief procurator of the Wuhan Procuratorate.

As a major Party and government official in Wuhan, Chang was in a vulnerable position in the fall of 1951 when a major case of corruption was exposed in the Party press.[2] Known as the "Sung Ying case" (named after the deputy director of the Wuhan Government Public Health Bureau), it involved several persons—including Party veterans—who had been accused of malfeasance and corruption in a letter written under an assumed name to Mao Tse-tung by a local Party member. The letter exposed irregularities that occurred in 1950, but as the case developed, other charges were brought against the alleged offenders, including accusations that they had allowed an innocent person to be jailed for eight months for stealing funds from a hospital. Stimulated by authorities in Peking, an investigation was begun by the Central-South Party Bureau under whose jurisdiction Wuhan fell. When the Bureau pressured the Wuhan Party Committee to look into the matter, Chang P'ing-hua, as the Committee's chief secretary, became involved in the case. The Wuhan Committee conducted its first investigation as early as May 1951, with Chang in charge. But his Committee failed to assign the blame for the theft upon the culprit (although the latter had already been brought under suspicion), chiefly because the Committee could not bring itself to consider a veteran Party member guilty of stealing. Not satisfied with the results, the Central-South Bureau again pressured Chang for further investigations. Five times, it was claimed, he had received but ignored Bureau directives. In December 1951 he presided over a meeting called to conduct wider investigations; now troubled by the censure from the regional Bureau, Chang criticized his handling of the case and promised to do better. However, his self-criticisms were not severe enough to satisfy the regional authorities, who subsequently called a meeting of the CSMAC in February 1952. The meeting was attended by 137 "high-level cadres" and 52 members of the CSMAC, many of them Party members. Teng Tzu-hui (q.v.), vice-chairman of the CSMAC and second to Lin Piao in charge of political affairs in central-south China, conducted the meeting. Criticisms and self-criticisms were the order of the day. Chang was again forced to censure himself. But the results were still not entirely successful, for the meeting found that "though directly responsible for the mistaken handling of the case," Chang "had carried out examinations and discussions in a strict manner." Accordingly, he was punished "with leniency," and given a "verbal censure." He was, however, demoted to deputy secretary of the Wuhan Party Committee, being replaced by Li Hsien-nien (q.v.), a high-ranking Party official. Other important figures implicated in the case included Wuhan Mayor Wu Te-feng (q.v.), Vice-mayor Chou Chi-fang (the husband of Sung Ying), and Hsieh Pang-chih, a member of the Wuhan Party Committee. Still others were dismissed from their jobs, expelled from the Party, or, in several cases, imprisoned.

Notwithstanding the apparent severity of the case, a number of the higher-ranking Party officials made political comebacks—most notably Wu Te-feng, Hsieh Pang-chih (who became ambassador to Bulgaria in 1962), and Chang P'ing-hua himself. The Sung Ying case coincided with the famous "three-anti" movement directed against the three "evils" of corruption, waste, and bureaucratism. The fact that some of the more important Party members involved ultimately moved on to higher positions in the hierarchy suggests that the Party used the case as a "model" to revitalize the sagging revolutionary fervor of Party members who had grown lethargic in the performance of their duties. In any event, Chang P'ing-hua was active again in his capacity as a Wuhan deputy secretary within three months of the February 1952 meeting when the Sung Ying case was settled. Although he was not re-elected to membership on the CSMAC when it was reorganized in early 1953, he continued to serve as the second-ranking Party official in Wuhan and, finally, in November 1954 he was promoted to the first secretaryship, replacing Wang Jen-chung (q.v.).

At the same time that Chang became Wuhan first secretary, he was also identified as third secretary of the Hupeh Provincial Party Committee; he advanced to second secretary by March 1956 and then in October 1956 he was identified simply as secretary (although this was still the second-ranking post under First Secretary Wang Jen-chung). In March 1955 Chang had also become chairman of the Wuhan CPPCC Committee, but by this time he had assumed more important posts at the provincial level, and it appears that by the end of 1955 he was largely removed from Wuhan municipal affairs. He was reported in the press regularly in the mid-fifties, often in the company of the CCP's top leaders, as when Li Fu-ch'un visited Wuhan in October 1957 and when Mao was there in April 1958.

In May 1958 Chang received his first national Party post when he was elected an alternate member of the Central Committee at the second session of the Eighth National Congress. A month later he was made a deputy leader of a group appointed to inspect production in Hupeh at the beginning of the period of the Great Leap Forward. In September 1959, after spending a decade in Hupeh, Chang was assigned to his native Hunan, where he succeeded Chou Hsiao-cou (q.v.) as first secretary of the Hunan Party Committee. Chou, probably a victim of the Great Leap, was removed from all his Hunan posts. Thus, Chang P'ing-hua succeeded Chou in December 1959 when the former was elected chairman of the Second Hunan Committee of the CPPCC, and by April 1960 he had also replaced Chou as political commissar of the Hunan Military District. Chang continued to make numerous appearances in Hunan as he had previously in Hupeh, speaking before provincial Party meetings, conducting inspections throughout the province, and engaging in similar duties that normally occupy the time of top provincial leaders. In September 1964 he became chairman of the Third Hunan Committee of the CPPCC and in the same month he was also elected as a member of the Hunan Provincial People's Government Council. Chang spent most of his time in Hunan, but he made one important trip abroad in January 1963 when he went to East Germany to attend the Sixth Congress of the German Socialist Unity (Communist) Party. The Congress served as a platform for mutual denunciations between the Chinese and the Russians as part of the continuing Sino-Soviet ideological dispute (see under Wu Hsiu-ch'üan, the delegation leader).

In June 1966 Chang was identified as a member of the Party's Central-South Bureau. But then in the following month he was brought to Peking to become a deputy director of the Party's Propaganda Department. At approximately this same time T'ao Chu, who had been the first secretary of the Central-South Bureau, was also transferred to Peking to become director of the Propaganda Department. The new assignments for both T'ao and Chang came in the midst of the 1966 "cultural revolution" and coincided with the removal of Lu Ting-i and Chou Yang (qq.v.) as director and deputy director, respectively, of the Propaganda Department. Assuming that Chang remains in Peking, he will probably relinquish all his posts in Hunan, where, since 1959, he had been the top Communist official.

1. *SCMP* 3027, pp. 1–6.
2. *CB* 256.

Chang Su

(c.1909–   ; Wei-hsien, Hopeh). Specialist in judicial affairs; member, NPC Standing Committee; alternate member, CCP Central Committee.

Chang Su was probably born about 1909 or a few years earlier. He hails from an area in present-day Hopeh that was under the jurisdiction of Chahar Province during its existence from 1928 to 1952. Chang is a graduate of Peking Normal College, and in 1927, possibly while a student there, he joined the Communist Youth League. Until 1933 he worked as a school teacher, reportedly having taught during these years at middle schools in Peking, Yü-lin in Shensi, and in Chekiang, as well as at a normal college in Hopeh. By 1933 he had returned to his native province (then Chahar), where he worked with the army of Feng Yü-hsiang, the famous "Christian General." Chang participated in Feng's Allied Anti-Japanese Army, established at Kalgan (Chang-chia-k'ou) for the alleged purpose of countering Japanese advances toward the Great Wall in the Jehol and Chahar areas. This effort soon petered out, and Chang was reported later in the same year (1933) to be teaching at a middle school in Kalgan.

Chang apparently remained in Chahar and was serving there as a hsien magistrate when war with Japan broke out in mid-1937. In January 1938 Chang took part, as a representative of Yü hsien in Chahar, in the formation of the important Chin-Ch'a-Chi (Shansi-Chahar-Hopeh) Border Region Government (see under Sung Shao-wen), the first Communist-sponsored government behind Japanese lines. He was named to the governing nine-member Chin-Ch'a-Chi Administrative Committee,[1] as well as to the directorship of the Border Region's Industry Department, positions he held until about 1945. At some time during the war he was also appointed director of the Region's Finance Department and general manager of its bank, holding both posts until 1944 when he became chairman of the Hopeh-Chahar Administrative Office.

At the close of the war the Communists began to establish civil administrations in those areas previously occupied by their guerrilla forces. Now, however, they began to employ the traditional provincial designations rather than "border regions." A case in point was the province of Chahar, of which Kalgan was the capital. This important city was taken by the Communists in August 1945, after which Chang was named as the provincial governor as well as the Kalgan mayor. He remained as Chahar governor until the end of 1951 but lost his position as mayor of Kalgan when the Nationalists successfully occupied the city from October 1946 until December 1948. When the Communists recaptured the city in the last days of 1948, Chang was named to head the Municipal Military Control Commission, a post he retained until 1949.

In addition to municipal and provincial administrations, the Communists began the formation of larger, multi-provincial governments in the postwar period. Such a governmental unit had existed in Manchuria from 1946. In August 1948 the Chin-Ch'a-Chi (Shansi-Chahar-Hopeh) and the Chin-Chi-Lu-Yü (Shansi-Hopeh-Shantung-Honan) Border Region Governments were combined into a new North China People's Government (NCPG) under the chairmanship of Party veteran Tung Pi-wu. The NCPG lasted only 14 months, its functions being absorbed by the Central People's Government in October 1949. But while it existed it was an active organization, particularly after it moved from Shih-chia-chuang to Peking in early 1949. Chang served as one of the 27 members of the NCPG as well as head of the Pei-yüeh Administrative Office, one of the subdivisions of the NCPG covering a large area which lay south of Kalgan and west of Peking.

Chang remained until the end of 1951 in Chahar, where he served from September 1950 as head of the provincial Finance and Economics Committee in addition to his post as governor.

In the interim, he also took part in the establishment of the central government in the fall of 1949. Chang attended the first session of the CPPCC (September 1949), the organization that brought the PRC into existence, as a delegate from the north China "liberated areas." He also served on the *ad hoc* committee that drafted the Organic Law of the Central People's Government, one of the key documents adopted at this time; the committee was headed by Tung Pi-wu, under whom he was still working in the North China People's Government. From October 1949 to December 1954 Chang was also a member of the First Executive Board of the Sino-Soviet Friendship Association.

Chang was brought from Chahar to Peking in late 1951 to assume two new and important posts. In December 1951 he was named both as a vice-chairman and as secretary-general of the North China Administrative Committee (NCAC), the governmental administration with jurisdiction over the five provinces of Hopeh, Shansi, Chahar, Pingyuan, and Suiyuan. He relinquished the secretary-generalship in late 1952 but retained the vice-chairmanship until the NCAC was abolished in August 1954, just prior to the establishment of the constitutional government. Paralleling this executive position, Chang was named (April 1952) as the Chief Justice of the north China branch court under the Supreme People's Court. From that time onward, Chang has played an increasingly active role in Peking's judicial and quasi-judicial affairs, a field where a background of administrative experience and Party service can sometimes substitute for more formal legal training. In April 1953 he served as a member of the presidium (steering committee) for the meeting that inaugurated the Political Science and Law Association of China, although it was not until later that he became formally affiliated with this organization (see below). At about the same time he also became chairman of the Political and Legal Affairs Committee under the NCAC, and in 1954 he chaired a special committee to promote the discussion in north China of the draft constitution. In August 1954 Chang was promoted to a vice-presidency of the Supreme People's Court, concurrently with his position as Chief Justice for north China. Rather oddly, however, he relinquished both posts in the following month. The one known Party post held by Chang in these years was that of second deputy secretary of the North China Bureau; he held this post by early 1954, but no later than August 1954, at which time the Bureau was abolished.

In September 1954 Chang attended the inaugural session of the First NPC and from that time has been one of the key officials in this legislative body. At the close of (and shortly after) the sessions he was given four important assignments. He was named to NPC Standing Committee membership, as well as being made a deputy secretary-general (under Secretary-General P'eng Chen) and director of the Standing Committee's Staff Office. Finally, Chang was named to head the permanent NPC Bills Committee, responsible for the drafting of legislation for submission to the Congress. Chang was appointed again to all these posts when the Second NPC was formed (1959), but he was removed as a deputy secretary-general in September 1962. He was once again named to the Standing Committee and Bills Committee at the close of the initial session of the Third NPC (January 1965), but it is not certain if he continues to head the Staff Office.

Chang's work was given recognition in May 1958 at the second session of the Eighth Party Congress when he was elected an alternate member of the Party Central Committee. In August 1958 he was elected a member of the Third National Council of the Political Science and Law Association of China, the organization he had helped to found in 1953. Six years later, in October 1964, he was boosted to a vice-presidency when the Fourth National Council was formed. As already noted, Chang was removed as a deputy secretary-general of the NPC in September 1962. The reason, apparently, was to allow more time for a new and important assignment; he was appointed at this time as a deputy procurator general of the Supreme People's Procuratorate, serving here under veteran Party leader Chang Ting-ch'eng. The Procuratorate, responsible to the NPC, has broad investigative powers to carry out its functions of ensuring the nationwide observance of the law.

Between 1956 and 1964, Chang made six trips abroad. He accompanied Sung Ch'ing-ling (Mme. Sun Yat-sen) on a goodwill visit to Indonesia in August 1956, traveling via Burma. In August–September 1959 he was secretary-general of a group led by Politburo member Lin Po-ch'ü, that visited Mongolia, and in February 1961 Chang led a delegation to Moscow to take part in the celebrations marking the 11th anniversary of the signing of the Sino-Soviet Treaty of Friendship, Alliance and Mutual Assistance. In May of 1962 he accompanied Politburo member P'eng Chen to North Korea for a visit described as a "goodwill" tour, but one that occurred as the Chinese and Soviets fought for the allegiance of the Koreans in the continuing Sino-Soviet ideological struggle. On a somewhat similar mission, and again accompanying P'eng Chen, Chang visited North Vietnam in September–October 1962. Finally, in September 1964, Chang again toured North Korea, this time as leader of a small delegation of the China-Korea Friendship Association. In addition to the contacts he has made while abroad, Chang has doubtless come to know many other foreigners owing to the fact that he is very often on hand in Peking to receive and entertain the many foreign visitors to the national capital.

---

1. *K'ang-chan chung-te Chung-kuo cheng-chih* (Chinese politics during the resistance war; Yenan, 1940), p. 454.

Chang Ta-chih

(1911–   ; Feng-hsiang hsien, Shensi). Commander, Lanchow Military Region; alternate member, CCP Central Committee.

Chang Ta-chih, a career military officer, has spent his entire career in northwest China and has been an alternate member of the Party Central Committee since 1956. He was born in 1911 in Feng-hsiang hsien, located in west Shensi just north of the Wei River. By 1932 he had joined Communist guerilla units in north Shensi, probably in association with Liu Chih-tan (q.v.), the leading Communist military and political figure in Shensi during that period. In 1932 Chang was a member of the Party's North Shensi Special Committee, but nothing further is known of his work until early 1936 when he became director of civil transport of the Political Department in the 15th Army Corps. This Corps had been established a year earlier by a merger of forces led by Liu Chih-tan with those under the command of Hsu Hai-tung who had come to Shensi from the Communists' Hupeh-Honan-Anhwei (Oyüwan) Soviet. In mid-1936 the Communists in Shensi, who now included Mao Tse-tung's Long Marchers, re-established the Red Army Academy in north Shensi. Chang was a student in the first class.

Nothing further is known of Chang until 1942 by which time he had become a deputy political commissar of a cavalry unit in Inner Mongolia, which operated in the Tach'ing Mountains north of Huhehot (formerly Kweisui). Seven years later, when the Communists were completing the conquest of the mainland, Chang was an army commander in P'eng Te-huai's First Field Army in northwest China, and by 1950 he was a deputy chief-of-staff of this force. Working in the military headquarters in Lanchow, Kansu, Chang was primarily involved in military affairs in the early fifties. However, following the establishment of the Northwest Military and Administrative Committee (NWMAC), the governing organ for the northwest, Chang was made director of the NWMAC's Public Security Department (July 1952 to March 1953), replacing Kan Szu-ch'i (q.v.). About the same time he also became a member of the Northwest Labor Employment Committee, and in January 1953 he was appointed to membership on the Northwest Administrative Committee, the successor to the NWMAC. In September 1954, with the creation of the constitutional government and the dis-

solution of regional administrations, Chang received his first position in the central government when he became a member of the newly created National Defense Council. He was reappointed to the Council in April 1959 and January 1965.

When the Communists bestowed personal military ranks in September 1955 Chang was made a lieutenant-general, the equivalent of a two-star U.S. Army general, and at the same time he received one or one more of the decorations that were given for military service from the birth of the Red Army in 1927 to 1950. A year later, in September 1956, he was elected an alternate member of the CCP Central Committee at the Party's Eighth National Congress. Chang was identified as commander of the Lanchow Military Region in September 1958 (although some reports suggest that he held this post as early as 1956). The Lanchow headquarters has jurisdiction over military affairs in Shensi, Kansu, Tsinghai, and Ninghsia. Since 1956 Chang has been quite prominent in Kansu and Lanchow, where he is a frequent participant in political and military functions; for example, it fell to him to make a report on the military situation to Defense Minister Lin Piao when the latter visited Lanchow in November 1960. The outline of Chang's activities suggests close ties with the Kansu Party machinery, although he has never been specifically identified in any post. He was, however, identified in February 1964 as a secretary of the even more important Northwest Party Bureau. The Bureau, headed by Liu Lan-t'ao (q.v.), was created by the Ninth Party Plenum in January 1961 and includes in its jurisdiction the same provinces that fall under the Lanchow Military Region (Shensi, Kansu, Tsinghai, and Ninghsia) in addition to Sinkiang.

Chang T'ai-lei

(1898–1927; Ch'ang-chou, Kiangsu). A founder of the Socialist Youth League; Comintern official; participant in the Canton Uprising; member, CCP Central Committee.

Chang T'ai-lei has gone down in Chinese Communist history primarily as the martyred hero of the Canton Commune of December 1927. One of the earliest CCP members, he was a liaison official with the Comintern in the early twenties and then the key figure in the Socialist Youth League. A native of Ch'ang-chou, Kiangsu, Chang came from a family that ran a small business. His original name was Chang T'ai-lai, which in his native dialect, sounded like Chang "T'ai-lei," the name he adopted after he began to participate in revolutionary work. Prior to this time he was also known as Chang Ch'un-mu.

Not much is known about him in the years before he became a Party activist. However, it is known that he lost his father at an early age and was brought up by relatives. He was a classmate of Ch'ü Ch'iu-pai (q.v.) at the Ch'ang-chou Middle School; Ch'ü was also to rise to prominence in the CCP, and the early ties probably account in part for the closeness between them in the Party. Chang also appears to have attended Soochow University briefly, but a chance meeting with a Peking University professor got him into the Law School of Peiyang University in Tientsin. One of the most important assets he possessed was a mastery of English, which he developed at this time and which made him an important early liaison official of the CCP with the Russians. In China he worked closely with Comintern agent Gregory Voitinsky and Soviet adviser Michael Borodin. Like Ch'ü Ch'iu-pai, he seldom questioned the policies laid down in Moscow.

As in the case of most of his contemporaries, Chang began his revolutionary career with the nationalistic convulsions of the May Fourth Movement. In February 1919 he founded the Society for Social Reconstruction, a student organization in Tientsin. He once engaged Bertrand Russell, then lecturing in China, in a public debate, defending the view that the "menial proletariat," rather than the "mental proletariat" (intelligentsia) was the foremost class that would bring about social progress. At this time he was deeply immersed in the investigation of labor conditions and the study of the labor movement. In several articles in the short-lived Communist tabloid *Lao-tung chieh* (Labor circles), published in Shanghai by the Communists, he urged workers to organize themselves into labor unions. Meantime, as a member of Li Ta-chao's Society for the Study of Marxism in Peking, he developed an interest in Marxism.

In August 1920 Chang was in Shanghai and was one of the founding members of the Socialist Youth League. In September he was also present as one of the nine individuals, led by Voitinsky and Ch'en Tu-hsiu (q.v.), who formulated plans for the formation of a central Communist Party organization as well as for a foreign language school to prepare students who wanted to go to Russia to enroll in the University of the Toilers of the East. Then in October he returned to Tientsin, where he initiated the Tientsin branch of the Socialist Youth League, which was peculiarly free of anarchist dissensions plaguing so many other early Communist-oriented groups; Chang was made its first secretary.

In the following two years, 1921 and 1922, Chang's activities were connected with the Comintern. In the spring of 1921 he reported to the Comintern's Far Eastern Secretariat in Irkutsk and set up the Chinese section that was to act as the liaison between the Chinese Communists and the Comintern. He was designated as its secretary. As a Comintern functionary, he

was named to its Organization Bureau in charge of preparing for the formation of the Korean Communist Party, and at its founding congress of May 4, 1921, Chang delivered a report entitled "The Japanese proletariat and the Korean poor."

In June 1921, with another young Chinese Communist sent from Shanghai, he proceeded to Moscow to attend the Third Congress of the Comintern, held in June–July 1921. Chang and his colleague were the first Chinese delegates to have come from a *bona fide* Communist Party in China. (Delegates at earlier congresses were representatives of an émigré Chinese organization in the Soviet Union.) The Congress adopted a set of theses drafted by Chang on national and colonial questions, echoing Lenin's theses of the second congress. Sharing the frustration of M. N. Roy and other Asian delegates, he urged the Russians to pay more attention to the East. After the Congress, with Japanese Communist Katayama Sen and others, he laid the groundwork for the convocation of a congress of revolutionary organizations in Asia and penned the appeal to these organizations to send delegates. Returning to China, he was assigned to assist Comintern emissary Maring, who sent him to Japan to recruit delegates for the Congress of Toilers of the East. The congress was originally scheduled to be held at Irkutsk to coincide with the opening of the Washington Conference on November 11, 1921, but the Russians, deciding to give it more substance than a propaganda show, moved the venue to Moscow, where the Congress lasted from January 21 to February 1, with a closing session in Petrograd on February 2. Representing the Socialist Youth League, Chang was among some 43 delegates, mostly students, drawn from various organizations in China. He delivered one of the key speeches and took part in the drafting of the manifesto of the Congress.

After the Congress, he returned to China and was put in charge of the Shanghai Masses' Girls' School (Shanghai P'ing-min Nü-hsiao), an institution sponsored by the CCP, whose faculty members included Ch'en Wang-tao and Shen Yen-ping (q.v.). In July 1922 Chang was present at the Second CCP Congress as an observer. Later in the year he appears to have accompanied Ch'en Tu-hsiu and Liu Jen-ching to Moscow to attend the Fourth Comintern Congress held in November–December 1922. His Ch'ang-chou Middle School schoolmate Ch'ü Ch'iu-pai, whom he had initiated into the Moscow branch of the CCP, was also present as an interpreter.

Chang returned home in the early part of 1923 and in the middle of the year he joined Shanghai University, which was founded that year under KMT-CCP sponsorship. In July he went to Canton to attend the Third CCP Congress, meeting for the first time as a legal organization. At the Congress he sided with Li Ta-chao, Ch'ü Ch'iu-pai, Teng Chung-hsia (q.v.), among others, who approved the Comintern line of forming a "bloc within" in collaboration with the KMT, beating down the opposition led by Chang Kuo-t'ao that resisted the merger. In August 1923 he was in Nanking for the Second National Congress of the Socialist Youth League, which was attended by some 30 delegates representing a membership of about 6,000. The Congress endorsed the Third CCP Congress resolution to implement the policy of the "bloc within" theory of cooperation with the KMT. At the First Congress of the Socialist Youth League, held in May 1922 during Chang's absence in the Soviet Union, he had been elected a member of the Central Committee along with Ts'ai Ho-sen and Teng Chung-hsia. Now, at the Second Congress, he was elected secretary-general of the Socialist Youth League, with Yün Tai-ying and Teng Chung-hsia, among others, on the Central Committee.

Chang was one of the first Communists to enter the KMT. After its reorganization in the early part of 1923, he was made a member of the Propaganda Department. In August 1923 he was a member of the mission sent by Sun Yat-sen to the Soviet Union, which included Chiang Kai-shek, Wang Teng-yun, and Shen Ting-i; the purpose of the group was to study Soviet military institutions and obtain Soviet aid. The delegation set out on August 16 and stayed in Russia for three months. Chang appears to have remained in Moscow and spent the year 1924 at the Communist University of the Toilers of the East.

Chang was present at the Fourth CCP Congress in January 1925 and was elected an alternate member of the Central Committee. At the Third Congress of the Socialist Youth League held in the same month in Shanghai, he was re-elected secretary of the Central Committee, which he remained until the Fourth Congress in May 1927 when Jen Pi-shih (q.v.) succeeded him. After his return from the Soviet Union, he worked mainly in Canton as chief interpreter in Borodin's office. He was one of the editors of the Communist journal *Jen-min chou-k'an* (People's weekly) and participated actively in the organization of the Hong Kong–Canton strike and boycott against the British in response to the May 30th Incident in Shanghai.

In October 1926 he moved to Hankow with Borodin, serving as his secretary until the spring of 1927; concurrently, he was chief of political work in the National Revolutionary Army. Here his activities encompassed both the peasant associations and the trade unions as well. In the spring of 1927 he was appointed secretary of the Hupeh CCP Provincial Committee. At the Fifth CCP Congress in April–May 1927 he was a staunch supporter of Ch'ü Ch'iu-pai in his challenge to the Ch'en Tu-hsiu-P'eng Shu-chih leadership. He became a full Central Committee member at the close of the congress, and in

July, as Ch'en Tu-hsiu was being eased out of power, Chang was named to a newly constituted Provisional Politburo.

Chang was present at the August 7 Emergency Conference, at which Ch'ü Ch'iu-pai succeeded Ch'en Tu-hsiu as Party chief; Chang was appointed secretary of the Kwangtung CCP Provincial Committee and at the same time head of the South China Bureau. Joining the expedition led by Yeh T'ing and Ho Lung (qq.v.), which headed southward after the failure of the Nanchang Uprising, he was entrusted with the organization of peasant soviets. At Swatow and Ch'ao-chou these forces were routed by Chang Fa-k'uei, the Kwangtung general, in September 1927.

After the debacle at Swatow and Chao-chou, Chang returned to Shanghai and attended a meeting of the CCP Central Committee, which resolved to foment further insurrections where opportunity permitted. It decided that Kwangtung was promising in view of the impending clash between Chang Fa-k'uei and Li Chi-shen, two local militarists. During that crisis the workers and peasants of Kwangtung were supposed to rise and seize power in the entire province. As it turned out, the showdown between the two militarists occurred on November 17, with Canton falling into the hands of Chang Fa-k'uei. Chang T'ai-lei rushed back to Canton to take things in command. In the ensuing weeks an opportunity presented itself when Chang Fa-k'uei withdrew most of his forces from the city to the front to meet Li Chi-shen's reinforced army. On November 26, the Kwangtung CCP Provincial Committee resolved that the time was ripe for an armed insurrection. A five-man Revolutionary Military Council was created, with Chang T'ai-lei as chairman and Yeh T'ing as commander-in-chief. (Yeh arrived in Canton only a few hours before the insurrection began.) Heinz Neumann, who temporarily replaced Lominadze (then in Moscow attending the 15th C.P.S.U. Congress), was on hand to furnish funds and direction, while the Soviet Consulate in Canton also took an active part in the preparations.

On December 7 the Provincial Committee met and scheduled the insurrection for December 13 and nominated a "soviet" of 15 members. Su Chao-cheng (q.v.), the proletarian labor leader, was accorded the honor of the chairmanship, but being absent, Chang T'ai-lei acted on his behalf. Chang also held the post of commissar of the Army and Navy. Other members of the "soviet" included:

Huang P'ing	People's commissar of the Interior
Yang Yin	People's commissar for Suppression of Counterrevolution
Chou Wen-yung	People's commissar of Labor

P'eng P'ai	People's commissar of Land (P'eng being occupied at the Hai-lu-feng Soviet, Chao Tzu-hsuan officiated in his absence.)
Yun Tai-ying	Secretary General
Yeh T'ing	Commander-in-Chief of the Workers' and Peasants' Red Army

An information leak forced the Communists to advance the uprising to December 11, and on the following day they were surrounded on all sides by KMT forces, and Chang himself was killed in the fighting.

Among the most useful sources for Chang's career are: (1) B. Z. Shumiatskii, "Iz istorii Komsomola i Kompartii Kitaia (Pamiati odnogo iz organizatorov Komsomola i Kompartii Kitaia tov. Chang T'ai-lei)" (On the Communist Youth and the CCP. In memory of one of the organizers of the Communist Youth and the CCP, Comrade Chang T'ai-lei); *Revoliutsionnyi Vostok,* nos. 4–5: 194–230 (1928). (2) [Ch'ü] Ch'iu-pai, "In Memory of Comrade Chang T'ai-lei," *Bolshevik,* no. 12:385–386. (3) N. Fokin, "In Memory of the Organizer of the Canton Rising—Comrade Chang T'ai-lei," *Communist International,* March 15, 1928, pp. 155–156. (4) Wang I-chih, "I T'ai-lei" (In memory of T'ai-lei), *Hung-ch'i p'iao-p'iao* (Red flag fluttering, Peking, 1957), no. 5:13–19.

Chang Te-sheng

(1909–1965; Yü-lin hsien, Shensi). Northwest Party leader; alternate member, CCP Central Committee.

Chang Te-sheng spent his entire career in the Communist movement as a Party official in his native northwest. He was born in 1909 in Yü-lin hsien in northern Shensi. It was in Yü-lin that such prominent Communists as Liu Chih-tan and Kao Kang (qq.v.) studied during their school days in the 1920's, and it may have been through contacts with Liu or Kao that Chang began his revolutionary activities. (For a longer discussion of Communist activity in Shensi during the twenties, see under Chia T'o-fu.) Chang joined the Communist Youth League in 1927 and three years later was admitted to the CCP.

According to Chang's obituary (the source for most of the information about his career prior to 1949), he spent the years from 1930 to 1934 as an underground worker, serving first in Fu-ku hsien in northeast Shensi (not far from Yü-lin) as head of the Party's Organization Department. He was subsequently head of the Organization Department of the Kansu-Ninghsia-Tsinghai Special Party Committee and later the director of the Propaganda Department of the Han-chung Special Party Committee. (Han-

chung is the name of an area along the Han River that includes portions of Shensi, Szechwan, and Hupeh.) When Chu Te and Mao Tse-tung arrived in the northwest at the end of the Long March, Chang engaged in political work among those portions of the First and Fourth Front Armies of the Chinese Peasants' and Workers' Red Army that Chu and Mao commanded.

Chang's rise in the CCP continued during the Sino-Japanese War. Specializing in Party activities, he first headed the Party's Shensi Provincial Committee. Later, he was secretary of the Kuan-chung District Party Committee; Kuan-chung, located in southern Shensi, was one of the five major subdivisions of the Shensi-Kansu-Ninghsia (Shen-Kan-Ning) Border Region that was established in 1937. In addition to his Party post in Kuan-chung, by the spring of 1943 he was also political commissar of the Kuan-chung Military Sub-district.[1] Under the Party's Northwest Bureau, he also served during the war as secretary-general of the Bureau and as head of its United Front Work Department. In April 1946, when the first session of the Third Assembly of the Shen-Kan-Ning Border Region Government met in Yenan, Chang attended as a deputy from Hsin-ning hsien (located in southern Shensi in the above-mentioned Kuan-chung District).

From 1947 to 1949, during the course of the civil war with the Nationalists, Chang was a deputy director of the Political Department of the First Field Army, a position that placed him under political officer Kan Szu-ch'i (q.v.), the head of the Political Department for most of this period. After P'eng Te-huai's First Field Army captured Lanchow, the Kansu capital, in August 1949, Chang served briefly under Chang Tsung-hsun (q.v.) as a deputy director of the Lanchow Military Control Commission. More important, however, he became the ranking secretary of the Kansu Party Committee, his major post for the next five years. Chang also held several positions within the Kansu Provincial People's Government after it was established in January 1950. He was a Kansu vice-governor from 1950 to 1954 and also headed two of this government's most important subordinate bodies, the Finance and Economics Committee (1950–1954) and the Land Reform Committee (1951–1954). Although Chang did not receive any post of importance in the national government that was established in the fall of 1949, he served as a member of the preparatory committee (representing the First Field Army) of the All-China Athletic Federation from October 1949 to June 1952.

During the early years of the PRC, both the CCP and the government had regional subdivisions; in the northwest, the government administration covering the provinces of Shensi, Kansu, Ninghsia, Tsinghai, and Sinkiang was known as the Northwest Military and Administrative Committee (NWMAC). From its formation in January 1950 Chang served as one of the members of the NWMAC that was chaired by P'eng Te-huai. He was reappointed to membership when the NWMAC was reorganized into the Northwest Administrative Committee in January 1953, continuing in this post until the regional administrations were dissolved in 1954. In the Northwest Party Bureau, he was a deputy director of the Organization Department by 1951 and head of the Bureau's United Front Work Department by 1954, presumably holding these posts until the Bureau was abolished in mid-1955. In 1954 (to an uncertain date) Chang became chairman of the preparatory committee for the Northwest Branch of the Academy of Sciences. Although his main tasks in the early fifties kept him in Lanchow, the Kansu capital, Chang's assignments in the Party's Northwest Bureau and the NWMAC (NCAC) took him on occasion to Sian where they were headquartered.

From 1953 to 1954, Chang headed the Kansu Election Committee, which was given the task of preparing for the elections to the NPC. When the provincial elections were held in mid-1954, he was elected as a Kansu deputy to the First NPC (1954–1959). At approximately the same time these elections were held, Kansu and Ninghsia Provinces were merged (and thus a "new" Kansu Provincial Party Committee had to be formed). Chang was replaced as the Kansu Party secretary by another veteran from the northwest, Chang Chung-liang (q.v.). Chang Te-sheng, in turn, was transferred to his native Shensi. In March 1955 he was elected as the chairman of the Shensi Committee of the CPPCC; his term in this office is uncertain, and by May 1962 Fang Chung-ju was serving as the chairman. More important, by April 1955 he was identified as the Party first secretary in Shensi, replacing P'an Tzu-li (q.v.), who had been appointed as ambassador to North Korea in late 1954. Chang continued to head the Party Committee in Shensi until his death a decade later.

Chang played an active role at the Party's Eighth National Congress in September 1956, serving as a member of both the Congress Presidium (steering committee) and the Credentials Committee. He addressed the Congress on agricultural cooperatives and agricultural production in Shensi and at the close of the sessions was elected as an alternate member of the Party Central Committee. From the mid-fifties until about a year before his death, Chang's activities in Shensi received frequent and rather full coverage in the Chinese press. As the Shensi Party first secretary, he participated in a number of meetings sponsoring Party policies, particularly in connection with the "rectification" campaign in 1957–1958 and with the Great Leap Forward launched in 1958. He attended the Second Session of the Eighth Party Congress in May 1958, as well as the important Sixth Party Plenum held in Wuhan in late 1958 when it was decided to curb some of the excesses of the Great Leap.

At the Ninth Plenum of the Party Central Committee held in January 1961, the decision was taken to re-establish the regional Party Bureaus to "strengthen leadership over the Party Committees in the various provinces, municipalities, and autonomous regions." There were, however, suggestions that the bureaus had already been established by late 1960—at a time when the effects of the failures of the Great Leap Forward were being felt throughout China. These suggestions seem to have been borne out in Chang's obituary, which states that he became Second Secretary of the Northwest Party Bureau by 1960, a post that placed him under First Secretary Liu Lan-t'ao. It was also noted in the obituary that when Chang died he was concurrently first political commissar of the Shensi Military District.

In early 1965 Hu Yao-pang (q.v.) was identified as the acting first secretary in Shensi, suggesting (in retrospect) that Chang was in ill health. He died in Sian on March 4, 1965, at the age of 56. The memorial services in connection with his death were in accord with those normally granted to a person of Chang's stature in the CCP.

---

1. *Hsing-huo liao-yuan* (A single spark can start a prairie fire; Peking, 1961), VI, 65.

Chang T'i-hsueh

Party and government administrator; Hupeh governor.

A brigade commander during the Sino-Japanese War, Chang T'i-hsueh has been an official in Hupeh provincial administration since 1949 and governor of the province since 1955. His first known association with the Chinese Communists was in east-central China during the war years. By the last year of the war he was commanding the 14th Brigade in the Fifth Division of the New Fourth Army. The division was commanded by Li Hsien-nien (q.v.), later a Politburo member, and was operating in the Hupeh-Honan-Anhwei Military Region, an area roughly coinciding with the old Oyüwan base (see under Chang Kuo-t'ao), one of the most important "soviets" during the late twenties and early thirties. Chang has remained in this general area for well over 20 years, an exceptional case among Chinese Communist leaders, whose work has been notably peripatetic.

By early 1946 Chang was in charge of the Communists' East Hupeh Military District, which was subordinate to the larger Central Plains (Chung yuan) Military Region, and concurrently he commanded the Second Brigade. He was imprisoned briefly by the Chinese Nationalists in 1946. Although the circumstances surrounding this event are not known, they may have been related to the arrest of his wife, Lin Shao-nan, in the early part of the year. Lin had been arrested while visiting her parents in Wuhan, but, presumably owing to the brief interlude of KMT-CCP cooperation that existed during the early days of the Marshall Mission (see under Yeh Chien-ying), the Communists protested and were able to gain Mme. Chang's release.[1] After his own release Chang returned to his command assignment in eastern Hupeh, where presumably he remained throughout the civil war with the Nationalists.

With the Communist conquest in 1949, Chang remained in Hupeh to become, with the passage of years, one of the senior political figures in this important industrial and agricultural province. By early 1950 he was already the executive officer of the Hupeh Party Committee; he was then promoted to deputy secretary (1953–1954), first deputy secretary (1954–1956), and finally to secretary (1956). During this period after 1950, Chang served under Hupeh Party Secretary Li Hsien-nien (Chang's former superior in the 1940's), and then under First Secretary Wang Jen-chung after Wang replaced Li in 1954. Chang continues to hold this position.

Chang's rise in the governmental hierarchy in Hupeh parallels his ascent in Party circles. When the Hupeh Government was first formally organized in March 1950, he was named as a member of the Government Council, once again serving under Li Hsien-nien, the governor. Just five years later (in January–February 1955, at a session of the Hupeh Congress for which Chang served on the presidium, or steering committee), he was promoted to vice-governor under the new governor, Liu Tzu-hou. Then, one year later (January 1956), Liu was transferred and Chang was named to succeed him as governor, a post he continues to hold. At the national level he served as a Hupeh deputy to the First (1954–1959) and Second (1959–1964) NPCs and was then reelected for the Third NPC, which held its first session in December 1964–January 1965. The annual sessions of the NPC have, of course, brought him to Peking. Furthermore, he attended the Eighth National Party Congress as a deputy from Hupeh. However, aside from these trips, he has spent virtually all his time in Hupeh.

Like many provincial officials of Chang's stature, he has participated in numerous campaigns and movements, often as head of quasi-official organizations of brief duration. For example, in late 1955 Chang was named to chair the Hupeh provincial committee to prevent and cure schistosomiasis, a crippling disease that has plagued many areas of China for centuries. Shortly after, in early 1956, he was named as head of the Hupeh committee to eliminate illiteracy,

and in May 1958 became chairman of the newly formed Hupeh Scientific and Technical Work Committee. Aside from these somewhat formalized positions, Chang has constantly been in the news from the mid-1950's in his capacity as a senior Hupeh official, mainly engaged in the management of the provincial government. In addition, he spends a great deal of time hosting both foreign and domestic guests visiting Wuhan. Apart from being the Hupeh capital, Wuhan is also the locale of China's greatest showpiece of progress under the Communists, the Yangtze River Bridge. This bridge provides, for the first time in Chinese history, an unbroken link across the great river that bisects China. When the bridge opened in October 1957 Chang was on hand for the ceremonies and was one of the main speakers. Aside from having this impressive bridge, Wuhan is the main industrial center of central China and thus the object of frequent inspection visits by China's political elite (e.g., Chou En-lai in October 1959).

Already well entrenched in the Hupeh government and Party ranks, Chang received a significant new post by January 1963, when he was first identified as the Political Commissar of the Hupeh Military District, a position he still holds. Thus, although not a Party Central Committee member, Chang is probably the most important figure in Hupeh with the exception of Party First Secretary Wang Jen-chung. Nothing is known of Chang's personal life aside from the fact that he is married to Lin Shao-nan.

1. *Chin-Ch'a-Chi jih-pao* (Shansi-Chahar-Hopeh daily), Kalgan, March 3, 1946.

Chang Ting-ch'eng

(c.1898–   ; Yung-ting hsien, Fukien). Chairman, former West Fukien Soviet; a commander, the former New Fourth Army; Procurator-General, Supreme People's Procuratorate; member, CCP Control Commission and Central Committee.

Chang Ting-ch'eng comes from southwest Fukien, where he studied and taught in primary schools before he became active in work with the peasants and joined the CCP in 1927. He was an important leader of the Communist Movement in Fukien, organized one of the first Communist soviets there, and remained behind with the Fukien guerrillas in the mid-1930's when Mao Tse-tung and Chu Te led their armies on the Long March. During the Sino-Japanese War Chang was a top commander in the Communists' New Fourth Army, his troops harassing the Japanese in the strategic area south of Nanking. He became the first governor of Fukien when the Communists took over there in August 1949 and has been procurator-general of the PRC since

1954. He has also been known by the name of Chang Ting-hsin.

Chang was born in Chin-sha village, Yung-ting hsien, a rural area in southwest Fukien not far from the Kwangtung border. Communists were actively working there with the peasants from the late 1920's and the area was traversed by Red armies making their way to Swatow after the Communists' defeat at Nanchang in August 1927. Although Chang was of poor peasant origin, he received some education in rural schools in Fukien and later seems to have taught for a brief time in a primary school in his native Chin-sha village. According to Japanese sources, he went to Canton to study at the Peasant Movement Training Institute about the year 1925. The Institute opened in 1924 under KMT auspices (but mainly staffed by CCP members) for the training of revolutionary cadres to work among the peasants, and the students recruited for its first three classes that were held in the first year and a half of the Institute's brief existence are all presumed to have been recruited from Kwangtung. Hence, the date when Chang attended classes there cannot be definitely established. According to one report he joined the KMT before becoming a Communist.[1] Both events may have occurred while he attended classes at the Peasant Movement Training Institute. Again the record is obscure, but it suggests that he returned to southwest Fukien during the year 1925 to teach again in a primary school. This was a primary school in Feng-lang village in Shang-hang hsien, the neighboring county to Yung-ting. The latter information is drawn from a biography of Liu Yung-sheng, a fellow radical from Shang-hang hsien who later commanded local forces in Yung-ting belonging to the army of Chang Ting-ch'eng. Liu became a Party member in 1928 and is today a commander of the Fukien Military District. According to his biography his first introduction to the radical political ideas of the day came from his teacher, Chang Ting-ch'eng, who was then at the Feng-lang primary school.[2]

After the split between the CCP and the KMT following the Nanchang Uprising of August 1927, Chang went to work with the peasants in southwest Fukien. He may have been engaged in this work when the Red armies traveled close to his native area on their way to attempt the coup at Swatow in September 1927. That year he joined the CCP and the following year, in collaboration with Liu Yung-sheng and Teng Tzu-hui (q.v.), he organized a peasant uprising in Yung-ting. All three men came from adjoining areas in southwest Fukien and were to remain active there until the outbreak of the Sino-Japanese War. Their respective skills and training must have complemented one another; all were of rather humble origin, though Teng, a middle school graduate, had had a year's study in Japan. Both Liu and Chang had had only

primary school training. Chang, the son of a peasant, had been to the revolutionary training institute for peasant organizers, while Liu, who earned his living making charcoal before becoming a Communist, joined the Party when he entered the Fukien Red guerrilla forces in 1928 as a common soldier. Soon after the peasant uprising took place in Yung-ting, the Communists established a base there and Chang, in 1928, became chairman of the local Communist administration in this part of Fukien. By sometime in 1930, when the seat of the soviet government in west Fukien was located at Hu-kang near the capital of Yung-ting hsien, the soviet had within its boundaries both a Red Army school (for West Fukien) located at Lung-yen to the north and a military hospital in Shang-hang hsien.[3] Chang was the commander of a 21st Red Army in 1931. Almost nothing is known about this army, but it may have been allied with the 12th Red Army, as were some of the guerrilla units in southwest Fukien in about 1930.[4] The 12th Army, commanded by Lo Ping-hui and T'an Chen-lin (qq.v.), fought in west Fukien, especially in the area around Ch'ang-t'ing to the north of Yung-ting in the early 1930's.

In November 1931, when the Communists created the Chinese Central Soviet Republic with its capital in southeast Kiangsi at Juichin, Chang was made a member of the soviet's governing body, the Central Executive Committee (CEC). In addition, he was made "People's Commissar for Land," the equivalent of a cabinet post. Both T'an Chen-lin and Teng Tzu-hui were also elected to the CEC, and Teng was made Commissar for Finance in the government. Only Chang was re-elected to full membership on the CEC at the meeting of the Second All-China Congress of Soviets of January–February 1934; Teng was dropped to an alternate CEC member at this time. In addition, at the 1934 Congress, Chang and Teng were both dropped from their cabinet posts. No reasons have been given for Chang's demotion, but those of Teng and T'an relate to the attack made at the time upon the so-called Lo Ming line with which the two men were associated (see under Teng Tzu-hui).

Chang and his associates remained in Fukien when the Communist armies commanded by Mao Tse-tung and Chu Te left southeast Kiangsi to begin the Long March. When Juichin fell to the Nationalists late in 1934, Chang's small West Fukien Soviet had established its capital in Szu-tu in Ch'ang-t'ing hsien, located in Fukien due east of Juichin. After the Long Marchers left, Chang and his forces continued to carry out guerrilla operations in Yung-ting and Shang-hang hsien. In 1934 Liu Yung-sheng was sent south from Szu-tu to command Red forces over the border in northeastern Kwangtung in the Ta-p'u area and to coordinate Communist operations there with those in Fukien.[5] Chang was joined by Teng Tzu-hui and T'an Chen-lin in August 1935 when the Southwest Fukien Military and Administrative Committee was set up. Chang became the Committee's chairman and Teng and T'an the vice-chairmen. At this time one of the bases for Communist operations in southwest Fukien was again in the Lung-yen area where Teng Tzu-hui was in charge.

During the next three years Red guerrilla forces continued to operate in west Fukien. They centered especially in the southwest from Ch'ang-t'ing to Shang-hang, Yung-ting, and Lung-yen, and also south across the Kwangtung border into the area around Ta-p'u. These forces were never large in number and by the start of the Sino-Japanese War they were said to have numbered no more than 2,000 men.[6] For a time in 1937 after the start of the Sino-Japanese War the Communist forces in these areas were known as the Southwest Fukien People's Anti-Japanese Volunteers, commanded by Chang with T'an and Teng as his deputies.

Once the war broke out the Communists entered into negotiations with the Nationalists to allow for the continuation of the Red armies. First they created the Eighth Route Army to operate in north China; then in September 1937 negotiations were begun for the creation of a Communist army that was to operate in east-central China in the plain of the lower Yangtze Valley. Early in 1938 Yeh T'ing, the commander of this New Fourth Army, established his headquarters in Nanchang, the Kiangsi capital. By the spring, contact had been made with all the scattered units of Red guerrilla forces operating south of the Yangtze. Thus the New Fourth Army went into operation with four major detachments, only one of which was initially active north of the river. Chang Ting-ch'eng was given command of the Second Detachment, a force that included his own troops from southwest Fukien, plus those of Su Yü, who had been operating north of Chang's territory along the borders of Fukien and Chekiang. Chang brought all the units under his command together and in March 1938 left Lung-yen, his old west Fukien soviet base.[7]

When the New Fourth Army went into the field of battle in May 1938, it moved into strategic areas along the important railroads connecting the industrial cities Shanghai, Wuhu, and Hangchow with Nanking. For the first year of its existence Chang's Second Detachment made its headquarters not far south of Nanking city at Chin-t'an north of Tao Lake, while his forces scattered over a territory immediately south of the Yangtze and Nanking, stretching from Tang-t'u hsien in southern Anhwei (through which the Nanking-Wuhu railroad crossed) into south Kiangsu around Tan-yung and Chü-jung on the Grand Canal (and crossed by the railroad running from Nanking to Shanghai). As political

commissar of the Second Detachment Chang had Su Yü, and for a time from early 1939 Lo Ping-hui served as his deputy commander. Lo's troops from the Second Detachment were among the first units of the New Fourth Army to be moved north of the Yangtze (see under Yeh T'ing), a move that Lo had completed by May of 1939.[8] A year later, at the end of June 1940, Ch'en I, commander of the New Fourth Army's First Detachment, brought his own detachment and some troops from the Second Detachment north of the Yangtze to give the Communists control of north Kiangsu east of the Grand Canal.[9] At about this time Ch'en established his new headquarters at Yen-ch'eng, in the central part of north Kiangsu. Thus, by mid-1940, a large part of Chang's force had been brought north of the Yangtze into the area that became the new headquarters for Ch'en I and his army. Some units from Chang's Second Detachment, however, remained south of the Yangtze and were not moved north until late 1940 when they accompanied the headquarters forces commanded by Yeh T'ing.

This move, which resulted in the New Fourth Army Incident of January 4, 1941, is more fully described in the biography of Yeh T'ing. Briefly, Yeh's headquarters' troops, plus the remnants of Chang Ting-ch'eng's Second Detachment were the last segments of the New Fourth Army to move north, units that did not begin the move until late December 1940. Under circumstances that are not entirely clear (see under Ch'en I), these troops were at Mao-lin southwest of their old headquarters in Ching, south Anhwei, when they were surrounded by Nationalist troops and all but annihilated in early January 1941, at the time of the New Fourth Army Incident.[10] The New Fourth Army was reorganized in February 1941, with Ch'en I named as acting commander in place of Yeh T'ing, who was captured during the Incident. At this time the army's forces were regrouped into new units composed of seven divisions instead of the former detachments (see under Ch'en I). The whereabouts of Chang Ting-ch'eng are uncertain at the period of the New Fourth Army Incident, but sometime in 1940 he went to Yenan, possibly in June when most of his force accompanied Ch'en I to north Kiangsu. In the 1941 reorganization he was given command of the new Seventh Division, with Tseng Hsi-sheng (q.v.) as his political commissar. Meanwhile, one of Chang's former deputy commanders, Teng Tzu-hui, became head of the New Fourth Army Political Department. From 1941 the Seventh Division operated in central Anhwei in what was known to the Communists as the Central Anhwei Military Region (see under Tseng Hsi-sheng).[11] Chang was division commander from 1941 until about the early part of 1944. During most of this time he was also commander of the Kiangsu-Anhwei Border Military Region. It appears that Chang returned to Yenan again in about 1942 when the Party Center was conducting the intra-Party "rectification" (*cheng-feng*) campaign under the personal direction of Mao Tse-tung. Chang's presence in Yenan is strongly suggested in an article entitled "Rectification at the Yenan Central Party School," which was published in 1961 in a volume of wartime reminiscences.[12] When the CCP met for its Seventh National Party Congress in Yenan in the spring of 1945 (April–June), he was elected for the first time to membership on the important Party Central Committee.

With the end of hostilities in the summer of 1945, Chang remained with the forces of the New Fourth Army. Continuing to serve in military affairs for the next few years, by 1949 he began to assume other responsibilities with the government and Party administrations. He spent the winter of 1945 in the Kiangsu-Anhwei Border Region in charge of the field army group stationed there. In 1946 the Communists designated their principal armies as regional branches of the People's Liberation Army. At this time Ch'en I's former New Fourth Army became the East China PLA; at a later date it was called the East China Field Army and by early 1949 the Third Field Army. During the year 1945–1946 Ch'en led a major portion of his army into Shantung Province, but Chang Ting-ch'eng was left in charge of his PLA forces in central China, the command area known as the Central China (Hua-chung) Military Region. Chang headed the command in 1946 and had Su Yü as his deputy commander, while former associates Teng Tzu-hui and T'an Chen-lin served respectively as political commissar and deputy political commissar.[13] With special responsibility also at this time for Anhwei Province, Chang was concurrently the commander of the Central Anhwei Military District and secretary of the Central Anhwei CCP District Committee (subordinate to the Central China Bureau of the CCP).

Chang was one of the deputy commanders of the East China PLA from 1947 to 1948, serving in this post with Su Yü, Chang Ai-p'ing, and T'an Chen-lin. He held the same position from early 1949 with the newly renamed Third Field Army. In this capacity he took part in the battle for Huai-hai in north Kiangsu late in 1948, the campaign that proved a major turning point in the civil war between the Communists and the Nationalists. When it was concluded early in January 1949, Ch'en I's Third Army and the Second Field Army of Liu Po-ch'eng continued their coordinated operations, moving south to the Yangtze Valley to conquer Nanking in April 1949. At Nanking the two armies separated; Liu turned into the southwest and Ch'en's army continued down the coast to take over the rest of Kiangsu and move into Chekiang and Fukien.

The army began its march into Fukien in June, capturing Foochow on August 17 and Amoy on October 17.

From the fall of Fukien to the Communists in 1949 until 1954, Chang was the dominant figure in his native province. He immediately assumed the three most important posts in Fukien, becoming secretary of the provincial CCP Committee, the provincial governor, and political commissar of the Fukien Military District, retaining all three positions until his transfer to Peking in 1954 (see below). Within the provincial government he also chaired the Land Reform Committee from April 1951 to 1954, and in 1952 he was also identified as chairman of the provincial chapter of the Sino-Soviet Friendship Association.

At approximately the same time that the provincial administration was being established in Fukien, the new central government was being organized in Peking at the first session of the CPPCC (September 1949). Although Chang apparently did not attend these meetings, he was named to membership on the CPPCC's First National Committee, retaining this position until the Second CPPCC was formed in late 1954. In October 1949, he was also appointed as a member of the Overseas Chinese Affairs Commission under the Government Administration Council (the cabinet). His appointment to this post was probably made on the basis of the relatively heavy concentration of overseas Chinese whose families come from Fukien. In spite of these two appointments in the national government, there is little indication that Chang spent much time in the early fifties in the national capital. Most of his activities in the early years of the PRC, as indicated above, were devoted to his work in east China. In addition to his major role in Fukien, he also served on the multi-provincial governmental committee responsible for east China—known as the East China Military and Administrative Committee (ECMAC) from its formation in January 1950, and as the East China Administrative Committee (ECAC) from December 1952 until its dissolution in 1954. Chang was a member of the ECMAC and was then promoted to a vice-chairmanship under the ECAC; moreover, from September 1952 until 1954 he served concurrently as chairman of the Political and Legal Affairs Committee. In addition, from early 1953 to 1954 he was also the fourth secretary of the Party's East China Bureau. Among his colleagues on the ECAC and the Party Bureau were Ch'en I, T'an Chen-lin, and Su Yü, all former associates from their days together with the New Fourth Army. Because both the Party Bureau and the ECAC had their headquarters in Shanghai, Chang was frequently there in 1953–1954. As a consequence, Yeh Fei (q.v.) began to assume some of Chang's tasks in Fukien. Finally, when Chang transferred to Peking in 1954, Yeh formally replaced Chang as the leading CCP and government leader in Fukien.

In early 1953 Chang was named to head the east China branch of a nationwide committee to implement the Marriage Law, an assignment that lasted through 1954. In a rare disclosure, the Chinese press revealed that Chang had missed a plenary session of the ECAC in October 1953 because of ill health. This was apparently short-lived, because he was back in public by early 1954.

In 1954 Chang was elected to the First NPC, the body that inaugurated the constitutional government at its initial session in September 1954. He sat in the NPC as a deputy from Fukien and was re-elected to the Second and Third NPC's, which opened their first sessions in April 1959 and December 1964, respectively. At the close of the September 1954 Congress, Chang succeeded Lo Jung-huan (q.v.) as procurator-general of the Supreme People's Procuratorate, the approximate equivalent of the U.S. Attorney-General's Office. Chang has continued in this position, having been officially reappointed in April 1959 and January 1965. The post of the procurator-general is one of the most important within the PRC government, standing on a par with the premier of the State Council and the chief justice of the Supreme People's Court. In theory, the Procuratorate has the right to protest any decision made by the State Council (over which the premier presides). Similarly, the procurator-general is specifically enjoined to attend the meetings of the Supreme Court's Judicial Committee and has the right to protest any decision taken. Disputes between the Procuratorate and the State Council or the Supreme Court must be resolved by the NPC (or the NPC Standing Committee). As procurator-general, Chang is also required to report on the work of the Procuratorate before the NPC. Consequently, he has made periodic reports before the NPC Standing Committee and the sessions of the full NPC that meet approximately once a year.

Chang attended the Party's historic Eighth National Congress in September 1956 and during the meetings served on both the Presidium (steering committee) and the Credentials Committee. At the close of the Congress he was re-elected to the Party Central Committee and at the First Plenum of the new Central Committee (held the day after the Congress closed), he was named to membership on the Party's Central Control Commission. Thus, as procurator-general in the government and a member of the Control Commission, Chang is in a pivotal position in terms of the inner workings of two key organs deeply involved in matters of security, supervision, and control of the Chinese Communist system.

Aside from meetings of the NPC, Chang makes relatively few public appearances. He has, however, served on occasion as a host for visiting foreign judicial delegations. Chang had never been abroad until November 1964 when he spent two weeks in North Vietnam as leader of a procurators' delegation that had been invited there by Chang's counterpart in the North Vietnamese Government. Among Chang's writing is an article that reviewed procuratorial work for the previous decade; this appeared in the Party's top journal, *Hung-ch'i* (Red flag, issue of October 16, 1959), on the occasion of the 10th anniversary of the PRC.

1. *Who's Who in China* (Shanghai, 1950), p. 251.
2. Biographic Service, Union Research Institute (URI), Hongkong, 1963, biography no. 759.
3. *Flame on High Mountain* (Peking, 1959), pp. 60–121.
4. *Ibid.,* p. 77.
5. URI, biography no. 759.
6. Wang Shu-jen, *Min-hsi jen-min chien-ch'ih tou-cheng erh-shih-nien* (The west Fukien people's hard twenty-year struggle; Shanghai, 1951), pp. 2, 17.
7. Chalmers A. Johnson, *Peasant Nationalism and Communist Power* (Stanford, Calif., 1962), pp. 76, 214.
8. *Ibid.,* p. 127.
9. *Ibid.,* pp. 136–137.
10. *Ibid.,* p. 138.
11. *Ibid.,* p. 145.
12. *Hsing-huo liao-yuan* (A single spark can start a prairie fire; Peking, 1961), VI, 1–18.
13. Chang-chia-k'ou, *Chin-Ch'a-Chi jih-pao* (Shansi-Chahar-Hopeh daily), March 4, 1946.

Chang Tsung-hsun

(c.1898–   ; Wei-nan hsien, Shensi). Deputy chief-of-staff, PLA; alternate member, CCP Central Committee.

An officer in the Red Army since its birth in 1927, Chang Tsung-hsun made the Long March and participated in both the Sino-Japanese War and the civil war against the Nationalists in the late 1940's. After serving in the northwest in the early years of the PRC, he was transferred to Peking to become a deputy chief-of-staff of the PLA, a post he still holds. Chang was elected an alternate member of the Party Central Committee in 1945, a position to which he was re-elected 11 years later at the Eighth CCP Congress.

Chang was born about 1898, although some sources report the year as 1904. He comes from Wei-nan hsien, east of Sian in Shensi Province, an area that witnessed Communist-led uprisings in the mid-1920's (see under Liu Chih-tan). In 1927 he was a cadet in the Wuhan branch of the Whampoa Military Academy. The branch of the well-known Nationalist military institute was established when the left-wing of the KMT made the city its headquarters during the Northern Expedition; it was more influenced by the Communists than its parent organization in Canton. It is probable that Chang was a CCP member by the time the Communists and Nationalists broke off relations in the summer of 1927; shortly thereafter he joined Mao Tse-tung in organizing the Autumn Harvest Uprisings in Hunan. Chang was one of the few commanders in Mao's greatly depleted First Red Division who escaped the counterattacks provoked by the Autumn Harvest Uprisings. Serving as commander of the Sixth Company of the First Division's First Regiment,[1] he fled with Mao's forces to the safety of the Chingkang Mountain retreat on the Hunan-Kiangsi border. In the next years he came to command the 64th Division of the Communist 12th Army (see under Lo Ping-hui) in western Fukien. This army joined units led by Mao, Chu Te, and P'eng Te-huai for the attack on Changsha (directed from the CCP Headquarters then under the influence of Li Li-san) in the summer of 1930, but when this failed the army returned to the Kiangsi-Fukien border where Chang seems to have become the army commander.

About 1933 Chang was reported to have been a cadet at the Red Army Academy at Juichin, Kiangsi, the capital of the Communists' Chinese Soviet Republic. By the start of the Long March in 1934 he was reportedly a divisonal commander with the Seventh Army, which formed part of the First Front Amy under Chu Te and Mao Tse-tung. When the Chu-Mao army reconnoitered with the army of Chang Kuo-t'ao and Hsu Hsiang-ch'ien in western Szechwan in the summer of 1935 (see under Chang Kuo-t'ao), Chang Tsung-hsun was with Mao's army. But he left Mao's forces at this juncture to move into Sikang with Chang Kuo-t'ao and became chief-of-staff of an army in Chang's Fourth Front Army. These units did not re-join Mao in north Shensi until late 1936.

After the Sino-Japanese War broke out in mid-1937, the Communists established the Eighth Route Army. Chang was assigned to Ho Lung's 120th Division, one of the three major elements of the Eighth Route Army. Chang's wartime activities are poorly documented, but it appears that he served for a brief time as commander of the 120th Division's 358th Brigade. He was soon replaced by Hsiao K'o (q.v.) who in the winter of 1938–39 led the 358th eastward from Shansi into Hopeh. Chang, in the meantime, was given command of the Second Military Sub-district of the Chin-pei (North Shansi) Military District, a post he may have continued to occupy throughout the war.

When the Seventh Party Congress met in Yenan from April to June 1945, Chang was elected one of the 33 alternate members of the CCP Central Committee. In the immediate postwar period he continued to be occupied with mil-

itary responsibilities. From 1946 to 1947 he commanded the 120th Division in the Shansi-Suiyuan Military Region, and from 1947 to 1949 he led the First Column of the Northwest PLA headed by P'eng Te-huai. These forces were responsible for the takeover of Kansu, Tsinghai, and Sinkiang. Concurrently Chang was a deputy commander of the Northwest PLA.

Early in 1949 P'eng's forces were redesignated the First Field Army, and Chang was made commander of its Second Army Group. From the same year to 1952 he was also a deputy commander of both the First Field Army and the Northwest Military Region. Chang's troups helped to capture Lanchow in late August 1949; he was appointed vice-chairman of the Lanchow Military Control Commission, but before the year had ended he was promoted to the chairmanship. Following the consolidation of nationwide rule the Communists inaugurated regional governments during the winter of 1949–50, and thus in early 1950 Chang became a member of the Northwest Military and Administrative Committee (NWMAC), which was headquartered in Sian. Soon afterwards, in March 1950, he was made a vice-chairman of the NWMAC's Finance and Economics Committee, but he relinquished this post in August of the same year. He may have stepped down from this post in order to become, in June 1950, chief procurator of the Northwest Branch Office of the Supreme People's Procuratorate.

When the NWMAC was reorganized into the Northwest Administrative Committee in January 1953, Chang was reappointed a member, and he also continued to be chief procurator for the northwest until May 1953. In fact, however, both posts were nominal by the early fall of 1952 when he was transferred to Peking. There, in October 1952, he was identified as deputy chief-of-staff of the highest military organ of that period, the People's Revolutionary Military Council. He continues in this post, though since 1954 it has been directly subordinate to the PLA Headquarters, and as of the mid-1960's he was the ranking deputy chief-of-staff in terms of length of service. In September 1954, with the inauguration of the constitutional government, Chang was appointed to membership on the National Defense Council, a position to which he was reappointed in April 1959 and January 1965. The Defense Council was established in 1954 at the inaugural session of the First NPC. Chang served as a deputy from the Northwest Military Region to the First NPC (1954–1958), but he was not re-elected to the Second Congress, which first met in 1959. For the second through the fifth sessions of the First NPC he also served as a member of the *ad hoc* Motions Examination Committee.

Since his transfer to the capital in 1952, Chang has made most of his rather frequent public appearances in his capacity as deputy chief-of-staff, and on numerous occasions he has been reported in connection with visiting military delegations. In March 1953 he took his first trip abroad, accompanying Chou En-lai to Moscow for Stalin's funeral. He received recognition for his lengthy military career when the PRC first awarded military decorations in September 1955; he was given the nation's three highest awards—the Orders of August First, Independence and Freedom, and Liberation. Personal military ranks were also inaugurated in 1955, with Chang being made a colonel-general (a three-star rank). A year later, in the August 28, 1956, issue of the *Chieh-fang-chün pao* (Liberation army news), he was identified as a deputy director of the PLA General Training Department, but the lack of later information about this post suggests that he did not hold it for long.

For reasons that are not clear, Chang was not promoted from alternate to full membership on the Party's Central Committee when the Eighth CCP Congress was held in September 1956. Among those who held alternate membership on the eve of the Congress, only Chang, Ku Ta-ts'un, and Wan I (qq.v.) were re-elected as alternates rather than being advanced to full membership. Nonetheless, there is little evidence over the next decade to suggest that his career was adversely affected. In fact, he continued to appear at a variety of military functions and meetings in Peking and in 1959 and 1960 made two rather important visits abroad. The first of these was from late April to mid-June 1959 when he was a member of P'eng Te-huai's 12-man military delegation to Mongolia and East Europe. The group visited Poland, East Germany, Czechoslovakia, Hungary, Rumania, Bulgaria, and Albania, returning to China via the USSR and Mongolia. While in Albania he was given a military decoration known as the "Guerrilla Band." A year later, from late September to the end of October 1960, Chang led a military delegation to the United Arab Republic. After spending almost a month there his group visited briefly in Albania before returning home.

1. *Hui-i Ching-kang-shan ch'ü te tou-cheng* (Recollections of the struggles in the Chingkang Mountains; Peking, 1956), p. 13.

Chang Tzu-i

(Hunan). Deputy director, Propaganda Department, CCP; member, Control Commission, CCP.

A native of Hunan, Chang Tzu-i has become one of the more significant propagandists within the CCP. Little is known of his early career except for the important fact that he is a veteran of Chingkangshan, where Mao Tse-tung and Chu Te gathered the remnant guerrilla forces on the Hunan-Kiangsi border in 1928 after the dis-

astrous defeats of the Communists in the previous year. He is also known to have made the Long March in 1934–1935 as a member of the Second Front Army (see under Ho Lung).

After the outbreak of the Sino-Japanese War in 1937, the Chinese Communists sent a number of rather important Party leaders to Sinkiang during the time when Sinkiang Governor Sheng Shih-ts'ai was collaborating with the Communists (see under Ch'en T'an-ch'iu). Chang was among these men. However, in 1942 Sheng pledged his loyalty to the central government in Chungking and subsequently arrested a number of the Communists, Chang among them.[1] Many of these persons, including Ch'en T'an-ch'iu and Mao Tse-tung's brother Mao Tse-min, were executed by Sheng, but Chang was among the more fortunate who lived through the imprisonment.

After his return to Communist-held areas in the mid-1940's, Chang was assigned to the Shansi-Suiyuan area, where he served as a deputy secretary of the Party Committee, presumably in close contact with important Party leaders in the area such as Lü Cheng-ts'ao (q.v.). By the closing stages of the civil war, in 1949–1950, Chang was serving in Liu Po-ch'eng's forces, which pushed from central-south China into the southwest. He was a deputy director of the Political Department of Liu's Second Field Army, and after the southwest was conquered he held an identical post in the Southwest Military Region. The political commissar for the Military Region was Teng Hsiao-p'ing (q.v.). In May 1950 the Communists established the Southwest People's Revolutionary University in Chungking, with seven branches throughout the southwest. Chang was appointed vice-president of the school under President Liu Po-ch'eng, but because Liu spent relatively little time in the area it is probable that Chang was the *de facto* president. The Southwest Military and Administrative Committee (SWMAC) was set up in July 1950 to govern the provinces of Szechwan, Kweichow, Yunnan, and Sikang; from 1953 to 1954 it was known as the Southwest Administrative Committee (SWAC). Chang was a member of the SWMAC–SWAC, again under Liu Po-ch'eng. Subordinate to the SWMAC–SWAC were several important organs, one of which was the Culture and Education Committee, chaired by Ch'u T'u-nan (q.v.), a former professor. Inasmuch as Ch'u was not a Communist, it seems probable that Chang was in fact the actual head of the region-wide committee.

Chang also held an important post in the Southwest Party Bureau as well as in one of the more important mass organizations. By at least late 1952 until 1954 he served as director of the Party's regional Propaganda Department and as a member of the Southwest Party Bureau in 1954. He was also a vice-chairman of the southwest branch of the Sino-Soviet Friendship Association from 1951 to 1954. At about the end of

1954, Chang was transferred to Peking, apparently being assigned to the Party Center. When the Second National Committee of the CPPCC was established in December 1954, he was named as a Party representative. By June 1957 he was a deputy director under Lu Ting-i of the Party Propaganda Department, a position he still holds. In April of 1959 he was reelected as a Party representative to the Third CPPCC and, moreover, was elevated to the Standing Committee. He was again elected to the Fourth CPPCC in 1964, and when the Fourth National Committee held its first session in December 1964–January 1965, he was once more elected to the Standing Committee.

Although the Party Propaganda Department is one of the most important of the central Party organs, Chang has made relatively few appearances since going to Peking in the mid-1950's. One of the more important of these occurred in 1960, when he served as a vice-chairman of the preparatory committee for a national conference of "outstanding workers" in culture and education and, when the conference was held in June 1960, he served on the presidium (steering committee). For one who is an important Party propagandist, he seems to have written very little. However, his article for the January 3, 1958, issue of *Hsueh-hsi* (Study), then the Party's most important journal, provides an exception. It was one of the first exhortations in the Great Leap Forward (then just beginning). Entitled "Concerning the Question of Intellectuals in the Countryside," the article stressed the necessity for intellectuals to be both "red and expert," a goal that could be gained with greater speed by going to the countryside to work closely with the peasants.

At the 10th Plenum of the Party Central Committee, held in September 1962, it was decided to "strengthen the work of the Party Control Commissions at all levels" and to add new members to the Central Control Commission. Although Chang has made rather few appearances and has written little, any doubt of his importance was dispelled when he was added as a member. Very little is heard of the Commission; yet it is patently one of the key organs of discipline and inspection within the CCP. Membership appears to be on a functional basis, with Chang apparently serving as a representative of the propaganda organs.

1. *Hung-ch'i p'iao-p'iao* (Red flag fluttering; Peking, 1959), X, 127–148.

Chang Wen-t'ien

(c.1898–   ; Nan-hui, Kiangsu). Important ideologue during 1930's; CCP general secretary, 1935–c.1939; alternate member, CCP Politburo.

Chang Wen-t'ien, often known by his pen name Lo Fu, was awakened to an interest in Marxism during the May Fourth Movement. Before becoming a highly influential polemicist for the CCP, he worked in the United States and studied in Moscow during the 1920's. In the Soviet Union he became a leader of the "28 Bolshevik" group, which played so important a role in the political controversies which led to Mao Tse-tung's becoming the head of the CCP. Chang was named to the Party Politburo in 1931 and succeeded to the position of Party general secretary four years later during the course of the Long March. He relinquished the post to Mao sometime after the Communists concluded the March. Chang's chief importance in Chinese Communist history rests on the fact that he was one of the Party's leading propagandists in the period before Mao came to power; he wrote prolifically on important matters of theory and policy until silenced by the preparations for the Party's first major ideological remolding campaign, which began in 1942. Despite his ensuing eclipse, he continued to hold high Party and diplomatic posts in the postwar years, serving as China's second ambassador to the USSR and as her representative (though in name only) to the United Nations. Chang's political life seems to have ended abruptly in 1959.

Chang was born on the outskirts of Shanghai, into a well-to-do peasant family. After attending a middle school in nearby Woosung, he went to Nanking where he enrolled at the Ho-hai School of Engineering. In an interview with American journalist Nym Wales in 1937, Chang said that all his instructors at Ho-hai had been educated in the United States.[1] This was obviously an overstatement, for the faculty member who seems to have influenced him the most was French-educated Tso Shun-sheng. Chang was in school at the critical time just prior to the outbreak of the May Fourth Movement and was influenced by some of those who played a part in it. Tso belonged to the Young China Association organized in Peking in mid-1919 by a group of politically minded students, many of whom had formerly studied in Japan. Among the Association's founders was Li Ta-chao (q.v.) who was later one of the giant figures in the history of the Chinese Communist Movement. Through the efforts of Tso Shun-sheng, who was actively recruiting for the Young China Association in the Nanking-Shanghai area, Chang joined the organization during the winter of 1919–20.[2] In doing so, he came in touch with such prominent young leftists (and latter-day Communists) as Mao Tse-tung, Li Ta-chao, Teng Chung-hsia, and Yun Tai-ying (qq.v.). Chang began at once to contribute to the Association's journal, *Shao-nien Chung-kuo* (Young China), where some of his earliest writings are found. Published from mid-1919 to the spring of 1924, it was edited for a time by Chang's former teacher, Tso Shun-sheng.

Chang had originally gone to Nanking to study the natural sciences, but under the influence of the new intellectual awakening he began to read widely (mostly from Western source materials) in literature, philosophy, and the social sciences. In 1919, joining with a friend from Shanghai, Shen Tse-min (q.v.), he left the engineering school to pursue more literary interests. They soon found positions in Shanghai with the Commercial Press, China's largest publishing house, where they probably got work with the aid of Mao Tun (Shen Yen-ping; the elder brother of Shen Tse-min), who was gaining recognition as a writer. In Shanghai Chang also held a position with the Chung Hua Book Company, editing a new series of cultural publications. In the fall of 1920 Chang and Shen went to Japan to study, but they returned to China after six months. Chang's many-faceted interests apparently drew him for a time to Buddhism, because an item in *Shao-nien Chung-kuo* revealed that he was living in a Buddhist temple by the West Lake in Hangchow.[3] However, he soon returned to the political scene and in mid-1921 attended the initial conference of the Young China Association in Nanking. Reports that he went to the United States in 1921 (including Chang's own account to Nym Wales) are apparently erroneous, for in the summer of 1922 he was living in Shanghai. He often visited the home of Kuo Mo-jo in Shanghai, where short story writer Yü Ta-fu was living.[4] Yü had been studying at Tokyo Imperial University in 1921, probably while Chang was in Japan. Yü, Kuo, and Chang were close friends and all three belonged to a literary group, the Creation Society, which Yü and Kuo founded in 1921 with the aid of other Chinese students who had studied in Japan.

Chang apparently sailed for the United States in the latter half of 1922. He worked for a time in San Francisco as a translator for a Chinese newspaper, *Ta-t'ung jih-pao* (Universal daily). Founded in 1902 by a disciple of K'ang Yu-wei, the paper later supported Sun Yat-sen and was very well known among overseas Chinese in America. While there, Chang also had a part-time job in a library connected with the University of California at Berkeley and may have attended some university courses. A little is known of Chang's life in America from a letter he wrote to Yü Ta-fu from the United States, which was published in the Creation Society's *Ch'uang-tsao chi-k'an* (Creation quarterly). Written in November 1922, Chang's letter was tinged with romanticism and a rather morbid introspection. He described a life in which he did a half-day's work in the library but would have been as happy if he never had to leave. He was surrounded by many Chinese students but he found few with whom he could communicate. "Life is fundamentally boring," Chang wrote, "and even art and literature are manifestations of the same," with suicide "the best way to rid one's self of all frustrations." "Ta-fu, the masses cannot be reformed.

This is something I have long since known, but from time to time I like to have a try." He confessed to his friend that "we must be able to be a minority" and "we must not fear being rejected by the masses because we have long since rejected them."[5]

Chang was back in Shanghai by 1923, and from there he went to Szechwan where for the next two years he taught in normal schools and started a newspaper. By his own testimony he was working with Communists in Szechwan, but he had still not joined the Communist Party. However, he returned in 1925 to Shanghai and joined the Party. Chang worked for a period in Shanghai and Soochow; he gave up his literary pursuits and turned to writing Party polemics, and for over a decade wrote frequently for the leading CCP journals. In 1926 Chang went to Moscow, where for the next few years he attended the revolutionary Sun Yat-sen University and taught at the Lenin School.[6] The latter institute had been set up to provide advanced training for Communists and was under the direct control of the Comintern. Chang is reported to have attended the CCP's Sixth Congress, which was held in Moscow in mid-1928.[7] Prior to his return to China in 1930, Chang had become associated with a group of fellow students who were to return to China and take over the principal Party organizations. This group, widely known as the "28 Bolsheviks" or the "returned students" clique, studied at Sun Yat-sen University from the mid-twenties until the spring of 1930, when they returned to China in the company of Pavel Mif, their chancellor and a Comintern official. Chang's old friend Shen Tse-min was a member of the group. Their succession to power at the time of the Fourth Party Plenum in January 1931 is described in the biography of Ch'in Pang-hsien, one of their principal leaders. At the Fourth Plenum, both Chang and Shen became Central Committee members; Chang was also named to the Politburo. Initially he directed work with peasants. In June 1931, when Party chief Hsiang Chung-fa (q.v.) was caught and executed by Nationalist police, Ch'en Shao-yü assumed his role for a brief time. In the ensuing months Chang took over the Organization Department and Shen Tse-min became propaganda chief, but Shen could not have been in this work for long, because he was dispatched to Oyüwan about this time (see under Chang Kuo-t'ao), and it is possible that some of his work fell to Chang. By September 1931 Ch'in Pang-hsien had taken over the position of CCP general secretary and Ch'en Shao-yü had either left or was about to leave for Moscow to rejoin the Comintern.

Because of the dangers from the KMT police, Party work in Shanghai was carried on at great risk between 1931 and 1933 and therefore little is known about it. The period also witnessed a struggle for control between the CCP leaders in

Shanghai and those in the rural hinterlands, and because the controversy did not come to light until many years later (see under Ch'en Shao-yü) it remains all the more obscure. In these years Mao and Chu Te were building a strong Communist base in the rural areas of southeast Kiangsi, and largely because the KMT continued to close in on the CCP apparatus in Shanghai, a number of the Party's leaders found their way to the Mao-Chu base during the year 1931. By 1932 Ch'in Pang-hsien and Chang Wen-t'ien were left as the principal leaders in charge of the Party office in Shanghai. Control stemming from this office was fairly well limited to the urban areas controlled by the KMT, and although there continued to be some contact between Shanghai and the hinterlands, it is questionable how much authority Ch'in and Chang could exert there. The later writings of Mao, which serve to introduce the controversy between himself and Shanghai to his followers, present the matter only from Mao's side. As regards Chang's position, the question becomes more complicated, because from some of the available documentary material surviving from the early thirties, Chang would appear to have been on Mao's side, or at least on the side that Mao later claimed as his. Thus, writing under the pseudonym Szu Mei for the official *Hung-ch'i chou-pao* (Red flag weekly), in an article entitled "The Present Political Situation and Our Tasks," Chang called for an expansion of guerrilla warfare, the development of mass organizations (in the rural bases), and the establishment of a Central Soviet Government.[8] The last-mentioned proposal did in fact take place in November 1931, some months after the article was published. However, there remains no doubt that from 1931 the major burden of Party work shifted from Shanghai to the countryside, and it was in Shanghai that Chang's authority was strongest. His importance in Shanghai at the time is suggested by one piece of evidence from the year 1932; in that year, as a representative from the Party Center in Shanghai, he journeyed to north China for a conference of the North China Party Bureau, which took place during four days in late February or early March. Here, as one of the two presiding officers, he led the conference attended by leading Party officials from Honan, Hopeh, Shantung, Shensi, and Manchuria, areas where at this time Party organizations were admittedly small, but where a thread of contact with the Center was being maintained. It is notable that the conference considered the basic question of the weakness of CCP work in north China, and more especially in Manchuria where the Japanese had been in complete control since 1931.

By his own statements Chang worked in the Shanghai headquarters for two years, until his whereabouts were reported to the police by an imprisoned colleague, forcing him to flee "to the Soviet districts."[9] A further description of the Party organization in Shanghai is contained in the biography of Ch'in Pang-hsien. Chang left Shanghai in 1933, the year often given as the official closing date of the Party headquarters there. Once in Juichin, the capital of the southeast Kiangsi base, he formally assumed the directorship of the CCP Propaganda Department, although quite possibly he had already been carrying on this work in Shanghai for his friend Shen. Chang also became editor of the Kiangsi edition of the official Party journal, *Tou-cheng* (Struggle), published there in the thirties before the Long March. The editor's post was a logical one for the Party propaganda head, and while he retained it Chang contributed a number of articles on Party policies.[10] Holding a post on the Party's Central Committee and Politburo, he of course attended the Fifth CCP Plenum held at Juichin in January 1934 (see under Ch'in Pang-hsien). Chang's report at the Plenum, "The Chinese Soviet Movement and Its Tasks," was one of the three conference reports. A few days after the Plenum closed, the Second All-China Congress of Soviets was convened in Juichin January 22–February 1). Although the speeches from the Congress appear to be more in harmony with what Mao has later said were his views than with those given at the earlier Party Plenum, the Second Congress witnessed a significant shift of leading government posts in favor of the "28 Bolshevik" group. For the first time a 17-member Presidium was elected to run the affairs of the larger governmental Central Executive Committee (CEC) when the latter was not in session. Both the CEC and the Presidium were headed by Mao. Chang, who attended the Congress as a delegate from Fukien, was given a seat on both bodies. But more significantly, the day after the Congress closed, he was named chairman of the People's Commissars of the Chinese Soviet Republic, in effect, the cabinet of the Communist government in the hinterlands. He assumed this post on February 3, 1934, taking it over from Mao who had been named to it at the First Congress in 1931. Chang held all his government posts until he embarked upon the Long March in October 1934.

In January 1935, as the Red Armies were crossing northern Kweichow, they captured the small town of Tsun-i and paused there for an important conference on policy matters. During the meetings, called an Enlarged Conference of the Politburo, Mao Tse-tung claims that he brought forth two major charges against the Russian-returned students who were heading the Party. The first was a charge from the recent past; Mao found fault with the leadership for not having supported the revolt in Fukien, which broke out against the KMT in November 1933 (see below). The second charge was directed against the military strategy that had controlled the

Red Army prior to and during the first lap of the Long March. Ch'in Pang-hsien and his followers, Mao said, were fighting a positional war instead of adopting more mobile guerrilla tactics.[11] The failures of military strategy had forced the Communists to abandon their bases in Kiangsi and were losing them men and supplies during the March. Mao felt that it was imperiling the Red Army and China's revolutionary cause.[12] The importance of the Tsun-i Conference is that it marked the turning point in the careers of Mao and his opponents, for it was then, according to the official Maoist view, that Mao put down his opposition and was elevated to supremacy over the CCP.

Though it is generally accepted that at Tsun-i Ch'in Pang-hsien ceased, in Maoist terms, to be the person responsible for the "Provisional Center" of the Party, what actually happened is difficult to reconstruct from the available evidence and the reported results leave a number of questions unanswered. When Ch'in was demoted, Chang Wen-t'ien was said to have taken his place, presumably as CCP general secretary, although the position could in no sense equate to that of head of the Party. The best date for the transfer of posts from Ch'in Pang-hsien to Chang Wen-t'ien can be assigned to Mao; it is he who states that Ch'in ceased to head the "provisional leadership" of the CCP at Tsun-i, though Mao does not mention Chang as the successor. However, there are other reports making Chang Wen-t'ien heir to the post of general secretary, first among them the statements of the important Communist defector Chang Kuo-t'ao (q.v.). Yet Chang seems to be in some doubt as to the date of the transfer, for in one interview he dated it to the Tsun-i Conference,[13] whereas in an earlier interview he reported that it took place at the Fifth Plenum in January 1934.[14] There is still another report, although not of the highest reliability, that also states that Chang assumed the post in 1934,[15] and when American journalist Nym Wales saw and interviewed Chang in 1937 she described him as "National Secretary of the Central Committee," a post she seemed to think was equated to chief of Party administration and which she said he had held since 1934.[16]

From the available writings of Chang Wen-t'ien in the early thirties he appears to have sometimes sided with and sometimes against Mao. Good examples of Chang's position are drawn from an article he wrote for *Tou-cheng* in February 1933 in which he was strongly critical of the so-called Lo Ming line, a controversial policy of the provincial Party secretary in Fukien[17] (see under Lo Ming). Mao now supports the Lo Ming line and has come out against its detractors in contemporary times. But at a later date, probably while the Fifth Plenum was in session, Chang seems to have been in harmony with Mao in the matter of the Party's treatment

of the Fukien rebels. Again the question of how Mao stood on the Fukien rebellion in 1934 is obscured by Mao's stand on Fukien today when he states that the actions of the Party in 1934 were wrong. However, documentary evidence from the early thirties would seem to prove otherwise. The Fukien insurgents, led by Ts'ai T'ing-k'ai, Li Chi-shen, and other militarists, broke with the KMT in November 1933 and established a short-lived government at Foochow, capital of Fukien. Not long before the outbreak of the rebellion, the CCP apparently had entered into negotiations with the rebel leaders, but later the Party gave them no support and allowed them to be crushed by Chiang Kai-shek's army (January 1934). Then in the aftermath of defeat, probably while the Fifth Plenum was meeting, the CCP found it necessary to review its position on the rebellion, and it fell to Chang Wen-t'ien and another of the "28 Bolsheviks," K'ai Feng (q.v.), to give the Party a report on Fukien and to justify the fact that the CCP had given no support to the insurgents, its reason being that their reliability as revolutionaries was not considered sufficient. At this time, despite his later attitude, Mao Tse-tung and Chu Te showed themselves in agreement with Chang's and K'ai's reports on the situation in Fukien and the Party's response to it.[18]

For whatever reason Mao allowed one of his supposed opponents to assume the post of Party general secretary at Tsun-i, Chang seems to have retained it until after the start of the Sino-Japanese War. There is one report indicating that by 1939 it had been taken over by Mao,[19] but Chang continued to be very much in evidence in Yenan at least until the beginning of the *cheng-feng* period in early 1942. In 1936, when Edgar Snow was in Pao-an, the Communist capital in north Shensi after the completion of the Long March, Chang was a lecturer at the Hung-chün ta-hsueh (Red Army academy), and he gave Snow a résumé of CCP history that was the accepted one of the time. A year later, when Snow's wife visited Shensi, she too interviewed Chang whom she knew as "Lo Fu," and he told her that he had written a history of the Chinese Revolution that was being used in all Communist schools. Later Mao himself referred Mrs. Snow to Chang for an analysis of the historical stages of development in the Chinese Communist Movement.[20] Hence, it is not surprising to find that by 1940 Chang was identified as president of the Marx-Lenin Institute, evidently a training school for higher Party cadres. It was in the early forties too that Chang took charge of the reference room of the *Chieh-fang jih-pao* (Liberation daily), which began publication in 1941 and was directed by his colleague Ch'in Pang-hsien.

Chang is one of the few among the Party's top leadership who can claim literary distinction. As noted, he first contributed to the journal of the

Young China Association in his student days. In the mid-twenties, when he returned to China from America, he tried his hand at a number of translations from the works of such a wide-ranging group of Western writers as Henri Bergson (*Le Rire*), Oscar Wilde (*The Ballad of Reading Gaol*), and Russian dramatist Leonid Andreyev (*The Waltz of the Dogs*); all were published by the Commercial Press. Meanwhile, the Chung-hua Book Company published his translations of two novels, *Gioconda* by Gabriele L. D'Annunzio and *The Blind Musician* by V. G. Korolenko. In October 1923 the *Ch'uang-tsao chou-k'an* (Creation weekly) published an article by Chang on the Lebanese poet Kahlil Gibran.[21] Chang also translated works by Tolstoy and Turgenev and, as mentioned, wrote a novel and a play of his own. But upon joining the CCP he ceased his literary efforts and wrote only polemics, his articles in the early thirties appearing in *Shih-hua* (True words), the official organ published by the CCP in 1930 and 1931, in *Hung-ch'i chou-pao* (Red flag weekly), and in *Tou-cheng* (Struggle). Chang wrote especially for the edition in Kiangsi, which he edited for a time. During the first years of the Sino-Japanese War he was one of the Party's most prolific writers on the question of the united front and the anti-Japanese resistance, and many of his articles are found in the literature of this time.[22] As a writer and polemicist Chang used the names of Lo fu and Szu Mei, the latter especially in the thirties.

At the Party's Seventh National Congress, held in Yenan from April to June 1945, Chang served on the presidium (steering committee), made a speech, and was re-elected to both the Central Committee and the Politburo. Toward the end of the summer of 1945, as the war was drawing to a close, the CCP sent some of its top leaders to Manchuria, a group that included Kao Kang, P'eng Chen, Lin Piao, Ch'en Yun, Li Fu-ch'un (qq.v.), and Chang Wen-t'ien. Chang was initially assigned to Hokiang (Ho-chiang) province, a province with its capital in Chia-mu-szu (Kiamusze) and absorbed by Heilungkiang province when the Communists came to power in 1949. He served in Hokiang (1945–46) as the provincial Party Committee secretary and as political commissar of the Hokiang Military District. To govern those portions of Manchuria controlled by them, the Communists established the Northeast Party Bureau and a governmental body known as the Northeast Administrative Committee (NEAC). In the Party Bureau, Chang was a Standing Committee member from 1945 to about 1950, and it appears that he was also an important official (possibly the director for a brief period) of the Bureau's Organization Department. Within the NEAC, he was by 1949 a vice-chairman of the Finance and Economics Committee. This important body was chaired by

Ch'en Yun, and Li Fu-ch'un was one of Chang's fellow vice-chairmen.

By 1949, at which time all of Manchuria was in Communist hands, Chang had been assigned to Liaotung Province, the province bordering on Korea and with its capital at Antung on the Yalu River. There he served until 1950 as the provincial Party Committee secretary. In August 1949, when the NEAC was reorganized into the Northeast People's Government (NEPG) under the chairmanship of Kao Kang, Chang was named to NEPG membership, nominally retaining this post until November 1952. As of this time he was still referred to as Lo Fu in official CCP publications.

Unlike virtually every other top Party leader— including those serving in the provinces—Chang received no post in the central government established by the Communists on October 1, 1949. Though this can be interpreted as part of Chang's continuing difficulties under the Maoist leadership, such an interpretation must be viewed in the light of his appointment in January 1950 when he was named as head of the PRC's delegation to the United Nations and as its representative on the U.N. Security Council. After it became clear that there was little hope the PRC would gain entry into the United Nations, Chang was given a new assignment. In March 1951 he was named to succeed Wang Chia-hsiang (q.v.), another of the "28 Bolsheviks," as Peking's ambassador to the Soviet Union. He presented his credentials in Moscow in April 1951 and remained there for almost four years. Most of the basic groundwork for the Sino-Soviet alliance had been laid during the ambassadorship of Wang Chia-hsiang, but a number of important questions remained unsettled. To deal with two of these, the Chinese sent Chou En-lai to Moscow in August–September 1952. Thus, as an official member of Chou's delegation, Chang participated in the negotiations that led to an agreement to a transfer to China of the Chinese Changchun Railway in Manchuria and to another agreement providing for the extension of the joint use of the Chinese naval base at Port Arthur. Similarly, he probably participated in the lengthy trade and aid negotiations conducted in Moscow by important economic specialists Li Fu-ch'un and Yeh Chi-chuang (q.v.) from the fall of 1952 to the spring of 1953. Shortly before the talks were concluded Stalin died in Moscow; Chang served as a member of Chou En-lai's delegation attending the funeral.

On April 14, 1954, Chang was appointed a vice-minister in Chou En-lai's Foreign Ministry. The reason he was named to this post while still abroad became apparent a few days later when he was named as the senior member of Chou's delegation to the Geneva Conference, the conference that brought an end to hostilities in French Indochina. When the conference closed in July,

Chang accompanied Chou on brief stops in Berlin and Warsaw. Chou then proceeded to Moscow with Chang, but the latter remained in his Moscow post when Chou left for home after a few days of talks with Soviet leaders.

Chang's last major task in Russia was to represent the Chinese Communists at the Preparatory Conference of the European Security Conference, held in Moscow in November–December 1954. This meeting paved the way for the establishment of the famous "Warsaw Pact" in May 1955 (see under P'eng Te-huai). Because the Chinese were never members of the Warsaw Pact, Chang participated in the 1954 Moscow meeting only in an "observer" capacity.

In January 1955 Chang was recalled from Moscow and replaced by Liu Hsiao (q.v.). In anticipation of his return home, Chang had been elected from his native Kiangsu to the First NPC and, although he was not in China to attend the inaugural NPC session in September 1954, he was elected to membership on the permanent NPC Standing Committee. He was again elected from Kiangsu to the Second NPC (1959–1964), serving again on its Standing Committee. Another appointment received prior to Chang's return from Moscow was membership on the Second Executive Board of the Sino-Soviet Friendship Association (December 1954). He was also elected to the Third Board formed in May 1959. When Chang returned to Peking in early 1955, he assumed his duties as the ranking vice-minister in the Ministry of Foreign Affairs (MFA). Aside from Chou En-lai, Chang was then the only Politburo member in the MFA. On two occasions he was officially appointed as acting foreign minister—when Chou went to the Bandung Conference in April 1955 and again when he visited Southeast Asia, the Soviet Union, and East Europe in the period from November 1956 to February 1957.

A few weeks after Chang's return from Moscow he was present at the Party Conference in March 1955 when Politburo member Kao Kang and Party Organization Department Director Jao Shu-shih were purged for allegedly engaging in "anti-Party" activities. Chang was among the top elite who delivered an "important" speech at the Conference, but the text was not released. His participation in these events is worth noting in view of the oft-cited (but undocumented) theory that the "28 Bolsheviks" (Chang among them) and Kao Kang shared a common characteristic, namely, a so-called "pro-Soviet" orientation.

As one of Peking's top specialists in foreign affairs, Chang frequently participated in talks with visiting delegations during the middle and late fifties, particularly those from the Soviet Union and the East European Communist countries. One of the more important of these took place in December 1955 when East German Otto Grotowohl visited Peking. Chang participated in the talks (led by Chou En-lai) that culminated in the signing of the Sino-German Treaty of Friendship and Cooperation as well as several lesser agreements. Later, on January 23, 1956, it fell to Chang to deliver the official report on the negotiations before a meeting of the NPC Standing Committee.

At the Party's Eighth National Congress in September 1956, Chang was re-elected to the Central Committee. The day after the Congress closed the new Central Committee elected a new Politburo. For reasons that are not clear (but that may relate to Chang's long-standing differences with the Maoist leadership), he was demoted from full to alternate membership on the Politburo. K'ang Sheng (q.v.) was also demoted to alternate status at this time, but there seems to be no direct link between Chang and K'ang to explain this. Chang's demotion initially suggested that he would be quickly eased out of positions of authority, but for the next three years he was quite active in foreign affairs and made three trips abroad. The first of these took him to Pakistan and Indonesia in May 1957, where he reportedly went to "inspect" the embassies. More important were two journeys in 1958 and 1959, the first of which was with Chou En-lai's delegation to North Korea in February 1958 when it was decided to withdraw the "Chinese People's Volunteers," which had remained in Korea after the war there ended in mid-1953. The other trip took him to Poland where he represented Peking at the Foreign Ministers' Conference of the Warsaw Pact countries in April 1959.

Immediately prior to Chang's trip to Warsaw he had been re-elected to the NPC Standing Committee at the initial session of the Second NPC. However, in September 1959, during a major reshuffle of government personnel, he was dropped as a vice-minister in the Foreign Ministry. In retrospect, it seems that his dismissal may have resulted from the visit to Warsaw in April. It is noteworthy that Chang and Defense Minister P'eng Te-huai had gone to Poland on the same day, Chang going there for the foreign ministers' meeting and P'eng as head of a military delegation that subsequently toured the other East European nations and the Soviet Union. Details are not available on Chang's activities in Poland, but as regards P'eng, strong suggestions were made during the Sino-Soviet polemics of the early sixties that he had attempted to get support for his viewpoints regarding the management of the PLA. (A more detailed discussion of P'eng's activities at this time is contained in his biography.) It is significant that both men were removed from their top government posts in September 1959 (P'eng being replaced by Lin Piao in the Defense Ministry). After a prolonged absence, Chang reappeared in April 1960 at celebrations marking the 90th anniversary of Lenin's birth, and six weeks later he took part in memorial services for Politburo member Lin Po-ch'ü (q.v.), services in which P'eng Te-huai also participated. More than a year passed before Chang again appeared in public, this time on June 30, 1961, at a rally commemorating the 40th CCP anniversary. In view of his rapidly declining political status, his appearance at these ceremonies was probably a gesture by the CCP elite to show its solidarity, particularly in view of Chang's position as one of the early Party leaders. In any event, it was his last public appearance. He continues to be listed in official handbooks as an alternate Politburo member, but virtually all doubt about his political demise was removed in 1964–65 when he failed to be re-elected to the NPC and its Standing Committee. P'eng Te-huai has been denounced by name, but never Chang. If, in fact, P'eng and Chang were in league, the Party elite probably felt it had more to fear from P'eng, who might have been able to rally the powerful PLA to his side. In any case, Chang's career as a significant Party leader seems to have ended after his mission to Warsaw in 1959.

In 1937 Nym Wales described Chang as "tall and thin, looking much overworked." He wore thick glasses and had "thoughtful, irregular features." Chang spoke very good English and in fact conducted the interviews with both Snows in English. Chang has been married to Liu Ying since at least the mid-thirties. Liu, a Hunanese, was born about 1908 and like her husband studied in Moscow in the late twenties. She was among the relatively few women who made the Long March and by 1936 was a member of the Communist Youth League's Central Committee. When Miss Wales interviewed Liu in Yenan in mid-1937, she described her as being fully occupied with youth work. Liu was in Moscow with her husband in the early fifties and upon her return home with him was appointed (January 1955) as an assistant minister of Foreign Affairs. However, unlike most Foreign Ministry officials, very little was heard of her in the ensuing years, and finally, about 1960, she was dropped from her Foreign Ministry. It is normal practice for the PRC to announce the dismissals of top governmental personnel, but Liu's removal from office was only revealed with the publication of the *1961 Jen-min shou-ts'e* (People's handbook) when, in contrast to the previous issue, her name had been deleted from the Foreign Ministry roster. Significantly, it coincided almost exactly with the political downfall of her husband. Liu had served as a Honan deputy to the Second NPC (1959–1964), but she was not, of course, re-elected to the Third NPC, which opened in late 1964.

---

1. Nym Wales, *Inside Red China* (New York, 1939), p. 227.

2. *Shao-nien Chung-kuo* (Young China), February 15, 1920, p. 66.

3. *Ibid.,* June 15, 1921, p. 63.

4. Kuo Mo-jo, *Ko-ming Ch'un-ch'iu* (Revolution in spring and autumn; Shanghai, 1956), p. 132.

5. *Ch'uang-tsao chi-k'an* (Creation quarterly), 1.4:22–23 (January 23, 1923).

6. Wales, p. 228.

7. Conrad Brandt, Benjamin Schwartz, and John K. Fairbank, *A Documentary History of Chinese Communism* (Cambridge, Mass., 1952), p. 124.

8. William F. Dorrill, unpublished manuscript, "Mao Tse-tung and the Chinese Communist Movement: 1927–35."

9. Wales, p. 228.

10. Chün-tu Hsüeh, *The Chinese Communist Movement, 1921–1937* (Stanford, Calif., 1960), p. 80.

11. Robert C. North, *Moscow and Chinese Communists* (Stanford, Calif., 1953), p. 166.

12. Ho Kan-chih, *A History of the Modern Chinese Revolution* (Peking, 1960), p. 269.

13. Modern China Project, Columbia University, New York, Howard L. Boorman, director.

14. North, p. 164.

15. *Chung-Kung chung-yao jen-wu* (Peiping, 1949), p. 11.

16. Wales, p. 227.

17. Tso-liang Hsiao, *Power Relations within the Chinese Communist Movement, 1930–1934* (Seattle, 1961), p. 236.

18. Dorrill.

19. Ke Han, *The Shansi-Hopei-Chahar Border Region* (Manila), quoting from the New China Information Committee Bulletin, no. 9 (Chungking, 1939).

20. Wales, p. 229.

21. Modern China Project.

22. Chün-tu Hsüeh, *The Chinese Communist Movement, 1937–1949* (Stanford, Calif., 1962), *passim.*

Chang Yen

Deputy director, Foreign Affairs Office of the State Council.

In the fall of 1939 American journalist Agnes Smedley encountered a "Chang Yen" during her visit in central Anhwei to the headquarters of the Fourth Detachment of the New Fourth Army. Inferential evidence suggests that this is the same man considered in this sketch, particularly because Chang is known from other sources to have worked in the New Fourth Army during the war. When Smedley met Chang Yen, he was teaching elementary science at one of the Red Army training camps. He explained to her that when the Japanese attacked Shanghai in 1937 he took part in the retreat as a Red Cross worker and in November was badly wounded, barely escaping death from a serious sword wound on the face and neck. A Catholic priest succored him for three weeks, and then peasants led him toward the interior. Then, according to Chang: "After a number of weeks I reached south An-hwei and heard that the New Fourth Army was being formed to fight the enemy in the rear. I volunteered to fight as a soldier, but the Army said the soldiers needed knowledge. So I began to teach natural science because I had been a science-teacher at Woosung [near Shanshai] before the war."[1]

At some later point in the war Chang was known to have been serving as dean of a military school (presumably in the New Fourth Army area), and then Japanese sources report him in 1940 as political commissar of a unit known as the Su-wan (Kiangsu-Anhwei) Column, subordinate to the New Fourth Army, which was commanded after 1941 by Ch'en I. It was probably about this time that Chang came to know Ch'en I, presently a Politburo member and the foreign minister, under whom Chang would serve for many years.

Chang apparently remained in east-central China throughout the Sino-Japanese War and through the civil war with the Nationalists in the late 1940's. He was still in this region in early 1950 when he was serving as secretary of the Communist Party "local work committee" for the Sung-chiang district, located in southern Kiangsu. When the Communists took power in 1949–1950, a few of the provinces were divided for administrative purposes; Kiangsu was one of these, being partitioned into North and South Kiangsu. By February 1951 Chang was already a member of the Party Committee for South Kiangsu area, and in that same month was appointed as a Land Reform Committee member for the South Kiangsu People's Administrative Office (the name given to the governmental apparatus for South Kiangsu until the two portions were merged to form Kiangsu Province in November 1952). Kiangsu came under the jurisdiction of the larger governmental organization, the East China Military and Administrative Committee (ECMAC), renamed the East China Administrative Committee (ECAC) in December 1952. Under this organization, Chang served from February 1950 to June 1954 as a member of the Land Reform Committee, headed by T'an Chen-lin (who became a Party Politburo member in 1958).

By mid-1953 Chang was transferred to Shanghai, where he became secretary-general of the East China Bureau of the CCP; the bureau was then headed by Jao Shu-shih (q.v., purged in 1955), with Ch'en I as the Second Secretary. A Chinese familiar with Chang at this time has stated that he worked directly under Ch'en I and was considered to be his protégé.[2] Chang remained in Shanghai until April 1955 when he

was posted to Peking to become a deputy director of the Office of the Premier of the State Council, an administrative office designed to serve the needs of the premier. Interestingly, this appointment came soon after Ch'en I was appointed a vice-premier (September 1954), after which he spent most of his time in the capital. Chang held the position until April 1958 by which time he had received a far more important post.

Until early 1956, there was nothing in Chang's career to suggest future work in foreign relations. Nonetheless, he was to spend most of the next several years in this field. His first appointment in this line of work came in February 1956 when he was appointed as a member of the newly founded Asian Solidarity Committee of China (renamed "Afro-Asian" in 1958). In November of that year, Chou En-lai embarked on an extended goodwill tour of Southeast Asia. It was clear that the Chinese were concerned about the bad image created by the Russians during the Hungarian Revolt and were anxious to portray a "softer" image as represented by Peking. From mid-November to January 1957, the delegation (of which Chang was a member) toured North Vietnam, Cambodia, India, Burma, and Pakistan. Chang again accompanied Chou (as well as Ch'en I) on another important mission in February 1958 when Chou and Ch'en visited Pyongyang for the purpose of negotiating the withdrawal of the Chinese Army from Korea, where it had remained since the end of the Korean War in mid-1953.

Just prior to the mission to North Korea, the State Council had created a new organ under its jurisdiction, the Foreign Affairs Office, headed by Foreign Minister Ch'en I and apparently charged with coordinating the work of foreign affairs (including the work done by the Foreign Ministry). In March 1958 Chang was named as one of the deputy directors; the stature of the other three deputy directors, Liao Ch'eng-chih, Liu Ning-i, and K'ung Yuan (qq.v.), was sufficient to illustrate the importance of this new organ of government. In the following month Chang was removed as a deputy director of the Office of the Premier. As a result of this transfer, Chang was once again working directly under Ch'en I. Apart from this government post, Chang holds two quasi-official posts related to foreign affairs. He was named to the Standing Committee of the China Peace Committee in July 1958, and to the Executive Council of the China-Africa People's Friendship Association, established in April 1960.

In 1960 and 1961 Chang made two additional trips abroad, one with both Chou En-lai and Ch'en I and the other with Ch'en alone. The 1960 trip took place in April–May and was concerned chiefly with settling border disputes with neighboring countries. The nations visited were

Burma, India, and Nepal; and then after returning briefly to south China the two men visited Cambodia and Vietnam. In May 1961 Chang accompanied Foreign Minister Ch'en I as member and, concurrently, secretary-general of the delegation to the Geneva Conference on Laos. When it became apparent that the conference would be prolonged, Ch'en left for home in July, taking Chang Yen with him; Chang Han-fu (q.v.) remained behind to head the delegation. Ch'en I returned to Geneva for the final stages of the conference in July 1962, but Chang Yen did not accompany him. Since that time Chang has been mentioned in the national press mainly in connection with visiting dignitaries, especially those from Laos. In 1964 he was elected as a Shantung deputy to the Third NPC, which held its first session in December 1964–January 1965.

Little is known of his personal life aside from the fact that he was married by at least 1962.

(A man with the same name was serving as deputy secretary-general of the All-China Federation of Journalists in the mid-1950's, but apparently this is a different person.)

1. Agnes Smedley, *Battle Hymn of China* (New York, 1945), pp. 325–327.
2. Interview in Hong Kong, 1963.

Chang Yu-yü

(c. 1899–   ; Ling-shih, Shansi). Lawyer, journalist; vice-chairman, Political Science and Law Association of China.

Chang Yu-yü is a lawyer by training, but his main contribution to the Chinese Communist movement before 1949 was in the field of journalism. Throughout most of the 1950's he was a leading government and Party official in Peking and since that time has devoted his time mainly to the legal profession and the NPC. Chang was born about 1899 into a peasant family in Ling-shih, central Shansi. He graduated from the law school at Peking University and then received further training at the Tokyo Law College. In the twenties and thirties Chang divided his time between the field of journalism (reporting for papers in both Shanghai and Peking) and law. He taught law at such prominent schools as Peking and Yenching Universities.

Chang's first contact with the left-wing movement in China apparently came through the National Salvation Association, an organization that was particularly active in the mid-thirties in its attempts to arouse the Chinese populace against the repeated incursions of the Japanese into north China. In 1937 he worked briefly in Peking for the 29th Army, commanded by General Sung Che-yuan and ostensibly under the control of the Nationalist Government. In fact, however, Sung had a large degree of autonomy and his forces were apparently heavily infiltrated at the lower levels by young left-wing students in the Peking-Tientsin area, many of whom were under the influence of the CCP-dominated National Liberation Vanguard of China (see under Li Ch'ang). When the Sino-Japanese War broke out in 1937, Chang fled to the Communist Shansi-Chahar-Hopeh Border Region, apparently making his first direct contact with the Communists. In view of his later career it seems likely that he had joined the Party by this time.

Chang went from the Shansi-Chahar-Hopeh Border Region to Hong Kong in 1940, then still under British control. For about a year he was the editor of the *Hua-shang Pao* (China commercial news). When Hong Kong fell to the Japanese (just after Pearl Harbor), Chang went to Chungking, the wartime capital of the Nationalists, where he worked as a reporter for the important Communist newspaper, the *Hsin-hua Jih-pao* (New China daily). By 1945 Chang was the editor of this newspaper, as well as a deputy secretary of the CCP Szechwan Committee, director of the Propaganda Department of the same committee, and an alternate member of the Party's Chungking Committee. Although the Party committees were covert at this time, their existence was probably known to the Nationalists. Chang's work in these years probably brought him into close contact with Chou En-lai, Tung Pi-wu, Wu Yü-chang, and Wang Wei-chou, all important Communist leaders who were working in the Communist mission in the Nationalists' capital.

On January 10, 1946, the cease-fire agreement worked out by U.S. Special Envoy George C. Marshall was signed, thus bringing about a brief cessation of hostilities between the Communists and the Nationalists. On the same day, the Political Consultative Conference opened in Chungking, attended by such top CCP leaders as Chou En-lai and his wife, Tung Pi-wu, and Lu Ting-i (qq.v.). Chang served as an adviser to the Communist delegation, but shortly after the conference adjourned in late January he was briefly detained by the Nationalist authorities. After his release, Chang returned to the Communist-held regions in north China, being assigned to the Shansi-Hopeh-Shantung-Honan (Chin-Chi-Lu-Yü) Border Region. He served in this government for about two years as a vice-chairman and secretary-general. In these positions Chang served directly under Border Region Chairman Yang Hsiu-feng who, like Chang, had been a professor in Peking during the thirties. Concurrently, Chang was also the secretary-general of the Party's North China Bureau, a position he held until at least 1951.

Like so many of the officials in the Chin-Chi-Lu-Yü Government, Chang took part in the administration of the north China cities as they were captured by the PLA in 1949. Thus, when Tientsin fell to the Communists in January 1949, he was named as the vice-mayor. It is quite possible that Chang was acquainted with the mayor, Huang Ching (q.v.), who had been an active Party organizer among students in Peking during the thirties. Chang only held the Tientsin post briefly before he was reassigned (April 1949) to Peking, where he would spend the next nine years as a top government and Party official. He was named as a vice-mayor, a post that placed him directly subordinate to three of the most important of the Communist leaders, Mayors Yeh Chien-ying (1949), Nieh Jung-chen (1949–1951), and P'eng Chen (the mayor after early 1951). Chang was also engaged in a wide range of other activities, as the following positions indicate: director, Labor Bureau (1949–?); chairman, Finance and Economics Committee (1949–1950); vice-chairman, same committee (1950–?; he was replaced as the chairman by the more senior P'eng Chen); vice-chairman, Planning Committee (1950–?).

Chang also held critical posts in the Party's Peking Municipal Committee, serving by 1952 as a member of the Standing Committee, as a deputy secretary from 1956 to 1957, and from 1957 to 1958 as a secretary—all of which placed him under ranking Secretary P'eng Chen. During the fifties he also served in a number of lesser (or *ad hoc*) posts. For example, from 1949 he was a vice-chairman of the Peking chapter of the Sino-Soviet Friendship Association, then a highly active organization. In 1953 he was named to chair the municipal committee to implement the marriage law, and in the following year he became the chairman of the Peking committee to discuss the draft (national) constitution. Chang's only position in the national government in the early years of the PRC was a member of the First National Committee of the CPPCC (1949–1954); he was not re-elected to the Second CPPCC in 1954 but returned in later years to this organization (see below).

Until the constitutional government was inaugurated by the NPC in 1954, China was divided into six large administrative areas. From 1953 to 1954 Chang served as a member of the North China Administrative Committee headed by veteran Party leader Liu Lan-t'ao. When the NPC was established in 1954, Chang was elected as a deputy from Peking and since that time has been one of the NPC's more active members. He was re-elected to the Second NPC (1959–1964) and to the Third NPC, the first session of which opened in December 1964. In this legislative body, the PRC has utilized Chang's training as a lawyer by placing him on the Motion's Examination Committee (which serves for the life of each annual NPC session) and the permanent Bills Committee. Chang served as a member of the former committee for the sessions held in 1956 through 1958, and since 1959 he has chaired the committee. On the Bills Committee,

he served as a vice-chairman from 1959 to 1964. In his dual capacity as a Peking Government official and as a NPC deputy, Chang served as a member of the Peking Government–NPC delegation that visited the U.S.S.R., Rumania, Czechoslovakia, Bulgaria, Albania, and Yugoslavia from November 1956 to January 1957 (see under P'eng Chen, the delegation leader).

Coincidental with his more active role in the legislative affairs of the NPC, Chang relinquished his posts in the Peking government and municipal Party Committee in 1958 and entered, in effect, upon a new phase in his career, becoming involved with mass organization work. This reorientation probably derives from the fact that the fields of political science and law were found to be staffed by persons who, from the Party viewpoint, were considered untrustworthy—a situation that was brought into the open during the 1957–1958 "rectification" movement. A large number of officials, mainly non-Communists, were sharply criticized during the movement and were subsequently purged from their posts in various professional organizations and institutions of higher learning. It was in this atmosphere that Chang was named as a vice-chairman and as a member of the newly created Secretariat of the Political Science and Law Association of China (PSLAC) in August 1958. The elderly Party veteran Tung Pi-wu nominally continued to head the PSLAC, but the real authority passed to Wu Te-feng, the first secretary of the Secretariat. Wu's authority was made more explicit in 1964 when he succeeded Tung as the chairman, while continuing also as the first secretary. By the middle of 1959 Chang had been identified in two further posts closely related to the work of the PSLAC. By April he had become the director of the Institute of Jurisprudence, one of the many institutes subordinate to the Academy of Sciences. Within two months he was also identified as a deputy director of the Philosophy and Social Sciences Department of the Academy, one of its four major academic departments and the one that coordinates the work of all subordinate institutes (such as the Institute of Jurisprudence) in the social sciences. As a further reflection of his new assignment to work with social scientists, Chang was named to the Third National Committee of the CPPCC in April 1959 as a representative of social science organizations. (As described above, Chang had served on the First National Committee, 1949–1954, but had not been re-elected to the Second Committee in 1954.) He was once again named to represent social scientists when the Fourth CPPCC was formed in late 1964.

Since 1959 Chang has also been fairly active in China's international relations. His first assignment in this field came in November 1959 when he was elected president of the China-Burma Friendship Association, replacing Cheng Chen-to, who had died in an air crash a year earlier. It was probably because of his affiliation with this organization that he was assigned to take part in a parliamentary delegation, led by Kuo Mo-jo, that visited Indonesia and Burma in August–September 1961. Also in this capacity Chang is often present to entertain visiting Burmese leaders, as he was in October 1961 when Burmese Prime Minister U Nu was in China. He was given still another assignment in the foreign relations field in April 1962 when he was named to the national council of the newly-formed Asia-Africa Society of China, an organization ostensibly devoted to academic research.

Apart from his visit to Burma and Indonesia in 1961, Chang has been abroad on three other occasions. In October 1960 he led a delegation of jurists to the Seventh Congress of the Communist-dominated International Association of Democratic Lawyers (IADL), to which the Chinese Political Science and Law Association is affiliated. In June of the following year he was reported returning from Moscow as the deputy leader of an Academy of Sciences delegation led by physicist Wu Yu-hsun, an Academy vice-president. From March 1961 Wu had toured through Hungary, Czechoslovakia, Bulgaria, and Rumania before visiting in the U.S.S.R.; presumably Chang was also with him for these portions of the trip. In October 1962 Chang led another delegation of Chinese jurists to the Second Afro-Asian Lawyers' Conference held in Conakry, Guinea. Chang's increasing international contacts were probably useful to him when the Chinese held the Peking Scientific Symposium in August 1964. The symposium was attended by 367 delegates from 44 nations, mainly in Asia, Africa, and Latin America. Chang served as one of the six deputy leaders of the large Chinese delegation to the conference, which held panels on both the natural and social sciences.

As a leading administrator in the field of social sciences, Chang often attends academic meetings and forums in Peking. An example occurred in the spring of 1962 when the Political Science and Law Association sponsored a series of academic discussions on law. A speech by Chang at one of these sessions, emphasizing the necessity of applying Marxist-Leninist theories to the study of law, was reprinted in the Association journal, *Cheng-fa yen-chiu* (Political science and law research, issue number 3, 1962). He is also the author of an article for the Party's most important journal, *Hung-ch'i* (Red flag, July 1, 1962) with the self-descriptive title "The falsehood of parliamentary democracy."

Chang has been married to Han Yu-t'ung since 1931. Born in 1908 in Ning-an, Heilungkiang, and of Hui nationality, Han (like her husband) was trained at the Peking University law school and in Japan. She participated in revolutionary work from her student days, activities for which

she was twice imprisoned. Han was with her husband in Hong Kong just before Pearl Harbor and was also with him in Chungking during the war. She has served as a Heilungkiang deputy to the three NPC's and has been a member of the Executive Committee of the National Women's Federation since 1957. Among the numerous positions she has held, the most important was a vice-presidency of one of the divisions of the Supreme People's Court (1952–1959). Beginning in 1947, when she participated in the Communist World Congress of Women in Budapest, Han has attended several international conferences abroad, most of them related to the field of law. The most dramatic of these took place in March–April 1964 when she led the Chinese delegation to the Eighth Congress of the International Association of Democratic Lawyers in Budapest. Although still members of this organization, since the Sino-Soviet ideological split of the early sixties the Chinese have used these international meetings principally to denounce the Russians. At the conference in question, a Chinese resolution denouncing the United States was defeated, whereupon Han walked out of the final plenary session. In a parting speech, widely reported in the international press, Han is reported to have shouted: "Come on, attack us. This does not worry us. We fight to the last."[1] Her actions, of course, were approved by the CCP, a fact made completely evident by the favorable coverage given to her delegation by the Chinese Communist press.

1. *New York Times* (international edition), April 7, 1964.

Chang Yun

(Anhwei?). Prominent woman leader; alternate member, CCP Central Committee.

One of the most important women members of the CCP, Chang Yun has been active in the Communist Party since the 1920's. From then until the early 1950's she worked in east China, after which she was transferred to Peking where she has been particularly prominent in the work of the All-China Federation of Democratic Women. Chang has been an alternate member of the Party Central Committee since 1956.

The birthplace of Chang Yun is uncertain, varying between Anhwei and the city of Wu-hsi (Wusih) in Kiangsu. She attended Futan University in Shanghai and was active in the May Fourth student movement, possibly while enrolled there. Six years later, in 1925, Chang was reported to be a student in Hankow. By this time she had joined the Party and was active in its underground, serving as director of the Women's Department of the CCP Committee in Hankow between 1925 and 1927. After the Nationalists and Communists broke relations in the summer of 1927, she engaged in Party underground work in Wuhan, Nanking, Shanghai, and Hunan Province, and when the Sino-Japanese War broke out in 1937 she joined the Communist guerrillas. By 1941 she was identified as secretary of the Party Committee in the Second Sub-district of the CCP-controlled central Kiangsu administrative district, a territory held by the New Fourth Army. She held this post through 1948, and by 1949 was president of the Institute for Women Cadre Workers, a school established to train women activists attached to the Third Field Army, the force that took over most of the coastal provinces for the Communists.

From the spring of 1949 until her transfer to Peking in 1952, Chang was occupied with organizational tasks in east China, particularly those related to women's activities. During this three-year period she headed the "democratic women's" organizations for both east China and Shanghai, and in this capacity was in Peking in March–April 1949 for the women's congress that established the All-China Federation of Democratic Women (ACFDW). At this congress she was elected to the First Executive Committee of the ACFDW. She was again in Peking in December 1949 leading a delegation from Shanghai to the large "Asian Women's Conference," one of the first of many such regional conferences that Peking was to hold in the years ahead.

In the early 1950's, China was divided for administrative purposes into six large military-political regions, the one for east China being known as the East China Military and Administrative Committee (ECMAC). When this was formally established in January 1950, with Shanghai as the capital, Chang was named to ECMAC membership, and in the following month was also appointed a member of the ECMAC Land Reform Committee. There is little information on her during the early 1950's, although she did serve on a special committee for the "study of Mao Tse-tung's thought" that was established in December 1951, and by the next month she was also serving as head of the Women's Work Department of the East China Bureau of the CCP. Then, by September 1952, she was transferred to Peking to become secretary-general of the Women's Federation, thereby surrendering her various posts in east China.

Soon after her arrival in the capital, Chang was very active in the affairs of the ACFDW. She gave a report before a "women's work conference" of the Federation in November–December 1952, and then served on the Presidium (steering committee) for the Second All-China Women's Congress in April 1953. At the close of this congress Miss Chang was re-elected to the Executive Committee, and also to membership on the Standing Committee. Most important, however, was her election to a vice-chairmanship under Chairman Ts'ai Ch'ang (Mme. Li Fu-ch'un), the most important woman leader in China. Soon thereafter, Chang served as a deputy leader of the Chinese delegation to the Communist World Congress of Women, held in Copenhagen in June 1953. Another task that engaged the time of Chang in 1953–1954 was membership on the committee to implement the marriage law, the important statute promulgated in April 1950.

In 1954, elections were held for the First NPC, the legislative body that inaugurated the constitutional period in September 1954. Chang was elected as a deputy from Anhwei, and when the first session was held in September 1954 she was named as a member of the NPC Bills Committee, one of the permanent committees of the Congress. Chang was re-elected from Anhwei to the Second NPC (1959–1964) and to the Third NPC that held its first session in December 1964–January 1965. In both cases, she was also re-elected to the Bills Committee. Also in 1954, Miss Chang was elected as a representative of the Women's Federation to the legislative advisory body, the CPPCC, that held the first session (of the Second National Committee) in December 1954. She was named again in 1959 to the Third National Committee, and when it first met in April 1959 she was also appointed to the Standing Committee. She was once more named to the Standing Committee at the first session of the Fourth CPPCC in December 1964–January 1965.

Chang's stature within the Women's Federation was notably enhanced in April 1955 when the organization created a small (eight-member) Secretariat to conduct the day-to-day activities of this important organization. Chang was named to the Secretariat and continued to hold the post until the next congress of the Federation in 1957. In March 1956 she was named to membership on the National Association for the Elimination of Illiteracy, an organization subordinate to the State Council and headed by Vice-Premier Ch'en I. Miss Chang's career reached a new peak in September 1956 when she was elected an alternate member of the Party Central Committee at the Eighth National Congress. At that congress only four women were elected to full membership, and only four more as alternates. Still another indication of her stature within Party circles came about in June 1957 when she was identified as the third secretary of the Party's Women's Work Committee, of which the above-mentioned Ts'ai Ch'ang is the first secretary and Teng Ying-ch'ao (Mme. Chou En-lai) is the second secretary.

At the Third Women's Congress, held in September 1957, Chang gave the keynote report, a lengthy statement that was reprinted in consecutive issues of the *JMJP* (September 10–11, 1957). At the close of the Congress, she was re-elected a vice-chairman (but not to membership on the Secretariat). Apart from her trip to

Denmark in 1953, Chang's work in the women's movement has also taken her abroad on three other occasions, journeys that are summarized as follows: 1954—leader, women's goodwill mission to France for 10-day visit, December; 1957 —member, "working people's" delegation led by Liu Ning-i to the 40th anniversary celebrations of the Soviet Union, November; 1958—leader, women's delegation to Vienna to attend the Fourth Congress of the Women's International Democratic Federation, arriving May 28th, leaving June 9, going via Prague to Poland (June 10–23).

As her position on the Party Central Committee indicates, Chang is one of the foremost leaders in women's work in China. Until 1960 she was particularly active in this field, but since that time (possibly owing to age) she has not been frequently mentioned in the national press. Aside from re-elections to the NPC and the CPPCC, the only new assignment that she received after 1957 occurred in July 1958 when she was named to the National Committee of the China Peace Committee.

Chang was married to an early revolutionary, Li Yun-sheng, who was killed. A child by that marriage was arrested in the 1920's.

Chang Yun-i

(c.1891–   ; Wen-ch'ang, Hainan Island, Kwangtung). Former Red Army commander; deputy secretary, CCP Central Control Commission; member, CCP Central Committee.

A military officer before the establishment of the CCP, Chang Yun-i joined the Communist movement in the mid-1920's. For the next three decades he participated in many of the keynote events in Chinese Communist military history, including the Long March. During the latter war years he was deputy commander under Ch'en I of the Communists' important New Fourth Army that operated in the lower Yangtze River Valley. He was the top Communist official in Kwangsi after the establishment of the PRC in 1949, but he has worked in Peking since the mid-fifties. Chang has been a Party Central Committee member since 1945 and a deputy secretary of the CCP Central Control Commission since 1962.

Chang was born in the small town of Wen-ch'ang in northeastern Hainan Island. He began his formal education in Canton at a military primary school, later seeking further military training in the well-known military academy at Paoting, where so many of China's military leaders of the Republican period (1911–1949) were trained. Chang graduated in 1919 as a member of the sixth class (see under Yeh T'ing). Having been a member of the revolutionary T'ung-meng hui before attending Paoting and a participant in the 1911 Revolution, upon graduation he continued his military career. He returned to south China where he served for three years (1919–1921) in the army of a local Kwangsi warlord before becoming a staff officer in the First Division of the Kwangtung Army. Chang remained for at least a year in the Army's First Division, serving under Li Chi-shen, the chief-of-staff, who later became an influential leader in south China. Chang's career is not documented for the next few years during which time he may have continued to take part in the military exploits conducted by Li's army in south China.

Chang was serving with the Kwangtung Army when the Nationalists embarked in mid-1926 on the Northern Expedition to unify China under the KMT Government. Some reports state that he joined the CCP that year. In mid-1925 Li Chi-shen's Kwangtung Army had been renamed the Fourth Nationalist Army, and as such it participated in the Northen Expedition. Chang, by this time a staff officer with the rank of lieutenant-colonel, moved north with the army into the Yangtze Valley region in the latter half of 1926. The Fourth Army was mostly composed of Cantonese soldiers; initially commanded by Li Chi-shen, it had two other south Chinese leaders serving successively as commanders-in-chief after the Northern Expedition began. Ch'en Ming-shu, the first of the two, was contemporary in age to Chang and was also a graduate of the Paoting Military Academy. In the summer of 1927 the Fourth Army reached an area north of Nanchang, the Kiangsi capital, and made its headquarters at Chiu-chiang (Kiukiang). It then became known as the Fourth Army Group (or the Second Front Army), and by this time was commanded by Kwangtung General Chang Fa-k'uei. Because it contained a large component of officers recruited from the revolutionary Whampoa Military Academy at Canton (whose president was Chiang Kai-shek), service with this army gave Chang Yun-i an opportunity to work with the young men who had come from the disbanded Workers' Guard, a Communist organization formed among the Whampoa cadets.[1] Consequently, it may have been at this time that he joined the Party. When the Second Front Army reached Chiu-chiang, Chang was serving as the chief-of-staff of the 25th Division, which made its headquarters at Te-an on the rail line between Chiu-chiang and Nanchang, a strategic location in relation to Nanchang. When the Second Front Army's pro-Communist units received the signal to rebel, they, with the help of Chu Te's garrison force guarding the city, were able to capture the Kiangsi capital (August 1, 1927). All relations between the CCP and the KMT were immediately broken, the Party center was forced to go underground, and after five days Chang Fa-k'uei drove the Communists out of Nanchang.

The course of their evacuation and the route that they followed south through Kiangsi and Fukien are episodes covered in the biographies of Chu Te and Ho Lung, who were among the top leaders of the routed Communist army. After the Communists' defeat at Nanchang, Chang Yun-i followed Chu Te south into the North River area of Kwangtung, where they remained on the outskirts of Swatow when, at the end of September, Ho Lung and others captured the city. Then, when the Communists suffered a second defeat at Swatow, Chu retreated across Kwangtung and into southern Hunan and formed a unit of the Chinese Workers' and Peasants' Red Army in which Chang assumed command of the Third Division.

Chang's next assignment took him to Kwangsi Province, possibly to resume contact with some of the provincial military forces he may have known during the period of the Northern Expedition. He arrived in Kwangsi during the year 1928–1929, possibly sent there by the Party center at Shanghai, which was then controlled by Li Li-san (q.v.). Political feuding between the lesser and smaller provincial leaders in Kwangsi gave the Communists an opportunity to exploit the uneasy balance of power, and Chang was able to infiltrate forces of one of the lesser warlords, Li Ming-jui, whose headquarters were at Nanning in southeast Kwangsi. Li Ming-jui's political loyalties had already shifted several times. During the Northern Expedition he had been a deputy commander to powerful Kwangsi leader Li Tsung-jen, serving in the latter's Seventh Army. (There is also a report that Chang Yun-i served briefly as a high-ranking officer on the Seventh Army staff during the Northern Expedition). Later, however, Li Ming-jui came to oppose the stronger leaders Li Tsung-jen and Pai Ch'ung-hsi, both of whom came originally from Kweilin in northeast Kwangsi. By the time Chang arrived in Kwangsi, Li Ming-jui was described as "somewhat anti-Chiang Kai-shek."[2] Thus the Communists found him willing to cooperate temporarily in their plans to organize military forces in western Kwangsi. Li Ming-jui's army was the easier for the Communists to penetrate because he had on his staff two cousins of high officer rank, both of whom were favorably disposed to the CCP. One of them, Yü Tso-po, had been with the Seventh Army on the Northern Expedition and had worked with the Communists before that as head of the Kwangsi provincial Bureau of Agriculture; the other man, Yü's brother Yü Tso-yü, had already been recruited into the Party.

According to a Communist account, once in Nanning, Chang Yun-i took charge of a Fourth Brigade of the training corps of the Kwangsi Garrison Army (of Li Ming-jui) and Yü Tso-yü took charge of the Fifth Brigade. These two units soon moved into different sections of west-ern Kwangsi, Chang Yun-i going to the area near Pai-se close to the Yunnan border, while Yü went to Lung-chou, a small town in southwest Kwangsi near the Indochina border that was strategically located above the important rail line linking Nanning with Hanoi.[3] The Pai-se region on the Yu Chiang (Right River) is sometimes referred to as the Right River Base, and Lung-chou on the Tso Chiang (Left River) as the Left River Base.

Maoist historians have paid scant attention to the small Red bases established in Kwangsi under the auspices of Li Li-san. The Li Li-san period was one of tense inner-Party conflicts and much of its history has been rewritten in official contemporary accounts. At the same time existing source materials give only an indication of what actually happened when the CCP tried to establish soviet areas in Kwangsi. For a time in the late 1920's the CCP apparently worked in alliance with Li Ming-jui, an alliance that allowed them to get a toehold in western Kwangsi. Li apparently left Kwangsi when the Red armies evacuated the province; he marched toward Wuhan with the Red armies (after September 1930), but subsequently became involved in intrigues and was killed by the Communists somewhere north of Kwangsi. However, prior to this event, when the Fourth and Fifth Brigades of Li's former army left Nanning under Communist leadership to go into western Kwangsi, they met with varying success in their efforts to establish small soviets and military bases. Under Yü Tso-yü an Eighth Red Army was formed about February 1930. It occupied eight hsien centering around Ping-hsiang and Lung-chou hsien, but could not hold out for long and in about six months was driven from the Lung-chou area. With what remained of his Eighth Army (some of it seems to have deserted), Yü moved north into the territory of the Yu Chiang soviet where Chang Yun-i had temporarily been more successful in establishing a military base. Yü was probably killed sometime in 1930 or 1931, presumably in the fighting in Kwangsi.

Chang Yun-i had had more success when he led the Fourth Brigade into the Pai-se area along the upper reaches of the Yu Chiang. Establishing a small base there, he had been able to expand his territory to include the Communist base to the northeast, which centered around Tung-lan. In this area, which was chiefly populated by the non-Han minority, the Chuang, Wei Pa-ch'ün (a Chuang member of the CCP) had been active since the mid-1920's. Wei, born in Tung-lan hsien in 1894, had been active in his native hsien reorganizing the peasants of the Yu Chiang region. A brief description of developments in the Pai-se area is contained in the biography of Teng Hsiao-p'ing, a young CCP political agent who had been sent to Kwangsi from the Party center in Shanghai. Teng first came to Kwangsi in 1929, apparently not long after Chang arrived there. Party writers, always eager to link historic events to the anniversary of a prior well-known incident, state that on December 11, 1929 (the second anniversary of the Canton uprising; see under Chang T'ai-lei), the Yu Chiang Soviet was established and the Seventh Red Army activated. Chang Yun-i was named commander of the Seventh Army, and Lei Ching-t'ien headed the soviet government. (Lei remained with the Communists and died in 1959 while holding the post of president of the Shanghai Academy of Social Sciences.) The capital of the Yu Chiang government was at P'ing-ma, near Pai-se on the Yu River. When the Tung-lan base was included under Chang's territory, the larger area was sometimes referred to as the Pai-se Soviet.

Chang's exit from Kwangsi and his move north toward Wuhan on the orders of Li Li-san in Shanghai are described in the biography of Teng Hsiao-p'ing. On its way north, the Seventh Army lost many of its troops in battles or through desertions. After they left Kwangsi the Seventh Army commanders learned that the Communists had been defeated in the Wuhan area and at Changsha, where they were routed by the local military forces for a second time in mid-September 1930. After learning of the defeats, Chang decided to turn his troops toward Juichin to join Mao. According to some reports the two men met at Hsing-kuo in central Kiangsi in mid-1931. Once a member of Mao's army, Chang was given important assignments to perform. He was named director of the Operations Bureau of the Revolutionary Military Council, a post he held from 1931 to 1937. When the First All-China Congress of Soviets met at Juichin, Kiangsi, in November 1931, Chang was elected as a member of the Central Executive Committee (CEC), the executive arm of the new Chinese Soviet Republic. However, for reasons that are not clear, when the Second Congress was held in January–February 1934, he was not re-elected to the CEC.

There are few references to Chang's activities in the latter years of the Kiangsi period, which ended in October 1934 when the Communists began the Long March. Chang was probably in Fukien in the year before the March began, for there is a report that as of November 1933 he was one of two emissaries whom the Party at Juichin sent to Foochow, the Fukien capital, to act as Juichin's representatives to the rebel Fukien government headed by one of Chang's former military chiefs, Li Chi-shen.[4] The other emissary was said to be P'an Han-nien, a former Comintern representative (who served as a vice-mayor of Shanghai from 1949 to 1955 when he was purged from the CCP and imprisoned). Following the Fukien visit Chang was reported to have been sent to join Fang Chih-min (q.v.),

commander of Red guerrillas on the northern Kiangsi-Fukien border. After fighting there for a time he apparently returned to south Kiangsi about mid-1934 when Fang moved his forces north from Kiangsi into Anhwei. After rejoining Mao Tse-tung's army, Chang made the Long March, arriving with the Mao army in north Shensi in the fall of 1935.

Chang's stature grew considerably during the Sino-Japanese War. For a brief time before war began he was based in north Shensi where, in August 1936, he was identified as chief-of-staff of the Revolutionary Military Council, the top organ of the Party with jurisdiction for military affairs. The Council was headed by Mao Tse-tung, but it is not known how long Chang continued to serve as Mao's chief-of-staff. The position was held by T'eng Tai-yuan as of 1940; Chang must have relinquished it before that date because soon after the Sino-Japanese War broke out he was assigned to other duties outside of north China. From 1937 to 1938 he was said to have acted as a CCP liaison officer with Nationalist military officers in south China and Fukien, probably with the Kwangsi leaders with whom he had once associated.

Soon after the war began the Communists entered into negotiations with the Nationalists to gain official permission to operate an army in east-central China (in addition to the Eighth Route Army in northwest China). This force, known as the New Fourth Army, came into being early in 1938 with Yeh T'ing as its commander, and soon afterwards Chang must have been assigned to the new army. He was commander of its Fourth Detachment by the late fall of 1939 when American author Agnes Smedley visited Communist military bases in central China and interviewed Chang.[5] According to Chang, he had first been sent to investigate the Fourth Detachment late in 1938 after Kao Chün-t'ing, the commander, had become "a local militarist." The Fourth Detachment of the New Fourth Army had had a history somewhat different from the other three detachments, which were staffed by guerrilla forces that had been fighting in central China for some time. In 1938 the first three New Fourth Army units were established south of the Yangtze below Nanking, in a region that extended roughly from Tan-yang on the Grand Canal in southwest Kiangsu to Wu-hu in Anhwei, while the Fourth Detachment (a force of some 1,000 men) was sent directly from Hankow in March 1938 to an area north of the Yangtze around Huang-an in northwest Hupeh. Huang-an had been part of the Communists' base at Oyüwan in the early 1930's (see under Chang Kuo-t'ao). During 1938 the detachment increased its strength by local recruitment and in January 1939, probably about the time that Chang Yun-i assumed command, it moved its headquarters eastward to Shu-ch'eng hsien in central Anhwei. Units from this Fourth Detachment soon split off to form a Fifth Detachment based at Lu-chiang in Anhwei (see under Lo Ping-hui), while the Fourth Detachment continued to function largely as a unit to train other forces. In April 1939 the Fourth Detachment moved its base from Shu-ch'eng to an area near the small town of Ting-huan, not far to the southeast of Huai-nan (see under Fang I). Then early in 1940 the Detachment ran into serious opposition from the Kwangsi forces commanded by Chang Yun-i's former protagonist, Li Tsung-jen, commander of the Nationalists' Fifth War Zone, whose army was then acting as a semi-independent unit allied with Chiang Kai-shek's forces. So severe were the pressures put upon the Fourth Detachment, not only by Li's army, but also by the Japanese, that the unit lost contact with the rest of the New Fourth Army south of the Yangtze, and by mid-1940 it again moved its headquarters eastward, crossing the Tientsin-Pukow railroad into north Kiangsu to settle near Hsu-i on the shores of Lake Hungtse.[6] Chang presumably continued to head the Fourth Detachment all this while, although by November 1939 he also assumed other and more important posts with the headquarters command of the New Fourth Army.

As of about July 1939 the New Fourth Army was expanded and its organization table enlarged as the total forces were divided into two commands, one south and the other north of the Yangtze. Each command was composed of three detachments, the First through the Third placed under Ch'en I (of the South Command), the Fourth through the Sixth Detachments commanded by Chang Yun-i (north of the Yangtze). This latter post gave Chang direction of Red military forces in an area that extended from the Ko-yang region in northern Anhwei where the Sixth Detachment made its headquarters, across northern Anhwei and beyond the Tientsin-Pukow Railroad to the region around the Hungtse and Kao-yu Lakes in northern Kiangsu where the Fourth and Fifth Detachments were settled.[7]

As of January 1940 the organization table for the new Fourth Army, reflecting the newly created commands, indicated that Chang's stature as a military-political leader was continuing to grow. He was now given a post in the top command of the New Fourth Army, namely, as chief-of-staff under Yeh T'ing, the Army commander whose headquarters were south of the Yangtze. However, the position must have existed mainly on paper, because beginning in June 1940 much of the New Fourth Army began to move north of the Yangtze. The move, led by Ch'en I (q.v.), brought the First and Second Detachments into north Kiangsu late in June. Later, when T'an Chen-lin (q.v.) led the Third Detachment across the Yangtze into Anhwei, only the New Fourth Headquarters Staff headed

by Yeh T'ing and Hsiang Ying, the deputy commander, remained at Ching-hsien in Anhwei, south of the Yangtze. For a brief time before Ch'en I started to move north, Chang was the most important New Fourth Army commander north of the river, probably a reason for his being named chief-of-staff for the whole army. Then as of about October 1940, having established himself north of the Yangtze, Ch'en I created a new north Kiangsu command, which he headed. Apparently this succeeded the command held by Chang Yun-i whose troops, the Fourth, Fifth, and Sixth Detachments continued to operate in north Anhwei. Between October 1940 and February 1941 when the New Fourth Army was reorganized (see below), Chang's detachments plus troops from the Third Detachment now also fighting in north Anhwei, were savagely attacked both by the Japanese and by the KMT.

Following the serious defeat suffered by Yeh T'ing's units in their attempt to move north of the Yangtze, the New Fourth Army Incident of January 1941 (see under Yeh T'ing), Yenan announced a new command staff for the New Fourth Army. With Yeh a prisoner of the Nationalists, and Hsiang Ying killed, Ch'en I became the army's acting commander, and Chang Yun-i was elevated to the position of deputy commander. As the chief-of-staff he was succeeded by Lai Ch'uan-chu (q.v.), Chang's chief-of-staff in the former Fourth Detachment. At the same time that the Communists appointed a new chain of command for the New Fourth Army, they reorganized the former six detachments and, by adding a former independent guerrilla column commanded by Li Hsien-nien (q.v.), they created seven new divisions. The Fourth and the Fifth Detachments of the New Fourth Army were merged to form the Second Division, with Chang as the commander. Lo Ping-hui (q.v.), who had been the commander of the Fifth Detachment, was Chang's political commissar. Lo succeeded Chang as the Division commander about 1942. For the remainder of the war the Second Division controlled a critical area in Anhwei and west Kiangsu, traversed by the important rail line that linked Nanking and Tientsin. This area, known as the South Huai Military District, was bounded by the Yangtze on a line from Nanking to Hofei on the south, by a line between Hofei and Pang-fou on the west, by the Huai River on the north, and by the Grand Canal on the east.

Chang remained with the New Fourth Army until the close of the war, journeying occasionally to Kweilin in the years between 1941 and 1944 to contact Li Chi-shen who was then in charge of the Kweilin office of Chiang Kai-shek's Military and Political Headquarters. During the Sino-Japanese War Kweilin became a center for Communist front activities (see under Li K'o-nung). Chang was said to have gone there to aid Li in carrying out the united front policy under the terms of which the Communists and the KMT were working together to fight the Japanese. In view of Li's long history of disagreement with the KMT, and perhaps influenced by his contacts with Chang, it is not surprising that he went over to the Communists in the spring of 1949 as the latter were preparing to establish the central PRC government.

Chang's services to the Party during the war were given recognition at the Seventh CCP Congress in Yenan from April to June 1945 when he was elected to the Central Committee as a full member. He was re-elected to this post at the Eighth CCP Congress of September 1956.

Though he made occasional visits to Kweilin in the last years of the war, Chang worked primarily as the deputy commander of the New Fourth Army and as a member of Ch'en I's headquarters staff. Thus his military operations in the last years of the war were probably very similar to those of his commander. The headquarters of the New Fourth Army were located around Yen-ch'eng in eastern Kiangsu from sometime in 1940, but by 1946 these had moved to Lin-i in southeastern Shantung (see under Ch'en I). The army, commanded by Ch'en, was largely responsible for capturing Shantung in the years from 1946 to 1949. Known by 1947 as the East China PLA, the army was called the Third Field Army by early 1949. It took Shanghai in May 1949 and then established Communist headquarters there. When it completed its conquests, the Army exercised military control over the coastal provinces of Shantung, Kiangsu, Chekiang, and Fukien, as well as the inland province of Anhwei. Its period of military expansion is described in the biography of Ch'en I. During this time Chang was deputy commander and chief-of-staff of the East China PLA from 1947 to 1948 and deputy commander of the Third Field Army in 1949. While Ch'en's army conquered Shantung, connecting the province with the Communist-held area in the Hopeh-Shantung-Honan border area, where Lo Jung-huan and Hsiao Hua had been stationed with units of the 115th Division commanded by Lin Piao (qq.v.) before the end of the war, Chang became one of the principal military commanders in Shantung, identified in 1946 as the deputy commander of the Shantung Military District and commander of the East Front Army Group in Shantung. Eventually he became commander of the Shantung Military District. Then late in 1947 Ch'en I led some of the East China PLA forces out of Shantung and into Honan, and in the next year these cooperated with the army of Liu Po-ch'eng to capture the area around Cheng-chow and Kaifeng. Early in November 1948 Ch'en's and Liu's forces began the decisive battle for Huai-hai, which, when completed in January 1949, opened the way for the Communist armies to move south into central China. Chang took part in the battle for Huai-hai and for Shanghai in May 1949. But when the Third Army had established its Shanghai headquarters, he was transferred elsewhere.

Before proceeding to his new and major assignments in south China, Chang went to Peking to participate in the formation of the national government, which was established by the first session of the CPPCC held in September 1949. He attended as a representative of the PLA forces in South China and served on the Presidium (steering committee) for the CPPCC meetings. In the following month, when the major assignments in the central government were made, Chang was named as a member of the People's Revolutionary Military Council (under the chairmanship of Mao Tse-tung) and as a member of the Overseas Chinese Affairs Commission of the Government Administration Council (the cabinet). On paper the most important assignment he received at this time was membership on the Central People's Government Council (CPGC), an organization that had legislative, executive, and judicial responsibilities and which, in 34 meetings between 1949 and 1954, passed on virtually all the vital national legislation adopted in these first critical years of the new government. However, because Chang was stationed in south China, he attended very few of the 34 CPGC meetings and none after 1950. It was also in October 1949 that Chang was named to membership on the newly organized Sino-Soviet Friendship Association, one of the most active of the mass organizations in the early years of the PRC. He was not, however, reappointed to the Association when it was reorganized in December 1954.

Although Chang held major positions in the central government from 1949 until the constitutional government was inaugurated in 1954, his major contributions during these years were in south China, especially in his native Kwangsi. The two major Kwangsi cities, Kweilin and Nanning, fell to the advancing Communist armies in November and December 1949, respectively. Chang immediately assumed virtually all of the key assignments within the province, becoming Kwangsi governor, both commander and political commissar of the Kwangsi Military District, and the ranking secretary of the Party Committee. Although he remained as governor and secretary until early 1955, he relinquished the military posts to others by the early fifties. Within the Kwangsi Government Chang was also chairman of the provincial Finance and Economics Committee from 1950 to 1953.

In the period from 1949 to 1954, central-south China was organized somewhat differently from the other five large regions in which the country was then divided. Thus, in this area there were special sub-districts covering Party and military organizations in south China that covered the two provinces of Kwangtung and Kwangsi. Chang was the deputy commander of the South China Military Region from the early fall of 1949 and by the end of that year was also the second secretary of the Party's South China Sub-bureau. However, unlike most of the key personnel in south China who spent much of their time in either Wuhan or Canton (e.g., Yeh Chien-ying), Chang remained in Kwangsi most of the time. At the regional level, covering the six provinces of Hupeh, Honan, Hunan, Kiangsi, Kwangtung, and Kwangsi, Chang was a member of the governmental Central-South Military and Administrative Committee (CSMAC) that made its headquarters in Wuhan. The CSMAC began its operations in February 1950, and when it was reorganized into the Central-South Administrative Committee in January 1953, Chang was promoted to a vice-chairmanship, a position he held until the regional administrations were abolished in 1954. Subordinate to the CSMAC, he was also a member of the South China Sub-committee of the Finance and Economics Committee from September 1951.

The paucity of Chang's public appearances in the early fifties for a leader of his stature lends credence to otherwise undocumented KMT press reports that Chang spent part of this time in North Vietnam as head of a Chinese Communist military aid program to Ho Chi-minh's forces in the fight against the French. On occasion, Kwangsi government proclamations were issued in Chang's name, as in May 1953 when a directive concerning natural disasters was published. But for the most part, Ch'en Man-yuan (q.v.), serving as the acting secretary of the Kwangsi Party Committee, attended and spoke before most of the meetings that Chang might normally have addressed as the senior Kwangsi leader. Ultimately, in early 1955, Ch'en Man-yuan replaced Chang as the Party first secretary and Wei Kuo-ch'ing replaced him as the provincial governor. But by this time Chang had already been transferred to Peking.

Chang was elected in 1954 as a Kwangsi deputy to the First NPC; when the first session of the Congress was held in September 1954, he was named to membership on the Standing Committee, a position to which he was re-elected in April 1959 for the Second NPC and in January 1965 for the Third NPC. He was also named in September 1954 as a member of the new National Defense Council (NDC), the successor (though less important) organization to the People's Revolutionary Military Council. He also continues to sit on the NDC, having been re-elected in April 1959 and January 1965. In September 1955, when the PRC first gave its officer corps personal military ranks and decorations, Chang received the Orders of August First,

Independence and Freedom, and Liberation, awards for service in the Red armies covering the period from 1927 to 1950. He was also made a colonel-general at this time (the equivalent of a three-star general in the U.S. Army), and by 1963 had been promoted to senior general (only one rank below that of marshal).

As already described, Chang had been a member of the Party Central Committee from the Seventh Congress in 1945. When the Eighth Congress was held in September 1956, he served on the Congress Presidium (steering committee) and was elected at the close of the proceedings to membership on the new (Eighth) Central Committee. Since that time, however, Chang has been mentioned in the Party press infrequently. Inferential evidence suggests that one of his continuing assignments may be to keep watch over the state of affairs in his native Kwangsi. For example, in April 1957 he participated in talks in Peking related to the change of Kwangsi from a province to the Kwangsi-Chuang Autonomous Region (a step formally taken in March 1958—see under Wei Kuo-ch'ing). Similarly, in March 1963 he was in Kwangsi to attend the celebrations marking the fifth anniversary of the Region, and in November 1964 he was once again reported there (although the nature of his activities was not revealed).

Although Chang has been infrequently in the public eye in the period after the Eighth Congress (1956), his importance as a senior Party leader was again illustrated at the Party Central Committee's 10th Plenum held in September 1962. It was decided then to strengthen the work of the important Party Control Commission and to expand its membership. Chang was named as a deputy secretary (under Secretary Tung Pi-wu), in effect, replacing Deputy Secretary Liu Lan-t'ao (q.v.), who was transferred away from Peking and therefore relinquished this position. There are only five deputy secretaries on the Control Commission, among them such important persons as Party Central Committee members Hsiao Hua and Wang Ts'ung-wu (qq.v.). Chang's major contributions to the Chinese Communist movement were made from the late twenties to the fifties, but his presence on the Control Commission suggests that he remains a political figure of some importance, even though he is one of the more elderly members of the CCP Central Committee.

1. F. F. Liu, *A Military History of Modern China: 1924–1949* (Princeton, N. J., 1956), p. 34.

2. *SCMM* 285, pp. 33–40.

3. *Ibid.*

4. Kung Ch'u, *Wo yü hung-chün* (The Red army and I; Hong Kong, 1954), p. 364.

5. Agnes Smedley, *Battle Hymn of China* (New York, 1945), pp. 317ff.

6. Chalmers A. Johnson, *Peasant Nationalism and Communist Power* (Stanford, Calif., 1962), pp. 124ff.

7. *Ibid.*

Chao An-po

(1915–　　; Chekiang). Specialist in Japanese affairs.

Chao An-po was born in January 1915 in Chekiang. He has risen within the Chinese hierarchy to be one of the top specialists on Japanese affairs and is so regarded by influential and knowledgeable Japanese. Chao is fluent in Japanese, probably because he lived in Japan at least long enough to attend a Japanese high school. Japanese sources state that Chao was "reportedly" a staff member of the Social Affairs Department of the CCP Central Committee (long the euphemism for Chinese Communist intelligence) and was then both the deputy head of a section of the "foreign affairs" bureau of the Northeast People's Government and head of a "Northeast committee to control overseas Japanese." None of these items are dated, but the terminology suggests that they refer to the latter stages of the Sino-Japanese War and the postwar period in Manchuria, where tens of thousands of Japanese were prisoners of the victorious allies, including the Chinese.

Chao's entry onto the national scene in contemporary Chinese Communist politics occurred in early 1953 when he was identified as an adviser to the Red Cross Society of China, a position he continues to hold. The apparent unimportance of this title is deceptive; one of the major issues in Sino-Japanese affairs in the early and mid-1950's was the return of the above-mentioned thousands of Japanese left on the China mainland after the war (many, but not all of whom, were military men). Lacking diplomatic relations, both sides resorted to various semi-official devices to negotiate for the release of these men. The Red Cross Society served as a useful instrument, and thus Chao has been intimately connected with the society for many years. It was in this capacity that he was twice a member of Red Cross delegations to Japan led by Red Cross President Li Te-ch'üan in October–November 1954 and December 1957–January 1958. And in June 1956 in Peking, he was one of the Chinese signatories to a joint communiqué signed with quasi-official Japanese repatriation specialists on the release of Japanese "war criminals."

By 1955 Chao was involved in another field that is of great sensitivity to Japan, namely, the fishing industry. Here again it was necessary to use an ostensibly unofficial organization, and thus Chao became an adviser to the China Fishery Association, another position he continues to retain. He took part in negotiations in 1955 with Japanese fishery experts leading to the signing on April 15, 1955, of an agreement on fishing in the Yellow Sea and the East China Sea, and a year later he participated in discussions that led (on May 8, 1956) to the signing of an extension of this agreement for another year. Also, in November–December 1956, he visited Japan as a member of a delegation led by the chairman of the China Fishery Association.

Chao's increasingly important role in foreign affairs was given official recognition in July 1955 when he was elected to the Standing Committee of the Board of Directors of the Chinese People's Institute of Foreign Affairs, the most important of the technically unofficial instruments of foreign policy in Communist China. He was re-elected to this position as late as December 1964 at the fourth congress of the Institute. In August 1955 Chao was again in Japan, on this occasion for the first World Conference Against Nuclear Weapons as a member of a delegation led by Liu Ning-i, a top Party international liaison official and a Central Committee member since 1956. These conferences became annual events and Chao attended three more of them after the first one in 1955. He was a deputy leader to the sixth conference in August 1960, secretary-general to the eighth conference in August 1962, and deputy leader to the ninth conference in August 1963.

From the late 1950's, Chao began to receive increasing attention in the national press. In particular, he has very often been on hand to entertain and negotiate with the many Japanese visitors to the mainland and frequently was a witness (or signatory) to a joint communiqué signed with one Japanese group or another. To cite a random but typical example, Chao was one of the Chinese signers to a joint statement dealing with peace and "American imperialism" signed in Peking on October 12, 1962, with a visiting Japan-China Friendship Association delegation. In the late 1950's and 1960's he received (and continues to hold) several new appointments. He was named in July 1958 to the National Committee of the China Peace Committee; by January 1961 he was a deputy secretary-general of the Chinese People's Relief Administration. At a far more important level he was identified in September 1963 as a "leading functionary" of a department under the Party Central Committee. Peking has never openly identified a Party organ dealing with foreign affairs, but some such "international liaison department" obviously exists. It is probable that such a department has sections dealing with different areas of the world; almost certainly Chao has responsibilities regarding Japan within some such Party organization. Still another post that Chao holds is that of secretary-general of the Japan-China Friendship Association, created in October 1963 under the chairmanship of Liao Ch'eng-chih, generally regarded as Peking's leading specialist on Japanese affairs.

Chao made his eighth trip to Japan in February 1964 when he led a delegation of the Afro-Asian Solidarity Committee of China for a tour of Japan at the invitation of a counterpart organization in Japan. During this visit he met with members of the Central Committee of the Japan Communist Party. Five months later, in July 1964, Chao was denied entry into Japan to attend the 10th World Conference Against Nuclear Weapons; reportedly, he was officially declared by the Japanese to be an "undesirable person" (along with Wang Chao-hua, a youth leader also en route to Japan). The Chinese issued a series of bitter denunciations of this "extremely unfriendly act," which would "have an adverse effect" on Sino-Japanese relations. Chao was further described as a man who had "done much in the past ten years . . . to strengthen the . . . relations" between China and Japan. In retrospect, Chao's troubles with the Japanese authorities appear to stem from two earlier sessions of the annual "Conference Against Nuclear Weapons." By the early 1960's these meetings had become forums for the airing of Sino-Soviet disputes, with complex ramifications within Japanese Communist, left-wing, and peace movements. Thus, at the close of the August 1962 conference, Chao issued a blistering denunciation of "some officials" of the Japanese Socialist Party and the General Council of Trade Unions of Japan (SOHYO) who, he charged, had "slandered" the Chinese delegation for the "alleged" attempt by the Chinese to impose its views on other delegations. Exactly a year later (August 1963), at the next conference, Chao bitterly protested the signing by the Americans, Russians, and British of the nuclear test ban treaty on the eve of the opening of the conference in Japan, and throughout the stormy conference Chao issued a number of volatile statements.

Apparently all these activities led the Japanese to the conclusion that Chao should be barred from the country. Nonetheless, he continues to specialize in Japanese affairs within China, as evidenced by his participation in talks with the General Secretary of the Japanese Communist Party in September 1964 and with a delegation of the Japanese Socialist Party in the following month.

Chao has on occasion served as a Japanese interpreter for important Chinese leaders, including Mao Tse-tung. He is regarded by well-placed Japanese as second only to Liao Ch'eng-chih (q.v.) in dealing with Japanese affairs.

Chao Chien-min

(c.1910–   ; Shantung). Secretary, Yunnan CCP Committee; alternate member CCP Central Committee.

Chao Chien-min served with guerrilla units in Shantung during the Sino-Japanese War and then held government posts in the southwest in the early 1950's. In 1953 he became a vice-minister of Railways. By 1955 he had been transferred from the southwest to Shantung, where he was governor and a secretary in the Provincial Party Committee until 1958 when he was purged. He has since reappeared as a secretary of the Yunnan Provincial Party Committee.

Chao was born into a landlord family in Shantung about 1910.[1] By 1936 he was a Party member, working in northern Honan in the area adjacent to western Shantung. Early in 1936 he was sent from Honan into west Shantung, where he is credited by the Communists with having established the CCP Shantung Provincial Work Committee, which soon became the Provincial Party Committee.[2] He apparently remained in the Shantung area, because by 1938 he was a Party organizer in guerrilla units commanded by Fan Chu-hsien. Fan had been a nationalist government official in western Shantung. When the war began in mid-1937 he had refused to retreat and instead had organized guerrilla forces, which included some Communists, to resist the Japanese in Shantung and southern Hopeh.[3] After Fan was killed in 1938 and his guerrilla units were decimated, Chao and others reorganized some of the remnant forces.[4] In early 1939 these were merged with a "vanguard" unit (subordinate to the 129th Division of Liu Po-ch'eng, q.v.), led by Li Chü-k'uei, that had been sent into northwest Shantung to assist the local resistance (see under Li Chü-k'uei and Yang Hsiu-feng). Little else is known about Chao's wartime activities aside from the fact that he was commanding an independent brigade in southern Hopeh in 1945 when the war ended.

Liu Po-ch'eng's Second Field Army (largely composed of his old 129th Division) had pushed into the southwest by the end of 1949. In July 1950 the Communists formed the Southwest Military and Administrative Committee (SWMAC) to control Kweichow, Szechwan, Yunnan, and Sikang. At that time Chao was appointed to head the SWMAC Communications Department and was also named a member of its Finance and Economics Committee under Teng Hsiao-p'ing, then the chief political figure in the southwest. Until the latter part of 1950 Chao was mainly occupied with the construction of the important rail line between Chengtu and Chungking, Szechwan's two most important cities.[5] Then, after Chinese forces entered the Korean War in October 1950, Chao was briefly assigned to the "Chinese People's Volunteers," apparently in his capacity as a specialist in logistics.[6] He was back in the southwest by mid-1952. His work in the field of transportation probably attracted the attention of the authorities in Peking, for in January 1953 he was named a vice-minister of railways. Though the overwhelming majority of cabinet-level personnel work in Peking, Chao was an exception. He may have been kept in the southwest because that area was a principal center of railway construction.

When the regional government in the southwest was abolished in late 1954, Chao was transferred to his native Shantung. At a provincial congress that ended in March 1955 he was elected governor, replacing K'ang Sheng (q.v.). Soon thereafter, Chao became one of the secretaries of the Shantung Party Committee, serving under First Secretary Shu T'ung. In mid-1956 he was named as a Shantung deputy to the First NPC to replace a deceased colleague, and when the Congress held its third session in June 1956 he spoke on the development of provincial industry and agriculture. He was not, however, re-elected a deputy to the Second NPC (1959–1964), undoubtedly because of the serious political difficulties he encountered in late 1958 (see below).

Chao's work in the southwest and Shantung was rewarded at the Eighth Party Congress held in September 1956 when he was elected to alternate membership on the Party Central Committee. During the next two years he made frequent public appearances in Shantung. For example, he inspected PLA units stationed in Shantung and attended provincial congresses of "progressive" workers, as well as meetings of the Party Committee. In May 1957 he was made head of a "rectification" committee for Shantung to help carry out the nationwide "rectification" campaign against the "rightists." A year later he reported to a meeting of Party cadres in Shantung on the work of the second session of the Eighth Party Congress (May 1958), which he presumably had attended.

In late 1957 or early 1958 Chao was removed as a vice-minister of railways. He appeared regularly in Shantung until August 1958, when he suddenly disappeared from the national press. The explanation was not long in coming. At a Shantung Government congress in October–November 1958 Chao came under a severe attack that made it clear that the Great Leap Forward and the development of the communes had caused a serious shake-up in the Shantung Party Committee. Certain Committee members and provincial government officials, including Chao, had apparently opposed the Great Leap, arguing that Shantung lacked the agricultural resources to sustain the tremendously accelerated pace in production. Prior to the congress the seriousness of the situation had apparently motivated Mao Tse-tung to visit Shantung, and he had urged the development of the communes and the accelerated production drive of the Great Leap.

T'an Ch'i-lung (q.v.), a fellow Party secretary in Shantung, was the man who brought the principal charges against Chao. In two reports to the 1958 provincial congress T'an described the "errors" committed by Chao Chien-min. The gist of the criticism was that Chao had been reluctant to promote the communes and the Great Leap and undermined Party authority. Specifically, T'an said that as early as 1956 Chao had displayed insufficient enthusiasm in the programs for socialization, disavowed the necessity for continuing class struggle, and opposed the CCP Provincial Committee "on all issues." As a member of the landlord class he had defended its interests; neither Chao's family, nor he as provincial governor had ever joined one of the agricultural cooperatives, which were the forerunners of the communes. Further, he had been reluctant to have surplus grain sold to the government and had sought a restoration of the landlords' old position. Consequently, he was accused of "not working for socialism" but "defending capitalism and feudalism." Moreover, he had sympathized with "anti-Party" and "rightist" elements, not bringing their activities to the attention of the authorities. (This charge probably referred to the period when Chao headed the provincial anti-rightist campaign.) Nor had he attempted to wipe out evidences of parochialism among the people of Shantung. "I am a native of Shantung, and I am for the people of Shantung and the cadres of Shantung," Chao is quoted as saying. The most serious charge was that Chao stood for the division of Party and government responsibilities, even urging some degree of independence for the latter, thereby gravely challenging the authority of the Party and weakening the CCP's influence in the Provincial Government. Such "errors" were said to reflect "emphatically his vile, bourgeois individualistic thoughts and aims." Finally, he was linked with Hsiang Ming, a leading figure in the so-called anti-party case that led to the purge of Kao Kang and Jao Shu-shih in 1955 (see under Kao Kang), one of the most serious purges in the history of the CCP. Hsiang was an important east China Party leader in the early fifties and was the acting secretary of the Party's Shantung Sub-bureau at the time of his purge. The charge against Chao, who arrived in Shantung shortly before the Kao-Jao purge was revealed, was that he had "always doubted and opposed the verdict" and had wanted Hsiang exonerated. In spite of all this public criticism, however, T'an hoped that Chao "would come to know his errors, correct them, and return to the stand of the Party."[7]

At the close of the provincial congress, T'an Ch'i-lung replaced Chao as Shantung governor. Although the latter lost all his Shantung posts, he was not removed as an alternate member of the Party Central Committee. Over four years passed before anything further was heard of Chao. Then in April 1963 he reappeared in the southwest, the region where he had worked in the early 1950's. His new assignment was as secretary of the Yunnan Provincial Party Committee under First Secretary Yen Hung-yen (q.v.). This pattern of accusation-purge-reappearance is not peculiar to Chao Chien-min. Other persons of equal stature (e.g., P'an Fu-sheng) underwent a similar cycle.

Since his identification in Yunnan in 1963, Chao has received rather substantial press coverage, partly because the Yunnan capital, Kunming, is a point of entry to and exit from China for both foreign visitors and Chinese leaders traveling in Southeast Asia. For instance in July 1964 Chao was on hand to bid farewell to Chou En-lai, then en route to Burma. In addition to the provincial Party secretaryship, in January 1965 Chao received one other rather minor post when he was named to the preparatory committee for the Second National Sports Meet held later in 1965.

---

1. Interview with Chinese newspaperman familiar with Chao, Hong Kong, July 1964.
2. Ch'i Wu, *I-ko ko-ming ken-chü te ch'eng-chang; k'ang-Jih chan-cheng ho chieh-fang chan-cheng shih-ch'i te Chin-Chi-Lu-Yü pien-ch'ü kai-k'uang* (The establishment and growth of a revolutionary base; a general account of the Shansi-Hopeh-Shantung-Honan Border Region during the anti-Japanese war and the war of liberation; Peking, 1958), p. 203.
3. *Ibid.*, p. 28.
4. *Ibid.*, pp. 28, 306.
5. Interview, see note 1.
6. *Ibid.*
7. *SCMP* 1924.

Chao Erh-lu

(c.1905–1967; Yuan-p'ing hsien, Shansi). Veteran military officer; specialist in machine building industries; vice-chairman, State Economic Commission; member, CCP Central Committee.

A Party member since 1927, Chao Erh-lu was a military commander and political officer in the Red Armies from the late twenties. He made the Long March and continued as a military leader throughout the Sino-Japanese War and the postwar years. Chao spent most of the years after the establishment of the PRC as a government administrator specializing in the machine building industries and military affairs. A colonel-general in the PLA, he was a Party Central Committee member from 1956 until his death in 1967.

Chao was born about 1905 in Yuan-p'ing hsien, 60 miles north of Taiyuan, Shansi. A graduate of a middle school in Taiyuan, he began his career as a revolutionist in June 1927 and was admitted into the CCP two months later. In the following year Chao went to Chingkangshan on the Hunan-Kiangsi border, where he served as the Party representative in a company of the 28th Regiment, one of the six regiments in the Fourth Red Army established by Chu Te and Mao Tse-tung in the spring of 1928. (A brief history of the Fourth Army is contained in the biography of Chu Te.) At sometime prior to the end of 1929 Chao was promoted to the post of Party representative in the Communists' First Column and then took command of the Fourth Red Army's 29th Regiment. In the early thirties he was chief of a regimental-level supply department within the Chu-Mao First Army Corps. Chao is reported to have attended a military academy in the early thirties, possibly the Red Army Academy that opened near Juichin in 1933.

Chao made the Long March in 1934–1935 as director of the Supply Department of Lin Piao's First Army Corps. After arriving in north Shensi, he attended the first class of the Anti-Japanese Military Academy in mid-1936. A year later, when war with Japan broke out, Chao was assigned to Lin Piao's 115th Division, one of the three divisions of the Communists' Eighth Route Army. He spent most or all of the war years as a commander and political officer in the Shansi-Chahar-Hopeh (Chin-Ch'a-Chi) base (see under Nieh Jung-chen). The exact dates are not available, but Chao's obituary revealed that he held the following positions: commander and political commissar of the Second Sub-district of the Chin-Ch'a-Chi Military Region, commander and political commissar of the Hopeh-Shansi Column, and chief-of-staff of the Chin-Ch'a-Chi Military Region. He remained in this area in the immediate postwar period and by 1947 was identified as a member of the Chin-Ch'a-Chi CCP Central Bureau. In the meantime, in 1946, when General George C. Marshall's Peking Executive Headquarters was attempting to implement the terms of the cease-fire agreement (January 1946) between Communists and Nationalists, Chao was the Communist member of the truce team sent by the Executive Headquarters into the area around Chang-chia-k'ou (Kalgan), the capital of Chahar Province. As a truce team member he had the simulated military rank of a major-general.

In August 1948 the Communists established the North China People's Government to administer those areas of north China then under their control. The government lasted only until October 1949 when the PRC came into being and absorbed the North China Government. From 1948 to October 1949 Chao held three posts in north China; he was chief-of-staff of the North China Military Region, a member of the North China People's Government Council, and a member of the Council's Finance and Economics Committee headed by the veteran Tung Pi-wu.

At some time in 1949 Chao transferred to Lin Piao's Fourth Field Army, the Communist force that had conquered the Nationalists in Manchuria and had captured Tientsin and Peking in January 1949. In the spring of 1949, with Hsiao K'o (q.v.) as chief-of-staff of both the Fourth Field Army and of the Central-South Military Region (CSMR), this army moved into Hupeh, Kiangsi, and Hunan, and later into Kwangtung and Kwangsi. Chao served under Hsiao as deputy chief-of-staff of the CSMR and of the Fourth Field Army. He was also a member of the Wuhan Military Control Commission subsequent to the Communist takeover of that important Yangtze River city in May 1949. In 1950 Chao succeeded Hsiao as chief-of-staff of both the CSMR and its field army, continuing in these posts until 1952. Concurrently, Chao was the garrison commander of Wuhan. During these same years he was a member of the Central-South Military and Administrative Committee (CSMAC), the governmental organ for the area under the jurisdiction of the Military Region. In addition, he was a member of the CSMAC's Finance and Economics Committee. He received two further assignments when he was named as vice-chairman of both the Central-South Flood Prevention Headquarters and the Central-South Anti-Epidemic Committee, two organizations formed in the spring of 1952, the first under important Party leader Teng Tzu-hui (q.v.).

After approximately three years in central-south China, Chao was transferred in 1952 to Peking, where he was given administrative posts in accordance with his background as a military leader. He was made director in 1952 of the Ordnance Department of the Rear Services Department under the People's Revolutionary Military Council, the military advisory branch of the PRC Government. In a reorganization of some of the government ministries, the Communists took offices away from the Ministry of Heavy Industry in August 1952 and from these created the First and Second Ministries of Machine Building. Chao was made minister of the Second Ministry of Machine Building (while continuing to hold the Ordnance post). His Ministry was said to deal with munitions production. After six years in this post, Chao's responsibilities were considerably widened during another partial reorganization of the State Council in February 1958. The First and Second Ministries of Machine Building were merged, and to them was added the former Ministry of Power Equipment to form a single First Ministry of Machine Building; there was, in addition, a new Second Machine Building Ministry. Chao was made chief of the First Ministry, holding the post until September 1960 when he was succeeded by Tuan Chün-i (q.v.). On the same day that Chao relinquished the ministerial post, he was assigned to the State Economic Commission as one of the vice-chairmen. He continued to hold this post, his principal governmental responsibility, until his death in 1967.

In September 1954, with the creation of the constitutional government, Chao was given a seat in two of the national advisory councils, the National Defense Council and the CPPCC. He was named to membership on the National Defense Council in September, when that organization was created, and was reappointed in April 1959 and in January 1965. From 1954 to 1959 he was also a member of the Second CPPCC, representing the CCP, but he was not re-elected to the Third CPPCC that opened in April 1959. Chao was not a member of the First NPC, which had inaugurated the constitutional government in 1954, but he was elected to the Second NPC (1959–1964) and was re-elected to the Third NPC, which opened in December 1964. During the term of the Second NPC he had represented Szechwan, but he was transferred to the Kwangsi-Chuang Autonomous Region for the Third NPC.

In September 1955, when national military honors were first awarded, Chao received all three top decorations: the Orders of August First, Independence and Freedom, and Liberation, awards that covered military service during the period from 1927 to 1950. Personal military ranks were also designated for PLA officers for the first time in 1955. However, it was not until July 1963 that Chao was identified as a colonel-general, the equivalent of a three-star general in the U.S. Army. Chao's long career in the CCP was given official recognition in September 1956 when he was elected a member of the Party Central Committee at the Eighth Party Congress. He was one of only 33 men elected to full membership who had been neither an alternate nor a full member of the Seventh Central Committee elected in 1945.

From the mid-fifties to 1960 Chao's name appeared in the press with some regularity, particularly in connection with conferences related to the machine building industries. He was a featured speaker, for example, at the first "National Second Machine Industry Advanced Producers Conference" held in April 1956. However, after he relinquished his ministerial portfolio in the First Ministry of Machine Building in 1960 he was mentioned in the press almost exclusively in connection with military affairs, as on July 31, 1963, when he took part in celebrations marking the anniversary of the PLA. Chao's obituary revealed that at the time of his death he was holding three important posts in organizations theretofore not mentioned in the Communist press. The first of these was a deputy directorship of the State Council's National Defense Industry Office (Kuo-fang kung-yeh pan-kung-shih), an organization that seems to parallel several other offices (e.g., the Agriculture and Forestry Office) that direct and coordinate the work of subordinate commissions and ministries. Secondly, Chao had been director of the Party Central Committee's National Defense Industry Political Department, an organ in the Party apparatus paralleling the above-mentioned office. Finally, he was deputy director of the National Defense Committee under Communist China's most important military organ, the Party's Military Affairs Committee.

Chao wrote at least four articles for the Party press, all dealing with the machine building industries. These appeared in *Hung-ch'i* (Red flag, issues of December 1, 1958, and April 1, 1960) and the *JMJP* (May 31, 1958, and September 24, 1959). He remained an active member of the Party elite until his death on February 2, 1967, at the age of 62. He was given the honors normally accorded to a leader of his stature, including a memorial service four days after his death.

Chao I-min

(c.1905– ; Hopeh). Specialist in international Party liaison work; alternate member, CCP Central Committee.

From the Sino-Japanese War to the mid-fifties, Chao I-min was an important propaganda and education official, first in northwest and north China and later in the central-south area. Since the mid-fifties he has been one of the most prominent officials of the CCP in its relations with foreign Communist parties. Chao was born about 1905 in Hopeh Province in north China. His early background is not recorded, but it is probable that he was a Party member by the start of the Sino-Japanese War. According to a Communist source, during the war four men served successively as the head of the Lu Hsun Fine Arts Academy, an important propaganda training institute established in Yenan in 1938. The four men, in the order listed, were dramatist Sha K'ofu, Chao, Wu Yü-chang (q.v.), and Chou Yang (q.v.).[1] In the latter stages of the war Chao served as vice-president and then as president of Yenan University, a school established in 1941 through the merger of the Lu Hsun Academy and six other institutes in Yenan.

In the postwar period Chao continued in the educational field, being named to the presidency of the Hopeh-Chahar-Jehol-Liaoning Associated University when it was established in 1947.[2] He was among the first officials to enter Peking after its fall to the Communists in early 1949. Throughout the spring and summer of 1949 Communist officials in Peking were engaged in the preparatory work that culminated in the fall in the formation of the central government and many of the "mass" or "people's" organizations. Chao's principal task at this time was apparently to contact leading literary and artistic figures (most of them non-Communists), many of whom were arriving in Peking from all parts of China and from abroad. For example, in March 1949 Chao attended a meeting to welcome re-

turning literati, which was sponsored by the North China People's Government and the North China Literary and Artistic Circles Association.[3] He apparently remained in Peking through the fall of 1949; at any rate, he was named to membership on the First Executive Board of the Sino-Soviet Friendship Association (SSFA), which was formed in early October, just a few days after the new central government was established. He retained his post in the SSFA until the end of 1954.

By no later than the end of 1949 Chao was assigned to central-south China, which had just been conquered by the advancing Communist armies. There he headed both the Party's Central-South Bureau's Propaganda Department and the Youth Work Committee, posts he retained until the Bureau was abolished in late 1954. The governmental administration for this area (covering Honan, Kiangsi, Hupeh, Hunan, Kwangtung, and Kwangsi) was set up in February 1950 under the name Central-South Military and Administrative Committee (CSMAC). The headquarters of both the CSMAC and the Party Bureau were located in Wuhan, and both organizations were headed by Lin Piao (q.v.). Chao was named to membership on the CSMAC and in March 1950 was given concurrent assignments as director of the CSMAC's Culture and Education Committee and its Culture Department. Three years later (January 1953), when the CSMAC was reorganized into the Central-South Administrative Committee (CSAC), he was reappointed as a member of the CSAC and director of its Culture and Education Committee (although he relinquished his post in the Culture Department). Thus, in the years from 1949 to 1954, Chao was one of the principal officials concerned with the development of cultural-propaganda affairs both in the Party and civil administrations throughout the six-province area. For example, it fell to him to deliver a major report on cultural and educational work in the region when the CSMAC met for its second meeting in Wuhan in September 1950. And in May 1952, to commemorate the 10th anniversary of Mao Tse-tung's famous address on literature and art (delivered in Yenan), Chao reported on ideological remolding in central-south China, a talk in which he criticized Party cadres who were becoming estranged from the life of the workers and peasants.

Like most major political figures in the early years of the regime, Chao also received extracurricular assignments that lay outside his major areas of responsibility. In March 1952 he received two such assignments, a vice-chairmanship of the Central-South Anti-Epidemic Committee and membership on the Ching River Flood-harnessing Committee. Within the "people's" organizations, he headed the China Peace Committee's Central-South Branch from 1951 and was from the following year a vice-chairman of both the Central-South and Wuhan branches of the SSFA (to which, as described above, he was affiliated at the national level). He was also identified in mid-1952 as the secretary of the New Democratic Youth League's Central-South Work Committee.

In 1954 Chao was given an assignment that was a forerunner of much of his activity in latter years. In July of that year he was sent to Chile as head of a delegation to attend the birthday celebrations for a Chilean Communist poet, Pablo Neruda; his delegation visited Argentina briefly before returning to China in September. Chao is one of the very few ranking Chinese Communists who have visited Latin America (exclusive of Cuba). The regional administration in central-south China was abolished in 1954; as a consequence, soon after returning from Latin America, Chao was transferred to Peking. Since then he has devoted his time almost exclusively to two closely related activities—international liaison on behalf of ostensibly non-governmental organizations (such as the China Peace Committee) and liaison work between the CCP and other Communist parties throughout the world. In the former category he received his first major assignment in March 1955, when he was named as a vice-chairman of the Chinese People's Association for Cultural Relations with Foreign Countries (CPACRFC), an important mass organization whose activities are directed mainly toward nations that do not maintain diplomatic relations with Peking. In this capacity, for example, Chao was one of the signers in November 1955 of a joint communiqué with a Japanese delegation representing the National League for the Protection of the (Japanese) Constitution. In the following years Chao devoted much of his time to the CPACRFC; although he relinquished his vice-chairmanship in April 1959, he retains his seat on the organization's Standing Committee. In June 1955 Chao was elected *in absentia* to the World Peace Council (WPC) at the World Peace Congress held in Helsinki. He was named to the Standing Committee of the China Peace Committee, the Chinese affiliate of the WPC, in July 1958, and in June 1965 he was promoted to a vice-chairmanship. Still another liaison organization with which Chao has been affiliated is the Asian Solidarity Committee of China, an organization formed in February 1956 and renamed the Afro-Asian Solidarity Committee in May 1958 to reflect Communist China's growing interest in Africa. Chao became a member of the organization's National Committee upon its formation and in June 1965 was elevated to the Standing Committee.

In the meantime, Chao had received an even more important assignment, a fact revealed in July 1955 when Vietnamese leader Ho Chi-minh visited China. At that time Chao was identified as a "responsible official" in one of the departments of the Party Central Committee. Although the specific post has never been identified, inferential evidence strongly suggests that it is in a department relating to international Party liaison (possibly the International Liaison Department —see under Wu Hsiu-ch'üan). Since 1955 Chao has dealt with scores of foreign Communist Party delegations that have visited Peking; it is a rare occasion, in fact, when he is not present for talks with such groups. His work in this field was given official recognition at the second session of the Party's Eighth National Congress in May 1958 when he was elected an alternate member of the CCP Central Committee. In the same month he left Peking as a member of Party veteran Tung Pi-wu's delegation to Communist Party congresses in Bulgaria, Czechoslovakia, and East Germany and returned to Peking in August. Two years later, in July 1960, Chao was back in Europe to attend the funeral of British Communist Party Chairman Harry Pollitt. He returned to England in March 1961 to represent the CCP at the 27th Congress of the British Communist Party.

Between Chao's 1961 trip and his next trip in late 1962, the already tense atmosphere in the international Communist movement had grown far more severe—a situation illustrated in October 1961 by Chou En-lai's walkout from the Russians' 21st Party Congress as a protest against the attacks upon the Albanian Communists, by then Peking's major ideological ally in Europe. The Sino-Soviet ideological dispute reached a new peak of intensity over the winter of 1962–1963 at five Party congresses held in Europe. It was probably an indication of the CCP elite's trust in Chao that he was given the task of leading their delegation to one of these meetings, that held in Italy in December 1962. (See under Wu Hsiu-ch'üan for details of the other four congresses.) At the Rome meetings Chao openly castigated Tito and "modern revisionism" (then an euphemism to describe Soviet policies). He called for wars of national liberation in colonial areas and protested the "attacks" made at the Congress on both the Albanian and Chinese Communist Parties. Chao's performance at the Italian Congress received wide coverage in the international press—he was "coldly received" by the delegates and, contrary to normal Communist practice, he failed to receive the customary ovation at the close of his speech.[4]

From the Italian Congress of 1962 to mid-1965, Chao was abroad on four more occasions. In October–November 1964 he was a member of Foreign Minister Ch'en I's delegation to Algeria for the 10th anniversary of the Algerian Revolution, and later in November he accompanied Liao Ch'eng-chih (q.v.) to Rome. Ostensibly the group went to Italy as a China Peace Committee delegation, but the significance of the mission rests on the fact that the Chinese were able to gain permission to open a permanent commercial mission in Rome (officially opened in early 1965 —see under Lei Jen-min). Chao returned to Europe in March 1965 as a member of Chou En-lai's delegation to the funeral of Rumanian Party First Secretary G. Gheorghiu-Dej. Afterwards the group visited briefly in Albania, Algeria, the United Arab Republic, Pakistan, and Burma before returning home in April. The following July Chao led a large delegation to the World Peace Congress in Helsinki; like virtually every Communist-sponsored meeting since the early sixties, this one quickly became a forum for airing the Sino-Soviet dispute. During the course of these meetings Chao rejected American offers of "unconditional negotiations" to end the war in Vietnam and warned the world to "remember Korea."[5]

Chao's activities in connection with international liaison work since the mid-fifties place him among a group of top Party officials who constantly deal in this work—nobably Liu Shao-ch'i, P'eng Chen, Wu Hsiu-ch'üan, Liu Ch'ang-sheng, and Liu Ning-i (qq.v.). All these men are full members of the Party Central Committee and far outrank Chao (an alternate member) in the Party hierarchy, thereby making his role all the more singular. Although his activities have been almost exclusively related to international affairs, he has received additional posts since the mid-fifties in the domestic governmental structure— positions that are probably largely nominal. Chao was a member of the Second and Third National Committees of the CPPCC; in the Second CPPCC (1954–1959) he was a representative of the CCP and in the Third (1959–1964) he represented "organizations for peaceful and friendly relations with foreign countries." In 1964 he was elected as a Honan deputy to the Third NPC, and at the Third NPC's First Session in December 1964– January 1965 he was elected a member of the NPC Standing Committee.

1. *Chung-hua ch'üan-kuo wen-hsueh i-shu kung-tso-che tai-piao ta-hui chi-nien wen-chi* (Commemorative articles of the All-China Congress of Literary and Art Workers; Peking [?], 1950), p. 235.

2. *Ibid.*, p. 238.

3. *JMJP,* March 4, 1949.

4. *New York Times* (international edition), December 5, 1962.

5. *New York Times,* July 13, 1965.

Chao Po-p'ing

(1909–   ; Shensi). Party and government administrator; alternate member, CCP Central Committee.

Chao Po-p'ing, a native of Shensi, was born in 1909. He was first identified in May 1944 as a member of the Drama Committee of the Yenan Literary and Art Association. This was probably one of the groups of entertainers sponsored by the CCP to which numbers of Chinese students belonged during the Sino-Japanese War and which brought many young people to the Yenan area to entertain and indoctrinate the soldiers and peasants. Chao was a deputy from Ch'un-yao hsien to the first session of the Third Assembly of the Shensi-Kansu-Ninghsia (Shen-Kan-Ning) Border Region Government that met in April 1946. Ch'un-yao hsien is some 40 miles north of Sian and was located in the southernmost section of the Border Region. At the close of the assembly session he was made deputy director of the Border Region Government's Education Office. He apparently remained in the northwest, because when Nationalist forces evacuated the city of Sian in May 1949, Chao was appointed to the Communist-established Sian Military Control Commission. From this date it became apparent that he was important as a Party and government leader in Sian, in Shensi Province, and later in the over-all administration for the northwest region to which Shensi belonged, the Northwest Military and Administrative Committee, inaugurated in January 1950.

As a Party official in the northwest, Chao was a deputy secretary of the Sian Party Committee for about two years from June 1949. He became the ranking secretary of the Sian Committee by June 1951, a position that was redesignated as first secretary in 1954. At the provincial level, he became second secretary of the Shensi Provincial Party Committee by April 1955, and a full secretary in November 1956, serving under First Secretary Chang Te-sheng (q.v.). At the time Chao became a full secretary in Shensi (1956) he relinquished his Party post on the Sian Municipal Committee to Fang Chung-ju. The other Party post that Chao was known to have held in the early 1950's was as director of the Propaganda Department of the Northwest Bureau, a position he occupied from early 1953 to 1954.

In addition to these assignments directly under the jurisdiction of the CCP, Chao also held several posts in the civil administrations at the municipal, provincial, and regional level. For the municipal government in Sian, he served as head of the Finance and Economics Committee from 1950 to about 1953. From December 1949 to January 1953 he was a member of the Shensi Provincial People's Government Council. However, his major activities in civil government centered around the Northwest Military and Administrative Committee (NWMAC). He was named to head the NWMAC's Labor Department in March 1950 and at the same time was appointed as a member of its Finance and Economics Committee. Later, in November 1950, he was named to membership on the NWMAC's Land Reform Committee. Chao held the Labor

Department post until March 1953 and the other two until mid-1954. When the NWMAC was reorganized in January 1953 and renamed as the Northwest Administrative Committee, he was named to membership and continued to hold it until the NWAC was abolished in 1954.

In that year Chao received his first assignment at the national level when he was elected as a deputy from Sian to the First NPC (1954–1959). He was elected to the Second NPC (1959–1964) from Shensi, which in the interim had absorbed the Sian constituency. Chao was once more elected to represent Shensi at the Third NPC, which held its initial session in December 1964–January 1965. In the meantime, Chao rose to higher levels within the Shensi Provincial Government. In December 1954 he was elected as a vice-governor, nominally subordinate to a former KMT General, Chao Shou-shan. Chao Po-p'ing was probably actually running the provincial government from that time onward; in fact he served for most of the period between late 1956 to mid-1959 as the acting governor. Finally, in July 1959, after Chao Shou-shan was transferred to Peking, Chao Po-p'ing was elected to succeed him as governor.

Chao's labors in the northwest for the Party and government were rewarded in May 1958 at the second session of the Eighth Party Congress. At this session, 25 men were added as alternate members of the Party Central Committee, Chao among them.

Like many of his prominent Party colleagues, Chao has given extracurricular time to the affairs of the Sino-Soviet Friendship Association (SSFA) and the Communist-sponsored peace movement. He was identified as a vice-president of the SSFA's Sian branch in March 1953 and as president of the branch in December. In December 1950 he was identified as chairman of the Sian Branch of the China Peace Committee, a position he retained as late as September 1957. In July 1958 the China Peace Committee was reorganized, with Chao named to the organization's national committee.

Because Sian is an important rail and commercial center in China's northwest, many important persons visit the city, foreigners as well as Chinese. Chao, as a high Party official in the area, attended a large number of social functions. In the period after 1956 he was especially active in welcoming distinguished foreign visitors to Sian; in 1957 he was deeply involved in the meetings and rallies staged for the "rectification" campaign.

After at least two decades in the northwest, Chao was transferred in January 1963 to Peking to become a deputy secretary-general of the NPC Standing Committee, serving under Politburo member P'eng Chen, the secretary-general. At the close of the first session of the Third NPC (January 1965), Liu Ning-i, a Central Committee member and specialist in international liaison work, replaced P'eng Chen as Chao's superior. Because of Chao's transfer to Peking in 1963, his post as Shensi governor was assumed by Li Ch'i-ming, first as the acting governor and then in December 1963 as the newly elected governor.

Chao P'u-ch'u

(c. 1908–   ; Anhwei). Vice-Chairman, Chinese Buddhist Association.

Chao P'u-ch'u, born in about 1908 in Anhwei, is the most prominent lay Buddhist leader in Communist China. He reportedly studied at Soochow University and by 1937 was engaged in the transport and storage business in Shanghai. Also in the 1930's Chao was assistant head of the Pure Karma Society (a large lay Buddhist group in Shanghai) and, after the Japanese attack in 1937, worked in Chinese refugee camps and with the International Red Cross in various relief endeavors in east China. He apparently remained in Shanghai during the Sino-Japanese War, for in 1943 he was serving as a vice-chairman of the board of a Buddhist nursery in that city.

After the Communist conquest of Shanghai in May 1949, Chao served as secretary-general of the Shanghai Federation for Emergency Relief and later in that year was active in the establishment of the central government in Peking. The government was established at the first session of the CPPCC, which met initially in September 1949; Chao attended as a delegate from religious circles and during this session served on the Committee to Draft the Organic Law of the CPPCC, one of the principal documents adopted at that time. At the close of the meetings, he was named to the CPPCC First National Committee; he was subsequently elected to membership on the Second, Third, and Fourth National Committees, which opened their initial sessions in December 1954, April 1959, and December 1964, respectively. At the close of the first meeting of the fourth CPPCC (January 1965), Chao was also named to the Standing Committee, the CPPCC organ that meets when the full National Committee is not in session.

In October 1949 he was named to the newly established China Peace Committee. When this committee was reorganized in July 1958 he was elevated to membership on the Standing Committee, and then in June 1965 he was promoted to a vice-chairmanship. In April 1950 he was elected to Central Committee membership in the China Association for Promoting Democracy, one of the eight "democratic" political parties and one consisting mainly of persons in cultural or educational work. In subsequent years Chao was re-elected to the Central Committee and in February 1956 was promoted to the Standing Committee, a position he continues to hold. Also in April 1950, Chao took part in the formation of the Chinese People's Relief Administration and was named to its Executive Committee, another post he continues to retain.

In mid-1950 Chao participated in a meeting in Peking where the possibility of forming a nation-wide Buddhist association was discussed. It was decided that such an association would be pre-mature. Two years later, however, a Preparatory Office of the Chinese Buddhist Association was established (November 1952), and Chao was named as the director. At the May–June 1953 meeting when the Association was formally established, Chao was named as a vice-chairman and concurrently as secretary-general, posts he still holds. Inferential evidence suggests that Chao has been the actual head of this leading association, leaving the titular leadership to polit-ically lesser figures. Specific evidence is not avail-able that Chao is a CCP member, but once again inferential evidence suggests that he is. Because the Communist authorities would prefer that he remain ostensibly a non-Communist Party mem-ber, it is unlikely that Party membership will ever be made public. Chao has participated in many Buddhist activities sponsored by the Association, both domestically and abroad. For example, in August 1955 he was appointed as a member of a committee to prepare for the establishment of a Chinese Buddhist Theological Institute in Peking, and when it was founded in September 1956 he became the vice-president. Once more this serves as an example of the *de facto* versus titular leadership; the Institute president, Shirob Jaltso (q.v.), is an elderly Buddhist monk of little political significance. Chao has been par-ticularly active in representing Chinese Buddhists in dealing with foreign Buddhists. On scores of occasions he has received and entertained visiting Buddhist dignitaries in China. And from 1955 to early 1965 he made at least 21 trips abroad to nine different nations. Of these 21 trips, 11 were directly concerned with Buddhist affairs. A typi-cal and important example occurred in Novem-ber 1961 when he attended the Sixth Conference of the World Fellowship of Buddhists in Phnom Penh, Cambodia. Ostensibly Chao was the deputy leader under Shirob Jaltso, but observers at the conference were confident that Chao was in fact the head of the group. Chao displayed a good knowledge of parliamentary procedures dur-ing the conference, and his hotel room seemed to be the headquarters for the Buddhist delegations from various Communist countries.[1] At the close of this conference he was elected a vice-president of the World Fellowship of Buddhists, a post he lost when he boycotted the 1964 Conference in India. Other trips abroad involving Buddhist affairs have taken him to Burma (April–May 1955, October 1955, January 1960, December 1960–January 1961), Japan (May 1963), India (March 1956, November 1956), Nepal (Novem-ber 1956), Ceylon (April–May 1957 and June 1961), and Indonesia (March–April 1965).

Chao's 21 trips abroad have most often taken him to Japan (seven times), where he seems to have specialized in attending the annual (from 1955) World Conference Against Nuclear Weap-ons. He attended the first, third, sixth, seventh, ninth, and tenth conferences held, respectively, in 1955, 1957, 1960, 1961, 1963, and 1964. Somewhat more miscellaneous trips have in-volved meetings devoted to promoting Commu-nist-backed peace movements (Sweden in May 1959 and India in March 1961), a disarmament meeting (Sweden, July 1958), and the First Afro-Asian Solidarity Conference held in Cairo in December 1957–January 1958. On occasion Chao has gone abroad merely as a member of a large delegation, but in 15 instances he has been either the leader or a deputy leader.

Although Chao's chief value to the Commu-nists has been within the sphere of Buddhist affairs, he has also held a multitude of other offi-cial and semi-official positions. Some if not most of these have had little meaning beyond the value of his name (as a leading lay Buddhist) to mem-bership rosters; this is particularly true after the mid-1950's when the bulk of his time has been demonstrably devoted to Buddhist affairs. A few examples will suffice to illustrate the range of his ostensible assignments. From 1950 to 1951 he was a deputy director of the Civil Affairs Depart-ment of the East China Military and Administra-tive Committee (ECMAC) and then from 1951 to 1952 was deputy director of the ECMAC Personnel Department. From 1954 to the present he has served from his native Anhwei on the NPC, being elected to the First (1954–1959), Second (1959–1964) and Third (1964 to date) terms of this legislative body. He was added to the Board of Directors of the China-India Friendship Association (FA) in August 1955; in November 1959 he became a vice-president of the China-Burma FA, and when the China-Ceylon FA was established in September 1962 he was named to the board, as he was in March 1963 when the China-Laos FA was formed. Finally, when the China-Japan FA was set up in October 1963 he was named as a vice-president. Thus Chao holds membership on five friendship associations, each vis-à-vis a nation with a signif-icant Buddhist population. He has also been a vice-president of the Chinese Red Cross Society from October 1961, and when the Asia-Africa Society of China was formed in April 1962 as a learned society, he was named as a member of the council.

Chao can be regarded as one of the leading devotees of Buddhism in China. It was in this spirit that he was named in February 1956 to membership on an editorial committee to com-pile a Chinese encyclopedia and to help Buddhists in Ceylon compile the Chinese section of their international Buddhist encyclopedia (the preparation of which coincided with the 2,500th anniversary of the Nirvana of Buddha). In the following year (1957) the Chinese Buddhist Association published a 56-page pamphlet by Chao entitled *Buddhism in China,* which was, in fact, an expanded version of his report to the Fourth Conference of the World Fellowship of Buddhists in Nepal in 1956.

1. Interview with a person who attended the conference, San Francisco, 1961.

Chao Shih-yen

(1901–1927; Yu-yang hsien, Szechwan). Early CCP leader; member, CCP Central Committee.

Chao was one of the earliest members of the CCP and was among the important group of leaders trained in both France and the Soviet Union in the twenties. Returning to China in 1924 he worked first in Peking and then in Shanghai, where he played a leading role in the dramatic events that culminated in the April 1927 suppression of the Communists by Chiang Kai-shek. Chao was elected to the Party Central Committee in the spring of 1927 but was captured and executed by the Nationalists two months later. Throughout his career he was among the more significant contributors to the literature of the May Fourth Movement and to CCP publications. He frequently wrote under the names Ch'in Sun, Shih Ying, and Shih Yang.

Chao was born in the town of Lung-t'an in Yu-yang hsien, located in southeast Szechwan. Influenced by the new culture movement and the dangers many young intellectuals felt were imperiling China's existence, he went to Peking, where in 1917 he enrolled in the French Language Institute (Fa-wen chuan-hsiu kuan), which was then headed by Wu Yü-chang (q.v.). The purpose of the Institute was to prepare students to go to France on a work-and-study basis, and within a few years a number of similar schools were established, especially in Peking and Chungking.[1] At the end of 1919 Chao was editing a short-lived semi-monthly that belonged to the literature of the May Fourth period; known as *Kung-tu* (Work and learning), it was published by an organization of students mainly from Szechwan, who were enrolled at the French Institute.[2] Judging from publications to which Chao contributed, he may also have attended the middle school of the Peking Higher Normal College. He wrote for *Shao-nien* (The youth), a publication issued by a student society at the Normal College, as well as for *P'ing-min chiao-yü* (Mass education), published by another group at the school.[3]

While attending the French Language Institute

Chao presumably became acquainted with many other Szechwanese students, for the intellectual ferment was strong in Szechwan, where the provincial government had promoted the program by offering financial assistance for European study. Of the 1,600 students who went to France in 1919–1920 for the work-and-study program, the largest number who ultimately became Communists came from Hunan and the second largest from Szechwan.[4] Chao was among a group that left for France in May 1920. There he met other Chinese students who had preceded him, including the Hunanese group. Many of the latter had belonged to the Hsin-min hsueh-hui (New people's study society) in Changsha, which had been founded in April 1918 by Ts'ai Ho-sen (q.v.) and Mao Tse-tung. Chao also met Hsiang Ching-yü, whom Ts'ai married in France, and Ts'ai's sister, Ts'ai Ch'ang (q.v.). Ts'ai and the others spent much of their time at a college south of Paris, but Chao seems to have remained in the capital for most of his three years in France.

Although most of the Chinese students were not Marxists upon their arrival in France, they were strongly attracted to communism, socialism, and other revolutionary doctrines, and within a brief time had established a number of leftist-oriented groups and societies. In an account written by Chao's former teacher Wu Yü-chang, the latter claims that Chao was among those who established a Communist small group (hsiao-tsu) in February 1921—at approximately the same time that other small groups were being formed in China. Then, after the establishment of the CCP in July 1921, Chao became the Paris correspondent for the Party in China. Over the winter of 1921–1922, Chao's small group evolved into the Young Chinese Communist Party, and then, after several changes in designation, it became in effect the French branch of the CCP in mid-1922 with Chao as its secretary.[5] He and Ch'en Yen-nien (q.v.), the son of the CCP's first general secretary Ch'en Tu-hsiu (q.v.), were the only two full-time workers on the staff of six or seven functionaries in the Paris office.[6]

By late 1922 Chao and his colleagues began to learn of opportunities for further study in the U.S.S.R., where the new Communist University of Toilers of the East had just opened a three-year course. In early 1923 Chao joined the exodus of students going from France to Moscow. He remained there for about a year and a half and in the company of Li Ta-chao, a CCP founder, he attended the Fifth Comintern Congress in June–July 1924. In the fall Chao returned to Peking, where he became secretary of the Party's Peking Committee. Late in the following spring, under the leadership of Li Ta-chao, the CCP established the North China Regional Committee with jurisdiction over the entire area, including Peking. In addition to his responsibilities within the Peking apparatus, Chao now assumed new tasks under Li's Regional Committee; he was made Propaganda Department chief and secretary of the Labor Movement Committee, activities that frequently took him to nearby Tientsin and T'ang-shan.[7] He also edited *Cheng-shih sheng-huo*, a journal that published many of Li Ta-chao's writings,[8] and contributed articles to *Chung-kuo kung-jen* (Chinese laborer), a publication that Chang Kuo-t'ao and Teng Chung-hsia (qq.v.) had inaugurated in late 1924.[9]

While working in Peking in 1925 Chao married Hsia Chih-hsu, who had joined the Socialist Youth League in 1922 and the CCP underground soon afterwards. He also renewed his friendship with Wu Yü-chang when Wu went to Peking. It was through Chao's "introduction" that Wu joined the CCP in 1925. Chao remained in Peking long enough to participate in the student demonstrations led by Li Ta-chao on March 18, 1926, events described in Li's biography. Shortly afterwards, he was transferred permanently to Shanghai, but only after attending the Third Congress of the All-China Federation of Labor held in Canton in May (see under Su Chao-cheng).

At this juncture the Nationalists launched the Northern Expedition, moving their armies north from Canton and transferring their government out of south China in an attempt to extend their authority throughout China. Shanghai became a focal point in the drive northward, thus increasing its importance to the Communists, who, though still allied with the KMT, already had a well-established network in Shanghai. When Chao Shih-yen arrived in Shanghai he went to work for the Party's Kiangsu-Chekiang Regional Party Committee, which was led by Lo I-nung (q.v.). Chao became director of the Committee's Organization Department and, concurrently, secretary of the Party unit within the Communist-led Shanghai General Labor Union, which Li Li-san (q.v.) and others had established a year earlier. Among Lo's and Chao's more important colleagues in Shanghai at this time were Ch'ü Ch'iu-pai and Wang Jo-fei (qq.v.), both of whom played key roles in the dramatic events that were about to unfold. Chao and his associates helped organize Shanghai workers for the explosive demonstrations staged on May 30, 1926, the first anniversary of the outbreak of the serious Shanghai strikes. Throughout the latter half of 1926 and the first months of 1927 they continued their campaign to organize factory workers in Shanghai.

By early 1927 the Shanghai labor movement had grown to impressive proportions and thus provided one more element in the power struggles occurring in the city as the Northern Ex-

peditionary forces approached and prepared to take over from military leader Sun Ch'uan-fang. The Nationalist forces were under the command of Chiang Kai-shek, who had split from the left-wing KMT Government established at Wuhan; Chiang was allied with the banking and comprador groups in Shanghai, who feared the growing strength of the Communists and the Communist-led Shanghai General Labor Union. Surging ahead in its organization and agitation among workers, the CCP, acting through the labor union, was sufficiently strong to call a general strike on March 21, 1927. This quickly turned into an insurrectionary movement, through which the workers momentarily got the city largely in their control. They seized police stations, the military arsenal, and even units of the municipal garrison force. Only the International Settlement and the French Concession remained relatively undisturbed when a "people's government" for Shanghai was proclaimed by the workers. Communist accounts credit Chao, who was with the "command headquarters" in the northern section of the city, with a major role in these endeavors.[10] Writing under the name Shih Ying, he also reported on the labor movement for Party journals in 1926–1927, including the important *Hsiang-tao chou-pao* (Guide weekly).[11]

The Shanghai workers' supremacy did not last long, for on March 26, 1927, Chiang Kai-shek's troops entered the city and, assisted by the anti-labor elements, wiped out the insurrection. His campaign to take over the city actually opened on April 12. It enormously increased the dangers for all Communists, especially those assigned to the headquarters and holding official positions. At this point Lo I-nung, head of Party affairs in Shanghai, was sent to the CCP headquarters in Wuhan. Wang Shou-hua, head of the Shanghai General Labor Union, was killed by Chiang's forces and Chao succeeded him. On April 27, after Chiang had put down the workers' government and driven Chao and his associates underground, the CCP opened its Fifth Congress in Wuhan. Chao was unable to attend, but he was elected to the new Central Committee. In June, after the Congress closed, the Kiangsu-Chekiang Regional Committee was reorganized into separate Chekiang and Kiangsu Provincial Committees. Ch'en Yen-nien, Chao's old colleague in France, was sent to Shanghai to become secretary of the Kiangsu Committee. In the latter part of June Ch'en was arrested by the Nationalist authorities and executed. Chao Shih-yen's presence in Shanghai was revealed by a Communist who had been arrested with Ch'en Yen-nien. And thus Chao was apprehended on July 2 and executed on July 19, 1927.

As noted above, in 1925 Chao married Hsia Chih-hsu, who was born in 1907 in Hai-ning hsien, Chekiang. From the early twenties she engaged in revolutionary activities and continued to work in the Party underground in Shanghai after her husband's death. After spending two years in Moscow (1929–1931) with her two children, Hsia was imprisoned in Shanghai in 1932 and held until the outbreak of the Sino-Japanese War five years later. During the war years she worked for the Communists in Hankow and Yenan, and after the Communists came to power in 1949 she worked for the CCP Organization Department in Wuhan. Since 1954 Hsia has served in various administrative positions in Peking, holding a vice-ministerial post in the Ministry of Light Industry since 1960.

1. Conrad Brandt, *The French-Returned Elite in the Chinese Communist Party,* reprint no. 13 (Institute of International Studies, University of California, Berkeley, 1961).
2. *Ibid.*
3. Chow Tse-tsung, *Research Guide to the May Fourth Movement* (Cambridge, Mass., 1963), *passim.*
4. Brandt.
5. *JMJP,* July 19, 1962.
6. Brandt.
7. *JMJP,* July 19, 1962; *Hung-ch'i p'iao-p'iao* (Red flag fluttering; Peking, 1957), V, 6.
8. Modern China Project, Columbia University, New York, Howard L. Boorman, director.
9. Jean Chesneaux, *Le Mouvement ouvrier chinois de 1919 à 1927* (Paris, 1962), p. 357.
10. *Hung-ch'i p'iao-p'iao,* p. 6; *Ti-i-tz'u kuo-nei ko-ming chan-cheng shih-ch'i te kung-jen yun-tung* (The workers' movement during the period of the first revolutionary civil war; Peking, 1963), *passim.*
11. *Hung-ch'i p'iao-p'iao,* pp. 11–12; *JMJP,* July 19, 1962.

Chao Shou-shan

(c.1893–1965; Hu-hsien, Shensi). Former KMT general; former governor of Tsinghai and Shensi.

Chao Shou-shan was one of the more important KMT generals who left the armies of Chiang Kai-shek in the 1940's and thereafter served the Communist cause. He was born about 1893 in a poor peasant family in Hu-hsien, just a few miles southwest of Sian, the capital of Shensi. Nothing is known of his education aside from the fact that he attended a surveying school, after which he served in the forces under Yang Hu-ch'eng, a warlord and onetime governor of Shensi. By the mid-1930's Chao was in charge of the garrison command in Han-chung, southern Shensi. In 1936 his troops were transferred to an area north of Sian to fight against the Communists, who were gaining strength in the area following the arrival of the first of the Long Marchers a year earlier. On

December 12, 1936, dissident KMT Generals Chang Hsueh-liang and Yang Hu-ch'eng kidnapped Chiang Kai-shek in Sian on the grounds that he was not offering sufficient resistance to continuing Japanese incursions into north China; the kidnapping has come to be known as the Sian Incident. At this juncture, Chao's forces were transferred to Sian to take up garrison duties. In the Communist-written obituary, Chao is credited with having "played an active role" in this famous incident.

After the release of Chiang Kai-shek (late December 1936), Yang Hu-ch'eng was arrested, whereupon Chao was appointed as commander of the Nationalist's 38th Army, previously one of Yang's units. Chao spent the remainder of the war in the Hopeh-Shansi-Honan area fighting Japanese forces. The Communist account of Chao's political activities in the post-Sian incident days reads as follows: "He worked for the Party on his own initiative, protecting the Communist organizations and other anti-Japanese patriotic elements of the troops under his command." Finally, "In 1942, Comrade Chao joined the CCP and, under the leadership of the Party, continued to serve in the KMT Army and engage in the revolutionary work." Although this date for entering the CCP cannot be corroborated, it does not seem unlikely in view of the concerted efforts by the Communists to woo many of the sympathetic officers stationed in the Northwest and in view of the fact that Chao was one of the earliest of the KMT officers to defect to the Communists after the war.

Chao continued to serve in the Nationalist Army in Shensi for a brief time after the war. However, in 1947 he was recalled to Nanking, then the Nationalist capital, for his failure to prosecute the anti-Communist campaign. There he was named to a nominal post as a councillor to the Military Council and ordered to make an "inspection tour" abroad. Instead, Chao flew to Tientsin and then made his way into the Communist-held territories in the spring of 1947. Taking advantage of his intimate familiarity with the northwest, the Communists assigned him to the Northwest People's Liberation Army (NWPLA), where he became a deputy commander under P'eng Te-huai. (When the NWPLA was redesignated as the First Field Army in early 1949, Chao continued to hold this post.)

Although Chao's entire career had been spent in military life, his service to the Communists after 1949 was almost exclusively devoted to civil administration. His first post with an essentially civilian orientation was given to him in May 1949 when the Communists captured Sian; Communist military leader Ho Lung was named as the chairman of the municipal Military Control Commission, with Chao and two other veteran Communist military men (Chia T'o-fu and Kan Szu-ch'i, qq.v.) serving as Ho's deputies.

In September 1949 Chao was in Peking for the meetings of the CPPCC that formally brought the central government into existence. Chao attended as one of the representatives of the First Field Army and, in a brief speech, castigated Chiang Kai-shek's "reactionary government." He also served on the *ad hoc* committee charged with the task of selecting the PRC flag, the new capital city, and national day (October 1). At the close of the meetings he was named to membership on the First National Committee of the CPPCC, holding the post until the Second Committee was established in December 1954. Although the CPPCC has been only marginally important since 1954, it was an organ of considerable importance from 1949 to 1954; altogether four plenary sessions of the First National Committee were held between 1949 and 1954, with Chao returning from the northwest to attend each of these sessions.

Following the establishment of the central government in Peking in the early fall of 1949, Chao returned to the northwest. Now, however, the Communist armies had pushed beyond Sian where he had previously been posted. Therefore, he was sent to Tsinghai Province, where he became the first Communist governor; he was officially appointed in early December 1949, although the provincial government was not established until January 1, 1950. At the same time that he received this provincial appointment, he was also named to the regional government administration known as the Northwest Military and Administrative Committee (NWMAC), responsible for the provinces of Shensi, Kansu, Ninghsia, Tsinghai, and Sinkiang. The NWMAC was formally inaugurated in January 1950, and when it was reorganized in January 1953 into the Northwest Administrative Committee, Chao was reappointed to membership. During his time in Tsinghai, he held at least two other positions; in July 1951 he was named to membership on the provincial Land Reform Committee and in May of 1952 he was identified as a member of the Northwest branch of the China Peace Committee, one of the more active of the "people's" organizations, especially in the early 1950's.

In 1952, Chao was transferred to his native Shensi, relinquishing his gubernatorial post in Tsinghai to Chang Chung-liang, later to become an alternate member of the Party Central Committee. Chao was named in November 1952 as the new Shensi governor, replacing Ma Ming-fang, one of the most important Party officials in the northwest in the early 1950's. For about half of the nearly seven years that he served as the Shensi governor, Chao was rather active in the functions normally exercised by a provincial official of that rank—making inspections of industrial and agricultural projects, speaking before the sessions of the provincial government

council, and attending rallies to mark one or another of the Communist holidays. Chao seems to have been particularly involved in water and soil conservation projects. For example, in October 1955 he was named as chairman of a special Shensi committee to "support the Sanmen Gorge project," a multi-purpose scheme on the always troublesome Yellow River (see under Liu Tzu-hou). Also, in June 1956 at a session of the NPC, Chao spoke on water and soil conservation in the Yellow River area, claiming that over 6,700 square kilometers of usable land had been added between 1955 and 1956. It was also in 1956 that Chao attended the Party's Eighth National Congress as a deputy from Shensi.

From October to December 1952 Chao was abroad for the first time, traveling to North Korea as a deputy leader of Ho Lung's large delegation to inspect and "comfort" Chinese Communist troops there. Three years later (September 1955), the Chinese Communists awarded their military officers with orders covering the period from the birth of the Red Army in 1927 to the eve of the Korean War in 1950. Chao was among those receiving the awards, although the specific order he received was not published. (Presumably he received at least the "Order of Liberation," covering the period of the civil war with the Nationalists in the late 1940's.)

Although Chao was not originally elected to the First NPC in 1954, he was named in 1956 to fill a vacancy, serving as a deputy from Shensi. He was elected again from Shensi to the Second NPC (1959–1964) as well as the Third NPC that opened in December 1964. After the latter part of 1956, Chao began to make only infrequent appearances in Shensi. In fact, Vice-governor Chao Po-p'ing (q.v.), a politically more important man than Chao Shou-shan, served for most of the period from late 1956 to mid-1959 as the acting governor. Nonetheless, Chao was re-elected as the Shensi governor in August 1958. In the following April he was named to membership on both the NPC Standing Committee and the military advisory organ known as the National Defense Council. Shortly thereafter (July 1959), Chao "requested his release from the duties of governorship because of his transfer to the central leadership." The governorship of Shensi fell to Chao Po-p'ing, the man who had been serving as the acting governor. From that time to the end of Chao Shou-shan's life, he spent all his time in Peking. His last services for the Chinese Communists seem to have taken place in 1958 and 1959 when he was sent abroad on two occasions. In November 1958 he was a deputy leader under Liu Lan-t'ao of the Chinese delegation to the celebrations in Moscow marking the 41st anniversary of the Russian Revolution, and in October 1959 he accompanied Marshal Nieh Jung-chen to East

Germany for the festivities commemorating the 10th anniversary of the founding of the East German Government. After this last journey, Chao seldom appeared in public. He was again appointed to membership on the NPC Standing Committee and the National Defense Council in January 1965, but in view of his inactivity in the last five years of his life, these appointments were probably *pro forma*. In any event, Chao died in Peking on June 20, 1965, at the age of 72. A memorial service held three days later was attended by over 600 persons, including several senior Party officials. In a eulogy delivered by Central Committee member Liu Ning-i, the point was emphasized that even though Chao had fought in non-Communist armies, he had correctly appraised the "incorrect" policies of Chiang Kai-shek and had worked with the Party from a relatively early date. Although the Party's trust in Chao must have been limited, his career suggests that he enjoyed its confidence to a degree probably far beyond that enjoyed by the ex-KMT generals who surrendered at the eleventh hour.

Chao Tzu-yang

First secretary, Kwangtung Party Committee.

Chao Tzu-yang has been described by a former Kwangtung Party official as a "northerner," but from the Kwangtung viewpoint that might cover any area from Hunan northward. This same person has described Chao as well-versed in Marxism-Leninism, suggesting that he may have received some training in a Party school prior to the Communist conquest in 1949.[1] His only known position before 1949 was as the Communist Party secretary for the Nan-yang local Committee in southwestern Honan, where he may have come under the jurisdiction of the forces commanded by Li Hsien-nien (q.v.), a top commander in central China in that period. Late in 1949 Li's forces became part of the Fourth Field Army of Lin Piao.

As Lin Piao's army swept through central China in 1949, Chao was apparently assigned to it as a civilian cadre, for by 1950 he was known to be working for the South China Party Sub-bureau, a special sub-bureau (believed to have had jurisdiction over Kwangtung and Kwangsi) that was subordinate to the larger Party Central-South Bureau. During the life of the South China Sub-bureau (1950–1955), Chao held a series of posts in it. Initially in 1950 he was only a member of the Standing Committee, but then from 1951 to 1954 he served as the secretary-general, one of the key positions in the day-by-day activities of the bureau. He assumed the directorship of the Rural Work Department in 1953, and then became third secretary in 1954, holding both these positions until the sub-bureau was abolished in mid-1955. South China, an important but rather difficult area to control, has always been staffed with important leaders by the Chinese Communists. For this reason Chao has worked directly under some key Party officials, including Yeh Chien-ying, T'an Cheng, and T'ao Chu (qq.v.). He is, in fact, reported to be a close protégé of T'ao,[2] presently the first secretary of the CCP Central-South Bureau. His chief activities in the early 1950's were centered around the training of Party cadre and the management of agriculture. In addition to his involvement in such matters for the South China Sub-bureau, Chao received a series of appointments in both the Kwangtung Party and provincial government channels. In 1951 he was serving as a vice-chairman of the Kwangtung Government's Land Reform Committee and in 1955 was elected as a member of the Kwangtung Provincial People's Council (a government post he may still retain). But his most significant tasks have been performed for the Party structure in Kwangtung, one of China's most populous provinces. In 1955 he was only a third deputy secretary. But he was promoted in the same year to a deputy secretaryship and then to a secretaryship in 1957. By early 1962 he was the second secretary. This portion of his career was climaxed in early 1965 when he became the first secretary, thereby replacing T'ao Chu, under whom he had served in the Kwangtung Party Committee for a decade. He still remains directly below T'ao in the Party hierarchy, however, because T'ao is first secretary of the Central-South Party Bureau and Chao was identified as a secretary of the Bureau in July 1965.

Aside from these permanent positions, Chao has held a number of *ad hoc* positions over the past years. For example, he was a member of the Kwangtung Election Committee in 1953–1954, the organization charged with preparing for elections to the NPC in 1954. And in August 1955 he was named to chair a special committee for the exploitation of the sub-tropical resources on Hainan, the large island under the jurisdiction of Kwangtung. Canton, the Kwangtung capital, is very frequently transited by the many foreign visitors to China, and many government Party and government leaders stationed in Canton have had to devote time to the entertainment of these visitors. In general, Chao seems to have been exempted from most of these duties, because he has not been frequently reported in the company of visitors. However, he has been mentioned in the press with great frequency since the early 1950's as being present at events related to internal Kwangtung problems, especially those involving agriculture. For example, he is almost always reported at the many conferences of "advanced" agricultural workers held in Canton and is often reported as making inspections of agricultural areas in Kwangtung. This strong emphasis on agriculture culminated in June 1965 when he was named as Chairman of the Kwangtung Association of Poor and Lower-middle Peasants, a newly formed organization that places considerable weight on Party purity as determined by class background. A year earlier, in January 1964, Chao received still another appointment when he was identified as the political commissar of the Kwangtung Military District. If Chao were stationed in almost any other province than Kwangtung, his authority would probably be greater than it has come to be in the mid-1960's. However, his stature in Kwangtung is overshadowed by men of higher Party rank, like T'ao Chu, Ch'en Yü (the Kwangtung governor), and Wang Shou-tao, all of whom are full members of the Party Central Committee. Chao's career is noteworthy, nonetheless, because he is one of the few men to have risen to a provincial first secretaryship without being a member of the CCP Central Committee.

Chao has been a rather frequent contributor to the Party press. He wrote an article based on an inspection trip for the important journal *Hung-ch'i* (Red flag, August 16, 1958), and has contributed several articles on agriculture for the *JMJP* (e.g., the issues of May 30, 1958, November 18, 1958, June 4, 1959, and July 23, 1960) and for *Chung-kuo nung-pao* (China agricultural bulletin, February 23, 1959). The above-mentioned ex-Kwangtung official has suggested that Chao may have written articles on occasion for T'ao Chu, noting that Chao is better educated than T'ao.[3] Chao had still another connection with the field of journalism since at least 1959 in the capacity of Party secretary for one of Canton's most important dailies, the *Yang-ch'eng wan-pao*.[4]

1. Interview, Hong Kong, July 1965.
2. *Ibid.*
3. *Ibid.*
4. *Current Scene,* Hong Kong, July 1, 1963, p. 8.

Ch'en Ch'ang-hao

(c.1910–   ; Hupeh). Oyüwan Soviet leader.

Ch'en Ch'ang-hao was a key member of the Oyüwan Soviet in the early thirties, but he faded into relative obscurity after the Long March. He was born about 1908 in the vicinity of Hankow, Hupeh Province. Ch'en joined the Communist Youth League in Hankow, and through this organization was drawn into the CCP. By the late twenties he was attending Sun Yat-sen University in Moscow, where he became associated with the group of students known as the "28 Bolsheviks" or the "Russian-returned" students. Ch'en and his student colleagues were

protégés of Pavel Mif, a Russian expert on China and chancellor of Sun Yat-sen University from 1927 to 1930. While Ch'en was in Moscow he is said to have continued to specialize in Party youth work. He was sufficiently fluent in Russian to act as an interpreter for other Chinese students at the university, and he frequently translated classroom lectures for his friends, as did Chang Ch'in-ch'iu (q.v.), his wife.[1]

In the spring of 1930 Mif became the Comintern representative to China. A number of his student protégés (including Ch'en) arrived in China with him in the spring or early summer of 1930. The CCP was then dominated by Li Li-san (q.v.), who was leading the Party in a course of action that Moscow later attacked. Mif and his "28 Bolsheviks" began to make concerted efforts to replace the Li Li-san leadership (see under Ch'en Shao-yü). In January 1931, at the Party's Fourth Plenum, they succeeded in having Li's policies repudiated and in removing him and his followers from positions of authority. Li's group was succeeded by three leaders of the "28 Bolshevik" clique, Ch'en Shao-yü, Chang Wen-t'ien, and Shen Tse-min (qq.v.). All three men received even more important positions after April 1931 when the Party met for a high-level conference in Shanghai. Ch'en Ch'ang-hao at that time seems to have been assigned to youth work. He was identified in 1936 as a member of the Communist Youth League's Central Committee,[2] but he had probably held this post from an earlier date.

At the Shanghai conference the Party's new leadership decided to send some of the Russian-returned students to reorganize political work in rural areas where the Party, under Li Li-san's direction, had established bases a few years earlier. In 1931 Chang Kuo-t'ao (q.v.), who had also been in Moscow (but who did not belong to the "28 Bolsheviks" group), was sent to the Oyüwan (Hupeh-Honan-Anhwei) base. He took with him two of the most important Bolsheviks—Shen Tse-min and Ch'en Ch'ang-hao. Ch'en was engaged in youth work as secretary of the Oyüwan Youth League, and he was also political commissar of the military forces led by Hsu Hsiang-ch'ien (q.v.). These four men—Chang, Hsu, Shen, and Ch'en—were probably the four principal Oyüwan leaders.[3] Within a year or so of his arrival Ch'en seems to have been involved in the suppression of a dissident element within the Red Army in Oyüwan. In this connection he published an article for a leading Party journal in early 1932 that dealt with an alleged "counter-revolutionary" plot that had been planned for September 1931. As a consequence of the actions taken by Ch'en and his colleagues, more than a thousand Oyüwan military commanders and political workers were purged.[4]

Ch'en was with Chang Kuo-t'ao and Hsu

Hsiang-ch'ien when the Communists were forced to retreat in the face of Chiang Kai-shek's Annihilation Campaigns (see under Chang Kuo-t'ao). With the greater part of the Communists' Fourth Front Army Ch'en moved westward to the small base established in the spring of 1933. By the next year Ch'en was identified as political commissar of the Fourth Front Army and head of the Political Office for what the Communists called the Northwest Military District.[5] Again on the march in early 1935, Ch'en was with the Fourth Front Army when it moved to the small west Szechwan town of Mao-kung to rendezvous with the forces of Mao Tse-tung and Chu Te, which arrived there on the Long March in the early summer of 1935. When differences of opinion over future strategy created a split between Mao and Chang Kuo-t'ao, Mao moved his armies north toward Shensi while Chang Kuo-t'ao and his troops, now joined by Chu Te, went west into Sikang Province. Chang's units spent the winter of 1935–1936 in the small Tibetan trading center of Kan-tzu. Ch'en Ch'ang-hao was then a political adviser to Chu Te.

In Kan-tzu, Chang Kuo-t'ao was joined in mid-1936 by another retreating Communist force, the Second Front Army led by Ho Lung and Jen Pi-shih, which was withdrawing from its rural base on the borders of Hunan, Hupeh, Szechwan, and Kweichow. The two armies joined forces and proceeded north to join Mao Tse-tung. As they passed through the Kansu Corridor, Chang's part of the army was disastrously defeated by the troops of Moslem leader Ma Pu-fang, who controlled the area. According to Chang Kuo-t'ao, Ch'en was his political commissar during the Kansu misfortune, and Chang claims that it was Ch'en who made some of the military decisions that resulted in the disaster.[6] After the defeats Chang continued north and finally rejoined Mao in late 1936. But Ch'en fled to Hankow and remained there until early 1938 when he too went to Yenan, where he was subjected to severe criticism from the Maoist leadership.

Like many of the "28 Bolsheviks" Ch'en's importance as a political leader declined sharply after the mid-thirties. Virtually nothing was reported about his activities during the war and postwar years, and unlike almost every other member of the CCP elite he received no assignment when the PRC was established in 1949. Finally, in May 1953 he was identified as a lecturer in a special class to train instructors for a program of theoretical study, which the Party was then about to launch. By the next year he had become a deputy director of the Central Committee's Editing and Translation Bureau of the Works of Marx, Engels, Lenin, and Stalin. In this capacity he wrote an article for the *JMJP* (November 28, 1955) commemorating

the 135th anniversary of Engels' birth and relating the "upsurge" of agricultural producer cooperatives to his teachings. However, nothing has been heard about him since that time. Ch'en's eclipse must be partially related to his close ties with the Russian-returned student group, and it may also reflect his unwillingness to submit to criticism. Chang Kuo-t'ao speaks of Ch'en's frequent clashes during the Oyüwan days with the military commander, Hsu Hsiang-ch'ien. Chang has described Ch'en as aggressive, quick, adventuresome, and ambitious; he was overly eager to command troops, undaunted by the lack of sufficient preparations. More favorably, Chang reported that Ch'en had a good command of Russian, spoke persuasively, and wrote well.

Sometime prior to 1936 Ch'en is said to have written a history of the Red Army,[7] and although he was not very active politically after the mid-thirties he continued to publish and translate books and articles until the 1950's. He was a contributor to collections of articles published in 1938 and 1940, one entitled *K'ang-Jih yu-chi chan-cheng te i-pan wen-t'i* (General problems in the anti-Japanese guerrilla war) and the other *Hsiang-ch'ih chieh-tuan te hsing-shih yü jen-wu* (The situation and our tasks during the stalemate). In 1939 he published *Chin-tai shih-chieh ko-ming shih* (A history of revolution in the modern world). In the 1940's Ch'en edited a Chinese-Russian dictionary. His *Cheng-tang lun* (On political parties) was published in Harbin in 1949; in the same year *Wu-ch'an-chieh-chi te cheng-tang* (Proletarian political parties) was brought out in Hong Kong and republished in Shanghai in 1950. Ch'en's last known major work was a translation from M. I. Kalinin, published in Peking in 1953 under the title *Lun kung-ch'an-chu-i chiao-yü* (On Communist education).

As already noted, Ch'en was once married to Chang Ch'in-ch'iu, but they were subsequently divorced. He has also been married to another of the "28 Bolsheviks," Tu Cho-ch'iang, who studied at Sun Yat-sen University in the twenties. The couple had one son.

---

1. *Tsa-chih* (Magazine; Shanghai), 4.3:59 (April 1939).

2. Edgar Snow, *Random Notes on Red China, 1936–1945* (Cambridge, Mass., 1957), p. 52.

3. Tso-liang Hsiao, *Power Relations within the Chinese Communist Movement, 1930–1934* (Seattle, Wash., 1961), p. 195.

4. *Ibid.*, pp. 193–195.

5. Norman Hanwell, "The Chinese Red Army," *Asia*, 36.5:319 (May 1936, New York).

6. Modern China Project, Columbia University, New York, Howard L. Boorman, director.

7. Hanwell, p. 318.

Ch'en Cheng-jen

(c.1905–   ; Kiangsi). Minister, Eighth Ministry of Machine Building; alternate member, CCP Central Committee.

A native of Kiangsi, Ch'en's birth year is probably about 1905, although it has also been reported as 1900. He had joined the CCP by 1928 when he was identified as a deputy secretary of the local Party committee in the Hunan-Kiangsi Border Area Base, the headquarters of Mao Tse-tung and his followers who fled with him to Chingkangshan in the fall of 1927. Mao's forces were joined by those under Chu Te in the following spring, forming the nucleus of the Chinese Communist Army. Mao Tse-tung, in his *Selected Works,* describes the establishment of a Party Committee for the Hunan-Kiangsi base. The committee was formed in the spring of 1928 at a congress of Party groups and was reorganized in October of that year, at which time a 19-member Special Committee was elected, numbering Mao, Chu Te, T'an Chen-lin, and Ch'en Cheng-jen among its members. Five of the 19 were members of the Standing Committee, which was headed by T'an Chen-lin with Ch'en as his deputy. Mao's writings indicate that Ch'en is of bourgeois origins, for T'an is spoken of as a representative of the workers, but Ch'en is called a representative of the "intellectuals."[1]

The next reports of Ch'en's activities place him in Kiangsi in 1930 by which time, to judge from other positions he held, he must have been a leading member of the Kiangsi Provincial Party Committee. According to an interview of American journalist Edgar Snow with Ch'in Pang-hsien, a leader of the "28 Bolshevik" clique, Ch'en headed the first Soviet government established in Kiangsi in 1930 and was later succeeded by Tseng Shan (q.v.).[2] This report requires some explanation, and because of the obscurity surrounding political events in Kiangsi at this time, Ch'en's position is a matter of conjecture. There is good evidence that at least by December 1930 the chairman of the Kiangsi Provincial Soviet was Tseng Shan. However, the soviet was created in October 1930 when the Red Army commanded by Chu Te captured Chi-an (Kian) on the Kan River (see under Tseng Shan), and hence it is possible that Ch'en held the chairmanship briefly when the government was first organized. On the other hand it is possible that Ch'in's report refers to yet another Communist government in the hinterlands, a short-lived Southwest Kiangsi Soviet (about which very little is known), which came into being following a local Party conference held in south Kiangsi early in February 1930 to plan for the establishment of soviets in other Communist-held areas in China. How long this organization in southwest Kiangsi existed is not known,

but some of its functions may have been taken over by the one at Chi-an later in the year. In May of 1932 the Communists held the first congress of the reestablished Kiangsi Provincial Soviet in central Kiangsi, and at that time Tseng Shan was named soviet chairman and Ch'en became a vice-chairman. Then at the end of December 1933 a second congress of the Kiangsi Soviet was held; again the principal officers changed. An unknown Communist from Kiangsi named Liu Ch'i-yao became soviet chairman, Tseng became a vice-chairman, and Ch'en was dropped from all positions.

Over a decade passed before the threads of Ch'en's career were again picked up. It seems likely that he made the Long March, for by at least early 1942 he was in Yenan. No details of his activities are available, but it is known that he was associated socially with Party veterans Lin Po-ch'ü and Hsiao Ching-kuang. Lin was at that time head of the Shensi-Kansu-Ninghsia Border Region Government and Hsiao was head of the Rear Office of the Eighth Route Army.[3]

It is probable (but undocumented) that Ch'en was in the forces led by Liu Po-ch'eng in the civil war with the Nationalists in the late 1940's. In any event, he was with Liu's units when they captured Nanchang in Ch'en's native Kiangsi in late May 1949. When the Communists captured major cities during their conquest of the mainland, the first administrative act was always the establishment of a military control commission to govern the city. Thus, in early June 1949, Ch'en became the chairman of the newly established Nanchang Military Control Commission, a post he held until his transfer in late 1952 (see below). Subordinate to him in this post were Vice-Chairmen Ch'en Ch'i-han and Shao Shih-p'ing (qq.v.). From June 1949 Ch'en Cheng-jen was also political commissar of the Kiangsi Military District, which was commanded by Ch'en Ch'i-han, and at approximately this same period Ch'en Cheng-jen also became the ranking secretary of the Kiangsi CCP Committee. These two posts alone probably made him the most powerful leader in Kiangsi from 1949 to 1952; the only others who could have rivaled him were Governor Shao Shih-p'ing and Military District Commander Ch'en Ch'i-han.

Like almost all major provincial officials in the early 1950's, Ch'en was given assignments in the provincial government in addition to his positions in the military and Party hierarchies. Thus, in March 1950, he was named to membership on the Kiangsi Provincial People's Government Council, and in the following September he was appointed as chairman of this government's Finance and Economics Committee. Still another position that he held during the takeover period in Nanchang was that of president of the August First Revolutionary College, a school named for the founding date of the Red Army in 1927. In 1950 this college was amalgamated with others to form Nanchang University, with Ch'en retaining the presidency. Finally, at the multi-provincial level, Ch'en was also a member of the Central-South Military and Administrative Committee (from February 1950), the administrative body that governed Honan, Hupeh, Hunan, Kiangsi, Kwangtung, and Kwangsi. Owing to his transfer in 1952, he was not reappointed to this committee when it was reorganized in early 1953.

Ch'en relinquished all his positions in Kiangsi in late 1952, with the most important one (the secretaryship of the Kiangsi Party Committee) being assumed by Yang Shang-k'uei, a fellow native of Kiangsi whose career also reaches back to the pre-Long March days of the Chinese Communist movement. Ch'en surrendered these posts in order to assume new and more important duties in Peking at the ministerial level. In preparation for the inauguration of the First Five-Year Plan (1953), a number of changes were made in the central government. One of these changes was the establishment of a Ministry of Building (sometimes translated as "construction engineering"), a Ministry that had been carved out of sections of the Ministry of Heavy Industry. Ch'en assumed this portfolio in November 1952. He remained as the minister until another reorganization of the central government in September 1954, at which time he was replaced by Liu Hsiu-feng (q.v.). Shortly thereafter, Ch'en entered into a new career, that of agricultural planning and production. This began in December 1954 when he was selected for membership on the Second National Committee of the legislative advisory body, the CPPCC, as a representative of the peasants (*nung-min*). He was also named to the CPPCC Standing Committee, charged with handling the work of the National Committee when the latter is not in full session. A more important assignment was revealed in the summer of 1955 when he was identified as a "responsible member" under the Party Central Committee; in view of the fact that he was specifically identified as a deputy director of the important Rural Work Department by July 1956, it may be inferred that he was associated with this organization from at least 1955. He continues to hold this post under Teng Tzu-hui, one of Peking's top specialists in agricultural affairs. In November 1955, Ch'en received a closely related position when he was appointed as a deputy director of the State Council's Seventh Staff Office, redesignated the Agriculture and Forestry Office in September 1959. He also served in this post under Teng Tzu-hui until November 1962, and thereafter under Politburo member T'an Chen-lin, his immediate superior in the Hunan-Kiangsi Party

Committee over 30 years earlier. The Agriculture and Forestry Office, in which he continues to serve, is charged with the task of coordinating the activities of the several State Council commissions, ministries, and bureaus engaged in agricultural work.

Ch'en's steady climb in both the government and Party agencies concerned with agriculture received official recognition at the Eighth National Party Congress held in September 1956 when he was elected an alternate member of the Party Central Committee. In the following May, he was given still another assignment closely related to agriculture, being named to chair the newly formed Water and Soil Conservation Committee, a special committee under the State Council but not at the level of the commissions or ministries. Relatively little has been heard about this committee, although Ch'en gave a report before a national conference of the committee held in Peking in September 1958 and attended by nearly 500 delegates.

Already deeply involved with important posts in the agricultural sector, Ch'en received another ministerial portfolio in August 1959 when he was appointed to head the new Ministry of Agricultural Machinery. He continues to lead the Ministry, known since January 1965 as the Eighth Ministry of Machine Building. Not surprisingly, Ch'en has attended many conferences related to agriculture and has written for important journals on agricultural affairs. He gave a major report, for example, at an agricultural cooperation conference held in Lanchow in June–July 1958, and he spoke on the problems of rural villages before a national conference of "young activists in building socialism" in November 1959. At the official government level, in his capacity as Minister of Agricultural Machinery, he gave a two-part report before consecutive meetings of the NPC Standing Committee in February 1963, describing the work of the Ministry in three previous years. His writings include two articles for China's most important journal, *Hung-ch'i* (Red flag, issues dated January 16, 1959, and February 16, 1960). The former dealt with the "rectification" movement in the communes, whereas the latter outlined the pace at which China hoped to proceed in the mechanization of agriculture. Ch'en claimed that overall mechanization and electrification would be completed within 10 years (i.e., about 1970).

As already described, Ch'en served as a representative of the peasants on the Second National Committee of the CPPCC (1954–1959). He was again named to represent the peasants on the Third National Committee (1959–1964) and once more served on the Standing Committee. However, like a large number of other officials, he was changed from the CPPCC to the NPC in 1964, being elected as a deputy from his native

Kiangsi to the Third NPC. It was at the close of the First Session of the Congress (January 1965) that his Ministry was redesignated the Eighth Ministry of Machine Building.

1. *Selected Works of Mao Tse-tung* (London, 1954), I, 97–98.
2. Edgar Snow, *Random Notes on Red China, 1936–1945* (Cambridge, Mass., 1957), p. 18.
3. *Hung-ch'i p'iao-p'iao* (Red flag fluttering, Peking, 1958), VI, 10.

Ch'en Ch'i-han

(c.1898–　　; Kiangsi). Vice-president, Supreme People's Court, member, CCP Central Control Commission; alternate member, CCP Central Committee.

A member of the Red Army from its birth in 1927, Ch'en Ch'i-han was an active military officer for the next 25 years. He has been an alternate member of the Party Central Committee since 1956, a vice-president of the Supreme Court since 1957, and a member of the Party's Control Commission since 1962. Ch'en was born in Kiangsi about 1898 (though Japanese sources say it was about 1905). He graduated from the Nationalists' Whampoa Military Academy in the mid-twenties and then took part·in the Northern Expedition, which began in mid-1926, as a member of Yeh T'ing's (q.v.) staff. In July of the following year he was an instructor in the training regiment of the Nationalists' Third Army, a Yunnanese army led by Chu P'ei-te, whose headquarters was in Nanchang, the Kiangsi capital. A number of the Third Army soldiers, Ch'en among them, participated in the revolt against the Nationalists on August 1, 1927, an event known in Communist histories as the Nanchang Uprising (see under Yeh T'ing). At some time in the next three years he was a staff officer in Huang Kung-lueh's (q.v.) Third Red Army and the Kiangsi Military District, as well as an instructor in a Red Army military school in Kiangsi.

In the early 1930's Ch'en was a regimental commander with the Communist forces that supported the Chinese Soviet Republic established in November 1931 at Juichin in southeast Kiangsi. In late December 1933, at the Second Congress of the Kiangsi Provincial Soviet (not to be confused with the larger Chinese Soviet Republic, often popularly called the "Kiangsi Soviet"), Ch'en was named to the 67-member Provincial Executive Committee. The Kiangsi Provincial Soviet had been in existence at least since 1930 (see under Tseng Shan). Ch'en presumably made the Long March to north Shensi, for in November 1935 he was serving in Hsu Hai-tung's (q.v.) 15th Army Corps.

Little is known of Ch'en's activities during the Sino-Japanese War aside from the fact that he was a staff officer of the Revolutionary Military Council (the highest Communist military organ) and an official in the Party's intelligence network. In the late forties, during the civil war with the Nationalists, he once again served as a staff officer, this time in the Hopeh-Jehol-Liaoning area. In 1949, as the Communists began their final conquest of the mainland, Ch'en commanded an army corps, and he was with the troops that captured Nanchang on May 22, 1949. In June he was appointed a vice-chairman of the Nanchang Military Control Commission, then headed by another native of Kiangsi, Ch'en Cheng-jen (q.v.). In the same month Ch'en Ch'i-han was also appointed commander of the Kiangsi Military District, a post he held until 1954. For a part of that time (1949–1952) Ch'en Cheng-jen was the political commissar. Their careers in the regional and provincial governments ran somewhat parallel for a time. In December 1949 both were appointed to the regional administration that governed Kiangsi, the Central-South Military and Administrative Committee (CSMAC), and both held this post until the CSMAC was reorganized early in January 1953, at which time they were dropped. From March 1950 to September 1954, Ch'en Ch'i-han was also a member of the Kiangsi Provincial People's Council.

In July 1954, Ch'en was elected a Kiangsi deputy to the First NPC (1954–1959). By September, when the Congress convened its first session, he had been transferred to Peking. The Congress elected Ch'en to membership on the National Defense Council, a post he still holds. Exactly a year later (September 1955), when the Communists first awarded military decorations, Ch'en was given one or more of the three orders that cover military service from 1927 to 1950. Personal military ranks were also given at that time, but it was not until October 1958 that he was identified as a colonel-general, the equivalent of a three-star U.S. Army general. In the meantime, at the Party's Eighth National Congress in September 1956, Ch'en was elected an alternate member of the Central Committee. In the following April he was appointed a vice-president of the Supreme People's Court. In this capacity he has served under Presidents Tung Pi-wu (to 1959), Hsieh Chueh-tsai (1959–1965), and Yang Hsiu-feng (since 1965). In October 1958, while on an inspection tour in Inner Mongolia, Ch'en was identified in another judicial post—the presidency of the Supreme Military Court (which comes under the jurisdiction of the Supreme People's Court). He was not mentioned in this post after 1958, and in any event the 1963 *Jenmin shou-ts'e* listed it as vacant.

Ch'en was a CCP representative to the Third CPPCC, which opened in April 1959; he was not, however, elected to the Fourth CPPCC, which was first convened in December 1964. At the Party's 10th Plenum in September 1962 the decision was made to expand the important Central Control Commission to 38 full and 22 alternate members. Ch'en was named to full membership. His affiliation with the Commission, charged with discipline and supervisory functions, may account for the fact that he is seldom in the news. As described above, Ch'en was a Kiangsi deputy to the First NPC (1954–1959). Though not elected to the Second Congress, he was selected to represent the PLA in the Third NPC, and at the close of its first session in January 1965 he was elected a member of the NPC Standing Committee, the governing body between sessions of the full Congress. At that same time he was again reappointed a member of the National Defense Council.

Ch'en Chia-k'ang

(1911–   ; Kuang-chi, Hupeh). Diplomat; vice-minister of Foreign Affairs.

A long-time associate of Premier Chou En-lai, Ch'en Chia-k'ang is one of Peking's most senior diplomats. His ten-year tour as ambassador in Egypt (later the United Arab Republic) is the longest single tour of an ambassador in the history of the PRC. Ch'en was born in 1911 into a family of moderate means from Kuang-chi, a small town near the Yangtze in southeastern Hupeh. His education included two years in the study of the Chinese classics, after which he entered Wuhan University (c.1931). His principal professor at the university was Wang Shih-chieh who later became the foreign minister of the Republic of China. Ch'en joined the CCP in 1931 and, because he engaged in Party affairs, was expelled from the university in 1933.

Ch'en spent the years from 1936 to 1938 in Shanghai, where he was active in forming anti-Japanese activities among college students. At about the time Shanghai fell to the Japanese (November 1937), Ch'en became the personal secretary to Chou En-lai and served in this capacity in Hankow (1938), Chungking, and Yenan until 1945. In about 1940, Ch'en was purportedly the CCP contact man in the efforts of the Party to get in touch with and control Korean Communist leaders in Chungking. The Chinese Communists were successful in persuading the small group of Koreans, who had been under KMT control in the Chungking area, to move their cadres and military forces to CCP-controlled areas in north China.[1] Ch'en's fluency in English probably accounts for his assignment in 1943–1944 as an interpreter to work with the American military observation team in Yenan, where he became acquainted with a number of Western journalists as well as the U.S. military personnel. (He also has some knowledge of Russian, although there is nothing in his career that suggests he has had opportunities to use the language.)

In the period after the war, Ch'en acted, in effect, as a roving ambassador for the Chinese Communists, a task that kept him abroad for long periods of time and that also provided him with useful experience for his later diplomatic assignments. In 1945, when the Communists and the KMT were ostensibly cooperating, CCP veteran Tung Pi-wu attended the United Nations Conference on International Organization in San Francisco (April–May) as a member of the official Republic of China delegation (see under Tung Pi-wu). Ch'en accompanied Tung as the latter's secretary and then remained in the U.S. until November 1945 when he went to London to attend the first congress of the Communist-dominated World Federation of Democratic Youth (WFDY). Ch'en attended as a delegate from the Chinese Liberated Areas Youth Federation and at the close of the meetings was named to the WFDY Executive Committee, a position he held until 1950. Later in the same month he was an adviser to labor leader Teng Fa (q.v.), who headed the CCP delegation to the 27th International Labor Conference in Paris.

By 1946 Ch'en was back in China, where he served as an economist in the CCP mission in Nanking (headed by Chou En-lai), as an official Party spokesman in Shanghai, and as a writer for the Shanghai Party organ *Ch'ün-chung* (The masses). During his time in Shanghai (1946–1947) he was also a member of the Shanghai Party Committee. After the collapse of the cease-fire that had been worked out by U.S. Special Envoy George C. Marshall, the Communists were evacuated to Communist-held areas. Thus, Ch'en was sent to Yenan in March 1947 but was soon transferred to Chefoo (Yen-t'ai) in Shantung, where he engaged for a brief time in Party organizational work. He was back in Europe once again in mid-1947 to attend the First World Youth Festival in Prague, and then in February 1948 he was a delegate to a WFDY Executive Committee meeting in Rome. That spring he joined a WFDY delegation that toured Finland, Sweden, Norway, and Denmark.

Ch'en was in China again in the spring of 1949 participating in the organization of newly established student and youth organizations formed in Peking after that city was surrendered to the Communists in January 1949. He attended the All-China Students' Congress in March and was named to the Preparatory Committee. In the next month he was elected to the Central Committee of the New Democratic Youth League (NDYL) and was also made an alternate member of its Standing Committee. Ch'en's work abroad with the WFDY was reflected in the fact that he was also appointed as the deputy director of the NDYL International Liaison Department. (However, by 1951 he was removed from both the Standing Committee and the Liaison Department owing to a new assignment in the Foreign

Ministry—see below.) Within a month after the formation of the NDYL, Ch'en was named to the National Committee of the All-China Federation of Democratic Youth, as well as a deputy secretary-general. When both these major youth organizations held their next congress in mid-1953, he was removed from all his posts, having by that time become an important Foreign Ministry official.

Just as Ch'en was receiving these new assignments in the youth and student organizations, he was once again sent abroad, this time to Prague to attend the World Peace Congress in April 1949. Three months later he was again in Europe to attend the Second Congress of the WFDY in Budapest, after which he toured briefly in Bulgaria and Poland. It was also in 1949 that Ch'en became affiliated with two other organizations related to international affairs, being named in October 1949 to membership on the China Peace Committee (until 1950) and to membership on both the Executive Board and the Executive Committee of the Sino-Soviet Friendship Association (until 1954). However, after the spring of 1950, when he was named as a deputy director of the Foreign Ministry's Asian Affairs Department, Ch'en devoted little time to his other assignments. Shen Tuan-hsien (Hsia Yen) was the nominal head of the Asian Affairs Department from 1949 to 1952, but because he remained in Shanghai most of the time and never actively assumed the post, Ch'en or his colleague Ch'iao Kuan-hua (q.v.) often served as the acting director. Then, in August 1952, Ch'en formally assumed the directorship of the Asian Affairs Department. For a few months in 1955, the Department was divided into the First and Second Asian Affairs Departments, with Ch'en heading the former. To judge from latter years, the First Department apparently dealt with non-Communist Asian nations whereas the Second Department was concerned with relations with Asian Communist countries. However, in the latter part of 1955 the two sections were amalgamated and Ch'en resumed the directorship, a post he held until assigned to Cairo in 1956.

In April 1951 there was reorganization of the Board of Directors of the Chinese People's Institute of Foreign Affairs (CPIFA), an organization ostensibly devoted to research in international relations, but frequently utilized to deal with nations not having formal diplomatic relations with Peking. Ch'en was named to the Board in 1951 and continues to serve on it; he was also named to the Board's Standing Committee in July 1955.

Ch'en made his first trip abroad as a Foreign Ministry official in August 1952, a few days after his elevation to the directorship of the Asian Affairs Department. He accompanied Chou En-lai to Moscow for negotiations that led to an agreement (September 1952) to transfer complete control of the Chinese Changchun Railway to China and to extend the joint use by China and Russia of the naval facilities at Port Arthur, an extension that was justified in Chinese eyes by the Korean War. (The railway transfer took place at the end of 1952, but the joint use of the Port Arthur facilities was not terminated until 1955—see under Ouyang Ch'in.) From the end of 1953 to April 1954 Ch'en also assisted in the talks that led to the signing of a treaty concerned with the status of Tibet (see under Chang Han-fu, the chief Chinese negotiator). Ch'en also accompanied Chou En-lai to the Geneva Conference (April–July 1954), which brought about a temporary settlement of the Indochinese War; he served as an adviser to Chou and was with him when the latter made brief visits to East Germany, Poland, the U.S.S.R., and Mongolia en route home.

Ch'en's work in the Foreign Ministry was rewarded in October 1954 when he was named as an assistant-minister (not to be confused with the higher post of vice-minister), a position he held concurrently with the directorship of the Asian Affairs Department until 1956. A few days later (November 1954), serving under Chang Han-fu, he began the preliminary negotiations related to the question of the dual nationality of Chinese residing in Indonesia (see under Huang Chen). One of his last major assignments before going abroad in 1956 was in April 1955 when he again served as an adviser to Chou En-lai, who led the Chinese delegation to the Afro-Asian ("Bandung") Conference in Indonesia.

In May 1956 China and Egypt agreed to establish diplomatic relations, thereby allowing the Chinese to establish their first diplomatic mission in the Middle East. In June Ch'en was relieved of his Foreign Ministry posts and appointed as Peking's first ambassador to Cairo, presenting his credentials there in July. (He continued to be the ambassador after Egypt and Syria merged to form the United Arab Republic in February 1958 and also remained as ambassador in Cairo after Syria split away from the Republic in September 1961.) Soon after his arrival in Egypt, Peking and the Yemen established diplomatic ties at the legation level. Although Ch'en was listed in the official 1957 Chinese handbook as Peking's minister, he did not formally present his credentials until April 1958. Then, when both nations agreed to raise their representation to the ambassadorial level in February 1963, Ch'en became the ambassador and held this concurrent post until Wang Jo-chieh was named as the first resident ambassador to the Yemen in February 1964. Although Ch'en visited the Yemen on occasion, he spent most of his time in Cairo, probably the most important Chinese diplomatic post in the Middle East and Africa.

During Ch'en's decade in Cairo, he served as host for the numerous Chinese delegations that visited there and also arranged for a large number of persons and groups to visit China. In the late 1950's and the early 1960's he served, in effect, as the ambassador to the "Provisional Government of the Republic of Algeria," many of the officials of which spent much of their time in Cairo. He also used Cairo as a base to make contacts with African countries, especially after 1960 when so many of the African nations received their independence. One of his first trips from Cairo occurred in December 1958 when he went to Khartoum (immediately after China and the Sudan established diplomatic relations), apparently to make arrangements for the establishment of the Chinese diplomatic mission. Ch'en was also in the Congo (Brazzaville) in August 1960 as an observer to the Foreign Ministers' Conference of African States. The highlight of Ch'en's tour in Cairo occurred in late 1963 and early 1964 when Chou En-lai and Ch'en I made an extended tour of Africa, a trip that was designed to enhance Chinese influence and, in part, to counter similar Soviet efforts. The tour began with a week's visit to Cairo, during which time Ch'en participated in talks with United Arab Republic leaders. Chou and Ch'en I then proceeded to visit several nations in north and west Africa before returning to east Africa in late January 1964. Ch'en Chia-k'ang preceded them to Ethiopia (a nation without diplomatic relations with Peking), where he made preparations for the visit by Chou and Ch'en. Although no tangible results came of the talks with the Ethiopians, the latter gave indications of their intentions to establish diplomatic relations with Peking.

Although Ch'en's long tour in Cairo can probably be regarded as successful, Sino-Egyptian relations underwent some difficult periods that naturally involved Ch'en. The most serious of these occurred in the fall of 1959 when a Syrian Communist leader was allowed to attack the United Arab Republic (UAR) in Peking in a speech given in the presence of UAR diplomats. For a brief period there was talk of a possible break in diplomatic relations, but the tension ebbed when the Chinese apologized.[2] The other notable instance of friction occurred in mid-1965 and early 1966 (coinciding with Ch'en's departure for home) when the Cairo press expressed displeasure with various aspects of Chinese foreign policy, including Peking's persistence in wanting to hold the Asian-African Solidarity Conference in Algiers (a tactic that the UAR opposed). Cairo's irritation was exacerbated by alleged Chinese contacts with Communists in the UAR, men who were later arrested by the UAR government.[3]

Ch'en left Cairo for home in December 1965 and was officially replaced in Cairo by career diplomat Huang Hua (q.v.) in January 1966. Ch'en was immediately named as a vice-minister of Foreign Affairs. His long tour abroad in one

post, lasting nine and a half years, is rivaled only by that of Wang Ping-nan, who was in Poland for nine years, and Yao Chung-ming (qq.v.), who spent seven and a half years in Burma.

A Western diplomat who knew Ch'en in Peking in the early fifties described him as "very bright" and a man with an active sense of humor.[4] In private life, Ch'en is married to Hsu K'o-li, a former writer for the *Hsin-hua jih-pao* (New China daily), the CCP organ in Chungking during the war years. Since 1957 she has been a member of the Executive Committee of the National Women's Federation of China. As of 1947 the Ch'en's had two minor children.

1. Chong-sik Lee, "Korean Communists and Yenan," *The China Quarterly,* no. 9:182–192 (January–March 1962).
2. *New York Times,* October 1, 2, 4, 5, 10, 13, and 26, 1959.
3. *Ibid.,* January 31, 1966.
4. Interview with Western diplomat, San Francisco, June 1961.

Ch'en Chung-ching

(1915–   ; Kiangsu). Former youth leader; vice-chairman, Commission for Cultural Relations with Foreign Countries, State Council.

Ch'en Chung-ching is one of the more important Chinese Communist officials engaged in the field of international cultural liaison. He was first involved in left-wing activities as a student at Peking University in the mid-thirties. Although he worked for non-Communist organizations in the late thirties and early forties, he was almost certainly then a covert Communist. Ch'en studied in the United States in the late forties, after which he joined the Chinese Communist government as an official in the Foreign Ministry.

Ch'en was born in November 1915, but the place of his birth is uncertain. It is known that his family comes from Kiangsu (either Su-chou or Ch'en-chiang), but a person well-acquainted with Ch'en believes he may have been born in Shansi, where his father, for many years an officer in the Nationalist army, was serving as a private secretary to Hsu Yung-ch'ang, a former governor of Shansi.[1] Ch'en's mother died when he was an infant. His father remarried, but Ch'en did not get along well with either his father or his stepmother. He graduated from a middle school in Nanking in about 1934 and then studied at Peking University (Peita) from 1934 to 1937. Ch'en was at Peita in December 1935 when thousands of students from Peita and other schools in north China vented their anger at the Nationalist Government for continuing to countenance Japanese incursions into north China. Their protest demonstrations, staged on December 9, mark the beginning of a movement known as the December Ninth Movement, from which followed the inauguration of the National Liberation Vanguard of China (NLVC) in 1936 (see under Li Ch'ang). Ch'en was among the leaders of the NLVC, an organization that came under Communist control by mid-1936. This was probably his first direct contact with the CCP, although it is not specifically known if he joined the Party at this time.

Like most NLVC members, Ch'en fled the city when the Sino-Japanese War broke out in mid-1937. Going south to Hunan, he enrolled in the Changsha Provisional University (Ch'ang-sha lin-ta), in effect a refugee school made up of former departments from Peking, Tsinghua, and Nankai Universities. He was there in 1937 and 1938. In 1938, when Nationalist General Hu Tsung-nan was withdrawing westward in the face of a Japanese attack in east China, he sought recruits from colleges to bolster his depleted officer corps. It was in these circumstances that Ch'en joined the Third Corps of the Hunan Youth Field Service Corps, of which he became a deputy commander. Among those who joined with him were Shen Chien and Hsiung Hsiang-hui, both of whom became prominent in the 1960's as Foreign Ministry officials (Shen serving as ambassador to Cuba, and Hsiung as the chargé d'affaires in London).[2]

In 1938 Ch'en was sent to Sian in Shensi, where he attended a short course for political workers held in a military academy under the jurisdiction of General Hu Tsung-nan. After this Ch'en served as a political cadre in a political workers' training corps that was closely affiliated with the military academy where he had studied. It is said that in about 1938, he and others "confessed" their CCP membership to General Hu, assuring him that they had renounced the Communists. In reality, however, they probably retained their affiliation with the CCP.[3] In about 1940, when he was 25, Ch'en became head of the Organization Department of the Shensi chapter of the Nationalist-sponsored San-min Chu-i Youth Corps, the principal youth organization of the KMT. By 1941 he had risen to deputy provincial secretary of the Youth Corps. The Shensi corps was then nominally headed by Hu Tsung-nan but in fact was led by a KMT follower, with whom Ch'en constantly quarreled. When Hu learned of this he arranged for Ch'en to be transferred to Kunming for further study.[4]

In Kunming, Ch'en studied at the Southwest Associated University and was also a part-time employee of the Kunming Broadcasting Studio in 1943. Although almost certainly then a Communist Party member, he returned to Shensi in 1943, where he resumed work in the San-min Chu-i Youth Corps, and by 1945 was serving as a member of the Corps' National Committee. Also, in 1946, he became an executive member of the Shensi Provincial KMT Headquarters. Like his wartime friends Shen Chien and Hsiung Hsiang-hui, Ch'en went to the United States after

the war. Shen and Hsiung enrolled in Western Reserve University in Cleveland, but Ch'en studied economics at Columbia for about two years and returned to China in 1948 or 1949.

When Ch'en joined the Communist government he was assigned to the Ministry of Foreign Affairs. Possibly because of his experience in the U.S., he was given an important assignment in in November–December 1950 serving as a technical counselor to Special Representative Wu Hsiu-ch'üan (q.v.) when Wu led a delegation to the United Nations to present China's case regarding the Korean War. (Just one month before Wu, Ch'en, and the others arrived in New York, Chinese Communist forces had entered the Korean War.) After returning to China, Ch'en continued to work in the Foreign Ministry, but then in October 1951 he was assigned as a deputy director of the Liaison Bureau for Cultural Relations with Foreign Countries, then headed by playwright Hung Shen. The bureau was then subordinate to the Culture and Education Committee of the Government Administration Council (the cabinet). In the fall of 1954 (when the government was reorganized), the bureau was placed directly under the State Council; Ch'en continued to serve as a deputy director and, following the death of Director Hung Shen in August 1955, he became the acting director. In the meantime, in May 1954, the Communists had formed a "people's organization" with a title almost identical to that of the government bureau: the Chinese People's Association for Cultural Relations with Foreign Countries. In this association Ch'en served first as a member of the Standing Committee (1954 to date), as the secretary-general from 1954 to 1959, and since 1961 as a vice-chairman. The governmental organ and the "people's organization" seem to differ in that the former deals with nations having diplomatic relations with Peking, while the latter works mainly with nations having no formal diplomatic ties with the Chinese. Ch'en's major assignment appears to be the governmental organization that, in February 1958, was elevated to a commission (paralleling the ministries) under the State Council. When this reorganization took place, Ch'en became the secretary-general of the commission. The commission is nominally chaired by non-Party member Chang Hsi-jo (q.v.), but two former employees of the commission claim that Ch'en and Chang Chih-hsiang (q.v.), an important Party member, are in fact the persons of real authority within the organization.[5] Ch'en received still another promotion within the commission in April 1964 when he was promoted to a vice-chairmanship (concurrent with his post as secretary-general).

Like most officials deeply immersed in foreign affairs, Ch'en has been abroad on several occasions. In March and April 1958 he led a delegation to Bulgaria, Yugoslavia, Hungary, and Rumania; in each nation he signed agreements covering cultural exchanges. In July 1959 he took a music and dance ensemble to Iraq in commemoration of the first anniversary of the Iraqi revolution. In the summer of 1960 Ch'en led a Chinese classical theater group to Cuba where they remained for about two months; the Chinese press noted that the group had also toured Venezuela and Colombia, but it is not clear whether Ch'en visited these two countries with the group. On July 23, while he was in Havana, he signed a cultural cooperation agreement with the Cubans covering a five-year period. Ch'en then took the 90-odd member troupe to Canada, where they spent two months (August–October) on a visit described by the Chinese as the first artistic group to visit Canada. En route home, the theater group performed in Switzerland.

Closely related to his travels abroad and his work in international cultural liaison is Ch'en's membership in four of the friendship associations vis-à-vis foreign countries. From its formation in May 1952 he has served on the Standing Committee of the China-Burma Friendship Association (FA). Similarly, he has been on the Executive Councils of the China–Latin American FA and the China–African People's FA from their formation in March and April 1960, respectively. He was also identified in April 1961 as an Executive Council member of the China-Hungary FA (originally formed in September 1958). He received a closely related appointment in July 1958 when he was named to the Standing Committee of the reorganized China Peace Committee. As a corollary of his work abroad, Ch'en makes numerous appearances in Peking, particularly as a host for foreign visitors. For example, he was on hand to greet the president of Toronto University in April 1962 and a Mongolian cultural delegation in June 1964. In the latter instance, he signed the annual 1964 plan for cultural exchanges with the Mongols on June 17, 1964. Although Ch'en does not seem to have played any role of importance in domestic affairs, he has served as a deputy from Kiangsu to the First, Second, and Third NPC's, which first met in 1954, 1959, and 1964.

Ch'en has been described as an intelligent and capable person.[6] He married a woman surnamed Li in about 1938, and by 1946 they had two children. Like her husband, Li was also a student in the political course at the school controlled by Hu Tsung-nan in Sian.

---

1. Interview with a former subordinate of General Hu Tsung-nan, Hong Kong, January 1964.
2. *Ibid.*
3. *Ibid.*
4. *Ibid.*
5. Interview with former Commission staff members, Hong Kong, May 1964, and Cambridge, Mass., June 1965.
6. Interview, see note 1.

Ch'en Hsi-lien

(c.1913–   ; Hupeh). Commander, Shenyang Military Region; alternate member, CCP Central Committee.

Ch'en Hsi-lien, a Red Army commander since the late twenties, is a veteran of the Long March and the Sino-Japanese War. After brief service in Chungking at the time of the Communist conquest of the mainland, he commanded the PLA Artillery Force from 1951 to 1959, and since the latter date he has been the top military commander in Manchuria. Ch'en was elected an alternate member of the Party Central Committee in 1956.

Ch'en, whose original name was Ch'en K'ai-ch'u, comes from eastern Hupeh, probably from Nan-hsiang in Huang-an hsien, which is also the native district of Politburo member Li Hsien-nien. Other reports state that he came from Ma-ch'eng hsien farther to the east, where there was Communist activity from the 1920's. He was born about 1913 to a peasant family that was apparently able to give him little formal schooling. In his youth he is reported to have worked as a cowherd.

Little is known about Ch'en in this early period, but later references connect him with Li Hsien-nien, Hsu Hai-tung, and Hsu Hsiang-ch'ien by the late 1920's and early 1930's when the latter were all active Communists. The three are high-ranking Party members today and are associated with the Hupeh-Honan-Anhwei (Oyü-wan) Soviet in the early thirties (see under Chang Kuo-t'ao). As Ch'en was associated with them at various times his experiences probably ran somewhat parallel to theirs.

After serving with Li Hsien-nien and Hsu Hai-tung between 1927 and 1930, Ch'en reportedly went about 1930 to Oyüwan where he joined Hsu Hsiang-ch'ien's forces, which were designated the Fourth Front Army in 1931. By Ch'en's own account he was fighting with Hsu's army in eastern Szechwan in 1932 in an area near the Ta-pa Mountains in northeast Szechwan, where he was serving as a "political instructor of the signal corps of the 263rd Regiment of the 88th Division," commanded by Wang Lieh-shan. According to this account he was wounded in battle in February 1933 and his commander was killed.[1] The fighting occurred near Hsuan-han just east of the Ch'u River. During the Long March Ch'en served first with the Fourth Front Army, moving successively from platoon, to company, and finally to battalion commander. In mid-1935, when the Fourth Front Army from western Szechwan met Mao's army from southeast Kiangsi (see under Chang Kuo-t'ao), Ch'en must have switched to the forces of Mao. At that time he was promoted to divisional commander. He reached north Shensi with Mao's forces in the fall of 1935. Once in Shensi he attended the Red Army Academy, perhaps remaining until 1937 when it was renamed the Anti-Japanese Military and Political Academy (K'ang-ta).

When the Sino-Japanese War began in mid-1937 Ch'en was assigned to command the 769th Regiment in Liu Po-ch'eng's 129th Division, one of the three divisions subordinate to the Communists' Eighth Route Army. Ch'en moved with the 129th Division into Shansi in the early fall of 1937 and took part in the fighting against the Japanese. In the late thirties or early forties he was promoted to the command of a brigade (possibly the 385th) in the 129th Division, and by war's end he was in command of a column of the division operating in the Shansi-Hopeh-Shantung-Honan Military Region. In the postwar period Ch'en remained with Liu Po-ch'eng's forces, serving as commander of both the Third Column of the Central Plains People's Liberation Army and the West Anhwei Military District. In the latter part of 1948 he took an active part in the important Huai-Hai Campaign in north-central Anhwei.[2] During the following year, as Liu Po-ch'eng's forces, now known as the Second Field Army, moved into central-south China and then into the southwest, Ch'en led the Third Army Corps' 11th Army and then the Third Army Corps itself.

Since 1949 Ch'en's career has continued to center around military activities, though he has also held positions on some important government councils. In December 1949 Liu Po-ch'eng's Second Field Army occupied Szechwan; Ch'en was named a vice-chairman of the Chungking Military Control Commission and was identified in this post as late as December 1951. At the same time he served as mayor of Chungking until he was succeeded by Ts'ao Ti-ch'iu (later a secretary of the Shanghai Party Committee) in April 1951. There are also reports that Ch'en was a secretary of the Chungking CCP Committee in 1949, but these have not been confirmed. At the regional level, he was a member of the Southwest Military and Administrative Committee from 1950 to 1952.

Ch'en nominally retained posts in the southwest until 1952, but by February 1951 he had been transferred to Peking to assume the important position of commander of the PLA Artillery Force. Reports placing him in Korea in 1950 and on the Vietnam border in 1952 were never confirmed by Chinese Communist sources, and in any case, beginning in late 1952 he began to make frequent appearances in Peking at events normally attended by military leaders (e.g., receptions given by foreign military attachés). Ch'en served from 1954 to 1959 as a deputy from the Southwest Military Region to the First NPC, and at the first session of the Congress in September 1954 he was made a member of the newly created National Defense Council, a position he still retains. A year later, when the Communists first awarded military decorations and gave their

officers personal ranks, Ch'en was made a colonel-general (a three-star rank) and was given high but unspecified military decorations.

Ch'en received Party recognition in September 1956 when he was elected an alternate member of the Central Committee by the Eighth National Party Congress. The following year he was among 12 military leaders under P'eng Te-huai who formed the "goodwill" delegation of the mission that Mao Tse-tung took to Moscow to celebrate the 40th anniversary of the U.S.S.R. P'eng's group remained in the Soviet Union from November 6 to December 3.

Ch'en was last identified as PLA Artillery commander in March 1959 when he addressed a national conference of "outstanding artillery men" in Peking. He remained in the capital until the fall when he was transferred to the position that has subsequently been his principal post, that of commander of the Shenyang (Mukden) Military Region, the command responsible for all of Manchuria. Ch'en replaced Teng Hua (q.v.), who was apparently removed for political reasons. Paralleling the Shenyang Military Region is the Northeast Party Bureau which was re-created in January 1961 in accordance with a decision taken at the Ninth Party Plenum. By June 1963 Ch'en was identified as one of the secretaries of this Bureau, which position placed him under the veteran Hunanese Communist, First Secretary Sung Jen-ch'iung (q.v.).

Ch'en visited Korea briefly in November and December 1960 as a member of the military "goodwill" mission led by Ho Lung, and on at least two occasions he has been reported back in Peking (1961 and 1962). Otherwise, since his appointment to Mukden, Ch'en's activities have been confined to that city where he has been quite regularly identified in attendance at the various social functions that require his presence by virtue of his position as commander of the military region. In private life he is married to Wang Hsuan-mei, whose antecedents are unknown.

1. *Flame on High Mountain* (Peking, 1959), pp. 122–131; *Hung-ch'i p'iao-p'iao* (Red flag fluttering; Peking, 1957), III, 89–95.

2. *The Great Turning Point* (Peking, 1962), pp. 172–174.

Ch'en I

(1901–   ; Lo-chih, Szechwan). Former commander, New Fourth Army; minister of Foreign Affairs; member, CCP Politburo.

Ch'en I was a top Red Army commander in the three decades after the birth of the Red Army in 1927. He was with Mao in the Chingkang Mountains and the central Soviet areas in Kiangsi from 1928 to 1934, and he was among those who remained behind when the Long March began in

1934. After the Sino-Japanese War began he headed a detachment in the New Fourth Army, and from 1941 to the end of the war he was the army's commander. In the ensuing civil war Ch'en's armies conquered the coastal provinces, and in the early years of the PRC Ch'en and Jao Shu-shih were the leading Communist officials in east China. A vice-premier since 1954, Ch'en became foreign minister in 1958. He was elected to the Party Central Committee in 1945 and to the Politburo in 1956.

Ch'en was born into an "old family of scholars"[1] in Lo-chih, 50 miles east of Chengtu, the Szechwan capital. He spent a few years of his childhood in Hunan where his father was a district magistrate during the last years of the Ch'ing dynasty. Returning to Szechwan, Ch'en studied at a vocational training institute in Chengtu. In 1918 he enrolled in a new school which had been established to encourage young Chinese to prepare themselves for further training in France. Early in 1919 Ch'en won a provincial government scholarship, and in the summer he left for Paris to take part in the work-and-study program (see under Ts'ai Ho-sen). He is reported to have studied in St. Germain and Grenoble and to have earned his living as a dishwasher and by loading barges.

Few of the young Chinese in France had arrived with a clear-cut political ideology, and it is doubtful if Ch'en differed from the group in this respect. Nonetheless, he and his colleagues were political activists, and in short order they formed various politically oriented associations which ultimately led to the establishment of a French branch of the CCP (after Ch'en's departure from France). Although documentation is lacking, it is probable that Ch'en was affiliated with the Kung-hsueh hu-chu she (Work and study cooperative society), which was established by Ts'ai Ho-sen (q.v.) and others. In any event, he was constantly in touch with a corps of young intellectuals whose chief interests were neither in study nor work, but in politics. Speaking with unusual candor to a group of foreign language students four decades later, he remarked that when "we went to study in France . . . , some of us were busy with the organization of political campaigns, the discussion of Marxism and the printing of publications, and had no time to study the French language."[2] In speaking of "political campaigns" he may have had in mind an incident in the first part of 1921 when a number of these students demonstrated in front of the Chinese legation in Paris in connection with their protests over the termination of financial aid to the students. In the same year the Institut Franco-Chinois, with some support from the French government, was founded in Lyons for Chinese students in France. This school was a branch of the Université Franco-Chinoise in Peking, which Ch'en was to attend a few years

later. Thinking they would be admitted to the school, Ch'en, Ts'ai Ho-sen, Hsiang Ching-yü, Li Li-san (qq.v.), and others went to Lyons. However, when the Chinese sponsors barred their admission, Ch'en and his colleagues occupied the buildings by force on September 21 (only a few weeks before the school officially opened). The French gendarmarie immediately moved in and placed the students in jail for a few weeks. The school at Lyons continued in existence for many more years, but the Li-ta yuntung (Lyons University movement), as the Communists have termed it, proved to be a failure for the 104 students, Ch'en among them, who were deported from Marseilles in October.

By 1922 Ch'en was back in his native Szechwan, and after a brief stint in the headquarters of Szechwan warlord Yang Sen, he was associated in 1922–23 with the *Hsin-shu jih-pao* (New Szechwan daily). This newspaper was then edited by Hsiao Ch'u-nü (q.v.), one of the most important Youth League leaders and ideologues in the early history of the Communist movement. In 1923 Ch'en went to Peking where he joined both the CCP and the KMT. In the same year he enrolled in the Université Franco-Chinoise, a school whose purpose was to prepare students for study in France, but which was also attended by a number of students who had already studied in France. A Russian biographic sketch of Ch'en asserts that in the 1923–24 period he worked in the "youth movement" in Peking;[3] this may refer to the activities in connection with the Socialist Youth League or with one of the numerous Marxist-oriented youth organizations that sprang up in the wake of the May Fourth Movement under the guidance of Li Ta-chao (q.v.) and other important early Communists.

In 1926 Ch'en went to Canton, then the revolutionary center of China. There he joined the staff of his former colleague in France, Chou En-lai, who was then a top official in the Whampoa Military Academy's Political Department. As the Northern Expedition was getting underway in mid-1926, many recruits were drawn from Whampoa. The National Revolutionary Army was then modeled after the Soviet Red Army, and therefore it had "party representatives"—the equivalent of political commissars—at various levels within its hierarchy. Ch'en, still a member of both the KMT and the CCP, served as a KMT representative, probably in some unit under the well-known Independent Regiment led by Communist Yeh T'ing (q.v.). By the fall of 1926 the Northern Expeditionary forces had taken Wuhan, where the KMT government was soon to make its headquarters. In 1927 Ch'en became secretary of the CCP Committee of the Military-Political Academy (in effect, the Wuhan government's branch of the Whampoa Academy).[4] However, on the eve of the Nanchang Uprising, now celebrated as the birth of the Red Army (see under Yeh T'ing), Chen was with the 73rd Regiment, which was headquartered not far north of Nanchang. Ch'en's role in the insurgency is not known, but the important part played by this regiment is described in the biography of Chou Shih-ti, the regimental commander.

The Communists were quickly routed from Nanchang, after which their military forces moved southward to Swatow on the Kwangtung coast, led by Yeh T'ing and Ho Lung, and, to a lesser degree, by Chu Te. Yeh and Ho led their men into Swatow where they were quickly defeated by KMT forces. In the meantime, the men under the command of Chu Te and Chou Shih-ti (probably including Ch'en I), remained north of Swatow as a rear guard force. After the failure at Swatow, the remaining Communists, who had now dwindled to about 2,000 men,[5] were forced to flee to the interior hinterlands. The complications of this difficult westward trek, including a serious case of defections within the ranks (see under Chou Shih-ti), are smoothed over in orthodox Maoist accounts, which uniformly associate Ch'en with Chu Te and Lin Piao as the three key men who led the survivors of the Swatow debacle to their ultimate merger with the forces led by Mao Tse-tung on the Kiangsi-Hunan border.

Late in 1927, as the Chu-Ch'en-Lin forces moved across southwest Kiangsi, they reorganized their troops. Now down to 600–700 poorly equipped men, they formed a column (*tsung-tui*) under Chu Te, with Ch'en I as his deputy.[6] Despite the Nanchang and Swatow insurrections, the Chu Te force still maintained the fiction that it was fighting under the "KMT banner," an arrangement that enabled the Communists to get some supplies from Yunnanese General Fan Shih-sheng. Fan, whose 16th Army held the area for the KMT, had been acquainted with Chu Te several years earlier when both men were soldiering in Yunnan. One hostile account (by ex-Communist Kung Ch'u) describes this as a capitulation to the KMT and one to which Ch'en had agreed.[7] Maoist historians, on the other hand, assert that this was a clever ruse by Chu and Ch'en to gain a breathing spell, get additional supplies, and to induce members of Fan's army to join the Communist cause.[8] In any case, the Chu-Fan "truce" did not last long, because in early 1928, when Chu's army moved into southern Hunan and took I-chang, the agreement with Fan was broken and Chu's men now declared themselves to be a Communist army. The subsequent series of uprisings in south Hunan led by Chu, Ch'en, and Lin Piao in the early part of 1928 are described in orthodox accounts as an integral part of a series of revolts against KMT authority, which began at Nanchang and which include the Autumn Harvest Uprisings, the establishment of the Hai-lu-feng Soviet in Kwangtung, and the Canton Commune.[9]

The subsequent merger of the forces led by Chu, Ch'en, and Lin with those under Mao Tse-tung's command is treated in detail in the biography of Chu Te. These complex political and military maneuverings took part in the spring and summer of 1928. The details surrounding the establishment of the Fourth Red Army during this period are a matter of historical dispute; some accounts claim this was done in May 1928, others in August. In any case, the Chu-Mao forces were gathered together by the spring of 1928 in the Chingkang Mountains on the Hunan-Kiangsi border, and it is evident that Ch'en was one of the major figures in establishing the Fourth Red Army.[10] Chu Te was the Army commander, Mao was the Party representative, and Ch'en served under Mao as head of the Political Department.

Coincident with the establishment of the Fourth Army, the First Party Congress of the Hunan-Kiangsi Border Area was convened at Mao-p'ing in Ning-kang hsien (May 20, 1928). Ch'en took part in the meeting, and at that time or shortly thereafter he became secretary of the Army Committee of the Party.[11] He probably also became a member of the Party's Border Area Special Committee, of which Mao was secretary. The Special Committee was then, in effect, the highest authority in the border area. Mao Tse-tung has reviewed many of the events in this period in his famous essay "The Struggle in the Chingkang Mountains." This piece is no model of clarity, but it is evident that he was plagued both by attacks from local military forces and by the political maneuverings of his own provincial CCP committee, which was not enthusiastic about developments in Mao's territory. Later in the year, when it appears that Mao had matters in control, a Second Special Committee was elected at the Second Border Area Party Congress (October). Mao, Chu, and Ch'en were all made committee members,[12] but a month later, when a new Army Committee of the Party was established, Chu Te replaced Ch'en as the secretary. Soon after this, Ch'en was with Mao and Chu when they abandoned the Chingkang Mountain base and moved eastward toward the Kiangsi-Fukien border over the winter of 1928–29. Writing a quarter of a century later, Ch'en also reviewed the events in Chingkangshan in 1928, and predictably, he aligned himself with Mao's "correct" actions.[13]

There is little information on Ch'en's activities or whereabouts for the next two years. However, in November 1930 he was one of the speakers at a meeting of the Central Executive Committee of the Kiangsi Provincial Soviet, which met in Chi-an (Kian). According to Ch'en, a recently adopted and controversial land law had been countermanded on orders of the Kiangsi

Southwest Special Action Committee, an opposition group headed by Li Wen-lin and others, who were allegedly from the rich peasantry. He further claimed that Li's supporters had prevented the division of land in many parts of Communist-held territory in Kiangsi.[14] It was Li and his Southwest Special Action Committee that openly rebelled against Mao in December 1930 (the Fu-t'ien Incident; see under P'eng Te-huai). According to Chang Kuo-t'ao, Ch'en initially wavered in his support of Mao during the incident, but he ultimately upheld Mao and took a direct hand in the bloody suppression of the rebels.[15]

When the Chinese Soviet Republic was established in November 1931 at Juichin, Ch'en was elected a member of the republic's highest organ, the Central Executive Committee (CEC). This took place at the First All-China Congress of Soviets, and when the Second Congress met in January–February 1934, he was reelected to the CEC. Just prior to the Second Congress, Ch'en was elected (December 1933) to the Executive Committee of the Kiangsi Provincial Soviet. His colleagues in this organization included such prominent figures as Tseng Shan, Li Fu-ch'un, and Ts'ai Ch'ang (qq.v.).

In the meantime, during the early thirties Ch'en commanded the 12th Division, and later both the Kiangsi Military District and the 22nd Red Army. In contrast to the other units subordinate to the Chu-Mao military establishment, relatively little is known about the 22nd Red Army. To judge from an essay written in commemoration of his colleague P'eng Hsueh-feng (q.v.), Ch'en apparently took an active part in the Third and Fourth Annihilation Campaigns (1931–1933), fighting in southeast Kiangsi in the former campaign and in the central portion of the province in the latter.[16] During the fifth and final campaign, which ended in the fall of 1934 when the Red Army left Kiangsi on the Long March, Ch'en was commanding troops in Hsing-kuo hsien, which by then was on the western border of the much-contracted "central soviet." According to Chu Te, it was decided to leave Hsiang Ying (q.v.) and Ch'en behind as a rear-guard element for the Long Marchers. In Chu's words, Hsiang was to be the "party leader and political commissar of all the armed forces and political cadres," and Ch'en was to be the "supreme military commander."[17]

The effective forces left under the Hsiang-Ch'en command, which never numbered more than a few thousand, were routed from the Juichin base soon after the main Long March columns left the area. They then led their remnants to the Wu-ling Mountain Range in the region where Hunan, Kiangsi, and Kwangtung merge, arriving there in the spring of 1935. It is clear from a number of sources that Ch'en remained in this area for the next two and a half years. Hsiang, on the other hand, appears to have spent most of this time on the Kiangsi-Fukien border. It should also be noted that the Maoist historians have tended to slight Hsiang's role in those difficult years (for reasons explained in Hsiang's biography). Ch'en's role, on the other hand, is presented in heroic and romantic terms, particularly in the book published in 1961 by Yang Shang-k'uei (q.v.) entitled *The Red Kiangsi-Kwangtung Border Region,* as well as in Yang's condensation, which appeared two years later (*The Unquenchable Spark*). Despite their shortcomings, Yang's writings provide a valuable source on the careers of Ch'en and his colleagues in the post–Long March period. As Yang explains it, the essence of the Communist strategy was to "preserve the backbone of the Party during the period when the revolution had sustained a setback" and to "tie down a part of the enemy in the Kiangsi-Kwangtung Border Region."[18] The border area offered both physical and political advantages: the rugged terrain was suitable to guerrilla skirmishes and the area was also the border between regions controlled by Chiang Kai-shek and those dominated by Kwangtung warlords who, though opposing the Communists, were reluctant to place themselves under the complete control of Chiang. Ch'en's men, operating out of a narrow base that stretched for only 30-odd miles, were virtually independent of higher Party authority. Yang notes that as of early 1937 they had been out of contact with the Party Central Committee for over two years and that most of their information about their comrades in Shensi, Mao's base, came from local newspapers.[19] They were also beset by serious defections, the most important of which is mentioned in Yang Shang-k'uei's biography.

Ch'en and his associates were ultimately rescued from their difficult situation by the outbreak of the Sino-Japanese War in July 1937. From the end of 1936 the KMT and the CCP had moved cautiously toward a rapprochement in order to resist the Japanese more effectively. These steps were hastened when war erupted; top-level negotiations were carried out in the Nationalist capital at Nanking by Ch'in Pang-hsien (q.v.) and others, while at the same time local KMT commanders were authorized to negotiate with the scattered Communist bands in central-south and east China. In the latter half of 1937 Ch'en took part in a series of lower-level talks, first at Ta-yü in southern Kiangsi, and finally at Nanchang, the provincial capital.[20] The talks were consummated in October 1937 when, under the official auspices of the Nationalists, the Communists' New Fourth Army was created.

The New Fourth Army Headquarters were established in Nanchang in January 1938. Yeh T'ing was the commander and Hsiang Ying was his deputy, and both men, in turn, were ostensibly responsible to Nationalist General Ku Chu-t'ung, the commander of the Third War Zone along the Yangtze Plain. Yeh and Hsiang quickly organized four detachments from the various Communist guerrilla bands in central-south and east China. Ch'en was put in command of the First Detachment, Chang Ting-ch'eng (q.v.) of the Second, and T'an Chen-lin (q.v.) of the Third. These three units moved into the field in the spring of 1938; they were initially stationed around She-hsien in south Anhwei, but by June 1938 they had moved north and established their headquarters in the Mao-shan Range just south of Nanking. Ch'en described his military and political operations in a fact-laden article published in the November 30, 1939, issue of *Ch'ün-chung* (The masses), an important Communist journal published in Chungking. In that same month these three detachments were organized into the South Kiangsu Command (sometimes known as the South Yangtze Command).[21] Ch'en was put in charge of this command and he also continued to head the First Detachment, while the North Yangtze Command was placed under the direction of Chang Yun-i (q.v.).

The area Ch'en commanded was east and south of Nanking, extending from Tan-yang in Kiangsu to Fan-ch'ang in Anhwei. Tan-yang was controlled soon after the outbreak of the war by local Communists led by Kuan Wen-wei and his brother who were native to the area. Kuan, a former elementary school teacher, began to organize the peasants and by late 1939, with the help of Ch'en's forces, he had established a corridor through which the Communists could cross the Yangtze into north Kiangsu. In response to increasing Nationalist pressures to have the Communists evacuate the area south of the river, Ch'en began to move his men across the Yangtze in the spring of 1940 and, augmented by local guerrilla forces, they pushed north to Yen-ch'eng hsien. This locale in north-central Kiangsu east of the Grand Canal was to be his headquarters for most of the remaining war years. By October 1940 he had reorganized his units into four columns, which were designated the North Kiangsu Command. This became the major Communist force north of the Yangtze, replacing in importance Chang Yun-i's North Yangtze Command, which had been battered by the Japanese in Anhwei to the west of Ch'en's territory. Ch'en's new force consisted of his former First Detachment, part of the Second Detachment (see under Su Yü), the headquarters staff from his former South Kiangsu Command, and two local guerrilla units. One of the guerrilla bands was the Kiangnan Advance Column, the above-mentioned force from the Tan-yang region organized by Kuan Wen-wei; the other guerrilla unit was composed of elements from the Kiangnan Anti-Japanese Patriotic Army, a Communist-affiliated force operating in south Kiangsu about

midway along the rail line connecting Nanking and Shanghai.[22] At the same time Ch'en was joined by an important force of some 15,000 men from the Communists' Eighth Route Army. Led by Huang K'o-ch'eng (q.v.), it had established itself in early 1940 at Fou-ning, some 40 miles north of Ch'en's headquarters at Yen-ch'eng. Huang's men, who had come from Shansi, linked up with Ch'en's columns after the latter had arrived in the Yen-ch'eng area.[23]

In November 1940 the Communists established the North Kiangsu Provisional Administrative Committee at Yen-ch'eng, with Kuan Wen-wei as chairman. This was the first important civilian base under Communist control in east-central China. At this same time the Communists began to take over the extreme eastern end of the north bank of the Yangtze in Kiangsu, an important and fertile peninsula. This was organized as the Fourth District Guerrilla Command after the Communists had driven out the Nationalists, who had had their own administration there operating behind Japanese lines. The prime operative in the district was Chi Fang (q.v.), a CCP member, who cooperated with the elements of Ch'en I's forces sent there to help win over the peasantry. Late in January 1941 the district declared its allegiance to Kuan's North Kiangsu Provisional Administrative Committee and to the North Kiangsu Command headed by Ch'en I.[24]

At this juncture the New Fourth Army underwent a devastating blow when, in January 1941, it lost several thousand men during the famous New Fourth Army Incident (see under Yeh T'ing). Commander Yeh was captured by the Nationalists and Hsiang Ying, the political commissar and secretary of the CCP Southeast Bureau, was killed in the fighting. At the time of the incident, Ch'en and his troops were far north of the Yangtze, and thus he was not directly involved. However, the annotators of Mao's *Selected Works* have singled out Ch'en for praise in connection with a May 1940 Central Committee directive which was designed to strengthen the New Fourth Army and to increase the Party's contacts with the local populace. The annotation (written many years after the event) asserts that Hsiang's failure to carry out these orders played a major role in causing the New Fourth Army Incident. In contrast, Ch'en was praised for having put the directive into effect "immediately."[25] At that time Ch'en was a member of Hsiang Ying's Southeast Bureau, which was in charge of Party work in Kiangsu, Chekiang, Anhwei, Kiangsi, Hupeh, and Hunan provinces.

Following the 1941 Incident, the Communists immediately reorganized the New Fourth Army and the Party apparatus for the army's area of operations. Liu Shao-ch'i (q.v.) became the political commissar, and Ch'en was named acting commander. (Yeh T'ing remained in Nationalist prisons until after the war.) In the new hierarchy, Chang Yun-i became deputy commander, Lai Ch'uan-chu (q.v.) was made chief-of-staff, and Teng Tzu-hui (q.v.) became director of the Political Department. The Party apparatus underwent a similar reorganization. The new organ, known as the Central China Bureau (Huachung chü), was headed by Secretary Liu Shao-ch'i. Jao Shu-chih (q.v.), who was to be closely associated with Ch'en for well over a decade, became deputy secretary, and Ch'en was made a member.

In addition to the changes in the New Fourth Army's high command, the rest of the Army underwent a major reorganization. Seven divisions were activated to absorb the former detachments, as well as other units that had been operating semi-independently. Ch'en's First Detachment became the First Division under Su Yü (q.v.). The Second through the Seventh Divisions were commanded, respectively, by Chang Yun-i, Huang K'o-ch'eng, P'eng Hsueh-feng, Li Hsien-nien, T'an Chen-lin, and Chang Ting-ch'eng (qq.v.). The significance of this impressive cluster of military leaders under Ch'en can be gauged in part by the fact that in 1945 they were all elected to the Party Central Committee at its Seventh Congress (excepting only P'eng Hsueh-feng, who was killed in action prior to the Congress). Each of the divisions operated in separate areas, with the result that the Communists controlled much of the territory surrounding the large cities in Kiangsu and Anhwei and had a strategic toe-hold in the old Hupeh-Honan-Anhwei (Oyüwan) guerrilla base north of Wuhan. These areas witnessed considerable fighting in the closing years of the war, when the Communists engaged in guerrilla warfare against the Japanese and also fought a number of skirmishes with KMT troops. Basically, the territories held by the New Fourth Army remained in Communist hands after the war, and from them the Communists expanded from 1947 to 1949 when they conquered east-central China.

Ch'en remained in the field with his New Fourth Army until 1944 when he was called to Yenan; it took him three months to make the difficult trip through Japanese lines.[26] By the time he reached the Communist capital, a United States Army observers' mission had been established there. He was interviewed by various American newsmen, and in August he gave a lecture to the observers' mission on the New Fourth Army. Later in the year an American diplomat in Yenan described him as a man of "commanding presence, evident vigor and determination."[27] Ch'en was still in Yenan when the CCP held its Seventh Party Congress from April to June 1945. He served on the Congress presidium, delivered an address, and at the close of the proceedings was elected one of the 44 full members of the CCP Central Committee. Afterwards, he returned to the field in his capacity as acting commander of the New Fourth Army, which then consisted of about 150,000 men. Units from his command had already begun to move north into Shantung, where they were able to link up with forces led by Lo Jung-huan, Hsiao Hua (qq.v.), and others who had been operating there for several years. Thus, by mid-1944 Ch'en was already political commissar of the Shantung Military District,[28] and by early 1946 (and probably earlier) he was also the district commander. In both positions he replaced Lo Jung-huan, who went to Manchuria at the end of the war. Moreover, following the death in an air crash of New Fourth Army Commander Yeh T'ing in April 1946 (immediately after his release from prison), Ch'en formally succeeded to the command of the army.

The Communists' position in Shantung in the postwar period was of particular strategic importance: control of the province would enable them to interdict the key north-south rail line connecting Tientsin and Nanking and thus prevent the consolidation of Nationalist forces in the Yangtze area with those in north China. The province had a further importance in the early postwar period, because it was through its northern ports that the Communists were able to move portions of Lin Piao's army into Manchuria. As early as the first part of 1946 Ch'en had moved his headquarters north from Kiangsu into Lin-i in southeast Shantung. His troops took part in heavy fighting beginning in early 1947, by which time the civil war with the Nationalists was in full swing. As he drew his New Fourth Army into Shantung, Ch'en also recruited new forces there, and after some reorganization the Army was redesignated in 1947 the East China Liberation Army. During the winter of 1948–49 it was renamed the Third Field Army, and it continued in existence until the field armies were abolished in the 1954–55 period. In early 1947, while Ch'en was still in south Shantung, he gave an interview to an American journalist which contains a useful exposition of Ch'en's ideas on guerrilla tactics.[29] He was, at this point, in command of about 200,000 troops.[30]

Despite the demands of the battlefields, Ch'en was again called to the Yenan area in mid-1947 to attend a military conference,[31] apparently to prepare for the great campaigns which lay ahead. By the time Ch'en attended the conference he was able to report a number of successes in the Shantung area. In a series of operations coordinated with the army of Liu Po-ch'eng (q.v.), they had been able to disrupt the important Lunghai Railway running east-west from Shantung into Honan. Much of Shantung was now in Communist hands, and the stage was set for the major campaigns in 1948 on the north China plains. By the end of May 1948, once more in coordination with Liu Po-ch'eng, the Communists threatened Kaifeng, the Honan capital and a key rail juncture, and the city fell to them for a time in June 1948. Then, as the fighting grew more intense, Ch'en slipped away and returned to Shantung. In a two-month battle from November 1948 to January 10, 1949, Ch'en and Liu Po-ch'eng once again collaborated to win the Huai-Hai Campaign, which is described in Communist accounts as one of the three greatest battles of the civil war. After this victory, the crossing of the Yangtze was only a matter of time. On April 21 the Liu-Ch'en armies began to move across the Yangtze along a 300-mile front. Nanking, the former Nationalist capital, fell two days later. Thereafter, the two armies took separate routes; Liu moved to the south and west, while Ch'en began to converge on Shanghai to the east.

Ch'en and his political commissar Jao Shu-shih moved into Shanghai in late May 1949, and within a short time they assumed the lion's share of the key posts in Shanghai and east China. On the day that Shanghai was "completely liberated," May 27, Ch'en was made chairman of the Shanghai Military Control Commission, and on the next day he became the mayor. In the Party's East China Bureau he served as second secretary under Jao. Within the military establishment he continued to head the Third Field Army, as well as the newly created East China Military Region, whose boundaries coincided with those of the field army—namely, Shantung, Kiangsu, Anhwei, Chekiang, and Fukien provinces. These provinces also formed the boundaries of the governmental body known as the East China Military and Administrative Committee (ECMAC), established in Shanghai during the winter of 1949–50. Ch'en was a member of the ECMAC, and when it was reorganized into the East China Administrative Committee in late 1952, he was reappointed a member, continuing in this post until the organization was dissolved in the summer of 1954. Ch'en's various speeches and reports represent an important source of information on the early period of Communist rule in east China in general and Shanghai in particular.[32]

Although his prime responsibilities were in east China in the early years of the PRC, Ch'en also held a number of posts in the national government. In this connection, as a representative of the East China Liberated Areas, he went to Peking in September 1949 to participate in the meetings of the CPPCC, the body which brought the national government into existence on October 1. Ch'en served on the *ad hoc* committee that drafted the Organic Law of the central government, one of the key documents adopted at that time, and at the close of the sessions he was elected a member of the Central People's Government Council (CPGC), the highest organ of government (chaired by Mao Tse-tung). Over the next five years most of Ch'en's visits to Peking were for the purpose of attending the meeting of the CPGC, which, in its 34 sessions, passed on virtually all vital measures adopted by the national government. At the time the government was established, he was also made a member of the People's Revolutionary Military Council, the government's top military organ (and for a brief period in 1954 he served as one of its vice-chairmen). In the same month (October 1949), he was made an Executive Board member of the Sino-Soviet Friendship Association (SSFA), then one of the most active of Peking's "mass" organizations. Ch'en sat on the SSFA board until 1954 and concurrently (from 1951) headed the Shanghai chapter.

Most of the heavy fighting in east China ended in the latter half of 1949, but as late as the early part of 1950 troops under his jurisdiction were still engaged in mopping-up operations and assaults (not all of them successful) on a number of offshore islands. Most important, Taiwan, which was nominally a part of the Communists' military and political structures, remained "unliberated." During the 1949–50 period some preparations were carried out for an invasion (which was to have been led by Ch'en's deputy, Su Yü), but the undertaking was quietly shelved when the Korean War broke out in June 1950 and the United States' Seventh Fleet was sent into the Taiwan Straits to prevent Taiwan from falling into Communist hands.[33]

As already indicated, Ch'en spent most of his time prior to 1954 in Shanghai where he attended a singularly large number of government, military, and CCP meetings, received a constant stream of foreign visitors to Shanghai, and appeared at the numerous ceremonial functions required of a man of his stature. By May 1952 he had replaced Jao Shu-shih as the ranking Party secretary in Shanghai, and in October of that year he was a member of Liu Shao-ch'i's delegation to the 19th CPSU Congress, the last one held during Stalin's lifetime. In January 1953 he was named to membership on a committee to draft the national Election Law, which led, in turn, to nationwide elections and the convocation of the First NPC in September 1954. Ch'en attended as a Shanghai deputy, and at the close of the NPC session he was made a vice-premier of the State Council and a vice-chairman of the newly established National Defense Council. By this time Ch'en had been transferred to Peking, and therefore relinquished his various east China-Shanghai posts, excepting only the mayoralty of Shanghai. He was re-elected mayor in January 1957, but the news release which accompanied this announcement made it plain that Ts'ao Ti-ch'iu was to be the acting mayor. Finally, in November 1958, K'o Ch'ing-shih (q.v.) formally replaced Ch'en.

In October 1954 Ch'en spent two weeks in East Germany as head of the Chinese delegation to the celebrations marking the fifth anniversary of the German Democratic Republic. Before returning home he spent a few days in Warsaw where he held talks with top Polish officials. In the following December he was elected a Standing Committee member of the CPPCC and a member of the Second Executive Board of the Sino-Soviet Friendship Association. He was abroad again in April 1955 as the senior member of Chou En-lai's delegation to the famous Afro-Asian Conference in Bandung, Indonesia. In September the Communists gave their officers personal military ranks and also awarded decorations for past services. Ch'en was made one of the 10 marshals, the highest rank, and he also received the three highest awards—the Orders of August First, Independence and Freedom, and Liberation.

In early 1956, in rapid-fire succession, Ch'en received new posts in three newly established organizations. In February he was made chairman of the Central Work Committee for the Popularization of Standard Spoken Chinese (*p'u-t'unghua*), and in March he became chairman of the National Association for the Elimination of Illiteracy. The third appointment was related to the initial steps toward the adoption of a 12-year plan for the development of science; to implement this program the State Council created the Scientific Planning Commission in March, with Ch'en as the chairman. At first glance it appeared that Ch'en's career was undergoing a rather sharp reorientation toward the educational and scientific field. In fact, however, the first two appointments quickly turned into *pro forma* positions, and in May 1957, when the Scientific Planning Commission was reorganized, Nieh Jung-chen (q.v.) replaced Ch'en. In the meantime, Ch'en was given still another assignment in March 1956 when he was named to head a huge delegation to Lhasa to attend the inauguration in April of the Preparatory Committee for the Tibet Autonomous Region (see under Chang Ching-wu). Ch'en spent six weeks in Tibet. In September he delivered the keynote speech on foreign affairs at the Party's Eighth Congress. In retrospect, this appears to have been one of the first major indicators that he was to become Peking's foreign minister a year and a half later. Ch'en was reelected to the Party Central Committee, and at the first plenum of the new Central Committee, held the day after the congress closed, he was elected a member of the Politburo, which then consisted of 17 full and six alternate members.

In 1958 Ch'en was one of China's more famous leaders, but he was known abroad mainly by specialists in Chinese Communist affairs. This situation changed quickly after February 1958 when he replaced Chou En-lai as foreign minister. A few days after receiving this appointment he accompanied Chou to Pyongyang where they negotiated the withdrawal of the large Chinese Communist military force (the "Chinese People's Volunteers") which was still in North Korea nearly five years after the Korean War had ended. In the next month Ch'en was named director of the Foreign Affairs Office, which is in charge of coordinating the work of the various commissions, ministries, and bureaus under the State Council that have overseas activities. These two appointments had the ostensible effect of elevating Ch'en to the number one position* in foreign affairs, but there is a considerable body of inferential information to suggest that Chou En-lai retains his long-held supremacy in this field, particularly in regard to policy making.

Since assuming the Foreign Ministry portfolio, Ch'en has spent a great deal of time abroad. Most of his trips have been to Asian or African countries, and most of them, in effect, have been part of the heated contest with the Soviet Union to exercise influence in these developing nations. In April 1960 he accompanied Chou En-lai on a goodwill visit to Burma, India, and Nepal, and in each nation they held talks on border issues. After returning to south China for a few days, he and Chou visited briefly in Cambodia and North Vietnam in May, and from May 27 to June 1 he was again with Chou on a goodwill visit to Mongolia. In August 1960 Ch'en went to Kabul to attend independence day ceremonies, and while there he signed the Sino-Afghan Treaty of Friendship and Mutual Non-aggression.

Ch'en spent most of the first half of 1961 abroad. In early January Chou En-lai and Ch'en arrived in Burma leading one of the largest delegations ever sent to a foreign country by the Chinese. They attended ceremonies marking the 13th anniversary of Burma's independence, exchanged the instruments of ratification of the Sino-Burmese Boundary Treaty (see under Yao Chung-ming), and held a series of talks with top Burmese leaders. Six weeks later Ch'en went to Indonesia where he signed a treaty of friendship and a cultural cooperation agreement (April 1), and en route home he held talks with Burmese Prime Minister U Nu in Rangoon (April). In May Ch'en went to Geneva for what was probably the highlight of his career as a diplomat. From mid-May to early July Ch'en led the Chinese delegation in the first round of talks that was ultimately to lead to a settlement of the smoldering situation in Laos. Ch'en left the delegation in the care of Chang Han-fu (q.v.) in July, but exactly a year later he returned to Geneva to sign the final accords. These extended negotiations, and Ch'en's part in them, are covered in detail in a book by Arthur Lall, who headed the Indian delegation to the conference.[34]

Ch'en was back in Southeast Asia in April 1963 as a member of Liu Shao-chi'i's goodwill delegation to Indonesia and Burma, and, after a short return trip to China, they visited Cambodia and North Vietnam. In December 1963 Ch'en led Peking's delegation to Kenya to attend independence ceremonies. However, rather than return home, Ch'en went to Cairo where he joined Chou En-lai at the beginning of Chou's much publicized 11-nation tour. Over the next six weeks (until early February 1964) they visited the following African countries: the United Arab Republic, Algeria, Morocco, Tunisia, Ghana, Mali, Guinea, Sudan, Ethiopia, and Somalia. In addition, they made a short visit to China's leading East European ally, Albania. One of the major themes stressed by the Chinese was the need to convene a Second Afro-Asian ("Bandung") Conference; other agenda items included the status of Taiwan, the issue of China in the United Nations, and Chinese economic assistance. Following a brief return trip to China, Chou and Ch'en undertook a similar tour in February 1964 in Burma, Pakistan, and Ceylon. Ch'en pursued the question of the Second "Bandung" Conference in April 1964 when he led the Chinese delegation to Indonesia to attend a meeting to prepare for the conference.

In July 1964 Chou En-lai and Ch'en again visited Rangoon where they held talks with leading Burmese officials on international affairs. In October–November Ch'en led a Chinese delegation to Algeria for celebrations commemorating the 10th anniversary of the Algerian Revolution, and a few days later he was in Cambodia for that nation's 11th anniversary of independence. In late November and early December Ch'en was in Indonesia where he again discussed preparations for the Second Afro-Asian Conference, which was scheduled to be held in Algeria. (Ultimately, despite intensive efforts to convene the conference, it was indefinitely postponed in 1965.)

In addition to these numerous trips Ch'en has, of course, seen hundreds of foreign visitors in Peking and signed a number of agreements with foreign envoys. The very nature of his foreign ministry portfolio has projected him to the forefront in the news media, and with the probable exception of Chou En-lai, no other Chinese leader has been mentioned more frequently in the press since 1958. Similarly, few books and articles on Chinese foreign affairs since 1958 fail to treat his activities and statements in detail. However, it should be noted that he has played a relatively minor role in intra-Communist bloc party relations (as opposed to state relations). He has never attended, for example, any of the Communist "summit" meetings, such as the one held in Moscow in 1960 (see under Teng Hsiao-p'ing).

Ch'en's assumption of the two State Council foreign affairs positions in 1958 were his last major appointments. However, he has continued to receive lesser posts, as in October 1961 when he was made president of the Institute of International Relations (*wai-chiao hsueh-yuan*), and in December 1964 when he and Chou En-lai were elected honorary chairmen of the Chinese People's Institute of Foreign Affairs, an organization which frequently deals with nations not having formal diplomatic relations with Peking. Ch'en also continues to serve as a Shanghai deputy to the NPC, and at the close of the inaugural sessions of the Second and Third NPC's (April 1959 and January 1965), he was reappointed vice-premier, foreign minister, and vice-chairman of the National Defense Council. Since April 1959 he has also been a vice-chairman of the CPPCC.

Few Chinese leaders see foreigners with any regularity, and when they do it is usually in a highly bureaucratized manner. In contrast, Ch'en's massive exposure to outsiders, both at home and abroad, has provided an opportunity to gauge his personal qualities. Most accounts indicate that he is an outspoken man of considerable intelligence and wit, a capable negotiator, and not particularly given to expressing himself in Marxian language. Other accounts note that he is a gourmet and has a rather active interest in the arts (which is further demonstrated by his penchant for writing poems, many of which have been published in the Communist press). Foreign diplomats may find some significance in the fact that Ch'en is honorary chairman of the Chess (*wei-ch'i*) Federation of China.

Ch'en's first wife was killed in Kiangsi in 1934. In 1947 he had two children, apparently by his first wife. Since at least the 1950's he has been married to Chang Ch'ien, who is obviously much younger than Ch'en. The fact that she was a member of a drama society attached to Ch'en's New Fourth Army during the war years, suggests that he met her at that time. She remained in the background until the mid-1950's, but since then she has assumed a number of minor and presumably honorific posts. Chang has been a member of the National Women's Federation's Executive Committee since 1957, a vice-chairman of the China-Cambodia Friendship Association since 1960, and a deputy from Hupeh to the NPC since 1964. She has accompanied her husband on many of his trips abroad.

---

1. Agnes Smedley, *The Great Road* (New York, 1956), p. 221.

2. *SCMP* 2713, p. 3.

3. *Bol'shaya Sovetskaya Entsiklopedya* (Large Soviet Encyclopedia), XLVII, 488 (April 1957).

4. *Ibid.*

5. Wang Shih, et al., *A Brief History of the Chinese Communist Party* (Shanghai, 1958); translated in JPRS no. 8756, August 16, 1961, p. 104.

6. *Chung-kuo kung-ch'an-tang tsai chung-nan-ti-ch'ü ling-tao ko-ming tou-cheng te li-shih tzu-liao* (Historical materials on the revolutionary struggles led by the CCP in central-south China; Wuhan, 1951), I, 130.

7. John E. Rue, *Mao Tse-tung in Opposition, 1927–1935* (Stanford, Calif., 1966), pp. 86–87.

8. *Chung-kuo kung-ch'an-tang tsai chung-nan-ti-ch'ü ling-tao ko-ming tou-cheng te li-shih tzu-liao*, p. 130; Wei Hung-yun, ed., *"Pa-i" ch'i-i* (The "August First" uprising; Wuhan, 1957), p. 27.

9. Wang Shih, p. 105.

10. Wei Hung-yun, p. 29.

11. *Selected Works of Mao Tse-tung* (Peking, 1965), I, 75.

12. *Ibid.*, p. 96.

13. *CB* 208, pp. 9–16.

14. Rue, p. 228.

15. Modern China Project, Columbia University, New York, Howard L. Boorman, director.

16. Hua Ying-shen, ed., *Chung-kuo kung-ch'an tang lieh-shih chuan* (Biographies of Chinese Communist Party martyrs; Hong Kong, 1949), p. 188.

17. Smedley, p. 308.

18. *The Unquenchable Spark* (Peking, 1963), p. 7.

19. Yang Shang-k'uei, *The Red Kiangsi-Kwangtung Border Region* (Peking, 1961), pp. 130–133.

20. *The Unquenchable Spark*, p. 34.

21. Chalmers A. Johnson, *Peasant Nationalism and Communist Power* (Stanford, Calif., 1962), p. 128; *K'ang-Jih chan-cheng shih-ch'i chieh-fang-ch'ü kai-k'uang* (A sketch of the liberated areas during the Anti-Japanese War; Peking, 1953), p. 113.

22. Johnson, p. 141.

23. *Ibid.*, pp. 135–136.

24. *Ibid.*, pp. 142–144.

25. *Selected Works of Mao Tse-tung* (Peking, 1965), II, 432.

26. Gunther Stein, *The Challenge of Red China* (New York, 1945), p. 345.

27. *Foreign Relations of the United States; Diplomatic Papers, 1944*, vol. VI, *China* (Washington, D.C., 1967), pp. 528, 753.

28. *Ibid.*, p. 623.

29. Hong Kong, *China Digest*, no. 10:13–14 (May 6, 1947).

30. *Ibid.*, no. 9:7–8 (April 22, 1947).

31. *Hung-ch'i p'iao-p'iao* (Red flag fluttering; Peking, 1957), III, 355.

32. Hong Kong, *China Digest*, no. 5:17 (June 14, 1949); *ibid.*, no. 12:8–9 (September 21, 1949); *Hsin-hua yueh-pao* (New China monthly), no. 1:97 (August 15, 1949); *ibid.*, no. 2:261–262 (June 15, 1950); *ibid.*, no. 4:744 (August 15, 1950); *ibid.*, no. 1:25–28 (November 25, 1950); Shanghai, *China Monthly Review*, no. 4, pp. 1–2 of supplement (December 1950).

33. John Gittings, *The Role of the Chinese Army* (London, 1967), pp. 41, 44.

34. Arthur Lall, *How Communist China Negotiates* (New York, 1968).

Ch'en Keng

(1904–1961; Hsiang-hsiang hsien, Hunan). Veteran Red Army leader; member, CCP Central Committee.

For almost four decades Ch'en Keng was one of the Communists' most outstanding military leaders. Trained at Whampoa, he took part in many of the landmark events in Chinese Communist history, including the August 1, 1927, uprising at Nanchang and the Long March. He also spent a few years working in the intelligence network in Shanghai and was among the more important commanders in the Oyüwan Soviet in the early thirties. In the 13 years from the outbreak of the Sino-Japanese War until he led his troops into Yunnan in 1950, Ch'en was an active and highly successful field commander. He was a deputy commander of the Chinese Communist forces in the Korean War and afterwards served as PLA deputy chief-of-staff and vice-minister of National Defense. The significance of his career rests mainly on his role as a field commander, but he also held a seat on the Party Central Committee from 1945 until his death in 1961.

Ch'en was born in 1904 in Hsiang-hsiang hsien, approximately 50 miles southwest of Changsha, the Hunan capital. Ch'en came from a landlord family with strong military ties. In the Ch'ing era his grandfather had been a prominent commander at Shan-hai Pass, the famous gateway to Manchuria. After a brief exposure to traditional Chinese education, Ch'en ran away from home at the age of 13 to join the army of Hunan military leader Lu Ti-p'ing. He served with Lu until 1922 when his army was defeated by northern warlord Wu P'ei-fu. He then began to work for the Hankow-Canton Railway. This was about the time that strikes were being organized on the Chinese railways following a successful one on the Peking-Hankow line in May 1922. Sympathy for the railroad workers encouraged Ch'en to join first the Socialist Youth League and then the CCP that year, thereby making him one of the earliest members of the Communist Party. Returning to his native Hunan, he participated (in the words of his obituary) in the "national salvation movement by the students in Changsha."

Ch'en soon returned to his military career, entering a military school in 1922 in Canton, then the revolutionary center of China. In the late spring of 1924 he enrolled in another Canton military school, the newly opened Whampoa Military Academy headed by Chiang Kai-shek. His classmates included Hsu Hsiang-ch'ien, Hsiao Ching-kuang, Tso Ch'üan, and Huang K'o-ch'eng (qq.v.), and serving on the staff were such important Communists (or latter-day Communists) as Chou En-lai and Yeh Chien-ying (qq.v.).

He graduated from the Whampoa infantry course with the first class of cadets in 1925. In the fall of that year he took part in a successful drive by Chiang Kai-shek's forces against Ch'en Chiung-ming called the Second Eastern Expedition. It is reported that Ch'en personally saved Chiang's life during the fighting. This incident was to be recalled ten years later when Ch'en met Chiang under very different circumstances (see below).[1] By the time the campaign ended Ch'en Chiung-ming's forces and several other dissident groups had been defeated.

In August 1926 the Party sent Ch'en Keng to Moscow, where he studied until December. Returning to China in 1927, he joined the Eighth Army of Hunan militarist T'ang Sheng-chih, whose troops fought for the Nationalists in Hunan and Hupeh during the Northern Expedition. Ch'en led a special service battalion. As the summer of 1927 approached and tensions between the CCP and the KMT increased, Ch'en left the Eighth Army for Nanchang, the capital of Kiangsi, to take part in the Communist uprising of August 1. Leaving Hankow in mid-July he arrived in Nanchang on the same boat as Chou En-lai, a leader of the uprising.[2] During the five days the Communists held the city, Ch'en and Li Li-san were given the task of arresting "counterrevolutionaries" and dealing with the Kiangsi Provincial Bank. Concurrently, Ch'en commanded the Sixth Regiment of the Third Division in Ho Lung's 20th Army.[3]

After the Nanchang failure Ch'en was with Ho Lung's troops, which retreated southward to attempt another coup at Swatow in late September 1927 (see under Ho Lung). Ch'en's account of the march south was published in the *Kuang-ming jih-pao* (Kuang-ming daily) of May 26, 1961.[4] When the Red troops got to Juichin in late August, some of Ho's forces commanded by Chou I-ch'ün (q.v.) engaged Nationalist troops in Hui-ch'ang, a small town southwest of Juichin. The Communists took the town for a few days, but during the fighting Ch'en was seriously wounded and was taken to a small mission hospital in Ch'ang-t'ing, Fukien, as the Red army continued south. He was treated by Dr. Fu Lien-chang (q.v.), who saved his life.[5] Ch'en was then sent to a Japanese hospital in Swatow but could not stay there after the Nationalists recaptured the city. He escaped to Hong Kong and then to Shanghai, where he spent the next three years working in the Communist underground. Using the alias Wang, he seems to have been a key figure in intelligence and counterintelligence work against the Nationalists.

In early 1931 Ch'en was sent to join his Whampoa classmate Hsu Hsiang-ch'ien, the commander of the Red Army units in the Oyüwan Soviet in the Hupeh-Honan-Anhwei border area. Ch'en assumed command of the 38th Regiment, a component of the Fourth Army's 13th Division, but he was later placed in command of the Fourth Army's 12th Division. Chiang Kai-shek's Fourth Annihilation Campaign, begun in mid-1932, had serious consequences for the Oyüwan Communists. Ch'en was wounded in the leg in the early fall, and when Hsu's forces began their withdrawal in October 1932, Ch'en began the march toward northern Szechwan as chief-of-staff of Hsu's forces, now known as the Fourth Front Army. However, he was soon forced to leave his troops and, after a series of misadventures and hardships, he made his way to Shanghai in late 1932 or early 1933. Ch'en gave an account of the next stage of his career to Edgar Snow in 1936, an account that substantially agrees with another one published in a PLA journal in 1961 (after Ch'en death).[6] While seeking medical attention in Shanghai in early 1933, he was recognized by renegade Communist Ku Shun-chang and turned over to the Nationalist police. His fellow prisoners included an old friend from Canton, Liao Ch'eng-chih, and an important early Communist, Lo Teng-hsien (qq.v.). He was sent to Nanking and then Nanchang, where he allegedly refused an offer made personally by Chiang Kai-shek to join the Nationalists. Returned to Nanking, Ch'en escaped and immediately made his way to the central soviet area in Kiangsi.

Having reached Juichin, Ch'en was given command of a division and was president of the Red Army School (Hung-chün hsueh-hsiao), not to be confused with the more important Red Army Academy (Hung-chün ta-hsueh). A year later he set out on the Long March as commander of the Red Cadres' Regiment (Kan-pu t'uan), with Sung Jen-ch'iung (q.v.) as his political commissar. His unit was drawn largely from cadres of "two military academies" (presumably those mentioned above), and it had the task of "protecting the leaders and organizations" of the Party Central Committee, including Mao Tse-tung.[7] One description of the Long March indicates that Ch'en took part in some of the strategy conferences that included Mao.[8]

Having arrived in north Shensi in late 1935, Ch'en was placed in charge of the First Division that was subordinate to Lin Piao's First Army Corps. In early 1936 he led his Division on the "anti-Japanese" thrust into Shansi, where the Communists engaged the forces of Shansi Governor Yen Hsi-shan and Nationalist troops sent to aid Yen. This foray into Shansi was designed in part to obtain men and supplies for the badly depleted Red Army units (see under Liu Chih-tan, who was killed in this campaign).[9] A year later, after war with Japan began in mid-1937, the Communists reorganized their armies. In north China they created the Eighth Route Army comprising three divisions, one of which was the

129th commanded by Liu Po-ch'eng. Ch'en was placed under Liu's division as commander of the 386th Brigade, with Hsieh Fu-chih (q.v.) as his political commissar. From this time until he was sent to the Korean War in 1951 Ch'en remained on Liu's staff, participating in many important battles during the Sino-Japanese War and the postwar conflict with the Nationalists. In the earlier period he fought in Shansi, Honan, Hopeh, and Shantung. Units of the 386th Brigade penetrated Shantung as early as the spring of 1938, arriving in the Liao-ch'eng area in west Shantung (north of the Yellow River) in May. Later that year other units of the brigade may have come from southern Hopeh, occupying northern Shantung farther to the east and making contact with the local guerrillas in the Lo-ling area. From August to December 1940 Ch'en's forces participated in the "100 Regiments Offensive," a major campaign in five north China provinces against the Japanese. Communications networks were the special target and by August 1940 members of Liu Po-ch'eng's 129th Division, including Ch'en's brigade, had succeeded in cutting the Peking-Hankow Railroad.[10]

From about 1940 Ch'en was commander of the T'ai-yueh Military District in Shansi. The district was one of two important military divisions of the territory controlled by the 129th Division and organized politically as the Shansi-Hopeh-Shantung-Honan Border Region (see under Hsieh Fu-chih). In the T'ai-yueh District, Ch'en came in contact with other important Party officials who were later to become members of the top elite, including economic specialist Po I-po and Party organization expert An Tzu-wen (qq.v.). Ch'en's lengthy service in the Red Army was acknowledged at the Seventh National Party Congress held in Yenan (April–June 1945), when he was made an alternate member of the Central Committee. The next year he represented the Communists on the field team sent to Taiyuan, the Shansi capital, to implement the terms of the January 1946 Cease Fire Agreement which had been worked out through the mediation efforts of U.S. Special Envoy George C. Marshall. The various field teams, each of which had American, Nationalist, and Communist representatives, were responsible to the Peking Executive Headquarters, where Yeh Chien-ying (q.v.) was the chief Communist representative. The Communists did not then have personal military ranks, but at the Taiyuan field headquarters Ch'en held the simulated rank of lieutenant-general.

Heavy fighting between the Nationalists and Communists began in mid-1946 and the cease-fire arrangements were abandoned by all sides early in 1947. Ch'en returned to his 386th Brigade, which in the ensuing civil war con-

tinued to operate under Liu Po-ch'eng's army. Both forces underwent a series of name changes. The 129th Division became the Shansi-Hopeh-Shantung-Honan PLA and the 386th Brigade became its Fourth Column. Sometime in 1947 the former became the Central Plains Liberation Army and the latter the Fourth Army Corps, and finally, in early 1949, the Central Plains Liberation Army became the Second Field Army. Each of these changes coincided with the expansion of Communist-held territory. After participating in the unsuccessful defense of Yenan against the Nationalists in March 1947, Ch'en's Brigade was with Liu's forces as they began to advance rapidly to the east in August. Part of Ch'en's troops, apparently now called the Fourth Column of the Shansi-Hopeh-Shantung-Honan PLA (to correspond with their new location), crossed the Yellow River and advanced into western Honan; they "wiped out more than 40,000 enemy troops and built base areas on the Honan-Shensi-Hupeh border and in southern Shensi, completely isolating Loyang, the enemy's strategic centre in western Honan Province, and threatening T'ung-kuan"[11] (on the Yellow River where Shensi, Shansi, and Honan converge). This move was coordinated with the rest of Liu's army, enabling it to reach the Ta-pieh Mountains on the borders of Hupeh, Honan, and Anhwei, which became the heart of the Central Plains Liberated Area. During 1948 Ch'en took part in attacks in Honan and in the Huai-hai area (the Huai River basin of northern Kiangsu and Anhwei). At this juncture Ch'en was temporarily assigned to Ch'en I's (q.v.) Third Field Army, and in May 1949 he was with the troops that marched into Shanghai. From then until July he headed the Public Security Department under the Shanghai Military Control Commission. Returning to Liu Po-ch'eng's Second Field Army, he served briefly as a member of the Changsha (Hunan) Military Control Commission after the city was surrendered to the Communists in August. In the latter part of the year, serving now as a deputy commander of Liu's Second Field Army as well as commander of its Fourth Corps, Ch'en took part in the thrust into the southwest. Accompanied by his political commissar, Sung Jen-ch'iung, Ch'en's units captured Kunming, the Yunnan capital, in February 1950. A few days later, in early March, Ch'en was appointed chairman of the Kunming Military Control Commission and in the same month he also became the provincial governor. In the provincial Party apparatus, Sung Jen-ch'iung was made the ranking secretary, with Ch'en as his second secretary. By this time Ch'en was also commander of the Yunnan Military District and deputy commander of the Southwest Military Region, and in July 1950 he was also appointed to membership on the Southwest Military and Administrative Committee. This impressive array of positions in the Yunnan and the southwest administrations placed Ch'en in the echelon just below the senior leaders in the area—Teng Hsiao-p'ing, Liu Po-ch'eng, and Ho Lung.

Ch'en officially retained some of the above positions until the 1954–1955 period, but he did not remain long in Yunnan. In 1951 he was transferred to the Korean battlefront, where he and Teng Hua (q.v.) were deputy commanders of the "Chinese People's Volunteers" (CPV) under Commander P'eng Te-huai. Ch'en and Teng had previously served together in the First Army Corps during the Yenan period. Ch'en was seldom mentioned in the press during the next three years, although he is known to have been back in Peking briefly in October 1952 when he addressed a meeting to commemorate the second anniversary of the CPV's entry into the Korean War. He remained in Korea until shortly after the armistice in July 1953. Returning to Peking, he was placed in charge (by February 1954) of an unnamed department subordinate to the People's Revolutionary Military Council, the military advisory arm of the PRC Government. The Council was abolished in September 1954 with the advent of the constitutional government and the creation of the National Defense Council (NDC). Ch'en became a member of the NDC, an organ that meets rarely but has considerable prestige. A far more important appointment was given to Ch'en shortly thereafter when he was named a deputy chief-of-staff of the PLA General Staff, a position he held until his death. When Chief-of-Staff Su Yü was absent from his post from the spring of 1956 to early 1957, Ch'en served as acting chief-of-staff.

In 1955 the Communists created personal military ranks and made their first awards for distinguished military service. Ch'en received all three top military honors: the Orders of August First, Independence and Freedom, and Liberation. He was also made a senior (four-star) general in the PLA, a rank given to only a few officers. A year later (September 1956) he was promoted to full membership on the Central Committee at the Eighth National Party Congress. From May 1957 to November 1958 Ch'en was a member of the State Council's Scientific Planning Commission, and in September 1959, during a partial reorganization of the government, he was appointed a vice-minister of National Defense, a post he still held when, at the age of 58, he died suddenly in Shanghai on March 16, 1961, of a heart disease.

Ch'en's 39 years of service in the Communist movement were acknowledged in funeral and memorial services. In Peking on March 25, Chief-of-Staff Lo Jui-ch'ing eulogized Ch'en's career at services attended by virtually every top Communist leader. Little is known of Ch'en's personal life except that he was survived by his wife, Fu Ya, and sons and daughters.

1. Edgar Snow, *Random Notes on Red China, 1936–1945* (Cambridge, Mass., 1957), pp. 94–95; *SCMM* 281, pp. 1–11.

2. J. Guillermaz, "The Nanchang Uprising," *The China Quarterly,* no. 11:164 (July–September 1962).

3. *Ibid.;* Wei Hung-yun, ed., *"Pa-i" ch'i-i* (The August First Uprising; Wuhan, 1957), p. 12.

4. Guillermaz.

5. Nym Wales, *Red Dust* (Stanford, Calif., 1952), p. 171.

6. Snow, pp. 92–99; *SCMM* 281.

7. *The Long March, Eyewitness Accounts* (Peking, 1963), p. 51.

8. Ch'en Ch'ang-feng, *On the Long March with Chairman Mao* (Peking, 1959), p. 68.

9. *Shan-hsi ko-ming tou-cheng hui-i-lu* (Reminiscences of revolutionary struggles in Shansi; Taiyuan [?], preface dated 1961), p. 32.

10. Chalmers A. Johnson, *Peasant Nationalism and Communist Power* (Stanford, Calif., 1962), p. 58.

11. *Selected Works of Mao Tse-tung* (Peking, 1961), IV, 216.

Ch'en Kung-po

(1892–1946; Canton, Kwangtung). A founding member, CCP; leader, Canton branch, CCP.

Ch'en Kung-po's direct participation in the CCP was limited to its first two or three years, but his career highlights the factionalism within Chinese Communism in its formative stage. He is usually identified as the key figure in the Canton faction of the CCP, which favored an alliance with Kwangtung general Ch'en Chiung-ming over an alliance with Sun Yat-sen, but for the rest of his life he sought to refute and obliterate this episode, doubly embarrassing because his subsequent career came to be identified with the KMT of Sun Yat-sen, whose followers quickly apotheosized him while they simultaneously condemned Ch'en Chiung-ming for "betraying" the father of the Chinese Revolution.

Ch'en Kung-po was born in Canton in October 1892 into a Hakka family. His father was a leader of the anti-Manchu secret society, the *San-ho hui,* and played a prominent role in the unsuccessful revolt of 1907, for which he was arrested and not released until after the 1911 Revolution. In his youth Ch'en combined a classical education with martial calisthenics, the latter a hallmark of Chinese secret societies. In 1908 he entered a modern school, the Yü Ts'ai Academy in Canton, where he studied English for three years. In 1914 he entered the Canton Law College, graduating in the summer of 1917.

Then he went to Peking to enroll in the Philosophy Department at Peking University, where he met two fellow-provincials and future comrades, T'an P'ing-shan and T'an Chih-t'ang. He appears to have divorced himself from much of the organized student activity, and the May Fourth Movement practically passed him by, although he followed the events as a reporter.

Ch'en graduated in the summer of 1920 and with the two T'an's returned to Canton. With a capital of 3,000 Chinese dollars they published a newspaper called *Kuang-tung Ch'ün-pao* (Kwangtung masses). Ch'en was editor-in-chief, and T'an P'ing-shan and T'an Chih-t'ang were the news and literary editors, respectively. At this point his fateful connection with Ch'en Chiung-ming began when the latter, in cooperation with Sun Yat-sen, was on the verge of retaking Canton from the Kwangsi generals. Apparently wanting to turn the *Ch'ün-pao* into his own mouthpiece, Ch'en Chiung-ming offered a monthly subsidy of $300 to the editors in return for the appointment of two of his protégés. The negotiation was effected, although Ch'en Kung-po later asserted that he declined the subsidy except as a salary for the two men who were put in charge of details of the enterprise while Ch'en Kung-po and T'an P'ing-shan each held separate teaching positions. Ch'en and his colleagues may have considered Ch'en Chiung-ming's offer highly desirable in view of the fact that, imbued as they were with the "new culture," Ch'en Chiung-ming had gained a wide reputation as an enlightened administrator and a progressive general while he was based in Changchou, southern Fukien.

Sometime in 1920 Ch'en Kung-po and his *Ch'ün-pao* colleagues met two Russian agents, disguised as merchants, who proposed that the group should establish a Communist Party in Kwangtung, starting with a youth league to spread the ideas of socialism. Sharing the widely prevalent interest in the Russian Revolution, and discovering that Ch'en Tu-hsiu had formed the first Communist cell in Shanghai in May with Comintern assistance, Ch'en Kung-po and his friends readily accepted the proposal and began recruiting teachers and students in the schools where they taught. The burgeoning movement was reinforced by the arrival of Ch'en Tu-hsiu himself in December 1920 as provincial commissioner of education in Ch'en Chiung-ming's Kwangtung Government (see under P'eng P'ai). Ch'en Tu-hsiu appointed Ch'en Kung-po to be chief of a publicity bureau with the purpose of promoting Communist propaganda and organizational work. As in other centers, the Kwangtung Communist group now entered a period of bitter struggle with anarchists, converting some and dissociating themselves from the rest, but the problem persisted for some time because Canton was an anarchist stronghold.

In July 1921 Ch'en attended the founding CCP Congress in Shanghai. Comintern agent Maring was present, and as he had instructions to effect in China the Second Comintern thesis of a united front with the national revolutionary movement, he had evidently placed the question of the CCP's attitude toward other political parties on the agenda. Some accounts—Chang Kuo-t'ao's and Ch'en T'an-ch'iu's, for instance—make it appear that the Congress resolution on this subject was entirely in accord with the Comintern line, namely, that the CCP should support Sun Yat-sen's revolution while pursuing independent proletarian goals. On the other hand, Ch'en's account of 1924 (in his master's thesis at Columbia University; see below) records an attitude of "independence, aggression, and exclusion" on the part of the Congress; it was felt neither the Northern Government of Hsu Shih-ch'ang nor the Southern Government of Sun Yat-sen was worthy of support, and that both were equally responsible for popular misery by prolonged civil war. In his 1943 account Ch'en Kung-po took pains to record that he objected to the passage of the resolution that criticized Sun Yat-sen, and after the resolution was passed, he sought out other delegates to repair the situation. Some accounts also linked Ch'en with Li Han-chün (another CCP founder) in resisting the impatience of others to get down to practical work and to carry out the program of organizing the proletariat in order to seize power under the guidance of the CCP. Ch'en's view that members should concentrate on theoretical study and not immediately rush into practical activity represented a distinct pattern in the Communist movement at the time and one with which Li Ta-chao also appears to have been identified. Some evidence indicates that Comintern rejection of this view led to several early withdrawals (see under Li Han-chün), though perhaps not in Ch'en's particular case.

Returning to Canton, Ch'en was placed in charge of the Organization Department of the Kwangtung CCP branch; T'an P'ing-shan was secretary, and T'an Chih-t'ang headed the Propaganda Department. The branch concentrated on agitation among labor unions and was active in the Hong Kong seamen's strike of January–March 1922 (which was largely led by the KMT; see under Su Chao-cheng).

Meanwhile, differences between Sun Yat-sen and Ch'en Chiung-ming broke into the open in the spring of 1922. The latent rivalry between them, persistently fomented by followers on either side, was combined with a difference of strategy: Ch'en Chiung-ming, reflecting widely prevalent localist (Kwangtung) sentiments and no doubt also mindful of his own power interests, openly espoused federalism whereby a provincial regime would occupy itself solely with the welfare of Kwangtung. He planned to set up a model provincial government for other provinces to emulate, which in turn would serve as a base for future expansion into other provinces. On the other hand, Sun Yat-sen insisted on national unification by military force (no doubt aware of the weakness of his own authority, inasmuch as his sphere of authority almost coincided with Ch'en's provincial government, which controlled virtually all sources of power in Kwangtung), and he took steps to enter into an alliance with Manchurian warlord Chang Tso-lin. Chang was then preparing a campaign to eliminate his powerful rival Wu P'ei-fu, who also bade fair to vie with Sun Yat-sen for claims to national leadership. Sun was to attack Wu from the south and Chang from the north. Sun's scheme, however, would have committed the meager provincial resources of Kwangtung to a national undertaking and was therefore deeply resented by the local population, particularly the commercial class.

The conflict between Ch'en Chiung-ming and Sun Yat-sen presented the Canton branch of the CCP with a dilemma: whether to support Ch'en or Sun. Initially, the Party Center in Shanghai was prepared to wait and see, but it soon came out in support of Sun; the position of Ch'en Kung-po and the Canton branch is obscure and remains a puzzle in view of the conflicting evidence. In his 1943 account, Ch'en states that about this time he was losing interest in Communism and had made up his mind to pursue further studies in the United States. He denied he was in any way involved with Ch'en Chiung-ming and was therefore outraged when Ch'en Tu-hsiu demanded his presence in Shanghai to answer charges that he was assisting Ch'en. Refusing to obey Ch'en Tu-hsiu's order, he convened a conference of the Canton branch, whose members were also enraged and proposed making the Kwangtung CCP Committee independent of Shanghai. However, other accounts—for example, Chang Kuo-t'ao's and Ch'en T'an ch'iu's—assert that Ch'en Kung-po persisted in helping Ch'en Chiung-ming despite repeated warnings from Shanghai; he and others continued to work for the Ch'ün pao and wrote in favor of Ch'en Chiung-ming. After the Second CCP Congress in July 1922 the Central Committee again warned the Canton branch about its intransigence and, failing to secure its compliance, finally expelled T'an Chih-t'ang, suspended T'an P'ing-shan from his duties as secretary, and delivered Ch'en Kung-po a stern rebuke, whereupon the latter withdrew from the CCP. The CCP formally expelled him in January 1923.

Once again, judging from the context of the times, it would not have been surprising if Ch'en Kung-po and his colleagues had in fact sided with Ch'en Chiung-ming. The latter seemed the wiser and more realistic to them, and his achievements as an administrator in Kwangtung were

impressive to Chinese and foreigners alike. In the eyes of many foreigners and Chinese, Sun was a perpetual troublemaker, using Kwangtung's resources for goals too far out of reach. Few foresaw that Sun Yat-sen would stage one more of his many political comebacks and that after his death he would become canonized by a movement with which Ch'en Kung-po himself, only three years later, would become identified and in which power and seniority depended to a great extent on one's degree of loyalty and length of association with the deceased leader.

In November 1922 Ch'en sailed for the United States. From February 1923 to February 1925 he studied at Columbia University, where he wrote the above-mentioned master's thesis. Returning home in the spring of 1925, he joined the KMT and was in close association with Liao Chung-k'ai. After the latter's death in August he worked closely with Wang Ching-wei. In fact, Ch'en was associated with Wang for almost the whole of the next 20 years, first in the Wuhan government in 1927, then in the anti-Chiang "Reorganization Clique" in 1928–1932, and finally in the Japanese-sponsored government in 1939–1945, excepting only the 1932–1935 period when he served in Chiang's Nanking government. At the end of the War he was extradited from Japan and executed on June 3, 1946, at Soochow.

Ch'en's master's thesis at Columbia, entitled "The Communist Movement in China" was edited by C. Martin Wilbur and published in monograph form in 1960 by Columbia's East Asian Institute. The appendices to Ch'en's thesis contain important documents on the early years of the Communist movement, and Wilbur's introduction provides the best brief source for Ch'en's career.

Ch'en Man-yuan

(1907–   ; Meng-shan hsien, Kwangsi). Vice-minister, State Farms and Land Reclamation; alternate member, CCP Central Committee.

Red Army veteran Ch'en Man-yuan made the Long March and served in Hopeh and the Shansi-Suiyuan border area during the Sino-Japanese War. He was a key Party official in Kwangsi from 1949 until 1957 when he was denounced for the mismanagement of food supplies. He reemerged in 1960 as president of Peking Agricultural University, and since late 1963 he has been a vice-minister of State Farms and Land Reclamation. Ch'en has been an alternate member of the Central Committee since 1956.

Ch'en was born in Meng-shan hsien in eastern Kwangsi, some 70 miles south of Kweilin. Ch'en's family of wealthy landlords sent him to a middle school in Wu-chou, an important Kwangsi trading center near the Kwangtung border situated not far south of Meng-shan. While attending the middle school Ch'en is said to have had family disagreements, and when his father cut off his allowance he ran away to join the Communists. Ch'en joined the Seventh Red Army, commanded by Chang Yun-i (q.v.), which was organized in Kwangsi about 1929. The army provided the military support for the small Communist soviet established at Lung-chou in southwest Kwangsi near the Vietnamese border. Sometime prior to mid-1930 the Party headquarters, then under the direction of Li Li-san, ordered this army to join other Red forces which were being mobilized in central China for an attack upon the major industrial cities. On its way north the Seventh Army met with serious defeats and only a handful of survivors under Chang Yun-i were able to make their way to Juichin, the capital of the Chinese Soviet Republic (formed in November 1931), where Mao Tse-tung and Chu Te had their headquarters. Ch'en made his way to Juichin with the remnants of the Seventh Army. In Juichin, Ch'en enrolled at the Red Army Academy, which graduated its first class in 1933, and he was among the Academy cadets who made the Long March from Kiangsi to the northwest in the fall of 1934.

Not long after Mao Tse-tung and his troops reached north Shensi in October 1935, Ch'en was posted in the 15th Army Corps (see under Hsu Hai-tung), which had been organized shortly before Mao reached the northwest. It was formed from groups of indigenous Shensi guerrillas under the command of Liu Chih-tan (q.v.) and others, plus the forces that Communist military leader Hsu Hai-tung had been ordered to bring to north Shensi from the Hupeh-Honan-Anhwei (Oyüwan) Soviet.

During the early years of the Sino-Japanese War Ch'en was a regimental commander in the Eighth Route Army's 115th Division, which was led by Lin Piao and Nieh Jung-chen. Soon after the war started in mid-1937 this division moved from the Shensi headquarters into the Wu-t'ai Mountains of eastern Shansi near the Hopeh border. Nieh, the acting commander, divided the new base into four sub-divisions: the main headquarters in Wu-t'ai hsien, Shansi, a base in I and Man-ch'eng hsien, western Hopeh, and two others in P'ing-shan hsien and T'ang-hsien, also in western Hopeh. Ch'en commanded the T'ang-hsien base, headquartered about 50 miles west of Paoting and not far west of the Pinghan (Peking-Hankow) Railroad. When the Shansi-Chahar-Hopeh (Chin-Ch'a-Chi) Border Region was established in early 1938 (see under Sung Shao-wen) it contained two distinct areas, one of which was Nieh's east Shansi–west Hopeh base. The other part of the border region, composed of approximately 29 hsien on the plains of central Hopeh, was protected by Manchurian

military leader Lü Cheng-ts'ao (q.v.), who had organized strong anti-Japanese resistance there.[1] Lü was not a Communist initially. However, when he began to suffer military defeats, he sought assistance from Nieh's headquarters and soon joined the Party. In late 1937 Nieh despatched political agents working in nearby hsien to affiliate with Lü's forces. T'ang-hsien was not far from Lü's headquarters and thus Ch'en may have become associated with Lü at this time. In any case, by the fall of 1943, when Lü was transferred to Ho Lung's Shansi-Suiyuan base (see under Ho Lung) to replace Ho as the commander there, Ch'en was identified as Lü's chief-of-staff. The Shansi-Suiyuan Military Region was strategically important to the Communists because it was a communications link between Yenan and other military fronts. When American journalist Harrison Forman visited the Shansi-Suiyuan Region in late 1944, he interviewed both Lü and Ch'en on the military situation there.[2] His conversations with Ch'en suggest that by 1944 he might have been in the district for a few years; if so, he would have preceded Lü there.

When the war ended Ch'en remained in the northwest at least until the spring of 1946,[3] but after that there is conflicting information concerning his whereabouts. Some reports suggest that he joined the Communist units fighting in the central plains, but others claim that he went to Manchuria to serve in Lin Piao's forces. In any event, he was with Lin's Fourth Field Army by 1949, serving as a deputy commander of an army corps. Lin's men pushed south to Kwangtung and Kwangsi by the end of 1949. Prior to these last military thrusts into south China, the Communists convened the first session of the CPPCC in September 1949 to inaugurate the central government. Ch'en attended as a delegate of the South China PLA and served on the *ad hoc* committee chaired by Chou En-lai to draft the Common Program, the precursor of the 1954 Constitution. When the session closed he was named to membership on the First National Committee of the CPPCC, but he was not re-elected to the Second Committee formed in late 1954.

Immediately after the meetings in Peking, Ch'en returned to the south to participate in the formation of civil administrations in the wake of Communist victories over the Nationalists. When Kweilin, in Ch'en's native Kwangsi, fell on November 22, 1949, he became chairman of the Kweilin Municipal Military Control Commission, apparently only briefly holding the position. In early December he was appointed a vice-governor of Kwangsi under Governor Chang Yun-i, Ch'en's former military superior in the Seventh Army back in the 1920's. (This assignment presumably meant that he was transferred to Nanning, the capital of Kwangsi.) Ch'en also held senior positions on two of the more important committees of the Kwangsi Government. From November 1950 he chaired the provincial Land Reform Committee, and in the following month he became a vice-chairman of the Finance and Economics Committee; he was promoted to chairman in January 1953, replacing Chang Yun-i.

Besides holding his Kwangsi government posts, Ch'en was also one of the top provincial Party leaders. By 1951 he was second secretary of the Party Committee, another post he held under Chang Yun-i, and after mid-1952 he was the acting secretary. Although his principal responsibilities were to the Party and the Kwangsi Government from the early 1950's, he also served from 1951 to 1954 as political commissar of the Kwangsi Military District. In addition, Ch'en was a member of the multi-provincial Central-South Military and Administrative Committee from its establishment in February 1950. When it was reorganized into the Central-South Administrative Committee in January 1953, he was reappointed, serving until it went out of existence in November 1954.

By 1952–53, Governor and Party Secretary Chang Yun-i was infrequently reported in Kwangsi, and Ch'en began to assume most of the important duties in the province. As already noted, he was the acting Party secretary by mid-1952 and by the fall of 1953 he was also serving as the acting governor. In 1955 Ch'en formally replaced Chang as the ranking Party secretary and at approximately the same time relinquished most of his duties within the Kwangsi Government. Although he had been serving as the acting governor, he was not elected a member of the Kwangsi Provincial People's Council until in February 1955 when the government was reorganized. The new governor elected at that time was Wei Kuo-ch'ing (q.v.), another native of Kwangsi and a member of Kwangsi's large ethnic minority, the Chuang. In February 1955, Ch'en also became chairman of the First Kwangsi Committee of the CPPCC.

At the national level, Ch'en participated in the formation of the constitutional government in 1954. He chaired the Kwangsi Provincial Committee, formed in 1953 to supervise the provincial elections. Subsequently, he was elected a deputy from Kwangsi to the First NPC, which met initially in September 1954. Far more important, however, was his participation in the Eighth Party Congress in September 1956. He submitted a report to the congress on agricultural production in Kwangsi, and at the close of the proceedings was elected an alternate member of the Party Central Committee. In the remaining months of 1956 and the first half of 1957, the press regularly reported his activities in Kwangsi. For example, in April 1957 he met with a group of "democratic personages" to discuss Mao Tsetung's February 1957 speech on the "correct

handling of contradictions." A few days later he spoke on the same subject to a meeting of cadres working for the Kwangsi Government.

Then, quite suddenly, in mid-June 1957 Ch'en was removed from the Kwangsi Government and as the Party first secretary. He and 10 other officials were charged with failure to arrange for the adequate distribution of food supplied by the government to overcome local shortages in the spring of 1956—that is, one year before his denunciation and removal. Unlike most cases resulting in dismissals, the charges against Ch'en and his colleagues seemed to be devoid of ideological content; their mistakes were presented as misfeasance. Ch'en remained completely out of the news until 1960, being replaced as Kwangsi first Party secretary by Liu Chien-hsun (q.v.) by September 1957. Although stripped of all his Kwangsi posts, technically he continued to hold alternate membership on the Party Central Committee.

After two and a half years of apparent inactivity, Ch'en was brought to Peking to become president of the Peking Agricultural University (January 1960). Virtually nothing was heard about him in the early 1960's, but in December 1963 he was appointed a vice-minister of State Farms and Land Reclamation, a ministry headed by Party veteran Wang Chen. Following this new assignment, he was removed from Peking Agricultural University (June 1964). He received still another position in the fall of 1964 when he was elected a deputy from Szechwan to the Third NPC, which held its initial session in December 1964–January 1965. Despite these posts, Ch'en's political career seems to have been permanently damaged as a result of his troubles in Kwangsi in 1956–57.

Two examples of Ch'en's writings published in his most active period are: "Implement the Principles of Being Concerned about Life of the Masses, and Pay Attention to the Working Style in Our Work," *JMJP*, January 27, 1954; and, "How Did Socialist Agricultural Cooperativization Expand in Kwangsi Province?" *Hsüeh-hsi* (Study), June 2, 1956.

1. Chalmers A. Johnson, *Peasant Nationalism and Communist Power* (Stanford, Calif., 1962), p. 102.

2. Harrison Forman, *Report from Red China* (New York, 1945), pp. 201–202.

3. *"Szu-pa" pei-nan lieh-shih chi-nien-ts'e* (In memory of the martyrs who died in the accident of "April Eighth"; Chungking [?], 1946), p. 537.

Ch'en P'ei-hsien

(1911–   ; Foochow, Fukien). First secretary, Shanghai CCP Committee; alternate member, CCP Central Committee.

Ch'en P'ei-hsien began his career with the CCP in the Kiangsi Soviet in the early thirties.

He remained behind in central-south China in 1934 when the Long March began, and during the Sino-Japanese War he fought with the Communists' New Fourth Army, which operated in east-central China. From the early 1950's he has been a ranking official in Shanghai and, following the death of K'o Ch'ing-shih in 1965, Ch'en became first secretary of the Shanghai Party Committee.

Ch'en was born in 1911 in Foochow, the capital of Fukien. By the early 1930's he was serving in the Kiangsi Soviet as secretary of the "Children's Bureau" (Erh-t'ung chü) under the Party Central Committee.[1] He was among those ordered to remain behind to conduct guerrilla warfare in central-south China after the main Communist forces led by Chu Te and Mao Tse-tung left on the Long March in the fall of 1934. Shortly afterward, Nationalist pressures forced Ch'en and others to fight their way out of the Central Soviet area; over 80 per cent of the 1,800-man force was annihilated by the time it had reached the Kiangsi-Kwantung border area over the winter of 1934–35. By early 1935, Ch'en was serving as secretary of the Communist Youth (Shao-kung) organization, which was subordinate to the South Kiangsi Provincial CCP Committee.[2] In the early spring of 1935 important Party leaders Hsiang Ying and Ch'en I (qq.v.) arrived in the area to take command. For the next two years, Ch'en P'ei-hsien served in this area as a guerrilla leader and Party organizer. The Communist forces were small, badly armed, and largely ineffective. One measure of their ineffectiveness as guerrilla leaders comes from the fact that some of the most important leaders, including Yang Shang-k'uei (q.v.), were forced to take up simple trades in order to make a living. Ch'en and his colleagues were also completely out of contact with the main Communist forces; it was nine months after the completion of the Long March that they first heard of it, and for over two years they were out of contact with the Party Central Committee.[3]

About the time the Sino-Japanese War began in mid-1937, Ch'en went north to Kiangsu where he became secretary of the Su-chung (Central Kiangsu) District CCP Committee, a post he held until the Communist victory in 1949. As such, he was an important political figure in the New Fourth Army area of operations, and as of early 1941 he was known to be taking instructions directly from Liu Shao-ch'i, the political commissar for the entire New Fourth Army.[4] (For a discussion of the Central Kiangsu District, see under Su Yü, the military commander.) In addition to his Su-chung post, Ch'en was also connected with the "Southeast Youth Bureau," which may have been subordinate to the Party's Southeast Bureau headed by Hsiang Ying.

Ch'en remained in Kiangsu during the civil war with the Nationalists in the late forties, and when the Communist armies captured Wu-hsi

(Wusih) in the spring of 1949 he was made chairman of the Wu-hsi Military Control Commission. Until Kiangsu was restored to its traditional boundaries in November 1952, the province was divided into northern and southern sectors. Ch'en was the top Communist official in southern Kiangsu from the 1949 takeover until 1952. He headed the South Kiangsu District CCP Committee and was also political commissar of the Military District. The governmental organ, with its capital at Wu-hsi, was known as the South Kiangsu People's Administrative Office (SKPAO); Ch'en was a member of the SKPAO from its formation in late 1949 and was also chairman of the SKPAO Finance and Economics Committee. Lesser posts held by Ch'en from 1949 included membership on both the Standing Committee of the South Kiangsu General Labor Union and the South Kiangsu Branch of the Sino-Soviet Friendship Association.

Although he worked mainly in south Kiangsu in the early years of the PRC, he also held positions in organizations at the national and regional level. He was a Central Committee member of the nationwide New Democratic Youth League from April 1949 until mid-1953. And when the regional government organ known as the East China Military and Administrative Committee (ECMAC) was established under the chairmanship of Jao Shu-shih (q.v.) in January 1950, Ch'en was appointed as a member. He was reappointed in December 1952 when the ECMAC was reorganized into the East China Administrative Committee (ECAC), holding this position until the dissolution of the ECAC in 1954.

Ch'en was transferred to Shanghai in early 1952 and has held ranking posts there from that time. For a brief time in 1952 he was third deputy political commissar of the Shanghai-Woosung Garrison. More important was his position as fourth secretary of the Shanghai CCP Committee, a post that placed him under First Secretary Ch'en I, Second Secretary Liu Hsiao, and Third Secretary Liu Ch'ang-sheng (qq.v.). By early 1955 he was elevated to second secretary, a post that now placed him under the new Shanghai first secretary, K'o Ch'ing-shih (q.v.). Ch'en's title was redesignated as secretary in the early fall of 1956, but in fact he remained as the second-ranking Party official in Shanghai under K'o. By 1954 Ch'en was also a member of the Party's East China Bureau, a post he presumably held until the Bureau was abolished in mid-1955. In February 1955 he was given an additional assignment as a member of the Shanghai Municipal People's Council, a position to which he was re-elected in January 1957 and November 1958.

Ch'en attended the Party's Eighth National Congress in September 1956 and spoke on the use of the "working masses" to improve industry. At the close of the Congress he was elected an alternate member of the Party Central Committee. In November 1958 he received still another post in Shanghai when he was elected chairman of the Second Shanghai Committee of the CPPCC, and in July 1962 he was named to chair the Third Committee. From mid-1960 to about mid-1964 he was also political commissar of the PLA Shanghai Garrison Command. Ch'en has also been associated with the Party's East China Bureau, which was re-established in accordance with a decision taken at the Party Central Committee's Ninth Plenum in January 1961. By May 1963 he was identified as one of the secretaries of the Bureau, then headed by K'o Ch'ing-shih.

Since the mid-fifties Ch'en has been constantly reported in the press, very often in connection with the many foreigners who visit Shanghai. On many occasions he acted for Shanghai CCP First Secretary K'o Ch'ing-shih when the latter was not in Shanghai. Then, when K'o died in April 1965, Ch'en replaced him as first secretary, a position he continues to hold. His only known trip abroad was in April–May 1961 when he led a delegation to Leningrad to attend May Day celebrations. His contributions to the press include two articles for the Party's leading journal, *Hung-ch'i* (Red flag, issues of October 16, 1959, and February 16, 1960).

1. Yang Shang-k'uei, *Hung-se Kan-Yueh pien* (The Red Kiangsi-Kwangtung border [region]; Peking, 1962), p. 25.

2. *Ibid.,* pp. 25–26.

3. *Ibid.,* p. 127.

4. Chalmers A. Johnson, *Peasant Nationalism and Communist Power* (Stanford, Calif., 1962), p. 230.

Ch'en Po-ta

(1904–   ; Hui-an hsien, Fukien). Ideologue and "interpreter" of Mao Tse-tung; vice-president, Academy of Sciences; deputy director, CCP Propaganda Department; Politburo member.

Ch'en Po-ta, the leading interpreter of the "thought of Mao Tse-tung," has been a Communist since the mid-twenties. He was a relatively obscure professor and a member of the Communist underground in north China in the thirties, but he emerged as a leading Maoist ideologue and polemicist in the early forties. A key figure in the Propaganda Department since then, Ch'en was elected to the Central Committee in 1945 and advanced to the Politburo in 1956. He has also been the leading Party official in the Academy of Sciences since the Communists came to power. One of Ch'en's major tasks in the early PRC years was to interpret Mao's contributions to Marxism, and in particular to reconcile them in light of Stalin's writings and policies. A prolific author, Ch'en has ranged in his writings

from anti-KMT tracts to the justification of the "people's communes."

Ch'en was born into a poor peasant family in Hui-an hsien. He graduated from the Chip Bee (Chi-mei) School near Amoy, which Ch'en Chia-keng (better known as Tan Kah-kee) had founded in 1913. Ch'en Chia-keng, a Singapore millionaire who gave considerable assistance to Sun Yat-sen, founded a number of schools in his native Fukien in the early years of the century. Semi-official Communist biographies state that Ch'en Po-ta also attended the "Shanghai Labor University," presumably a reference to Shanghai University, which existed from 1923 to 1925 and produced a number of top Communist leaders (see under Ch'ü Ch'iu-pai).

In the mid-twenties Ch'en worked as a clerk in Fukien army units and in 1927 engaged in political work during the Northern Expedition among forces led by KMT General Chang Chen. That year he joined the CCP and went to Moscow where he enrolled in Sun Yat-sen University (redesignated the Communist University of the Toilers of China during his stay there). According to a biography of Ch'en in *Bol'shaya Sovetskaya Entsiklopedya* (Large Soviet Encyclopedia; vol. 47, April 1957), he returned to China in 1930, after which he engaged in Party and propaganda work in Fukien province and north China, editing Party newspapers and journals. The same source asserts that he was imprisoned in 1931–32 by the KMT, but no further details are supplied. Upon his release he taught philosophy and history at China University (Chung-kuo ta-hsueh) for a few years and worked in the Party underground. Ch'en was at the University in December 1935 when thousands of students in Peking schools demonstrated against KMT policies which they regarded as ineffectual in resisting the steady encroachments of the Japanese into north China. (This student unrest, known as the December Ninth Movement, is described in the biography of Li Ch'ang.) According to an account by a participant in the movement, Ch'en was then a "responsible official" in the Party's North China Bureau and was known by the alias Ch'en Chih-mei.[1]

Ch'en had already begun to write by this time; as early as 1934 he had published *Lun T'an Szu-t'ung* (On T'an Szu-t'ung), but his career as a Party historian and ideologue did not begin until he went to Yenan at the outbreak of war in 1937. He was immediately put to work as an instructor in the Central Party School and he also became director of the Propaganda Department's Research Section. He was a regular contributor to the leading Yenan newspapers and journals and served for a time as Mao Tse-tung's political secretary. His rise to prominence began about 1941 when, while working at the Central Research Institute, he came into conflict with Wang Shih-wei.[2] A prominent Communist writer-translator, Wang opposed the use of literary forms familiar to the masses and accused the Party hierarchy of a variety of faults that are reviewed in the biography of Chou Yang. With the launching of the *cheng-feng* (rectification) movement in 1942, Wang became one of the chief targets of the Maoist ideologues, among whom Ch'en, Chou Yang, Fan Wen-lan, and Ai Szu-ch'i (qq.v.) were the most prominent. In assessing the rise of Mao Tse-tung to supremacy within the CCP, one writer has observed that after 1937 leading policy statements "came more and more from Mao, Chou En-lai, and rising theoreticians Liu Shao-ch'i, Ch'en Po-ta, and Ch'en Yun." In contrast, after the 1942 rectification movement, Ch'en Shao-yü, Chang Wen-t'ien, and Ch'in Pang-hsien (qq.v.), key members of the "28 Bolshevik" group, "lost their voice."[3]

Having successfully carried out the rectification campaign in north Shensi by mid-1942, several key propagandists were sent to other areas to spread the movement. Ch'en was dispatched to Chungking in 1942, where for about a year he was an editor of the Communists' *Hsin-hua jih-pao* (New China daily) and the Sheng-huo (Life) Book Company. He returned to Yenan in 1943 and in the middle of that year wrote a caustic critique of Chiang Kai-shek's famous *China's Destiny*, which had just been published. Ch'en charged that Chiang's political ideas were "fascist" and did no more than preserve the facade of Sun Yat-sen's "three principles." This attack was published in book form in 1948 under the title *Jen-min kung-ti Chiang Kai-shek* (Chiang Kai-shek, the people's enemy). Following his return to Yenan, Ch'en worked in the Party Propaganda Department and wrote five of his more important works. The first two, both written in 1944, were translated a decade later under the titles *Notes on Mao Tse-tung's "Report of an Investigation into the Peasant Movement in Hunan"* and *Notes on Ten Years of Civil War, 1927–1936*. In 1945 he wrote and published *Ch'ieh-kuo ta-tao Yuan Shih-k'ai* (Yuan Shih-k'ai, the traitorous thief). Ch'en's *A Study of Land Rent in Pre-Liberation China* was written in 1945–46, published in 1947, and translated into English several years later. *Chung-kuo szu-ta chia-tsu* (China's four big families), published in 1947, was a propaganda attack on Chiang Kai-shek, T. V. Soong (Sung Tzu-wen), H. H. Kung (K'ung Hsiang-hsi), and the famous brothers of the "C-C" clique (Ch'en Kuo-fu and Ch'en Li-fu).

At the Party's Seventh National Congress, held in Yenan from April to June 1945, Ch'en was elected the third alternate member of the Central Committee. He was elevated to full membership sometime after mid-1946 by which time three full members of the Central Committee had died. Ch'en went to Peking after its sur-render to the Communists in January 1949 and in the spring and summer was very active in organizing the numerous "mass" and professional societies. In July he was one of the founders of both the China New Philosophy Society and the China New Economic Research Society; in the latter he was made chairman of the Preparatory Committee. In the same month he spoke at the All-China Congress of Literary and Art Workers and was elected a vice-chairman of the Preparatory Committee for the China Social Science Workers' Conference. He was also identified in two key Party posts: as a deputy director of the Party's Propaganda Department and as a vice-president of the CCP's most important school, known then as the Marxist-Leninist Institute. He continued in the Institute until at least 1953 and still holds his position in the Propaganda Department.

Heading the delegation of representatives from the social science conference, in September 1949 Ch'en attended the initial session of CPPCC, the body that brought the new central government into existence on October 1. When the major governmental appointments were made later in October, he became a vice-chairman of the Culture and Education Committee which was one of the four key committees under Chou En-lai's Government Administration Council. Non-Communist Kuo Mo-jo was the Committee chairman, and two of the other vice-chairmen, Education Minister Ma Hsu-lun and Culture Minister Shen Yen-ping, were also non-Communists. As a consequence, the real political power fell to Ch'en and Lu Ting-i (q.v.) who was both a vice-chairman and Ch'en Po-ta's immediate superior in the Party Propaganda Department. Ch'en's role as a senior Party operative was even more evident in the Academy of Sciences when it was reorganized (also in October 1949). Here he again nominally served under Academy President Kuo Mo-jo, and the other three vice-presidents, Li Szu-kuang (q.v.), T'ao Meng-ho, and Chu K'o-chen, were all non-Communist natural scientists. Ch'en received three further appointments in professional and "mass" organizations in October 1949, serving on the national committees (or councils) of the China Peace Committee (to 1950), the Association for Reforming the Chinese Written Language (to 1952), and the Sino-Soviet Friendship Association (to 1954).

Immediately after the establishment of the PRC in October 1949, Ch'en made a quick trip to Moscow where he discussed with S. I. Vavilov, the president of the Soviet Academy of Sciences, scientific planning problems and particularly the role and organization of the Soviet Academy.[4] Two months later (December 1949) Ch'en was back in Moscow, this time accompanying Mao Tse-tung on the historic visit that led to the signing of the Sino-Soviet Treaty of

Friendship, Alliance, and Mutual Assistance on February 14, 1950. Ch'en was the only key leader to arrive with Mao. A month later Chou En-lai joined them, bringing with him several other top leaders. Mao, Chou, Ch'en, and the others were, of course, received by Stalin and virtually all the other important Soviet leaders before their departure for home on February 17.

In the early years of the PRC, Ch'en faced the rather delicate task of being the chief eulogizer of Mao Tse-tung while at the same time reconciling Mao's "thought" and political career with Stalin's writings (and, implicitly, the Comintern orders to the CCP dating back to the 1920's). One of Ch'en's first efforts in this regard appeared in the journal of the Sino-Soviet Friendship Association the day before Mao and he arrived in Moscow. This article, "Stalin and the Chinese Revolution," was a prelude to a far more important piece that was published to coincide with the 30th anniversary of the CCP (July 1951). It appeared in the two most authoritative Party organs, the *JMJP* and *Hsueh-hsi* (Study), under the title: "Mao Tse-tung's Thought Is the Synthesis of Marxism-Leninism and the Chinese Revolution." The April 12, 1952, issue of the *JMJP* carried Ch'en's "In Commemoration of the 25th Anniversary of the Comrade Stalin's Great Work, *The Problem of the Chinese Revolution.*" Finally, in 1953 (after Stalin's death), the above-mentioned "Stalin and the Chinese Revolution" was expanded into a book of the same title.

As one of Mao's major ideologues and in his capacity as a vice-president of the Academy of Sciences, Ch'en made a major report before the Academy in July 1952. This speech was probably the Party's definitive statement as of that time on its attitude toward scientists (most of whom were then not Party members) and the role they were expected to play in developing the economy. It was translated into English and published the next year under the title *Speech before the Study Group of Research Members of Academia Sinica*. In January 1953 the Communists took one of their first major steps toward the establishment of a constitutional government when they set up a special committee to draft the national constitution. Chaired by Mao and including Ch'en among its members, the committee drafted a constitution that was adopted at the first session of the First NPC in September 1954.

Like several other prominent Party leaders, Ch'en was not elected to the First NPC. But three months later (December 1954) he was named to represent social science organizations on the National Committee of the Second CPPCC, as well as being given a seat on the Standing Committee. He continued to hold both posts in the Third CPPCC (1959–1964); he was once again named to hold these positions when the Fourth CPPCC was inaugurated in December 1964–January 1965, but on this occasion he was selected to represent the CCP rather than social science organizations. In 1955 he received two further assignments in the Academy of Sciences. In June he became a member of the newly established Department of Philosophy and Social Sciences and in October a member of a special committee to select social and natural scientists to be given prizes for their research. He received still another appointment in scientific administration in March 1956 when he was made a member of the State Council's Scientific Planning Commission, retaining this post until the Commission was reorganized in November 1958.

In mid-1955, as the PRC began to step up the pace of agricultural collectivization, Ch'en was identified as a deputy director of the Party's Rural Work Department, a post he was to hold for about two years concurrently with his post in the Propaganda Department. In October of that year he presented the official explanations at the Central Committee's Sixth Plenum of the "draft decisions on agricultural cooperation." This important address, in effect, offered the ideological justification for Mao's well-known speech given on July 31, 1955, which sharply advanced the speed at which collectivization was to take place. Ch'en spoke in a similar vein in February 1956 when he addressed the CPPCC, a speech that contained the remarkable statement that there was "no sign of overpopulation" and that China could "find room for at least another 600 million people." He was to play an even more important role in connection with the communes in 1958 (see below), but before then, in September 1956, he was re-elected to the Central Committee at the Eighth Party Congress. On the day following the Congress, a new Politburo consisting of 17 full and six alternate members was elected. Lu Ting-i and Ch'en, by then the top propagandists, were both elected alternates. A year later, in November 1957, Ch'en accompanied Mao Tse-tung to Moscow for celebrations marking the 40th anniversary of the Bolshevik Revolution. (Ch'en is the only member of the CCP elite who was with Mao on both of his trips abroad.) Mao and his large delegation also joined in the important talks held among the many world Communist leaders then assembled in Moscow. These discussions were summarized in a joint communiqué, but the Sino-Soviet polemics of the early sixties revealed that serious disagreement had arisen during the talks over the "correct paths to socialism" to be fostered by the Communist powers.

Ch'en's stature in the Party hierarchy was further enhanced in the spring and summer of 1958 in connection with the second session of the Eighth Party Congress and the Fifth Plenum (both held in May), as well as the development of the commune movement and the initiation of the international campaign against "revisionism" (initially directed against Yugoslavia and later, in explicit terms, against the Soviet Union). At the Plenum the decision was made to establish *Hung-ch'i* (Red flag) as the Party's leading theoretical journal, with Ch'en as the editor. (Later in 1958 *Hsueh-hsi*, which had previously been the top Party organ, was disbanded.) In the initial issue of *Hung-ch'i* (June 1), Ch'en fired one of the opening shots in the long and vitriolic campaign against Tito's form of socialism. More important were his articles for the third and fourth issues of *Hung-ch'i* (July 1 and 14, 1958) in which he mentioned the "people's communes." The Communists later claimed that the communes had already (and "spontaneously") begun to operate in the spring of 1958 as a major component of the "Great Leap Forward," but Ch'en's reference in July appears to be the first time the term was used.[5] Significantly, his article in the third *Hung-ch'i* issue was entitled "Entirely New Society, Entirely New People." In the next issue Ch'en elaborated on this, crediting Mao with having said that China should organize "industry, agriculture, commerce, education and soldiers (namely, the militia)" into single large communes. One writer has observed that "Ch'en's remarks were pervaded" by a stress "on the independence of Mao's new 'conclusion' and on the warrant given for striking out boldly with original ideas: Marx, Engels, and Lenin 'could not provide each country . . . with a detailed plan' and held that Marxist theory 'should be enriched and developed uninterruptedly.'"[6] Ch'en's remarks also carried a special significance in terms of Sino-Soviet relations because they represented a Chinese challenge to Soviet supremacy in the underdeveloped world. As another writer observed: "The implications were clear: the path to Communism in the East would differ considerably from that in Europe, and Mao had discovered the special path for the East."[7]

In 1958 Ch'en was elected a Shanghai deputy to the Second NPC (1959–1964) and he was returned from the Shanghai constituency to the Third NPC, which opened in December 1964. He continued to write on ideological questions (e.g., for the 13th and 22nd issues of *Hung-ch'i* in 1959) and to take part in meetings, such as the large and important conference of "outstanding" cultural and educational workers in June 1960. In October 1962 he was made a vice-chairman of the State Planning Commission, a position he still holds. However, in spite of these activities and new assignments, he seemed to play a somewhat less important role than he had in the middle and late 1950's. If in fact this is true, it may have been related to the serious dislocations caused by the Great Leap Forward with which he had been associated. Nonetheless, his career took a significant and dramatic turn

in the early stages of the Great Proletarian Cultural Revolution in 1966 when he became the head of the "group in charge of the cultural revolution" and was elevated to the Standing Committee of the Politburo. These changes had the effect of placing Ch'en among the top leaders, and probably in the fourth-ranking position behind Mao, Lin Piao, and Chou En-lai.

1. Chiang Nan-hsiang *et al., The Roar of a Nation* (Peking, 1963), p. 5; Li Ch'ang *et al.,* "*I-erh-chiu*" *hui-i-lu* (Reminiscences of "December Ninth"; Peking, 1961), p. 39.

2. Merle Goldman, *Literary Dissent in Communist China* (Cambridge, Mass., 1967), pp. 37–38.

3. Boyd Compton, *Mao's China* (Seattle, 1952), p. xxxviii.

4. John M. H. Lindbeck, "The Organisation and Development of Science," *The China Quarterly,* no. 6:103 (April–June 1961).

5. Roy Hofheinz, "Rural Administration in Communist China," *The China Quarterly,* no. 11:154–155 (July–September 1962).

6. Arthur A. Cohen, *The Communism of Mao Tse-tung* (Chicago, 1964), p. 176.

7. Donald S. Zagoria, *The Sino-Soviet Conflict, 1956–1961* (Princeton, N.J., 1962), p. 105.

Ch'en Shao-min

(c. 1900–   ; Shou-kuang hsien, Shantung). Vice-chairman, All-China Federation of Trade Unions; member, CCP Central Committee.

Ch'en Shao-min is the outstanding woman trade union leader in China and one of only four women to have reached full membership on the Party Central Committee. She was born about 1900 in Shou-kuang hsien in north-central Shantung. Her father, a poor peasant, had been a soldier during the 1911 Revolution. From 1913 to 1924 Ch'en was a lace factory worker in Shantung. Although already in her twenties, she attended primary school in Shantung from 1924 to 1926, and then in 1927 studied briefly at a middle school in Wei-hsien, not far southeast of her native Shou-kuang. It was apparently while she attended the middle school that Ch'en had her first contact with Communist activities, joining the Communist Youth League in 1927 and the CCP two years later.

By 1930 Ch'en was back in the textile mills, active this time as a Communist political worker. Work of this sort took her to Peking, Tientsin, and Tsingtao. At about this time her husband, Jen Kuo-cheng, one-time secretary of the Shantung Party Committee, was executed (1931). A child of this marriage died in 1932. In the years from 1930 to 1933, Ch'en continued her political work until arrested and briefly imprisoned by the Nationalist authorities in 1933. Sources are conflicting about Ch'en's activities during the period from her release from prison in 1933 to the beginning of the war in 1937. Non-communist sources assert that she engaged in Party organizational work in Hopeh, Shantung, and Honan. The Communists, however, have described her "heroic" feats on the Long March from Kiangsi to Shensi in 1934–35. In any event she was in Yenan in 1937 where she attended a conference of CCP organizations in Nationalist-controlled areas and also attended a Party school for a brief period.

In 1938 Ch'en was assigned to united front work in Nanchang, the Kiangsi capital, for a brief period. But in the latter part of the same year she was sent to Honan and remained in the central China area for the remainder of the war. In Honan she directed the Party's Organization Department in 1938, but in the following year she joined guerrilla leader Li Hsien-nien (q.v.) in Hupeh to help organize the Hupeh-Honan guerrilla base. Ch'en is also credited with having commanded guerrilla units and, during and immediately after the war, is known to have held the following posts: director, Organization Department, CCP Central China Bureau; deputy secretary, Central China Bureau; acting chairman, Hupeh-Honan Border Region Government. It is possible that her work in the Central China Bureau brought her into contact with Liu Shaoch'i, the Bureau secretary in the early 1940's.[1]

At the Party's Seventh Congress, held from April to June 1945 in Yenan, Ch'en was elected an alternate member of the Central Committee, possibly *in absentia*. At this Congress, only three women were elected as full or alternate members, the two others being Ts'ai Ch'ang (Mme. Li Fuch'un) and Teng Ying-ch'ao (Mme. Chou Enlai). Ch'en's activities in the postwar years are not documented. She may have remained in east-central China where, with the civil war between the Nationalists and the Communists still in progress, she was elected in February 1949 (at an undisclosed location) to membership on the Executive Committee of the East China Women's Association. Moreover, she was also named as a delegate to the First National Congress of Women held two months later in Peking. At this congress the Chinese formed the All-China Federation of Democratic Women (ACFDW); Ch'en was elected to the Executive Committee and was later re-elected to this position at the congresses held in 1953 and 1957. (At the 1957 congress the ACFDW was renamed the National Women's Federation of China.)

At the first session of the CPPCC, held in Peking in September 1949 to form the new government, Ch'en attended as a representative of the All-China Federation of Labor (ACFL). She served on both the presidium (steering committee) and an *ad hoc* committee to draft the declarations published in connection with the work of the CPPCC. At the close of the CPPCC

meetings Ch'en was elected as a member of the First National Committee representing the ACFL. She again represented the Labor Federation on the Second and Third National Committees (1954–1964), serving also as a Standing Committee member. Although she was named again to the Fourth Committee, she was not re-appointed to the Standing Committee when the first session ended in January 1965 (probably owing to the fact that she had been transferred to the NPC Standing Committee at that time— see below). When most of the assignments were made to the new central government in October 1949, Ch'en was named to membership in the Supreme People's Procuratorate (the approximate equivalent to the office of the U.S. Attorney General), then headed by Lo Jung-huan. She held this post until the constitutional government was inaugurated in the fall of 1954.

In the earliest days of the PRC, the Communists set about to organize a number of constituent trade unions under the jurisdiction of the ACFL (which Ch'en had represented at the CPPCC meetings). One of the first to be organized was the All-China Textile Workers' Trade Union (ACTWTU); a preparatory committee was set up in December 1949 followed by the convocation in January 1950 of a conference to elect the leading officials. Ch'en's long experience in textile factories, plus the fact that this industry had always employed a great number of women, made her a logical choice for the chairmanship of the Preparatory Committee. When the ACTWTU was established on a permanent basis at a conference held in July 1950, Ch'en was the dominant figure, making the keynote speech on past work and future tasks and being elected to the union's chairmanship. At the next congress, held in Tientsin (an important textile city) in August 1953, she again made the keynote address and was re-elected to the chairmanship. In December 1957, however, probably because she had by then assumed more important responsibilities, Ch'en relinquished the chairmanship to another person (although she has continued to serve on the National Committee of the ACTWTU).

Ch'en's work with the textile union was given further recognition at a plenum of the parent ACFL in January 1953 when she was named to membership on the ACFL Executive Committee. Three months later, at the Seventh Congress of the ACFL, she was re-elected to the Executive Committee and was also given membership on the important Presidium and Secretariat, the two bodies that run the ACFL when the Executive Committee is not in session. She was re-elected to the Executive Committee and Presidium at the next congress (December 1957); more important, Ch'en was also elected as a vice-chairman of the All-China Federation of Trade Unions (as the ACFL was now known)—the first woman to have reached this post in the long history of this union.

Internationally, the ACFL (ACFTU) is affiliated with the Communist-dominated World Federation of Trade Unions (WFTU). From 1950 (to an uncertain date) Ch'en was a member of the Executive Committee of the Trade Union International of Textile and Clothing Workers, an affiliate of the WFTU. In October 1952 she led the Chinese delegation to the second congress of the organization held in East Berlin. Moreover, from 1953 to 1957, she served as an alternate member of the Executive Committee of the WFTU. Ch'en's only other known trip abroad also occurred in connection with trade union work when, in June 1952, she was deputy leader of the Chinese delegation to the 11th congress of the All-Union Central Council of Trade Unions in Moscow.

Since November 1951, Ch'en has been a member of the Chinese People's Committee in Defense of Children and from June 1952 to October 1956 she was a Standing Committee member of the All-China Athletic Federation. In both cases she represented the ACFL, but there are no indications that she has devoted much time to either organization. Ch'en received her next important assignment in 1954 when the NPC was formed. She was elected as a deputy from her native Shantung to the First NPC (1954–1959) and to the Second NPC (1959–1964). She was once again elected from Shantung to the Third NPC, and when it held its first session (which closed in January 1965), she was elevated to the NPC Standing Committee, the committee in charge of congressional work between the annual sessions.

Ch'en's position as one of the most important women Communists was illustrated by the events surrounding the historic Eighth Party Congress held in September 1956. At the Seventh Congress in 1945, Ch'en had been elected as the eighth-ranking alternate member of the Central Committee. However, in the intervening years, several deaths among the members of the Central Committee had had the effect of raising her to full membership by the time the Eighth Congress was held in 1956. Then, at the close of the Eighth Congress she was elected to full membership on the new Central Committee. Aside from a few women who reached Central Committee membership in the early history of the CCP (e.g., Hsiang Ching-yü, q.v.), in more contemporary times Ch'en is one of only four women to have reached this level, the others being Ts'ai Ch'ang, Teng Ying-ch'ao, and Ch'ien Ying (qq.v.). (There are also four women who are alternate members: Chang Yun, Li Chien-chen, Ou Meng-chueh, and Shuai Meng-ch'i, qq.v.) Ch'en attended the Eighth Congress as a delegate from Hupeh (where she had worked many years earlier); she also served as a member of the Congress presidium (steering committee) and as one of the executive chairmen for two of the daily sessions.

Relatively little was heard about Ch'en in the late fifties and early sixties, although she appeared from time to time in public (most frequently when a foreign trade union delegation was visiting Peking). At one of these public occasions, in July 1961, she was identified as a Council member of the China-Mongolia Friendship Association, although her membership in this rather unimportant organization must be regarded as largely *pro forma*. However, her continuing importance in the Party hierarchy was reaffirmed at the Central Committee's 10th Plenum held in September 1962, when it was decided to expand the powers and membership of the Central Control Commission. In this expansion, which roughly tripled the size of the Commission, Ch'en was added as a member. Although the Communists have never spelled out the details regarding the qualifications for Commission membership, it is clear that representation is by functional groups (e.g., the military, youth organizations). Thus, it is evident that Ch'en represents the labor movement on this important Commission.

There are reports, apparently incorrect, that Ch'en was the wife of Politburo member Li Hsien-nien. If true, this must have been prior to 1964 when Li was known to be married to Lin Chia-mei.

1. Modern China Project, Columbia University, New York, Howard L. Boorman, director.

Ch'en Shao-yü

(1904–   ; Liu-an, Anhwei). Leader of the Russian-returned student faction in the CCP; member, CCP Central Committee.

Ch'en Shao-yü, often known as Wang Ming, was the leader of the Russian-returned student group, which triumphed over the Li Li-san leadership in a major intra-Party struggle for power in 1930–31. He was the CCP representative to the Comintern from 1931 to 1937, and during his years in Moscow he gained a worldwide reputation within the Communist movement as a proponent of the anti-Japanese united front policy. Ch'en continued to be a major spokesman for the united front during the early years of the Sino-Japanese War. He was stripped of his authority by the Maoist leadership during the early 1940's, and he later became a leading target of CCP historians, who charged him with responsibility for crucial errors in policy during the early 1930's. Ch'en continued to hold nominally important posts into the 1950's, but by the middle of that decade he was in Moscow where, in effect, he was living in exile.

Ch'en was born in Liu-an in west-central Anhwei, an area that was in the early 1930's a part of the Communists' Oyüwan Soviet (see under Chang Kuo-t'ao). He came from a family of well-to-do peasants. There are varying reports about his middle-school years (some suggested he studied in Anhwei, others Wuhan), but by about 1925 he was enrolled in Shanghai University (see under Ch'ü Ch'iu-pai), one of the most important recruiting grounds for young Communists in the mid-1920's. Ch'en joined the CCP in 1925.

Ch'en himself records that he arrived in Moscow in November 1925 among a group of 50-odd Chinese students to attend Sun Yat-sen (Chung-shan) University.[1] The school opened the month Ch'en arrived. Because this was a period of rather close KMT–CCP cooperation in China, it was supported in part by funds from wealthy KMT members; in fact, the initial class had far more KMT than CCP members, a point disregarded in later Communist histories. The students, who were subsidized, went through a two-year course oriented toward the social sciences, and they also took field trips to factories, courts, and other institutions. The first rector was Karl Radek, but he was later replaced by one of Moscow's best-known China specialists, Pavel Mif,[2] a man destined to play a critical role in Ch'en's future career.

Ch'en learned Russian well during his stay at the university, and, according to his own account, in 1926 he was elected chairman of the university's "student commune" (*hsueh-sheng kung-she*). There were a number of other Chinese students there who were to become part of the group known as the Russian-returned students, or "28 Bolsheviks," and which included Ch'in Pang-hsien, Chang Wen-t'ien, Shen Tse-min, Wang Chia-hsiang (qq.v.), and Ch'en's wife-to-be (in 1929), Meng Ch'ing-shu. In early January 1927 Ch'en left for home on a temporary assignment to take part in "secret work." This coincided with the beginning of the serious deterioration in KMT–CCP relations, and thus, for the next half year, Ch'en was an eyewitness to some of the most dramatic and disastrous events in CCP history. He went to Wuhan, then the center of Communist activities, and there, in April–May, he served as interpreter for Mif at the CCP's Fifth National Congress. Ch'en returned to Moscow in early August. He went back to Sun Yat-sen University, possibly still as a student or perhaps as an instructor.

At the CCP's Sixth National Congress, held in Moscow in June–July 1928, Ch'en's ability in Russian won for him the assignment as chief interpreter for the many observers who were there. Some reports maintain that Ch'en returned to Shanghai in 1929 to engage in Party and trade union work, but Chang Kuo-t'ao, who knew Ch'en and who was then himself in Moscow, claims that he remained in the Soviet capital until 1930. In any case, he was in the Soviet Union in the early part of 1930, and in the spring returned to China where, within the next year, he was to become a major actor in one of the most celebrated intra-Party struggles in CCP history. It is generally accepted that the returned student group was steadfastly loyal to Stalin and, more particularly, to Pavel Mif, who in 1930 became the Comintern's representative in China. It is also usually accepted that Ch'en's group had been sent to China to take control of the CCP from Li Li-san, or, at a minimum, to rein in the headstrong Li. In the period after the Sixth Congress in Moscow, Li had emerged as the most powerful CCP figure in China, and in the early part of 1930 he had set in motion a train of events which were to climax during the summer in abortive attempts to capture the key cities in the Yangtze Valley.

In 1930 a complex set of factors surrounded Li Li-san's control of the CCP and affected his policies. On the positive side, from Li's point of view, a short-term and divisive war had broken out between Chiang Kai-shek on the one hand and north China warlords Yen Hsi-shan and Feng Yü-hsiang on the other. On the negative side, Li was faced with serious policy disagreements from a faction in the CCP headed by labor leaders Ho Meng-hsiung and Lo Chang-lung (qq.v.) in Shanghai. Ho and his colleagues felt that Li's impetuous policies would ruin the slim chance the Party had to build up a Communist-dominated labor movement. Perhaps more seriously, Li was frustrated in his efforts to win the forthright allegiance of the hinterland guerrilla armies, which was vitally important if these forces were to carry out the assaults on the key cities in central China. In particular, he was unable to get firm commitments from the most important guerrilla force—the one led by Mao Tse-tung and Chu Te in southeast Kiangsi. Thus, the arrival of Ch'en Shao-yü and his group presented Li with one more contending faction and one viewed by many Party members as a group of untested youths who were unaware of the hard realities of being a revolutionary activist. It is indeed true that Ch'en and his colleagues were young. Most of them were only in their mid-twenties. And it is also true that few of them had first-hand experience in China during the years immediately prior to 1930 when so many of their Communist colleagues lost their lives.

The details of the struggle for power are contained in the biographies of Li Li-san, Ho Meng-hsiung, Lo Chang-lung, and Ch'in Pang-hsien (the last mentioned being Ch'en Shao-yü's most important protégé within the returned student faction). In brief, Li was initially strong enough to fend off and even chastise his critics in the spring and summer of 1930. Ch'en, for example, was placed on probation as a Party member for half a year and relegated to a propaganda post in the Kiangsu Party apparatus.[3] Moreover, Li Li-san was able to engineer the capture of Changsha, which was temporarily held by forces led by P'eng Te-huai (q.v.). However, P'eng was quickly driven from Changsha, and other military ventures along the Yangtze were blunted by the Nationalists. Thus, by the time of the important Third Plenum in September 1930, Li was on the defensive. Over the ensuing weeks his position was seriously eroded, and toward the end of the year he was "exiled" to Moscow. Then, despite the vigorous opposition of the Ho-Lo labor group, the returned students, strongly backed by the Comintern and Mif, were able to capture control of the key Party posts at the Fourth Plenum in January 1931 or in the weeks and months thereafter. Ch'en emerged from these intricate maneuvers as a member of the Central Committee and Politburo. At this juncture, operations in Shanghai were becoming increasingly precarious as the KMT vigorously sought to destroy the Communist underground apparatus. It was under these conditions that Hsiang Chung-fa (q.v.) was captured and executed in June. Throughout the period when Li Li-san was at the height of his powers, Hsiang had been the nominal chief of the CCP in his capacity as Party general secretary. As part of the reorganization of the Party hierarchy at the Fourth Plenum in early 1931, Hsiang had been retained as the general secretary. But there is near unanimity among students of this period that Hsiang was no more than a figurehead and that the real power was held by Ch'en and his colleagues. After Hsiang's death, Ch'en assumed the post of general secretary (or, according to some reports, acting general secretary).

The assumption of the key Party posts in Shanghai during the first half of 1931 did not mean that Ch'en's group had become the undisputed masters of the CCP. By this time much of the strength of the Party lay in the rural areas where Mao, Chu Te, Ho Lung, and others had built up formidable military units. Mao and the others had already learned much about guerrilla warfare through trial and error, and they were often unreceptive to directives from the young men in control in Shanghai. The returned student leadership, in an effort to assert their authority over the hinterland Red armies, dispatched a number of important political figures to various regions. For example, Hsia Hsi (q.v.) was sent to the Hunan-Hupeh border to join Ho Lung's troops. Ch'en himself soon left China for Moscow (see below), but the policies he and his followers pursued have been the subject of scores of books and articles by non-Communist writers, and an even greater number of polemical attacks by Maoist historians. Ch'en in particular, and his colleague Ch'in Pang-hsien to only a slightly lesser degree, are accused in orthodox Maoist works as the perpetrators of the "third leftist deviation," which is said to have existed from the Fourth Plenum in early 1931 until the Tsun-i Conference in January 1935 when Mao assumed a commanding, if not the commanding, position in the CCP. Party historian Hu Ch'iao-mu (q.v.) provides a typical attack on Ch'en and Ch'in. They "flatly denied the important changes which the Japanese invasion [of Manchuria in 1931] had brought about in China's domestic political situation and regarded the various cliques in the Kuomintang and the middle groups as equally counter-revolutionary." Consequently, Hu continued, they "demanded that the Party should wage a 'life-and-death struggle' against all of them without distinction." Moreover, they "opposed . . . Mao Tse-tung's ideas of guerrilla warfare and mobile warfare and persisted in demanding that the Red Army seize all key cities. On the question of the Party's underground work in the Kuomintang-controlled areas, they opposed the view of utilizing legal forms and accumulating revolutionary strength . . . and continued to carry out the adventurist policies which isolated them from the masses. Under this erroneous leadership, almost all Party organizations in the Kuomintang-controlled areas were finally destroyed." Finally, according to Hu, their "incorrect" military policies ultimately made the rural bases untenable in the face of continuing KMT attacks and forced the Communists to abandon them and undertake the Long March.[4]

There is doubtless a measure of truth in these charges, but the nature of Ch'en's role in CCP policies after mid-1931 remains unclear. Sources differ on when Ch'en left for Moscow to become chief CCP representative to the Comintern (leaving the Party apparatus under the control of his returned students' colleagues, especially Ch'in Pang-hsien and Chang Wen-t'ien). It would appear that he left about September 1931, but in any case it is clear that he was in Moscow by the late fall.[5] This meant he was not present for the First All-China Congress of Soviets held in Juichin, Kiangsi, in November 1931. (At this congress Ch'en was elected *in absentia* to membership on the Central Executive Committee, which was established as the major political organ of the newly formed Chinese Soviet Republic, and he was re-elected to this position at the Second Congress in January–February 1934.)

The reason for Ch'en's departure from China has never been adequately explained. Whatever the reason, his new assignment with the Comintern represented a major turning point in his checkered career. In the words of Benjamin

Schwartz, "His return to Moscow was more in the nature of an exile from the sources of power in the Chinese Communist movement than a climb to new heights of power. It must . . . be emphasized that the power of the Chinese Communist leaders after 1931 did not derive solely from the mandate of Moscow, but was solidly based on the control of a military force, a territorial base, and a government apparatus. [Ch'en] had no access to this 'real power' . . . in Moscow."[6] The next few years of Ch'en's career were characterized by an endless stream of articles by him, principally on Comintern policies in colonial areas and on events in the Chinese Soviet Republic. In March 1932 in Moscow, he republished a much-cited work entitled *Wei chung-kung keng-chia pu-erh-se-wei-k'o-hua erh tou-cheng* (Struggle for the more complete bolshevization of the CCP). This had been originally published in Shanghai 13 months earlier under the title *Liang-t'iao lu-hsien* (Two lines), and it was reissued once again in Yenan in 1940. This work, an important source for the Li Li-san period and the rise of the returned student leadership, contained major additions in the Moscow edition. These additions espoused policies which, many years later, were sharply attacked by Maoist historians.[7]

Two works written by Ch'en in 1933, *Su-wei-ai Chung-kuo* (Soviet China) and *Chung-kuo Su-wei-ai cheng-ch'üan ti ching-chi cheng-ts'e* (The economic policy of the Chinese Soviet Government), suggest that he was able to keep in relatively close touch with developments in the soviet areas in China. Earlier, in September 1932, he attended the 12th Plenum of the Executive Committee of the Comintern (ECCI), and in December 1933 he spoke at the 13th Plenum. His 1933 speech, together with one delivered by K'ang Sheng (q.v.), was published in New York in 1934 under the title *Revolutionary China Today*. Ch'en stressed the need for the continued struggle against imperialism (the main thrust of the Comintern line at that time) and against the KMT and Chiang Kai-shek in particular. However, somewhat in keeping with earlier calls by the Chinese Communists in the Kiangsi Soviet for cooperation with military forces willing to take up arms against Japan, Ch'en also mentioned the possibilities of "working among the armed forces of the enemy" (that is, KMT troops). Continuing in this vein, he called for work among the "soldier masses," adding that "today we must also pay attention to work among the lower and even the middle commissioned and non-commissioned officers." Taking cognizance of the rising wave of anti-Japanese sentiment in China (the "national salvation" movement; see under Sung Ch'ing-ling), he also spoke of the need to win over disaffected elements among the "petty bourgeois intellectuals." Such language, although a subordinate

part of Ch'en's address, was soon to be a major theme in Comintern and Chinese Communist pronouncements. Moreover, despite the anti-imperialist tone of the 12th and 13th ECCI Plenums, it should be noted that the Kremlin was in the midst of diplomatic maneuvers to cope with the rising threat from Nazi Germany and Japan. Thus, between the two Comintern Plenums, Moscow established diplomatic relations with the Chiang Kai-shek government (December 1932) and received formal diplomatic recognition from the United States (November 1933), and in September 1934 the Soviet Union joined the League of Nations.

As late as June 1934, in an article published in a Kiangsi journal, Ch'en continued to maintain that the returned students' leadership was bringing great successes to the CCP.[8] On the scene in China, however, the Communist leadership found itself in an increasingly dangerous situation as Chiang Kai-shek's Fifth Annihilation Campaign was closing the net. The final capitulation took place in October when the Red Army evacuated the Juichin base and started on the one-year Long March to north Shensi. Soon after this began, Ch'en advanced the view that the forced retreat was in fact a maneuver to "achieve a more fluid defense," to "participate in the anti-Japanese defense in north China," and to "replenish the Red Army's reserves from new territories."[9] The Long March was still in progress in July–August 1935 when the Seventh Comintern Congress was held in Moscow. This historic meeting, in effect, brought the Comintern into harmony with the above-described efforts of the Kremlin's Foreign Ministry by adopting as the primary Comintern goal the international united front against fascism. In a long and important speech entitled "The Revolutionary Movement in the Colonial Countries," Ch'en advocated a united front between the CCP and "bourgeois" groups to oppose Japanese aggression. He called on the CCP Central Committee and Chinese Soviet Government to "issue a joint appeal to the whole nation, to all parties, groups, troops, mass organizations and all prominent political and social persons, to organize together with us an all-China united people's government of national defense." In organizational terms, Ch'en emerged from the Seventh Congress as a major figure in the international Communist movement. He, Mao, Chou En-lai, and Chang Kuo-t'ao were elected full members of the ECCI, and K'ang Sheng (in Moscow with Ch'en) and Ch'in Pang-hsien (a key figure among the returned students) were elected alternates. Ch'en was also elected a member of the ECCI Presidium and a candidate member of the Comintern's Secretariat.[10]

In the months following the Seventh Comintern Congress Ch'en deluged the Comintern press and Chinese-language publications (both in China and abroad) with articles on the need for a united front. As early as November 1935 he specifically asserted that if Chiang Kai-shek concentrated on defeating the "Japanese imperialists" instead of the CCP, the Communists would be willing to cooperate with Chiang's army.[11] In a series of five articles for *Inprecorr,* published from late December 1935 to early February 1936, Ch'en repeated this theme and elaborated on the need to conciliate various classes in China (the petty bourgeoisie and even rich peasants and some landlords) to secure their participation in the united front.[12]

The relationship between the Comintern policy of united front as enunciated by Ch'en and that of the CCP leaders in Shensi continues to be debated. Some scholars argue that Russian fear of a Japanese invasion of Mongolia made the Kremlin far more amenable to compromise with the KMT than the Shensi Communists, whereas others hold that Mao and his colleagues arrived at fundamentally the same view by themselves. The issue is further complicated by the famous Sian Incident in December 1936 (see under Chou En-lai), when Chiang Kai-shek was kidnapped by two dissident generals, Chang Hsueh-liang and Yang Hu-ch'eng. Although the full story surrounding the incident has never been revealed, it appears that the Communists played a major role in having Chiang released. Ch'en, of course, was still in Moscow at that time, and thus he only witnessed from a distance the subsequent steps which led to a gradual reconciliation between the KMT and the CCP. Nonetheless, in later years he was charged by Maoist scribes with an abject willingness to surrender Communist autonomy to the Nationalists during these years. In any event, the rush of events temporarily settled the issue—within a few weeks after the beginning of the Sino-Japanese War in July 1937, a united front was worked out between the KMT and the CCP.

After some six years in Moscow, Ch'en left for home in the fall of 1937. En route he and K'ang Sheng held discussions in Sinkiang with Sheng Shih-ts'ai concerning his cooperation with the CCP (see under Teng Fa and Ch'en T'an-ch'iu).[13] Ch'en was in Yenan in time to attend a Politburo meeting in December, when he reiterated the primacy of the united front policy. In the same month he told a Western correspondent that he had seen Stalin shortly before his departure from Moscow and had returned specifically to confer with Chiang Kai-shek about the possibility of closer KMT–CCP cooperation, especially the question of Communist representation in the national government.[14] Because the degree of cooperation with the KMT was then a vital matter to the CCP, such statements were of course not unnoticed by Mao. In later years CCP historians have de-emphasized Mao's willingness to cooperate with

the Nationalists, so perhaps Mao did not then take exception to Ch'en's comments to an outsider. However, a case can be made that Ch'en's return to China was not a matter for rejoicing by Mao and some of his colleagues. The authority of the Comintern had been considerably diluted in contrast to earlier CCP history, but Ch'en evidently arrived on the scene with considerable prestige because of his close ties to Moscow. In organizational terms, he was apparently still a member of the CCP Politburo.[15] Whatever Ch'en's power within the CCP, it was not sufficient to unseat the Maoist leadership, if, in fact, he ever attempted to do so.

Ch'en was an obvious candidate to head the Party's United Front Work Department, and it was equally obvious that much of the united front work had to be carried out at the Nationalist capital. Thus, in the early days of 1938 Ch'en went to Hankow, which had become the temporary national capital after the fall of Nanking shortly before. Concurrently with his United Front Department post, Ch'en now took charge of the Party's Yangtze Bureau. The CCP apparatus in the Yangtze Valley had been dormant for several years, but it was rapidly reactivated in the early months of the war. Apart from Ch'en's presence there, a number of top Communists (for example, Chou En-lai and P'eng Te-huai) regularly visited Hankow and other Yangtze cities for conferences with the Nationalists on measures to stop the onrushing Japanese armies. During the spring, in a conciliatory gesture, the Nationalists announced that a consultative body known as the People's Political Council would be established. The seven-member CCP delegation consisted of Mao (never more than a nominal member), Ch'en Shao-yü, Lin Po-ch'ü, Tung Pi-wu, Wu Yü-chang, Ch'in Pang-hsien, and Chou En-lai's wife, Teng Ying-ch'ao (qq.v.).

By the time the People's Political Council held its inaugural session in July 1938, tensions had again arisen between the KMT and the CCP. Some KMT members hostile to Communist participation in the government proposed that China come to an understanding with Germany and Italy (who in turn would presumably bring pressure upon Japan to cease its aggression). According to one account, Ch'en "hotly replied that Germany and Italy were allies of Japan and that any rapprochement with them would lead to capitulation to the Japanese." When Ch'en described Moscow as the "natural ally" of China, a Nationalist delegate demanded of Ch'en: "Are you a Chinese or a Russian?" A scuffle was narrowly avoided.[16] KMT–CCP disputes were also evident in the attempts by each party to mobilize support for the defense of Wuhan. Ch'en and his colleagues established a "defense committee" and likened the situation to Madrid, then under seige by Franco. But this was an uneven struggle; the Nationalists had troops on the scene, the Communists none. Thus, in August 1938, when the Nationalists dissolved the defense committee as well as a number of Communist-oriented mass organizations (see under Li Ch'ang), there was little the CCP could do but comply.

In the fall of 1938 Ch'en returned to Yenan. He continued to be a member of the People's Political Council through the mid-1940's, but after the September 1939 meeting of the Council, which he attended, his membership was nominal. Ch'en was on hand in Yenan for the CCP's Sixth Plenum in October–November 1938. The plenum is often characterized (for example, in the annotations to Mao's *Selected Works*[17]) as a major turning point in Mao's efforts to assert the "proletarian leadership" within the united front, as opposed to the "capitulationists" led by Ch'en. However, the author of a detailed study of this period has written that it is his "tentative conclusion that Mao's move against Ch'en was more a matter of factionalism than of doctrinal disagreement."[18] Whatever the exact nature of their disputes, it is evident that Ch'en was not immediately cast into political oblivion. He is known at that period to have had major responsibilities in one of the Party's top schools in Yenan,[19] and, from at least 1939, he was president of the Yenan Chinese Women's University. Later, in 1941, this school was amalgamated with several others to form Yenan University (see under Wu Yü-chang). Ch'en was also entrusted to represent the CCP in Chungking during the latter part of 1939 (temporarily replacing Chou En-lai, who was then in Moscow);[20] he also continued to head the United Front Work Department for a period, but toward the latter part of the war this post was taken over by K'o Ch'ing-shih (q.v.).

No precise date can be given for Ch'en's downfall as a Party leader of consequence. It appears, however, that the process began in 1940 when he was only in his mid-thirties. For example, Ch'en had been one of the most consistent contributors to Yenan's leading journal, *Chieh-fang* (Liberation), from his return from Moscow until early 1940, but after that time his once prolific pen came to a virtual standstill. Two years later Mao launched the famous *cheng-feng* (ideological remolding) movement with an attack on "Party formalism." Neither Ch'en nor his returned student colleagues were mentioned by name, but they were obviously the intended targets of the assertion that "great harm" had been done by "foreign formalism" and "foreign dogmatism." Elaborating on this point, Mao declared that "a Communist Party member living in China who divorces himself from the practical necessities of the Chinese situation in speaking of Marxism is a false Marxist, even though he reads ten thousand Marxist books a thousand times." During the next two years senior CCP officials held a series of discussions on the Party's history. These were summarized by Mao in April 1944, and exactly a year later, on the eve of the Seventh Party Congress, the "Resolution on Certain Questions in the History of Our Party" was adopted. This resolution, now a part of Mao's *Selected Works,* spells out in considerable detail the Maoist interpretation of Ch'en's so-called "dogmatist errors." Reviewing this period, Boyd Compton has written that after 1937 "leading policy statements came more and more from Mao, Chou En-lai, and rising theoreticians Liu Shao-ch'i, Ch'en Po-ta, and Ch'en Yun" (qq.v.), and that after the *cheng-feng* "attack," Ch'en and his colleagues "lost their voice." Compton has further observed that Ch'en and the other returned students "were not in any sense purged." Rather, "what they actually lost was control of the highest Party offices and their positions as principal Party spokesmen."[21]

At the Party's Seventh National Congress, held from April to June 1945, 44 persons were elected to the Central Committee. It was obviously no accident that Ch'en was given the 43rd place and his colleague Ch'in Pang-hsien the 44th. Not surprisingly from that time until preparations began for the establishment of the Communists' central government in 1949, virtually nothing was heard of Ch'en's activities, although during this period he did serve as chairman of the Party Central Committee's Law Commission. Nor is much known about his whereabouts during this period; he was in Yenan in the spring of 1946, and presumably remained in northwest and north China during the civil war.

Ch'en re-emerged to some degree of prominence in the summer and fall of 1949 as the first organizational steps were taken to establish the various "mass" organizations and the new central government. In June of that year, at the founding conference of the China New Legal Research Society, he spoke on the rules and regulations for the society and was elected as a vice-chairman of the Preparatory Committee and chairman of its Standing Committee. In the next month he attended a meeting to establish the China New Philosophy Research Society, and at still another conference he was named to Standing Committee membership on the China Social Science Workers' Conference Preparatory Committee. It was in the latter capacity that he attended the inaugural session in September 1949 of the CPPCC, the organization that brought the new government into existence (October 1). While the CPPCC was in session, he served on the committee to draft the Organic Law of the CPPCC, one of the basic state documents adopted at that time. At the close of the meetings, Ch'en was elected a member of the

CPPCC's First National Committee, nominally retaining this seat until the Second CPPCC was formed five years later.

When the major assignments in the new government were made in October 1949, Ch'en received posts in the executive and judicial branches. In the former, known from 1949 to 1954 as the Government Administration Council (GAC), he was appointed a vice-chairman under Tung Pi-wu of the Political and Legal Affairs Committee (PLAC). The PLAC, in turn, had jurisdiction over five ministries and commissions, one of which, the Law Commission, was headed by Ch'en. Additionally, he was named to membership on the Supreme People's Court. Also in October 1949 Ch'en was made a member of the Sino-Soviet Friendship Association's First Executive Board. He was fairly active during the first half of 1950, particularly in connection with the passage of the important Marriage Law (promulgated April 30). In May he reported before the GAC on the work of his Law Commission, and in the next month he attended the second meeting of the CPPCC National Committee, a meeting that saw the passage of the critical Land Reform Law. A month later Ch'en gave a major speech on legal work at the First National Judicial Conference, but after this virtually nothing was heard of him until early 1954 when he made a nominal appearance in Peking. In the meantime, as early as September 1951, Law Commission Vice-Chairman Hsu Te-heng (q.v.) began to act for Ch'en as head of the commission. Ch'en's career as an active political figure in China ended for all practical purposes in the early fall of 1954 when the central government was reorganized. He was stripped of all his government posts, and a few months later he was also dropped from the Sino-Soviet Friendship Association—an ironic action by the Maoist leadership in view of Ch'en's close ties with the Soviet Union.

By the spring of 1956 Ch'en was being openly castigated by the Chinese press for his "errors," which were dated back to the early thirties. Although he was re-elected to Central Committee membership at the Eighth Party Congress in September 1956, the circumstances of his election were humiliating to a man who had once been a top CCP leader. Ch'en was placed last on the list of the 97 Central Committee members; only Li Li-san (q.v.) was subjected to greater humiliation in making an abject confession of his previous political "errors." Ch'en's failure to address the congress was almost certainly the result of the fact that he was no longer resident in China. (The day after the Congress ended, all but one of the Central Committee members attended the new Central Committee's First Plenum—presumably Ch'en was the missing man.) According to unverified but seemingly reliable reports, he has been living in the Soviet Union since the mid-fifties, and in view of the continuing attacks on Ch'en in the Chinese press and the intensity of the Sino-Soviet dispute, his residence abroad is probably equivalent to political exile. Nonetheless, he continues to be listed in the latest available (1965) Jen-min shou-ts'e (People's handbook) as a Central Committee member.

There are few Chinese Communists who have been mentioned more frequently in histories of the CCP, but there is surprisingly little information about his personal character and abilities. In this sense, U.S. military observer Evans Carlson is one of the rather few Westerners who met and commented upon Ch'en. Carlson saw him in Hankow in 1938 and described him as having a "pleasing and disarming manner" and as being "exceptionally articulate."[22]

Ch'en is married to Meng Ch'ing-shu. They both attended Sun Yat-sen University in Moscow, and it was probably there that they married. Meng served as head of the Party's Women's Work Department during the period of her husband's primacy in the CCP (1931), and in the late thirties and forties she was with Ch'en first in Hankow and then in Yenan where she taught at the Yenan Chinese Women's University, an institute headed by her husband. Edgar Snow met Meng during the war years, and wrote a brief but useful account of the school where she taught.[23] Meng also served under Ch'en in the forties in the Party's Law Commission, and she worked under him once again after 1949 as a member of the central government's Law Commission. Like the wives of most men who have been politically disgraced, Meng disappeared from the political scene with the fall of her husband in the early fifties.

1. *Lieh-shih chuan* (Biographies of martyrs; Moscow, 1936), pp. 62–74.

2. Jane Degras, ed., *The Communist International, 1919–1943* (London, 1960), II, 182; Xenia Joukoff Eudin and Robert C. North, *Soviet Russia and the East, 1920–1927* (Stanford, Calif., 1957), pp. 86–87.

3. Tso-liang Hsiao, *Power Relations within the Chinese Communist Movement, 1930–1934* (Seattle, Wash., 1961), p. 133.

4. Hu Ch'iao-mu, *Thirty Years of the Communist Party of China* (Peking, 1952), pp. 34–35.

5. Charles B. McLane, *Soviet Policy and the Chinese Communists, 1931–1946* (New York, 1958), p. 38; Agnes Smedley, *Red Flood over China* (Moscow, 1934), p. 387.

6. Benjamin I. Schwartz, *Chinese Communism and the Rise of Mao* (Cambridge, Mass., 1951), pp. 186–187.

7. Hsiao, pp. 202–207.

8. *Ibid.*, p. 290.

9. McLane, p. 54.

10. *Ibid.,* p. 61.

11. Lyman P. Van Slyke, *Enemies and Friends* (Stanford, Calif., 1967), pp. 57–58.

12. Dorothy Borg, *The United States and the Far Eastern Crisis of 1933–1938* (Cambridge, Mass., 1964), p. 209.

13. Allen S. Whiting and Sheng Shih-ts'ai, *Sinkiang: Pawn or Pivot?* (East Lansing, Mich., 1958), pp. 55, 186.

14. McLane, p. 113.

15. I. Epstein, *The People's War* (London, 1939), p. 138.

16. Lyman P. Van Slyke, *The Chinese Communist Movement: A Report of the United States War Department, July 1945* (Stanford, Calif., 1968), p. 65.

17. *Selected Works of Mao Tse-tung* (Peking, 1965), II, 213–214.

18. Van Slyke, *Enemies and Friends,* p. 107.

19. Edgar Snow, *Random Notes on Red China, 1936–1945* (Cambridge, Mass., 1957), p. 24.

20. McLane, p. 122.

21. Boyd Compton, *Mao's China* (Seattle, Wash., 1952), pp. xxxviii–xxxix.

22. Evans Fordyce Carlson, *Twin Stars of China* (New York, 1940), p. 279.

23. Edgar Snow, *The Battle for Asia* (New York, 1941), pp. 273–278.

Ch'en Shih-ch'ü

(1909–   ; Ching-men hsien, Hupeh). Veteran PLA officer; commander, Engineer Corps, PLA.

Ch'en Shih-ch'ü has been a member of the Red Army since its establishment in 1927. He fought with Mao Tse-tung's forces during the Autumn Harvest Uprisings and was a member of Mao's small band, which survived the rigors of the winter of 1927–28 in the Chingkang Mountains. Since then he has devoted his entire career to the military establishment, serving as commander of the PLA Engineer Corps since 1952. Ch'en was born in 1909 in Ching-men hsien, Hupeh, a rural area about 100 miles west of Wuhan. The information on Ch'en's life through the 1920's is drawn largely from an autobiographical account given to a correspondent of the *Chung-kuo ch'ing-nien pao* (China youth newspaper) in 1961.[1]

The son of an office worker, Ch'en received his early schooling in Peking until his education was cut short by the financial difficulties of his family after he graduated from primary school. Upon leaving Peking and returning to his native Ching-men, he was adopted into the family of a landlord. He soon tired of his adopted parents and went to work in the nearby town of Sha-yang as an apprentice in a general store. According to Ch'en's autobiography, he did not last long at the Sha-yang store and on New Year's Day

of 1927 found himself dismissed for inciting his fellow workers against the management. In early 1927 Wuhan was the capital of the left-wing KMT government from which agents of both the KMT and the CCP were being sent to organize industrial workers in the cities and the peasants in the rural areas. Ch'en, influenced by such activity, left Sha-yang for northern Hupeh to help organize the peasantry. Soon, however, the peasants had become sufficiently aroused to provoke actions on the part of KMT-controlled military forces, and in April 1927 General Hsia Tou-yin (later the Wuchang garrison commander and an important KMT official) sent his troops to put down the dissident elements. Ch'en was forced to seek safety in Wuchang, which offered revolutionaries more obscurity, and it was there that he joined the Communist Youth League.

After a brief period of training at the "Hupeh Student Military Training Class" (a Youth League school sponsored by the Hupeh CCP Committee), Ch'en joined a unit of the Wuchang garrison force, which was commanded by Lu Te-ming, a Communist. Lu's men, alerted to the Communists' plans to stage an uprising at Nanchang at the beginning of August 1927, embarked on a Yangtze River steamer for Nanchang in late July. Fearing apprehension by Nationalist guards, who were checking passengers at Chiu-chiang (Kiukiang) before the steamer reached its destination, the Communists disembarked at Huang-shih (midway between Wuhan and Chiu-chiang) and began their march overland to Nanchang. However, before reaching Nanchang, Communist troops led by Yeh T'ing and Ho Lung (qq.v.) had already staged their uprising (August 1) and had been driven from the city five days later. Therefore, Lu Te-ming, Ch'en, and the others turned westward and moved into the mountainous regions of northwest Kiangsi. At this juncture their forces were reorganized into the First Regiment of the First Division of the Workers' and Peasants' Revolution Army; Ch'en was assigned to a guards company for the division headquarters. Soon afterwards these troops moved into Hunan where, after joining forces with units led by Mao Tse-tung, they launched an abortive attack on P'ing-chiang in northeast Hunan, thus initiating a part of the Autumn Harvest Uprisings (September 1927). After the insurrection at P'ing-chiang failed, Ch'en participated in the retreat led by Mao, who led the badly battered Red troops south into Kiangsi. After these units, composed of fewer than 1,000 men, reached the Chingkang Mountains on the Hunan-Kiangsi border in the latter part of 1927, Ch'en became a member of the CCP.

Ch'en was thus among the hard core of troops that remained with Mao from the difficult winter of 1927–28 at Chingkangshan through the period of the Kiangsi Soviet dating from 1931 to

1934. During the latter years of the Kiangsi period he became a battalion commander with the forces led by Lin Piao (q.v.). Ch'en made the Long March, which started from Kiangsi in the fall of 1934. During the March he was commander of a training battalion under Lin Piao's First Army Corps. This was probably the special regiment of Red Army cadets commanded by Ch'en Keng and Sung Jen-ch'ing (qq.v.), which acted as a special guard for the Party leadership during the March.

In 1937 Ch'en studied at the Anti-Japanese Military and Political Academy in Yenan. Immediately following the outbreak of the Sino-Japanese War in July 1937 he became a member of the 115th Division of the Eighth Route Army. Ch'en served as chief-of-staff of the 343rd Brigade, which, under Division Commander Lin Piao, won the famous battle at P'ing-hsing Pass in northeast Shansi (September 1937), defeating a major portion of one of the strong Japanese invading forces (see under Lin Piao). Ch'en also took part in a battle in Wu-ch'eng in western Shansi in early 1938. He was then promoted to chief-of-staff of the 115th Division, and in this capacity he was with elements of the division that moved eastward into Shantung in the early part of 1939. Ch'en was serving at this time under Hsu Hsiang-ch'ien (q.v.), the deputy commander of another key Communist division, the 129th, which was cooperating with the 115th Division. Little is known about Ch'en's activities during the middle years of the war, but it appears that he remained in the Shantung area. In any case, from 1944 to 1946 he was in command of the Communists' Pin-hai Military District; located in the coastal area southwest of Tsingtao, the Pin-hai region was one of the five sections into which the Shantung Military Region was then divided. In 1945 Ch'en assumed the concurrent post of commander of the Second Advance Column of Communist forces in Shantung. At the end of the war Ch'en I's New Fourth Army came to be the principal Communist force in Shantung. In 1946 Ch'en I made his headquarters at Lin-i in southern Shantung, and by that time Ch'en Shih-ch'ü was serving as chief-of-staff of both the New Fourth Army and the Shantung Military District.

In January 1946, through the mediation efforts of U.S. Special Envoy George C. Marshall, the Communists and Nationalists signed a cease-fire agreement. Under the terms of the agreement an Executive Headquarters was established in Peking where representatives from the Communists, Nationalists, and the United States attempted to supervise the truce. Ch'en was assigned to this headquarters where, holding the simulated rank of major general, he served directly under Lo Jui-ch'ing (q.v.), the chief-of-staff of the Communist delegation. He is also known to have spent some time in the spring of 1946 in Chungking, which, during the truce period, was a rather important center for Communist political operations.[2] However, when the truce arrangements collapsed in the latter part of 1946 and early 1947, Ch'en returned to the Shantung area, where in 1947 Ch'en I's New Fourth Army had been redesignated the East China PLA. Under this force Ch'en Shih-ch'ü served until 1949 as chief-of-staff.

In 1947 and 1948 Ch'en spent most of his time in the field commanding an army corps subordinate to the East China PLA. During this period he was closely associated with T'ang Liang (q.v.), his political commissar. In fact, their well-known unit is commonly referred to in Communist histories as the "Ch'en-T'ang Army Corps." After waging a number of successful campaigns in Shantung, the corps moved into Honan, where, in a drive coordinated with forces led by Liu Po-ch'eng, it converged on Loyang and Kaifeng in mid-1948. Ch'en also played an important role in the battles these armies fought during the critical Huai-hai Campaign from early November 1948 to mid-January 1949 (see under Liu Po-ch'eng). Heading the 11th Army Corps of the Third Field Army (the new designation for the East China PLA), Ch'en is credited by the Communists with having commanded troops that won important victories in north Anhwei, not far from Hsu-chou (Suchow), the main target of the Huai-hai Campaign.[3] These victories during the Huai-hai operations dealt a decisive blow to the power of the Nationalists.

Nanking fell to the Communist forces in late April 1949, a victory of great psychological value because the city had been the capital of the Nationalist Government. Ch'en was immediately named to command the Nanking Garrison, and by November he was serving as a member of the Nanking Military Control Commission under Chairman Su Yü (q.v.). For at least a time in 1949 Ch'en was also the vice-president of the East China Military and Political University located in Nanking. Because President Ch'en I was fully occupied in Shanghai, it is likely that Ch'en Shih-ch'ü was the principal Party figure connected with this school.

Ch'en went to Peking in September 1949 to attend the First CPPCC, the organization that brought the new PRC government into existence. He attended the meetings as a representative of the Third Field Army and also served on an *ad hoc* committee (chaired by Kuo Mo-jo) to draft the public declaration on the work of the CPPCC. In 1949–50, not long after these meetings were held and as the Communists began to consolidate their victories, regional governments were formed to administer the newly conquered areas. Ch'en became a member of the one formed for east China, the East China Military and Administrative Committee (ECMAC). He held this post until the ECMAC was reorganized in late 1952, although by that time he was already working in the national capital.

By the fall of 1952 Ch'en was in Peking where he became commander of the Engineer Corps of the PLA, the post that has probably occupied most of his time since that date, although it receives little attention in the Chinese press. In 1954 he was elected a deputy to the First NPC. He was also elected to the Second NPC (1959–1964) and again to the Third NPC, which opened its first session in December 1964. He was a deputy from Honan to the First NPC, but at the Second and Third Congresses he represented the Foochow Military Region. Although a man's representation in the NPC is an uncertain guide to his actual place of work, it is often suggestive. Thus the shift in Ch'en's NPC constituency suggests that as commander of the Engineer Corps he has been involved in the erection of the military fortifications in Fukien opposite Nationalist-held Quemoy Island. In this connection it may be noteworthy that Ch'en was first elected to the NPC from the Foochow Military Region in mid-1958—a date coinciding with the outbreak of the "off-shore island crisis," which has continued into the 1960's.

At the close of the first session of the First NPC (September 1954), Ch'en was named to membership on the National Defense Council (NDC), an organization with limited power and authority, but one with considerable prestige. He was subsequently reappointed to membership in April 1959 and January 1965. One year after his appointment to the NDC, the PRC awarded military orders to PLA veterans and also gave ranks to its officer corps. Ch'en received the Orders of Independence and Freedom and of Liberation, granted for service from 1937 to 1945 and from 1945 to 1950, respectively. At the same time he was made a colonel-general, equivalent to a three-star general in the U.S. Army.

Ch'en has appeared in public quite regularly since 1953. He has been noted most frequently in Peking where he attends ceremonies for PLA holidays (such as August 1), or acts as host for visiting foreign military delegations. He only rarely appears at conferences, although he did appear at one sponsored by the Second Ministry of Machine Building (then engaged in making munitions) in April 1956. Ch'en has occasionally contributed to the Chinese press. An essay describing the Huai-hai battle in which he participated appeared in *Chung-kuo ch'ing-nien* (China youth, December 1, 1960) and was reprinted in a collection of essays.[4] He is also the author of an article in the *JMJP* (May 11, 1964) entitled "The Doctrine of Class Struggle Is the Essence of Marxism-Leninism."

1. *SCMP* 2567, pp. 1–5.
2. *Chui-tao "szu-pa" yü-nan lieh-shih chi-*

nien-ts'e (In memory of the martyrs who died in the accident of "April Eighth"; Kalgan, 1946), p. 281.
3. *The Great Turning Point* (Peking, 1962), p. 173.
4. *Chieh-fang chan-cheng hui-i-lu* (Reminiscences of the liberation war; Peking, 1961), pp. 241–259.

Ch'en T'an-ch'iu

(1896–1943; Hupeh). CCP founder; member, CCP Central Committee.

Ch'en T'an-ch'iu was a delegate to the founding congress of the CCP in 1921. He helped organize in Wuhan one of the small Communist groups that antedated the organization of the national Party. Ch'en devoted most of his early career to Party affairs in Hupeh and then worked in the Shanghai underground. He was first elected to the Party Central Committee in 1927. He was active in Fukien before the Long March and remained there with Communist guerrilla units when Mao Tse-tung left the area in 1934. In the late thirties Ch'en went to Sinkiang as a special envoy of the CCP. He was arrested during the purge of Communists there in 1942 and executed a year later.

Ch'en was born in Hupeh in 1896,[1] but little is known of his early years. Because of his close association with Tung Pi-wu (q.v.), he may have had much the same training as Tung, who was reared and educated in Wuhan, the Hupeh capital. Tung joined Sun Yat-sen's revolutionary T'ung-meng hui in 1911, the year the Manchus were overthrown. Ch'en also joined the T'ung-meng hui and later the KMT. He then became a teacher in Wuchang and by about 1920 was among a group of eight men teaching in a middle school that Tung Pi-wu had founded with their assistance. The school was modern for its day and offered some of its courses in *pai-hua* (the contemporary, non-classical language). It soon became a nucleus for radical Hupeh students and teachers, a number of whom turned to Marxism in the next few years (see under Tung Pi-wu). Among the most influential in converting Hupeh students was Li Han-chün (q.v.), who had been introduced to Marxism while studying in Japan. Li converted Tung Pi-wu to Marxism in late 1920 when he went to Wuhan to confer with Tung and his associates about the possibilities of founding a Communist Party in China. Resulting from the discussions was a provisional Communist branch established by Tung and Ch'en toward the end of 1920,[2] apparently with assistance and guidance from I. K. Mamaev, the secretary of Comintern representative Gregory Voitinsky, and Sergei A. Polevoy, a radical member of the Peking University faculty (see under Yang Ming-chai).[3]

By mid-1921 the Hupeh radicals were meeting

frequently at Tung Pi-wu's middle school and at the Social Benefit Book Store, established by Yun Tai-ying (q.v.) and his associates in 1919 to distribute literature of the May Fourth period. In July 1921 Tung and Ch'en T'an-ch'iu were the two Hupeh delegates to the founding congress of the CCP in Shanghai. Ch'en's account of the congress, published in the mid-thirties under Comintern auspices, is one of the few eye-witness reports. It was published under the name Chen Pan-tsu.[4]

After the First Congress Ch'en returned to Wuhan, and from that time until 1926 he was secretary of the Party's Hupeh Provincial Committee. During these same years he spent some of his time as an English language teacher at the Hupeh Provincial Girls' Normal School. He also helped Tung Pi-wu and others to establish labor unions that the Party was sponsoring in the important Wuhan industrial region. The CCP took a special interest in organizing the workers of the important Peking-Hankow Railway. Hsiang Ying (q.v.), another leading Party operative in Wuhan, mentions in his autobiography that he began to organize the railway workers under Ch'en T'an-ch'iu's direction. Hsiang and Ch'en were among those promoting the trade union movement on this rail line when their efforts were suppressed by northern warlord Wu P'ei-fu in February 1923.[5] In the next year Ch'en worked in the peasant movement with Tung Pi-wu and Hsiao Ch'u-nü.[6] This took place in Chin-chai hsien, located in western Anhwei near the borders of Hupeh and Honan, an area that became a part of the Oyüwan Soviet several years later (see under Chang Kuo-t'ao).

Apart from his work in Hupeh, Ch'en also continued to play a role in the national Party organization. According to Soviet sources, he took part in the Second, Third, and Fourth Party Congresses.[7] Chinese Communist sources conflict on both the date and locale of the Second Congress, but it was probably held in Shanghai in July 1922. The Third and Fourth Congresses were held in Canton (June 1923) and Shanghai (January 1925), respectively. Each of these was attended by an average of only 20 delegates, an indication of the relatively small size of the CCP during those years. Ch'en also attended the Party's Second Enlarged Plenum in July 1926 in Shanghai. The Plenum adopted a series of resolutions designed to steer the difficult middle path between continued cooperation with the KMT and the efforts of the Communists to strengthen their position within peasant, trade union, student, and other organizations. In April–May 1927, back in Wuhan, Ch'en attended the Party's important Fifth Congress, held in the wake of the suppression of the Communists by Chiang Kai-shek, particularly in Shanghai. At this Congress he was elected for the first time to membership on the Party Central Committee. In the same year Ch'en became head of the Organization Department of the Kiangsu Party Committee, which had its headquarters in Shanghai.[8] He apparently assumed this post in mid-1927 after Kuo Po-ho, who had been the Organization Department chief under Kiangsu Party Secretary Ch'en Yen-nien (q.v.), was executed by KMT police.

The documentation on Ch'en's activities for the next few years is somewhat conflicting, but apparently he fled from Shanghai to Moscow where he was a student when the CCP held its Sixth Congress in mid-1928. He seems to have been re-elected to the Central Committee at this time. Returning to China, Ch'en went to the central soviet area to join Chu Te and Mao Tse-tung at their base on the Kiangsi-Fukien border. He was wounded in the fighting in 1930 during the Nationalists' First Annihilation Campaign against the Communists and returned to Moscow for medical treatment.

Ch'en was back in China by no later than mid-1932. From that time until at least through the first half of 1933 he worked in the extremely precarious Shanghai underground. During this period he was in charge of a training class conducted under the auspices of the Party's Kiangsu Provincial Committee.[9] He also spent part of this time in jail, but apparently the KMT did not know his identity; if they had it is unlikely that he would have been released. Like so many of the other CCP members in Shanghai in the early thirties, Ch'en was ultimately forced to leave the city, making his way to the central soviet area on the Kiangsi-Fukien border. He was assigned to Fukien where he was secretary of the Party's Provincial Committee, possibly assuming the post from Lo Ming (q.v.), who had come under fire for his conduct of Party affairs. Lo was considered "defeatist" and "opportunistic" by the Russian-returned leadership of the CCP, the men who controlled the Party headquarters in Shanghai (see under Ch'in Pang-hsien). According to an article in the Party's journal *Tou-cheng* (Struggle) in January 1934, Ch'en T'an-ch'iu was one of four high-ranking cadres censured by the central Party leadership in December 1933 because they had not been sufficiently active in a campaign to expand the Red Army. The drive had been promoted that month to stem the Nationalists' Fifth Annihilation Campaign (see under Lo Ming). Subsequently, as a result of what was considered "wavering opportunism" (a tendency affecting several areas of Party activity because of the influence of Lo Ming), Ch'en was removed as the Fukien Party chief.[10] Several other officials accused of following the "Lo Ming line" failed to receive important positions when the Second All-China Congress of Soviets met in January–February 1934 to elect a new Central Executive Committee (CEC) for the Chinese Soviet Republic (see under Teng Tzu-hui).

Ch'en, in contrast, was named to the government's new CEC and was also appointed People's Commissar for Food, an important post at a time when the Communists were feeling the effects of the Nationalist blockade.

When the Long March began in 1934, Ch'en was among those who remained behind to lead the small Red guerrilla forces that continued to harass the Nationalists in the territory of the former Chinese Soviet Republic. In the next year he was with Teng Tzu-hui and T'an Chen-lin (q.v.) in west Fukien where he worked at the Communist base established in the mountains of Ch'ang-t'ing hsien along the Fukien-Kiangsi border in late 1934 (see under Chang Ting-ch'eng). According to one account he went from Chang Ting-ch'eng's headquarters to address a group of Red Guards stationed in the mountains along the Fukien-Kwangtung border to the south of Chang's base. Ch'en was described as a CCP Central Committee member, an indication that he had retained this post after 1928, during the period of tense political struggle that ensued after the Sixth Congress (see under Li Li-san). Ch'en's visit to the Red Guard unit probably took place in the first half of 1935. He was then en route to Hong Kong and was seeking the Guards' assistance in crossing the mountainous region around Ta-p'u in northeast Kwangtung.[11] From the date of this episode Ch'en's activities are unreported until the early years of the Sino-Japanese War, but inferential evidence suggests that he returned once again to Moscow.

In 1938 or 1939 (Communist accounts conflict), Ch'en went from Moscow to Tihwa, the Sinkiang capital, to replace Teng Fa as head of the Sinkiang Staff office of the Communists' Eighth Route Army and as the CCP's chief representative in the province.[12] (The complex political situation in Sinkiang at this time is described in the biographies of Saifudin and Burhan.) Ch'en arrived during the period when Governor Sheng Shih-ts'ai was working more closely with the Soviet and Chinese Communists than with the Chinese Nationalist Government. At approximately the time of Ch'en's arrival a large number of Chinese Communists were sent there (from both Moscow and Yenan) to serve in Sheng's government. Ch'en, in effect, was for several years the chief of this advisory group. Sheng Shih-ts'ai has written an account of his relations with the Chinese Communists, but it is an account that strains credulity in many ways.[13] According to his version, he became deeply suspicious of the Chinese Communists, particularly Ch'en T'an-ch'iu (known to him as Hsu Chieh) and Mao Tse-min (q.v.), a younger brother of Mao Tse-tung and also an adviser in Sinkiang. Sheng felt his suspicions were confirmed when his younger brother died under mysterious circumstances in March 1942. He then moved quickly to break relations with the Communists and to round up a number of suspects, both the advisers from Yenan and alleged agents native to Sinkiang. According to Sheng, 656 persons were apprehended and 88 executed; the Communists use far higher figures. Ch'en, Mao Tse-min, and others were placed under what amounted to house arrest in the spring of 1942 and were formally imprisoned that September. A year later (September 27, 1943), Ch'en and Mao were executed, but this was so well concealed that when the CCP met in Yenan in 1945 for its Seventh National Congress Ch'en was re-elected to the Central Committee. According to the official announcement of the election, Ch'en was listed as one of the three persons then in jail.

The Party apparently did not learn of Ch'en's death until mid-1946 when over 100 CCP members imprisoned in Sinkiang were released and returned to Yenan. In early 1950 the Chinese press reported that the man most directly responsible for the death of Ch'en and Mao had been arrested. He was taken to Sinkiang in 1952 and executed a year later. Another group implicated in the death of Ch'en and Mao was executed in 1951. The Communists published a long account of Ch'en's imprisonment in 1959,[14] and Sinkiang Party leader Saifudin wrote a similar but much shorter account for the September 1963 issue of *Min-tsu t'uan-chieh* (Nationalities unity).

Ch'en was married to Hsu Ch'ien-chih in 1924. She had been one of his students at the Hupeh Girls' Normal School and was with him in Shanghai in 1927. Arrested there, she was taken to Nanking where she was executed. Ch'en married again and his second wife was with him in the Shanghai underground in the 1932–33 period. She too lost her life, but the circumstances are not known.

1. *Bol'shaya Sovetskaya Entsiklopedya* (Large Soviet Encylopedia), vol. 47, April 1957, p. 488.

2. Hsi-wu lao-jen [Tung Pi-wu], *"Erh-ch'i" hui-i-lu* (Reminiscences of "February Seventh"; Peking, 1957), pp. 25–26; SCMM 274, p. 13.

3. Chow Tse-tsung, *The May Fourth Movement* (Cambridge, Mass., 1960), p. 249.

4. Chen Pan-tsu, "Reminiscences of the First Congress of the Communist Party of China," *Communist International*, American edition, 13.10:1361–1366 (October 1936); cited in C. Martin Wilbur, ed., *The Communist Movement in China, an Essay Written in 1924 by Ch'en Kung-po* (New York, 1960), p. 49.

5. *"Erh-ch'i" hui-i-lu, passim.*

6. *Kung-ch'ing-t'uan, wo-te mu-ch'in* (The Communist Youth League, my mother; Peking, 1958), p. 17.

7. *Bol'shaya Sovetskaya Entsiklopedya*, p. 488.

8. *Hung-ch'i p'iao-p'iao* (Red flag fluttering; Peking, 1957), V, 149.

9. *Chung-kuo ch'ing-nien* (China youth), no. 67, June 25, 1951, p. 29.

10. Tso-liang Hsiao, *Power Relations within the Chinese Communist Movement, 1930–1934* (Seattle, Wash., 1961), pp. 246–247.

11. *Flame on High Mountain* (Peking, 1959), pp. 116–117.

12. *Hung-ch'i p'iao-p'iao,* V, 150; *Hung-chi p'iao-p'iao* (Peking, 1959), X, 122.

13. Allen S. Whiting and Sheng Shih-ts'ai, *Sinkiang: Pawn or Pivot?* (East Lansing, Mich., 1958), *passim.*

14. *Hung-ch'i p'iao-p'iao,* X, 132–155.

Ch'en Tu-hsiu

(1879–1942; Huai-ning, Anhwei). First CCP General Secretary.

Ch'en Tu-hsiu occupies a position of great significance in China's intellectual modernization as one of the prime movers of the May Fourth Movement. Having helped found the CCP in 1921, he was its chief in the turbulent phase from 1921 to 1927. A man of impassioned nature and great moral courage, he began his career as a classical scholar, then in the decade from 1910 to 1920 became one of the foremost iconoclasts. He led the Chinese Communist movement from its nascent stage, and under Russian guidance he directed it falteringly through a storm of events which ended in a tragic debacle in 1927. Without absolving himself from responsibility for the failure, Ch'en nevertheless defied the Stalinist attempt to make him the scapegoat of the failure and identified with Trotskyism. After several years of imprisonment by the Nanking government he returned to a democratic outlook and to classical studies.

Ch'en Tu-hsiu was born on October 8, 1879, a scion of a fairly wealthy and prominent scholar-official family. His father, a military official in Manchuria, died before Ch'en was a year old. He was reared by his grandfather and an elder brother and was given a strict classical education. In 1896 he took the *Hsiu-ts'ai* degree and in the following year the *Chü-jen,* but he developed an aversion toward the civil service examinations, a sign of rebellion against the traditional order. He was drawn to Liang Ch'i-ch'ao's *Shih-wu pao* (Current affairs), which was first published in 1896, and soon developed a profound admiration for Liang.

Ch'en's modern education began with his enrollment in Ch'iu-shih shu-yuan (Truth-seeking school) in Hangchow, Chekiang, where he studied naval architecture in the French language. He had to flee after making a speech against the Manchus, taking refuge briefly in Nanking. In 1902 he went to Japan and enrolled at the Higher Normal School in Tokyo. There, with Chang Chi, Feng Tzu-yu, and others, he organized the Chinese Youth Society (Chung-kuo ch'ing-nien hui). In the same year he returned to China

and in 1903, with Chang Shih-chao, a prominent Chinese scholar, Chang Chi, and others, established a revolutionary daily, *Kuo-min jih-jih pao* (National daily news).

In 1904 Ch'en returned to Anhwei where he engaged in educational and journalistic work. He taught at the Anhwei Academy in Wuhu, a revolutionary institution with which Anhwei military leader Po Wen-wei and the scholar Liu Shih-p'ei were associated. He also founded a secret, quasi-military organization, of which Po Wen-wei was also a member. In 1906 he was again in Japan, but he returned the same year to teach in Wusih, Kiangsu, where he started the *Wu-hsi pai-hua pao* (Wusih vernacular magazine) with journalist-educator Chang Shih-chao and Liu Shih-p'ei. Exactly when he left for France is uncertain (probably 1907), but he was there until 1910 and found in French culture much that he felt could overcome China's cultural weaknesses. French political and literary thought, particularly ideas concerning the rights of man, Social Darwinism, assertiveness, socialist thought, and scientism, prepared him for the role of one of China's great intellectual modernizers. Returning to China in 1910, he taught school briefly at Hangchow, took some part in the 1911 Revolution, and in 1912 was named chief secretary to his former associate Po Wen-wei, then the military governor of Anhwei. In 1913 he took part in the so-called second revolution against Yuan Shih-k'ai, and after its failure fled to Shanghai and thence to Japan, where he remained until 1915.

The failure of the Chinese Revolution and the deepening chaos which ruled in China profoundly disappointed Ch'en. At 37 he embarked on his new role as one of China's foremost intellectual modernizers by launching the *Ch'ing-nien tsa-chih* (Youth magazine) on September 15, 1915 (renamed *Hsin ch'ing-nien* [New Youth] in 1916). Its avowed purpose was to eliminate Chinese tradition and introduce Western ideas. China's youths were reminded of their mission to revitalize the nation and were urged to discard the old morality for a new code of ethics: to be independent, progressive, assertive, cosmopolitan, utilitarian, and scientific. Ch'en was the sole editor of the *New Youth* until January 1918 when an editorial board of six, which included himself, Li Ta-chao, and Hu Shih, took over. In the next few years the journal attracted the cream of China's young intelligentsia and espoused a bewildering variety of novel ideas touching every sphere of Chinese life.

In 1917 Ch'en was named dean of the School of Letters of Peking University by the new chancellor, Ts'ai Yuan-p'ei. The appointment proved to be highly strategic for Ch'en's leadership of the renaissance movement. At the nation's foremost educational institution, Ch'en provided much of the needed guidance to the best elements of China's youth who shared his revolt against the old order. He led or lent support to a variety of undertakings by colleagues and students, which profoundly impinged upon traditional Chinese culture—the best known being Hu Shih's call for a literary revolution in 1917.

As Ch'en mustered all available forces to destroy the old, he was simultaneously engaged in the quest for a new philosophy, which led him eventually to Marxism-Leninism. Initially in 1915–1917 he thought 19th-century European liberalism was the best antidote to China's problems, but he was basically a man of action. He realized China's problems were deep-rooted; her cure involved nothing less than a fundamental overhaul in her basic culture. In the course of the 1917–1920 period, he veered toward socialism as the panacea. This interest was interrupted briefly by the spell of John Dewey, who lectured in China from May 1919 to July 1921. Ch'en was attracted to Dewey's conception of democracy as a system not easily imposed from above, but one that required a grass-roots transformation of Chinese society. However, under the impact of the May Fourth Movement, and more especially of the Russian Revolution, he seized upon Marxism-Leninism as the formula that offered not only an all-embracing modern world-view, but also a program of action.

In December 1918, with Li Ta-chao's assistance, he founded the *Mei-chou p'ing-lun* (Weekly critic), which signalled a rift in the Chinese intelligentsia between the politically oriented activists and the culturally oriented gradualists. In the pages of this weekly, Li Ta-chao and Hu Shih, representing the two camps, engaged in a crucial debate on "Problems and Isms." Ch'en's attack on tradition stirred up a swarm of opposition, and in March 1919 he was forced to resign from Peking University. He played a leading role in the May Fourth Incident, which occurred two months later. He was arrested on June 11 and imprisoned for almost three months for distributing handbills denouncing the Anfu militarists who ruled in Peking.[1]

In the spring of 1920 Ch'en left Peking for the freer atmosphere in Shanghai where he continued to publish *New Youth*. Here began a new chapter in his career: the organization and leadership of the CCP. In April 1920 he met Comintern official Gregory Voitinsky and other members of his mission, which included Yang Ming-chai (q.v.) and Voitinsky's secretary, I. K. Mamaev. Voitinsky suggested that a Communist party be formed from the progressive publicists in Shanghai, namely, Ch'en himself, Tai Chi-t'ao, Shen Ting-i, and Li Han-chün of the KMT's *Hsing-ch'i p'ing-lun* (Sunday critic), Shao Li-tzu of the KMT's *Min-kuo jih-pao* (Republic daily), and Chang Tung-sun of the Progressive Party's *Shih-shih hsin-pao* (Current

news). After preliminary discussions the first Communist nucleus was formed in May 1920, and it established a provisional Central Committee with Ch'en as secretary. In August a unit of the Socialist Youth League (SYL) was also formed. The Communist movement now entered its developing period; Voitinsky and Mamaev helped organize nuclei of the CCP and the SYL in other major cities, while Yang Ming-chai and Mme. Voitinsky taught Russian to a group of students to be sent to Moscow for training. The early "Communists" were in fact a group of socialists of many hues and included also a number of anarchists. The anarchists soon rose to challenge the more Marxian-oriented elements. On November 7, 1920, the monthly *Kung-ch'an tang* (Communist) appeared and declared war on the anarchists, who were resisting the Bolshevik concept of a Communist party and proletarian dictatorship as the ideal which the Chinese Marxists should espouse.

On December 16, 1920, Ch'en Tu-hsiu departed for Canton to assume the position of provincial educational commissioner on the invitation of the new Kwangtung governor, Ch'en Chiung-ming. He immediately made use of the opportunity to initiate a Communist nucleus. By January 1921 he had recruited his former students from Peking University, T'an P'ing-shan, Ch'en Kung-po (q.v.), and T'an Chih-t'ang, to organize the Kwangtung Party nucleus and publish *Lao-tung-che* (The proletariat); a SYL unit was also organized and its members included Lo Ch'i-yuan (Lo I-yuan) and Juan Hsiao-hsien. In February 1921 Ch'en also transferred *New Youth* to Canton. Not long afterward, in July 1921, twelve Chinese Communists representing six groups in China and one in Japan convened the first CCP Congress in Shanghai. Ch'en was then in Canton, but he was consulted on the Party constitution and manifesto and was elected Party general secretary.

Ch'en's involvement in Ch'en Chiung-ming's government later proved to be a disadvantage to his Party's effort to collaborate with Sun Yat-sen's KMT. The fact that he was an appointee of Ch'en Chiung-ming and that the Canton Communists worked for the latter's organ, *Kuang-tung Ch'ün-pao* (Kwangtung masses), antagonized Sun's personal followers, who were fomenting a showdown between Sun and Ch'en Chiung-ming (see under Ch'en Kung-po). In August 1921 Ch'en resigned his post in Canton and returned to Shanghai to assume leadership of the CCP. Almost from the beginning his relations with the Comintern were strained. He objected to what he thought was Comintern official Maring's excessive interference in CCP affairs and was offended when Maring offered Comintern funds for CCP expenditures. The pressure of events forced him to alter his attitude, however; in September 1921, along with his wife and fellow Communists Yang Ming-chai, Pao Hui-seng, K'o Ch'ing-shih (q.v.), Li Ta, and Chou Fo-hai, he was arrested by the Shanghai Settlement authorities on the charge of propagating Bolshevism in *New Youth*. Maring hired a French lawyer and bailed out Ch'en after a day and a half (at a cost of 50,000 Chinese dollars to the Comintern), and the others remained in jail for a few more days until they were released after being fined $5,000, also at Comintern expense.[2]

The fundamental issue which caused tension in Ch'en's relations with the Comintern and on which his leadership disastrously foundered in 1927 was that of collaboration with the KMT in the form required by Sun Yat-sen and imposed on the CCP by the Comintern, namely, the Communists were to enter the KMT as individuals, be loyal to KMT principles, and be subject to KMT discipline. Until after the Second CCP Congress of July 1922 Ch'en had assumed that CCP support of Sun's national revolutionary movement implied no organizational bondage for the Party. He therefore viewed with deep misgivings the form under which the collaboration was to take place, but again the pressure of events and of Comintern authority compelled him to acquiesce. In August 1922 Maring had Ch'en call a plenum of the Central Committee in Hangchow to endorse' the policy. There is conflicting testimony on the subject, but it appears that with the exception of Li Ta-chao (q.v.), Maring's proposal was strenuously resisted by Ch'en Tu-hsiu, Chang Kuo-t'ao, Ts'ai Ho-sen (qq.v.), and Kao Yü-han. These men felt that the principle of working within the KMT (often referred to as the "bloc within") would cause confusion in the CCP as a class organization and a loss of freedom to pursue independent policies. However, Maring forced through his proposal by a display of Comintern authority, but not before Ch'en secured an understanding from him that the KMT would be reorganized along less rigid lines.

Sun Yat-sen, then marooned in Shanghai after his ouster by Ch'en Chiung-ming in June 1922, welcomed the cooperation of the Communists because of their great influence over China's youths, but perhaps more important was the Soviet aid that he knew would follow CCP cooperation. In the latter part of August 1922, along with Li Ta-chao, Ts'ai Ho-sen, and Chang T'ai-lei (q.v.), Ch'en, sponsored by KMT veteran Chang Chi, was inducted into the KMT. On September 6, Ch'en was appointed by Sun as a member of a nine-man committee to work out the plans for KMT reorganization. But he was soon called away to lead the CCP delegation to Moscow to attend the Fourth Comintern Congress in November–December 1922. Among the Chinese Communists present were Liu Jen-ching, Ch'ü Ch'iu-pai (q.v.), and Chang T'ai-lei. Ch'en

was elected to the Executive Committee of the Comintern (ECCI) at the Congress. The Chinese delegates received a stern rebuke from the caustic tongue of Comintern Secretary Karl Radek for their utopian optimism concerning the imminence of socialism in China and for their excessive emphasis on theoretical study and reluctance to cooperate with the KMT in practical work.

Back in China the Chinese Communists were still profoundly divided over the issue of cooperation with the KMT. Having discovered for himself the Comintern's sentiments on the matter and having been convinced of the weakness of the Chinese proletariat by the February 7, 1923, "massacre" of the Peking-Hankow Railway workers (see under Teng Chung-hsia), Ch'en became more compromising. Whereas earlier he believed the Chinese proletariat, leading the peasantry and following the footsteps of the world proletariat, would in the near future inaugurate a socialist order in China, his analysis of the Chinese class forces now recognized that the bourgeois democratic revolution was a necessary stage in China's evolution and that it should be led by the national bourgeoisie (the KMT) with proletarian and peasant support. Collaboration within the KMT as a policy of the CCP was endorsed by the Third CCP Congress held in Canton in June 1923. It was implemented with Michael Borodin's arrival in early October 1923. Although Ch'en was nominated by Sun as a delegate from Anhwei to the First KMT Congress in January 1924, he stayed away, partly because his presence was likely to be controversial among KMT delegates and partly on account of an earlier tacit agreement among the Communists that the key CCP leaders should stay out of the KMT.

Nevertheless, Ch'en continued to be uneasy with the development of the KMT-CCP collaboration. Leading the Party Center in Shanghai, he found the Kwangtung Regional Committee, headed by his eldest son Ch'en Yen-nien (q.v.), becoming increasingly less subordinate to the center and taking orders from Borodin, who usually bypassed not only Ch'en but also Voitinsky, the Comintern representative attached to the Shanghai Party Center. It also became increasingly apparent that the Soviet Union, in the interest of preserving the alliance, was committed to supporting Sun Yat-sen's KMT even at the cost of subordinating the CCP's real interest in mass agitation.

In July 1925 the KMT leader Tai Chi-t'ao published his pamphlet "The National Revolution and the KMT," which among other things demanded that the Communists dissolve their party and become pure KMT members if they were to be sincerely committed to the KMT-led revolution. At the CCP plenum held in Peking in October 1925, Ch'en voiced apprehension that Tai's views represented a trend within the KMT. He proposed that the CCP should prepare for withdrawal at the appropriate moment in order to preserve its identity, lead the masses, and not be bound by the KMT. However, being opposed by Voitinsky and other members of the Central Committee, Ch'en dropped his proposal.

Ch'en's fears were confirmed by the March 20, 1926, Incident (see under Chou En-lai) when Chiang Kai-shek arrested certain Communists among the Whampoa cadets and disarmed the Hong Kong–Canton Strike Committee. They were further confirmed by the resolutions of the KMT Central Executive Committee in May 1926, which ousted Communists from high-level KMT posts, forbade Communist criticism of Sun Yat-sen's doctrines, and demanded the roster of Communists who held KMT membership. Yet the CCP, under Kremlin orders, had to comply so as not to undermine the Soviet alliance with the KMT-led national revolutionary movement. It was feared a weakening of the alliance would endanger Soviet interests in the Far East, or alternatively, lend force to the Trotskyite attack on the Stalinist leadership, which Trotsky accused of damaging the Chinese Revolution. Ch'en Tu-hsiu and his colleagues in Shanghai, notably P'eng Shu-chih and Lo I-nung (q.v.), proposed that the CCP should develop independent military power to resist Chiang. P'eng was sent to Canton to lay the plan before Borodin, but the latter refused to allocate a portion of the arms supplied to Chiang and other generals by the Soviet Union on the grounds that arming the peasantry would arouse the suspicions of the KMT and incite peasant resistance to the KMT. P'eng was bluntly told that the CCP was at the stage where it should be rendering coolie service to the KMT.[3]

After the March 20 Incident, Ch'en wrote the Comintern a report presenting his personal views and proposing that instead of trying to cooperate as members of the KMT, the CCP should withdraw and cooperate as a separate Party alongside the KMT. If this were not done, Ch'en argued, the CCP would not be able to execute its independent policies and gain the confidence of the masses. Bukharin, representing the Comintern, responded with a rebuke in an article in *Pravda*. The Comintern further ordered Voitinsky to keep Ch'en in line.

When the Northern Expedition began in July 1926, Ch'en criticized its harmful effects upon the CCP. He felt that it weakened the workers' movement in the south; for instance, the Canton–Hong Kong strike and the boycott against the British were to be called off in the interests of the Northern Expedition, and the KMT would need to make heavy demands upon the peasantry to defray the costs of the military venture. In addition, the workers in Shanghai were on the verge of staging an insurrection to drive out the Chihli and Shantung militarists. If they should succeed, Ch'en argued, a dispute would certainly arise between the CCP and the KMT as to which side would inherit the political power that the workers might gain. Ch'en expressed his views in a resolution he drafted for the CCP Plenum in July 1926: "There are two paths for the Chinese revolution to follow, namely: (1) the proletariat is to lead the revolution, or (2) the bourgeoisie is to lead, but since it is bound to betray the revolution midway, the CCP should prepare to capture hegemony even though, temporarily, it should cooperate with the bourgeoisie." Voitinsky again opposed Ch'en's views, fearing they might influence the Communists to make a premature break with the KMT. He also told Ch'en that, should the Shanghai workers succeed, all power should go to the KMT.

Shortly before Chiang's forces entered Shanghai on March 22, 1927, Ch'en anticipated that Chiang would repress the mass movements. Hence P'eng Shu-chih was sent to Wuhan to see Borodin and some leading Communists to present the Party Center's viewpoint and to discuss plans to overcome or counter Chiang. P'eng found his colleagues too absorbed with problems in Wuhan to be concerned about the events in Shanghai. Furthermore, the Comintern wired Ch'en to get the Shanghai workers to bury their arms, to avoid stirring up trouble in the International Settlement, and to avoid conflict with Chiang Kai-shek's troops. In March 1927 the prominent KMT and Wuhan leader Wang Ching-wei arrived back in China and conferred with Ch'en about the state of the two-party alliance. On April 5 they issued a joint declaration from Shanghai favoring KMT-CCP collaboration. Then on April 10 Wang went to Hankow, and on April 12 Chiang Kai-shek's troops forcibly took over Shanghai and drove the Communists and labor leaders underground. Forced to evacuate Shanghai, Ch'en and the Party Center moved to Wuhan where he was distressed to find that Wang Ching-wei was showing himself quite opposed to the Communists, a number of whom held positions in his government and in the Wuhan armies. With Chiang Kai-shek having broken completely with the Communists and with the "Left-KMT" at Wuhan becoming more and more disenchanted with their actions, Ch'en found himself in a difficult position. This was not made easier by the attitude of Stalin, who had not yet agreed to abandon attempts at collaboration with the KMT. The Soviet leader was then locked in a battle with Trotsky, who was making Stalin's China policy one issue of their conflict. Still banking on Wang Ching-wei's support, Stalin sent the Indian Communist M. N. Roy to China as a Comintern representative whose task was to articulate the Stalin view of revolution and to pressure the CCP to maintain the alliance with the KMT. Arriving in Wuhan in mid-April, it was Roy who urged Ch'en to call the Fifth CCP Congress. This opened in Hankow on April 28. The Congress heard confusing and differing opinions, not the least of the confusion arising because Roy and Borodin, who attended in the capacity of Moscow's chief adviser to the KMT, each had his own interpretation of the Moscow line. The debates covered a number of problems, several of them notably affecting Ch'en. Borodin called for a temporary retreat into the hinterlands and Roy rebutted him. One writer has stated that Borodin was "inclined to go even further than Stalin himself in conciliating the Left Kuomintang leaders, and Ch'en Tu-hsiu supported him in this."[4] This Ch'en did when he presented Borodin's plan to move to the hinterlands as the "Northwestern theory." The theory assumed, in the words of Mif (who opposed it), that the revolution could not develop in major industrial centers such as Wuhan, Shanghai, nor Canton because of the strength of the "imperialists" and the Chinese bourgeoisie in those cities. Rather, the revolutionary forces should be shifted to the northwest provinces where imperialism was weaker and where the Communists could build up their forces for a later assault on "imperialist strongholds." The scheme was vetoed by the Congress, apparently on orders from Moscow.[5]

Another matter for debate at the Fifth Congress was the agrarian reform program, an issue that very directly concerned Ch'en. Here he found himself facing the opposition of Mao Tse-tung, who had been directing peasant affairs in Hunan and who had just presented his report on "An Investigation into the Peasant Movement in Hunan" before the KMT Land Committee in Wuhan. Mao later told Edgar Snow that the report was never allowed to come up for discussion at the Fifth Congress, largely because Ch'en disagreed with its proposals.[6] But Ch'en was well aware of it, because Mao's quite radical thesis for land reform had already caused dissension in the KMT, as well as within the ranks of the CCP where many members, like Ch'en, felt that such schemes would only further antagonize members of the KMT (see under Hsia Hsi). After he had attended the Fifth Congress for a few days Mao grew disgusted and withdrew. No doubt this gesture received the support of a number of his Hunan Party colleagues, although there were still others who favored Ch'en's view (see under Li Wei-han). However, Ch'en was opposed more openly by Ch'ü Ch'iu-pai and other members of the Kwangtung Regional Committee who partially sided with Mao on the land issue, but who also had personal grudges against Ch'en (see under Ch'ü Ch'iu-pai). Notwithstanding this serious opposition, Ch'en was reelected Party general secretary.

After the Congress the political situation rapidly worsened. A local Hunanese militarist, acting on orders from Chiang Kai-shek, attacked Changsha on May 21, 1927 (see under Li Wei-han). Once again the Party was caught in the dilemma of what to do about continued support to the Wuhan government. The Politburo held an emergency meeting to decide the matter and Ch'en, who was now discouraged with efforts at cooperation, reverted to his initial fears that they would not work and vigorously proposed a complete break with the KMT. In his report to the Politburo he noted that collaboration with the KMT had become daily more dangerous and that the KMT was demanding the entire leadership of the revolution. Thus he felt that the CCP had before it only two alternatives, either abandon its leadership of the mass movements or break with the KMT altogether. When he received no conclusive reaction from his colleagues, he appealed to Borodin, who agreed with him but stated that "Moscow will never permit it."[7] Unable to restrain himself any longer, Ch'en tendered the Central Committee a letter of resignation, stating as his main reason for resigning: "On the one hand the Comintern wants us to carry out our own policies, and on the other it does not permit us to withdraw from the KMT. There is really no way out; I really cannot continue my work."[8]

Ch'en's letter was ignored and meantime, in the interest of preserving face for Stalin and the Comintern, an effort was begun by some Party members to make Ch'en the scapegoat for the failure of the Chinese revolution. The more active of these were Ch'ü Ch'iu-pai, Ts'ai Ho-sen, and Jen Pi-shih (qq.v.), all of whom were not without personal reasons for challenging their leader. Nine years later, when he spoke to Edgar Snow about Ch'en Tu-hsiu, Mao stated that Ch'en had been guilty of a "wavering opportunism [that] deprived the Party of decisive leadership." He had been much influenced by Ch'en and his writings when he was a younger political leader, but regarding the Fifth Congress Mao spoke critically about Ch'en's lack of aggressiveness. "Ch'en was really frightened of the workers and especially of the armed peasants. Confronted at last with the reality of armed insurrection he completely lost his senses."[9]

A period of confusion and worsening relations continued until mid-July when the Wuhan government completely severed its ties with the Communists. Depressed by the failure of a policy for which he had never been totally enthusiastic, Ch'en withdrew to Shanghai where despite Chiang Kai-shek's control of the city, police surveillance was not yet so efficient that Communist operatives could not function with some degree of safety. Thus Ch'en was not on hand in Wuhan for the final debacle in KMT-CCP relations when on August 1, 1927, the Nanchang garrison force revolted and brought off the rebellion planned by members of the Central Committee who had remained in central China. The capture of the Kiangsi capital, known as the Nanchang Uprising (see under Yeh T'ing and Ho Lung), is officially viewed as a major turning point in Communist developments. From the time of the Fifth Congress Ch'en's control of CCP affairs had virtually ended and it was the group that planned the Nanchang Uprising that would now carry on the CCP leadership and direct the flight from Nanchang when the Communists were quickly driven from the city.

On August 7, 1927, Ch'en's rival Ch'ü Ch'iu-pai and members of his faction called an emergency conference and had Ch'en deposed, *in absentia*. As the Party's elder statesman, Ch'en's prestige was still high, but for all practical purposes his role in Chinese Communism ended with this conference, although from time to time he criticized CCP policies. In November 1929, unable to tolerate Ch'en's vexatious criticisms, Li Li-san, the newly emerged leader of the CCP, found a pretext to have Ch'en expelled from the Party. In early 1930 Ch'en refused to go to Moscow to answer charges that he had sabotaged Comintern policies and had thereby caused the failure of the Chinese Revolution, charges which were brought forward at the Sixth CCP Congress held in Moscow in mid-1928. Rather, Ch'en identified himself with the Trotskyites and proceeded to weld the various splintered anti-Stalinist groups in China into a Trotskyist party. In October 1932 he was arrested by the French Concession police and turned over to the Nationalist government. He was imprisoned until August 1937, and after his release he devoted the remaining five years of his life to classical studies. A series of private letters to his friends indicate that Ch'en had returned to his original democratic outlook in his last days. He died on May 27, 1942, in Chiang-chin (Kiangtsing), a small town on the Yangtze near Chungking.

Ch'en was married in 1897 and had three sons and a daughter (Yen-nien in 1898, Ch'iao-nien in 1901, Sung-nien in 1903, and Yü-ying in 1900). Both Ch'en Yen-nien and Ch'en Ch'iao-nien were very active in the Communist movement and both lost their lives as "revolutionary martyrs" in the turmoil of the 1920's.

---

1. Chow Tse-tsung, *The May Fourth Movement* (Cambridge, Mass., 1960), p. 172.

2. Hsi-Wu lao-jen [Tung Pi-wu] "Chung-kuo Kung-ch'an tang ch'eng-li ch'ien-hou ti chien-wen" (A personal account of the establishment of the CCP), *Hsin kuan-ch'a* (New Observer), no. 13 (July 1, 1957), pp. 16–18.

3. Ch'en Tu-hsiu, *Kao Ch'üan-tang t'ung-chih shu* (A letter to all Party comrades; Shanghai, 1929), p. 3.

4. Stuart Schram, *Mao Tse-tung* (New York, 1966), p. 97.

5. Conrad Brandt, *Stalin's Failure in China* (Cambridge, Mass., 1958), pp. 122–123.

6. Edgar Snow, *Red Star over China* (New York, 1938), p. 145.

7. Brandt, p. 129.

8. Ch'en Tu-hsiu, p. 10.

9. Snow, pp. 132, 147–148.

Ch'en Yen-nien

(1898–1927; Huai-ning, Anhwei). Early Party leader; member, CCP Central Committee.

Ch'en Yen-nien, son of the famous Ch'en Tu-hsiu, was one of the early members of the CCP and a key figure in the establishment of a French branch of the Party in 1922. He later went to Moscow and after two years of study returned home to become an important Party leader in Canton and Shanghai. He was apprehended and executed by the Nationalists in mid-1927, only a few weeks after he had been elected to the Party's Central Committee.

The Ch'en family was native to Huai-ning (now An-ch'ing), a river port in southern Anhwei on the north bank of the Yangtze. Ch'en Yen-nien grew up in large cities, accompanying his father to Shanghai, Peking, and Canton. He probably received part of his schooling in each of these cities. Exposed to the ideas of his father and his father's many intellectual friends, young Ch'en was particularly influenced by anarchist doctrines. Ch'en Tu-hsiu was an ardent Francophile, a fact that may have influenced his sons, Yen-nien and Ch'iao-nien, to go to France for further study in 1920. They joined a group of Chinese enrolled in the work-and-study program (see under Chao Shih-yen) that had sponsored students in France since the early days of the Chinese Republic. Like many of the Chinese students in France, Ch'en devoted more of his time to political activities than to his academic work. He, Chao Shih-yen, and Ts'ai Ho-sen (q.v.) formed a "trio of brilliant propagandists" who promoted the cause of Chinese Communism through "sheer force of personality and power of persuasion."[1] Ch'en and his colleagues established small but active political organizations, which by mid-1922 became, in effect, the French branch of the CCP. Of the six or seven functionaries in the French branch, only Chao Shih-yen and Ch'en were full-time workers.[2] Ch'en was also the editor of a mimeographed publication known as *Shao-nien* (Youth), put out first by the Chinese Socialist Youth League and later by the CCP unit in Paris. This began in the summer of 1922 and continued for a few years (renamed *Ch'ih-kuang*, Red glow, in 1923). In this enterprise he was assisted by his brother. Their audience was largely the worker-student groups in France and Belgium, but copies of *Shao-nien* were circulated in Canada through the Chinese Labor Union of Canada and in Shanghai through the New Youth Society.[3]

After two years in France Ch'en left for Moscow in late 1922 or early 1923 to enroll in the newly established Communist University of the Toilers of the East, a school also attended by his friend Chao Shih-yen. Ch'en returned to China in early 1925 and went to Canton to join his father, then the Party general secretary. In Canton he was said to have been on good terms with Borodin, the Soviet adviser to the KMT, and Liao Chung-k'ai, the left-wing KMT leader who was assassinated in August 1925. Not long after his arrival Ch'en was chosen to head the CCP's Kwangtung Regional Committee, which was in charge of Party affairs in both Kwangtung and Kwangsi. Ch'en's Committee was the largest of the Party's regional units, and from its headquarters in Canton it had a direct influence on the many CCP members who were working in KMT organs and the Nationalist Army. By 1925 it had developed an organizational structure that included six departments—organization, propaganda, military, women's, labor, and peasant affairs. The Regional Committee also had its own publication, the *Jen-min chou-k'an* (People's weekly).[4] While Ch'en was in charge of Party affairs in Kwangtung, the important Canton-Hong Kong strike began in the wake of the May 30th Incident in Shanghai (1925). The strike, which affected industrial establishments in the southern coastal cities in 1925–26, is discussed in the biography of labor leader Su Chao-cheng.

When the Northern Expedition began in mid-1926, a number of Communist leaders from Canton followed the armies to Wuhan to take part in the transfer there of the left-KMT government in late 1926. Ch'en, however, remained in Kwangtung where he continued to direct Party operations. In early 1927 the Communists in Shanghai began to step up the pace of their activities in order to help the advancing armies led by Chiang Kai-shek with whom the CCP was still cooperating. According to an account by the wife of Ch'ü Ch'iu-pai (q.v.), a decision was made at this juncture to transfer Ch'en to Shanghai to help strengthen the leadership of the Kiangsu-Chekiang Regional Committee. But rather than proceeding to Shanghai it appears that Ch'en went directly to Wuhan where in April–May the Communists held their Fifth National Congress.[5] In the meantime Chiang Kai-shek's forces had moved into Shanghai in late March with the assistance of the Communists, but then in mid-April he suppressed the CCP apparatus in Shanghai, killing a large number of Communists and forcing the others underground. Ch'en was elected to the Party Central Committee at the Fifth Congress and immediately afterwards was sent to Shanghai where, in effect, he replaced Lo I-nung who had been head of the Kiangsu-Chekiang Committee. Now, however, to improve the Party apparatus in this area separate provincial committees were established.

Ch'en Yen-nien was made secretary of the Kiangsu Committee. Subordinate to him were Chao Shih-yen, who was in charge of the workers' movement, and Han Pu-hsien, the secretary-general of the Committee. In the latter part of June, Ch'en and Han were arrested by the Nationalists; according to the Communists' account, Han revealed the identity of Ch'en who was immediately executed.[6]

Ch'en Yen-nien's rise in the Party hierarchy was very rapid during the last two years of his life, while his father was still the CCP general secretary. In Maoist histories he is credited with having opposed the "opportunism" of his father and although his father left the Party by 1929, Ch'en had been generally accepted as a Communist in good standing. In the first decade of the Party's growth he was one of its leading theoreticians and displayed good organizational ability.

Ch'en Yen-nien's younger brother, Ch'iao-nien, also played a role of some significance in the Communist movement. He was born in 1901 and probably had much the same upbringing as his older brother. He too went to Paris in 1920 and helped to organize the French branch of the CCP. In addition to working on *Shao-nien*, Ch'iao-nien worked in a Paris factory, thus enabling his brother to devote himself to political affairs without the need to seek outside employment.[7] He probably went to Moscow with his brother, but by the mid-1920's he was working in Peking under Chao Shih-yen when the latter was secretary of the Party's Peking Municipal Committee.[8] Ch'iao-nien later went to Canton and then, after the KMT–CCP split in 1927 he was a leading official in the Communist underground in Hupeh. He was captured and executed in January 1928.

1. Conrad Brandt, *The French-Returned Elite in the Chinese Communist Party,* reprint no. 13 (Institute of International Studies, University of California, Berkeley, Calif., 1961).

2. *Ibid.*

3. Chow Tse-tsung, *Research Guide to the May Fourth Movement* (Cambridge, Mass., 1963), p. 113.

4. C. Martin Wilbur and Julie Lien-ying How, *Documents on Communism, Nationalism, and Soviet Advisers in China, 1918–1927* (New York, 1956), p. 96.

5. *Hung-ch'i p'iao-p'iao* (Red flag fluttering; Peking, 1958), VIII, 39; *Chung-kuo kung-ch'an-tang tsai chung-nan-ti-ch'ü ling-tao ko-ming tou-cheng te li-shih tzu-liao* (Historical materials on the revolutionary struggles led by the CCP in central-south China; Wuhan, 1951), I, 183.

6. *Hung-ch'i p'iao-p'iao* (Peking, 1957), V, 11.

7. Modern China project, Columbia University, New York, Howard L. Boorman, director.

8. *Hung-ch'i p'iao-p'iao,* V, 5.

Ch'en Yü

(1916–   ). Specialist in international trade union liaison work; member, Secretariat, World Federation of Trade Unions.

Ch'en Yü is one of Peking's leading liaison officials with the World Federation of Trade Unions (WFTU), the Communist-sponsored organization established at a congress in Paris in September 1945. A delegation from the Chinese Communist "liberated areas" attended the Paris congress under the leadership of Teng Fa (q.v.), then the top Chinese Communist labor official. It is not known if Ch'en attended this congress, but this seems likely in view of the fact that he was elected an alternate member of the WFTU General Council. Because Ch'en is so closely associated with the WFTU, a note of explanation is necessary to explain its internal organization. In descending order of importance, the WFTU consists of the following positions and organs: chairman, vice-chairmen, Secretariat, Executive Committee, General Council. The chairman, the vice-chairmen, and members of the three subordinate organs are elected at congresses held every four years.

Ch'en's whereabouts in the late forties and early fifties are not documented, but apparently he spent most of this period at the WFTU Headquarters, then in Vienna. He was not reported in China until May 1953 when he was elected a member of the Executive Committee of the All-China Federation of Trade Unions (ACFTU) at the Seventh Labor Congress. In this same month he was also identified as a member of the Asian and Australasian Liaison Bureau of the WFTU; by November 1953 he had become secretary-general of the Bureau, a post he held until at least the end of 1956. However, rather little was heard about the Bureau and it apparently lapsed into inactivity by the mid-fifties.

Although Ch'en had returned to China by 1953, he was to spend much time abroad in the ensuing years, usually traveling under the auspices of either the WFTU or the ACFTU and very frequently in the company of either Liu Ning-i or Liu Ch'ang-sheng (qq.v.). The two Liu's, both politically more important than Ch'en, have held high posts in the WFTU. It is evident that Ch'en's career is intimately linked with these two leaders, both of whom are CCP Central Committee members. Thus it was as a member of a delegation led by Liu Ning-i that Ch'en attended the Third WFTU Congress in Vienna in October 1953 when he was re-elected an alternate member of the General Council. He was next abroad in March–April 1955 as an adviser to the WFTU delegation sent to Japan for a meeting of the Economic Commission for Asia and the Far East (ECAFE), a regional organization subordinate to the United Nations. In the interim, reflecting his activity in international relations,

Ch'en was made a member in May 1954 of the Board of Directors of the newly formed Chinese People's Association for Cultural Relations with Foreign Countries, a position he probably still retains.

In December 1956 Ch'en was identified as a deputy director of the ACFTU's International Liaison Department, a logical assignment in view of his background. Within less than a year he was serving as acting director, and by September 1958 he had become the director. In the meantime he had gone abroad again, attending a congress of the Indonesian Plantation Workers' Union in January 1957. In July of that year he left Peking for Hong Kong en route to Tokyo to attend a congress of the General Council of Trade Unions of Japan, better known by its Japanese contraction, "SOHYO." Ch'en stayed 10 days in Hong Kong but returned to China when the Japanese refused to give him a visa. In October 1957 he was once again elected an alternate member of the WFTU General Council at the Fourth WFTU Congress in Leipzig, East Germany. He was, in addition, elected an alternate member of the smaller but more important WFTU Executive Committee. The Chinese delegation was led by Liu Ch'ang-sheng, but it is not certain if Ch'en attended the Congress. When the Eighth ACFTU Congress was held in December 1957, Ch'en served as one of the deputy secretaries-general of the Congress presidium (steering committee), and at the close of the meetings he was re-elected to the Executive Committee, a position he still holds. Several years later, in April 1966, he was identified as a secretary of the ACFTU Secretariat, the body in charge of the routine work of the Federation when the Executive Committee is not in session.

Throughout the 1950's the activities of the WFTU had been conducted in a spirit of unanimity; more bluntly, the WFTU was essentially a mouthpiece for the policies of the Soviet Union. However, beginning about 1960, as a by-product of the Sino-Soviet ideological dispute, the WFTU was used by both the Chinese and the Russians to denounce each other. It was in this changing atmosphere that Ch'en attended the 11th Session of the WFTU General Council in Peking in June 1960. The meetings were characterized by only slightly veiled recriminations between the Chinese and the Russians. (For a more detailed treatment of this important meeting, see under Liu Ch'ang-sheng, the head of the Chinese delegation.) In July–August 1960 Ch'en was in Japan as a member of Liu Ning-i's delegation sent there to attend the 10th anniversary of the SOHYO as well as its 15th Congress. In addition, the same delegation also participated in the Sixth World Conference for the Prohibition of Atomic and Hydrogen Weapons. In October of the same year Ch'en was a member of Liu Ch'ang-sheng's trade union delegation to

Australia; their appearance there was greeted with open hostility by the Australians (see under Liu Ch'ang-sheng).

Between 1961 and 1965 Ch'en attended three more WFTU meetings. These were held in East Berlin (February 1961); Sofia, Bulgaria (March 1964); and, Moscow (January 1965). During this same period he was promoted within the WFTU hierarchy; he was elevated to full membership on the WFTU General Council in 1961 and to full membership on the Executive Committee by 1964. Most important, he became a member of the WFTU Secretariat in 1965, replacing K'ang Yung-ho (q.v.) who, like Ch'en, is a specialist in international liaison activities. Apart from these trips to WFTU meetings, Ch'en has made two others. In July 1964 he went to Japan for a SOHYO congress and in October–November 1964 he led a trade union delegation to Algeria for the 10th anniversary of the Algerian Revolution. From there he proceeded to the Congo (Brazzaville) where he attended a Congolese trade union congress.

As already noted, Ch'en had become director of the ACFTU International Liaison Department in 1958. In this capacity, aside from his numerous trips abroad, he has been very frequently in contact with the many foreign trade union delegations that have visited China. He remained as Liaison Department director until the spring of 1963 when he was replaced by Li Yun-ch'uan whose activities have been quite similar to Ch'en's. In the late fifties and early sixties Ch'en also received new posts, most of them related to some aspect of international relations. Since July 1958 he has been a member of the Afro-Asian Solidarity Committee of China and a Standing Committee member of the China Peace Committee. In March 1960 he was named to Standing Committee membership on the newly established China-Latin America Friendship Association. He has also been affiliated with the CPPCC since the Third National Committee was formed in April 1959. Representing the ACFTU he was a member of the Third Committee (1959–1964), and he was again named to the Fourth Committee that opened its initial session in December 1964.

Ch'en Yü

(1902–   ; Pao-an hsien, Kwangtung). Labor leader; governor of Kwangtung; member, CCP Central Committee.

Ch'en Yü was an important labor leader in the early years of the Chinese Communist Movement. He faded into relative obscurity in the thirties and forties, but after the PRC was established in 1949 he held key ministerial posts in Peking. Transferred to Kwangtung in 1957, he has been governor and a Party secretary there since that time.

Ch'en was born in Pao-an hsien, located in Kwangtung on the eastern shore of the Pearl River estuary near Hong Kong. He was a sailor in his youth, and like many of his fellow seamen in south China he was a member of Sun Yat-sen's KMT. He first achieved some degree of prominence as a participant in the famous two-month long Hong Kong seamen's strike, which began in January 1922 under the leadership of Su Chao-cheng (q.v.). The strike was led by the Chinese Seamen's Union, which had been established in 1921. Ch'en was a "responsible official" in the union, but the exact nature of his duties is not known. He was again associated with Su in the long Hong Kong-Canton strike, which began in June 1925 to support the May 30th Movement (see under Su Chao-cheng). By this time Ch'en had joined the CCP and was a member of the Kwangtung Regional Committee headed by Ch'en Yen-nien (q.v.), a son of Ch'en Tu-hsiu.[1] In December 1927 Ch'en Yü was one of the key figures in the armed uprising in Canton and the establishment of the short-lived Canton Commune (see under Chang T'ai-lei). Under the "soviet government" that was to have ruled Canton, Ch'en served as People's Commissar of Justice.[2]

A half-year after the Canton debacle the CCP held its Sixth Congress in Moscow (June–July 1928). It is not known if Ch'en attended, and there are conflicting reports regarding his election to the Central Committee and Politburo. Some sources assert that he was elected to the Central Committee; others claim he was elected only as an alternate member. Similarly, various reports indicate that he was elected to alternate or full membership on the Politburo. In any event, he had risen to a rather high position in the CCP by the latter part of 1930 when Li Li-san was deposed as the de facto head of the CCP. Of the two major factions opposing Li, one was led by Ch'en Shao-yü (q.v.) and his "28 Bolsheviks," the other by top labor leaders Ho Meng-hsiung and Lo Chang-lung (qq.v.). Ch'en Yü is said to have sided with the labor faction in the struggle that culminated at the Fourth Plenum in Shanghai (January 1931), when Ch'en Shao-yü's group gained control of the Party apparatus. Ch'en Yü reportedly recanted shortly afterwards, and at the behest of Chou En-lai issued a statement denouncing the labor faction as "rightists." He was identified at this time as secretary of the CCP group within the Seamen's Union.[3] If in fact Ch'en had been a Politburo member or alternate, it appears that he was dropped during or shortly after the Fourth Plenum.

Ch'en remained in Shanghai through the spring of 1931, but as the KMT suppression of the CCP grew more severe many Communists left for Juichin, Kiangsi, where Chu Te and Mao Tse-tung had built a sizable military base. Ch'en was apparently among them, because in November 1931 at the First All-China Congress of Soviets he was elected a member of the Central Executive Committee (CEC), the ruling organ of the Chinese Soviet Republic. However, he was not re-elected to the CEC at the Second Congress two years later (early 1934). His whereabouts and activities during the next few years are not known, but in the early stages of the Sino-Japanese War he was working in the Yenan area as an assistant to Ch'en Yun (q.v.) in economic affairs. At the Seventh National CCP Congress, held in Yenan from April to June 1945, Ch'en was elected one of the 33 alternate members of the Central Committee.

In the summer of 1945 Ch'en became a member of the newly established Preparatory Committee of the Liberated Areas Trade Union Federation in Yenan. In the early autumn he was nominated as a Federation delegate to attend the inaugural congress of the Communist-dominated World Federation of Trade Unions. Teng Fa (q.v.) led the Chinese Communist delegation to Paris, but it is not known if Ch'en accompanied him. In the postwar period he was among the many Party leaders sent from Yenan to Manchuria where, by 1948, he was deputy director of the Industry Department subordinate to the Northeast Administrative Committee, the governmental body that administered those areas of Manchuria under Communist control. In August of the same year Ch'en attended the Sixth National Labor Congress in Harbin after having served on the Congress Preparatory Committee. He gave a report on the nearly 400 proposals put before the Congress, and at the close of the meetings he was elected a member of the Executive Committee of the All-China Federation of Labor (ACFL).

After the fall of Mukden to the Communist armies in November 1948, Ch'en was transferred there to become a member of the Mukden Military Control Commission, which was chaired by Ch'en Yun. In the following spring and summer he served concurrently as director of the Industry Department of the Northeast Administrative Committee. At the end of the summer Ch'en was transferred to Peking to become chief of the Fuel Industry Division of the North China People's Government (NCPG). However, he held this post for only a brief time, for the NCPG was abolished shortly after the Communists established the central government. The new national government was brought into existence by the CPPCC, which held its inaugural session in September 1949. Ch'en attended these meetings as a representative of the Labor Federation, and when the major administrative assignments were made in October, he was given the portfolio for the Ministry of Fuel Industry. In addition, he was made a member of the Finance and Economics Committee, the most important economic body in the central

government until 1954; in this post Ch'en again served under Ch'en Yun.

Ch'en's Ministry of Fuel was responsible for three basic industries—coal, electric power, and petroleum. During the six years he headed the ministry he gave a number of reports before government organs and government-sponsored conferences concerned with these industries. He also received several new appointments in the early years of the PRC, mainly in the economic field. In May 1950 Ch'en was appointed one of the supervisors of the Communications Bank, a specialized bank under the Finance Ministry, which handles the state's investments in joint state-private enterprises. From July 1951 to January 1955 he was president of the China Institute of Mining and Metallurgy. He was on a special committee established in December 1951 to investigate the economy and to propose austerity measures. In August–September 1952 Ch'en was a member of a high-level delegation led by Premier Chou En-lai to Moscow where they negotiated the return of the Chinese Changchun Railway to China and the extension of the joint use of naval facilities at Port Arthur. Several months later, in January 1953, Ch'en signed the Sino-Rumanian Technical and Scientific Cooperation Agreement in Peking. He was presumably selected to lead these negotiations because his ministry would have the greatest interest in the technical assistance for the petroleum industry that the Rumanians might be able to offer.

Ch'en's primary responsibilities after 1949 were in the field of economic administration, but he still retained his ties with the labor movement for a few years. From the end of 1949 to the spring of 1955 he was a member of the Standing Committee of the Chinese Seamen's Trade Union's Preparatory Committee. Moreover, at the Seventh Labor Congress in May 1953 Ch'en was again named to membership on the Executive Committee of the Labor Federation, a post he held until the next congress in late 1957. He also represented the Federation on the Second National Committee of the CPPCC from December 1954 to April 1959. In September 1954, when the constitutional government was inaugurated at the First NPC, Ch'en was reappointed to the Fuel Industry Ministry. However, in July 1955 the ministry was divided into ministries of Coal Industry, Electric Power Industry, and Petroleum Industry. Ch'en assumed the ministerial post in the first one, and Liu Lan-po and Li Chü-k'uei (qq.v.) became the ministers of the last two.

Ch'en attended the Eighth Party Congress in September 1956 and presented a report on the coal mining industry. At the close of the Congress he was promoted from alternate to full membership on the Central Committee. The following August he was assigned to his native Kwangtung to replace T'ao Chu (q.v.) as governor, and a month later he was officially replaced as minister of Coal Industry by Chang Lin-chih (q.v.). Shortly after Ch'en's arrival in Canton he was identified as one of the secretaries (under First Secretary T'ao Chu) of the CCP Kwangtung Committee. In the years that followed, Ch'en was frequently mentioned in the press, very often in connection with the many foreign visitors who transit Canton to and from Peking. He represented the province in the Second NPC, which first met in April 1959, and was again elected to the Third NPC, which opened in December 1964.

Ch'en's primary responsibilities in Kwangtung have been mainly in connection with domestic affairs, but he has also made two trips abroad. He spent two weeks in March 1959 in Hanoi as head of a commercial delegation that concluded an agreement on supplementary trade orders for 1959. Thirteen months later he was the CCP delegate to the National Conference of the New Zealand Communist Party in Auckland (and is thus one of the extremely few Chinese Communists to have visited that nation). He was also scheduled to accompany P'eng Chen (q.v.) to Japan in November 1964 as a member of the CCP delegation to the Ninth Congress of the Japanese Communist Party, but the trip was cancelled when the Japanese Government refused the delegation permission to enter the country. Also in connection with foreign affairs, Ch'en was named as a vice-chairman of a special committee for the "reception and settlement of Chinese nationals victimized in India." This committee was formed in April 1963 in the wake of the Sino-Indian border conflict in late 1962 when many Chinese were forced to leave India.

At the Ninth Plenum of the Party Central Committee in January 1961, the regional bureaus were re-established. By October of that year Ch'en was identified as one of the secretaries of the Central-South Bureau, again serving under T'ao Chu, the first secretary. By 1965 he had been promoted to third secretary. Thus, by the mid-sixties, Ch'en was one of the major regional leaders in China, presiding over the government apparatus in south China's most important province and holding a key post in the regional Party bureau.

Ch'en is married to Yuan P'u-chih who worked with her husband in the late forties in Manchuria, where she was director of a workers' school under the Manchurian government's Industry Department. In August 1950 she became deputy director of the Personnel Division in her husband's Fuel Industry Ministry. Accompanying Ch'en to Kwangtung, she has been a deputy director of the provincial government's Higher Education Bureau since at least 1960.

1. Li Kuang, ed., *Ti-liu-tz'u ch'üan-kuo lao-tung ta-hui* (Sixth All-China Labor Congress; Hong Kong, 1948), p. 59.

2. *Ti-erh-tz'u kuo-nei ko-ming chan-cheng shih-ch'i shih-shih lun-ts'ung* (Accounts of the second revolutionary civil war; Peking, 1956), p. 29.

3. Warren Kuo, "Chinese Communist 6th CC's 4th Plenum and Party Rift," *Issues and Studies,* 2:37–47 (September 1966).

Ch'en Yun

(c.1900–　　; Ching-p'u hsien, Kiangsu). Early labor leader; economic expert; vice-chairman, CCP Central Committee; member, Politburo Standing Committee.

Ch'en Yun, one of the few proletarians in the CCP elite, began his career as a Party labor organizer in the mid-twenties. Elected to the Central Committee in 1934, he spent two years in Moscow and then headed the Party's Organization Department in Yenan in the early war years, during which he wrote a major tract on Party membership. In the middle war years he emerged as the Communists' top economic expert, continuing in this capacity in Manchuria in the postwar years and during the first decade of the PRC. During approximately these same years he was considered to be one of the half-dozen most important CCP leaders. He suffered a serious political setback with the inauguration of the Great Leap Forward in 1958, and for the next several years, although never specifically denounced, there were no indications that he had regained his once vast powers in the economic apparatus.

Ch'en was born in Ching-p'u hsien, which lies a few miles west of Shanghai, in Kiangsu province. His original name was Liao Ch'en-yun, and he has also been known by the name Liao Ch'eng-yun. In his early years Ch'en worked as a typesetter for the famous Commercial Press in Shanghai. He joined the CCP in 1924 and played his first important role in Party affairs the next year as a participant in the May 30th Movement (see under Li Li-san). At this juncture the Communists set up the Shanghai General Trade Union under Li Li-san's direction; Communist historians credit Ch'en with having been one of the organizers of this key union. At the same time a trade union organization was established in the Commercial Press, and sometime within the next two years Ch'en was elected its chairman. During the ensuing months he worked with Li Li-san, Liu Shao-ch'i and others, and in February–March 1927 he assisted Chou En-lai and Chao Shih-yen (qq.v.) in organizing insurrectionary strikes. These were designed to gain control of Shanghai in advance of the arrival of the Northern Expeditionary forces, which were converging on the city. The CCP continued to maintain its uneasy alliance with the KMT after Chiang Kai-shek led his troops into Shanghai in late March. However, on April 12 he turned on the Communists, killing many of them and forcing others to go underground or flee the city.

Ch'en fled to his native Ching-p'u, organizing peasant uprisings there and in neighboring Sung-chiang hsien to the south, presumably in co-ordination with the uprisings being led by Mao Tse-tung and others in central China.

Ch'en's activities during the next few years are unrecorded, but by 1931 he had gone to the Kiangsi-Fukien border area where Chu Te and Mao Tse-tung had built up a sizable military force. Until the Long March began in 1934, Ch'en was chiefly occupied with Party organi-zational work and as chairman of the labor federation in the central soviet area. He also contributed to *Tou-cheng* (Struggle) and other Party journals in those years. Inferential evidence suggests that he occasionally made covert trips to Shanghai and other major cities; a semi-official biography of Ch'en asserts that he was "responsible" for labor affairs in KMT-controlled areas, and he spoke on this subject at the Party's Fifth Plenum held in Juichin, Kiangsi, in January 1934.[1] At this same Plenum he was elected to the Party's Central Committee. Ch'en is one of the very few Communists still active in the mid-sixties who has continuously held a Central Committee seat since 1934.

A few days after the Fifth Plenum the Second All-China Congress of Soviets was convened in Juichin. Ch'en was elected a member of the Central Executive Committee (CEC) of the Chi-nese Soviet Republic, and on February 3, 1934, when the CEC held its first session, he was elected to its 17-member presidium, which was chaired by Mao. In the fall of 1934 Ch'en set out on the Long March with the Chu-Mao forces, and by the first part of 1935 he had been made a member of the important Revolutionary Military Council, one of the key organs of the CEC. However, he did not complete the long trek to Shensi, for he left the Long Marchers and went to Moscow where in July–August 1935 he attended the Seventh Comintern Congress. He was elected to the Comintern Credentials Committee, but unlike Mao Tse-tung, Ch'en Shao-yü, Chou En-lai, and Chang Kuo-t'ao, he was not elected to the more important Com-intern Executive Committee.

Ch'en remained in Moscow for about two years, but by the early part of 1937 he went to Sinkiang. At this juncture Sinkiang warlord gov-ernor Sheng Shih-ts'ai was cultivating ties with both the Moscow and Yenan Communists in spite of Nanking's opposition to such moves. Ch'en served as a liaison officer with Soviet officials in Tihwa (the Sinkiang capital). It is possible, though undocumented, that he played some role in the establishment in Sinkiang of a permanent CCP liaison mission, which was set up in that year when Teng Fa (q.v.) arrived from Yenan. In the spring of 1937 Ch'en was ordered by the Party Center in Yenan to contact remnants of the Long Marchers who had been driven up the Kansu Corridor and were moving toward Sinkiang. Ch'en rendezvoused with these men on May 1, 1937, in the small town of Hsing-hsing-hsia on the Kansu-Sinkiang border. He then accompanied them back to Tihwa,[2] but before long they turned around and made the long journey to join the Maoist elements in north Shensi. Ch'en reached Yenan before the end of 1937, and at that time, or early in 1938, he became director of the Party's Organization De-partment. He seems to have succeeded Liu Shao-ch'i in this post and continued to hold it until about 1940.

Ch'en was apparently elected to the Politburo in 1940 (although some sources use 1945) by which time he had moved into the inner circle of the Maoist leadership. One writer, comment-ing on Mao's rise to supremacy in the late thirties and early forties, observed that after 1937 lead-ing policy statements "came more and more from Mao, Chou En-lai, and rising theoreticians Liu Shao-ch'i, Ch'en Po-ta, and Ch'en Yun." Coinciding with this ascendancy, the key leaders of the "28 Bolsheviks" group, Ch'en Shao-yü, Chang Wen-t'ien, and Ch'in Pang-hsien (qq.v.), began to lose their influence in the Party hier-archy, particularly after the 1942 *Cheng-feng* (rectification) movement. In 1939, Che'n Yun had published *Tsen-yang tso i-ko kung-ch'an tang yuan* (How to be a Communist Party mem-ber). It came out only a few weeks before Liu Shao-ch'i published his famous *How to Be a Good Communist*. Whereas Liu "discusses the 'cultivation' of the best-quality members," Ch'en's work deals with formal requirements (e.g., age qualifications, probationary membership) and stresses that "workers should be the 'founda-tion' " of the Party, although the Party "should also pay attention to poor peasants, intellectuals, and women."[3] One writer has summarized Ch'en's primary membership conditions as: "struggle all one's lifetime for communism; place revolutionary interests above everything; obey party discipline and keep party secrets; carry out decisions unflinchingly; be an example for the masses; and study."[4]

These long essays by Ch'en and Liu were two of the key documents of the 1942 rectification movement, which finally consolidated the posi-tion of Mao as the undisputed leader of the CCP. The membership qualifications they outlined were, in essence, incorporated into the Party Constitution adopted at the Seventh Congress in 1945. The "chief significance" of these tracts "lies in the fact that the Party chose to re-emphasize its basic principles during this period, in an evident determination to maintain its Leninist foundations in the midst of all the changes brought about by the war-time shift to the united front." Both men simply ignored the fact that the CCP had had little contact with the urban proletariat for over a decade. This awkward problem was skirted by an "inversion of certain Marxist presuppositions." Rather than "deducing ideological tendencies from class affiliations," they argued that class affiliations could be deduced from "ideological tendencies."[5]

By the time of the 1942 rectification movement, Ch'en was devoting most of his time to economic questions. His first specific assignment in this field was related to the disintegration of the wartime KMT-CCP cooperation, that had become evident by the 1939–40 period. To combat the KMT economic blockade of the Communist regions in north China, the CCP adopted a series of measures, one of which was the creation of a special office to manage and coordinate financial and economic affairs in the Shensi-Kansu-Ninghsia and the Shansi-Suiyuan Border Regions. Ch'en was made its director, retaining the post throughout the remaining war years. Concurrently, he headed the Party Central Committee's Finance and Economics Department, with Li Fu-ch'un (q.v.) as one of his key assistants. From this period through the first decade of the PRC Ch'en was the Communists' top economic expert.

At the Party's Seventh National Congress, held in Yenan from April to June 1945, Ch'en served on the 15-member presidium (steering committee) and was re-elected to the Central Committee. He was elected (or possibly re-elected) to the Politburo and made an alternate member of the Secretariat. The latter body was, in effect, the "inner" or "super" Politburo until the new Party Constitution was adopted in 1956. The exact membership of the Secretariat in the late 1940's is not known, but it apparently included only Mao, Liu Shao-ch'i, Chou En-lai, Jen Pi-shih, Chu Te, and possibly one or two more. Ch'en remained an alternate member until sometime after Jen's death in 1950 when he was elevated to full membership.

With Japan's surrender in August 1945, the CCP immediately dispatched several of its most senior leaders to Manchuria to organize military forces and gain political control of this vital area. Among those who went were Ch'en, P'eng Chen, Lin Piao, Kao Kang, Li Fu-ch'un, and Lin Feng (qq.v.). During Ch'en's three years in Manchuria he continued to concentrate on economic affairs in his capacity as chairman of the Finance and Economics Committee (1946–1949) of the Northeast Administrative Committee (NEAC). The NEAC, chaired by Lin Feng, was the chief governmental organ for those sections of Manchuria controlled by the Communists. It was paralleled in the Party hierarchy by the Northeast Bureau of which P'eng Chen was the secretary and Ch'en a member. In August 1948, in an effort to resuscitate the relatively dormant labor movement, the Communists held the Sixth All-China Labor Congress in Harbin —the first one in nearly two decades. As one of

the Party's most experienced labor leaders, Ch'en was given the place of honor on the Congress presidium. Although the documents from the meetings indicate that Li Li-san (recently returned to China from Moscow) was the most active Party leader at the Congress, Ch'en was elected chairman of the All-China Federation of Labor (ACFL). Liu Shao-ch'i, even more senior in the Communist labor movement, was made honorary chairman. Ch'en remained the official head of the ACFL until the Seventh Congress in May 1953, but he was soon preoccupied with more important assignments, leaving most of the Federation's work to Li Li-san, Liu Ning-i, and Lai Jo-yü (qq.v.).

Mukden, the last of the great Manchurian cities captured by Lin Piao's armies, fell in early November 1948. Ch'en was appointed chairman of the Municipal Military Control Commission, an interim administration set up before the inauguration of a "people's government." He remained there only briefly, however, going to Moscow in April 1949 as a delegate to the 10th Congress of the Soviet Union's nationwide labor organization. Returning home, Ch'en went to Peking where in June he attended meetings chaired by Mao Tse-tung to prepare for the establishment of the central government. In September 1949, representing the CCP, he attended the inaugural session of the CPPCC, which brought the new national government into existence on October 1. Aside from some military commanders who were still fighting the Nationalists, most of the CCP hierarchy was then assembled in Peking. But few of them received such an impressive array of posts as Ch'en Yun. He was made a member of the Central People's Government Council, the highest governmental organ until the constitution was adopted five years later. In the cabinet, known to 1954 as the Government Administration Council (GAC), Ch'en was one of four vice-premiers under Chou En-lai and chairman from 1949 to 1954 of one of its four key committees, the Finance and Economics Committee. He was also appointed minister of Heavy Industry, but this post was relinquished to Li Fu-ch'un in April 1950. Ch'en was also a member of the CPPCC First National Committee from 1949 to 1954, but in contrast to his other posts this was largely an honorary assignment. Like many of the Party's senior leaders, he was elected to the Executive Board of the Sino-Soviet Friendship when it was established in the early days of the PRC.

Ch'en's dominance in the field of economics during the early PRC years can scarcely be exaggerated, particularly during the period of "reconstruction and rehabilitation" (1949–1952), that preceded the First Five-Year Plan. He was the keynote speaker at virtually every important economic conference and made innumerable reports on economic affairs before the leading government bodies. His speeches and reports were regularly carried in the leading newspapers and journals and were frequently reprinted in pamphlets (published in both Chinese and English). In addition to his positions in the permanent economic apparatus, Ch'en even chaired several *ad hoc* bodies. For example, before the PRC was a month old he was heading a special committee for "take-over work," that is, to take over the materials, personnel, and so on, from KMT organs. One of his most notable achievements as China's new economic "czar" was to halt the runaway inflation that had so badly crippled the KMT in its final years on the mainland.

Mobilizing managerial talent and excess capital was given priority attention in the early years of the PRC. Mao Tse-tung addressed himself to this problem in June 1950 at the second session of the CPPCC when the Communists were still willing to deal quite cautiously with the bourgeois elements. At this same meeting, Ch'en elaborated on this question, indicating that because of China's "backwardness" it would be "progressive" to allow the "national capitalists to develop industry and make investments in it for a long time." However, the Party subjected the "capitalists" to the rigorous "five-anti" campaign in 1951–52 (against alleged corruption, etc.). Then in the early part of 1952 the Communists all but admitted that the campaign had been pushed too vigorously, and it appears that Ch'en was called upon to reassure the business elements that, within carefully defined limits, the Party was still willing to cooperate with them. This important speech, which set the tone for "communist-capitalist" relations for the next three years, was made in June 1952 at the preparatory meeting of the All-China Federation of Industry and Commerce (see under Hsu Ti-hsin).

In August–September 1952 Ch'en was Chou En-lai's senior deputy on a mission to Moscow. The visit was of particular importance because it resulted in the first modification of the 1950 Sino-Soviet Treaty of Alliance. An agreement was reached to return to complete Chinese control the important Chinese Changchun Railway in Manchuria. However, because the Korean War was still being fought, both sides agreed to the extension of the joint use of the naval facilities at Port Arthur-Dairen. Two months after returning home Ch'en was made a member of the State Planning Commission, which was established in anticipation of the First Five-Year Plan (1953–1957). In view of Ch'en's preeminence in the economics field, it seems somewhat unusual that the chairmanship fell to Kao Kang. And, in fact, Ch'en's role in economic affairs diminished in 1953.[6] However, Kao fell from power in early 1954, and by the middle of the year Ch'en was identified as a "close com-

rade-in-arms" of Mao Tse-tung, an accolade reserved for the favored few. He was by now the fifth-ranking leader (behind Mao, Liu Shao-ch'i, Chou En-lai, and Chu Te), a position he was to hold for three more years. In September–October 1954 Ch'en once again assisted Chou En-lai in negotiations with the Soviet Union. These took place when Soviet leaders Khrushchev and Bulganin led what was probably the most important delegation to visit Peking after 1949. A wide range of questions vital to both nations was reviewed, and several new agreements were reached that markedly altered the Sino-Soviet relationship (e.g., the USSR agreed to turn over to China the Port Arthur-Dairen naval facilities and several "joint" stock companies were given to the Chinese).

In 1953–54 Ch'en served on the committee that drafted the national constitution, and when it was adopted at the first session of the First NPC in September 1954, he attended as a deputy from Shanghai. (He was subsequently re-elected from Shanghai for the Second and Third NPC's, which opened in 1959 and 1964, respectively.) Under the reorganization of the central government in September 1954, Ch'en was made the first of 10 vice-premiers under Chou En-lai. In 1955 and again in 1956, he was specifically designated as acting premier in Chou's absence from the country. Although the First Five-Year Plan had ostensibly been in operation from 1953, it was not then publicly presented to the nation. This was done by Ch'en in March 1955 at a national conference of the CCP (the same conference that exposed the Kao Kang "anti-Party" plot). His place in the inner-elite was reconfirmed 18 months later when the Party held its Eighth National Congress (September 1956). He was elected again to the Central Committee. More important, at the First Plenum of the new Central Committee (held the day after the Congress closed), he was re-elected to the Politburo and newly elected a vice-chairman of the Central Committee and a member of the Politburo Standing Committee. The Standing Committee, in effect, replaced the Secretariat to which Ch'en had previously belonged. In brief, Ch'en retained his position as the fifth-ranking leader.

During the mid-fifties Ch'en was primarily occupied with commercial problems (e.g., the supply of consumer goods, problems of grain distribution). He delivered lengthy reports on these questions at the annual NPC sessions and also at the Party's Second Plenum in November 1956. The day after this Plenum closed he replaced Tseng Shan as minister of Commerce (renamed First Ministry of Commerce in February 1958). The evidence suggests that by this time Ch'en had come to be regarded as an economic "conservative" or "gradualist" and headed a loosely defined "opinion group," which stood at odds with a Maoist element that wanted to develop the national economy at a faster pace. The issue, apparently, hung in the balance for about a year—until the Party's Third Plenum in September–October 1957. In summarizing the intra-Party arguments that prevailed in the latter part of 1957, one writer has commented that the Maoist group 'advocated a policy of *social mobilization* in order to achieve rapid economic growth. Another group, headed by Ch'en Yun, advocated a policy of *material incentives* in order to achieve a more balanced, though slower, economic growth."[7]

The triumph of the Maoist group found its expression in the launching of the Great Leap Forward in 1958. Ch'en's fall from effective political power can be dated from late 1957 and early 1958, but the differences of opinion were never openly articulated in terms of personalities. Yet his decline became apparent in a relatively short time. In September 1958 he was removed from the Commerce Ministry (which had already lost many of its broad powers), and although he was appointed at this time to head the newly formed State Capital Construction Commission, virtually nothing was reported of his work in this body. Finally, in January 1961, the Commission was abolished, with its functions assumed by the State Planning Commission under Li Fu-ch'un, the man who seems to have benefited most directly from Ch'en's decline in the sphere of economics. One of Ch'en's last important assignments was undertaken in May 1958 when he went to Moscow as Peking's "observer" to meetings of the Council for Mutual Economic Assistance (the economic arm of the Warsaw Pact nations). The day after the meetings closed he attended the one-day session of the Warsaw Pact, again as an observer. At this point the Chinese were beginning to differ with the Soviet Union on policies vis-à-vis the non-Communist world, and thus the tone of Ch'en's address was markedly different from that of Khrushchev. Stressing the growing strength of the "socialist camp" (in the wake of the recently demonstrated Soviet missile capability), he scorned the United States as a "paper tiger" and repeated the then-current phrase that the "east wind was prevailing over the west wind." His address, in brief, as one writer observed, repeated the essence of Mao's famous November 1957 speech in Moscow at ceremonies marking the 40th anniversary of the Russian Revolution.[8]

As already suggested, after 1958 Ch'en seems to have lost his once authoritative voice in policy-making decisions, and by 1961 he had lost his last substantive administrative post. He no longer made keynote reports before government or Party organs, and aside from an article on problems of capital construction for *Hung-ch'i* (no. 5, March 1, 1959), he does not seem to have written anything of substance. A particularly telling indication of his steady decline took

place in January 1959 when Ch'en I, in the absence of Chou En-lai, served as acting premier —a role that had previously fallen to Ch'en Yun. Superficially, he continued into the early and mid-1960's as a key leader, as suggested in 1959 when he was again appointed as the ranking vice-premier under Chou at the Second NPC. Yet even this was denied him in January 1965 when, at the close of the first session of the Third NPC, Lin Piao became the ranking vice-premier, with Ch'en being dropped to the second vice-premiership.

The Chinese *volte-face* in 1959–60 in the wake of the disorders caused by the Great Leap Forward suggested that Ch'en's more conservative economic policies were more appropriate for Chinese economic development. Yet several years later there were still no substantive indications that he had been returned to his once exalted place in the Party's inner-elite. Though far less dramatic than the political fall of some other CCP veterans, Ch'en's decline symbolized crucial changes in basic economic policies in the second decade of the PRC. These changes and their effects on other key economic personnel are discussed in several other biographies, most notably T'an Chen-lin, Teng Tzu-hui, Li Fu-ch'un, and Hsueh Mu-ch'iao.

1. Li Kuang, ed., *Ti-liu-tz'u ch'üan-kuo lao-tung ta-hui* (Sixth All-China Labor Congress; Hong Kong, 1948), p. 54; Tso-liang Hsiao, *Power Relations within the Chinese Communist Movement, 1930–1934* (Seattle, 1961), pp. 261, 264.

2. *Hung-ch'i p'iao-p'iao* (Red flag fluttering; Peking, 1959), X, 106–111.

3. John W. Lewis, *Leadership in Communist China* (Ithaca, New York, 1963), p. 104.

4. *Ibid.*

5. Conrad Brandt, Benjamin Schwartz, and John K. Fairbank, *A Documentary History of Chinese Communism* (Cambridge, Mass., 1952), pp. 319–320.

6. *CB* 290, p. 24.

7. Franz Schurmann, *Ideology and Organization in Communist China* (Berkeley, Calif., 1966), p. 196.

8. *SCMP* 1787, pp. 49–51; Donald S. Zagoria, *The Sino-Soviet Conflict, 1956–1961* (Princeton, N.J., 1962), pp. 187–188.

Cheng Sen-yü

(1910–   ; Chekiang). Specialist in "international peace movement."

Cheng Sen-yü, a specialist in international affairs, is one of the most extensively traveled of the Chinese Communist leaders. Between 1952 and 1964 he made over 25 trips abroad, visiting Austria, Ceylon, Cuba, Egypt, Finland, East Germany, Hungary, India, Japan, Rumania,

Sweden, and the USSR. Many of these trips have involved the Communist-sponsored World Peace Council or related organizations.

Cheng was a journalist by profession. He was lecturing on journalism at the Chinese Spare-Time School in Hong Kong in 1938. Between the outbreak of the Sino-Japanese War in 1937 and the attack on Pearl Harbor in 1941, Hong Kong was the scene of considerable CCP activity, particularly in the propaganda field. It is possible, though undocumented, that Cheng moved in these circles. By mid-1948 he was in Shanghai (still under KMT control) where he was one of the signers of an open letter from cultural circles charging the United States with aggression against China. In May of the following year (the month Shanghai fell to the Communists), Cheng took part in establishing a Preparatory Committee for the China New Economics Research Society; two months later in Peking a national Preparatory Committee was formed under the chairmanship of Ch'en Po-ta (q.v.), but it is not known if Cheng played any part in this endeavor. In February 1952 Cheng attended a meeting of the Chinese People's Institute of Foreign Affairs of which he was a member. This was his first identification in the field of foreign affairs, an activity to which he has devoted the rest of his career. During 1952 he received two more appointments, both related to international relations. In May he was named to the Standing Committee of the newly formed China-Burma Friendship Association, and the following September he was appointed to the Board of Directors of the newly established "China News Service," which was organized to report on overseas Chinese affairs (not to be confused with the well-known New China News Agency). Then in late 1952 or early 1953 Cheng was assigned to work in the headquarters of the World Peace Council (WPC) in Prague. In this connection he was a delegate to the World Peace Congress held in Vienna in December 1952. In March 1953 he returned to Vienna for another "peace" meeting at which time he was identified as a member of the World Peace Council's (WPC) International Committee. In June and again in November he was a delegate to sessions of the WPC in Budapest and Vienna.

In the spring of 1954 the WPC headquarters was moved to the Russian zone of Vienna where it was situated until February 1957 when the Austrian authorities forced it to close; it was then moved back to Prague. At least as late as mid-1954 Cheng was still posted at the headquarters. Between February and April 1955 Cheng was in New Delhi serving first on the Preparatory Committee for the Asian Countries' Conference and then as a Chinese delegate to it. This conference (not to be confused with the famous Bandung Conference held later in April 1955) was a Communist-sponsored meeting and

the predecessor of the First Afro-Asian Solidarity Conference (see under Yang Shuo), which was held in Cairo in December 1957–January 1958 and which Cheng also attended. In June 1955 he was back in Europe for a WPC meeting held in Helsinki. Then in August he made the first of several trips to Japan as secretary of the Chinese delegation to the First World Conference for the Prohibition of Nuclear Weapons. From the fall of 1955 until late summer 1956, Cheng was present at several functions in Peking, suggesting that he was no longer stationed in Vienna. However, by November 1956 his travels had apparently begun again because he attended the All-India Peace Congress in Calcutta.

After the Vienna headquarters of the WPC was closed in 1957, the Communists established a thinly disguised front group known as the "International Institute for Peace" in that city. Cheng attended one of the Institute's meetings in November 1957 and in December 1963 he was elected to its Executive Committee. During the late 1950's he also continued his activities in connection with the WPC. In March–April 1957 he attended a WPC Standing Committee meeting in East Berlin and in June he was a Chinese delegate to the WPC meeting in Colombo, Ceylon, where he was elected to the WPC Secretariat. Afterwards, he returned to Peking, but in August he was in Tokyo for the second time as secretary-general of the six-man Chinese delegation to the Third World Conference for the Prohibition of Nuclear Weapons. He attended a similar meeting in Sweden in July 1958 as a member of Kuo Mo-jo's (q.v.) delegation to the Conference on Disarmament and International Cooperation. The same month he became a WPC Council member at the same time that he held his post on the Secretariat. He apparently retains both positions. During 1958 Cheng attended two other WPC meetings in New Delhi (March) and Helsinki (December). By February 1959 he was apparently temporarily back in Vienna, because when Liao Ch'eng-chih (q.v.) left Peking for a WPC Standing Committee meeting in Moscow, it was mentioned that Cheng would go there from Vienna to meet the Chinese delegation. In May–June 1959 Cheng was in Stockholm for a WPC meeting celebrating the 10th anniversary of the "world peace movement."

Although in the 1960's Cheng continued to be quite active in the WPC (attending meetings in Sweden, May 1960; Rumania, November 1960; India, March 1961; Sweden, March 1963; Hungary, April–May 1964), he became increasingly involved in Chinese relations with Japan. During this period he visited Japan four times and was frequently on hand to confer with Japanese visitors to China. In July–August 1960 Cheng was in Japan for a convention of the General Council of Trade Unions of Japan (SOHYO) and the Sixth World Conference for

Prohibition of Atom and Hydrogen Bombs and for Disarmament. He also attended the Seventh World Conference the following year (August 1961) and the Ninth World Conference held in August 1963. At the latter meeting, which witnessed Chinese and Soviet delegates exchanging insults, Cheng took part in the polemics. He asserted that the conference had "unmasked the ugly features of the tiger in sheep's skin," an obvious reference to the Soviet Union which had just signed the famed partial nuclear test ban with the United States and the United Kingdom, a treaty violently opposed by the Chinese. In October 1963 the China-Japan Friendship Association was formed and Cheng became a member of its Standing Council. Then in August 1964 he was the deputy leader of a delegation of the China Peace Committee's Peking branch, which visited Japan on the invitation of the Japan National Peace Committee and the Tokyo Peace Committee.

Cheng's participation in the polemics of the Sino-Soviet dispute was not limited to meetings in Japan. In May 1964 he and another Chinese delegate issued a statement at the above-mentioned WPC meeting in Budapest "refuting the slanders made by . . . Tass" as part of a Chinese statement which denounced Soviet foreign policy, particularly a Soviet proposal to renounce force in settling territorial disputes.

Besides specializing in Japanese affairs, Cheng is frequently on hand for negotiations with visiting "peace" or "friendship" delegations from other countries. He has also played a role in Sino-Cuban affairs, having visited Havana in December 1960–January 1961 to celebrate the second anniversary of Castro's victory and being appointed to the Council of the China-Cuba Friendship Association when it was established in December 1962.

Aside from his work for the WPC and the "friendship" associations, Cheng serves in other organizations that clearly fit into his career pattern, the most important of which are the China Peace Committee and the Afro-Asian Solidarity Committee of China. Cheng was identified as a member of the former in September 1955, and the next month he was identified as a deputy director of its Liaison Department. In July 1958, when the China Peace Committee was reorganized, he became a member of the National and Standing Committees, as well as one of the deputy secretaries-general. Seven years later (June 1965), during another reorganization, Cheng was returned to the National and Standing Committees, appointed one of the secretaries of the newly formed Secretariat, and most important, he was made one of the organization's vice-chairmen. His role in the Afro-Asian Solidarity Committee has paralleled the above. This Committee, known as the Asian Solidarity Committee before 1958, was formed in February 1956 at

which time Cheng became a member and a deputy secretary-general. After the July 1958 reorganization he retained his membership but was dropped as a deputy secretary-general. Finally, in June 1965 he became a member of the organization's Standing Committee. As mentioned above, he was identified as a member of the Chinese People's Institute of Foreign Affairs in 1952; he was identified as a member of the Institute's Board of Directors in October 1964, but it is not known if he retained this post after the Institute held its fourth congress in December 1964. Cheng was also a deputy secretary-general of the All-China Journalists Association in August 1960, but there is no further information about his work with this organization.

Although Cheng's work has been almost exclusively with the various "people's" organizations, he has held quasi-governmental posts since 1959. In April of that year he was named to the Third National Committee of the CPPCC as a representative of "peace and friendship associations with foreign countries" and was then reappointed to the Fourth National Committee in 1964.

Ch'eng Tzu-hua

(1904–   ; Hsia-hsien, Shansi). Former Red Army political officer; specialist in supply and marketing cooperatives; vice-chairman, State Planning Commission; member, CCP Central Committee.

Ch'eng Tzu-hua was a Red Army political officer from the early thirties through the Sino-Japanese War and a troop commander in Manchuria in the postwar period. For a brief time after the establishment of the PRC in 1949 he was the senior Party official in Shansi, and then from the early to mid-fifties Ch'eng devoted most of his time to the cooperative movement. He was elected an alternate member of the CCP Central Committee in 1945 and promoted to full membership in 1956. Since 1961 Ch'eng has been a vice-chairman of the State Planning Commission.

According to the account of his life given by Ch'eng to Nym Wales,[1] he was born in 1904. He came from a family of middle peasants in Hsia-hsien, southwest Shansi. His father and a brother were merchants, and another brother was a doctor in the Nationalist army. Ch'eng's original name was Szu, but he took the married name of a maternal aunt, who adopted him because she had no son of her own. Although his adopted parents were poor, he was able to begin a traditional Chinese education in his eighth year. Two years later he changed to a primary school where modern studies were taught, and in 1916 he graduated after two years there. When he was 13 he ran away to enter a "free school" in the nearby town of Yun-ch'eng.

In 1921 Ch'eng graduated from the Yun-ch'eng school and went to Taiyuan, the Shansi capital, to attend the Kuo-min Normal School headed by Chao Tai-wen. Chao, a Japan-trained follower of Sun Yat-sen, was a confidant of Shansi warlord Yen Hsi-shan and "represented the conservative, Japanese-oriented element in Yen's regime."[2] Ch'eng, who claims to have been deeply influenced by the May Fourth Movement, became one of the most politically active students at the normal school. In mid-1925, in the wake of the May 30th Incident in Shanghai, which raised the student movement throughout China to new levels of activism, a student association was formed at the normal school with Ch'eng as its chairman. In the latter part of 1925 the students were able to have the conservative Chao Tai-wen replaced by the more liberal Chao P'i-lien, another leading Shansi official in Yen's government.

Ch'eng joined the CCP in 1926 while he was still a student. In December of that year he left Shansi for Wuhan where the Nationalist Government had just been moved during the course of the Northern Expedition. There Ch'eng entered the Wuhan branch of the Whampoa Military Academy, which Chiang Kai-shek had organized in Canton two years earlier. In early 1927 Ch'eng and some of his fellow cadets became members of a training regiment in Chang Fa-k'uei's Fourth Army. He was still with the regiment in mid-1927 when the final split between the CCP and the left-KMT occurred. But after the Communists' August First Uprising at Nanchang, Ch'eng made his way to Canton and in December he participated with the more radical members of his former training regiment in the Communists' Canton Commune (see under Chang T'ai-lei). The Communists held the city for less than three days, after which the survivors, Ch'eng among them, fled to Kwangtung's East River District where P'eng P'ai (q.v.) had organized a small Communist soviet in the adjoining seacoast hsien of Hai-feng and Lu-feng. Before P'eng's soviet was crushed by the Nationalists in early 1928, Ch'eng received a permanently disabling wound on his left hand.

Up to this time Ch'eng had been a common soldier with the newly recruited and badly organized Red armies, and he had probably experienced the demoralization felt by many ordinary soldiers as their leaders tried unsuccessfully to capture Nanchang, Swatow, and Canton. Following each defeat many soldiers deserted and went home. Ch'eng's autobiographical account suggests that he too may have felt a moment of disillusionment after the Canton failure, for he left the Red forces and made his way to his native Shansi. He quickly discovered that old friends and classmates had left or been arrested, and as an order for his own arrest had been issued, he was forced to hide in his grandmother's house. Escaping from Shansi he went to Nanyang in eastern Honan and joined the troops of the local warlord, forces that were fighting against Feng Yü-hsiang. Here he met a former schoolmate, a battalion staff officer, who helped him to become a platoon commander. Ch'eng spoke of himself and his former schoolmate as having lost contact with the Party and operating for a time on their own. In 1929 Ch'eng went with his warlord's troops to Hupeh to fight the forces of Chang Fa-k'uei. Now allied to the Nationalists, Ch'eng's regiment encountered P'eng Te-huai's Fifth Red Army at Ta-yeh, near Wuhan. Ta-yeh was an iron-mining region that P'eng's forces were trying to capture in December 1929. Ch'eng, then a squad leader and political worker, made this possible by bringing over his troops to join the Communists. In the account that Ch'eng gave to Nym Wales, he accorded himself full credit for leading the successful uprising at Ta-yeh.

Ch'eng remained with P'eng's forces during the first half of 1930, and he was once again wounded in a battle in Kiangsi. In mid-1930 he was sent to Shanghai to recuperate, remaining there until January 1931, when he went to the central soviet district in Kiangsi where he became a regimental and later a division commander in the 35th Red Army. In December 1931 major elements of the Nationalists' 26th Route Army defected to the Communists at Ning-tu in eastern Kiangsi. The Communists immediately reorganized these forces into the Fifth Army Corps in which Hsiao Ching-kuang (q.v.) was the political commissar. Subordinate to the Fifth Corps Ch'eng Tzu-hua was political commissar and later commander of the 41st Division. Later, in 1932 or 1933, he was transferred to the 14th Division. In the latter part of 1933 Ch'eng was sent to Juichin, the capital of the Chinese Soviet Republic in Kiangsi, where he enrolled in the Red Army Academy (Hung-chün ta-hsüeh).[3] He studied in a class established for high-level military cadres, which was taught by P'eng Hsüeh-feng (q.v.). After graduation he became commander of the 22nd Division and then chief-of-staff of the Kwangtung-Kiangsi Military Region.

In 1934 Ch'eng was sent to the Oyüwan Soviet area on the borders of Hupeh, Honan and Anhwei Provinces to contact what was left of the leadership there. He carried instructions to the Party secretary in East Hopeh, Cheng Wei-san (q.v.), ordering him to evacuate Oyüwan.[4] Oyüwan was the second largest of the Communist soviets in the early 1930's and one that operated with a certain amount of independence from Kiangsi. It had been so strongly attacked by the Nationalist armies that most of its personnel had been forced to evacuate in late 1932. Chang Kuo-t'ao, Hsu Hsiang-ch'ien (qq.v.), and the Fourth Route Army had moved west into Szechwan, but Hsu Hai-tung's (q.v.) 25th Red

Army had been left to cover the retreat and to continue guerrilla operations in the Oyüwan area. It was this army that Ch'eng joined in 1934. He told Nym Wales that he commanded the 25th Army and that Hsu Hai-tung was the deputy commander, but some accounts state that Hsu was the commander and Ch'eng the leading Party functionary.[5]

The 25th Red Army's 1934–35 march to Shensi is described in the biography of Hsu Hai-tung. In September 1935 their units joined forces with the Red guerrillas that had been operating there for several years under the command of Liu Chih-tan (q.v.) and others. The merged forces, known as the 15th Army Corps, were commanded by Hsu Hai-tung. Liu Chih-tan was the deputy commander, Ch'eng the political commissar, and Kao Kang the director of the Corps' Political Department. At the same time a political reorganization took place and a "Central Committee Representative Body" was set up with Ch'eng as one of its members.[6] In October 1935 Ch'eng was among those present to welcome to Shensi the units of the First Front Army led by Mao Tse-tung and P'eng Te-huai.[7] In early 1936 Ch'eng participated in the Communists' thrust across the Yellow River into Shansi, a short-lived campaign described in Liu Chih-tan's biography. Ch'eng was wounded again during the fighting in Shansi.

Immediately after the outbreak of the Sino-Japanese War in mid-1937 the 15th Army Corps became part of Lin Piao's 115th Division, one of the major components of the Eighth Route Army. The division moved from Shensi across the Yellow River into Shansi where Ch'eng served briefly as director of the Shansi Mobilization Office of the Eighth Route Army. Later in 1937 he was transferred to Hopeh and from then until about 1944 he was political commissar of the Central Hopeh Military District. As a military sector, the Central Hopeh District was one of two areas subordinate to the Wu-t'ai-shan military base, the general headquarters of the 115th Division. Politically, the area was under the Shansi-Chahar-Hopeh (Chin-Ch'a-Chi) Border Region Government organized in early 1938. The history and the strategic significance of the Central Hopeh Military District is discussed in the biography of Lü Cheng-ts'ao, the commander there during the years when Ch'eng served as the political commissar.

Late in the war Lü Cheng-ts'ao was transferred to the Shansi-Suiyuan Border Region. At approximately this time Ch'eng became deputy political commissar of the Chin-Ch'a-Chi Military Region that was commanded by Nieh Jung-chen (q.v.). When the Party's Seventh National Congress was held in Yenan from April to June 1945, Ch'eng was elected one of the 33 alternate members of the Central Committee. After the Sino-Japanese War he moved into Manchuria

with Lin Piao's forces and commanded units of the Shansi-Chahar-Hopeh PLA that were operating in the Hopeh-Jehol-Liaoning border area. By the latter part of 1948, when Lin Piao's army was completing its conquest of Manchuria, Ch'eng commanded the Second Army Group in operations along the Tientsin-Mukden rail line. When all of Manchuria fell to the Communists in the winter of 1948–49, Ch'eng moved south with Lin's forces, and in early February 1949, immediately after Peking was surrendered, he was named commander of the Peking Municipal Garrison Command Headquarters.

Ch'eng remained in Peking only briefly, for after the fall of Taiyuan, the capital of his native Shansi, he was sent there to take charge of installing the provincial Communist administration. He became the ranking secretary of the Shansi CCP Committee, and when the Shansi Provincial People's Government was formally established in August, he was appointed governor. He was also appointed commander and political commissar of the Shansi Military District, and thus held all four of the major political-military posts in the province. Ch'eng summarized developments in Shansi in a report delivered in Peking before the Government Administration Council (the cabinet), which was published in the May 20, 1950, issue of the *JMJP*. Toward the end of 1950 he was permanently transferred to Peking, his major political posts in Shansi being assumed by Lai Jo-yü (q.v.). A Japanese report states that Ch'eng participated in the Korean War, but in view of his frequent public appearance in Peking during the early fifties this seems most unlikely.

Ch'eng's transfer to Peking was presaged in July 1950 when he was made a member of the Provisional Board of the All-China Federation of Cooperatives (ACFC), the organization to which he devoted most of his time until about 1957. The purpose of the Federation, regarded by the Chinese as a "mass" organization, is to promote agricultural and handicraft production and to ensure the flow of commodities between the urban and rural areas. When the Provisional Board held its first meeting in November 1950, Ch'eng was elected as the ranking vice-chairman under Po I-po (q.v.). In the same year Ch'eng also became president of the Federation's Cadres School. Concurrent with these assignments, he received a new appointment (October 1950) as director of the Central Cooperative Enterprises Administration (CCEA), the governmental counterpart of the Federation. Ch'eng retained the CCEA directorship until September 1952 when the organ was abolished. The CCEA was subordinate to the cabinet's Finance and Economics Committee, of which Ch'eng was a member from October 1950 until it too was abolished in September 1954.

When the ACFC held its next major meeting,

July 1952, Ch'eng gave the keynote speech. The Provisional Board at this time brought a permanent organization into existence; Ch'eng continued as a vice-chairman and then in 1953 he became acting chairman. In July 1954, when the ACFC was reorganized and renamed the All-China Federation of Supply and Marketing Co-operatives, he became the chairman. Ch'eng made his first trip abroad in connection with the Federation when he led a 28-member delegation to the Soviet Union in August 1954 at the invitation of the Central Union of Soviet Consumers' Cooperatives. In addition to his reports at Federation meetings, Ch'eng wrote an important article on the cooperative movement for the August 3, 1955, issue of the Tientsin *Ta-kung pao,* which was reprinted in the *1956 Jen-min shouts'e* (People's handbook). Ch'eng continued as the most active figure in the Federation until about 1957 when he became more occupied in other posts; from then on Chang Ch'i-lung (q.v.), one of the vice-chairmen, became the *de facto* head of the organization. Finally, in 1963, still another man, P'an Fu-sheng (q.v.), formally succeeded Ch'eng Tzu-hua as the chairman.

Apart from his work with the cooperative movement in the early and mid-fifties, Ch'eng was engaged in other tasks. In June 1952 he took part in the organization of the All-China Federation of Industry and Commerce, a mass organization established to maintain liaison with "capitalist" enterprises and to assist in their "transformation" into state organizations. From mid-1952 to 1954 he was a member of the central government's Labor Employment Committee, and from 1953 to 1954 he served as a member of the Central Election Committee that was set up to prepare for the elections to the NPC. When the elections were held in 1954 Ch'eng became a Shantung deputy to the First NPC, and at the close of its inaugural session in September 1954 he was elected to the important NPC Standing Committee. He was also a member (and later vice-chairman) of the NPC's Budget Committee. Ch'eng did not serve in the Second NPC (1959–1964), but he was again elected to the Third NPC, which opened in late 1964, this time as a deputy from his native Shansi.

At the Party's Eighth National Congress in September 1956, Ch'eng was promoted from alternate to full membership on the Central Committee. Exactly two years later he received his first cabinet appointment when he was named to head the Ministry of Commerce, which had existed briefly from February to September. In April 1959, at the first session of the Second NPC, Ch'eng spoke on commercial work and was reappointed as minister. However, he was succeeded in February 1960 by Yao I-lin (q.v.). This change came the day after Ch'eng was appointed a vice-chairman of the State Council's Commission for State Capital Construction. The Commission, headed by economic expert Ch'en Yun (q.v.), was abolished in January 1961. Once again, however, Ch'eng received another assignment, this time as a vice-chairman of the State Planning Commission, a position he continues to hold under Li Fu-ch'un (q.v.). Related to these top-level economic assignments, Ch'eng has also been associated with the State Council's Finance and Trade Office, which coordinates the work of the numerous commissions, ministries, and bureaus in the State Council that deal with financial and commercial work. He served as a vice-chairman of the Office under Li Hsien-nien from September 1959 to December 1961.

Most of Ch'eng's public appearances throughout the fifties and early sixties were in connection with domestic economic affairs, quite often in places other than the national capital where he spends most of his time. Although he has not been frequently identified in connection with foreign affairs, he was sent to East Germany in June 1957 as head of the CCP delegation to a congress of the East German Socialist Unity (Communist) Party. Similarly, although he has had virtually no association with military affairs since the Communist takeover in 1949, he was appointed a member of the central government's National Defense Council in January 1965.

1. Nym Wales, *Red Dust* (Stanford, Calif., 1952), pp. 143–147.
2. Donald G. Gillin, *Warlord Yen Hsi-shan in Shansi Province, 1911–1949* (Princeton, N. J., 1967), pp. 44–45, 73–74.
3. *Hung-ch'i p'iao-p'iao* (Red flag fluttering; Peking, 1957), III, 46.
4. *Ibid.,* p. 174.
5. Mark Selden, "The Guerrilla Movement in Northwest China," *The China Quarterly,* no. 29:74 (January–March 1967).
6. *Ibid.*
7. *Hung-ch'i p'iao-p'iao,* III, 46.

Cheng Wei-san

(c.1901–   ; Huang-an, Hupeh). Former military political leader; member, CCP Central Committee.

Cheng Wei-san has been almost completely inactive since the mid-1940's, but his career is important because he was one of the founders of the Oyüwan Soviet in the early 1930's. He was born about 1901 (though some sources use 1896) in the small town of Huang-an, located about 100 miles northeast of Wuhan in Hupeh province. Several important Communists also came from Huang-an, among them Tung Pi-wu and Li Hsien-nien (qq.v.), and during the late 1920's Huang-an hsien witnessed considerable peasant unrest, much of it fomented by the CCP. Later, in the early thirties, Huang-an became part of the Oyüwan (Hupeh, Honan, and Anhwei) Soviet, the second in importance to the "central" soviet in Kiangsi, which was established in 1931.

After receiving the equivalent of a university education at about the time of the May Fourth Movement in 1919, Cheng joined the CCP. He may have become a Communist shortly after the Party was founded in 1921, for by 1923 he was already working among the peasantry in Hsin-chi hsien (now Hsin-hsien), southeast Honan, inciting them against the local landlords and the high taxes. It is not clear if Hsin-chi hsien fell within the territory that was later a part of the Oyüwan Soviet; if not, it was close by. In any case, during the first 10 years of his career as a Communist, Cheng was active in and around the Oyüwan area.

By 1926 Cheng was working as a Party functionary in Wuhan, the Hupeh capital. The importance of Wuhan at this time was rapidly increasing, especially when major elements of the Nationalist government were transferred there during the winter of 1926–27 in the wake of the Northern Expedition. And it became even more important from the Communist viewpoint when the CCP was vigorously suppressed in Shanghai in the spring of 1927, an action that caused the Party to transfer many of its activities to Wuhan. Cheng was presumably in or near Wuhan on August 1, 1927, when the Communists mutinied at Nanchang, the Kiangsi capital. The uprising signaled a complete break in the uneasy relations between the Communists and the KMT, and it forced the CCP to go underground. In the succeeding months many CCP activists in central China were dispatched to the countryside to continue (or start anew) the work of organizing the peasants. In 1927, following the uprising at Nanchang, Cheng was serving as the secretary of the CCP Committee in his native Huang-an. Together with Wang Shu-sheng (q.v.) and others, he led a series of peasant uprisings in and around Huang-an and Ma-ch'eng hsien.[1] These activities were part of a wider campaign in central-south China rural areas known as the Autumn Harvest Uprisings. Cheng and his colleagues established a unit subordinate to the Workers' and Peasants' Red Army known as the Seventh Army (not to be confused with the Seventh Army established in 1929 by Chang Yun-i in Kwangsi). After undergoing a number of reorganizations, the Seventh Army was ultimately incorporated into the units led by Hsu Hsiang-ch'ien (q.v.) in the Oyüwan area in the early thirties. In the post-1927 period Cheng was probably working also in conjunction with Hsu Hai-tung who later became a colleague of Cheng during the Oyüwan period.

Early in 1930, in association with Wang Shu-sheng, Cheng took a leading part in guerrilla operations in Hsin-chi hsien where he had begun his revolutionary career several years earlier. Efforts to organize the peasantry intensified during the next year, and then in the spring of 1931 the CCP Headquarters in Shanghai sent several high-ranking leaders to bolster the operations in the Oyüwan area. The most notable of these men was Chang Kuo-t'ao, whose biography contains the details of the developments in Oyüwan. Chang immediately established the Party's Central Sub-bureau for the Oyüwan area, and later in the year the Oyüwan Soviet was set up as the government apparatus. Chang headed the Party Sub-bureau and Cheng was a member of the Sub-bureau and director of the Finance Department of the Soviet government. Chang has described Cheng Wei-san as "virtuous, peaceable, and fair-minded" with a scholarly appearance.[2]

Late in 1932 Chang Kuo-t'ao and Hsu Hsiang-ch'ien, the senior military figure in Oyüwan, were forced by Nationalist military strength to evacuate the area. Leading their military units, known as the Fourth Front Army, they sought refuge in west Szechwan. However, some military units were left behind in Oyüwan under the command of Hsu Hai-tung's 25th Red Army. For the next two years Cheng remained in the Oyüwan area where he carried on Party work clandestinely. When the Second All-China Congress of Soviets was convened under the chairmanship of Mao Tse-tung in Juichin, Kiangsi, in January–February 1934, Cheng was elected a member of the governing Central Executive Committee (CEC). It is quite possible, however, that this position was more nominal than real, for in view of the Nationalists' blockade of the "central soviet" in Kiangsi it is unlikely that Cheng actually attended the Congress. Nonetheless, he was in touch with the top leadership in Juichin, and in September 1934 (immediately prior to beginning of the Long March by Mao and his men), Cheng received an important directive from the "Party Center." Cheng was then serving as secretary of the CCP Hupeh District Committee. The directive was delivered from Kiangsi by Ch'eng Tzu-hua (q.v.), and upon its receipt Cheng Wei-san sent an emissary to Hai-tung's 25th Red Army, which was then in western Anhwei Province. The directive ordered Hsu to move his army into eastern Hupeh before moving north from Oyüwan to Shensi.[3] Hsu carried out the order, and then he, Ch'eng Tzu-hua, and Cheng Wei-san led the 25th Army to Shensi, arriving there a year ahead of Mao Tse-tung, who arrived in Shensi in the fall of 1935.

Upon arriving in Shensi, Hsu Hai-tung and his political officers began to organize and arm the peasants in the southern part of the province. Early in 1935 Cheng became secretary of the Party's South Shensi Special Committee. Moreover, a small soviet was established. Journalist Edgar Snow, who visited Communist territories in 1936, described this as a "provisional Soviet Government" with Cheng, a "member of the Cheka of Shensi province, as chairman."[4] By 1936 Cheng had left south Shensi for the northern part of the province where the main Communist leaders and military units were stationed. From that time until midway through the Sino-Japanese War, nothing is recorded of his activities, but it appears that he was assigned to the New Fourth Army, which operated in the lower reaches of the Yangtze. In any case, early in 1941, at the time of the disastrous defeat of New Fourth Army units by the Nationalists (see under Yeh T'ing), Cheng was political commissar of Chang Yun-i's (q.v.) Second Division of the New Fourth Army.[5] He was soon succeeded by Lo Ping-hui (q.v) and was transferred to the old Oyüwan area where, in collaboration with Li Hsien-nien, he played a key role in establishing the new Fourth Army's Fifth Division.[6] Li commanded the Division, and by the latter part of the war (and probably earlier), Cheng was the political commissar. By 1944 he was head of the Communists' Honan-Hupeh Border Region Assembly; in 1945 he was deputy secretary and then secretary of the Party's Central Plains Bureau, serving concurrently as head of the Bureau's Organization Department and deputy political commissar of the Central Plains Military Region. Thus by the closing stages of the war Cheng was among the Party's leading figures in central China. He gained additional stature in 1945 when, at the Party's Seventh Congress held in Yenan from April to June, he was one of only 44 persons elected a full member of the Party Central Committee. In view of his assignments in central China, Cheng was probably elected in absentia.

As the Red Armies began to expand over China in the postwar period, they integrated the scattered wartime guerrilla bases into larger territorial divisions which served as bases of operation for Communist forces. Thus, the former Oyüwan area was incorporated into the Central Plains Liberated Area. The military unit, the Central Plains Liberation Army, was led by Li Hsien-nien. By 1946 Cheng was Li's political commissar, and during the first half of that year the two men fought under extremely difficult circumstances, surrounded as they were by large Nationalist armies. In the middle of the year they were forced to break through a Nationalist encirclement and fight their way to the Shensi-Hupeh border area. Their activities during this period are referred to in highly favorable terms in Mao Tse-tung's Selected Works.[7] At approximately this time Cheng was taken ill and had to return to north Shensi to recuperate. It appears that he never fully recovered, for during the next two decades he virtually disappeared from the political scene. In September

1949 he did, however, attend the inaugural session of the CPPCC (as a representative of the CCP), the organization that brought the national government into existence (October 1). During the term of the Second CPPCC (1954–1959), he served as a member of the National Committee, on this occasion representing the "peasants." He has also been a member of the Third and Fourth National Committees (again representing the CCP), which held their initial sessions in April 1959 and December 1964–January 1965, respectively. Since the formation of the Second CPPCC in 1954, Cheng has also been a member of the governing Standing Committee, but he seems to have done little except lend his name to the list of delegates. Far more important—and virtual proof that his "illness" is physical and not political—Cheng was present in Peking in September 1956 for the Party's Eighth National Congress. He served on the Congress Presidium (steering committee) and was one of the presiding executive chairmen for one of the daily sessions. At the end of the meetings he was re-elected to full membership on the Party Central Committee. He is not known to have made a public appearance since then, presumably because of continuing ill health.

1. Chung-kuo kung-ch'an-tang tsai chung-nan-ti-ch'ü ling-tao ko-ming tou-cheng te li-shih tzu-liao (Historical materials on the revolutionary struggles led by the CCP in central-south China; Wuhan, 1951), I, 275.
2. Modern China Project, Columbia University, New York, Howard L. Boorman, director.
3. Hung-ch'i p'iao-p'iao (Red flag fluttering; Peking, 1957), III, 174.
4. Edgar Snow, Red Star over China (New York, 1938), p. 202.
5. Kōain, Sohoku kyōsan chiku jitsujō chōsa hōkokusho (Investigation report on the current situation in the North Kiangsu Communist region; Shanghai, 1941), chart following p. 142.
6. Chung-kuo kung-ch'an-tang tsai chung-nan-ti-ch'ü ling-tao ko-ming tou-cheng te li-shih tzu-liao, I, 5.
7. Selected Works of Mao Tse-tung (Peking, 1961), IV, 115–118.

Chi Ch'ao-ting

(1903–1963; Fen-yang, Shansi). Economist; vice-chairman and secretary-general, China Committee for the Promotion of International Trade.

American-educated Chi Ch'ao-ting, an economist of international reputation, was among the most important foreign trade officials in the PRC until his death in 1963. He was born in Shansi, a province famed for having produced a large number of bankers and financial experts. His father, Chi Kung-ch'üan, was a scholar-official who served in the Shansi government under Yen Hsi-shan and, after the Communists came to power, he continued in this government in a minor capacity. Chi Ch'ao-ting studied law and diplomacy at Tsinghua University, graduating in 1924. He is said to have been influenced by the May Fourth Movement (1919); he was an active student and a regular participant in debating and public speaking societies. His sense of nationalism at this time is perhaps best illustrated by the fact that he won first prize in the English oratorical contest with a speech entitled "Save Mongolia." In the year of his graduation he went to the United States where he continued his study of law at the University of Chicago (J.D., 1928). While in Chicago Chi became associated with various left-wing organizations, most notably the Anti-Imperialist League. In a eulogy delivered at a memorial service for Chi in 1963, it was revealed that he had joined the CCP in 1927 and was among the first Chinese students in the United States to do so. In that same year he left for Europe where he attended the first and second congresses of the Anti-Imperialist League (in Brussels, February 1927 and Frankfurt, January 1929). He also spent about a year in Moscow where he was an interpreter for the Chinese who had fled to Moscow at the time of the CCP–KMT split in 1927. Chi took part in the work of the CCP delegation to the Sixth Comintern Congress in Moscow in mid-1928, and he worked with the Chinese Communist delegation that was affiliated with the Red Trade Union International (Profintern). He returned to the United States in 1929 and for the next 12 years lived principally in New York City where he was active in leftist circles and was a frequent contributor (often using a pseudonym) of articles on China. In the obituarial materials regarding Chi it was revealed that after 1929 he worked for the *Daily Worker* and the China Bureau of the Communist Party of the United States. Some of these activities were, of course, carried on covertly, while others were well known in American intellectual circles. In the meantime, Chi had enrolled at Columbia University and in 1936 he received his doctorate in economics. His highly regarded though controversial doctoral dissertation won Columbia's Seligman economic prize and was published in England in 1936 under the title *Key Economic Areas in Chinese History*. During his many years in the United States Chi was perhaps best known in connection with the Institute for Pacific Relations. In 1936 he was a member of the Chinese delegation led by the distinguished scholar Hu Shih to an IPR conference held in Yosemite, California, and from 1937 to 1940 he was a member of the IPR Research Staff in New York.

Sometime in the thirties Chi came to know Frank Coe and Solomon Adler, both of whom were U.S. Treasury Department officials and both of whom ultimately were to work for the PRC after the Communists took power in 1949. Few other Chinese Communists have had such close connections with U.S. Government officials, and in the decade prior to 1949 Chi was able to put these contacts to good use for the CCP. His contacts with Coe and Adler won him a job as a secretary to K. P. Chen (Ch'en Kuang-fu), a top Chinese Nationalist financier who was posted in the United States to handle negotiations related to American aid to the Chinese Nationalist Government. After some 17 years abroad, Chi finally returned to China in 1941 where for the next few years he held important economic posts with the Nationalist Government in Chungking. Chi's political agility was impressive; already a CCP member (though covertly) and already well known among senior American Government officials, Chi was now able to become (1944) a confidential secretary to H. H. K'ung, the brother-in-law of Chiang Kai-shek, one of the key Nationalist officials and their top economic expert. When Chi died in 1963 the Communists openly boasted that after his return to China in 1941 he served as a covert liaison agent for them, presumably feeding them information through the CCP liaison mission in Chungking headed by Chou En-lai. Serving as secretary-general of the delegation led by H. H. K'ung, Chi attended the important International Monetary and Financial Conference held at Bretton Woods, New Hampshire, in 1944. Also in 1944 Chi had become administrative director of the Economic Research Department in the Central Bank of China of which H. H. K'ung was governor. He worked at this post first in Chungking and then, after the war ended, in Shanghai.

Even by mid-1948, when the Nationalists were on the brink of defeat, Chi was able to serve as an adviser to the Nationalist delegation to the third session of the United Nations' Economic Council on Asia and the Far East (ECAFE) in Octacamund, India (June), and again at the fourth session in Lapstone, Australia (December). Upon his return to China Chi immediately went to Peking, which was within days of being surrendered to the Communists by KMT General Fu Tso-i. When it fell on the last day of January 1949 and Chi formally joined the Communist regime, he was quickly given a variety of tasks befitting his broad background in economics and international banking; he became economic adviser to the People's Bank (the financial institution in charge of China's international banking) and director of its Research Department, as well as manager of the People's Insurance Company. Then, following the surrender of Shanghai in May, he temporarily served as assistant general manager of the Shanghai Branch of the Bank of China.

When the PRC was inaugurated in October 1949, Chi was brought back to Peking to assume key posts in the financial hierarchy that was being established. He became a member of the Government Administration Council's Finance and Economics Committee (FEC), the most important economic body in the PRC until its dissolution in 1954, serving also from 1949 to 1952 as director of the FEC's Foreign Capital Enterprises Control Bureau and from 1951 to 1952 as a deputy director of its Central Financial and Economic Planning Committee, the predecessor of the important State Planning Commission formed in the fall of 1952. From December 1949 until his death Chi was also a Board member of the Chinese People's Institute of Foreign Affairs. Had the Chinese Communists gained admission to the United Nations, Chi would have been their top economic representative; in early 1950 he was appointed as the PRC representative to the Economic and Social Council (ECOSOC), and later in 1950 and again in 1951 he was designated to represent the PRC at ECAFE meetings in Bangkok and Lahore. All these efforts were in vain.

China's initial frustrations in gaining entry into the world of international finance were exacerbated shortly after the outbreak of the Korean War (July 1950) when the Western allies clamped an embargo on the sale of strategic goods to the Communist Bloc. Seeking to counter this move, the Communists convened the International Economic Conference in Moscow in the spring of 1952; trade relations were openly courted with business firms in the non-Communist world and, to institutionalize the processes, the Conference created a Committee for the Promotion of International Trade and each of the Communist nations created national branches. Chi was deeply involved in these developments, attending the Moscow conference as secretary-general of the Chinese delegation led by Nan Han-ch'en (q.v.) and, when the PRC created the China Committee for the Promotion of International Trade (CCPIT) in May 1952, he became its secretary-general. The CCPIT, in effect, is a semi-official arm of the PRC's Foreign Trade Ministry—the Ministry deals with nations having diplomatic relations with Peking and the CCPIT handles trade with countries not having diplomatic ties with the PRC. Chi (until his death) and Chairman Nan Han-ch'en were the two key Chinese officials in the CCPIT.

From his trip to Moscow in 1952 until his death 11 years later, Chi Ch'ao-ting spent a great deal of time abroad—33 missions took him to 20 different nations throughout the world. Most frequently he traveled as a top CCPIT official—leading trade negotiation delegations, attending international trade fairs and economic seminars, or supervising Chinese exhibitions that displayed the economic growth of "New China." In the fifties most of these visits were to nations in West Europe: Austria, 1952, 1956, 1957, and 1959;

Italy, 1956; France, 1956; Switzerland, 1956, 1957, 1958; West Germany, 1957; England, 1957; and, Belgium, 1957. Then, as China's economic relations expanded, Chi's trips took him to the following countries: India, 1959; Iraq, 1960; Burma, 1961; Brazil, 1962; and, Mexico, 1963. It is a noteworthy reflection of the aims of the CCPIT that the above-mentioned trips took Chi to seven nations that did not recognize Peking. In view of this work it is not surprising that in 1955 Chi, already the secretary-general of the CCPIT, was named concurrently as a vice-chairman, and in the following year as chairman of the CCPIT's newly established Foreign Trade Arbitration Committee.

In the meantime, Chi had received a number of new posts, which, for the most part, reflected his deep involvement in international affairs. From the spring of 1950 to at least mid-1952 he was a deputy manager of the Bank of China, and from 1952 to an uncertain date he was a deputy director of the Finance Ministry's International Economic Affairs Bureau. In the spring of 1952 he was also identified as a "senior expert" in the Academy of Sciences, presumably in connection with one of the Academy's institutes engaged in economic research. From November 1956 to at least 1960 he was an Executive Committee member of the All-China Federation of Industry and Commerce, an organization that includes among its members China's most experienced banking, economic, business, and industrial figures (see under Hsu Ti-hsin). He also served from May 1954 to his death as a Standing Committee member of the Chinese People's Association for Cultural Relations with Foreign Countries, and from December 1954 until he died as a member of the CPPCC's Second and Third National Committees, serving here as a representative of "people's organizations for peaceful and friendly relations with foreign countries."

In the mid-fifties Chi took on a new assignment as a delegate to some of the international conferences of the Communist-dominated World Peace Council (WPC). He attended WPC-sponsored meetings in Sweden in 1954, 1958, and 1959, and in Ceylon in 1957. He became a Standing Committee member of the China Peace Committee, an affiliate of the WPC, in July 1958. Rather closely related to his work with the WPC were Chi's activities in connection with the Afro-Asian "solidarity" movement. This movement initially appeared to be no more than a regional offshoot of the WPC, but with the emergence of many new African and Asian nations in the late fifties and early sixties and the growing tension in Sino-Soviet relations, it was gradually transformed (in Chinese eyes) into a movement that held great potential for spreading Chinese influence. The first Afro-Asian Solidarity Conference, the background of which is explained in the biography of Chu Tzu-ch'i, took place from late December 1957 to early January 1958. It was decided at this conference, which was attended by Chi, to establish a permanent Afro-Asian People's Solidarity Organization (AAPSO), with headquarters in Cairo, and plans were laid for establishing an auxiliary body to deal with economic problems. The next step was the convocation in Cairo of a preparatory meeting for an Afro-Asian Economic Conference in August 1958. Chi led the Chinese delegation to this meeting, and then in December he was a deputy to Nan Han-ch'en at the first Afro-Asian Economic Conference, also held in Cairo. During the remainder of his life Chi spent a good deal of time attending AAPSO-sponsored meetings (Guinea, 1960; Lebanon, 1960; and Tanganyika, 1963) and, more important, meetings of the Afro-Asian Organization for Economic Cooperation (AAOEC). The latter took him to Jakarta in 1959, Cairo in 1960 and 1962, and New Delhi in 1961. Chi's speech at the Cairo meeting in May 1962 is suggestive of the Chinese Communist view of the Afro-Asian solidarity movement. The AAOEC was then exploring the possibility of gaining consultative status in ECOSOC (to which Chi himself had been the PRC representative-designate 12 years earlier). Chi grasped this occasion to denounce any such affiliation, commenting that despite the increase of Afro-Asian votes in the United Nations, "the basic character of the United Nations Organization as an instrument of United States foreign policy has not been changed." He went on to point out that any further steps to establish relations with ECOSOC or any of its subordinate agencies would have "no binding force on China."

When Chi was not abroad he spent much of his time in Peking conferring with visiting trade groups and on several occasions signed joint statements and agreements related to trade and financial matters. Similarly, it was a logical extension of his numerous foreign connections that Chi's name was placed on the roster of six "friendship associations" vis-à-vis the Soviet Union (1954), Iraq (1958), Latin America (1960), Africa (1960), Ceylon (1962), and Cuba (1962). He was named to the national council in each case, and in the China-Latin America Friendship Association he served also as a vice-chairman. He was also named to the national Council of the Asia-Africa Society of China, established in April 1962 to promote scholarly research on these two continents. Chi was extremely active until the last days of his life; on August 2, 1963, just one week before he died, he welcomed a delegation of Colombian parliamentarians in Peking. Then on August 9 he died of a cerebral hemorrhage at the age of 60. In death as in life, there was an international atmosphere surrounding the funeral and memorial arrangements made for Chi. His funeral

committee, headed by Foreign Minister Ch'en I, included five foreigners, among them Chi's friends from his days in the United States, Solomon Adler and Frank Coe, as well as the American Communist author Anna Louise Strong. In addition, over the next several days the Chinese reported the receipt of scores of messages of condolence from foreign trade organizations throughout the world.

Chi was married three times and is probably the only important Chinese Communist to have had an American wife. Harriet Levine became Chi's first wife in Paris in 1927, and she is the mother of two sons, both American citizens. Harriet Chi was in Shanghai in 1947, but she separated from her husband and returned to the United States where she continues to reside, as do the sons, Emile and Carl. Chi's second wife was Lu Yu-chen, a Stanford graduate who also studied at Sun Yat-sen (Chung-shan) University in Moscow. Although the details of his third marriage are not known, at the time of his death it was revealed that his widow was Lo Ching-i. Nothing is known of Lu Yu-chen's activities in the post-1949 period, but since the mid-fifties Lo Ching-i has been fairly active in work similar to that of her late husband. She is a member of the national Council of the China-Latin America and the China-Cuba Friendship Associations, and she has also been the secretary-general of the China-Pakistan Friendship Association since its formation in 1956. Mme. Chi is also a deputy director of the Propaganda Department of the State Council's Commission for Cultural Relations with Foreign Countries, and in late 1964 she was elected to the Fourth National Committee of the CPPCC. Chi is also survived by his father who had a long-standing acquaintance with the K'ung family and was a friend of H. H. K'ung, a native of Shansi. In the early fifties Chi Kung-ch'üan was a member of the Shansi Provincial People's Government Council and a vice-chairman of its Culture and Education Committee. He has also served as a vice-chairman of the Shansi chapter of the CPPCC since 1955, and in August 1958 he was elected to the Third National Council of the Political Science and Law Association of China. He was re-elected to the Council at the Fourth Congress of the Association held in October 1964, a year after his son's death.

Chi Fang

(c.1893–   ; Hai-men hsien, Kiangsu). Former military leader of the New Fourth Army; chairman, Chinese Peasants' and Workers' Democratic Party.

Chi Fang was an important independent guerrilla leader in Kiangsu who placed his forces under the command of the Communist New Fourth Army in 1940 and continued to serve in this area until the PRC was established in 1949. Chi's most important contribution to the PRC has been his leadership of the Chinese Peasants' and Workers' Democratic Party, one of the eight non-Communist political parties that ostensibly share in political power in Communist China.

Chi Fang has also been known by the name Chi Cheng-ch'eng; he was born in Hai-men hsien, located in Kiangsu on the north bank of the Yangtze River estuary north of Shanghai. After graduating from the sixth class of the Paoting Military Academy (see under Yeh T'ing), he went to Canton in 1924 and by the following year was an instructor at the Whampoa Military Academy, the Republican Chinese equivalent of West Point, which was created and headed by Chiang Kai-shek. Chi participated in the Northern Expedition (1926–27), serving as head of the Organization Section of the General Political Department, which was headed by Teng Yen-ta, a man with whom Chi was to be associated over the next few years (see below). A supporter of the left-wing KMT Government (the "Wuhan Government"), Chi went to Shanghai in 1927 where he helped to found a number of political periodicals. More important, however, he participated in the founding of the China Revolutionary Party, which soon evolved into the Third Party (Ti-san tang). Led by Teng Yen-ta, the party stressed Sun Yat-sen's Three Principles and the interests of the peasants and laborers.[1] In 1929–30 the Third Party was reorganized into the Provisional Action Committee of the KMT, although until 1949 it continued to be popularly known as the Third Party. Chi apparently did not take an active part in the work of the party after the early thirties, but in the late forties he was again to become deeply involved (see below).

In late 1933 and early 1934 Chi participated in the short-lived Fukien People's Government, an administration established by dissident KMT leaders Ts'ai T'ing-k'ai, Chiang Kuang-nai, and Li Chi-shen and backed militarily by the 19th Route Army. Following the collapse of this government in January 1934, Chi returned to Shanghai where he was briefly imprisoned. After his release he again engaged in anti-KMT and anti-Chiang Kai-shek activities and was once again arrested and shortly after released. According to a semi-official handbook, Chi was sent by Li Chi-shen to the Kiangsu-Chekiang area to lead a "people's movement" and to organize guerrilla forces following the outbreak of the Sino-Japanese War in the summer of 1937. He probably remained in the border area where some of the guerrillas from his "people's movement" may have come in contact with the scattered bands of Communist guerrillas that operated along the provincial borders under the direction of Su Yü (q.v.). When war broke out, Su's guerrillas were incorporated into the Red military unit com-

manded by Chang Ting-ch'eng (q.v.) from the Communist soviet in southwest Fukien. Nothing further is known about the group with which Chi was working, but by 1940 he emerged as an active guerrilla organizer of the peasants in the Kiangsu peninsula north of Shanghai.

In late 1940 Chi merged his guerrilla force from the Fourth Administrative District of North Kiangsu with the Communists' New Fourth Army. Prior to this, Chi had apparently been working clandestinely to organize the local peasants quite independently of the KMT inspector (or commissioner), who exercised authority over the Fourth District as the local representative of Nationalist General Han Te-ch'in, governor of Kiangsu. The Fourth Administrative District of Kiangsu was made up of the hsien of Nan-t'ung, Ch'i-tung, Hai-men (Chi's native hsien), and Ju-kao, with its capital city in the small town of Chueh-chiang, a riverport town not far from the coast. A fertile and comparatively rich area on the Kiangsu peninsula, the district was strategically located along the mouth of the Yangtze near Shanghai. Thus it was one of the first objectives of the Communists when their New Fourth Army troops, which had been initially concentrated south of the Yangtze, began to move north in 1940.

A major segment of the New Fourth Army was brought north of the Yangtze under command of Ch'en I (q.v.) beginning in June 1940. Governor Han's Nationalist forces had already had clashes with elements of the Communist New Fourth Army, which were stationed north of the Yangtze, but conflict increased when Ch'en's troops entered north Kiangsu. In early October, in a second battle at Huang-ch'iao, Han was roundly defeated, and once the Nationalist opposition in the area was knocked out, the Communists began expanding eastward into the coastal area of north Kiangsu. In a two-pronged drive, forces went toward Yen-ch'eng under Ch'en I and in a more southerly direction toward the Fourth District under one of Ch'en's commanders, T'ao Yung. T'ao was a Communist military leader from Szu-hsien, north Anhwei. Separated from the main army of Ch'en I after the successful battle at Huang-ch'iao and moving south to enter the peninsula, he led his troops through Ching-chiang and Nan-t'ung hsien. Early in November 1940 he was able to displace the KMT inspector at Chueh-chiang and set up his own headquarters there, but the town remained the administrative seat of the Fourth Administrative District. Then in mid-November, T'ao's force, known as the Third Column of the New Fourth Army, was joined at Ma-t'ing (about 10 miles west of Chueh-chiang) by the independent Fourth District Guerrillas headed by Chi Fang. At this time Chi's force was the most important group of anti-Japanese guerrillas in north Kiangsu and had been organized independently of Communist efforts. Hence he brought a recognizable fighting unit to the side of the Communists.

In taking over the Fourth Administrative District in Kiangsu the Communists retained much of the existing government structure, but they put a number of their own men into office. The area became a model of Communist wartime administration and a show place of collaboration between the CCP and the local peasantry. Full use was made of the development of mass associations (under Communist direction) to increase the participation of the inhabitants in resisting the Japanese. Here was a field in which Chi had had considerable experience. Whether he was or was not a covert Party member at the time, he could play a more useful political role in the guise of a non-Communist cooperating with the Communist-led resistance to the Japanese. When he joined forces with T'ao, an avowed Communist, Chi became the principal local district military commander, and T'ao was made the deputy commander of the local military force. At the same time the post of inspector of the Fourth District was given to a Communist named Chi Ch'iang-ch'eng. When this slate of local officials had been established, it was then given legal sanction by a congress of federated mass associations for the area, convened under the auspices of the political department of Chi's Fourth District Guerrilla Command. The congress met on January 23, 1941, and approved the above slate of officials, at the same time declaring its support for the new Communist government of north Kiangsu. This government is extensively treated in Chalmers A. Johnson's *Peasant Nationalism and Communist Power,* from which the information on Chi Fang's career at this time is drawn.[2] In brief, the Fourth Administrative District of Kiangsu or, as it was officially called, the Fourth District Administrative Inspectors' Office (under Chi Ch'iang-ch'eng), belonged to the "Central Kiangsu Military Area" (Su-chung Chün-ch'ü), located between Yen-ch'eng and the Yangtze in north Kiangsu. The Military Area, "the most highly developed Communist guerrilla base in central China," was the headquarters of the New Fourth Army staff under Ch'en I (after January 1941) and the base of operations for the Army's First Division (commanded by Su Yü). The structure of Communist and Communist-sponsored institutions in the Su-chung region included "Army, government, and mass organs" —the most influential in terms of work with the local population being "the mass-movement sections of the political departments attached to the New Fourth Army units in the area." For the duration of the war, Chi's Fourth District Guerrilla Command continued to be one of the Communists' principal military strengths. The closeness with which Chi worked with Communist personnel at this time is illustrated by the official slate in the Fourth Administrative District where

both his military deputy's post and the position of inspector were held by Communists. But he also held an administrative post which tied him even more closely into the political machinery that functioned in the "Central Kiangsu Military Area," over which the Communists' First Division (under Su Yü) and Ch'en I's military headquarters had control. This military area contained two political units, one in the Kiangsu peninsula where (as described) Chi was top military man, and the other the area to the north of this centering around Yen-ch'eng where Ch'en's headquarters were located. The latter area was administered by the North Kiangsu Provisional Administrative Committee under Kuan Wenwei, a local Kiangsu CCP leader from Tan-yang, and on this Administrative Committee Chi served as the vice-chairman.

In the postwar period Chi remained in the Kiangsu area, serving the Communists as director of the North Kiangsu Administrative Office, and as vice-chairman of both the North Kiangsu People's Government and the Kiangsu-Anhwei Border Region Government. It was also in the postwar years that the Third Party was resuscitated, after which Chi became one of its most important members. At a meeting held in February 1947 in Shanghai the Third Party was renamed the Chinese Peasants' and Workers' Democratic Party (CPWDP), and Chi was elected to membership on the Central Executive Committee. He also participated in the establishment of the new national government, the formation of which began in June 1949 when the Communists set up a preparatory committee headed by Mao Tse-tung that was responsible for convening the CPPCC in September 1949. Chi was a member of the preparatory committee and also attended the September 1949 meetings as a representative of the "East China Liberated Areas." Shortly after the central government was inaugurated on October 1, 1949, Chi was named as a vice-minister of Communications where he served until September 1954 under Minister Chang Po-chün, then head of the CPWDP. The Ministry of Communications is responsible for river and highway transportation (but its jurisdiction includes neither railways nor telecommunications). Chi also served from 1949 to 1954 as a member of the Executive Board of the Sino-Soviet Friendship Association, then one of the more active of the mass organizations.

In December 1949 Chi became a member of the Central Committee of the China Democratic League (CDL), another of the non-Communist political parties. However, although he remains a CDL Central Committee member, his principal activities have continued to center around the CPWDP. When the CPWDP was structurally reorganized in December 1951, Chi emerged with enhanced stature within the party. He was re-elected to the Central Committee (the new name for the Central Executive Committee) and to the smaller and more powerful Central Executive Bureau (CEB). At this time he also became head of the Personnel Section and a deputy secretary-general. Chairman Chang Po-chün continued as the dominant figure in the CPWDP until the 1957–58 "rectification" campaign, which resulted in the near total elimination of the CPWDP hierarchy. In fact, no other "democratic" party was so badly hit as the CPWDP by the purges that were formally implemented at its Seventh Congress in December 1958. For a year and a half prior to the congress, Chi had headed a special committee to direct an internal "rectification" campaign. He had, moreover, served as the party's acting chairman from April 1958. Finally, at the congress itself, he delivered the keynote speech, the major portion of which was devoted to a denunciation of the alleged "rightist alliance" headed by CPWDP Chairman Chang Po-chün. Predictably, Chi emerged from the congress as the chairman of the party, a position he still retains.

In the intervening years, Chi had participated in the establishment of the constitutional government that was formed at the first session of the First NPC in September 1954. He was a deputy from his native Kiangsu to the First NPC, and was re-elected to the Second NPC (1959–64) and to the Third NPC, which first met in December 1964–January 1965. Furthermore, to replace a deceased colleague, he was named to the NPC's Standing Committee in July 1957; he has continued to sit on the Standing Committee since that time, having been re-elected in April 1959 and January 1965. Although Chi had spent most of the early years of the PRC in Peking, he was reassigned to Kiangsu in 1955, serving there as a vice-governor from February 1955 to October 1958. It is evident that he relinquished this post in 1958 to assume the leadership in the CPWDP in Peking in place of the purged Chang Po-chün.

Relatively little has been heard of Chi's activities since he assumed the leadership of the CPWDP in 1958. In large part, the scant attention paid to "democratic" party leaders since the 1957–58 "rectification" campaigns seems to reflect the CCP's conviction that the non-Communist parties can no longer be usefully employed in the service of the state. Chi does, however, participate in various ceremonial tasks that require the presence of senior members of the non-Communist parties. He was, for example, a member of the presidium for a rally held in September 1959 to commemorate the 10th anniversary of the PRC. He has also been fairly active in the affairs of the NPC. In addition to serving on the NPC Standing Committee since 1957, he has been a member of the presidium (steering committee) for each of the annual NPC sessions since 1960. Chi has also participated in the work

of the CPPCC. As described above, he served on the CPPCC Preparatory Committee in 1949. In 1954 he became a member of the CPPCC's Second National Committee, and in 1959 and 1964 respectively, he was elected to the Third and Fourth National Committees. In each case he represented the CPWDP, and since 1959 he has also served on the CPPCC Standing Committee.

Chi's career differs so greatly from that of most of the so-called "democratic" leaders that the suspicion arises that he may have been a covert Party member for some time—even perhaps from the early days of his cooperation with the New Fourth Army. A typical course of activity for most of the "democratic" leaders is to have joined the CCP at the eleventh hour in 1949 after having spent most of the war years engaged in political in-fighting in Chungking and the postwar years in Shanghai or Nanking jockeying for political power as the Communist and Nationalist armies fought. In contrast, Chi has spent a considerable part of his life working with Communist-sponsored and leftist organizations, and during the Sino-Japanese War he saw active service with one of the major Communist armies.

1. Ch'ien Tuan-sheng, *The Government and Politics of China* (Cambridge, Mass., 1950), pp. 355–356.

2. Chalmers A. Johnson, *Peasant Nationalism and Communist Power* (Stanford, Calif., 1962), chap. 5.

Chi Ya-t'ai

(Jiyadai). (c.1907–   ; Tumet Banner, Inner Mongolia). Vice-chairman, Inner Mongolia Autonomous Region; member, CCP Central Control Commission.

Chi Ya-t'ai is a native of the village of San-liang in the Tumet Banner in Inner Mongolia[1] (see under K'uei Pi). Chi Ya-t'ai is the sinicized form of his Mongol name, Jiyadai. He was among the first group of Mongols to join the Communist Party and has been a long-time associate of Ulanfu (q.v.), a Politburo alternate member since 1956. The combined stimuli of Communism and nationalism apparently were the catalysts that brought Chi into the ranks of the revolutionary movement. According to his own account, "In the summer of 1923, our group of youths devoted to the cause of national liberation, who were awakened by the salvo of the October Revolution and were under the impact of the 'May Fourth' movement, arrived in Peking from . . . Inner Mongolia."[2] This group included Ulanfu and K'uei Pi (q.v.), another significant Mongol, who has risen to the level of the Party Central Committee. They enrolled in a school for Mongols and Tibetans in Peking and by the latter part of 1923 were in contact with Li Ta-chao, a founder of the CCP and then head of the North China Bureau of the Party.[3]

Almost immediately after these initial contacts with Li, the young Mongols joined the Party. In Chi's words: "Our group of Mongolian youths, including Comrades Ulanfu, K'uei Pi, . . . and myself, gloriously joined the great CCP in 1923–1924. Thus, the first group of Mongolian members was found in the CCP."[4] Chi was associated with Li Ta-chao for at least the next two years. Early in 1925 the Party sent him to Inner Mongolia (Suiyuan) to organize an "Association for the Promotion of the National Assembly," an act that was in response to Sun Yat-sen's proposal to convene such an assembly in order to thwart the machinations of warlord Tuan Ch'i-jui. Chi has also claimed that in the fall of 1925 Li Ta-chao gave him instructions on the founding of the "Inner Mongolia People's Revolutionary Party" (see under K'uei Pi), as well as another organization formed at about the same time under the name "Great League of Workers, Peasants, and Soldiers." The latter, led by Li Ta-chao, was established at Kalgan (Chang-chia-k'ou).[5]

The threads of Chi's career are again picked up in the early 1940's when he was known to be working at the Nationalities Institute in Yenan. Among his associates there were Ulanfu and Kao K'o-lin (q.v.). There is also evidence that from 1942 to 1945 he was in Ulan Bator, the capital of Outer Mongolia, engaged in the training of young Chinese for underground work in China. It is probable (though undocumented) that he engaged in underground work among Mongols in north China during the remainder of the 1940's.

In the days and weeks immediately following the establishment of the PRC in October 1949, the other Communist nations recognized the new government in Peking. The Mongolian People's Republic (Outer Mongolia) was naturally among those granting diplomatic recognition. Chi was named as Peking's first ambassador, a post he was to hold for four years. He was appointed in late June 1950, arrived in Ulan Bator a few days later, and presented his credentials there July 10, 1950. During the first two years Chi was in Mongolia, Sino-Mongolian relations were not particularly active—as is suggested by the unusual fact that no known government-to-government agreements were signed during this period. Chi's activities, therefore, were almost exclusively of a ceremonial nature; an outstanding illustration is his attendance in February 1952 at the state funeral for Marshal Choibalsan, Mongolia's top leader. This relative inactivity in relations was probably connected with the paramountcy of Russian influence in Mongolia in those years. However, the situation was somewhat altered in 1952 when Mongolian Premier Tsedenbal journeyed to Peking with an important delegation

(September–October). The negotiations headed by Tsedenbal with the Chinese led to the signing (October 4, 1952) of the Sino-Mongolian Agreement on Economic and Cultural Cooperation under which China agreed to give substantial aid to Mongolia. Coinciding with the events in Peking (the explanation of why Chi did not accompany the Mongolian premier to China), was the staging of a "China-Mongolia Friendship Week" in Ulan Bator. Peking sent a delegation led by writer Chou Li-po to take part in these activities, and Chi was reported frequently in his capacity as host for Chou's delegation.

After an appearance in Ulan Bator in December 1952, Chi does not appear to have remained in Mongolia. On several occasions in 1953 and early 1954 he was represented there by a chargé d'affaires—occasions he would normally have attended in his capacity as ambassador. Also, an American Consulate General (Hong Kong) list of ambassadors, current as of October 1953, indicated that Chi was absent from his post.[6] In any event, he was officially removed in June 1954, being replaced in Ulan Bator by Ambassador Ho Ying (q.v.).

Following his return to China, Chi was assigned to his native Inner Mongolia where he has since remained as one of the most influential Party and government leaders. His first appointment (by August 1954) was as director of the Party's United Front Work Department, the post to which he has devoted the major portion of his time. (The Party organization in Inner Mongolia in 1954 was known as the Inner Mongolia Sub-bureau, but was changed to the Inner Mongolia Autonomous Region Party Committee in 1955.) One of the chief tasks of the United Front Department is to gain the acquiescence of minority nationalities to rule by Han Chinese. In spite of the name "Inner Mongolia Autonomous Region," the Mongols make up only a small minority of the total population, numbering approximately one million of the six million inhabitants. By mid-1961 Chi was also serving as a member of the Standing Committee of the Party Committee for Inner Mongolia, a post he continues to hold.

At the same time that Chi took up his post in united front work, he was also named (August 1954) as a member of the Inner Mongolia Autonomous Region Government. Exactly six years later, in August 1960, he was promoted to a vice-chairmanship of the region, a position he still retains. In December 1954, as a representative of the national minorities, he attended the second national conference of the Sino-Soviet Friendship Association. It was in this same month that Chi, again representing the minority groups, was named to membership on both the Second National Committee and the Standing Committee of the CPPCC. He was named to the Third CPPCC (which opened in April 1959) as well as the Fourth CPPCC (opening in December 1964) and on both occasions was again selected for membership on the Standing Committee.

Like many leaders in the national CPPCC organization, Chi has also been a senior official at the provincial-regional level. Thus, when the First CPPCC Committee was organized in Inner Mongolia in February 1955, he was selected as one of the vice-chairmen and was again named to this post when the Second and Third Inner Mongolia Committees were formed in 1960 and 1965. As in the case of his positions in both the Regional Party and government organizations, Chi serves under Ulanfu, the dominant figure in Inner Mongolia since its formation in 1947. However, in contrast to many provincial-regional officials, Chi's *de facto* authority is probably enhanced owing to the fact that Ulanfu is frequently in Peking where, as a Politburo member, he is often involved with high-level policy affairs. Nonetheless, Chi is politically overshadowed in Inner Mongolia by his lifetime colleague, K'uei Pi, who holds positions equal to and higher than those held by Chi and is also an alternate member of the Party Central Committee. Unlike Ulanfu, both Chi and K'uei spend almost all their time in Huhehot, the Inner Mongolia capital.

Chi made a significant political stride in 1962 when he was named as a full member of the Party's Central Control Commission, charged with intra-Party disciplinary and inspection functions. The Commission was reorganized and enlarged in accordance with the 10th Plenum of the Party Central Committee in September 1962. Under the reorganization, the Control Commission had 38 full members and 22 alternates. Chi has the distinction of being the only non-Han Chinese to be named to the organization.

Like most leaders of his stature, Chi devotes some of his time to extracurricular activities. Logically, his principal activity in this vein has been with the China-Mongolia Friendship Association (CMFA), formed in September 1958. He is a vice-president of this organization and, from at least July 1961, has been the president of the Inner Mongolia chapter—probably the most important and active of the provincial-regional branches. It was in his capacity as an official in the CMFA that Chi made his only trip abroad since returning from Ulan Bator in 1954. This occurred in September–October 1960 when he served as a deputy leader of a "friendship" delegation that visited Outer Mongolia for over two weeks to celebrate China's National Day (October 1). He has also served from at least November 1963 as vice-chairman of the Inner Mongolian chapter of the China Peace Committee.

Chi has been an occasional contributor to the Communist press. The historical article dealing with his early relations with Li Ta-chao has already been cited. In addition, he is the author of an important article related to his special field—united front work—which appeared in the April 30, 1962, issue of the *Kuang-ming Jih-pao*.

1. *SCMM* 269.
2. *Min-tsu t'uan-chieh* (Nationalities unity), 7:10–12 (July 6, 1961).
3. *Ibid.*
4. *Ibid.*
5. *Ibid.*
6. *CB* 266.

Ch'i Yen-ming

(c.1906–   ; Wan-p'ing hsien, Hopeh). Government administrator.

Ch'i Yen-ming is a Mongol; he was born in Wan-p'ing hsien, Hopeh, a few miles west of Peking. His courtesy name is Chen-hsun. Sources differ on his education, but apparently he graduated from Yenching University; he is reported to know English, French, and some Russian. Sometime in the 1920's, Ch'i began his career as a teacher, working first in the First Peking Municipal Girls Middle School and then at Ta-t'ung Middle School. In about 1930 he joined the CCP, probably in secret. He continued his teaching career in Peking, serving as a lecturer in the department of literature at the Sino-French University in 1933–34. Then from 1934 to 1937 he taught at China Institute (presumably *Chung-kuo kung-hsueh,* a school that was disbanded after the outbreak of the Sino-Japanese War[1]). Though Ch'i may not have been openly identified as a Communist, he was already known as a "progressive" during this period. Apparently he played some role in provoking student action against the authorities during the "December Ninth" movement, a youth movement begun by demonstrations in Peking on December 9, 1935, in opposition to Japanese incursions into north China (see under Li Ch'ang). Many years after the events, a participant described a meeting in Peking of leftist students in May 1936. One of the decisions reached at the meeting was that "progressive professors" such as Yang Hsiu-feng (q.v.) and Ch'i, who had "high prestige" among the students, were invited to give lectures on international and domestic affairs which would thus "expose" the "insidious propaganda and shameless plots of the Kuomintang reactionaries."[2]

When the war broke out in mid-1937 with Japan he fled to Yenan where he became dean of a political training institute. His activities in Yenan during the war are undocumented, but presumably he was engaged in teaching. In 1945 he served as a deputy secretary-general of the preparatory committee for a "People's Assembly of the Liberated Areas" held in Yenan, but further information on this meeting is lacking.

There can be little question that during the Yenan period Ch'i gained the confidence of the Party leaders. Proof of this was evident by the winter of 1945–46 when he accompanied the Communist delegation led by Chou En-lai to Chungking to participate in the Political Consultative Conference (held in January 1946). Three years later, in April 1949, a Nationalist delegation came to Peking to conduct peace negotiations with the Communists—talks that inevitably ended in failure as the Communists had by then conquered most of China north of the Yangtze. Ch'i served as the secretary-general of the Communist side for these negotiations.

By mid-1949 Ch'i was busily engaged in preparations for establishing the Communist government and mass organizations. In July he was a member of the preparatory committee for the First All-China Scientists Conference and in the same month he was also one of the convenors of the Social Science Workers Conference. Out of these two conferences grew several of the more important mass organizations formed in the early days of the PRC (e.g., the All-China Federation of Scientific Societies and the Political Science and Law Association of China). More important was Ch'i's participation in the formation of the central government. The first formal steps were taken in June 1949 when a preparatory committee was formed for the "new" Political Consultative Conference, a committee chaired by Mao Tse-tung. Party veteran Li Wei-han was named as the secretary-general of the committee, with Ch'i serving as one of the deputy secretaries-general. From the work of the preparatory committee came the Chinese People's Political Consultative Conference (CPPCC). The first session of the CPPCC was held in September, immediately after which the PRC was brought into existence. While these meetings were in session, Ch'i served as one of the deputy secretaries-general of the CPPCC presidium (steering committee) under Secretary-general Lin Po-ch'ü. When the central government was fully staffed in October 1949, Ch'i received two important administrative posts. He was named as head of the Staff Office of the Central People's Government Council (CPGC), the supreme organ of state power until the constitutional government was inaugurated in 1954 and a body under the direct leadership of Mao Tse-tung. Standing below the CPGC was the cabinet-like organ known from 1949 to 1954 as the Government Administration Council (GAC); the other post Ch'i received in October 1949 was that of a deputy secretary-general of the GAC. He continued as a deputy secretary-general after the GAC was renamed the State Council in 1954, and until he was removed in March 1965 he was the only man who had served continuously in this post from the formation of the central government in 1949. During this period of over

15 years Ch'i served as the immediate subordinate of three important Party leaders: Li Wei-han, Hsi Chung-hsun, and Chou Jung-hsin. Moreover, from December 1949 to March 1952, Ch'i also headed the Secretariat of the GAC, an organization that dealt with security matters. Ch'i's involvement in the security field was well illustrated in June 1951 when he delivered a report (which was approved) before the 87th GAC meeting on the "preservation of state secrecy" and on regulations for the organization of "security committees" at all levels of government.

By 1951 he was serving as secretary-general of the Party's United Front Work Department headed by Li Wei-han (until 1965), who was also Ch'i's superior in the GAC. The duration of Ch'i's tenure in this post is not known. In view of his background as an intellectual, he would be a logical candidate for work in the United Front Department, the organization charged with gaining maximum cooperation from China's non-Party personages, particularly the intellectuals and minority groups.

Ch'i's work during the early and mid-1950's was mainly along administrative lines, as the titles of his many positions suggest. He continued in this type of work even after the constitution was inaugurated in September 1954 at the first session of the First NPC (which Ch'i attended as a deputy from his native Hopeh). As already noted, he was reappointed as a deputy secretary-general of the State Council during this governmental reorganization (fall 1954); in addition, he was appointed to head the Staff Office of the Premier (Chou En-lai), a position he held until April 1958. It was as a senior administrative official in the State Council that Ch'i took part in the talks with the Soviet Union which led to the signing in December 1954 of the Sino-Soviet Air Service Agreement, formalizing civil air service between the two Communist powers. In October 1956, Ch'i received still another high-level administrative assignment when he was made director of the State Council's Bureau of Experts Administration, an organ apparently responsible for the placement of senior scientific personnel (but one which should not be confused with the "Bureau of Foreign Experts").

In May 1957, when the State Council's Scientific Planning Commission was reorganized, he was named as a member, holding this position until the commission was merged with another in November 1958. After this, the scope of Ch'i's activities changed somewhat, giving greater emphasis to cultural as opposed to purely administrative work. For example, in 1958 he served as head of a section under the Scientific Planning Commission devoted to the classification and publication of ancient Chinese classics. This new emphasis on cultural affairs culminated in February 1960 when he was named as a vice-minister of Culture under Shen Yen-ping (Mao Tun) and, after January 1965, under Lu Ting-i. In August 1960, Ch'i was a member of the presidium (steering committee) for the third congress of the All-China Federation of Literary and Art Circles (ACFLAC). At the close of the congress he was named to the ACFLAC National Committee and in the same month became a member of the Standing Committee of one of the affiliates of the ACFLAC, the Union of Chinese Drama Workers.

On December 12, 1960, the Chinese formed the China-Cambodia Friendship Association, just prior to a visit to China by Prince Norodom Sihanouk of Cambodia. Ch'i was named as president of this organization and, owing to the increased ties with Cambodia in the years after 1960, he has been involved in a great number of activities (such as banquets or tours) sponsored by the association for Cambodian visitors to China. Logically, Ch'i was present in December 1960 when Prince Sihanouk signed the Sino-Cambodian Treaty of Friendship and Mutual Non-aggression in Peking at the close of his visit.

Further evidence of Ch'i's growing role in cultural affairs was provided in 1961 and 1962. In March 1961 he was named as chairman of the Committee on the Culture of Minority Nationalities (Ch'i himself being a Mongol) under the Ministry of Culture and two months later (May 1961) was elected as secretary-general of the Peking Society of Philosophy at its inaugural meeting. He was among the speakers at a national forum in Canton in March 1962 which dealt with the writing of plays and "modern" operas, a forum attended by such top Party leaders as Chou En-lai and Ch'en I. In the following month in Peking he presided over a meeting concerned with the problems of training writers and artists of minority nationalities and of compiling minority folk art.

As already noted, Ch'i was elected from his native Hopeh as a deputy to the First NPC (1954–1959). He again served from Hopeh to the Second NPC (1959–1964) and then in October 1964 was re-elected from Hopeh once more for the Third NPC, which held its initial session in December 1964–January 1965. Aside from numerous positions already mentioned, Ch'i has participated in the work of many other *ad hoc* bodies and meetings, or organizations of minor importance. For example, since August 1956 he has been an executive committee member of the China Welfare Institute (headed by Sung Ch'ing-ling); in September 1959 he served on the preparatory committee for celebrations marking the 10th anniversary of the PRC; and in September 1961 he served on the preparatory committee for commemorating the 50th anniversary of the 1911 Revolution.

In the first half of 1965 Ch'i was removed from two important positions, losing his post as a deputy secretary-general of the State Council (March) and as a vice-minister of Culture (April). Shortly before this Shen Yen-ping (q.v.) had been removed as minister of Culture. Another long-time superior of Ch'i's, Party veteran Li Wei-han (q.v.), also came under a political cloud over the winter of 1964–65. Moreover, during the first half of 1965 Ch'i played no apparent role in the affairs of the China-Cambodia Friendship Association, an organization in which he had previously been quite active in his capacity as its president. These suggestions of political difficulties in 1965 were confirmed in the next year when he was attacked by name during the early phases of the Great Proletarian Cultural Revolution.

1. *China Handbook, 1937–1943* (New York, 1943), p. 373.

2. Chiang Nan-hsiang *et al.*, *The Roar of a Nation* (Peking, 1963), p. 162.

Chia T'o-fu

(c.1904–   ; Shen-mu, Shensi). Early Party leader in the northwest; economic administrator; member, CCP Central Committee.

Chia T'o-fu, one of the earliest members of the CCP in Shensi Province, was an important Party leader in the northwest from the 1920's until his transfer to Peking in the early fifties. He was deeply involved in economic administration, particularly in the fields of light industry and economic planning, until his apparent fall into political disfavor in the late fifties. Chia has been a member of the Party Central Committee since 1956.

Chia, who has also used the names Chia Ming-kuang and Chia Yao-tsu, comes from Shen-mu, an old city on the Great Wall about 100 miles north of Sui-te where he attended normal school in the middle 1920's. In 1926, probably during his student days, he joined the Communist Youth League. At that time a number of the urban schools in Shensi felt the impact of the May Fourth Movement, which had erupted in Peking and Tientsin in May 1919 and which had been brought back to Shensi by former students enrolled in Peking or Tientsin universities. After getting a generous exposure to the unsettling ideas of modernization engendered by the Movement, some of these students became teachers in the Shensi schools. A group of them teaching in the middle schools of Yenan, Sui-te, Mi-chih, and Yü-lin formed a teachers' alliance, which soon came into conflict with the provincial authorities. In the early 1920's many of the radical teachers in Shensi were imprisoned or dismissed from the schools. The newly founded CCP, quick to realize this discontent among students and intellectuals, had sent its own agents into Shensi to organize small Party cells among the intellectuals in the cities and the poorer peasants in the countryside. During this time Chia is reported to have been a leader of the student movement in Sui-te, but by 1928 he had become connected with other Shensi leaders who had been working among the peasants. Capitalizing upon local unrest, Liu Chih-tan led an uprising among the peasantry in 1928. This event, known to the Communists as the Wei-Hua Uprising, is described in the biography of Liu Chih-tan. It appears that Chia took part in the revolt. In any case, before the year had ended he was serving under Liu as a member of the CCP North Shensi Special Committee. In addition, at some time between 1928 and 1934 Chia directed the CCP Shensi Committee's Organization Department and worked in the Party underground in north Shensi and Sian.

Chia went to Kiangsi in 1934, possibly at the time of the Second All-China Congress of Soviets held in Juichin, Kiangsi, in January–February 1934. There he reportedly directed the "sabotage" division of the Red Army Political Department. Later he is said to have returned to Shensi with the Long March armies of Mao Tse-tung. Arriving in the fall of 1935 he was immediately given work on the Grain Supply Committee of Mao's First Front Army. At the same time he continued to work in the Army's Political Department. In October 1935 Chia was sent to contact the headquarters of the 15th Army Corps, based in north Shensi not far from Pao-an where Mao had his headquarters. The 15th Army Corps had been created in September 1935 from the two local 26th and 27th Armies of Liu Chih-tan and Kao Kang, plus Hsu Hai-tung's 25th Army, which had come from central China late in 1934. Thus when Mao came to Shensi at the end of the Long March he had to make contact with a Communist army already active in the province and somewhat larger than his own. The two armies met and joined forces in the fall of 1935, and it is noteworthy that Chia (who knew both groups) was one of the liaison officers who brought them together.

There is little reporting of Chia's activities during the Sino-Japanese War. He is said to have returned for a time to the CCP underground in Sian, apparently in addition to the legal CCP activity undertaken in agreement with the Nationalist Government controlling the city. He was said also to have been a member of the Northwest CCP Bureau; presumably this post dated from the late 1930's and continued until sometime in 1952. According to an unconfirmed report, from about 1937 Chia was also secretary-general of the Northwest Bureau. In December 1949 he was identified as secretary of the Bureau's "Workers' Work Committee."

In April 1946 Chia was a deputy to the Third Assembly of the Shensi-Kansu-Ninghsia Border Region from Chia-hsien in Shensi. The capital of Chia-hsien, bordered by the Yellow River, is located mid-way between Chia T'o-fu's native Shen-mu and Sui-te where he went to middle school. In his position as chairman of the Finance and Economics Committee of the Border Region Government, Chia reported in April 1946 to the Assembly on financial and economic questions. A Communist pamphlet published in 1948 details a "high level cadre" meeting, held a year earlier under the auspices of the Northwest CCP Bureau, at which he addressed the cadres on matters of land reform.[1] Chia admitted to weaknesses among Party cadres, where tendencies toward what the Communist call "petty bourgeoisism," "bureaucratism," and "individualism" had hindered Party-directed programs in the financial and economic sectors in the northwest.

In August 1948 the Communists created the first of their administrations to govern north China, the North China People's Government (NCPG), located in the vicinity of Shih-chia-chuang in western Hopeh. Chia was apparently transferred there, because in September he was appointed a member of the Government's Finance and Economics Committee, headed by Tung Pi-wu (q.v.). Chia nominally continued in this post until the NCPG was absorbed by the central government in October 1949, but after the fall of Sian in May of that year he transferred back to the northwest. He served briefly in 1949 as secretary of the Sian Party Committee and as a vice-chairman of the Sian Military Control Commission. Moreover, from May 1949 until June 1950 when he was replaced by Fang Chung-ju, Chia was mayor of the city.

Aside from his positions in Sian, Chia was also the vice-chairman of the Finance and Economics Committee of the Northwest Liberation Region, an administration created in February 1949 by the merger of the Shensi-Kansu-Ninghsia and the Shansi-Suiyuan Border Regions. The Northwest Liberated Region, headquartered in Sian, gave way in January 1950 to the Northwest Military and Administrative Committee (NWMAC). Chia was a member of the NWMAC from its inauguration. He also chaired the NWMAC's Finance and Economics Committee from March to August 1950, when he was replaced by P'eng Te-huai; from that date until 1953 Chia served as a vice-chairman under P'eng. Like many prominent regional leaders in the early years of the PRC, Chia also held various other less important positions. Thus from 1950 he was a member of the Executive Committee of the Northwest Branch of the All-China Federation of Labor, and he was the chairman by 1952. In December 1951 he became vice-president of the newly established Northwest Branch of the Sino-Soviet Friendship Association, and in February 1952 he was appointed chairman of a special committee to increase production and to prevent droughts.

After a career spent almost exclusively in China's northwest, Chia was transferred to Peking toward the end of 1952. In December of that year he spoke before the National Labor Protection Work Conference, and in May 1953 he addressed the Seventh All-China Labor Congress on the subject of industrial development in China. In June, in his capacity as chairman of the Chinese group of the Sino-Czech Joint Committee on Scientific and Technical Cooperation, he signed a protocol for the first session of the Committee. When Chia had arrived in Peking his only national-level post was membership on the Government Administration Council's Finance and Economics Committee, a post he had held from the formation of the central government in the fall of 1949. Then, in September 1953, he received a significant appointment when he and economic expert Li Fu-ch'un were made vice-chairmen of the State Planning Commission. Previous to this date the only vice-chairman had been Teng Tzu-hui (q.v.). Chia held this post under Chairman Kao Kang, his former colleague in Shensi.

Chia was a deputy from Honan Province to the First NPC which, at its inaugural session in September 1954, brought the constitutional government into existence. In the reorganized central government he relinquished his post on the Planning Commission, but at the same time he was given the portfolio for the Ministry of Light Industry, replacing non-Communist Huang Yen-p'ei. In the following month he was made director of the Fourth Staff Office, which was charged with coordinating the work of the various State Council commissions, ministries, and bureaus involved with light and consumer industries. Chia continued in his ministerial post until he was replaced by Sha Ch'ien-li (q.v.) in May 1956, and he directed the Fourth Staff Office until September 1959 when it was merged with two others. During the middle and late 1950's Chia was among the more active economic administrators; he was, for example, a featured speaker at four of the five annual sessions of the First NPC held between 1954 and 1958, and he also made major addresses at important national conferences, such as the First National Congress of Handicraft Cooperatives in December 1957.

During the middle and late fifties Chia also received new and important assignments in the Central Government and the CCP. From March 1956 to May 1957 he was a member of the State Council's Scientific Planning Commission. When the Party held its Eighth National Congress in September 1956, Chia was one of the few members of the presidium (steering committee) who was not already a member of the Central Committee. He addressed the Congress on the development of light industry, and at the close of the meetings he was elected a full member of the Party Central Committee. Two months later he became a vice-chairman of the State Council's State Economic Commission under Chairman Po I-po (q.v.). This commission handles annual planning, in contrast to the State Planning Commission which is in charge of long-range (five year) plans. Chia was the ranking Economic Commission vice-chairman from the time of his appointment until he was removed from the post in September 1959 during another reorganization of the national bureaucracy. Exactly one year before his removal from the Economic Commission he was for the second time appointed a vice-chairman of the State Planning Commission. He was the ranking vice-chairman on this commission as he had been on the Economic Commission previously.

Representing the CCP, Chia was a member of the CPPCC's Third National Committee, which met for the first time in April 1959. At the close of these meetings he was elected to membership on the CPPCC Standing Committee. In the same month the Second NPC held its first session, with Chia once more serving as a deputy from Honan. In the previous month (March 1959) he had been listed as a member of the Preparatory Committee for the National Conference of Advanced Workers. However, though most Preparatory Committee members served on the Conference Presidium when it opened in October 1959, Chia was not among them. It appears that in the interim he had fallen into political disfavor. As previously noted, he had been dropped from the State Council's Fourth Staff Office and the Economic Commission in September 1959, although he continued to be a vice-chairman of the State Planning Commission. Chia continued to be listed as a Planning Commission vice-chairman in the 1960 and 1961 editions of the *Jen-min shou-ts'e* (People's handbook), but his name was dropped from the 1962 edition. He continued to be a nominal member of both the NPC and the CPPCC until 1964, but in that year he was dropped from both organizations. In fact, Chia has not made a public appearance since the spring of 1959, and it seems that his political career ended in that year.

Chia was a rather frequent contributor to the press during the 1950's. Among his more important articles and reports are: a report on economic work in the northwest in 1950 and plans for 1951, excerpted in *Hsin-hua yueh-pao* (New China monthly), May 25, 1951; "The Advance of China's Industry," *People's China*, June 1, 1952; "The Obligations that Agricultural Cooperativization Places upon Light Industry," published in *Hsueh-hsi* (Study), December 2, 1955, and reprinted in the 1956 *Jen-min shou-ts'e*; "Several Questions on the Development of Light Industry" (Chia's speech at the Eighth Party Congress), published in the 1957 *Jen-min shou-ts'e*; Chia's address to the Congress of Handicraft Cooperations, printed in the 1958 *Jen-min shou-ts'e* and translated in *CB* 488.

---

1. *Wei ch'un-chieh tang-te tsu-chih erh tou-cheng* (Struggle to purify the Party organization; Hong Kong, 1948), p. 65.

Chiang Hua

(Hupeh). First secretary, Chekiang CCP Committee; alternate member, CCP Central Committee.

Chiang Hua, a veteran political officer in the Red Army, has been a key Party official in Chekiang since the Communist conquest of the mainland in 1949. He was elected an alternate member of the Party Central Committee in 1956. Chiang was working in the Anhwei-Kiangsu area by mid-1940 with the guerrilla forces of the Communists' New Fourth Army. At this time his troops joined with Huai-pei guerrillas of Chang Ai-p'ing (q.v.) in Anhwei north of the Huai River to make an attack upon Nationalist troops commanded by Wang Kuang-hsia. A year later, in October 1941, having apparently joined forces with some of the Communist Eighth Route Army troops which Yenan had infiltrated into Shantung Province, he was identified as a senior political officer of the Shantung Military District. In the late 1940's, again as an important political officer, Chiang took part in the fighting to capture southern Manchuria from the Nationalists.

Early in May 1949 the Communist armies took possession of Hangchow, the capital of Chekiang, and in late August Chiang replaced T'an Chen-lin (q.v.) as mayor. In 1949 Chiang also became commander of the Hangchow Garrison Headquarters and the ranking secretary of the municipal Party Committee. He continued as the Hangchow major and garrison commander until 1951. In November 1952 he was identified as a deputy secretary of the Chekiang Provincial Party Committee, and at approximately this time or not long thereafter he relinquished the lower-ranking post as secretary of the Hangchow Party Committee. Chiang had become a member of the Chekiang Provincial People's Government Council in 1951 and has been twice re-elected (January 1955 and November 1958). He continues to hold the post.

As Chiang's stature in the provincial Party Committee grew, his activities were more frequently reported in the press. Since late 1952 he has often been mentioned in connection with CCP-sponsored conferences and propaganda efforts. In the first two years (1952–1954) he was especially involved with propaganda directed toward the military forces stationed in east China and with the Communist-sponsored "peace" campaign. By May 1954 he had become chairman of the Chekiang chapter of the China Peace Committee, a position he may still retain. He was first identified as the ranking secretary of the provincial Party Committee in mid-1955, replacing T'an Ch'i-lung (q.v.), another veteran of the New Fourth Army, who had been transferred in late 1954 to Shantung. Chiang's senior Party post in Chekiang was redesignated in 1956 as first secretary, a position he continues to hold. In February 1955 he was elected chairman of the First Chekiang Committee of the CPPCC. Chiang was elected to head the Second Chekiang Committee in November 1958 and was presumably selected to chair the Third Committee formed in September 1964. In the latter part of 1956 he also became political commissar of the Chekiang Military District, another position he continues to retain.

Chiang addressed the Eighth Party Congress in September 1956 on agricultural cooperatives, and at the close of the proceedings was elected an alternate member of the Central Committee. In 1957–58 he was deeply involved in the nationwide "rectification" campaign against "rightists." The first indications of trouble in Chekiang occurred in December 1957 at a meeting of the Chekiang Party Congress when a number of leading Chekiang officials were "exposed" and criticized for "anti-Party and rightist" activities. Chiang delivered the major report about the "rightists," a speech published in the December 28, 1957, issue of the *JMJP*.[1] The chief victim of the ensuing purges was Sha Wen-han (q.v.), then the governor of Chekiang. Chiang also reported the need for accelerated production in agriculture and industry; he referred to a "leap" in production in the language that was to become so familiar as part of the Great Leap Forward that began in 1958. In the *JMJP* of May 19, 1958 (while the second session of the Eighth Party Congress was in session), Chiang published another article written in the spirit of the Great Leap Forward. He also attended the important Sixth Party Plenum held at Wuhan in November–December 1958 at which time the pace in the development of the "people's communes" was slowed down.

Chiang's political structure in Chekiang is particularly accentuated by the fact that the governor since 1958 (Chou Chien-jen, q.v., a brother of Lu Hsun) is not a Communist. He is consistently reported in the press in his Party, governmental, and military duties, where he presides over most important meetings, makes numerous inspections of agricultural and industrial production, and attends the celebrations marking Communist holidays. Moreover, because Hangchow is an attraction for foreign visitors, he is often reported in the company of visitors. A random but typical example occurred in July 1961 when he served as a host for North Korean leader Kim Il-sung.

Chiang's wife, Wu Chung-lien, is also a veteran Party member. She has been president of the Chekiang Higher People's Court since 1955 and concurrently secretary of the Court's Party Committee. While her husband was making his "anti-rightist" charges against Governor Sha Wen-han, she directed similar attacks against her deputy, the vice-president of the Chekiang Higher People's Court.

---

1. *CB* 487.

Chiang I-chen

North China guerrilla leader; Vice-Minister of Agriculture.

Chiang I-chen was associated with the Chinese Communists by the early 1930's when he was serving in the Red Army medical school in the Kiangsi Soviet. He subsequently made the Long March to Shensi (1934–35) and was then assigned to the Shansi-Chahar-Hopeh (Chin-Ch'a-Chi) Border Region in 1938 where he worked under Norman Bethune, a Canadian surgeon and a veteran of the Spanish Civil War who was serving with the Chinese Communist forces until his death in November 1939. In Bethune's honor, the Communists renamed the Chin-Ch'a-Chi Military District medical school as the Bethune Medical College. This college was formally inaugurated in early 1940 with Chiang as its president. From a modest beginning of 18 students in 1940, the college trained and sent out to border regions some 700 medical workers by 1943, and in that same year had nearly 1,000 students in training. The pressure of the Japanese on the Communists forced the latter to shift the location of the college from time to time. A Communist-authored article describes one such move in 1942, noting that the medical authorities were then on the move in Fou-p'ing and Hsing-t'ang hsien in western Hopeh. Fou-p'ing had been the original seat of the Chin-Ch'a-Chi Border Region when it was formed in January 1938 (see under Sung Shao-wen) and Hsing-t'ang was not far north of Shih-chia-chuang, one of the most important rail heads in North China. The Bethune College continued to operate throughout the war with the Japanese as well as the civil war with the Nationalists, and presumably Chiang was connected with it during all those years. He was definitely known to head the college in 1942 and 1943 at which time he was described as a "good practical surgeon" and a member of an 18-man faculty.[1]

Chiang was next mentioned in 1951 in Fukien where he was to remain for nearly a decade. However, he had no connections at that time with the field of medicine. Instead, his career in the 1950's was strongly oriented toward agricultural affairs.

In April 1951 he was appointed as a vice-chairman of the provincial Land Reform Committee under chairman Chang Ting-ch'eng, who was also the provincial governor and a veteran Party leader. In December of that year Chiang was elected to the provincial People's Government Council and in the second half of 1952 became both director of the Forestry Department and member of the Labor Employment Committee. He probably held all these government posts until February 1955 when the province was partially reorganized. Chiang also held three quasi-governmental posts in the early and mid-1950's

when he served as a vice-chairman of the Fukien Peasants Association (by 1952), as chief of a "production and drought-prevention office" (a position to which he was named in March 1952), and as president of the Fukien Agricultural Institute (from January 1955 to April 1957). Several of these positions, it should be noted, illustrate a deep involvement in agricultural affairs which was to culminate in the 1960's when Chiang served in two national ministries dealing with agricultural affairs.

In Party activities Chiang began quite modestly in 1952 as a member of a Committee for the Exchange of Commodities under the Fukien Provincial Party Committee. By April 1954 he was a member of the Standing Committee in the Party structure in Fukien and was then a deputy secretary from 1955 to 1956; he was made a secretary under first secretary Yeh Fei by the early fall of 1956. He served in still another post under the Fukien Party structure when he became chairman of the Planning Committee, a post he held by January 1956. As a Fukien Party Secretary, Chiang moved in rather exclusive company when, in September 1956, he spoke before the historic Eighth Party Congress in Peking on the subject of improving the "old revolutionary bases," the phrase the Communists use to describe their former guerrilla and "soviet" areas dating back to the late 1920's.

As already noted, Fukien underwent a government reorganization in February 1955. At that time, Chiang was elected as a vice-governor, serving under Governor Yeh Fei (elected at the same time), who was also Chiang's superior in the provincial Party hierarchy. However, for unexplained reasons Chiang was not listed in this post in the official annual handbooks for 1956 through 1958. Yet during this same period he was mentioned in the press rather frequently and in April 1956 succeeded Tseng Ching-ping, a former alternate Central Committee member, as Chairman of the First Fukien CPPCC, a post Chiang held until February 1959 when he was replaced by Yeh Fei.

In January 1959 Chiang was deputy leader of a Fukien "10,000-man inspection corps to tidy up" the communes, as the Communists described it. In the following month he replaced Yeh Fei as Fukien governor. He was a Fukien deputy to the Second NPC and at its first session in April 1959 spoke of the "victories in production" as well as the "frontline battle." The latter term referred to the continuing struggle with the Chinese Nationalists over the off-shore islands of Matsu and Quemoy. Although Chiang had long been a senior official in Fukien, he had not often been associated with the off-shore islands, apparently leaving such matters to Yeh Fei, the provincial Party first secretary.

Immediately after the April 1959 NPC session, Chiang dropped completely out of the news.

Moreover, the 1960–1962 editions of the official handbook did not carry his name as Fukien governor. This is highly unusual and suggests some political difficulties, possibly related to the Great Leap Forward. However, after more than three years of official silence on Chiang, he was transferred to Peking and named as a vice-minister of State Farms and Land Reclamation in October 1962. Two months later Wei Chin-shui was elected as Fukien governor, with the official news agency merely noting that Chiang had been transferred. Even after this appointment very little mention was made of Chiang in the national press. For two years after his October 1962 appointment he was only mentioned on two rather insignificant occasions. Then in October 1964 he was appointed as a vice-minister of Agriculture, and two months later was removed as vice-minister of State Farms and Land Reclamation. Chiang, who had served as a Fukien deputy on the Second NPC (1959–1964), was re-elected from Fukien to the Third NPC, which held its first session in December 1964–January 1965, during which he submitted a written report.

1. Kang Ke, "Bethune Medical School in Guerrilla Days," *China Reconstructs* (September 1963), pp. 29–31; *In Guerrilla China* (Chungking, n.d.), pp. 27–29; Stuart Gelder, *The Chinese Communists* (London, 1946), p. 230.

Chiang Ming

Vice-minister of Foreign Trade; director, Customs Administration.

Chiang Ming, a foreign trade specialist, was a youth leader in north China in the mid-1930's and very probably a participant in the "December Ninth Movement," which began in 1935. The name derives from the date in December 1935 when students in Peking held large demonstrations in opposition to Japanese encroachments in Manchuria and north China (see under Li Ch'ang). In early 1936 a number of these students established the National Liberation Vanguards of China (NLVC), which came under Communist domination within a few months. A year later (February 1937), when the NLVC held its first congress, Chiang was elected one of the 39 members of the Vanguards' Executive Committee. Liu Shao-ch'i and P'eng Chen (qq.v.) were among the top CCP leaders then in contact with the NLVC. Many of the Vanguards' leaders went to Yenan after the outbreak of the Sino-Japanese War in mid-1937, but nothing is known of Chiang's career until late 1941 when he was working with Liu Shao-ch'i in the CCP's Central China Bureau, then headed by Liu. Following the New Fourth Army Incident of early 1941 (see under Yeh T'ing), Liu was sent from Yenan to reorganize this army. Chiang may have accompanied him to the New Fourth Army areas, but in any event, when Liu made his way through enemy lines back to Yenan over the winter of 1941–42, Chiang accompanied him.[1] He was not heard of again until the late 1940's when he was identified as a deputy director of the North China Foreign Trade Control Bureau, apparently one of the organs subordinate to the North China People's Government, which was the governing body for north China from August 1948 to the formation of the central government in October 1949.

When the central government was established in the fall of 1949, the principal economic organ of government was the Finance and Economics Committee headed by chief economic specialist Ch'en Yun. Subordinate to this was a Central Financial and Economic Planning Bureau, in many respects the predecessor of the important State Planning Commission established in 1952. Under this bureau Chiang headed the Trade Planning Department from June 1950 until the Planning Bureau (and thus Chiang's department) was abolished in August 1952. Concurrently, he was appointed (November 1950) to the directorship of the Industry and Commerce Department of the Ministry of North China Affairs (which had approximately the same responsibilities and structure of the previously mentioned North China People's Government). He relinquished this post in early 1952. In 1951 Chiang took up a new position in still another organ of the central government, the Ministry of Trade, at that time concerned with both foreign trade and domestic commerce. He became a deputy director of the Foreign Trade Department and since then has devoted his time almost exclusively to this field of work.

In August 1952 the Ministry of Trade was divided into the Ministries of Commerce and Foreign Trade. Although Chiang was not immediately identified in either ministry, he almost certainly was assigned to the Foreign Trade Ministry; by 1954 he was identified in this ministry as head of the First Bureau, and then in June 1955 was promoted to a vice-ministership, a position he continues to hold. As of early 1965, only two other vice-ministers (Lei Jen-min and Li Ch'iang, qq.v.) have served longer than Chiang. Since 1953 he has negotiated and signed in Peking or abroad a large number of trade agreements for the Chinese government. The pattern of this activity indicates that he has been mainly concerned with trade within the Communist Bloc, although from August 1955 to January 1956 he was in the Middle East, where he held trade discussions and negotiated some agreements in Syria, Lebanon, and Saudia Arabia, and again in September–October 1956 he was in Cairo where he signed a trade protocol. The bloc nations he has visited are the USSR

(December 1953–January 1954); Mongolia (July 1956 and January 1959); North Korea (February–March 1960); Rumania (December 1964); and, Poland (February–March 1965). Chiang led the delegations to each of these nations except the one to Moscow and the July 1956 mission to Mongolia (which was the only one not connected with trade—the delegation was in Ulan Bator for the 35th anniversary of the Mongolian Revolution). In the fall of 1964 Chiang assumed a new post in the Foreign Trade Ministry when he became (by October) Director of the Customs Administration, replacing Lin Hai-yun, a fellow vice-minister of Foreign Trade.

Chiang holds positions in one or possibly two semi-official organizations which are closely related to his work in the foreign trade or foreign affairs field. In August 1955 he was identified as a member of the China Council for the Promotion of International Trade, an organization established in 1952 mainly for the purpose of stimulating trade with non-Communist nations. However, issues of the annual handbooks after 1955 have not listed Chiang in this position, suggesting he has dropped his affiliation. The other position is membership on the Council of the China-Syria Friendship Association (CSFA) from its formation in September 1957; owing to the merger of Egypt and Syria into the United Arab Republic (UAR) in February 1958, the CSFA was merged with a counterpart organization for Egypt into a new China-UAR Friendship Association, with Chiang retaining membership on the Council. The reason for his selection to this organization is fairly clear; in the mid-1950's the Chinese Communists had extremely few people with even the slightest background in Middle Eastern affairs, and thus Chiang's long trip to the Middle East in 1955–56 presumably made him something of a Middle East "specialist" among the leaders in Peking.

1. *Chung-kuo ch'ing-nien* (Chinese youth), May 1, 1959, July 1, 1959, and September 16, 1960.

Chiang Nan-hsiang

(c.1915–   ). Minister of Higher Education; president, Tsinghua University; alternate member, CCP Central Committee.

A former youth leader, Chiang Nan-hsiang has risen in the PRC to become one of the most important Party education officials. To judge from the development of his career, Chiang was probably born about 1915. He is known to have entered Tsinghua University in 1933 and is believed to have graduated in 1937.[1] He was an important leader in the student movement known as the "December Ninth Movement" (see under Li Ch'ang); the name derives from the date in 1935 when students in Peking staged demon-strations in opposition to continuing Japanese encroachments in Manchuria and north China. At that time Chiang was a "responsible person" in the Tsinghua branch of the National Liberation Vanguard of China (NLVC), an organization established in February 1936 in the wake of the December Ninth Movement.[2] It was also in February 1936 that the police briefly detained Chiang on the Tsinghua campus. However, his fellow students managed to free him, after which he went into hiding in Peking and then made his way to Shanghai.[3] By this time he was already a Party member. There are conflicting Communist accounts of when he returned to Peking; in Chiang's own account he claimed he returned in July 1936, but Li Ch'ang has stated that he was already back by May, when Chiang was instrumental in reorganizing one of the many student organizations—the Peiping Students' Federation for National Salvation—in which he "took part in the leadership work of the Party organization" within the Federation.[4]

When the Sino-Japanese War broke out in July 1937, Chiang and other colleagues fled Peking, going first to Tientsin where a debate was held among the students on their future course of action. Subsequently, some of the students went north to engage in guerrilla warfare against the Japanese, and others went south to "arouse the masses."[5] Chiang, among the latter, went to Nanking together with Tuan Chün-i (q.v.), a fellow student in Peking and presently the minister of the PRC's First Ministry of Machine Building. In Nanking, then still outside the fighting zone, Chiang and the others were apparently hampered by the Nationalists in carrying on youth and Party activities. As a consequence, he left Nanking in late 1937 and made his way to Lin-fen in southern Shansi, where both the Party's North China Bureau and the headquarters of the NLVC had withdrawn in the face of the Japanese capture of Taiyuan, the Shansi capital 150 miles to the north. It was apparently at Lin-fen that Chiang had his first contact with ranking Party leaders, most notably Liu Shao-ch'i, Chou En-lai, and Yang Shang-k'un. For a brief period, in cooperation with the CCP, Chiang edited a small, mimeographed newspaper to carry war news and "spread the Party's policies."[6] When Lin-fen also fell to the Japanese, the NLVC headquarters (and presumably Chiang) withdrew to Sian, capital of Shensi. Not long after, in mid-1938, Chiang was in Wuhan along with other such Party youth leaders as Li Ch'ang and Huang Hua (qq.v.). There, under the guidance of the Yangtze Bureau of the Party, Chiang again engaged in youth work. He remained in Wuhan until at least September 1938 (one month before the city fell to the Japanese), but by January 1939 he was working for the Party in Chungking.[7] Although Chiang's activities in Chungking are undocumented, it is probable that he came under the jurisdiction of Chou En-lai's liaison mission to the Nationalist Government. Then, in 1941, Chiang went to Yenan, the Communist capital.

During the war years in Yenan, Chiang worked with Hu Ch'iao-mu (q.v.) as co-editor of *Chung-kuo ch'ing-nien* (China youth) magazine. He was also a delegate to the legislative body of the Shensi-Kansu-Ninghsia (Shen-Kan-Ning) Border Region Government, attending sessions of the Second Assembly in November 1941 and December 1944 as a "representative of those engaged in work for the Border Region Government."[8] According to one report, in September 1945, immediately after the end of the war, Chiang went to Manchuria with Sung I-p'ing (a colleague in the youth work from the thirties and presently a vice-chairman of the Commission for Cultural Relations with Foreign Countries).[9] Sent by top Party leader Jen Pi-shih, Sung and Chiang's group of youth workers consisted of over 90 persons; a year later (1946) they were instrumental in founding the Northeast Democratic Youth League, formed in accordance with a CCP Central Committee directive of September 1946 as a preparatory step for the establishment of the nationwide New Democratic Youth League (see below). By early 1949 Chiang was head of one of the departments of the Youth Work Committee of the CCP. With the convocation in April 1949 of the first Congress of the New Democratic Youth League (NDYL), he came to prominence along with a number of colleagues from his student days in the mid-1930's, including Li Ch'ang, Jung Kao-t'ang, and Lu P'ing (qq.v.). He delivered one of the major addresses at the Congress, speaking on the League's draft constitution, and was elected a member of the NDYL Central Committee and Standing Committee, as well as a deputy secretary. As originally organized, the NDYL had a secretary, Feng Wen-pin (q.v.), and two deputy secretaries, Liao Ch'eng-chih (q.v.) and Chiang. Two and a half years later (November 1951), this structure was slightly altered with the formation of a Secretariat (in place of the secretary and deputy secretaries). Chiang was named at this time as one of the secretaries, still serving under Feng Wen-pin and Liao Ch'eng-chih. For a brief period after the first NDYL Congress, Chiang also headed the Central League School, the Organization Department, and the Research Office. In short, most of Chiang's time in the early days of the PRC was devoted to the NDYL. In addition, from May 1949 to June 1953 he was also a member of the National Committee of the other important youth organization, the All-China Federation of Democratic Youth.

As a delegate of the NDYL, Chiang attended the first session of the CPPCC in September 1949, at which time the PRC central government was formed. During the CPPCC sessions he served on the *ad hoc* committee that drafted the public statements on the work of the CPPCC in forming the new government. He was elected to the first National Committee of the CPPCC and was elevated to its Standing Committee in February 1953. (He was not, however, re-elected to the Second National Committee, formed in December 1954.) In the new central government, Chiang was a member (October 1949–September 1954) of the Culture and Education Committee (headed by Kuo Mo-jo), one of the most important subordinate bodies of the Government Administration Council (the cabinet). In December 1949, representing the NDYL, he was appointed to the Preparatory Committee of the All-China Athletic Federation, holding this post until the Federation was permanently established in June 1952. In 1950, he was made a member of the Cinema Guidance Committee under the Ministry of Culture, and in October of that year he was named to the Standing Committee of the China Peace Committee, a post he held until a reorganization in July 1958. One year later (October 1951), he became a member of both the Executive Board and the Executive Committee of the Sino-Soviet Friendship Association, posts he held until the end of 1954.

Chiang's work in educational and cultural fields was given recognition in November 1952, when he was appointed president of his alma mater, Tsinghua University, one of China's most famous educational institutions. He was identified by 1957 as secretary of the Party Committee at Tsinghua. With this new responsibility, he became less active in other fields, particularly in the Youth League. At the mid-1953 youth congress he was dropped as a secretary, although he retained his posts as member of both the Standing Committee and Central Committee. Then, four years later (at the Third Youth League Congress in 1957), Chiang was only named to the Central Committee of the renamed Communist Youth League; at this juncture it could be considered mainly an honorary post. In 1954 he was elected as a deputy from Peking to the First NPC (1954–1959); he also served in the Second NPC (1959–1964) and was again elected to the Third NPC, which held its first session in December 1964–January 1965. Chiang reached a new peak in his career at the Eighth Party Congress in September 1956 when he was elected an alternate member of the Central Committee. He addressed the Congress on the necessity of raising the quality of higher education.

Two years later, on the eve of the PRC's ninth anniversary, the Chinese formed a number of "friendship associations" related to the Bloc nations (September 1958). Chiang was named to head the China-Albania Friendship Association (CAFA). From about 1960 this seemingly unimportant post became one of the most active owing to the formation of the Sino-Albanian "axis," which opposed the alleged "revisionism" of the Soviet Union. In recent years his name has appeared constantly in the Chinese press in connection with CAFA activities—to the point, in fact, that Chiang's work with the CAFA would seem to hamper his work as president of Tsinghua and (from 1960) in the Ministries of Education and Higher Education (see below). It was in connection with the Albanian Friendship Association that Chiang made his only trip abroad when, in February 1961, he went to Albania in a dual capacity—as a member of the CCP delegation led by Politburo member Li Hsien-nien to attend the Fourth Albanian Labor (Communist) Party Congress and as head of a five-member delegation of the CAFA.

In January 1960 Chiang was appointed vice-minister in the Education Ministry; he was the ranking vice-minister, being the only man within the Ministry of Central Committee rank aside from Minister Yang Hsiu-feng (q.v.). In June–July 1964 the Ministry was divided into the Ministries of Education and of Higher Education. Chiang remained in the Ministry of Education, but then in January 1965 Yang Hsiu-feng was transferred to the Supreme Court and Chiang replaced him as the minister of Higher Education, a post he continues to hold. (Soon after, in April 1965, he was formally removed as a vice-minister of Education.)

Over the course of the years Chiang has regularly contributed to the Chinese press, almost always in connection with educational policy. Among his articles is one on higher education, which appeared in the Party's most important journal, *Hung-ch'i* (Red flag, issue of September 16, 1958). He also contributed an essay to a collection of articles (published in both Chinese and English) commemorating a fellow student at Tsinghua University and a colleague in the "December Ninth Movement."[10]

---

1. Interview with former classmate of Chiang's, Hong Kong, April 1964.
2. *SCMM* 296, p. 31.
3. Chiang Nan-hsiang *et al., The Roar of a Nation* (Peking, 1963), p. 157.
4. *Ibid*. SCMM 296, p. 34.
5. *SCMM* 297, p. 36.
6. *Ibid*., p. 38.
7. Li Ch'ang *et al., "I-erh-chiu" hui-i-lu* (Reminiscences of "December Ninth"; Peking, 1961), p. 186.
8. *Shen-Kan-Ning pien-ch'ü ts'an-i-hui wen-hsien hui-chi* (Collection of documents of the Shensi-Kansu-Ninghsia Border Region Assembly, Peking, 1958), pp. 170, 268.
9. Union Research Service, Hong Kong, Biographic Service, report no. 990, June 11, 1965.
10. Li Ch'ang, pp. 146–159. Chiang Nan-hsiang, pp. 176–186.

Chiang Wei-ch'ing

(Kiangsu). Political commissar, Kiangsu Military District; first secretary, CCP Kiangsu Committee; alternate member, CCP Central Committee.

Chiang Wei-ch'ing, an important Party official in Kiangsu Province since the mid-1940's, has been an alternate member of the CCP Central Committee since 1956. Information is lacking on his early career, but toward the end of the Sino-Japanese War or immediately thereafter he was director of the Communists' South Kiangsu Administrative District. At approximately this same time (until 1946) he served as political commissar of both the Sixth Division of the New Fourth Army and the South Kiangsu Military District, a district probably covering the same area as the Administrative District. (The wartime history of the Sixth Division and the Military District is discussed in the biography of T'an Chen-lin.)

In 1946 Chiang moved toward the southwest into Anhwei Province where he was an official under the jurisdiction of the Party's Central China Bureau. He remained in this general vicinity during the late forties as a political officer in the Communist armies, and when Nanking fell in April 1949 he became a member of the Nanking Military Control Commission under Liu Po-ch'eng and a deputy secretary of the city's Party Committee. He went to Peking in the fall of 1949 to attend the inaugural session of the CPPCC, the organization which brought the new central government into existence on October 1. Chiang attended these meetings as a representative of Ch'en I's Third Field Army, which had occupied most of the coastal provinces earlier in the year.

Returning to Nanking, the Kiangsu capital, Chiang soon assumed new responsibilities. His principal new posts were: chairman of the Nanking Federation of Trade Unions, 1950–1953; commander of the Nanking Garrison Headquarters, 1950–c.1952; chairman of the Finance and Economics Committee of the Nanking Government, 1951–1953; and member of the Political and Legal Affairs Committee of the Nanking Government, 1951–1953. In addition, from February 1950 to September 1954 he was a member of the People's Supervision Committee of the regional administration known until 1952 as the East China Military and Administrative Committee and from 1952 to 1954 as the East China Administrative Committee. Finally, in November 1952 he was appointed a member of the Kiangsu Provincial People's Government, a position to which he was re-elected as late as September 1964.

By March 1953 Chiang had been promoted to higher Party responsibilities when he became second secretary under K'o Ch'ing-shih (q.v.) of the CCP Kiangsu Committee. Before long Chiang had relinquished all his posts in Nanking, the provincial capital. In January 1955, when K'o was transferred to Shanghai, Chiang succeeded him as the ranking secretary in Kiangsu. The position was redesignated first secretary by July 1956, and it continues to be Chiang's principal post. From April 1955 he also chaired the Kiangsu Committee of the CPPCC, a position he still holds. When the Party met for its Eighth National Congress in September 1956 Chiang submitted a report on the need to follow the "mass line" in the management of agricultural producers' cooperatives. At the close of the Congress he was elected an alternate member of the Party Central Committee. For a long period afterward there was no mention of Chiang's activities and Liu Shun-yuan served as the acting first secretary for Kiangsu. Ill health may have been the reason for his absence. However, in June 1958 he reappeared as the first secretary, and since then he has been regularly reported in a variety of activities commensurate with his Party status. For example, he has been frequently mentioned in the company of visitors to Nanking, both Chinese leaders from Peking and foreign guests. In February 1960 he was identified as first political commissar of the Kiangsu Military District, and since then he has made a number of talks before military groups in the province. Chiang's writings include an article entitled "Promote the Mass Line and the Down-to-Earth Working Style" for the *JMJP* of January 5, 1959, and another on studying the thought of Mao-Tse-tung for *Hung-ch'i* (Red flag; no. 2, January 16, 1960).

Ch'iao Kuan-hua

(1914–   ; Yen-ch'eng, Kiangsu). Journalist; propagandist; diplomat; vice-president, Chinese People's Institute of Foreign Affairs; vice-minister, Ministry of Foreign Affairs.

Ch'iao Kuan-hua is one of Peking's more important diplomats, having served in the Foreign Ministry since the Communist conquest of the mainland in 1949. A veteran journalist and propagandist, he and his wife Kung P'eng have been closely associated with Chou En-lai since the early forties and both were well known to Western journalists, scholars, and diplomats in China during the war and postwar years. He was born in March 1914 in Yen-ch'eng hsien, in eastern Kiangsu. Propagandist Hu Ch'iao-mu also comes from Yen-ch'eng, and both men have used the same *nom-de-plume,* Ch'iao Mu. To distinguish between them the Communists nicknamed Hu as Pei ("north") Ch'iao-mu and Ch'iao Kuan-hua as Nan ("south") Ch'iao-mu. Fortunately, the confusion between the two men

ended after 1949 when both men dropped "Ch'iao Mu" as pen name. Ch'iao Kuan-hua was also known by the pen name Yü Huai during the Sino-Japanese War years. He received his education at Tsinghua University in Peking, graduating in 1933 with a bachelor's degree in philosophy. He then traveled briefly in Japan and France before enrolling at the University of Tübingen in Germany, receiving his doctorate in philosophy in 1936. Ch'iao is one of the very few Chinese Communist leaders to hold a doctorate and also one of the few educated in Germany. As a result of his extensive education, he is among the most accomplished linguists in the PRC. Fluent in English and German, he reportedly also speaks Japanese, Russian, and French, skills that served him well in later years as a diplomat.

Upon the outbreak of the Sino-Japanese War in mid-1937, Ch'iao returned to China, where from 1937 to 1938, during a period of relatively good KMT–CCP relations, he engaged in propaganda work for the KMT Propaganda Department in the Nationalists' Seventh War Zone (the Wuhan area). He probably joined the CCP during this period. From 1938 to 1941 he worked as a propagandist and journalist in Hong Kong where as a writer on international affairs he quickly gained fame for his articles in such journals at *Ta-chung sheng-huo* (Masses' life), edited by the well-known leftist journalist Tsou T'ao-fen.[1] Other prominent leftist or Communist journalists working in Hong Kong at this time include Chin Chung-hua and Hu Yü-chih (qq.v.). When the city fell to the Japanese at the end of 1941 Ch'iao escaped and took refuge with Communist guerrillas in the Tung-chiang (East River) area of Kwangtung (see under Tseng Sheng).

From Kwangtung Ch'iao made his way in 1942 to Chungking where he became a secretary to the CCP delegation there headed by Chou En-lai. This was apparently Ch'iao's first contact with Chou, an association that has lasted since that time. Ch'iao was also the international news editor for the Communists' *Hsin-hua jih-pao* (New China daily) and he contributed articles to *Ch'ün-chung* (The masses), a journal published at irregular intervals.[2] In the 1943–45 period he was identified as a member of the Party's Propaganda Department, working both in Chungking and Yenan. Over the winter of 1945–46, Ch'iao was a secretary to Chou En-lai when the latter was negotiating in Chungking with the Nationalists about the cessation of hostilities and the terms under which the Communists would participate in the Nationalist-convened Political Consultative Conference (held January 1946). Ch'iao spent most of the first half of 1946 in Nanking and Shanghai working as a CCP propagandist; the Communists were able to operate openly at this time as a result of the January 1946 Cease-Fire Agreement that had been worked out through the cooperation of U.S. Special Envoy George C. Marshall. A number of articles on international relations written by Ch'iao at this time appear in *Wen-ts'ui* (Digest), a Shanghai weekly that was closed down by the KMT in March 1947 when virtually all CCP periodicals in Nationalist-held areas were suppressed.[3]

By the fall of 1946 Ch'iao went to Hong Kong where he remained for the next three years. Although suffering from tuberculosis at this time, he directed the activities of the Communists' New China News Agency and served as a member of the CCP's South China Bureau, then headed by Liao Ch'eng-chih (q.v.). During this period Ch'iao continued to write regularly for CCP-supported publications.[4] As a consequence of Ch'iao's work in Hong Kong during this period he came to be regarded by both Chinese and Westerners in Hong Kong as the leading Communist liaison official there, a status noted by K. M. Panikkar, India's last ambassador to the Nationalist Government and its first to the PRC.[5] Ch'iao remained in Hong Kong until the late summer of August 1949, by which time much of the mainland was already in Communist hands.

By the time Ch'iao left Hong Kong for the mainland, he was one of the best-known Chinese Communist leaders among the Western diplomats, journalists, and scholars concerned with China. His knowledge of Westerners, of course, stemmed from his extensive experience in cities with a significant Western diplomatic, press, and scholarly community, namely, Chungking, Nanking, Shanghai, and Hong Kong. Much the same could also be said about his wife, Kung P'eng (see below), who was with him most of this time. During these years most of Ch'iao's Western friends and acquaintances knew him by the name of Ch'iao Mu.

Even before he reached Peking in September 1949, Ch'iao had been given several assignments in the "mass" organizations that the Communists were busy establishing in the spring and summer. In May of that year he was elected a member of the First National Committee of the All-China Federation of Democratic Youth. Then 35, Ch'iao held this position until mid-1953. In July 1949 he was named to the Preparatory Committee headed by Hu Ch'iao-mu of the All-China Journalists' Association, retaining this post until the organization was established on a permanent basis in 1954. Also in July 1949 he was named as one of the conveners of a large conference of social science "workers," and in September he gained membership on the Standing Committee of the China New Political Science Research Association's Preparatory Committee. However, it seems that Ch'iao devoted little of his time to these organizations, for when the central government was established in September–October 1949, he received important administrative posts, which apparently occupied him fully in the ensuing years.

In September 1949 Ch'iao was present in Peking for the First Session of the CPPCC, the organization that brought the new government into existence (October 1). He attended as a representative of the South China Liberated Area and while the CPPCC was in session served on an *ad hoc* committee that prepared the press releases on the results of the meetings. In October he was appointed as one of the deputy directors of the Staff Office of the Central People's Government Council (CPGC), the highest organ of state in the PRC that operated under the chairmanship of Mao Tse-tung. Ch'iao worked in the Staff Office under Director Ch'i Yen-ming (q.v.) until the CPGC was abolished in 1954 with the inauguration of the constitutional government. He was identified in October (although not officially appointed until December 1949) as the vice-chairman of the Foreign Ministry's Foreign Policy Committee. Chou En-lai headed both the Ministry and its subordinate Policy Committee, but little was heard of the latter's activities and apparently it went out of existence in the early fifties. Ch'iao received a closely related appointment in December 1949 when he became director of the International News Bureau under the Press Administration, an organization one level below a ministry in the Government Administration Council (the cabinet). The Press Administration, headed by Hu Ch'iao-mu, was abolished late in the summer of 1952, and it is probable that some of the functions of the International News Bureau were placed under the Foreign Ministry's Information Department, a department headed by Ch'iao's wife, Kung P'eng.

During the latter part of 1949 Ch'iao was also given new assignments in three important "mass" organizations. From October 1949 until a reorganization one year later, he served as a National Committee member of the China Peace Committee. Also from October 1949 he was a member of the First Executive Board of the Sino-Soviet Friendship Association, holding this post until the Association was reorganized in December 1954. Most important was Ch'iao's election as a vice-president of the Chinese People's Institute of Foreign Affairs (CPIFA) in December 1949. The CPIFA, officially described as an "organization devoted to the study of international relations," has been utilized by the PRC as an unofficial arm of the Ministry of Foreign Affairs (MFA). Headed by non-Communist Chang Hsi-jo (q.v.), the CPIFA's leadership consists mainly of highly educated men with considerable experience abroad. With the exception of Ch'iao and his colleague Hu Yü-chih, another vice-president, most of the other Institute leaders are non-Communists. In practice the CPIFA has been used largely to promote ties with nations not having diplomatic relations with the PRC. Thus, in his numerous dealings with foreigners, Ch'iao has acted as either an Institute official or as a Foreign Ministry official—depending upon the state of diplomatic relations of the nations involved. Within the CPIFA he also served as head of the Translation Committee from 1952 to 1955.

On various occasions in 1950 Ch'iao served as acting director of the Foreign Ministry's Asian Affairs Department, and from the same year until the end of 1952 he was editor of *People's China*, an English-language publication. In November–December 1950, immediately after the entry of Chinese forces into the Korean War, he was in New York as a member of the special PRC delegation sent to the United Nations to present the Chinese case regarding the alleged aggression of the United States in Korea and Taiwan (see under Wu Hsiu-ch'üan, the delegation leader). As such, he is one of a handful of Chinese Communist officials to have been in the United States since 1949.

Ch'iao was abroad again in the spring and summer of 1954 as an adviser to Chou En-lai's delegation to the famous Geneva Conference, which brought an end to the fighting in Indochina between the French and the Communist forces of Ho Chi-minh. During a recess in the conference in June, Ch'iao accompanied Chou on goodwill visits to India and Burma. The delegation proceeded to Peking for a short stay and then returned to Geneva. When the conference closed in July, Ch'iao accompanied Chou en route home on brief visits to East Germany, Poland, the Soviet Union, and the Mongolian People's Republic. Soon afterwards, in October 1954, he was appointed an assistant minister (one rank below a vice-minister) in the Ministry of Foreign Affairs.

Ch'iao was once more an adviser to Chou En-lai when the latter led a delegation in April 1955 to the historic Bandung Conference in Indonesia, and again from November 1956 to early January 1957 when Chou led a group on visits to North Vietnam, Cambodia, India, Burma, and Pakistan. He was a member of still another delegation led by Chou in April–May 1960 to Burma, India, Nepal, Cambodia, and North Vietnam, a mission whose main purpose was to discuss border disputes with officials of these nations. He spent much of the year 1961–62 in Geneva as a member of Foreign Minister Ch'en I's delegation to the so-called Geneva Conference on Laos. The group arrived in May, and Ch'iao remained in Geneva after July under acting delegation leader Chang Han-fu (q.v.) when Ch'en I returned to Peking. Over the winter of 1961–62 Chang and Ch'iao returned to Peking, but then both men went back to Geneva in mid-1962 for the conclusion of the conference.

In the ensuing years Ch'iao continued to accompany top Chinese leaders abroad. There are few officials, in fact, who have participated in as many important delegations as Ch'iao, the balance of which are summarized as follows: member of the delegation led by Liu Shao-ch'i and Ch'en I to Indonesia, Burma, and North Vietnam, April–May 1963; member of the delegation led by Liu Shao-ch'i to North Korea, September 1963; member of the group led by Chou En-lai and Ch'en I to 10 nations in Africa (United Arab Republic, Algeria, Morocco, Tunisia, Ghana, Mali, Guinea, Sudan, Ethiopia, Somalia), to Albania, and to Burma, Pakistan, and Ceylon, December 1963–February 1964; member of Ch'en I's delegation to the Preparatory Meeting for the Second Afro-Asian ("Bandung") Conference in Indonesia, April 1964; member of Chou En-lai's delegation to Moscow for celebrations marking the 47th anniversary of the Russian Revolution, November 1964; member of a delegation led by Chou En-lai and Ch'en I to Jakarta for celebrations commemorating the 10th anniversary of the Bandung Conference, April 1965.

In the meantime, Ch'iao received two new assignments, the first of these, largely ceremonial, in October 1963 when he was appointed to Council membership on the newly established China-Japan Friendship Association. Far more important was his promotion to a vice-ministership in the Foreign Ministry in April 1964. Although Ch'iao is outranked in the Ministry by men of greater political importance (e.g., Liu Hsiao, q.v.), there are few others who have served longer in the Chinese Communist foreign service —both the official ministry established in 1949 and the "unofficial" ministry that existed under Chou En-lai's aegis since the Sino-Japanese War. In this regard, Ch'iao's career closely parallels those of other key members of Chou's entourage, including Chang Han-fu and Ch'en Chia-k'ang (q.v.). He is regarded by those who have known him as an intelligent and capable man who has an affable personality.

Ch'iao has been married to Kung P'eng since the latter part of the Sino-Japanese War, and by 1945 they had a son named Paris. Kung is as well known to Western diplomats, scholars, and journalists as her husband. She was born into a Christian family about 1917 in Shanghai where she was educated in an Episcopalian girls' school. Under her original name, Kung Wei-hang, she studied in the Chinese language and literature department at Yenching University in Peking, graduating in 1937. Since the war years, Kung's career has been quite similar to that of her husband; she too worked for Chou En-lai in Chungking and was a propagandist-journalist in Shanghai and Hong Kong. She also joined the Foreign Ministry in 1949, serving as head of the Information (Intelligence) Department until 1964 and since then as an assistant minister. She has accompanied her husband abroad on several of the delegations described above, including those to Geneva (1954 and 1961) and to Africa (1963–64). Kung's sister, Kung P'u-sheng, is married to Foreign Ministry Vice-minister Chang Han-fu and has also held important positions in the Chinese foreign service (see under Chang Han-fu).

1. Chün-tu Hsüeh, *The Chinese Communist Movement, 1937–1949* (Stanford, Calif., 1962), p. 54.
2. *Ibid.*, p. 6.
3. *Ibid.*, p. 218.
4. *Ibid.*, pp. 7–8, 182.
5. K. M. Panikkar, *In Two Chinas* (London, 1955), p. 64.

Ch'ien Chün-jui

(1908–   ; Wu-hsi, Kiangsu). Specialist in Sino-Soviet relations; alternate member, CCP Central Committee.

Ch'ien Chün-jui, a Party member since the mid-1920's, has specialized in education and the promotion of Sino-Soviet relations. He was elected an alternate member of the Party Central Committee in 1956, but little has been heard of him since 1960 when his political fortunes began to decline. Born in September 1908 in Wu-hsi (Wusih), a rice-marketing town in southern Kiangsu, Ch'ien graduated from the Third Normal School of Kiangsu and the provincial Education Institute in Wu-hsi. In about 1926 he joined the CCP, subsequently engaging in Party underground work in Shanghai. There he was one of the founders of a leftist study group, the China Rural Economic Research Association (1934), serving as chief editor of the Association's *Bulletin.* Among others associated with him in founding the Association was economist Sun Hsiao-ts'un, who remained on the China mainland after 1949.

On the eve of the Sino-Japanese War Ch'ien was reported to have been a professor at Shansi University, but the possibility of his having been there long (if at all) seems unlikely in view of the fact that he was very actively engaged in founding the Sino-Soviet Cultural Association (SSCA), the predecessor of the Sino-Soviet Friendship Association. The SSCA was established in 1935, with a Shanghai chapter formed in March 1936. Ch'ien worked with the Association for the next few years, possibly operating from clandestine headquarters after the Japanese attacked Shanghai in August 1937. At about this time he was also said to have been engaged in anti-Japanese work among intellectuals. Some confirmation of this comes from one report that he had attended an anti-Fascist Congress in Paris in 1936.[1] The following year he was a delegate to the Brussels Youth Conference, which was sponsored by the Soviet Communist Party. After the meeting he wrote *The Brussels Youth Conference,* one of six books published in Shanghai in the fall of 1937 in a "National Salvation Series" designed to arouse popular resistance to the Japanese invasion. Speeches by Chiang Kai-shek and Madame Sun Yat-sen's *China Will Never Be Conquered* were other volumes in the series.[2] Ch'ien was also one of eight editors of the *Chiu-wang shou-ts'e* (Salvation handbook), a left-wing, anti-Japanese work published in Shanghai in January 1938.

It is not known how long Ch'ien remained in Shanghai after the outbreak of war, but at some-time in the late thirties he was associated with a Chungking periodical entitled *Li-lun yü hsien-shih* (Theory and reality). In any event, he spent most of the early war years in east-central China at the headquarters of the Communists' New Fourth Army (see under Yeh T'ing). In the early war years he was secretary-general of the New Fourth Army Headquarters, and in the latter years (1941–1945) he was director of the Army's Propaganda Department. By 1941 Ch'ien was also head of the Culture and Education Affairs Committee of the CCP's Central China (Hua-chung) Bureau.[3] Liu Shao-ch'i was then secretary of the Bureau and Jao Shu-shih was the deputy secretary as well as director of the Bureau's Propaganda Department.

At the end of the war Ch'ien went to Yenan for a brief period but was soon transferred to Peking where he remained for most of 1946 carrying out various assignments for the CCP. He was manager of the Peking office of the New China News Agency (NCNA) and a Party representative at the Executive Headquarters for the Marshall Mission (see under Yeh Chien-ying). Late in 1946, as the civil war between the Communists and Nationalists intensified, Ch'ien returned to Yenan where he assumed the editorship of both the NCNA and the *Chieh-fang jih-pao* (Liberation daily), the leading Communist newspaper of that period and the predecessor of today's *JMJP.*

When the Communists occupied Peking in January 1949, Ch'ien was among the first civil officials to go there. He was immediately assigned as chairman of the Cultural Control Committee under the Peking Military Control Commission, the first of his many posts related to cultural and educational affairs. He was already dean of Education of North China University, an institution for cadre training established by the Communists soon after they occupied north China. With the arrival of the Communists in Peking, Ch'ien also had a hand in their takeover of the well-known Tsinghua University, and prior to the establishment of the PRC in October 1949 he was made a vice-chairman of the Higher Education Committee in the Communists' administration governing north China, the North China People's Government. He was also a vice-chairman and secretary-general of the Preparatory Committee for the National Educational Workers' Conference (July 1949), which ultimately established the All-China Educational Workers Trade Union in August 1950.

Although Ch'ien was over 40 when the Communists took Peking, he served as one of the principal officials from 1949 to 1953 in the two most important youth organizations, the New Democratic Youth League (NDYL) and the All-China Federation of Democratic Youth, established in April and May 1949, respectively. In the Youth League he was a member of the Standing Committee (1949–1953) and director of the NDYL Department of Culture and Education from 1949 to 1950. In the Youth Federation he served as a vice-chairman of the First National Committee. Ch'ien was dropped from both organizations when they held their second congresses in mid-1953 and their initial periods of development were over, but by this time he had taken on other important responsibilities.

In the spring of 1949 he took his first extensive trip outside China, traveling widely in the Soviet bloc countries of Eastern Europe. As the secretary-general of Kuo Mo-jo's delegation to the World Peace Congress, he left China for Paris where the conference was held, only to find at the last moment that the French government had refused entry to the 10 delegations from Communist countries. They were therefore forced to hold a "rump" Peace Congress in Prague in April. The following month Ch'ien attended the Ninth Congress of the Czech Communist Party as well as the Second Congress of Polish Trade Unions in early June. Later in June the group (apparently including Ch'ien) started for Italy to attend the Second World Congress of Trade Unions in Milan, but the Italian government, following the French example, refused them entry. Hence, a "rump" congress of trade unions from the Communist countries was held in Warsaw. After the congress closed, the delegation visited Hungary, Bulgaria, Rumania, and the USSR. Nine years later, when he sent public birthday greetings to American Negro Paul Robeson, he spoke of their first meeting in Prague in 1949, and of later meetings in Warsaw and Moscow.[4]

After his return to China, Ch'ien took an active part in the establishment of the central government that was formed under the aegis of the First CPPCC in September 1949 (and formally inaugurated on October 1). Representing the National Educational Workers' Conference, he attended the meetings in September, serving as a member of the *ad hoc* committee to draft the Common Program, the document that served as the equivalent of a constitution until 1954. When the government organs were staffed in

October 1949, Ch'ien was named to membership on the Government Administration Council's Culture and Education Committee, a committee headed by cultural leader Kuo Mo-jo. He was also named as a vice-minister of Education, serving concurrently (from December 1949 to November 1950) as head of the Ministry's Higher Education Office. Ch'ien's political position within the Ministry was accentuated by the fact that neither the minister (Ma Hsu-lun) nor the other vice-minister (Wei Chueh) belonged to the Communist Party. In November 1952 the Education Ministry was split into the Ministry of Education and the Ministry of Higher Education, but Ch'ien was not reappointed to either. However, he was promoted to the post of secretary-general of the Culture and Education Committee, replacing Party historian Hu Ch'iao-mu.

Like most of the important government leaders, Ch'ien was given a number of semi-official assignments in the latter part of 1949. In October he was made a member of the Association for the Reform of Written Chinese (to 1954) and of the China Peace Committee (to 1958). It was also in October 1949 that he became a member of the All-China Athletic Federation as a representative of the Education Ministry (but he did not serve in this organization after it was fully organized in June 1952). Two months later, in December 1949, he was named to the Board of Directors of the Chinese People's Institute of Foreign Affairs, a position to which he was re-elected in 1951 and 1955.

Despite the many government and semi-government responsibilities that Ch'ien assumed in 1949, he probably devoted more time to the Sino-Soviet Friendship Association (SSFA) than any other single activity during the period from 1949 to 1961. On July 16, 1949, a large conference was held in Peking to prepare for the establishment of the SSFA, the direct successor of the Sino-Soviet Cultural Association. At the meeting, attended by such top leaders as Liu Shao-ch'i and Chou En-lai, Ch'ien served on the presidium (steering committee), gave a report on the purposes of the organization, and was named to head an 18-member group charged with the task of establishing the organization on a full-time basis. When the SSFA was inaugurated in October 1949, Ch'ien was named as a member of the Executive Board and as general secretary (secretary-general after 1954). Although Liu Shao-ch'i was the nominal head of the Association until 1954 and Sung Ch'ing-ling (Mme. Sun Yat-sen) thereafter, Ch'ien was the most active of the top leaders; for the next 12 years (to 1961), he attended many conferences of the organization, wrote for its publications, and traveled abroad on its behalf (or for other purposes closely related to Sino-Soviet relations). Setting the tone for the intimate relations with Moscow during the early years of the PRC,

Ch'ien wrote an article for the most important Party periodical of this period, *Hsueh-hsi* (Study; no. 4, December 1949), entitled "An Important Symbol of Internationalism: The Friendship of the Soviet Union." In another article, written for the English-language *People's China* (November 16, 1952), he summarized the activities of the SSFA from its formation. In spite of his long involvement with Soviet cultural relations, Ch'ien does not know Russian. He does, however, know English.

Re-elected secretary-general at the Second SSFA Conference in December 1954, and again at the Third Conference in May 1959, he made six trips abroad after 1949 on behalf of the Association or its allied interest. In November 1950 he traveled via Moscow to the Second World Peace Congress held in Warsaw; in March 1953 he was a member of the delegation led by Premier Chou En-lai to Stalin's funeral; in 1954 he led a group to Moscow for the May Day celebrations; and in November 1957 he was a deputy leader of the "working peoples' " delegation, which Liu Ning-i took to Moscow for the celebrations marking the 40th anniversary of the founding of the USSR. On two other occasions he was in Moscow negotiating Sino-Soviet cultural cooperation agreements (June 1956 and November 1959). Earlier, in Peking, Ch'ien had acted in a similar capacity in negotiations with the East Germans, signing the 1954 plan for the implementation of the Sino-German Cultural Cooperation Agreement on November 28, 1953.

With the inauguration of the constitutional government in September 1954, Ch'ien continued to serve in a number of important governmental roles as shown in the following list of his principal posts after 1954: member, First and Second NPC's, 1954–1964, serving as a deputy from Kiangsu; member of the NPC Bills Committee, 1954–1959; deputy director, Second Staff Office, State Council, October 1954–September 1959 (after this office was renamed the Culture and Education Office in 1959, he continued as a deputy director until July 1965); vice-minister of Culture, October 1954–September 1963 (from June to December 1955, September excepted, he served as acting minister); member, Second National Committee, CPPCC, December 1954–April 1959; member, Third National Committee, April 1959–December 1964 and, concurrently, a member of the Standing Committee; member of the Fourth National Committee (which first met in late 1964) but not re-elected to the Standing Committee; member, Scientific Planning Commission, State Council, March 1956–May 1957; member, State Council's Spare-Time Education Committee, January 1960. He presumably continues to hold this post.

In addition to these government posts, Ch'ien received additional assignments in the "people's" organizations. In May 1954, when the Chinese People's Association for Cultural Relations with Foreign Countries was formed, he was named to the Board of Directors. This very active organization underwent a reorganization in 1959, and since that date it is not certain if Ch'ien is still a board member. In August 1960 he was elected to National Committee membership in the All-China Federation of Literary and Art Circles, a position he continues to hold.

In addition to the above, Ch'ien has worked with the Communist program for adult education and has been associated with the plans to phoneticize written Chinese and to standardize the pronunciation. In this connection he has been a member of the State Council's National Association for the Elimination of Illiteracy since its establishment in March 1956, a member of the State Council's Committee for the Phoneticization of the Chinese Language since its inception in October 1956, and a member of the presidium of a conference for "advanced" cultural and educational workers in June 1960. He has also attended a number of conferences and meetings on behalf of each of these organizations.

Some insight into Ch'ien's views on certain Communist practices can be gained from an account describing the living conditions of students at Peking University in 1950. Speaking of their state of health, one student reported that news had "trickled down" to them that Ch'ien had addressed a special meeting of the Culture and Education Committee on the subject. He made "a moving and emotional plea," citing as an example his own daughter who had gone in good health to the Northeast College of Medicine in Mukden, only to be sent home suffering from tuberculosis. This condition had been brought on, he said, because she had been overworked and had been forced to attend too many meetings at the college in addition to her heavy assignments.[5] In a 1956 interview with French statesman Edgar Faure, Ch'ien asserted that though art must serve the workers, it need not be political propaganda. This view, of course, was in accord with the Party policy of that time—the famed Hundred Flowers Movement. Faure described Ch'ien as follows: "He gives an impression of intellectual and physical vigour and, ... of frankness. The information that he gave me, especially on the problem of the illiterates, had no suggestion of bluff."[6]

Ch'ien's long service to the Communist movement was given formal recognition at the Eighth Party Congress in September 1956 when he was elected an alternate member of the Party Central Committee. However, after years of intensive activity in the promotion of Party-directed programs for education and cultural exchange with the Soviet Union, his political fortunes declined suddenly in the fall of 1960 when Chang Chihhsiang (q.v.), another specialist in cultural relations, became acting secretary-general of the

SSFA. Ch'ien's last public appearance was in February 1961 when he bade farewell to a visiting Soviet cultural delegation. Since that time, as already described, he has been removed as a vice-minister of Culture (September 1963) and as a deputy director of the important Culture and Education Office (July 1965). The only appointment he has received since his political troubles began was in late 1964 when he was named to membership on the Fourth National Committee of the relatively unimportant CPPCC. Because there is no other apparent reason for his sudden political decline, it is probably related to the worsening of Sino-Soviet relations.

1. Edgar Faure, *The Serpent and the Tortoise* (New York, 1959), p. 125.
2. Israel Epstein, *The People's War* (London, 1939), p. 108.
3. *Sohoku kyōsan chiku jitsujō chōsa hōkokusho* (Investigation report on the current situation in the North Kiangsu Communist Region; Shanghai, 1941), chart following p. 222.
4. *Peking Review,* April 15, 1958.
5. Maria Yen, *The Umbrella Garden* (New York, 1954), p. 80.
6. Faure, p. 125.

Ch'ien Hsin-chung

(1911–   ; Wu-sung, Kiangsu). Minister of Public Health.

Ch'ien Hsin-chung, a medical doctor, joined the Communist movement in the early thirties and has served since then in the public health field. In Edgar Snow's *Random Notes* he records an interview in Kansu in 1936 with a "Ch'ien Tsung-hsin" who, from the internal evidence of his career, is almost certainly the same person as the subject of this biography. According to Snow's material, Ch'ien was born in 1911 in Wu-sung (Woosung), Kiangsu, immediately north of Shanghai. He was educated in Wu-sung schools and then entered T'ing-chi University, also in Wu-sung, in 1925 where he studied engineering. After a year there the lack of funds forced him to drop out, whereupon he worked in a hospital in Shanghai as a nurse, holding the job for five years. Ch'ien left the hospital in 1931 to join the Nationalist Army, motivated by the Japanese attack on Shanghai in that year. He became dissatisfied with the Nationalists and deserted.

After Ch'ien left the Nationalist Army he sought out the Communists. The latter, however, thought him to be a spy and imprisoned him. He was released in 1933 and began to work in the "Red Army General Hospital" (the locale of which is not mentioned in Snow's account). He was then assigned as director of hospital work in the 25th Red Army led by Hsu Hai-tung (q.v.), a force that remained in the Oyüwan

Soviet base until late 1933 or early 1934 when it marched to Shensi. After the 25th Red Army reached Shensi it was merged with other Communist units and was designated the 15th Army Corps. When Snow interviewed Ch'ien in Kansu in the late summer of 1936 he identified him as director of the 15th Army Corps' Public Health Bureau. He also described Ch'ien as being "angry over the non-resistance policy in Manchuria" and as a "convinced Marxist."[1] Nothing further was heard of him until September 1949 when he attended the first session of the CPPCC in Peking as a delegate from the Second Field Army, the force led by Liu Po-ch'eng, which was at that time poised for its final thrust into southwest China. During the course of the CPPCC meetings Ch'ien served on the *ad hoc* committee headed by Chou En-lai to draft the Common Program, the document that served as the constitution until a formal constitution was adopted five years later.

After the CPPCC meetings Ch'ien proceeded to the southwest where he became director of the Health Department of the Southwest Military Region. However, by mid-1950 he was switched from military to civil work with the establishment of the Southwest Military and Administrative Committee (SWMAC), the body headed by Liu Po-ch'eng, which was responsible for administering the provinces of Szechwan, Sikang, Kweichow, and Yunnan. When the SWMAC was formally established in July 1950, Ch'ien was named as a SWMAC member, as well as director of the subordinate Public Health Department and as a member of the Culture and Education Committee. In August 1950 he was named to the Standing Committee of the All-China Federation of Scientific Societies when the federation was inaugurated. Eight years later (September 1958), this organization was merged with another scientific body to form the China Scientific and Technical Association, with Ch'ien as one of the National Committee members, a position he still holds.

When the SWMAC was reorganized in the Southwest Administrative Committee in early 1953, Ch'ien was not reappointed to membership. The reason, apparently, was that a decision had been made to send him to Moscow for further training. For about three years he was in the Soviet Union studying public health administration at an institute subordinate to the Ministry of Public Health. While still in Moscow, Ch'ien was appointed in February 1955 as a standing committee member of a "medical science research committee" under the Chinese Ministry of Public Health. This was an indication that following his return to China (1956) he was scheduled for assignments in Peking in the field of science and public health. In May 1957 he received his first Peking post, membership on the State Council's Scientific Planning Commission when the Commission was reorganized and expanded. He retained the post until the Commission was again reorganized in November 1958. At about this same time he also assumed the position of a deputy director of the Health Department under the PLA's General Rear Services Department. However, with the press of additional assignments in the government structure, Ch'ien apparently did not hold this military post for a long period. In October 1957, he was named as a vice-minister of Public Health under Miss Li Te-ch'üan. In the next month he returned to Moscow, this time in the scientific delegation led by Kuo Mo-jo to the 40th anniversary celebrations of the Russian Revolution (although it is clear that Kuo's large scientific group engaged in lengthy scientific discussions quite apart from the anniversary celebrations).

Apparently to take advantage of his familiarity with the Soviet scientific world, Ch'ien was assigned by the early fall of 1961 to work on the Sino-Soviet Commission on Scientific and Technical Cooperation, meetings of which are held approximately semi-annually. He took part in the 11th session of this commission in Peking under the direction of science administrator Wu Heng (q.v.). Less than two years later, in June 1963, he took part in negotiations, again in Peking, leading to the signing of a protocol to the 13th session. In 1961 Ch'ien received two further assignments related to the medical field. He was named to a vice-presidency in the China Medical Society, one of the many learned organizations subordinate to the above-mentioned China Scientific and Technical Association in which he serves. Also, in October 1961, he was named to the Standing Committee of the Red Cross Society of China, an organization chaired by Li Te-ch'üan, then his superior in the Ministry of Public Health.

Between 1962 and 1964, Ch'ien was abroad on three occasions. Back in the Soviet Union in July 1962, he led a delegation of cancer specialists to the Eighth International Cancer Conference in Moscow. From November 1963 to January 1964 he was in North Korea heading a public health delegation visiting the country in accordance with a Sino-Korean cultural cooperation agreement. He was abroad once again in October 1964 as the head of a medical delegation to Cairo for the First Afro-Asian Medical Conference, and en route home stopped for a week's visit in Pakistan (November). During this same period he was elected from his native Kiangsu to the Third NPC. At the first session of the Third NPC, held in December 1964–January 1965, Ch'ien served as a member of the presidium (steering committee), and on the closing day was named to succeed Li Te-ch'üan as minister of Public Health. Four months later (April 1965) he succeeded Li in another post when he became chairman of the Red Cross So-

ciety. Thus by 1965 Ch'ien could be considered the senior PRC official in the field of public health and related activities.

As with many present-day leaders, Ch'ien holds a number of *pro forma* positions of apparently little significance. He is a member of the Council of the China-Africa People's Friendship Association (from April 1960) and a vice-president of the China-Ceylon Friendship Association from its establishment in September 1962. He makes rather frequent appearances to entertain foreign visitors who have interests in the field of medicine, and he also appears often at scientific meetings. In late 1961, for example, he spoke in Shanghai at a national conference on schistosomiasis, a parasitic disease which has plagued China for centuries, and in September 1963 he made the closing speech before a congress of surgeons. He played an important role at a more politically oriented conference in August 1964 when the Chinese staged the huge "Peking Scientific Symposium." The symposium, attended by 367 delegates from 44 countries (almost all in Asia, Africa, or Latin America), was held in direct defiance of the Soviet-backed World Federation of Scientific Workers, It was, therefore, one more example of the widening Sino-Soviet split. Ch'ien served as one of the six deputy leaders of the Chinese delegation and, like all the Chinese delegates, signed on August 31 a "protest against United States imperialist aggression in Vietnam."

Ch'ien has been married at least twice. When he was working in the southwest in the early 1950's, his wife died, leaving him with four children.[2] Then, while in Moscow, he married a doctor surnamed Shen (in about 1956), a woman some 15 years younger than he. She is the mother of two children by Ch'ien, and following their return to China in 1956 she worked in a mental hospital in Peking. Ch'ien is said to be a man with an easy-going character and a sense of humor.[3] His only known writing of significance is an article that appeared in *Peking Review* (February 28, 1964) under the title "Chinese Medicine: Progress and Achievements."

---

1. Edgar Snow, *Random Notes on Red China, 1936–1945* (Cambridge, Mass., 1957), p. 131.

2. Interview with former employee of the Ministry of Public Health, May 1964, Hong Kong.

3. *Ibid.*

Ch'ien Li-jen

Youth leader; specialist in liaison with Afro-Asian nations.

Although Ch'ien Li-jen did not emerge in the Communist movement until after the establishment of the PRC in 1949, he had become one of the most significant youth leaders by the mid-fifties. He began his public career in Shanghai in 1949 as a member of the New Democratic Youth League (known as the Communist Youth League after 1957). Little is known about Ch'ien in the early days of the PRC aside from the fact that in 1952 he was a judge on the Shanghai "People's Court" and in the same year took part in organizing celebrations in East China to mark the third anniversary of the PRC.

Ch'ien first reached a level of national prominence in 1953 when both the Youth League and the All-China Federation of Democratic Youth held their second congresses. In the more important Youth League he served as a Central Committee member from 1953 to 1964, and during the 1960–1964 period he was also a member of the Standing Committee, the committee responsible for managing League affairs when the Central Committee is not in full session. His rise in the All-China Federation of Democratic Youth (known as the All-China Youth Federation after 1958) approximates his role in the Youth League. He went from membership on the National Committee in 1953 to a vice-chairmanship in 1962, serving also as a deputy secretary-general (1953–1958) and then as secretary-general from 1959 to 1962. However, none of these posts were as important as his part in the international liaison work of both youth organizations. Like most important organizations in Communist China, both the Youth Federation and the Youth League have extremely active international liaison departments. Until the deterioration of Sino-Soviet relations in the early 1960's, the liaison activities of both organizations were strongly oriented toward the Soviet Bloc nations and such Communist-dominated organizations as the World Federation of Democratic Youth. In both the Federation and the League, Ch'ien was one of the key international liaison figures from the early fifties to the early sixties. He began to take an active part in these affairs in June 1953 when he was named as deputy director of the Youth Federation's International Liaison Department at the close of the second Federation Congress. He succeeded to the directorship of the Department by 1959 and held the post until about 1962. Paralleling this assignment, he was a deputy director of the Youth League's International Liaison Department by 1957 and the director by 1959; he held this position until 1964.

In addition to serving as host for numerous youth delegations visiting China in the fifties and sixties, Ch'ien's important role in international youth liaison work was most clearly manifested by the large number of trips made abroad on behalf of one or both of the youth organizations. Between 1953 and mid-1965, Ch'ien made no less than 13 journeys abroad, trips that took him to 16 different nations. In general, his travels can be divided into two categories—those to Communist countries (or to events dominated

by Communists) and, secondly, to the Afro-Asian nations. Thus, Ch'ien participated in delegations sent by China to meetings or youth "festivals" sponsored by either the World Federation of Democratic Youth (WFDY) or the International Union of Students (both Communist-backed) in Rumania (July–August 1953), Sweden (January 1954 and February 1961), the U.S.S.R. (July–August 1957 and July 1961), Austria (July–August 1959), Finland (February 1961 and July–August 1962), and Czechoslovakia (November 1961). It was while he was in Rumania in July 1953 that he was elected as a secretary of the WFDY (at the third congress of this organization). It is not certain how long he held this position, but presumably he relinquished it by the middle or late fifties.

As the Chinese Communists became more involved with the Afro-Asian nations in the mid-1950's, they naturally began to participate in (and often initiate) meetings to gather together peoples from the Afro-Asian world. One of the first endeavors in this field was the 1955 Asian Countries Conference (see under Yang Shuo), later altered to "Afro-Asian Solidarity Conferences" (see below). It was in this vein that Ch'ien led a group to Jakarta in May–June 1956 to attend meetings of the International Preparatory Committee for the Afro-Asian Students' Conference. He went in his capacity as secretary-general of the All-China Students' Federation, although he does not appear to have had any later affiliation with this organization. Perhaps his most important assignment in promoting Afro-Asian relations occurred over the winter of 1963–64 when he led a "youth friendship" delegation to six African nations. From late November 1963 to the end of January 1964 the group toured Mali, Ghana, Senegal, Tanganyika, Kenya, and Somali, visits that took place at a time when the Chinese were vigorously attempting to garner support for their policies in Africa. It is also noteworthy that these visits took place just a few weeks or days before Chou En-lai visited three of these nations (Mali, Ghana, and Somali).

Ch'ien's next two trips into the Afro-Asian world were at a higher level than youth "friendship" tours. In May 1965 he was a member of the Chinese delegation to the Fourth Afro-Asian People's Solidarity Conference in Ghana. The Chinese group was led by Central Committee member Liao Ch'eng-chih, one of Peking's most influential figures in the promotion of Afro-Asian ties. In the following month, Ch'ien served as an adviser to the government delegation led by Premier Chou En-lai to the Second Afro-Asian Conference scheduled to be held in Algiers. Whereas the "Solidarity" conferences have ostensibly been non-governmental, the Afro-Asian Conference was to be the direct heir of the famous governmental Bandung Conference of 1955. However, owing mainly to a coup in Algiers just prior to the scheduled opening of the conference, it was not held. The Chinese delegation, therefore, never proceeded beyond Cairo.

Apart from those trips already described, Ch'ien also led a youth delegation to the Fourth National Conference of the Cuban Socialist Youth League in April 1960. Early in the next month he took his group to Chile at the invitation of Chile-China Cultural Institute to attend a celebration sponsored by the Institute to commemorate the anniversary of the famous Chinese May Fourth Movement. Ch'ien was to have made a trip in May–June 1964 to Japan at the invitation of the Japan-China Friendship Association (in Tokyo). However, because the Japanese authorities would not permit the entry of Ch'ien's group into Japan, the visit was cancelled.

In view of this extensive record of contacts abroad, it is not surprising that Ch'ien has assumed several positions in the many organizations in Peking devoted to one or another aspect of foreign relations. A list of these posts is as follows: member, Afro-Asian Solidarity Committee of China, July 1958. Promoted to a vice-chairmanship, June 1965; member, Board of Directors, China-Iraq Friendship Association, September 1958 to date; member, Standing Committee, China-Latin American Friendship Association, March 1960 to date.

He also served on an *ad hoc* committee formed in April 1963 to "receive and settle Chinese nationals victimized in India," which, as the title suggests, pertained to the aftermath of the Sino-Indian border conflict of late 1962 following which a number of Chinese nationals in India emigrated to Communist China. Ch'ien has also held one position in the national government, serving on the Third National Committee of the CPPCC as a representative of the All-China Youth Federation. He was elected to the post in 1959, but he was not returned to the Fourth Committee that opened in December 1964.

In 1964 and 1965 both of the major youth organizations underwent major changes of top echelon personnel. Ch'ien lost all his posts in both of the Youth League and the Youth Federation. However, as already described, it was after these events that he made the two important trips to Africa in 1965 in the company of such top leaders as Liao Ch'eng-chih and Chou En-lai. It is apparent, therefore, that he has advanced to a level of authority beyond the youth organizations. His long ties in international liaison work suggest that he will continue in this line of activity, possibly in some capacity in the Foreign Ministry or in a Party organization related to foreign affairs.

Ch'ien San-ch'iang

(1913–   ; Shao-hsing, Chekiang). Nuclear physicist; director, Institute of Atomic Energy, Academy of Sciences.

Ch'ien San-ch'iang (often romanized as Tsien San-tsiang) is Communist China's leading nuclear physicist. Trained in France, he has been a leader in the program that led to the detonation of China's atomic device in 1964 and has been a senior figure in the Academy of Sciences. Ch'ien was born in October 1913. There is conflicting information about his birthplace; some sources list Peking whereas others give Shao-hsing, Chekiang. However, a student directory published in 1937 by Ch'ien's alma mater, Tsinghua University, states that he comes from Wu-hsing, Chekiang, the birthplace of his father, Ch'ien Hsuan-t'ung, who was a scholar and one of the leaders of the May Fourth Movement. Young Ch'ien graduated from the Physics Department of Tsinghua University in 1936, and after engaging briefly in research work in Peking he went to France to pursue his study of nuclear physics. There, from 1937 to 1944, he studied at the famous Curie Laboratory, receiving his doctorate in 1943. Ch'ien remained in Paris until 1947 where he continued his research; in 1946 he won the physics award from the French Academy of Sciences. It was also in 1946 that he served as a technical expert to the Republic of China's delegation at the UNESCO General Conference in Paris, and in this same year he joined the board of directors of the Communist-front World Federation of Scientific Workers.

Ch'ien returned to China in 1948 where he assumed a teaching post in physics at Peking University. He remained in Peking in 1949 when the Communists came to power and in April of that year was a member of the delegation to the Communist World Peace Congress in Prague, visiting the Soviet Union en route. In the next month he was elected to the Standing Committee of the All-China Federation of Democratic Youth, a post he held until the Third Congress of the Federation in 1958. In the same year he became a member of the World Federation of Democratic Youth, the international organization to which the Chinese Federation is affiliated.

In the summer of 1949 the Communists began detailed preparations for the establishment of the central government as well as for many professional organizations. Ch'ien served on the Preparatory Committee of the CPPCC, which was established in June under the chairmanship of Mao Tse-tung; he subsequently became a member of the First National Committee of the CPPCC from its first session September 1949 when the central government was inaugurated. In early 1953 he was elevated to the Standing Committee, the governing body of the CPPCC when the National Committee is not in session. More important, however, was his participation in the initial steps to reorganize the Chinese scientific community. This was begun in July 1949 at a nationwide conference of scientists, at which time a preparatory committee was established with Ch'ien as one of the members. One year later (August 1950) the All-China Federation of Scientific Societies was brought into being at another conference of scientists. Ch'ien was named to the Standing Committee of this organization, as well as to the Planning Committee. In September 1958 the Federation was merged with another scientific organization to form the China Scientific and Technological Association; from that date to the present he has been a member of its National Committee. Subordinate to the Federation (and later the Association) are a number of professional societies, one of them the China Physics Society of which Ch'ien has been a vice-chairman since January 1952.

It was also in 1949 that Ch'ien joined two of the most active of the "people's" organizations, the China Peace Committee and the Sino-Soviet Friendship Association. He served on the National Committee of the former until 1958 and on the Executive Committee of the latter until 1954. In October 1949 he received his first post under the new government when he was appointed to membership on the Culture and Education Committee of the Government Administration Council (the cabinet). By the spring of 1950 he was known to be the head of the Physics Department at his alma mater, Tsinghua University.

Since the spring of 1950 Ch'ien has held a series of important posts in the Academy of Sciences. The first was as deputy director of the Planning Bureau; he was appointed to this post in May 1950 and by 1954 had become the director, a position he may still hold. It was also in May 1950 that he was named as deputy director of the Institute of Modern Physics, and in March 1951 he was promoted to the directorship. (In 1958 the Institute was renamed the Institute of Atomic Energy.) In 1954 he became a secretary-general of the Academy, but by 1959 another man succeeded to this post and Ch'ien was made one of the deputy secretaries-general, a post he still holds. Since June 1955 he has also been a member of the Academy's Department of Physics, Mathematics and Chemistry, and from October of the same year he has served as a member of Science Awards Committee. For the *Kuang-ming jih-pao* of July 21, 1953, Ch'ien wrote an article summarizing the growth of the Academy of Sciences; a very similar article by him appeared in the English-language *People's China* (issue of September 16, 1953).

Although he is one of China's top scientists, Ch'ien has had to devote much of his time to politics, particularly in the early fifties. For example, he attended the Second World Peace Congress in Warsaw in November 1950 and in the same month he participated in a Communist youth conference in Vienna. The year 1952 was the high point of his involvement in political activities. In the spring of that year he was a member of a Communist-sponsored group that was charged with the task of investigating the alleged use by the United States of bacteriological warfare in the Korean War, although he himself did not go with the investigation group to Korea. In March 1952 he spoke at a meeting of the World Peace Council in Oslo where he reiterated the charges about "germ warfare." He visited Sweden briefly and then in May–June he attended a meeting in Austria of the Communist World Federation of Scientific Workers. In October he was an official member of the Chinese delegation to the Asian and Pacific Regions Peace Conference in Peking; at the close of the meeting he was one of the signers of a conference-sponsored declaration condemning the United States again on the "germ warfare" charges. In December 1952 he attended another World Peace Congress held in Vienna. From 1953 to 1955 he was a member of the World Peace Council, the permanent organization of the Communist international "peace" movement.

From February to May 1953 Ch'ien was in Moscow as head of a 26-member scientific delegation sent to study Soviet science and "to strengthen ties and cooperation" in scientific matters. This was the first large delegation of Chinese scientists to visit the Soviet Union. When Stalin died in March 1953, while Ch'ien was in Moscow, he was named to the official Chinese delegation led by Chou En-lai to attend the funeral. Several months after his return from Russia he presented a major report on his visit to the Soviet Union before a meeting of the Government Administration Council (January 1954).

Ch'ien was a deputy to the First NPC from Shantung. He was not elected to the Second NPC (1959–1964) but was again named as a Heilungkiang deputy to the Third NPC, which opened in December 1964. Although there are exceptions (see below), it appears that Ch'ien has been allowed to devote most of his time to scientific matters following his rather extensive political activities of the early 1950's. Early in 1956 the PRC adopted a broad scale 12-year scientific development plan. To implement this, the Scientific Planning Commission was established in March 1956, and from that date until November 1958 (when it was reorganized) Ch'ien served as one of the members under Chairman Ch'en I and, later, Nieh Jung-chen. It was also in March 1956 that Ch'ien was in

Moscow to attend a Bloc conference dealing with the establishment of the Joint Institute for Nuclear Research, which was set up at Dubna near Moscow. Apparently Ch'ien played a major role in this institute, because in May 1957 he spoke before a meeting in Peking of the Academy of Sciences, which dealt with China's participation in the Dubna Institute.

In mid-1957 Ch'ien participated in the "rectification" campaign when he severely criticized fellow intellectuals Tseng Chao-lun and Ch'ien Wei-ch'ang. In November 1957 he was a deputy leader of a "working people's" delegation sent to the USSR to commemorate the 40th anniversary of the Russian Revolution. Among the other delegations sent to the Soviet Union at the same time was a scientific group led by Kuo Mo-jo—there is little doubt that Ch'ien took part in the extensive negotiations that were conducted with Soviet scientists at this time. He was again in the Soviet Union at the end of 1960 to attend another meeting held at the Dubna Nuclear Institute.

In recent years, the fact that Ch'ien has not been frequently in the news suggests that he has been devoting most of his time to purely scientific matters. On occasion, however, he has lent his name to such ceremonial committees as one established in September 1961 to commemorate the 50th anniversary of the 1911 Revolution. In addition to his purely scientific writings, he is also the author of articles on science for popular consumption — as in the *JMJP* of October 11, 1959, when he wrote on the developments in China of atomic energy for peaceful purposes. Similarly, in mid-1962, he was mentioned among a group of prominent scientists who had been giving public lectures in Peking. He has also occasionally served as a host for scientific visitors to China; for example, in October–November 1962 he was mentioned several times in the press in connection with the visit to China of the head of the Theoretical Physics Institute in Copenhagen.

Since his days in France he has worked closely with his wife, Ho Tse-hui, a prominent physicist in her own right, said to be the co-disoverer with Ch'ien of new techniques to split uranium atoms, which were developed during their days in France. For her work in China, she was awarded a third class prize in 1956 by the Academy of Sciences. Like her husband, she has been partially involved in political work under the PRC. From 1953 to 1957 she was an alternate member of the Executive Committee of the All-China Federation of Democratic Women, and since 1957 she has been a full member. In June 1953 she attended the Communist-sponsored World Congress of Women in Copenhagen. She has also been a member of the National Committee of the China Peace Committee since 1958 and a deputy from Honan to the Second NPC (1959–1964) and the Third NPC (1964 to date).

Ch'ien Ying

Important woman leader; deputy secretary, CCP Central Control Commission; member CCP Central Committee.

A guerrilla leader in central China during the Sino-Japanese War, Miss Ch'ien Ying was active during the early years of the PRC in central-south China where she specialized in Party and government supervisory and disciplinary work. She has continued this activity since her transfer to Peking in 1952 and has been a member of the Party Central Committee and a deputy secretary of the Central Control Commission since 1956.

Ch'ien is said to have joined the CCP in 1933. She was then imprisoned for a time at the headquarters of the Nanking gendarmerie because of her radical political activities. In 1938 she was among a small group of Party workers trying to establish a rural CCP base in Central Hupeh. Two of her associates there were T'ao Chu (q.v.) and Yang Hsueh-ch'eng, a former Tsinghua University youth leader who joined the CCP in 1936 and died of tuberculosis on the Hupeh front in 1944. According to Ch'ien, in 1938 the Party cell in central Hupeh was very small and was armed with only "eight rusty old guns."[1]

Ch'ien was not reported again until December 1949 when she was identified as a deputy director of the Organization Department of the CCP's Central-South Bureau and as the secretary of the Bureau's Women's Work Committee. She was in central-south China from that time until late 1952, holding posts with the Central-South Military and Administrative Committee (CS-MAC; the regional government established in February 1950), as well as with the Party Bureau. She was a member of the CSMAC until November 1952, a vice-chairman of its People's Supervision Committee from March 1950 until February 1951, and director of its Personnel Department from September 1951 until November 1952. Ch'ien's work for the latter two organs was complemented by her Party post as a deputy secretary of the Central-South Bureau's Discipline Inspection Committee (c.1951–1952). The regional Inspection Committees were the predecessors of the more authoritative Control Commissions which were set up at the March 1955 Party Conference, when Kao Kang's (q.v.) purge was announced. By June 1952 Ch'ien had been promoted from deputy director to director of the Bureau's Organization Department, succeeding Li Hsueh-feng (q.v.).

During her time in central-south China Ch'ien was also active in the mass organization for women, the All-China Federation of Democratic Women. She became a member of its national Executive Committee in 1950 and by August 1951 was chairman of its Central-South branch.

Ch'ien was transferred to Peking in November

1952 when she was appointed a vice-chairman of the People's Supervision Committee of the Government Administration Council (the cabinet). From 1953 she held a parallel, national-level position as deputy secretary of the CCP Discipline Inspection Commission. She probably relinquished this post at the Party Conference in March 1955 when the Discipline Inspection Commissions were replaced by Control Commissions (as noted above).

Ch'ien was a deputy from Shantung to the First NPC (1954–1959), which established the constitutional government in September 1954. During the second through fifth sessions (1955–1958) she served on its Motions Examination Committee. As part of the government reorganization in 1954 the People's Supervision Committee on which Ch'ien had served was abolished and its functions were transferred to the newly created Ministry of Supervision. Ch'ien was given the new portfolio and for the next five years devoted much of her time to this post. In this capacity she made major reports at the annual national supervisory conferences. Her role in reorienting the mechanisms of control over Chinese industry is discussed at length in Franz Schurmann's *Ideology and Organization in Communist China*.

At the Party's Eighth Congress in September 1956, Ch'ien's importance in the CCP elite was reaffirmed. She was a member of the Congress presidium (steering committee) and spoke on the "struggle against bureaucracy." At the close of the meetings she was one of only four women elected to full membership on the Central Committee. The measure of her importance can be gauged from the group in which she was now included: Mmes. Li Fu-ch'un (Ts'ai Ch'ang) and Chou En-lai (Teng Ying-ch'ao), and Miss Ch'en Shao-min (qq.v.), three of the top women leaders of the CCP. At the First Plenum of the new Central Committee, held the day after the Congress closed, Ch'ien was made a deputy secretary of the Party's Central Control Commission, which is headed by Party veteran Tung Pi-wu (q.v.). At the time of her appointment she was the only woman among the five deputy secretaries. When a Standing Committee within the Control Commission was created in 1961, Ch'ien was made one of its members.

In June 1957 Ch'ien delivered an important report before the State Council on a case of mismanagement in Kwangsi, which had led to widespread starvation, and as a consequence Kwangsi Party First Secretary Ch'en Man-yuan (q.v.) was removed from his post. Ch'ien's only recorded trip abroad took place in November 1958 when she attended celebrations in Moscow marking the 41st anniversary of the Russian Revolution. She was a deputy leader of the delegation led by Liu Lan-t'ao (q.v), a fellow deputy secretary of the Central Control Commission.

Miss Ch'ien also continued her involvement in women's work. In April 1953, at the Second Congress of the All-China Federation of Democratic Women, she was again elected to the Executive Committee. During the same year she was a member of the Committee to Implement the Marriage Law. When the Women's Federation held its Third Congress in 1957, Ch'ien was re-elected to the Executive Committee.

Ch'ien was re-elected to represent Shantung in the Second NPC (1959–1964), and during its second, third, and fourth sessions she again served on the NPC Motions Examination Committee. At the inaugural session of the NPC, held in April 1959, her Ministry of Supervision was abolished. However, at this same time she received a comparable post when she succeeded Party veteran Hsieh Chueh-tsai (q.v.) as minister of Internal Affairs, but then in November 1960 she was replaced by Tseng Shan (q.v.). Since then she has been reported in the press only infrequently. Most of her time has probably been spent in connection with the Control Commission, an organ rarely mentioned in the press. However, in late 1964 she was elected a deputy from Hupeh to the Third NPC. At the close of its initial session in January 1965, Ch'ien was elected to the NPC Standing Committee.

Ch'ien is the author of a brief but useful historical essay on the role of the CCP in central-south China from the twenties to the early 1950's. Written for the July 1, 1951, issue of the *Ch'ang-chiang jih-pao* (Yangtze daily) to commemorate the 30th anniversary of the CCP, it was reprinted in an important collection of articles published in the same year.[2]

---

1. Chiang Nan-hsiang *et al., The Roar of a Nation* (Peking, 1963), pp. 152–153.
2. *Chung-kuo kung-ch'an-tang tsai chung-nan-ti-ch'ü ling-tao ko-ming tou-cheng te li-shih tzu-liao* (Historical materials on the revolutionary struggles led by the CCP in central-south China; Wuhan, 1951), I, 3–8.

Chin Chung-hua

(1902–   ; Chia-hsing, Chekiang). Vice-chairman, All-China Journalists' Association.

· Chin Chung-hua is one of Communist China's more prominent journalists, a profession he has followed since the thirties. He spent the war and postwar years in Shanghai, Hong Kong, Kweilin, and Chungking, and since the establishment of the PRC he has worked principally in Shanghai. In postwar years he has traveled abroad on numerous occasions, usually to attend meetings of the World Peace Council or the International Organization of Journalists.

Chin was born in February 1902 in Chia-hsiang, in northern Chekiang midway between Shanghai and Hangchow, the capital of Chekiang.

After receiving his B.A. degree from Hangchow Christian College, he engaged in editorial work in Shanghai for the Commercial Press and the K'ai-ming Book Company, two of China's most important publishing firms. Perhaps his most important work in Shanghai was as an editor of *Shih-chieh chih-shih* (World knowledge), a semi-monthly (later a weekly) that published articles for popular consumption on international affairs. Together with Hu Yü-chih (q.v.), also a left-leaning journalist, he worked with *Shih-chieh chih-shih* from its founding in September 1934 until it was evacuated to Wuhan in January 1938 in the wake of the Japanese attack on China. In later years (see below), Chin was again associated with this journal.

For a brief period in 1936 Chin was in Hong Kong with leftist journalist and publisher Tsou T'ao-fen publishing the *Sheng-huo jih pao* (Life daily). Chin soon returned to Shanghai, however, where he became associated with still another publication, the *Kuo-min chou-k'an* (National weekly). Among his colleagues on the latter were the well-known lawyer, Chang Chih-jang (q.v.), and Miss Shen Tzu-chiu, later the wife of Hu Yü-chih. Chin spent the years from 1938 to 1941 in Hong Kong, where he was chief editor of the influential *Hsing-tao jih-pao*. From 1939 to 1941 he was also a member of the International Committee of the Chinese Industrial Cooperatives, better known by its abbreviated name "Indusco," an organization that attempted to stimulate the manufacture of small producer and consumer goods in China after the loss of the main industrial centers to the Japanese (see under Meng Yung-ch'ien). When Hong Kong fell to the Japanese in late 1941, Chin went to Kweilin, where from 1942 to 1944 he edited a daily. The fall of Kweilin to the Japanese in November 1944 again forced Chin to move, this time to Chungking, where from 1944 to 1946 he was in charge of translation for the Press Monitoring Section of the U.S. Office of War Information (OWI). An American colleague of his at this time asserts that he was completely fluent in English.[1] After the war ended he went back to Shanghai, where from 1946 to 1948 he continued to be in charge of translation, now with the U.S. Consulate General. In this same period he again served as an editor for the *Shih-chieh chih-shih* that had resumed publication in Shanghai at the end of 1945. Chin stayed in Shanghai until 1948 when he went to Hong Kong, where he worked as a free-lance writer. Although he had long been associated with "progressive" or left-inclined publications, the exact date he joined the CCP is not known. Eric Chou, a former writer for the Communist *Ta-kung pao,* claims that Chin was already a Party member when he worked for the Americans in Chungking.[2]

Chin left Hong Kong and made his way to Communist-controlled areas in north China in March 1949 and by the following month was in Peking. His first assignment was to accompany Kuo Mo-jo to Prague to attend the World Peace Congress in April. Upon his return home he was assigned to Shanghai, where he had worked for many years. There he became a cultural and educational adviser to the Shanghai Military Control Commission. He returned to Peking to participate in the formation of the "mass" organizations and the central government in the summer and fall of 1949. Chin attended the meeting in July 1949 that established the Preparatory Committee of the All-China Journalists' Association (ACJA); he was elected at this time to membership on the Preparatory Committee, and in this capacity attended the inaugural session of the CPPCC in September, the organ that brought the new central government into existence (October 1). He was elected a member of the First National Committee of the CPPCC, holding this post until the Second Committee was formed in December 1954. Chin also received posts in two important "mass" organizations. In October 1949 he was elected a National Committee member of the China Peace Committee, an affiliate of the World Peace Council in which he has been quite active. Almost 16 years later (June 1965), he was elevated to a Peace Committee vice-chairmanship. Also in 1949 he was appointed to membership on the Board of Directors of the Chinese People's Institute of Foreign Affairs upon its establishment in December, another post he still holds.

By the latter part of 1949 Chin was back in Shanghai where, aside from occasional trips to Peking, he has since worked. To govern east China the Communists formed in early 1950 the East China Military and Administrative Committee (ECMAC), known from December 1952 until its dissolution in 1954 as the East China Administrative Committee (ECAC). During this four-year period Chin was a member of the ECMAC-ECAC, a deputy director of the Culture Department, and a member of the Culture and Education Committee. Closely related to his work in culture and education was his assignment from 1949 as a vice-chairman of the Shanghai chapter of the Preparatory Committee of the nationwide ACJA. Moreover, he once again became associated with *Shih-chieh chih-shih* when it resumed publication in Shanghai in September 1949, serving briefly as the editor, but presumably relinquishing the post when the publication was moved to Peking in 1950. Concurrently, he was chief editor of the Shanghai *Hsin-wen jih-pao* (News daily) from 1949 to 1952, after which he became managing director. An English-language version of this paper, known as the *Shanghai News,* was also published under Chin's editorship from mid-1950 until it was closed down at the end of 1952.

As already described, Chin had gone to the

World Peace Congress in Prague in 1949. Over the next decade and a half he made numerous other trips abroad and by the mid-sixties had become one of the most widely traveled Chinese Communist leaders. Because of Chin's extensive experience in dealing with foreigners and his journalistic background, most of his journeys were related to either the promotion of the Communist-backed international "peace" movement or to the activities of the international front organization for journalists, the International Organization of Journalists (IOJ). Including his 1949 trip to Czechoslovakia, Chin led or was a member of 26 delegations between 1949 and 1964. These trips are summarized as follows:

1950: member, delegation led by Kuo Mo-jo to the Second World Peace Congress, Warsaw, November; 1952: member, delegation led by Sung Ch'ing-ling to the Congress of Peoples for Peace, Vienna, December; 1953: deputy leader, fourth sub-group of the delegation led by Ho Lung to "comfort" the CPV in North Korea, October–November; member, delegation led by Shen Yen-ping to a World Peace Council (WPC) meeting, Vienna, November; 1954: member, delegation led by Kuo Mo-jo to an extraordinary session of the WPC, East Berlin, May; member, delegation led by Liu Ning-i to a WPC meeting, Stockholm, November–December; 1955: member, delegation led by Kuo Mo-jo to the Asian Countries Conference, New Delhi, April; 1956: leader, delegation to the International Meeting of Journalists (sponsored by the IOJ), Helsinki, June; 1957: member, delegation led by Kuo Mo-jo to Afro-Asian Solidarity Conference, Cairo, December 1957–January 1958; 1958: leader, delegation to the Fourth Congress of the IOJ, Rumania, May; member, delegation led by Kuo Mo-jo to the Conference on Disarmament and International Cooperation, Sweden, July; 1959: member, delegation led by Liao Ch'eng-chih to the All-India Afro-Asian Solidarity Conference, Calcutta, April; member, delegation led by Kuo Mo-jo to an extraordinary session of the WPC, Stockholm, May; presumably attended a session of the Executive Committee of the IOJ, Varna, Bulgaria (at which time he was elected an IOJ vice-president), July; 1960: attended the Third Iraqi Peace Congress, March–April; member, delegation led by Liao Ch'eng-chih to the Second Afro-Asian People's Solidarity Conference, Conakry, Guinea, April; leader, delegation to "Second World Journalists' Gathering" (presumably sponsored by the IOJ, but not to be confused with an IOJ Congress), Baden, Austria, October; attended celebrations marking the 43rd anniversary of Russian Revolution, Moscow, November; 1961: member, delegation led by Liu Ning-i and Liao Ch'eng-chih to a WPC meeting, New Delhi, March; 1962: member, delegation led by Chu Tzu-ch'i (q.v.) to a presidential committee meeting of World Peace Council, Vienna, March;

deputy leader, delegation led by Shen Yen-ping to the World Congress for General Disarmament and Peace, Moscow, July; leader, delegation to Fifth Congress of the IOJ, Budapest, August; 1963: leader, friendship delegation to Cuba, July–August; 1964: leader, art troupe that toured in France, West Germany, Switzerland, Italy, Belgium, and the Netherlands, February–July; leader, peace delegation to Japan, November–December.

In 1952 Chin assumed two additional journalistic assignments. In that year the well-known English-language monthly *China Reconstructs* was established; Chin has been an editor since the journal began and since 1955 he has also chaired the Editorial Board. In October 1952 the China News Service (Chung-kuo hsin-wen she) was inaugurated with Chin as director. This news agency, not to be confused with the better-known New China News Agency, directs most of its dispatches toward the overseas Chinese community. It was probably for this reason that Chin was appointed in March 1957 to membership on the State Council's Overseas Chinese Affairs Commission, a position he continues to hold. In the middle and late fifties he received still more journalistic posts. In September 1954 he was elected a vice-chairman of the All-China Journalists' Association, and by 1955 he was chairman of its Shanghai branch. When he attended the IOJ meeting in Helsinki in mid-1956, he was elected a member of the IOJ Executive Committee; three years later, at the IOJ meeting in Bulgaria, Chin replaced Teng T'o (q.v.) as the Chinese vice-president of the IOJ. During the 1957–1958 "rectification" movement, Chin denounced numerous "rightists" in the field of journalism, and when Hsu Chu-ch'eng was purged in March 1958 as director of the important Shanghai *Wen-hui pao,* Chin replaced him. Like Chin, Hsu was a veteran journalist and had also worked for the U.S. Government in Shanghai. Already a top Communist journalist, with the assumption of this post on the important *Wen-hui pao,* Chin clearly moved to the forefront of journalism in the PRC's largest city—long the publishing center of China.

Although Chin's major assignments since 1949 have been in quasi-official organizations, he has also held governmental posts, both in Shanghai and in the national government. He became a vice-mayor of Shanghai in February 1953 and since 1954 has represented Shanghai in the NPC, serving in the First and Second NPC's (1954–1964), as well as in the Third NPC, which opened in December 1964. He has also been a vice-chairman of the Shanghai Committee of the CPPCC since 1955.

Reflecting Chin's extensive experience in foreign relations, he has held executive positions in five internationally oriented organizations since their formation: vice-president, China-Rumania

Friendship Association (FA), September 1958; Standing Committee member, China-Latin America FA, March 1960; Executive Committee member, China-Africa People's FA, April 1960, Council member, Asia-Africa Society of China, April 1962; and, Standing Committee member, Afro-Asian Solidarity Committee of China, June 1965. Representing one of these organizations, or Shanghai branches of such bodies as the China Peace Committee of the Sino-Soviet Friendship Association, Chin has been constantly in the news since the PRC was established in 1949. He is almost invariably a member of the many *ad hoc* committees set up to commemorate national or international Communist holidays (e.g., May Day), and he is frequently in the news when foreign visitors tour Shanghai. In fact, the very frequency with which he is reported in the press probably tends to inflate his actual importance as a political leader. In political terms he ranks considerably below many Chinese leaders who have served in Shanghai since 1949—such men as Ch'en I, Jao Shu-shih, K'o Ch'ing-shih, T'an Chen-lin, Tseng Shan, and Ch'en P'ei-hsien (qq.v.), all of whom have reached membership on the Party Central Committee. However, as a newsman of long experience he is unquestionably a journalistic figure of considerable stature and has apparently been one of the PRC's most effective spokesmen, both at home and abroad.

1. Interview held in Hong Kong, January 1964.
2. Eric Chou, *A Man Must Choose* (London, 1963), p. 140.

Chin Ming

(c.1903–   ; Shantung). Finance specialist; secretary, central-South China Bureau, CCP.

Chin Ming was a political and military leader in north Kiangsu during the Sino-Japanese War and a key Party official in Hunan in the early years of the PRC. After serving for eight years in Peking as a vice-minister of Finance he returned to the central-south region to work in the Party's Central-South Bureau.

Born about 1903 in Shantung, Chin reportedly received no more than a middle school education.[1] He has been in ill health for many years, but this has not prevented a rather active career that reaches back to at least the early 1940's. A 1958 Communist press report stated that he had long suffered from pleurisy and had "never quite recovered" from the "difficult days of his revolutionary work."[2] This statement probably referred to the early forties when Chin was secretary of the Party's Huai-Hai Committee and political commissar of the Huai-Hai Military District.[3] This area, located south of the Lunghai Railway and east of the Grand Canal in northern

Kiangsu, was under the control of Ch'en I's New Fourth Army. It was strategically important as a link between the areas controlled by the New Fourth Army and the Communist units in north China. Liu Shao-ch'i passed through the Huai-Hai district en route to Yenan in the spring of 1942; his discussions with the senior Huai-Hai officials are described in the biography of Liu Chen.

Nothing further was heard of Chin until the Communist conquest of Hunan in early August 1949. Late in that month the Hunan Military District was established, with Hsiao Ching-kuang as commander and Huang K'o-ch'eng as political commissar. Chin was one of the deputy political commissars under Huang. Aside from this military post, he held many other positions over the next three years in the Hunan government and Party organizations. In 1950 he became a member of the Hunan Provincial People's Government Council and chairman of its Land Reform Committee. In February 1952 he was promoted to vice-governor. In the Party he was a deputy secretary by October 1952, and when ranking secretary Huang K'o-ch'eng was transferred in late 1952, Chin replaced him. At about the same time he was made a member of the regional administration for this part of China, the Central-South Military and Administrative Committee, continuing in this post when it was redesignated the Central-South Administrative Committee in early 1953.

Few details are available about Chin's activities in central-south China aside from a press report that he spoke in January 1952 to a group of students and teachers who had participated in "land reform" work in Hunan. Yet his work must have attracted some attention in Peking, for in September 1953 he was transferred to the capital to become a vice-minister of Finance, a post he held for over eight years, serving briefly under Teng Hsiao-p'ing, and then under Li Hsien-nien (qq.v.). A former Finance Ministry employee asserts that he and his colleagues regarded Chin as the most important vice-minister, a supposition supported in the annual editions of the *Jen-min shou-ts'e* (People's handbook), which listed him first among the several vice-ministers. This same person claims that Chin specialized mainly in economic construction work and spent much of his time outside the Ministry coordinating with other government and CCP groups. He was regarded as adept in working with the Party apparatus—in short, he was a good "organization man."[4]

During Chin's tenure as vice-minister he was reported regularly in the press. He often attended conferences in connection with financial matters, as for example a conference on investments in July 1958, one of directors of finance departments in April 1959, and still another on "technical innovations" held in May 1960. Interviews of Chin occasionally appeared in the press,[5] as did articles by him, most notably one for *Hung-ch'i* (Red flag, November 16, 1960) entitled "How the Finance Work of People's Communes Serves Distribution," and another for the *JMJP* of December 1, 1960, "Effectively Supporting Agriculture Is a Political Task for Finance Departments."

In January 1961, at the Party Central Committee's Ninth Plenum, regional Party bureaus were re-created, apparently to regain some of the political and economic control that had been lost because of the excesses of the Great Leap Forward. In the next year or two a number of key leaders from many fields were transferred from Peking to serve in these bureaus. Presumably because of his familiarity with financial matters, Chin was sent to Canton, where by October 1961 he was identified as a deputy secretary of the Central-South Bureau under T'ao Chu (q.v.). (Two months later Chin was removed as a vice-minister of Finance.) By the early spring of 1965 he had been promoted to a full secretaryship in the Central-South Bureau, still serving under First Secretary T'ao.

Chin served as a deputy from his native Shantung to the Second NPC (1959–1964). However, because of his transfer, he was elected to represent Kwangtung in the Third NPC, which opened in December 1964. When the China-Laos Friendship Association was established in March 1963, a "Chin Ming" was appointed a member of the Council, but this probably referred to the Chin Ming who is one of the secretaries in the Union of Chinese Dance Workers.

---

1. Interview with former Finance Ministry employee, Hong Kong, July 1964.
2. *Builders of the Ming Tombs Reservoir* (Peking, 1958), p. 102.
3. *CB* 777, pp. 17–24.
4. Interview, see note 1.
5. Peking *Ta-kung pao*, August 18, 1959.

Ch'in Pang-hsien

(1907–1946; Wu-hsi, Kiangsu). A leader of the Russian-returned student clique; general secretary, CCP, 1931–1935.

Ch'in Pang-hsien was a leader of the "28 Bolshevik" clique of Chinese students who studied at Sun Yat-sen University in the second half of the 1920's, and he had close contact with the Comintern for a time. He was the Party's general secretary from 1931 to 1935 and participated in some of the major revolutionary episodes of the first two decades of CCP history. He was important as a Party theorist in the early thirties, and his career has become significant because Mao Tse-tung, in later times, made him a chief protagonist in the drama of his own rise to power.

The family of Ch'in Pang-hsien was native to

Wu-hsi, an important south Kiangsu city located on the Grand Canal, but Ch'in may have been born in Ning-po, Chekiang, where his father was a hsien magistrate for a number of years. When the boy was ten his father died and the family returned to the ancestral home in Wu-hsi, where Ch'in was brought up by his mother. After attending primary school in his native city he went to the Second Provincial Technical School in nearby Soochow and spent the years from 1921 to 1924 there, becoming president of the student union and joining the KMT and the Socialist Youth League. Indeed, Ch'in became so involved in student politics while he was in Soochow that he almost failed to graduate from the middle school. In the fall of 1924 he enrolled in the English Department at Shanghai University, an institution founded under the joint auspices of the KMT and the CCP in 1923 (see under Ch'ü Ch'iu-pai). In a short while Ch'in left the university to engage in full-time political work with Shanghai laborers; this plus his earlier university connections brought him in touch with Ch'ü Ch'iu-pai, Ch'en Tu-hsiu, Yun Tai-ying, and other young Communists who were then active in the city. Working also in the Propaganda Department of the KMT's municipal office, he joined the CCP about this time. The Communist Party sent him to Moscow in 1926 (according to Ch'in's official obituary), where he enrolled at Sun Yat-sen University. He became fluent in Russian during his four years in Moscow. Ch'in was also very interested in the theoretical courses on Communism offered at Sun Yat-sen and was one of only four Chinese students selected to attend courses at the "Red Institute of Teachers" for teacher training in the field. At the institute his Chinese colleagues were Ch'en Shao-yü, Chang Wen-t'ien, and Wang Chia-hsiang (qq.v.). In a sense the political careers of all four began while they were in Moscow, for it was there that their associations began and they first became leaders of the favored students of Comintern agent and Sun Yat-sen chancellor Pavel Mif. The group was afterwards known as the "28 Bolsheviks."

Ch'in was in Moscow for the Sixth CCP Congress of 1928. At the congress the impetuous young Hunanese Li Li-san became head of the CCP Propaganda Department and from this post came to dominate the Party in the next two years. Li's activities in China were not favorably viewed in Moscow by Stalin and the Comintern; hence it was to counter Li that Mif and his "28 Bolsheviks" returned to China late in the spring of 1930. Once in China, Ch'in went to work in the Shanghai office of the All-China Federation of Labor, headed by Lo Chang-lung (q.v.) and affected by the policies of Li Li-san. No sooner had they returned than the "28 Bolsheviks" made their opposition to Li felt in Communist circles. In June of 1930 four of them, Ch'in, Ch'en,

Wang Chia-hsiang, and Ho Tzu-shu, tried to get Li to alter certain of the views that he wished to make public in the form of a Politburo resolution. The attempts were unsuccessful and the resolution was published on June 11. Following this the four dissenters were said to have again strongly opposed Li at a top Party conference held in late June or early July. All four were subsequently censured for their actions, Ch'in being sent to "study."[1] However, by the end of the year he was more active than ever in the affairs of the Labor Federation, serving in its Propaganda Department and editing two labor newspapers in Shanghai.

The "28 Bolsheviks" attended the Third CCP Plenum called by Ch'ü Ch'iu-pai and Chou En-lai in September 1930 at Lu-shan, Kiangsi. Both men had returned from Moscow with the blessing of the Comintern not long before the plenum opened. Before the meetings closed Ch'ü and Chou capitulated to Li, leaving the Russian-returned students without sufficient support to block him, although Li had had strong opposition from labor leaders Lo Chang-lung, Ho Meng-hsiung (qq.v.), and their supporters. But in November 1930, through the combined efforts of the Comintern and its agent Mif, and assisted by his students and by Lo, Ho, and their followers, Li was finally ousted from high Party office and exiled to Moscow. In January 1931 the Fourth CCP Plenum was called in Shanghai by Mif and his students. While the plenum was in session in the first two weeks in January, the "28 Bolsheviks" took control of the principal Party offices, removing such Li Li-san supporters as Li Wei-han, Kuan Hsiang-ying (qq.v.), and Ho Ch'ang from the Party Central Committee. All three men soon joined forces with Mao Tse-tung in Kiangsi; Ho Ch'ang, who had been a leader of the CCP in the North China Bureau, became deputy chairman of the Red Army Political Department in Kiangsi (then headed by Wang Chia-hsiang) and was killed during the Long March. At the plenum it became evident that not only were Mif's protégés in opposition to Li Li-san's supporters, but they also did not wish to tolerate such political rivals as Ho Meng-hsiung, Lo Chang-lung, or Lin Yü-nan, a cousin of Lin Piao who was a supporter of Ho and Lo. Thus these men also left the Central Committee. Chou En-lai and Ch'ü Ch'iu-pai were forced to admit mistakes they had made in supporting Li at the Third Plenum but were then allowed to retain their Central Committee seats. So sharp did the political tensions become that, after the Fourth Plenum closed, Lo Chang-lung (who had persistently opposed calling the session in the first place), attacked the dictatorial and undemocratic spirit that had existed during the meetings, going so far as to request that the Comintern recall Mif to Russia.[2]

Despite the intensity of personal antagonisms

exhibited at the Fourth Plenum, little is known about the meetings themselves. They were held in secret for fear of Nationalist police, attendance must have been small, and, moreover, a number of the Party's important leaders were not in Shanghai to attend the sessions. Among those absent were such leaders as Mao Tse-tung, Chu Te, Ho Lung, and other young military activists who had already gone to the rural hinterlands and were building up Red military bases among the peasants. The Fourth Plenum achieved a major shift in top Party officers in Shanghai. It also chose an important Party bureau of 16 members and alternates to take charge of CCP operations at the Party headquarters. The nature of the new Party bureau remains uncertain. Mao Tse-tung in later times referred to it as a "provisional" Politburo. The Party headquarters in Shanghai continued to be the seat of the Central Committee; one source has likened this organization to a secretariat or standing committee formed to operate as a *de facto* Party organ.[3] The leading officers of the Shanghai Party bureau included Ch'en Shao-yü, generally thought to have been chief of the "28 Bolsheviks" group at this time. Serving with him was Ch'in, who became director of the Party Youth League's Propaganda Department. Shen Tse-min headed the Propaganda Department of the Party, and Chang Wen-t'ien at first took charge of work with the peasants but later took over organization work. At the Fourth Plenum, Ch'en, Ch'in, Chang, Shen, and Wang Chia-hsiang all became members of the Central Committee; the first three were also elected to the Politburo. The general secretary was Hsiang Chung-fa, a holdover from the Sixth Congress of 1928 who had been named to the post under Mif's direction because the Party needed a compromise candidate. Hsiang was weak and inoffensive, but retaining him in office may have given an air of continuing authority to the new leadership. Under his nominal direction the young "Bolsheviks" proceeded to launch a wide "reshuffle" of Party personnel at all levels, the changes becoming most apparent in Shanghai.

Ch'in Pang-hsien was 24 when the "28 Bolsheviks" took control of Party affairs in the urban centers where the headquarters could exercise its authority. The new leaders were young intellectuals from the privileged classes, fresh from four or more years of Marxian indoctrination in Moscow. Well versed in theory, they had had little revolutionary practice and any experiences they had gained in China were gained while working in the large cities. None of the group had worked with the peasants or undergone military training in the field, and in both of these areas other leaders of the Party were fast becoming experts. With such wide differences of training and background between the leadership in Shanghai and in the rural areas, it is perhaps not surprising that conflicts should develop between the two groups. In recent years Mao has made much of the rivalry that developed between his branch of the Party in Kiangsi and Shanghai.

In April 1931 Ch'in took over the position of secretary of the CCP Youth League, but he was to assume a more important role in the course of the year. In the spring of 1391 the head of the "special affairs unit" of the CCP, Ku Shun-chang, was arrested while on a visit to Wuhan. Ku turned traitor and disclosed the names of many of his colleagues. Thus in June Hsiang Chung-fa was captured and executed. These events forced Party workers in Shanghai to carry on at an even greater risk and a number of them were forced to leave Shanghai and join their comrades in the hinterlands. In 1931 Chou En-lai and a number of others went to southeast Kiangsi to join Mao Tse-tung and Chu Te. For a brief interval following the death of Hsiang it is generally believed that Ch'en Shao-yü took over chief responsibilities in Shanghai. But in a short time Ch'en and his wife returned to Moscow to continue work with the Comintern, and by September 1931 the Shanghai Party office was left to Ch'in Pang-hsien and Chang Wen-t'ien. We learn of the time of the change through the writings of Mao Tse-tung made public in the mid-forties. These speak of Ch'in as "the head . . . of the Party's provisional leadership in Shanghai" from September 1931,[4] which seems to be a euphemism for the post of CCP general secretary, although by this time it did not carry the power that it had had prior to the Sixth CCP Congress in 1928. Whatever the exact nature of the post, the importance of Ch'in's career is that he became a chief protagonist in a political controversy with Mao. At the time that Ch'in took over the Shanghai office, the Party headquarters served as the chief contact between the CCP and the Comintern, but from 1931 the importance of this contact diminished, and after the Fourth Party Plenum the Comintern was never again able to exert such influence over the internal affairs of the CCP.

The details of the conflict between the Party's Shanghai leadership and Mao remain unclear, with certain of the basic questions still unanswered. Not only is documentary evidence from the period meager, but the controversy did not even come to light until Mao Tse-tung chose to publicize it, and then he presented it in his own interests. The Russian-returned students have never publicly spoken in their own defense. In an earlier version of the translated works of Mao Tse-tung, Ch'in is described as the head of the CCP's "Provisional Central Political Bureau in Shanghai."[5] The word "provisional" obviously represents Mao's view that the bureau was chosen at a time when the Party did not hold a regular election. The most recent translations of Mao's writings reduce Ch'in's stature even more, naming him "head of the Party's provi-

sional central leadership in Shanghai."[6] Whatever his title, it is evident that when Ch'in took office in Shanghai the Party headquarters had come to be but a "pale shadow" of the growing authority and strength beginning to be exhibited by Mao and his supporters in southeast Kiangsi.[7] Two questions remain: if Ch'in, an inexperienced intellectual of 24, was only head of a "provisional leadership" how did he threaten Mao so seriously, and why has Mao chosen to make him an important figure in the political drama of the thirties?

Among the documents that contain evidence of a feud, there is a September 1, 1931, letter from the Party Central to the leaders of the Soviet Areas which was evidently meant especially for those leaders in Kiangsi. (It is notable that Mao dates Ch'in's ascendency over the Shanghai headquarters from September 1931.) This document would appear to mark the opening of the political struggle between the Ch'in leadership and Mao. Attributing the weaknesses of policies in the soviet areas to the continuing influence of "Li Li-sanism," it criticizes the absence of a clear and definite class line, among other things, and notes the lack of proper military strategy. In brief, the letter found that the Central Soviet Areas had been too lenient toward the rich peasant and too disposed to use guerrilla tactics instead of positional warfare.[8] Stuart Schram finds the struggle between Kiangsi and Shanghai "to have the same two basic themes that had characterized Mao's debates with the Central Committee ever since 1927: agrarian policy; and the relation of guerrilla tactics to revolution in the cities."[9] Writing two years later for the Party journal *Tou-cheng* (Struggle; an edition published in Kiangsi in February 1933), Ch'in advanced ideas that have since formed part of Mao's reason for attacking him. Ch'in was critical of the so-called Lo Ming line. Lo Ming (q.v.), the provincial Party secretary in Fukien, had been fighting savage Nationalist attacks against his provincial Red troops and had been advocating certain policies less aggressive than the Ch'in leadership desired. This group considered Lo Ming "defeatist" in military tactics, and not sufficiently aggressive in his agrarian policy.[10] Ch'in's definition of the correct Party line, which he termed the "forward and offensive line," has been one of the major points criticized by Mao in recent times.

It is matter of record that Ch'in contributed frequently to the CCP literature in the Shanghai period and in the years before the Long March. Using his Party name, Po Ku, he wrote many theoretical articles of the kind already cited. A number of his writings also dealt with previous political controversies that had split the CCP in the middle 1920's when the Party was under the leadership of its first general secretary, Ch'en Tu-hsiu (q.v.).[11] While he was in Shanghai there is little reporting about his political activities, largely because of the need to conduct these underground. In July 1936, in an interview with American journalist Edgar Snow in north Shensi, Ch'in stated that while in Shanghai he led an organization of volunteer workers to join the 19th Route Army, the army that defended the city against the Japanese in 1932. He also reported that he organized strikes in the Shanghai cotton mills, which were broken up by the Japanese.[12]

Maoist historians date the closing of Party headquarters in Shanghai and the subsequent transfer of headquarters personnel to the Kiangsi Soviet as occurring sometime in early 1933. Presumably Ch'in moved to Kiangsi about this time, for it is known that Chang Wen-t'ien was forced to flee from Shanghai to Kiangsi early in 1933 and assumed that Ch'in did likewise. With the move to Kiangsi, evidence of political rivalry with the Mao leadership becomes visible in the shifting of important government and Party posts in favor of the "28 Bolsheviks." According to Mao, Ch'in now became head of the CCP "Central Political Bureau of the Red Base Areas."[13] Another "Bolshevik," K'ai Feng, arrived in Kiangsi early in 1933 to become secretary of the CCP Youth League. Ch'in was named to this post (as noted) in April 1931, so presumably K'ai took it over from his colleague when both transferred to Kiangsi. Chang Wen-t'ien now became chief of Party propaganda. In May 1933, Chou En-lai, who had been supporting Ch'in's "forward and offensive" line in military tactics, took over the post of political commissar of the Chu-Mao First Front Army. This shift must have dealt a blow to the Mao leadership, for the post had previously belonged to Mao himself.

Early in 1934 many of the CCP leaders were gathered in Juichin for two important meetings at which evidence of political conflict became even clearer. The Fifth Party Plenum (in session on January 18) was undoubtedly chaired by Ch'in as CCP general secretary. Mao gave none of the important speeches and one source suggests that he may not even have attended the Plenum.[14] Ch'in and Chang Wen-t'ien gave two of the key speeches, Ch'in's entitled "The current situation and the tasks of the Party." This dealt with policy matters, some of which Mao was later to cite as major issues in the controversy between the "28 Bolsheviks" and himself, one particular point being the Fukien Rebellion (that had just been put down by Chiang Kai-shek) and the Party's refusal to cooperate with the insurgents (see under K'ai Feng). According to Chang Kuo-t'ao, other issues between Mao and Ch'in were aired at the Plenum where Ch'in made an open attack upon Mao's agrarian policies in the Kiangsi Soviet as well as upon his concern with tactics of guerrilla warfare.[15] However, this information must be viewed with some reservation as Chang was not then in Kiangsi.

The second meeting in Juichin, the Second All-China Congress of Soviets, met in January–February 1934. Mao, as head of the Chinese Soviet Republic, chaired these meetings and gave the keynote and opening address, and Ch'in, on behalf of the CCP Central Committee, was spokesman for the Party. If there was conflict between the two groups at this congress it is not readily apparent from the available speeches, but the shifts of personnel in high government posts certainly suggest rivalry. Earlier, in November 1931 at the First All-China Congress of Soviets, only three of the more prominent "28 Bolsheviks" had been named to the newly created government organ, the Central Executive Committee (CEC). The three were Ch'en Shao-yü, Shen Tse-min, and Wang Chia-hsiang, who opened the first congress. Wang was probably the only "Bolshevik" to attend the congress. But when the second congress met, several "Bolsheviks" were named to the CEC, including Ch'in and his wife, Ch'en, Chang Wen-t'ien, and Wang Chia-hsiang. All but Ch'en were present. It is significant that both Ch'in and Chang were included on the new Presidium (a 17-member body in charge of daily government affairs when the larger CEC was not in session). But it is even more notable that Chang Wen-t'ien now succeeded Mao as chairman of the Council of People's Commissars—in effect, the head of the cabinet. At the same time, three men who had previously held cabinet posts but who in the meantime had been associates of Lo Ming in Fukien, were demoted or dropped. These men were Chang Ting-ch'eng, Teng Tzu-hui, and T'an Chen-lin (qq.v.).

According to one report the formal initiative for embarking upon the Long March was taken by the "28 Bolshevik" group.[16] Although their importance in engineering the March may be somewhat exaggerated, Mao has subsequently held the returned-student leadership responsible for errors in military strategy that almost doomed the expedition to failure on its first lap while the Red armies were crossing Kiangsi and southern Hunan into Kweichow. When the marchers reached Tsun-i in northern Kweichow in early January 1935, the military strategy was changed and Mao took charge of the conduct of the remainder of the March. The enlarged Politburo Conference at Tsun-i is now regarded as the moment when Ch'in was forced to surrender his high Party post. Here, according to the Maoist historians, steps were taken to reverse the mistaken "third left line" for which Mao has held the "28 Bolsheviks" responsible, and in the official view Mao was finally elevated to actual leadership of the CCP. The Communist accounts make much of Mao's becoming actual head of the CCP at Tsun-i, but they do not state what position he assumed nor explain why another of the "28 Bolsheviks," Chang Wen-t'ien, apparently took over the Party general secretaryship from Ch'in (see under Chang Wen-t'ien).

At an unspecified date in 1934, often thought to have been during the Long March, Ch'in is said to have taken over from Yang Shang-k'un (q.v.), another of his "28 Bolshevik" colleagues, as director of the Political Department of the First Front Army, the principal military force that accompanied Mao Tse-tung to north Shensi. But according to some of these reports, upon completion of the march in 1935, Yang resumed responsibility for the Political Department. However, as the dates of these changes are not specific, possibly Ch'in headed the Political Department from the time of the Fifth Plenum and the Second All-China Congress of Soviets and relinquished the post to Yang at Tsun-i. In either case, it remained in the hands of the defeated political group, possibly because at that time Mao could not get control of the entire power structure of the Red Army.

In the summer of 1935 while Mao Tse-tung and Ch'in were making the Long March, the Comintern held its Seventh Congress in Moscow. Although some of the Chinese who were named to the Seventh Comintern Executive Committee (ECCI) were not present for the meetings, six Chinese were elected. Ch'en Shao-yü, who was in Moscow and an official Chinese delegate, was made a full ECCI member. Ch'in became an alternate. He was very much in evidence in north Shensi when Edgar Snow visited there in the summer of 1936, giving him several long interviews from which much of the data on his early life has been taken. According to Snow, Ch'in was then "the youngest member of the Politburo," and the "minister of foreign affairs" as well as the "chairman" of the Northwest Government (evidently a forerunner to the Shen-Kan-Ning Border Government of 1937; see under Chang Kuo-t'ao). Both Snow and his wife Nym Wales, who saw Ch'in when she visited north Shensi a year later, were well aware that he had once been "secretary" of the CCP, which they seemed to equate with head of the Party apparatus. But it is noteworthy that in talking to Snow, Ch'in did not mention this and only said that in the Shanghai period he had belonged to the Party Central Committee. It was Snow's impression that at this time Ch'in was not very popular with the army and played no role in military affairs.[17]

Ch'in participated in the negotiations at Sian in December 1936 to release Chiang Kai-shek when he had been taken into custody by Chang Hsueh-liang and his Manchurian army. Chou En-lai, leader of the Communist negotiating team, did much of the work to bring about the General-issimo's release, and was assisted by Communists Yeh Chien-ying, Li K'o-nung (qq.v.), and Ch'in. The work of negotiator was to concern Ch'in for the remainder of his life. But before he turned to this work on a full-time basis, he returned to Yenan and for a brief time in 1937 served as director of the Party's Organization Department, relinquishing the post in the same year to Liu Shao-ch'i (q.v.). By the time the Sino-Japanese War began in mid-1937, Ch'in had been assigned to Nanking as one of the principal liaison officials with the Nationalists. There, before the city fell to the Japanese in November 1937, he conducted negotiations for the creation of the New Fourth Army, the Communist army to operate in central China. When Nanking fell, Ch'in followed the Nationalist government to Hankow, but he left the city before it was evacuated (October 1938) and preceded the government's move to Chungking, arriving there by the spring of 1938. In Chungking Ch'in was a member of the Party's Yangtze Bureau, which was then under the direction of Ch'en Shao-yü. Later Ch'in became chief of the CCP South China Bureau and director of the latter's Organization Department. However, these positions were somewhat nominal because the Communist Party was not very strong in south China during wartime, and the Party side of Ch'in's life while he was at the Nationalist capital was secondary to his role as a liaison official. From 1938 he served as a CCP delegate to the People's Political Council (PPC) where attempts were made to settle the growing political differences between the Communists and the KMT. In the later war years the CCP boycotted most of the PPC sessions, but Ch'in carried on his work for a time as a member of Chou En-lai's staff in Chungking. In this connection he was known to diplomats and foreign residents who were in Chungking during the war. Early in 1940 Ch'in took part in some of the negotiations with Nationalist General Ho Ying-ch'in, the War Minister, which were held outside the PPC and attempted to settle political differences with the Communists.

Late in 1940 Ch'in returned to Yenan to assist in a Party program to improve work in information and propaganda. As part of the program the *Chieh-fang jih-pao* (Liberation daily) was created in May 1941 as the key Party newspaper. Ch'in was appointed chief editor, and he also became director of the New China News Agency, which had been established in the late summer of 1937. In retrospect, it seems that Ch'in may have been recalled to Yenan in connection with the *cheng-feng* (or ideological remolding) movement which began in February 1942. When Mao opened the campaign he first began to attack publicly the "28 Bolshevik" group. However, he did not then refer to them by name and spoke in somewhat guarded terms, calling them foreign "dogmatists" (see under Ch'en Shao-yü). But as the campaign developed, the attack upon the Russian-returned student leadership became more open. According to Maoist historians the *cheng-feng* movement led the CCP cadres into long discussions held between 1942 and 1944 when the history of the Party was carefully reviewed, especially that period from 1931 to 1934 before the conference at Tsun-i when Mao established his superiority over Ch'in and the "28 Bolsheviks."[18] When Mao gave his speech entitled "Our Study and the Current Situation" before a meeting of senior cadres in Yenan in April 1944 (cadres who had undoubtedly been involved in the previous study meetings on Party history), he could afford to be more explicit. Speaking in a spirit of "learning from past mistakes to avoid future ones," and of "curing the sickness to save the patient," he pointed out that, from the Fourth Party Plenum to the Conference at Tsun-i, the leadership of the Russian-returned students had committed certain serious errors. (Later in the speech he said that these had cost the CCP "about 90 percent of the revolutionary forces" they had "built up with so much toil.") But he also conceded that not everything had been wrong. He granted legality to Ch'in's "provisional central leadership" formed in Shanghai in 1931 and to his leadership at the CCP's Fifth Plenum (January 1934), but Mao noted that the "procedures for the election" at these meetings were "inadequate" and should serve as object lessons for future Party leaders. The essence of Mao's thinking was adopted as a Party resolution by the CCP's Seventh Plenum held just prior to the Seventh Congress of April–June 1945.[19] Now the final blow was delivered. Ch'in Pang-hsien and Ch'en Shao-yü were named by name and said to have been guilty of left "dogmatist errors," a so-called "third left line" that had cost the Party so dearly in the period before the Long March. And though there was some distinction made between the actions of the two men in that Ch'en Shao-yü was held responsible for originating the mistaken line whereas Ch'in was criticized for carrying it out between September 1931 and the conference at Tsun-i, both were said to have opposed the "correct" policies that Mao had been trying to implement.

A year before the Seventh Congress Ch'in was one of the Party leaders who gave interviews to Chinese and foreign correspondents who flew from Chungking to Yenan in May 1944, the first large group of non-Communists to visit the Communist capital. Four months later Ch'in was interviewed by an American Foreign Service Officer in Yenan (September 1944) who identified him as a Politburo member and "in charge of propaganda" for the CCP. Ch'in, further described as "one of the Party's active policy makers," outlined the Communist views on the postwar treatment of Japan in the interview.[20] Notwithstanding this rather high estimate of Ch'in's role in the Party hierarchy, the important period of his career had clearly ended. By 1945 Lu Ting-i (q.v.) had succeeded to the directorship of the Propaganda Department, and Ch'in was re-elected only to the Party Central Committee at the Seventh Congress in 1945. It is noteworthy that his name was placed last on the list of 44 full Central Committee members.

In February 1946 Ch'in flew to Chungking to aid in the negotiations to release the former head of the Communist New Fourth Army, Yeh T'ing (q.v.), who had been a prisoner of the Nationalists since the disastrous New Fourth Army Incident of January 1941. Yeh was released in March and in the next month he, together with Party leaders Wang Jo-fei, Teng Fa, and Ch'in, enplaned from Chungking; on the way to Yenan the plane crashed in Shansi (April 8, 1946). At the time of his death a number of commemorative articles appeared in the Communist press,[21] indicating that although Ch'in's importance as a political leader had diminished, his record as a revolutionary was still honored.

In addition to his participation in many of the major developments of the first two decades of Chinese Communism, he contributed a substantial amount to the Party literature of the thirties, not only articles for the leading CCP journals but also a number of translations from Russian and English. These included the *Communist Manifesto, History of the Communist Party of the Soviet Union,* and works by Engels, Georgy Plekhanov, and Lenin's *Karl Marx.* Among his journalistic writings those on the earlier CCP controversies have been mentioned. A summary of some of the available writings of the Party Central when it was headed by Ch'in, as well as some of his articles and speeches written in the early thirties, is contained in Tso-liang Hsiao's *Power Relations within the Chinese Communist Movement, 1930–1934.* In prewar times Ch'in wrote for the edition of *Tou-cheng* published in Shensi (1936) and from March 1938 to early 1940 for issues of *Ch'ün-chung* (The masses) published in Hankow and in Chungking. However, any theoretical writing of significance by Ch'in ended before the opening of the *cheng-feng* movement. According to one writer, the last major appearance in print of the Russian-returned group was in 1939 when Ch'in and Ch'en Shao-yü "wrote articles on the 'imperialist war' in Europe and the United Front in China."[22]

Edgar Snow described Ch'in as one of the more "personable and interesting of the Communist leaders" whom he met. Above average height, thin and wiry, he had a high nervous laugh, and moved with tense, jerky bodily movements. "His mind was very quick and as subtle as, and perhaps more supple than, Chou En-lai's." He spoke Russian and some English and read English with ease.[23]

Ch'in was twice married and had seven children. His first wife, Liu Ch'ün-hsien, a native of Wu-hsi like her husband, had once been a worker in a cotton mill. They met while both were students at Sun Yat-sen University and she too belonged to the "28 Bolsheviks." Married in Moscow, she presumably returned to China with her husband in the spring of 1930. She was again with him in the Kiangsi Soviet and was elected a member of the Second CEC in January 1934. She also made the Long March. Sometime after 1936 the Ch'in's were divorced. Later he married Chang Yueh-hsia who has been a Standing Committee member of the All-China Federation of Supply and Marketing Cooperatives since mid-1954, and since the latter part of that year she has represented the cooperatives on the CPPCC National Committee. Chang was elected a member of the Asian Solidarity Committee of China in February 1956, and since September of the following year she has been a member of the Executive Committee of the National Women's Federation. At the time of Ch'in's death in 1946, three of his children lived in Yenan and four in Shanghai, but it is not known how many of these may have been the children of his second marriage.

---

1. Tso-liang Hsiao, *Power Relations within the Chinese Communist Movement, 1930–1934* (Seattle, Wash., 1961), pp. 133–134.
2. *Ibid.*, p. 135.
3. William F. Dorrill, unpublished manuscript, "Mao Tse-tung and the Chinese Communist Movement: 1927–35."
4. *Selected Works of Mao Tse-tung* (Peking, 1965), III, 222.
5. *Selected Works of Mao Tse-tung* (London, 1956), IV, 341.
6. *Selected Works* (Peking, 1965), III, 222.
7. Dorrill.
8. Hsiao, pp. 159ff.
9. Stuart Schram, *Mao Tse-tung* (New York, 1966), p. 137.
10. Hsiao, p. 232.
11. Chün-tu Hsüeh, *The Chinese Communist Movement, 1921–1937* (Stanford, Calif., 1960), *passim*.
12. Edgar Snow, *Random Notes on Red China, 1936–1945* (Cambridge, Mass., 1957), p. 17.
13. *Selected Works* (Peking, 1965), III, 222.
14. Charles B. McLane, *Soviet Policy and the Chinese Communists, 1931–1946* (New York, 1958), p. 41.
15. Nym Wales, *Red Dust* (Stanford, Calif., 1952), p. 14.
16. Robert C. North, *Moscow and Chinese Communists* (Stanford, Calif., 1953), p. 174.
17. Snow, p. 17.
18. *Selected Works* (Peking, 1965), III, 163.
19. *Ibid.*, pp. 177–225.
20. *Foreign Relations of the United States; Diplomatic Papers, 1944,* Vol. VI, *China* (Washington, D.C., 1967), pp. 585–587.
21. *"Szu-pa" pei-nan lieh-shih chi-nien-ts'e* (In memory of the martyrs who died in the accident of "April Eighth"; Chungking [?], 1946), *passim*.
22. Boyd Compton, *Mao's China* (Seattle, 1952), p. xxxvii.
23. Snow, pp. 15–18.

Ch'iu Ch'uang-ch'eng

(c.1912–   ; Juichin, Kiangsi). Military leader; specialist in artillery; minister, Fifth Ministry of Machine Building.

A veteran Red Army officer, Ch'iu Ch'uang-ch'eng was a top commander of the PLA Artillery Force in the 1950's, and since 1963 he has been minister of the Fifth Ministry of Machine Building. He was born in Juichin, Kiangsi, the famous Communist capital before the Long March began in 1934. He apparently had little or no formal education, for he was apprenticed to a carpenter when he was 11 years old. In the late twenties, when Ch'iu was in his teens, he joined the Red Army, presumably about the time that Mao Tse-tung and Chu Te made Juichin their headquarters. In the fall of 1933 he was a cadet in the first class of the newly established Red Army Academy (Hung-chün ta-hsüeh).[1] Ch'iu was a student in the Academy's Political Department together with Liu Tao-sheng (q.v.), who later became an important Chinese Communist naval officer. Ch'iu's whereabouts for the next nine years are not known, except for the fact that at sometime in this period he studied in a military academy in Moscow where he specialized in artillery.

Ch'iu was back in China by 1942 and in the ensuing years he reportedly served as a deputy commandant of a military school in Yenan and then as a deputy commander of an army corps. After the Sino-Japanese War ended he was assigned to Lin Piao's forces in Manchuria as an artillery officer, presumably serving under Chu Jui, who headed the artillery units until his death in 1948.

Nothing further was heard of Ch'iu until October–November 1951 when he was in Peking for the third session of the CPPCC. He attended the meetings as a representative of the PLA. Less than a year later, in August 1952, his association with the PLA was clarified when he was identified as a PLA Artillery Force deputy commander under Commander Ch'en Hsi-lien (q.v.). In the same month he was a member of a delegation led by Chou En-lai to Moscow, one of the most important groups sent abroad in the early years of the PRC. From mid-August to the end of September Chou and his colleagues negotiated for the return of the Chinese Changchun Railway and for the extension of the joint use by China and the Soviet Union of the naval facilities at Port Arthur.

In December 1954 Ch'iu was a PLA delegate to the Second National Conference of the Sino-Soviet Friendship Association. Less than a year later the Communists awarded military decorations and personal ranks. Ch'iu was given the Order of Liberation in September 1955 for his services in the postwar period (1945–1950), and in the next month he was identified as a lieutenant-general, the equivalent of a two-star U.S. Army general. He was identified as Artillery Force deputy commander as late as May 1955; concurrently, he became deputy political commissar by February 1954 and then, in March 1956, the political commissar. He was identified in the last-mentioned post as late as March 1957. According to an unconfirmed but plausible report Ch'iu succeeded to the command of the Artillery Force in 1959 when Ch'en Hsi-lien was transferred to Manchuria. The lack of information about Ch'iu in the late 1950's may have been due to a possible temporary transfer to Fukien opposite the Nationalist-held offshore islands, for in mid-1958 he was elected a deputy to the Second NPC from the Foochow Military Region. During the "Quemoy Crisis" of late summer and early fall 1958, the only real military force which the Communists brought to bear was artillery shelling. Ch'iu, an artillery specialist, may have been in command of these operations. In any case, he was back in Peking by the spring of 1960 and has presumably remained there since then. Then in September 1963 he was appointed minister of the newly established Fifth Ministry of Machine Building. No definition of the Ministry's functions has been published, but Ch'iu's background suggests that it may be in charge of some phase of armaments production. (Similar inferences can be drawn regarding the Fourth and Sixth Ministries of Machine Building which were also established at that time—see under the respective ministers, Wang Cheng and Fang Ch'iang.)

As noted above, Ch'iu was a PLA deputy to the Second NPC (1959–1964). However, in 1964 he was elected from his native Hunan to the Third NPC, which held its first session in December 1964–January 1965. At the close of the session he was reappointed to his ministerial post and was also named to membership on the National Defense Council, an advisory body with considerable prestige but little real authority. If in fact Ch'iu succeeded to the command of the Artillery Force in 1959, it seems likely that he relinquished it when he was given his ministerial portfolio in 1963. In any case, he was definitely replaced as the Artillery Force political commissar by February 1961, and by mid-1965 another man was identified as the commander.

Ch'iu's only known publication is an article in the Peking *Kuang-ming jih-pao* (Kwangming daily) on March 14, 1957, entitled "The Growth of the People's Artillery."

---

1. *Hung-ch'i p'iao-p'iao* (Red flag fluttering, Peking, 1957), III, 46.

Chou Chien-jen

(c.1887–   ; Shao-hsing, Chekiang). Biologist; vice-chairman, China Association for Promoting Democracy; governor, Chekiang Province.

Chou Chien-jen is not politically important in Communist China, but he holds a place of prominence owing to the fact that he is the younger brother of Lu Hsun (Chou Shu-jen), China's most famous 20th-century writer and a supporter of left-wing causes until his death in 1936. Chou's other brother, Chou Tso-jen, is an essayist and professor who headed the Education Department of the Japanese-sponsored North China puppet government during the Sino-Japanese War. Chou Chien-jen was born in Shao-hsing, Chekiang. Shao-hsing is the home of his two brothers and also of such prominent Chinese intellectuals as Ch'ien San-ch'iang and Fan Wen-lan (qq.v.). Chou came from a wealthy landlord-scholar family, which lost its money in 1894. Despite the family misfortunes, the three Chou brothers received university training, Chou Chien-jen as a biologist.

In contrast to his more famous brothers, Chou lived in relative obscurity until he went to Communist-controlled areas in the late 1940's on the eve of the Communist takeover of the China mainland. He spent most of these years as a biology professor and researcher in various universities, principally in Shanghai where he came into contact with the left-wing circles that included his brother Lu Hsun and the writer Mao Tun (Shen Yen-ping; q.v.).[1] During his years in Shanghai he also served as an editor for the Commercial Press, China's largest publishing house. Chou remained in Shanghai throughout the Japanese occupation (1937–1945) and then spent the year 1947–48 in Hong Kong. In 1948 he went to Communist-controlled north China where he was assigned to be a vice-chairman of the Textbook Editing Committee under the North China People's Government's Education Department.

Chou accompanied the North China People's Government when it moved to Peking shortly after the city fell to the Communists in January 1949. In the summer of that year the Communists initiated the first major steps toward establishing the new national government. In June, under the chairmanship of Mao Tse-tung, a Preparatory Committee for the CPPCC was established. Chou served as a member of this committee and was also named to a small sub-committee given the task of drafting the "Organic Law" for the new government, the law that was to serve as the constitution of the PRC until a formal constitution was adopted in 1954. When the first session of the CPPCC was convened in September 1949, he attended as a representative of the China Association for Promoting Democracy. It is one of the non-Communist political parties whose existence is intended to lend credence to the claims that the PRC is governed by a "united front" of political groups. Five years later (December 1954), Chou was named to membership on the Second National Committee of the CPPCC as well as on its Standing Committee; he served in a similar capacity under the Third CPPCC (1959–1964). When the Fourth CPPCC was formed at the end of 1964, Chou was again named as a representative of the China Association for Promoting Democracy, but he was not reappointed to the Standing Committee, probably because he was named at this same time to the Standing Committee of the more important NPC (see below).

When the new government and mass organizations were formed in the fall of 1949, Chou was given three assignments (all in October). He was named to the National Committee of the China Peace Committee (to July 1958) and to the First Executive Board of the Sino-Soviet Friendship Association (to December 1954). Under the Government Administration Council (the cabinet), he was appointed as a deputy to Hu Yü-chih (q.v.) in the Publications Administration, a body that existed until the constitutional government was inaugurated in 1954. From 1951 to 1954, Chou also headed the Publication Administration's Periodicals Office.

From the earliest days of the PRC, Chou has been a prominent figure in two of the non-Communist parties. In addition to the above-mentioned China Association for Promoting Democracy (CAPD), he has been associated with the China Democratic League (CDL). Both parties were formed in the forties (before the CCP came to power) and the membership of both is drawn largely from cultural and educational circles; the principal task of each is officially described as "uniting and remoulding intellectuals." In the CDL, Chou has been a Central Committee member since December 1949 and a Standing Committee member since December 1958. Also, from 1949 (presumably to date) he has been deputy director of CDL's Culture and Education Department. Within the CAPD, he had been a Standing Committee member since April 1950 and a vice-chairman since mid-1955. In addition, he has headed the CAPD's Culture and Education Department since April 1950.

As a trained biologist, the PRC has called upon Chou to lend his talents to the major efforts of the regime to promote the development of science. In June 1949 he was appointed to a preparatory committee for a large conference of scientists held the following month in Peking. From these efforts two national scientific organizations were established in August 1950—the All-China Federation of Scientific Societies and the All-China Association for the Dissemination of Scientific and Technical Knowledge (ACADSTK). Chou was named to Standing Committee membership on the latter, retaining this post until September 1958 when the two societies were merged (by which time he had been transferred to Chekiang—see below). Within the ACADSTK, he also headed the Propaganda Department from 1950 to 1958. In addition to his association with this ostensibly non-governmental society, Chou has also been affiliated with both national and provincial scientific bodies. At the national level he was a member of the State Council's Scientific Planning Commission from May 1957 to November 1958, and within Chekiang he has headed both the Chekiang Government's Scientific and Technical Work Committee and the provincial branch of the Academy of Sciences since 1958.

Although Chou was working in Peking at the time, he was appointed a vice-governor of his native Chekiang in February 1951. He relinquished the post in the fall of 1954 but later returned to become the governor (see below). In 1952 he made his only known trip abroad when, as a biologist, he was a member of the "mission for the investigation of American imperialists' crimes of bacteriological warfare" in North Korea. Led by Public Health Minister Li Te-ch'üan (q.v.), the mission visited Korea for three weeks in March–April 1952 when the Korean War was still in progress. The large delegation's visit was a major component of one of the most extensive propaganda campaigns ever staged by the PRC.

Chou was elected a deputy from Chekiang to the First NPC (1954–1959), the Second NPC (1959–1964), and the Third NPC that held its first session in December 1964–January 1965. For the First and Second NPC's he also served as a member of the governing Standing Committee, and then in January 1965 he was promoted to a vice-chairmanship of the Standing Committee. He has been a rather active NPC member, serving several times on the presidiums (steering committees) established to manage the affairs of the annual sessions. From October 1954 to February 1958 he was a vice-minister of the State Council's Ministry of Higher Education where he worked under Minister Yang Hsiu-feng (q.v.); he relinquished this position just one month after becoming the Chekiang governor. Also under the State Council Chou has been a member of a special committee formed in February 1956 to phoneticize the Chinese language, and from March 1958 to September 1959 he was a member of the Commission for Cultural Relations with Foreign Countries. There is also a counterpart "people's" organization—known as the Chinese People's Association for Cultural Relations with Foreign Countries—in which Chou has served as a Standing Committee member since December 1956.

Chou's rather unusual position within the PRC was illustrated during the "rectification" campaign of 1957–58. In the spring of 1957 he criticized certain practices of the CCP that he claimed had created a "gulf" and a "wall" between Party members and non-Communists. Many other non-Party intellectuals who spoke out in a similar vein were pilloried by the Party press throughout much of 1957–58. It is reasonable to assume that the regime has allowed Chou a greater latitude mainly because he is the brother of Lu Hsun whom the CCP has persistently attempted to picture as an ardent supporter of CCP policies prior to his death.

In late 1957, Chekiang Governor Sha Wen-han (q.v.), a Party member, was charged with "anti-Party activities" and purged as the provincial governor. Shortly after, in January 1958, Chou was made the new governor, a position he still holds. It is clear, however, that political authority in Chekiang does not rest in Chou's hands. Major political decisions in Chekiang undoubtedly pass through the provincial CCP Committee headed by alternate Central Committee member Chiang Hua (q.v.). Moreover, Chou spends more time than most governors in the national capital where, for example, he continues to devote some time to the China Association for Promoting Democracy or the China-Nepal Friendship Association that he has headed since its formation in September 1956. Even when in Chekiang he appears to spend most of his time in greeting visiting dignitaries, many of whom are sent to the province to visit the scenic capital at Hangchow.

Like his two brothers, Chou has been a rather prolific writer. In 1947 he translated Darwin's *The Origin of Species* (although it was not published until 1955), and in the following year he published a booklet on eugenics and racial discrimination and translated a work by Marx and Engels. Since the PRC came into existence he has also written on scientific subjects. In September 1949, for the inaugural issue of the important Party journal *Hsueh-hsi* (Study), he wrote an article on the contributions made to biology by T. D. Lysenko, the famous and controversial Soviet scientist who was supported in his theories by Stalin. Another typical article that he wrote appeared in the *Kuang-ming jih-pao* (April 2, 1964), the organ of the eight non-Communist parties in China; here Chou argued for the necessity to cast aside religious and superstitious beliefs.

Chou is married to Wang Yun-ju.

---

1. T. A. Hsia, *Enigma of the Five Martyrs* (Berkeley, Calif., 1962), pp. 40, 110.

Chou En-lai

(1898–   ; Huai-an, Kiangsu). Red Army veteran; ex-Foreign Minister; Premier; vice-chairman, CCP Central Committee.

Chou En-lai is one of the great political figures of modern China. He has an international reputation for his great skill as a negotiator, an art he has practiced for much of his career. Trained in Japan and France, Chou's early years in the CCP were primarily related to military affairs. Involved in the founding of the Red Army in 1927, Chou was the chief political officer for a portion of the Kiangsi Soviet period. After making the Long March, he spent most of the Sino-Japanese War years in Chungking as the senior liaison official to the national government, and he was also the senior Communist official in the postwar negotiations with the KMT. Chou has been premier of the PRC since 1949, and from 1949 to 1958 he was concurrently foreign minister. He gained world-wide attention at the Geneva Conference in 1954 and the Bandung Conference of 1955. Chou has been a CCP Politburo member since 1927 and is presently a vice-chairman of the CCP Central Committee. For most of the period from the late 1920's he has ranked among the three or four most powerful figures in the Communist movement.

Chou was born to a well-to-do gentry family. His parents had ties in both Shao-hsing, Chekiang (the ancestral home), and in Huai-an, Kiangsu, and it was in Huai-an that Chou was born. He was reared by uncles during his youthful and teenage years in Shanghai and Mukden. In his elementary school years in Mukden, Chou became acquainted with the works of reform-minded Chinese and Western political thinkers, and then from 1913 to 1917 he studied at the Nankai Middle School in Tientsin. One of his friends there was Ma Chün, who later became one of the earliest members of the CCP in Tientsin and who worked closely with Chou during the May Fourth period. Ma studied at Sun Yat-sen University in Moscow in the mid-1920's; he was secretary of the CCP Peking Committee in the fall of 1927 when he was apprehended and executed.[1]

In the fall of 1917 Chou went to Tokyo for further study. Wang Jo-fei (q.v.), who was for many years closely associated with Chou, also arrived in Tokyo at that time, but it is not known if they became acquainted then. Chou studied Japanese and audited courses at Waseda University (where Wang also studied), and then in 1918 he went to Kyoto. He was reportedly deeply influenced by the writings of Kyoto University socialist scholar Kawakami Hajime, but he apparently did not formally enroll at the school. Like so many of the politically motivated Chinese students in Japan, Chou returned home in the immediate wake of the May Fourth

(1919) Incident. He became a nominal student at Nankai University, but most of his time was spent in political work in Tientsin and, to a lesser degree, in Peking, two of the major centers of May Fourth activity. (For a description of Tientsin at this period, see under Teng Ying-ch'ao, who later became Chou's wife.)

For much of the next year and more, Chou was deeply involved in writing for and editing various student publications which sprang up in profusion during the May Fourth period. In September 1919 he was instrumental in setting up the Chueh-wu she (Awakening Society), which began to publish *Chueh-wu* (The awakening) in January 1920. The Awakening Society bore a marked resemblance to other organizations formed before and after the May Fourth Incident, including one established by Ts'ai Ho-sen and Mao Tse-tung in Changsha and another by Yun Tai-ying (qq.v.) in Wuhan. All these organizations later served as nuclei for the CCP, established in mid-1921, and most of them advocated work-and-study programs to help students study abroad (see under Ts'ai Ho-sen). Chou was also in touch with Party founder Li Ta-chao (q.v.) and his many student colleagues in Peking. Because of his agitation against police for the manner in which they handled student demonstrators, Chou was jailed in Tientsin for a few months in the early part of 1920.

Sometime in the latter half of 1920 Chou left for Paris as one of the students in the work-and-study program. He soon became acquainted with Ts'ai Ho-sen, Wang Jo-fei, Li Li-san, Li Wei-han, Ts'ai Ch'ang, Li Fu-ch'un, Nieh Jung-chen (qq.v.), and several other latter-day members of the CCP. Few of these young men and women were then Marxists, but within a brief time they became increasingly drawn to Communist doctrines. The work-and-study groups evolved in the 1921–22 period into French branches of the Socialist Youth League and the CCP. Chou spent little time in formal study or gainful employment but a great deal of time in various forms of political agitation among Chinese students. He was involved, for example, in attempts to get more funds from Chinese diplomats for the students and in the celebrated Lyons University demonstrations in 1921 (see under Wang Jo-fei and Li Li-san). The latter incident brought about the expulsion of many of the students, including Ts'ai Ho-sen and Li Li-san.

Chou was among the contributors to *Shao-nien* (Youth), a journal established in Paris in August 1922 and described in the biography of Ch'en Yen-nien. Chou then used the pseudonym Wu Hao, as he did in late 1924 in contributing articles to the important CCP journal *Hsiang-tao chou-pao* (Guide weekly). He joined the CCP in 1922 and, according to remarks made in Hanoi many years later, he also met Ho Chi Minh in Paris. Ho was "already a mature Marx-

ist," Chou commented, "and I had just joined the Communist Party. He is my big brother."[2] In addition to France, Chou also spent some time in England, Belgium, and Germany. Chu Te has related that in October 1922 in Berlin he sought out Chou, who assisted him in joining the CCP. Many of the students were also active members of KMT branches in Europe, and Chou is credited with being one of the more important members of branches in both France and Germany. KMT membership, at this stage, was probably more useful than CCP membership for those students who wished to return home to participate in revolutionary activities; Sun Yat-sen was still alive, and his progress in creating a revolutionary base in south China was growing more hopeful with each passing month. In this atmosphere Chou left for home in mid-1924.

When Chou went to Canton in 1924 the city was the center of activities for both the KMT and the CCP. The short-term goal was the consolidation of authority in Kwangtung and the long-range priority was the annihilation of the northern government in Peking and the various north China warlords. KMT–CCP cooperation was at a high point, and the city was alive with Russian military advisers and Comintern representatives. Chou quickly won assignments in both KMT and Communist organizations. Within the CCP apparatus he became secretary of the important Kwangtung Regional Committee (see under Ch'en Yen-nien, who succeeded Chou in 1925), as well as head of its Military Committee. He also served as a sometime aide to General Vassily Blücher (known then as Galen), the Soviet military adviser to Chiang Kai-shek. But Chou is best known in this period for his work in the Political Department of the KMT-established (May 1924) Whampoa Military Academy, of which Chiang Kai-shek was the commandant. The important KMT leader Tai Chi-t'ao initially headed the Political Department, but because he was occupied with other tasks Chou often acted for him; then, by the latter part of 1925 Chou became the director[3] and continued as the dominant figure in the department until the Chung-shan Incident of March 1926 (see below). Owing in part to the influence of Soviet advisers, political training was given priority attention, and thus Chou was in a pivotal position to influence the Whampoa cadets. Among his Communist colleagues on the Academy staff were Yeh Chien-ying, Yun Tai-ying, Hsiao Ch'u-nü, and Nieh Jung-chen (qq.v.).

Kwangtung could not serve as a secure base until the Nationalists were able to subdue the forces of Kwangtung warlord Ch'en Chiung-ming, whose center of authority lay in east Kwangtung. The subjugation of Ch'en was accomplished in two "Eastern Expeditions," the first of which took place in February–March 1925. Chou quickly won a name for himself as a senior political officer at the front where two training regiments from Whampoa were engaged. Immediately after this campaign he was recommended by Chiang Kai-shek to head the Academy's Martial Law Office, and later in the year he became head of the Political Department of the National Revolutionary Army's First Army. In this capacity, as well as KMT representative to the First Army,[4] he played an even more important role in the second Eastern Expedition in October–November 1925. Chou's influence in the First Army reportedly enabled him to put CCP members in charge of political work in four out of the army's five divisions, and, in his new post as special commissioner of the East River District, to appoint the provisional chairman of the Municipal Council in Swatow, one of the key cities captured by the Eastern Expedition forces.[5]

In the meantime, the death of Sun Yat-sen (March 1925) and the assassination of left-KMT leader Liao Chung-k'ai (August 1925) brought about increased tensions between the political left and right in Canton. The forces of the left had the upper hand at the time of the Second KMT Congress in January 1926 (when Teng Ying-ch'ao, who had married Chou in 1925, was elected an alternate member of the Central Executive Committee). Not long afterwards, however, there was a sharp turn to the right, dramatized by the celebrated (though still not fully understood) Chung-shan Incident of March 1926, which took its name from a gunboat in the small Nationalist Navy. The details of the incident are obscure, but it was apparently caused by Chiang Kai-shek's fear that the CCP and the KMT's Russian advisers were growing too powerful. When Li Chih-lung, a CCP member who was acting chief of the Navy Bureau and the Chung-shan captain, readied his ship for use near Canton, Chiang assumed a coup was planned. He immediately seized the ship, placed the Russian advisers' residence under guard, and had loyal troops occupy labor union headquarters, railway stations, and the central bank. He also declared martial law in Canton and arrested some 50 CCP political workers in the First Army (including Chou, who was then apparently still in Swatow). Having demonstrated his power, Chiang withdrew his troops the same day; he apologized to his Russian advisers and said only a few CCP members had been involved. Chou was quickly released.

The Chung-shan Incident marked the first open break in the united front between Chiang and the CCP. The influence of the Communists was sharply diminished during the ensuing weeks (see under Lin Po-ch'ü) when Chou was removed from his various posts in the KMT. Chiang's bold move had caught the CCP off guard and precipitated a heated debate within the CCP regarding the proper response. Some wished to make a complete break with the KMT, but others felt that such an action would be premature in view of the relative weakness of the Communists. Chou supported the latter position and in doing so placed himself on the side of the Comintern which, despite Chiang's actions, felt it could still manipulate Chiang and the KMT. The Comintern was particularly anxious for continued KMT–CCP cooperation in view of the fact that preparations for the Northern Expedition were in the final stages, and consequently brought great pressure on the CCP leadership to abide by its wishes.

Chou's activities in the post–Chung-chan months are not well documented, but he is known to have lectured on military affairs and the peasant movement at the Peasant Movement Training Institute (see under P'eng P'ai) after Mao became head of the school in the spring of 1926. He is also reported to have been director (or deputy director) of political training classes attended by CCP members and commissars who had been removed from the army following the incident. According to one source, Chiang Kai-shek set up these classes as a gesture of compromise toward the CCP, because he too wished to avoid an open break at this time.[6]

When the Northern Expedition began in mid-1926, many Communists held important posts in various units of the National Revolutionary Army (see under Yeh T'ing and Lin Po-ch'ü), and some reports assert that Chou was a political officer in the First Army Corps, which moved along a coastal route to bring it to Shanghai in the early spring of 1927. If so, he apparently soon left the army and returned to Kwangtung or went to Wuhan, which was captured in October 1926. In December Chou delivered a military report (presumably at a special conference of the CCP held in Wuhan) in which he exhorted his colleagues to "go into [the National Revolutionary Army], strengthen it, raise its fighting ability, but do not carry on independent work there."[7] At this juncture, Stalin and his Comintern representatives in China still clung to the belief that the KMT was the major vehicle for the success of the revolution against the northern warlords and foreign imperialism and that the CCP should at all costs avoid clashes with the KMT. Thus, Chou's admonition to shun independent work—even at this late stage—was no more than an espousal of Comintern policy. It was at approximately this time—late 1926 or early 1927—that Chou became head of the CCP's newly established Military Department.

The above-mentioned fall of Wuhan in October 1926 was followed in the next month by the capture of Nanchang and Kiukiang in Kiangsi province. This made Shanghai one of the next major targets. Communist operatives in Shanghai led by Lo I-nung (q.v.) and others had already tried to facilitate the takeover of the city by a workers' uprising in late October. This was crushed by warlord Sun Ch'uan-fang, as was an uprising on February 22, 1927. Many accounts state that Chou took part in the abortive February attempt, but Ch'ü Ch'iu-pai's wife, who was an eyewitness to these events, tells a somewhat different story. According to her, an emergency meeting was held immediately after the February uprising, which decided to transfer Chou from Kwangtung to "strengthen military leadership."[8] Chou arrived soon thereafter and took up new posts as director of the Military Department and the Organization Department of the Kiangsu-Chekiang Regional Committee,[9] of which Lo I-nung was the secretary. After intensive organizational work, especially with the labor unions, a successful armed strike involving several hundred thousand workers was staged on March 21 when Chiang Kai-shek's troops were in the outskirts of the city. In a few days Shanghai was in the hands of the Northern Expedition forces. Chou and his colleagues Lo I-nung and Chao Shih-yen (whose biographies contain further details about these events) are singled out in most orthodox accounts as the leading actors in the March uprising. However, these same accounts ignore the important role played by Ku Shun-chang for the simple reason that Ku later defected to the Nationalists (see below). Chou was also immortalized by André Malraux's *Man's Fate,* published a few years later, in which one of the characters (although a Eurasian) was supposedly modeled after him.

Chiang Kai-shek was happy to have Communist cooperation in capturing Shanghai, but he was increasingly apprehensive about their power and thus, on April 12, 1927, he staged his famous anti-Communist coup. Chou, Lo, and Ku barely escaped with their lives, but Chao Shih-yen was soon apprehended and executed. From Shanghai Chou went to the new center of Communist power, Wuhan, where the CCP was still working closely with the left-KMT. There, in late April and early May, he attended the CCP's controversial Fifth National Congress (see under Ch'en Tu-hsiu). Chou emerged from the congress as a member of the Central Committee and Politburo. He is unique in being the only man to serve continuously on the Politburo from 1927 to the post-1949 period. In the weeks following the Fifth Congress there was a serious deterioration in relations between the CCP and the left-KMT, and by mid-July the CCP was virtually an outlawed party in Wuhan. At this emergency juncture a five-man provisional Politburo was established, consisting of Chou, Chang T'ai-lei, Chang Kuo-t'ao, Li Li-san, and Li Wei-han (qq.v.). This restructuring of the hierarchy pointedly omitted former Party head Ch'en Tu-hsiu, who was being eased out of

authority (or, as many accounts put it, was being made the scapegoat for the catastrophic events of the spring and early summer).

The Communist response to the break with the left-KMT was the celebrated Nanchang Uprising on August 1, 1927. Chou was one of the major planners of the uprising (see under Yeh T'ing) in his capacity as secretary of the Front Committee.[10] Immediately after the troops led by Yeh T'ing, Ho Lung, and Chu Te took control of the city, they established a Revolutionary Committee, of which Chou was a member. Moreover, he and Liu Po-ch'eng were the key figures on the Military Directorate (*ts'an-mou-t'uan*), one of the subordinate organs of the Revolutionary Committee.[11] The rebel forces held Nanchang for only a few days, after which they moved southward to Kwangtung where in late September they briefly held Swatow. However, it was quickly recaptured by KMT units, and Chou and his colleagues were forced to flee. At this point Chou became seriously ill with malaria and was barely able to make his way on a small boat to Hong Kong in the company of Yeh T'ing and Nieh Jung-chen. Chou's career and the Communist movement had reached a disastrous low.

Chou's whereabouts and activities for the latter part of 1927 and early 1928 are poorly documented. Some reports suggest that he worked in the Party underground in Hong Kong and then Shanghai, but in any case he was in Moscow by June–July 1928 to attend the Sixth CCP National Congress. The congress dealt with the difficult problem of reconstituting the CCP; it decided that the immediate overthrow of the KMT was impossible and therefore efforts should be concentrated on developing guerrilla warfare in the countryside and continuing underground work in the cities. Chou was re-elected to the Central Committee and the Politburo and, according to a Soviet biography of Chou,[12] he was also elected a secretary of the Secretariat. Chou continued to head the Party's Military Department, and for a year or so after the Sixth Congress he also directed the Organization Department (after which he was succeeded by Li Wei-han). Ch'ü Ch'iu-pai was deposed as the top Party leader, being replaced by Hsiang Chung-fa (q.v.). However, most sources agree that Hsiang was only nominally the leader, and that Li Li-san soon emerged as the most powerful figure in the new Politburo. Similarly, there is general agreement that Chou was second only to Li at this juncture. In addition to Chou's impressive array of posts in the CCP, he was also elected a candidate member of the Executive Committee of the Comintern (ECCI) at the Sixth Comintern Congress, held in Moscow from July to September 1928.[13]

When Li Li-san, Chou, and the others returned to Shanghai in late 1928, Party fortunes were still low. Red Army guerrilla units in the countryside were just beginning the formidable task of creating strongholds, and at CCP headquarters in Shanghai there was constant bickering about the best means to reconstitute Party strength in urban areas. (Party membership had fallen from 58,000 in early 1927 to 40,000 at the time of the Sixth Congress.) Chou spelled out many of these problems in an article of April 1929 in which he conceded the extreme difficulties of "recapturing" the "proletarian base" of the Party.[14] Li and Chou were faced with the further problem of relating the often unrealistic demands of the Comintern to the concrete situation in China. For example, there were genuine problems for the Shanghai leadership in conveying their own or Comintern directives to guerrilla units, the leaders of which (like Mao Tse-tung) had their own ideas about tactics and strategy.

Chou's relations with Li Li-san, known for his volatile personality, have been discussed by many writers. Chou initially seems to have been a faithful aide to Li, but as time passed the relationship became more ambiguous. It appears that differences existed by the winter of 1929–30 as the Li Li-san "line" of assaulting the major cities arose—differences, it should be added, which may well have been aggravated by the continual problem of interpreting the sometimes ambiguous and often contradictory directives from Moscow. In any case, Chou left China in the early part of 1930 for Moscow and, according to one source, became the effective head of the CCP delegation to the Comintern,[15] which was watching the situation in China with growing concern. In early July he addressed the 16th CPSU Congress; in essence Chou expressed agreement with a basic point of the Li Li-san policy that the Red Army must move to capture major cities. Three weeks later P'eng Te-huai (q.v.) was carrying out this very policy when he captured Changsha, the Hunan capital. The Comintern immediately hailed this as a "new chapter in the history of the Chinese revolution,"[16] but no sooner were these words in print than P'eng was routed from Changsha.

The failure at Changsha called for a scapegoat (ultimately Li Li-san) and emissaries to lay down a new policy for the CCP. To this end Chou and Ch'ü Ch'iu-pai returned to China and soon afterwards, in late September 1930, convened the famous Third Plenum. Chou's oft-quoted speech (the so-called "Shao-shan" report, after one of Chou's pen names) was equivocal regarding Li Li-san's "mistakes." He claimed, in essence, that Li had differed from the Comintern in tactics, but not in basic strategy. The Third Plenum left many issues unsolved, including control of the Party's central apparatus. In the following months there was an intensive intra-Party struggle, which was not resolved until the Fourth Plenum in January 1931 (see under Li Li-san and Ho Meng-hsiung). By then Li had been deposed (November 1930) and sent to Moscow in virtual exile, but at the Fourth Plenum Chou, with his usual agility in surviving crises, managed to retain his place on the Politburo and Secretariat after a confession of past errors. Moreover, in the restructured hierarchy dominated by Ch'en Shao-yü and his returned student colleagues, Chou continued to head the Military Department. At this juncture the Party also established the Central Bureau of the Soviet Areas, in which Chou became one of the dominant figures (see under Hsiang Ying). This organ was supposed to strengthen ties with, and control over, the various guerrilla forces in the hinterlands—one of the major goals of the new leadership.

The dangers and difficulties for those working in Shanghai were exacerbated in the spring of 1931 when the KMT apprehended Ku Shun-chang, who four years earlier had worked closely with Chou in Shanghai. Ku's revelations to his captors resulted in the apprehension of important Communist leaders, and many accounts (especially from hostile sources) assert that Chou masterminded a vengeful annihilation of Ku's relatives. Sometime later in 1931 (there are many conflicting dates) Chou left Shanghai for Juichin, the headquarters of the First Front Army commanded by Chu Te and Mao Tse-tung in southeast Kiangsi. At the First All-China Congress of Soviets, held in November, Chou was elected a member of the Central Executive Committee (CEC) of the newly established Chinese Soviet Republic, and to membership on the Central Revolutionary Military Council, an organ of the republic chaired by Chu Te.

Orthodox Maoist histories uniformly ignore Chou's role during the Kiangsi period, but other research indicates contention with Mao on a number of issues, especially those related to military affairs. Mao held that enemy forces should be lured deep into soviet territory, after which they would be destroyed piecemeal. Beginning in the latter part of 1931 the returned student leadership, strongly supported by Chou, argued that this "guerrillaism" was antiquated in view of the growing strength of the Red Army. Instead, they urged that the Kiangsi soviet area should be enlarged and linked with other Communist bases. The debate was temporarily settled at the Ning-tu Conference in August 1932 when Chou succeeded Mao as political commissar of the First Front Army. This appointment was reaffirmed in May 1933, at which time Chou was also made political commissar for the entire Red Army (although, in terms of the Kiangsi soviet, this amounted to the same thing as the First Front Army).[17] A few years later, when Mao had achieved control of the CCP, he replied in caustic terms to the charges against "guerrillaism," but Chou was not mentioned by name.[18]

Mao–Chou relations were doubtless further strained in 1933 during the campaign against the "Lo Ming line" (see under Lo Ming), which most historians view as an indirect attack on Mao. The essential point of the charges against Lo was that he embodied a spirit of "defeatism" in the struggle against the KMT and in military terms that he stressed a "defensive" rather than an "offensive" posture. In this regard, Chou was again allied with the returned student leadership, especially Ch'in Pang-hsien (q.v.). Chou retained his position as one of the two or three key leaders at the Party's Fifth Plenum, held in January 1934. Immediately afterwards, at the Second All-China Congress of Soviets, he was re-elected to the CEC and as a member of the CEC's 17-member Presidium. In addition, he was promoted to a vice-chairmanship on the Central Revolutionary Military Council. The council then had Chu Te as its chairman and Chou and Wang Chia-hsiang (q.v.) as the two vice-chairmen. (In becoming one of the vice-chairmen, Chou in effect replaced a previous vice-chairman, P'eng Te-huai.)

In the winter, spring, and summer of 1934 Chou worked feverishly to strengthen the Red Army, which was then under the relentless attacks of the Nationalists' Fifth Annihilation Campaign. Much of his work took the form of exhortations in various Party and Red Army journals to rally every available force to the defense of the soviet base. When all else failed the high command decided on the retreat from Kiangsi—known in Communist annals as the Long March. The army units left Kiangsi in October 1934, and by January 1935 they reached Tsun-i in Kweichow province where they paused to hold a vitally important meeting. The full story of the Tsun-i Conference has never been told, but it appears that Mao was able to gain control of the Party apparatus from the returned student faction (notably Ch'in Pang-hsien) and, to a lesser degree, from Chou. The returned students never regained their past pre-eminence, but despite Chou's previous disagreements with Mao he once again retained his position as a top leader. However, in fact if not in name, Chou did relinquish to Mao the post of chief political officer in the Red Army. Moreover, Mao also succeeded Chou as head of the Party's Military Affairs Committee (or department). From that point Chou served as a vice-chairman of the latter organ. (The Military Affairs Committee and the Central Revolutionary Military Council were apparently merged and placed under the Party's jurisdiction during the Long March; Chou continued as a vice-chairman through the civil war period of the late 1940's, by which time it was known as the People's Revolutionary Military Council.) A half year after Tsun-i, Mao's forces met Chang Kuo-t'ao's Fourth Front Army on the Szechwan-Sikang border. Chou was among those who supported Mao in his controversy with Chang (which is described in Chang's biography). Chou was so seriously ill during the latter part of the march to north Shensi that he had to be borne on a stretcher.

In July–August 1935, while Mao and Chou were still on the Long March, the important Seventh Comintern Congress was held in Moscow. Mao, Chou, Ch'en Shao-yü, and Chang Kuo-t'ao were all elected members of the ECCI. The congress endorsed the international united front against fascism (see under Ch'en Shao-yü), a policy which would have a profound effect upon Chou's work in the years immediately ahead. After the Long Marchers arrived in north Shensi in October 1935, Chou continued to serve as a senior Red Army commander for another year. When American journalist Edgar Snow arrived in north Shensi in the early summer of 1936 he had a lengthy interview with Chou, describing him as the commander of the Eastern Front, that is, the areas along the Yellow River opposite Shansi province.[19] However, by the latter half of 1936, when the Red Army position in Shensi was relatively secure, Chou in effect abandoned his army role and turned to the difficult task of exploiting the growing national sentiment for domestic peace in order to present a united front against Japan. The Japanese militarists inadvertently cooperated by their continual encroachments upon Chinese sovereignty in north China. Chou was also aided by the fact that two nearby KMT units were led by Generals Chang Hsueh-liang and Yang Hu-ch'eng, who were lukewarm in their support of Chiang Kai-shek and who were persuaded that Chinese should turn their guns on Japan and not other Chinese.

Numerous reports indicate that Chou was secretly in contact, both directly and indirectly, with Generals Chang and Yang during 1936, and it was common knowledge that Red Army troops often fraternized with the supposedly hostile Chang–Yang units. Chiang Kai-shek soon learned of these developments and went to Sian to make a personal investigation. This set the stage for the celebrated Sian Incident of December 1936, when Chiang was kidnapped by his two dissident generals. As with the Chungshan Incident of a decade earlier, the full details about the Sian Incident have never been revealed, even though Communist, Nationalist, and neutral observers have recounted the events on scores of occasions. On the Communist side, one of the more interesting accounts suggests that Mao and Chou wanted to put Chiang on trial but were countermanded by Moscow.[20] In any case, the Communists were deeply involved in the negotiations during the two weeks that Chiang was held captive. In the complex negotiations, in which the two dissident KMT generals and Chiang and his wife were involved, Chou led the Communist side, assisted by Yeh Chien-ying, Lin Po-ch'ü, Ch'in Pang-hsien, Li K'o-nung, Wang Ping-nan, Feng Wen-pin, and Li T'ao (qq.v.). There is considerable controversy regarding the "terms" of Chiang's release by Chang Hsueh-liang on December 25. Yet the main contention of the Communists—that Chiang agreed to cease military operations against the Red Army and to concentrate all energies against Japan—seems borne out by the developments of the post-Sian period.

In the early months of 1937, with war clouds on the horizon, Chou traveled back and forth between Yenan, Sian, and Nanking as the KMT and the CCP inched toward a united front. The basis for Chou's negotiations was apparently a program outlined by the CCP Central Committee in a message to the Third Plenum of the Fifth KMT Central Executive Committee, which met in Nanking in February. The Communists offered to stop their program to overthrow the National government and to incorporate the Red Army into the National Revolutionary Army. In return, their demands included a cessation of civil war and preparations for a "war of resistance" against Japan. The talks continued for several months, and then in June–July, when Chou was conferring with Chiang Kai-shek in Lushan, Kiangsi, war with Japan erupted. The various points of contention were quickly swept aside, and the program above, in broad outline, was accepted by the two sides. In the following month, August 1937, Chou continued these talks in Nanking with top KMT military leaders. The next few months found Chou in Shansi where the Communists' Eighth Route Army was engaging the invading Japanese forces, but by early 1938 he was in Hankow (the temporary capital after the fall of Nanking) to assume what was to be his major wartime role: chief CCP liaison official to the National government. In the spirit of the united front, Chou was given a nominally high position in the Nationalist hierarchy in February 1938 as deputy director of the Political Training Board of the National Military Council (a post he held until 1940). The department was headed by the important KMT military figure Ch'en Ch'eng. Chou was even reinstated in the KMT and in this capacity was on the 17-member presidium for the Extraordinary KMT National Congress held in March–April 1938 in Hankow.

By mid-1938 Wuhan had become an important center for Communist activities. The Party was already publishing the *Hsin-hua jih-pao* (New China daily) and the journal *Ch'ün-chung* (The masses), and a number of publishing houses did a thriving business turning out the speeches and articles of Chou and his colleagues, as well as those by top leaders in Yenan. In addition, the CCP held seven seats on the newly established consultative organ known as the People's Political Council (see under Lin Po-ch'ü), which first met in July 1938. This placed on the scene in Wuhan CCP stalwarts Lin Po-ch'ü, Wu Yü-chang, Tung Pi-wu, Ch'en Shao-yü, Ch'in Pang-hsien, and Teng Ying-ch'ao (Chou's wife). (Mao was the seventh member, but this was purely nominal and he never attended a council session.) Various Communist-backed "mass" organizations also established branches in Wuhan, including the National Liberation Vanguard of China (NLVC), a youth association. The initial harmony in Wuhan soon gave way to a number of disputes. Chiang responded in August by closing down the NLVC and other organizations (see under Li Ch'ang); he also placed restrictions on the non-KMT press, but the Communists' newspaper and journal were allowed to continue.[21] In the same month Chou returned to Yenan and in October–November attended the CCP's Sixth Plenum, the first held since January 1934. Despite the growing tensions which Chou had witnessed in Wuhan, the spirit of wartime cooperation was still strong enough for Mao to speak of the KMT and Chiang Kai-shek in glowing terms and for the meeting to resolve that Communists should join the KMT.[22] Chou immediately returned to the Nationalist capital, which because of the fall of Wuhan was now in Chungking. He advanced the proposal about KMT membership to Chiang, but to judge from the generalissimo's scornful recounting of their conversation this was apparently turned down.[23]

The year 1939 marked a turning point in wartime collaboration. The Communists charged the Nationalists with provoking incidents against Eighth Route Army units and liaison offices in KMT-held territory, and the KMT made similar countercharges. Chiang expressed his dislike of the Communists' "attitude" to Chou on June 10.[24] Two days later the P'ing-chiang Incident took the lives of six Communist officials at a New Fourth Army liaison office in Hunan (see under Yeh T'ing). Chou responded to this in print with a piece in the Yenan journal *Chieh-fang* (Liberation; no. 81, August 20, 1939), and then in mid-September he flew to Moscow. The P'ing-chiang and other incidents were much too minor to necessitate a trip to Moscow for a man of Chou's stature, and it is not likely that medical treatment for an arm injury (the officially explained reason) was sufficient to keep him in Moscow for half a year. It is probable, though undocumented, that he was sent to learn more about the critical events which were unfolding. In August the Nazi–Soviet pact was signed; on September 1 war in Europe broke out; and in mid-September a truce was agreed to between Moscow and Tokyo after a brief undeclared war on the border between Manchuria and Mongolia. Whatever Chou may have learned about Soviet attitudes concerning these events, he presumably reported to Mao and his colleagues in Yenan, where he spent the period from March to June 1940 before returning to his post in Chungking.

Chou had been away from Chungking for nearly a year before his return in mid-1940. In the interim the KMT had been pressing the Communists for a clear demarcation of war zones to avoid confusion and clashes. In September Chou gave the impression to an American observer that an agreeable solution had been reached, and, apparently as a gesture of good faith by the KMT he was made deputy director of a Nationalist government agency to control Chinese political affairs in areas occupied by the Japanese.[25] However, the clash between the Communists' New Fourth Army and government troops in south Anhwei in January 1941—the famed New Fourth Incident (see under Yeh T'ing)—plummeted KMT–CCP relations to a new low. The united front was in effect dead, but neither side was willing to bring upon itself the opprobrium of breaking the alliance against the hated Japanese. Under this difficult situation Chou remained in Chungking for two and a half years more.

After America's entry into the war in December 1941, the United States pushed for closer KMT–CCP collaboration to help the war effort. A notable movement in this direction took place in 1942–43 when Lin Piao joined Chou in Chungking for talks with Chiang and the KMT military high command (the details of which are given in Lin's biography). During these same years Chou built up a large and talented staff in Chungking, which in the post-1949 period formed the nucleus of the PRC Foreign Ministry. Similarly, many editors and correspondents for the *Hsin-hua jih-pao* and *Ch'ün-chung* held top posts in Peking's journalistic circles after 1949. Chou and his colleagues were also indefatigable in maintaining contacts with the increasingly vocal non-Communist left in Chungking. Many of these people, deeply disenchanted with the KMT, joined the PRC in 1949 and thus brought to the Communists sorely needed talents in administration, education, and commerce. Finally, Chou exerted himself to make a favorable impression on foreign diplomats and journalists, an effort which most observers agree was accomplished with consummate skill. In sum, Chou's semi-official endeavors in the middle and later war years were probably of far greater value to the Communist movement than his official liaison task in Chungking. After the above-mentioned Chou–Lin talks in 1942–43, the two men left for Yenan in mid-

1943. For the balance of the war Tung Pi-wu, sometimes aided by Lin Po-chü, served as Yenan's principal spokesman in Chungking.

On August 1, 1943, a reception was given to mark Chou's return to Yenan. His speech on this occasion gave witness to the more independent path upon which the Communists were now embarking, including some scoffing remarks to refute anti-Communist "slanders" that Communism was "no longer fit for China." Also noteworthy were his comments about the Comintern, which had just been dissolved by Stalin: "After the dissolution . . . , one thing should be made clear—that is, that the Chinese Communist Party will be more responsible and independent to solve the problem of the Chinese revolution."[26] In March 1944 Chou articulated further demands when he indicated that the CCP wanted KMT agreement to the reorganization of Communist forces into 18 divisions, grouped into six armies—in contrast to demands of the previous year for 12 divisions in four armies. Moreover, on the political front, the Communists began to make serious demands for a coalition government. To this end Lin Po-ch'ü held talks with the KMT in Sian and Chungking for several months in 1944. Chou punctuated Communist demands for a coalition government in a major address on October 10, 1944 (the anniversary of the 1911 Revolution). Lin Po-ch'ü, having made no progress in Chungking, returned to Yenan in early November, accompanied by President Roosevelt's personal representative in China, General Patrick J. Hurley, who was known for his ardent desire to bring the feuding Chinese sides together. Chou returned to Chungking with Hurley for a month of fruitless talks, which included conversations with Chiang Kai-shek. Chou was in Chungking again for three weeks in January–February 1945. The results were the same and, in fact, there were no further top-level talks until immediately after Japan's surrender when Mao and Chou flew to Chungking (see below).

Chou followed up his contacts with Hurley by urging upon him CCP representation on the Chinese delegation to the forthcoming (April 1945) conference in San Francisco which established the United Nations. Chou suggested himself, Ch'in Pang-hsien, and Tung Pi-wu as delegates, but ultimately only Tung went (see under Tung). From April to June Chou attended the Party's Seventh National Congress in Yenan. At the congress and the plenum which followed, he was reaffirmed as a Central Committee member, a Politburo member, a secretary of the Central Secretariat, and a vice-chairman of the Revolutionary Military Council. In sum, Chou continued as one of the three or four top men within the hierarchy.

KMT–CCP talks were resumed at the highest level in the days immediately after the war ended. In late August 1945, accompanied by Chou and Wang Jo-fei, Mao flew to Chungking for six weeks of intensive talks with Chiang Kai-shek. After eight years of a disastrous war, there were strong pressures from all strata of society to avoid a civil war between the two most powerful forces in China, and therefore both Chiang and Mao attempted to give every appearance of reasonableness in working toward solutions of important differences. In sum, the Communists muted their demand for a coalition government, and instead pressed for the convocation of a Political Consultative Conference (PCC) to "exchange views on national affairs and discuss questions relating to peaceful national reconstruction and the convocation of the National Assembly."[27]

Although Mao and Chiang had moved toward the settlement of some differences, there were many other critical issues still outstanding when Mao returned to Yenan on October 11. As a consequence, Chou remained in Chungking to continue the talks. Washington's deep concern over the events in China soon led to the appointment of General George C. Marshall as special envoy to China. Marshall arrived in Chungking in late December, and played a major role in bringing about a cease-fire between KMT and CCP military units and convocation of the PCC. The cease-fire agreement of January 10, 1946, was arranged by the so-called Committee of Three—General Marshall, Chou, and Nationalist General Chang Ch'ün—which was further charged with enforcing the truce throughout China. On the same day the PCC was convened; the Communist delegates were Chou, Tung Pi-wu, Wang Jo-fei, Yeh Chien-ying (later replaced by Ch'in Pang-hsien), Wu Yü-chang, Lu Ting-i, and Chou's wife, Teng Ying-ch'ao (qq.v.). During the three-week conference (January 10–31) several committees were established to deal with the various issues; Chou served on the Military Affairs Committee and the Committee to Draft the Constitution.

Assisted by Tung Pi-wu, Wang Ping-nan, and others, Chou spent the better part of 1946 in negotiations with his American and Nationalist counterparts. Initially working in Chungking, Chou accompanied the Nationalist government when it moved the capital back to Nanking in the spring of 1946. He also maintained a headquarters in Shanghai, and from time to time he made trips to Peking and Yenan. While Chou held policy-level talks in the national capital, the most important attempts to carry out the truce on a day-to-day basis were being acted out in Peking where Yeh Chien-ying headed the large Communist team at the tripartite Executive Headquarters (see under Yeh).

While Chou negotiated with his American and KMT counterparts, the realities of the situation were being acted out on battlefields throughout north China and Manchuria. Temporary truces were quickly broken by one side or the other, and by mid-1946 it was clear that ultimate solutions would be found only through a nationwide test of arms. Chou's departure from Nanking for Shanghai in September marked the effective end of the tripartite arrangements. He remained at his post to mid-November, but then, despite pleas from General Marshall, Chou left for Yenan. From the abundant documentation of the 1946 truce efforts,[28] it is apparent that Chou and Marshall got along well and respected each other. But in January 1947, Chou and other senior Communists (notably Lu Ting-i, q.v.) denounced the American efforts as a subterfuge to aid Chiang Kai-shek. At almost the same moment the United States officially terminated the Marshall mission. Soon afterwards the KMT ordered all Communist delegates still in Nationalist territory to leave for Communist-held areas (see under Yeh Chien-ying), and then in mid-March the Nationalists captured Yenan. Two decades of struggle between the KMT and the CCP was now transferred to a nationwide civil war.

Chou had only been in Yenan four months when, as noted, Yenan was captured in March 1947. Except for harassing actions by the PLA, the Communists did not contest the city. In what appears to have been an effort to provide for an extreme emergency, the inner-elite of the CCP was divided into two groups. One, which included Liu Sao-ch'i and Chu Te, set out for P'ing-shan hsien in west Hopeh, and the other, which included Mao, Chou, and Jen Pi-shih, moved by a slow and circuitous route through north Shensi and Shansi and finally joined Liu and Chu in P'ing-shan in the spring of 1948. During this year-long march the Mao group was guarded by only a small PLA force, and on a number of occasions they remained only a step ahead of pursuing Nationalist troops. Because of the inherent dangers, Chou went by the pseudonym Hu Pi-ch'eng during this period,[29] and because he became seriously ill he had to be carried on a stretcher for a portion of the trip. There is little specific documentation on Chou's work in the two-year period from the Yenan evacuation to his arrival in Peking with Mao in 1949. Most of the directives issued in this period were signed by Mao as head of the Party or by Chu Te as PLA commander, but given Chou's stature it may be presumed that he was involved in the major strategic decisions.

The early months of 1949 again found Chou cast in the role of chief negotiator, only this time he negotiated from a position of strength. The resounding defeats of Nationalist armies during the winter of 1948–49 led to eleventh-hour KMT efforts to salvage their increasingly desperate situation. On February 22, in Shih-chia-chuang, Mao and Chou received an un-official "peace" negotiation team sent from Shanghai, but nothing came of this. In the next month Chou attended the Party's Second Plenum near Shih-chia-chuang, immediately after which he and Mao moved to Peking. They arrived on March 25, and on the following day Chou was designated head of a six-man delega-tion to negotiate with an official delegation sent by the acting president of the national gov-ernment, Li Tsung-jen. When Chou offered what amounted to surrender terms, Li Tsung-jen instructed his delegates, on April 20, to reject them. The hopelessness of the National-ists' position was well illustrated when the three top KMT negotiators chose to remain with the Communists in Peking. Within a few days Com-munist armies crossed the Yangtze, and by the end of the year the mainland was in Commu-nist hands.

Chou's role as negotiator with other Chinese ended at long last in the spring of 1949 and he could now turn to the task of chief diplomat in China's dealings with foreign countries and chief administrator of a huge state bureaucracy. This began in June 1949 when he became a vice-chairman under Mao of the CPPCC Pre-paratory Committee, as well as head of a special group to draft the Common Program (the equivalent of a constitution until 1954). He was also a featured speaker on several occasions during the summer as the Communists estab-lished a number of "mass" organizations. As a representative of the CCP, Chou attended the inaugural session in September 1949 of the CPPCC, the organization which brought the PRC into existence on October 1. He reported on the Common Program and, predictably, in the new government he received top appoint-ments. He became premier of the Government Administration Council (the cabinet—known as the State Council from 1954) and minister of Foreign Affairs, the two positions which quickly brought him international fame. He was also elected in October as a member of the Executive Board of the Sino-Soviet Friendship Association, and in December he was appointed chairman of the Foreign Ministry's Foreign Policy Committee and honorary chairman of the newly established Chinese People's Institute of Foreign Affairs (see under Chang Hsi-jo).

In the earliest days of the PRC Chou estab-lished himself as the ubiquitous political figure. It is difficult to overstate the extraordinary pace and variety of his activities. For example, al-though complete details are not available, he apparently attended the overwhelming majority of the 34 meetings of the Central People's Gov-ernment Council and the 224 meetings of the Government Administration Council (the cab-inet) held between 1949 and 1954. His innu-merable reports before these two bodies would fill many volumes, and many more would be required to include still other addresses before the CPPCC National Committee, various "mass" and professional organizations, and national conferences of "progressive" workers and peas-ants. Many of these reports were technical in nature and only of passing interest, but many others represented the official Chinese position on key domestic and foreign issues. Collectively, Chou's speeches and reports, especially during the first decade of the PRC, provide one of the richest sources of basic data about China, and most of them are readily available in the major Chinese and foreign-language publications.

In mid-December 1949 Mao went to Moscow for talks with Stalin. He took with him only a small group, but on January 20, 1950, Chou arrived with a large delegation which consisted principally of specialists in economic affairs. A month later Mao and Chou concluded a series of agreements which formed the cornerstone of Chinese foreign relations during much of the next decade. On February 14 Chou and Andrei Vyshinsky signed the Sino-Soviet Treaty of Friendship, Alliance, and Mutual Assistance. The crucial clause read: "In the event of one of the Contracting Parties being attacked by Japan or any state allied with her and thus being in-volved in a state of war, the other Contracting Party shall immediately render military and other assistance by all means at its disposal." The hypothetical ally of Japan was, of course, the United States, a point which Chou made clear in the fall on the eve of Chinese entry into the Korean War. Other agreements affirmed the independent status of Mongolia, pro-vided for the joint administration (and ultimate transfer to China) of the Chinese Changchun Railway, Port Arthur, and Dairen, and estab-lished a five-year credit to China amounting to $300,000,000. Other matters, such as trade and the establishment of joint stock companies to exploit Chinese natural resources, were left to subordinates (see under Yeh Chi-chuang and Wang Chia-hsiang).

In the early weeks and months of the PRC, Chou communicated with many nations regard-ing the establishment of diplomatic relations. Initially, most of these concerned other Com-munist nations, but many measures were also exchanged with non-Communist countries; these were uniformly worded to emphasize that "New China" was the complete master of its own house and would tolerate nothing less than abso-lute equality in its foreign relations. Chou also attempted to undercut the international stand-ing of the Nationalist government, then exiled in Taiwan. On several occasions he sent notes to the United Nations denouncing the "illegality" of the Nationalist delegation, and he also noti-fied the United Nations that a PRC delegation had been appointed (see under Chang Went'ien). These endeavors were simply the beginning of Peking's unaltered policy to deny the existence of "two Chinas." Chou's efforts in this regard might have succeeded, but they were seriously eroded in June 1950 with the outbreak of the Korean War and with the entry of China into the war in the fall. For the next three years his work in foreign affairs revolved around bolstering the Chinese war effort in Korea and working out the complex details that culminated in the truce of July 1953.

Chou is credited with intense efforts to avert a direct Sino-American confrontation in Korea,[30] but once this began he issued innumerable official statements denouncing the United States, the United Nations, the Nationalist government on Taiwan, and the American negotiations which led in 1951 to the signing of a peace treaty with Japan. By the same token, massive Soviet aid to both North Korea and China during the Korean War dictated close liaison between Moscow and Peking. Consequently, in mid-August 1952 Chou led a top-level group to Moscow. It was composed of specialists in war-related industry and senior military figures, including a PLA deputy chief-of-staff, the Air Force commander, and deputy commanders of the Navy and the Artillery Force. A month of talks led to agreements to return to Chinese jurisdiction the Chinese Changchun Railway, to extend the time limit for joint use of the naval facilities at Port Arthur, and to construct a rail line from Tsining (Chi-ning) to Ulan Bator (which, when completed in 1956, cut the rail distance from Peking to Moscow by several hundred miles). Of equal importance was the question of further Soviet economic aid; this was not settled by Chou, but rather by Li Fu-ch'un (q.v.), one of his top aides, who remained in the Soviet capital for many months to complete the negotiations. Chou's journey to Moscow also provided a historic footnote; it was the last time he saw Stalin, a man he had been dealing with for a quarter of a century.

In early March 1953 Chou returned to Moscow for Stalin's funeral, and a few days later he was in Prague for another funeral following the death of Czech leader Klement Gottwald. His trip to the USSR symbolized what might be considered the end of the first phase of Sino-Soviet relations. To this point China's top three leaders—Mao, Liu Shao-ch'i, and Chou—had gone to Moscow, but no significant Soviet official had visited Peking. Stalin's death opened the way for the conclusion of the Korean War. No sooner had Chou returned to Peking in late March than agreement was reached with the United Nations Command in Korea on the repatriation of prisoners-of-war, and this quickly led to an armistice in July (see under P'eng Te-huai, the commander of Chinese forces in Korea). In the meantime, Chou was equally occupied with domestic affairs. He had a prominent voice in several of the various campaigns and movements of the early 1950's, such as one dealing with the ideological "remolding" of intellectuals in 1951 and the major "three-anti" campaign of 1951–52 against corruption, waste, and bureaucracy. Chou dealt with these and other domestic and foreign affairs in what amounted to a state-of-the-union address in October 1951 at the third session of the CPPCC. A year later the period of "rehabilitation and reconstruction" (1949–1952) gave way to the era of the five-year economic plans and the initial steps to convene a national legislature and to adopt a constitution. In this connection Chou was appointed in January 1953 as chairman of a committee to draft the constitution. In the next month he delivered another lengthy political report at the fourth session of the CPPCC, which dealt with the First Five-Year Plan and the forthcoming NPC.

Chou played the key role from 1952 to 1954 in cementing China's ties with its three Asian Communist neighbors. In October 1952 he signed in Peking the Sino-Mongolian Economic and Cultural Cooperation Agreement with Prime Minister Y. Tsedenbal, and in November of the next year he led the Chinese side in talks with Korean leader Kim Il Sung. On November 23 in Peking Chou and Kim signed the Sino-Korean Economic and Cultural Cooperation Agreement which provided for large-scale aid to assist war-ravaged Korea to restore its economic base. The closer China–North Vietnam relationship resulted from the famous Geneva Conference, convened in April 1954, to which Chou led a top-flight delegation of foreign affairs specialists. The "final declaration," signed by China, the USSR, Great Britain, France, Cambodia, North Vietnam, and Laos, brought an end to the hostilities in Indochina. Chou utilized a temporary adjournment of the Geneva Conference to great advantage by making brief visits to India, Burma, and North Vietnam. In New Delhi on June 28 and in Rangoon on the next day, he signed joint statements with Prime Ministers Nehru and U Nu, which advocated the Five Principles of Peaceful Co-existence. This phrase, which became the hallmark of Peking's self-described foreign policy for years to come, had been initially set forth in a Sino-Indian agreement two months before, but it did not gain international currency until Chou and his fellow Asian prime ministers signed these statements.

From Rangoon Chou went to Hanoi for talks with Ho Chi Minh, and after a few days in Peking he returned to Geneva (via Moscow) on July 12 for the concluding phase of the Geneva Conference. (In later years Chou traveled widely in Africa, Asia, and East Europe, but excluding his student days in Japan and West

Europe, his visit to Switzerland was the only time through the mid-1960's that he visited an industrialized Western democracy.) Immediately after the conference, Chou made brief visits to East Germany, Poland, the USSR, and Mongolia, holding talks in each country with the top leaders. He arrived home on August 1, 1954, having emerged from the Geneva Conference as a world statesman of the first magnitude. His skillful performance in Geneva had done much to allay an impression of a "bellicose" China, an image nurtured by the world's non-Communist press during the Korean War period. Chou also became the first senior Chinese to rub shoulders with the major Western statesmen of the postwar world, like Anthony Eden and Pierre Mendes-France (and he even found time to pay a visit on comedian Charlie Chaplin in Geneva).

As a deputy representing the city of Peking, Chou attended the inaugural session of the First NPC in September 1954. (He was returned from Peking for the Second and Third NPC's, which opened their first session in April 1959 and December 1964, respectively.) Chou delivered a lengthy and fact-laden report on the progress of the PRC since 1949, and he was confirmed as premier and foreign minister in the reorganized central government.

The PRC now had a national legislative body, and thus the CPPCC, which had previously "acted as the provisional" legislature, was reorganized in December 1954 to "function as the organization of the people's democratic united front." Mao had chaired the First CPPCC (1949–1954), but in 1954 he became honorary chairman and Chou succeeded him as chairman of the Second CPPCC. (Chou was re-elected to this post in the Third and Fourth CPPCC's, in April 1959 and January 1965.) As already mentioned, Chou's reports before various government bodies provide a key source of data about China, and few are more important than his speeches before the NPC and the CPPCC. The dates of his NPC speeches are September 1954, July 1955, June 1956, June 1957, February 1958, April 1959, April 1960, March 1962, December 1963, and December 1964. The dates for the CPPCC from 1954 are December 1954, January 1956, and March 1957. After the last-mentioned date, all subsequent sessions of the CPPCC were held concurrently with the NPC sessions listed above, and as this fact suggests the CPPCC became a less important platform for major pronouncements in the post-1957 period. In short, whatever Chou's day-to-day relationship to these two bodies, he was the dominant figure in the sense of being the major spokesman when the NPC and the CPPCC held their national meetings.

In late September 1954 the first important Soviet delegation to China, led by Nikita Khrushchev and N. A. Bulganin, arrived in Peking to attend the PRC's fifth anniversary celebrations and to hold talks with Peking's officialdom. Chou led the negotiations for China, which changed Peking's relationship to Moscow from that of a junior partner to a more equal one. The Russians agreed to a large loan, the withdrawal of Soviet forces from Port Arthur (completed in May 1955), and the transfer to China of four joint-stock companies which the two nations had been operating. A scientific and technical cooperation agreement was also concluded, as well as a plan to build a Lanchow–Urumchi–Alma Ata rail line (which, because of the deterioration of Sino-Soviet relations, was later shelved).

Chou's speech to the NPC in September 1954 (delivered just before Khrushchev's visit) suggested an expansive and independent mood in Chinese foreign relations. Among other things, he stated a willingness to establish "peaceful relations" with "any country in Europe, South and North America, and Australia, provided that it has the same desire and sincerity." Three months later he reported that talks concerning the establishment of diplomatic relations were being conducted with Yugoslavia, a nation hitherto the object of scorn from Peking. During this same period Nehru and U Nu both visited China as Chou's guests. In early 1955 Chou's talks in Peking with United Nations Secretary-General Dag Hammarskjöld led to the release of American military personnel imprisoned in China and helped pave the way for Sino-American ambassadorial talks, which began later in the year (see below). But these gestures were paralleled by a series of actions and reactions by the United States and China which for a time seemed to be a serious threat to peace in Asia. On the one side the United States sponsored the formation of the Southeast Treaty Organization (SEATO) in September 1954 and signed a mutual security treaty with Nationalist China in December; both actions were characterized by Chou as provocations against China. On the other side, Chinese shelling of various Nationalist-held off-shore islands beginning in September 1954 and the capture of one of them (off the Chekiang coast) in January 1955 was regarded in Washington as proof of Peking's oft-stated intention to assault Taiwan.

The "Taiwan crisis" was a matter of grave concern to many Asian countries. Taking the initiative, the five Colombo Powers (India, Burma, Indonesia, Pakistan, and Ceylon) decided to hold a conference of Afro-Asian nations and issued invitations to this effect in mid-January 1955. Rather surprisingly, it took Chou almost a month to respond to the invitation. In any case, he led the Chinese delegation to the 29-nation Afro-Asian (Bandung) Conference which met for a week in April. In addition to such Afro-Asian notables as Nehru, Nasser, and Sukarno, Chou found himself in the company of delegations from the three Asian members of SEATO, Pakistan, Thailand, and the Philippines. The conference proved to be a diplomatic showcase for Chou's talents, which exceeded his impressive performance a year earlier in Geneva. One writer has commented that his "skill . . . in championing both peaceful coexistence and anti-imperialism succeeded in creating an impression that there existed a united front of Communists and neutralists, based on the common conviction that Western colonialism and Western military pacts were the only real dangers threatening the independence of the new nations of Asia and Africa."[31] In a somewhat different fashion Nehru summed up the spirit of the conference with the rhetorical question—Why should we be dragged into [the] quarrels and wars [of Europe and America]?—and with his reference to "our new dignity, our new independence, our new freedom, our new spirit."[32] More specifically, the Bandung Conference endorsed universal United Nations membership, the reduction of armaments, the elimination of nuclear weapons, and ten principles designed to foster international cooperation and peace.

For China, the concrete results from the conference were marginal, but it opened a new range of diplomatic contacts to be explored. Chou used the occasion to move toward solutions of two other problems. He signed an agreement with Indonesia regarding the centuries-old problem of the nationality of overseas China (see under Huang Chen). Secondly, in a *démarche* that captured world headlines, he expressed a willingness to negotiate with the United States on the "question of relaxing tension in the Far East, and especially the question of relaxing tension in the Taiwan area." Hopes for fruitful talks with the United States were also heightened on May 13 when Chou, for the first time, referred to the willingness to "strive for the liberation of Taiwan by peaceful means so far as it is possible." Moreover, he repeated the "peaceful liberation" formulation in July at a session of the NPC. Soon afterwards, on August 1, the Sino-American ambassadorial-level talks began in Geneva (see under Wang Ping-nan).

Utilizing the momentum of the Bandung Conference, Chou moved quickly to advance China's position in Asia and, for the first time, to gain meaningful contacts in the Middle East. The visit of Indonesian Prime Minister Ali Sastroamidjojo to China in May 1955 was only the first in a series of trips to Peking by Asian heads of state or government during the next year and a half. Among the visitors were the prime ministers of Cambodia, Laos, Nepal, India, Burma, and Pakistan, and President Sukarno of Indonesia. During the same period China established formal diplomatic relations with Nepal, Egypt, Syria, and Yemen. The increasing contacts set the stage for Chou's extended goodwill tour of south and southeast Asia in 1956. In the meantime, however, there had been a marked change of relationships within the Communist bloc, which was most dramatically illustrated by the restiveness in Poland in mid-1956 and the Hungarian Revolt in the fall. Peking had stood by Moscow in the sense of maintaining bloc solidarity, but there were numerous suggestions of Chinese displeasure with Moscow's handling of the situation in both Poland and Hungary. As a consequence, Chou's frequent disavowal of "great nation chauvinism" during his Asian tour was widely interpreted as an indirect slap at Moscow. He had begun his trip in mid-November 1956 by spending a few days in North Vietnam. From there he went to Cambodia and then to India for talks with Nehru. Chou toured around India, visited briefly in Burma and Pakistan, and returned to New Delhi in late December for further talks with Nehru. Chou's itinerary called for visits to Nepal and Afghanistan, but at this point he was summoned back to Peking where he arrived in early January 1957.

The reasons for the interruption of Chou's tour were not discussed in Chinese media, but they were clearly linked to the aggravated relations between Moscow and its allies in East Europe. After a few days in Peking Chou left for Moscow on what seems to have been a mission to restore some degree of harmony with the Communist bloc. In Moscow, from January 7 to 10, he held talks with Russian, German, and Hungarian leaders. He then spent a few days in Warsaw and one day in Budapest, after which he returned to Moscow for further talks. The various communiqués issued during this series of talks all stressed the solidarity of the bloc. Chou then resumed his Asian tour, arriving in Afghanistan on January 19. Over the next two weeks he held talks with government leaders in Afghanistan, India, Nepal, and Ceylon. The emphasis during this portion of Chou's Asian tour was on peaceful coexistence. However, in contrast to the first leg of the tour, he avoided any reference to "great nation chauvinism"—apparently as a result of an explicit or implicit understanding reached during his talks in Moscow.

While Chou was promoting the "spirit of Bandung" abroad, he was, as usual, also deeply involved in domestic affairs. In the latter part of 1955 the CCP apparently decided to heighten the participation in public affairs of the non-Communist intellectuals, many of whose acknowledged talents were underemployed. Chou endorsed this theme in an important speech delivered in mid-January 1956 at a special Central Committee meeting attended by nearly 1,300

Party members from all walks of life. His address, in effect, launched the Hundred Flowers campaign, which is described in the biography of Lu Ting-i. In September of the same year, just prior to Chou's 11-nation tour of Asia and Europe, he delivered a detailed report on proposals for the Second Five-Year Plan at the Party's Eighth National Congress. His speech conveyed a spirit of buoyant confidence, but he also discussed with considerable candor a number of defects. Chou's senior position in the Party was once again reconfirmed at the congress. He was re-elected to the Central Committee, and the day after the Congress he was re-elected to the Politburo. Under the terms of the revised Party constitution, he now became a vice-chairman of the Central Committee and a member of the Politburo Standing Committee. The Standing Committee, in effect, replaced the Secretariat (to which Chou had previously belonged) as the single most important organ in the CCP and consisted then of only Mao, Liu Shao-ch'i, Chou, Chu Te, Ch'en Yun, and Teng Hsiao-p'ing. (In 1958 Lin Piao was added.)

In February 1958, after nearly a decade as foreign minister, Chou relinquished this post to Ch'en I. No explanations were given for the change, but the killing pace required of the foreign minister—especially in the period after the Geneva and Bandung Conferences—suggested that it was merely a common sense move to conserve Chou's energies. In any case, there was no indication during the ensuing years that Chou's voice in China's foreign affairs was diluted. In fact, just a few days after this change, Chou made one of his more important trips abroad when, in the company of Ch'en I and other top diplomatic and military figures, he traveled to Pyongyang. There, on February 19, he signed a statement providing for the withdrawal by the end of 1958 of the large number of Chinese troops which were still in Korea well over four years after the war had ended there. In the summer and early fall China and the United States became involved in another crisis regarding the Taiwan Straits (which is described in the biography of P'eng Te-huai). Chou made a number of pronouncements during the crisis, but perhaps the best known was a statement of September 6 expressing willingness to renew the then suspended Sino-American ambassadorial talks—a position which aided in cooling off the crisis.

Chou was abroad again in January–February 1959 when he went to Moscow for the 21st CPSU Congress. While there, on February 7, he signed an agreement with Khrushchev providing for the expansion of Soviet economic and technical aid for the 1959–1967 period. In retrospect, this was a landmark in Sino-Soviet relations; it was the last commitment of large-scale aid to China, and by the middle of the next year relations had deteriorated so sharply that Soviet technicians were withdrawn from China. Other top Chinese officials would visit Moscow again (including Chou himself), but Chou's 1959 trip was the last visit marked by an air of cordiality. Only a few weeks after Chou's return home, the Dalai Lama fled from Tibet to India where, to the annoyance of Peking, he was permitted to live in exile. The subsequent deterioration of Sino-Indian relations was paralleled by border disputes in other areas, most notably on the Burmese border. As a consequence, Chou and Ch'en I devoted considerable time to these issues during the next few years. In January 1960, during Premier Ne Win's visit to China, Chou signed the Sino-Burmese Treaty of Friendship and Mutual Non-aggression and a boundary agreement. Two months later in Peking, Chou signed boundary and economic aid agreements with the visiting Nepalese premier, and then in April and May Chou and Ch'en made goodwill visits to Burma, India, Nepal, Cambodia, and North Vietnam. Chou returned home with a Sino-Nepalese Treaty of Peace and Friendship, but in New Delhi he could only gain agreement that Chinese and Indian officials would meet at a later date to continue talks on the thorny border disputes. Two weeks later, May 27–June 1, 1960, Chou and Ch'en were in Ulan Bator where Chou signed the Sino-Mongolian Treaty of Friendship and Mutual Assistance and an agreement to provide Mongolia with economic and technical aid.

In the first days of 1961 Chou and Ch'en I went to Rangoon to attend Burmese independence celebrations and to exchange the instruments of ratification of the Sino-Burmese Boundary Treaty (which Chou had signed in Peking in October 1960). Chou took with him over 400 persons, the largest government delegation ever sent abroad by the PRC. On January 9 he signed an economic and technical cooperation agreement providing for a 30 million pound non-interest loan for the 1961–1967 period. In July 1961, in Peking, Chou signed the Sino-Korean Treaty of Friendship, Cooperation, and Mutual Assistance with Kim Il Sung, thereby matching a similar agreement which Kim had signed a week earlier in Moscow. These two agreements were suggestive of the competition in which Peking and Moscow were then engaged to get support for their respective positions in the steadily widening Sino-Soviet ideological dispute. The conflict became further aggravated in October 1961 when Chou led a delegation to Moscow for the 22nd CPSU Congress. Angered by Khrushchev's attack on Albania, then Peking's only ally in East Europe, Chou left for home before the congress ended, leaving P'eng Chen in charge of the delegation. This was Chou's last visit to Moscow during

Khrushchev's rule, but in November 1964, immediately after his fall from power, Chou went to the USSR for the 47th annversary of the October Revolution. He held talks with the new leaders, L. I. Brezhnev and A. N. Kosygin, but it was obvious that Sino-Soviet differences were not settled, and within a brief time the Chinese press was describing Brezhnev and Kosygin as "new Khrushchevs."

In the intervening years, Chinese domestic affairs had undergone profound changes. Almost exactly at the time of Chou's relinquishment of the Foreign Ministry portfolio (February 1958), the CCP launched the Great Leap Forward. Chou's role in this program, and his attitude toward it, is ambiguous; as so often in his past, he seems to have maintained a guarded neutrality which would allow him to shift with the currents as events unfolded. However, in speaking to the NPC in February 1958, he did endorse one of the themes which became a major component of the early phase of the Great Leap, namely, that China intended to surpass Great Britain in iron and steel production within 15 years. He attended the Party's Sixth Plenum (November–December 1958), which cut back some of the Great Leap program, but he was not listed as one of the speakers. In the following April, at another NPC session, Chou emphasized the need for centralized leadership over local industry and a still more pressing need to consolidate the system of the people's communes. In general, by that time he seems to have taken a rather conservative view of the Great Leap.

In August 1959 further adjustments were made in Great Leap programs at the Party's Eighth Plenum. Later in the month Chou reported to the NPC Standing Committee on the situation. He was given the embarrassing task of publicizing dramatic cutbacks in past claims and future goals. For example, the claim was made in late 1958 that grain output for that year was a staggering 375 million tons, and that it would reach an even more staggering 525 million tons in 1959. Chou now conceded that the 1958 grain figure should have been 250 million tons and that the projected 1959 figure would reach 275 million tons. Similarly, he lowered the 1959 target for steel from 18 to 12 million tons. Further difficulties in the economy led to a reordering of priorities in January 1961 at the Party's Ninth Plenum, when it was decided to emphasize agriculture and de-emphasize industry. This policy shift—sloganized as "taking agriculture as the foundation and industry as the leading factor"—was "crystallized further during the course of 1961, until it was articulated in a more nearly final form" by Chou when he presented a report at the NPC session in March 1962.[33] In the period when the Great Leap Forward faltered in the late 1950's, and

continuing into the early and middle 1960's when a notable economic recovery was made, the PRC displayed a marked reluctance to issue detailed public documents. This was particularly true regarding economic statistics. As a consequence, Chou's 1962 speech to the NPC was far less fact-laden than his reports of the 1950's. Much the same can be said about his address before the NPC in December 1964, but it was probably still the most thorough report on domestic and foreign affairs in the year preceding the Great Proletarian Cultural Revolution.

Chou and his colleague Ch'en I were abroad again in 1963–64 on a tour which received world-wide press coverage. From mid-December 1963 to early February 1964 they held talks with top officials in 11 nations: the United Arab Republic, Algeria, Morocco, Albania, Tunisia, Ghana, Mali, Guinea, Sudan, Ethiopia, and Somalia. Because Peking was still dueling with Moscow for influence in the Middle East and Africa, a major theme was the need to convene a Second Afro-Asian (Bandung) Conference (which, they made quite plain, should be held without Soviet participation). Other items discussed included the status of Taiwan, the issue of China in the United Nations, and Chinese economic assistance. The long trip was not one of Chou's finer moments—and the basic purpose, to gain support for a second Bandung meeting, foundered in the following year. The one immediate gain was the agreement by the Tunisians to establish diplomatic relations with the PRC. After returning to south China for a brief rest in early February 1964, Chou and Ch'en undertook a visit to Burma, Pakistan, and Ceylon in the last two weeks of the month. The basic themes were the same as those on the 11-nation tour. In July the two leaders were again in Rangoon; this was described simply as a "visit," but the resulting joint communiqué indicated that their talks with Burmese officials centered on the deteriorating situation in Vietnam and Laos.

Chou's wide-ranging travels in the post-1949 years are unmatched by any other senior Peking official, and they are all the more remarkable in view of his gargantuan responsibilities as chief administrator of the national bureaucracy. Chou was again reaffirmed as premier in January 1965 at the close of the inaugural session of the Third NPC. He was as active as ever when the Great Proletarian Cultural Revolution began in 1966, and although many of his subordinates in the State Council became victims of this important political movement, Chou himself remained as a key figure in the inner-elite.

With the exception of Mao Tse-tung, Chou is the best known Chinese Communist of the twentieth century, and he far surpasses Mao in his knowledge of the world's statesmen, political leaders, and journalists. No serious book on the Communist movement in China fails to mention him, and there are scores of descriptions which attest to his charm and superior intelligence. Many of these accounts have been deftly sifted in Kai-yu Hsu's biography of Chou published in 1968. Chün-tu Hsüeh's two-volume bibliography of the Communist movement is a major source for Chou's numerous pre-1949 speeches and articles.[34]

Chou's younger brother, Chou En-shou, participated in the Northern Expedition,[35] but nothing further is known about him. Chou En-lai and his wife, Teng Ying-ch'ao, are childless. In terms of the political importance of both the husband and the wife, the Chou–Teng couple is matched in CCP annals only by Li Fu-ch'un and his wife, Ts'ai Ch'ang.

1. *Lieh-shih chuan* (Biographies of martyrs; Moscow [?], 1936), pp. 62–74.

2. *SCMP* 1418, p. 12.

3. Kai-yu Hsu, *Chou En-lai: China's Gray Eminence* (Garden City, N.Y., 1968), p. 216.

4. *SCMM* 281, p. 8.

5. C. Martin Wilbur and Julie Lien-ying How, eds., *Documents on Communism, Nationalism, and Soviet Advisers in China, 1918–1927* (New York, 1956), p. 218; Jean Chesneaux, *The Chinese Labor Movement, 1919–1927* (Stanford, Calif., 1968), p. 311; Kai-yu Hsu, p. 44.

6. Kai-yu Hsu, pp. 52–53.

7. Harold R. Isaacs, *The Tragedy of the Chinese Revolution* (Stanford, Calif., 1961, 2nd rev. ed.), pp. 115–116; Robert C. North and Xenia J. Eudin, *M. N. Roy's Mission to China* (Berkeley, Calif., 1963), p. 73.

8. *Hung-ch'i p'iao-p'iao* (Red flag fluttering; Peking, 1958), VIII, 39.

9. *Lieh-shih chuan*, pp. 83–84.

10. C. Martin Wilbur, "The Ashes of Defeat," *The China Quarterly*, no. 18:3–54 (April–June 1964); Wei Hung-yun, ed., *"Pa-i" ch'i-i* (The "August First" uprising; Wuhan, 1957), pp. 8–16.

11. *Ti-erh-tz'u kuo-nei ko-ming chan-cheng shih-ch'i shih-shih lun-ts'ung* (Accounts of the second revolutionary civil war; Peking, 1956), p. 3.

12. *Bol'shaya Sovetskaya Entsiklopedya* (Large Soviet encyclopedia; Moscow, 1957), XL, 352–353.

13. *Ibid.*

14. Benjamin I. Schwartz, *Chinese Communism and the Rise of Mao* (Cambridge, Mass., 1951), pp. 128–132.

15. Tso-liang Hsiao, *Power Relations within the Chinese Communist Movement, 1930–1934* (Seattle, 1961), pp. 62–63.

16. Schwartz, p. 144.

17. Stuart Schram, *Mao Tse-tung* (New York, 1966), pp. 141–145; *Bol'shaya Sovetskaya Entsiklopedya*, XL, 352–353.

18. *Selected Works of Mao Tse-tung* (Peking, 1965), I, 214–223.

19. Edgar Snow, *Red Star over China* (New York, 1938), pp. 43–44.

20. Edgar Snow, *Random Notes on Red China, 1936–1945* (Cambridge, Mass., 1957), pp. 1–14.

21. Lyman P. Van Slyke, ed., *The Chinese Communist Movement: A Report of the United States War Department, July 1945* (Stanford, Calif., 1968), pp. 67–68.

22. Stuart R. Schram, *The Political Thought of Mao Tse-tung* (New York, 1963), pp. 159–160; Charles B. McLane, *Soviet Policy and the Chinese Communists, 1931–1946* (New York, 1958), p. 114.

23. Chiang Kai-shek, *Soviet Russia in China* (New York, 1957), pp. 87–88.

24. *Ibid.*, pp. 92–93.

25. Van Slyke, pp. 78–79.

26. Stuart Gelder, *The Chinese Communists* (London, 1946), pp. 173–180.

27. Tang Tsou, *America's Failure in China, 1941–50* (Chicago, 1963), pp. 316–324.

28. United States Department of State, *United States Relations with China: With Special Reference to the Period 1944–1949* (Washington, D.C., 1949), *passim*.

29. *Hung-ch'i p'iao-p'iao* (Peking, 1957), III, 345.

30. Allen S. Whiting, *China Crosses the Yalu* (New York, 1960), pp. 68–115.

31. Richard Lowenthal, "China," in Zbigniew Brzezinski, ed., *Africa and the Communist World* (Stanford, Calif., 1963), p. 151.

32. O. Edmund Clubb, *Twentieth Century China* (New York, 1964), p. 345.

33. Alexander Eckstein, *Communist China's Economic Growth and Foreign Trade* (New York, 1966), p. 38.

34. Chün-te Hsueh, *The Chinese Communist Movement, 1921–1937* (Stanford, Calif., 1960), and *The Chinese Communist Movement, 1937–1949* (1962).

35. Josiah W. Bennett, "A Poet with the Northern Expedition," *The Far Eastern Quarterly*, no. 2:159, 166 (February 1944).

Chou Hsiao-chou

(c.1912–   ; Changsha, Hunan). Former Hunan Party official; alternate member, CCP Central Committee.

Chou Hsiao-chou, a Party veteran from the thirties, was the top CCP official in Hunan Province from 1953 until his apparent purge in 1959. He was born in Changsha, the capital of Hunan. Chou is reported to have made the Long March and was serving as a personal secretary to Mao Tse-tung when the Communists moved to Yenan in 1936. According to fragmentary reports, he was engaged in guerrilla warfare in Hopeh and his native Hunan at some period during the Sino-Japanese War. However, he apparently spent part of the time in Sinkiang, because an account by General Sheng Shih-ts'ai, the powerful governor of Sinkiang with whom the Communists cooperated during the early years of the war, mentions that Mao Tse-tung sent Chou there "to tell us of the difficulties besetting the Eighth Route Army during the winter of 1940 . . ." Chou's mission was reportedly to get assistance from Sheng; the latter claims that in response to Chou's requests he sent money and 50,000 "fur coats" to the Communists in Yenan. Another of Sheng's references suggests that Chou may have been in Sinkiang as late as early 1942.[1] (See also under T'eng Tai-yuan.)

Nothing further is known of Chou's wartime or postwar activities, but he must have held posts of some significance within the CCP, for by the early fifties he had emerged as a leader of prominence in his native Hunan. His most important positions were under the jurisdiction of the Hunan Party Committee. By early 1950 he was head of the Hunan Propaganda Department (a post he held to about 1952), and from about 1952 to 1953 he was secretary of the West Hunan CCP District Committee. In the early fall of 1953 the ranking Hunan Party Secretary, Chin Ming (q.v.), was assigned to a post in the central government. Chou replaced Chin as the Human secretary (redesignated as "first" secretary in 1956), a position he retained until mid-1959 (see below).

In addition to his role in the Hunan Party hierarchy, Chou also participated in the work of the Hunan government. He was a member of the Hunan Provincial People's Government Council from early 1950 until his promotion to a vice-governorship in February 1955. In addition, from July 1950 he served under Chin Ming as a vice-chairman of the government's Land Reform Committee. In February 1955 Chou was also named as chairman of the Hunan Committee of the CPPCC, and in September of the next year he attended the Eighth National Party Congress in Peking where he presented a written speech on the subject of strengthening agricultural producers' cooperatives. The peak of Chou's career was clearly reached in the years from 1956 to 1958 when, as the key Hunan Party official, he was constantly reported in the Chinese press—making inspection tours of the province, speaking before conferences, and presiding over rallies marking important national holidays.

In the spring of 1958 Chou was identified in still another position of importance, the political commissarship of the Hunan Military District. He was identified in this post when he accompanied Mao Tse-tung on an inspection tour of a military unit in Changsha. In the following month (May 1958), at the second session of the Eighth Party Congress, Chou was elected an alternate member of the Party Central Committee. Two months later, at a session of the Hunan Provincial People's Congress, Chou gave the keynote report on Hunanese governmental affairs. At the same time he requested to be relieved as a vice-governor owing to the "complicated and heavy" work of the Hunan Party Committee. Chou continued to play an active role in Hunanese affairs through 1958 and was among those who attended the Party's Sixth Plenum in Wuhan (November–December 1958) at which time the goals of the "Great Leap Forward" were sharply cut back.

After the Sixth Plenum in 1958, Chou made only a few more appearances in the first half of 1959, the last in June. Within less than a year Chang P'ing-hua (q.v.) replaced Chou in the latter's three major positions in Hunan—as Party first secretary, chairman of the Hunan Committee of the CPPCC, and political commissar of the Hunan Military District. The reason for Chou Hsiao-chou's political fall has never been made public. It might have had some relation to the Great Leap Forward. The timing of his disappearance might also suggest some connection with the purge of Defense Minister P'eng Te-huai who faded from the public scene at approximately the same time as Chou. However, there is no evidence to support this. Whatever the reason, Chou's purge seems to have been more serious than other Central Committee-level provincial leaders who fell from power during the Great Leap period (e.g., P'an Fu-sheng, Chao Chien-min, Shu T'ung). In virtually all cases these men made a comeback after three or four years of political oblivion. However, there has been no mention of Chou since 1959 even though he nominally continues to be an alternate member of the Party Central Committee.

1. Allen S. Whiting and Sheng Shih-ts'ai, *Sinkiang: Pawn or Pivot?* (East Lansing, Mich., 1958), pp. 231, 245.

Chou Huan

(1904–   ; Liaoning). Secretary, Liaoning Party Committee; alternate member, CCP Central Committee.

Chou Huan, who has spent most of his career in his native Manchuria, served as a political officer in the Red Army from the 1930's until 1959. He became an alternate member of the Party Central Committee in 1956 and a secretary of the Liaoning Party Committee in 1959. '

Chou's activities are not recorded until the early 1930's when he was serving as a political officer with a Red Army unit commanded by Huang Kung-lueh (q.v.). This was probably the Third Army (subordinate to the First Army Corps of Chu Te and Mao Tse-tung), which Huang headed in central Kiangsi from 1929 until he was killed in 1931. In mid-1930 the First Army Corps was renamed the First Front Army; Chou apparently remained with it because he took part in the Long March to north Shensi, which began in 1934.

The only report about Chou's activity during the Sino-Japanese War was that by 1938 he was serving in the Communist Eighth Route Army, which had been formed in north and northwest China after the start of the war. He was a deputy chief of the Liaison Section of the Army's General Political Department. At the end of the war he returned to his native Manchuria, accompanying Communist troops under Lin Piao, which began infiltrating from China proper at the time of the Japanese surrender. These forces united with the local resistance army, which had been operating in Manchuria under Communist military leader Chou Pao-chung (q.v.) to form the Northeast Democratic Allied Army in January 1946. Lin became the commander of this new army which in the next three years was responsible for the conquest of Manchuria.

By 1948 Chou had become a deputy director of the Northeast Military Region's Political Department. The main elements of Lin Piao's forces moved into China in the winter of 1948–49, but Chou remained in Manchuria where he assumed an increasingly important role as a political-military leader. In 1949 he advanced to the directorship of the Political Department, and in August of that year, on the eve of the establishment of the PRC, Chou was appointed a member of the Northeast People's Government (NEPG), the civil administration for Manchuria, headed by Kao Kang (q.v.). Kao was also commander and political commissar of the Northeast Military Region, and thus when Chou was promoted to deputy political commissar by December 1952 he was again directly subordinate to Kao. The NEPG was reorganized in the Northeast Administrative Committee (NEAC) in January 1953; Chou was reappointed to membership, retaining this post until the NEAC was abolished in 1954. Concurrently, from April 1950 to September 1954, he was a member of the NEPG–NEAC People's Supervision Committee.

Chou's prominence in the northeast enabled him to participate in the inauguration of the PRC. He made one of his few trips away from Manchuria to attend the inaugural session of the First CPPCC in September 1949 as a representative of the "Northeast Liberated Areas." Five years later, when the Communists were preparing to establish their constitutional government, committees were set up throughout China to discuss the draft constitution and Chou was chosen as a vice-chairman of the one in Manchuria. Subsequently, when the First NPC was convened (September 1954), he was a deputy from the Northeast Military Region. He continued to serve in the First NPC, but was not re-elected to the Second NPC, which first met in 1959.

In 1955 personal military ranks were established for the first time in the PLA and military orders were conferred for outstanding service in the period between 1927 and 1950. Though Chou may have been given a rank at this time, he was not identified as a colonel-general in the PLA (equivalent to a three-star general in the U.S. Army) until late 1957. However, he did receive one or more of the orders, although it is not known which ones. The fact that Chou received any national citation in 1955 is significant, since he and one other man were the only recipients among the seven top military leaders who had been active in the Northeast Military Region in the early 1950's. The omission of the others was due to the alleged "anti-Party" plot led by Kao Kang, which had been "uncovered" in Manchuria in 1954–55. In addition to Kao, who was Chou's immediate superior and the most important figure in the region, one of Chou's fellow deputy political commissars, Chang Hsiu-shan, was among those implicated. Chou had served under Chang when the latter chaired the People's Supervision Committee of the NEPG. Although it is not known if Chou played any role in the downfall of Kao Kang and Chang Hsiu-shan, it is obvious that he was not implicated in the "plot" and he clearly profited from their purge.

At about the same time as Kao Kang's purge in early 1955, the Northeast Military Region was redesignated as the Shenyang (Mukden) Military Region, the territorial boundaries remaining unchanged. By the latter part of the year Chou had become political commissar of the region, in effect replacing Kao Kang. A year later, at the Eighth Party Congress in September 1956, Chou was elected as an alternate member of the Party Central Committee. During this period he was mentioned rather frequently in the press because Shenyang is often visited by leading Chinese and foreign officials. For example, Chou served as a host for East German Prime Minister Otto Grotewohl during the latter's tour of Shenyang in December 1955, and he was on hand to welcome Chou En-lai back from North Korea in February 1958.

By September 1959 Chou had become a secretary of the Liaoning Provincial Party Committee. Two months later Lai Ch'uan-chu (q.v.) replaced him as political commissar of the Shenyang Military Region and at the same time Ch'en Hsi-lien replaced Teng Hua (qq.v.) as the commander. Since then, both Chou and Teng have fallen into relative obscurity, which suggests that they have encountered political difficulties. Only a short time before the Shenyang commands were changed, Defense Minister P'eng Te-huai was removed from his post and fell into political disfavor. Teng Hua's career had been closely linked to P'eng's, and it is probable that Chou Huan had been an associate of P'eng in the early 1930's. Nonetheless, this circumstantial evidence is tempered by the fact that Chou continues to serve as a secretary of the Liaoning Party Committee.

Chou I-ch'ün

(c.1898–1931). Early CCP leader.

Chou I-ch'ün was an early Party leader who took a prominent part in a number of important military campaigns between 1927 and 1931. He appears to have had an influence in bringing veteran military leader Ho Lung into the Communist Movement. Chou was probably a native of Kweichow,[1] but he is said to have been related to Ho Lung, who comes from Sang-chih in northwest Hunan. He graduated as a logistics officer from the second class of the Whampoa Military Academy in Canton in June 1925 when he was about 27. That same year the KMT sent him to western Hunan to convince Ho Lung (q.v.), already noted for his military exploits, to join the Nationalists. The attempt was successful and when the Northern Expedition began in mid-1926, Ho became commander of an independent regiment in Chang Fa-k'uei's Fourth Nationalist Army. Chou was made the regiment's chief political officer. At that time Chou was a CCP member, but Ho was not. The two men worked together during the Nanchang Uprising on August 1, 1927 (see under Yeh T'ing), when the final split occurred between the KMT and the CCP. Although he was not a Party member until after the Nanchang defeat, Ho had a major role in the uprising and Chou continued as one of his political officers. After the failure at Nanchang, Ho Lung's 20th Red Army joined the southern march to Swatow along with Yeh T'ing's 11th Army and Chu Te's Nanchang garrison regiment. In addition to his political work Chou commanded the Third Division of the 20th Army on the march. He entered Swatow with the Red forces in late September 1927. The next month he wrote an article for a leading Party journal criticizing some of the campaign strategy and commenting: "In the 20th Army, party work was most advanced in [Chou's own] 3rd Division." During the Swatow campaign, he wrote, "Ho Lung and Kuo Mo-jo . . . found it best to join [the CCP] because they had no other future."[2]

Chou commanded some of the operations to take and hold Swatow. When the campaign failed in the last days of September he led some of the surviving troops out of the city. It was not until he secretly returned to Swatow and boarded a steamer for Shanghai on October 5 that he learned that the Communist defeat had been complete, that the particularly strong 24th Division of Yeh T'ing's 11th Army had suffered heavy losses, and that Yeh himself had been wounded.[3]

Not long after these events he went to southwest Hupeh where, with a local partisan leader named Tuan Te-ch'ang, he organized the Sixth Red Army. Ho Lung was organizing the Second Army across the border in northwest Hunan at about the same time. The two armies fought together under Ho Lung's command in mid-1930 when Li Li-san, then the most influential leader of the Party headquarters in Shanghai, ordered the Red forces in central China to move from their rural bases into the Wuhan area for an attack on the major cities of China's industrial heartland. Ho's joint force attacked Wuhan and suffered heavily (see under Ho Lung). When the campaign ended, the Sixth Army withdrew to the south. Chou I-ch'ün, however, remained in west Hupeh where he directed political work in the West Hunan-Hupeh Soviet, which Ho Lung headed. In the spring of 1931 Chou was the acting Party secretary of the West Hupeh District.[4]

At this time Party work in the rural base areas was often disastrously affected by the confusion and political tensions which existed among the highest CCP leaders, especially those at the Party headquarters in Shanghai. There a number of personnel changes had resulted in the ouster of Li Li-san in the fall of 1930. By January 1931 the Party hierarchy had been taken over by the "Russian-returned students" (see under Ch'en Shao-yü), sometimes known as the "28 Bolsheviks." Ho's West Hunan-Hupeh area did not escape the effects of these power struggles. In March 1931 Hsia Hsi (q.v.), an emissary of the Russian-returned student group, arrived there to succeed Teng Chung-hsia (q.v.) as the key political leader. Hsia and his supporters are said to have expelled Chou I-ch'ün from the leading Party organs in the West Hunan-Hupeh Soviet. Shortly afterward, in May 1931, Chou lost his life while on an inspection trip in the area.[5]

The circumstances of Chou's death have never been explained and reports on the subject conflict. One supposition is that Hsia Hsi was responsible, while renegade Communist Li Ang states that Chou's death was arranged by Mao Tse-tung.[6] A Japanese source suggests that Chou was a close follower of Chou En-lai and was also somewhat influenced by Li Li-san. However, this report does not indicate which political faction caused Chou's downfall.[7]

---

1. *Huang-p'u t'ung-hsueh tsung-ming-ts'e* (Whampoa student directory; n.p., 1933).
2. C. Martin Wilbur, "The Ashes of Defeat," *The China Quarterly,* no. 18:24–31 (April–June 1964).
3. *Ibid.*, p. 30.
4. *JMJP*, February 1, 1962, p. 5.
5. *Ibid.*
6. Wilbur, p. 5.
7. Benjamin I. Schwartz, *Chinese Communism and the Rise of Mao* (Cambridge, Mass., 1951), p. 181.

Chou Jung-hsin

Secretary-general, State Council.

Chou Jung-hsin is a prominent government administrator who, with the exception of a three-year tour in Chekiang, has worked in Peking in the central government. He presently serves as the secretary-general of the State Council under Premier Chou En-lai. When the Communists came to power in 1949, Chou was working as deputy secretary-general of the Party's North China Bureau, which was then headed by Secretary Po I-po, one of the PRC's leading economic specialists. He was promoted to second secretary of the Bureau by mid-1950, but by late 1951 he may have been replaced in this post by Nieh Jung-chen. When the central government was established in the fall of 1949, Chou was assigned to the Government Administration Council's Finance and Economics Committee (FEC), a key organ of government headed by Ch'en Yun (q.v.) that was in charge of coordinating the work of several ministries and commissions. Within the FEC he was deputy secretary-general (October 1949–August 1952) and concurrently head of the FEC's Staff Office (December 1949–November 1950).

Chou's rise to prominence occurred in 1951–52 when he received several important positions in rapid succession. From August 1951 to September 1954 he was a member of the Government Administration Council's Nationalities Affairs Commission, although there is little evidence that he was active in this organization. In December 1951 he was named as a deputy secretary-general of the national government's Central Austerity Examination (or Inspection) Committee chaired by Po I-po. The establishment of this committee was an outgrowth of decisions taken at the important third session of the CPPCC's First National Committee held a few weeks earlier and attended by Chou. At this session considerable stress was placed upon the necessity (growing out of the pressures of the Korean War) to economize on a nationwide basis. For similar reasons a committee to facilitate the productivity of government organizations was also set up in February 1952; Chou was named to membership on this committee, retaining it until the body was dissolved in 1954. Not long after, in May 1952, the PRC formed the China Committee for the Promotion of International Trade. Ostensibly a non-governmental "people's" organization, the Committee has played a major role in stimulating trade with nations not having formal diplomatic relations with the PRC (see under Nan Han-ch'en, the chairman).

Chou received his first ministerial-level post in August 1952 when he was appointed to the newly established Ministry of Building (sometimes translated as "engineering construction") as a vice-minister, a post he was to hold for nearly six years under ministers Ch'en Cheng-jen and Liu Hsiu-feng (qq.v.). He received a closely related appointment a year later when the China Architectural Society, a professional organization, was established at a national congress held in October 1953. Chou was named as the chairman and continued in this position until about 1961 or 1962 when he was replaced by Yang Ch'un-mao, another vice-minister of Building. In this capacity Chou spoke before the Society's second national conference (February 1957) that centered on the problems concerned with the construction of industrial cities and city planning.

Chou made his only known trip abroad in November 1957 when he joined a delegation led by Kuo Mo-jo to the USSR. The delegation, composed of a large group of scientists, was one of several groups (the most important headed by Mao Tse-tung) that visited the Soviet Union to attend celebrations in connection with the 40th anniversary of the Russian Revolution. The scientific group remained in Moscow for several weeks and was known to have carried on extensive negotiations with their Soviet counterparts. Not long after returning from Moscow, Chou was removed from the Ministry of Building (March 1958) and posted to Chekiang Province where he was to remain for the next three years. His initial appointment there was as president of Chekiang University; by mid-1958 he also served as a member of the provincial CCP Committee's Standing Committee, and in November 1958 he was also appointed as a member of the Chekiang Provincial People's Government Council.

In July 1961 Chou was transferred back to Peking to become a vice-minister of Education, serving under Minister Yang Hsiu-feng. Relatively little was heard of Chou's activities in the Ministry, although on occasion he appeared with senior Party leaders in connection with foreign visitors—as in November 1961 when he accompanied Chou En-lai to receive a delegation from Ghana.

In March 1963 Chou was removed from the Education Ministry and named as a deputy secretary-general of the State Council. Ostensibly, Chou served under Secretary-general Hsi Chung-hsin (q.v.). In fact, however, Hsi dropped completely from the public scene in the fall of 1962, and by July 1963 Chou was serving as the acting secretary-general. For the next year and a half he made numerous public appearances in this capacity, and then in January 1965 (at the close of the first session of the Third NPC), Chou formally replaced Hsi as the secretary-general. In view of the heavy schedule of Premier Chou En-lai and of the vice-premiers, the State Council's secretary-general presumably attends to much of the daily routine of this important organization. The significance of the position is illustrated by the fact that Chou Jung-hsin's two predecessors (Li Wei-han and Hsi Chung-hsun) are of Central Committee rank.

In the meantime, Chou had received another position under the State Council. In the spring of 1963 the State Council created the State Establishment Committee (*kuo-chia pien-chih wei-yuan-hui;* sometimes translated "State Committee on Government Organization") at one level below the ministries and commissions. The directorship of the Committee was vacant until November 1963 when Chou was named to that post, a position he still retains. The nature of the Committee's activities has not been divulged, but to judge from the powers exercised by an "Establishment and Wages Committee" that existed in 1955,[1] the present Committee apparently has authority to retrench government organs and reassign government personnel.

1. 1956 *Jen-min shou-ts'e* (People's handbook), p. 235.

Chou Lin

(Kweichow). Former Kweichow Party leader.

Chou Lin was the most prominent Party leader in Kweichow Province from the mid-fifties to the mid-sixties. Little is known about his early career; according to Japanese sources he graduated from Kweichow University. He first came to prominence in December 1948 when the Communist forces led by Liu Po-ch'eng and Ch'en I (qq.v.) captured Hsu-chou (Suchow) in northwestern Kiangsu, one of the major targets of the Communist armies during the important Huai-hai campaign. Chou served there briefly as a member of the municipal Military Control Commission and as the mayor. Soon after, however, he transferred to Shanghai when that city fell to the advancing Communist armies in May 1949. There Chou was initially a deputy secretary-general of both the Shanghai Military Control Commission and the Shanghai Municipal People's Government. He was promoted to the secretary-generalship in both organs of government in the latter part of 1949, retaining these posts until transferred to Kweichow in late 1951.

In October 1951 Chou was elected to two important posts in the southwest. He was made a vice-governor of his native Kweichow and was named to membership on the Southwest Military and Administrative Committee (SWMAC), chaired by Liu Po-ch'eng under whom he had worked during the Huai-hai campaign. When the SWMAC was reorganized into the Southwest Administrative Committee in February 1953, Chou was reappointed to membership, continuing in this post until the regional governments were dissolved in 1954. In Kweichow, Chou served under Governor Yang Yung (q.v.) until Yang was transferred to North Korea in 1954 where he was the deputy commander of the

Communist forces that remained after the Korean War. Shortly afterwards, Su Chen-hua, the ranking Party official in Kweichow, was transferred to Peking. Thus, by mid-1954, Chou was probably the most important Communist official in Kweichow. Chou's primacy in the Kweichow government structure was formalized in February 1955 when he was elected as the provincial governor to replace Yang Yung. Similarly, he apparently took over the leadership of the Kweichow Party Committee following Su Chen-hua's departure in mid-1954, although Chou was not specifically identified as the Kweichow Party first secretary until 1956.

Chou Lin received his first post in the national administration in 1956 when, in by-election, he was named to replace a deceased colleague as a deputy from Kweichow to the First NPC. Immediately he was also appointed (at the third session of the First NPC in June 1956) to membership on the NPC Nationalities Committee. Although Chou is a Han Chinese, he owed his seat on the Nationalities Committee (representing non-Han peoples) to the large concentration of minority peoples residing in Kweichow whom a provincial deputy ostensibly represents. He also served as a Kweichow deputy to the Second NPC (1959–1964) and was again named to its Nationalities Committee. He was once again elected a Kweichow deputy to the Third NPC that opened in December 1964, but he was not reappointed to the Nationalities Committee. In addition to annual trips to Peking to attend NPC sessions, Chou is known to have attended important Party meetings in Peking and elsewhere outside Kweichow. For example, he attended the Eighth Party Congress in September 1956 where he submitted a written speech on the development of mountainous regions in Kweichow. He was also at the Second Session of the Eighth Party Congress in May 1958, as well as the important Sixth Plenum of the Party Central Committee (held in Wuhan, November–December 1958) when it was decided to curb some of the excesses of the commune movement.

During the decade after the mid-fifties when Chou became the key Party leader in Kweichow, his activities were frequently reported in the Chinese press. He was often reported, for example, making inspection tours of national minority areas, delivering keynote reports before Party and government meetings, or accompanying senior Party leaders (as in May 1960 when Chou En-lai visited an iron and steel factory in Kweiyang, the Kweichow capital). He was identified in August 1958 as the political commissar of the Kweichow Military District but apparently held this position for only a brief time. Chou's position as the ranking Party-government leader in Kweichow was unusual in two respects. First, he was one of the relatively few Party first secretaries and governors who did not belong to the

Central Committee, and second, he was one of the few men who (after the mid-fifties) held the post of provincial governor and Party first secretary concurrently.

Until the turn of the year 1964–65, Chou's career gave every indication of a man rising steadily in the Party hierarchy. Although he was elected to the Third NPC in late 1964, he was not (as already noted) reappointed to the NPC Nationalities Committee. In this connection, a mitigating factor was his election as a representative of minority nationalities to membership on the Fourth National Committee of the CPPCC that met simultaneously with the opening session of the Third NPC (December 1964–January 1965). However, in the first half of 1965 Chou lost both his key positions in Kweichow—the Party first secretaryship and the governorship. He was replaced in the former post by alternate Party Central Committee member Li Ta-chang (q.v.) in February 1965 and by Li Li, formerly a Honan Party official, as the Kweichow governor in July 1965. It has been normal Chinese Communist practice for leaders who fall ill to be carried in their official positions for rather lengthy periods (with another person serving, for example, as the acting governor). But as Chou was rather quickly removed, it appears that he may have run into political difficulties, being allowed to retain only his post in the NPC and the rather unimportant CPPCC.

Chou Pao-chung

(1902–1964; Ta-li, Yunnan). Leader of Manchurian resistance, 1931–1945; alternate member, CCP Central Committee.

Chou Pao-chung was one of the most important Communist resistance leaders in Manchuria from 1931 until the end of the Sino-Japanese War. His original name was either Hsi Shao-huang or Yü Shao-huang; the former is used in a semi-official Communist biography.[1] He used his Party pseudonym, Chou Pao-chung, from the time he entered Manchuria to work with the resistance in 1931.[2] Chou was from Ta-li in western Yunnan, an important military-government center for a remote region that was traversed by the ancient caravan route to Burma. Ta-li was the capital of a kingdom that in the seventh and eighth centuries A.D. covered most of present-day Yunnan. The city is still the center for the descendents from the ancient kingdom, the Min-chia minority peoples (also known as the Pai) who are rice farmers on the Ta-li plain. The Min-chias, to which Chou's family belonged, continue to speak their own language, but they have long been politically assimilated with the Han Chinese. When some of the Min-chias moved to the city, they became artisans and small shop owners. Chou's father was a shoemaker and his mother a peasant woman. Chou

was the youngest son in the family; he finished primary school and then went to a junior middle school before joining the army about 1915. Within three years he had become a company commander. Then in 1921 he decided to further his military education by entering the Yunnan Military Academy, the school that Chu Te had graduated from 10 years earlier. Chou graduated with distinction in military engineering in 1923. After leaving the Yunnan academy, he then went to Moscow for two years of study at the Communist University of the Toilers of the East (1923–1925).[3] Other accounts claim that he studied in the USSR somewhat later, attending the Red Army Staff College between 1928 and 1931.[4] In any case, Chou was known to have been in China in 1925 when he was on the staff at the Whampoa Military Academy in Canton. Entering the Nationalist army from Whampoa, at the start of the Northern Expedition in mid-1926 he became a deputy commander and concurrently the chief-of-staff of a regiment in the Sixth Army of Hunanese General Ch'eng Ch'ien (who defected to the Communists in 1949). At Whampoa, Chou must have met some active Party members, because there were a number on the teaching staff as well as among the cadets. Possibly he followed one of his colleagues, Party veteran Lin Po-ch'ü, into the Hunanese Sixth Army. In 1926 Lin was head of the Political Department with the army. Ch'eng Ch'ien's army captured Nanking for the Nationalists in 1927. Chou joined the CCP that same year, but he continued to be a member of the Nationalist military forces, and in 1928 became a deputy commander of the 18th Division and concurrently the garrison commander of eastern Hunan. However, when he failed to suppress some of the Communist-led peasant uprisings in eastern Hunan, he was relieved of these posts with the Nationalist armies. He then managed to escape to Shanghai where he is said to have worked with the CCP underground until after the Japanese entered Manchuria in September 1931. The period is also one in which there are reports that he went to the USSR and may have attended the Red Army military school.

The notable years of Chou's career were those he spent in Manchuria fighting the Japanese and later the Nationalists from about 1931 to 1948. The Party sent him into Manchuria immediately after the Mukden Incident (September 1931) to make contact with other Communists who were working there. It was then that he took the name Chou Pao-chung by which he came to be well known in the Manchurian resistance by the end of the Sino-Japanese War. Chou was assigned to work under Lo Teng-hsien (q.v.), then in the Harbin area as secretary of the Manchurian Provincial Committee of the CCP.[5] Accounts of Party activity in Manchuria at this time are sketchy, but there was known to have been considerable opposition to the CCP's working there on the part of Korean Communists who were also active in and around Harbin. Chou's connections with the Korean Communists are not known, but in addition to his contacts with Lo's CCP group, he worked with the non-Communist National Salvation Army of Li Tu and became Li's chief-of-staff. In the early 1930's Chou was active in the resistance around Ning-an hsien in eastern Kirin (now southeastern Heilungkiang), an area not far south of the important city of Mu-tan-chiang and about 100 miles from the Russian border. Most of the Manchurian resistance suffered severe losses in combat with the Japanese in 1932–1933. Resistance leaders such as Li Tu were forced to leave the area (Li fled across the Soviet border); Lo Teng-hsien left for Shanghai in late 1932, and eventually Chou seems to have assumed Lo's post with the Manchurian CCP Committee.

In spite of these defeats, by the summer of 1933 Yang Ching-yü, a CCP member from Honan, who was killed by the Japanese in 1940, and other Chinese Communists had begun to reorganize the Manchurian resistance. During 1933 and 1934 the Northeast People's Revolutionary Army (Tung-pei jen-min ko-ming chün) was created, including six armies operating in north, south, and east Manchuria. There were Korean Communists in all of them. Chou Pao-chung became the commander of the Fifth Army, which was formed in 1933 and operated in eastern Manchuria under the Chi-tung (East Kirin) Bureau of the CCP Manchurian Provincial Committee. During 1934 Chou's forces fought in Kirin as well as along the Mu-tan River (traversing Heilungkiang and Kirin) and into the Ch'ang-pai Mountains, which form the boundary of eastern Kirin and Korea. There his forces were joined at one point by Korean resistance units led by Kim Il-sung (see under Chu Te-hai). In 1935–36 the Northeast People's Revolutionary Army was united with other resistance forces to form the Northeast Allied Anti-Japanese Army (later "Northeast" was dropped in the title). The commander-in-chief was Yang Ching-yü. By 1938 the Allied Army had been expanded and reorganized into three route armies. Chou commanded the Second Route Army and continued to fight in eastern Kirin. After the head of the Third Route Army was killed in 1942, Chou took over his command, but Japanese attacks forced his army to retreat temporarily into the Soviet Maritime Provinces north of Khabarovsk. There the Allied Army set up a field school for about 200 men with Chou as its head. Just prior to the cessation of hostilities in August 1945, the Allied Army was re-named the Northeast Self-Defense Army, with Chou as its commander as well as its political commissar. Chinese Communist sources claim that this army cooperated with the Russians in fighting the Japanese after the USSR entered the war.

By 1945 Chou had emerged as the leader of Communist resistance in Manchuria, thereby serving as a focus for the Communist vanguard that began to infiltrate Manchuria at the time of the Japanese surrender in August 1945. When the CCP dispatched elements of the former Eighth Route and New Fourth Armies into Manchuria, these forces came together with Chou. Lin Piao was in charge of these forces moving in from China proper, with two deputy commanders who were veteran Communists, Hsiao Ching-kuang (now head of the PLA Navy) and Manchurian-born Lü Cheng-ts'ao. Soon Chou's army formed a part of the larger Northeast Democratic Allied Army organized by Lin Piao in 1946, with Chou, Hsiao, and Lü as his deputy commanders. When he joined Lin, Chou was assigned to the Kirin-Liaoning Military Region established under the army's control; in this area he became top military commander as well as commander of the garrison force in the principal city of Changchun. He held both posts from 1946 to 1947.

Because the Communists were in wide control in Manchuria almost from the moment that hostilities ended, they were able to establish regional and provincial governments there a few years before such governments were in operation in China proper where the CCP was not in complete control until 1949–50. In 1946 the Northeast Administrative Committee (NEAC) was established under the chairmanship of Lin Feng (q.v.) as the government organ for Manchuria. Chou was named as a NEAC member, and by 1947 he became governor of Kirin (subordinate to the NEAC), a post he held until 1949. In 1948 he was the deputy commander of the Northeast (Manchuria) Military Region.

When the last two Manchurian cities held by the Nationalists fell to the Communists in the fall of 1948 (Changchun, October; Mukden, November) the conquest of Manchuria was completed. Lin Piao then moved his army into north China, surrounding Peking and Tientsin in December; the cities were taken over by Lin's army in January 1949 by which time the army was redesignated as the Fourth Field Army. Lin's army did not pause long around Peking and Tientsin but soon began preparations to expand into central and south China. As it moved south the army saw considerable fighting before it finally completed its conquests on Hainan Island in April 1950. Chou went with Lin as far as Peking and participated in the negotiations for the takeover of the city, which was surrendered peacefully by KMT General Fu Tso-i. Chou remained in Peking where he participated in the formation of the new PRC national government, which was established at the First CPPCC in September 1949. He attended the CPPCC meetings as a representative of the Northeast Liberated Areas and also served on the ad hoc committee that drafted the Common Program, the document serving as the constitution until the formal constitution was adopted by the NPC in 1954. When the Sino-Soviet Friendship Association was established a few days after the inauguration of the national government (October 1949), Chou was named to membership on the Executive Board (although he was not re-elected to the Second Executive Board formed in 1954). While in Peking Chou was found to have serious heart trouble. Nonetheless, according to his wife's account after his death, Chou participated in the preparations for the conquest of the southwest and also took part in the operations led by Liu Po-ch'eng's Second Field Army in Yunnan in December 1949.[6] It is also probable that the Party preferred to have Chou back in his native Yunnan where his Min-chia origins could be especially useful. The Min-chia, already well assimilated into Chinese political life, could be expected to be less hostile to the coming of the Chinese Communists than other less assimilated minority nationality groups. Thus, Chou's kinship with a relatively assimilated group could be exploited in order to influence other minorities to cooperate with the Communists.

Soon after the arrival of the Communists in the southwest, they began to establish their usual pattern of Party, military, and civil administrations to govern the province and the entire southwest region. In view of Chou's ill health it is not clear how active he was in political life. Nonetheless, from the end of 1949 to 1954, Chou held an impressive array of positions in Yunnan and the Southwest Military and Administrative Committee (SWMAC) to which Yunnan belonged for administrative purposes. His military assignments were largely concerned with staff work because by the time he reached Yunnan the active military campaigns had ended. As mentioned, Chou's most useful work was probably in the field of minority affairs, but the following lists of his principal posts indicates the wide scope of his activities (insofar as illness allowed him to perform them): 1949–?: deputy commander, Yunnan Military District; 1950–?: vice-chairman (under Chairman Ch'en Keng), Kunming Military Control Commission; 1950–1952: vice-governor, Yunnan Provincial People's Government (YPPG); vice-chairman, Finance and Economics Committee, YPPG; chairman, Nationalities Affairs Committee, YPPG; 1950–1954: member, SWMAC, 1950–1953 (known as the Southwest Administrative Committee from 1953 to 1954).

In 1951 he became president of the Yunnan Nationalities Institute and spoke at the institute's inaugural ceremonies on August 2, 1951. By the winter of 1952 Chou's health took a turn for the worse; according to his wife's account he had been much overworked in Yunnan.[7] Hoping that a change of scene might relieve the pressures of work, the CCP sent him to Chungking, Szechwan, the capital for the southwest regional gov-

ernment. There his health continued to worsen. Then, in mid-1954 he was forced to return to Peking for medical treatment.

Shortly after his death in 1964, Chou's widow, Wang I-chih, wrote an account of his life making it evident that the last nine years of his life were marked by chronic ill health.[8] In 1959 he was hospitalized and confined to the hospital or his home for most of the time until his death. In view of this it is noteworthy that the records at the time made it appear that he was still fairly active. In 1954 he was elected a Yunnan deputy to the First NPC (1954–1959) and was re-elected in the same capacity to the Second NPC (1959–1964). In both congresses his Min-chia origins won him a seat on the NPC Nationalities Committee. In September 1954 he was named a member of the newly created military advisory National Defense Council and was reappointed in 1959. When national military honors were created in 1955, Chou received all three top national awards (the August First, the Independence and Freedom, and the Liberation Orders, covering military service for the period from 1927 to 1950). Personal military ranks were designated for officers that same year; Chou was made a lieutenant-general, equivalent to a two-star general in the U.S. Army.

When the CCP held its Eighth National Congress in September 1956, Chou was made an alternate member of the Central Committee. In 1958 he was able to journey as far as Tung-hua in Kirin, Manchuria, to attend a memorial service held for his former commander in the resistance, Yang Ching-yü. In April 1959, when the Third CPPCC met for its opening session, Chou was named to the new National Committee. And although he was now critically ill, he was also named to the governing body of the Third CPPCC, its Standing Committee. He was holding all the above posts at the time of his death. In June of 1961 Chou's contribution to the Communists' wartime history was published in the fourth volume of Red Army memoirs: *A Single Spark Can Start a Prairie Fire*.

Chou died in Peking on February 22, 1964. Politburo member P'eng Chen headed his funeral committee, which numbered 52 top-ranking CCP officials. These included 10 members of the Politburo, among them CCP General Secretary Teng Hsiao-p'ing, Premier Chou En-lai, and Foreign Minister Ch'en I.

To judge from Wang I-chih's memorial account, she and Chou must have been married by the late 1930's, a time when Chou was fighting with the Manchurian resistance. She noted that Chou had been wounded in battle five times, three of them during the days of the resistance movement in Manchuria. Wang gives no information about their personal lives but does mention that they had children. In 1959 she became a member of the Overseas Chinese Affairs Commission of the PRC State Council and was named as an overseas Chinese representative to the CPPCC. She was reappointed to both posts in 1965.

---

1. *Hsin Ming-tz'u Tz'u-tien* (New terminology dictionary; Shanghai, 1949), international section, pp. 68–69.
2. Howard L. Boorman, ed., *Men and Politics in Modern China, Preliminary 50 Biographies*, I (Columbia University, New York, 1960), p. 43.
3. *Ibid.*
4. *Hsin Ming-tz'u Tz'u-tien*, p. 69; Union Research Service, Hong Kong, biographic report no. 607, October 10, 1961.
5. Howard L. Boorman, p. 43.
6. Wang I-chih, "In memory of Comrade Chou Pao-chung," *JMJP*, May 6, 1964, translated in JPRS 25,072, June 15, 1964, *Translations on Political and Sociological Information on Communist China*, no. 169, pp. 8–12.
7. *Ibid.*
8. *Ibid.*

Chou P'ei-yuan

(1902–   ; I-hsing, Kiangsu). Physicist; president, China Physics Society; vice-chairman, China Scientific and Technical Association; vice-president, Peking University.

American-educated Chou P'ei-yuan is one of the most prominent scientists in Communist China. For many years a professor of physics at Tsinghua University, China's leading scientific institution, he has played a major role in scientific research and the administration of science since the Communists came to power in 1949. He has represented the Chinese scientific community abroad on many occasions, particularly at meetings of the Communist-sponsored World Federation of Scientific Workers.

Chou was born in I-hsing hsien, located in southern Kiangsu on the western shore of Lake T'ai. He comes from a landlord family and, by his own account, led an "easy life" as a youth.[1] He attended Tsinghua University in Peking, graduating in 1924 with a degree in physics. In the following year he went to the United States, where he earned a bachelor's (1926) and a master's degree (1927) from the University of Chicago, and then received his doctorate at the California Institute of Technology in 1928. He returned to China in 1929, taking up a post at his alma mater as a physics professor. He was again in the United States for the 1936–37 academic year as a member of the Institute for Advanced Study at Princeton, New Jersey. Returning to China he rejoined Tsinghua, which during the war years was temporarily merged with Peking and Nankai Universities and relocated in Kunming, Yunnan, under the name National Southwest Associated University. Chou remained in Kunming until the end of 1943

when he went to the United States once more. In a "confession" during an "ideological remolding" campaign in 1952, Chou stated that he arranged this trip through his contacts with Tsinghua classmates and American Consulate personnel in Kunming (whom he described as "special agents of the U.S. State Department").[2] He began to work on U.S. Government military projects in early 1945 and during his stay took a year-and-a-half "research course on the subject of launching torpedoes from planes" and attended a scientific conference held under U.S. Navy Department auspices. After more than three years in the United States, Chou returned to Peking and his teaching post at Tsinghua in the spring of 1947.

In the fall of 1948 Chou was in London attending an international conference on dynamics. Before the year ended he had returned to Peking, remaining there when the Communist forces marched into the city at the end of January 1949. In his 1952 "confession" he admitted that he had been deeply suspicious of the CCP and of its willingness to allow "freedom of scientific research." Nonetheless, he quickly threw in his lot with the Communists and within a brief period held a number of important posts in the Chinese intellectual and scientific community. In mid-1949 he was named to membership on the preparatory committee for the First All-China Conference of Scientific Circles; a year later (August 1950), at the close of the conference, the Communists established the All-China Federation of Scientific Societies (ACFSS), the national organization that oversees the activities of China's professional scientific societies. Chou was named to the ACFSS national Council and to membership on its [International] Liaison Committee, and two years later he became director of its Organization Department. One of the more important societies under the ACFSS is the China Physics Society; Chou had already been president of the society since 1948 (prior to the Communist takeover), and after the Communists took power he was in effect reappointed to this position (although in the early days of the PRC he was referred to simply as the "responsible member" of the Physics Society).

When the Communists came to power Chou continued at Tsinghua as a physics professor, and in 1949 he became dean of studies. In his confession he stated that he agreed to take the latter post in return for a promise from the Communist authorities to assist in having one of his daughters return to Peking from south China. The daughter had been one of thousands of youths sent to south China in 1949 to help administer the newly conquered territories in the wake of the advancing PLA. In 1953 Chou was transferred to Peking University where he first became dean of studies and then, in November 1956, a university vice-president, a position he still retains. In 1954 he received his first governmental post, a seat in the First NPC as a representative of his native Kiangsu. He was subsequently re-elected to serve in the Second NPC (1959–1964), and again to the Third NPC, which opened in late 1964.

Chou's participation in the NPC has been peripheral to his continuing participation in scientific research and science administration. Thus, when the Academy of Sciences established four major academic departments in May–June 1955, he was named to the Standing Committee of the Department of Physics, Mathematics, and Chemistry, and in October of the same year he became a member of the Academy's Scientific Awards Committee. In February 1957 he became a Council member of the newly established China Dynamics Society, and by the next year he had become a vice-president. This society, like the China Physics Society, came under the aegis of the national Federation of Scientific Societies. The latter was merged with another scientific organization in September 1958 to form the China Scientific and Technical Association (CSTA). Chou was appointed as one of the secretaries of the CSTA, but he was removed from this post and promoted to a vice-chairmanship in 1964. He held still another post in the field of science administration from 1957 to 1958, serving as a member of the State Council's Scientific Planning Commission.

In addition to his numerous scientific responsibilities in China, Chou has also been called upon to represent the PRC abroad on many occasions. His travels abroad have been for two specific purposes, to attend scientific meetings and to participate in political activities sponsored by various international Communist front organizations (for example, the World Peace Council). His first two trips after the Communists came to power fell into the latter category. In October 1950 he was a member of a "friendship" delegation led by Liu Ning-i (q.v.) to England, and in the next month he was among the members of Kuo Mo-jo's delegation to the Second World Peace Congress in Warsaw. Similarly, he was with Hsu Ti-hsin's (q.v.) "cultural" delegation visiting Italy, England, and Switzerland in March–June 1958; in March 1961 he was in New Delhi as a member of a group led by Liu Ning-i and Liao Ch'eng-chih to a World Peace Council meeting; and in August 1961 he led the Chinese delegation to the Seventh World Conference Against Atomic and Hydrogen Bombs in Tokyo. For his work in the international "peace" movement Chou was made a member of the World Peace Council in July 1958 (a position he presumably still holds) and a vice-chairman of the China Peace Committee in June 1965.

Chou's travels abroad in the interests of science have often centered around the activities of the World Federation of Scientific Workers (WFSW). Throughout the 1950's the WFSW was essentially a Soviet-dominated organization, but with the emergence of a large number of new African and Asian nations in the sixties (and their subsequent admission into the organization), it was gradually transformed into a more open and professional organization. And, although the political content of the Federation's meetings is still high, it now hears serious scientific papers read before its gatherings by distinguished scientists from both Communist and non-Communist nations. Chou's first association with the WSFW took place in September 1953 when he attended its third congress in Budapest. Immediately afterwards he was in Poland to attend meetings commemorating the 410th anniversary of the death of Copernicus. Over the next decade he attended eight other WSFW meetings held in: East Berlin, September 1955; Helsinki, August 1957; Warsaw, September 1959; Budapest, October 1960; Sofia, April 1961; Geneva, September 1961 and February 1963; and Moscow, September 1962. Chou has been an honorary secretary of the WFSW since September 1955 and a vice-president since September 1962.

Apart from WFSW meetings, Chou has been abroad on nine other occasions directly or indirectly related to science. He was in the Soviet Union in June 1955 for the 200th anniversary of Moscow University, and in September of the next year he read a scientific paper before the Ninth International Conference on Applied Mechanics in Brussels. In July 1957 he attended the first "Pugwash Conference" that brought together distinguished scientists from both Communist and non-Communist nations, a notable meeting in that it was one of the few in which both Americans and Chinese Communists participated. The conference drew its name from the small village in Canada that is the birthplace of American industrialist Cyrus Eaton, the initiator and sponsor of the original Pugwash meetings. Chou was back in Canada in March–April 1958 for the Second Pugwash Conference, held this time at Lac Beauport, Quebec, and in November–December 1960 he was in Moscow with Yü Kuang-yuan (q.v.) for the Sixth Pugwash meeting. Earlier, in November 1957, he was a member of the important scientific delegation led by Kuo Mo-jo to Moscow; ostensibly, the group was in the Soviet Union to celebrate the 40th anniversary of the Russian Revolution (with the main PRC delegation led by Mao Tse-tung), but Kuo's delegation remained for several weeks to negotiate a number of scientific cooperation agreements with Soviet officials. In January 1960 Chou attended a scientific congress in New Delhi, and he led still another group to a scientific meeting in Albania in November–December 1962. Leading a delegation composed of scholars from Peking and Futan Universities, he went to Rumania in October 1964 for the centenary celebrations of Bucharest University. Chou was also invited to New Zealand in June 1964 by the New Zealand-China Society, but he was unable to go when the government there refused him a visa.[3]

Related to his work in the promotion of international contacts, Chou has participated in a number of conferences in China and has lent his name to various organizations with strong foreign interests. He was, for example, an observer at the Asian and Pacific Regions Peace Congress held in Peking in October 1952, a meeting that devoted the bulk of its time to the denunciation of the alleged use by the United States of bacteriological warfare in the Korean War. He has also been an Executive Council member of the China-Africa People's Friendship Association since its formation in March 1960, as well as a Council member of the China-Japan Friendship Association from its establishment in October 1963. These posts, however, are largely *pro forma;* Chou clearly spends a rather large amount of time with foreign visitors, but most such liaison work is done in connection with visiting scientists. In this regard, one of the high points of his career took place in August 1964 when the PRC sponsored the so-called 1964 Peking Scientific Symposium, a meeting attended by 367 delegates from 44 nations, mainly in Africa, Asia, and Latin America. Chou was given the honor of heading the Chinese delegation, which consisted of 61 official members and 32 "specially invited" delegates, among them some of China's top natural and social scientists. While the meetings were not without political content (see under Fan Ch'ang-chiang, one of the deputy heads of the Chinese group), many of the scientific papers read at the conference were reported to be of high quality.[4]

Since September 1952, Chou has been a Central Committee member of the Chiu San Society, an organization consisting mainly of intellectuals drawn from cultural, educational, and scientific circles. Although called a "society," the organization is treated by the Chinese Communists as one of the eight "democratic" political parties that ostensibly shares political power with the CCP. (For further details about the Society, see under Hsu Te-heng, the chairman.) Chou was promoted to a vice-chairmanship in December 1958, and at the same time became director of the Society's Organization Department, positions he still retains. Representing the Chiu San Society, he was elected to the Third and Fourth National Committees of the CPPCC that held their initial sessions in April 1959 and December 1964–January 1965, respectively, and in each case he was also named to the Standing Committee that is in charge of CPPCC affairs between National Committee meetings.

Chou seems to have fared better than many intellectuals who have worked with the Communists in the post-1949 period, although Western-

ers familiar with him are quick to testify to his "bourgeois tastes." Like many outstanding social and natural scientists, he was forced to make a self-confession in 1952, but there is little indication that this was detrimental to his career. Five years later found Chou with the attackers— during the 1957 "Rectification" campaign, he was among those who condemned the alleged "rightist" activities of Ch'u An-p'ing, a prominent journalist-intellectual who was then a fellow member of the Chiu San Society and editor of the *Kuang-ming jih-pao,* the newspaper that ostensibly serves as the organ for the eight non-Communist political parties. Less than two years later, by which time the "Rectification" campaign had come to an end, Chou was admitted to candidate membership in the CCP (February 1959). He described his admission into the Party in the March 13, 1959, issue of the *Kuang-ming jih-pao,* an article that repeated many of the self-accusations he had made in 1952. Chou's formal association with the CCP occurred at a time when a number of China's top intellectuals were also admitted to the Party (for example, geologist Li Szu-kuang, q.v.). Party membership for Chou and his fellow intellectuals cannot be taken seriously in the sense that it has enhanced their political power, but it does suggest they are considered among the more trustworthy intellectuals by the CCP hierarchy.

Throughout his career Chou has regularly published in scientific journals, both in China and abroad. His work has been extolled in the Chinese press, which has been anxious to describe the research of Chinese scientists with solid reputations abroad. In 1963, for example, the New China News Agency reported that Chou had been working in the field of turbulence since 1938 and that an article he published during the Sino-Japanese War "received international attention." The same news item noted that he had made important advances in his special field and that a paper he presented at a 1963 symposium in Peking had "won great interest" from his scientific colleagues. It was further stated that he has three assistants and two graduate students working for him and that a special laboratory was to be built for his research work.[5] At least one important Western study of science in Communist China indicates that his contribution to the PRC has been a significant one.[6]

---

1. *SCMP* 1981, pp. 1–4.

2. *CB* 213, pp. 26–31.

3. Hong Kong, *The China Sunday Post-Herald,* June 14, 1964, quoting Reuter, June 13, 1964, Auckland, New Zealand.

4. Charles Warner, "Developing Science," *Far Eastern Economic Review,* 46.2:68–70.

5. *SCMP* 3004, pp. 11–12.

6. Sidney H. Gould, ed., *Sciences in Communist China* (Washington, D.C., 1961), *passim,* esp. p. 648.

Chou Shih-ti

(c.1902–   ; Hainan Island, Kwangtung). Military leader; member, CCP Central Control Commission.

Chou Shih-ti, a Party member since the mid-twenties, has served in the Communist armies since the Nanchang Uprising in 1927. After making the Long March he was a staff officer in Ho Lung's 120th Division during the Sino-Japanese War. He continued as a staff officer in the war against the Nationalists in the late forties. Since the early fifties Chou has held important military positions in Peking, and he has been a member of the Party's Central Control Commission since 1962.

Chou was born on Hainan Island (probably in Lo-hui in eastern Hainan). He graduated from primary school in Kwangtung and then entered a military school run by KMT military leader Ch'eng Ch'ien, who had come from his native Hunan to Kwangtung about 1920 to join the Kwangtung Army. This army, then under the over-all command of Ch'en Chiung-ming, was one of the training grounds for young revolutionaries, many of whom soon joined either or both the KMT and the CCP. Some of the army's staff became officers and instructors at Whampoa Military Academy, opened by the KMT in Canton in June 1924. Chou was a member of Whampoa's first graduating class (February 1925). This was a group of special usefulness to Whampoa's commandant, Chiang Kai-shek, who recruited many of its cadets into his army prior to their graduation. Chou was apparently among those chosen for military service. First he was sent from Canton in late December 1924 with the special Armored Division, which went to Kuang-ning in west Kwangtung to support the Peasant Association's work there. A month later he participated in Chiang's First Eastern Expedition (February 1925) to suppress Ch'en Chiung-ming, who was then threatening KMT supremacy and rivaling Sun Yat-sen for control of Kwangtung. In the first months of 1925 Chiang Kai-shek's army succeeded in driving Ch'en from Swatow, Chao-an, and the East River District of Kwangtung, areas that had been his special stronghold. Chou had joined the CCP at some time prior to 1925, perhaps under the influence of a friend from the Kwangtung Army or from Whampoa (see under Chou En-lai).

When the First Eastern Expedition was completed, Chou Shih-ti entered another military unit under Nationalist government auspices, a regiment then being prepared for the Northern Expedition by Yeh T'ing (q.v.). Yeh had first joined the Kwangtung Army and then studied in Moscow where he joined the CCP in 1925. When he returned to China later that year, Nationalist military leaders Li Chi-shen and Chang Fa-k'uei recruited him into their newly organized (November 1925) Fourth Nationalist Army. Yeh was

made commander of the 34th Regiment (soon to be known as the Independent Regiment) and Chou Shih-ti was his chief-of-staff. For the next two years Chou was closely associated with Yeh. Although the Northern Expedition was not formally launched until July 1926, the Independent Regiment, led by Yeh and Chou, moved north in May to assist forces in Hunan, which were under attacks from the northern warlords. Not long after Wuhan fell to the Northern Expeditionary forces in October 1926, Yeh's Independent Regiment was expanded into the 24th Division. At approximately this time, Yeh and Chou separated; Yeh assumed command of the new 24th Division, but Chou was made commander of the 73rd Regiment under the 25th Division. Chou was stationed just south of Kiukiang (Chiu-chiang) on the rail line connecting Kiukiang with Nanchang. He was not immediately informed of the Nanchang Uprising, staged on August 1, 1927, by his colleague Yeh T'ing, but within a matter of hours Nieh Jung-chen (q.v.) was dispatched to see Chou, and together the two men staged their own uprising. One Communist account claims that they wiped out five to six hundred men from Chang Fa-k'uei's 25th Division before taking the men of Chou's 73rd Regiment south to join the revolt at Nanchang, and a Western writer has observed that of the various units in Chang Fa-k'uei's 25th Division, only Chou Shih-ti's 73rd Regiment "appears to have taken part to a man" in the uprising.[1] The revolt at Nanchang marked a complete break in CCP-KMT relations and, because the rebels were driven out of Nanchang within a few days, it represented a defeat for the Communists. When the Communists regrouped their forces after the defeat (still, ostensibly, under the Nationalist banner), their troops were reorganized into different units, among them the 20th Army led by Ho Lung and the 11th Army under Yeh T'ing. The 11th Army was composed of the 24th and 25th Divisions. Yeh seems to have retained command of the 24th, and Chou took command of the 25th Division. For the next two months the two units moved southward together to Swatow; these events are described in Yeh T'ing's biography. But when the Communists neared Swatow, Chou and Yeh were separated, Chou's 25th Division remaining at San-ho-pa, 75 miles to the north of the coastal city, and Yeh took the remainder of his force into Swatow (September 24, 1927).

When Chou's 25th Division was left at San-ho-pa it numbered somewhat above 2,000 men, who were left to fight rear guard actions for the advancing Communist troops that took Swatow.[2] Chu Te, whose units at Nanchang had also taken part in the uprising there, was also near San-ho-pa. As the Communists fought to hold Swatow they were under attack not only from local forces but also from a portion of Chang Fa-k'uei's army, which had come south after the events at Nanchang to defend Swatow. After a week of fighting the Red forces were routed. The battered troops of Yeh T'ing and Ho Lung fled to the East River District of Kwangtung where they joined forces with P'eng P'ai (q.v.), who had been working with the peasants in the area for some time (see under Yeh T'ing). During the retreat Yeh and Ho's men lost contact with Chu Te and Chou Shih-ti at San-ho-pa, and for a time Chu and Chou also became separated. Chu Te escaped from San-ho-pa to Jao-ping on the coast, while Chou Shih-ti took a more northern route via Chao-an to Chang-chou over the Fukien border.

Chu Te's men encountered great difficulties after they left the San-ho-pa area. Fleeing in haste, they did not learn of the defeat at Swatow until informed by stragglers from Ho Lung's Student Training Detachment, who joined forces with Chu at Jao-ping. Later, when Chu reached the Fukien-Kiangsi border, he held a strategy conference. By this time he had been joined by Chou Shih-ti's 25th Division. The conference is described by Agnes Smedley, based on her interview with Chu Te in 1937. Smedley has some noteworthy comments about Chou Shih-ti (whom she describes as chief-of-staff to Chu Te) at this period. A defeatist spirit seems to have prevailed at the conference. In spite of the numbers of his forces that were turning back into Kwangtung, Chu Te proposed that the Communists march westward into southern Hunan. He was opposed by Chou Shih-ti and others. Chou, it seems, was "so discouraged that he proposed the army be disbanded."[3] However, Chu Te persisted in his march across Kiangsi; opposition continued until they reached Hsin-feng in southwest Kiangsi in late 1927 where Chu held another conference. He now suggested that any man wanting to leave his army do so at once. Among those who opted to stay were Lin Piao and Ch'en I, but Chief-of-Staff Chou Shih-ti was the first to go. "Even in 1937, ten years later," Smedley wrote, "Chu spoke of this 'desertion' with hatred."[4]

There is no conclusive information about Chou Shih-ti's activities for the next six years. After leaving Chu Te he apparently went to Hong Kong and then to Japan. Returning to China he joined the Third Party, which had been organized in Shanghai early in 1928 (see under Chi Fang). When Third Party leader Teng Yen-ta was captured and executed by the KMT (November 1931), Chang Po-chün, a Communist before the 1927 CCP-KMT split, took over the affairs of the Third Party. Chang was one of the leaders of the short-lived rebellion in Fukien (November 1933–January 1934) against the authority of Chiang Kai-shek's central government. (The complex attitude of the Communists toward the Fukien insurgents is described in the biography of K'ai Feng.) According to one report Chou Shih-ti commanded a regiment in the insurrec-

tionary military force during the Fukien Rebellion, but when it failed he is said to have escaped to Communist-held territory in west Fukien. If Chou was in fact associated with the insurgents, he appears to have been the only figure of importance among the Fukien insurgents who joined the Communists in Kiangsi at this time.

After 1933 Chou's career is clearly connected with the Communists in southeast Kiangsi. Before the Long March he was an instructor at the Red Army Military Academy that opened in 1933. He then made the Long March, arriving in north Shensi in the fall of 1935 with the main force commanded by Mao Tse-tung. He soon became affiliated with the 15th Army Corps (see under Hsu Hai-tung), a Communist unit that was already in north Shensi before Mao's arrival.

When the Sino-Japanese War broke out in mid-1937, Chou became chief-of-staff of the 120th Division of the Eighth Route Army, one of the three divisions of the Communists' army in north China. The division was commanded by Ho Lung (q.v.). Chou held his position until sometime in 1946. Ho was in command of the Shansi-Suiyuan Military Region and in the early war years his headquarters was in north Shansi, but by about 1942 he was brought to the Communist capital at Yenan to take charge of the new Joint Defense Command composed of the military regions in the Shansi-Suiyuan and the Shensi-Kansu-Ninghsia border areas. For the remaining war years, while Ho was in charge of the 120th Division in addition to his joint command post, his place in the Shansi-Suiyuan Military Region was taken over by Lü Cheng-ts'ao (q.v.). After Lü assumed command, Chou worked under him, and by 1944 he was serving as chief-of-staff and deputy political commissar of the Shansi-Suiyuan Military Region. In 1945 he became Lü's deputy commander as well. He presumably held all three positions until 1946, when the military commands began to be enlarged, concurrently remaining as chief-of-staff of the 120th Division.

Chou continued to work mainly with Ho Lung's army from 1946 until the early fifties, and although his activity is not recorded in detail, it can be traced in outline from a brief account of Ho's army during those years. Ho was in charge of protecting Yenan, which the Nationalists planned to capture in early 1947 after negotiations broke down completely between the KMT and CCP. The Communists were prepared for the attack and made a rather well-planned retreat from their headquarters, moving north into Shansi. From there he continued to operate in the Shansi-Suiyuan area during 1947–48. With the gradual expansion and assistance of Communist troops from armies in Suiyuan and Inner Mongolia, the PLA began to take over Shansi. By May 1947 the entire province was in their hands, excepting only some territory along the

Peking-Suiyuan Railway and the capital city of Taiyuan. The latter continued to be held by Shansi warlord Yen Hsi-shan.[5]

From 1947 to 1949 Ho Lung's army, sometimes termed the Shansi-Suiyuan-Shensi-Kansu-Ninghsia PLA, was subordinate to P'eng Te-huai's Northwest PLA that operated to the west of Ho in Kansu. At the same time Ho also fought some engagements in conjunction with Nieh Jung-chen's North China PLA that operated in north Hopeh. For at least a brief time in 1948–49 Chou Shih-ti was assigned to the North China PLA in which he served under Hsu Hsiang-ch'ien (q.v.) as deputy commander and deputy political commissar of the First Army Group.[6] Chou remained with Hsu and took part in the capture of Taiyuan in the early spring of 1949. Hsu was appointed to head the Taiyuan Military Control Commission and Chou was made a Commission member.

In the campaigns of the second half of 1949, units of P'eng Te-huai's First Field Army led by Ho Lung began to push into the southwest from Shansi and Shensi. In coordination with the forces of Liu Po-ch'eng's Second Field Army that had been operating in the Hupeh-Honan-Anhwei area, these two large armies swept into the southwest in a pincer-like drive—Liu's units moving into the area through Kweichow and Ho's driving from the north into western Szechwan and Sikang. During these operations Chou Shih-ti commanded the First Field Army's 18th Corps. He had as his political commissar Li Ching-ch'üan (q.v.), with whom he had previously served in the Shansi-Suiyuan Military Region. The Chou-Li forces were largely responsible for the capture of Chengtu, Szechwan, on December 27, 1949. The fall of Chengtu was of historic significance, for it was there that the Nationalist Government made its final stand before fleeing to Taiwan.

On the first day of 1950 the Communists established the Chengtu Military Control Commission with Chou as the vice-chairman under Li Ching-ch'üan. They also established the civil government, the Chengtu Municipal People's Government, making Chou the mayor. By the following month he was identified as commander of the West Szechwan Military District, and at approximately this time he was serving concurrently under Ho Lung as a deputy commander for the entire Southwest Military Region, a command structure that had control over Szechwan, Kweichow, Yunnan, and Sikang. The Communists established a civil government paralleling this military command in July 1950, which was known as the Southwest Military and Administrative Committee (SWMAC). The SWMAC, chaired by Liu Po-ch'eng, had Chou as one of its members, a post he nominally held until it was reorganized in early 1953. However, by the time he received this appointment other plans

had been made for his future work. In June 1950 he was removed as the Chengtu mayor and in the same month Chou En-lai cabled the occupation authorities in Japan that Chou Shih-ti was to be Peking's representative on the Allied Council for Japan, the political advisory body to General Douglas A. MacArthur's headquarters in Tokyo. It is doubtful that the Communists expected the Allied Powers to accept Chou Shih-ti as a representative; rather, they were apparently attempting to assert their rights as the legal successor to the Chinese Nationalist Government (that was represented on the Allied Council). This gesture was in vain, as was a similar one in August 1950 when Chou was named as a delegate to the Fifth Session of the United Nations' General Assembly, a position in which he would have served under chief delegate Chang Wen-t'ien.

By 1951 Chou had been permanently transferred to Peking, assuming in that year the post of head of the Air Defense (anti-aircraft) Force. He retained it until 1956 and in the meantime he was identified on one occasion in 1953 as director of the Militia Department. The latter was one of the major sections under the People's Revolutionary Military Council (PRMC), the top PRC military organ until its dissolution in 1954. Chou was infrequently mentioned in the Communist press during the early fifties, one of the few instances occurring in October–November 1951 when he attended the Third Session of the CPPCC as a representative of the PLA. Most of his other public appearances were ceremonial, as in March 1953 when he paid his respects at the Soviet embassy in Peking following Stalin's death. In the next year Chou was elected as a PLA deputy to the First NPC, and at its inaugural session in September 1954 he was elected to membership on the National Defense Council, the successor to the PRMC but a less powerful body. Chou retains Council membership, having been reappointed in April 1959 and January 1965.

In 1955 the Communists gave their officers personal military ranks and created military orders for past services. In view of the controversies surrounding Chou's military record after 1927, it is noteworthy that he was awarded the Order of August First, a decoration given for service in the years from 1927 to 1937. Moreover, he was given the Orders of Independence and Freedom and of Liberation for his military service from 1937 to 1950, and he was also made a colonel-general, the equivalent of a three-star U.S. Army general. From 1956 to about 1959 he was a deputy director of the PLA's Armed Forces Supervision Department (the equivalent of an inspectorate-general in Western military forces), serving here under veteran military leader Yeh Chien-ying (q.v.). Chou was not re-elected to the Second NPC, which opened in

April 1959, but at that time he was named as a CCP representative to the Third National Committee of the CPPCC, and was re-elected to the Fourth National Committee, which first met in December 1964–January 1965. On both occasions he was also named to membership on the Standing Committee, which is in charge of the work of the CPPCC between sessions of the National Committee.

The relative infrequency of public appearances by Chou since the early fifties may result from some unreported role involving military security and control functions. His assignment with the Armed Forces Supervision Department suggests this, as does his membership on the Party Central Control Commission. Chou was named to the Commission following the decision to expand its size taken at the Party Central Committee's 10th Plenum in September 1962.

1. J. Guillermaz, "The Nanchang Uprising," *The China Quarterly,* no. 11:163 (July–September 1962); Wei Hung-yun, ed., *"Pa-i" ch'i-i* (The "August First" uprising; Wuhan, 1957), p. 14.

2. C. Martin Wilbur, "The Ashes of Defeat," *The China Quarterly,* no. 18:37, *passim* (April–June 1964).

3. Agnes Smedley, *The Great Road* (New York, 1956), p. 210.

4. *Ibid.,* p. 212.

5. Lionel Max Chassin, *The Communist Conquest of China* (Cambridge, Mass., 1965), p. 137.

6. Li Kuang, ed., *Ti-liu-tz'u ch'üan-kuo lao-tung ta-hui* (Sixth All-China Labor Congress; Hong Kong, 1948), p. 50.

Chou Yang

(1908–   ; I-yang, Hunan). Former literary theorist and deputy director, Propaganda Department, CCP; purged 1966.

Chou Yang, a literary theorist, was the principal spokesman for education and cultural policies in Communist China until purged in 1966. His steady rise to prominence after the 1930's was due to his obedience to the Communist Party and to his organizing ability rather than to any literary achievement. His orthodox approach to Party policy gave him authority over his less single-minded colleagues. Because literary intellectuals have played a significant part in the Communist political scene, Chou, as the chief organizer of this group, wielded power out of proportion to the number he represented. He proclaimed a cultural credo adroitly adopted to the shifts in the Party line, and he served as the official watchdog for any deviation in the intellectual and literary realm.

Chou was born into the family of a rich landlord in I-yang, just south of Tung-t'ing Lake in Hunan, but little is known about his childhood.

His courtesy name is Chou Ch'i-ying, a name he used until the early thirties. After completing his secondary education in Hunan in 1926, he entered Ta-hsia (Great China) University in Shanghai where he studied English literature and became acquainted with Marxist ideology. He left the university in 1928 and went to Japan where he learned more about Marxism and Western literature. During these years he learned both English and Russian. In 1929 he was arrested for participating in leftist demonstrations and was subsequently released. He returned to China in 1930 and settled in Shanghai where he published literary criticism. He also translated Tolstoy's *Anna Karenina* (from English) and some short works by Soviet writers, and wrote articles on new Russian literature. As early as the 1930's, he began to espouse theories which, with minor variations, later became the basis of Communist policy in literature and art. He believed that literature was primarily a political weapon and that a writer should create only with this aim in view. Nevertheless, he also felt that art must have its own language, and should not be merely a repetition of political policy.

Chou expressed these theories in articles and debates on the popularization of literature and he figured prominently in the controversies over mass literature, which engrossed the literary world from 1930 to 1932. Along with Ch'ü Ch'iu-pai, he argued that the literary revolution following the May Fourth Movement had not been completed and that the *pai hua* (common speech) style of writing could be understood only by the middle classes. A further revolution was necessary to produce literature in forms accessible to the ordinary people. He advocated "national forms" which were actually short, simple stories and poems in popular, old literary styles, written in the colloquial language. Chou denied that this popularization would debase literature as some of his opponents claimed; rather it would educate the people and make them aware of class problems. This utilitarian concept of literature and art as a transmitter of educational propaganda was a recurring theme in all of Chou's pronouncements. The mass language movement of 1934 implemented many of Ch'ü Ch'iu-pai's and Chou's ideas. Their views that writers should describe the life of workers and peasants, use "national forms," and emphasize popular content over artistic criteria were later restated as orthodox doctrines by Mao Tse-tung in his Yenan Talks in 1942.

Chou rose in the literary hierarchy not only because of his utilitarian literary views but also because of his maneuvers in the Party's cultural organization. He apparently joined the Party in the early 1930's. From 1931 to 1936 he was secretary-general of the League of Left-Wing Writers. The League was ostensibly under the direction of Lu Hsun, but the actual policy-makers were Party officials, principally, Ch'ü Ch'iu-pai. After Ch'ü left Shanghai over the winter of 1933–34 for Kiangsi, Chou became the real authority in the League. Because Lu Hsun and his followers sought to maintain an independent attitude not only toward literature but also toward the Party organization, they clashed with Chou and his associates, among them the playwright T'ien Han and the writer Hsia Yen. These two groups competed with each other in a fierce struggle for the leadership of left-wing intellectuals.

Their sharpest controversy occurred in 1936 over the slogan "Literature of National Defense." After the formation of the united front against Japan, Chou disbanded the League and replaced it with another organization, the Association of Chinese Writers. Instead of confining its activities as the old organization had done to a small left-wing group within a limited geographical area, Chou sought to unite as many people as possible on a nation-wide scale. His association brandished the "classless" slogan, "literature for national defense," which called for a realistic style of writing whose special theme would be national defense. Writers with different political views were encouraged to enroll, but once members of the association they were expected to conform to its requirements. Chou urged writers to engage in free debate and criticism but only as a means of resolving differences of belief and imposing the Party's ideology. As early as the 1930's, the techniques of the "rectification" campaigns of later years were beginning to evolve.

Because of political and personal differences with Chou, Lu Hsun and some of his disciples, among them Hu Feng (q.v.) and Feng Hsueh-feng, refused to join Chou's association or to accept its aims. Fearing the dilution of the revolutionary spirit, they set up their own organization, the Chinese Literary Workers, made up of a small group of left-wing writers. It adapted a more revolutionary slogan, "people's literature for the national revolutionary struggle." Because of the refusal of Lu Hsun's group to join the Association of Chinese Writers, Chou enticed one of Lu Hsun's close colleagues, Hsu Mou-yung, to write a letter to Lu Hsun insinuating that his actions and those of his associates were against the Party. Lu Hsun responded by publishing Hsu's letter and attaching an angry retort in which he defended his associates and accused Chou of labeling people traitors to enhance his own position. The disagreement between these two groups brought to light a fundamental question which was later to trouble the Party—the relation of art and politics. Lu Hsun's group maintained that writers should keep their creative independence while supporting the political resistance against Japan; Chou and his circle insisted that in such a crucial period it was essential to have cultural as well as political unity. Already Chou appeared as the self-appointed champion of political control over literature and art.

In 1937, when war broke out, Chou left Shanghai for Yenan where he quickly rose to prominent positions in the education and propaganda organizations. In addition to his political orthodoxy, the fact that he was one of the first intellectuals to arrive in Yenan aided his swift promotion. When the Shensi-Kansu-Ninghsia Border Region Government was established in 1937 he became head of the Education Department, retaining this post throughout the war years. In the spring of 1940 he was appointed vice-president of the Lu Hsun Art Academy and two years later he advanced to the presidency. Concurrently, he was dean of education at Yenan University and by 1944 he had replaced Wu Yü-chang (q.v.) as president of this school. These two institutions supposedly specialized in higher education in the arts, literature, and education, but were primarily training centers in Party ideology.

Chou's ideas about education, as he expressed them in Yenan, were similar in spirit to his literary views. His anti-intellectual, anti-Western approach foreshadowed the tone of the Party's educational policies in the 1950's. Because to Chou education was inextricably linked to politics, he emphasized the need for mass indoctrination. He disapproved of any stress on technical and intellectual achievement because it diverted people from practical political demands. He declared that educational specialization was a result of Western middle-class influence. Instead he fostered "proletarian education," which was largely the study of Marxist-Leninism and its practical application.

An important element in the Yenan educational system was the ideological remolding movement by which the Party sought to impose control through training and indoctrination. Chou played a leading role in this program, particularly in the campaign against the author Wang Shih-wei in the spring and summer of 1942. Wang Shih-wei, in an article entitled "The Wild Lily," sharply criticized the Party's policies in Yenan. He charged the Party with perpetuating the old class system except that at the top there were now Party bureaucrats. In Wang's view, these bureaucrats were becoming as divorced from the needs of the masses as the old upper class had been. In another article, Wang also demanded that the intellectual and cultural realm be the preserve of the writers and the scholars, not of the Party.[1] Wang became the negative example with which the Party propelled its first *cheng-feng* movement. Chou gave the final summation of this case in July 1942. Thereafter, he increasingly enunciated the Party's case for political control of intellectuals. He repeatedly articulated the

Party's views that the majority of intellectuals were petty bourgeois and therefore required ideological remolding in order to make them more obedient to the Party's will.

Next to Mao, Chou was the principal policy-maker for literature in the liberated areas. He was chairman of the All-China Literary and Art Resistance Association, whose members included such well-known writers as Ting Ling and Ai Ch'ing. Chou and Ting Ling established the Border Area Cultural Association, which was primarily designed to carry out propaganda in the villages and the army.

During the Yenan period, Chou edited several books, a compilation of essays by Marx, Lenin, Engels, and Stalin with a statement by Mao on literature, and an anthology of stories and reports from the liberated areas. He also translated into Chinese *The Aesthetic Relationship between Art and Reality* by N. G. Chernyshevsky, a Russian populist writer of the 1860's. He presented his theories most fully in *The New Age of the Masses* in which he elaborated on Mao's literary doctrine. He particularly emphasized Mao's tenet that a new literature be created in traditional folk styles. He also gave prominence to Mao's dictum that intellectuals participate in the struggle of the masses. Here, he may have been influenced as much by his study of Chernyshevsky as by Mao. He urged writers to go to the villages, factories, and front lines in order to establish an organic relationship between their creative work and the practical world of the peasants and soldiers. The creativity and intelligence of the masses above other groups was an article of faith for Chou.

After hostilities against Japan ended in 1945 Chou was transferred to Kalgan, capital of the Shansi-Chahar-Hopeh (Chin-Ch'a-Chi) Border Region where, as in Yenan, he became one of the dominent figures in cultural and educational fields. From 1946 to 1948 he was vice-president of the North China Associated University (Hua-pei lien-ho ta-hsueh) and during approximately this same period he headed the Propaganda Department of the Party's North China Bureau. Moreover, he was a Council member of the North China Literary and Art Circles Federation from its formation in August 1947. A year earlier Chou was one of four Communist cultural leaders chosen to tour the United States on the invitation of the State Department, but he was forced to return to Kalgan from Shanghai when the Nationalist Government refused to issue him a passport.

Chou was one of the first Communist leaders to arrive in Peking after its surrender in January 1949, and he immediately assumed new and more important positions in the cultural sphere. Until its dissolution in the fall of 1949 he was a vice-chairman of the Higher Education Committee of the North China People's Government and a member of the Government's Cultural and Arts Committee. He was one of the dominant figures at the All-China Congress of Literature and Arts attended by some 800 persons in July 1949; at the close of the proceedings he became vice-chairman of the All-China Federation of Literary and Art Circles (ACFLAC), a position he held until his political fall in 1966. Moreover, he also became a Standing Committee member of the All-China Association of Literary Workers (known after 1953 as the Union of Chinese Writers) and a member of the All-China Drama Reform Association's Preparatory Committee. In the fall of 1953 he advanced to a vice-chairmanship in the Writers' Union and by the end of 1954 he was in control of the Party's principal cultural publications: the literary section of the *JMJP, People's Literature, Poems,* and *Harvest.* He controlled these magazines through his loyal followers from the Yenan days, among them Yuan Shui-p'o, literary editor of the *JMJP,* Lin Mo-han, chief of the literary division of the Writers' Union, and Shao Ch'üan-lin, who became secretary of the Writers' Union.

Chou's political posts were even more numerous. From 1949 to 1954 he was a member of the First National Committee of the CPPCC, and when the government was formed in the fall of 1949 he became a vice-minister of Culture and director of the Ministry's Art Bureau (1949–1951). Moreover, from at least 1951 until he left the Ministry in 1954, he was also secretary of its CCP Committee. From 1949 to 1954 Chou served concurrently as a member of the central government's Culture and Education Committee, and during these same years he was an Executive Board member of the Sino-Soviet Friendship Association. Still another post that he received in the fall of 1949 was membership on the China Peace Committee, then one of the most active of the "mass" organizations; he retained this position until the Committee was reorganized in mid-1958. Probably his most important post was as a deputy director of the Party's Propaganda Department, which formulates the policies of the Ministry of Culture; Chou served in the Department from at least 1951 until 1966. He was also a Kwangtung deputy to the First, Second, and Third NPC's, whose initial sessions opened in 1954, 1959, and 1964, respectively. At the Eighth Party Congress in September 1956, after delivering a speech on socialist literature and art, he was elected an alternate member of the Central Committee. In 1955 he was elected a member of the Academy of Sciences' newly-established Philosophy and Social Sciences Department, and from 1956 to 1958 he was a member of the central government's Scientific Planning Commission.

However, Chou's official positions in no way connote the power he wielded in the literary and intellectual sphere. His chief function during the first decade and a half of Chinese Communist government was his unofficial responsibility for an evolving pattern of ideological control, not only in literature, but also in the social sciences and the humanities. He was to insure that "bourgeois survivals" in Western-educated intellectuals and left-wing writers and artists did not assert themselves while at the same time he educated them in the current orthodoxy. Throughout the fifties he organized ideological remolding campaigns, which tightened the Party's control over the creative arts and scholarship. In the first nation-wide remolding movement of the new regime, Chou and his colleagues, supposedly at the instigation of Mao, used a film, "The Story of Wu Hsun," to warn intellectuals of the peril of heterodoxy. The hero of the film was the 19th century educator Wu Hsun, who attempted to educate the poor by setting up schools. Chou attacked the film for stressing education and evolutionary change rather than the class struggle. He insisted that the revolutionary masses, not a small circle of educated individuals, would be the creators of a better world.

In 1954, Chou was one of the leaders of the campaign against Western-educated Hu Shih and Yü P'ing-po and their interpretation of the 18th century novel, *The Dream of the Red Chamber*. Chou insisted that a popular literary work such as this should be reinterpreted as a description of the class struggle. Here again, he was concerned with Chinese tradition for political purposes. This campaign led to an attack at the end of 1954 on Feng Hsueh-feng, chief editor of one of the most important cultural journals, *Wen-i pao* (Literary gazette), ostensibly because he had defended the non-Communist analysis of *The Dream of the Red Chamber*. The attack was personally directed by Chou and seems to have been motivated as much by Chou's past conflict with Feng and other disciples of Lu Hsun from the Shanghai days as by ideological differences. Moreover, as Lu Hsun's closest associate, a Party member for 25 years, and a highly regarded Marxist literary theorist, Feng apparently did not submit readily to Chou's direction. Consequently, this campaign gave Chou and his associates the opportunity to remove Feng and his assistant editor, Ch'en Ch'i-hsia, from *Wen-i pao* and replace them with Chou's followers. Now, all the major literary journals were under Chou's and the Party's complete control. The attack on Yü P'ing-po and Feng Hsueh-feng soon led into a national campaign against literary critic Hu Feng. Although the campaign was based on political expediency, again it was probably motivated also by personal animosity. Most of Chou's pronouncements in 1955 were devoted to assaults on heterodox thinking as exemplified by Hu.

With the inauguration of the Hundred Flowers policy of liberalization in 1956, Chou conformed to the new Party line. As during periods of regimentation, he was vocal in enunciating Party policy. Contradicting his views of a few months earlier, he now endorsed the writer's right to choose his own subject and he urged assimilation of the best of Western culture. Although socialist realism was still considered the most advanced form of art, Chou acknowledged that other forms could portray life. A great culture could develop, he declared, from the competition of diverse forms of art. He even asserted that literary and artistic development might be impeded by Party intervention and called for recognition of artistic values and of the independent nature of literary creativity.

When in June 1957 the Party launched the "anti-rightist" campaign in an effort to halt the criticisms against it, Chou was one of its directors. A major victim of this campaign was the novelist Ting Ling. Once more, Chou hounded a writer with whom he had disagreed in an earlier period. Ting Ling had been a supporter of Wang Shih-wei in Yenan. In 1955 she was secretly labeled a counterrevolutionary by Chou's followers in the Writers' Union. During the Hundred Flowers period, she and her colleagues denied these charges, which they imputed to clique jealousies, and sharply criticized Chou for his bureaucratic control of culture. This later charge was voiced loudly by several young writers who looked to Ting Ling for leadership. The anti-rightist movement enabled Chou to eliminate Ting Ling and her associates as rivals in leading the intellectual community.

Chou's main theoretical work of the second half of the 1950's was "The Great Debate in the Literary Front," which was presented on March 11, 1958, at the conclusion of the anti-rightist campaign against writers. It was an effort to update Mao's Yenan "Talks" of 1942 in response to the criticism of them during the Hundred Flowers movement. Actually, Chou's work added little to Mao's original concepts other than to provide them with examples of more recent vintage. Nevertheless, this work served a similar purpose of indoctrinating writers in the Party's official line. After it was published, writers and intellectuals in the creative arts gathered together in study groups to discuss it, write related essays, and criticize themselves accordingly.

With the introduction of the Great Leap Forward in 1958, Chou became a leader of the mass poetry movement. He provided the ideological framework for this movement by introducing a purportedly new literary theory of Mao's—the union of revolutionary realism with revolutionary romanticism. Actually, it was merely a restatement of the original Soviet concept of socialist realism, which decreed that literature focus on happenings to come rather than on existing problems.

Because of the failure of the Great Leap Forward and the withdrawal of Soviet scientists and technicians, the Party eased the pressure on intellectuals in the early 1960's in order to gain their cooperation in remedying China's economic difficulties. Though Chou spoke out against "revisionism," he once more was active in promoting the Party's switch in policy. In line with the relaxation in the intellectual sphere, Chou emphasized professional criteria. Also, because the Party at this time encouraged an aggressive nationalism which took pride in China's past, he too at the Third National Conference of Writers and Artists (July–August 1960) ordered writers to follow in the footsteps of China's ancient writers and poets. He encouraged writers and playwrights to deal with historical themes and to turn back to the relatively creative period of the 1930's for inspiration.

Although Chou's principal tasks were in domestic cultural affairs, he also played a role of some importance in international relations. From the spring of 1954 to at least 1959 he was a Board member of the Chinese People's Association for Cultural Relations with Foreign Countries (see under Chang Hsi-jo), and in December 1954 he led the Chinese delegation to the Second National Congress of Soviet Writers. In December 1956 he was in New Delhi to attend the Conference of Asian Writers, and in October 1958 he traveled to Tashkent for the Afro-Asian Writers Conference. In both cases he was officially a deputy to the non-Communist Minister of Culture Shen Yen-ping, but it was evident that Chou was the *de facto* leader. As an outgrowth of Peking's increasing interest in Africa and Asia, the Chinese laid plans in the spring of 1959 to form the Asian-African Society of China, ostensibly to conduct research on these two continents. Chou was one of those responsible for establishing the new organization, and when it was officially inaugurated in April 1962 he became its chairman. He was abroad once again in December 1962 when he led a cultural delegation to Cuba where he attended First National Congress of Culture, remaining there long enough to attend the celebrations on January 1, 1963, marking the fourth anniversary of Fidel Castro's assumption of power. He was thus a logical member to win a seat on the Standing Committee of the China-Cuba Friendship Association when it was formed in December 1962 while he was still in Havana.

When the Party in September of 1962 shifted again to regimenting the intellectuals, Chou once more was in the forefront, particularly in the denunciation of Soviet "revisionism." His speech on October 26, 1963, before the Philosophy and Social Sciences Departments of the Academy of Sciences was treated as the authoritative reformulation of the Party's attitude toward Soviet culture. He launched a frontal attack on every aspect of Chinese intellectual output in the past decade, which could be interpreted as evading the class struggle and as expressing sympathy with the Soviet brand of Communism. He denounced the Soviet ideological position that new processes emerge under socialism, which turn contradictions into unity, and enunciated the opposing doctrine that everything tends to divide itself into two, making it impossible, therefore, to have any compromise in the class struggle and the dictatorship of the proletariat.

However, there was evidence that Chou and his associates were losing some of the fervor of their earlier days. Though Mao called for renewed class struggle at the Party's 10th Plenum in September 1962, unlike the anti-rightist campaign, this campaign got underway rather sluggishly in the cultural realm. A "socialist education" campaign was launched in literary circles but the intensity of the campaign against Hu Feng or of the denunciations of Feng Hseuh-Feng were lacking. In June 1964 Mao attacked the "high and mighty bureaucrats in literary circles," and a rectification of writers was carried out in the latter half of 1964. Some of Chou's closest followers, Hsia Yen and Shao Ch'üan-lin, were attacked. Though Chou prepared a self-criticism that attacked his old colleagues, it was evident his position was undermined by this attack on his underlings.

Despite these suggestions of troubles to come, Chou's political position in the mid-sixties seemed secure. He had served on the Third CPPCC Standing Committee from 1959 to 1964, and at the end of 1964 he was re-elected to this post for the Fourth CPPCC. He also served on the Presidium (steering committee) and the important Credentials Committee for the inaugural session of the Third NPC held from December 1964 to January 1965. And even in 1965, when the Party stressed the need for more works of art from amateur writers and artists (rather than the professional writers), Chou seemed to be capable of bending to this new directive. It was he, for example, who delivered a keynote address before the national conference of "Young Activists in Amateur Literary and Artistic Creations" in the closing days of 1965. But then in the spring of 1966 an unnamed deputy director of the Propaganda Department came under scathing attack for his alleged defense of a play by historian-playwright Wu Han. Within a few days it was revealed that this anonymous deputy director was Chou Yang, who, by the early summer of 1966, had become a major target of the "great proletarian cultural revolution," an attack that coincided with the fall of Chou's superior in the Propaganda Department, Director Lu Ting-i (q.v.).[2] The attack on Chou was apparently a reflection of Mao's frustrations with the intellectuals, particularly the literary intellectuals. Chou was blamed for the fact that after almost 25 years of unceasing indoctrination and thought reform, intellectuals still resisted Mao's direction.

Mao lashed out at the very one most conspicuous in implementing his policies toward the intellectuals. In line with the doctrinairism of the cultural revolution, the Party held Chou responsible for those periods in its past when it was conciliatory toward the intellectuals. Therefore, he was blamed for the united front of the 1930's and the relaxation during the Hundred Flowers and the early 1960's. In fact, Chou was attacked for faithfully implementing the Party's orders. His efforts to establish a united front, the regime charged in 1966, was not the policy of Mao but of Ch'en Shao-yü (q.v.). In reality, the united front policy which Chou implemented was the official policy of the Party at the time. Similarly, he was blamed for the intellectual ferment and criticism of the Party during the Hundred Flowers, but here again, he was attacked for carrying out Mao's orders. Likewise, the regime disassociated itself from the relaxation of the early 1960's by holding Chou responsible. In an Orwellian rewriting of history, Chou was blamed for policies in a more moderate period, which were antithetical to the Party's emphasis on "struggle" in the cultural revolution. In addition to his identification with the Party's unsuccessful program for the intellectuals, the choice of Chou as a scapegoat may also have been due to his maneuvers in the power structure. As Lin Piao and the General Political Department of the PLA began to assume some of the duties of the Propaganda Department and direct literary activity, Chou, along with the head of the Propaganda Department, Lu Ting-i, apparently resisted this intrusion.

Thus, Chou, the faithful servant of the Party, who for over 30 years had ruthlessly purged the ranks of China's most creative writers and campaigned against unorthodox thinking, suffered the same fate as his victims in the summer of 1966. This master of the *volte-face* who had been a major force in implementing the Party's cultural policy and in twisting art to suit Party ends found that not even he could be trusted to carry out the cultural revolution.

1. Merle Goldman, "Writers' Criticism of the Party in 1942," *The China Quarterly,* no. 17: 205–228 (January–March 1964).

2. Merle Goldman, "The Fall of Chou Yang," *Ibid.,* no. 27:132–148 (July–September 1966).

Ch'ü Ch'iu-pai

(1899–1935; Ch'ang-chou, Kiangsu). Early Party leader; CCP chief, 1927–1928; political theoretician.

A key figure in the early years of the Chinese Communist movement, Ch'ü Ch'iu-pai was a man of many parts. Beginning his career as a translator of Tolstoy, he was in the Soviet Union in 1921–22, part of the time as special correspondent for the Peking *Ch'en-pao* (Morning post). By the time he returned to China in early 1923, he was something of an expert in Russian and Russian affairs, and a major channel for Soviet ideological influences, as seen in his new role as editor of Party journals and instructor of Party cadres. By August 1927 he had replaced Ch'en Tu-hsiu as the Party chief and during his brief incumbency presided over the policy of armed urban and rural insurrections. Having failed in this policy, he temporarily faded from the China scene and for about two years (mid-1928 to mid-1930) achieved some fame in Moscow as an international Communist under the name of Strakhov. He returned from Moscow in the summer of 1930 and for the next half year was involved in a power struggle with Pavel Mif. He lost in the tussle and was ousted from the Politburo in January 1931. From then until his departure for the Soviet government in Juichin, Kiangsi, in late 1933, he led an underground existence in Shanghai, struck up a friendship with Lu Hsun, directed the left-wing Literary Movement, and vigorously plunged into the field of Marxist-Leninist literary theory. From early 1934 until the beginning of the Long March late in the year, he occupied the position of commissar of Education in the Juichin government. His execution on June 18, 1935, by the Nanking government ended his brief but varied career. As Party chief, he is the only predecessor whom Mao's regime has accorded apotheosis.

Ch'ü Ch'iu-pai was born into an impoverished gentry family in Ch'ang-chou, Kiangsu, on January 29, 1899. His grandfather, Ch'ü Keng-shao, was financial commissioner of Hupeh and for a while acting governor of that province; the fortune he left to the family had afforded Ch'ü a rather comfortable childhood but was quickly dissipated by Ch'ü's father, Ch'ü Chih-pin, a shiftless individual who smoked opium and indulged in occult Taoism. He finally abandoned his wife and six children, of whom Ch'ü Ch'iu-pai was the oldest, and went to Shantung to serve as a family tutor. Ch'ü's mother, Chin Heng-yü, the daughter of a one-time salt-intendant of Kwangtung and a woman of some education, had no means of maintaining the family other than to pawn or sell the family's meager possessions. Nevertheless, Ch'ü attended school, first at the Kuan-ying Primary School and later at the Ch'ang-chou Middle School. Among his classmates at the latter was Chang T'ai-lei (q.v.), the future hero of the Canton Uprising, and until his death a staunch supporter of Ch'ü in the intra-Party power struggle. Barely within graduation, Ch'ü was forced to leave school for financial reasons, after which he taught primary school for a while. Then in February 1915 the most tragic event of his youth occurred when his mother took her own life in despair over her grim poverty. Whereupon Ch'ü, his brothers, and sister were divided among various relatives as wards. It is evident that these years of misery in his youth engendered the impulse of his subsequent renunciation of his "genteel" past and made him a most implacable iconoclast.

In 1915 he went to Wuchang to live with his second cousin, Ch'ü Ch'un-pai. For a few months he studied English at the Foreign Language College at Hankow. He gave that up and then went to live with another cousin, Chou Chün-liang, who encouraged him in composing Chinese poetry for which he had developed a taste in school, as well as in studying Buddhist scriptures. Buddhism was then providing a refuge for many a contemporary from the toils and bewilderment of ubiquitous chaos and was to have some influence on his outlook.

In 1916 he moved to Peking with Ch'un-pai and hoped to continue his education at Peking University. He passed the entrance examination but could not pay the fees although he was allowed to audit. He took the examination for civil servants but was unsuccessful. Finally, in the summer of 1917, he gained admission to the Russian Language Institute, a tuition-free school established by the Peiyang government for the training of personnel for diplomacy and positions in the Chinese Eastern Railway. Ch'ü selected the literature department and studied Russian and French. Here began a long and abiding interest in Russian literature, which, to his subsequent regret, he gave up in exchange for a consuming and abortive political career. He was particularly drawn to Tolstoy, his brand of anarchism, and Gogol, whose works he attempted to translate. For a brief time Buddhism and Tolstoyan anarchism kept his mind occupied, but he was soon carried along in the rising tide of nationalism and "new culture," and he immersed himself in the plethora of journals, carriers of every conceivable wisp of new ideas, which shaped the minds of many of his generation. He actively engaged in the May Fourth student movement and led a group of students of the Russian Language Institute in the June 5 demonstrations. He was arrested and imprisoned for three days along with many others. According to him, he sustained an internal injury in the violence that broke out, which accounted for the periodic bloodspittings which punctuated his hectic career.

Among his associates of student life were his uncle, Ch'ü Shih-ying, a student of philosophy at Hui-wen College, who later received his Ph.D. at Columbia, taught philosophy at Yenching University, and actively supported the rural reform movement under James Yen; Cheng Chen-to, the future literary historian, who was studying at the School of Railway Management; Hsu Ti-shan, another prominent literary scholar, who later taught at Hong Kong University; and Keng Chi-chih, a classmate at the Language Institute, who later won fame as translator of Russian literature. With the cooperation of these men and the sponsorship of the YMCA, he launched the *Hsin she-hui* (New society), a ten-day periodical, which lasted for 18 issues from November 1919 to April 1920. It had the avowed purpose of "rallying all forces in the interest of social reconstruction" and was subsequently banned on charges of containing socialist propaganda. Undaunted, he and his friends launched *Jen-tao* (l'Humanité), a monthly which was again repressed after its first and only issue.

In March 1920 Ch'ü joined the She-hui chu-i hsiao-tsu (Socialist study group), which Li Ta-chao had organized at Peking University, and he developed toward Marxism, although his final conversion took place only after he had been in Soviet Russia. For a brief time he displayed some interest in the emancipation of women. In April 1920, he finished a translation of *Socialization of Society*, by the German socialist August Bebel (1840–1913).

Upon graduation from the Institute, he accepted the appointment of special correspondent in Moscow for Peking's leading daily, *Ch'en-pao*. He regarded it as a unique opportunity to continue his study of the Russian language and literature as well as to visit the "promised land." On October 16, 1920, he left Peking in the company of two other correspondents, Yü Sung-hua and Li Tsung-wu. The party finally reached Moscow on January 25, 1921, after months of dark bread and the rigors of the Siberian winter. The long trip provided the opportunity for an introspective autobiography *O-hsiang chi-ch'eng* (A journey to the land of hunger), which depicted his progression from the dark despair of his past to the new-born hope of the October Revolution, and distant Moscow, the Holy City, had a hypnotic effect on him. He conceived of his mission as that of ripping open the curtain of darkness over China to let in the new rays.

During his two-year sojourn in Moscow his activities were varied. He investigated and wrote about conditions and developments in the "new" Russia, which appeared from time to time in *Ch'en-pao* as well as in the *Shih-shih hsin-pao* (Current news) of Shanghai. These reports constituted the earliest on-the-spot observations by a Chinese of their kind on a country about which the reading public craved information. Subsequently, he put his amassed materials into a book, which he called *O-lo-szu ko-ming lun* (On the Russian Revolution).

He also applied himself to the study of the Russian language and literature with the aid of a tutor, one of the results of which was a historical survey of Russian literature before the October Revolution, the earliest of its kind in Chinese. This was incorporated by Chiang Kuang-tz'u, another specialist in Russian literature, in his volume *O-lo-szu wen-hsueh* (Russian literature).

In June 1921 he attended the Third Congress of the Comintern, still in the capacity of a correspondent, and his classmate, Chang T'ai-lei, now secretary of the Socialist Youth League, represented the CCP. Another Chinese present was Kiang (Chiang) K'ang-hu, who attended the Congress in the name of his Chinese Socialist Party. However, he had gone to Soviet Russia primarily to investigate conditions there and to formulate a program for his projected party.

In the fall of 1921, a group of more than 60 Chinese students arrived in Moscow to enroll at the Communist University of the Toilers of the East, an institution sponsored by the Commissariat of Nationalities with the purpose of training cadres to work among Asian peoples, both within and outside the boundaries of the Soviet state. Among these students were future CCP luminaries Liu Shao-ch'i, P'eng Shu-chih, and Jen Pi-shih. Although they had begun Russian at Yang Ming-chai's (q.v.) Foreign Language Institute at Shanghai, their training proved to be inadequate; a special Chinese class was formed and Ch'ü Ch'iu-pai was invited to be the lecturer-interpreter in charge of the class. Here he had the opportunity, which many of his future Communist colleagues lacked, to make a concentrated study of Marxism-Leninism and learn the art of indoctrination.

Late in 1921 he experienced the first attack of tuberculosis and on December 12 was confined to a sanatorium. Some weeks later he was well enough to attend the Congress of the Toilers of the East where some 42 Chinese delegates were present, representing all sorts of social organizations in China. Ch'ü served as the interpreter at the congress. In February 1922 he underwent what must have been a mere formality of affiliating himself to the Moscow branch of the CCP, done on the recommendation of Chang T'ai-lei and Chang Kuo-t'ao. In the spring of 1922 he had a relapse of his illness, and during his confinement to a sanatorium he compiled a sequel to his *Journey to the Land of Hunger*, consisting of descriptions of his moods, thoughts, and observations which he had made earlier from time to time; he entitled this *Ch'ih-tu hsin-shih* (Thoughts in the Red capital).

At the Fourth Comintern Congress (November–December 1922), Ch'ü again served as the interpreter for the Chinese delegation, which comprised Ch'en Tu-hsiu and Liu Jen-ching, the latter being one of the founding members of the CCP who, like Ch'en, became a Trotskyite in the 1930's. After the congress Ch'ü returned to China with Ch'en Tu-hsiu, and during January–June 1923 he was reported in Peking, the exact nature of his work there being unclear. He was, at this time, without doubt the outstanding Russian expert of the CCP; he knew the language well and was known to the leaders at the head-

quarters of the world revolution, and he had had some grounding in Marxist-Leninist theory and could interpret Comintern strategy and tactics. He was the first to translate into Chinese Lenin's "Theses on National and Colonial Questions," passed at the Second Comintern Congress in 1920.

In June 1923 Ch'ü attended the Third CCP Congress in Canton, and played a key role in drafting the Congress manifesto. He was elected a member of the Central Committee, which post he retained to the end of his life. Soon after the congress he went to Shanghai and headed the Social Science Department of newly established Shanghai University, a cadre school with quasi-KMT support. The president of the university was KMT veteran Yü Yu-jen; the dean of studies was Teng Chung-hsia (q.v.). The Communist movement being in its most inceptive stage, when theoretical study and indoctrination were considered immediate goals, it is not surprising that some of the finest elements of the Party were found here engaged in cadre indoctrination. On the faculty were Yun Tai-ying, Shih Ts'un-t'ung, Chang T'ai-lei, Ts'ai Ho-sen, Hsiao Ch'u-nü, among others. (The university was closed down by the Settlement authorities on June 4, 1925, following the May 30 Incident, in which it played a crucial role.)

In addition to teaching, Ch'ü occupied another and equally important role as Party propagandist. He was editor-in-chief of *Hsin ch'ing-nien* (New youth), once the vehicle of the "new culture" movement, which now reappeared as a CCP organ; he was also one of the editors of *Hsiang-tao chou-pao* (Guide weekly), the Central Committee organ. Moreover, he was editor-in-chief of a new Party journal, *Ch'ien-feng* (Vanguard). Writing under innumerable pseudonyms (in all he had about 50) he wrote prolifically; his writings ranged from expositions of the Party line and translations of Comintern documents to vitriolic attacks on the "reactionaries," such as Tai Chi-t'ao.

In January 1924, Ch'ü attended the reorganization congress of the KMT in Canton and was elected an alternate member of the KMT Central Executive Committee. About this time, he married a woman by the name of Wang Chien-hung, of whom Ch'ü said nothing and little is known beyond the fact that she was of poor health and died in July of the same year.

In October 1924, he was wanted by the Settlement authorities because of his activities at Shanghai University; he went underground, now and then emerging surreptitiously to teach at the university. Meantime, the Party cell at the school was developing substantial liaison with the workers of Shanghai and was conducting workers' evening classes.

On November 5, 1924, quite a stir in Shanghai society was caused by the appearance of three simultaneous announcements in the *Min-kuo jih-pao* (Republic daily), one concerning the divorce by mutual consent of Shen Chien-lung (the son of Shen Ting-i, a founding member of the CCP, an instructor at Shanghai University, and later a right-wing KMT member), and Yang Chih-hua (a student at Shanghai University and a member of the Socialist Youth League, who was attached to the Women's Department of the Shanghai branch of the KMT). Another announced the marriage of Ch'ü Ch'iu-pai and Yang Chih-hua, and the third was a pledge to maintain comradelike cordiality between Ch'ü Ch'iu-pai and Shen Chien-lung.

The May 30 Movement (1925) derived much of its leadership from the young Communists at Shanghai University; prominent among the leaders were Li Li-san, Ts'ai Ho-sen, Yun Tai-ying, and Ch'ü Ch'iu-pai. As usual, Ch'ü was most effective with the pen, and he edited the *Jo-hsueh jih-pao* (Ardent daily), which began on June 4 and ran for 24 issues before it was closed down by the police.

In the spring of 1926 Ch'ü was laid up by another relapse of tuberculosis, but by August he was in Canton lecturing at Mao Tse-tung's Peasants' Movement Training Institute on the subject of "The Peasant Problem in the National Revolution." At the end of the year he was back in Shanghai and played a key role in planning the Shanghai uprisings in February–March 1927, which enabled the workers to take Shanghai. After this, he was ordered to Wuhan in March 1927 to be political instructor at the Wuhan branch of the Central Military Academy (formerly the Whampoa Academy).

His arrival at Wuhan made him the center of rallying forces hostile to the Ch'en Tu-hsiu–P'eng Shu-chih leadership of the CCP. The dissensions within the CCP in the early half of 1927 leading virtually to a breakdown of Party discipline and paralysis at the top were, in retrospect, more results of personal issues than matters of principle. Ch'ü lined up behind himself the Communist Youth League, led by Jen Pi-shih, which had been impatient with the limitations imposed by the nature of the KMT-CCP alliance. He also had the support of P'eng P'ai, Lo Ch'i-yuan, and especially Mao Tse-tung, who were exasperated by Ch'en Tu-hsiu's seeming lack of appreciation of the rural upsurge; Mao demanded a policy of total confiscation of land. Earlier, according to Yang Chih-hua, it seemed that P'eng Shu-chih, an editor of the *Hsiang-tao chou-pao* (no doubt acting at the behest of Ch'en Tu-hsiu), had declined to publish Mao's third installment of his renowned "Report of an Investigation into the Peasant Movement in Hunan" in the interest of maintaining surface harmony with the KMT. Ch'ü, however volunteered to publish the full text as a book, and even wrote a preface for it. Yet another source of support came from Ts'ai

Ho-sen, who evidently was settling a personal score with P'eng and Ch'en—the former having seduced his wife and the latter having failed to discipline his protégé.

Ch'ü's own cause for discontent seemed to stem from the frustration of his vaulting ambitions. He had returned from Moscow with Ch'en Tu-hsiu with high hopes, but Ch'en preferred P'eng Shu-chih, once Ch'ü's student at the Communist University of the Toilers of the East, and gave him the position of chief of the Propaganda Department instead. Ch'en may have been reluctant to make greater use of Ch'ü in the Party apparatus as a result of the latter's chronic ill health; probably more important was the fact that Ch'ü was of an independent nature, rather vain and hard to work with, and, moreover, he was too outspokenly critical of the KMT, thus making CCP-KMT relations all the more difficult.

In any event, when the Fifth CCP Congress was held at Hankow, in April–May 1927, soon after Chiang Kai-shek's anti-Communist coup, a veritable storm broke out as the opposition openly challenged the Ch'en-P'eng leadership. Ch'ü circulated a pamphlet entitled *Chung-kuo ko-ming chih cheng-lun wen-t'i* (Controversial questions of the Chinese revolution) in which he placed the blame of the disaster of the Communists on the Menshevism of the Ch'en-P'eng leadership, i.e., their subordination of the CCP and its leadership of the workers' and peasants' revolution to the bourgeoisie and their appeasement of the KMT by pursuing a compromising policy on the agrarian question. The flimsiness of the charge, of course, was evident in the light that the CCP was expected to execute contradictory orders of the Comintern, i.e., to remain inside the KMT and assert hegemony over a party backed by military might. Inasmuch as Chiang had vigilantly stamped out any attempt on the part of the Communists to subvert the Whampoa cadets and had succeeded in turning them into his personal instrument, the fate of the Communists was sealed.

The upshot of the intra-Party struggle was that Ch'ü was elected to the Politburo, Ch'en Tu-hsiu retained his position as general secretary but lost all his initiative of action in the face of rapidly unfolding events. And when the Wuhan KMT broke with the Communists, and the Kremlin decided to make Ch'en the scapegoat for its own failure, Ch'ü was the obvious candidate to replace Ch'en. An emergency conference was called on August 7, 1927, in Kiukiang at which Ch'en was deposed, Ch'ü became secretary (not general secretary) of the Party, while Besso Lominadze, a young Georgian who enjoyed Stalin's trust, replaced Borodin and virtually took over the full reins of CCP affairs as Stalin's personal representative. The Lominadze-Ch'ü leadership was marked by a radical shift of the Party line of united front from above to open urban and rural insurrections, the call to seize power and organize soviets.

Rampant violence expressed in the Autumn Harvest Uprisings and the Canton Insurrection was met by equally unbridled repression, and the lack of success exposed Ch'ü to the charge of "left opportunism" or putschism at the Ninth Plenum of the Executive Committee of the Comintern (ECCI) in February 1928. Because of probable KMT repression, as well as the Russians' desire to exert more direct control over the CCP, the Sixth Congress of CCP was held in Moscow in June–July 1928. Accordingly, Ch'ü left for the Soviet Union in April 1928, and at the congress he presented a report entitled "The Chinese Revolution and the CCP," which reviewed the events of the 1925–1927 period. He was stripped of his post as secretary (but remained a member of the Politburo), which was now given to Hsiang Chung-fa, a Communist leader of proletarian origin who in the course of time was eclipsed by the more dynamic and assertive propaganda chief, Li Li-san.

Ch'ü's loss of influence within the Chinese Communist movement inside China was offset by his gain of a position of some prestige in the international Communist movement where he was known by his Russian name, Strakhov (a Russian translation of his surname, both meaning "fear"). He was made chief of the Chinese delegation to the Comintern, which included four other members: Teng Chung-hsia, Chang Kuo-t'ao, Huang P'ing, and Yü Fei. Ch'ü was also a member of the Presidium of the ECCI.

In August 1928, at the Sixth Comintern Congress, he delivered a co-report on the national and colonial question entitled "The Lessons of the Chinese Revolution." In connection with the Comintern, he attended the Anti-Imperialist Congress in Paris in the fall of 1929 and the Conference of the Unemployed in Berlin in the summer of 1930.

Another area in which he achieved some reputation while in the Soviet Union was the field of Chinese linguistics. In 1928 he was elected a member of the Institute of Scientific Research on China, which was attached to Sun Yat-sen University and which in the following year was engaged in the project of devising a latinized Chinese alphabet (the purpose being to facilitate the education of Chinese domiciled in Siberia). Ch'ü worked with two Soviet Sinologues, V. S. Kolokolov and A. A. Dragunov, and two other Chinese, Lin Po-ch'ü and Wu Yü-chang (qq.v.). Ch'ü's study was the subject of a conference on May 23, 1930, at the institute, and was published in the same year in Moscow under the title *Chung-kuo Latinxua tzu-mu* (Chinese latinized alphabet).

While in Moscow, he was involved in one of the fiercest but little known factional fights, sometimes referred to as the Sun Yat-sen University case. In brief, it involved, on the one hand, Pavel Mif and his protégés (see under Ch'en Shao-yü) and on the other hand Ch'ü Ch'iu-pai and the Chinese delegation to the Comintern. Pavel Mif, who was Stalin's China expert during 1925–1927, had by the end of 1927 replaced Karl Radek as rector of Sun Yat-sen University and as chief of the Chinese Section of the Comintern's Far Eastern Bureau. At the Sixth CCP Congress, two evenly balanced groups, the "left," consisting of Chou En-lai, Ch'ü Ch'iu-pai and Li Li-san, and the "right," consisting of Ts'ai Ho-sen, Hsiang Ying, and Chang Kuo-t'ao, vied for the post of general secretary and control over the CCP. Mif resolved the deadlock by choosing Hsiang Chung-fa without satisfying all the leaders. Ch'ü was as keen to make a political comeback in China as Mif was to dominate the Chinese Communist movement. The latter's strategy was to plant his Chinese protégés, the so-called Russian-returned students or the "28 Bolsheviks," in China as the new power group. At Sun Yat-sen University these men had gained control of the CCP branch and their high-handed policies (as well as Mif's education and administrative policies at the university) had alienated a considerable part of the student body. Thus, by attacking Mif's policies in the university, Ch'ü, Chang Kuo-t'ao, and others of the Chinese Comintern delegation were in effect lining up the enemies of Mif and his Chinese protégés for a showdown.

Exact details of the showdown are unavailable, but by the spring of 1930 Mif had succeeded in obtaining Comintern action to push the Chinese delegation aside and have their duties assumed by his appointee, Chou En-lai, whom he sent for from China. The struggle between Mif and Ch'ü now shifted to China as they both went there to handle the Li Li-san affair. On arrival, Ch'ü easily resumed control of the Party apparatus and took charge of the Third Plenum in September 1930. He drafted a resolution on the Li Li-san line to the effect that Li had erred, not in strategy, which was in harmony with the Moscow line, but in tactics, that is, in the assessment of the "objective" conditions for revolution; Mif's objection was rudely brushed aside. However, Moscow backed Mif and wrote the CCP Politburo on November 16, 1930, about its disagreement with the resolution, even though the Li Li-san line had ceased in practice with the Third Plenum. In January 1931, with the support of Moscow, Mif sponsored the Fourth Plenum and succeeded in eliminating Ch'ü Ch'iu-pai from the Politburo and in entrenching his protégés in power.

From January 1931 to the end of 1933, when he left to join the Juichin government, Ch'ü led a precarious underground existence in Shanghai and was engaged in a sphere of literary activities which made possible his posthumous apotheosis by the CCP. He was the guiding spirit and policy-maker of the League of Left-Wing Writers in this period, because of his eminence as a Party member and his reputation as a writer. He engaged in ruthless polemics with such figures as Hu Ch'iu-yuan and Su Wen, both advocates of greater cultural freedom.

His posthumous reputation was, to a large degree, connected with his relationship with Lu Hsun, another key figure in the League, whose ideological affiliation then could at best be described as "fellow traveler." A genuine friendship appears to have grown out of shared interests in literary matters and mutual respect for each other's abilities, which was cemented by certain mutual advantages that the relationship afforded. Living underground, hounded by tuberculosis and the KMT, Ch'ü, with his wife, was dependent on Lu Hsun for occasional cover and all kinds of other assistance. In return, Chü supported Lu's position as nominal spokesman of the League. He also wrote a highly favorable critique of Lu's intellectual development in the form of a long preface to a collection of Lu's *feuilletons*, entitled *Lu Hsun tsa-kan-lu hsuan-chi hsu-yen* (Preface to a selection of Lu Hsun's random thoughts), in which he showed the progression of Lu's intellectual evolution from Social Darwinism to class theory. This evolution may have paved the way for Mao's elevation of Lu Hsun a few years later at the Yenan literary forum.

Part of the time Ch'ü was also engaged in translations, largely of views on the literature of Marx, Engels, Lenin, Plekhanov, Lafargue, Zola, and Gorky. He also translated several works of Gorky, Serafimovich, and Lunacharsky. Yet another area of his concern was literature for the masses (*ta-chung wen-i*), for which he agitated in 1932. This literature was to be revolutionary, using old forms but new content. It was in this connection that he called for a language reform and urged the use of the "common vernacular" (*p'u-t'ung-hua*), which he believed to be the evolving and living language of the masses as the medium for mass literature. Mao's regime has followed with some success Ch'ü's recommendations about the manufacture of a single literature for the masses, the use of folk art forms, and folk speech.

In December 1933 Ch'ü left Shanghai for Juichin. In January–February 1934 he attended the Second All-China Congress of Soviets and was re-elected a member of the Central Executive Committee, and in early February he was made commissar of Education. (He had been elected to both these positions at the First Congress in November 1931, but he was not present at Juichin to fill them). On April 1, he was appointed head of the Shen Tse-min University. Poor health prevented too many exertions, so the results of his work, according to his own accounts, were meager. He established a system of Leninist primary schools, edited teaching materials, organized literacy classes, and founded a Leninist teachers' college to train primary school teachers.

In October 1934 the Soviet government and the Red Army evacuated Juichin and set out on the Long March. Ch'ü was too ill to accompany them and was left behind in Kiangsi as chief of the Propaganda Department, along with Hsiang Ying, vice-chairman of the Kiangsi Soviet, Teng Tzu-hui, chairman of the Fukien Soviet, and Ho Shu-heng, an old Party veteran who with Mao Tse-tung formed the Hunanese delegation at the founding Congress of the CCP in July 1921. By February 1935 the pressure of KMT troops had made their position on the Fukien-Kiangsi border highly untenable. In the course of seeking refuge, Ch'ü was captured at Shang-hang in southwestern Fukien on March 20 and was kept at the prison in T'ing-chou (Ch'ang-t'ing), western Fukien, where he spent about three months. Lu Hsun and Ts'ai Yuan-p'ei interceded in vain on his behalf. During that period he wrote the third part of his introspective trilogy, entitled *To-yü ti hua* (Superfluous words), in which he reflected on his past, especially on the events of his political career. Along with the several lyrics which he composed in prison, one discerns that he had returned to his earlier Buddhist outlook although he felt unable to renounce his Marxist beliefs. On June 18, he was executed at the age of 36.

Except for a few rare omissions, Ch'ü Ch'iu-pai's writings are listed chronologically, with useful annotations, in Ting Ching-t'ang and Wen Ts'ao, *Ch'ü Ch'iu-pai chu-i hsi-nien mu-lu* (A chronological catalog of Ch'ü Ch'iu-pai's writings and translations; Shanghai, 1959). The bulk of his literary works has been collected in the four-volume *Ch'ü Ch'iu-pai wen-chi* (Collected works of Ch'ü Ch'iu-pai; Peking, 1953). Yang Chih-hua has written a useful reminiscent account of her husband in volume 8 of *Hung-ch'i p'iao-p'iao* (Red flag fluttering; Peking, 1958), and T. A. Hsia contributed a stimulating study of Ch'ü's autobiographical writings in *The China Quarterly* (no. 25, January–March 1966).

Ch'ü's wife, Yang Chih-hua, continued to have an active career after the death of her husband. She was imprisoned for a few years before 1946 by Sinkiang warlord Sheng Shih-ts'ai (see under Ch'en T'an-ch'iu). Since the Communists came to power in 1949 she has been particularly active in the Trade Union and Women's Federations, serving in the latter as a vice-chairman since 1957. She has been a member of the Party's Central Control Commission since 1962 and was elected in January 1965 as a member of the NPC Standing Committee.

Chu Te

(1886–   : I-lung hsien, Szechwan). "Father" of the Red Army; Politburo member.

Chu Te is one of the great military figures of modern East Asian history. A CCP member since 1922, Chu brought to the Party military skills which he had learned from many years of campaigning in southwest China. In the years after 1928, in close association with Mao Tse-tung, he built a small band of soldiers into an effective fighting unit in the famed Kiangsi Soviet. Chu made the Long March and then commanded the Communist armies during the Sino-Japanese War and the civil war with the Nationalists during the late 1940's. His major contributions to the Communist movement were made before 1949, but after the establishment of the PRC he continued to play an active role for about a decade.

Chu was born on November 30, 1886, in a village in I-lung hsien, located in a hilly and isolated section of north Szechwan some 120 miles north of Chungking. He came from a large farming family, but their economic status is a matter of dispute. Edgar Snow was told by a member of Chu's staff that his family were landlords, but a year later Snow's wife was told by Chu that his family were "poor tenant farmers."[1] Agnes Smedley, whose biography of Chu is a major source of information about his career,[2] accepts the version that he came from humble origins. Because Chu's forebears had come to Szechwan from Kwangtung, his generation was reared with a knowledge of both the Cantonese and the Szechwanese dialects.

Chu began his education in his fifth year at a private school. In 1906, when he was 20, he went to nearby Shunking (Shun-ch'ing, now Nanch'ung) where he attended a middle school. In the next year he went to Chengtu to study physical education at a higher normal school. After graduating in 1908 he returned home to teach physical education at a higher primary school, but he left within the same year for Yunnan. In 1909 Chu embarked upon his half-century long military career by enrolling in the newly established Yunnan Military Academy. The school had been set up under the auspices of the Manchu government, but the faculty included many members of Sun Yat-sen's T'ung-meng hui and the academy soon became a center of anti-Manchu activities. Chu had already come under the influence of Sun's revolutionary ideas, and soon after entering the academy he secretly joined the T'ung-meng hui. At approximately the same time he also secretly joined the Ko-lao-hui, the important secret society which had a large following in southwest China. His membership in both organizations proved to be useful in advancing his career during the ensuing years. Chu graduated with the first class

in mid-1911, after which he was assigned as a platoon commander in forces commanded by Hunanese military leader Ts'ai O, who maintained close ties with T'ung-meng hui members in Kunming.

On October 30, 1911, just three weeks after the uprising in Wuchang which triggered the Revolution of 1911, Chu took part as a company commander under Ts'ai O in the revolt in Kunming, which brought down the Manchu authorities in Yunnan. A half-century later, on the anniversary of the 1911 Revolution, Chu wrote a lengthy description of these events for the *JMJP*. During the decade after the revolution he was a middle-ranking officer in the provincial army which operated in Yunnan and Szechwan. In 1912 Chu joined the KMT and from 1912 to 1913 he was a detachment commander and instructor at the Yunnan Military Academy. Once again under Ts'ai O's command, Chu took part as a regimental and then a brigade commander in the campaign of 1916 to thwart Yuan Shih-k'ai's attempt to restore the monarchy. In describing these events to Agnes Smedley, Chu stressed the help his troops received from peasants who were members of the Ko-lao-hui. After Yuan's death in June 1916, Ts'ai O became the Szechwan governor, and he in turn appointed Chu to command a brigade of the Yunnan Army in Szechwan. For the next few years Chu spent most of his time in southwest Szechwan, operating out of his headquarters in Lu-chou (Lu-hsien).

In the years before 1920 Chu, in the apt words of Agnes Smedley, "was caught in the net of warlordism without recognizing it as such." He led an unproductive and dissolute life and smoked opium. However, he had met Sun Ping-wen during the anti-Yuan campaign of 1916, and during the next few years Sun had an important influence on Chu's intellectual and political development. Sun, a graduate of Peking University, was from a scholarly Szechwanese family and had worked with Sun Yat-sen in Japan. Through Sun and his friends, Chu was introduced to some of the revolutionary literature which was beginning to find a nationwide audience in the period before the May Fourth Movement of 1919. Sun later accompanied Chu to Europe (see below) where he joined the CCP; he worked in the Whampoa Military Academy in the mid-1920's and was killed in Chiang Kai-shek's anti-Communist coup in 1927.

In 1920 Chu found himself caught between contending warlord elements in Yunnan and Szechwan. At the end of that year he returned to Yunnan where he backed elements opposed to T'ang Chi-yao. They were initially successful, and Chu was rewarded in 1921 with the post of commissioner of Public Security in the provincial government. However, T'ang soon returned to power and Chu was forced to retreat to the Szechwan-Tibet border area. By coincidence he followed part of the route that the Long March troops followed 13 years later. In early 1922 Chu made his way to Chungking and then to Shanghai. In his own words, he went to Shanghai to "make preparations to go to Russia or Germany to study." First, however, he placed himself under medical care to break the opium habit. He made brief visits to Nanking, Peking, and Suiyuan and then returned to Shanghai with his friend Sun Ping-wen. There he met the "long-admired" Sun Yat-sen. Chu also sought out CCP founder Ch'en Tu-hsiu (q.v.) in hopes of gaining admission to the Communist Party. Chu found Ch'en to be "cool and reserved," and Ch'en in turn was suspicious of Chu's background with warlords. He informed Chu that admission to the Party depended upon his willingness to submit to a long period of study and a "sincere application" of his talents to the "workers' cause." Chu was dejected; he had "knocked on the door of the future and it had refused to open to him."

In September 1922 Chu, then in his mid-thirties, embarked on a new phase of his career when he sailed for France. In the next month, after a brief stay in Paris, he arrived in Berlin. He soon met Chou En-lai and joined the CCP, apparently with Chou as his sponsor. Chu's background was strikingly dissimilar to the majority of the earliest members of the CCP; not only was he several years older than the average member, but he was also one of the very few who had military academy training and several years experience as a troop commander. His military experience was probably not appreciated in 1922 to the extent it would be later when the CCP first took up arms to maintain its very existence. Chu spent the next months studying Marxist works and German, and then for about a year (1923–24) he attended lectures in the social sciences at the University of Göttingen. Partly because of his inadequate knowledge of German, he regarded his formal study at Göttingen as a waste of time and far less useful than trips to many German cities where he visited factories, mines, and places of cultural interest. In 1924 he returned to Berlin where he edited the *Cheng-chih chou-pao* (Political weekly), which was published under the auspices of the German chapter of the KMT. Many politically active Chinese students in Germany and France participated in the work of both the KMT and the CCP at this period. Chu, in fact, was elected in 1924 to alternate membership on the Central Executive Committee of the Berlin chapter of the KMT.[3]

In 1925 Chu was twice arrested for political activities, but on each occasion he was immediately released. There are conflicting accounts concerning his whereabouts and work in 1925–

26; the Smedley biography asserts that he was deported from Germany in 1926, but other and apparently more reliable accounts claim that he was deported in July 1925 after which he spent some time in the USSR. There, according to Edgar Snow, he studied at the Communist University of the Toilers of the East. Chu returned home in mid-1926 just as the Northern Expedition was getting underway from Kwangtung. The Nationalists and Communists were still working together closely, and one of their chief tactical goals was to woo warlords to the cause of the revolution or, failing that, to neutralize them. As a consequence, because of Chu's previous ties to General Yang Sen, then the most powerful figure in east Szechwan, he was sent to Szechwan to convince Yang to join the revolutionary cause. Yang agreed to join the Northern Expedition, and for a brief time in late 1926 Chu headed the Political Department of Yang's 20th Army. Almost immediately afterwards, however, Yang became suspicious of the Communist influences among his troops. Chu, barely managing to escape arrest, left Szechwan for Nanchang, Kiangsi, then a key center of revolutionary activity.

Chu arrived in Nanchang over the turn of the year 1926–27. There he contacted Chu P'ei-te, the commander of the Third Army of the National Revolutionary Army, who had been Chu Te's student at the Yunnan Military Academy many years earlier. Chu Te was placed in command of an officers' training regiment and made the head of a military training school. A few months later Chu P'ei-te made him chief public security officer in Nanchang, and by the middle of the year Chu Te was also deputy commander of the Ninth Army (a unit under Chu P'ei-te's overall command). During this same period—the first half of 1927—the tenuous Communist alliance with the Right-wing KMT, led by Chiang Kai-shek, came to an abrupt end when Chiang engineered his anti-Communist coup in April. And soon thereafter, Communist ties with the Left-KMT elements, headquartered in Wuhan, sharply deteriorated; a final break became inevitable in mid-July when the Communists were expelled from the Left-KMT government in Wuhan.

By the last half of July 1927 the Communists came to believe their only hope lay in a coup which would bring intact to them a significant military force—the stage was set for the famous Nanchang Uprising of August 1 (see under Yeh T'ing). The standard formulation by Communist historians is that the uprising was led by Chou En-lai, Yeh T'ing, Ho Lung, and Chu Te. Chu's pivotal positions in Nanchang were of doubtless value, but his troop strength was far less than that of Yeh and Ho. Nonetheless, Chu did take part in the planning, and when the rebels captured the city he was named to the 25-member Revolutionary Committee. Chu's relatively minor role is also emphasized in the new order of battle; when driven from the city a few days later Ho's 20th Army consisted of three divisions, Yeh's 11th Army had two divisions and elements of another, but Chu's Ninth Army (which he now commanded) consisted of only one regiment.

From Nanchang the rebel forces pushed southward to Kwangtung. The march (see under Yeh T'ing) ended in disaster when they were thoroughly routed at Swatow in late September. Chu's troops had remained as a rearguard force around San-ho-pa, 70 miles north of Swatow, and were thus able to retreat northward with about 2,000 men and then westward to the Kwangtung-Kiangsi-Hunan border area. This difficult march, which was marred by serious defections (see under Chou Shih-ti), reduced Chu's forces to 6–700 poorly armed troops, but among them were two first-rate junior officers, Ch'en I and Lin Piao (qq.v.). Chu's forces continued to maintain the fiction that they were still fighting under the "KMT banner," and this in turn enabled them to get some badly needed supplies from Fan Shih-sheng, a KMT commander in this area whom Chu had known many years earlier in Yunnan. Soon afterwards Chu received orders to march southward to assist in the Communist uprising planned for Canton. However, the march was halted in northern Kwangtung when the famous Canton Commune was crushed (see under Chang T'ai-lei). At about this time Chu was reprimanded by the Party Central Committee in Shanghai for his "alliance" with KMT General Fan Shih-sheng. This phenomenon of belated cooperation with the KMT, as Stuart Schram has noted, was so widespread among a number of Communist groups that the Central Committee issued a directive on December 31, 1927, to cease such practices.[4] Chu quickly broke with Fan and led his troops toward I-chang in southern Hunan. The city was captured in early January 1928 and the I-chang "soviet" was established. At this point Chu's forces openly proclaimed themselves to be a Communist unit.

In the meantime, Mao Tse-tung had been operating with great difficulty from his base in the Chingkang Mountains on the Hunan-Kiangsi border. Mao and Chu had made abortive attempts to contact one another, but it was not until the spring of 1928 that they joined together when Mao led troops into south Hunan to assist Chu. In doing so, Mao abandoned the Chingkangshan base to the enemy, and thus the celebrated meeting of the two leaders took place in south Hunan, and not in Chingkangshan as suggested in most accounts. The merger of the two units brought their forces to about 10,000 men, but only a fifth were armed.[5] The Chu–Mao troops soon reoccupied Chingkangshan and

formally established the Fourth Red Army; Chu was the commander and Mao was the Party representative. The Communists officially date the birth of the Red Army from the 1927 Nanchang Uprising, but in fact it was the Fourth Red Army which provided the core of Communist power in the late twenties and early thirties.

The Fourth Army was originally organized into three divisions, but these were quickly abandoned in favor of six regiments, numbered from the 28th through the 33rd. A few weeks later the army was depleted when soldiers of the 30th and 33rd Regiments deserted and went home. The next several months witnessed extreme hardships for the Fourth Army as it fought a series of defensive actions on the Hunan-Kiangsi border and in areas of northern Kwangtung, but there were some successes in organizational work on the Hunan-Kiangsi border where the initial steps were taken to establish a government apparatus. It was also during this period, in October 1928, that the Second Border Area Party Congress was held at Mao-p'ing in Ning-kang hsien. Chu was elected a member of the Second Special Committee, and in the next month, at the Sixth Party Congress of the Red Army, he was elected secretary of the Standing Committee of the Army Committee of the Party (replacing Ch'en I). The Special Committee and the Army Committee were both subordinate to the Front Committee, and when this was reorganized in early November with Mao in the ranking post as secretary, Chu was named a member.[6] The net effect of these elections and reorganizations was to make Mao the leading figure in the border area and, although detailed evidence is lacking, it appears that Chu supported Mao, who was then at odds with other provincial Party authorities.

The Chu–Mao forces were temporarily strengthened in the fall of 1928 when P'eng Te-huai (q.v.) arrived from the north after staging an uprising within the KMT ranks at P'ing-chiang a few months earlier. But when the KMT pressed the attack against the Ching-kangshan base over the turn of the year 1928–29, Chu and Mao moved eastward toward Fukien, while P'eng was left behind with his Fifth Red Army. Several weeks later P'eng's battered forces marched to southeast Kiangsi where they once again joined the Chu–Mao forces, but soon afterwards P'eng returned to the Hunan-Kiangsi border area and the Chu–Mao Fourth Army continued to campaign in Kiangsi. Because of fighting between Chiang Kai-shek and various warlord forces, the Fourth Army gained occasional respites. Nonetheless, the Chu–Mao elements only totalled about 5,000 (half of them armed) by the late summer of 1929.[7]

While Chu and Mao were slowly building their base in and around Juichin in southeast

Kiangsi—the well-known Kiangsi Soviet—most of the key CCP leaders were working underground in Shanghai, the headquarters of the Party. The Shanghai group, led by Li Li-san (q.v.), began to devise a grand strategy in late 1929 and early 1930 to launch major assaults on the key cities of central China. This plan necessitated a high degree of cooperation between Li and the various rural-based guerrilla units, of which the Chu–Mao forces were the most important. Chu and Mao, however, regarded Li's plans as ill-conceived, and throughout the spring of 1930 they resisted his promptings to prepare to move north for the attacks on major cities. Chu expounded to Agnes Smedley on his reasons for opposing Li's strategy, but noted that apart "from Mao and myself, there was very little opposition to the Li Li-san line. We had no choice but to accept it." Thus, in June 1930, the Fourth Army was joined with the Third, 12th, and 21st Armies to form the First Army Corps. In this new formation Chu was the commander and Mao the political commissar. At this same time the Revolutionary Military Council was established. This organ, in Chu's words, was the "forerunner" of the Chinese Soviet Republic (see below); it consisted of all commanders and commissars of the various Red Army units, but Chu candidly commented that it was "little more than a theory at the time because our communications . . . were so poor." Hsiang Ying (q.v.) was the council chairman, and by no later than 1931 Chu was a vice-chairman.

The famed Li Li-san line reached its zenith in mid-1930 when P'eng Te-huai's Third Army Corps captured and held Changsha, the Hunan capital, for a few days. Coinciding with this attack, Chu and Mao began their own assault on Nanchang, the Kiangsi capital. Quickly repulsed, they led their men westward to the Kiangsi-Hunan border. There, in August, they joined with P'eng's retreating forces to form the First Front Army. In the new formation Chu was the commander and Mao the political commissar; in addition, Chu retained his command of the First Army Corps (until January 1932 when Lin Piao became the corps commander). The combined forces consisted of some 40,000 men, but fewer than half had arms.[8] In early September they began a second assault on Changsha, but then in apparent defiance of Li Li-san, Chu and Mao called off the attack and retreated toward Chi-an (Kian) in central Kiangsi. Chi-an was captured in October and held for a few weeks before it was abandoned.

The second failure at Changsha in September 1930 marked the effective end of the Li Li-san line. In response to this development, the CCP Central Committee held its Third Plenum in Lu-shan, Kiangsi. Most of the CCP hierarchy attended the Plenum, with the important exception of such top field commanders as Chu, Mao, and P'eng Te-huai. Li Li-san was not immediately stripped of his authority, but a few weeks later he was deposed and sent in virtual exile to Moscow. Chu was among those elected to the reconstituted Party Central Committee, but there is no indication that he played an even indirect role in the disputes which characterized the Third Plenum. These were not settled until the Fourth Plenum in January 1931 when the Russian-returned student leaders (see under Ch'en Shao-yü) took control of the key Party organs.

The closing weeks of 1930 were a time of grave concern for Chu and his colleagues in Kiangsi. Not only had the Red Army suffered a defeat at Changsha, but in early December the Chu–Mao forces were rocked by a revolt within their ranks. This episode, known as the Fu-t'ien Incident, is described in the biography of P'eng Te-huai. The anti-Mao rebels attempted to gain Chu's support, but the available evidence suggests that Chu sided with Mao. Coinciding with the Fu-t'ien Incident, Chiang Kai-shek was positioning troops for an assault on the Communist strongholds in Kiangsi. This attack—the first of the famous Annihilation Campaigns—lasted only a brief period in the final days of 1930 and the first days of 1931, and it was successfully repulsed by the Red Army. While Chu was pushing back the KMT forces, the CCP was holding its Fourth Plenum in Shanghai (early January 1931) where, as mentioned above, the returned student leadership took control of the Party hierarchy. There are many conflicting reports about Politburo membership at this period in CCP history, and according to many accounts Chu was not elected to this important body until 1934. However, a Russian biography of Chu published in 1957 asserts that he was elected in 1931[9] (presumably at the Fourth Plenum). At the same time the Party created the Central Bureau of the Soviet Areas, with Chu as one of the members. Interpretations vary regarding the purposes and importance of the Central Bureau, but in general it seems to have been established to provide more effective liaison with and direction over the numerous Communist military units which were scattered over a wide area of central-south China.

In the period from 1931 to 1934 Chu was principally occupied commanding the Red Army as it sought to fend off the successive attacks by KMT armies. Most of this time was spent in central and southeast Kiangsi, and in the western portion of Fukien. Chu seems to have felt most comfortable when he was on the front lines with his troops, and he is probably due much of the credit for building the Red Army into a formidable force. At its peak, the army totalled about 200,000 men, and through the skills of Chu and his fellow officers, including P'eng Te-huai, Huang Kung-lueh, and Lin Piao (qq.v.), the Red Army was successful in defeating the Second, Third, and Fourth Annihilation campaigns (1931–1933).

The Communists institutionalized the Kiangsi Soviet in November 1931 at the First All-China Congress of Soviets. Chu was elected a member of the Central Executive Committee (CEC), the highest political body of the newly established Chinese Soviet Republic. The Council of People's Commissars (the cabinet) was set up under the CEC, and in this organ Chu was appointed People's Commissar for Military Affairs. He was also made chairman of the important Central Revolutionary Military Council, where he was assisted by two vice-chairmen, Wang Chia-hsiang (q.v.) and P'eng Te-huai. In effect, Chu replaced Hsiang Ying as council chairman, but according to Hsiang's own account, he sometimes acted as the chairman when Chu was at the front during the next few years. Finally, at the 1931 congress, Chu's role as commander of the entire Red Army was reconfirmed. Two years later, at the CCP's Fifth Plenum in January 1934, Chu was elected (or perhaps, as noted above, re-elected) to the Politburo. In the same month, at the Second All-China Congress of Soviets, Chu made one of the keynote speeches. This dealt with the build-up of the Red Army in face of the Fifth Annihilation Campaign, which had already begun. He was re-elected to the CEC, and he was also elected a member of the 17-man Presidium, which acted for the CEC when it was not in session. Chu was again reconfirmed in his other top military posts at the first session of the CEC, held in early February 1934 immediately after the congress.

By the spring of 1934 the situation in Kiangsi reached crisis proportions as the KMT began to close the net around the embattled Communist armies. In May, Chu issued a call for a further build-up of the Red Army, in which he stressed the growing dangers to the Communist base. Then in July he and Mao issued another directive announcing a "northward march" by elements of the Red Army for the ostensible purpose of engaging the Japanese. This abortive foray was led by Fang Chih-min (q.v.), and in retrospect it appears that it was the first substantive step on the Long March. By October 1934 the Red Army was whittled down to a force of about 100,000, and in that month the famed Long March was begun. Chu set out with the Long Marchers as commander-in-chief. Chou En-lai was then chairman of the Military Affairs Committee. This was a Party organ, as distinguished from the Revolutionary Military Council, the government apparatus which Chu Te had chaired in 1931. However,

from the period of the Long March the two organs were apparently merged and placed under the Party. During the Long March Mao replaced Chou En-lai as the chairman, and Chu became one of the vice-chairmen. Chu seems to have continued as a vice-chairman through the civil war period (1946–1949), by which time it was known as the People's Revolutionary Military Council.

The heaviest losses on the Long March were sustained during the first two months as the Red Army fought its way across south and southwest China. The Party hierarchy paused briefly in Tsun-i, Kweichow, in early January 1935 to regroup and consider future strategy. It was then, according to most accounts, that Mao assumed control of the CCP. Chu continued as the overall commander-in-chief of the Red Army. From Tsun-i the army moved in a generally northwestward direction to the Szechwan-Sikang border area. There, in the early summer of 1935, they rendezvoused with the Fourth Front Army, led by Chang Kuo-t'ao and Hsu Hsiang-ch'ien (qq.v.). The disputes over strategy and tactics are described in Chang's biography. In brief, a decision was reached to divide the two principal elements of the Long March forces—that is, the Chu–Mao troops and the Chang–Hsu troops—into two columns. Moreover, the leadership groups were also divided, and thus Mao, P'eng Te-huai, and Chou En-lai proceeded directly north to Shensi where they arrived in the fall of 1935. But Chu and other commanders who had begun from Kiangsi remained with Chang Kuo-t'ao, after which Chang decided to remain in the Szechwan-Sikang area rather than moving north to Shensi. Orthodox Maoist historians assert that Chu was "detained" by Chang and was thus forcibly separated from Mao for more than a year. However, Charles McLane has noted that as late as May 1936 a Russian journal indicated that there had been widespread "gossip" that the real dispute had been between Mao and Chu and that this resulted in Mao's "separation from the main forces of the Red Army."[10]

Chu remained in the Szechwan-Sikang border area with Chang Kuo-t'ao until mid-1936 when still another element of the Long March—the Second Front Army led by Jen Pi-shih, Ho Lung, and Kuan Hsiang-ying (qq.v.)—arrived from Hunan. At this juncture, to quote again from orthodox CCP accounts, it was only due to the "persevering efforts" of Chu, Jen, Ho, and Kuan that Chang Kuo-t'ao was forced to relent and push northward to join Mao in Shensi. Under these circumstances Chu arrived in north Shensi in the fall of 1936, where he once again assumed overall command of the Red Army. At this stage in his career Chu was not a familiar name in international affairs, but he was already well known in China and to readers of Comintern journals. His importance in Comintern eyes is perhaps best illustrated in a "special number" on China of *The Communist International,* published in New York in February 1936. In a section dealing with Chinese Communist leaders, there are biographies of only three men: Mao, Chu, and Fang Chih-min.

By the time Chu reached Shensi, the flagrant Japanese incursions into north China had aroused strong national sentiment for Chinese of all political persuasions to join in a united effort to resist Japan. This was abetted by the famous Sian Incident of December 1936 (see under Chou En-lai) when Chiang Kai-shek, in effect, agreed to concentrate the nation's resources on resisting Japan rather than eliminating the Communists. The difficulties involved in agreeing to a united effort were quickly swept aside after the Sino-Japanese War began in July 1937. In August Chu and Chou En-lai flew to Nanking where an agreement was concluded, which, in theory, placed the Red Army under the jurisdiction of the national government. Chu was appointed deputy commander of the Second War Zone, which nominally made him a subordinate of Shansi Governor Yen Hsi-shan, the zone commander. More important, the agreement provided that the Red Army would be renamed the Eighth Route Army, with Chu as commander and P'eng Te-huai as deputy commander. The major units under the Eighth Route Army were the 115th, 120th, and 129th Divisions, commanded by Lin Piao, Ho Lung, and Liu Po-ch'eng, respectively. The history of the other principal wartime Communist force, the New Fourth Army, is described in the biographies of Yeh T'ing and Ch'en I.

In September 1937 the three Eighth Army divisions crossed the Yellow River into Shansi to engage the invading Japanese who were moving down the province from the north. Chu established a temporary headquarters in the Wu-t'ai Mountain area of northeast Shansi. By the turn of the year he was forced to transfer his headquarters to the southwest portion of the province, but many Eighth Route Army troops remained behind Japanese lines to conduct guerrilla warfare (see under Nieh Jung-chen). In the early days of the war there was relatively close KMT–CCP cooperation, and thus in January 1938 Chu and P'eng Te-huai went to Lo-yang in north Honan to confer on war strategy with Chiang Kai-shek, then on an inspection tour of the northern front. At this same period, once again in the spirit of the times, Chu was among the key CCP leaders readmitted to the KMT. Similarly, when the Nationalists established the Supreme National Defense Council as the highest political organ for the duration of the war, Mao, Chu, and Chou En-lai were reportedly appointed as members.[11]

Chu spent much of the year 1938 at the front where, at least for a while, he commanded his own troops as well as KMT units and some forces drawn from Yen Hsi-shan's provincial units in Shansi. From scattered reports Chu seems to have spent most of this period in southeast Shansi where the 129th Division was based. In the fall he went to Hankow, then the provisional capital of the Nationalists, for talks with Chiang Kai-shek. Then he went to Yenan to attend the CCP's Sixth Plenum (October–November 1938). Chu was back with his troops again through most of 1939, this time in the T'ai-hang Mountains on the Shansi-Hopeh border. At the end of 1939 Chu was ordered back to Yenan, and from then until the end of the war he spent most of his time there. This left Deputy Commander P'eng Te-huai as the top military figure in the field for the next few years.

Chu's return to Yenan during the winter of 1939–40 coincided with the marked deterioration of KMT–CCP relations. From the Communist viewpoint, the situation was sufficiently serious for them to redeploy many front-line troops back to the Yenan area in order to counter the pressures from nearby KMT forces. The situation reached a climax in January 1941 at the time of the New Fourth Army Incident (see under Yeh T'ing). New Fourth Army commander Yeh T'ing was captured, deputy commander Hsiang Ying was killed, and several thousand Communist troops were put out of action. Mao and Chu responded with a declaration demanding Yeh's release and a promise that the Nationalists would not further molest the New Fourth Army; failure to meet these terms, according to Mao and Chu, would end the united front. In fact, the united front was already dead. Pressed by both the Japanese and the Nationalists, the Communists were forced to turn their attention during the early and mid-1940's to concerted efforts to become more self-sufficient. For example, some Eighth Route Army units in the Shensi-Kansu-Ninghsia (Shen-Kan-Ning) Border Region spent much of their time cultivating crops. These activities were given strong support by Chu and other top leaders who, from time to time, engaged in manual labor as an example for all to follow. Similarly, the theme of self-sufficiency ran through the speeches and articles by Chu during this period, many of which are listed in Chün-tu Hsüeh's bibliography of the Communist movement.[12]

The isolation of the Communists was partially alleviated in 1944 when a number of foreign journalists were allowed to visit Yenan and when the U.S. Army was allowed to establish an observation team there. Chu gave a number of interviews to newsmen and he held several talks with American diplomats. He tried to impress upon the American diplomats the alleged weakness of the KMT and the use-fulness of supplying arms directly to Commu-nist forces. He also requested a loan of $20 million from the United States to procure the defection of Chinese puppet troops and to en-courage acts of sabotage by these same troops against the Japanese.[13] These overtures were turned down by the Americans. From the scores of talks Chu held with journalists, diplomats, and military observers during the war, he emerges as one of the more vivid personalities of the Communist movement. Most accounts, such as those by Edgar Snow, Evans Carlson, and Harrison Forman, stress his close ties with the troops he led, a fondness for sports, and an affable and unassuming manner. He seems to have struck most Western observers as far less politically oriented and dogmatic than many of his highly politicized colleagues, an assumption which may account for Chu's relative lack of involvement in the many political controver-sies throughout the history of the CCP.

From April to June 1945 Chu was among the 752 full and alternate delegates who attended the Party's Seventh Congress in Yenan. He was listed second only to Mao on the congress pre-sidium (steering committee). The delegates heard three major speeches: a political report by Mao, a speech on military affairs by Chu, and a report on revisions to the Party Constitu-tion by Liu Shao-ch'i. Chu's address, published in English in 1952 under the title *On the Battle-fronts of the Liberated Areas,* represented the official Party version of the Sino-Japanese War. Aside from a brief section on "future military tasks," it is perhaps most useful for its exposi-tion of the growth of the Red Army and sta-tistics on friendly and enemy casualties. At the close of the congress Chu was re-elected to the Central Committee, and immediately afterwards, at the inaugural plenum of the new Central Committee, he was re-elected to the Politburo and elected for the first time to the Secretariat (a kind of inner-Politburo). In the most official sense, Chu was then the second-ranking member of the CCP. But in reality he was probably al-ready a notch below both Liu Shao-ch'i and Chou En-lai. For example, when Mao went to Chungking later in 1945 to talk with Chiang Kai-shek, it was Liu—not Chu—who was made acting chairman of the Party. By 1952 even the most official listings of the inner-elite placed Chu in the fourth position after Mao, Liu, and Chou. This same sequence, as noted below, was maintained after the Eighth Party Congress in 1956.

In August 1945, immediately after Japan's surrender, Chu issued a series of orders to his troops to occupy areas held by Japanese and Chinese puppet troops and to disarm them. He also issued a directive to the Japanese com-mander-in-chief to surrender peacefully. These orders were countermanded by the Nationalists, and during the next few months both sides raced to achieve their objectives. While these develop-ments were taking place in the field, gestures were being made to prevent a nationwide civil war. In the late summer and early fall Mao held talks with Chiang Kai-shek in Chungking, and in January 1946, with the assistance of United States Special Envoy George C. Mar-shall, a truce was arranged. This lasted only a few months, and by mid-1946 civil war raged in many parts of China. By this time the Eighth Route Army, the New Fourth Army, and vari-ous other Communist units had assumed a new name—the People's Liberation Army (PLA)—with Chu as the commander-in-chief. At this early stage in the civil war, Chu and other top Communists openly acknowledged their strategy of a mobile war of attrition in which the PLA would concentrate on destroying KMT man-power rather than attempting to hold cities, in-cluding the Communist capital at Yenan.[14]

In mid-March 1947 the Nationalists captured Yenan. Anticipating this, the Communist hier-archy divided the Party Secretariat into two groups. One, which included Mao, Chou En-lai, and Jen Pi-shih, remained in the Shen-Kan-Ning Border Region. The other, known as the "Working Committee" and consisting of Liu Shao-ch'i (the head), Chu Te, and a number of Central Committee members, made its way into the Shansi-Suiyuan Liberated Region, and from there to the Shansi-Chahar-Hopeh Lib-erated Region. In the summer Liu, Chu, and their colleagues arrived in southwest Hopeh, not far from Shih-chia-chuang, a key communica-tions center. They set up their headquarters in the village of Hsi-pai-po in P'ing-shan hsien, where the Working Committee continued to op-erate until Mao arrived in May 1948. By this date the momentum of the civil war had swung to the Communists, and in the last months of 1948 and early 1949 the PLA won a series of battles which gave them almost undisputed control of Manchuria and much of north China.

Soon after the fall of Tientsin in mid-January 1949, Chu was among the top leaders who went there for the victory celebrations. He then re-turned to Hsi-pai-po to attend the Party's Second Plenum (March 5–13) when Mao out-lined the shift in emphasis from the countryside to the cities which the PLA was capturing in rapid succession. Less than two weeks later the Central Committee and the PLA Headquarters were transferred to Peking which, several months later, was to be designated the new capital. Like most of the key leaders, except those still in direct command of troops in the field, Chu participated in the preparations which culminated in the establishment of the PRC on October 1. He was among the speakers on the opening day (April 11) of the youth congress which set up the New Democratic Youth League. In June, when Mao convened the Preparatory Committee of the CPPCC, Chu attended as the ranking member of the seven-man PLA Headquarters' delegation. Then in September, in this same capacity, he attended and delivered two brief speeches at the inaugural session of the CPPCC, the organization which brought the national government into existence. While the CPPCC was in session, Chu served as a member of the standing committee of the presidium (steering committee), and he was also a member of the special committee which drafted the Organic Law of the central government, one of the key documents adopted then. After more than two decades in the hinterlands, he was among those given a place of honor on October 1 when Mao proclaimed the PRC to be in existence. Chu officially reviewed the troops which took part in the ceremonies and he issued the order-of-the-day to the PLA. He was then almost 63 years old.

In the new government hierarchy, Chu received top posts in three key organs, each chaired by Mao. He was appointed a member of the Standing Committee of the CPPCC, one of the six vice-chairmen of the Central People's Government Council, and one of the five vice-chairmen of the People's Revolutionary Military Council. In addition, he continued as commander-in-chief of the PLA. He retained all these posts until September 1954 when the central government was reorganized, and during these same years Chu was also an Executive Board member of the then active Sino-Soviet Friendship Association. During the formative years of the PRC he spent most of his time in Peking. For the period after 1949 Chu is often characterized as one of the "grand old men" of the Party who played only a peripheral role in affairs of state. There may be some truth in this assumption, but the public record indicates that he continued to be very active. For example, although complete attendance records are not available, he is known to have participated in the majority of the 34 meetings between 1949 and 1954 of the highly important Central People's Government Council. He also attended and frequently spoke at many national conferences sponsored by the government or "mass" organizations. Such meetings were especially frequent in the first year or two of the PRC as the Communists set about organizing and formulating plans for many segments of Chinese society. During the year 1950, for example, Chu attended at least 15 national conferences; predictably, several of these concerned the PLA, but others dealt with such varied topics as the textile industry, the Academy of Sciences, export trade, and publishing. During these same years he also delivered speeches or wrote ar-

ticles about the history of the Red Army, the most useful of which was published in 1952 to mark the 25th anniversary of the Red Army.[15]

In early 1953 the PRC took the first major steps toward drafting a national constitution and convening a national legislature. Thus, in January, the Committee for Drafting the Constitution was set up, and in the next month the Central Election Committee was established. Chu was a member of both committees, and when elections were held in 1954 he was elected a deputy from Szechwan to the First NPC. (He was returned from Szechwan to the Second and Third NPC's, which first met in 1959 and 1964, respectively.) At the inaugural session of the NPC, held in September 1954, he became the sole vice-chairman of the PRC in the reorganized central government. Previously, as already noted, he had been one of the six vice-chairmen, but under both the old and the reorganized structure, he served under Chairman Mao. The NPC also set up the National Defense Council; this was also chaired by Mao, and Chu was appointed the first of the 15 vice-chairmen. At this same time the post of PLA commander was abandoned, and Chu thus relinquished the post he had held under one title or another for a quarter of a century. A year later, in September 1955, military ranks were established and decorations were awarded for Red Army veterans. Chu was made a marshal (a five-star rank), and he was given the Orders of August First, Independence and Freedom, and Liberation.

In the meantime, in late September and early October 1954, Chu participated in negotiations with a Soviet delegation led by Nikita Khrushchev. The talks led to a number of important agreements, including a large loan to China and the withdrawal of Soviet troops from Port Arthur (which was completed in May 1955). Chu went abroad for the first time in 30 years when he spent two weeks in North Korea in August 1955 heading a delegation which took part in celebrations marking the 10th anniversary of the defeat of Japan. Four months later, in December, he went to Bucharest for the Second Congress of the Rumanian Workers' (Communist) Party. On January 1, 1956, Chu and his delegation arrived in East Berlin for the celebrations in connection with the birthday of President Wilhelm Pieck. Two weeks later the group visited Hungary for four days, and then from Budapest the delegation traveled to Czechoslovakia. While in Prague, Nieh Jung-chen, a member of Chu's delegation, spoke before a meeting of the Warsaw Pact, but Chu himself apparently did not participate. Then in late January and early February he spent a few days in Poland.

On February 4, 1956, Chu arrived in Moscow from Warsaw to attend the landmark 20th CPSU

Congress, which featured Khrushchev's famous denunciation of many aspects of Stalinism. The men touring with Chu left for home at this time, but another top-level group, consisting of Teng Hsiao-p'ing, T'an Chen-lin, and Wang Chia-hsiang (qq.v.), arrived from Peking to assist Chu. Chu's speech before the congress was replete with praise of the Soviet Union, the "shining example" for the CCP. He also read a message of similar tone from the CCP Central Committee, which was signed by Mao. Mao's favorable mention of Stalin stood out, in retrospect, when Khrushchev delivered his indictment of Stalin a few days later. For a month after the congress Chu traveled extensively in the Soviet Union, and when Polish United Workers' (Communist) Party First Secretary Boleslaw Beirut died in mid-March, Chu went to Warsaw for the funeral. He then returned to Moscow for further talks with Soviet officials. He left for home on March 20, stopping en route for visits to several cities in Siberia. Chu arrived in Ulan Bator, the capital of Mongolia, on March 28; he conferred with senior Mongolian officials and, after more than three months abroad, he left for home on the 31st. It may not have been coincidental that Peking delayed its initial full-scale response to the 20th CPSU Congress until a few days after Chu's return home. This was published in the April 5 *JMJP* in the famous editorial, "On the Historical Experience of the Dictatorship of the Proletariat." At one level of analysis the Chinese endorsed the 20th Congress. However, they apparently attempted to limit the attack on Stalin so that it would not be expanded into an "attack on the Communist system in general" and to "protect Mao from the charge that he was following in Stalin's footsteps."[16]

At the CCP's Eighth National Congress held in September 1956, Chu delivered a brief speech which reiterated the major themes enunciated in keynote addresses by Liu Shao-ch'i and Teng Hsiao-p'ing, and at the close of the meetings he was re-elected to the Central Committee. On the following day, at the First Plenum of the new Central Committee, Chu was re-elected to the Politburo. On the same day Liu Shao-ch'i, Chou En-lai, Chu, and Ch'en Yun were elected vice-chairmen of the Central Committee; this was a new post created in accordance with the revised constitution adopted at the congress. The new constitution also provided that the Central Committee vice-chairmen would automatically be vice-chairmen of the Politburo. Finally, Liu, Chou, Chu, and Ch'en, in addition to Chairman Mao and General Secretary Teng Hsiao-p'ing, were elected members of the Politburo Standing Committee. The Standing Committee was another innovation, and it replaced, in effect, the Secretariat as the apex of political authority in

China. (Lin Piao was added to the Standing Committee in 1958, but no other personnel changes were made through the mid-1960's.)

In the middle and late 1950's and the early 1960's, Chu's activities underwent a gradual change. In contrast to the early PRC years, he appeared at fewer national conferences, although, like many Politburo members, he frequently "received" delegates to these conferences. On the other hand, he undertook a new but probably informal function by a series of brief tours throughout China. He is known to have made at least 23 trips in the period from 1956 to 1964. Many of these were described as inspection tours, but a few were in connection with prominent visitors; for example, in April 1957 Chu accompanied Soviet leader K. E. Voroshilov on a tour of Manchuria. Chu made his last trip abroad in March 1959 when he led a delegation to Poland for the Third Congress of the Polish United Workers' Party. He then spent a week in Hungary taking part in celebrations commemorating the 40th anniversary of the establishment of the Hungarian Soviet Republic, the short-lived Communist government headed by Bela Kun in 1919.

In April 1959 the Second NPC convened its first session. A number of changes were made in the government hierarchy, the best known of which was the retirement of Mao as chairman of the PRC. Chu Te also stepped down from his post as the sole vice-chairman of the PRC; two persons, Tung Pi-wu and Sung Ch'ing-ling (Mme. Sun Yat-sen), were now named to this post. Liu Shao-ch'i replaced Mao as PRC chairman, and because Liu vacated the chairmanship of the NPC Standing Committee, Chu was named to succeed him. (In January 1965 Chu was elected to chair the Standing Committee of the Third NPC.) Moreover, in April 1959, Chu was not reappointed a vice-chairman of the National Defense Council. He had, as noted, relinquished the command of the PLA in 1954, and now five years later he was removed from his only remaining formal position in the military establishment. Chu did retain his rank as marshal, and during the ensuing years he occasionally attended, or received delegates to, military conferences, but there is little to suggest that he played a significant role in military affairs after the middle or late 1950's. In fact, by the 1960's, when Chu was to reach his 80th birthday, his role in state and Party affairs seems to have been essentially ceremonial.

Like so many other CCP leaders, Chu's turbulent revolutionary career is reflected in his personal life. In 1912 he married a woman from Szechwan, who was a normal-school teacher with "progressive ideas." A son was born to them in 1916, and soon afterwards his wife died. In the next year he married a woman from a well-to-do scholarly family, who was also active in the Revolution of 1911. They apparently lived a pleasant life together, but Chu never saw her again after his departure for Europe. In the mid-1930's she and Chu's son were allegedly murdered by warlords. In 1928 Chu married a woman from Changsha, whom he described as a writer and a member of an intellectual family that had been active in the revolution. She was soon captured and beheaded, and then in 1929 Chu married K'ang K'o-ch'ing. Then in her late teens, K'ang was a leader of a partisan unit in the Red Army, and she later made the Long March. Since 1949 she has been one of the more politically active women in the PRC, especially in the National Women's Federation, of which she has been a vice-chairman since 1957. A sketch of her early life is contained in Nym Wales' *Red Dust* (Stanford, Calif., 1952).

1. Edgar Snow, *Red Star over China* (New York, 1938), p. 346; Nym Wales, *Inside Red China* (New York, 1939), p. 113.

2. Agnes Smedley, *The Great Road* (New York, 1956).

3. *Chung-kuo Kuo-min-tang chou-k'an* (China Kuomintang weekly), Canton, no. 40:7 (September 28, 1924).

4. Stuart Schram, *Mao Tse-tung* (New York, 1966), pp. 117–118.

5. Chün-tu Hsüeh and Robert C. North, "The Founding of the Chinese Red Army," in E. Stuart Kirby, ed., *Contemporary China, 1962–1964* (Hong Kong, 1968), VI, 59–83.

6. *Selected Works of Mao Tse-tung* (Peking, 1964), I, 96.

7. Hsüeh and North.

8. *Foreign Relations of the United States, 1930* (Washington, D.C., 1945), II, 185.

9. *Bol'shaya Sovetskaya Entsiklopedya* (Large Soviet encyclopedia; Moscow, 1957), XLVII, 354–355.

10. Charles B. McLane, *Soviet Policy and the Chinese Communists, 1931–1946* (New York, 1958), pp. 59–60.

11. Lyman P. Van Slyke, *The Chinese Communist Movement: A Report of the United States War Department, July 1945* (Stanford, Calif., 1968), pp. 62–63.

12. Chün-tu Hsüeh, *The Chinese Communist Movement, 1937–1949* (Stanford, Calif., 1962).

13. *Foreign Relations of the United States, 1944, China* (Washington, D.C., 1967), VI, 542, 752–755; *United States Relations with China: With Special Reference to the Period 1944–1949* (Washington, D.C., 1949), pp. 86–87.

14. John Gittings, *The Role of the Chinese Army* (London, 1967), p. 11.

15. *CB* 208, pp. 30–36.

16. Donald S. Zagoria, *The Sino-Soviet Conflict, 1956–1961* (Princeton, N.J., 1962), p. 43.

Chu Te-hai

(1910–   ; Hoeryŏng, North Hamkyŏng, Korea). Chairman and principal Party official, Yenpien-Korean Autonomous Chou, Kirin; alternate member, CCP Central Committee.

Chu Te-hai (Korean transliteration: Chu Tŏkhae) is head of the Party Committee and chairman of the Yenpien-Korean Autonomous Chou, which is the PRC's largest autonomous area for Korean nationals. He was active in Manchuria during the twenties and thirties in the anti-Japanese resistance movement. After a period of study in the Soviet Union he worked in Yenan from 1939 to 1945. Returning to Manchuria in the postwar period, he has worked mainly in Yenpien, located in eastern Kirin where the borders of China, Korea, and Soviet Union meet. For many years Korean nationals have made up the majority of the population in the Yenpien area, and in some periods there has been easy communication between Koreans on both sides of the Manchurian-Korean border. Chu is said to have been born on the Korean side, in Hoeryŏng, a town on the Tumen River that forms part of the boundary between Kirin and Korea. Although this birthplace cannot be verified and he may have been born of Korean parents in Kirin (as some accounts assert), it is certain that he has spent most of his career in Manchuria.

Chu had his first contact with the Communist movement through the Korean Communist Party (KCP), which had been active from the early 1920's in eastern Kirin. He may well have known Kim Il-sung there. Kim, today head of the North Korean Party, was in Manchuria from at least the early twenties. The two men are contemporaries; Kim was born in 1912 in Pyongyang, Korea. Taken by his parents to Kirin in his early youth, Kim Il-sung joined the Chinese Communist Youth League there in the late twenties. He was said to have been a secretary of the Youth League in eastern Manchuria in 1929, the year Chu Te-hai joined the KCP. (Kim Il-sung remained in Manchuria until 1941 when he was driven into Russia by the Japanese.) From the late 1920's the Chinese Communist Party began to operate in Manchuria, but its activists often ran into opposition from Korean Communists working there independently. Chu joined the Chinese Communist Youth League in Manchuria in 1930, becoming a secretary of a local league branch in Kirin that same year. After 1931 he was for a time secretary of a larger regional committee of the League but it is not clear whether this position had any relation to the Youth League unit to which Kim Il-sung belonged. In 1931, when the Japanese invaded Manchuria, a number of Korean Communists working there joined the Manchurian branch of the CCP, as Chu was said to have done in 1931. The various anti-Japanese resistance forces in

Manchuria were decimated by the Japanese in 1933, but they were soon reorganized into units in which the Communists had a greater role than they had prior to 1933. From the mid-1930's these forces were known as the Northeast Allied Anti-Japanese Army (see under Chou Pao-chung) and were active in the Ning-an area of eastern Kirin (now southeastern Heilungkiang). Chou Pao-chung was a commander in the army and Chu was also associated with it. In the mid-1930's Kim was commander of the Sixth Division of its First Army, which fought in the Ch'ang-pai Mountains south of Ning-an on the Manchurian-Korean border. Chu was reported to be fighting in the Ning-an area at this time. He left Manchuria in 1936 to study in the Soviet Union.

In 1939 Chu returned to the Communist capital at Yenan, where he spent the remaining years of the Sino-Japanese War. During this period he was attached to the Communist Eighth Route Army and also studied at an educational institution in Yenan, possibly the Nationalities Institute, which opened in September 1941. In that same year the Korean Communists in China established the Yenan branch of the North China Korean Independence League under Kim Tu-bong (then known as Kim Paek-yôn). Kim was one of the most important Koreans during the war and postwar years until his purge in North Korea in 1958. Japanese intelligence documents indicate that Chu Te-hai was serving as an assistant to Kim in 1944 in the Yenan branch.[1] Also in 1944 Chu was head of the administrative section of a small academy run by the Koreans in Yenan.

At the time of the Japanese surrender in 1945, the Communists began to infiltrate elements of their wartime armies into Manchuria where they joined forces with local resistance groups like those led by Chou Pao-chung. They soon formed an army known as the Northeast Democratic Allied Army (NEDAA) under the command of Lin Piao. Chu served as a political commissar with a detachment of the NEDAA between 1945 and 1948 and concurrently as director of the Bureau of Nationality Affairs, probably a bureau under the regional government that the Communists established in Manchuria (the Northeast Administrative Committee). However, on his return to Manchuria, Chu's main activity was with the Kirin Korean minority. The Communists point with pride to the regime they have established for the Koreans in Manchuria, a model for similar governments created for other non-Han ethnic groups living within China. The area of Chu's activity, Yenpien, includes the city of Yen-chi (Yenki) and six hsien in eastern Kirin. It is south of Ning-an (now in Heilungkiang) where Chu and Chou Pao-chung had carried on guerrilla operations during the war. Koreans had inhabited this part of Manchuria, formerly called Chien-tao, for many years. After the Japanese

defeat of the Korean "Righteous Army" about 1912, parts of the army retreated to Chien-tao and established military centers from which Korean guerrilla forces continued to cross the border to harass the Japanese. In the spring of 1920 Korean translations of the *Communist Manifesto* were distributed to Korean communities in this area.[2] Yenpien, with a population (in 1964) of about one million, of whom over half are Korean, contains the largest part of China's Korean minority, 75 per cent of whom live in Kirin Province. Largely a rice-growing area before the war, the Communists have developed its industry and opened mines.[3]

In 1948 Chu was the CCP secretary of the Yen-chi District. (Yen-chi is a hsien as well as the principal city of Yenpien.) In 1949 he was director of the Special Administrative District Office for Yenpien, a part of the Kirin Provincial Government; this was redesignated the Korean Autonomous District People's Government in September 1952. In December 1955 the name was changed to the Yenpien-Korean Autonomous Chou. Since 1952 Chu has been the chairman of the governmental organization as well as the ranking Party secretary.

Beyond Yenpien, Chu has carried his specialization in nationality affairs into other branches of the provincial, regional, and national governments. In June 1949, in preparation for the opening of the CPPCC, which inaugurated the central government, the Communists established a Preparatory Committee to organize the CPPCC. Chu was named to this Committee as a representative of the national minorities and also attended the first meeting of the CPPCC in September. Speaking at the session, he stressed the need for the Korean minority groups to "unite" with the Han Chinese. At the close of the meetings, he was elected to membership on the First National Committee. He was re-elected to the Second National Committee, which opened in December 1954 and served on its governing Standing Committee. However, he was not re-elected to the Third CPPCC, which opened in April 1959.

In addition to his position in the CPPCC, a legislative body, Chu represented national minorities in the executive branch, serving from October 1949 as a member of the Nationalities Affairs Commission of the Government Administrative Council (GAC). He held this position until the constitutional government came into being in September 1954 at the first meeting of the First NPC. Chu was a deputy from Kirin to the First and Second NPC's (1954-1964), and was re-elected to the Third NPC, which first met in December 1964. When the Communists established their constitutional government in 1954 they created committees under both the legislature (the NPC) and the executive branch (known since 1954 as the State Council). Whereas Chu had served to 1954 on the executive organ devoted to nationalities questions, since 1954 he has been a member of the NPC Nationalities Committee.

Chu has been a fairly active member of the NPC and at the April 1959 session he delivered a speech entitled "The Indian Aggressors Cannot Save the Tibetan Rebels," an address that came in the wake of the March 1959 rebellion in Tibet against Han Chinese rule. His familiarity with Tibet may have been gained from his membership on the PRC delegation led by Vice-premier Ch'en I, which attended the ceremonies marking the establishment of the Preparatory Committee for the Tibet Autonomous Region in April 1956. Several months earlier Chu had attended the inauguration of another national minority government—the Sinkiang-Uighur Autonomous Region government, which was formally established in Urumchi in October 1955.

Besides his work for the national government, Chu has represented Yenpien in the larger provincial and regional administrations under whose jurisdiction it falls. From 1949 to 1953 he was a member of the Northeast People's Government, which had been established in August 1949. In January 1953 he became a member of the successor to this government, the Northeast Administrative Committee (NEAC) in which he was also a vice-chairman of its Nationalities Affairs Committee; he held these positions until the dissolution of the NEAC in 1954. In May 1950 he was named as a member of the Kirin Provincial People's Government; he was promoted to a vice-governorship in August 1954, a position he continues to hold, having been re-elected in February 1955, July 1958, and December 1963.

Chu has, of course, assumed more peripheral responsibilities to which every Party member is required to devote some time. Such activities include his being a member of the First National Committee, All-China Federation of Democratic Youth, 1949–1953; a member of the Council for the Reform of the Chinese Written Language, 1949–1954; and a delegate from the national minorities to the Second National Conference of the Sino-Soviet Friendship Association in December 1954. In addition, Chu has been president of Yenpien University since June 1951. The school was established two years earlier and offers all its courses in Korean; by 1955 it had an enrollment of over 1,000 Korean students. Chu was elected an alternate member of the Party Central Committee at the Eighth Party Congress in September 1956. He is the only Korean serving on the Central Committee.

1. "Saikin ni okeru Chūkyo oyobi Chukei kankei" (The relationship of the Chinese Communists and Chungking in the recent period), *Gaiji geppo* (External affairs monthly; Tokyo, March 1940), pp. 88–90.

2. Robert A. Scalapino and Chong-sik Lee, "The Origins of the Korean Communist Movement," *The Journal of Asian Studies*, 20.1:9–31 (November 1960).

3. *Economic Geography of Northeast China* (1959), JPRS translation no. 15,388, p. 297.

Ch'u T'u-nan

(1899–   ; Wen-shan hsien, Yunann). Non-Communist; specialist in international cultural relations; president, Chinese People's Association for Cultural Relations with Foreign Countries.

A former university professor and a non-Communist, Ch'u T'u-nan has been active in left-wing and revolutionary activities since his days as a college student during the May Fourth Movement. He taught in Kunming during the Sino-Japanese War, and in the early years of the PRC he specialized in cultural and educational work in southwest China. Most of his time since the mid-fifties has been devoted to the promotion of Peking's international "cultural" relations and the international "peace" movement. As a consequence of these activities, he is one of the most widely traveled men in China and is one of the few representatives from Peking who has visited South America.

Ch'u was born in February 1899 in Wen-shan hsien. Wen-shan, also known as K'ai-hua, is located some 40 miles from the Indochina border in southeastern Yunnan, and the hsien capital is located on the P'an-lung River, a tributary of the Red River. He completed middle school in Yunnan and then attended Peking Normal University, graduating as a history major in 1923. While at Peking Normal, Ch'u was a member of an organization for the study of Marxism, one of the many such organizations that flourished in the twenties in the wake of the May Fourth Movement (see under Chang Kuo-t'ao). He was also a contributor to the monthly *Kung-hsueh* (Work-and-study), described by Chow Tse-tsung as a "significant student magazine." It was published by the Kung-hsueh hui (The Work-and-Study Society), established in May 1919.[1]

Ch'u taught at a middle school in Peking for a brief time after graduation and then returned to his native Yunnan where he was a middle school teacher until 1928. In that year he was forced to flee Yunnan by the KMT authorities; he proceeded to Manchuria where he was arrested and imprisoned until 1931. From 1931 to 1937 Ch'u taught in middle schools and universities in Peking, Shanghai, Shantung, and Honan, but when the war broke out in mid-1937 he returned to Yunnan to become a professor at Yunnan University in Kunming. He remained there until 1946, and during a portion of this period was head of the University's History Department. In 1945 he joined the important China Democratic League (CDL) and in October of that year was elected to the League's Central Committee. The League was founded during the war by middle-of-the-road political figures; in the latter stages of the war and during the postwar period it became increasingly oriented to the political left and was finally outlawed by the KMT in 1947 and taken over by the Communists in 1949 as a minority party. In addition to CDL Central Committee membership, Ch'u also became chairman of the Yunnan branch in 1946.

In July 1946 well-known CDL leaders Wen I-to and Li Kung-p'u were assassinated in Kunming. Because Ch'u himself was allegedly marked for assassination, he fled to Shanghai where he taught in the Shanghai College of Law and Commerce (1946–47). In 1948 he made his way to Communist-held areas and by 1949 he was in Peking. There Ch'u taught at Peking Normal University (his alma mater), and in the summer of 1949 was active in the preparations that led to the establishment of the many "mass" organizations and the central government. Representing the CDL, Ch'u was a member of the CPPCC Preparatory Committee established under the chairmanship of Mao Tse-tung in June 1949. Later in that month he became a member of the Preparatory Committee of the China New Legal Research Society, and in July he attended two large conferences, one of literary and art "workers" and the other of philosophers. At the former meeting the All-China Federation of Literary and Art Circles was founded, and although Ch'u was not then named to the permanent National Committee, he was elected to the organization's Third National Committee in August 1960. In 1949 Ch'u was also advanced in the hierarchy of the CDL. He was promoted from Central Committee to Standing Committee membership in 1949; a decade later (December 1958) he was elected a vice-chairman, a position he still retains.

In September 1949 Ch'u attended the inaugural session of the CPPCC, the organization that brought the PRC Government into existence (October 1). He attended as a CDL delegate and was elected to the First National Committee (1949–1954). In October he became an Executive Board member of the Sino-Soviet Friendship Association, one of the most active of the "mass" organizations in the early years of the PRC. Ch'u was affiliated with the Association until it was reorganized in late 1954. Soon after the central government was formed he was assigned to the southwest and, except for his attendance at the third session of the CPPCC National Committee in October–November 1951, he remained there for the first three years of the PRC's existence. From 1950 to 1952 he was the "special representative" of the CDL in the southwest, and when a Southwest branch Preparatory Committee of the League was formed in 1952, he became chairman. From 1950 to 1954 Szechwan, Sikang,

Kweichow, and Ch'u's native Yunnan were governed by the Southwest Military and Administrative Committee (SWMAC), known in 1953 and 1954 as the Southwest Administrative Committee. When the SWMAC was established in July 1950 Ch'u was named as a member. Concurrently, he was appointed chairman of the SWMAC Culture and Education Committee as well as director of the Committee's Culture and Education Department, the two posts that occupied most of his time until his transfer to Peking in late 1952.

To judge from the number of major reports that Ch'u delivered before meetings of the SWMAC, he seems to have been the dominant figure in the field of culture and education in the southwest. However, as a non-Communist, there is little doubt that he was subordinate to leading Party figures (e.g., Chang Tzu-i, q.v., an important propagandist and ostensibly subordinate to Ch'u on the Culture and Education Committee). In 1951–52 he was a member of the SWMAC's Land Reform Committee and chairman of the Southwest branch of the China Peace Committee; the latter post seems to have been a prelude to his work in the international Communist-sponsored "peace" movement in the fifties and sixties. In February 1953, when the SWMAC was reorganized into the Southwest Administrative Committee, Ch'u was reappointed to membership. He nominally retained this post until 1954 when the Committee was abolished, but in fact he was transferred to Peking in November 1952 to become chairman of the Commission for the Elimination of Illiteracy, a body that existed under the Government Administration Council (the cabinet) until the constitutional government was inaugurated in September 1954. Though little is known of the work of the Commission, Ch'u was singled out for praise in a mainland China journal in early 1953.[2] His work in 1953–54 was apparently devoted principally to the Commission, as suggested by his report to a meeting of the Government Administration Council in May 1953 and by his speech in August 1954 at a national conference to promote culture and education among peasants.

In 1954 Ch'u was elected a deputy from Yunnan to the First NPC, which brought the constitutional government into existence at its first session in September 1954. At the close of this session he was named a member of the NPC Standing Committee. He has continued to be a Yunnan deputy, serving in the second term of the NPC (1959–1964) and then being elected to the Third NPC, which held its first session in December 1964–January 1965. He has also continued to be a member of the NPC Standing Committee, and in addition, he was made a member of the NPC Credentials Committee in December 1964. The year 1954 also witnessed Ch'u's first trip abroad—the first of many he was to make in the ensuing years. These extensive travels are outlined below: 1954: member, delegation led by Kuo Mo-jo to the "Conference for the Relaxation of International Tension" (sponsored by the World Peace Council), Sweden, June; 1955: member, delegation led by Kuo Mo-jo to the Asian Countries Conference, India, April; member, delegation led by Shen Yen-ping to the World Peace Congress, Finland, June; leader, classical opera theater group touring Finland, Sweden, Norway, Denmark, Iceland, and the Soviet Union, September–December; 1956: leader, folk art troupe touring Chile, Uruguay, Brazil, and Argentina, August–November. (Some members of the troupe were killed in an air crash in Switzerland en route home.) 1957: leader, cultural delegation to Nepal, June; deputy leader, delegation led by Kuo Mo-jo to the Afro-Asian Solidarity Conference, Egypt, December 1957–January 1958. (The conference was held as an outgrowth of the Asian Countries Conference that Ch'u had attended in 1955.) 1958: member, delegation led by Kuo Mo-jo to an extraordinary session of the World Peace Council (WPC), Sweden, May; 1959: leader, cultural delegation to North Korea, February; member, delegation led by Kuo Mo-jo to a special session of the WPC, Sweden, May; 1960: leader, cultural and friendship delegation to Burma, January–March; 1961: leader, friendship delegation to Cuba, April–May 1961; leader, cultural and friendship delegation to Japan, November–December; 1963: leader acrobatic troups to Pakistan and Burma, November–December.

Though these trips are largely self-explanatory, a few points deserve further elaboration. Ch'u's trip to Iceland in 1955 and to the four South American countries in 1956 places him among the extremely few Chinese leaders who have visited these nations, none of which have diplomatic relations with the PRC. His extensive travels since the mid-fifties also place him among a coterie of persons who have devoted a major portion of their time to the development of "peaceful" and "cultural" ties abroad, a group that includes Kuo Mo-jo, Shen Yen-ping, and Ch'en Chung-ching (qq.v.). Logically, his travels have also been reflected in his assignments in Peking. Whereas Ch'u had represented the China Democratic League in the First CPPCC, he has been a member of the Second, Third, and Fourth National Committees (which opened in December 1954, April 1959, and December 1964, respectively) as a representative of "organizations for peace and friendship with foreign countries." Moreover, since 1959 he has headed the CPPCC's International Problems Section. Ch'u has also been associated with several "mass" organizations related to international relations. He was elected president of the Chinese People's Association for Cultural Relations with Foreign Countries (CPACRFC) upon its formation in May 1954. This organization, one of the most active in China, is normally used to deal with nations not having diplomatic relations with the PRC. In early 1958 the Chinese established a governmental counterpart to the CPACRFC known as the Commission for Cultural Relations with Foreign Countries. Ch'u has been a Commission vice-chairman since March 1958. Depending on the circumstances, he represents the CPACRFC or the Commission. Thus, when he negotiated a cultural cooperation agreement in February 1959 with the North Koreans (with whom the PRC has diplomatic relations), Ch'u signed the agreement as a Commission official, but when in October 1961 he signed a joint statement with cultural delegation leaders from Japan (with whom the PRC does not have relations), he acted in his capacity as head of the "unofficial" CPACRFC.

A member of the World Peace Council since June 1955, Ch'u has also been a Standing Committee member of the China Peace Committee, an affiliate of the international organization, since July 1958. In March and April 1960, respectively, he was appointed president of the China-Latin American Friendship Association and a Standing Committee member of the China-Africa People's Friendship Association. In addition, he has been a vice-president of the Asia-Africa Society of China since its formation in April 1962; established on the seventh anniversary of the Bandung Conference, the Society is ostensibly a research organization. He has also been affiliated with two "friendship" organizations, serving as a Standing Committee member of the China-Cuba Friendship Association (formed in December 1962) and as a Council member of the China-Japan Friendship Association (established in October 1963).

Ch'u seems to have fared better politically than a large number of non-Communists who have worked for the PRC since 1949. For example, he was apparently untouched by the 1957–58 "rectification" campaign, which toppled many non-Communists. During this intensive movement the CDL was hard hit by purges of such prominent figures as Chang Po-chün and Lo Lung-chi. Ch'u, on the other hand, was promoted to a CDL vice-chairmanship shortly after the "rectification" campaign ended. The CCP has apparently felt that his services in the promotion of quasi-official cultural ties abroad have been a useful adjunct to the policies of the PRC Government.

1. Chow Tse-tsung, *Research Guide to the May Fourth Movement* (Cambridge, Mass., 1963), p. 49.

2. Lin Han-ta, "The Drive Against Illiteracy," *People's China*, no. 3:6 (February 1, 1953).

Chu Tzu-ch'i

(c.1912/1917–   ). Secretary-General, Afro-Asian Solidarity Committee of China.

Chu Tzu-ch'i, one-time journalist, first came to attention in December 1949 when he covered the visit to Moscow by Mao Tse-tung, which led to the signing of the historic Sino-Soviet Treaty of February 1950. An article by Chu entitled "December in Moscow" (Shih-erh yueh Mo-szu-k'o) appeared in the *Hsin-hua yueh-pao* (New China monthly) of February 15, 1950. Five years passed before Chu was mentioned in the national press again, but since that time he has been one of the most active persons in the Communist-backed "peace" movement, as well as in the campaign to establish closer ties with the Afro-Asian nations.

Aside from Cairo, where he was stationed for about four years, Chu's work has taken him to at least the following 15 nations between 1955 and 1964: Algeria, Austria, Ceylon, Cyprus, Finland, Guinea (four times), India, Indonesia, Japan (four times), Lebanon, Sweden (three times), Syria, Tanganyika, Tunisia, and the USSR (three times). He began these extensive travels in April 1955 when he accompanied Kuo Mo-jo to the Asian Countries Conference in New Delhi, a meeting held just prior to the Afro-Asian Conference (better known as the Bandung Conference) and designed to promote a leftist influence at the proceedings to be held at Bandung. The New Delhi conference itself was not very important, but out of this meeting grew the Afro-Asian People's Solidarity Organization (AAPSO) in which Chu has been so active. This organization has held three large-scale meetings, each attended by Chu. The first was in Cairo in December 1957–January 1958, the next in Guinea in April 1960, and the third in Tanganyika in February 1963.

The AAPSO has had a permanent secretariat in Cairo since the first Afro-Asian Solidarity Conference of December 1957–January 1958. Yang Shuo (q.v.) was the first Chinese representative on the Secretariat, but then from 1959 to 1963 Chu served in this capacity and spent most of those years in Cairo. Chu's first affiliation with the Afro-Asian Solidarity Committee of China, the Chinese national chapter of the AAPSO, began in July 1958 when he was named secretary-general of this committee, a post he continues to hold. It is suggestive of his stature that the man he replaced as secretary-general was Liu Ning-i, a Party Central Committee member and a leading figure in the "peace" and Afro-Asian movements.

During these same years of the mid-1950's when Chu was becoming an important figure in Afro-Asian affairs, he was also developing his ties with the "peace" movement. By August 1955 he was a deputy-director of the Liaison Department of the China Peace Committee (CPC). When the CPC was reorganized in July 1958, Chu received significant promotions; he was named a Standing Committee member and one of the deputy secretaries-general, positions he still holds.

Chu has also been a member of the World Peace Council (with which the CPC has been affiliated) since July 1958. This activity in the Communist-sponsored peace movement has meant attendance at many meetings of the world organization. For example, he attended the World Peace Congress in Helsinki in June 1955, a meeting of the World Peace Council in Ceylon in June 1957, a Council-backed conference on disarmament in Sweden in July 1958, and a special session of the Council called in May 1959 in Stockholm to mark the 10th anniversary of the "world peace movement."

As already noted, Chu spent much of the 1959–1963 period in Cairo as a secretary of the AAPSO Secretariat. It was during these same years that two developments affected his activities. First, many African colonies gained their independence (mainly from France in 1960); and, second, the smoldering Sino-Soviet conflict burst into the open, often in the presence of Asians and Africans at functions sponsored by the AAPSO or similar organizations. Thus, for example, Chu was an observer at the Second All-African People's Conference held in Tunis in January 1960 and used the occasion to present to Congolese (Leopoldville) leaders copies of resolutions issued by China in support of the "struggle for independence." To quicken the pace of Afro-Asian "solidarity," the AAPSO established the "Afro-Asian Solidarity Fund Committee" at a meeting attended by Chu in Guinea in February 1961; he was named a vice-president of the Fund Committee and continues to hold the post. As late as October–November 1963 he attended another meeting of this Committee, again in Guinea.

Chu has been a highly active participant in the Sino-Soviet conflict. He attended meetings in 1962 and 1963 where Sino-Soviet differences arose, but his personal role in the proceedings is unknown. However, in two conferences in 1963 and one in 1964, he became involved in a very personal manner. At the Ninth World Conference Against Atomic and Hydrogen Bombs in Hiroshima in August 1963, Chu openly castigated the Russians for having signed the atomic test ban treaty with the United States and Britain.

According to the official Chinese news agency, Chu was then "vilified" by the Soviets, but he in turn spoke and gave the Soviet delegate a "severe rebuff" for his "preposterous statement." In the next month, at an AAPSO meeting in Cyprus, Chu again tangled with Soviet delegates, accusing the Soviets of giving India military aid and of "instigating India's attack on China" (a reference to the Sino-Indian border conflict in the fall of 1962). Again, in Algeria in April 1964, Chu granted an interview to the Algerian press corps and accused the Soviets of having "sown discord" at a session of the Afro-Asian People's Solidarity Council held in Algiers in March 1964.

Beginning with the Sino-Soviet Friendship Association in 1949, the Chinese established a large number of similar organizations vis-à-vis other nations in which they have an interest. Chu belongs to four such bodies: the China-Nepal Friendship Association (September 1956); the China-Iraq FA (September 1958); the China-Africa People's FA (April 1960); and the China-Japan FA (October 1963). In each of these he is a member of the national council, and in the China-Africa organization also serves on the governing Standing Committee. As might be expected from membership in these organizations, Chu is often reported in the national press in connection with the innumerable visits to China by Asians and Africans. He often greets such groups at the Peking airport, will occasionally tour China with them, or attend the many rallies and banquets given in their honor.

Chung Ch'i-kuang

(1909–   ; Mei-hsien, Kwangtung). Former political commissar, Nanking Military Academy; alternate member, CCP Central Committee.

Chung Ch'i-kuang is a veteran political officer whose origins are obscure. He was born in 1909 in Mei-hsien (Ka-ying). Mei-hsien is located about 80 miles northwest of Swatow in Kwangtung Province, not far from areas in southwest Fukien where such prominent Communist leaders as Chang Ting-ch'eng, Teng Tzu-hui, and T'an Chen-lin (qq.v.) were active in establishing Communist bases in the late twenties and early thirties. Each of these men later became important figures in the New Fourth Army when that force was activated in early 1938 following the outbreak of the Sino-Japanese War in the previous summer. It is possible, though undocumented, that Chung first became associated with the Communist movement in the Fukien area.

By no later than the fall of 1940, Chung was a political officer in Ch'en I's (q.v.) New Fourth Army forces operating around the city of Yench'eng near the coast in central Kiangsu. There, in November 1940, the Communists established the North Kiangsu Provisional Administrative Committee, an executive organ of government that has been described as the "highest civilian agency in the evolving guerrilla base" that "marked the first step in bringing the civilian population of north Kiangsu into the Communist war effort."[1] Ch'en I and Chung were both

members of this important Committee which was headed by Kuan Wen-wei, a Party leader from south Kiangsu who is currently a vice-governor of the province. In this same month Chung was identified as deputy director of the North Kiangsu Command's Political Department, and by the following month (December 1940) he was the director. After the New Fourth Army Incident of January 1941 (see under Yeh T'ing), Chung was assigned to direct the Political Department in Su Yü's First Division. (For details on the work of this division and its area of control, see under Su Yü.) The importance of Chung's Political Department can be judged in part from the names of the eight sections under his jurisdiction: organization, propaganda and education, "people's" movements, "enemy work" (i.e., intelligence), youth work, battleline services, military law, and general affairs. Chung's role in the army can also be judged from the number of directives he co-signed with such figures as Ch'en I and Su Yü, such as a February 1941 appeal to the troops under the command of KMT General Han Te-ch'in (see under Lo Ping-hui) urging them to come over to the Communist side in the fight against the Japanese. Chung was also connected with two of the more important publications put out by the Communists in Kiangsu; he is known to have contributed to the magazine *Chiang-Huai* (Yangtze-Huai [Rivers]) in late 1940 and to have been involved in the editing of *K'ang-ti chou-pao* (Resistance weekly), which began in January 1941.[2]

Chung remained with the First Division throughout the Sino-Japanese War and in the postwar period he continued with elements of the New Fourth Army in their fight against the Nationalists. The New Fourth Army units eventually evolved into the Third Field Army, a designation adopted in early 1949 as this army was in the process of conquering Nationalist-held areas in east China and preparing for the takeover of the important cities of Nanking and Shanghai. In view of Chung's rather extensive experience with the Communists, it is somewhat surprising that he was not given a political position of importance in east China following the conquest of the mainland in 1949–50. In the early fifties he was reportedly a commander in the Third Field Army, but nothing more specific was known about his activities until February 1954 when he was identified among a group of Third Field Army commanders and commandants of military schools in Nanking; it is probable that Chung belonged to the latter category because by 1956 he was deputy commandant and deputy political commissar of the PLA Military Academy in Nanking, and by 1957 he was the political commissar. The academy is China's equivalent to a Western command and staff college.

In 1955 Chung was political commissar of the East China Naval Headquarters, but it is not known how long he retained this post. It was also in 1955 that the PRC first awarded military orders and gave personal ranks to the officer corps. Although the citation Chung received is not known, it is probable that he was awarded the Order of Independence and Freedom and the Order of Liberation, the two awards covering the Sino-Japanese War and the civil war with the Nationalists. He was given the military rank of colonel-general, the equivalent of a three-star general in the U.S. Army. Chung received political recognition for his past work at the Eighth Party Congress in September 1956 when he was elected as an alternate member of the Party Central Committee. He remained in Nanking until mid-1961 when he was transferred to Peking (presumably relinquishing his posts in Nanking). His public appearances in the capital have been confined almost exclusively to receptions and social functions held to celebrate important military holidays (such as Red Army day on August 1) or to fete visiting military delegations from abroad. Despite the lack of information on a specific assignment, it is probable that Chung holds some political post in the PLA hierarchy.

1. Chalmers A. Johnson, *Peasant Nationalism and Communist Power* (Stanford, Calif., 1962), p. 142.

2. Kōain, *Shohuku kyōsan chiku jitsujō chōsa hōkokusho* (Investigation report on the current situation in the North Kiangsu Communist region; Shanghai, 1941), pp. 49, 53, 138, 316, and the charts following pages 141 and 222.

Chung Fu-hsiang

(c.1901–   ; Kwangsi). Vice-minister of Posts and Telecommunications.

Chung Fu-hsiang is a telecommunications specialist. Until the Communist conquest in 1949 his name was unknown except for the fact that he participated in the Long March (1934–35) from south Kiangsi to Shensi. When the Telecommunications Bureau of the People's Revolutionary Military Council was formed in May 1949, he was appointed as a deputy director under telecommunications specialist Wang Cheng (q.v.); at the same time he was named to head the Tientsin Telecommunications Bureau. By 1950 he had given up these posts and was transferred to Canton where he became director of the Telecommunications Control Department under the Canton Military Control Commission. Concurrently, he served from September 1950 to sometime in 1953 as head of the Central-South Posts and Telecommunications Control Bureau, an organ subordinate to the national Ministry of Posts and Telecommunications. In the interim, Chung had been elected a national committee member of the National Postal and Telegraph Workers' Trade Union at the first congress of

the union in March 1950. It is not known how long he remained affiliated with this union.

Information on Chung's work in central-south China is not available, but obviously he was engaged there in communications work. It was therefore not unexpected in September 1953 that he was transferred to Peking to become a vice-minister of Posts and Telecommunications under the non-Communist minister Chu Hsueh-fan. Subsequently, Chung has served in several ministries, each calling for rather specialized technical knowledge. In his capacity as a vice-minister, he led a delegation to Bulgaria in August–September 1955 to take part in the 16th International Fair at Plovdiv, Bulgaria. On September 14, prior to leaving Sofia, he signed an agreement to improve posts and telecommunications service between China and Bulgaria. Then Chung led his five-member group to Prague where he attended an international stamp exhibition in late September. Not long after his return to China he was named (November 1955) as president of the Peking Posts and Telecommunications College, a position held until September 1957.

Chung was removed from the Posts and Telecommunications Ministry in January 1957, but four months later (May 1957) he was appointed a vice-minister of the Second Ministry of Machine Building under Minister Chao Erh-lu. The ministry was known to have at least partial responsibility for the manufacture of munitions. In February 1958 it was merged with two other ministries and renamed the First Ministry of Machine Building, still under Chao Erh-lu. Some notion of Chung's work during this period can be gained from the fact that in September 1958 he attended the opening of the Wuhan Heavy Machine Tools Plant and in December 1958 he spoke at the test flight ceremony of an aircraft produced by the Peking Aeronautical Engineering School. In 1959 and 1960 Chung spoke at conferences which stressed the importance of the link between education and machine building; one was in Nanchang, Kiangsi, in April 1959 and the other in Taiyuan, Shansi, in May 1960.

In September 1960, Chung was once again transferred, this time to become a vice-minister of the newly formed Third Ministry of Machine Building. Finally, after holding this post for just over two years, he was transferred back (October 1962) to the position of vice-minister of Posts and Telecommunications, a post he continues to hold. In the fall of 1964 he was elected as a deputy from the Kwangsi-Chuang Autonomous Region (his native area) to the Third NPC, which held its first session in December 1964–January 1965.

Unlike most of his colleagues, Chung is seldom called upon to engage in the heavy protocol activities (e.g., receiving foreign guests) that occupy so much of their time. Nor does he belong to the many organizations devoted to Communist-sponsored causes such as peace or international relations. In brief, he appears to be a technocrat, concerned almost entirely with technical problems.

Fan Ch'ang-chiang

(c.1908–   ; Nei-chiang, Szechwan). Journalist; vice-chairman, Scientific and Technological Commission.

Fan Ch'ang-chiang was one of China's most famous journalists in the thirties and early forties. He joined the Communists midway through the Sino-Japanese War and for the next decade was one of their more important journalists and propagandists. He continued in these activities during the early years of the PRC but since 1956 has devoted virtually all of his time to the field of science administration.

Fan Ch'ang-chiang, whose original name was Fan Hsi-t'ien, was born in the city of Nei-chiang, which lies midway between Chungking and Chengtu, the Szechwan capital. He comes from a landed gentry family and his father, once an army company commander, served as a local government official in the Fan home town. Young Fan attended a middle school in Chengtu, studied at a KMT-sponsored academy in Nanking, and also studied privately and attended some classes at Peking University. He began to free-lance as a journalist while studying in Peking about 1930. He joined the famous Tientsin *Ta-kung pao* in the early thirties and quickly became one of China's most famed journalists. He spent much of the early and mid-thirties traveling in north and northwest China (including a trip to the Communist headquarters in Yenan in early 1937) and from these travels produced numerous articles and books, many of them describing and exposing Japan's continuing encroachments in these areas. He covered the early phases of the Sino-Japanese War in north China, and then went to Changsha, Hunan, where he helped establish the *Kuo-chi hsin-wen she* (International news agency) in 1938. When Changsha fell to the Japanese in 1939, he moved the *Kuo-chi hsin-wen she* to Kweilin, Kwangsi. There Fan became closely associated with Communist circles, and it was probably about the year 1940 that he joined the CCP. In any event, by 1941 Fan was taking instructions from Communist officials in Kweilin. (For a discussion of the large Communist organization in Kweilin at this time, see the biography of Li K'o-nung.) Following the New Fourth Army Incident in January 1941 (see under Yeh T'ing), the Communist liaison office in Kweilin was ordered out of the city by the KMT. Apparently fearing the arrest of their men and supporters in Kweilin, the CCP ordered them to flee. Under direct instructions from Chou En-lai, Fan went to Hong Kong.[1] About this same time (1941), he severed his connections with the *Ta-kung pao,* allegedly because of ideological differences. In Hong Kong he helped establish and edit the *Hua-shang pao* (Commercial newspaper) and also continued to direct the *Kuo-chi hsin-wen.* According to Western journalist Israel Epstein (who ultimately joined and worked for the Communists), the dispatches of the *Kuo-chi hsin-wen* were an important source of news about China for the overseas Chinese press, as well as the Western press.[2]

Fan was in Hong Kong less than a year when it fell to the Japanese in the closing days of 1941. By 1942 he was sent to the Kiangsu-Anhwei Border Region, an area under the control of Ch'en I's New Fourth Army. There Fan worked with the central China branch of the New China News Agency (NCNA) and also directed a school of journalism at Huai-yin, Kiangsu. After the war ended in 1945 he was sent to Shanghai where he worked briefly as a spokesman for the Communists. From 1946 to early 1947 he headed the NCNA office in Nanking where the Communists operated openly as nominal participants in the affairs of the Nationalist Government. However, when the truce between the CCP and KMT completely broke down in early 1947, all Communist officials were ordered to leave Shanghai, Nanking, and other major cities. Like most Communists Fan went to Yenan to continue his work with the NCNA. However, almost immediately after he arrived in Yenan it fell to Nationalist armies. He apparently remained with Communist units in north Shensi, but by the winter of 1948–49 he was editing the *JMJP* in the Shih-chia-chuang area in western Hopeh. The *JMJP* was then the organ of the Party's North China Bureau, but after it moved to Peking in early 1949 it became the main organ of the Party Central Committee. In May of that year Fan was elected a member of the National Committee of the All-China Federation of Democratic Youth, then headed by Liao Ch'eng-chih (q.v.) who, as another prominent official in the NCNA, had probably been associated with Fan for several years. Fan was not re-elected to the Second National Committee of the Youth Federation in 1953, but by that time he was holding more responsible positions with the central government.

Fan was temporarily reassigned to Shanghai following the surrender of that city to Communist forces in late May 1949. There he served as a vice-chairman of the Culture and Education Committee under the Shanghai Military Control Commission and as chairman of the Shanghai branch of the All-China Journalist Workers' Association's Preparatory Committee. When the national Preparatory Committee of the Journalists' Association was formed in Peking in July 1949, Fan was named to Standing Committee membership, retaining this post until 1954. Perhaps his most important assignment in Shanghai was as director of the Shanghai *Chieh-fang jih-pao* (Liberation daily), the organ of the

Party's East China Bureau. Fan's work in Shanghai was of short duration, and by the time assignments were being made to the the newly formed central government (October 1, 1949), he was back in the capital. He was made a deputy director of the Press Administration under the Government Administration Council (the cabinet). The Administration was headed by top propagandist Hu Ch'iao-mu (q.v.) and had jurisdiction over the NCNA and nationwide radio broadcasting. Fan retained this post until the Administration was abolished in August 1952. Also in October 1949 he was named to two of the most active "mass" organizations, the China Peace Committee and the Sino-Soviet Friendship Association; Fan was a National Committee member of the former until 1958 and an Executive Board member of the latter until 1954. In December 1949 he was also appointed to head the Peking Journalism School, but it is not known how long he held this assignment.

By 1950 Fan had returned to the *JMJP*, but now as the director rather than in his previous capacity as editor. He assumed the directorship from Hu Ch'iao-mu. It is not clear how long he retained this position; he was identified as late as May 1952 and may even have continued until 1957 when Teng T'o (q.v.) assumed the post. Fan's last direct assignment in the field of journalism was as chairman of the Preparatory Committee of the Chinese Journalists, Publishers, and Printers Trade Union, a post he assumed in 1951 and held until at least 1953. In this capacity, it fell to Fan to issue a protest to British authorities in Hong Kong in March 1952 concerning what the Chinese regarded as the "oppression" of Chinese journalists in that city. His association with this union probably accounts for his membership from 1953 to 1957 on the Executive Committee of the All-China Federation of Trade Unions.

In April 1952 Fan was assigned to the Culture and Education Committee (CEC) of the Government Administration Council, and for the next 13 years he devoted much of his time to this organization and its successors. Until 1954 he was a CEC deputy secretary-general, here again serving under Hu Ch'iao-mu and later Ch'ien Chün-jui (q.v.). Then, following the establishment of the constitutional government, Fan was named a deputy director of the Second Staff Office as it was now known. He was reappointed in September 1959 when the name changed again, this time to the Culture and Education Office. Serving under two of the PRC's most important education-cultural specialists, Lin Feng and Chang Chi-ch'un (qq.v.), Fan held the deputy-directorship until July 1965. It was in his capacity as a CEC official that Fan signed a Sino-German cultural cooperation agreement in East Berlin in February 1953. He had

gone to Germany after attending the Communist-sponsored World Peace Congress in Vienna in December 1952, serving as deputy secretary-general of the Chinese delegation led by the widow of Sun Yat-sen, Sung Ch'ing-ling (q.v.).

In May 1954, upon the formation of the Chinese People's Association for Cultural Relations with Foreign Countries (CPACRFC), Fan was appointed to the Association's Standing Committee and still retains the position. In December of the same year he was named to the National Committee of the quasi-legislative CPPCC; in conjunction with his association with the China Peace Committee and the CPACRFC, Fan was named to the CPPCC as a representative of "public bodies for peace and friendship with foreign countries." Also in conjunction with this aspect of his activities, he has been a Standing Committee member of the China-Latin American Friendship Association since its formation in March 1960 and president of the China-Mongolia Friendship Association since August 1961.

Fan's career underwent a major change in 1956 when he entered the field of science administration, a role that has brought him into continuing contact with such important science administrators as Nieh Jung-chen, Wu Heng, Chang Chin-fu, P'ei Li-sheng, and Tu Jen-sheng (qq.v.). Fan's initial assignment was as deputy secretary-general of the State Council's Scientific Planning Commission, established in March 1956. Fourteen months later he replaced Chang Chin-fu as secretary-general, retaining this post until the Commission was merged with the State Technological Commission in November 1958 to form the Scientific and Technological Commission. Since the 1958 merger Fan has been a vice-chairman under Chairman Nieh Jung-chen. Two months prior to this merger, two professional scientific societies were also merged to form the China Scientific and Technical Association. Here Fan serves as a vice-chairman under Chairman Li Szu-kuang (q.v.), who also heads the Ministry of Geology. As described above, Fan had served in the Second CPPCC (1954–1959) as a representative of "peace and friendship" associations, but as a consequence of his career reorientation he was named to membership on the Second National Committee (1959–1964) as a delegate from the Scientific and Technical Association. He again represented the Association on the Fourth National Committee, which held its first session in December 1964–January 1965, and in early 1965 he was also appointed as a deputy director of the CPPCC's Scientific and Technical Section, which is charged with the task of stimulating scientific inquiry among the CPPCC members, many of whom are highly qualified non-Communist scientists.

Most of Fan's time since the mid-fifties has been devoted to the administration of science, both domestically and in the promotion of scientific ties with foreign countries. One of his earliest assignments in this field took place in November–December 1957 when he was secretary-general of the large delegation of natural and social scientists to the Soviet Union, led by Academy of Sciences President Kuo Mo-jo. The ostensible purpose of the journey was participation in the 40th anniversary celebrations of the Russian Revolution, but in fact the group stayed several weeks and negotiated important agreements with their Soviet counterparts. Fan was among those present in Moscow on December 11 for the signing of a five-year cooperation agreement between the Academies of Sciences of China and the USSR. Earlier in the same year he had participated in the attacks on scientists accused during the "rectification" (*cheng-feng*) campaign. Among the "rightists" criticized by Fan were the prominent educator Tseng Chao-lun and nuclear physicist Ch'ien Wei-ch'ang.

Fan frequently participates in conferences related to science. For example, in November 1962 he spoke before a national conference on the use of science films for educational purposes, and in February 1964 he was a featured speaker at the inauguration of the Chinese Society of Aeronautics. In 1963–64 he was very active in the establishment of the Peking Center of the World Federation of Scientific Workers (WFSW). The Communist-dominated WFSW, of which the Chinese Scientific and Technical Association is a member, initially endorsed the plan to establish the Peking Center as an Asian branch of the WFSW. However, reflecting the rapidly worsening Sino-Soviet relations, the Chinese quickly began to transform the Center into a pawn in the dispute, a fact that became fairly evident in August 1964 when the Chinese staged the "1964 Peking Symposium," attended by 367 delegates, almost all of them from Asian, African, and Latin American countries. Although the meetings were not without scientific merit, the general atmosphere at the Symposium reflected the continuing attempt by the Chinese to emphasize various aspects of their foreign policy. For example, a major theme stressed throughout the meetings was the necessity of the underdeveloped nations to rely upon their own endeavors, the inference being that these nations could not rely upon the "developed" nations (e.g., the Soviet Union) to assist them. The large Chinese delegation that attended the Symposium was composed of both qualified scientists and Party science administrators; delegation leader Chou P'ei-yuan (q.v.) typified the former category and Fan the latter.

Closely related to his assignment as a science administrator, Fan holds two other positions of importance. He has been a member of a special committee to popularize "standard spoken Chinese" (*p'u-t'ung-hua*) since it was formed in

February 1956, and he has also served as a member of the State Council's Spare-Time Education Committee since its establishment in January 1960. Although Fan is a writer by profession, his contributions to the national press since 1949 have been marginal. A typical example appeared in the October 4, 1962, issue of the *JMJP* in which Fan wrote a prosaic summary of Sino-Mongolian relations to mark the 10th anniversary of the signing of the Sino-Mongolian Economic and Cultural Cooperation Agreement.

In private life, Fan has been married to Shen P'u since the early forties. His wife is the daughter of Shen Chün-ju, a prominent lawyer and educator who joined the PRC government in 1949 and from that year to 1954 served as president of the Supreme People's Court. Predictably, when Fan's father-in-law died in June 1963, Fan was a member of his funeral committee and a participant in the memorial services held in his honor.

1. *SCMP* 2813, p. 11.
2. Israel Epstein, *The Unfinished Revolution in China* (Boston, 1947), p. 149.

Fan Wen-lan

(1893–1969; Shao-hsing hsien, Chekiang). Historian; professor; director, Institute of Modern History, Academy of Sciences; alternate member, CCP Central Committee.

Fan Wen-lan is generally regarded as one of Communist China's most prominent historians. As such his concern has not been with the history of the Chinese Communist movement, but rather with the Marxian interpretation of all of Chinese history. Academically trained prior to the Sino-Japanese War, Fan has been active in the Communist Party since the Yenan period and he has been an alternate member of the CCP since 1956. He was born in Shao-hsing hsien, the native hsien of such other well-known intellectuals as Chou Chien-jen and Ch'ien San-ch'iang (qq.v.). After graduating from a middle school in P'u-tung (in greater Shanghai), he earned a degree in liberal arts from Peking University. From the twenties until the mid-thirties when he joined the Communists in Yenan, Fan taught Chinese history at Nankai University in Tientsin and at Peking and Peking Normal universities, and he was also engaged in these years in the writing of history, particularly commentaries on Chinese classics. In 1935 he was briefly detained as a "political criminal" by the Nationalist authorities, after which he taught for a short time at Honan University in Kaifeng before going to Yenan where he became president of the Central Research Institute, a school described by the Communists in 1941 as a "higher research organ for the training of the Party's theoretical cadres."[1] Fan won his spurs as a trusted Party ideologue during the *cheng-feng* ("rectification") campaign launched by Mao Tse-tung in 1942. He was among the leading critics of some of the dissident intellectuals in Yenan, particularly the important Party writer-translator Wang Shih-wei.[2] Like many other leading CCP authors, Fan was among those called upon to write the Party's reply to Chiang Kai-shek's famous treatise, *China's Destiny,* following its publication in 1943.[3]

Fan was primarily engaged during the Yenan years as a writer and ideologue, but he also served, at least nominally, in the legislative body of the Shensi-Kansu-Ninghsia (Shen-Kan-Ning) Border Region. He was elected as a delegate from Fu hsien to the Second Assembly of the Shen-Kan-Ning Government, and when its inaugural session was held in November 1941, Fan served on the presidium (steering committee). He was also among those who attended the second session in December 1944. In the meantime, in 1941, *Chung-kuo t'ung-shih chien-pien* (A brief general history of China) was published as a text in Yenan, with Fan as the principal author. This important work, dealing with Chinese history from the earliest times to the Opium War, has been described as "one of the earliest Chinese Communist attempts to apply Marxist conceptions, especially the Marxist interpretation of feudalism, to the whole sweep of Chinese history."[4] It has since been slightly revised and reprinted on several occasions in the forties and fifties. What amounted to a companion volume was published in 1947 by Fan, using the pseudonym Wu P'o, under the title *Chung-kuo chin-tai shih* (Chinese modern history); this work, dealing with the period from the Opium War in 1840 to 1905, was "one of the first Communist interpretations of the modern period."[5]

When the Communist armies began to expand over parts of north China in the middle and late forties, a number of the Yenan-based intellectuals were dispatched to other Communist border regions. Thus, in 1946, Fan was sent to the Shansi-Hopeh-Shantung-Honan (Chin-Chi-Lu-Yü) Border Region to assume the presidency of the newly established Northern University (Pei-fang ta-hsueh). Upon the merger of this school in 1948 with North China Associated University (Hua-pei lien-ho ta-hsueh) to form North China University (Hua-pei ta-hsueh), Fan became vice-president under President Wu Yü-chang (q.v.). In August of the same year he was elected as a member of the newly founded North China People's Government (NCPG), headed by Party veteran Tung Pi-wu. When the NCPG moved from Shih-chia-chuang, Hopeh, to Peking in early 1949 (after the city fell to the Communists in January), Fan went to Peking, and in June he became a member of the newly established NCPG Higher Education Committee. He re-

tained these posts until the NCPG was abolished and absorbed by the new central government in the fall of 1949.

In mid-1949 Fan became the secretary-general of the All-China Social Science Workers' Conference, and in this capacity he attended the inaugural session in September 1949 of the CPPCC, the organ that brought the new government into existence (October 1). From October 1949 until 1954 he served on the Standing Committee of the Association for Reforming the Chinese Written Language, but his major activities since the early fifties have centered around the continuing endeavors of the Chinese Communists to organize the social scientists. In the early days of the PRC a special office (pan-shih-ch'u) was established to oversee the formation of five societies dealing, respectively, with philosophy, history, economics, political science, and law. Fan was chairman of this office, and concurrently he and Wu Yü-chang were vice-chairmen under Kuo Mo-jo (q.v.) of the China New History Research Society's Preparatory Committee. When the new societies were established in the early fifties, the special office that Fan had headed went out of existence, but he has retained his vice-chairmanship of the historical society since its formal establishment in July 1951. He received a closely related appointment in May 1950 when he became director of the Academy of Sciences' Institute of Modern History. He continues to head the Institute, which was known for a period in the fifties as the Third Office of the Institute of Historical Research.

From October 1950 until July 1958, Fan was a National Committee member of the China Peace Committee, but there are few indications that he devoted much time to this "mass" organization. Rather, most of his public appearances have been in connection with symposia related to problems of historical research or with meetings convened to criticize intellectuals whose "thought" is inimical to Chinese Communist interests. A typical example of the latter occurred in December 1954 when Fan was one of the convenors of a series of forums held to criticize the "thought of Hu Shih." He has also been deeply involved in the Chinese editorial world, helping to organize intellectual journals and serving on their editorial boards. In the fall of 1953, for example, he was among the organizers of *Li-shih yen chiu* (Historical research), the most important journal in the field of history (which began publication in 1954). He has also been on the editorial boards of *Hsin chien-she* (New construction) since 1954 and *K'ao-ku hsueh-pao* (Journal of archaeology) since 1959.

In May 1954 Fan was named to the Board of Directors of the Chinese People's Association for Cultural Relations with Foreign Countries, a position he may still retain, and soon afterward he was elected as a deputy from Honan to the First NPC, which inaugurated the constitutional government when it first met in September 1954. He served throughout the term of the First NPC as a Honan representative, but in the Second NPC (1959–1964) he represented Shantung. Then, when the Third NPC was elected in late 1964, he was elected from his native Chekiang. He has also served as a Standing Committee member of the Academy of Sciences' Department of Philosophy and Social Sciences since it was established in May–June 1955. Fan received recognition for his contributions to the Party when the CCP held its Eighth Congress in September 1956 and elected him to alternate membership on the Central Committee.

In April 1959 Fan was named as a representative of social science "workers" to the Third National Committee of the CPPCC, and he was also named to membership on the CPPCC Standing Committee. Then in mid-1959 the CPPCC established the Research Committee on Cultural and Historical Materials, with Fan as chairman. The Committee's task was to collect materials from the members of the CPPCC, many of whom were participants in the major historic events early in the century (e.g., the 1911 Revolution). By the spring of 1960 it was claimed that half a million words of original materials had been collected and another 2,400,000 words of historical materials had been written by participants in the project.[6] By mid-1961 Fan was involved in a similar project; it was revealed then that he had attended a series of discussions in his capacity as a member of the Nationalities History Research Advisory Committee. The meetings had discussed the compilation of a series of books on the history of China's national minority groups. Fan continued to serve in the CPPCC until the Fourth National Committee was formed in December 1964–January 1965. However, at this same time he was elevated to membership on the Standing Committee of the more important NPC, a position he still holds.

As might be expected, Fan is frequently reported in the press in connection with anniversaries of importance to Chinese Communist historiography, as in April 1961 when he spoke before a forum convened to commemorate the 90th anniversary of the Paris Commune, or in the next month when he addressed a meeting held to mark the 110th anniversary of the Taiping Rebellion. Similar examples were provided later in 1961 when he served on the presidium for a meeting to commemorate Lu Hsun's 80th birthday and when he was named to the preparatory committee to celebrate the 50th anniversary of the 1911 Revolution. Apart from these tasks, Fan apparently continues to devote much of his time to the writing of history. In addition to the works mentioned above, he has also written, edited, or contributed to important studies dealing with the problem of periodization in Chinese history, the question of feudalism in China's past, as well as the Taiping and Nien rebellions.[7] He has also written numerous articles for learned journals such as *Li-shih yen-chiu,* and he is the author of two articles for the Party's top journal *Hung-ch'i* (Red flag, issues of June 16 and November 1, 1958), both dealing with the need to eliminate superstition in Chinese society.

In the broadest sense Fan Wen-lan can be regarded as a polemicist, but his contributions to the Chinese Communist movement have a sophistication that is lacking among other Chinese Communist Party historians—men like Ch'en Po-ta and Hu Ch'iao-mu (qq.v.), who are more accurately described as propagandists. Fan's role was summarized in 1951 by Professor Owen Lattimore who wrote that he was the "first historian to be recognized by the new regime as worthy of setting standards of historical interpretation for colleges and universities" and that he was a "scholar who instead of coming up through Communist Party ranks declared himself a convert to Marxism only rather late in life, after he had won recognition as an historian along orthodox lines."[8] Writing 13 years later, two authorities on Chinese Communist historiography characterized Fan in somewhat different terms. These writers distinguished three groups of historians at work in China: "the older generation of non-Marxist trained scholars, the middle-aging party liners, and the new hotheads." Fan was placed in the middle group among those who "learned their Marxist lessons early and often too well, and in some cases [they] have not always been able to keep up with changes in the text. Thus, for example, Fan Wen-lan has had to confess his doctrinal tardiness with every revision of his general studies of Chinese history."[9] On the whole, however, Fan seems to have been able to avoid the political difficulties that have beset so many of China's intellectuals, a supposition that seems to be borne out by the fact that he is one of the few intellectuals who has risen to Party Central Committee membership.

Relatively little is known about Fan's personal life. His wife (as of 1945) was a woman named Tai Lao,[10] but nothing further is known of her. Two Westerners who spoke with Fan in Chin-Chi-Lu-Yü in late 1947 reported that his work in Yenan had been seriously hampered by failing eyesight,[11] but to judge from his productivity in the ensuing years, this difficulty seems to have been overcome.

[Fan died in Peking on July 29, 1969.]

1. Boyd Compton, *Mao's China: Party Reform Documents, 1942–44* (Seattle, Wash., 1952), p. 75.

2. Merle Goldman, "Writers' Criticism of the Party in 1942," *The China Quarterly,* no. 17:

205–228 (January–March 1964); Chün-tu Hsüeh, *The Chinese Communist Movement, 1937–1949* (Stanford, Calif., 1962), p. 37.

3. Chün-tu Hsüeh, p. 17.

4. Albert Feuerwerker and S. Cheng, *Chinese Communist Studies of Modern Chinese History* (Cambridge, Mass., 1961), p. 2.

5. *Ibid.*, p. 35.

6. *Ibid.*, p. xvii.

7. *Ibid.*, pp. 15, 23, 93, 97.

8. Owen Lattimore, *Inner Asian Frontiers of China* (Boston, 1962), p. xxviii.

9. Harold Kahn and Albert Feuerwerker, "The Ideology of Scholarship: China's New Historiography," *The China Quarterly*, no. 22:8 (April–June 1965).

10. *The Great Turning Point* (Peking, 1962), p. 4.

11. Marion Menzies and William Paget, "Communist Education Policies in Certain North China Rural Areas, 1948," in Michael Lindsay, *Notes on Educational Problems in Communist China* (New York, 1950), p. 155.

Fang Ch'iang

(c.1907–   ; Hunan). Former naval officer; minister, Sixth Ministry of Machine Building.

Fang Ch'iang, a veteran of the Red Army since its establishment in 1927, was a leading naval officer during the first decade of the PRC. He has been minister of the Sixth Ministry of Machine Building since it was set up in 1963. Born about 1907, Fang is a native of Hunan. He was a soldier in Chu Te's (q.v.) garrison force in Nanchang in 1927. The revolt there on August 1, 1927—the famous Nanchang Uprising —brought about the final break between the Communists and the KMT (see under Yeh T'ing). After the defeat of the Communists at Nanchang, Fang was assigned to units led by Lin Piao, serving under him as a company, battalion, and regimental commander. Fang made the Long March (1934–35) with the Red Army from Kiangsi to north Shensi as a political officer at the division level (possibly the 22nd Division).

During the early part of the Sino-Japanese War Fang was in the USSR where he underwent training at the Red Army Academy. By September 1942 he was back in Yenan, the capital of the Communist-held areas in northwest China. There are no further reports of Fang's activities until after the war when he apparently went to Manchuria with the forces of his former commander, Lin Piao. In 1948 he was commander of the 44th Army in Lin's forces, which, by early 1949, were known as the Fourth Field Army. This large army was responsible for the takeover of Peking and much of the Yangtze Valley. It then pushed south into Kwangsi and Kwangtung, occupying Canton in October 1949.

After Canton was captured Fang became a deputy commander of its garrison force, as well as a deputy commander of the South China Military Region, which was responsible for Kwangtung and Kwangsi Provinces. In 1951 he was identified as commander of the Fourth Field Army's 15th Army Corps, and in the same year he assumed his first post in the Chinese Navy as commander of naval forces for the Central-South Military Region. He held the latter post at least until March 1953. Like most of the leading military figures in the early years of the PRC, Fang was concurrently assigned to civil posts. In January 1950 he was appointed a member of the Kwangtung Provincial People's Government Council, and in June 1951 he became a member of the Central-South Military and Administrative Committee. He was not reappointed to the latter when it was reorganized in January 1953 and was soon after transferred to Peking.

By the early fall of 1953 Fang had become a deputy commander of the Chinese Navy under Hsiao Ching-kuang (q.v.). He held this post at least until 1958 and possibly 1960. Personal military ranks were established by the Chinese Communists in 1955, and it was during that year that Fang was first identified by his present rank of vice-admiral, equivalent to a two-star admiral in the U.S. Navy.

By 1957 he had been transferred from Peking to command the East China naval units headquartered in Nanking. The following year Fang went to India with a 12-man delegation led by Marshal Yeh Chien-ying (January–March 1958). In January 1960 he was appointed a vice-minister of the First Ministry of Machine Building. He probably moved back to Peking, but he was apparently no longer holding the post by 1961, because the 1961 edition of the *Jen-min shou-tse* (People's handbook) did not list him with the ministry. His responsibilities in the Machine Building Ministry were never specified, but because the ministry included the Bureau of Shipbuilding it is assumed that Fang, who had had nearly a decade of naval service, was involved with its naval shipbuilding program. When the Communists created the Sixth Ministry of Machine Building in September 1963, the new portfolio fell to Fang; he continues to head this ministry about which very little is known. The scope of his present assignment can perhaps be surmised from the fact that there were two other new ministries of Machine Building (the Fourth and the Fifth) created in 1963. Judging from the backgrounds of their chiefs, these ministries probably deal with communications or electronics machinery and with the production of military equipment. To draw a similar inference on the basis of Fang's background, it seems likely that the Sixth Ministry is involved in the production of naval equipment.

In late 1964 Fang was named to membership on the Fourth National Committee of the quasi-legislative CPPCC as a representative of the China Scientific and Technical Association. Shortly afterwards, at the close of the first session of the Third NPC (January 1965), he was named as a member of the National Defense Council, the military advisory body with considerable prestige but little authority. At this same time he was also reappointed to head the Sixth Ministry of Machine Building.

Fang Chih-min

(1899–1935; I-yang hsien, Kiangsi). Early CCP leader and a founder of the Fukien-Chekiang-Kiangsi Soviet; member, CCP Central Committee.

Fang Chih-min was a leading figure in both the CCP and the KMT organizations in Kiangsi during the mid-1920's. After the KMT–CCP split in 1927 he became a founder of the Communist base in northeast Kiangsi which developed into the Fukien-Chekiang-Kiangsi Soviet in the early 1930's. Fang's 10th Army Corps attempted to break through the encirclement by Nationalist troops in mid-1934, not long before the major components of the Red Army began the Long March. Captured by the Nationalists in January 1935, he was executed six months later.

Fang was born on July 16, 1899, in I-yang hsien, about 100 miles east of Nanchang, the Kiangsi capital. His father, Fang Kao-chu, farmed 20 *mou* of land in Hu-t'ang village. One of three children, Fang Chih-min was sent at age seven to a small private school for a traditional education, and in his 17th year he enrolled in the I-yang Higher Primary School in the hsien capital. There he became acquainted with Shao Shih-p'ing (q.v.), also a native of I-yang. The young men became close friends and were closely associated until Fang's death. They participated in student demonstrations against the Japanese in 1918, and in the summer of that year Fang graduated from the school. In the fall he went to Nanchang to study at the Kiangsi Provincial First Higher Industrial School, and he was there in May 1919 when the May Fourth Movement broke out in Peking. Like so many youths of his generation, Fang responded to this event by political activism. Under the auspices of the Nanchang Student's Federation, he took part in demonstrations and made speeches advocating the boycotting of Japanese goods. After a year's study in the preparatory department of the school (1918–19), Fang enrolled as a first-year student in the mechanical engineering course, and in the evenings he studied English and mathematics. Fang was motivated by a growing commitment to revolutionary ideas, gained in part from the pages of Ch'en Tu-hsiu's (q.v.) *Hsin ch'ing-nien* (New youth) and was instrumental in setting up a student organization. His activities on behalf of the

student group led to his expulsion from the industrial school, probably in late 1920.

In 1921 Fang became associated with a group of young Marxists at the Second Middle School in Nanchang. Among this group were Yuan Yü-ping and Huang Tao, both of whom later became Communists. By the time Fang joined them they had already established the Kiangsi Reformation Society (*kai-tsao she*) which, in May 1921, launched a journal known as the *Hsin Chiang-hsi* (New Kiangsi). It originally contained articles by Liang Ch'i-ch'ao and other reformers but became increasingly dominated by the Communists. Fang and his colleagues Yuan and Huang contributed to this journal, which under a slightly different title was published in Nanking as late as 1924.[1] In the meantime, in the fall of 1921, Fang went to Chiu-chiang (Kiukiang) where he enrolled in William Nast College, known in Chinese as the T'ung-wen shu-yuan, a school established by American missionaries. He entered as a second-year student in the middle school.

Fang was dissatisfied with conditions at the Kiukiang school (particularly the compulsory religious exercises) and as a result he organized a reading club during the winter of 1921–22, which later developed into a Marxist group. He soon got into trouble with the school authorities, who, it is alleged, were eager to have him expelled. In any case, Fang left school in the summer of 1922 of his own accord. He then went to Shanghai where, through the introduction of Chao Hsing-nung (also known as Chao Kan), he joined the Socialist Youth League. According to Miao Min, Fang's wife and biographer, Chao Hsing-nung was a major influence in Fang's life. He too was a native of Kiangsi, and when he was captured and executed in 1925 or 1926, Fang was deeply affected, both personally and professionally. Miao has written that while Fang was in Shanghai he audited classes at Shanghai University, a school that had on its faculty a number of top Communists (see under Ch'ü Ch'iu-pai). Fang may well have had some association with the university, but his wife mistakenly placed this in the year 1922, whereas the school did not open until 1923.

By the late summer of 1922 Fang and Chao Hsing-nung returned to Nanchang where they set up the Kiangsi branch of the Socialist Youth League. This group, initially consisted of only seven members, including Fang, Chao, and Yuan Yü-ping. Fang and his colleagues established the New Culture Bookstore (Hsin wen-hua shu-tien), which, like similar enterprises established by Mao Tse-tung in Changsha and by Ch'en T'an-ch'iu (qq.v.) in Wuhan, served as a center for disseminating "progressive" and Marxist literature. The store sold such important journals as *Chung-kuo ch'ing-nien* (Chinese youth), *Chieh-fang yü kai-tsao* (Emancipation and reconstruction), and *Hsiang-tao chou-pao* (Guide weekly). Fang managed the bookstore, and together with Yuan Yü-ping he published and edited a tabloid to popularize the revolutionary movement. Aside from these activities, and notwithstanding his chronic ill health, Fang also audited lectures at a college in Nanchang.

The activities of the Nanchang group quickly expanded and led to the establishment of a Marxist research society and a league for civil rights. However, their work was severely circumscribed by the provincial authorities, and by 1923 some of the group, including Yuan Yü-ping, had been jailed and others had gone into hiding. Fang was then hospitalized, but when he heard his colleagues had been arrested he fled to Nanking and soon afterwards to Shanghai where he was rejoined with Chao Hsing-nung. Prior to leaving Nanchang, Fang had joined the CCP (March 1923), once again upon the recommendation of Chao. The two of them were not long in Shanghai before they were ordered back to Kiangsi where they proceeded to establish an underground Party organization in the latter part of 1923. The KMT had also formed a covert branch in Kiangsi in 1923, and because the two parties were then beginning to work together quite closely, both Chao and Fang were admitted to the KMT. In fact, Chao was a delegate to the First KMT Congress, which was held in Canton in January 1924, and two months later the KMT Central Executive Committee made him the ranking figure in the KMT organization in Kiangsi.[2] The initial congress of the KMT organization in Kiangsi was held in the summer of 1924. Chao was made one of the leading officials, and Fang became a member of the provincial Executive Committee and director of the Peasants' Department (nung-min pu).

In the course of the next year, often in collaboration with Chao Hsing-nung, Fang was engaged in a wide variety of activities designed to foster the revolution. The two of them set up a middle school in Nanchang, and when he returned to his native village in I-yang, Fang founded a primary school as well as a night school for the poor. Using these schools as a nucleus, he also formed a preparatory committee for a peasants' association. Further, at the I-yang hsien capital he organized a student youth association at his alma mater, the I-yang Higher Primary School. At this juncture (1925–26), as already noted, Fang's friend Chao Hsing-nung was captured and executed.

In May 1926 Fang was sent to Canton, then the revolutionary center of China, where he attended the Second Congress of the Kwangtung Peasants' Association. While there he met P'eng P'ai (q.v.), one of the Party's leading experts in agrarian affairs, and from P'eng he reportedly learned a great deal about the peasants' movement. En route back to Kiangsi Fang once again fell ill; he was forced to get medical treatment in Shanghai for two months, after which he spent

another three months in a sanatorium in Ku-ling, a mountain resort in Kiangsi. He was still bedridden in the fall of 1926, by which time the Northern Expeditionary forces had already captured many important Yangtze Valley cities. Fang soon returned to Nanchang; his responsibilities were now particularly heavy because Chao Hsing-nung was already dead and Yuan Yü-ping was then studying in the Soviet Union. Fang was once again elected to the Executive Committee of the Kiangsi chapter of the KMT, and he was also put in charge of the work of the provincial peasant associations. Agnes Smedley's biography of Chu Te notes that Fang was director of a peasant training school in Nanchang at this time, and that some 600 of the students took part in the Nanchang Uprising in mid-1927.[3]

In early January 1927, by which time the KMT–CCP alliance had become more tenuous, the third congress of the Kiangsi branch of the KMT was held. Fang's biographer asserts that concerted efforts were made to weaken the position of the Communists but that Fang nonetheless presided over the meetings and was re-elected to the Executive Committee. In the last week of February the Kiangsi Peasants' Congress was convened. Chiang Kai-shek was among the speakers at the congress, which established the Kiangsi Provincial Peasants' Association. Fang was elected secretary-general and a member of the association's Standing Committee. In the previous month, however, the KMT forced Fang's dismissal from his post as director of the Kiangsi KMT Peasants' Affairs Department.[4] At this time Fang held the counterpart post within the provincial CCP apparatus (serving as secretary of the Peasants' Committee) and he reportedly received instructions directly from Mao Tse-tung, then deeply immersed in agrarian affairs, to resist KMT efforts to oust the Communists from positions of importance in Kiangsi.

After Chiang Kai-shek's famous anti-Communist coup in Shanghai in early April 1927, Communist operatives in Kiangsi found themselves in an increasingly precarious position. Presumably because of this situation, Fang went to Wuhan, the center of CCP activities after Chiang's coup. There, also in April, he was elected a member of the 13-man Provisional Executive Committee of the All-China Peasants' Association, a committee which excluded six Communists, among them Mao Tse-tung and P'eng P'ai.[5] Communist scribes, following Mao himself, have portrayed the association as a creation of the CCP. But Stuart Schram has demonstrated that the left-KMT played at least an equal role, and Schram has further commented that the primary function of the organization was "in restraining the peasants in order to prevent the disruption of the alliance" between the CCP and the left-KMT.[6] In any case, after a brief period in Wuhan Fang was assigned to south Kiangsi where he was supposed to launch a peasants' movement. He again met and conferred with P'eng P'ai, and in the summer he married Miao Min. A few days later he went secretly to Kian (Chi-an) in central Kiangsi, and for a brief time there and in neighboring hsien to the north and west he continued his work in the peasant movement. While Fang was thus engaged, the Communists staged the Nanchang Uprising on August 1 (see under Yeh T'ing). In the words of his wife, Fang was "totally in the dark" about the uprising, but he quickly learned about the events, including the retreat of the Communists from Nanchang, and was forced into hiding for two weeks.

Like so many of the Communists in the period after the Nanchang Uprising, Fang returned to the countryside; but now Party policy stressed the establishment of armed forces with which to fight the Nationalists. Fang went back to his native I-yang hsien about early September 1927, and from then until his death eight years later he devoted himself principally to the task of organizing armed forces and developing base areas from which these military units could operate. Beginning with only a rudimentary CCP apparatus and virtually no arms, he soon established a number of Party branches and formed a "peasants' revolutionary corps," which claimed a membership of 5–6,000 members. In the early fall Fang was made secretary of the CCP Committee in Heng-feng, a hsien a few miles east of I-yang; he was given this post because it was felt an appointment in I-yang would attract too much attention from the authorities. The counterpart post in I-yang was given to Huang Tao, his colleague in the Nanchang student group several years earlier.

Over the turn of the year 1927–28, Fang led a peasant revolt in Heng-feng, but this was suppressed in rather short order. At this juncture, Shao Shih-p'ing, Fang's boyhood classmate, was sent to Heng-feng, and Fang in turn was transferred to I-yang. Fang, Shao, and Huang Tao then united their forces to form the I-yang–Heng-feng Guerrilla District. The base reportedly consisted of some 50 villages in the two hsien, but the Communist troops were still very poorly armed. The year 1928 was a bitter one for Fang and his colleagues, and from Miao Min's account it is clear that dissension was rampant within the ranks of the ill-equipped troops. Miao also makes the point that Fang and his colleagues had no prior military experience. In October 1928 Fang went to Hu-k'ou, a Yangtze River port city, where he attended a Kiangsi CCP Congress where the results of the Sixth National CCP Congress that had been held in Moscow during the previous summer were discussed. At the Moscow congress Fang was elected in absentia a member of the CCP Central Committee.

Despite considerable hardships, the area in which the Communists operated was expanded during the 1928–1930 period to form the Fukien-Chekiang-Kiangsi base, and the growing Communist forces were designated a regiment in the spring of 1929. During the latter half of 1929 Fang became secretary of the Party Committee in I-yang and neighboring Kuei-hsi hsien, both of which were located on the Hsin-chiang River. In December of that year the first congress of workers, peasants and soldiers was held, and this resulted in the formation of the so-called Hsin-chiang Soviet Government. Fang was elected the chairman, and its 33-member Executive Committee included Shao Shih-p'ing and Huang Tao. The new government passed provisional laws regarding marriage, labor, and land questions, and schools for cadres and military cadets were also established. Soon afterwards, in February 1930, Fang received his first formal military post as chairman of the Northeast Kiangsi Military Committee (Kan tung-pei chün-shih wei-yuan-hui), subordinate to which was only one regiment. In the previous month Fang had been praised by Mao Tse-tung in a letter Mao wrote to Lin Piao (which is now known in Mao's *Selected Works* under the title "A Single Spark Can Start a Prairie Fire"). Mao railed against those who "merely" advocated "roving guerrilla actions" to advance the revolution; in contrast, he noted the "undoubtedly correct" policy of Fang Chih-min, "that is, the policy of establishing base areas; of systematically setting up political power; of deepening the agrarian revolution; of expanding the people's armed forces by a comprehensive process of building up first the township Red Guards, then the district Red Guards, then the county Red Guards, then the local Red Army troops, all the way up to the regular Red Army troops; of spreading political power by advancing in a series of waves."[7]

In the spring of 1930 the Communists in northeast Kiangsi were able to expand their operations. This was due in part to warfare between Chiang Kai-shek against north China warlords Feng Yü-hsiang and Yen Hsi-shan. As a consequence of the growth of the Communist units in northeast Kiangsi, the above-mentioned regiment was redesignated the 10th Red Army in July 1930, and Chou Chien-p'ing was placed in command. This coincided with the grandiose policy of Li Li-san (q.v.), then the leading CCP figure, to capture the major cities in central China. The various Red Army units which Li called into action in mid-1930 were generally unsuccessful, and there is little evidence that the 10th Red Army made any significant progress in its intended capture of Kiukiang. In fact, at the very moment when P'eng Te-huai (q.v.) was fighting desperately but futilely to hold Changsha, Fang and his colleagues were meeting in I-yang where the Hsin-chiang Soviet Government was transformed into the Northeast Kiangsi Soviet Government, and a new body, the Northeast

Kiangsi Revolutionary Committee, was also established. Fang was made chairman of both organizations, but the relationship between them is not clear.

Toward the end of 1930 the various Communist forces in central-south China braced themselves for the first of Chiang Kai-shek's famous Annihilation Campaigns. At that time Fang was engaged chiefly in government work, but then in March 1931 he was transferred to the 10th Army to serve as acting political commissar. In the ensuing months he campaigned in northern Fukien against the Nationalists. The 10th Army later returned to northeast Kiangsi, but by September 1932, when the army was ordered into Fukien again, Fang had been made the political commissar. Chou Chien-p'ing was then still commander of the 10th Army. Moreover, to expand Communist control in north Fukien and to establish a direct link with this area and northeast Kiangsi, Fang was chosen to take charge of all military operations. In the meantime, in November 1931 Fang and his colleague Shao Shih-p'ing were elected members of the Central Executive Committee (CEC) of the newly established Chinese Soviet Republic. This took place at the First All-China Congress of Soviets, held in Juichin in southeast Kiangsi. At the Second Congress, held a little over two years later (January–February 1934), both men were re-elected to the CEC. Moreover, a fact which is indicative of Fang's importance in the Communist movement at that time, he was elected one of the 17 members of the CEC's Presidium, the organ in charge of government affairs when the CEC was not in session.

The English version of Miao Min's biography of Fang refers to the Second Congress of Workers, Peasants, and Soldiers of the Fukien-Chekiang Soviet, which, from context, was held in late 1931 or early 1932. At that time Fang was elected chairman of the Soviet, and he was also made secretary of the CCP committee for that area. Miao also quotes a speech made by Fang at the Congress in which he mentions the figure of 900,000 workers and peasants in the soviet area. As already noted, the 10th Red Army had been actively campaigning through the latter part of 1932. The army continued to press the attack in the early months of 1933; in a series of wide-ranging forays, P'u-ch'eng in north Fukien and Chiang-shan in southwest Chekiang were captured, and the important city of Kiukiang in north Kiangsi was threatened. But late in the year the tide began to turn with the inauguration of Chiang Kai-shek's Fifth Annihilation Campaign. The fall of Kuang-ch'ang in east-central Kiangsi had the effect of cutting off the 10th Army from the Central Soviet area in the southeast portion of the province. This took place in late April 1934. At this juncture the Communist high command in Juichin decided that the 10th Army should move from northeast Kiangsi into Chekiang and Anhwei.[8]

Fang's move to the east and north has been characterized by the Communists as the first stage in an advance against the Japanese in Manchuria, and in mid-July 1934 Mao Tse-tung and Chu Te in the central headquarters issued a proclamation to that effect.[9] Given the vast distance from Kiangsi to Manchuria, this is hardly an acceptable interpretation; it is more probable that the move was designed to relieve the pressure on the beleaguered elements of the Red Army in southeast Kiangsi, and in one sense it can be described as the first stage of the Long March. Beginning in July, the 10th Army moved by a circuitous route to T'ai-p'ing in southern Anhwei. There it was reinforced by the Seventh Army, led by Hsun Huai-chou, which had been sent from Juichin. The two armies were merged into the 10th Army Corps. In the amalgamated force Fang was chairman of the Corps' Political Committee, Liu Ch'ou-hsi was the Corps commander and concurrently head of the 10th Army, and Hsun Huai-chou led the Seventh Army as well as its 19th Division. Fang, Liu, and Hsun, as well as Wang Ju-ch'ih, who later succeeded Hsun, had all been elected to the CEC of the Chinese Soviet Republic earlier in the year. Other important Communists included Chief-of-Staff Su Yü (q.v.) and Liu Ying, who both later fought with the New Fourth Army during the Sino-Japanese War.

Despite the addition of the Seventh Army, which according to one source brought the total force to some 10,000 men,[10] Fang and his men met with little success over the next few months. In the early fall of 1934 Seventh Army commander Hsun Huai-chou was killed in south Anhwei. To curtail his losses, Fang decided to retreat to Kiangsi. Part of the total force, numbering some 800 men, was led by Su Yü into the Fukien-Chekiang border area, and Fang Chih-min made his way to Te-hsing (not far from I-yang in northeast Kiangsi) where some 2,000 troops were fighting. By that time 10th Army Corps commander Liu Ch'ou-hsi was wounded. The troops were soon depleted to such an extent that they were reorganized into a regiment under the command of Ch'iao Hsin-ming. But then in late January 1935 Fang, Ch'iao, and others were surrounded in the vicinity of Shangjao (a few miles east of I-yang) and captured. Fang was soon afterwards taken to Nanchang where, fettered and placed in an iron cage, he was paraded through the streets. Finally, on July 6, 1935, just ten days before his 36th birthday, he was executed.

In all, there were few survivors from the 10th Army Corps debacle, and it may be that there were more casualties in the Fukien-Chekiang-Kiangsi Soviet than in any other Communist base in that period. The following, all of whom were important enough to be elected to the Second Central Executive Committee in early 1934, were killed in battle or died in prison with Fang: Liu Ch'ou-hsi, Wang Ju-ch'ih, Wan Yung-ch'eng, Chan I-chin, Hung Shui, Tseng Hung-i, and T'u Chen-nung. There were, however, some survivors who went on to have significant careers. The above-mentioned Su Yü and Liu Ying continued to lead guerrilla forces for the next few years and later became important officers in the Communists' New Fourth Army. Two other men, Ch'iao Hsin-ming and Tseng Ju-ch'ing, survived the prison ordeal with Fang, and after war with Japan broke out in 1937 they were released. Both joined the New Fourth Army; in the post-1949 period Ch'iao rose to the position of political commissar of the Air Force Rear Services Department of troops stationed in Nanking before his death on September 4, 1963; Tseng served as a deputy political commissar of the Kiangsu Military District in the late 1950's and early 1960's. Wang Chin-hsiang (q.v.) later became a top public security official, and Yueh Shao-hua who had been political commissar of the 10th Army Corps and also a member of the Second Central Executive Committee, was a minor official in Manchuria in the early 1950's. Huang Tao, one of Fang's oldest colleagues, also survived for a time. When the Sino-Japanese War broke out he became a member of the Party's Southeast China Bureau (see under Hsiang Ying) and concurrently director of the Bureau's Propaganda Department and United Front Department. He was also director of the Communists' Staff Office in Kiangsi. Huang fell ill in 1939 and while recuperating he is purported to have been poisoned by a doctor who had been bribed by the Nationalists.

While still in prison Fang wrote a number of essays and letters which he managed to smuggle out. During the Sino-Japanese War these were published in Shanghai under the title *Fang Chih-min tzu-chuan* (The autobiography of Fang Chih-min), and again in 1951 under the title *K'o-ai te Chung-kuo* (Beloved China). A half a year after Fang's death, a short sketch of his life was published in New York in a "Special Chinese Number" of *The Communist International* (vol. XIII, February 1936), an organ of the Comintern. Although written in romantic terms, this brief sketch of Fang's career is fairly accurate. Many other biographies of Fang were published in later years, especially after 1949. The most important of these is the above-mentioned one published by his wife Miao Min in 1958. Entitled *Fang Chih-min chan-tou te i-sheng* (A life of Warrior Fang Chih-min), it was published with minor changes in English in 1962 under the title *Fang Chih-min*. A shorter but more substantial sketch of Fang's career and the Fukien-Chekiang-Kiangsi Soviet was published by Fujita Masanori in

Ajia Kenkyu (Asian research), vol. 6, no. 4, 1960.

Fang was survived by his wife, four sons, and a daughter. His wife, who has written of the "low political and cultural level" of her own background, was imprisoned for a time in P'o-yang while Fang was working in Heng-feng in 1927. Shortly before Fang was executed in 1935 she was again arrested by the Nationalists. Later released, she went to Yenan where she attended a women's training class. In 1960 Miao was serving as a deputy director of the Kiangsi Government's Public Health Department. Fang's mother, Chin Lien-hsiang, and his sister, Fang Jung-nien, were both active in the peasant movement in I-yang hsien in the years when Fang was operating there, and both women helped him carry out his work. His mother was arrested in 1934, but she was released and died on the mainland in October 1957.[11] Fang's younger brother, Fang Chih-hui, also joined the Communists and was killed in the late twenties or early thirties while commanding a Red Army regiment. Fang Chih-min's cousin, Fang Chih-ch'un, participated in peasant uprisings in Kiangsi with Fang during the 1920's. After the Communists came to power in 1949 he became one of the most important Party and government officials in Kiangsi. Serving as a provincial vice-governor from 1949, he became acting governor following the death of Shao Shih-p'ing in March 1965, and then in September he was elected governor. He has also served since the mid-fifties as a secretary of the CCP Kiangsi Committee.

1. Chow Tse-tsung, *Research Guide to the May Fourth Movement* (Cambridge, Mass., 1963), pp. 96–97.

2. *Hung-ch'i p'iao-p'iao* (Red flag fluttering; Peking, 1958), IX, 10; Li Yun-han, *Tsung jung kung tao ch'ing tang* (From the admission of the Communists to the purification of the [Nationalist] Party; Taipei, 1966), p. 271.

3. Agnes Smedley, *The Great Road* (New York, 1956), pp. 187, 203.

4. Roy Hofheinz, "The Peasant Movement and Rural Revolution: Chinese Communists in the Countryside (1923–7)," Ph.D. diss. (Harvard, 1966), p. 76.

5. *Ibid.*, p. 78.

6. Stuart Schram, *Mao Tse-tung* (New York, 1966), pp. 93–94.

7. *Selected Works of Mao Tse-tung* (Peking, 1964), I, 118.

8. Tso-liang Hsiao, *Power Relations within the Chinese Communist Movement, 1930–1934* (Seattle, Wash., 1961), p. 286.

9. Stuart R. Schram, *The Political Thought of Mao Tse-tung* (New York, 1963), pp. 152–154.

10. Nym Wales, *Inside Red China* (New York, 1939), p. 310.

11. *Hung-ch'i p'iao-p'iao*, IX, 13–14.

Fang Fang

(1904–   ; P'u-ning hsien, Kwangtung). Former guerrilla leader and Party official in Kwangtung; vice-chairman, Overseas Chinese Affairs Commission.

A Party member since the mid-twenties, Fang Fang was an important guerrilla leader in Kwangtung until the Communist conquest of the province in 1949. In the early years of the PRC he was a top Party official in Kwangtung, and since 1954 he has worked in Peking where he is one of the leading specialists in overseas Chinese affairs. Fang was born into the family of a petty merchant in a village of P'u-ning hsien near Swatow in eastern Kwangtung, an area that witnessed much peasant strife in the period from the twenties to 1949. A relative of Fang's has been described as one of the biggest landlords in the province.[1] While a student at a middle school Fang became active in the May Fourth (1919) Movement and was chairman of the hsien's students' association when still in his middle teens. This was apparently the catalyst that brought him into the revolutionary movement. By 1923 he was a member of a peasants' association formed by P'eng P'ai (q.v.) in Hai-feng hsien, and in the following year Fang joined the KMT. He rose quickly in the Nationalist organization, serving in 1925–26 as secretary of the KMT branch in P'u-ning. He also gained military experience at this time as a participant in Chiang Kai-shek's two "Eastern Expeditions" against Kwangtung militarist Ch'en Chiung-ming. In about 1926 he enrolled in the Peasant Movement Training Institute in Canton, and was probably there when Mao Tse-tung headed the school.[2]

In March 1926 Fang was implicated in an allegedly Communist-inspired plot against Chiang Kai-shek (the Chung-shan Incident—see under Chou En-lai). When this was suppressed by Chiang, Fang was among those who withdrew from the KMT and joined the CCP, and for the next year he organized peasants and laborers in the Chao-chou and Swatow areas. In the summer of 1927 Communist units led by Chu Te, Yeh T'ing, and others had tried to capture and hold Nanchang, the Kiangsi capital. When this failed they withdrew their forces and marched southward to the Swatow area where Fang had been working. Presumably because of his knowledge of the area, he was named as the CCP representative of the Third Regiment of Communist Red Guards, which, under the leadership of Ho Lung and Yeh T'ing, captured and briefly held Swatow in September 1927. This operation also failing, the remaining Communist units moved westward to P'eng P'ai's Hai-lu-feng Soviet, but Fang remained in the vicinity of Swatow where for the next three years he undertook guerrilla war operations against the Nationalists. In the fall of

1927 Li Li-san reviewed for a Party journal the Nanchang disaster and the equally disastrous events that followed. In a report that is replete with criticisms of many leading Communists, it is noteworthy that Li spoke in favorable terms about "Comrade Fang" (almost certainly a reference to Fang Fang). In describing the actions in and around Swatow he wrote: "Only the peasant army led by Comrade Fang of Ch'ao-yang [immediately to the south of Swatow] extensively slew counter-revolutionaries after the capture of the city, and the peasants welcomed him in an extraordinary way."[3]

In 1930 Fang moved his units northward to join the forces operating in west Fukien under the leadership of Teng Tzu-hui, Chang Ting-ch'eng, and T'an Chen-lin (qq.v.). Over the next four years he held a number of military, Party, and quasi-governmental posts in the west Fukien region. A fuller description of the work of the Communists in Fukien during these years is found in the biographies of Teng and Chang. Fang was among those who attended the Chinese Soviet Republic's Second All-China Congress of Soviets at Juichin, Kiangsi, in January–February 1934, but he was apparently not important enough to be elected to the Republic's Central Executive Committee.

When the Long March began in the fall of 1934, Fang remained behind and for the next three years engaged in guerrilla operations in Fukien. He is reported to have gone to Yenan in early 1937 to be briefed on CCP policies as they pertained to his Fukien guerrillas. He returned to the Fukien region in the same year— which was also the year that war with Japan erupted. After hostilities began, most of the Fukien guerrillas moved north and were incorporated into the Communists' New Fourth Army (see under Su Yü), but Fang remained throughout the war in the Fukien-Kwangtung-Kiangsi border area where he and his men were credited in a 1951 Party history with having engaged in valuable guerrilla skirmishes under difficult conditions in more than 20 hsien.[4] In the fall of 1943 Fang was called to Yenan for a period of study, and early in 1946 he was assigned as a political adviser to Yeh Chien-ying (q.v.), a fellow native of Kwangtung, who headed the Communist team at the Peking Executive Headquarters, which had been set up in January in accordance with the Cease-Fire Agreement signed in that month through the mediation efforts of U.S. Special Envoy George C. Marshall. Later in the same year he was sent to Canton to serve as the Communist representative on the Executive Headquarters' field team in that city. But when the truce collapsed in early 1947, Fang was sent to Hong Kong, then the center of CCP activities in south China. Although Fang was one of the Party's key officials in Hong Kong, he was probably taking orders at this time from

Liao Ch'eng-chih (q.v.), a man under whom he worked again in later years in Peking. Under the pseudonym of Yeh Ts'ao, Fang published a book in Hong Kong (1948) describing conditions in Fukien in the mid-thirties when he had been a guerrilla leader there.

Fang returned to the mainland in 1949 and took part in coordinating the operations of the Communist guerrillas in Kwangtung with the forces of Lin Piao, which pushed into Kwangtung in the early fall and captured Canton in October. Fang's long career in Kwangtung won for him a number of key appointments in the government and Party apparatus in south China. In October he was named to membership on the Canton Military Control Commission and became a provincial vice-governor. At approximately this same time he also took up the post of third secretary for the CCP South China Sub-bureau (responsible for Kwangtung and Kwangsi), serving in all three posts under his former superior, Yeh Chien-ying. From early 1950 to 1953 he was also a member of the Central-South Military and Administrative Committee, and he continued as a member (1953–54) when it was reorganized into the Central-South Administrative Committee. Fang's tasks were mainly provincial in scope during the early years of the PRC, but he also held two posts in national organizations. From 1949 to 1954 he was a member of the CPPCC's First National Committee, a body of considerable significance. The second national-level post held by Fang was that of membership on the central government's Overseas Chinese Affairs Commission (1950–1954). Though there is little to suggest that Fang was active in overseas Chinese work in the early fifties, after 1954 it was to become his principal occupation.

In the early days after the Communist conquest of Kwangtung, Fang was one of the Party's prime assets there. Not only was he thoroughly familiar with many sections of the province, but he was also aided in his work by his knowledge of Mandarin, Cantonese, and the Hakka dialect, a relatively rare qualification in the early PRC period. During his many years as a guerrilla leader Fang had built up a wide and devoted following, most of whom were fellow natives of Kwangtung.[5] But from the viewpoint of the central authorities in Peking, these virtues ultimately became vices when the Party sent thousands of "northern" cadres into Kwangtung to take up key posts—a move that was almost bound to create friction.

In the fall of 1950 Fang was named to head the Kwangtung Government's Land Reform Committee, one of the most important posts within provincial administrations during the early PRC years. At a major meeting in October of that year he gave the keynote address inaugurating land reform in Kwangtung, a speech that was characterized by its relatively moderate tone, stating that land reform should proceed in a gradual and orderly fashion. Soon after this, however, Party policies stiffened; accordingly, Fang spoke again on the subject in January 1951 in Canton, noting that land reform was "not simply a division of land" but that it also involved a "political struggle."[6] Despite his seeming accommodation to this sterner political approach, Fang's work was apparently viewed by higher authorities to be less than satisfactory. This was initially suggested at a cadres meeting in April 1951 when Fang told his audience that it was necessary for "local" (i.e., Kwangtung) cadres to subordinate themselves to the thousands of northern Party workers who had come south and who were rapidly taking over a high percentage of the key jobs in Kwangtung.[7]

By early 1952 dissatisfaction with Fang's work became more pronounced. Consequently, to get the agrarian reform moving at a faster pace, T'ao Chu was brought into Kwangtung where, within a short period, he replaced Fang as the leading spokesman on agrarian questions, a changeover that is described in greater detail in T'ao's biography. By the fall of 1952 Fang had fallen from third to fifth secretary in the South China Party Sub-bureau. In addition to his other difficulties, he was forced to make a written confession that appeared in May 1953. He accused himself of having shown a lack of consideration for salt workers when he had closed down an important salt mine in the spring of 1952; secondly, he had unnecessarily refused to allow the masses to sell certain commodities in late 1952, which would have permitted them to buy goods needed for New Year's celebrations; and finally, he wrote that he had been too harsh on teachers during a campaign in the spring of 1953, thus alienating the intellectual classes in Kwangtung.[8]

This combination of alleged failures had relegated Fang to minor officialdom by mid-1953, and for the next year very little was heard of his activities in Kwangtung. It was widely believed among Party cadres in the province that he had spent at least part of this time in "study"[9] (i.e., an ideological retraining program). In mid-1954, however, Fang was elected as a Kwangtung deputy to the First NPC, which held its initial session in September 1954. At approximately this same time he was permanently transferred from his native province to the national capital, and soon after the close of the First NPC he was appointed (in October) a vice-chairman of the State Council's Overseas Chinese Affairs Commission, a position that has since occupied the preponderance of his time. When Fang took up this post he was serving under Ho Hsiang-ning, the widow of famed left-wing KMT revolutionist Liao Chung-k'ai. Probably of greater importance was the fact that Fang was subordinate to Ho's son, Liao Ch'eng-chih, also a Commission vice-chairman, a Party Central Committee member, and the PRC's most prominent figure in overseas Chinese affairs. In the spring of 1959 Liao succeeded his mother as Commission chairman, and since then Fang has been the ranking vice-chairman. Yet because Liao is so constantly occupied with other tasks, Fang has probably been the most important PRC official dealing with the day-to-day problems of overseas Chinese affairs since the middle or late fifties. It is usually he, for example, who makes the keynote report before meetings of the Commission or other organizations dealing with overseas Chinese. One of his first major speeches was made in May 1956 before the Standing Committee of the CPPCC, a talk that outlined what the Chinese government expected of returned overseas Chinese and what it would do for them in turn. Fang's speech, made at a time when Chinese policy was relatively liberal, had a rather moderate tone setting forth policies that were in general rather favorable to the repatriates. Not long before this, in January 1956, he had been elected to replace a deceased overseas Chinese as a member of the CPPCC's Second National Committee. He was again named to represent overseas Chinese on the Third CPPCC (1959–1964), concurrently heading the CPPCC Overseas Chinese Section, a permanent body that is empowered to act between sessions of the CPPCC National Committee.

In contrast to such key social and political programs as land reform, the mobilization of the overseas Chinese on a national scale was a relatively late development in the PRC. Thus it was not until June 1956 that the Preparatory Committee of the All-China Federation of Returned Overseas Chinese (ACFROC) was set up. The PRC's most prominent overseas Chinese, Ch'en Chia-keng (better known as Tan Kah-kee), was made the chairman, but he was already well over 80 and clearly no more than a nominal leader. Moreover, when Ch'en died five years later he was replaced by Chuang Hsi-ch'üan, also very elderly and like Ch'en a non-Communist. Fang served on the Preparatory Committee as a vice-chairman, retaining the post when the Federation was established on a permanent basis in October 1956. From the outset he has been the dominant Party figure in the ACFROC and is frequently the principal speaker at its meetings. Exactly five years after the Federation was inaugurated, Fang was identified as a deputy director of the Party Central Committee's United Front Work Department. This important department has a wide range of tasks (e.g., religious questions, national minority problems), and it is evident that each of the several deputy directors works in a fairly specific area of specialization. Fang is clearly the principal man involved in overseas Chinese questions. In summary, he holds the key posts concerned with overseas Chinese affairs in the government Commission, the "mass" organization, and the Party organ.

Because of Fang's intense involvement in overseas Chinese affairs, his various speeches and articles are the source of many of the available statistics on the subject. Speaking in 1959, for example, he revealed that nearly 5,500 overseas Chinese from 50 different countries had returned to China for visits and that 48 overseas Chinese "tourist service centers" had been established to accommodate them. He also claimed that between 1955 and 1958 nearly 116,000 overseas Chinese, including students, had returned permanently.[10] In contrast, Fang, writing four years later, asserted that over 400,000 had returned to stay in China.[11] The reason for this startling increase is to be found in the bitter disputes with the Indonesians (1959–60) and Indians (1962–63); the controversy with the Indonesians centered largely on policies adopted by the Jakarta government, which overseas Chinese regarded as discriminatory, whereas the exodus of Chinese from India was a direct result of the brief Sino-Indian War in late 1962. In response to these problems, the PRC established *ad hoc* committees in both instances to handle the huge influx of overseas Chinese; Liao Ch'eng-chih headed both committees, established in February 1960 and April 1963, respectively. On the former Fang was a member and director of the Staff Office, and on the latter he was one of three vice-chairmen. In both cases the Chinese press gave extensive coverage to the events surrounding the return of the repatriates, and to judge from the frequency with which Fang was mentioned it appears that he, rather than Liao, was the CCP member with the principal responsibilities for handling the problems of resettling the returnees.

As noted above, Fang was a Kwangtung deputy to the First NPC. However, as a result of his new assignment he was selected to represent overseas Chinese in the Second NPC (1959–1964) and was once more named as an overseas Chinese representative to the Third NPC, which opened in late 1964. Because the overwhelming majority of overseas Chinese have settled in south China (especially Kwangtung and Fukien), Fang frequently visits this area on inspection tours, but otherwise he spends most of his time in Peking. Because the PRC has taken great pains to foster a favorable image among overseas Chinese, Fang has often been reported at ceremonial functions related to them. A typical example was in connection with the death of the above-mentioned Ch'en Chia-keng in August 1961; Fang served on the funeral committee, attended the memorial services, and one year later he was a member of a committee formed to erect a memorial hall honoring Ch'en at the Overseas Chinese University in Ch'üan-chou, Fukien. Similarly, Fang has been a frequent contributor to the authoritative *Ch'iao-wu pao* (Overseas Chinese affairs bulletin), established in late 1956. He has been a member since mid-1958 of the China Peace Committee's National Committee, but there is little to indicate that he has been active in this organization.

In private life Fang is married to Su Hui, whose career since 1949 has closely paralleled that of her husband. In the early fifties she was a member of both the Canton Government Council and its People's Supervision Committee, serving also as a vice-chairman of the Kwangtung chapter of the All-China Federation of Democratic Women (ACFDW) and as chairman of its Canton committee. At the national level, Su has been an Executive Committee member of the ACFDW since 1953. She transferred to Peking with her husband in 1954 and has worked closely with him since then in overseas Chinese affairs. She has been a Standing Committee member of the All-China Federation of Returned Overseas Chinese since 1956; Su was also an overseas Chinese deputy to the Second NPC (1959–1964) and was elected again to the Third NPC, which opened in late 1964. In addition to this legislative post, she has worked on a related assignment in the PRC's executive arm, serving since September 1959 as a member of the State Council's Overseas Chinese Affairs Commission.

1. Ezra F. Vogel, *Canton under Communism* (Cambridge, Mass., 1969), p. 105.

2. Eugene Z. Hanrahan, "The Birth of the Chinese Red Army," M.A. thesis (Columbia, 1953), p. 26; John E. Rue, *Mao Tse-tung in Opposition, 1927–1935* (Stanford, Calif., 1966), p. 269.

3. C. Martin Wilbur, "The Ashes of Defeat," *The China Quarterly,* no. 18:21 (April–June 1964).

4. Wang Shu-jen, *Min-hsi jen-min chien-ch'ih tou-cheng erh-shih nien* (The West Fukien people's hard 20-year struggle; Shanghai, 1951), p. 2.

5. Vogel, p. 97.

6. *Ibid.,* p. 111.

7. *Ibid.,* p. 112.

8. *Ibid.,* p. 120.

9. *Ibid.,* pp. 120–121.

10. *ECMM* 176, pp. 21–23.

11. *SCMM* 392, p. 8.

Fang I

(1909–   ; Foochow, Fukien). Chairman, Commission for Economic Relations with Foreign Countries, State Council; alternate member, CCP Central Committee.

Fang I is an important economic administrator. In view of the fact that Japanese sources claim that he "understands" Japanese, German, English, and Russian, it may be surmised that he is a man of some higher education. In addition, he is known to have been an editor in the 1930's of the famous Commercial Press in Shanghai. Fang had joined the CCP by 1936 when he was reported to have become a member of the Provincial Party Committee in Hupeh.

With the outbreak of the Sino-Japanese War in 1937, portions of Anhwei and Kiangsu Provinces traversed by the Tientsin-Pukow Railway (connecting Tientsin and Nanking) became the scene of intense fighting as the Japanese advanced toward Nanking. They won control of the entire rail line in the spring of 1938. The Communists established the New Fourth Army in early 1938 (see under Yeh T'ing) and immediately began to infiltrate units along the territory around the railroad. In April 1939, Tai Chi-ying, a CCP leader from Hupeh, established a headquarters for his Fourth Detachment of the New Fourth Army in Ting-yuan hsien, Anhwei. Ting-yuan lies a little to the west of the Tientsin-Pukow Railway, about 30 miles east of the Huai River city of Huai-nan in north Anhwei. At about this time the forces of Lo Ping-hui (q.v.) moved to the east side of the railway in north Kiangsu. Thus, by the middle of 1940, Communist guerrilla forces held virtually all the territory bordering the railroad in both provinces. It is in this general area that Fang was active in 1939 as a "deputy director of the office of the Mutual Defense Commander in Tung-ku hsien in the Tientsin-Pukow Railway Liberated Area." During the remainder of the war he served the Party in various capacities and in 1944 was director of the Huai-nan Administrative Office, an area south of the Huai River which included Ting-yuan and the headquarters of other New Fourth Army detachments. The term "administrative office" was used by the Communists at this time for the civil government in the guerrilla-occupied areas. These offices were staffed by civilians rather than military leaders and proved to be a training ground for many of the younger generation of Communist administrators.

Within the next year Fang had risen to an important administrative post in the Kiangsu-Anhwei Border Region Government of which he was a vice-chairman (1945–46). Now concentrating in the field in which he was to make his career, he was also the secretary-general of the Government's Finance and Economics Committee. In 1946 he was appointed director of the Finance Department of the Shantung-Anhwei Border Region Government. This administrative experience made Fang a logical candidate for work under the important North China People's Government (NCPG) established in 1948. This government, formed mainly from the Shansi-Hopeh-Shantung-Honan (Chin-Chi-Lu-Yü) and Shansi-Chahar-Hopeh (Chin-Ch'a-Chi) Border Region Governments, was established in August 1948. Until the PRC was formally inaugurated in October 1949 it was the closest approximation that the Communists had to a "central" government. Its officials included such prominent men as Tung Pi-wu (the chairman), P'eng Chen, Po I-po, and Nieh Jung-chen (qq.v.). The capital of this government moved from Shih-chia-chuang in western Hopeh to Peking in February 1949. Fang served in this government as secretary-general of the Finance and Economics Committee, a committee chaired by Tung Pi-wu. Although Fang ostensibly remained with the government until its dissolution in October 1949, it is apparent that he was detached from active service and assigned as a high-level cadre to administer the areas being conquered by the advancing Red Armies. In March 1949 he was assigned to Shantung as a vice-governor but was transferred to his native Fukien in August 1949, the same month that the provincial capital (Foochow) was captured by Communist troops. He was immediately assigned as a member of the Foochow Military Control Commission and as a provincial vice-governor, serving under Party-military leader Chang Ting-ch'eng (q.v.). Fang remained in Fukien for almost three years, concentrating on his special field of finance and economics. He headed both the provincial Finance and Economics Committee (October 1950–July 1952) and the Finance Office (October 1950–September 1951), in addition to holding membership on the provincial Land Reform Committee (April 1951–July 1952). While in Fukien, Fang also served in 1951–52 as a deputy commander of the provincial military district and as a council member of the provincial branch of the Sino-Soviet Friendship Association.

Concurrent with his responsibilities in Fukien from 1949 to 1952, Fang also held posts at the regional level. Prior to the establishment of the East China Military and Administrative Committee (ECMAC) in January 1950, the Communists had established a temporary Finance and Economics Committee in September 1949 under the jurisdiction of the East China Military Region, with Fang as one of the vice-chairmen. Then, when the ECMAC came into existence as the regional government for the provinces of Shantung, Chekiang, Fukien, Kiangsu, and Anhwei (January 1950), Fang was named as a member, as well as continuing as vice-chairman of the Finance and Economics Committee, now under the jurisdiction of the ECMAC. In this economics post, Fang served under Chairman Tseng Shan, another Party leader initiated into civil administration through his work in the areas controlled by the New Fourth Army. For reasons that are not clear, Fang was removed from ECMAC membership (although he retained his economics post) in August 1952 but was then reappointed to membership on the East China Administrative Committee (as the ECMAC was known after it was reorganized in January 1953).

He retained these posts until the regional governments were abolished in 1954 with the advent of the constitutional government.

Although Fang was not officially removed from his various positions in Fukien until July 1952, he was already working in Shanghai, the capital of the ECMAC–ECAC, by March 1952, being identified at that time as the vice-chairman of the Shanghai Spring Epidemic Prevention Committee. His permanent transfer to Shanghai was confirmed in July 1952 when he was given two new assignments there which were similar in scope to work he had done in Fukien. For about a year he served as a vice-mayor of Shanghai (under Ch'en I) and as chairman of the city's Finance and Economics Committee. Then, in September 1953 he received his first assignment in the national government, being named as a vice-minister of Finance. Virtually nothing was reported in the press about Fang's role in the Finance Ministry, and when the constitutional government was established in September 1954 he was not reappointed. Almost two years passed before Fang was again identified—this time in North Vietnam where he was mentioned in June 1956 as the "representative of the Vietnam Office of the Economic Affairs Liaison Bureau of the Foreign Trade Ministry," a position he was to hold for about four and a half more years. Fang's lengthy background in the financial and economic field made him a logical choice for this work, and it is noteworthy that since his return to China in 1960 (see below) he has remained a specialist in foreign economic liaison. It is also of interest that in no other instance have the Chinese stationed a full-time economic liaison official abroad (excepting, of course, commercial attachés, who are in most Chinese embassies).

There is a paucity of information concerning Fang's long stay in Hanoi. One event in June 1956 was suggestive of his role in the Chinese aid program to Vietnam—Fang was on hand at the port of Haiphong to attend ceremonies when China formally handed over two ships to the North Vietnamese Government. But his most important appearance probably related to Chou En-lai's visit to Hanoi in May 1960. Although officially described as a "friendship" visit, the composition of the official delegations for both Vietnam and China (among whom Fang was included) suggested that economic relations were discussed in detail. Fang returned home by the latter part of 1960, and then in June 1961 was awarded (in Peking) the "Order of Labor," first class, by the North Vietnamese ambassador.

While Fang was still in Vietnam, he was made an alternate member of the Party Central Committee at the Second Session of the Eighth National Party Congress in Peking (May 1958), apparently an indication of his value as an economic administrator as well as for the work he had done in Vietnam, one of Peking's closest allies.

Since Fang's return to China in late 1960, he has become one of the PRC's most important economic officials, especially in economic relations with foreign nations. Immediately upon his return he was named (January 1961) a vice-chairman of the State Council's State Planning Commission, serving under Politburo member Li Fu-ch'un. Four months later in April 1961, he received two other posts under the State Council. The first was as a deputy director of the Foreign Affairs Office, an organization headed by Foreign Minister Ch'en I and charged with the task of coordinating the activities of the various ministries, commissions, and bureaus of the State Council involved in foreign affairs. At the same time he was named director of the Bureau for Economic Relations with Foreign Countries, whose activities are related to the Chinese aid program (as opposed to the Foreign Trade Ministry, which deals mainly with trade). This bureau was created in January 1960 but remained without a director until Fang was named to the post. In June 1964 it was elevated to the commission level, with Fang continuing to serve as its head.

Fang's stature rose considerably in 1963–64 during which time he visited seven countries and signed agreements or protocols with nine countries. With one exception (Albania), these visits and agreements involved either an Asian or African country and thus reflected the emphasis that the PRC has placed on courting the Afro-Asian nations in the early and mid-1960's. His first trip was to North Vietnam in May 1963 as a member of Liu Shao-ch'i's goodwill delegation, which remained for a week. The presence on this mission of Fang, China's most experienced official in Vietnamese economic affairs, suggests that economic relations were an important agenda item. In 1963–64, Fang spent almost three months (October 1963–January 1964) leading government delegations to Algeria, Albania, Mali, and Guinea. At the conclusion of each visit he signed agreements or protocols involving some aspect of economic and technical cooperation or trade. In June 1964 he led a government delegation to Geneva where he took part in a meeting to prepare for the discussion of economic questions at the Second Afro-Asian Conference. Fang addressed the gathering, emphasizing the theme that the "developing" nations must rely on their own efforts, thereby following the Chinese example. In August–September 1964 he spent three weeks in North Korea as head of an economic and goodwill delegation; however, no agreements were signed. In addition to the agreements signed abroad, Fang has negotiated and signed several more in Peking, each involving economic and technical cooperation. They were signed with officials from: Syria, February 1963; the Yemen, June 1964; Algeria, September 1964; the Congo (Brazzaville), October 1964; and Mali, November 1964. Moreover, Fang has served as an official negotiator on several other occasions (when the actual documents of agreement were signed by others). For example, he took part in the talks in Peking with the Nigerian Finance Minister in June 1961 and with Ibrahim Abboud (the head of the Sudanese Government) in May 1964.

Fang Ming

Vice-chairman, China Educational Trade Union.

Fang Ming is Peking's delegate to the World Federation of Teachers' Unions and in this capacity has become one of the more widely traveled Chinese leaders. Within China he has been a vice-chairman of the China Educational Trade Union (CETU) since its formation in August 1950. The elderly Wu Yü-chang has been the CETU chairman since 1950, but Fang Ming has in fact been far more active than Wu and might fairly be considered the acting chairman. In terms of the CETU's international ties, Fang Ming has completely dominated this aspect of the work.

The World Federation of Teachers' Unions was formed in Paris in 1946 as a member union of the Communist-sponsored World Federation of Trade Unions. In 1949 the Chinese joined the former, and from that date Fang has been the Chinese delegate, serving as a vice-chairman. It is not known if he attended a meeting abroad in 1949 when he was elected a vice-chairman of the international organization, but since at least 1950 the work of this body has taken him abroad on six different occasions. He has attended congresses of the federation or meetings of its executive bureau in: Vienna, August 1950; Bulgaria, February 1951; Vienna, July 1953; Poland, August 1957; and Guinea, July 1960. Furthermore, he represented the international federation in Ceylon in August 1962 when two Ceylonese educational unions held an amalgamation conference.

Apart from these trips directly connected with the international federation, Fang has led (or been a member of) delegations to 10 other countries between 1954 and 1964. Following is a summary of them.

1954–1955	Indonesia	Congress of Indonesian Teachers' Association, November 1954–January 1955.
1956	India	Congress of All-India Primary School Teachers' Association, May–June.
1958	England	Meeting of the National Union of Teachers of Britain, April.
1959	USSR	Visit at invitation of the Trade Union of Workers of College and Scientific Institutions, November.
1961	Japan	Congress of Japan Coal Mine Workers' Union, January–February.

	Bulgaria	Congress of the Trade Unions of Bulgaria, November.
1963	Brazil	Teachers' Congress of the American States as well as a students' forum and a professors' seminar on education in China, June–July.
	Mali	Congress of the National Union of Workers of Mali, July.
1964	Algeria	Meeting of the Afro-Asian Solidarity Council; tour of Algeria, March–April.
	United Arab Republic	Invitation of International Confederation of Arab Trade Unions, April.

Fang led all these delegations except the one to Japan in 1961. He was also scheduled to visit Japan in January 1956 but the Japanese government refused the group visas. Like virtually every Chinese leader who has traveled to international meetings in the 1960's, Fang has come into open conflict with Soviet (or pro-Soviet) delegates. In his case, this occurred in Brazil in July 1963. He was attending a students' seminar on the underdeveloped world, which was soon characterized by open Sino-Soviet polemics; the Indians joined in, taking the occasion to attack the Chinese over the Sino-Indian border conflict in 1962. Fang tried to retort to these charges but was "denied" the floor by the chairman even though, according to the Chinese account, he was "entitled" to it.

Fang's intimate ties with international Communist liaison activities have been reflected in numerous other ways. From about 1953 to 1956 he served as a deputy director of the International Liaison Department of the All-China Federation of Trade Unions; in February 1957 in Shanghai he signed an agreement with a visiting Japanese teachers' union on the strengthening of ties between Chinese and Japanese teachers; and in September 1960 he signed a joint statement with a Cuban teachers' group which also proposed increased ties. By December 1961 Fang was serving as an alternate member of the General Council of the World Federation of Trade Unions, the parent organization of the World Federation of Teachers' Unions with which he has been so active; he continues to hold this position. He was named to the national council (and standing committee) of the China-Ceylon Friendship Association, which was formed in September 1962 (just a few days after Fang had returned to China from Ceylon, as already noted), and when a China-Japan Friendship Association was established in October 1963, he was named to the national council. In addition, Fang is almost always a participant in the negotiations with and festivities for visiting educational groups; he has been particularly associated with visiting Japanese delegations and, from about 1960, with visiting Africans. He was therefore a logical candidate for participation in the Peking Scientific Symposium, held in August 1964 and attended by 367 delegates from 44 nations, mainly African, Asian, or Latin American countries. And at the close of the symposium, Fang was among those who signed a "protest" against American "imperialist aggression" in Vietnam.

Although Fang's work has been overwhelmingly international in orientation, he has taken a limited part in domestic affairs. From May 1951 to an undetermined date he served as a member of the Shanghai government's Culture and Education Committee; in December 1951 he was named to membership on an East China committee to study the thought of Mao Tse-tung; and at the seventh and eighth congresses of the All-China Federation of Trade Unions (held, respectively, in May 1953 and December 1957), he was elected an alternate member of the Federation's executive committee; he continues to hold the post. In August 1956 he was elected to the Fourth Central Committee of the China Association for Promoting Democracy, one of the eight "democratic" (or non-Communist) political parties in China; he was re-elected to the central committee in December 1958 and was elevated at the same time to the standing committee. Though most members of the "democratic" parties are not Communist Party members, there are a number of important exceptions. Although specific evidence is lacking, it would seem almost certain that Fang (so often entrusted to represent Peking abroad) is a Party member. In 1964 he was elected a deputy from Shanghai to the Third NPC, which held its first session in December 1964–January 1965. As already mentioned, Fang worked in Shanghai in the early 1950's. This further association with Shanghai in 1964 suggests that he may be native to Shanghai or some other part of East China.

Feng Pai-chü

(c.1901–   ; Ch'iung-shan hsien, Hainan Island, Kwangtung). Former guerrilla leader on Hainan Island; vice-governor, Chekiang; alternate member, CCP Central Committee.

Feng Pai-chü, who joined the CCP in 1926, is best known for the guerrilla operations he conducted on his native island for some 20 years before the Communists took possession there in 1950. His original name was Feng Chi-chou, and he comes from the small village of Ya-tai in Ling-chiao hsiang on Hainan Island, where his family were stonecutters, not far from Ch'iung-shan, the principal city of the northeastern hsien of the same name. In 1925 Feng graduated from the Sixth Normal School in Ch'iung-shan and then sought further education on the mainland, going to Shanghai, where from 1925 to 1926 he studied at Ta-hsia University. He was expelled from the university in 1926 for his participation in the student movement, possibly in connection with the May 30th (1925) Movement, which initiated a period of unrest among student groups throughout China.

After his expulsion from Ta-hsia, Feng returned to Hainan where in 1926 he joined the CCP. In the next year he became chairman of a sub-committee subordinate to the Hainan (Ch'iung-yai) District Committee, the highest organ of the CCP in Hainan, which was then under the direction of Huang Hsueh-tseng. Feng immediately began organizing guerrilla units among the Hainan peasantry. The next three years of tension and conflict within the Party membership on the mainland were reflected in Hainan. Sometime between 1927 and 1929 Huang Hsueh-tseng was arrested and executed by the Nationalist authorities, leaving Feng to eliminate rival groups and put his own in power. Having initially become a member of the Hainan District Committee (1927), in 1929 he succeeded in gathering a group of his own supporters and convened a conference in Ting-an hsien (to the south of Ch'iung-shan) at which he organized his own Hainan Special Party Committee. The timing of these actions coincided or followed closely upon the expulsion from the CCP on the mainland of Ch'en Tu-hsiu, the first Party general secretary, and when Feng finally gained control of the Party Committee in Hainan, he expelled his rivals as "Trotskyites."

Feng remained in Hainan for some 20 years, making his base of operations a hideout in the remote forests of the Five Finger Mountain Range, which dominates the island. At times he lived in retreat there, at others he sent his men to harass the authorities in control, either the Nationalists or the Japanese. Eventually, his troops were organized into an army numbering some 10,000 to 12,000 men. Never well armed, and consequently unable to challenge the authorities directly, they nonetheless persisted in conducting attacks upon communication lines and thus served as a continuing threat until the arrival of major Communist forces on the island in April 1950.[1] It was during his early years as a guerrilla fighter, probably about 1928, that Feng dropped his original name and adopted Feng Pai-chü, by which he has since been known. His base in Hainan is described by the Communists today as one of the 14 "liberated areas" in which Communist bases were left when the main Red armies were forced to evacuate central China and make the Long March to the northwest (1934).[2] However, despite the rather tenuous connections with Yenan implied by this claim, central Party control over Feng's guerrillas in remote Hainan must have been very slight indeed.

Realizing the need to maintain contact with Feng's operations while Party headquarters were in central China, the headquarters sent an emissary to visit Hainan in 1930. Thus, quite soon after his return from the Soviet Union in the summer of 1930, Teng Fa (q.v.) went to Hainan to help organize Feng's army. Teng had been elected to the Party Central Committee in 1930 and was a logical person to send to contact Feng, because prior to his visit to the USSR he had held various posts in the Party apparatus for the Canton-Hong Kong area under which supervision of Hainan fell. As a result of this visit, in 1930 Feng organized an independent division of the Chinese Workers' and Peasants' Red Army, the Mao-Chu Army of central China, and for the next six years he harassed the Nationalist headquarters on the island with his guerrilla troops. During the Long March he is said to have lost touch completely with Party headquarters, and he did not re-establish contact until the spring of 1936 when the Communist capital was in north Shensi. Later in 1936 Nationalist forces arrested Feng and his wife, Wang Hui-chou, who had been a fellow guerrilla fighter in Hainan, but Feng was released upon the outbreak of the Sino-Japanese War (July 1937), and he set about immediately regrouping and recruiting for his original forces, said to number now only some 200 men.[3] In 1938 the Nationalists recognized him as the commander of an independent unit of the People's Anti-Japanese Self-Protection Corps, a militia-like organization, which fell under the command of their 14th Area Command in Kwangtung.

In February 1939 a Japanese brigade invaded Hainan and within two weeks the island was conquered. Japanese estimates at the time numbered the Chinese forces on the island at some 3,600 troops, many of whom they killed, leaving only a very few men to escape to the mountains. In 1939 Feng's guerrillas established their base in Ch'iung-shan hsien, to which he was native, and the adjoining Yai-hsien. The latter is today part of the Li and Miao Nationalities Autonomous Chou, the government organized to give identity to these two small groups of non-Chinese ethnic minorities. Sometime in 1941 Feng's supporters spread out to establish a base of operations at Mei-hou but were soon forced to retreat back to Ch'iung-shan. In November 1941 Feng's guerrillas convened the Northeast Hainan Conference of People's Representatives at Ch'iung-shan, and established the Northeast Hainan Anti-Japanese Democratic Government, which was soon cooperating with Li tribesmen living in the Five Finger Mountains, led by Wang Kuo-hsing. In 1944 Feng reorganized this government into the Hainan Provisional Government with himself as chairman, and his guerrillas into the Hainan Column, making himself the Column commander and political commissar. This unit consisted of five battalions, which he led until April 1950 when a unit of Lin Piao's Fourth Field Army commanded by Teng Hua (q.v.) reached Hainan.

Immediately following his arrival from the mainland, Teng was made chairman of the Hainan Military and Administrative Committee, and Feng was named vice-chairman. He held this post until July 1951 when he became chairman after Teng was transferred to Korea. In addition, Feng was made the principal Party representative in Hainan, becoming first secretary of the Hainan CCP Committee in 1950 and holding the post until about 1953. He was also: vice-chairman of the Hai-k'ou (the Ch'iung-shan port city) Military Control Commission, April 1950–February 1953; chairman of the Hainan Finance and Economics Committee, 1950–c.September 1951; commander of the Hainan Military District, 1950–February 1953. Concurrently, Feng held positions in the China mainland administrations, some of which he received several months before the conquest of Hainan in the spring of 1950. By the end of 1949 he was identified as third deputy political commissar of the Kwangtung Military District and he became a member of the Kwangtung Provincial People's Government Council, inaugurated in January 1950; in the latter he also served from December 1951 as a member of the Land Reform Committee. From 1950 he held membership on the multi-provincial administration known as the Central-South Military and Administrative Committee (CSMAC) until 1953 and as the Central-South Administrative Committee from 1953 until it was abolished in 1954. He also served as a member of its special south China sub-committee in charge of finance and economics. Following the example of a number of Party officials in the early fifties, as soon as a Kwangtung branch of the Sino-Soviet Association was formed in November 1952, Feng became a member.

In the first half of 1953 Feng was transferred to Canton, the Kwangtung capital, after which he relinquished his posts in Hainan. In May of that year he was identified as a Kwangtung vice-governor and in June as director of the United Front Work Department of the CCP's South China Sub-bureau, the organ in charge of Party affairs in Kwangtung and Kwangsi. The assignment in the United Front Department may have resulted from Feng's rather long experience in dealing with the Li and Miao minority groups in Hainan. In 1953 he was also appointed as a member of the Kwangtung Election Committee, and when elections were held in the following year he became a Kwangtung deputy to the First NPC, which, at its inaugural session in September 1954, established the constitutional government in Peking. At the close of this same session he was elected to membership on the newly established military advisory body, the National Defense Council. A year later, in September 1955, he was among the large group of military veterans who were awarded the newly created

decorations; Feng received the three top honors, the August First, the Independence and Freedom, and the Liberation Orders for his military achievements during the period from 1927 to 1950. By mid-1955 Feng had advanced in the Party hierarchy to the post of deputy secretary of the Kwangtung CCP Committee, and by November of the next year he had become one of the several secretaries under First Secretary T'ao Chu (q.v.). Two months before this, at the Party's Eighth National Congress, he was elected an alternate member of the CCP Central Committee.

As the Communists extended their control over China, the central authorities remained very sensitive to the dangers inherent in strengthening regional factions, an element which had always played so strong a part in Chinese politics, and they were especially alert to those which might develop within the Party itself. With Feng's long record of exercising a local command, it was perhaps not surprising that he should have found it difficult to submit to central authority once the CCP was firmly in control. Feng's struggles with higher authority, which had apparently gone on for some time, finally became public knowledge in May 1958 at the Second Session of the Eighth CCP Congress when he and Ku Ta-ts'un (q.v.) were accused of fostering "localist activities." Both Feng and Ku were then members of the provincial Party Secretariat and vice-governors of Kwangtung, as well as alternate members of the CCP Central Committee. Subsequently, an article published in an official Kwangtung CCP journal made the charges very specific.[4] They were all the more significant for having been written by the then director of the Kwangtung Party's Organization Department, Miss Ou Meng-chueh, who was herself also a CCP veteran and an alternate member of the national Party Central Committee. The charges against Feng went back some time, to "long ago, before the liberation," when, though nothing was specific, it was apparent that Feng had been making himself into a local hero. His actual resistance to Peking had allegedly begun in 1952, but had first come to a head in 1956. Around the time of the Eighth Party Congress (September 1956), he and his group were accused of trying to insinuate themselves into the good graces of the Party Center in Peking in an effort to make the Kwangtung Party Committee "give in" to their wishes. A major point of difference, the article stated, was over the land reform program. Miss Ou noted that only three per cent of the Hainan population had been classified as landlords, but she charged that Feng had argued that this figure was too high and that he had constantly clamored for enquiries into the "deviations" that had been committed during the land reform movement. As a supporter of the "localist" view, Feng had rejected the guidance of the Provincial Party

Committee as being "too left." Further, he was said to have obstructed the work of the political cadres accompanying the Fourth Field Army troops to Hainan when these officials attempted to carry out the Party's land reform measures. Possibly the most serious charge—and certainly the most dramatic—was that Feng had had a role in plotting a "miniature Hungarian incident" during the spring of 1957 in Lin-kao hsien in northern Hainan (although it was not clear from Ou's article that any revolt had actually taken place).

After listing these and many other charges (see under Ku Ta-ts'un), Ou Meng-chueh stated that the Party had taken into account the 30-year-long revolutionary careers of both Feng and Ku, and as a result the decision had been made to allow them to retain their Party membership as well as a part of their duties, but that they would be relieved of "their more important posts." Both men were removed as Kwangtung vice-governors and as secretaries of the Kwangtung CCP Committee, but they retained their status as alternate members of the Party Central Committee. Considering the seriousness of the charges, Feng's eclipse was rather brief—by September 1958 he was re-elected as a Kwangtung vice-governor, and although he was not re-elected a Kwangtung deputy to the Second NPC when it held its first session in April 1959, he was reappointed to membership on the National Defense Council. In general, however, Feng's activities in Kwangtung were seldom mentioned after 1958. Then, after more than 35 years of service in Kwangtung, he was transferred to Chekiang where in December 1963 he was elected as a vice-governor. Feng's transfer to Chekiang may well have resulted from a decision by the Party to remove him from Kwangtung where at least among certain quarters he is probably regarded as a local hero. It is also probable that he has considerable difficulty understanding the very distinctive Chekiang dialect which, if true, would tend to isolate him all the more. In any event, it is evident that Feng's political career had already come to an effective end in 1958 when he was so severely chastised by the Party. This was made all the more evident at the close of the first session of the Third NPC in January 1965 when he was among the very few men not re-elected to membership on the National Defense Council, thereby being stripped of his only remaining post on the national government level.

1. A. Doak Barnett, *China on the Eve of Communist Takeover* (New York, 1961), p. 302.
2. Mao Tse-tung, *Selected Works* (New York, 1954), I, 316.
3. *Hsin-hua yueh-pao* (New China monthly), 2.1:252 (June 15, 1950).
4. *SCMP* 1899, pp. 16–23.

Feng Wen-pin

(c.1911–   ; Chu-chi, Chekiang). Purged youth leader.

Feng Wen-pin, a CCP member from the twenties, was the Party's most important youth leader from the mid-thirties to the early fifties when he was removed and subsequently purged. He was born about 1911 in Chu-chi, about 30 miles southwest of Shao-hsing, Chekiang, a rail center not far from the provincial capital. In 1919 he was taken by his family to Shanghai where he received one or two years of primary school training and also studied in a night school. Afterward, he worked in a match factory and, together with his father and sister, joined the Communist Youth Corps (or League) in 1927; subsequently, he became an apprentice in a coal company and participated in trade union activities. Japanese sources claim that in 1926 Feng had joined the KMT—at a time when a number of Communists belonged to both the CCP and the KMT, a situation abruptly changed following the CCP-KMT split of 1927. In 1927 Feng went to Wuhan where he enrolled in the Peasant Movement Training Institute (headed there for a brief period in 1927 by Mao Tse-tung). In the following year Feng joined the CCP, and in July of that year he was in Hunan where he participated in the P'ing-chiang Uprising led by P'eng Te-huai and T'eng Tai-yuan (see under T'eng Tai-yuan) as a member of the "Red Guards."

Sources are conflicting on the whereabouts of Feng in the two-year period following the failure of the P'ing-chiang Uprising. He apparently went to Kwangtung in 1929 where he joined Communist guerrillas fighting in the East River (Tung-chiang) area (see under Ku Ta-ts'un) and then made his way to western Fukien where the Communists were gradually establishing base areas. There Feng belonged to the Red Fourth Army, the military force commanded by Chu Te. He is next reported to have been involved in Communist underground work in Shanghai in 1930. Because Feng was later a member of a telecommunications unit in the Red Army (see below), it is possible that during this period in Shanghai he was among CCP members who received training in a secret telecommunications school set up by the Communists (see under Li Ch'iang). In American authoress Nym Wales' brief biography of Feng, she claims that he went to the soviet areas in 1930.[1] He apparently returned to the Fourth Army (subordinate to the First Army Corps); the Fourth Army was then led by Lin Piao and the Corps by Chu Te and Mao Tse-tung. In early 1931 he was instrumental in the establishment of a small unit to train radio and telecommunications personnel in Kiangsi; the unit was commanded by Wang Cheng and Feng was the political commissar (see under Wang Cheng). Also, according to a Communist-published biography of Feng, it is claimed that he worked in the Communist Youth League during the Kiangsi Soviet period prior to the Long March.[2] The League was then headed by Kuan Hsiang-ying (q.v.). Feng's work with the Youth League at this time was indicative of his major activity in the years ahead. However, during the Kiangsi days Feng's chief responsibilities apparently continued to center on military and political duties. By 1932 he was head of a "political guards" unit in the Third Army Corps (commanded by P'eng Te-huai and T'eng Tai-yuan), and in the following year he was secretary of the CCP Committee in Fukien.

Although Feng was not a member of the Central Executive Committee of the Chinese Soviet Republic, he did attend the Second All-China Congress of Soviets held in Jui-chin, Kiangsi, in January–February 1934. Deputies (e.g., Mao Tse-tung from Kiangsi) attended this congress as representatives of the different Communist-run Soviet bases, but there was a special category, Red Army representation, which included Feng, together with such important Communists as Chu Te and Chou En-lai.[3] Prior to the beginning of the Long March in 1934, certain Youth League members were organized into a special division, with Feng as its political commissar; he remained in this post throughout the march.

In July 1936, Feng succeeded K'ai Feng (q.v.) as secretary of the Youth League.[4] By this time, however, the CCP Central Committee had already decided (in November 1935) to divide "the Youth League into several broadly representative and mass anti-Japan and national salvation youth bodies," a shift in strategy in accord with the Comintern's united front policy decided upon at the Seventh Comintern Congress in mid-1935.[5] Thus, in the spring of 1937 the Communists began a series of moves that had the nominal effect of dissolving the Youth League (although youth activities undoubtedly continued to come under the direction of the Party Central Committee). The first of these steps was taken in April 1937 when the Communists convened the "First Conference of Representatives of Youths in the Northwest," a meeting attended by some 300 delegates and described as the first large meeting held by the Youth League since its Fifth Congress held in Moscow in 1928.[6] At the 1937 conference the Northwest National Salvation Association of Youth was created. Feng assumed the chairmanship of the Association and retained it throughout the Sino-Japanese War.[7] In the fall of 1937 another youth congress was held at which time the "Joint Office of China Youth Organizations for National Salvation" was formed to coordinate the activities of all youth organizations under Communist control (such as the National Liberation Vanguards of China—see under Li Ch'ang). It is probable that Feng was the major figure involved in the wartime activities

of the Joint Office. The Communists have claimed that the various youth organizations in the Communist-held areas had a membership of one million by 1940.[8]

In the meantime, Feng had accompanied Chou En-lai to Sian in December 1936 immediately after Chiang Kai-shek had been arrested by dissident generals under his nominal command (the Sian Incident: see under Chou En-lai). After the war broke out in mid-1937, Feng was associated with Hu Ch'iao-mu (q.v.) in directing a youth training class in north Shensi, and by 1938 he was also a senior official at the important Anti-Japanese Academy (K'ang-ta) in Yenan.[9]

Feng's wartime and postwar activities are not well documented, but it is evident that he continued to be the top youth leader. According to Japanese sources he was head of the Party Central Committee's Youth Work Committee by about 1944, but it is more likely that he held this post from the mid-thirties. In August 1948, the Communists held their Sixth National Labor Congress in the Manchurian city of Harbin. Although it is not certain that Feng attended the meetings, he was elected to the Executive Committee of the All-China Federation of Labor (ACFL), retaining this position until the next congress in 1953. (From May 1949 to about 1951, he was also head of the ACFL's Youth Workers' Department.) At the time of his election to the ACFL, he was identified as the chairman of the Preparatory Committee of the Alliance of Democratic Youth in Liberated Areas, an organization that apparently grew out of a youth work conference held in mid-1947, which was convened to prepare for the re-establishment of the Youth League. Further steps leading to the formation of the League were taken in the fall of 1948 (presumably with Feng's participation), when the Central League School was established as well as the semi-monthly *Chung-kuo ch'ing-nien* (China youth). Finally, at a major congress held in Peking in April 1949, the League was re-established under the name New Democratic Youth League (NDYL), retaining this title until the traditional name Communist Youth League was adopted in 1957. At the 1949 congress, Party leader Jen Pi-shih (q.v.), who could be considered the spiritual father of the NDYL, delivered the keynote political speech. But aside from Jen's speech, Feng's addresses before the meetings were the most important; one talk concerned the responsibilities and work of the League and another summarized the work carried out at the congress. At the close of the meetings he was elected to the League's Central Committee as well as the League secretary. Feng's two immediate subordinates were Deputy Secretaries Liao Ch'eng-chih and Chiang Nan-hsiang (qq.v.).

In the period from the formation of the League in 1949 until 1951, Feng was the dominant figure in the organization. Almost without exception, he gave the keynote reports before the many meetings of the Youth League in this formative period. He also was often the main speaker before the subordinate organizations of the League, as in April 1950 when he addressed a cadres' work conference of the Young Pioneers. In addition, when conferences were held requiring League representation, it was frequently Feng who attended them; for example, at a PLA Youth Work Conference held in October 1950, he spoke on the experience of the League in local districts of China. Similarly, when a series of articles were released in mid-1951 to commemorate the 30th anniversary of the CCP, Feng was chosen to write a piece entitled "The CCP is the inspirer, organizer, and leader of Chinese Youth." This article, as well as another written by Feng in 1951 to commemorate the second anniversary of the League, provide useful summaries of the history of the Youth League and its predecessors.[10] He was also serving as the president of the League School in late 1951, apparently having replaced Chiang Nan-hsiang in this capacity. Feng also led two youth delegations abroad, one to the USSR in the period from October 1950 to January 1951 and the other to Berlin to attend the Communist-sponsored Third World Festival of Youth and Students for Peace held in August 1951.

When the Communists marched into Peking on January 31, 1949, Feng was among the first of the important leaders to arrive with the Chinese Communist military forces. Indeed, on March 1 the CCP convened the All-China Students' Congress, at which Feng was the featured speaker. Then, after taking part in the youth congress described above, he actively participated in the processes leading toward the establishment of the central government in the summer and early fall of 1949. Under the chairmanship of Mao Tse-tung, a committee was established in June to prepare for the convocation of the CPPCC; Feng served both on this committee and on a sub-committee charged with the task of drawing up a list of those to participate in the CPPCC meetings. When the CPPCC was convened in September 1949, he served on the presidium (steering committee) and the Credentials Committee. At the close of the meetings, Feng (who had attended as a delegate of the Youth League) was named to the Standing Committee of the CPPCC First National Committee. In October 1949, when most of the major appointments were made in the new central government, he was named to membership on the Supreme People's Court.

Feng was also involved in the work of establishing three "mass" organizations in 1949–50. In mid-July 1949 he attended a meeting called to initiate work toward the establishment of the Sino-Soviet Friendship Association (SSFA) and

was named to the SSFA Preparatory Committee. When the SSFA was formally established in October 1949, Feng was named to the Executive Board. Later that month the Communists set up a preparatory committee chaired by Feng to establish the All-China Athletic Federation; he remained as the chairman until the Federation was permanently established at a national conference in June 1952. He was also a member of the Board of Directors of the All-China Federation of Cooperatives from its formation in July 1950 until its reorganization in mid-1954.

Feng was among the many national leaders who attended the third session of the CPPCC's First National Committee in October–November 1951. Because of a decision taken at these meetings to "increase production and practice economy," the central government established (December) the Central Austerity Committee under the direction of Po I-po, a top economic specialist. Feng was named to membership on this body and not long after (in February 1952) he was also appointed to the newly formed Study (Hsueh-hsi) Committee under the CPPCC, a committee established to organize and stimulate the study of Marxism-Leninism and the "thought of Mao Tse-tung." Feng continued to appear with regularity in Peking until mid-1952. But then, at a meeting of the Youth League in August–September 1952, suddenly and with no forewarning he was replaced as the League secretary by Hu Yao-pang (q.v.). Soon after this he was sent to Tientsin where he was placed in charge of the Industry Department under the Tientsin Municipal CCP Committee, an anticlimactic position after having headed one of China's more important political organizations.

Feng made a few more appearances in Tientsin, the last in February 1954 when he spoke before a conference of the Tientsin Trade Union Council. His complete disappearance from the public scene in China has been ascribed to his alleged attempt to expand the Youth League by lowering membership standards.[11] Whatever the merits of this assertion, it is clear that Feng's career as an important political official ended in the early fifties. With rare exceptions, the Communist historians have practically written Feng out of contemporary Chinese Communist history. Two among many examples serve to illustrate this point. First, in late 1951 he had been named as a youth representative to the rather unimportant Chinese People's Committee in Defense of Children; he was listed as a member as late as the 1955 *Jen-min shou-ts'e* (People's handbook), but was quietly dropped in the subsequent issue. Even more striking was the treatment of Feng in a historical review of the Youth League published in mid-1964 while a major youth congress was in session. Even though Feng had been the dominant youth leader from the mid-thirties until the early fifties, no mention whatever was made of his contributions (although many other youth leaders were cited by name). This treatment of Feng stands in contrast to the following description published by the Communists in 1950: "After twenty and more years of unceasing revolutionary work among the youths he is well known and respected by all young people in every part of China."[12]

1. Nym Wales, *Inside Red China* (New York, 1939), p. 99.
2. *China's Youth March Forward* (Peking, 1950), p. 68.
3. *Ch'ih-fei fan-tung wen-chien hui-pien* (A collection of Red bandit documents, Taipei [?], 1960), p. 651.
4. Wales, p. 99.
5. *CB* 738, p. 51.
6. Wales, p. 99; *ECMM* 77, p. 12.
7. *China's Youth March Forward*, p. 68.
8. *ECMM* 77, p. 12.
9. Edgar Snow, *Random Notes on Red China (1936–1945)* (Cambridge, Mass., 1957), p. 24.
10. *CB* 100, pp. 36–39; *Hsin-hua yueh-pao* (New China monthly), 4:1, 51–52 (May 25, 1951).
11. Union Research Service, Union Research Institute, Hong Kong, report no. 783, June 18, 1963.
12. *China's Youth March Forward*, p. 68.

Fu Lien-chang

(1895–   ; Ch'ang-t'ing, Fukien). Veteran Red Army doctor; president, Chinese Medical Association.

Fu Lien-chang was the first physician in the Red Army, joining the Communists in 1927 in Fukien. His entire career has been devoted to the field of medicine and includes service with the Communists during the arduous days of the Long March and the Yenan period when doctors were in extremely short supply. He has been president of the Chinese Medical Association since 1950 and holds a number of honorary posts in the medical field.

Fu was born in 1895 of a poor laboring family in Ch'ang-t'ing (T'ing-chou), located in western Fukien not far from the Kiangsi border, an area that served as a major Communist base in the late twenties and early thirties. His father was a stevedore by trade and the family were practicing Christians, being communicants of a local English Protestant mission. Fu was reared in an orphanage sponsored by the mission and was also given medical training at a school attached to the Gospel Hospital in Ch'ang-t'ing, which was run by the mission. He remained with the hospital after graduation and became superintendent of the medical school in 1925 when the

British missionaries evacuated the area following the May 30th Movement and the ensuing labor unrest, which broke out in Shanghai and quickly took on nationwide anti-foreign overtones. In his early years Fu was known as Nelson Fu, a name he had probably been given by the missionaries in Ch'ang-t'ing. He was a charter member of the Chinese Medical Club (Po-i-hui) organized by the famous surgeon, Sir William Osler.

After the failure of the Communists' Nanchang Uprising in August 1927, the date celebrated as the birth of the Red Army, retreating Communist forces led by Yeh T'ing and Ho Lung (qq.v.) made their way to Fu's native area in western Fukien and passed through Ch'ang-t'ing on their way to Swatow. This was presumably his first direct contact with Communism. He has stated that about this time he was also influenced by the writings of Ch'ü Ch'iu-pai (q.v.), one of the earliest CCP leaders, who later became a good friend. The Yeh-Ho forces left the Ch'ang-t'ing area, but Fu remained behind to care for wounded and ill Red Army soldiers, and at this same time secretly joined the CCP. Shortly afterwards, in 1928, he made his way to the Communists' stronghold at Chingkangshan, Kiangsi, and remained with them when they moved to Juichin, Kiangsi, only a few miles west of his native Ch'ang-t'ing, which was also under Communist control. Although Fu himself was already suffering from tuberculosis, an illness that has since remained with him, he was instrumental in setting up the first organized Communist medical establishment. In late 1931 he founded a Red Army school for nurses, and a year later he founded and became director of the Central Hospital and Medical School, located in Ch'ang-t'ing. Among Fu's earliest patients were Communist military leader Ch'en Keng and political leader Hsu T'e-li. He is also credited with saving Mao Tse-tung's life in 1929 when Mao contracted a serious case of malaria.[1]

Fu made the Long March, which began in October 1934, and because of his tubercular condition, he had to be carried part of the way. He arrived in north Shensi via Sikang and Kansu with the forces led by Chu Te in the fall of 1936, a year after the Long Marchers led by Mao had arrived there (see under Chu Te). By 1936 Fu was head of the Red Army Medical Corps, and from the following year until the end of the Sino-Japanese War he concurrently directed the work of the Central Medical Bureau in Yenan. He was interviewed by both American author Edgar Snow and his wife, Nym Wales, in 1936–37, and it is largely from Miss Wales' account that the details of Fu's early life are drawn.[2],

Although nothing is known of Fu's activities after the Sino-Japanese War, to judge from the fact that he was awarded the Order of Liberation in 1955 (see below), it is evident that he was with Communist military forces in north China during the civil war with the Nationalists in the late forties. When the PRC was established in 1949 Fu became deputy surgeon general of the People's Revolutionary Military Council, the highest military organ of the government from its formation until it was abolished in 1954. In August 1950, when the Communists reorganized the Chinese Medical Association (CMA), Fu was named president, a position he still retains. He has also been associated with two bodies subordinate to the CMA, the International Medical Exchange and Cooperation Committee and the Committee for the Exchange of Medical Knowledge between [Traditional] Chinese and Western Medicine [Practitioners]. He has been chairman of the former since about 1953 and vice-chairman of the latter since November 1953. The Communists also reorganized the National Red Cross Society in August 1950, and since that time Fu has been a member of its Board of Directors (known as the Executive Committee since 1961). In 1951–52 he was a member of the Planning Committee of the All-China Federation of Scientific Societies, and since November 1951 he has been a vice-chairman of the Chinese People's Committee in Defense of Children, a child-care organization headed by Sung Ch'ingling. He has also been honorary president of two other organizations: The China Pharmacy Association (since 1952) and the China Federation of Tuberculosis Prevention Societies (from 1953).

Nominally, Fu's most important position since the formation of the national government was with the Ministry of Public Health where he served as a vice-minister under Miss Li Te-ch'üan from April 1952 to September 1959. However, a former employee of the ministry has stated that Fu seldom came to work owing to his protracted illness.[3] There is further testimony to his bad state of health; an official of the International Planned Parenthood Federation who spoke with Fu in 1964 found him to be "thin and feeble."[4] As a consequence, Fu makes relatively few public appearances, even though he holds a large number of honorary and quasi-official positions. Perhaps his most active period was in the mid-fifties when he spoke on several occasions in connection with birth control problems. He has been one of the relatively few prominent officials to advocate birth control openly, and on one occasion in 1956 he endorsed induced miscarriages. At a March 1957 CMA meeting he announced the establishment of a "birth control technical guidance committee," and writing for the February 2, 1963, issue of Chung-kuo ch'ing-nien pao (China youth newspaper) he strongly advocated "late marriages," a favorite and oblique means the Communists have attempted to use to curb population increases.

Specifically, Fu urged that men marry no earlier than "about 30," and women "about 25." He again argued the cause for late marriages, as well as the virtues of having fewer children, in the April 1, 1963 issue of Chung-kuo fu-nü (Women of China).

Although it is evident that Fu has not been particularly active since 1949, the prestige of his name has been lent to a number of organizations. These are summarized below:

1954 to date?: member, Board of Directors, Chinese People's Association for Cultural Relations with Foreign Countries.

1954 to date: member, Second National Committee, CPPCC, as a representative of medical and public health circles. He also served on the Third and Fourth National Committees (as well as their Standing Committees) that opened, respectively, in April 1959 and December 1964. In addition, he has chaired the CPPCC's Medical and Health Section since 1959.

1956 to date: member, Asian Solidarity Committee of China (known since 1958 as the Afro-Asian Solidarity Committee).

1956: member, Standing Committee, Chinese People's Committee to Support Egypt Against Aggression (an ad hoc body established at the time of the Anglo-French-Israeli invasion of Egypt).

1964 to date?: vice-chairman of a committee to promote the circulation of popular scientific materials.

Fu was also the recipient of the Order of Liberation in 1955, an award given for military service between 1945 and 1950.

Although Fu is clearly not a figure of political significance, he has been honored by the Communists for his long services to them, particularly in the early and difficult days of the Kiangsi Soviet and the Yenan period. As the first physician to join the Communist guerrillas, he might well be regarded as the father of the Chinese Communist medical world. Little is known of his personal life aside from the fact that he is married and has had at least four children. According to Fu's claim, one of his daughters (as well as her husband) was executed by the KMT when she was 21. Fu has a limited knowledge of English (presumably learned from his days in mission schools) and as late as 1944 he still described himself as a Christian, but it is likely that he made this claim to ingratiate himself with Western journalists who visited Yenan.

———

1. Agnes Smedley, The Great Road (New York, 1956), p. 262.

2. Nym Wales, Red Dust (Stanford, Calif., 1952), pp. 171–173.

3. Interview in Hong Kong, April 1964.

4. Unpublished report by Temeyoshi Katagiri, regional secretary, Western Pacific Region, International Planned Parenthood Federation, n.d.

Han Che-i

(Shantung). Economic official: alternate secretary, East China Bureau, CCP.

Han Che-i is a native of Shantung, but nothing is known of his early life. Like many latter-day Communist officials he first emerged in the late 1940's as the Communists pushed to the fore a number of cadre to staff the many new positions which the mastery of the huge China mainland demanded. To administer those areas captured in north China, the North China People's Government was created in August 1948. This government, in turn, was divided into a number of sub-districts, one of them the Hopeh-Shantung-Honan Administrative Office where Han served in 1948 and 1949 as a deputy director. The North China Government was absorbed by the central government when it was formed in October 1949, but just prior to that time (in August 1949) Pingyuan Province was formed with its capital in Hsin-hsiang (in present-day north Honan). Han was transferred southward to join this new government as a vice-governor and concurrently as head of the Industry Department; the next year he was also made a vice-chairman of the provincial Finance and Economics Committee (August 1950). These two appointments in the field of economics were a harbinger of the type of work that Han would perform in the years ahead. He was also engaged in 1950–51 in the perennial problem of controlling the Yellow River, being named in 1950 as a deputy director of the Yellow River Flood Prevention Headquarters.

Apparently Han's work in Pingyuan gained favorable attention in Peking, because he was called back north at the end of 1951 when the North China Administrative Committee (NCAC) was established (December 1951); the NCAC was a multi-provincial governmental organ supervising the work in the five provinces of Hopeh, Shansi, Chahar, Suiyuan, and Pingyuan. It existed until the six regional administration committees were all abolished in 1954. A few days after his appointment to membership on the NCAC, Han was named (January 1952) as the NCAC Director of Finance. Within the next 18 months Han received two more important economic posts under the NCAC; in January 1953 he was appointed a vice-chairman of a committee to regulate warehouses in North China (a potentially important position in a nation where food storage is a critical matter), and in mid-1953 he was named a vice-chairman of the region's Finance and Economics Committee. He held these posts to the end of the summer of 1954 when he was transferred to work in the national government.

In August 1954 Han received two appointments in the central government, and from that time until transferred to East China in 1961 he held a series of important positions in the government's network of economic commissions and bureaus. Because of the complexity of these appointments, they are first summarized in tabular form, and then commented upon in the text that follows.

Member, State Planning Commission
August–October 1954

Director, State Supplies Allocation Bureau, State Planning Commission
August 1954–probably May 1956

Vice-chairman, State Planning Commission
October 1954–November 1956

Vice-chairman, State Economic Commission
November 1956–September 1959

Director, Administrative Bureau of Supplies, State Council
November 1956–probably September 1959

Vice-chairman, State Planning Commission
October 1958–c.1961

The State Planning Commission had been formed in late 1952 on the eve of the First Five-Year Plan, inaugurated in 1953. Han became associated with the Planning Commission in August 1954, just prior to the general reorganization of the central government in September–October 1954. At this time Li Fu-ch'un, a top economic specialist and later a Politburo member, was named as Chairman; it was also at this point that Han was elevated from membership on the commission to a vice-chairmanship. The growing complexities of the economy were such that in May 1956 the State Economic Commission was formed. It differed from the State Planning Commission in that it specialized in annual planning whereas the Planning Commission concentrated on long-range planning. This new commission has been headed from 1956 by Po I-po, a man who has ranked just below Li Fu-ch'un in the economic sphere.

Han's transfer from the State Planning Commission to a comparable post (vice-chairman) on the State Economic Commission in the fall of 1956 indicated that he was changing his emphasis from long-range economic planning to shorter-range planning. Two years later, he was reappointed to the State Planning Commission, so that from October 1958 to September 1959 he was concurrently a vice-chairman of the two top economic organizations. Moreover, from 1954 to 1959 Han also headed the government supply bureau, an organ charged with the allocation and distribution of many of the strategic materials needed by all sectors of the economy. It has been a fairly rare situation when one man has held such high posts within two or more closely related commissions and bureaus and thus seems a tribute to Han's abilities.

Very little was reported about Han after the general government reshuffling of personnel in

September 1959, thereby giving rise to the thought that he may have been among those "economic planners" who opposed the more extreme economic measures employed during the Great Leap Forward. But after receiving no publicity from 1959 to March 1961, he reappeared in East China as a "responsible official." Ultimately (July 1962) this description was refined to that of alternate secretary of the important East China Bureau of the Party Central Committee. Further evidence of Han's permanent transfer to east China in early 1961 came with the publication of the semi-official yearbook of 1961, which failed to list him as a vice-chairman of the State Planning Commission (although it was not until February 1963 that he was officially removed).

Han's transfer to east China came as an outgrowth of decisions taken at the Party's Ninth Plenum held in January 1961. At that time it was decided to re-create the six regional Party Bureaus which had been abolished in 1954–55. This also came at a period when the effects of the faltering Great Leap Forward had seriously dislocated the entire economy and thus demanded a number of transfers from Peking of capable personnel in all walks of life.

Although a senior economic official, Han has apparently written very little. However, he did write an article for the important Central Committee organ *Hung-ch'i* (Red flag), May 23, 1964. This dealt with a campaign then in progress that stressed the necessity for the less developed industrial regions to learn from the more advanced areas (such as Shanghai).

Han Hsien-ch'u

(1908–   ; Hunan). Commander, Foochow Military Region; alternate member, CCP Central Committee.

Han Hsien-ch'u is a career military man. He graduated from the Changsha Middle School in the capital of his native Hunan; to judge from his birth year this would have been in the mid-1920's. He was first known to be fighting with the Communists when he was an officer in a regiment commanded by Wang Shu-sheng (q.v.), belonging to the Fourth Front Army (see under Chang Kuo-t'ao). In 1933, when Han was a regimental commander and later a deputy divisional commander, this army was fighting in northeast Szechwan. There it established its headquarters in the T'ung-Nan-Pa Soviet, named for the three principal hsien which the Communists controlled in that area. The Fourth Front Army moved to the extreme western part of Szechwan in 1935 to meet the army of Mao Tse-tung, which was coming from Kiangsi on the Long March. Mao and Chang Kuo-t'ao, with their respective armies, met in the small town of Mao-kung in June. However, disagreements

arose between the two men over the eventual destination of the Red armies, and in August they separated, Chang turning west into Sikang, while Mao and his army went north to Shensi. Han remained with Chang Kuo-t'ao, becoming a divisional commander in Chang's army by 1936. The Fourth Front Army finally reached north Shensi and joined forces with Mao late in 1936. Once there, Han entered the second class at K'ang-ta, the military academy established by the Communists upon their arrival in north Shensi after completing the Long March.

After the outbreak of the Sino-Japanese War in mid-1937, Han was identified as a commander of Liu Po-ch'eng's 129th Division of the Communist Eighth Route Army. Liu's division, one of three major divisions of the Eighth Route Army, was made up largely of units that had earlier been part of the Fourth Front Army; therefore, Han's identification with the 129th Division suggests that he had remained with his former military associates. In the first year of the war he was stationed at the military base in the T'ai-hang Mountains of southeast Shansi where the division made its headquarters from about September 1937. By 1939 the 129th Division had expanded its operations into the bordering areas of Honan and Shantung, and another former Fourth Front Army man (Hsu Hsiang-ch'ien) was sent into Shantung to coordinate Communist guerrilla operations there. Han was also sent to Shantung in 1939 where he served as a brigade commander in the Po-hai area. Po-hai, one of four areas in the Communist war zone in Shantung, was located north of the Yellow River.

Sometime after the end of the Sino-Japanese War (1945) Han was transferred from the army of Liu Po-ch'eng to the army of Lin Piao. The latter entered Manchuria at the end of hostilities and joined forces with the local resistance there (see under Chou Pao-chung). In January 1946 all the Communist forces in Manchuria were reorganized into the Northeast Democratic Allied Army under Lin Piao. By 1947 Han was identified as a divisional and later a column commander of the Third and Fourth Columns of Lin's army. In September 1948 he participated in the battles to capture Linkiang (Lin-chiang), Kirin, situated on the Korean border at a bend in the Yalu River. Later, Han accompanied elements of Lin's army that occupied Chin-chou, Liaoning, in October 1948, finally arriving on the outskirts of Peking at the end of the year. By January 1949, when the Red Army commanders had completed the negotiations for the surrender of Peking, Lin's army was known as the Fourth Field Army. Han remained with the Fourth Field Army, serving as deputy commander of the 12th Corps (commanded by Hsiao Ching-kuang, q.v.) on the march through central and south China, culminating with the takeover of Hainan Island in April 1950. During this period, and for a short time after the Communists captured Hainan, Han held military posts in the territories over which the army was expanding. From August 1949 to June 1950 he was a deputy commander of the Hunan Military District, and in June 1950 he became a member of the Military and Administrative Committee for Hainan. In September 1949 Han represented the Fourth Field Army at the inaugural meeting of the CPPCC at which time the PRC was established. In the latter half of 1949 the expanding Fourth Field Army occupied Kwangtung, and in March 1950, soon after the Kwangtung Provincial People's Government Council was established, Han was named to membership. However, his membership in this government became nominal owing to a 1950 transfer.

The Korean War began in June 1950, with the Chinese Communist forces entering the conflict in October. The main Chinese force was composed of Lin Piao's Fourth Field Army troops, which had been brought back from south China. Han was transferred to the Korean front in late 1950, and by October of the next year he was a representative of the Chinese People's Volunteers (CPV) to the Panmunjom truce negotiations (which began in July 1951). He remained in Korea during much and perhaps all of 1952. In February 1952 he was in charge of a 20-member CPV delegation that attended the fourth anniversary of Korean Army Day; in August he headed a delegation to a Pyongyang rally marking the 25th anniversary of the PLA. In 1952, the year before the end of the Korean War, he was made deputy chief-of-staff of the CPV.

With the establishment of the constitutional government in 1954, Han became a member of the newly created National Defense Council, a military advisory body with little power but with considerable prestige. When personal military ranks were created in the PLA in 1955 Han was made a colonel-general, the equivalent of a three-star general in the U.S. Army. Military orders for service in the period from 1927 to 1950 were also awarded for the first time in 1955. Han was a recipient of one or more of these orders, but the exact ones are not known. It was also in the fall of 1955 that Han was reported attending the "PLA Academy," possibly the PLA Political Academy in Peking, Communist China's national war college.

In May 1958 Han was made an alternate member of the Central Committee at the Second Session of the Eighth Congress. His exact military duties were for a time obscured, probably for reasons of military security. Since about 1955 he has been in charge of troops stationed along the Fukien coast opposite the offshore islands of Quemoy and Matsu. This has been a particularly important command, especially during the period of heightened tension over the islands in 1958.

Since 1960 he has been commander of the Foochow Military Region, the larger military command which includes both Fukien and Kiangsi Provinces. In the Foochow Military Region, Yeh Fei (q.v.), who was formerly commander, is now the political commissar. Han continues to serve on the Defense Council and on the Party Central Committee as well as in the Foochow Military Region. The *JMJP* of July 31, 1962, published one of Han's infrequent articles, entitled "Carrying the Battle across the Sea."

Han Kuang

(c.1911–   ; Kirin). Science administrator; alternate member, CCP Central Committee.

Han Kuang fought against the Japanese in Manchuria during the early 1930's and then after spending a few years in the Soviet Union, Sinkiang Province, and Yenan, he returned to his native Manchuria, where he was an important official until 1956. Since his election to alternate membership on the Party Central Committee in 1956, Han has worked in Peking as one of the PRC's leading science administrators.

Han was born about 1911 in Kirin Province in Manchuria. He graduated from a middle school, presumably in Manchuria, and was admitted into the Communist Youth League in 1930. He joined the CCP in 1931, the year the Japanese invaded Manchuria. He remained there for a time working in the Communist youth movement, becoming successively a regional committee secretary, a special committee secretary, and a provincial secretary-general of the Manchurian branch of the Youth League. From 1933 to 1935 he was a member of the local resistance forces in Manchuria, where the Communists formed a very active nucleus. He was connected with the Allied Anti-Japanese Army (see under Chou Pao-chung), formed in 1935 from the various guerrilla units that had been operating in Manchuria. This Army had seven subordinate armies and five guerrilla units; Han served with both the First and Third Armies. The former was led by Yang Ching-yü, a prominent Communist who was killed in 1940.

In 1936 Han went to the Soviet Union where he reportedly studied at Moscow University. He knows Russian and is also said to have some understanding of English. Chu Te-hai (q.v.), a member of the Korean national minority group from Kirin, was also associated with the Manchurian branch of the Youth League and the Anti-Japanese Allied Army. Chu joined the CCP the same year as Han and also went to the USSR in 1936 to study. Available accounts do not connect the two men's activities, but it is possible that they were colleagues during those years. The duration of Han's stay in Moscow is not known, but by 1938 he was working for the Party in Sinkiang. There, using the alias of

Han Ming-kuang, he directed propaganda for the Anti-Imperialist Association organized by Sheng Shih-ts'ai, the Nationalist Governor of Sinkiang. He also served in Sinkiang briefly as a deputy magistrate of a hsien. From the mid-1930's to the 1942–43 period, Sheng Shih-ts'ai cooperated closely with both the Russian and Chinese Communists. Taking advantage of these relations, the Chinese Communists sent a number of top men to Sinkiang in the late 1930's and early 1940's, including Teng Fa, Ch'en T'an-ch'iu, and Mao Tse-min (Mao Tse-tung's brother). Most of these men were ultimately arrested and executed by Sheng (see under Ch'en T'an-ch'iu), but fortunately for Han Kuang he was ordered to Yenan in 1940, where he worked as a section chief and secretary-general of the Party's United Front Work Department, the organization charged with the task of gaining maximum cooperation from both non-Party intellectuals and the national minorities.

Han's whereabouts during the last years of the war are not clear. Apparently he was working in some underground capacity in his native Manchuria. Soon after the end of the war he was assigned to the Port Arthur-Dairen area. These important cities, situated on the Kwantung Peninsula, were occupied by the Soviet Union immediately after the war. Although the August 1945 treaty between the Chinese Nationalists and the Russians provided for joint control of Dairen and Port Arthur, the Russians effectively blocked any Nationalist participation in the management of the Kwantung Peninsula. Instead, the Russians allowed the entry of a number of Chinese Communist officials to set up Communist-controlled organizations. Han was among those officials, and between 1946 and about 1953 he was a key leader in the Kwantung Peninsula where he held a wide variety of positions. By 1946 he was serving as the head of the "Democratic Youth Federation" for Dairen, as secretary for the Party Committee in that city, and as president of the Construction (Chien-kuo) College in Dairen.

In 1947 Han became a vice-chairman of the Kwantung Administrative Office, the organization governing the Port Arthur-Dairen area; he succeeded to the chairmanship of this office in 1949. In the meantime, in 1948 he had assumed two additional posts of importance when he became head of the Port Arthur-Dairen Public Security Bureau and deputy secretary of the Party Committee for these two cities. From about 1949 Han served as second in command of this area under Ouyang Ch'in (q.v.), a Party veteran about 10 years senior to Han, who was the ranking Party secretary there. As already noted, Han became chairman of the Kwantung Administrative Office in 1949 (which in April of that year was redesignated the Port Arthur–Dairen Administrative Office), and in that same year also assumed the task of heading the

Office's Economic Planning Bureau. In November 1950, the Administrative Office was renamed the Darien-Port Arthur People's Government, with Han continuing to serve as the head of this government, a post he held until Ouyang Ch'in replaced him in February 1953.

In August 1949, just prior to the establishment of the national government in Peking, the Chinese Communists established the Northeast People's Government. Han was named as a member of this government, and when it was reorganized into the Northeast Administrative Committee in January 1953 he was reappointed to membership and also named a vice-chairman of its Finance and Economics Committee. He held both posts until the regional committees were abolished in 1954. The whereabouts of Han after his removal as mayor of Port Arthur-Dairen in February 1953 are not clear. The only clue comes from his election in mid-1954 as a deputy to the First NPC from the important industrial city of Fushun in present-day Liaoning. In any event, he could not have been there long, because in August 1954 he became governor of Heilungkiang in northern Manchuria. This appointment came just a few days after Han, identified simply as a "responsible person," had spoken at a meeting on August 1, 1954, in Harbin at which time Heilungkiang and Sungkiang Provinces were merged into a "new" Heilungkiang Province. At this same time, Han was also named as a deputy secretary of the Heilungkiang Party Committee, serving once again under Ouyang Ch'in, who had also been transferred to Heilungkiang.

The transfer of Ouyang and Han to Heilungkiang was not fortuitous. The previous ranking party secretary, Chao Te-tsun, was implicated in the Kao Kang "plot," which formally came to light in early 1955. However, it is clear that the activities of Kao (q.v.) and his accomplices were known to the Party center by at least mid-1954, thus necessitating the changes in the Heilungkiang hierarchy. Han was promoted to second secretary of the Heilungkiang Party Committee by January 1955, and then at the Eighth National Party Congress in September 1956 he was selected as an alternate member of the Central Committee. In the same month he was relieved from his posts in Heilungkiang, being replaced as governor by his long-time colleague Ouyang Ch'in, and shortly thereafter Han was transferred to Peking to enter a new phase in his career.

Although Han's past record gave little indication that he would qualify as a science administrator, he has devoted most of his time to this field since coming to Peking. First appointed a vice-chairman of the State Technological Commission in January 1957, he was also made a member in May of that year of the Scientific Planning Commission, serving under Vice-Premier Nieh Jung-chen. Both commissions were under the State Council. When Technological Commission Chairman Huang Ching (q.v.) died in February 1958, Han became the commission's acting chairman. He remained in that post until the two commissions were merged in November 1958 to become the Scientific and Technological Commission headed by Nieh Jung-chen, under whom Han has continued to serve as a vice-chairman. In April 1959 he was elected to the Third National Committee of the CPPCC as a representative of the China Scientific and Technical Association, and at the close of the first session he was named to membership on the CPPCC's Standing Committee. However, when the Fourth National Committee was formed in late 1964, Han was not reappointed. In the more important NPC Han has played a more significant role. As already described, he was elected from Fushun to the First NPC (1954–1959). He was transferred to the Liaoning constituency for the Second NPC (1959–1964) and once again transferred—this time to Heilungkiang—for the Third NPC, which held its first session in December 1964–January 1965. He served on the Budget Committee for this session and gave a speech on the need to apply the results of scientific research to industrial and agricultural production. Finally, at the close of the meetings (January 1965), he was elevated to the Standing Committee, the ruling body, which meets regularly between the annual sessions of the NPC. Since his arrival in Peking over the winter of 1956–57, Han has frequently taken part in meetings related to science and technology. To cite a random but typical example, he presided over a meeting in Peking in June 1964 at which more than 1,400 awards were given for new industrial products. He has also played a role of some significance in the promotion of scientific and technological ties with foreign countries. Specifically, he has signed at least three agreements providing for scientific cooperation with the Soviet Union (October 1959), North Vietnam (November 1960), and Rumania (June 1963). An article by Han entitled "Several Problems Concerning Technical Work in Industry" was published in the top Party journal, *Hung-ch'i* (Red flag, December 16, 1961),[1] and was also reproduced in the 1962 edition of the authoritative *Jen-min shou-ts'e* (People's handbook).

1. *SCMM* 295.

Han Nien-lung

(1910–   ; Jen-huai, Kweichow). Vice-minister of Foreign Affairs.

Han Nien-lung was born in Jen-huai, Kweichow, which is about 25 miles west of Tsun-i and lies directly astride the route which Mao Tse-tung's First Front Army followed during the Long March; Mao and his men were in that area in the early part of 1935. Although there is no corroborating information, it is possible that Han, then a young man of about 25, might have been recruited into the Red Armies as they passed through his native area. In any event, he apparently was a military figure of moderate stature during the Sino-Japanese War because in January 1946 he was assigned to the Peking Executive Headquarters with the rank of a colonel. The headquarters had been established in January 1946 to supervise the truce worked out (under the auspices of American diplomat-general George C. Marshall) between the Chinese Nationalists and Communists. From the headquarters in Peking, a number of special teams were sent into the field to keep the peace. For a time in 1946 Han served as the Communist representative to the 17th team stationed at Huai-yin (Ch'ing-chiang), Kiangsu, a city on the Grand Canal and in the heart of territories controlled by the New Fourth Army headed by Ch'en I.

The Executive Headquarters were dissolved in early 1947 following the renewal of the civil war, with the Communist representatives evacuated to Communist-held areas in the northwest. Han apparently took up duties as a political officer; this is inferred from the fact that he was assigned the post of deputy political commissar of the Woo-sung-Shanghai Garrison Headquarters (Woosung being a port city just north of Shanghai) following the Communist occupation of Shanghai in the spring of 1949. He held this post until early 1951 when he was given another assignment.

In May 1951 China and Pakistan agreed to the establishment of diplomatic relations, and at the same time Han was named as the first ambassador. He arrived in Pakistan in early September 1951 and presented his credentials on September 10. At the time Chinese news releases referred to him by his military rank of general. He remained in Pakistan for four and a half years, a relatively long assignment for a Chinese Communist ambassador. The relative paucity of news about Han during his tenure in Karachi derives, in part, from the rather cool relations between the two countries during this period. Broadly speaking, Peking policy was generally "pro-Indian" in the early and mid-1950's and thus by definition somewhat hostile to Pakistan, at that time a close ally of the United States and, for part of Han's stay in Pakistan, a member of the Southeast Asian Treaty Organization (SEATO). Therefore, most of Han's publicized appearances, for example, receptions marking the anniversary of the PRC, tended to be formalistic. Perhaps his busiest period occurred in late January 1956 when he was involved in the various activities arranged for Sung Ch'ing-ling (Mme. Sun Yat-sen), then in Pakistan on a goodwill visit.

In February 1956 Han was transferred to Sweden as ambassador, replacing Keng Piao (q.v.). In fact, the two men simply exchanged jobs, with Keng being assigned to Pakistan. Sino-Swedish relations were not particularly active, and thus Han was seldom mentioned in the Chinese press except in relation to such ceremonial duties as parties marking Peking's National Day. He did, however, sign a trade agreement on November 8, 1957, the first government-to-government agreement negotiated between the two nations. Despite the relative inactivity of Sino-Swedish relations, a diplomat familiar with Han's work in Sweden has claimed that he was rather well regarded by the Swedes.[1]

On December 20, 1958, Han was replaced in Sweden by Tung Yueh-ch'ien and on the same day appointed an assistant minister of Foreign Affairs. By mid-1959 he assumed (and may still hold) the concurrent post of head of the ministry's Staff Office, an office concerned mainly with the administrative tasks peculiar to any large governmental agency. Since his assumption of high office in the ministry, Han appears to be chiefly concerned with the non-Communist nations, presumably a result of his lengthy stay abroad in two non-Communist nations. This observation is drawn from the fact that the great majority of his public appearances in Peking are concerned with visits to China by persons from non-Communist countries. However, a notable exception to this pattern of activity occurred in May–June 1960 when Han accompanied Premier Chou En-lai and Foreign Minister Ch'en I to Mongolia. During this visit, an important treaty of friendship and mutual assistance was signed, in addition to a large (200-million ruble) long-term loan by China to Mongolia.

Han's thirteen years in the Ministry of Foreign Affairs were rewarded in April 1964 when he was promoted from assistant to vice-minister. In March–April 1965 he accompanied Foreign Minister Ch'en I as the senior member of a small delegation that visited Afghanistan, Pakistan, and Nepal. Ch'en signed agreements relating to the Sino-Afghan boundary, as well as to cooperation in cultural, economic, and technical fields. A Sino-Pakistani boundary protocol and a cultural cooperation agreement were signed in Pakistan, while a press communiqué issued in Nepal revealed that there had been discussions there relating to political and economic matters of mutual interest.

Nothing is known of Han's personal life aside from the fact that he is married to Wang Chen who is otherwise unknown.

1. Interview in Hong Kong, November 1964.

Ho Ch'ang-kung

(1900–   ; Hua-jung hsien, Hunan). Former Red Army officer; vice-minister of Geology.

A specialist in the fields of heavy industry and geology, Ho Ch'ang-kung began his interest in political affairs as a middle school student in Changsha during the decade that followed the 1911 Revolution. One of the Hunanese students who joined the work-and-study program to further his education in Paris, he belongs to the group that founded a French CCP unit while they were students in Paris. Although Ho was converted to Marxism along with the others, he was not on intimate terms with Ts'ai Ho-sen, Ch'en Yen-nien, and other members of this founding group. When he returned to China he took part in the campaigns of peasant insurrection, the Autumn Harvest Uprisings of mid-1927, and was among those who followed Mao Tse-tung to Chingkangshan when the campaigns failed. Ho made the Long March but separated from Mao to follow Chang Kuo-t'ao midway on the route and thus did not arrive in north Shensi until the year 1936–37. Since the creation of the PRC government he has become a middle-rank government official of some note, but he has never received the Party awards that have gone to many of those members of the elite who founded the CCP branch in France or who followed Mao Tse-tung to Chingkangshan.

Ho was born in northern Hunan in Hua-jung on the shore of Lake Tung-t'ing. With help from brothers and sisters, he received an early education in his native Hua-jung and then won scholarships for middle school study and for later study in Europe. Ho enrolled at the Third Middle School in the nearby town of Yueh-yang, a school jointly financed by Yueh-yang and three neighboring hsien, Hua-jung, Lin-hsiang, and P'ing-chiang. Ho was to engage in Party work in the last-named area a decade later. While in middle school he became a leader in a student organization that worked to expose the principal, who was involved in corrupt practices, and as a result was expelled from Yueh-yang. Although the corruption was later righted and Ho could have returned to school, he chose instead to go to the Chia-chung Technical School in the provincial capital of Changsha. There he came into contact with Mao Tse-tung's student colleagues as a member of the *Hsin-min hsueh-hui* (New people's study society—see under Ts'ai Ch'ang).[1] After about a year of specializing in mechanical engineering at Chia-chung (which he entered in 1917), he went to Peking to join the Hunan students led by Mao and Ts'ai, to embark upon the work-and-study program for university study in France (see under Ts'ai Ho-sen). Ho's own account of his student days (cited below) mentions that in Peking the students divided into three groups for this program, those who were in Peking proper, those who went for some preliminary study at Pao-ting, and those who were assigned to the Ch'ang-hsin-tien station workshops on the important Pinghan (Peking-Hankow) Railroad. The last-cited group, to which Ho belonged, was the only one having students who practiced for the work-and-study program before going to France; they worked in the railroad shop each morning and studied in the afternoons, often on their own. When the May Fourth Movement of 1919 broke out among the students in Peking and Tientsin, students at the Ch'ang-hsin-tien station joined with the railway workers in what was one of the first of the sympathy strikes in support of the May Fourth Movement with its demand for a boycott of the Japanese. Not only did these students hold combined labor and student demonstrations, but they began to engage in labor organizing.[2] In the next months Ho must have spent more time agitating for the strike movement than studying, but in the fall of 1919 he was able to take advantage of a public grant from the Hunan provincial administration, which assisted the Hunanese students in their program for study in France. Thus, in the fall or early winter of 1919, he embarked for France, as did Ts'ai Ho-sen and a number of others from the Changsha group.

Once in France most of the Changsha students went south of Paris to Montargis, where they enrolled at the Collège de Montargis, and there began to organize a chapter of the student association from which they had come in Changsha (see under Hsiang Ching-yü). Possibly because his connections with these students were not so strong (Ho having worked with the group at Ch'ang-hsin-tien) and possibly also to follow his desire to learn French, he cut himself off from the rest of his provincial colleagues and went to the west Normandy coast where he entered a church-sponsored school to study mechanical engineering. It so happened that both the school headmaster and his assistant were Communists. After about six months, Ho's money ran out and so in the summer of 1920 he returned to Paris to find work, taking on a number of menial and ill-paying jobs to help defray his expenses. One of these was in the Renault Motor plant outside of Paris where he spent four months. In the course of his stay in France Chou En-lai also worked there for a short time. During the year Ho joined the Work-and-Study Cooperative Society, an organization founded to help the Chinese students in France (see under Li Fu-ch'un), and once more he came into contact with Ts'ai, Wang Jo-fei, and Hsiang Ching-yü, and some of the others who later joined the CCP. By February 1921 this society had increased its membership to some 300 and formed a nucleus for the small CCP unit that was officially established in mid-1922.

During 1921 the Chinese students were involved in a series of demonstrations to protest political happenings at home where a weak and vacillating government was adhering to Japanese demands and negotiating loans with Western powers. After an attack upon the Chinese minister to France earlier in the year, and more violent demonstrations held before the embassy later, a number of the Chinese students were jailed and then deported. Among them were Ts'ai Ho-sen, Li Li-san, Ch'en I, and Hsiang Ching-yü. Although some students were forced to leave France, others remained to carry on their political work and to organize a unit of the CCP in the summer of 1922 in Paris. Among these founding members were Wang Jo-fei, Ch'en Yen-nien, and Chao Shih-yen, the last two the only fully paid Party officials there at this time. Ho, however, did not remain in Paris but instead returned to his Normandy School and under the guidance of the headmaster and together with some 20 of the Chinese students (by late in 1920 the Chinese student quota had increased to about 70), joined the French Socialist Youth Corps. Thus Ho now had contact with a number of leftist French students while at the same time he kept in touch with the affairs of his Chinese colleagues in Paris through the *Shao-nien* (Youth), the student periodical published there and edited by Ch'en Yen-nien. Ho became a Party member at this time although he does not seem to have been present at the CCP organization meetings.

In the winter of 1922–23 the Party selected Ho for advanced technical study in Belgium. He arrived there early in 1923 to enroll at the Université de Travail at Charleroi where the Belgium Socialist Party had got a scholarship for Nieh Jung-chen (q.v.) from about 1921 to 1923. Ho entered a program in architectural engineering but when he ran short of money he went to Zeebruge to find work in a shipyard. There he contracted tuberculosis and after several months, on the advice of his doctor, went home, arriving in China in the early winter of 1924.

Ho's career in the next two decades must be constructed from the very meager reporting of his activity. He is said to have been elected to the Party Central Committee at the Fourth CCP Congress held in early January 1925.[3] He probably worked as an undercover agent in the labor movement for the two following years; in any case, when American authoress Nym Wales met him on her visit to northwest China in the summer of 1937, he was known to her as having been active in labor organizing upon his return from France.[4] In 1927 Ho is mentioned as belonging to certain Nationalist military guard units, but there is no indication of how he came to be associated with these forces.[5] Following the break in KMT-CCP relations in August 1927, he became involved in the Party-directed peasant insurgency known as the Autumn Harvest Uprisings, campaigns with which Mao Tse-tung is closely connected. In this connection there are also indications that he may have belonged to the renegade unit from the troops of Hupeh militarist Hsia Tou-yin, which joined Mao during the Autumn Harvest Uprisings (August and September 1927).[6] This unit made an attack upon P'ing-chiang but was badly defeated and subsequently the regiment broke up, only a small number of its soldiers following Mao to his mountain base at Chingkang on the Hunan-Kiangsi border. Ho was among the few who followed Mao, and for about the next year he seems to have been at Chingkangshan.[7]

Ho joined the forces of P'eng Te-huai (q.v.) at some time in or shortly after 1928. P'eng's troops were left in charge of the Chingkangshan base when Mao and Chu Te had to retreat with their army into eastern Kiangsi and Fukien in early 1929. P'eng's army, first named the Fifth Army and in mid-1930 called the Third Army Corps, had control of operations in western Kiangsi and in the territory of the Chingkangshan base (which by about 1929 was reorganized, extended, and called the Hunan-Hupeh-Kiangsi base). In the years between 1928 and 1933 Ho was said to be in charge of the Communists' Eighth Army (not to be confused with the army of the same name in Kwangsi mentioned in the biography of Chang Yun-i). The Eighth Army operated in western Kiangsi and in the above-mentioned border area base and belonged to the force commanded by P'eng Te-huai. From the scattered references to its activities, none of which are very precise, a number of the Communists connected with the Hunan-Hupeh-Kiangsi border area base were officers in this army. Of these Wang Chen was at one time the political commissar and K'o Ch'ing-shih (qq.v.) headed the Political Department. The Army must have been badly decimated by Nationalist attacks directed against the Red bases in central China in the early thirties, and by about 1932 or 1933 the survivors were absorbed into the Sixth Red Army commanded by Hsiao K'o (q.v.). As of November 1933, Ho Ch'ang-kung was reported to have gone to Juichin where he was associated with the Red Army Military Academy.

In the early part of 1934, as a delegate from the Red Army, he attended the Second All-China Congress of Soviets held in Juichin and was elected a member of the governing Central Executive Committee of the Chinese Soviet Republic. By the time the Long March began in October 1934 he had become political commissar to Lo Ping-hui (q.v.). Ho made the first part of the march with Lo's force, which formed a unit of the Chu-Mao First Front Army. Lo's separation from Mao in west Szechwan in mid-1935 is described in his biography, as is his subsequent joining of forces with Chang Kuo-t'ao (q.v.) and his march west into Sikang to spend the winter of 1935–36 at Kan-tzu. Chang himself is the source for the statement that Ho followed his commander Lo and therefore attached himself to the Chang Kuo-t'ao army,[8] survivors of which eventually found their way to north Shensi to rejoin Mao and his army during the year 1936–37.

Once in Yenan, Ho returned to the Military Academy, by this time redesignated the Anti-Japanese Military and Political Academy (K'ang-ta). Lin Piao was head of the school, but Lin's health was very poor during the Sino-Japanese War and for long periods other persons took over his responsibilities (see under Lin Piao). When Miss Wales met Ho in 1937 she reported him to be "one of the directors" of K'ang-ta.[9] From approximately 1942 to 1945 he is reported to have served as a vice-president there. In view of Ho's lack of political recognition from the CCP, it is interesting that he is one of the few persons who refused to relate his personal history to Miss Wales, though she succeeded in getting his photograph.[10]

There is little reporting on Ho during the later war years, and significantly, when the Party met for its Seventh National Congress in April–June 1945, he was not among those elected to the Central Committee. Chang Kuo-t'ao suggests that Ho's apparent political decline was related to the fact that he suffered from poor health for a number of years, having received a serious leg wound prior to or during the Long March. However, when Miss Wales saw Ho she made no mention of this and wrote of him as one of the "three tallest and handsomest of the Red commanders."[11] Two very useful accounts written in later years by Ho are part of the extensive Party literature of personal reminiscences describing important revolutionary events. These include a number of details about Ho's life. One account describes his student days in Paris, and the other, entitled *Party life in the Eighth Army,* deals with his military experiences in the late twenties and early thirties.[12]

Like many important CCP leaders, Ho was sent to Manchuria when Japan surrendered in the late summer of 1945. He was interviewed by Communist journalist Liu Pai-yü (q.v.) in the following year in Hua-t'ung, a rail junction in the southern part of present-day Kirin Province.[13] Ho was then serving as vice-president of the Military and Political Academy, a school subordinate to the Northeast Democratic Allied Army, the designation for the main Communist force in Manchuria, commanded by Lin Piao. The Academy had several branches throughout Manchuria; Lin served as the president and Party leader P'eng Chen (q.v.) as political commissar. At some point in the late forties Ho was also head of the War Industry Department (Chün-kung pu), which was subordinate to the Northeast Military Region, and when the Northeast People's Government was established in the late summer of 1949 under the chairmanship of Kao Kang, Ho was appointed to membership on the Government Council. However, he held the latter post only for a short time, because when the Communists' central government was established in October 1949, he was brought to Peking to become a vice-minister of the Ministry of Heavy Industry and a member of the Finance and Economics Committee. Both the Ministry and the Committee were subordinate to Chou En-lai's Government Administration Council, the name given to the cabinet during the period from 1949 to 1954. Ho was most frequently mentioned in the press during the early PRC years in connection with the Ministry of Heavy Industry, which was first headed by Ch'en Yun and then by Li Fu-ch'un (qq.v.), two of Peking's most important economic officials. As the ranking vice-minister, Ho served on several occasions as the acting minister; from at least mid-1951 he concurrently headed the ministry's Aeronautical Industry Bureau and toward the end of 1951 he also became chairman of an *ad hoc* committee to increase production and promote austerity measures within the ministry.

During a partial reorganization of the national government in August 1952 Ho was transferred from the Heavy Industry Ministry to become the ranking vice-minister of the newly established Ministry of Geology, a position he still retains. He works under Minister Li Szu-kuang (q.v.), a prominent Western-trained scientist, but in political terms Ho is far more important than Li, as demonstrated by the fact that Ho was identified as secretary of the ministry's CCP Committee in 1958. He was reappointed to his vice-ministership in October 1954, and two months later, representing the CCP, Ho was named to membership on the CPPCC's Second National Committee. Five years later he was named again as a CCP delegate to the Third National Committee (April 1959), and on this occasion he was also selected as a member of the Standing Committee, which is in charge of CPPCC affairs when the National Committee is not in session. When the Fourth CPPCC first met in December 1964–January 1965, Ho was again named to both the National and Standing Committees, this time representing the China Scientific and Technical Association, a professional organization including in its membership many officials who work in technically oriented government departments.

Many of Ho's appearances from the mid-fifties through the early sixties were in connection with geological conferences, as in May 1956 when he addressed the First National Congress of the China Geological Workers' Trade Union in Peking. In September of the same year he presented a written report on geological work to the Eighth CCP Congress. From 1959 to 1964 he was a deputy from his native Hunan to the Second NPC, but he was not re-elected to the Third NPC, which opened late in 1964. Ho writes on occasion for the Chinese press, almost always dealing with the topic of geology. One such article appeared in the Party's leading journal, *Hung-ch'i* (Red flag, issue number 9–10, May 5, 1961). In a particularly useful article (*JMJP,* October 11, 1959), written to commemorate the 10th PRC anniversary, Ho claimed that the number of geological workers had risen from 800 in 1949 to over 400,000, of whom 50,000 were described as "geological technicians." Whatever the value of

these figures, they at least suggest the high priority given by the Chinese Communists to the part that geological explorations play in their developing economy.

1. John E. Rue, *Mao Tse-tung in Opposition, 1927–1935* (Stanford, Calif., 1966), p. 32.
2. Chow Tse-tsung, *The May Fourth Movement* (Cambridge, Mass., 1960), p. 162.
3. Modern China Project, Columbia University, New York, Howard L. Boorman, director.
4. Nym Wales, *The Chinese Labor Movement* (New York, 1945), p. 25.
5. Union Research Institute, *Who's Who in Communist China* (Hong Kong, 1966), pp. 194–195.
6. *Ibid.,* p. 195.
7. Rue, p. 93; *Hui-i Ching-kang-shan ch'ü te tou-cheng* (Recollections of the struggles in the Chingkang Mountains; Peking, 1956), p. 13.
8. Boorman.
9. Nym Wales, *Red Dust* (Stanford, Calif., 1952), p. 113.
10. *Ibid.,* pp. 113–114, 165.
11. Nym Wales, *Inside Red China* (New York, 1939), p. 82.
12. Ho Ch'ang-kung, *Ch'in-kung chien-hsüeh sheng-huo hui-i* (Reminiscences of work-and-study life; Peking, 1958); *Hung-chün ti-pa chün tang-te sheng-huo* (Party life in the Eighth Army; n.p., n.d.).
13. Liu Pai-yü, *Huan-hsing tung-pei* (Traveling in the northeast; Shanghai, 1946), p. 55.

Ho Ch'eng-hsiang

(c.1910–   ; Shansi?). Former director, Religious Affairs Bureau, State Council; vice-governor, Kansu.

Ho Ch'eng-hsiang, a CCP leader in Manchuria in the early thirties, was director of the central government's Religious Affairs Bureau from 1951 to 1961. He was born about 1910 and is probably a native of Shansi.[1] A former PRC official who heard Ho speak at a meeting in 1953 claims that he is obviously a well-educated person.[2] He was already a CCP member in 1931 when he was working in the Communists' Manchurian Provincial Committee (Man-chou sheng-wei), the headquarters of which were located in Mukden. Little is known of Party work in Manchuria at that time. The paucity of information seems to derive from the underground situation in which the Party worked, in addition to a number of policy conflicts that arose between the China-directed and the Korean- or Manchurian-directed Party workers—conflicts that were an embarrassment to latter-day CCP historians. Following the "Mukden Incident" of September 1931, after which the Japanese quickly won control of Manchuria, the CCP headquarters in Manchuria was transferred to Harbin. Ho also moved to Harbin at this time. The situation for the Party in Manchuria became extremely difficult after the Japanese takeover, and most of its energies were concentrated on building an "anti-Japanese" guerrilla force (see under Chou Pao-chung). Ho remained in Manchuria until mid-1934 when he went to Juichin, Kiangsi, then the major area of Communist activity in China and the place where Mao Tse-tung and Chu Te had their headquarters.[3]

Virtually nothing is known of Ho's activities for the next 15 years. The one clue comes from his identification in late 1949 as a "former" deputy director of the First Office of the CCP's United Front Work Department. At that time the First Office was responsible for managing the CCP's relations with the various non-Communist political parties (e.g., the China Democratic League). In December 1949, shortly after the PRC Government was established, Ho was named to head the Staff Office of the Culture and Education Committee (CEC). The CEC, chaired by Kuo Mo-jo, was one of the four major committees under the Government Administration Council (the cabinet). Ho remained in this post until 1951, by which time he had been transferred to the task that was to occupy him for the next decade. He received his new assignment in January 1951 when he was appointed to head the newly created Religious Affairs Bureau. For administrative purposes the Bureau was subordinate to the government's CEC, but in fact it took orders directly from the Party's Propaganda Department until 1952 and from the United Front Department thereafter.

When Ho became head of the Religious Affairs Bureau one of the major tasks was the formation of China's various religious groups into national organizations. Most of this work took place between 1952 and 1954 by which time all of the major religious denominations had set up national organizations such as the Chinese Buddhist Association. Though specific details are lacking, Ho's assignment in the Bureau suggests that he played a major role in these endeavors. For example, he was frequently reported at important religious meetings, as in mid-1954 when he was present at the First National Christian Conference. Inferential evidence is also found in the fact that he was identified in June 1953 as deputy chief of the Religious Affairs Section of the CPPCC, and by the spring of the following year he had become the Section chief. Soon after the constitutional government was inaugurated at the First NPC session in September 1954, the Religious Affairs Bureau was placed directly under the State Council, with Ho continuing as the Bureau director. However, as already noted, the real authority over the Bureau rested with the Party's United Front Work Department.

Ho was most frequently reported in the national press during the mid-fifties, a period when the Chinese Communists made a concerted effort to cultivate friendly relations with non-Communist governments (e.g., Indonesia), many of which strongly supported their own religious groups. As a consequence, Ho was often in attendance when top PRC officials feted foreign religious officials visiting Peking. Foreshadowing these new ties, the Communists had established in May 1954 the Chinese People's Association for Cultural Relations with Foreign Countries (CPACRFC). Ho was named a Board member of the Association, a position he may still hold. Paralleling this "mass" organization, the central government established the Commission for Cultural Relations with Foreign Countries under the State Council in early 1958. Ho became a Commission member in March of that year and still retains this post. Moreover, he belongs to three "friendship" associations subordinate to the CPACRFC; he was elected a vice-chairman of the China-Poland Friendship Association (FA) upon its formation in September 1958, he has been a Council member of the China-Nepal FA since mid-1959, and he was also named to Council membership in the China-Latin America FA when it was established in March 1960. Beginning in late May 1958, Ho spent two months abroad leading a religious affairs delegation on a tour of Hungary, Czechoslovakia, East Germany, and the Soviet Union.

After working more than a decade in the Religious Affairs Bureau, Ho was replaced in July 1961 by Hsiao Hsien-fa whose antecedents are unknown. His services in the Bureau spanned the years when China's religious groups were permanently established along organizational lines by the Communists. Ho's role seems to have been mainly that of an administrator; policy decisions almost certainly came from more important Communists—men such as Chang Chih-i (q.v.), a deputy director of the Party's United Front Work Department. Within two months of Ho's removal, he was identified as a vice-governor of Kansu, an assignment probably made because of the heavy concentration of Muslims (Hui) in that province. He continues to be involved in affairs at least indirectly related to religious groups, as in October 1963 when he went to Ninghsia (another stronghold of Muslim peoples) to attend meetings celebrating the fifth anniversary of the establishment of the Ninghsia-Hui Autonomous Region, or in July 1964 when he spoke at a festival held to promote spare time culture among the minority peoples in Kansu.

---

1. Interview with former PRC official, Hong Kong, June 1964.

2. *Ibid.*

3. *Hung-ch'i p'iao-p'iao* (Red flag fluttering; Peking, 1957), V, 119–122.

Ho Lung

(1896–   ; Sang-chih, Hunan). PLA marshal;
vice-premier, State Council; chairman, Physical
Culture and Sports Commission, State Council;
member, CCP Politburo.

Ho Lung, one of the foremost Red Army
commanders, joined the CCP in 1927 immediately after the Nanchang Uprising in which he
played a leading role. From 1928 to 1935 he was
the commanding officer of Communist troops in
their base on the Hunan-Hupeh border, and after
completing the Long March he led one of the
three divisions in the Eighth Route Army
throughout the Sino-Japanese War. He figured
prominently in the conquest of both northwest
and southwest China during the civil war against
the Nationalists. After serving in the southwest
during the early PRC years, he transferred to
Peking where he became a vice-premier. He was
first elected to the Party Central Committee in
1945, and in 1956 he was advanced to the Politburo.

Ho was born in March 1896. His father, a
minor military officer, belonged to the Ko-lao-
hui (Elder brother society), an important secret
society dating from the beginning of the Ch'ing
dynasty. Such connections contributed to the
prestige of the family name in the Sang-chih
community, and Ho was able to capitalize upon
them when he entered upon his own military
career. Both Communist and non-Communist reports have stressed his peasant origins, an emphasis perhaps overplayed in view of the fact
that his father belonged to the lower ranks of
the official class. Ho received no formal education, and as late as the 1930's he was still only
semi-literate. In his youth he was a cowherd in
his native hsien, a poor, undeveloped, and
sparsely settled region of northwest Hunan.
Peasant unrest had long been prevalent there,
and this intimately affected Ho's family. Two of
his sisters were Communist activists who were
killed in civil strife; one, a guerrilla fighter, was
killed in Hunan in 1934. A brother and Ho's
first wife were also killed.

Ho's early career treads that narrow line between bandit and revolutionist. One account
(based on interviews with Ho's colleagues in
Yenan during the Sino-Japanese War) claims
that an uncle had been killed by the local magistrate for tax defaults and that to avenge this
death Ho murdered the magistrate and "so became an outlaw."[1] This took place in Ho's twentieth year, and for the next two years he lived
the life of a bandit in rural areas. About 1918
he joined a provincial army in Hunan and rose
to the position of divisional commander. Sometimes described as a modern Robin Hood who
never enriched himself nor harmed the poor, Ho
had become an important local military figure
by the mid-1920's. In 1925 he was garrison com-

mander in a small town in northwest Hunan, an
area where he established a Communist guerrilla
base a few years later. In that same year a KMT
"propaganda committee" was sent to Ho's area
to try to win him over to the Nationalist cause.
Heading the committee was one of Ho's relatives,
Chou I-ch'ün (q.v.), a Whampoa graduate and
a CCP member. The attempt was successful; Ho
left Hunan and joined the Nationalist armies,
retaining Chou to head a KMT training school
in his new command. These initial contacts with
the KMT brought Ho into close touch with the
CCP, because many of the training school students were Communists.[2]

In the National Revolutionary Army, Ho successively commanded a regiment, the First Division of the Ninth Army, the Independent 15th
Division, and the 20th Army. The last two commands were subordinate to Chang Fa-k'uei's
Fourth Army (later redesignated the Second
Front Army), which was one of the major
Nationalist units on the Northern Expedition,
which began in mid-1926. By the end of that
year Ho was posted in the Wuhan area, and in
the spring of 1927 he was among those who
moved north with Chang to Honan on the so-
called Second Northern Expedition. However,
Chang soon returned to the Yangtze Valley, and
in July 1927 most of his troops were in north
Kiangsi between Nanchang and Kiukiang (Chiu-
chiang); Ho's 20th Army was concentrated between Kiukiang and Wu-hsueh (on the north
bank of the Yangtze nearby Kiukiang). CCP
cooperation with the right wing of the KMT
had ended in April 1927 with Chiang Kai-shek's
anti-Communist coup, and in mid-July the Communists' tenuous alliance with the left-wing KMT
government in Wuhan collapsed. The state was
thus set for the bold Communist counter-stroke:
the Nanchang Uprising.

Ho's 20th Army arrived in Nanchang on July
26, and on the following days he took part in
planning the revolt. Together with Yeh T'ing
(q.v.), then commander of the 24th Division,
Ho was one of the key leaders of the August
First uprising, the date celebrated as the birth
of the Red Army. A 25-member Revolutionary
Committee was immediately established, and to
preserve the illusion of a combined CCP and
KMT government, it included Chang Fa-k'uei,
as well as prominent members of the left-KMT
such as Mme. Sun Yat-sen and Ho Hsiang-ning
(the widow of KMT leader Liao Chung-k'ai).
Ho was a member of the Revolutionary Committee, as well as its seven-member Presidium.
Subordinate to the Presidium, he was one of the
members of the Military Directorate (ts'an-mou-
t'uan). Most important, he was made general
commander (tsung-chih-hui) of the reorganized
military units, and his colleague Yeh T'ing was
made front-line general commander. In the new
order of battle, Ho's 20th Army had three

divisions (one of which was commanded by Chou I-ch'ün), Yeh T'ing's 11th Army also had three divisions, but Chu Te's so-called Ninth Army consisted of only one regiment. The overall force consisted of some 20,000 men, and again, in keeping with the theory that it was truly the representative of the KMT, it retained the title of the Second Front Army.[3]

Ho had little opportunity to exercise his authority during the brief period (five days) that the Communists held Nanchang, but when they were defeated there and moved south to Kwangtung he took an important part in directing military operations.[4] Chang Kuo-t'ao, who also made the march, described Ho's 20th Army as an "old-fashioned army which showed sympathy" toward the Communists but which was by no means well disciplined. Chou I-ch'ün provided a more detailed description: it was composed of "five regiments of old soldiers" (dating from the period of Chang Fa-k'uei's command), a "sixth regiment of entirely new soldiers" whose officers had been "conscripted by force," a "four-battalion Training Regiment . . . composed of newly recruited students," plus another "two battalions recruited from reserves at Nanchang whose officers were all Whampoa students."

Ho and his colleagues marched from Nanchang through Fu-chou and Lin-ch'uan in Kiangsi where they held a conference which discussed the next stage of the route to follow. Chou I-ch'ün and others favored a course through central Kiangsi along the Kan River and from there to Canton. But Ho and his supporters wanted to follow a more easterly route along the Kiangsi-Fukien border where the terrain might afford greater protection and where it was hoped that peasants would feed and supply their men. The armies marched according to Ho's proposal (although this was later judged to have been a mistake), passing through Ning-tu and Juichin. When they reached Juichin on August 19, Ho decided to join the CCP.

From Juichin the army made one thrust into Hui-ch'ang to the south, then turned east into Fukien, passing through T'ing-chou (Ch'ang-t'ing) and down the Han River into Kwangtung. After moving through San-ho-pa, where Chu Te and Chou Shih-ti remained as a rear guard force (see under Chou Shih-ti), they captured Swatow toward the end of September. At least one Russian adviser was with Ho's army, and he had sided with Ho on the question of taking the route through eastern Kiangsi and Fukien. Chou I-ch'ün calls him Chi-kung (Zigon). Zigon, also known as Kumanine, was a Russian agent active in south China who was arrested by the Nationalists in December 1927.[5] Swatow was held only a few days before the Communist troops suffered a severe defeat. With some remnants from his 20th Army, Ho escaped to Lu-feng on the Kwangtung coast where P'eng P'ai (q.v.) was

organizing peasants into a small Communist soviet. The group of Communists who gathered there by early October 1927 included Ho, Chang Kuo-t'ao, Li Li-san, Lin Po-ch'ü, Liu Po-ch'eng (qq.v.), T'an P'ing-shan, and P'eng P'ai (q.v.). From Lu-feng Ho went to Hong Kong with Liu Po-ch'eng and Lin Po-ch'ü. At about this time the Party Center had already conducted its postmortem on the Nanchang Uprising and the march south to Kwangtung. Most of the blame was placed at the feet of those most directly concerned with Party affairs, but military commanders Yeh T'ing and Ho were also criticized for a number of errors in tactics and strategy.[6]

At this juncture Ho sought permission to go to the Soviet Union,[7] but instead he was sent to Shanghai, and from there to Wuhan. The Communists were then attempting to spark peasant uprisings in various parts of central and south China, and thus the Party Center ordered Ho, together with Hsu T'e-li (q.v.), Chou I-ch'ün, Kuo Liang, and Liu Chih-hsun, to proceed to Hunan to organize peasant guerrilla forces.[8] All of them had been with Ho during the Nanchang Uprising and the subsequent events. Because of illness, Hsu was not able to accompany Ho. Kuo, a 1922 graduate of the Hunan Normal School and a colleague of Mao Tse-tung, was made secretary of the CCP Hunan-Hupeh-Kiangsi Special Committee, but he was almost immediately arrested and then executed (March 1928). Liu Chih-hsun, another colleague of Mao and the former secretary-general of the Hunan Peasants' Association, did not immediately go with Ho, but he joined him later and was killed in Hupeh in 1933.

Ho began his operations in early 1928 with only a handful of men, some of them from the Ko-lao-hui.[9] By July 1929 he had 500 men under his control, and in the next month he and K'uang Chi-hsun from east Szechwan were able to set up a "soviet district."[10] (K'uang later became an important commander in the Oyüwan area—see under Hsu Hsiang-ch'ien.) Not long after this a partisan leader named Tuan Te-ch'ang (killed in 1933) organized a "government" in the vicinity of Lake Hung in southern Hupeh.[11] Tuan was cooperating with Chou I-ch'ün, Ho's relative, who was organizing partisan units farther to the west in Hupeh, and together they established the Sixth Red Army. By 1930 Ho was head of the Fourth Red Army (often, but erroneously, referred to as the Second Army), and in July of that year all these units were brought together to form the Second Red Army Corps under Ho's command. This took place at Kung-an, located on the south bank of the Yangtze River in southern Hupeh. According to a highly detailed account of these events published in the JMJP (February 1, 1962), Chou I-ch'ün's area in west Hupeh controlled over 10 hsien, and Ho's area on the Hunan-Hupeh border controlled six or seven. With this merger, the area became known as the West Hunan-Hupeh (Hsiang-o-hsi) Border Region (or "soviet").

Immediately after the formation of the Second Army Corps, Ho was ordered by Li Li-san (q.v.), then the dominant Party leader, to move against Wuhan in coordination with troops from the Hupeh-Honan-Anhwei (Oyüwan) base. At the same time Mao Tse-tung and Chu Te were supposed to capture Nanchang and P'eng Te-huai was to assault Changsha. Except for P'eng, who held Changsha for a few days from the end of July 1930, the grandiose Li Li-san plan soon collapsed and shortly thereafter Li fell from power and was "exiled" to Moscow. Ho's drive against Wuhan had ended in failure, and in a short time he witnessed his area of control shrinking to only two or three hsien in west Hunan. However, within the next half year or so he was able to expand his base until, in the spring of 1931, it included seven hsien and apparently a restoration of Communist strength around Lake Hung in southern Hupeh.[12]

In the period after mid-1930, Chou I-ch'ün directed political affairs in the West Hunan-Hupeh area, but then over the winter of 1930–31, after Li Li-san had been dismissed from top CCP leadership, the Party headquarters sent Teng Chung-hsia (q.v.) to take charge of political work. A former important labor leader who had just completed two years of study in the Soviet Union, Teng went to west Hunan soon after his return to China, but it is not clear what his relations were with the groups at Party headquarters then involved in the power struggle for Li's succession. After joining Ho, Teng remained in charge of political work for only a short time. His stay there coincided with some of the important advances made by Ho's army in the Lake Hung region, but there were also strategic retreats which were not approved by the Party headquarters in Shanghai. Late in 1931 Teng came under attack for his political direction of operations in the West Hunan-Hupeh Soviet. He was accused of "opportunism," a criticism stemming from his having favored relinquishing the base around Lake Hung, and at about this time he was retired from Ho's base.[13]

In the meantime, in March 1931, another political emissary was sent to join Ho. The new man was Hsia Hsi (q.v.), who was a leading member of the "28 Bolsheviks" faction, which had taken over control of the Party Center in early 1931. Hsia established the CCP Central Sub-bureau for the West Hunan-Hupeh Soviet, and as head of this organ he controlled both political and military affairs. In the same month that Hsia arrived, Ho's Second Corps was redesignated the Third Red Army, and it was not until 1934 that it reverted to the Second Army Corps. It is not known what relationship Hsia had with Teng Chung-hsia, but because the stay of the two political emissaries coincided for a time, it may have been some of Hsia's reports which caused Teng to be retired from the area under a political cloud later that year. Hsia's relationship to Chou I-ch'ün is clearer: he shunted him aside to lesser tasks, and soon thereafter Chou was killed while on an inspection trip (May 1931).

According to the more conservative of Communist estimates, Ho's troop strength was upwards of 20,000 men by the time Chiang Kai-shek opened the Fourth Annihilation Campaign in June 1932. The first three campaigns had been largely confined to the Red bases in Kiangsi and Fukien, but now, especially at the start of the campaign, the main targets of attack were the two Communist soviets that threatened the Wuhan area, the Oyüwan Soviet (see under Chang Kuo-t'ao) and the West Hunan-Hupeh Soviet of Ho Lung. The height of Ho's expansion came about August 1932 when his troops made their way from the Lake Hung area and vanguard units reached the vicinity of Wuhan to make contact with units from the Fourth Front Army from Oyüwan, thereby threatening Wuhan in a pincer-like movement from the north and south. But the tide began to turn in the Nationalists' favor by the fall of 1932. By mid-September Ho's forces had been driven back into the Lake Hung area where they were regrouped after having been overextended and badly shattered. Ho began a trek of many months, which took his forces through western Hupeh to southern Honan, then into southern Shensi, and eventually back again to the west Hunan-Hupeh border where, in early 1933, the Red forces again occupied Sang-chih in northwest Hunan and Ho-feng across the border in southwest Hupeh. Half a year later, in mid-1933, Ho's troops were driven from Sang-chih and Ho-feng; they moved in a southwest direction and established a new base in four hsien in northeast Kweichow.

Throughout this period Hsia Hsi, still the secretary of the Party Sub-bureau, was with Ho's troops, and in orthodox Maoist histories the many setbacks suffered by Ho were uniformly attributed to the series of "errors" on Hsia's part. Hsia's alleged mistakes in leadership are set in contrast with the "correct" policies advocated by Ho, Chou I-ch'ün, and still another political officer, Kuan Hsiang-ying (q.v.). Kuan had come to the area sometime over the winter of 1931–32 and ultimately came to be the political commissar of Ho's army. Kuan was apparently on good terms with Ho, and although the two men had not worked together before, their close working relationship endured until Kuan's death in 1946. Ho was primarily a military leader in these years, but he was elected to the Central Executive Committee (CEC), the leading political organ of the Chinese Soviet Republic established in November 1931 in Juichin at the First All-China Congress of Soviets.

He was re-elected to the CEC at the second congress held in January–February 1934, but there is no indication that he attended either congress. In addition to CEC membership, at the first congress Ho was also named a member of the CEC's Central Revolutionary Military Council, a post he held at least as late as 1937.[14]

The units led by Ho and Kuan, which were now known again as the Second Army Corps, were headquartered in Yin-chiang hsien in northeast Kweichow in October 1934 when they were joined by the Sixth Red Army Corps, led by Jen Pi-shih, Hsiao K'o, and Wang Chen (qq.v.). The Sixth Corps had been driven from its Hunan-Kiangsi border base several weeks earlier. The two units merged to form the Second Front Army, and under the new command structure, Ho was made the commander, Jen Pi-shih the political commissar, and Kuan Hsiang-ying the deputy political commissar. (Soon after this Ho and Hsiao K'o married sisters from Hunan, who had probably been guerrilla fighters in their armies.) In November 1934 the Second Front Army moved eastward into Hunan, but when they were unable to withstand KMT attacks in April 1935, they moved north into the western sector of Hupeh. During the course of these maneuvers they established the Hunan-Hupeh-Szechwan-Kweichow base (often described as a "soviet"), and Jen Pi-shih, already a Politburo member, was made the secretary of the CCP Sub-bureau for the four-province base.

While Ho and Jen were attempting to expand their base, there was apparently some degree of cooperation with the First Front Army, which had left Kiangsi in the fall of 1934 on the Long March. According to a contemporary description of the Long March (written before the march was completed and published in a Comintern journal), the battles fought in Kweichow by the Chu-Mao First Front Army in the early months of 1935 helped to relieve the pressure on Ho's men to the northeast.[15] When Mao's troops arrived in north Shensi in October 1935, Ho's main forces were once again in northwest Hunan, in and around Ho's native Sang-chih. In the next month the Second Front Army set out on its own leg of the Long March, and after moving south and east in Hunan, they doubled back and followed much of the route that Mao's troops had used, although in their northward march through Yunnan and Sikang they took a more westerly course. In June 1936 in Kan-tzu, Sikang, Ho's troops met the Fourth Front Army of Chang Kuo-t'ao and Hsu Hsiang-ch'ien (who had been joined by Chu Te and Liu Po-ch'eng from Mao's armies), which had gone there a year earlier. One source estimates that Ho's Second Front Army left Hunan in 1935 with 40,000 men, but by the time it reached Sikang a half year later the number had been reduced to 15–20,000.[16]

When the Second Front Army reached Chang Kuo-t'ao's encampment in Sikang, there was a dispute about future strategy. Orthodox Maoist histories link Ho with Jen Pi-shih, Kuan Hsiang-ying, and Chu Te for having displayed "persistent efforts . . . in the face of Chang Kuo-t'ao's opposition," which enabled them to bring their combined forces north to join Mao's units in Shensi.[17] The two armies left Sikang in July 1936, and toward the end of the year they arrived in Shensi. Ho's troops were posted in the area around Yao-hsien and Fu-p'ing, some 30 miles north of Sian, the provincial capital.[18] Then, immediately after the outbreak of the Sino-Japanese War in mid-1937, the Communists regrouped their forces into the Eighth Route Army, which consisted of three divisions. Ho was placed in command of the 120th Division, which was composed principally of the troops he had led on the Long March. Kuan Hsiang-ying served as Ho's political commissar; Hsiao K'o was division deputy commander and concurrently commander of one of the division's two brigades; Wang Chen headed the other brigade; and Chou Shih-ti was Ho's chief-of-staff.

In September 1937 Ho's division crossed the Yellow River into Shansi and moved to the northern part of the province to engage the advancing Japanese armies. Ho's troops took part in a number of battles in the earliest days of the war, but as the Japanese moved in additional troops, Ho settled into northwest Shansi (west of the rail line from Ta-t'ung to Taiyuan) where the 120th Division was headquartered throughout the war. He had begun the war with some 15,000 men, but within a few months he reportedly tripled this figure through enlistments from local peasants.[19] In the earliest years of the war, Ho's troops worked in rather close cooperation with the troops under the command of Shansi Governor Yen Hsi-shan, but by the winter of 1939–40 this collaboration had ended and thereafter Ho's troops operated independently in northwest Shansi (see under P'eng Shao-hui and Lo Kuei-po). In the meantime, important units under Ho's command moved eastward into Hopeh in 1938–39 (see under Sung Shih-lun and Hsiao K'o), and Ho himself was in Hopeh from the end of 1938 to 1940 where he was sent to assist the Third Column, led by Lü Cheng-ts'ao (q.v.), in battles against the Japanese, as well as a series of clashes fought against KMT-led guerrilla units.[20]

In addition to the troops moved eastward into Hopeh, other units from the 120th Division moved northward into Suiyuan, most notably a detachment led by Li Ching-ch'üan (q.v.). This laid the groundwork for the formation of the Shansi-Suiyuan Liberated Region and the parallel Military Region. Ho commanded the Military Region from 1940, and in the same year the Communists began to form what was called the

Joint Defense Command for the Shansi-Suiyuan and the Shensi-Kansu-Ninghsia regions. Ho became head of the Joint Command and thus spent most of the final years of the war in Yenan, while Lü Cheng-ts'ao was sent to replace him as commander of the Shansi-Suiyuan Military Region in 1943. In October 1942 Ho was elected a member of the Northwest Shansi Administrative Office,[21] a governmental organ, but this appears to have been a nominal post, and in any case Lin Feng (q.v.) was the chief Communist official in northwest Shansi in the latter war years. (Other important events in the history of Ho's 120th Division are dealt with in the biography of Wang Chen.)

By the end of the war Ho had emerged as something of a legend—one fed by accounts which Ho and his colleagues gave to Westerners who seem to have been intrigued by his rise from bandit to commander in the Red Army. Most such descriptions emphasize his personal bravery in battle; one account, for example, claims that when Ho received orders in 1938 to "threaten" Japan-held Taiyuan, he personally sneaked into the city to investigate the Japanese fortifications.[22] His value as a troop commander was given recognition when the CCP met for its Seventh Congress in Yenan from April to June 1945. Ho served on the Congress presidium (steering committee) and was elected one of the 44 full members of the Central Committee. In the postwar years he remained in northwest and north China as commander of the Shansi-Suiyuan PLA until 1948 and of the Northwest PLA in 1948–49. Aside from the primary task of garrisoning the Communist capital at Yenan, in the months immediately after the war, troops under Ho's jurisdiction moved in force into northernmost Shansi to secure the route for Communist troops and cadres then being moved into Manchuria. By the late summer of 1946 he had some 60,00 troops around Ta-t'ung, a vital rail center in north Shansi.[23] In March 1947, not long after the collapse of the cease-fire agreement between the Communists and the KMT, Yenan fell to the Nationalists. The Communists had anticipated the attack on Yenan and made no effort to defend the city. Rather, Ho fought a series of delaying actions in the Yenan area which were designed to tie down the maximum number of Nationalist troops. This, in effect, continued to be his strategy for the next year as his troops campaigned in Shensi, Shansi, and Suiyuan.

In 1948, as Nationalist strength in the north and northwest steadily diminished, the Communists stepped up their attacks. In cooperation with P'eng Te-huai (then Ho's superior), Ho took part in campaigns in Shensi that resulted in the recapture of Yenan in the spring and the isolation of Sian, the provincial capital. A year later some of Ho's troops took part in the capture of Taiyuan, a fierce struggle fought in collabora-

tion with troops under the North China PLA (see under Hsu Hsiang-ch'ien). Taiyuan fell in late April, and a month later Ho's troops marched into Sian. With the capture of these two key provincial capitals, serious Nationalist resistance in Shansi and Shensi came to an end. During this period Ho was also president of the Northwest Military and Political Academy and chairman of the Finance and Economics Committee of the Shensi-Kansu-Ninghsia Border Region Government. However, in view of his active command of troops in the field, it appears that both posts were largely nominal.

When Sian fell to the Communists in May 1949, Ho was named chairman of the Sian Military Control Commission. He apparently remained there until September when, as the senior representative of the First Field Army (the new name for the Northwest PLA), he went to Peking to attend the inaugural session of the CPPCC, the organization which brought the PRC into existence on October 1. Ho served on the standing committee of the CPPCC presidium (steering committee) and delivered a brief speech. In the new central government he was named a member of the Central People's Government Council, the top political organ of the PRC until it was abolished in 1954. He was also made a member of the People's Revolutionary Military Council; he was a vice-chairman of this body for a brief time in 1954 (June–September) before it too was abolished. Ho returned to the northwest immediately after the central government was created. However, a few weeks later Ho led units of the First Field Army into southwest China in a campaign coordinated with Liu Po-ch'eng's Second Field Army, which was converging on the area from the east. By the end of the year, all of southwest China (except Tibet) was under Communist control, and the Nationalists had transferred their seat of government to Taiwan.

When most of the southwest was consolidated under the Communists by early 1950, the Southwest Military Region (SWMR) was established. The principal positions fell to the three leading Communists in the region—Ho Lung, Liu Po-ch'eng, and Teng Hsiao-p'ing. Ho became the SWMR commander and Liu was commander of the Second Field Army, responsible for Szechwan, Kweichow, Yunnan, Sikang, and, later, Tibet. Teng Hsiao-p'ing was political commissar of both the Military Region and the Second Field Army. Similarly, these three men assumed the principal assignments in the regional government for the area, the Southwest Military and Administrative Committee (known as the Southwest Administrative Committee from 1953 to 1954). When the SWMAC was established in July 1950 at Chungking, Liu Po-ch'eng became the chairman, and Ho and Teng became two of the vice-chairmen.

Ho spent most of the early fifties in the southwest, but on occasion he went to Peking for meetings of the CPGC or the CPPCC. He has been credited by the Communists with having "personally planned" the military expedition into Tibet, which began in late 1950 (although he himself did not lead troops into Tibet.)[24] Like most prominent Communist leaders, he also held nominal assignments in the various "mass" organizations in the early years of the PRC; from 1949 to 1954 he was an Executive Board member of the Sino-Soviet Friendship Association, and when a southwest chapter was formed in February 1951, he became its chairman. Aside from his military duties, he received his most important assignment in the southwest in the fall of 1952 when he succeeded Teng Hsiao-p'ing (who had been transferred to Peking) as secretary of the Party's Southwest Bureau. At this same time he was also appointed to the newly established Physical Culture and Sports Commission in the central government, a position to which he devoted more of his time after his transfer to Peking in 1954.

In mid-1954 Ho was relieved of all his assignments in the southwest and transferred to Peking where he has since worked. As a deputy from the PLA he attended the inaugural session of the First NPC in September 1954 when the constitutional government came into being. (He also served as a PLA deputy to the Second and Third NPC's, which opened in 1959 and 1964, respectively.) With the reorganization of the central government in 1954, Ho became a vice-premier of the State Council and a vice-chairman of the less important military advisory body that replaced the PRMC, the National Defense Council. He continues to hold both posts. A year later, in September 1955, his long military career was given recognition when the PRC for the first time awarded national military honors and established military ranks. Ho was given the three top awards, the August First, the Independence and Freedom, and the Liberation Orders, and he was also made one of the 10 marshals.

At the Party's Eighth Congress in September 1956, Ho was re-elected to the Central Committee, and at its First Plenum, held the day after the Congress adjourned, he was elected a member of the Politburo. Aside from Marshal Ch'en I (whose duties as foreign minister have taken him abroad quite frequently), Ho is the most widely traveled member of the Chinese Communist military elite. He was abroad for the first time from October to December 1953 when he led a delegation to North Korea to "comfort" the Chinese troops still stationed there. In July–August of the following year he headed a group to Moscow to participate in a sports festival, and in mid-1955 he was in Warsaw leading a delegation sent there for the 10th anniversary of the establishment of the Polish People's Republic.

He led a similar group to Karachi in March 1956 to attend the inauguration of the Pakistani Islamic Republic, and en route home he stopped over in India where he conferred with leading officials, including Prime Minister Nehru. In November 1956 he embarked on what is probably his most important trip to date, accompanying Chou En-lai to southeast Asia on a good will mission. The delegation had visited North Vietnam, Cambodia, India, Burma, and Pakistan and was again in India when Chou and Ho were suddenly called back to Peking. Early in January 1957 they set out for Moscow, evidently to patch up difficulties following the outbreak of the Hungarian Rebellion in the fall of 1956. Stressing the theme of "socialist solidarity" in their public statements, Chou and Ho also made quick trips to Warsaw and Budapest before returning to Moscow for further talks with Soviet leaders. Then in the latter part of January they went directly from Moscow to Southeast Asia to resume their tour, visiting India, Afghanistan, Nepal, and Ceylon before returning home in February.

Ho was abroad once more in October–November 1960 when he spent three weeks in North Korea leading a military delegation, and a year later he led a group to East Germany to attend the 12th anniversary of the East German government. In June 1963 Ho was named to head a special committee to prepare for Chinese participation in athetic games under GANEFO auspices. GANEFO (Games of the New Emerging Forces) was set up in 1963 by Indonesia in response to the alleged discrimination against the Indonesians by the International Olympics Committee. The Chinese were quick to join GANEFO, and Ho, as head of the Sports Commission, was a fitting choice to lead the Chinese delegation to the First GANEFO, held in Indonesia in November 1963. In the following year, when the Chinese set up a permanent National Committee for the GANEFO (August 1964), Ho became honorary chairman. In November 1964 Ho was again in Moscow, this time as deputy leader of Chou En-lai's delegation to the 47th anniversary celebrations of the October Revolution.

Ho has also been a rather active participant in negotiations with visiting dignitaries, and in terms of domestic affairs he was frequently reported in the press during the 1950's and early 1960's in association with the highest leaders of state. His role in the military establishment after the mid-fifties has not been clear, but the fact that he was identified in early 1961 as a vice-chairman of the Party's highly important Military Affairs Commission indicates that he was then still a key member of the military elite. Ho's numerous activities were regularly reported in the press until late 1966 when, during the early phases of the Great Proletarian Cultural Revolution, he was suddenly attacked as an opponent of the Maoist leadership.

Ho has at least two children, a boy and a girl. The daughter, born in the mid-thirties, was a student in the mid-1950's at Peking University where she was said to have been on friendly terms with a number of foreign students.[25] In 1964 Hsueh Ming was identified as Ho's wife (and is not to be confused with the Hsueh Ming who has been an economic planning official in Manchuria since the early fifties).

Ho is generally and properly regarded as the military man-of-action, but some of his articles are worthy of note—particularly those published during the Sino-Japanese War. For the February 6, 1938, issue of Ch'ien-hsien (The front), published in Sian by the Eighth Route Army, he summarized the military situation in northwest Shansi. Articles of a broadly similar nature were published in Yenan in the Party's leading organ, Chieh-fang (Liberation), on August 5, 1939, and February 29, 1940. To commemorate Red Army Day (August 1) Ho wrote articles on the Nanchang Uprising and the subsequent growth of the Red Army for the JMJP of August 1, 1951, and August 1, 1958 (translated in CB 208 and 514); both pieces are standard Maoist interpretations. Another article on military affairs was reprinted in Ten Glorious Years (Peking, 1960), which was published to mark the 10th anniversary of the PRC.

---

1. Claire and William Band, Two Years with the Chinese Communists (New Haven, Conn., 1948), p. 244.

2. Edgar Snow, Red Star over China (New York, 1938), pp. 52–53.

3. Wei Hung-yun, ed., "Pa-i" ch'i-i (The August First uprising; Wuhan, 1957), pp. 8–25; Ti-erh-tz'u kuo-nei ko-ming chan-cheng shih-ch'i shih-shih lun-ts'ung (Accounts of the second revolutionary civil war; Peking, 1956), pp. 1–11.

4. C. Martin Wilbur, "The Ashes of Defeat," The China Quarterly, no. 18:3–54 (April–June 1964).

5. George Sokolsky, The Tinder Box of Asia (New York, 1932), p. 340.

6. Wilbur, pp. 38–44.

7. Ibid., p. 34.

8. Chou Shih-chao, Wo-men te shih-piao (Our model teacher; Peking, 1958), p. 54.

9. Snow, pp. 53–4.

10. Hung-ch'i p'iao-p'iao (Red flag fluttering; Peking, 1959), X, 58; Wu Min and Hsiao Feng, Tsung "wu-szu" tao Chung-hua jen-min kung-ho-kuo (From "May Fourth" to the birth of the People's Republic of China; Peking, 1951), p. 95.

11. Li Yu-shih, ed., Chung-kuo hsien-tai ko-ming yun-tung ku-shih (Episodes from China's modern revolutionary movement; Nanking, 1957), II, 16.

12. Tso-liang Hsiao, Power Relations within the Chinese Communist Movement, 1930–1934 (Seattle, Wash., 1961), p. 196; Wu Min and Hsiao Feng, p. 104.

13. Tso-liang Hsiao, p. 197.

14. Nym Wales, Inside Red China (New York, 1939), p. 343.

15. The Communist International, New York, special number, 13:130–131 (February 1936).

16. Edgar Snow, Random Notes on Red China, 1936–1945 (Cambridge, Mass., 1957), p. 100.

17. Hu Ch'iao-mu, Thirty Years of the Communist Party of China (Peking, 1952), pp. 36–37; Ho Kan-chih, A History of the Modern Chinese Revolution (Peking, 1960), pp. 272–273.

18. SCMM 297, p. 35; Wales, pp. 62–63.

19. Evans Fordyce Carlson, Twin Stars of China (New York, 1940), p. 118.

20. Lyman P. Van Slyke, ed., The Chinese Communist Movement: A Report of the United States War Department, July 1945 (Stanford, Calif., 1968), p. 74; Hung-ch'i p'iao-p'iao (Red flag fluttering; Peking, 1957), V, 228, 247.

21. K'ang-Jih chan-cheng shih-ch'i chieh-fang-ch'ü kai-k'uang (A sketch of the liberated areas during the Anti-Japanese War; Peking, 1953), p. 103.

22. Haldore Hanson, "Humane Endeavour" (New York, 1939), p. 286.

23. Lionel Max Chassin, The Communist Conquest of China (Cambridge, Mass., 1965), p. 87.

24. SCMP 2854, p. 2.

25. Interview with a Western student formerly at Peking University; San Francisco, June 1962.

Ho Meng-hsiung

(1903–1931; Hsiang-t'an, Hunan). Early labor leader; alternate member, CCP Central Committee.

Ho Meng-hsiung, one of the earliest members of the CCP, was a prominent labor leader in the first decade of the Communist movement in China. In 1930–31 he was deeply involved in a bitter struggle for power against two other major factions in the CCP. This led to his expulsion from the Party and, soon afterwards, to his arrest and execution in early 1931.

Ho was born in Hsiang-t'an, the capital of the hsien in east Hunan which is the birthplace of Mao Tse-tung. After graduating at age 16 from a higher primary school in Hsiang-t'an, he went to live with an uncle in Peking, who was then a member of parliament. Ho audited classes at Peking University where he became involved in the May Fourth Movement, which broke out first in Peking in May 1919. He seems to have come quickly under the influence of the more extreme leftist-minded students at Peking University, and he belonged to the group that included Chang Kuo-t'ao, Li Ta-chao, Teng Chung-hsia, and Lo Chang-lung (qq.v.), men who were active in forming a group to study Marxism and who became Party members as soon as the CCP was founded in 1921. Along with Lo, Teng, and others, he belonged to the Society for the Study of Marxism, which was officially formed at the University soon after the CCP was founded in Shanghai; again with Teng and Lo he was drawn into the labor movement about the time that he joined the CCP. In 1922 Ho helped organize the badly paid railway workers on the Peking-Hankow Railroad. Later he is credited with having taken the lead in organizing the union for railway workers on the Peking-Suiyuan rail line.[1]

When the CCP met for its Second Congress in Shanghai in July 1922, Ho was politically allied with Chang Kuo-t'ao, Lo Chang-lung, and for a time with the Party head, Ch'en Tu-hsiu. He was opposed by two of his former university colleagues, Li Ta-chao and Teng Chung-hsia, over the hotly debated issue before the Congress: whether or not to ally with the KMT. A year later, at the Third CCP Congress, when the decision was taken to form the alliance with the KMT, Chang was still opposed, Ch'en Tu-hsiu had changed his vote, but the records do not reveal where Ho stood.

In the next few years, when his activities are not recorded, Ho probably continued to work in the labor movement. He may have moved from Peking to Shanghai about 1923 when northern warlord Wu P'ei-fu put down the strikes on the Peking-Hankow Railroad and made it very difficult to organize railway workers in north China. By 1927 he had emerged as an important member of the Kiangsu Provincial Party Committee, which he seems to have headed, at least before September 1930. He also took part in labor organizing in the important industrial concerns centered at Shanghai. As a member of the Kiangsu Committee, Ho was in charge of work with the peasants of the province in 1927, but his concurrent post as secretary of a district Party Committee in Shanghai absorbed more of his time. There are unconfirmed reports that in mid-1928 he attended the Sixth Congress in Moscow. Ho was made an alternate member of the CCP Central Committee either at the congress or sometime within the following two years.[2]

While continuing to work as a labor organizer, Ho became increasingly influential in the Kiangsu Provincial Party Committee. After the Sixth Party Congress the CCP was torn by internal dissension, largely over the work of the controversial Li Li-san (q.v.), who had come away from the Sixth Congress as head of the Party Propaganda Department. Li's "highhanded behavior" in his efforts to control all the CCP organizations by his own machine began to meet stiff opposition from several quarters, not only from his colleagues in China but also from the Russians and the Comintern. One of Li's most vociferous opponents was the Kiangsu Provincial Committee (with Ho as one of its leaders), which "continued in its unruly tradition and frequently took issue with the Li Li-san leadership."[3] Then in the spring of 1930 the Comintern sent Pavel Mif, the chancellor of Sun Yat-sen University in Moscow, to China accompanied by some of his favorite Chinese students (who were sometimes known as the "28 Bolsheviks") to checkmate Li Li-san. At the time of their return the local Party committees in Shanghai, as well as the Kiangsu Provincial Committee, were fairly well controlled by Ho Meng-hsiung, who now began to be rivaled by Mif and his group as well as by Li Li-san and his followers.

The next years of Ho's career have been studied in some detail,[4] but because the documentation for the controversial episodes in which he was involved comes largely from CCP sources who were his opponents, much remains obscure. It appears that Ho openly opposed Li Li-san at least from early 1930 when the Kiangsu Provincial Committee held its second congress. He was again critical of his chief when Li called the important Conference of Delegates from the Soviet Areas in May and set up the Preparatory Committee for the All-China Soviet Congress. At the Shanghai conference Ho had one of his clashes with Li, but it was Li's policies that were adopted. Later that year Li's platform for a central Soviet government was criticized by the Comintern as partially Trotskyist in spirit.[5] Li continued to be victorious in his clashes with Ho through most of 1930, but meanwhile Ho's opposition was gathering supporters. In the summer certain Red armies directed by Li's headquarters in Shanghai unsuccessfully attempted to capture some of the important industrial cities in central China from stronger Nationalist forces. After taking Changsha, the capital of Hunan, at the end of July, the Communists were forced to evacuate the city on August 9, thereby losing many of their followers in the bloody battles. When the Party met in Shanghai on August 20 to consider these defeats, Ho not only attacked Li for his failure at Changsha but also accused him of "violating the Comintern line." Ho is also said to have denounced Li (evidently in his presence) at a meeting of Party secretaries from Shanghai on September 1. Among other things he accused Li of failure to build up a strong Red Army, and of having recruited some 70 per cent of his party membership from the peasantry, with a mere 5.5 per cent from labor.[6] This time Ho's attacks on Li struck home and on September 4 Ho was removed as secretary of the Central Shanghai District Committee. Presumably at this time he was also dismissed from his leading post in the Kiangsu Provincial

Committee, because in his letter of September 8, 1930, to the Party's central authorities he complained of having been demoted from all his positions and presented a 12-point criticism of the Li Li-san leadership. On matters of theory and policy these criticisms did not differ greatly from the criticism to be made two months later by the Comintern.[7] Ho Ch'ang, a Li Li-san supporter who later recanted, replaced him in the Provincial Committee.

With Li's position growing precarious, the central authorities (directed now by Ch'ü Ch'iu-pai) called the Third Plenum at Lu-shan, Kiangsi, on September 24, 1930. The Plenum met for four days, during which time the Li Li-san strategy was heatedly discussed. Ch'ü Ch'iu-pai and Chou En-lai (qq.v.), who had recently returned from Moscow to try to settle intra-Party disputes, both spoke at the Plenum. Because Ho had been stripped of his positions before the Plenum, he probably did not have a large part in its meetings. However, his challenge to the leadership could not have been overlooked and this may have been partly why Chou En-lai, who remained loyal to Li Li-san, persuaded Li that he would have to admit having made tactical, though not strategic, errors and indulge in at least some self-criticism in order to maintain his power.

Following the Third Plenum Ho's challenge to the CCP leadership continued with considerable vigor. In November the Party decided to act on the advice of the Comintern and dismiss Li Li-san, who was ordered to Moscow (see under Li Li-san). With Li out of the way tension between Ho Meng-hsiung and the Russian-returned student clique sharpened. The particulars about Ho's role in the controversy are difficult to uncover because they come from sources that are in themselves subject to prejudice—reports released by a Politburo in which the new Ch'en Shao-yü leadership and Li's supporters must still have been struggling for supremacy. From such sources it would appear that Ho had been forced to recant in October before Li was removed from his posts. Yet even with his apologies Ho had managed to make it clear that he objected to being called an opportunist and being left without work to do. Then in mid-December 1930, several weeks after Li had been dismissed, the Politburo apparently decided that Ho had been unjustly treated and earlier Party decisions inflicting penalties on him were reversed. Upon re-examining Ho's September 8 statement, the Politburo found it to be in line with Comintern views and its condemnation of Li's strategy to have been correct.

The Politburo reversal could not have been immediately implemented because on December 24, 1930, two weeks after the decision was made, Ho appears to have written to the Far Eastern Office of the Comintern complaining of having no work and asking that his previous statements concerning Li Li-san be made a matter of public record.[8] These were officially released early in January 1931 on the eve of the Fourth CCP Plenum held in Shanghai. However, it is not known whether or not Ho was reinstated in his former posts. If he was, it could only have been briefly, since he was expelled from the Party shortly thereafter.

Details of the Fourth Plenum are given in the biography of Lo Chang-lung, Ho's former colleague at Peking University who by this time had risen to be a leading figure in the All-China Federation of Labor as well as a Central Committee member. In brief, after putting up a determined struggle, Lo, Ho, and their followers were defeated by Ch'en Shao-yü and his Comintern-supported leadership. They subsequently withdrew from the Plenum and set up a separate organization of their own, whereupon the successful Ch'en Shao-yü group promptly expelled them from the Party.

While both Ho and Lo Chang-lung were actively engaged in organizing their separatists, Ho met with a "group of . . . older party members and trade unionists, and some younger men" in Shanghai on January 17, 1931.[9] It appears that the meeting dealt with the Preparatory Committee for the All-China Soviet Congress, because among the group were a number of left-wing writers who had been engaged in publicity work for the coming congress. However, Ho's presence suggests the separatist movement was also involved. Through a combination of circumstances that may cast suspicion on the Ch'en Shao-yü leadership, the British police learned of the meeting, interrupted it, and arrested 36 persons. They were turned over to the KMT and 25 of them were taken outside Shanghai to Lunghua and executed on February 7. Along with Ho Meng-hsiung the following also lost their lives: Lin Yü-nan; Li Ch'iu-shih (qq.v.); Jou Shih, a short-story writer and a founder of the League of Left-Wing Writers; Feng K'eng, an authoress who was on the Propaganda Committee of the Soviet Congress' Preparatory Committee; and Yin Fu, a left-wing poet.[10]

Although Ho had been expelled from the Party when he died, the Maoist "Resolution on Some Questions in the History of Our Party," which was adopted by the Seventh Plenum of the Central Committee in April 1945, stated that Ho, Lin Yü-nan, and Li Ch'iu-shih as well as many others had been wrongly condemned as "rightists" by the Ch'en Shao-yü leadership. It went on to say that they had performed "much useful work for the Party and the people" and after being arrested had "stood up firm to the enemy and became noble martyrs."[11]

1. *Selected Works of Mao Tse-tung* (London, 1956), IV, 341.

2. Modern China Project, Columbia University, New York, Howard L. Boorman, director.

3. Benjamin I. Schwartz, *Chinese Communism and the Rise of Mao* (Cambridge, Mass., 1951), p. 132.

4. Tso-liang Hsiao, *Power Relations within the Chinese Communist Movement, 1930–1934* (Seattle, Wash., 1961), chaps. 6, 7, and 9; T. A. Hsia, *Enigma of the Five Martyrs* (Berkeley, Calif., 1962), pp. 77ff.

5. Tso-liang Hsiao, p. 64.

6. *Ibid.*, p. 52.

7. *Ibid.*, p. 95.

8. *Ibid.*, pp. 95–96.

9. Harold R. Isaacs, *The Tragedy of the Chinese Revolution,* 2nd rev. ed. (Stanford, Calif., 1961), p. 334.

10. T. A. Hsia, pp. 4–5, 93.

11. *Selected Works of Mao Tse-tung,* p. 183.

Ho Shu-heng

(1874–1935; Ning-hsiang, Hunan). A CCP founder.

Ho Shu-heng was the oldest delegate present at the founding congress of the CCP in July 1921. He was never a significant Party leader, but he played a role of some importance in the early development of the Chinese Communist Movement in Hunan where he belonged to the small group of intimates of Mao Tse-tung. His record is still well regarded by the Party and his career is noteworthy as it illustrates the transition of the first CCP leaders from nineteenth-century China to the development of the Chinese Communist Movement. For two decades he remained in close association with Mao and was only separated from him after the Long March began in 1934.

Born in Ning-hsiang, the small industrial city a few miles west of Changsha, the Hunan capital, Ho had the traditional schooling before the 1911 Revolution. He passed the lowest rank of civil service examinations and gained the *Hsiu-ts'ai* degree in 1892, the year before Mao Tse-tung was born. During his formative years he became a close friend of Hsieh Chueh-tsai (q.v.), a radical intellectual who was some nine years junior to Ho and also from Ning-hsiang.

Ho was 37 when the 1911 Revolution took place and was then a teacher of Chinese literature. Just before the opening of the May Fourth Movement of 1919 he was a member of Mao Tse-tung's group in Changsha. There Mao and Ts'ai Ho-sen (q.v.) were organizing activities among the students and teachers of the First Normal School where Mao was a student between 1913 and 1918. His friends often met at the Ts'ai home where they planned the creation of the Hsin-min hsueh-hui (New people's study society), its membership mostly drawn from the First Normal School and the Hunan Students'

Union. Ho was one of the 13 members who officially brought the society into being on April 18, 1918. Hsiao San, Mao's official biographer, speaks of Ho as "the oldest among the early members" of the Hsin-min hsueh-hui.[1] After the May Fourth Movement began, the membership of the society grew to some 70 persons, a number of whom soon became Communists (see under Ts'ai Ho-sen). The organization aimed at strengthening China and training young intellectuals as future leaders. It was well-organized and continued to function for several years in Hunan, running regular programs, which included fortnightly meetings to discuss current affairs and specific problems of Chinese society. Its aggressive members often came into open opposition with the political authorities. After being society chairman for only a month, Mao left for Peking, but Ho remained to carry on in Hunan. When Mao returned to Hunan in mid-1920 Governor Chang Ching-yao, whom he had openly opposed, had just been replaced by T'an Yen-k'ai, an old associate of Sun Yat-sen. T'an was interested in reorganizing the provincial educational system and Mao was invited to teach at the First Normal School and to head the institution's primary school. He held these posts until the close of the 1922 school year. While Mao was in Changsha, Ho was one of his associates in a number of political events. In 1920 Mao and Ho prepared a petition on behalf of the Hunan Reconstruction Association, which was presented to Governor T'an. It called for the abolition of the post of military governor in Hunan and the establishment of a provincial constitution and democratic elections.[2] As a member of the New People's Study Society, Ho was a contributor to its publication, which was distributed from Mao's Wen-hua Bookstore in Changsha about 1921. Designed only for Society members, it was not for sale. It contained correspondence from Mao Tse-tung, Ts'ai Ho-sen, and others that discussed the questions of socialism and communism; its goal was to bring about social change not only in China but throughout the world.[3] In 1920 Ho also helped Mao organize a society for the study of Marxism, and this, like a number of similar groups then being organized in other provinces, provided the nucleus for the CCP.

Ho and Mao were the two delegates chosen from the Marxist group in Hunan to attend the founding congress of the CCP. All the orthodox Communist accounts agree that Ho was one of the men who founded the Party at its First Congress in Shanghai in July 1921. However, Chang Kuo-t'ao (among those who attended) has claimed that Ho had little grasp of the political questions that were to come before the delegates and that Mao contrived to send him back to Hunan before the Congress opened.[4] In any event Ho returned to Hunan in 1921 where he remained until 1927. Primarily an educator, he played a major role in the Hunanese school system, which proved to be a significant channel for spreading Communist propaganda because so many of the young teachers were Marxists. One of Ho's most notable contributions to Party work in the early twenties was in connection with the Self-Education College (Tzu-hsiu ta-hsueh), which he and Mao opened in Changsha in August 1921. The institution is described in the biography of Mao Tse-min who was a student there while Ho was on the faculty. The CCP used the school to convert a number of young Hunanese intellectuals to Marxism.

Following the break between the CCP and the KMT in mid-1927, Ho left for Moscow. In 1928, at the age of 54, he enrolled in Sun Yatsen University (known later as the Communist University of the Toilers of China). Among his classmates (also rather elderly) were Hsu T'e-li, Wu Yü-chang, and Lin Po-ch'ü (qq.v.).[5] After graduating in 1930, Ho returned to China and went to the Kiangsi Soviet where Mao Tse-tung and Chu Te had their headquarters. When the Chinese Soviet Republic was established in Juichin in November 1931 under the chairmanship of Mao, Ho was elected to the government's Central Executive Committee (CEC). He was also given the cabinet post of People's Commissar for Workers' and Peasants' Investigation. Half a year later, in mid-1932, Ho assumed another cabinet-level post when he became acting head of the CEC's Internal Affairs Department,[6] a position he held until mid-1933 when Liang Po-t'ai took over the post. It appears that Ho was active in training personnel in the central soviet areas; on one occasion in June 1932 he was described as the training supervisor of a group of "Soviet work personnel" when he delivered a report at their graduation exercises.[7] He was re-elected to the CEC at the Second All-China Congress of Soviets in January–February 1934, but at this time his post as People's Commissar for Workers' and Peasants' Investigation was given to Hsiang Ying (q.v.), who was also one of the two vice-chairmen of the Chinese Soviet Republic. Ho's loss of his cabinet post is almost certainly attributable to the fact that in 1933 he had been charged with following the so-called Lo Ming (q.v.) line.

Ho did not leave southeast Kiangsi in the fall of 1934 when the major portion of Mao Tsetung's forces embarked upon the Long March. At age 60 perhaps he was not up to the rigors that lay ahead of Mao's army. Instead he remained in the Kiangsi-Fukien area with the small group of leaders who were left behind (see under Chang Ting-ch'eng). Early in 1935 he was with Ch'ü Ch'iu-pai and Teng Tzu-hui (qq.v.) when the Communists were driven out of Kiangsi into the mountains of western Fukien. He was again with Ch'ü when the latter was captured by Nationalist troops, but refusing to be taken prisoner

he ended his life by jumping from a high cliff in the Communists' mountain retreat near Ch'ang-t'ing, Fukien.[8]

1. Emi Siao [Hsiao San], *Mao Tse-tung: His Childhood and Youth* (Bombay, 1953), p. 58.
2. Jerome Ch'en, *Mao and the Chinese Revolution* (London, 1965), p. 69.
3. Chow Tse-tsung, *Research Guide to the May Fourth Movement* (Cambridge, Mass., 1963), p. 99.
4. Modern China Project, Columbia University, New York, Howard L. Boorman, director; John E. Rue, *Mao Tse-tung in Opposition, 1927–1935* (Stanford, Calif., 1966), p. 295.
5. *Chung-kuo ch'ing-nien* (China youth), no. 12 (June 16, 1960), 14.
6. *Hung-se Chung-hua* (Red China; Juichin), June 16, 1932.
7. *Ibid.*
8. *Hu-nan ko-ming lieh-shih chuan* (Biographies of Hunan revolutionary martyrs; Changsha, 1952), pp. 82–83.

Ho Wei

(c.1910–   ; Honan). Former diplomat; minister of Education.

Ho Wei's 30-year career in the CCP has been exceptionally varied and includes service in the Red armies, the Party hierarchy, the diplomatic service, and the Ministry of Education. He was born about 1910 in a village near Ju-nan in southern Honan. His family enjoyed a better than average middle class income derived from land holdings. Unlike most Chinese Communists, he comes from a Christian family and was baptized into the Lutheran church. He also studied at Lutheran-sponsored schools and then took his degree in history from Hua-chung University, another missionary school, in Wuchang, Hupeh.

It was about 1935, while a student at Huachung University, that Ho joined the CCP. In that same year he went to Peking to help organize student demonstrations against the Japanese, an activity that was apparently connected with the December Ninth Movement (see under Li Ch'ang), which began in December 1935 when students in Peking staged large demonstrations in opposition to Japanese incursions into north China. He followed up his work in Peking by engaging in organizational work among students for the Party in Hankow in 1936–37 and then made his way to Shensi where he studied at the Anti-Japanese Military and Political Academy (*K'ang-ta*).

Ho spent at least part of the Sino-Japanese War serving as a battalion political commissar in the New Fourth Army (see under Ch'en I) in east-central China. In 1945, after hostilities ended, he was briefly active in Party circles in Hankow, an area with which he was familiar from his college days. However, when the civil war between the Nationalists and the Communists broke out in 1946, Ho was reassigned to the New Fourth Army, again serving as a political officer. Like many New Fourth Army officers, he took up political posts in areas in or near the operational sector of the Army as it swept over the mainland in 1949. In Ho's case, he served briefly in 1949 as acting secretary of the Hupeh Party Committee, as the ranking secretary of the Wuhan Party Committee, and as secretary-general of the Wuhan Military Control Commission following its occupation by the Communists in May 1949. However, he did not stay long in Hupeh but rather followed the Communist armies (presumably elements of Lin Piao's Fourth Field Army) as they advanced southward in the latter half of 1949.

Ho was assigned to Kwangsi where he was to remain for the next two and a half years. He served briefly as the secretary of the United Front Work Department of the South China Party Sub-bureau (responsible for Kwantung and Kwangsi), but his most important work in this period was in Kwangsi where he served in a wide variety of positions: 1950–1952: mayor of Kweilin; vice-chairman, Kweilin Military Control Commission; (ranking) secretary, Kweilin Party Committee; member, Kwangsi Provincial People's Government Council; 1951–1952: chairman, Land Reform Committee, Kwangsi Government; deputy-secretary, Kwangsi Party Committee; vice-president, Kwangsi People's Revolutionary University; chairman, Kwangsi Trade Union Council. Although Ho ranked below such senior Party veterans as Chang Yun-i and Ch'en Man-yuan (qq.v.) in Kwangsi affairs, he was among the more important provincial officials there from 1950 to 1952.

In mid-1952 Ho was transferred to Canton, south China's most important city and the headquarters of the South China Party Sub-bureau. He served briefly in 1952 as the second secretary of the municipal Party Committee but was promoted later in the year to the ranking secretaryship. In late December 1952 he also assumed the post of Canton mayor. Ho's transfer to Canton was apparently directly related to a serious case of mismanagement of an expensive organic fertilizer factory by Chu Kuang, a veteran Party member who had been serving as both acting mayor and acting Party secretary in place of Yeh Chien-ying (Yeh being occupied with higher-level duties in the South China Party Sub-bureau). The charges against Chu were aired in two important meetings of the Canton Party Committee held in March–April 1953, with Ho delivering the main attack on Chu's alleged mismanagement in Canton. Ho's charges were summed up with the statement that "Chu Kuang was to a considerable degree motivated by the ideology of the petty bourgeoisie, and this petty

bourgeois ideology had for a time replaced the ideology of the working class in assuming the major leadership in the Party, . . ."[1] (Although Chu Kuang was not purged from the Party and in fact has continued to hold a number of other positions in the government, his political career seems to have been permanently damaged by this case of mismanagement in Canton.)

In the same month that Ho assumed the mayoralty of Canton (December 1952), he was also identified as a member of the Standing Committee of the South China Party Sub-bureau having jurisdiction over Kwangtung and Kwangsi. Soon after, in January 1953, the regional governmental administration for the six provinces of Honan, Hupeh, Hunan, Kiangsi, Kwangtung, and Kwangsi was reorganized; formerly known as the Central-South Military and Administrative Committee, it was now changed to the Central-South Administrative Committee, with Ho named to membership on the new Committee. Other less significant positions that Ho held during his time in Canton include: 1952–1954: member, Executive Committee, Canton Federation of Trade Unions; member, Canton branch, China Peace Committee; 1954: chairman, Canton Committee for Discussing the Constitution of the PRC (adopted in September 1954).

In the fall of 1954, when the government constitution was promulgated, the central government underwent a reorganization at which time a number of provincial officials were called to Peking. Ho was among these and at this time (October 1954) entered into a new phase in his career when he was appointed as an assistant-minister of Foreign Affairs (one level below the vice-ministers). During the next three years he was often reported in the press media in activities normally attendant to such a position in the Foreign Ministry—conferring with many foreign visitors, taking part in negotiations with foreign diplomats and officials, and attending the innumerable banquets given in Peking. There is little to distinguish Ho's work in this period aside from the fact that he was a member of the Chinese team that negotiated with Polish counterparts in June 1955 as part of the Sino-Polish Scientific and Technical Joint Cooperation Commission, negotiations that led to the signing of a protocol on June 11 providing for continuing technological cooperation. In the following month he was named to the board of directors of the Chinese People's Institute of Foreign Affairs, a position he continues to retain.

In October 1957 Ho was removed as an assistant-minister of Foreign Affairs, thus paving the way for his assignment two months later as the ambassador to North Vietnam, one of Peking's most important posts abroad. Ho presented his credentials to Ho Chi Minh in Hanoi in January 1958 and then spent the next four and a half years in Vietnam—years that saw a dramatic escalation of the North Vietnam-supported war in South Vietnam. Perhaps owing to the proximity of Vietnam to China, Ho returned to Peking more frequently than most ambassadors that Peking sends abroad. Between 1958 and his recall in mid-1962, he returned to China four times; during three of these visits Ho took part in high-level negotiations between Chinese and Vietnamese leaders. He was also involved in important negotiations in Vietnam on several occasions, taking part in the talks in Hanoi during Premier Chou En-lai's visit in May 1960, when Marshal Yeh Chien-ying led a military mission there in December 1961, and when Foreign Trade Minister Yeh Chi-chuang led a trade mission to Hanoi that resulted in the signing of a protocol covering trade for 1962. Ho himself also signed trade, aid (from China to Vietnam), and cultural exchange agreements in January 1960 and April 1961.

It was during Ho's time in Hanoi that he became involved in the complex situation in neighboring Laos where pro-Communist, anti-Communist, and neutralist factions were fighting among themselves. In March 1961 a high Laotian official addressed an official note to Ho in Hanoi proposing the exchange of "economic and cultural missions" that would be "charged with the task of settling problems which may interest both countries." Ho immediately replied, expressing complete agreement. It was not until several months later (October 1961), however, that he was formally named as "Chief of the PRC Economic and Cultural Mission" in Laos. He arrived the following month in Xieng Khouang, Laos, where he presented his credentials to Prince Souvana Phouma, the prime minister. In effect, Ho can be considered as the first official envoy to Laos (although in formal diplomatic terms the first ambassador, Liu Ch'un, was not appointed until September 1962). Ho Wei, in fact, spent rather little time in Laos, although he returned there in January 1962 at which time he negotiated and signed two agreements, one providing for the construction of a highway to link Yunnan Province in China to the town of Phong Saly, long a Communist stronghold in Laos, and another agreement providing for civil air transport between China and Laos.

In late March 1962 Ho and his wife left Hanoi for home. He was formally removed as ambassador to Vietnam in July 1962, being replaced by Chu Ch'i-wen. In the following month he was identified as the second secretary of the Party Committee in his native Honan, serving there under First Secretary Liu Chien-hsun, an alternate member of the Party Central Committee. Rather little was reported about Ho's activities in Honan in the next two years, but this fact probably derives more from the paucity of source materials (in the wake of the Great Leap Forward and its aftermath) than from

Ho's apparent inactivity. In any event, in July 1964 he entered still another phase of his varied career when he was called to Peking to become the new minister of the Education Ministry. (In the previous month, June 1964, the "old" Ministry of Education had been divided into the ministries of Education and of Higher Education; the former minister of Education, Yang Hsiu-feng, was assigned to the new Ministry of Higher Education.) Later in 1964 Ho was elected from his native Honan to the Third NPC, which first met in December 1964–January 1965.

In 1965, Ho led two delegations abroad; the first of these was to Moscow for the 15th anniversary of the signing of the Sino-Soviet Treaty of Friendship, Alliance and Mutual Assistance. The other trip took place in August 1965 when he spent several days in Brazzaville for the second anniversary of what the Congolese call the "August Revolution," a revolt of 1963 that brought to power a government that was largely friendly to the PRC.

Ho has not apparently been a frequent contributor to the Party press. He did, however, write an article during his term of office in Hanoi for the Party's most important journal, *Hung-ch'i* (Red flag; issue of April 16, 1960), an article that described the achievements of the North Vietnamese government.

1. *CB* 253, p. 5.

Ho Ying

(c.1910–   ; Hainan Island, Kwangtung). Diplomat.

Ho Ying was one of the first diplomats the Chinese Communists sent to East Africa and is probably regarded in Peking as a leading specialist on this region. He was born about 1910 on Hainan Island. His career before 1949 is undocumented aside from the fact that he once lived in Malaya. By 1949 he was back in China serving as a division deputy political commissar with the Red Army; to have risen to this level Ho must have returned to China by at least the Sino-Japanese War period. By 1951 he was assigned to China's fledgling diplomatic corps, presumably because of his past experience abroad. His first assignment was a consul general (with the rank of minister) in Jakarta, a post he received in February 1951. In August 1951 he was given the concurrent position as minister-counselor of the PRC embassy in Indonesia. He returned to Peking late in 1951 but was not officially removed from his posts in Indonesia until August 1952.

It was also in August 1952 that Ho was made one of the deputy directors of the Asian Affairs Department of the Ministry of Foreign Affairs (MFA), a post that placed him under Department Director Ch'en Chia-k'ang (q.v.), a long-time colleague of Chou En-lai. Perhaps his most notable assignment while holding this position was as one of the negotiators of the Sino-Indian treaty regarding the status of Tibet (see under Chang Han-fu). The negotiations, led by Vice-foreign Minister Chang Han-fu, lasted from the end of December 1953 until the treaty was signed in Peking by Chang on April 29, 1954. Not long after, Ho was named as the ambassador to Mongolia where he succeeded Chi Ya-t'ai (q.v.). He was appointed in September 1954 and presented his credentials in Ulan Bator later that month.

Prior to Ho's tour in Mongolia, Sino-Mongolian relations had been relatively inactive. However, during his four-year stay in Ulan Bator, relations between Peking and Ulan Bator grew much closer. This was illustrated in several ways. For example, it was while Ho was in Mongolia that the first direct rail link between Peking and Ulan Bator was opened. This was known as the Tsining (Chi-ning)–Ulan Bator Railway, and when the rather elaborate ceremonies were held to celebrate the inauguration of the line in the closing days of 1955 and early January 1956, Ho was among those taking part. He was also an official member of the Chinese delegations to both the 12th and 13th Congresses of the Mongolian Party (November 1954 and March 1958), in each case under the leadership of Ulanfu, Peking's senior Mongol leader. Trade also increased sharply during Ho's time in Mongolia. For example, under the terms of a trade protocol that he signed in the Mongolian capital in February 1956, it was provided that Sino-Mongol trade in 1956 would be double that of 1955. A further indication of this trend was reported in the *JMJP* of October 4, 1957, which claimed that trade had risen nearly 40 times in 1956 when compared with 1952. But perhaps the most impressive indication of closer Sino-Mongol ties occurred under the terms of agreements negotiated in 1955 and 1956—large-scale Chinese aid to Mongolia was inaugurated, including the dispatch by China to Mongolia of an estimated 10,000 laborers to assist in a wide variety of construction projects.[1]

In August 1958 on the eve of his departure from Mongolia, Ho received the highest order bestowed by the Mongolian Government and early the next month was removed from his post. By early 1959 he was again working in a department within the MFA. Not long after his return from abroad, the Asian Affairs Department was divided into the First and Second Asian Affairs Departments. Ho was assigned as a deputy director of the First Department, the one devoted to the affairs of the non-Communist nations of Asia. He held this post for just one year; then in early 1960 was assigned to head the West Asian and African Affairs Department. Prior to this time,

this department had been one of the least active sections of the MFA. However, with the emergence in 1960 of many newly independent African countries, it rapidly emerged as one of the most important. Closely coinciding with Ho's appointment to this department, the China-Africa People's Friendship Association (April 1960) was created by the Chinese, with Ho being named to the Standing Committee. During the two years that he headed the West Asian and African Affairs Department, he frequently took part in negotiations with visitors from Africa. For example, he participated in talks with the Algerian president in October 1960 and with a visiting Nigerian economic delegation in June 1961.

In February 1962 Ho was named as Peking's first ambassador to Tanganyika, a nation with which China had established diplomatic relations in late 1961. He presented his credentials in Dar es Salaam in April 1962, and since that date has probably been the most important Chinese diplomat in East Africa. Following his arrival he negotiated the establishment of formal diplomatic relations with four other East African nations, the details of which require some elaboration. His first formal contact outside Tanganyika occurred in September 1962 when he was the official PRC representative to independence ceremonies in Burundi. However, because a Chinese Nationalist mission was also in Burundi, Ho departed—but not before issuing a press statement denouncing a United States' "two-Chinas" plot, while at the same time affirming Sino-Burundian friendship. However, 15 months later (December 1963), Ho was again in Burundi. On this occasion he successfully negotiated the establishment of formal diplomatic ties between the two nations. In the interim, he had succeeded in establishing diplomatic relations with three other nations, Uganda, Zanzibar, and Zambia. He performed this task vis-à-vis Uganda when he visited that country in October 1962; he subsequently became the first Chinese ambassador to Uganda (holding concurrently his post in Tanganyika), a position he held from April 1963 to April 1964. His task in Zanzibar was accomplished in December 1963 when he attended the independence ceremonies of that small island country. Not long after (April 1964), Tanganyika and Zanzibar merged to form Tanzania. After a short delay, Peking formally appointed Ho (July 1964) to head the Peking mission in this newly amalgamated nation, a position he continues to hold in 1965. In October 1964 Ho arrived in Lusaka, Northern Rhodesia, for independence ceremonies (after which this country became known as Zambia). Once again Ho succeeded in establishing diplomatic relations with this newly independent nation.

In January 1964 Ho made quick visits to both

Uganda and Kenya, apparently to prepare the way for Premier Chou En-lai (q.v.), who was making an extensive tour of Africa. However, the extremely unsettled political situation in East Africa (especially in Tanganyika where an abortive coup took place) forced Chou to postpone his visits to Uganda, Kenya and Tanganyika. But about a year later, Ho did participate in talks held in Dar es Salaam between Tanzanian President Julius Nyerere and Chou during the latter's visit in June 1965.

In addition to his visits to Uganda and Kenya in early 1964, Ho visited Nyasaland in March 1964, apparently attempting to lay the groundwork for recognition of the PRC after independence. Ho's mission to Nyasaland, however, was less than successful; when the new nation became independent in July 1964 (after which it was known as Malawi), the independence ceremonies were attended by a vice-minister of Foreign Affairs from Nationalist China, a fact vigorously denounced by the Chinese Communist press. Moreover, in September 1964, Malawi Premier Hastings Banda delivered a blistering attack on the Chinese Communists' interference in Malawian affairs in a speech before the Malawian parliament. He specifically accused Ho, then in neighboring Tanzania, of having tried to bribe members of the Malawi Government into forcing Banda to recognize the PRC.[2]

During his stay in Dar es Salaam, Ho has served as host for a large number of Chinese delegations that have visited East Africa. He has also negotiated agreements with his host country, one of the most notable, a protocol dealing with economic and technical cooperation, was signed in January 1965; at the same time he exchanged letters on the dispatch of Chinese experts and technicians to Tanzania. Ho has been called home on at least two occasions; the more important of these took place in February 1965 when he was in China to serve as one of the hosts for Tanzanian President Julius Nyerere, then on a state visit to the PRC.

Ho, who is accompanied by his wife and a teenage daughter in Tanzania, is known to have a fair understanding of English.[3] Unlike many Chinese ambassadors elsewhere, he circulates rather freely in the Tanzanian capital and has numerous contacts, not only with Tanzanian officials, but also with the numerous African revolutionary exiles in Dar es Salaam. He has achieved a degree of notoriety for driving the "largest and flashiest car anywhere in East Africa,"[4] and Ho and his staff have also gained a reputation in the international press for "living it up," a reference to the large and expensive facilities in which the Chinese diplomatic community lives and works.[5]

In private life, Ho has apparently been married at least twice. He was once married to Chung Chien-hua, but while he has been in East Africa his wife has been Wang Hao. Nothing is known about the antecedents of either of these women.

1. *The Wall Street Journal,* October 2, 1961.
2. *South China Morning Post* (Hong Kong), September 9, 1964.
3. Interview, Cambridge, Mass., with Western visitor to Tanzania, May 1965.
4. *Hong Kong Tiger-Standard,* September 3, 1963.
5. *The Christian Science Monitor,* June 4, 1965.

Hsi Chung-hsun

(1903–   ; Fu-p'ing, Shensi). Former Party leader in northwest; member, CCP Central Committee.

Hsi Chung-hsun was one of the early Party leaders in the twenties in Shensi where he was associated with such prominent CCP leaders as Liu Chih-tan and Kao Kang. He remained in the northwest until 1952 working mainly as a Party leader and an official in the Shensi-Kansu-Ninghsia (Shen-Kan-Ning) Border Region. In the decade after 1953 he was one of the most important government administrators in Peking, rising to the post of vice-premier of the State Council.

Hsi was born in Fu-p'ing, 30 miles north of Sian, the Shensi provincial capital. A graduate of a middle school in Fu-p'ing, Hsi attended the new Chung Shan Military and Political Academy in Sian in 1926 and it was there that he probably first became associated with Liu Chih-tan and Kao Kang (qq.v.), two of the most important leaders in Shensi prior to the arrival in the province of the forces from south China led by Mao Tse-tung. Hsi, like Kao, was a student and Liu was an instructor.[1] It was presumably about this time that Hsi joined the Communist Youth League and the following year (1927) he became a member of the CCP.

In the early thirties Hsi was a guerrilla leader in Hsun-i hsien, Shensi, some 50 miles northwest of his native Fu-p'ing near the Kansu border. The guerrillas were quite effective until mid-1933 when KMT forces decimated a crack regiment of the 26th Red Army, which was operating to the southeast. Subsequently, the center of guerrilla activity shifted north to a new area on the Shensi-Kansu border, which included Ch'ing-yang, Pao-an, and Ho-shui hsien. In early 1934 the Shensi-Kansu Border Region Revolutionary Committee was established to govern the new area. Hsi became chairman of the Committee and Liu Chih-tan was made chairman of the Military Committee.[2] Starting in 1934, the guerrilla movement in the border region began to have considerable success (see under Liu Chih-tan). In mid-1935 Liu Chih-tan's 26th and 27th Armies were merged with the 25th Red Army of Hsu Hai-tung (q.v.), one of the earliest elements of the Long Marchers to arrive in Shensi. Official Communist histories credit Hsi with a role in making contact with Hsu's forces.[3] At the time he was apparently still head of the Revolutionary Committee.

Soon after the arrival in north Shensi of Mao Tse-tung's Long Marchers in the fall of 1935, Hsi studied at the Central Party School in Wa-yao-pao, and then for a period he was a dean at this important institution. After the Long Marchers and the local Communists had consolidated their position in the northwest, the Shensi-Kansu-Ninghsia (Shen-Kan-Ning) Border Region Government was established (1937). In the ensuing years Hsi became one of its more important officials, working mainly in Kuan-chung, one of the five sub-divisions of Shen-Kan-Ning and the one in the southernmost sector of the Border Region. During the Sino-Japanese War he was secretary of the Kuan-chung CCP District Committee and principal of the Second Normal School. He represented two of the hsien within Kuan-chung (T'ung-i-yao and Hsin-cheng) in the Shen-Kan-Ning Second and Third Assemblies, which first met in Yenan in November 1941 and April 1946, respectively. Moreover, at the April 1946 session of the Assembly he was elected to the Assembly Standing Committee, the organ in charge of legislative matters when the full Assembly was not in session. The Assembly, as well as its Standing Committee, was under the direction of Kao Kang. Within the executive branch of the Shen-Kan-Ning government, Hsi was a member of the Finance and Economics Committee by 1949.

Although Hsi's principal duties were in connection with the Party and the Shen-Kan-Ning Government, he served at least briefly during the war as political commissar of the Second Independent Brigade, one of the units in Ho Lung's 120th Division. At the Seventh National Party Congress held in Yenan in April–June 1945, 44 full and 33 alternate members were elected to the Central Committee. Most of the new Central Committee members had served with Mao in Kiangsi and most had made the Long March. Hsi's place in the Party hierarchy at this juncture can be judged in part from the fact that only three men were elected from the Shensi group: Kao Kang (q.v.), a full member, and Ma Ming-fang (q.v.) and Hsi, both alternates. In the years immediately after the Congress Hsi continued to rise within the CCP elite. During the civil war with the Nationalists in the late forties he was political commissar of the Northwest PLA (1947–1949). In Mao's *Selected Works,* P'eng Te-huai, Ho Lung, and Hsi are singled out as the most significant leaders in major battles in the

northwest against the Nationalists in 1947 and 1948.[4] By the time of the collapse of the Nationalists in 1949, the Northwest PLA had been redesignated the First Field Army. Hsi continued as the political commissar of the field army, as well as the area it controlled, known as the Northwest Military Region (encompassing Shensi, Kansu, Ninghsia, Tsinghai, and Sinkiang provinces). He held these posts until his transfer to Peking in 1952.

In 1947 Hsi also assumed the secretaryship of the Northwest Party Bureau, his most important and active role in the northwest from that date until 1952. His place in the Northwest Party structure was approximately paralleled in the regional government when (in January 1950) he became the senior vice-chairman of the Northwest Military and Administrative Committee (NWMAC) under NWMAC Chairman P'eng Te-huai. P'eng was often in Peking in 1950, and not long after the Chinese entered the Korean War (October 1950) he was in North Korea commanding the Chinese forces fighting there. Thus P'eng's prolonged absence from the northwest in the early fifties had the effect of making Hsi the most important official in the CCP, the government, and military hierarchies there.

Subordinate to the NWMAC Hsi was also chairman of the Land Reform Committee; nominally, he retained this post after the NWMAC was reorganized into the Northwest Administrative Committee in January 1953, but by about that time he had been transferred to Peking (see below). In the period from 1949 to 1952 he presided over a large number of meetings in the northwest, made inspection trips, and was a frequent contributor to the national and local press. For example, on an inspection trip to the Kuan-chung district of Shensi (where he had worked in the thirties and forties), Hsi delivered a speech on Party work in rural areas, which was published in the Sian *Ch'ün-chung jih-pao* (The masses daily) of December 30, 1949, and his speech at the Northwest Party School in Sian on the training of cadres was carried in the *JMJP* January 4, 1950). Similarly, an article by Hsi for the *JMJP* of July 4, 1951 ("To follow Mao Tse-tung means victory") reviewed the situation in the northwest and gave a brief account of the history of the CCP movement there from the early 1920's.

Although Hsi spent most of his time in the early fifties in the northwest, he received important posts in 1949 when the national PRC government was inaugurated (October). The most important of these was membership on the Central People's Government Council (CPGC) from 1949 until 1954, when it was dissolved. Chaired by Mao Tse-tung, the CPGC had six vice-chairmen (including Hsi's colleague Kao Kang) and 56 members; in the period from 1949 to 1954, the Council passed on virtually every major item promulgated by the PRC. He attended few of the earlier CPGC meetings but after late 1952 became a regular participant. From 1949 to 1954 Hsi was also a member of the important People's Revolutionary Military Council (chaired by Mao) and of the Executive Board of the Sino-Soviet Friendship Association (SSFA). When the Northwest SSFA Branch was set up in December 1951, he was named president. Among his infrequent trips to Peking in the early fifties were ones made in the summer of 1950 and the fall of 1951 to attend sessions of the CPPCC National Committee, as well as another in February 1951 when he delivered a major report on work in the northwest before the 11th meeting of the CPGC.

Already the top official in one of the six major regions of China, Hsi began to receive a series of new and important national appointments in 1952–53—appointments that in retrospect, may have been related to the transfer of Hsi's long-time colleague Kao Kang to Peking from Manchuria at this same time. Hsi's first new national post was as a vice-chairman of the Culture and Education Committee, one of the four major committees subordinate to the Government Administration Council (the cabinet). Three months later (November 1952), in preparation for the inauguration of the First Five-Year Plan in 1953, the PRC created the State Planning Commission. As initially organized, the Commission had Kao Kang as the chairman, one vice-chairman, and 18 members, including Hsi and Jao Shu-shih. Jao and Kao were both purged in 1955 in one of the landmark events in the history of the CCP. Two of the first important steps leading toward the establishment of the constitutional government in 1954 were the creation in January and February 1953 of the Committee for Drafting the Constitution and the Central Election Committee, respectively. Hsi was named to both committees, and had Kao and Jao as fellow members on the one concerned with the drafting of the constitution. Even more important was Hsi's assumption by June 1953 of the directorship of the Party's Propaganda Department, one of the most important of the Central Committee organs. Here he replaced Party veteran Lu Ting-i, an intimate of Mao Tse-tung, who had headed the Department from 1945; Lu was lowered to the position of Department deputy director. By this time, of course, Hsi had already transferred to Peking—probably over the winter of 1952–53 or soon thereafter. He received still another important post in September 1953 when he replaced Li Wei-han as secretary-general of the Government Administration Council (GAC). One year later (September 1954), at the close of the initial session of the First NPC, Hsi was reappointed secretary-general of the State Council, the successor to the GAC (although he was dropped at this time from the State Planning Commission). Because the Premier of the State Council (Chou En-lai) and the vice-premiers (e.g., Teng Hsiao-p'ing) are so fully occupied with other tasks, it is probable that the secretary-general has a greater working knowledge of cabinet affairs than any other individual in this highly important organization. Some idea of the secretary-general's role can be gained from Hsi's candid and fact-laden speech before the second session of the First NPC in July 1955, an address dealing with measures taken by the government to retrench superfluous personnel from government organs and industrial units.[5] Until Hsi apparently ran into political difficulties in 1962 (see below), he remained as State Council secretary-general and made scores of public appearances in this capacity.

As described, Hsi succeeded Lu Ting-i as director of the Party's Propaganda Department in the first half of 1953, a date approximately coinciding with Jao Shu-shih's appointment as head of the Organization Department. At the Central Committee's important Fourth Plenum in February 1954, Kao Kang and Jao Shu-shih (though not then cited by name) came under attack. If it is true that Hsi had close ties with Kao, then it is noteworthy that by the second half of 1954 Lu Ting-i was reinstated as the chief of the Propaganda Department. Notwithstanding this possible coincidence of fact, Hsi was elected as a deputy from Sian to the First NPC (1954–1959) and was re-elected to the Second NPC (1959–1964) from Shansi. More important, at the Party's Eighth National Congress in September 1956, Hsi served on the Congress Presidium (steering committee) and was among the executive chairmen for one of the daily sessions. At the close of the Congress he was promoted from alternate to full membership on the Party Central Committee. Moreover, he played a rather major role in criticizing "rightists" during the nationwide "rectification" campaign of 1957–58, and in July 1957 he was appointed a vice-chairman of the government Central Relief Committee that was chaired by Teng Tzu-hui. The Committee was apparently established in response to severe criticisms of relief and disaster work that had been published in the *JMJP* on July 17, 1957.

At the close of the first session of the Second NPC in April 1959, Hsi received a significant new post when he was made one of the State Council's vice-premiers, a position he held concurrently with the secretary-generalship of the State Council. Shortly before this, in late February 1959, he made his first known trip abroad when he led a government delegation to the annual Leipzig Fair in East Germany. In the following month he joined a delegation led by Chu Te to celebrations in Budapest marking the 40th anniversary of the "Hungarian Soviet Revolution." Chu and Hsi returned to Peking in late March following a brief stopover in Moscow. He was back in Europe in August–September 1959 leading a delegation to an exhibition on Soviet economic achievements in Moscow and to the First International Brno Trade Fair in Czechoslovakia. One year later (September 1960) he led a group to East Germany to attend the funeral of East German President Wilhelm Pieck.

Throughout 1961 and most of 1962 Hsi was constantly in the news, often appearing with China's most important leaders, as in September 1961 when he took part in talks held between Liu Shao-ch'i and the president of Cuba. He appeared regularly in public until the fall of 1962 when Chou Jung-hsin (q.v.), one of the deputy secretaries-general of the State Council, became the acting secretary-general in his place. Chou continued in this capacity until January 1965 when he formally replaced Hsi as secretary-general.

Though there is no published evidence to explain Hsi's sudden disappearance from public affairs, it is possible that his past close ties with Kao Kang may have played a part in his downfall. Moreover, Hsi had worked closely with P'eng Te-huai (q.v.), who was ousted as Defense Minister in September 1959. In any case, events of 1964 and 1965 attest to the fact that he has fallen from power. He was not re-elected to the Third NPC in 1964 (after having served in both the First and Second NPC's), and at the close of the first session of the Third NPC in January 1965, he was not reappointed a vice-premier. (P'eng Te-huai was also formally removed as a vice-premier at this time.) In addition, as described above, Chou Jung-hsin replaced Hsi as the State Council's secretary-general at this same time. Although men of equal significance have been purged and made a subsequent comeback (e.g., Huang K'o-ch'eng, q.v.), it appears that Hsi's significance as a key Party-government leader ended in 1962.

---

1. Mark Selden, "The Guerrilla Movement in Northwest China: The Origins of the Shensi-Kansu-Ninghsia Border Region," pt. I, *The China Quarterly,* no. 28:67 (October–December 1966).

2. Mark Selden, "The Guerrilla Movement in Northwest China: The Origins of the Shensi-Kansu-Ninghsia Border Region," pt. II, *The China Quarterly,* no. 29:68 (January–March 1967).

3. *Hung-ch'i p'iao-p'iao* (Red flag fluttering; Peking, 1957), III, 181.

4. *Selected Works of Mao Tse-tung* (Peking, 1961), IV, 134, 217.

5. *1956 Jen-min shou-ts'e* (1956 people's handbook), pp. 235–236; translated in *CB* 347, pp. 1–5.

Hsia Hsi

(c.1900–c.1935; I-yang, Hunan). Early Party leader; active in the West Hunan-Hupeh Soviet.

Hsia Hsi, together with Mao Tse-tung, belonged to the small group which brought the CCP into existence in Hunan in the early 1920's, and he remained a key provincial figure until the KMT–CCP break in 1927. He was also active in those years in establishing the Hunan provincial organization of the KMT when the Nationalists and Communists were working together. After the split, Hsia took part in the Nanchang Uprising and then went to Moscow where he was elected to the CCP Central Committee in 1928. Hsia was a member of the Russian-returned student faction, which gained control of the CCP in early 1931, and in that same year he was sent to Ho Lung's West Hunan-Hupeh base where he worked as a top political leader until his death about four years later. In later years he was attacked by Maoist writers for his alleged "errors" in Ho Lung's base.

Hsia was a native of I-yang, a regional center in north Hunan not far south of Tung-t'ing Lake, and to judge from his student days he was probably born about the turn of the century or shortly before. In 1917 Hsia was at the Hunan First Normal School in Changsha where Mao Tse-tung was also a student.[1] In that year Mao and Ts'ai Ho-sen began to organize the *Hsin-min hsueh-hui* (New people's study society), which was formally inaugurated in April 1918. The majority of the founding members, Hsia among them, came from the normal school. Aside from Mao, Ts'ai, and Hsia, other founding members included such important latter-day Communists as Ho Shu-heng, Hsu T'e-li, and Li Wei-han (qq.v.). The radical student group in Changsha soon aroused the vigilance of Hunan Governor Chang Ching-yao who, when students demonstrated against Japanese influences (December 1919), broke up their rally with force. The students replied by circulating a manifesto against Governor Chang, which some 13,000 students signed, and they also decided to seek outside assistance. To this end, in early 1920 Mao visited Peking, while Hsia was sent to Heng-yang, in southern Hunan, then the headquarters of the powerful northern warlord Wu P'ei-fu, to solicit Wu's aid in ousting Chang.[2] It is doubtful if their endeavors were a significant factor in the downfall of Chang, but in any event he was driven from the province in mid-1920, and by the latter part of that year Chao Heng-t'i had become the dominant figure in Hunan.

In the latter half of 1920 several societies for the study of Marxism were established in major Chinese cities—groups which came to be the nuclei from which the CCP was established in mid-1921. The Hunan group was formed in September 1920, and its three most influential members were Mao, Lin Po-ch'ü (q.v.), and Hsia.[3] Soon afterwards, Mao, Hsia, and others established what amounted to a Hunan branch of the Socialist Youth League (see under Li Ta-chao), and with this act the New People's Study Society was disbanded (many of its key members joining the new youth organization).[4] During this period, and for the next several years, Hsia seems to have been most closely associated with Kuo Liang (1900–1928). According to Kuo's biographer, the two young men lived in the same dormitory at the Hunan Normal School, and because of their involvement in revolutionary activities they often missed classes. In 1921, according to the same biography, Hsia and Kuo organized a strike among ricksha pullers in Changsha, which was purportedly carried out under Mao Tse-tung's leadership.[5] It was also in 1921, immediately after Mao and Ho Shu-heng returned from the founding congress of the CCP in Shanghai in July, that Mao and Ho established the Self-Education College (Tzu-hsiu ta-hsueh) in Changsha to attract young intellectuals into the CCP. A year later, in September 1922, the college set up a preparatory class, in which Hsia and Li Wei-han both taught.[6] In 1922–23 Hsia was among the leaders in yet another organization with which Mao was associated, the Hunan Students' Union, headquartered in the same building as the Self-Education College. For a period Hsia was editor of the Students' Union organ, the *Hu-nan hsueh-sheng lien-ho-hui chou-k'an* (Hunan Students' Union weekly), and he was also associated then with Mao's younger brother, Mao Tse-min (q.v.), who headed the business department of the student organization.[7]

In March 1923, at the suggestion of the Hunan Students' Union, a national student conference was held in Shanghai to strengthen the student movement. Hsia apparently attended this meeting, because he was a contributor to a special publication which was put out during the life of the two-week conference.[8] One of the by-products of the conference was the establishment of the Hunan Association for the Support of Diplomacy in Changsha in April 1923. The aim of the organization was to agitate for the repeal of certain treaties with Japan which the students felt encroached on Chinese sovereignty, and among the association officials was Hsia's colleague Kuo Liang. It is not known if Hsia was an official in this organization, but he contributed in 1923 to its journal, *Chiu-kuo* (National salvation).[9]

Hsia had apparently joined the CCP at the time of its founding in 1921 or soon thereafter, and like so many Communists of that period he had joined the KMT by 1923 during the early phase of KMT–CCP cooperation. In April 1923, immediately after the above-mentioned student conference in Shanghai, Hsia and Liu Shao-ch'i (q.v.) were sent by the KMT to Changsha as organizers. As one observer has noted, the "fact that both men were dedicated Communists meant that from the beginning the KMT organization in Hunan during the national revolutionary period would have a more radical tint than in Kwangtung."[10] Hsia and Liu set up a joint KMT–CCP headquarters in Changsha, subordinate to which was a sub-section in nearby Ning-hsiang to the west and another one in P'ing-hsiang hsien across the border in Kiangsi. The CCP had already been working in these areas, and now with the additional backing of the KMT, Hsia was active in the next few years in building up a labor following in Changsha and engaged in similar activities among the railroad workers on the Chu-chou–P'ing-hsiang Railway and the miners in and around An-yuan and P'ing-hsiang, located just across the border in west Kiangsi. Thus, in the words of Li Jui (Mao's biographer), after 1923 Hsia was one of the "responsible persons" for the CCP Hunan Committee, and in the ensuing years he also "carried out important work for the KMT Hunan Headquarters."[11]

In January 1924, Hsia was included in the Hunan delegation which attended the First KMT Congress in Canton. It was indicative of the radical element in this group that five of its nine members were concurrently CCP members; among them, in addition to Hsia, were Mao, Lin Po-ch'ü, and Li Wei-han.[12] Mao and Lin were among the six Communists elected alternate members of the KMT Central Executive Committee (CEC). Hsia Hsi was not then made a CEC member, but when the Second KMT Congress met in January 1926, he joined Mao as a CEC alternate. Hsia's role in the KMT organization in Hunan was confirmed soon after the First KMT Congress; in March 1924, at the third meeting of the KMT CEC, he was appointed as the senior KMT official in Hunan.[13] Hsia returned to Hunan from Canton, and for the next two years he was engaged in organizational work; ostensibly this was done under the aegis of the KMT, but because his work was carried out in secret, it was a "boon to the Communists who had an extensive underground network."[14]

The importance of the work of Hsia and his colleagues was demonstrated in the early phase of the Northern Expedition. When the vanguard troops of Yeh T'ing (q.v.) captured Changsha in July 1926, he was assisted by military units organized among the peasantry in three hsien to the east of the city, units which were already in existence by the time Yeh's troops arrived there.[15] Immediately after the fall of Changsha, the KMT organization in Hunan convened a congress; the nine-member Executive Committee elected at that time included five Communists, one of whom was Hsia.[16] At the end of 1926 Mao returned to Changsha, and for the next few months he and Hsia worked together again, although apparently not in complete harmony. During this period, as both the CCP and the KMT struggled over questions of land tenure and taxation, which were making their cooperation increasingly difficult, Hsia and Mao disagreed publicly over a report Mao delivered to the KMT Central Land Committee. The committee, formed by the KMT CEC in Wuhan in early April 1927, had a membership of five, including Mao.[17] During that month the committee held meetings open to members of the "Left-wing" KMT government in Wuhan, as well as to political activists in the peasant movement (from both the CCP and the KMT). At a meeting on April 22, Mao presented a resolution calling for a rather drastic confiscation of the land holdings of rich peasants and absentee landlords. Mao's views encountered stiff opposition, not only from non-Communists but also from Party members, among them Hsia, who found Mao's resolution generally impracticable, "full of contradictions," and likely to lead to an "immediate struggle between the poor and rich peasants."[18]

Just ten days before the above-mentioned April 22 meeting, Chiang Kai-shek and the "Right-wing" KMT had staged its famous anti-Communist coup in Shanghai, and during the ensuing weeks the CCP's tenuous alliance with the "Left-wing" KMT also began to deteriorate markedly. Returning to Changsha after attending the Wuhan meetings, Mao, Hsia, Kuo Liang, and T'eng Tai-yuan (q.v.) were forced to flee to Kiangsi under fear of arrest by Left-KMT General T'ang Sheng-chih.[19] Hsia's activities over the next several weeks are not documented. However, after the complete break between the Left-KMT and the CCP in mid-1927, he was involved in planning the Nanchang Uprising on August 1 (see under Yeh T'ing) together with such important Communists as Chang Kuo-t'ao and Yun Tai-ying (qq.v.).[20] The insurgents were initially successful in holding Nanchang, and during the few days before they were driven from the city Hsia served as one of the 25 members of the Revolutionary Committee. Most of the participants in the Nanchang insurrection marched south to Swatow where, after another short-lived success, they were again badly defeated. Hsia's name has not been associated with the southward march, but by 1928 he and many of his colleagues had made their way to Moscow.

Hsia was elected to the CCP Central Committee at the Sixth Congress, held in Moscow in June–July 1928. He remained in the Soviet capital to study at Sun Yat-sen University where he came to be one of the more prominent figures in the group known as the Russian-returned student clique or the "28 Bolsheviks." These were the favored Chinese students of the university chancellor and Comintern official Pavel Mif, who went to China with his protégés in the

spring of 1930. In less than a year, with the help and guidance of Mif and the Comintern, the Russian-returned students ousted the strong Party leader Li Li-san (q.v.), and at the crucial Fourth Party Plenum in January 1931 they defeated another rival group led by Lo Chang-lung and Ho Meng-hsiung (qq.v.). After gaining control of most of the key Party organs, the new leadership under Ch'en Shao-yü and Ch'in Pang-hsien (qq.v.) quickly moved to extend its control to the rural Communist bases which still other leaders had been developing in the years after the 1927 debacle at Nanchang. Thus, in March 1931, Hsia was sent to join Ho Lung (q.v.) in the latter's West Hunan-Hupeh base.

The history of the West Hunan-Hupeh base is described at length in the biography of Ho Lung. It is difficult to assess Hsia's role over the next few years, particularly in view of the pejorative comments normally made by Maoist historians in dealing with the members of the returned-student group. When Hsia arrived in Ho's area two other important political figures were already at work there. One of them, Chou I-ch'ün (q.v.), had been with Ho from the earliest days of the base, whereas the other, Teng Chung-hsia (q.v.), had arrived only a few months before Hsia. Neither Chou nor Teng could be regarded as appointees of the returned-student leadership. Hsia immediately established the CCP Central Sub-bureau for the West Hunan-Hupeh Soviet, and as head of this organ he controlled both political and military affairs.[21] Chou I-ch'ün was killed not long afterwards (May 1931), and it appears that Hsia brought about the downfall of Teng, who was retired from the base toward the end of 1931.

At approximately the same time that Teng Chung-hsia left Ho Lung's base, still another political officer arrived. The new man, Kuan Hsiang-ying (q.v.), ultimately emerged as Ho's principal officer, but until at least 1933 Hsia continued to head the Party Sub-bureau. In the meantime, at the First All-China Congress of Soviets, convened at Juichin in November 1931, the Chinese Soviet Republic was established under Mao Tse-tung's chairmanship. Hsia was made a member of the leading political organ, the Central Executive Committee (CEC), and at the Second Congress, held in January–February 1934, he was again elected a CEC member. In both instances he was presumably elected *in absentia*. During the course of the early 1930's the West Hunan-Hupeh base was under incessant attack by the Nationalists. In a lengthy article published in the *JMJP* on February 1, 1962, which appears to be the definitive Maoist interpretation of the "errors" committed by the returned-student leadership insofar as they affected the West Hunan-Hupeh base, Hsia is blamed for virtually all the difficulties encountered by Ho Lung's troops. Furthermore, his work is set in contrast to the "correct" policies advocated by Ho, Chou I-ch'ün, and Kuan Hsiang-ying.

Although Hsia was re-elected to the CEC of the Chinese Soviet Republic in early 1934 (as noted above), little more is known of his work after that time. There is conflicting information about his death. One of Mao's biographers claims that he was drowned in 1934.[22] Another and probably more reliable biographer of Mao states that Hsia was killed during the Long March in 1935.[23] Nym Wales, on the other hand, has written that he was killed in battle in Kweichow in 1936.[24] Finally, when Edgar Snow interviewed Mao in north Shensi in mid-1936, the Communist leader spoke of Hsia as still being alive. In commenting upon the founding members of the *Hsin-min hsueh-hui*, Mao told Snow that many of them "were later to become famous names in Chinese Communism, and in the history of the Chinese Revolution. Among the better-known Communists," continued Mao, was "Hsia Hsi, now in . . . [Ho Lung's] Second Front Red Army [which had not yet completed its Long March to Shensi]."[25] As these lines suggest, Mao gave no indication that this former schoolmate and Party colleague would later become a target for orthodox Party historians.

---

1. Li Jui, *Mao Tse-tung t'ung-chih te ch'u-ch'i ko-ming huo-tung* (Comrade Mao Tse-tung's early revolutionary activities; Peking, 1957), p. 16.

2. *Ibid.*, pp. 117–118; Jerome Ch'en, *Mao and the Chinese Revolution* (London, 1965), p. 65.

3. Hu Hua, ed., *Chung-kuo hsin min-chu-chu-i ko-ming shih* (A history of China's new democratic revolution; Hong Kong, 1950), p. 44.

4. Li Jui, p. 146.

5. *Hu-nan ko-ming lieh-shih chuan* (Biographies of Hunan revolutionary martyrs; Changsha, 1952), p. 41.

6. Li Jui, pp. 156–157.

7. Chow Tse-tsung, *Research Guide to the May Fourth Movement* (Cambridge, Mass., 1963), p. 111.

8. *Ibid.*, pp. 117–118.

9. *Ibid.*, p. 121.

10. Roy Mark Hofheinz, Jr., "The Peasant Movement and Rural Revolution: Chinese Communists in the Countryside (1923–27)," Ph.D. diss., Harvard University, 1966, pp. 226–227.

11. Li Jui, p. 17.

12. Hofheinz, p. 394.

13. Li Yun-han, *Tsung jung kung tao ch'ing tang* (From the admission of the Communists to the purification of the [Nationalist] Party; Taipei, 1966), p. 271.

14. Hofheinz, p. 227.

15. *Ibid.*, pp. 237–238.

16. *Ibid.*, pp. 238, 396.

17. Stuart Schram, *Mao Tse-tung* (New York, 1966), p. 89.

18. *Ibid.*, p. 91.

19. Jerome Ch'en, pp. 115–116.

20. C. Martin Wilbur, "The Ashes of Defeat," *The China Quarterly,* no. 18:48 (April–June 1964).

21. *JMJP*, February 1, 1962.

22. Emi Siao [Hsiao San], *Mao Tse-tung: His Childhood and Youth* (Bombay, 1953), p. 58.

23. Li Jui, p. 17.

24. Nym Wales, *Inside Red China* (New York, 1939), p. 342.

25. Edgar Snow, *Red Star over China* (New York, 1938), p. 131.

Hsiang Ching-yü

(1895–1928; Hsu-p'u hsien, Hunan). Early Communist woman leader; member, CCP Central Committee.

Hsiang Ching-yü was one of the earliest members of the CCP and the most important woman leader in the early years of the Party. She became the first head of the Party's Women's Department in 1922 and was very active in the Communist movement until her execution in 1928. Married to Ts'ai Ho-sen while they were students in France, she, along with her husband, played a major role in the founding and growth of the CCP.

Hsiang was born in Hsu-p'u hsien in western Hunan about 130 miles west of Changsha, the Hunan provincial capital. She began with a traditional education, but through the influence of an older brother who had studied in Japan she was introduced to modern literature when she was 12. In 1912, when she was 17, she went to Changsha to attend a teachers' training school for women but, disliking it, she transferred to the "more progressive" Chou-nan Girls' School from which she graduated in 1915. During her last term she became interested in the contemporary political scene. She began to organize her fellow students and spoke in public against Yuan Shih-k'ai's tolerance of the harsh Japanese Twenty-One Demands and his attempts to restore the monarchy with himself as emperor. After graduation Hsiang returned to Hsu-p'u to start a co-educational primary school. Wang I-chih (the widow of Chou Pao-chung, q.v.), who has written a short biography of Hsiang, taught at the primary school a few years later.[1]

Hsiang continued to teach in Hsu-p'u for three years, but she apparently retained close connections with friends and colleagues in Changsha. Through her school mate Ts'ai Ch'ang (q.v.) she came to know the Ts'ai family, which made its home a meeting place for politically minded Hunanese students, among them Mao Tse-tung. Ts'ai Ch'ang's brother, Ts'ai Ho-sen, and Mao were the prime founders of the Hsin-min hsueh-hui (New people's study society), an association of young reformers formed in April 1918 in Changsha. Hsiang was one of its earliest members. Over the course of the next year she and Ts'ai Ch'ang were responsible for organizing the women's group among the Hunanese students who were preparing to go to France to take part in the work-and-study program. Roughly one fourth of all the Chinese students who went to France came from Hunan, many of them Hsin-min hsueh-hui members.[2]

The Changsha group set out from Shanghai in November 1919, and upon arriving, most of them went to Montargis, south of Paris, where they formed a branch of the Hsin-min hsueh-hui. Others in the group were Li Wei-han, Li Fu-ch'un (later the husband of Ts'ai Ch'ang), and Li Li-san (qq.v.). At Montargis Hsiang enrolled in a French course at a public school for women and worked part-time in a rubber plant and later a textile mill. She married Ts'ai Ho-sen in 1921 by which time he had become the acknowledged leader of the Hunan student group. However, neither academic life nor work was as important as politics to most of the Chinese students. Many of them had a taste of political agitating before going to France and they vigorously continued this work after their arrival. A number of their French teachers were interested in Marxism and taught them from the pages of *l'Humanité*, the organ of the French Communist Party.[3] In February 1921 Hsiang was briefly detained by the French police for demonstrating in front of the Chinese Legation in connection with a financial dispute between the students and the Chinese Government. A Socialist Youth League and a Communist Party branch for Chinese students in France eventually grew out of these activities (see under Ch'en I), but the Ts'ai's were deported some eight months before the French CCP branch was founded in mid-1922.

They returned to China in late 1921 or early 1922 to work for the CCP, which had been founded in Shanghai a half a year earlier. Hsiang immediately joined the CCP and became active in the women's and labor movements in Shanghai. In July 1922 the CCP held its Second National Congress in Shanghai. Hsiang and her husband were among the few delegates present and both were elected to the Central Committee. Hsiang was the first woman member of the Central Committee. She was also named to head the Party's Women's Department, which was organized at this time, continuing in this post until her departure for Russia in 1925. For almost four years Hsiang directed most of her attention to the women workers of Shanghai, and she is credited with having recommended to the Party most of the proposals regarding the women's movement in the early twenties.[4] She reportedly spent many hours visiting workers in their homes and organized and taught in night schools for them. In 1924 she took part in the strikes in the Shanghai silk mills and the Nanyang Tobacco

Plant. And in the next year Hsiang was active in the serious labor disturbances that broke out in May (see under Li Li-san) and soon spread to other industrial cities.

Although Hsiang was not on the faculty at the radical Shanghai University, she worked closely with many of its staff members, including Ch'ü Ch'iu-pai, Chang T'ai-lei, and Jen Pi-shih (qq.v.). In fact, she must have been well acquainted with virtually all the top Communists in Shanghai in the early twenties because, lacking a formal Party office, the CCP used the Ts'ai home as its headquarters in the early twenties. Hsiang is also credited with an important role in the training of two women Communists, Chang Ch'in-ch'iu (q.v.), presently a vice-minister of the Textile Industry Ministry, and the wife of Ch'ü Ch'iu-pai (Yang Chih-hua).[5]

Hsiang and her husband left for Moscow in late 1925 to attend the Sixth Plenum of the Comintern's Executive Committee (February–March 1926). Afterwards, they spent a little over a year in Russia where Hsiang studied at the Communist University of the Toilers of the East. They returned to China in the spring of 1927 and were on hand for the Fifth CCP Congress in Hankow in April–May. Ts'ai Ho-sen was elected to the Politburo and re-elected to the Central Committee. However, it appears that Hsiang was not re-elected to the Central Committee. In fact, it seems that after her election in 1922 she was not re-elected at the Third and Fourth Congresses, perhaps because her personal relationship with P'eng Shu-chih, a protégé of Party leader Ch'en Tu-hsiu, had angered other leading Communists (see under Ch'ü Ch'iu-pai).

After the Congress Hsiang remained in the Wuhan area where she worked as a propagandist for the Wuhan Federation of Trade Unions. In this capacity she may have attended the Fourth Congress of the Communist-backed All-China Federation of Labor, which was held in Hankow in June 1927. In any event, at this juncture the CCP and its affiliated organizations were rapidly moving toward an extraordinary crisis. Chiang Kai-shek had already delivered a devastating blow to the CCP two months earlier in Shanghai, and in Hupeh and neighboring provinces the Communist-led labor movement was being harassed by both Chiang's "Right-KMT" and elements from the "Left-KMT" in Wuhan. In fact, the Wuhan labor federation for which Hsiang had been working was disbanded in late June by Wang Ching-wei's Wuhan government, and in a few weeks Wang's "Left-KMT" broke all its ties with the Communists. The CCP was now an underground organization throughout China. In these circumstances, Hsiang was transferred to a propaganda post in the Hankow CCP Committee. Concurrently, she served as an editor of a Party journal entitled *Ch'ang-chiang* (Yangtze River), which was being published covertly, and within a brief time she replaced Huang Sung-ling (an important education official in the post-1949 period) as editor-in-chief. By this time Hsiang was also engaged in underground work for the Party's Hupeh Committee. She continued her work in Hupeh until the spring of 1928 when she was arrested in the French Concession in Hankow and executed on May 1.

Of the several sources on Hsiang's career, the best is probably a small volume published in Peking in 1958 entitled *Lieh-shih Hsiang Ching-yü* (Martyr Hsiang Ching-yü). This contains several sketches of Hsiang's career by her contemporaries, as well as five excerpts from her own writings in the twenties.

1. *China Reconstructs,* 14:24–26 (March 1965); *Women of China,* no. 2:22–25, 33 (1963).
2. Conrad Brandt, *The French-Returned Elite in the Chinese Communist Party,* reprint no. 13 (Institute of International Studies, University of California, Berkeley, 1961).
3. *Ibid.*
4. *Hu-nan ko-ming lieh-shih chuan* (Biographies of Hunan revolutionary martyrs; Changsha, 1952), p. 33.
5. *China Reconstructs; Hung-ch'i p'iao-p'iao* (Red flag fluttering; Peking, 1958), VIII, 24–56.

Hsiang Chung-fa

(c.1888–1931; Hupeh). General secretary of CCP, 1928–1931.

Hsiang Chung-fa was the Party general secretary from 1928 to 1931 but otherwise his role in the development of Chinese Communism was rather minor. Nothing is known about his family or his early education. A native of Hupeh, in all probability he came from the proletarian class and may have had his first contact with Communism through the night school indoctrination classes for the workers in the Wuhan area started soon after the CCP was founded in 1921. He is said to have been moved to join the Party while working in the shipyards of the Hanyang Arsenal through the influence of Shih Yang. (Hsiang's sponsor is not to be confused with Chao Shih-yen [q.v.] who sometimes used Shih Yang as a Party alias.) Shih also came from Hupeh; as a lawyer in Wuhan, he served as an adviser to the Wuhan labor unions. Before joining the CCP, soon after it was founded, he belonged to the KMT. He was killed in line of Party duty during the strike on the Pinghan (Peking-Hankow) Railroad that was put down by the army of northern militarist Wu P'ei-fu (February 7, 1923). It was under Shih's tutelage that Hsiang first became active

as an organizer on the Pinghan line and worked to bring about the strike.

After the death of his sponsor Hsiang turned to organizing the miners of the famous iron mines at Han-yeh-p'ing in the Wuhan area; by 1925 he had risen to the post of general secretary of the Han-yeh-p'ing General Labor Union. That same year, in recognition of his work as a labor organizer and probably also to give recognition to one of its few leaders with true proletarian origins, the CCP decided to send Hsiang to Moscow for further study. He remained there about two years but returned to China by the spring of 1927. In that year he became the chairman of the Hupeh General Labor Union, an important organization both for the CCP and the KMT because Hupeh and Wuhan were the industrial heartland toward which both parties directed their revolutionary forces. At the Fifth CCP Congress in April 1927 he was elected to the Party Central Committee. Despite his limited outlook and abilities, Hsiang was said to have been quite effective as a labor organizer. He could speak to a labor audience and had considerable support among the rank-and-file workers in Hupeh, a group with whom such intellectual Party leaders as General Secretary Ch'en Tu-hsiu (q.v.) did not have much following. When in August 1927 the final split occurred between CCP and KMT, and the Party held its emergency strategy conference on August 7, Hsiang Chung-fa was one of the small number called to the conference to help unseat Ch'en and allow Ch'ü Ch'iu-pai (q.v.) to assume his post.

Thereafter, Hsiang was among the top Party leaders who sought refuge in the Soviet Union. He was in Moscow and present at the Sixth CCP Congress held there in the summer of 1928. By this time there were rather strong opposing factions within the CCP leadership, and the Congress had a difficult time attempting to reconcile them. According to Chang Kuo-t'ao (q.v.), who also attended the Congress, the principal rivals were a leftist faction led by Chou En-lai and Ch'ü Ch'iu-pai and a faction whose policies were more to the right, which included Chang, Ts'ai Ho-sen, and Hsiang Ying (qq.v.). The Comintern, with Sun Yat-sen University Chancellor Pavel Mif as one of its chief spokesman, was anxious to pull the different factions together. Thus Mif singled out Hsiang Chung-fa, with his labor record and proper proletarian background, as a good candidate for general secretary to effect the necessary compromise.[1] During Hsiang's term of office other and stronger leaders were to become far better known than he (see under Li Li-san and Ch'in Pang-hsien). However, Hsiang proved himself sufficiently flexible and was thus able to retain the post of general secretary during the next three difficult years when Li Li-san was to emerge as the dominant Party leader and then to be ousted by the Russian-returned student clique led by Ch'en Shao-yü, Ch'in Pang-hsien, and Pavel Mif. The latter group took over the Party apparatus from Li's supporters at the Fourth CCP Plenum of January 1931, but after he had confessed to a certain amount of wrong-doing under the previous Li Li-san leadership, Hsiang was retained as the general secretary of the Party.[2] He remained in Shanghai where the Party maintained its headquarters, but the records do not suggest any special accomplishments during this time.

In April 1931 the Nationalist police arrested a Communist operative by the name of Ku Shun-chang, and under police treatment he turned traitor and reported on a number of his Communist comrades. Ku, who had also been elected (but *in absentia*) to the Party Central Committee at the Sixth Congress in 1928, had been a Li Li-san man who came to the fore during the strikes of 1926–27. He was taken prisoner while on Party business in Hankow. Ku subsequently identified Yun Tai-ying (q.v.) who was then executed. He is also said to have revealed the addresses of Chou En-lai, Ch'ü Ch'iu-pai, and Li Wei-han, but these men had by luck just left Shanghai so that the police could not find them. Then through relatives of Ku the police learned of Hsiang Chung-fa's whereabouts and he was arrested. He was executed in June; according to most sources this occurred on June 21, 1931, but one Communist source dates it June 24.[3] With Hsiang's death the position of Party general secretary fell to Ch'en Shao-yü (q.v.). A number of Hsiang's writings appearing in the official Party organs *Hung-ch'i* (Red flag) and *Hung-ch'i chou-pao* (Red flag weekly) in the years while he was Party general secretary are cited by Chün-tu Hsüeh in his bibliography, *The Chinese Communist Movement, 1921–1937*.

1. Tso-liang Hsiao, *Power Relations within the Chinese Communist Movement, 1930–1934* (Seattle, Wash., 1961), p. 61.
2. *Ibid.*, p. 115.
3. *Ibid.*, p. 147.

Hsiang Ying

(1898–1941; Wuchang, Hupeh). Early CCP member and labor leader; political commissar and deputy commander, New Fourth Army; member, CCP Politburo.

Hsiang Ying, whose name is frequently romanized as Han Ying in Western sources, is one of the relatively few members of the CCP elite from a proletarian background. He began his career as a labor leader in Wuhan and took part in many of the keynote events in the early CCP movement in Wuhan, Shanghai, and Canton. Elected to the Politburo in 1928, Hsiang held several top posts

in the Chinese Soviet Republic in Kiangsi during the early 1930's. He was among those left behind when the Long March began in 1934, and during the early years of the Sino-Japanese War he was political commissar and deputy commander of the Communists' New Fourth Army in the lower Yangtze Valley. Maoist historians have cast Hsiang in an unfavorable light and have placed upon him the major responsibility for the disaster of the New Fourth Army Incident of January 1941, in which he lost his life.

The information on Hsiang's early years and career is drawn chiefly from interviews he gave to journalist Edgar Snow in 1938 and a Communist account published in 1957; these accounts, though conflicting in some details, are in substantial agreement.[1] His father, an impoverished scholar, died when Hsiang was only 10, leaving a destitute widow and a son and daughter. Both children later became members of the CCP. Hsiang received four years of primary schooling, but, after graduating in his 15th year, a lack of funds forced him to become an apprentice for the next three years in a textile factory in Wuchang. After his apprenticeship he continued as a salaried worker. Hsiang stated that he had been badly treated, and this factor, combined with the Russian Revolution and the May Fourth Movement (1919) in China, led him to an interest in China's nascent labor movement. In 1920, according to his own account, he led the first textile strike in Wuhan, and in the same year he became acquainted with Marxism through an "intellectual" who was visiting factories in order to make contact with workers.

By late 1921 or early 1922 Hsiang was in touch with Tung Pi-wu and Ch'en T'an-ch'iu (qq.v.), two of the founders of the CCP, who were then attempting to establish a viable Party apparatus in Hupeh. Hsiang soon became even more deeply involved in the labor movement and organized iron and steel workers in Wuhan and nearby cities. In the early part of 1922 he was among the most active participants in the establishment of a workers' club (then a euphemism for a union) along the Peking-Hankow Railway. When the organization was formally set up in March 1922 he became the corresponding secretary and was placed in charge of educational work. In the following month he joined the CCP, and at the same time he gave up his original name, Hsiang Te-lung, in favor of Hsiang Ying.

Organizational work among the workers on the Peking-Hankow Railway made rapid strides, and in mid-1922 a preparatory conference was held in Chengchow to unify the various clubs into the Peking-Hankow Railway General Trade Union. Hsiang was made the general executive officer (*tsung kan-shih*) of the preparatory committee. Toward the end of the year plans were set for an inaugural conference to be held in February 1923. However, as explained in greater detail in the biography of Teng Chung-hsia, northern warlord

Wu P'ei-fu intervened and suppressed the union in a bloody episode which Communist historians call the February Seventh Incident. Hsiang barely escaped with his life; he went into hiding in Wuhan for a brief period, but for most of the next year his activities are undocumented. It appears that his major organizational affiliation at this period was with the Communists' Labor Secretariat[2] (see under Teng Chung-hsia), the forerunner of the All-China Federation of Labor.

In the period after 1923 a number of key Communist leaders held concurrent membership in the KMT, and Hsiang was apparently among them. After the February 7 debacle, he seems to have made his way to Canton, which was rapidly emerging as the revolutionary center of China. There, in January 1924, the KMT held its first congress. Hsiang may have been involved in some way with the congress, but his claim (made to Edgar Snow) that he was elected to the KMT Central Executive Committee is demonstrably false. After the congress he was sent to Shanghai to represent the Workers' Department of the CCP, and for the next year he worked as a labor organizer there and in Wuhan where the labor movement was undergoing a revival. By May 1925 Hsiang had returned to Canton to attend the Second Labor Congress. He was elected to the 25-member Executive Committee of the new All-China Federation of Labor (ACFL),[3] which, in effect, replaced the Labor Secretariat. Among his colleagues on the committee were such important Communists as Su Chao-cheng, Li Li-san, Liu Shao-ch'i, and Teng Chung-hsia (qq.v.). Almost immediately after the congress, the May Thirtieth Incident in Shanghai (see under Li Li-san) touched off a series of protracted strikes and boycotts in many major cities. In response to these events, the Labor Federation played a major role in conducting the famous Hong Kong–Canton strike and boycott, which began in June 1925 and lasted for nearly a year and a half. For a brief period Hsiang remained in the south to take part in the strike[4] (see under Su Chao-cheng, the head of the "strike committee"), but then he was sent to Shanghai. In Hsiang's words: "We had to fight strong suppression and our work became secret. Li Li-san left and I was the remaining workers' organizational leader." Hsiang's account of his life is anything but modest, but it is clear that he was in fact one of the major organizers of the labor movement in Shanghai in 1925–1927—a movement that was to play a vital role in the capture of Shanghai in March 1927 by the Northern Expeditionary Forces.

Hsiang was back in south China on at least two occasions in the first half of 1926. In March of that year, in order to strengthen the Hong Kong–Canton strike, the Hong Kong Transport Workers' General Union was inaugurated in the British colony. As one commentator has observed, the fact that such key Communist labor leaders as Su Chao-cheng, Teng Chung-hsia, Liu Shao-ch'i, and Hsiang went to Hong Kong for the inauguration indicates the importance placed on the cooperation of the transport workers, sailors, railway workers, and dockers in the strike-boycott.[5] Two months later, at the Third Labor Congress, which was held in Canton, Hsiang was again elected to the Labor Federation's Executive Committee. He then returned to Shanghai to continue his work in the labor movement; he was still in the city in March 1927 when it was captured by Chiang Kai-shek's Northern Expeditionary Forces, with a major assist from the Communist-led workers. Early in the next month Chiang staged his anti-Communist coup, which took the lives of scores of Communist and labor leaders. Hsiang returned to the Wuhan cities where he became organizing secretary of some half a million workers in Hupeh province. In the wake of Chiang Kai-shek's coup in Shanghai, the center of Communist strength was now in Wuhan where the CCP was able to maintain its uneasy alliance with the left-wing KMT through the spring and early summer of 1927. Thanks to the assistance of Yeh T'ing (q.v.), a Communist and key commander during the Northern Expedition, Hsiang was able to arm and train some of his trade union members. However, CCP General Secretary Ch'en Tu-hsiu was unwilling or unable to endorse a policy of forming Communist military units, and thus Hsiang's handful of armed workers were never called to action. In any event, the left-wing KMT broke relations with the Communists in mid-July, and on August 1 Yeh T'ing and others staged the famous Nanchang Uprising. Hsiang took ill just before the insurrection, and during the ensuing two months he was forced to remain in hiding, after which he escaped to Shanghai.

By early 1928 Hsiang had replaced Teng Chung-hsia as secretary of the CCP Kiangsu Committee. Hsiang's work in Shanghai was of relatively short duration, for by the middle of the year he had relinquished the post to Lo Teng-hsien (q.v.) and had departed for Moscow where in the summer of that year the CCP held its Sixth Congress and the Comintern its Sixth Congress. At the CCP Sixth Congress he was elected to the Party Central Committee and Politburo.[6] The CCP Congress also took up the question of the Party's new general secretary. According to Chang Kuo-t'ao, there were two roughly equal factions, one consisting of Chou En-lai, Li Li-san, and Ch'ü Ch'iu-pai, and the other of Ts'ai Ho-sen, Hsiang Ying, and Chang Kuo-t'ao (qq.v.). Because they could not reach an agreement, Comintern representative Pavel Mif selected Hsiang Chung-fa (q.v.) as a compromise general secretary[7] (although, in fact, Li Li-san soon emerged as the most powerful leader). At the Comintern meeting held immediately afterwards, Hsiang claims to have been elected a "supervisory member" of the Comintern.

Hsiang remained in Moscow for a brief period of study and then returned home in 1929. In November of that year he was elected chairman of the All-China Federation of Labor at the Fifth All-China Labor Congress, replacing Su Chao-cheng who had died earlier in the year. The Fifth Congress, held in secret in Shanghai, was the last national labor congress convened by the Communists until the Sixth Congress in Harbin nearly 19 years later. At the time of the 1929 congress, the Labor Federation purported to represent some 70,000 workers, but three fifths of them were in Communist bases in the hinterlands where there existed little of a true proletarian class.[8] Hsiang also replaced Su Chao-cheng (presumably about 1929) as China's representative to the Pan-Pacific Trade Union Secretariat, which had been set up in 1927 under the auspices of the Profintern.[9] Hsiang headed the Labor Federation only briefly, and by the latter part of 1930 Lo Chang-lung (q.v.) emerged as the key figure in the organization.

When Hsiang had returned to China in 1929 the CCP was led by the young labor leader Li Li-san. In the course of the next year Li's aggressive policies brought the Party to the brink of disaster. In particular, Li was the arch advocate of a policy to capture the major cities in the Yangtze River valley in central China. To carry this out, he ordered the various Red Army units in central and south China to move toward the Yangtze, and he also sent a number of Party and labor organizers to these key cities. Hsiang was dispatched to Wuhan to help organize a general strike intended to support P'eng Te-huai's (q.v.) military units, which captured Changsha, the Hunan capital, in late July 1930. P'eng was quickly driven from Changsha, and the strike effort in Wuhan proved to be equally abortive. In brief, within a few weeks Li Li-san's grandiose plans had collapsed, and in the latter half of the year he was removed from power and succeeded by the "28 Bolsheviks" (or Russian-returned student group) led by Ch'en Shao-yü (q.v.) and others, with the powerful backing of Comintern representative Pavel Mif. Ch'en and his colleagues consolidated their position at the Fourth Party Plenum, held in Shanghai in early 1931. This important meeting coincided with Chiang Kai-shek's First Annihilation Campaign against the Communist base in southeast Kiangsi where Chu Te and Mao Tse-tung were in command. Hsiang claims that after the debacle of mid-1930 he had been sent from Wuhan to Kiangsi, and that after the defeat of Chiang's attack he had become "chairman of the Revolutionary Military Committee" of the Red Army.

The nature of the Revolutionary Military Committee (or council) is not clear from available documentation. It was set up in mid-1930 in connection with Li Li-san's plans to capture the Yangtze cities; Chu Te described it as the "forerunner" of the Chinese Soviet Republic (see below), but he also commented that it was "little more than a theory at the time because our communications . . . were so poor."[10] In addition to this position, Hsiang also became secretary of the CCP's Central Bureau of the Soviet Areas, which had been established in mid-January 1931, just a few days after the above-mentioned Fourth Plenum. Like the Revolutionary Military Committee, there is a similar lack of clarity about the role and importance of the Central Bureau, whose nine members included such key figures as Hsiang, Chou En-lai, Jen Pi-shih, Chu Te, and Mao Tse-tung. It is fairly clear that it was intended to coordinate the activities of the scattered Red Army bases, but other sources assert that it was designed to "check" Mao's power in Kiangsi.[11]

In the early part of 1931 Hsiang seems to have taken an important part in settling the Fu-t'ien Incident[12] (see under P'eng Te-huai), and by his own account he also took part in a "number of battles" against Chiang Kai-shek's Nationalist armies—apparently a reference to the Second and Third Annihilation Campaigns in the spring and summer of 1931. In November 1931, at Juichin, the Communists convened the First All-China Congress of Soviets, which created the Chinese Soviet Republic. Hsiang was one of the featured speakers at the Congress; according to Agnes Smedley he was then "Secretary of the Central Revolutionary Committee of the Red Army," and "before the Congress he had been in charge of general affairs in the Kiangsi Central Soviet Region." Mao was elected chairman of the Central Executive Committee (CEC), the supreme political organ of the Republic, and Hsiang and Chang Kuo-t'ao were elected the two vice-chairmen (Chang in absentia.). Subordinate to the CEC was the Council of People's Commissars (the cabinet); Mao also headed this, and Hsiang and Chang were also the two vice-chairmen. At the same time that he held this post, Hsiang was People's Commissar for Labor, an appointment that reflected his past eminence in the labor movement.

The First Congress also established the Revolutionary Military Council, which was apparently a reorganized version of the body which Hsiang had previously directed. Chu Te was made chairman of the Council, as well as commander-in-chief of the Red Army. Hsiang described the next few years of his career to Snow: "Until that time Mao had been preoccupied with military duties and even afterward, until 1933, he spent most of his time at the front, while I remained in the rear as acting chairman of the Government. When Mao returned I acted as chairman of the Military Council, for Chu Te." Hsiang's assertion that he acted for Chu is also mentioned by Ts'ai Shu-fan (q.v.), who identified Hsiang in that post in mid-1933.[13] Hsiang then continued his comments to Edgar Snow: "In January [1934], the Second Congress was held and Chu Te returned, and remained at Juichin, as the Fifth Campaign of Annihilation was beginning." He went on to note that during the early thirties he had "acted as minister of various departments, including labor, land, finance, investigation, etc."

Hsiang was once more a featured speaker at the Second All-China Congress of Soviets, which met in January–February 1934. He and Chang Kuo-t'ao were again elected vice-chairmen of the CEC, and he was also elected one of the 17 members of the newly created Presidium, the organ in charge of government affairs between sessions of the CEC. Under the Council of People's Commissars, he relinquished the Labor portfolio, but he assumed new responsibilities as Commissar for Workers' and Peasants' Supervision. However, some eight months later (October 1934) the Kiangsi base was virtually abandoned when Chu, Mao, and most of the key military and Party leaders left on the Long March. A number of sources (particularly those hostile to Mao) assert that Hsiang was deliberately left behind to a hopeless cause. On the other hand, Chu Te provided a more commonplace and perhaps more reasonable explanation when he told Agnes Smedley that Hsiang and others had been ordered to serve as a rear-guard element. More specifically, Chu stated that Hsiang was designated the "party leader and political commissar of all the armed forces and political cadres," and Ch'en I (q.v.) was named "supreme military commander."[14]

The extraordinary difficulties that Hsiang, Ch'en, and their men endured during the next three years are described in the biography of Ch'en I. It should be further noted, however, that Maoist historians have uniformly underplayed Hsiang's role in those years. This appears to derive from the fact that during the pre-Long March period Mao and Hsiang differed on various political and military policies, and in later years Mao held Hsiang mainly responsible for the New Fourth Army Incident (see below). It was not until the early fall of 1937, not long after the start of the Sino-Japanese War, that Hsiang and his forces were rescued from their difficult situation by the new "united front" to resist the Japanese. Hsiang went to Nanchang for negotiations with Kiangsi Governor Hsiung Shih-hui and Nationalist Minister of War Ho Ying-ch'in. These talks, which led to the creation of the Communists' New Fourth Army, which was to operate in the lower Yangtze Valley, were completed soon afterwards in Nanking where Ch'in Pang-hsien (q.v.) led the Communist delegation. Before the negotiations were completed in mid-October, Hsiang went to Yenan where he "studied for several months" and "received new instructions from the Central Committee." According to journalist Nym Wales, who was in Yenan immediately before Hsiang's arrival, he was then one of the three vice-chairmen of the Revolutionary Military Council, which she described as second only to the Politburo in importance.[15] In view of the Maoist treatment of Hsiang's career, it is noteworthy that Miss Wales described Hsiang as the "No. 1 'proletarian' of the Chinese Communists" who "ranks next to Mao Tse-tung as a combination of political and military genius."[16]

The New Fourth Army was formally established in January 1938. Yeh T'ing was the commander, and Hsiang served as deputy commander and political commissar. Yeh had been a very important Communist leader in the 1920's, but he had left the Party in 1927. As a consequence, Hsiang was the senior Communist official in the New Fourth Army in its earliest days. In the latter half of 1938 Agnes Smedley, the American journalist who was on extremely close terms with scores of top Communist leaders, visited the New Fourth Army area of operations and interviewed both Yeh and Hsiang. According to her account, the two men were on very bad terms; she wrote that Hsiang and other Communist leaders had "conducted intrigues which prevented Yeh from exercising any control over the Army." She described Hsiang as having an "austere, unyielding personality" and as a "man who would adopt any method to reach his goal. His critics said that intrigue and craftiness had become a part of his nature." Further, Miss Smedley charged that Hsiang had been responsible for spreading the story that Yeh had left the CCP "after marrying a rich Hong Kong woman." After citing this and similarly damaging rumors, she wrote: "I happened to know that the highest Communist leaders in Yenan and Chungking were enraged by such rumors."[17] It is possible, though undocumented, that this situation contributed to the hostile attitude toward Hsiang adopted by latter-day Maoist historians.

An account of the first years of the New Fourth Army's operations is contained in the biography of Yeh T'ing. The army consisted initially of four detachments, three of which were operating south of the Yangtze River by mid-1938. These detachments were south and east of Nanking, in a region stretching from Tanyang to Kiangsu to Fan-ch'ang in Anhwei. The headquarters force to which Hsiang belonged was soon located at Ching-hsien, about 50 miles south of Wuhu. The New Fourth Army operated in the strategic countryside along the lower Yangtze through which ran vital communication lines to such important cities as Shanghai and Nanking. In the early part of the war the Nationalists and Communists cooperated in actions against both the Japanese forces and the Japanese-controlled Chinese "puppet" troops. However, by 1939 CCP–KMT relations had already become seriously strained, and the Nationalists exerted a variety of pressures to get the Communists to move their troops northward across the Yàngtze. The Communists yielded to these pressures, and by mid-1940 most of their troops were already north of the river. An important exception was the Yeh-Hsiang headquarters force, which remained at its Ching-hsien base in south Anhwei. After a series of proposals and counterproposals in the fall of 1940, the situation reached a dramatic climax in January 1941 when the Nationalists wiped out the Communist headquarters force. During the 10-day battle, known as the New Fourth Army or South Anhwei Incident (described in Yeh T'ing's biography), Hsiang and Political Department Director Yuan Kuo-p'ing were killed, and Yeh T'ing was captured and imprisoned.

Like other events in Hsiang's career, his contributions to the work of the New Fourth Army are not easy to assess. In spite of the above-quoted negative commentary by Agnes Smedley, she also wrote: "There was another side to this medal. Hsiang . . . had been one of the leaders responsible for the kind of organization and training that had made the New Fourth Army the most effective and intellectually enlightened military force" behind Japanese lines.[18] Moreover, the Maoist leadership had seen fit to give Hsiang not only two key posts in the New Fourth Army, but also to make him the secretary of the Party's Southeast Bureau, which, from 1938 to 1941, controlled Party affairs in Kiangsu, Anhwei, Chekiang, Kiangsi, Hupeh, and Hunan. (In addition, at the time of his death Hsiang was still a member of the Party Central Committee, although it appears that he had been dropped from the Politburo, presumably at about the time the Long March began in 1934.) The Communists, of course, immediately and vigorously protested the New Fourth Army Incident and Hsiang's death, but in a Party directive issued by Mao Tse-tung soon afterwards (May 1941), Mao attributed the severe defeat to Hsiang's "opportunism."[19] In later years the annotators of Mao's Selected Works elaborated on Mao's accusation. In May 1940, Mao issued a directive to Hsiang's Southeast Bureau, but Hsiang "held strong Rightist views and was irresolute in carrying out the line of the Central Committee. He did not dare fully to arouse the masses to action and to expand the Liberated Areas and the people's army in the Japanese-occupied areas, did not sufficiently realize the seriousness of the possibility of reactionary attacks by the Kuomintang, and was therefore unprepared for them mentally and organizationally." The annotators praised Ch'en I (q.v.), a top New Fourth Army commander, because Ch'en had allegedly put Mao's directive into effect immediately, but Hsiang had been "reluctant to do so. He made

no preparations against the attacks of the Kuomintang reactionaries so that he was in a weak and helpless position when Chiang Kai-shek staged the Southern Anhwei Incident in January 1941, in which nine thousand of our troops were annihilated and Comrade Hsiang Ying himself was killed."[20]

Photographs of Hsiang bear out Edgar Snow's vivid description of a man who looked "the part of a Treaty-Port foreigner's idea of a 'typical coolie.' His lips and nose are broad and thick; his teeth, some of which are missing, jut out irregularly and are unsightly; his hands are stubby and calloused; his big broad feet are most comfortable in peasant straw sandals. Everything about this wiry and muscular figure suggests primitive strength and a life of toil and sweat." Unlike so many of his Communist colleagues, Hsiang was apparently not a regular contributor to the Communist press. However, some of his speeches dealing with the early period of the New Fourth Army were published in 1939 under the title *Hsiang Ying chiang-chün yen-lun chi* (Collected speeches of General Hsiang Ying).

---

1. Edgar Snow, "Han Ying's 'Lost' Red Army," *Asia*, 39: 203–205 (April 1939); Edgar Snow, *The Battle for Asia* (New York, 1941), pp. 127–139; Nym Wales, *The Chinese Labor Movement* (New York, 1945), pp. 212–219; Hsi-wu lao-jen [Elder Hsi-wu], "*Erh-ch'i*" *hui-i-lu* (Reminiscences of "February Seventh"; Peking, 1957), pp. 62–104.

2. Wales, p. 30.

3. Teng Chung-hsia, *Chung-kuo chih-kung yun-tung chien-shih* (A short history of the Chinese labor movement; n.p., 1949), p. 175.

4. Jean Chesneaux, *Le Mouvement ouvrier chinois de 1919 à 1927* (Paris, 1962), p. 412.

5. *Ibid.*, pp. 419–420.

6. Wang Chien-min, *Chung-kuo kung-ch'an tang shih-kao* (An outline history of the Chinese Communist Party; Taipei, 1965), II, 3, 37.

7. Tso-liang Hsiao, *Power Relations within the Chinese Communist Movement, 1930–1934* (Seattle, Wash., 1961), p. 61.

8. Wales, p. 164.

9. *Ibid.*, p. 208.

10. Agnes Smedley, *The Great Road* (New York, 1956), pp. 275–276.

11. Tso-liang Hsiao, pp. 150–152.

12. *Ibid.*, p. 113.

13. Nym Wales, *Red Dust* (Stanford, Calif., 1952), p. 89.

14. Smedley, p. 308.

15. Nym Wales, *Inside Red China* (New York, 1939), p. 343.

16. *Ibid.*, p. 311.

17. Agnes Smedley, *Battle Hymn of China* (New York, 1943), pp. 257–259.

18. *Ibid.*, p. 259.

19. *Selected Works of Mao Tse-tung* (Peking, 1965), II, 465.
20. *Ibid.*, pp. 431–432.

Hsiao Ching-kuang

(c.1902–   ; Changsha, Hunan). Military leader; Chinese Navy commander; vice-minister, Ministry of National Defense; member, CCP Central Committee.

One of the earliest members of the Communist movement, Hsiao Ching-kuang received military and political training both in China and in the Soviet Union. He commanded troops in the Kiangsi-Fukien area in the early thirties and then made the Long March. During the Sino-Japanese War Hsiao saw relatively little action as a rear echelon officer in the Shansi-Kansu-Ninghsia Border Region, but in the civil war against the Nationalists he played a major role in commanding troops. He was elected an alternate member of the Party Central Committee in 1945 and was promoted to full membership 11 years later. Hsiao has been commander of the Chinese Navy since 1950.

Hsiao comes from a military family in Changsha, the Hunan capital. After receiving an elementary school education, he entered the First Middle School in Changsha (c.1918). Mao Tse-tung had studied at this school a few years earlier, before he entered the more famous Hunan Provincial First Normal School. Among Hsiao's fellow students was Jen Pi-shih (q.v.), who was destined to become one of the CCP's top leaders. Changsha was then a center of liberal and anarchist thought, and while Hsiao and Jen were in school the May Fourth Incident (1919) took place. Hsiao claims that he and Jen were deeply influenced by this famous incident, as well as by the short-lived *Hsiang-chiang p'ing-lun* (Hsiang River review), which Mao edited. Jen (and apparently Hsiao) graduated from the middle school in 1920. Mao was then sponsoring a program to encourage students to study in the Soviet Union, and it appears that Hsiao was in contact with him in this connection.[1] In any case, Jen and Hsiao went to Shanghai that year, where they studied Russian at a foreign language school set up by Comintern representative Gregory Voitinsky and his Chinese assistant, Yang Ming-chai (q.v.). Jen and Hsiao also joined the Socialist Youth League, founded at the instigation of Voitinsky in August 1920. It is not certain when Hsiao joined the CCP. One report states that he did not join until 1927, but it seems more likely that he followed the example of his companion Jen Pi-shih who joined in 1922.

In late 1920 or early 1921 Jen and Hsiao left for Moscow, traveling via Vladivostok, which was then still occupied by the Japanese. From 1921 to 1924 they studied at the Communist University of the Toilers of the East,[2] officially established in April 1921 and by the fall of 1922 offering a three-year program to some 800 Asian students. Hsiao was back in China in 1924 in time to enter the first class of the Whampoa Military Academy, where Chiang Kai-shek was the commandant. Among his classmates were Hsu Hsiang-ch'ien, Ch'en Keng, and Chou Shih-ti (qq.v.), all of whom became important Communist leaders in later years. From Whampoa, Hsiao entered the Hunan army of T'an Yen-k'ai, which was incorporated into the national revolutionary force in mid-1925 as the Second Army. In 1926–27 Hsiao participated in the Northern Expedition as a "party" representative attached to the Second Army's Fifth Division. The reference to the "party" might refer to the CCP, but it could refer to the KMT, which also had political officers, many of them Whampoa graduates.

After the final KMT-CCP break in mid-1927 Hsiao returned to the Soviet Union, where he studied at the Red Army Academy until 1931. Thus by 1931 he had spent a total of eight years in the USSR, a figure matched by few members of the CCP elite. There are conflicting reports about his activities after his return to China. Apparently he was active in west Fukien in 1931 as commander of the Seventh Red Army, and he may have been associated with a military academy there or in Juichin in southeast Kiangsi. But by the end of 1931 he was the political commissar of the Fifth Red Army Corps.[3] This Corps was organized in December 1931 from the troops that had defected from the Nationalists' 26th Route Army at Ning-tu in eastern Kiangsi.

In 1933 Hsiao was garrison commander of Li-ch'uan, a town in eastern Kiangsi on a tributary of the Fu River and a strategic point in the Kiangsi-Fukien base because of its location in the foothills of the mountain chain forming part of the provincial boundaries. When Li-ch'uan was lost to the Nationalists in September 1933 Hsiao was held responsible by the Party headquarters in Juichin. The accusations brought against him were connected with political policies which the Party leaders in Juichin called the Lo Ming line. Lo (q.v.), the acting secretary of the Fukien Party Committee in 1933, was carrying out policies in the Kiangsi-Fukien Soviet which he felt were necessitated by the special circumstances there. Apparently the peasants in the area had become apathetic if not hostile to the Communist programs, especially the aggressive land appropriation programs then being promoted by the group in control of the Party in Kiangsi (see under Ch'in Pang-hsien). Consequently, Lo favored a less aggressive program, which made him the target of attacks from such prominent Party leaders as Li Wei-han and Chou En-lai (qq.v.). In December

1933 Chou published an article in the Communist journal *Tou-cheng* (Struggle) describing Lo's principal mistakes as "retreat, escape, vacillation, and right opportunism." Hsiao was blamed for all the errors of the Lo Ming line as it affected military policy. This was a matter of grave concern to the Communists at a time when they were trying to stiffen their resistance in preparation for the Nationalists' Fifth Extermination Campaign. Chou's article described Hsiao as the "executer, leader, and promoter of the Lo Ming line in the Red Army."[4] It is not entirely clear where Mao stood in this controversy, but his later writings have repudiated Chou's and Li's position and approved of Lo and his supporters.[5]

Hsiao apparently returned to Juichin after his failure at Li-ch'uan in 1933. He was subsequently attached to the headquarters of the Chu-Mao First Front Army, with which he made the Long March in 1934–35. He was reported to have served as chief-of-staff of the Cadres' Regiment of the Red Army during the march. Not long after arriving in north Shensi, Hsiao participated in the Communists' thrust across the Yellow River into Shansi in early 1936, a campaign described in the biography of Liu Chih-tan. One of the major purposes of this operation was to recruit soldiers for the Red Army, whose forces had been badly depleted during the Long March. Hsiao helped recruit these men, whom the Communists formed into the 29th Independent Army, numbering about 8,000 under Hsiao's command.[6] The Communist campaign in Shansi ended in the spring of 1936 when they were driven back into Shensi. Hsiao continued to head the 29th Army until 1937, concurrently serving as chairman of the Kansu Soviet Government's Military Committee. He was interviewed by American journalists Edgar Snow and Nym Wales in 1936 and 1937 and also by U.S. Naval Observer Evans Carlson in 1938. Carlson described him as a "huge man with a hearty, boisterous manner" who was "considered to be an able tactician."[7]

During the Sino-Japanese War years Hsiao's main assignments were with the rear echelon of the Communists' Eighth Route Army and the Shensi-Kansu-Ninghsia (Shen-Kan-Ning) Border Region Government. As commander of the rear echelon, Hsiao's duties included the defense line demarcated by the Yellow River to the east of Yenan. Troops under his command clashed in December 1939 with the forces of the Nationalist governor of Kansu, Chu Shao-liang (the East Kansu Incident).[8] Although the fighting soon ended it has been characterized by the Communists as the Nationalists' "first anti-Communist upsurge." At some time in the early 1940's Hsiao served as second deputy commander of the Joint Defense Command, the

forces established to protect the Shansi-Suiyuan and Shen-Kan-Ning Border Regions (see under Ho Lung, the commander). Apart from his military duties, Hsiao represented Hsia-hsien (Shensi) in the Second Assembly of the Shen-Kan-Ning Border Region. At the Assembly's inaugural session in November 1941, Hsiao gave a report on military affairs and was elected to the Council, the executive branch of the Border Region Government. He was also present in December 1944 for the second session of the Assembly. When the CCP held its Seventh National Congress in Yenan from April to June 1945, Hsiao was elected one of the 33 alternate members of the Party Central Committee.

In the immediate postwar period Hsiao was one of the many military leaders sent to Manchuria, where Lin Piao established the Northeast Democratic Allied Army (known later as the Northeast PLA). Chou Pao-chung, Lü Cheng-ts'ao (qq.v.), and Hsiao were Lin's three deputy commanders. Hsiao served concurrently (c.1947–48) as commander of the North Manchurian Military Region and also as a member of the Party's Northeast Bureau. As the Communists completed their conquest of Manchuria and moved into north China in 1948–49, he participated in the battles for Changchun, Kalgan, and Tientsin. In February 1949, shortly after Tientsin fell, Hsiao was appointed as the garrison commander. When Lin's army (named the Fourth Field Army in early 1949) pushed southward into Hupeh, Hsiao became the Wuhan Garrison commander and a member of the Wuhan Military Control Commission (May 1949). Continuing their southward advance, the Communists won control of Hunan by the end of the summer. Hsiao, already a deputy commander of the Fourth Field Army, became chairman of the Changsha Military Control Commission and commander of the Hunan Military District. In the early part of 1950 he received two civilian posts, one as a member of the Central-South Military and Administrative Committee and the other as a member of the Hunan Provincial People's Government.

Hsiao remained in central-south China until the end of the summer of 1950 when he was transferred to Peking to assume command of the small Chinese Navy, which then consisted of only a few gunboats and other small ships. He continues to head the Navy, which in contrast to the other arms of the military establishment (e.g., the Air Force) is quite weak. Under a treaty signed in early 1950 in Moscow by Chou En-lai, the Russians retained rights (which were not relinquished until 1955) to use the naval facilities at Port Arthur-Dairen. Hsiao was presumably in regular contact with his Soviet naval counterparts, as suggested by several visits he made to the Port Arthur area in the early 1950's. In this regard his knowledge of Russian may have been a factor in his appointment as head of the Chinese naval forces.

In 1954 Hsiao was elected a Navy deputy to the First NPC, which, at its initial session in September, inaugurated the constitutional government. (He was not re-elected to the Second NPC in 1959, but he was again elected a Navy deputy to the Third NPC, which opened in December 1964.) In September 1954 he became a member of the newly created National Defense Council, a post he still retains. At this same time he was also made one of the vice-ministers of the newly established Ministry of National Defense, serving under P'eng Te-huai until 1959 and thereafter under Lin Piao. Of the 12 men who have been National Defense vice-ministers only Hsiao, Wang Shu-sheng, and Liao Han-sheng (qq.v.) have served continuously from 1954 to the mid-1960's. Since late 1954 Hsiao has also been a member of the Sino-Soviet Friendship Association's Executive Board.

In September 1955 the Communists first awarded national military honors and gave their officers personal military ranks. Hsiao was made a senior (four-star) admiral and was given the three top awards, the Orders of August First, Independence and Freedom, and Liberation—decorations covering military service from 1927 to 1950. Exactly a year later he was promoted from alternate to full membership on the Party Central Committee at the Eighth CCP Congress. In November–December 1957 Hsiao made his first postwar trip abroad as a member of P'eng Te-huai's 12-member delegation which was part of the larger entourage that Mao Tse-tung led to Moscow for the 40th anniversary of the Russian Revolution. Through the mid-sixties Hsiao continued to make a great many public appearances in Peking, although most of them seem to have been ceremonial in nature. He has also been reported in the press on occasion visiting coastal cities, presumably to inspect naval facilities. At the close of the first session of the Third NPC in January 1965, Hsiao was elected a member of the NPC Standing Committee. Thus, in addition to his Party, naval, and Defense Ministry posts, he became an official in the PRC's most important legislative body.

Hsiao's wife, who also studied in Moscow, was imprisoned in Shanghai in the early thirties and was not released until mid-1937.[9] In 1936 he told Edgar Snow that he had one son studying in Moscow and another in Shanghai.[10] Because of his very extensive military training in China and the Soviet Union, it might be expected that he would have regularly published articles on military policy or strategy. In fact, however, aside from a contribution to *K'ang-Jih yu-chi chan-cheng ti i-pan wen-t'i* (General problems in the anti-Japanese guerrilla war; Yenan, 1938),[11] he seems to have written very

little. The October 31, 1950, issue of the *JMJP* carried a brief piece by Hsiao commemorating his late colleague Jen Pi-shih; this was reprinted in *Hsueh-hsi Jen Pi-shih T'ung-chih* (Learn from Comrade Jen Pi-shih; Canton, 1950) and provides useful information on the early careers of both Jen and Hsiao.

1. Jerome Ch'en, *Mao and the Chinese Revolution* (London, 1965) p. 72.
2. *Hung-ch'i p'iao-p'iao* (Red flag fluttering; Peking, 1957), IV, 23.
3. Ch'en, p. 175.
4. Tso-liang Hsiao, *Power Relations within the Chinese Communist Movement, 1930–1934* (Seattle, 1961), pp. 245–246.
5. *Selected Works of Mao Tse-tung* (London, 1956), IV, 342.
6. Edgar Snow, *Random Notes on Red China, 1936–1945* (Cambridge, Mass., 1957), p. 32.
7. Evans Fordyce Carlson, *Twin Stars of China* (New York, 1940), p. 175.
8. Chalmers A. Johnson, *Peasant Nationalism and Communist Power* (Stanford, Calif., 1962), p. 122.
9. Nym Wales, *Inside Red China* (New York, 1939), p. 281; Snow, p. 32.
10. Snow, p. 32.
11. Chün-tu Hsüeh, *The Chinese Communist Movement, 1937–1949* (Stanford, Calif., 1962), pp. 78–79.

Hsiao Ch'u-nü

(1894–1927; Hupeh). Early Socialist Youth League leader; propagandist.

Hsiao Ch'u-nü was one of the Communist movement's leading ideologues in the 1920's and during his short career he was associated with top Party members in the youth movement and in Communist-dominated organizations like the Peasant Movement Training Institute. He lost both parents when still a child and grew up in poverty, working as a ship's steward, a clerk, and in various other jobs. He never had any formal schooling but apparently did a good deal of independent study. In the years before and after the May Fourth Incident (1919), Hsiao taught school in Wuhan, where he became involved in the "new culture" movement. In 1919 he edited the *Ta Han pao* (Great Han newspaper) there. Hsiao hoped to enroll at a Wuhan university but he was never able to accumulate enough money. Instead he audited classes at Chung-hua University in Wuchang. It was apparently at this time that he met Yun Tai-ying (q.v.) who attended the University from 1915 to 1919. Probably in association with Yun, Hsiao became very active in the Wuhan youth movement, and sometime between 1919 and 1921 his political activity cost him his job on the *Ta Han pao*. After being fired, he was invited to Hsiang-yang, a town about 150 miles northwest of Wuhan, to teach in the Hsiang-yang Provincial Normal School. However, he also lost this job for his continued political activities and a warrant for his arrest was issued. Returning to Wuhan, he lived as a fugitive in the Social Benefit Bookstore (see under Yun Tai-ying).

Hsiao contributed to *Wu-han hsing-ch'i p'ing-lun* (Wuhan weekly review), which was founded in Hankow in 1921 and which later became a Communist publication. In the late summer of that year he accompanied Yun and Li Ch'iu-shih (q.v.) to Lu-chou, Szechwan, where they taught at the Lu-chou Associated Normal School (see under Yun Tai-ying). Afterward, Hsiao left Yun to go to Chungking where he taught school and became editor of the *Hsin-Shu jih-pao* (New Szechwan daily). He also wrote articles for local newspapers, encouraging Szechwanese youths to adopt the "new thought" and propagandizing socialist theory. Hsiao was in Szechwan until the fall of 1923 when he was transferred to Shanghai to work on the Socialist Youth League Central Committee. At that time Yun Tai-ying was editing *Chung-kuo ch'ing-nien* (China youth), the League's organ, and Hsiao became a co-editor and contributor. He also lectured at the radical Shanghai University as did his fellow Communists Yun, Teng Chung-hsia, Chang T'ai-lei, and Ts'ai Ho-sen (qq.v.). After the Whampoa Military Academy was founded in May 1924 in Canton, Hsiao was sent there as a political instructor.[1] In the same year, with Tung Pi-wu and Ch'en T'an-ch'iu, he went to Chin-chai hsien, Anhwei, to lead the peasant movement and set up a CCP organization.[2] After the May 30th incident in 1925 he went to Honan where he engaged in propaganda work for Feng Yü-hsiang's Kuominchün.[3] Because Feng was then beginning to cooperate with both the Soviet and the Chinese Communists, quite a few CCP members were operating in his area (see under Wang Jo-fei).

Returning to Canton, Hsiao attended the Second Congress of the KMT in January 1926, and afterward served in the KMT Central Committee's Propaganda Department, headed by Mao Tse-tung. He also taught a course in the history of 19th-century social thought at the newly established Social Science Institute of Kwangtung University (later Sun Yat-sen University).[4] In March, Hsiao and Mao Tse-tung were members of the Committee for Peasant Movements of the KMT Central Peasants' Department. In that same month, *Nung-min yun-tung chiang-hsi-so ts'ung-shu* (Collected reprints of the Peasant Movement Training Institute) was compiled (although it was not published until 1927). The book included an article by Hsiao entitled "She-hui-chu-i chiao-shou ta-kang" (A teacher's outline of socialism).[5] Hsiao, Mao, Chang T'ai-lei,

and Teng Chung-hsia then worked at the Peasant Movement Training Institute in Canton during its sixth term (May–October 1926). Mao was the Institute's principal and the others were full-time teachers. Hsiao's courses were entitled "Imperialism," "The history of the Chinese people's revolutionary movement," and "Social problems and socialism."[6] During this period Hsiao was again a political instructor at Whampoa and in November 1926 the Academy's Political Department published a book entitled *She-hui k'o-hsueh kai-lun* (A summary of social science) by Hsiao.[7] In 1926 he was also co-editor with Li Ch'iu-shih of *Shao-nien hsien-feng* (Youth vanguard), published in Canton.

Hsiao's career was cut short in early 1927 when he became ill and entered the Sun Yat-sen University Hospital in Canton. On April 12, the right-wing KMT launched its coup against the Communists. Hsiao, still hospitalized, was unable to escape and was killed there on April 18. He was only 33 at the time.

In addition to the writings already mentioned, Hsiao is also said to have written two books. The first was *Hsien-wei-ching hsia kuo-chia-chu-i* (Focus on nationalism; 1924), written as an attack on Tseng Ch'i, a leader of the Young China Party who opposed the alliance with the Soviet Union and the admission of CCP members into the KMT. The second was *Kuo-min ko-ming yü Chung-kuo Kung-ch'an-tang* (The national revolution and the CCP; 1925). This was a criticism of Tai Chi-t'ao's *Kuo-min ko-ming yü Chung-kuo Kuo-min-tang* (The national revolution and the KMT; 1925), which attacked the KMT-CCP alliance. Apparently in an effort to preserve the alliance, Hsiao and Tai were restrained by their respective parties. Hsiao's book was not allowed to be sold and the Party allegedly placed him under observation (*ch'a-k'an*).[8]

1. Ch'en Po-ta, *Notes on Ten Years of Civil War* (Peking, 1954), pp. 107–108.

2. *Kung-ch'ing-t'uan, wo-te mu-ch'in* (The Communist Youth League, my mother; Peking, 1958), p. 17; *Chung-kuo Kung-ch'an-tang tsai chung-nan-ti-ch'ü ling-tao ko-ming tou-cheng te li-shih tzu-liao* (Historical materials on the revolutionary struggles led by the CCP in central-south China; Wuhan, 1951), I, 269.

3. T'an Kung, "Hsiao Ch'u-nü ti i-sheng" (The life of Hsiao Ch'u-nü), *Hsien-tai shih-liao* (Materials of modern history; Shanghai, 1935), IV, 317.

4. *Ibid.*, p. 318.

5. Chang Ching-lu, ed., *Chung-kuo hsien-tai ch'u-pan shih-liao* (Historical materials on contemporary Chinese publishing; Peking, 1954), p. 77.

6. *Ibid.*, p. 76.

7. Chang Ching-lu, p. 17 (photos).

8. T'an Kung, pp. 316–317.

Hsiao Fang-chou

(c.1910–   ). Vice-Chairman, China Council for the Promotion of International Trade.

Although Hsiao Fang-chou was not mentioned in the national press media prior to 1953, he had become an important foreign trade specialist by the 1960's. Photographs of Hsiao suggest a man born about 1910.

In September 1953, Hsiao led a team of specialists to Copenhagen to manage a Chinese industrial and agricultural exhibition. This was the first such exhibition to be held by the Chinese Communists in Denmark and was one of the first held in any non-Communist nation, taking place not long after the end of the Korean War during which the Chinese Communists had had extremely few contacts of this sort outside the bloc. The Copenhagen exhibition, which was held from September 25th to October 4th and was attended by a claimed 50,000 Danes, was the first of several such exhibits in which Hsiao took part.

By March 1955 Hsiao was identified as a deputy secretary-general of the Chinese Council for the Promotion of International Trade (CCPIT), the organization to which he would devote most of his time in the years ahead. The Council was established in May 1952 immediately after the Moscow International Economic Conference, a meeting held for the purpose of breaking out of the economic blockade of the Communist nations by the United States and its allies. Since the CCPIT is technically a non-official organ, it has been used mainly in negotiations with nations not having diplomatic relations with Peking. From its establishment the CCPIT has been headed by trade specialists Nan Han-ch'en (the chairman) and the late Chi Ch'ao-ting (the secretary-general).

Hsiao led another delegation abroad in August–September 1956 when he went to the Zagreb International Fair, thus becoming one of the few Chinese officials to have visited Yugoslavia (a visit made during the brief period when Sino-Yugoslav relations were relatively harmonious). Hsiao was abroad again in 1959 and 1963 on similar missions. In February–March 1959 he headed the Chinese exhibition at the Leipzig International Fair in East Germany, one of the most important annual fairs in the Communist world. And in August–September 1963 he was in Algeria in charge of the Chinese "economic construction" exhibition, the opening of which was attended by Algerian Premier Ben Bella.

In the interim, Communist China was expanding its contacts with the non-Communist world, and Hsiao was receiving a number of assignments directly or indirectly related to this work. In November 1956 he was named to membership on the council of the China-Egypt Friendship Association, and when this was merged with a China-Syria counterpart organization in February 1958 (reflecting the merger of Egypt and Syria), Hsiao was placed on the council of the new China-United Arab Republic Friendship Association. Not long after, in July 1958, the Afro-Asian Solidarity Committee of China was enlarged, with Hsiao appointed as one of the new members. He received a broadly similar appointment in April 1960 when he was named to the Standing Committee of the newly formed China-Africa People's Friendship Association.

By the late 1950's, it was clear that Hsiao was becoming a specialist in Sino-Japanese relations, with an emphasis on trade. He was very often on hand in Peking when Japanese visitors were there, and in March 1958 he took part in the negotiations (and was one of the signers) of an unofficial trade agreement between China and Japan providing for 35 million English pounds trade each way over a one-year period. Not long after, however, Sino-Japanese relations took a serious turn for the worse, with the result that this agreement was largely negated. Because of this sudden cooling off, Hsiao saw less of the Japanese for the next few years, but as relations improved in the early 1960's he was once again in the forefront of persons negotiating with visiting Japanese. It was logical, therefore, that when the China-Japan Friendship Association was established in October 1963 Hsiao was named to the Standing Committee. After this extensive association with Japanese affairs, it was also natural that he would lead an economic and trade exhibition to Japan in June and July 1964.

As Hsiao's stature as a foreign trade specialist was growing, he was also moving up the hierarchical ladder within the CCPIT. To handle disputes over maritime shipping, the CCPIT formed a "Maritime Arbitration Commission" in January 1959; Sun Ta-kuang (q.v.) was named as chairman and Hsiao as the vice-chairman. Then, in 1961, after having served several years as a deputy to CCPIT Secretary-General Chi Ch'ao-ting, Hsiao replaced him in this post. Apart from his secretary-generalship, Chi was also a CCPIT vice-chairman. After Chi's death in August 1963, Hsiao succeeded him in this post, being identified by March 1964. It was in this capacity that Hsiao signed semiofficial letters on May 5, 1964, with a visiting Dutch trade promotion delegation affirming a mutual desire to conclude a trade agreement at a later date.

From time to time Hsiao has written articles which, without exception, have dealt with foreign trade matters. For the *Kuang-ming jih-pao* of March 28, 1956, he wrote a piece on trade with Arab nations, and for the June 28, 1956, issue of the same newspaper he authored a denunciation of the United States trade embargo on China. He also wrote two articles for the English-language *Foreign Trade of the People's Republic of China;* for the December 1963 issue he wrote about his trip to Algeria in August–September of that year, and for the March 1964 issue he discussed the potentials of Sino-Japanese trade.

Hsiao Hua

(1914–   ; Hsing-kuo hsien, Kiangsi). Director, PLA General Political Department; member, CCP Central Committee.

Hsiao Hua has spent his entire career in the Red Army, almost all of it as a political officer. A veteran of the Long March, the Sino-Japanese War, and the civil war against the Nationalists, Hsiao served for well over a decade as a deputy director of the PLA General Political Department and then, following the death of Lo Jung-huan, he succeeded to the directorship in 1964. He is one of the youngest members of the CCP's top leadership.

Hsiao comes from a peasant family in Hsing-kuo hsien in east-central Kiangsi.[1] Hsing-kuo city, the hsien seat where Hsiao spent some of his early years, is a walled town in a rather isolated mountain area some 50 miles from the Fukien border. The area was fought over by the Communists a number of times in the late 1920's and the early 1930's. Living in Hsing-kuo, Hsiao probably witnessed some of the Red Army campaigns there such as those described by the American authoress Agnes Smedley, who talked with Chu Te about the battles he fought in Kiangsi before the Long March began. A number of young radicals were drawn to the city of Hsing-kuo in the late twenties by its good schools. One in particular, a middle school, had been the scene of local disturbances led by a young Communist and Whampoa graduate who incited an uprising in Hsing-kuo prior to the entrance into the city of the Communist army commanded by Chu Te and Mao Tse-tung in early 1929.[2]

The records do not associate Hsiao with the uprising, although he may have been influenced by it as his subsequent career suggests. In 1936, when he was in northwest China, American journalist Edgar Snow interviewed him and learned that he had joined the Communists at Chingkangshan at the age of 14.[3] It is possible that Hsiao had connected his career with Chingkangshan in order to indicate that he had been associated with Mao Tse-tung from the historic moment when Mao held together the small band of battle-weary soldiers who formed the nucleus of the Red Army. In fact, most of the Red Army led by Chu Te and Mao was driven out of Chingkangshan at the end of 1928 and on its route eastward toward the Fukien border had entered Hsiao's native Hsing-kuo (February 1929), where it established a short-lived Communist regime. At this time Mao opened a youth training class in Hsing-kuo, in which Hsiao is

said to have enrolled, so it may well have been at this moment that Hsiao first became formally connected with the Communists. Sometime in 1929 Hsiao became a member of the Communist Youth League and presumably he was admitted to the CCP soon afterwards. With only a month of training in Mao's youth class, Hsiao joined a Red Army military unit commanded by Lin Piao, then a very junior officer with the Chu-Mao force (the Fourth Red Army). He was, however, to continue to engage in youth work with the Red Army up to and through the period of the Long March. He had a number of rather important positions in the political training and youth departments of certain of the Red Army units in Kiangsi before the Communists left in the fall of 1934 on the Long March. In 1932 he was identified as director of a "young people's section" of the Political Department of the First Army Corps. This was the corps commanded by Lin Piao, which was subordinate to the First Front Army of Chu and Mao. In 1932 Lo Jung-huan was its principal political officer. Hsiao must have been closely associated with Lo from the moment he joined the Red Army, for in 1963 (in a eulogy for the deceased Lo) he commented that for "more than 30 years after I joined the Fourth Red Army, I spent the greater part of my time working under Marshal Lo's direct supervision."[4]

In September 1933 the Communists established the Young Communist International Division, with Hsiao as commander and political commissar. Hsiao, describing the division in an article written in 1957, claimed that it had more than 10,000 men, over 70 percent of whom were Communist Youth League members.[5] Early in 1934 he was reported to be political commissar of the 15th Division of the Red Army, but this identification is uncertain because the complete order of battle of this division is not known. Then, when the Long March began in 1934, Hsiao's "International Division" was incorporated into the First Army Corps; Nieh Jung-chen was by this political commissar of Lin Piao's Corps, and Lo Jung-huan was head of the Political Department. During the March, Hsiao served with these officers and also with Liu Po-ch'eng (q.v.), who commanded other vanguard troops.

When the Red armies entered southern Sikang in the spring of 1935 Hsiao was given a special assignment to contact the non-Han minority tribesmen (the Yi) who inhabited the area south of the Ta-tu River and to seek their permission to cross through their lands on the march north. Writing of this episode, Hsiao claims that it was he who made the initial contacts that enabled Liu Po-ch'eng to negotiate the agreement with the Yi. Now celebrated in Communist accounts, the agreement allowed the Red armies safe passage through Yi territory.[6]

Then, after reaching north Shensi with the main forces of Mao's armies in the fall of 1935, Hsiao (as political commissar of the Second Division of the First Army Corps) was sent with the Communist advance into Kansu in the spring of 1936. In his writings, Hsiao has described the battles his troops fought in eastern Kansu against the cavalry of Moslem warlord Ma Hung-k'uei, and tells of joining forces in October 1936 with the Second Front Red Army (see under Ho Lung) and the Fourth Front Red Army (see under Chang Kuo-t'ao), which were then making their way north from Sikang to join Mao Tse-tung in north Shensi.[7]

At the start of the Sino-Japanese War in mid-1937, Lin Piao's army became the 115th Division, one of the three important units of the Communists' Eighth Route Army in north China. Hsiao became director of the Organization Section of the Division's Political Department, and when the Division went into battle in September 1937 he was attached to the 343rd Brigade (said to be a favorite unit of Mao Tse-tung). In postwar times Hsiao was cited for "meritorious service" in the fighting during the early war years.

At the end of September 1937 Lin's 115th Division fought an important battle at P'ing-hsing Pass in northeast Shansi, defeating part of a major Japanese division. After the battle, Lin led two brigades of the 115th Division (the 343rd and the 344th) to the mountains of southeast Shansi, where he left them for a time to fight as semi-independent forces. (For descriptions of these brigades, see under Yang Te-chih and Yang Yung.) The 343rd Brigade, commanded by Ch'en Kuang (a secretary of the Kiangsu CCP Committee since 1956), made its headquarters in the border area of Shansi, Hopeh, and Shantung provinces, where it could command the route to Shantung. From the start of the war there were very active local resistance forces in western Shantung, which were at first able to harass the invading Japanese troops gaining control of the area. But when in November 1938 the Japanese turned upon the Shantung guerrillas in earnest, killing their commander, the resistance forces in western Shantung were temporarily broken up. Subsequently, in November 1938, the CCP decided to send troops to their rescue and called upon some of Lin's forces, which were stationed in eastern Shansi. In March 1939 Ch'en Kuang's 343rd Brigade, now also designated as the Eastern Advance Detachment (Tung-chin chih-tui), departed from the area along the Peking-Hankow (Pinghan) Railroad in southern Hopeh. By late spring it had established contact with local guerrillas in Yun-ch'eng, Shantung, some 50 miles south of Liao-ch'eng, where the resistance had been especially strong since the beginning of the war, though it too had suffered in the Japanese attacks of November 1938.[8]

Guerrilla operations in Shantung from the spring of 1939 were put largely under the command of the 115th Division and were led by a division officer, Lo Jung-huan. In March 1939, Lo led a major force from the division headquarters in Shansi to Shantung. There his job was to coordinate the work of local provincial guerrilla units; many of these had been influenced by the Communists either through their contact with Red military units or with groups from the National Liberation Vanguard, a militant student organization created in 1936, whose members were drawn from university circles in Peking and Tientsin (see under Li Ch'ang). It is not clear when Hsiao and his troops from the 343rd Brigade entered Shantung, but in 1939 they were under Lo's command. During his first years in the province Hsiao made his headquarters in an area west of Wei-shan Lake, possibly in the vicinity of Yun-ch'eng. In an account published by Hsiao in 1962, he claims that the Communist guerrilla forces in this area consisted initially of one brigade but by 1940 had grown to a force of some 60,000 men.[9] Still serving under the over-all command of Lo Jung-huan, Hsiao was commander of the West Shantung Military District from 1939 until sometime in 1941 (when succeeded by Yang Yung) and concurrently director of the West Shantung Administrative Office, the civil administration for the area. The latter post may have been held by Hsiao somewhat later than 1941. Young and able, Hsiao remained one of the principal officers on Lo Jung-huan's staff in Shantung during the war. It is not clear where the lines of authority in Shantung were divided between the 129th Division of Liu Po-ch'eng and the 120th Division of Lin Piao, but it is evident that elements from both forces were active there during the war.

The principal operations of Lin Piao's army as it fought to take over Manchuria are described in his biography. In these campaigns Hsiao played a significant role. In 1946 he was political commissar of the Liaotung Military District,[10] and from 1946 to 1948 the commander of the Jehol-Liaoning Military Region; in the latter post he had control of one of the important communication routes for the Communist armies entering Manchuria. Late in 1948, as the Communists fought the final battles to drive the Nationalists from Manchuria, he was also political commissar of the 12th Army Corps. This was the Communist force that took over Changchun on October 19, 1948. A month later Lin's army captured Mukden and all of Manchuria was in his control. He immediately moved south, putting his troops in the vicinity of Tientsin and Peking, where they joined the forces of Nieh Jung-chen for the final takeover of the two cities in January 1949. Hsiao Hua participated in all the campaigns of Lin's army during its Manchurian operations and then went south with it for the siege of Tientsin and Peking, which began at the end of 1948. But after the Communists had taken Peking in January 1949 and Lin's army (now designated the Fourth Field Army) prepared to move south to the Yangtze Valley, Hsiao remained in Peking where he was soon to become an important political officer in the PLA headquarters.

Hsiao, only 35 when the Communists came to power in 1949, spent the better part of that year engaged in youth work. He participated in the formation of two of the most important youth organizations, the New Democratic Youth League (NDYL) and the All-China Federation of Democratic Youth (ACFDY), established in April and May, respectively. He spoke on youth work in the PLA at the congress that set up the NDYL and at the close of the meetings was elected to membership on the NDYL Central Committee. He was promoted to Standing Committee membership in November 1951 but then relinquished all his posts in the League at its second congress in 1953. At the youth congress of May 1949, Hsiao became a member of the ACFDY's National Committee, another post he held until 1953. On behalf of the ACFDY, Hsiao went abroad in mid-1949 on an extended trip that took him to several countries in the Communist bloc. Led by youth leader Liao Ch'eng-chih (q.v.), with Hsiao as one of his deputies, the ACFDY sent a large delegation to the Second Congress of the Communist-dominated organization to which the ACFDY is affiliated, the World Federation of Democratic Youth (WFDY). The Congress was held in Budapest in August–September 1949; at the close of the meetings Hsiao was elected to the WFDY's Executive Committee, but it is not known how long he continued in this position. After the Congress, Liao Ch'eng-chih returned home, but Hsiao remained in Europe as leader of the delegation; the group visited Bulgaria, Hungary, Czechoslovakia, Poland, and the Soviet Union before returning to China in January 1950.

While Hsiao was abroad, the new central government was brought into existence at the inaugural session of the CPPCC in September 1949. He was elected to membership on the First National Committee of the CPPCC, a post he held until the Second CPPCC was formed in late 1954. And, when the Sino-Soviet Friendship Association was formed in October 1949, Hsiao was named as a member of the First Executive Council (a post he still retains, having been named to the Second and Third Executive Councils in December 1954 and May 1959, respectively). More important, however, over the winter of 1949–50 Hsiao became a deputy director of the important General Political Department, then subordinate to the People's Revolu-

tionary Military Council. Hsiao's superior in the Political Department was his long-time associate Lo Jung-huan. Within a brief time Hsiao had established himself as a major spokesman for the PLA, especially in relation to the political affairs of the military establishment. For example, he was the keynote speaker at a joint conference of "fighting heroes" and "labor models" held in September–October 1950, and in June 1951 he published a major article ("The CCP and the PLA") commemorating the 30th anniversary of the CCP.[11] A year later, to mark the 25th anniversary of the PLA, he published another important article in which he emphasized the necessity for the PLA to participate in construction work (e.g., dam building), a view he reiterated on many occasions.[12] From this period in the early fifties to the present, Hsiao has continued to be one of the most authoritative PLA spokesmen.

In January 1953 Hsiao became a vice-chairman of a short-lived committee to "implement" the Marriage Law. The following year he was elected as a PLA deputy to the First NPC, which opened in September 1954. (He was not, however, re-elected to the Second NPC in 1959.) In 1955, when the PRC awarded personal military ranks and military orders to its military veterans, Hsiao was made a colonel general (equivalent to a three-star general in the U.S. Army) and was given the Orders of August First, Independence and Freedom, and Liberation, covering service from 1927 to 1950. Throughout the fifties he was one of the more active PLA officers in the promotion of athletic activities—endeavors that the Communists regard as important in improving the physical condition of their soldiers as well as useful in promoting international relations. From June 1952 to October 1956 he was a vice-chairman of the All-China Athletic Federation, and in August 1952 he served as the chief judge of a nationwide PLA sports meet. He was also named as one of the vice-chairmen (January 1956) of the "Preparatory Committee for Participation in the 16th Olympic Games" in Melbourne. (The Chinese Communists, however, ultimately refused to take part in the games owing to the participation of Taiwan; see under Jung Kao-t'ang.) A month later (February 1956), Hsiao was named as a member of a committee established to promote the usage of "standard spoken Chinese" (p'u-t'ung-hua).

Hsiao's lifetime service in the Communist movement was given official recognition at the Party's Eighth National Congress in September 1956 when he was elected to the Central Committee. Then only 42, he was one of the youngest men elected to the Committee. At the First Plenum of the new Central Committee (held the day after the Congress closed), he was made a deputy secretary of the Party's important

Central Control Commission; of the five deputy secretaries, Hsiao was the only one on active military duty. Five years later, when a Standing Committee was formed within the Control Commission, Hsiao was named as a member. In December 1956 Lo Jung-huan relinquished his posts as director of both the PLA General Political Department and the General Cadres Department. T'an Cheng (q.v.) assumed the former post and Hsiao the latter. Thus, while heading one of the PLA departments, Hsiao continued to serve concurrently as a deputy director in the Political Department, now headed by T'an Cheng. Hsiao continued to hold both posts until about 1959 when the Cadres Department (in charge of promotion and movement of military personnel) was placed under the Political Department; at approximately the time this change was made, Hsiao apparently relinquished the Cadres Department directorship.

Although no precise date can be used, Hsiao began to eclipse T'an Cheng, his superor in the Political Department, in about the 1959–60 period. (See the biography of T'an for a discussion of his political decline.) Hsiao's rise was strikingly revealed in the secret PLA *Kung-tso t'ung-hsun* (KTTH; Bulletin of activities); issues of this highly important journal for the year 1961 were released by the U.S. Government in 1963. Although overshadowed by such prominent figures as Defense Minister Lin Piao and former Chief-of-staff Lo Jui-ch'ing, Hsiao's role in the internal workings of the PLA received a great amount of attention. Among other things, the *KTTH* revealed that Hsiao was both the deputy secretary-general (under Secretary-General Lo Jui-ch'ing) and a member of the Standing Committee of the Military Affairs Committee (MAC), the highest military organ of the CCP. A careful study of the secret documents by one authority disclosed nine members on the MAC Standing Committee, only two of whom (Hsiao and Lo Jui-ch'ing) were not PLA marshals.[13]

Hsiao's enhanced stature within the PLA was also indicated by his role in four important "political work conferences" held between late 1961 and early 1966. The conferences were held in response to Lin Piao's demand in October 1960 at a meeting of the Military Affairs Committee that greater attention be given to political work within the PLA. Hsiao was apparently the only man who spoke at all four conferences, each of which stressed the paramountcy of the CCP over the PLA. The above-mentioned decline of Political Department Director T'an Cheng was confirmed in September 1962, when, at the Party's 10th Plenum, he was removed as a member of the Central Secretariat. This removal had the effect of paving the way for Hsiao's assumption of the directorship of the PLA General Political Department, although it appears that former Director Lo Jung-huan again as-

sumed the assignment for a brief period in the early sixties. But then Lo died in December 1963, and nine months later (September 1964) Hsiao was officially appointed to the directorship. Not long afterward, at the close of the first session of the Third NPC in January 1965, Hsiao was made a member of the National Defense Council, a military advisory organ with little power but considerable prestige.

Hsiao has been among the most prolific writers of the PLA leaders. In addition to the articles already cited, he is the author of numerous others, including four in the Party's most important journal, *Hung-ch'i* (Red flag, issues of August 1, 1959, August 1, 1962, August 1, 1963, and May 23, 1964). In addition to his extended trip to Europe in 1949, Hsiao has been abroad on two other occasions. He was a member of P'eng Te-huai's military delegation that toured the seven East European satellite nations, the Soviet Union, and Mongolia in a seven-week period from April to June 1959. And in the last two weeks of December 1961 he was a deputy leader under Marshal Yeh Chien-ying of a delegation sent to Hanoi to attend the celebrations marking the 17th anniversary of the "Vietnam People's Army."

1. Edgar Snow, *Random Notes on Red China* (Cambridge, Mass., 1957), p. 131.

2. Agnes Smedley, *Red Flood over China* (Moscow, 1934), pp. 193ff.

3. Snow, p. 131.

4. *SCMP* 3133, p. 12.

5. *Kung-ch'ing-t'uan, wo-te mu-ch'in* (The youth corps, my mother; Peking, 1958), pp. 6–7.

6. *The Long March: Eyewitness Accounts* (Peking, 1963), pp. 74ff.

7. *Ibid.*, pp. 191ff.

8. Chalmers A. Johnson, *Peasant Nationalism and Communist Power* (Stanford, Calif., 1962), pp. 111–113.

9. *JMJP,* September 3, 1962.

10. Chou Erh-fu, *Tung-pei heng-tuan-mien* (Northeastern cross section; Hong Kong, 1946), p. 43.

11. *CB* 208, pp. 22–29.

12. Ellis Joffe, *Party and Army: Professionalism and Political Control in the Chinese Officer Corps, 1949–1964* (Cambridge, Mass., 1965), p. 86.

13. Ralph L. Powell, *Politico-Military Relationships in Communist China* (U.S. Department of State, Washington, D.C., 1963), p. 5.

Hsiao K'o

(1909–   ; Chia-ho hsien, Hunan). Veteran PLA officer; vice-minister, Ministry of State Farms and Land Reclamation; member, CCP Central Committee.

A member of the Red Army from its earliest

days, Hsiao K'o was an important officer during the Long March, the Sino-Japanese War, and the civil war with the Nationalists. In the first decade of the PRC he was a leading PLA officer, but since 1959 he has worked in the Ministry of State Farms and Land Reclamation. He was born in August 1909 in a village in Chia-ho hsien in southern Hunan; the capital of this rural hsien is about 25 miles from the Kwangtung border. In the 1920's and 1930's there was considerable peasant unrest in this area, including nearby I-chang, which Chu Te captured in early 1928 before joining Mao Tse-tung at Chingkangshan in the spring of that year.

According to the autobiography which Hsiao gave to journalist Nym Wales (the major source for Hsiao's early career), his family were impoverished gentry.[1] His father was a *Hsiu-ts'ai* degree holder, and Hsiao's two elder brothers had careers which he said "ran no more smoothly than my own." The eldest was executed in 1923 for his ties with "bandits," and the next brother joined the CCP in 1925 and was killed in 1933 while serving in the Red Army. These experiences deeply affected Hsiao, and partially in response to them, and partially to escape an authoritarian father, he ran away from home when he was about 17. By then he had received five years of training in the Chinese classics, three years in a higher primary school, and two and a half years in a normal school. While still in normal school, Hsiao became interested in military science. He says that he read from the works of both Chinese and foreign military writers, as well as works by the famous scholar-general of the late Ch'ing period, Tseng Kuo-fan.

Hsiao went to Canton in 1926 "because it was the center of the revolution" and because a cousin in a university there had been sending him "revolutionary books," including works by Sun Yat-sen. Despite the reports that Hsiao was a cadet at the Whampoa Military Academy, he specifically denied this, explaining that he had wanted to attend but had arrived in Canton a bit too late to enroll in the class for that year. However, he soon gained first-hand military experience, first as a noncommissioned officer in one of Chiang Kai-shek's gendarme regiments and later as a company-level political director in the 24th Division of Chang Fa-k'uei's Fourth ("Ironsides") Army. The division, commanded by Communist Yeh T'ing (q.v.), served as a vanguard on the Northern Expedition, which began in mid-1926. Hsiao, however, did not take part in the first phase of the expedition, because he did not join Yeh's division until it had already reached Wuhan. In June 1927, Hsiao joined the CCP after receiving a letter from his brother (a Party member) accusing Chiang Kai-shek of betraying the revolution. Two months later (August 1), Hsiao took part in the Communists' historic uprising at Nanchang (see under Yeh T'ing).

After the Communists were routed from Nanchang in early August, Hsiao took part in the southward march to Kwangtung where the Communists were again defeated at Swatow in September. The defeat at Swatow was so disastrous that many of the Red Army units were totally dispersed. Left to fend for himself, Hsiao joined a Nationalist Army unit in Kwangtung simply to get enough to eat. His identity as a Communist was, of course, unknown to the Nationalists, but after a month he returned to his native village in south Hunan. Hsiao soon learned (early 1928) that Communist units led by Chu Te were not far away; like Hsiao, Chu had taken part in the march south from Nanchang, but Chu had been able to hold together a small unit, which he led to the Hunan-Kwangtung border after the losses in the Swatow area. Even before Chu arrived, there had been Communist-backed partisan activity in this area (see under Li T'ao). Hsiao made contact with these partisans and campaigned with them for the next few months. Chu moved north to the Chingkangshan area in the spring of 1928 and, merging his men with those led by Mao Tse-tung, established the Fourth Red Army. A short time afterwards, Hsiao moved his small and badly equipped partisan band from south Hunan to Chingkangshan where he placed his men under the command of the Chu-Mao forces. Hsiao was placed in command of a company under the Fourth Red Army, and then over the turn of the year 1928–29 he was made a regimental commander. At that juncture, the Fourth Red Army left the Chingkangshan area, and for most of the next two years it fought against Nationalist troops in a wide area in central and southeast Kiangsi, southwest Fukien, and northeast Kwangtung. They passed several times through the area around Juichin (southeast Kiangsi), which later became the Communists' headquarters. By 1930 Hsiao had been promoted to a division commander, and from the end of that year through 1931 he took part in the battles to defend the Communist-held bases from the continual onslaughts of the Nationalist armies.

In September 1932 Hsiao was sent to command the Sixth Red Army, which was operating in the general vicinity of the old Chingkangshan base on the Hunan-Kiangsi border. In the next spring Jen Pi-shih (q.v.) was sent to join Hsiao as secretary of the CCP Hunan-Kiangsi Border Region Committee and as political commissar of the area's military region. Under severe attack from Nationalist armies in the fall of 1933, Hsiao's forces were reorganized and redesignated the 17th Division. In early 1934 they were forced to retreat from the base; they made a lengthy and circuitous march which took them in a northerly direction into Hupeh, before they returned to the Hunan-Kiangsi base. By approximately the time they returned, Hsiao's units were known as the Sixth Red Army Corps. In January–February

1934, while Hsiao was making this march, he had been elected a member of the Chinese Soviet Republic's Central Executive Committee at the Second All-China Congress of Soviets in Juichin.

By the summer of 1934 the encircling Nationalist armies were making the soviet bases in central-south China untenable. Therefore, the various Communist armies began to make the moves which eventually resulted in the Long March to the northwest. Hsiao's Sixth Army Corps was one of the first to leave its original base. In August 1934 Jen, Hsiao, and Wang Chen (the Sixth Corps' political commissar) received orders to leave the Hunan-Kiangsi base and to join Ho Lung's Second Army Corps in northeast Kweichow. The two armies met in October (the same month that Chu, Mao, and the others began the Long March from Kiangsi). The merged forces were designated the Second Front Army; Ho Lung became the commander, Jen Pi-shih the political commissar, and Kuan Hsiang-ying (formerly Ho's chief political officer) the deputy political commissar. Hsiao retained his command of the Sixth Army Corps. During the course of the next year the joint force expanded its area of control and established the Szechwan-Hupeh-Hunan-Kweichow base, and during this same period Ho Lung and Hsiao married sisters in Hunan.

In November 1935, a month after Mao Tse-tung's forces had already completed their Long March to north Shensi, the Ho-Hsiao armies left northwest Hunan. They crossed Kweichow, passing within a few miles of Kweiyang, the provincial capital which was a Nationalist stronghold, and from Kweichow they went north across Szechwan into eastern Yunnan, and then to Sikang where the Fourth Front Army was headquartered. This extended march had taken half a year and was not completed until June 1936. After a serious dispute concerning the destination of the Second and Fourth Front Armies (see under Chang Kuo-t'ao), the two large forces began to move northward in July 1936 to rendezvous with Mao in Shensi.

Early in 1937, not long after reaching Shensi, Hsiao was made commander of the 31st Army (about which little is known), but a few months later, in the summer of 1937, the Sino-Japanese War began. The Communists immediately reorganized their forces into the Eighth Route Army, composed of three divisions. Hsiao was appointed deputy commander of Ho Lung's 120th Division and concurrently commander of the division's 358th Brigade. In September 1937 Ho moved his division across the Yellow River into northwest Shansi. During the winter of 1938–39 Hsiao took the major elements of his 358th Brigade eastward into Hopeh on a mission to aid Communist guerrillas in east Hopeh where Sung Shih-lun and Teng Hua (qq.v.) had been sent half a year earlier. (The remaining elements

of Hsiao's brigade were left in northwest Shansi under the command of P'eng Shao-hui, q.v.) In east Hopeh the Communists had initially been able to mobilize peasant unrest against the Japanese with enough success to provoke savage counterattacks, and by the autumn of 1938 the main Sung-Teng force was almost "obliterated." After arriving in east Hopeh (not far from Peking), Hsiao contacted the two Red guerrilla leaders and together they began a program to rebuild Communist resistance. In August 1939 Hsiao presided over a meeting in Ning-ho hsien, Hopeh, some 30 miles northeast of Tientsin on the railroad leading to Manchuria. It was decided that Communist strategy in east Hopeh should henceforth depend more upon political than military operations; it was also decided to request that a greater number of political agents be sent to the area. With a less aggressive approach, the Communists managed to keep their agents in east Hopeh, a critical area to the Japanese throughout the Sino-Japanese War.[2] The guerrilla activities in this period were the base upon which the Communists' Hopeh-Jehol-Liaoning Liberated Area was built.[3] During the war years this base was subordinate to the more important Shansi-Chahar-Hopeh base (see under Nieh Jung-chen), but toward the end of the war it became an independent liberated area.

In 1940 Ho Lung withdrew most of his forces from Hopeh, returning them to the Shansi-Suiyuan border area. However, Hsiao remained in Hopeh, although he withdrew westward to the mountainous region just west of Peking where by 1941 he was commander of the West-of-Peking (Hsi-p'ing) Military District.[4] At the end of the war in 1945, together with Sung Shih-lung, Hsiao moved his guerrilla forces northward into Jehol province, the gateway to Manchuria; these operations were coordinated with the movement of troops led by Lin Piao into Manchuria. By early 1946 Hsiao was in command of the Hopeh-Jehol-Liaoning Military Region,[5] and before the year had ended he was also head of the Rear Services Department of the Northeast Democratic Allied Army (Lin Piao's army) and a member of the Party's Northeast Bureau.

Hsiao apparently remained in the Jehol area throughout the late forties as Lin Piao's army defeated the Nationalists in Manchuria. In the early days of 1949 Lin captured Peking, and at approximately that time Hsiao was deputy commander of the North China Military Region and vice-president of the North China Military Academy in Peking. After a brief pause, Lin's forces, now known as the Fourth Field Army, began to drive south, and by the end of 1949 virtually all of central-south China had been conquered. During this period Hsiao was chief-of-staff of the Fourth Field Army and the Central-South Military Region, both of which were commanded by Lin Piao. Hsiao relinquished both positions to Chao Erh-lu (q.v.) by the spring of 1950. Apart from his military posts in central-south China, Hsiao was also a member of the governmental organ which managed the region, the Central-South Military and Administrative Committee, from its establishment in early 1950. However, by the time he was officially removed from this post in June 1951, he had already been transferred to Peking.

Hsiao was apparently transferred to Peking by the early fall of 1950, because he was there then to attend a national conference of "fighting heroes" (that is, members of the PLA). In any case, he was definitely stationed in the capital by March 1951 when he was identified as director of the Military Training Department of the People's Revolutionary Military Council (PRMC). Except for a few ceremonial occasions, Hsiao was not often reported in the press during the early fifties, but from mid-1952 to 1956 he was a member of the National Committee of the All-China Athletic Federation. In this capacity Hsiao made his only trip abroad when in June–July 1955 he went to Prague to attend the First Czechoslovakian National Spartakiade.

In 1954 Hsiao was elected a deputy to the First NPC from the North China Military Region. When the NPC held its first session in September 1954, at which time the national government was reorganized, the PRMC was abolished and some of its functions were taken over by the PLA Headquarters. The General Training Department was placed under the PLA, and Liu Po-ch'eng (q.v.), a more senior military figure, succeeded Hsiao as director. According to unconfirmed reports, Hsiao served as a deputy to Liu; in any event, he once again assumed the directorship in November 1957. Hsiao was last reported in this post in early 1958, and it seems probable that he relinquished it by the fall of 1959 when he was relieved of all his active military assignments (see below). At the time of the 1954 government reorganization Hsiao was also made a member of the National Defense Council (the less important successor to the PRMC), and a vice-minister of National Defense. A year later, when the Communists created personal military ranks and awarded decorations to its officer corps (September 1955), Hsiao was made a colonel-general, the equivalent to a three-star U.S. Army general, and was awarded the Orders of August First, Independence and Freedom, and Liberation, the three top decorations. In September 1956, at the Party's Eighth National Congress, he was elected a member of the CCP Central Committee.

During the middle and late 1950's Hsiao was relatively active in protocol duties, particularly in connection with visiting military delegations. However, rather little else is known of his work in that period. Then in the fall of 1959 his career underwent a rather abrupt change. In September the national government was partially re-

organized and scores of persons were reshuffled throughout the bureaucracy. Defense Minister P'eng Te-huai and three of his vice-ministers, Hsiao, Huang K'o-ch'eng, and Li Ta (qq.v.), were all removed from the ministry. P'eng and Huang lost their posts for political reasons, and this gave rise to speculation that Hsiao might have been associated with them. However, unlike P'eng and Huang, Hsiao received a new post during the reorganization when he was appointed a vice-minister of State Farms and Land Reclamation. The ministry is headed by Wang Chen, Hsiao's colleague during the Long March period, and it maintains close ties with the PLA because some of the work on state farms is performed by military units. Nonetheless, although Hsiao continues to serve at the vice-ministerial level, it is apparent that the State Farms Ministry is considerably less important than the Defense Ministry. Hsiao continues to be a member of the National Defense Council (having been re-elected in 1959 and 1965), but his importance as a member of the Chinese Communist elite seems to have ended in the late 1950's.

Because many of the functions of the Ministry of State Farms and Land Reclamation are conducted outside the capital, Hsiao has been reported rather frequently in connection with these tasks. To cite two random but typical examples, in the fall of 1959 he was in Loyang for the inauguration of the First Tractor Plant, and in April–May 1960 he presided over a "propaganda and education" conference in Kiangsi in connection with state farms and reclamation work. On occasion he has served as acting minister in the absence of Wang Chen.

1. Nym Wales, *Red Dust* (Stanford, Calif., 1952), pp. 131–140.

2. Chalmers A. Johnson, *Peasant Nationalism and Communist Power* (Stanford, Calif., 1962), pp. 114–115.

3. *Kang-Jih chan-cheng shih-ch'i chieh-fang-ch'ü kai-k'uang* (A sketch of the liberated areas during the Anti-Japanese War; Peking, 1953), p. 27.

4. *Hung-ch'i p'iao-p'iao* (Red flag fluttering; Peking, 1957), I, 219.

5. Kalgan, *Chin-Ch'a-Chi jih-pao* (Shansi-Chahar-Hopeh daily), March 1, 1946.

Hsieh Chueh-tsai

(c.1883–   ; Ning-hsiang, Hunan). Elder statesman of the CCP; alternate member, CCP Central Committee.

Known as a serious, quiet, and scholarly person who is gifted as an author of prose and poetry, Hsieh Chueh-tsai is regarded in Communist circles along with Tung Pi-wu, Hsu T'e-li, Wu Yü-chang, and Lin Po-ch'ü (qq.v.) as one of the "elders" of the movement. He is one of the few Party leaders whose education and early training took place in the late Ch'ing period. Thus, his career bridges the gap between Imperial and Communist China. Having developed an interest in the reform movement at the turn of the century, Hsieh cooperated briefly with the KMT in the early 1920's before joining the CCP in 1925, when he was already over 40. During the late 1920's and early 1930's he worked in the Shanghai and Hankow underground and then in the guerrilla bases of Hunan and Kiangsi. After making the Long March with Mao's forces he was a leading official first in the Shensi-Kansu-Ninghsia Border Region and later in the North China People's Government. After the CPR was founded in 1949, Hsieh held many responsible posts, notably the portfolio of the Internal Affairs Ministry (until 1959). He was elected an alternate member of the Party Central Committee in 1956 but has been in virtual retirement since the mid-1960's.

Hsieh was born in Ning-hsiang, the small industrial city not far west of Changsha, the provincial capital. Ning-hsiang is also the birthplace of such Party notables as Ho Shu-heng and Liu Shao-ch'i (qq.v.). Hsieh comes from a landowning family sufficiently wealthy to have given their son the classical education necessary to pass the civil service examination for the *Hsiu-ts'ai* degree. He received the degree in about 1898 and in the same year was said to have been very interested in the brief reform movement initiated by the Kuang-hsu Emperor. During his youth Hsieh wrote poems modelled after the famous Tang poet, Tu Fu; to earn a living he taught school.

Little more is known of Hsieh's career until about 1920, when he was an editor of the Changsha *T'ung-su jih-pao* (The popular daily) and was associated with a politically active group of Hunan radicals. It was then that Hsieh met Mao Tse-tung, who was beginning to organize a Marxist study group in the city. In the early 1920's Hsieh also served as an adviser to T'an Yen-k'ai, the Hunan governor. In late 1923, in cooperation with Ts'ao Po-han and others, Hsieh helped establish the Hsiang-chiang Middle School. This school, at which Hsieh taught Chinese, was a continuation of the CCP-sponsored Self-Education College (see under Mao Tse-min and Li Wei-han), which had been closed by the provincial authorities. In 1924 he joined the newly reorganized KMT and for the next three years was active in its Hunan branch. He also joined the CCP (1925), keeping his membership a secret from his KMT colleagues. By this time Hsieh was already over 40 and considerably older than most of those then joining the CCP. From 1926 to 1927 he was a member of the KMT Hunan Executive Committee, chief editor of the provincial edition of the official KMT organ, the *Min pao* (People's

daily), and counsel for the special court established in Changsha to deal with legal problems arising from the Northern Expedition. In May 1927, when garrison commander Hsu K'o-hsiang took steps to quell Communist-led activity in Changsha, which had gained support from the student and labor groups within the city, Hsieh was forced to flee to Hankow and later to Shanghai where he joined the CCP underground. He spent the year 1928–29 in Mukden and then returned for another year in the Shanghai underground.

About 1931 he was sent to join a Hunanese colleague, Ho Lung, who in 1929 had established a small Communist guerrilla base in his native Sang-chih in western Hunan. Hsieh helped found another Party school there and was an editor of one of the local CCP publications, the *Kung-nung pao* (Workers and peasants news). A year after his arrival, the Communist guerrillas were driven from these remote headquarters and forced to move to the southeast near Hung Lake. In June 1932 the KMT opened its fourth "annihilation campaign" against the Communists in central China and Ho Lung's guerrillas were again forced to retreat (see under Ho Lung). KMT forces captured Hsieh during this second retreat but soon released him, deceived by his venerable scholarly appearance. He returned to Shanghai and Party work with the trade unions until sometime in 1933, when the vigilance of the KMT police made it necessary to close the Party headquarters and move to the remote area in south Kiangsi where Mao Tse-tung and Chu Te had established their base. In Kiangsi, Hsieh became secretary-general of the soviet government, and writing many years later he asserted that in 1933 he had also served as a secretary to Mao.[1]

Hsieh made the Long March (1934–35) and after arriving with Mao's forces in north Shensi he became one of the more important officials in the Shensi-Kansu-Ninghsia (Shen-Kan-Ning) Border Region Government, which was established in Yenan in 1937. He served for a brief time as the secretary-general of the Government, but his main work in the early years was as an economic administrator and as director of the Interior and Justice Departments. From 1941 until the Border Region Government went out of existence in early 1949, Hsieh was active in the legislative branch, serving as vice-chairman of the Shen-Kan-Ning Assembly. American journalist Nym Wales interviewed him in 1937; Hsieh, then in his sixties, was described as one of the Party's "patriarchs."[2]

Hsieh remained in the Yenan area until the Communists were driven out in early 1947 during the course of the civil war. Like many other senior Communist officials, he then made his way through Communist-held areas in Shensi and Shansi, and by the late summer of 1948 he was in west Hopeh where, in August, the Communists inaugurated the North China People's Government (NCPG) to administer the Communist-held areas until the central government was inaugurated a year later. During this period Hsieh served on the NCPG's Council and concurrently directed the Justice Department, thus paralleling his earlier role in Yenan. He moved to Peking after it fell to the Communists in early 1949, and despite his advanced years he was quite active in the summer of that year in the preparations for the creation of various professional organizations. Most notably, he was a vice-chairman of the China New Legal Research Society's Preparatory Committee established in June, an organization that evolved into the Political Science and Law Association of China four years later (see below). In July he attended a conference held to mobilize the talents of both Communist and non-Communist social scientists, and as a representative of social scientists he attended the inaugural meeting of the CPPCC, which established the new central government on October 1. While the CPPCC was in session in September, Hsieh served on the *ad hoc* committee that drafted the Central People's Government's Organic Law, one of the key documents adopted at that time. Then, when the government was formally staffed in October, he received four important assignments in the Government Administration Council (GAC; the cabinet). First, he became a member of the GAC itself, a body consisting of Premier Chou En-lai, four vice-chairmen, and 15 members. He was also named to membership on the Political and Legal Affairs Committee and the Law Commission, both subordinate to the GAC, but his most important assignment was as minister of Internal Affairs. Hsieh relinquished the first three posts when the central government was reorganized in 1954, but he retained the Internal Affairs portfolio for nearly a decade.

In China the Ministry of Internal Affairs is not, as in many Communist nations, in charge of security matters; these are assigned to the Ministry of Public Security. Instead, it is principally concerned with disaster relief work, the problems of veterans and their dependents, census-taking, and questions involving local government administration. Most of Hsieh's public appearances in the early PRC years occurred when he delivered reports on such problems before meetings of the GAC. For example, because disaster relief work was a topic of major concern to the new government, Hsieh spoke a number of times at GAC meetings on this subject, and he was also a logical selection for a vice-chairmanship of the quasi-official Chinese People's Relief Administration (CPRA) when it was established in April 1950. Similarly, from its inauguration in July 1953 to about 1959, Hsieh headed one of the CPRA's subordinate organizations, the China Association for the Welfare of the Blind.

Aside from his tasks in the Internal Affairs Ministry, Hsieh's activities during the first decade of Communist rule also involved legal and legislative matters. Thus, from its establishment in July 1951 until November 1956, he served under P'eng Chen as a vice-president of the Central Political and Legal Cadres Academy, and in early 1953 he was a member of a committee that drafted the national election law. When the law was drafted, he then became a member of the Central Election Committee, which was responsible for carrying out the elections to the First NPC. Also in 1953 Hsieh became a vice-chairman of the newly established Political Science and Law Association, retaining this post for over a decade.

The constitutional government was established in September 1954 at the inaugural meeting of the NPC, to which Hsieh had been elected as a deputy from Shantung. The central government was partially reorganized at this time, but Hsieh retained his Internal Affairs Ministry portfolio. A year and a half later, in February 1956, he received another central government post when he was named to serve as a member of the Central Work Committee for the Popularization of Standard Spoken Chinese. Finally, in September 1956 at the Eighth Party Congress, he was rewarded for a long career of service to the CCP by being elected an alternate member of the Central Committee.

When the Second NPC convened in April 1959, Hsieh again attended as a Shantung deputy. At this time Miss Ch'ien Ying (q.v.) took over his ministerial post. However, although in his mid-seventies, Hsieh was not yet to be retired. Rather, he replaced another of the Party "elders," Tung Pi-wu, as president of the Supreme People's Court. In contrast to both the executive and legislative branches of government, the organs of judicial authority are relatively inactive, and thus Hsieh's new assignment was probably not very taxing. Most of his public appearances since 1959 have been in connection with visits to China by foreign jurists, and he has been regularly given *pro forma* assignments on *ad hoc* committees that utilize his links with the past, as in September 1961 when he was appointed to a committee to commemorate the 50th anniversary of the 1911 Revolution.

By the mid-1960's Hsieh, then over 80, went into virtual retirement. In 1964 he was not re-elected to the Third NPC (which opened in December 1964), and in October 1964, at the Fourth Congress of the Political Science and Law Association, he was dropped as a vice-chairman. However, he and Tung Pi-wu were made honorary chairmen. Hsieh attended the first session of the Fourth CPPCC in December 1964–January 1965 as a representative of the CCP, and at the end of the meetings was made a vice-chairman of the CPPCC National Committee. However, this quasi-legislative organization is far less important than the NPC, and Hsieh's position in the CPPCC can probably be regarded as an honorary post. Most important, at this same time (January 1965), he relinquished the presidency of the Supreme People's Court to Yang Hsiu-feng (q.v.) and thus gave up his last important post in the central government.

Little is known of Hsieh's family. He claims to have had a son who was a peasant and a daughter who was a teacher.[3] One son about whom he has not reported was named Hsieh Hsuan-ch'u. Chang Kuo-t'ao, who knew this son personally, claims that he graduated in one of the first classes of the Whampoa Military Academy and later joined the CCP. He was wounded during the twenties and had to be hospitalized. Afterward, he defected from the Communists. When Chang next saw the son he was working in Shanghai in 1928. During the Sino-Japanese War he worked for Ho Chung-han of the Nationalist Government. Hsieh Hsuan-ch'u's present whereabouts are unknown.[4] Hsieh Chueh-tsai is married to Wang Ting-kuo, who reportedly works in the Supreme People's Court.

---

1. *SCMM* 273, p. 35.
2. Nym Wales, *Red Dust* (Stanford, Calif., 1952), p. 46.
3. *Ibid.*, p. 47.
4. Howard L. Boorman, director, Modern China Project, Columbia University, New York.

Hsieh Fu-chih

Hsieh Fu-chih (1898–   ; Hupeh). Veteran Red Army political officer; Minister of Public Security; commander and political commissar, PLA Security Force; member, CCP Central Committee.

Hsieh Fu-chih was one of the more important political officers in the Communist armies during the Sino-Japanese War and the civil war against the Nationalists in the late forties. In the first decade of the PRC he was a top political-military leader in the southwest, serving in both Szechwan and Yunnan. He was transferred to Peking in 1959 to head the Public Security Ministry and later became commander and political commissar of the PLA Security Force. Hsieh has been a Party Central Committee member since 1956.

Little is known of Hsieh's early career. However, he holds the first class Order of August First (see below), which was given for military service at the division level and above and which covers the years 1927 to 1937. This suggests that he was with the Chu-Mao forces on the 1934–35 Long March from Kiangsi to Shensi. He is said to have graduated from the Red Army Academy, but it is not known if this refers to the school

set up in Juichin in 1933 or to the period in 1936 when it wes re-established in north Shensi. At some time after his graduation Hsieh was reported to have been the political department director, a political committee member, and the commander of a Red Army regiment.

By 1938 Hsieh was political commissar of the 386th Brigade commanded by Ch'en Keng (q.v.). The brigade was subordinate to Liu Po-ch'eng's 129th Division, one of the three divisions in the Communist Eighth Route Army in north China. In 1938 the 386th Brigade was sent to southern Hopeh and by early fall it had advanced into the Lo-ling area (east of the Tientsin-Pukow Railroad) in northern Shantung where it joined forces with the local resistance.[1]

Two years later Hsieh was political commissar of the five brigades from Liu's 129th Division, which participated in the "100 Regiments Offensive." This Communist drive against Japanese forces in five provinces of north China lasted from August to December 1940 and was focused on the Japanese communications network. The units of the 129th Division were credited with cutting the Peking-Hankow Railroad late in August.[2] As of mid-1940 the main base of the 129th Division was in the Shansi-Hopeh-Shantung-Honan Border Region west of the railroad. The Region was divided into two major military sub-divisions, the T'ai-yueh Military District in west Shansi and the T'ai-hang Military District in east Shansi. In 1940 Hsieh was deputy commander of the former and by 1942 he had become head of the T'ai-yueh branch of the Anti-Japanese Military and Political Academy,[3] the successor to the Red Army Academy. He remained in the area for the rest of the war.

Hsieh stayed with Ch'en Keng and the 386th Brigade until the civil war against the Nationalists ended in 1949, and their troops saw considerable action as the Communists expanded over the mainland. The 386th Brigade continued to be subordinate to Liu Po-ch'eng's army, but both underwent a series of name changes (see under Ch'en Keng). Ch'en and Hsieh were so closely identified as a fighting twosome that many Communist accounts simply refer to the "Ch'en-Hsieh army." Almost immediately after the end of hostilities in August 1945, part of Liu's army, including the 386th Brigade, came into conflict with the forces of Yen Hsi-shan (the semi-independent warlord of Shansi allied with the Nationalists) in southeast Shansi near the towns of Ch'ang-chih, T'un-liu, Lu-ch'eng, and Hsiang-yuan. In September and October 1945 Ch'en and Hsieh (who was then Ch'en's deputy commander and probably also his political commissar) fought major battles with Yen's troops and reportedly destroyed a third of Yen's fighting strength.[4] By mid-1947 the troops of Ch'en and Hsieh, apparently now called the Fourth Column of the Shansi-Hopeh-Shantung-Honan PLA, were fighting supporting actions in Honan as Liu Po-ch'eng's forced moved toward their new base in the Ta-pieh Mountains north of Wuhan. These battles are described in the biography of Ch'en Keng.

In 1948 Hsieh was the deputy commander and political commissar of the Fourth Army Corps, the successor of the Fourth Column. However, sometime in the year 1948–49 Hsieh seems to have risen to command his own military unit, because he was then identified as commander of the 10th Army of the Third Army Corps. Hsieh's force still belonged to Liu's army, named the Second Field Army in early 1949. In November 1949 the Second Field Army took over Chungking. At about this time the close association between Ch'en and Hsieh ended, Ch'en leading his forces south into Yunnan (with a new political commissar, Sung Jen-ch'iung, q.v.) while Hsieh remained in Chungking to become a member of the Chungking Military Control Commission established on December 3, 1949. Hsieh was in Chungking for about two and a half years during which time one of his most important posts was as chief of the Chungking Party Committee (1949–1952). At about the same time (1950–1952) he was the ranking secretary of the Party Committee for East Szechwan, one of the four administrative units into which the Communists divided the province when they first took it over. Hsieh was also political commissar of the East Szechwan Military District, a member of the East Szechwan People's Administrative Office, and chairman of the Office's Finance and Economics Committee, holding these posts from mid-1950 until August 1952 when the four separate administrations for Szechwan were united to become one provincial government, the Szechwan Provincial People's Government. Hsieh's final post during his stay in Szechwan was as a member of the regional administration for the Southwest, the Southwest Military and Administrative Committee. He became a member when the administration was created in July 1950 and continued to hold the post when it was reorganized into the Southwest Administrative Committee in 1953–54.

Hsieh was probably transferred from Szechwan when the provincial reorganization took place in mid-1952, for by January 1953 he was the ranking secretary (later called first secretary) of the Party Committee in Yunnan, replacing Sung Jen-ch'iung. During the next six years, while he was the senior Party figure in Yunnan, Hsieh also held important posts in the military apparatus in the southwest. He was political commissar of the Southwest Military Region (SWMR) from 1953 to 1954, succeeding Teng Hsiao-p'ing. The SWMR then controlled military affairs in Szechwan, Yunnan, Kweichow, Sikang, and probably also Tibet. In 1954 the military regions throughout China were reduced

in size and redesignated; the SWMR was divided into the Chengtu and the Kunming Military Regions. In the latter, which had jurisdiction over Yunnan and Kweichow military units, Hsieh was political commissar from 1954 to 1959 and commander from 1954 to about 1956. Apart from his military posts at the multi-provincial level, Hsieh was political commissar (1953–1959) and commander (1957–1959) of the Yunnan Military District.

As the Yunnan Party first secretary and an important military leader in the area, Hsieh was the key official in Yunnan and one of the handful of top men in the entire southwest throughout much of the 1950's. Although far less important, from 1955 to 1959 he was also a member of the Yunnan Provincial People's Government Council and chairman of the First Yunnan Committee of the CPPCC. In addition, Hsieh served in the First NPC (1954–1959) as a deputy from Yunnan and was a member of its Nationalities Committee (headed by Liu Ko-p'ing), an important assignment for a Yunnan representative because of the large proportion of national minorities in the province. He was not re-elected to the Second Congress (1959–1964) but was again a deputy from Yunnan to the Third NPC (1964 to date).

While serving in Yunnan Hsieh received important recognition from both the military and the Party at the national level. When national military honors were created in 1955, he received the top three awards — the Orders of August First, Independence and Freedom, and Liberation for service in the Red Army from 1927 to 1950. Personal military ranks were also established at this time and Hsieh probably became a colonel-general (a three-star rank), although he was not identified as such until the spring of 1957. In September 1956, at the Eighth National Party Congress, Hsieh served on the Credentials Committee and was then elected to the Central Committee. He was one of 33 persons elected to full membership who had not previously served on the Central Committee, even as an alternate.

Because of his prominence in Yunnan, Hsieh's activities were frequently mentioned in the Chinese press (e.g., when he spoke at Party meetings or made inspections throughout the province). Moreover, because Kunming serves as a gateway to Southeast Asia, Hsieh was constantly involved in protocol activities, serving as a host for such prominent international leaders as Ho Chi-minh, Sukarno, and U Nu. For instance, in March–April 1957 he took part in talks held in Kunming between Chou En-lai and Burmese Premier U Nu. Later in April, at U Nu's invitation, he toured Burma and attended a national festival.

Hsieh's career took a major turn in September 1959 when the central government underwent a partial reorganization. He was called to Peking to succeed Lo Jui-ch'ing as minister of Public Security. In addition, he became director of the State Council's Political and Legal Affairs Office (formerly the First Staff Office, also headed by Lo Jui-ch'ing), which supervised the various State Council commissions, ministries, and bureaus (e.g., the Ministries of Public Security and Internal Affairs) concerned with political and legal problems. The Office was abolished about 1961, but was then re-established under the name Internal Affairs Office in May 1963, again under Hsieh's direction. Six months later he was identified as commander of the PLA Public Security Force. Chinese press media seldom mention security matters and there had been no mention of the Security Force chief after 1957 when Lo Jui-ch'ing held the post. Hsieh may well have succeeded Lo in this position in 1959 when he became minister of Public Security, but if so, the change was not made public then. In June 1964 Hsieh was further identified as political commissar of the Public Security Force. He thus holds four important posts in public security and political supervision work and is probably the most important person in these fields.

At the close of the Third NPC's first session in January 1965, Hsieh was appointed one of 16 State Council vice-premiers and a member of the National Defense Council. His dramatic rise in the hierarchy reached new heights in the early stages of the Great Proletarian.Cultural Revolution a year and a half later. In September 1966, shortly after the Party held its 11th Plenum, he was identified as an alternate member of the Politburo.

Hsieh is married to Liu Hsiang-p'ing, who by late 1956 was a secretary of the Party Committee in Kunming, the Yunnan capital. In 1964 she was elected a deputy from Yunnan to the Third NPC.

1. Chalmers A. Johnson, *Peasant Nationalism and Communist Power* (Stanford, Calif., 1962), pp. 112–113.
2. *Ibid.*, pp. 56–58.
3. *Chung-kuo ch'ing-nien pao* (China youth newspaper), November 8, 1960.
4. *The Great Turning Point* (Peking, 1962), pp. 55–57.

Hsiung Fu

Hsiung Fu (1916–   ; Szechwan). Former journalist; a senior official in international Communist party liaison work.

Hsiung Fu, a former journalist, was a Party propagandist in central-south China in the early PRC years. Since transferring to Peking in the mid-fifties he has devoted most of his time to international affairs, particularly relations with other Communist nations. Hsiung was born in Szechwan and by 1946 he was working in Chungking for the *Hsin-hua jih-pao* (New China daily), an organ of the CCP. He was apparently a senior official on the paper—very possibly the secretary of its Party committee.[1] Hsiung was probably working under the general direction of Party Central Committee member Wu Yü-chang (q.v.), then a top representative of the CCP in Nationalist-held Chungking.

By the winter of 1946–47 KMT-CCP relations had seriously worsened. At this juncture General Marshall, who had been attempting to mediate between the Nationalists and Communists, left China, thereby signaling the failure of the famous "Marshall Mission." The Nationalists then closed the *Hsin-hua jih-pao* on February 28, 1947, ordering all Communists in Chungking, Shanghai, and Nanking to return to Yenan. Wu Yü-chang led the Party contingent from Chungking, flying to Yenan on March 8; Hsiung left at about this same time. Within a few days the Nationalists attacked and captured Yenan. Although details are lacking, Hsiung must have left Yenan for the north China hinterlands along with all the other Party leaders.

Hsiung next appeared on the public scene in July 1949 when he was among some 650 delegates who attended the All-China Congress of Literary and Art Workers, which established the All-China Federation of Literary and Art Circles under the chairmanship of Kuo Mo-jo (q.v.). In the same month he attended a meeting which set up the Preparatory Committee of the All-China News Workers Association. Named to the Preparatory Committee, Hsiung held this post until the All-China Journalists Association was established in September 1954. By early 1950 he had been transferred from Peking to Wuhan to become a deputy director of the Propaganda Department of the Party's Central-South China Bureau, serving under Chao I-min (q.v.). It is not known how long he held this post, but certainly no later than the mid-1950's when the regional bureaus were dissolved. Another post assumed by Hsiung in 1950 was membership (until May 1953) on Chao I-min's (q.v.) Culture and Education Committee of the Central-South Military and Administrative Committee (CSMAC). Hsiung continued to be associated with Chao into the 1960's, both men being very active as liaison officials with foreign Communist party leaders. Hsiung held two further posts in the CSMAC structure; he was named in March 1950 as director of the News and Publications Bureau, a post he held until at least the latter part of 1952, and when a committee was formed in November 1951 to promote austerity in economic practices, Hsiung was appointed as a member under Chairman Teng Tzu-hui, an important official in economic work.

Still another position that Hsiung held after the Communist takeover was as director of the

Ch'ang-chiang jih-pao (Yangtze daily) in Hankow, a newspaper ranking with the Cantòn *Nan-fang jih-pao* (South China daily) as one of the two most important papers in central-south China. A somewhat related post Hsiung held from at least 1951 was that of chairman of the Central-South Branch of the All-China Federation of Literary and Art Circles.

In about 1954 Hsiung was transferred to the national capital. In May of that year he was named to the Board of Directors of the newly formed Chinese People's Association for Cultural Relations with Foreign Countries, a post he probably still holds. In February 1955, during one of Peking's frequent short-term campaigns, Hsiung served as a member and a secretary-general of the National Anti-Atomic Weapons Signature Campaign. And in December of the same year Hsiung journeyed to Japan as a deputy secretary-general of a scientific delegation led by Kuo Mo-jo to survey Japan's scientific world. Hsiung was identified simply as a "research worker" in the Third (modern) Institute of History of the Academy of Sciences, but it can be assumed that his role was more important than this modest title would suggest. The importance of the institute can be gauged from the fact that its director, Fan Wen-lan, is an alternate member of the CCP Central Committee and the Party's most important practicing historian.

In February 1956 Hsiung became a member of the newly formed Asian ·(Afro-Asian from May 1958) Solidarity Committee. But his really significant climb in the Party hierarchy became apparent by April 1956, when he was identified as the secretary-general of the Party's Propaganda Department, a field in which he had been active in central-south China in the early 1950's. In the following month he was identified as a "responsible member" of a department under the Party Central Committee, a designation that at first glance appeared to be a euphemism for his post in the Propaganda Department. Subsequent evidence, however, suggests that it is an assignment in still another Central Committee department. The Chinese Communists have never referred to a department devoted solely to liaison with foreign Communist parties, but in May 1959 a Polish source identified an "International Liaison Department." Hsiung's work since 1956 strongly suggests that he belongs to just such a department.

In mid-November 1956 Chou En-lai journeyed to Southeast Asia on a "friendship" tour. In late December he was suddenly called home and after a few days in Peking was dispatched to Moscow, apparently to act as mediator in the disputes Moscow was having with both the Poles and the Hungarians in the wake of the revolt in Hungary. Chou visited Warsaw and Budapest, went back to Moscow, and then returned to Southeast Asia to complete his tour there. Hsiung was not identified as a member of Chou's delegation by official Chinese sources. However, Japanese sources claim he made the first two legs of Chou's important tour, but British sources state that he only went to Moscow and Warsaw. In May 1961, acting as an "adviser," Hsiung accompanied Foreign Minister Ch'en I to Geneva for the conference on Laos. Although the conference lasted for well over a year (counting a few periods of adjournment), Ch'en and Hsiung left for home in July 1961. While in Geneva and Moscow, Hsiung was among those reported in the company of such famed Soviet leaders as Khrushchev and Gromyko.

If the mission to Geneva presented difficulties, they were probably minor compared to those encountered on two trips taken in late 1962 and early 1963, when Sino-Soviet relations had seriously deteriorated and denunciations by each side were openly polemical. It was in this atmosphere that Hsiung accompanied a Party delegation led by Wu Hsiu-ch'üan to party congresses in Bulgaria, Hungary, and Czechoslovakia from early November to mid-December 1962. The delegation returned briefly to Peking, only to return to Europe in mid-January 1963 for an East German party congress. At all four congresses the Chinese were roundly castigated; delegates (including Soviet participants) booed the Chinese speeches and engaged in other provocative gestures. While Wu and Hsiung were in Czechoslovakia, Hsiung's former associate in central-south China, Chao I-min, was at a Party Congress in Italy (December 1962), where he also faced the open hostility of most of the delegates.

This mission to East Europe further confirms Hsiung's role as an international Communist liaison official. Delegation leader Wu Hsiu-ch'üan is the director of the "International Liaison Department" of the Central Committee according to the above-cited Polish Communist source and may thus be Hsiung's immediate superior in the Party hierarchy. Hsiung's major responsibilities are within the Party apparatus, but since December 1964 he has also held a seat on the Fourth National Committee of the CPPCC as a representative of "organizations for peaceful and friendly relations with foreign countries."

Over the years Hsiung has been a leading contributor to a number of Party journals, including two of the most important, *Hsueh-hsi* (Study) and *Hung-ch'i* (Red flag). His articles include: "The System of Socialist Ownership Must Be Made the Sole Foundation of Our Society," *Hsueh-hsi,* February 2, 1954, translated in *CB* 285; "Learn Lessons from the Incident of the Kao Kang-Jao Shu-shih Anti-Party Alliance," *Chung-kuo ch'ing-nien* (China youth),

April 16, 1955, translated in *SCMP* 1036; "Communist Party Members—Advanced Fighters of the Working Class for the Communist Cause," *Hsueh-hsi,* May 2, 1955; "Oppose the Rightist Trend and Raise Our Vigilance to Liquidate All Counter-revolutionaries in Rural Villages," *Cheng-chih hsueh-hsi* (Political study), August 13, 1955; "The October Revolution Sheds Light on the Chinese People's Road to Victory (two-part article), *JMJP,* November 9–10, 1957; "The Road to Communism is Open," *JMJP,* November 7, 1958; and "The Indonesian People's Revolutionary Struggle and the Indonesian Communist Party," *Hung-ch'i,* May 20, 1963, excerpted in *SCMP* 2988.

1. *The Great Turning Point* (Peking, 1962), pp. 34, 36.

Hsu Chien-kuo

(Hupeh). Former public security official; diplomat.

Until he was made an ambassador in 1959, Hsu Chien-kuo, a native of Hupeh, had only worked in security affairs. He was first reported in 1938 serving as director of the Social Affairs Department of the Shansi-Chahar-Hopeh Border Region Sub-bureau, subordinate to the North China Party Bureau. "Social affairs" was the euphemism employed by the Communists until the early 1950's for intelligence and security work. Because he was involved in such work, it is not surprising that there was little reporting about Hsu during the difficult years of the Sino-Japanese War and the civil war with the Nationalists.

In August 1948, as the Communists were gaining control of North China, they formed the North China People's Government, which was ultimately absorbed by the central government in October 1949. When the senior officials were named to this government in September 1948, Hsu was appointed as director of the Public Security Department. Not long after, in January 1949, Tientsin fell to Communist forces, and Hsu took up a series of appointments in that key industrial city. He became a member of the Tientsin Military Control Commission and head of the Public Security Bureau in early 1949. When the Tientsin government was reorganized in January 1950, he was made a member of the government council and was promoted to vice-mayor of the city in March 1951. In September 1950 he was concurrently named as Chief Procurator of the Tientsin Procurators' Office, the office with a variety of investigative functions empowered to insure that local government regulations conform to the law and that the law is observed.

When the central government was formed in October 1949, Hsu was appointed a member of the important Supreme People's Procuratorate, a post he was to hold until the constitutional period was inaugurated in 1954. In November 1951, Hsu was transferred from Tientsin to Shanghai where he assumed several posts very similar to those he held in Tientsin. He immediately became head of the Shanghai Public Security Department and by 1953 was Chief Procurator for the city. More important than these Shanghai appointments, however, was his November 1951 appointment as head of public security for all of East China, under the organization administratively known as the East China Military and Administrative Committee (EC-MAC). This was a post he retained when the ECMAC was reorganized into the East China Administrative Committee in early 1953.

In February 1953, Hsu became a vice-mayor of Shanghai under Party leader Ch'en I; he held this position until appointed as ambassador to Rumania in 1959. All major cities of China have several vice-mayors, each with different responsibilities. In January 1957 the Communists described Hsu as the vice-mayor responsible for public security, judicial affairs, army recruiting, and air defense—all but the last assignment in accord with his past experience. Aside from the vice-mayoralty, he received two further Shanghai posts in 1953: chairman of the municipal election committee (in preparation for the elections to the NPC in 1954); and chairman of the Political and Legal Affairs Committee. From October to December 1953, Hsu was in Korea as a member of Ho Lung's "comfort" mission to the Chinese military forces posted there; these missions combined inspections with entertainment for the troops.

With the inauguration of the constitutional government in Peking in September–October 1954, Hsu was given a top assignment as one of the vice-ministers of Public Security. Vice-ministers of the State Council normally work in Peking, but the nature of the public security tasks may supply the reason why some Public Security vice-ministers work outside the national capital. In any event, Hsu did not transfer to Peking, but remained in Shanghai. Two years later, he assumed an additional post of importance in Shanghai when he became secretary of the Party Committee there, another post he held until his assignment abroad in 1959. By November 1957 Hsu had become a vice-president of the Shanghai chapter of the Sino-Soviet Friendship Association, but within a few years this organization was largely inactive owing to the Sino-Soviet rift. One of his final tasks in Shanghai was to deliver a report on economic work to a meeting of the municipal congress in November 1958.

In January 1959 Hsu was removed as a vice-minister of Public Security, and then four months later was appointed to replace K'o Pai-nien as ambassador to Rumania; he officially presented his credentials on June 12, 1959. One year later Hsu was a member of the delegation led by P'eng Chen to the Third Congress of the Rumanian Workers' (Communist) Party, one of the most significant held in a Bloc country in many years because it was one of the first open encounters between the Chinese and Soviet leaders (see under P'eng Chen). Hsu's stay in Bucharest was characterized by his participation in the normal protocol functions of Chinese ambassadors, and by negotiations involving trade and cultural matters. Thus he was reported signing trade agreements in July 1961 and April 1963, and cultural agreements in February 1962 and January 1964.

Hsu left for home in January 1964 and was officially replaced the following month by Liu Fang, a petroleum expert. One of his last acts in Bucharest may have been to convince Rumanian leaders to take a more sympathetic view toward the Chinese position in the Sino-Soviet dispute, because only a month after his departure a top-level Rumanian Politburo member (I. G. Maurer) visited Peking, and after that date Rumania clearly took a position less favorable to Moscow and more favorable to the Chinese. Even if Hsu did not take part in the initial diplomatic groundwork for this mission, his superiors were apparently satisfied with his work, because in August 1964 he was named to succeed Lo Shih-kao as ambassador to Albania. Ten years earlier this post would have been regarded as a minor one, but by the early 1960's Albania had become Peking's chief political and ideological ally in Europe. Hsu arrived in Tirana on September 3 and presented his credentials four days later. In November–December 1964, he served as an official member of the Party-Government delegation led by Politburo member Li Hsien-nien to the celebrations marking the 20th anniversary of the "liberation" of Albania from the Germans.

Nothing is known of Hsu's personal life aside from the fact that he was accompanied by his wife to Albania.

Hsu Chih-chen

(1898–1964; Han-shou hsien, Hunan). Vice-chairman, All-China Federation of Trade Unions.

Hsu Chih-chen, one of the early labor leaders in the Chinese Communist Movement, was a vice-chairman of the All-China Federation of Trade Unions from 1957 until his death seven years later. He was born in November 1898 in Han-shou hsien, located near the southwest edge of Tung-t'ing Lake in northern Hunan. Much of the information on Hsu's early career is drawn from his official obituary, and according to this source he participated in the May Fourth Movement (1919) and then joined the China Social-

ist Youth League in 1921 and the CCP in 1922. In the early twenties Hsu went to Moscow, where he attended the Communist University of the Toilers of the East, which had opened in 1921. Among Hsu's classmates at this institute were such leading Communists as Jen Pi-shih, Wang Jo-fei, Chao Shih-yen, and Hsiao Ching-kuang (qq.v.).[1]

In approximately the 1925–1927 period, according to his obituary, Hsu served successively as head of the Organization Department and then the Propaganda Department of the Hunan Party Committee, after which he was transferred to Hupeh, where he was secretary of the Hankow "Local Committee" and then chairman of the Han-yeh-p'ing Trade Union. Han-yeh-p'ing refers to the great iron and steel complex in and around Hankow, the largest in China proper. One source describes this union, organized by Li Li-san, Hsiang Ying, and Ts'ai Shu-fan (qq.v.), as the most powerful in China excepting only the railway workers' union.[2] Inasmuch as the Fourth All-China Labor Congress was held in Hankow in 1927, it seems probable that Hsu, in the area at the time, attended it. If so, he was doubtless in contact with Liu Shao-ch'i and Li Li-san, both of whom were at this congress. In any event, from this point in his career, he devoted most of the remainder of his life to trade union work.

According to Hsu's obituary, after the split between the Nationalists and Communists in 1927, he engaged in "progressive work" among Chinese workers living in the "Soviet Far Eastern districts." This cryptic statement may mean that Hsu was in the Maritime Province area; in view of the fact that he was involved in publishing work during the Sino-Japanese War, it is possible that he worked in Vladivostok to promote the use of a Latinized script for writing Chinese. In the mid-1920's there were an estimated 100,000 Chinese living in the USSR, of whom approximately 22,000 lived in Vladivostok.[3] Intensive efforts, led by Ch'ü Ch'iu-pai (q.v.), were made in this city to romanize Chinese. The "First Conference on the Latinization of Chinese" was held in Vladivostok in September 1931, and 13 months later a similar and better-attended conference was held in the same city. The work of these conferences brought about further educational efforts, including the publication of tens of thousands of new textbooks, which in turn led to near total literacy in the new script among Chinese in the USSR.[4] If in fact Hsu was in the Vladivostok area, he was probably also in contact with Liu Ch'ang-sheng (q.v.), one of the top Chinese Communist trade unionists.

Whatever his activities may have been in the Soviet Far East, Hsu was back to China during the Sino-Japanese War, where he was engaged in publishing and printing. He served as head of the Hopeh-Chahar Printing Press Workers'

Union and as director of a printing plant in the Shansi-Chahar area. During these wartime years there was a Central Publishing Bureau subordinate to the Party Central Committee, and Hsu served as its secretary-general. With three key positions in the fields of management, trade union leadership, and Party supervision, it is apparent that Hsu was a central figure in the publication world of Communist-held areas. He was also a co-translator in 1940 of a 1915 essay by Lenin entitled *Socialism and War*.[5]

In August 1948 the Communists convened the Sixth All-China Labor Congress in Harbin, the first held since a secretly convened congress in Shanghai in 1929. Hsu attended the Harbin congress and was elected to the Executive Committee of the All-China Federation of Labor (ACFL) as well as to the Standing Committee. In addition, he was named to head the Federation's Culture and Education Department, although he gave up this post in 1949. Hsu assumed three posts in 1949 that made him one of the most important ACFL leaders for the next few years, particularly in view of the fact that the Federation chiefs (like Ch'en Yun and Li Li-san) were occupied with several other activities aside from trade union work. First and most significant was Hsu's position as secretary-general, often the crucial post in Communist organizations. Closely related to this post was that of director of the Federation's Staff Office, the unit charged with the administrative work of the ACFL. Finally, he headed the Finance Section under the Staff Office. He held all these posts until 1952 and then was replaced in the most important one (the secretary-generalship) by Lai Jo-yü (q.v.), a senior Party leader.

In the interim, Hsu was an active participant in the establishment of "mass" organizations and the central government in the summer and fall of 1949. In June he was named to Preparatory Committee membership in the China New Legal Research Society, and in the next month he attended a large conference of social science "workers" held in Peking. Representing the ACFL, he also attended the CPPCC Preparatory Committee meetings in June (under the chairmanship of Mao Tse-tung), and when the CPPCC held its first session in September to bring the central government into existence, Hsu was again present as an ACFL representative. In the next month Hsu was appointed a member of the Supreme People's Court, a position he held until the constitutional government was inaugurated in the fall of 1954. In that same month he was named to the National Committee of the newly formed China Peace Committee but was dropped from membership when it was reorganized a year later. Also in October 1949 Hsu left Peking for Moscow as a member of a delegation led by writer Ting Ling to the 32nd anniversary of the Russian Revolution.

In January 1950, Hsu gave a report before a Standing Committee meeting of the ACFL on the attendance by Chinese trade unionists at meetings of the International Transportation Workers' Association in Rumania and the International Agricultural and Forestry Workers' Association in Poland (both affiliate unions of the Communist-led World Federation of Trade Unions). From the fragmentary information on this report, it is not clear if Hsu himself attended these meetings (possibly after his visit to Moscow), or whether he was simply acting as a spokesman for colleagues who had attended. At the same meeting, a Research Committee for the ACFL Constitution was formed, with Hsu as one of its members. This was obviously the prelude to his report on revisions to the Constitution given at the Seventh All-China Labor Congress in May 1953.

In October–November 1951, Hsu attended the third session of the First CPPCC, which stressed the need for austerity and economy to support the military effort in Korea. Interestingly, at a meeting of the ACFL held on January 1, 1952, shortly after the close of the CPPCC, Hsu subjected himself to mild self-criticism. The meeting was described as a "mobilization meeting for the struggle against corruption, waste, and bureaucracy." Yet it was clear that Hsu was not in any particular trouble, because in the same year he assumed still another key post in the ACFL when he became head of the Organization Department, a post he held at least until the close of the Seventh Labor Congress in May 1953.

The Seventh All-China Labor Congress was obviously a high point in Hsu's career. He served on the presidium (steering committee) for the Congress sessions and was also a deputy secretary-general of the Congress. Following the major report by Lai Jo-yü (elected chairman at this Congress), Hsu delivered the next most important address—a detailed speech on the revisions to the trade union constitution. At the close of the Congress he was re-elected to the Executive Committee, and when this body held its first meeting immediately after the Congress, Hsu was re-elected to the permanent Presidium (renamed from the Standing Committee) and to the Secretariat, then composed of only eight men. Four and a half years later (December 1957), Hsu was to play an almost identical role at the Eighth Congress of the All-China Federation of Trade Unions (ACFTU), as it was renamed (in English) following the 1953 Congress. Once again he served on the Congress presidium and was then re-elected to the Executive Committee, the Presidium, and the Secretariat. On this occasion, he was given still another post when he was named one of the vice-chairmen under Lai Jo-yü.

Although trade union work was Hsu's specialty, he was also involved in other tasks in the 1950's and 1960's. He was a Shantung deputy to the First (1954–1959) and Second (1959–

1964) NPC's, and in both he also served on the permanent Budget Committee. In extragovernmental organizations, he was named to the National Committee of the China Scientific and Technical Association when it was created from two other organizations in September 1958, a post he held until his death. In this same month a China-Vietnam Friendship Association was formed; Hsu may have been named to the National Council at that time, but at any rate he was identified in this post by May 1960. From March 1959 he served on a preparatory committee for a national conference of "advanced producers," and when it was convened in October of that year, he served on the conference presidium.

From 1959 to 1961, Hsu took three more trips abroad, each connected with trade union work. In May 1959 he attended the European Trade Union and Workers' Conference at Goerlitz in East Germany, and in August–September of the same year he led a trade union group to North Vietnam for the 14th anniversary of the "Democratic Republic of Vietnam." Finally, in February 1961 he led a small delegation to North Vietnam for the second national congress of the Vietnam General Confederation of Labor. Hsu remained fairly active in trade union work in Peking through 1962, but then dropped from public attention until he was re-elected in September 1964 as a deputy from Shantung to the Third NPC. However, he never served in this NPC because on October 26, 1964, just shy of his 66th birthday, he died in Peking. His funeral committee consisted of a number of leading Party figures and was headed by Politburo member P'eng Chen.

Hsu's only known writing was an article written on the eve of the Eighth Labor Congress, in which he summarized trade union work over the four previous years; this appeared in the Peking *Kung-jen jih-pao* (Daily worker), November 22, 1957.

1. *Hung-ch'i p'iao-p'iao* (Red flag fluttering; Peking, 1957), IV, 23.

2. Nym Wales, *The Chinese Labor Movement* (New York, 1945), p. 32.

3. John De Francis, *Nationalism and Language Reform in China* (Princeton, N.J., 1950), pp. 87–88.

4. *Ibid.*, pp. 99–100, 104.

5. Chang Ching-lu, ed., *Chung-kuo ch'u-pan shih liao pu-pien* (Supplementary historical materials on Chinese publishing; Peking, 1957), p. 461.

Hsu Hai-tung

(1900–   ; Huang-p'i, Hupeh). Red Army veteran; member, CCP Central Committee.

Hsu Hai-tung was an early guerrilla leader in north Hupeh, and from his and similar units the important Hupeh-Honan-Anhwei (Oyüwan) base was created in the late 1920's and early 1930's. In 1934–35 he was a top commander of the first major contingent of Long Marchers to arrive in north Shensi, and in the early part of the Sino-Japanese War he led troops in north Shansi. Hsu has been a member of the Party Central Committee since 1956, but poor health forced him into virtual retirement many years earlier. Most of the information on his early life is based on the extensive interviews recorded by American journalist Edgar Snow in 1936.[1]

Hsu was born in Huang-p'i (Huang-pei), an agricultural community not far north of Wuhan. Snow spoke of Hsu and Ho Lung as the two "pure proletarian" military leaders among the many he interviewed in 1936. Hsu's family had been pottery workers for generations, and in his grandfather's time they were landowners. But afterwards the combination of floods, droughts, and taxes had completely "proletarianized" the family. Hsu was the youngest of six sons and evidently intelligent, because the family pooled its meager resources to send him to school. He attended a primary school for about four years, but then left because of the injustices he felt he suffered there. Then only 11, he went to work at the family trade, becoming an apprentice to a potter. He won his journeyman's rating in his 16th year and, according to his own claim, was the highest paid potter among 300 fellow workers.

Hsu worked for five more years, but then after quarrelling with his family, he left for Hankow, and from there went to Kiangsi where he worked another year as a potter until he fell ill from cholera. He exhausted his savings while recovering, so instead of returning home he decided to join a warlord army in which he received "only beatings," instead of the small pay he had been promised. The army was infiltrated by Communists, and under their influence he defected and went south to Canton where he joined the KMT Fourth Army under General Chang Fa-k'uei. He remained with Chang's army until 1927, serving as a platoon commander during the Northern Expedition which began in mid-1926 and which reached the Wuhan area in the fall. When the "Left" and "Right" factions of the KMT began to split in the early part of 1927, Hsu, "siding with the radicals," was forced to flee to his native Huang-p'i. By then a CCP member, he set about organizing a Party branch and recruiting his own small peasant "army," which was modestly equipped with "one revolver and eight bullets" for its 17 men.

The next few years of Hsu's career belong to the period of Communist expansion in the rural hinterlands and are closely related to the development of the Hupeh-Honan-Anhwei (Oyüwan) base, which by the early 1930's grew to be second only in size to the Central Soviet area in Kiangsi where Chu Te and Mao Tse-tung were in command. The growth of the military strength of the Oyüwan base is described in the biography of Hsu Hsiang-ch'ien, a Whampoa graduate who was sent to the area in 1928 and who, in November 1931, became commander of the Fourth Front Army, the military arm of the base area. The two major components of the Fourth Front Army were the Fourth Army and the 25th Army; Hsu was by then or soon thereafter in command of the latter.

Despite a series of Annihilation Campaigns by the Nationalists in the early 1930's, the Oyü-wan base survived as a viable Communist stronghold until a campaign begun in mid-1932. By October, Chang Kuo-t'ao (q.v.), the top political leader, and Hsu Hsiang-ch'ien decided to evacuate the area and move westward into Szechwan. Chang and Hsu took the major elements of the Fourth Front Army with them, but Hsu Hai-tung and Shen Tse-min (q.v.), another top political figure, were left in Oyüwan to sustain a guerrilla operation and a Party organization. Chang Kuo-t'ao, who was, of course, an eyewitness to these events, claims that Hsu was left behind because he had been wounded in 1932.[2] In the course of the next two years Hsu and his men underwent extraordinary difficulties as they attempted to fight off continuing Nationalist attacks. These hardships, as well as a useful description of the military tactics employed by Hsu, are related in detail by Edgar Snow in a chapter in *Red Star over China*.[3]

In 1934, shortly before the Chu-Mao armies began the Long March from Kiangsi, Ch'eng Tsu-hua (q.v.) was sent to the Oyüwan base to convey orders that Hsu's 25th Army should move from Anhwei westward into Hupeh. As it turned out, this became an order to begin one of the phases of the Long March, which finally ended in north Shensi in the early fall of 1935. Many accounts state that Hsu led the 25th Army on this march, but according to Ch'eng Tsu-hua's version (as related to American authoress Nym Wales), Hsu was the deputy commander under Ch'eng at this time. Hsu himself has described the march of the 25th Red Army to Shensi in an account published in Peking in 1957.[4] The Oyüwan forces moved out with about 8,000 troops, but subsequent fighting and general hardship reduced these numbers to some 3,000 by the time the 25th Army joined forces in north Shensi (shortly before the arrival of Mao Tse-tung) with the Shensi guerrillas led by Liu Chih-tan (q.v.). Liu had conducted guerrilla campaigns for several years in Shensi. Prior to joining Liu, Hsu and his colleagues had set up a small soviet in south Shensi, but they soon moved from Shensi, leaving operations there to Cheng Wei-san (q.v.).

Leaving south Shensi, Ch'eng Tsu-hua and

Hsu moved into Kansu and then into north Shensi (constantly fighting guerrilla skirmishes en route). Finally, in September 1935, their units joined forces with Liu Chih-tan, after which they were known as the 15th Army Corps. Hsu was placed in command, Liu became deputy commander, Ch'eng Tzu-hua was the political commissar, and Kao Kang (q.v.) was put in charge of the Political Department. In the next month the 15th Corps was joined by the troops led by Mao Tse-tung. According to figures supplied to Edgar Snow by Chou En-lai in 1936, the Liu-Hsu combined armies had about 13,000 men (in contrast to Mao's troops who numbered some 7,000).[5] However, in Hsu's account he states that the combined strength of his and Liu Chih-tan's men came to about 7,000.

No sooner were the Mao-Liu-Hsu forces united when a decision was taken to launch a large-scale military expedition across the Yellow River into neighboring Shansi, controlled by Yen Hsi-shan, the famous warlord governor of the province. Hsu was among the participants in this endeavor, which began in February 1936. The Communists scored some initial successes, but when Yen was reinforced by troops from Chiang Kai-shek's armies, the Red Army was driven back across the Yellow River in the spring. (The campaign into Shansi is described in further detail in the biography of Liu Chih-tan, who lost his life at that time.) Hsu was then assigned to the garrison in Yü-wang hsien (then in Kansu, but now in Ninghsia), and it was there that Edgar Snow interviewed him in August 1936. A year later, journalist Nym Wales, who was also in the Communist-held northwest, reported that Hsu was a member of the Revolutionary Military Council, an organ second only in importance to the Politburo.

When the Sino-Japanese War began in mid-1937, the Communists immediately reorganized their forces into the Eighth Route Army, which consisted of three divisions. Most of Hsu's 15th Army Corps was incorporated into Liu Po-cheng's 129th Division, but Hsu himself was placed in command of the 344th Brigade in Lin Piao's 115th Division. Lin's first operation was to lead his division into battle at P'ing-hsing Pass in north Shansi (late September 1937), where, in conjunction with Nationalist forces, the Chinese scored a notable victory over the Japanese. A month later journalist-author Agnes Smedley, who was with the Red Army headquarters in northeast Shansi, reported that Hsu was conducting raids against the Japanese logistics network in the area.[6] Two months later (during the turn of the year 1937–38), U.S. military observer Evans F. Carlson, then on an inspection trip, visited Hsu's headquarters in northeast Shansi not far from the Hopeh border. Carlson was struck by Hsu's "qualities of leadership."[7]

Carlson was again in the northeast Shansi area

in mid-1938, but by then Hsu and his brigade had "gone south." By 1939 Hsu was identified as a deputy commander of the New Fourth Army's North Yangtze Command (Chiang-pei chih-hui-pu), the history of which is described in the biography of its commander, Chang Yun-i. In the same year Hsu was also identified as a member of the Party's bureau in Shantung province, but virtually nothing has been recorded about Hsu's work in the middle and late war years. Almost two decades later, the Peking *Ta-kung pao* (August 1, 1957) reported that Hsu had been bed-ridden for the 18 years—a date that coincides with Hsu's entry into the New Fourth Army's area of operations. The term "bed-ridden" may have been somewhat exaggerated, but it seems evident that he was largely incapacitated throughout those years. Fragmentary but unsubstantiated reports regarding Hsu in the late war years and the early postwar period place him in the Shantung-Kiangsu-Honan Military Region, southeast Shansi, and finally in the Mongolian People's Republic where he allegedly was deputy chief of a military liaison mission.

Despite Hsu's rather impressive military career throughout the 1930's, he was not elected to the Party Central Committee at the Seventh Party Congress in 1945, and when the PRC was established in 1949, Hsu did not receive any position in the government, nor even an honorific post in one of the many "mass" organizations. In fact, he was not reported in the press until June 1954 when he was added as a member of the PRC's People's Revolutionary Military Council (PRMC), the military advisory organ of the central government. Three months later, when the national government was reorganized, Hsu was made a member of the newly established National Defense Council (NDC), the successor to the PRMC. Hsu was twice reappointed to the NDC, in April 1959 and January 1965. In 1955 the PRC created personal military ranks for its officer corps and established three decorations to cover military service from the birth of the Red Army until 1950. Hsu's name appeared on a composite list of those receiving one or more of the three awards, and thus it is not known which he received. By mid-1957 he was identified as a senior general in the PLA, a rank equal to a four-star U.S. Army general and second only in the PLA to the highest rank of marshal.

At the Party's Eighth National Congress, held in September 1956, Hsu was elected a member of the Central Committee. He has been mentioned in the press very infrequently since then and usually in connection with ceremonial tasks— such as attending a reception in August 1957 to mark the anniversary of the PLA or serving as a member of a funeral committee for one of his former colleagues.

Based on his interviews of 1936, Edgar Snow has left a short but vivid characterization of

Hsu, a "battered veteran" who had been wounded eight times. Snow was impressed with his apparently boundless energy, and with his "naive, impulsive and at the same time shy" manner. "Wiry and tough," Hsu's "energy and attention to detail" were reflected, according to Snow, in the good physical condition and discipline of his army.[8] Even in a Communist movement marked by a high order of personal tragedy, few members of the Chinese elite witnessed such extraordinary family losses as Hsu. In his 1936 conversations with Snow, he claimed that two of three brothers serving in the Red Army had been killed, and that his wife had been sold as a concubine. In all, 27 near and 39 distant relatives were killed.

1. Edgar Snow, *Red Star over China* (New York, 1938), pp. 297–310.
2. Modern China Project, Columbia University, New York, Howard L. Boorman, director.
3. Snow, pp. 304–310.
4. *Hung-ch'i p'iao-p'iao* (Red flag fluttering; Peking, 1957), III, 174–186; an almost identical version appears in *Hsing-huo liao-yuan* (A single spark can start a prairie fire; Hong Kong, 1960), pp. 220–234.
5. Edgar Snow, *Random Notes on Red China, 1936–1945* (Cambridge, Mass., 1957), p. 100.
6. Agnes Smedley, *China Fights Back* (London, 1938), p. 86.
7. Evans Fordyce Carlson, *Twin Stars of China* (New York, 1940), pp. 112–113, 223.
8. Snow, *Random Notes,* p. 112.

Hsu Hsiang-ch'ien

(1902– ; Wu-t'ai hsien, Shansi). Military leader; marshal of the PRC; member, CCP Central Committee.

Hsu Hsiang-ch'ien, a graduate of the Whampoa Military Academy, was one of the major Red Army commanders in the two decades after its formation in 1927. He emerged as the top military leader in the Communists' Oyüwan base and commanded the Fourth Front Army during the Long March. Hsu led Eighth Route Army troops during the early years of the Sino-Japanese War, and in the civil war against the Nationalists in the late 1940's he was an important commander in Shansi province. He held a number of important posts in the PRC after 1949, but because of poor health he was relatively inactive until the mid-1960's. Hsu was elected to the CCP Central Committee in 1945.

Hsu was born in Wu-t'ai, a hsien in northeast Shansi near the Hopeh border, which was also the home of the prominent Shansi warlord Yen Hsi-shan. According to Hsu's account of his life given to journalist Nym Wales,[1] which is a major source of information about his career until the mid-thirties, his family were small landowners and Hsu's father, a *Hsiu-ts'ai* degree holder, taught school. Hsu had an older brother and three sisters. After six years of primary schooling in Wu-t'ai, he worked as a bookshop clerk before entering Taiyuan Normal School in the provincial capital. After graduation he taught in the primary school attached to a Wu-t'ai middle school founded by Yen Hsi-shan. His interest in "revolution," he told Miss Wales, dated back to his early teenage days when the Japanese presented China with the famous Twenty-One Demands in 1915, an act which had brought Hsu to lead an anti-Japanese student demonstration.

In 1924, in order to escape his father's conservatism, he left for Canton where he immediately joined the KMT and enrolled at the newly opened Whampoa Military Academy, whose commandant was Chiang Kai-shek. After about six months' training Hsu graduated from the first class (February 1925). Among his classmates were such prominent Communists (or latter-day Communists) as Ch'en Keng, Hsiao Ching-kuang, Huang K'o-ch'eng, and Tso Ch'üan (qq.v.). Hsu was married when he left home, but while he was at Whampoa his wife died, and he had lost touch with their daughter by 1937 when he was interviewed by Miss Wales. Immediately after his graduation in early 1925, Hsu took part in the First Eastern Expedition against Kwangtung warlord Ch'en Chiung-ming (see under P'eng P'ai). At approximately this time the KMT, with strong support from the Soviet Union, began to court northern warlord Feng Yü-hsiang, and by the spring of 1925 an agreement was reached which allowed the KMT to have political workers in Feng's famous Kuominchün (Nationalist Army). It was apparently under these circumstances that Hsu was dispatched to Honan as a political worker in the Second Kuominchün Army, commanded by General Hu Ching-i until his death in April 1925 and thereafter by General Yueh Wei-chün. For more than a year Hsu campaigned in several north China provinces, principally against warlord generals Chang Tso-lin and Yen Hsi-shan. Hsu was ill for a period and recuperated in Peking, and by the time he recovered, the Northern Expeditionary Forces had occupied Wuhan (fall 1926). He went to Wuhan where he became an instructor at the Central Political and Military Academy (in effect, a branch of the Whampoa Academy).

According to Hsu's own account, after his arrival in Wuhan he delved into and was influenced by Marxist works and, as a result, joined the CCP. (Hsu told Nym Wales that he joined in 1926, but the official biography of Hsu uses the year 1927.[2]) After the split between the KMT and the CCP in mid-1927, he worked covertly for a short time as an officer on Chang Fa-k'uei's general staff. He then "escaped" from Chang's army and made his way to Shang-

hai where the CCP assigned him to work in the labor movement in Canton. For the next several weeks Hsu secretly trained a group of ill-armed workers in preparation for the December uprising in Canton; because he could not speak Cantonese he was forced to use an interpreter. When the Canton Commune was established on December 11, 1927 (see under Chang T'ai-lei), Hsu was in command of a detachment of workers, but within less than three days the Communists were driven from Canton. Regrouping their 1,200 men north of the city, they established the Fourth Division of the Workers' and Peasants' Red Army, which consisted of three regiments.

The Fourth Division was commanded by Yeh Yung, the CCP representative was Yuan Kuop'ing, and Hsu was made the Party representative of the 10th Regiment. They first tried to link up with Chu Te's forces, which had come south to Kwangtung after the Nanchang Uprising in August 1927. However, when they could not locate Chu's men, they moved eastward where they joined the Communist stronghold in the Hai-lu-feng area (see under P'eng P'ai). The Fourth Division joined ranks with the Second Division, which consisted mainly of troops formerly led by Yeh T'ing and Ho Lung which had fled to Hai-lu-feng after the disastrous defeat at Swatow at the end of September 1927. However, the combined force of some 2,000 men was unable to withstand the assaults upon the Hai-lu-feng Soviet, and by the early spring of 1928 the Second and Fourth Divisions were all but destroyed. During this brief period Hsu rose to be chief-of-staff and then commander of the Fourth Division. (The original commander, Yeh Yung, was captured in June 1928 and executed.) In describing these events to Nym Wales, Hsu lamented that "our best revolutionary cadres were sacrificed" in Hai-lu-feng and claimed that there were only 60 survivors in his Fourth Division. Many years later he again recounted these events for the *JMJP* (July 30, 1958).

After the collapse of the Hai-lu-feng Soviet, Hsu escaped to Shanghai in March 1928. His statements regarding his whereabouts during the next year are seemingly contradictory; at one point he told Nym Wales that he left Shanghai for a Communist guerrilla base in Hupeh after only three weeks in Shanghai, and at another point he mentioned his arrival in Hupeh as being in June 1929. In any case, Hsu was one of the earliest Communist military men to arrive in the base, which was soon to grow into the Oyüwan (Hupeh-Honan-Anhwei) Soviet and which came to be second in importance only to the base formed by Chu Te and Mao Tse-tung in Kiangsi. The historians' task in unraveling the complex events in Oyüwan is complicated by the fact that Maoist histories have both neglected the base and distorted its history—principally because it came to be the political stronghold of Chang Kuo-t'ao (q.v.), one of Mao's greatest enemies, after Chang's arrival in Oyüwan in 1931. However, a rough reconstruction of the events can be made largely on the basis of Nym Wales interviews with Hsu and a lengthy article by Hsu in the *JMJP* (July 29, 1961).

The Oyüwan base had its origins in northeast Hupeh in the latter half of 1927. Working in and around Huang-an and Ma-ch'eng hsien, Hsu Hai-tung, Cheng Wei-san, Wang Shu-sheng (qq.v.), and others set up small guerrilla bands. These developments led to the establishment in July 1928 of the 31st Division of the 11th Red Army, and when Hsu arrived in Hupeh he was made deputy commander of this division and later the commander. The base was considerably expanded in the period from the end of 1928 to the beginning of 1930 by uprisings in Shang-ch'eng in southeast Honan and Liu-an and Huo-shan in southwest Anhwei. These, in turn, led to the formation of the 32nd and 33rd Divisions. At this juncture, in March 1930, the CCP Oyüwan Border Region Special Committee was established, and the above-mentioned divisions were reorganized into the First Red Army under the command of Hsu Chi-shen, a former Whampoa cadet. Hsu Hsiang-ch'ien's men, now designated the First Division, had some successes in attacking the Nationalists along the Peking-Hankow Railway north of Wuhan in mid-1930. These forays were carried out in conjunction with the plans of Li Li-san (q.v.), then the Party's dominant leader, who hoped to capture the major Yangtze Valley cities. In theory, Hsu was to cooperate with Ho Lung's forces in threatening Wuhan, while P'eng Te-huai's Third Army Corps was to capture Changsha and the First Army Corps under Chu Te and Mao Tse-tung was to assault Nanchang. P'eng Te-huai held Changsha for a few days, but otherwise Li Li-san's grandiose scheme collapsed and Li was soon "exiled" to Moscow.

By the fall of 1930 the First Red Army numbered about 5,000 men who had, in Hsu's term, "sovietized" portions of 10 hsien in Oyüwan. The Oyüwan forces were augmented by 2,000 men over the winter of 1930–31 when they were joined by the 15th Red Army, commanded by Ts'ai Shen-hsi, another Whampoa graduate. The 15th Army had been operating in eastern Hupeh, both north and south of the Yangtze. With this merger, the Communists established, in early 1931, the Fourth Red Army (some sources use Army Corps). Hsu was made the chief-of-staff, serving under K'uang Chi-hsun, who had earlier campaigned with Ho Lung in west Hunan and Szechwan. However, judging from Hsu's account, it appears that he soon replaced K'uang as Fourth Army commander.

While these developments were taking place in Oyüwan, important changes were being made in

the top Party leadership in Shanghai. At the Party's Fourth Plenum in January 1931, the Russian-returned student leadership (or "28 Bolsheviks") assumed control of the chief Party organs (see under Ch'in Pang-hsien and Ch'en Shao-yü). The new leadership soon dispatched a number of key political figures to the various Communist military bases. Thus, in the spring, Chang Kuo-t'ao arrived in Oyüwan, accompanied by two important members of the Russian-returned group, Ch'en Ch'ang-hao and Shen Tse-min (qq.v.). Under Chang's jurisdiction, a new Party organ was established—the Oyüwan Central Sub-bureau. Before long, in the late summer of 1931, the Oyüwan military structure was rocked by a major "counterrevolutionary plot," which led to wide-scale purges in the Fourth Army by the Chang Kuo-t'ao leadership (see under Ch'en Ch'ang-hao). Hsu attributed the direction of this conspiracy to the above-mentioned Hsu Chi-shen, but curiously he also asserted that Hsu Chi-shen was still one of his division commanders about three years later.

Hsu's position as the top military figure in Oyüwan was confirmed in the latter part of 1931. In November the Oyüwan forces were again reorganized; now known as the Fourth Front Red Army, it consisted of the Fourth and 25th Armies. Hsu was placed in command of the overall force, which was described in an official biography of Hsu as "one of the three main pillars of the Chinese Red Army."[3] In the same month, the First All-China Congress of Soviets met in Juichin, the headquarters of Mao Tse-tung and Chu Te, and elected the central Executive Committee (CEC) of the Chinese Soviet Republic. Chu Te was named chairman of the Central Revolutionary Military Council, subordinate to the CEC, and Hsu and Chang Kuo-t'ao were among its 15 members; Hsu continued to hold this post until at least 1937.[4] He did not attend the 1931 Juichin congress, but rather he remained in Oyüwan to direct the continuing battles against KMT troops. In the previous two years the Oyüwan troops had withstood three KMT Annihilation Campaigns. However, in mid-1932, the Fourth Front Red Army (then consisting of some 50,000 men) was subjected to the Fourth Annihilation Campaign. After a few months of intensive fighting, most of the army withdrew in October from the Oyüwan base. Hsu Hai-tung and Shen Tse-min remained behind, but Chang Kuo-t'ao, Hsu Hsiang-ch'ien, and Ch'en Ch'ang-hao marched their men through Hupeh, Honan, Shensi, and finally into north Szechwan where they established a new base at the end of 1932 and the early months of 1933 (see under Wang Hung-k'un).

Because the Oyüwan region was so close to vital KMT centers along the Yangtze, its destruction was given high priority by Chiang Kai-shek. Years later, Chiang wrote that even after Hsu's retreat into Szechwan, a "decisive victory was in sight," only to be thwarted in January 1933 when the government was forced to call off the campaign and to shift its troops to north China in response to new Japanese military incursions.[5] Another observer has written that the arrival of Chang Kuo-t'ao and Hsu in Szechwan had come at an "opportune time" when the "warlords of that province were busily fighting one of their many civil wars and Ho Lung was at the same time threatening the southeast corner of Szechwan."[6] In any case, Hsu had arrived with about 10,000 troops, and within about two years he was able to expand this to about 80,000 (although half of them were without arms).[7] During this period the Fourth Front Army was composed of five armies (the Fourth, Ninth, 30th, 31st, and 33rd). Serving under Hsu were a number of officers who later became important Party leaders; they include Li Hsien-nien, Wang Shu-sheng, Wang Wei-chou, Wang Hung-k'un (qq.v.), Ni Chih-liang (ambassador to North Korea in the 1950's), Tseng Ch'uan-liu (a vice-minister of Commerce from 1954 to 1963), and Chan Ts'ai-fang (a member of the National Defense Council since 1959). Norman Hanwell, a Western journalist who visited the area a few months after it was evacuated in 1935, wrote in admiration about the tactics employed by Hsu, emphasizing in particular the mobility of his troops and the excellence of their intelligence network.[8] Many years later, a Western military historian observed that it was in the Szechwan campaigns that Hsu "first established [his] reputation as an original and brilliant commander."[9]

Because of the great distance from northern Szechwan to Juichin it is unlikely that Hsu attended the Second All-China Congress of Soviets held in January–February 1934. Nonetheless, he was elected to membership on the Central Executive Committee, the principal political organ of the Chinese Soviet Republic. Later that year Chu Te, Mao Tse-tung, and the rest of the Long Marchers evacuated the Juichin base. In the following June, the Fourth Front Army under Chang Kuo-t'ao and Hsu, which had already begun to move westward from north Szechwan, met the Chu-Mao forces at Mao-kung in west Szechwan. From there the two forces moved north to Mao-erh-kai where in August 1935, after a bitter policy conflict, the leadership split (see under Chang Kuo-t'ao). Mao continued north to Shensi, but the Chang-Hsu troops, now joined by such top commanders as Chu Te and Liu Po-ch'eng (formerly with Mao), soon abandoned the northward march and instead moved west into Sikang province where they established their headquarters at Kan-tzu. There, in June 1936, they were met by the Second Front Army, led by Jen Pi-shih and Ho Lung (qq.v.), which had come from west Hunan (see under Ho

Lung). At this juncture there was another dispute, and according to orthodox Maoist histories, Chu Te, Jen Pi-shih, and Ho Lung "resolutely" opposed Chang Kuo-t'ao's policies, but no mention is made of Hsu's position. Chang himself claims that he was supported by Hsu.[10] In any case, the combined armies soon began to move northward, and in the fall of 1936 they rendezvoused in east Kansu with troops from Mao's army, which had been sent to help them make the final leg of the march to join Mao in north Shensi (see under Tso Ch'üan). However, still another dispute broke out, and as a result major elements from the Fourth Front Army were ordered to march westward toward far-off Sinkiang by way of the Kansu Corridor. Maoist historians claim that this westward march was ordered by Chang Kuo-t'ao, and that it involved more than 20,000 men. Chang himself went to north Shensi, but in the closing days of 1936 Hsu began his march up the Kansu Corridor. By the time his troops reached the vicinity of Chiu-ch'üan, about 400 miles northwest of Lanchow, Hsu and his men had suffered a series of disastrous setbacks which had left him with a force of fewer than 2,000 men. At this juncture, Hsu and a handful of others were ordered to turn back and proceed directly to Shensi.[11] The ultimate fate of the remaining troops in the Kansu Corridor debacle is described in the biography of Li Hsien-nien.

Hsu reached north Shensi in mid-1937, just before the Sino-Japanese War broke out. The Communists immediately reorganized their units into the Eighth Route Army, composed of three divisions. Hsu's Fourth Front Army was absorbed into the 129th Division under the command of Liu Po-ch'eng. Hsu was made deputy commander, as well as commander of the 385th Brigade. The other brigade, the 386th, was led by Ch'en Keng (q.v.). In September 1937 all three divisions crossed the Yellow River into Shansi, the 129th taking the southernmost route, moving south of Taiyuan toward the Hopeh and finally establishing its headquarters in the vicinity of Liao-hsien in east Shansi. The Communists soon sent political organizers into south Hopeh, and then in the spring and summer of 1938 Hsu led major elements from two regiments of his 129th Division and one regiment from the 115th Division across the Peking-Hankow Railway into Nan-kung and Chü-lu hsien in south Hopeh. There, combining with Yang Hsiu-feng's (q.v.) guerrilla units, they established the South Hopeh Military District, which proved to be of particular value as a communications route into Shantung.[12]

In the spring of 1939 Hsu was sent into Shantung to coordinate the activities of several guerrilla units, which became known as the First Column.[13] Hsu commanded this column, and his official biography credits him with a "leading part" in creating a base in Shantung. However, rather little is known about his activities after 1939 and it appears that the major responsibilities there fell to Lo Jung-huan, whose biography provides details on Communist-led guerrilla activities in Shantung during the early war years. Because of poor health Hsu left the front lines in 1941, and for the next year he was without an assignment. Then from 1942 to 1946 he was in Yenan as a deputy commander under Ho Lung of the Joint Defense Command, which controlled the military units subordinate to the Shansi-Suiyuan and the Shensi-Kansu-Ninghsia Border Regions. He is also reported to have been president in 1945 of the Anti-Japanese Military and Political Academy (K'ang-ta), apparently assuming the post from Lin Piao toward the end of the war.

When the Party held its Seventh National Congress in Yenan from April to June 1945, Hsu was one of only 15 men who served on the Congress Presidium (steering committee). At the close of the meetings he was elected one of the 44 full members of the Central Committee. He was still in the Yenan area in mid-1946, but by the end of 1947 he was in command of PLA units in the Shansi-Hopeh-Shantung-Honan Border Region, which, in coordination with P'eng Te-huai's Northwest Field Army, scored notable victories over Nationalist troops in southwest Shansi.[14] For the next year and a half Hsu campaigned in central and southwest Shansi. In 1948 his forces were incorporated into Nieh Jung-chen's North China Military Region; Hsu became a deputy commander of the region and concurrently the commander and political commissar of its First Army Group. With his deputy Chou Shih-ti (q.v.), Hsu fought a successful campaign against Yen Hsi-shan's forces, which began in the fall of 1948 and culminated after bitter fighting in the capture of Taiyuan, the Shansi capital, on April 24, 1949.[15] An unusual aspect of the battle for Taiyuan is that the city was defended by thousands of Japanese, as well as Chinese, troops. The Japanese were, in effect, mercenaries employed by Shansi Governor Yen Hsi-shan after the Sino-Japanese War. Moreover, when Yen fled Taiyuan in March, he left his troops under the command of a Japanese general, who, when the city fell to the Communists, committed suicide.[16]

In the meantime, to consolidate their gains in north China, the Communists established the North China People's Government (NCPG) in the Shih-chia-chuang area (west Hopeh) at a congress held in August 1948. Hsu's responsibilities were primarily in the military sphere during this period, but he was named a member of the government Council, which was headed by Tung Pi-wu (q.v.). The NCPG was dissolved in October 1949, immediately after the Communists' national government was established. When Hsu's troops captured Taiyuan in April 1949, he was named chairman of the Taiyuan Military Control Commission. However, inferential evidence suggests that his chronic ill health prevented any active military or political life for the next several years. Nonetheless, when the central government was established in September–October 1949 in Peking, Hsu received several key appointments. In September he was a delegate from the First Field Army to the CPPCC and was elected a member of the CPPCC National Committee (to 1954). In the next month he became a member of the People's Revolutionary Military Council (PRMC) and chief-of-staff of the PRMC. However, his deputy, Nieh Jung-chen, immediately began to serve as acting chief-of-staff and continued to do so until the PRMC was abolished in 1954. Hsu was also a member of the Central People's Government Council (CPGC), which was chaired by Mao Tse-tung. The CPGC, the highest organ in the PRC, held 34 meetings between 1949 and its dissolution in 1954, but Hsu did not attend a meeting until the end of 1953 (and only two meetings in all). Similarly, he is known to have been absent from the important first, second, and third sessions of the CPPCC National Committee (held in June 1950, October–November 1951, and February 1953).

Hsu appears to have partially recovered by late 1953, and from June to September 1954 he served as a vice-chairman of the PRMC. He was present at the CPGC meeting in early September, which tentatively approved the national constitution, and a few days later he attended the inaugural session of the First NPC, which formally adopted the document. He represented the PLA in the First NPC and was re-elected to the Second Congress (1959–1964) as well as the Third NPC, which opened in December 1964. In both the First and Second NPC's he was elected a member of the permanent Standing Committee and was advanced to a vice-chairmanship at the close of the first session of the Third NPC (January 1965). In recognition of his long military career, Hsu was also appointed in September 1954 a vice-chairman of the National Defense Council (a position he still retains), although this organ is less important than its predecessor, the PRMC.

In September 1955 the Communists awarded its officer corps personal military ranks and decorations. Hsu was made one of the 10 PLA marshals, the highest rank, and was given the three top decorations, the Orders of August First, Independence and Freedom, and Liberation, awards that covered three periods from the founding of the Red Army in 1927 through the victory over the Nationalists in 1950. Hsu's participation in military and political affairs, which had been virtually nil in the early fifties, picked up slightly in the middle and late fifties. At the Party's Eighth National Congress in September 1956 he was a member of both the presidium (steering committee) and credentials committee, and was one of the executive chairmen for two of the Congress sessions. He was re-elected to the Central Committee. Significantly, however, when the new Central Committee elected the Politburo on the day following the Congress, only three of the 10 PLA marshals failed to be elected to this key organ—Hsu, Nieh Jung-chen, and Yeh Chien-ying. Similarly, in May–July 1958, at an important conference of the Military Affairs Commission (MAC), the Party's highest military organ, Hsu was the only one of the 10 marshals who did not speak. A year earlier (March 1957), a Radio Peking broadcast described Hsu's simple life and love of books in terms that suggested that he was in virtual retirement. Chinese Communist media seldom comment on the state of health of the elite, but in the secret *Kung-tso t'ung-hsun* (Bulletin of activities) it was explicitly noted that Hsu had not taken part in inspections being conducted by top military leaders in early 1961 because of his "poor health." Nonetheless, this same journal revealed that by 1961 Hsu was a member of the MAC's Standing Committee, a group constituting the PRC's key military figures.[17]

Hsu continued to make only limited public appearances until the beginning of the Great Proletarian Cultural Revolution in 1966. Then, after nearly two decades of relative obscurity, he emerged as one of the apparent victors in the rapidly changing political situation. In January 1967 he was identified as a new member of the CCP Politburo and two months later as a vice-chairman of the Party's MAC.

Hsu worked very closely for five years with Chang Kuo-t'ao, who probably knew him better than any other major Communist leader. Chang has described Hsu as a capable military commander who had little interest in political affairs as such and one who was a good organizer and steady and cautious in his work methods.[18]

---

1. Nym Wales, *Red Dust* (Stanford, Calif., 1952), pp. 148–162; Nym Wales, *Inside Red China* (New York, 1939), pp. 132–141.
2. *SCMP* 1139, pp. 14–15.
3. *Ibid.*
4. *Hung-se Chung-hua,* December 18, 1931; Wales, *Inside Red China,* p. 343.
5. Chiang Chung-cheng (Chiang Kai-shek), *Soviet Russia in China: A Summing-up at Seventy* (New York, revised, abridged ed., 1965), p. 43.
6. Jerome Ch'en, *Mao and the Chinese Revolution* (London, 1965), p. 190.
7. Norman Hanwell, "The Chinese Red Army," *Asia,* no. 5:320 (May 1936); Wales, *Inside Red China,* p. 60.
8. Hanwell, pp. 317–322.
9. Samuel B. Griffith, II, *The Chinese People's Liberation Army* (New York, 1967), p. 53.
10. Modern China Project, Columbia University, New York, Howard L. Boorman, director.
11. *Hung-ch'i p'iao-p'iao* (Red flag fluttering; Peking, 1957), III, 211.
12. *K'ang-Jih chan-cheng shih-ch'i chieh-fang-ch'ü kai-k'uang* (A sketch of the liberated areas during the Anti-Japanese War; Peking, 1953), p. 48; Chalmers A. Johnson, *Peasant Nationalism and Communist Power* (Stanford, Calif., 1962), pp. 107–108.
13. Johnson, p. 113.
14. *Selected Works of Mao Tse-tung* (Peking, 1961), IV, 216.
15. *Ibid.,* p. 261.
16. Donald G. Gillin, *Warlord Yen Hsi-shan in Shansi Province, 1911–1949* (Princeton, N.J., 1967), pp. 285–288.
17. J. Chester Cheng, ed., *The Politics of the Chinese Red Army* (Stanford, Calif., 1966), p. 437.
18. Modern China Project.

Hsu Kuang-ta

(c.1902–   ; Changsha, Hunan). Vice-minister of National Defense; commander, PLA Armored Force; member, CCP Central Committee.

A veteran Red Army officer, Hsu Kuang-ta fought in central and north China from the twenties to the forties and has been commander of the PLA Armored Force since 1951. He became a member of the Party Central Committee in 1956 and a vice-minister of National Defense in 1959. Hsu, whose original name was Hsu Te-huai, has sometimes used the revolutionary pseudonym of Hsu Hao. He was born about 1902 in Changsha, the Hunan capital, of a well-to-do family. Hsu enrolled in the second class of Whampoa, the well-known Nationalist military academy, graduating with 449 other cadets in June 1925. When he left Whampao Hsu may have gone to the USSR for a brief period of study, but this cannot be confirmed. At some time shortly after graduation he entered the Nationalist army of Kwangtung general Chang Fa-k'uei, which was headquartered at Chiu-chiang (Kiukiang) north of Nanchang when the uprising broke out there on August 1, 1927, which severed all relations between the KMT and the CCP. Hsu, one of the insurgents from Chang's army, then joined the uprising led by Chu Te's garrison force within the city. Five days later, when the Communists were routed and forced to flee south, Hsu was a cadre in a battalion of the 75th Regiment of the 25th Division belonging to Yeh T'ing's 11th Army. Presumably he had joined the CCP by this time.

A description of the 11th Army in the immediate post-Nanchang period is contained in the biography of Yeh T'ing. The army was composed of two divisions, the 24th and the 25th, the latter with two regiments, one of which was the 75th, to which Hsu belonged. The Red forces fled south from Nanchang through eastern Kiangsi, passing by Kuan-ch'ang, Ning-tu, and Juichin, all towns that the Communists were to capture and fight in during the next few years. From Juichin they moved eastward into Fukien after passing T'ing-chou (Ch'ang-t'ing), turning south, and passing into Kwangtung above Ta-p'u, whence they made their way to Swatow. The Red armies were able to take and hold Swatow briefly toward the end of September 1927, but as they approached the city they left certain troops and the 25th Division at San-ho-pa, a point strategically important because it commanded the river and road communications to Swatow.[1] Chu Te was in over-all command of the troops left there, and Chou Shih-ti (q.v.) commanded the 25th Division. These forces were left at San-ho-pa to form a rear guard for the troops that entered Swatow. The siege of Swatow proved unsuccessful and the troops left at San-ho-pa were engaged in fighting, but after one week of battle Chu Te reported that he had lost half his regular units and was forced to retreat into Fukien.[2] In the fighting at San-ho-pa, Hsu was wounded but managed to escape.[3]

Hsu may have escaped to Hong Kong along with Ho Lung after the Swatow defeat. At any rate, when his activity is next reported (in the early 1930's), he was working in the west Hunan-Hupeh area controlled by the Second Army of Ho Lung. Communist activity in this area, located to the west and north of Tung-t'ing Lake, is described in Ho's biography. By the early thirties Ho had built a sizable army and was beginning to threaten Nationalist strongholds in the Wuhan area. He thus became the target of attack from Chiang Kai-shek's forces, which were attempting to drive the Communists from central China. In the fourth of a series of Annihilation Campaigns against the Communists (this one beginning in June of 1932), Ho's forces were driven out of the Tung-t'ing Lake area after suffering serious losses. The details of Hsu's connections with Ho Lung's army at this time are unknown, but his presence at Ho's base is known from a 1962 article in the authoritative *JMJP*, which Hsu wrote with two other PLA officers who were also there at the time (Wang Shou-tao and Wang Chen, qq.v.).[4] Describing the events there and mentioning the names of the principal Communists in the area at the time, the article is also quite critical of some of the military strategies that Ho was being advised to follow. It is the basis for much of the recent criticism that has been directed against one of Ho's political advisers, Hsia Hsi (q.v.).

Hsu probably made the Long March, but whether he accompanied the Long Marchers led from Kiangsi by Mao Tse-tung in the fall of 1934 or made the march a year later with the armies of Ho Lung is not known. Once in north Shansi he became associated with the Commu-

nist military academy, which in early 1937 was named the Anti-Japanese Military and Political Academy, abbreviated in Chinese as K'ang-ta. At about this time he was also reported to be working in Party intelligence.

By at least the latter years of the war Hsu was attached to the forces of Ho Lung, which fought along the Shansi-Suiyuan border. In 1942 he was identified as the commander of the Second Independent Brigade of Ho's 120th Division, and concurrently he was commander of a military district within the territory of the Shansi-Suiyuan Military Region. He continued to serve with the 120th Division throughout the war; in 1943 the military area over which he was in command was known as the Yen-pei Military District, Yen-pei being the region in northern Shansi to the north of the Yen-men-kuan (Yen-men Pass) in the Great Wall. Although Ho Lung commanded the 120th Division throughout the war, he moved his headquarters to Yenan in about 1943, and his post as commander of the Shansi-Suiyuan Military Region (which the 120th Division controlled) was taken by Lü Cheng-ts'ao (q.v.).

When the efforts of U.S. General George C. Marshall brought about the Cease-fire Agreement of January 10, 1946, the Peking Executive Headquarters was established to implement the agreement. Hsu, who was still in Shansi at this time, was made a member of the Headquarters' Truce Team, which operated out of Taiyuan, the provincial capital, but later in 1946 he was transferred to Manchuria where, with the simulated rank of major general, he headed Truce Team 29, which operated in Hai-lung in southern Kirin.

Sometime after the civil war broke out between the KMT and the CCP in 1946, Hsu returned to familiar territory in the northwest. In March 1947 the Nationalists captured Yenan, the Communist capital, and high-ranking Party officials were forced to evacuate the city. In moving from Yenan, the Communists divided the members of their governing Party Secretariat into two groups; the first group headed by Mao Tse-tung, who was aided by Chou En-lai and Jen Pi-shih remained in the Shensi-Kansu-Ninghsia Border Region (of which Yenan had been the capital) for a year, while the second group, led by Liu Shao-ch'i and Chu Te, made its way via the Shansi-Suiyuan border region into the Shansi-Chahar-Hopeh region and finally established headquarters in P'ing-shan hsien, west Hopeh. Mao and his group joined them there in May of 1948. In the evacuation from Yenan, P'eng Te-huai was in charge of a part of the Red Army, and in August 1947, when Mao's headquarters somewhere in the Shensi-Kansu-Ninghsia area was being threatened, he sent Hsu in charge of two brigades to offer him protection.[5]

Hsu was commander of the Third Army

Group in north China in 1948 and that same year was reappointed commander of the Yen-pei Military District. The following year the Communists created their important field armies from the armies that had previously been named for the geographic areas in which they were stationed. P'eng Te-huai was given command of the First Field Army (the former Northwest PLA), and Hsu remained in charge of his Third Army, but his troops were now called the Second Corps of the First Field Army. Concurrently in 1949 he was named the commander of the First Field Army's Armored Corps.

When civil administrations were formed in the northwest to control the areas conquered by the PLA, Hsu was given two assignments. He was named as a member of both the Kansu Provincial People's Government Council and the multiprovincial Northwest Military and Administrative Committee (NWMAC), which had jurisdiction over Kansu, Sinkiang, Tsinghai, Ninghsia, and Shensi. Both these governmental organs were inaugurated in January 1950. However, by the fall of 1950 he was transferred to Peking and as a consequence was removed from the Kansu Government post in early 1951 (although he remained a nominal member of the NWMAC until early 1953 when it was reorganized). Hsu was brought from the northwest to Peking to assume command of the Armored Force (the tank corps), a post he still holds. When he took command these forces were relatively insignificant, but as a result of large-scale Soviet aid during the Korean War, the Armored Force grew in both size and complexity of weaponry into one of the most important of the PLA service arms.

Hsu's appearances in the early fifties were rather infrequent, being confined mainly to national conferences involving the PLA, as in September–October 1950 when he attended a national conference for "fighting heroes" or in December 1953 when he spoke at the first "model representatives" conference of the Armored Forces. From 1954 to 1959 he was a PLA deputy to the First NPC, and at the end of the first session of the NPC (September 1954) he was elected to membership on the National Defense Council, a prestigious position but one with little power. He was reappointed to the Defense Council in 1959 and 1965. In 1955 the PRC gave its officers decorations as well as personal military ranks for past services. Hsu was made a senior general, the equivalent of a four-star general in the U.S. Army (and only one rank below the top rank of PLA marshal). In addition, he received the Orders of August First, Independence and Freedom, and Liberation for his service in the Red armies during three periods from 1927 to 1950. A year later, at the Party's Eighth National Congress (September 1956), Hsu was elected a member of the Party Central Committee. He was one of only 33 members elected to full membership who had been neither a full nor an alternate member of the Seventh Central Committee elected at the 1945 Party Congress.

Since the mid-fifties Hsu has appeared in Peking with great regularity—almost always in connection with PLA-sponsored conferences, festivities marking PLA holidays (such as the founding of the Red Army on August 1), or parties given by foreign military attachés stationed in Peking. In contrast to most high-ranking PLA officers, he has traveled abroad rather frequently. The first of these trips took place in November–December 1957 when he accompanied P'eng Te-huai to Moscow for the 40th anniversary of the Bolshevik Revolution; the delegation returned to China via Khaborovsk and Vladivostok. In September–October 1960 he led a Sino-Soviet Friendship Association delegation to Moscow to participate in celebrations marking the 11th anniversary of the PRC, and in March of the following year he headed a military group to Mongolia for the 40th anniversary of the founding of the Mongolian People's Army. In October–November 1962 Hsu spent three weeks in Algeria as head of a Chinese government delegation attending Algerian National Day celebrations, and while there he conferred with several top Algerian leaders, including Ben Bella and Ferhat Abbas. Finally, in May 1965 he led a military delegation to Moscow to take part in celebrations commemorating the 20th anniversary of the defeat of Nazi Germany.

Hsu assumed a new and important post when the top leadership of the Ministry of National Defense was reshuffled in September 1959, following the purge of Defense Minister P'eng Te-huai. P'eng was replaced by Lin Piao and at the same time one of the vice-ministers, Huang K'o-ch'eng (q.v.), was dropped from the ministry without being given another comparable post. Two other vice-ministers, Hsiao K'o and Li Ta (qq.v.), were also removed and given less important assignments. Simultaneously, Lo Jui-ch'ing, Su Yü, Ch'en Keng, Hsu Shih-yu, Liu Ya-lou (qq.v.), and Hsu Kuang-ta were named vice-ministers of Defense. As of the mid-sixties, only Hsu and Hsiao Ching-kuang (the Navy commander) among the vice-ministers concurrently headed one of the PLA service arms.

1. C. Martin Wilbur, "The Ashes of Defeat," *The China Quarterly,* no. 18:31 (April–June 1964).

2. Agnes Smedley, *The Great Road* (New York, 1956), pp. 308–309.

3. *Kuang-ming jih-pao,* July 31, 1957.

4. *JMJP,* February 1, 1962.

5. *Hung-ch'i p'iao-p'iao* (Red flag fluttering; Peking, 1957), III, 357, 359.

Hsu Li-ch'ün

Deputy-director, Propaganda Department, CCP; deputy editor-in-chief, *Hung-ch'i* (Red flag).

A leading propagandist, Hsu Li-ch'ün first gained a degree of national prominence in 1949 when he was selected for membership on the Central Committee of the New Democratic Youth League at the first congress of the league in April 1949. Later that year he was identified as head of the Peking chapter of the league. By 1950 Hsu was a deputy director of the league's Propaganda Department, and in November 1951 he was elevated to the Standing Committee of the Central Committee. He apparently held all these posts until the next congress of the league in mid-1953. It was as a youth leader that Hsu went to Hungary in April 1950 as a member of a Chinese delegation attending the celebrations marking the fifth anniversary of the "liberation" of Hungary. Hsu then broke off from the main delegation and led a portion of the group to East Germany in May 1950 to attend a congress of an East German youth organization. In June he attended a similar congress in Czechoslovakia and then returned home in mid-July 1950.

Apart from his work in youth affairs, Hsu also engaged in other activities in the early 1950's. When the central government was formed in the fall of 1949, he was named to membership on the People's Supervision Committee, an organ directly under the Government Administration Council (the cabinet); he held this post until the constitutional government was established in September 1954. He served on the National Committee of the China Peace Committee from October 1950 to July 1958, and on the Peking branch of this committee from November 1950.

Although Hsu has never been a member of the National Committee of the CPPCC, he has been active in the organization from 1951. In October–November of that year he attended the third session of the CPPCC, and when a Study (*hsueh-hsi*) Committee was formed in February 1952 under Politburo member Lin Po-ch'ü, Hsu was named to head the Staff Office, a position he apparently held throughout the life of the First CPPCC (to December 1954). The Study Committee is a body which organizes classes, schools, and special meetings attended mainly by non-Communists for the purpose of an intensive study of Marxism-Leninism and the thought of Mao Tse-tung. When the Second CPPCC was formed in December 1954, no Study Committee was established, but then in March 1956 it was re-created under Li Wei-han, then the head of the Party's United Front Department. Hsu was named as a member of the re-created committee and remained one until the close of the Second CPPCC (April 1959).

In 1954 he was elected as a Kiangsu deputy to the First NPC, but was not re-elected to the Second NPC, which opened in April 1959. Hsu's real move up the hierarchical ladder apparently began in about 1956. In September of that year the Party held its Eighth Congress; Hsu spoke at one of the sessions on the work of theoretical education for Party cadres. He addressed the congress, a rather singular honor for a man who was relatively unknown in that period, in his capacity as director of the Theoretical Propaganda Division of the Party's Propaganda Department, a position he may still hold. By September 1961 he was a deputy director of the Propaganda Department (under Director Lu Ting-i) and continues to hold this important position. Then, in September 1964, Hsu was identified as a deputy editor-in-chief of *Hung-ch'i* (Red flag), the most important Party journal, which is under the editorship of Ch'en Po-ta, an alternate member of the Party Politburo.

Since the Eighth Party Congress in 1956, Hsu has been rather active, particularly in the propaganda field. He was reported from time to time attending special meetings devoted to the study of some phase of Marxism-Leninism or the thought of Mao Tse-tung. For example, he spoke at a meeting in Peking in early May 1958 marking the first anniversary of Mao's famous speech "On the Correct Handling of Contradictions among the People." Similarly, he served on the preparatory committee and the presidium (steering committee) for a national conference of "advanced" workers in the field of culture and education held in Peking in June 1960. After he became a deputy director of the Propaganda Department (1961), he took an active part in the tasks of entertaining foreign dignitaries, especially those from Communist countries working in propaganda.

Hsu is the author of at least one book and several articles for important Communist journals. The book, entitled *Chung-kuo shih-hua* (Talks on Chinese history) was first published in Shanghai in 1947 and was subsequently re-issued in 1950 and 1952. His articles include:

"The Theoretical Strength of Comrade Mao Tse-tung's 'The Question of Agricultural Co-operativization,'" *Hsueh-hsi* (Study), December 2, 1955.

"The Leadership of the Communist Party Is the Decisive Factor for the Victory of Socialism," *JMJP*, October 12, 1957.

"Have We Already Reached the Stage of Communism?" *Hung-ch'i* (Red flag), November 16, 1958.

"On the Policy of Walking on Two Legs," *ibid.*, March 16, 1959.

Hsu Ping

(c.1899–   ; Nan-kung hsien, Hopeh). Director, United Front Work Department, CCP Central Committee; alternate member, CCP Central Committee.

Hsu Ping, an intellectual, has been for many years a senior figure in the Party's United Front Work Department, the organization whose principal task is to gain the cooperation of non-Party persons and groups. His original name was Hsing P'ing-chou, but he has been more widely known by his revolutionary pseudonyms: Hsu Ping and Hsing Hsi-p'ing. He was born into a well-to-do gentry family in Nan-kung hsien, located in southern Hopeh; one account describes the Hsing family as one of the wealthiest in Peking.[1] His father was a member of the Peking parliament in the first decade after the 1911 Revolution. Hsu Ping was born about 1899, and thus he must have had most of his primary schooling before the revolution. After his education in China, Hsu sought graduate training in Europe, being there in the early 1920's when a number of Chinese students, some already influenced by Marxism, were furthering their acquaintance with Western education by studying abroad. Most of the students went to France, though a smaller number, among them Chu Te, went to Germany. Hsu went to Berlin about 1920, enrolling at the University of Berlin to study economics. Like Chu Te, he joined the Communist Party while in Germany. From Berlin he went to the Soviet Union in the winter of 1925 and there enrolled at Chung-shan (Sun Yat-sen) University, which in the 1920's attracted a number of Chinese students coming to study about revolutionary activities. Hsu spent two years at Chung-shan, returning in 1927 to China, where he went to work for the CCP in Shantung. However, he was soon arrested by the provincial warlord, Sun Liang-ch'eng, who held him prisoner from about 1928 to 1930.

As soon as he was released, Hsu joined the Communist underground, first in Shanghai, later in Peking. While in Peking he was also a professor at Tung-pei (Northeastern) University, the former Manchurian institution which was moved to Peking after the Japanese invaded Manchuria in 1931 and which continued to enroll a number of former northeastern students, many of whom were sympathetic to Manchurian warlord Chang Hsueh-liang. American journalist Edgar Snow, who knew Hsu as a professor at Tung-pei in 1936, recounts a story of Hsu's bringing him a letter of introduction to Mao Tse-tung before he made the trip to Yenan, which resulted in his book Red Star over China. When he returned to China in 1960, Snow again saw Hsu and learned that the letter had been "authorized" by Liu Shao-ch'i, head of the Party Bureau for north China in 1936. It had been written by K'o Ch'ing-shih (q.v.), the late mayor of Shanghai, who was then an assistant to Liu in the North China Bureau.[2] Some sources claim that Hsu made the

Long March to northwest China (1934–35) before going to Peking, but what is known of his personal history prior to that time suggests that this is incorrect.

During the early stages of the Sino-Japanese War, Hsu apparently spent a good deal of time translating some of the major works of Marx, Engels, Lenin, and Stalin, including the Communist Manifesto and Stalin's Problems of Leninism.[3] At least three of his translations were published in Yenan (1938 and 1939), suggesting that he may have been working there then. However, by no later than 1940 Hsu was serving as a secretary to Chou En-lai, the Party's chief representative in wartime Chungking. While there, Hsu also worked for the Hsin-hua jih-pao (New China daily), the important Communist daily published in Chungking. In addition, he served as a contact between the CCP and Korean Communists then in Chungking, whom the Chinese Communists were attempting to influence. Through the efforts of Hsu and others, the CCP was able to have significant numbers of Korean Communists transferred to the Communist-held areas in north and northwest China, where many of them fought in the CCP-led armies.[4] In retrospect, however, it seems that Hsu's most important activity in Chungking may have been in gaining the acquaintance of political and intellectual leaders who belonged to neither the CCP nor the KMT; after the PRC came into existence in 1949 Hsu's principal task was in working with non-Party intellectuals, many of whom lived and worked in Chungking during the war.

After hostilities ended in 1945 and the Marshall Mission was established in the winter of 1945–46, Hsu was transferred to Peking to become secretary of the Communist delegation at the Peking Executive Headquarters. The Executive Headquarters were closed in early 1947 when relations between the Nationalists and Communists had broken down and it became evident that the terms of the January 1946 cease-fire agreement would not be implemented. Hsu was then transferred to Shantung, where the Communists were beginning to take over the entire province. He served there briefly in 1948–49 as a vice-mayor of the Communist Tsinan Municipal Government; concurrently, in the spring of 1948 he was secretary-general of the Wei-hsien People's Government in the Tsinan area.

Hsu played a major role in the earliest days of the Communist civil administration of Peking. On January 1, 1949, as the Communist armies stood poised at the gates of the city, they officially formed their municipal government. Veteran military commander Yeh Chien-ying was named as mayor and Hsu as his vice-mayor. Immediately after Peking was surrendered (January 31) and the Communists moved in, they formed a Joint Administrative Office to administer the city. Yeh was also named to head this special body, and under it the Communists established three committees. To gain maximum political support the CCP created a system of dual CCP-KMT leadership for each of the three committees. The Communist co-heads of the military and financial committees were, respectively, T'ao Chu and Jung Tzu-ho (qq.v.), while Hsu was named as the chief CCP representative on the political and cultural committee, ostensibly sharing leadership with Chiao Shih-tsai, who had been an assistant to General Fu Tso-i (q.v.), the KMT officer who peacefully surrendered Peking.

When the Communists convened the First CPPCC in September 1949 to establish the central government, Hsu attended as an alternate CCP delegate. Although his role in the First CPPCC was minimal in the early stages of this organization, in the period after 1952 he was to play an extremely active role (see below). In the same month that the central government came into existence (October 1949), Hsu was named as an Executive Board member of the newly created Sino-Soviet Friendship Association (SSFA), then a highly active organization. He retained this post until the second conference of the SSFA in December 1954. However, the most important post Hsu received in 1949 was that of a deputy directorship of the Party's United Front Work Department. Since then he has devoted the major portion of his time to the department and thus has been a key figure in the continuing efforts of the CCP to gain the allegiance of the non-Party intellectuals and of the leading figures in the eight non-Communist "democratic" parties—for example, the China Democratic League. Hsu's work in the Party's united front activities culminated in early 1965 when he replaced Li Wei-han as the department director (see below).

In the early fall of 1950 Hsu received a post which was apparently closely related to his united front work; in September 1950 the PRC created the Ministry of Personnel under the direction of An Tzu-wen, a top Party operative and then the deputy director of the Party's Organization Department. One of the vice-ministerships was given to Sun Ch'i-meng, a leader of the China Democratic National Construction Association, one of the eight above-mentioned "democratic" political parties. Hsu was given the other vice-ministership, suggesting that his role was to oversee the selection of personnel drawn from the non-Communist intellectual community. He held this post until September 1954 when the ministry was disbanded.

In early 1952 Hsu received still another assignment closely related to the activities of the non-Party intellectuals when he was made a member (February 1952) of the newly established Study (hsueh-hsi) Committee under the direction of Party elder Lin Po-ch'ü (q.v.). The

work of this committee has been involved mainly with the establishment of special forums and training institutes where non-Party persons are required to undergo certain periods of training. The committee was disbanded when the Second CPPCC was created in December 1954, but then it was re-created in March 1956 at which time Hsu was elevated to a vice-chairmanship, retaining the post until the creation of the Fourth CPPCC in January 1965; during this period (1956–1965) Hsu served under Li Wei-han, his superior in the Party's United Front Department. In the interim, Hsu had received new and significant assignments under the main CPPCC organization; by May 1953 he was identified as a deputy secretary-general of the CPPCC National Committee, which once again placed him under Li Wei-han, the secretary-general. Then, when the Second National Committee of the CPPCC was formed in 1954, Hsu was placed on the National Committee (as a Party representative) and, in addition, he replaced Li Wei-han as the secretary-general. He was again named to these two positions when the Third CPPCC was established in April 1959. Finally, when the Fourth CPPCC was created in January 1965, he was again named to a vice-chairmanship; however, he relinquished the secretary-generalship to another specialist in united front work, P'ing Chieh-san (q.v.).

Although the CPPCC was theoretically the supreme state organ prior to the inauguration of the constitutional government in 1954, at that time its legislative authority devolved to the NPC. Within the latter Hsu has served as a deputy to the three NPC's, which opened their initial sessions in September 1954, April 1959, and December 1964, respectively; he was a delegate from Shantung to the First and Second NPC's, but was changed to the Kweichow constituency for the Third NPC. Moreover, on each occasion he was named to membership on the NPC Standing Committee, which carries out the work of the Congress when it is not in session.

Hsu's long record as a CCP member was given official recognition at the Eighth National Party Congress held in September 1956 when he was elected an alternate member of the Party Central Committee. Apart from his work for the Party and the government legislative branches, Hsu has also been a fairly active participant in united front work in fields in which the CCP has special interests and wishes to secure the support of non-Party elements. For example, since the reorganization of the China Peace Committee in October 1950, he has been a member of the Standing Committee. Similarly, in another field, he was a deputy leader of a delegation led by military veteran Ho Lung to North Korea to inspect and "comfort" Chinese troops in October–December 1953. Also, from 1957 to 1958, Hsu took an active part in the Party-promoted "rectification" campaign, leading a number of forums that non-Party persons were required to attend. Because united front work is in many ways intrinsically linked with pre-1949 China, Hsu is also called upon to lend his name to various *ad hoc* committees established to commemorate past events or persons. A classic example of this occurred in 1956 when he served as a member of a preparatory committee established to commemorate Sun Yat-sen's 90th birthday, and exactly nine years later he was named as a vice-chairman of the committee preparing for similar events in 1966 marking the centennial of Sun's birth. Similarly, in September 1961 he was a deputy secretary-general of the preparatory committee formed to commemorate the 50th anniversary of the 1911 Revolution.

Hsu's career reached a peak in the early part of 1965 when he succeeded Li Wei-han, long his superior, as the director of the Party's United Front Work Department. Aside from his stature as an alternate member of the Central Committee, Hsu's long service in the department gave him a wide margin of seniority over the several other deputy directors. His succession to the directorship appears to be related with the political decline of Li Wei-han (q.v.), who lost at least two other positions within the PRC hierarchy shortly before Hsu was identified as the new director.

In his private life, Hsu is married to Chang Hsiao-mei, a woman about two years his junior. Like her husband, Chang was a friend of Edgar Snow in Peking in the mid-1930's, and she also met Snow when he revisited China in 1960. He has described her as the "vivacious little wife" of Hsu. When war broke out in 1937, Chang brought Teng Ying-ch'ao (Mme. Chou En-lai) to the Snow home in Peking; befriending the two women, Snow managed to get them safely past the Japanese guards and on to the "last train" to Tientsin, where they boarded a British ship for refuge in free China.[5] Chang was also with Hsu in Chungking and has been described as the leader of the women's movement there during the war.[6] She was again with Hsu in the Peking Executive Headquarters in 1946. From its inception in April 1949, she has been a member of the Executive Committee of the National Women's Federation and since at least 1951 has been chairman of the Peking chapter of this organization. Also like her husband, she has served in the three NPC's, in each case as a deputy from Peking.

1. A. Doak Barnett, *China on the Eve of Communist Takeover* (New York, 1963), p. 330.
2. Edgar Snow, *The Other Side of the River* (London, 1963), pp. 337, 544.
3. Chang Ching-lu, ed., *Chung-kuo ch'u-pan shih-liao pu-nien* (Supplementary historical ma-

terials on Chinese publishing; Peking, 1957), 448, 461, 471.
4. Chong-sik Lee, "Korean Communists and Yenan," *The China Quarterly*, no. 9:182–192 (January–March 1962).
5. Edgar Snow, pp. 74–75.
6. Chong-sik Lee, p. 189.

Hsu Shih-yu

(c.1906–   ; Hupeh). Commander, Nanking Military Region; vice-minister of National Defense; alternate member, CCP Central Committee.

Born of a peasant family in Hupeh, Hsu Shih-yu seems to have entered the Communist movement via the ranks of the peasant guerrilla armies. He was first identified when he was with the military forces of the Hupeh-Honan-Anhwei border area, the base where Hsu Hsiang-ch'ien and Chang Kuo-t'ao (qq.v.) were active in the early 1930's. While these forces were still in the border area, Hsu Shih-yu became one of their cadre workers. He was with them in 1932 when Nationalist attacks forced a retreat into northern Szechwan. There, under Hsu Hsiang-ch'ien and Chang, the Communists established another military base along the Szechwan-Shensi border. Now renamed the Fourth Front Army, Hsu Hsiang-ch'ien's troops controlled the Szechwan-Shensi base during the next two years. The move to north Szechwan had meant a quick rise for Hsu Shih-yu, who served as commander of the 25th Division of the Ninth Army and as deputy commander of the Ninth Army itself, the latter a component of Hsu Hsiang-ch'ien's Fourth Front Army.

After the start of the Long March in October 1934, Hsu Hsiang-ch'ien's Fourth Front Army moved west across Szechwan, joining the main Red forces commanded by Mao Tse-tung and Chu Te on June 16, 1935, at the small village of Mao-kung in the far western portion of the province. From there the combined forces proceeded northward to reach Mao-erh-kai, Szechwan, on July 10. At this time Hsu Shih-yu was identified as commander of a cavalry regiment fighting in western Szechwan and in eastern Sikang into which his regiment had crossed on its way to Mao-erh-kai. At Mao-erh-kai the Communist forces split, those commanded by Hsu Hsiang-ch'ien and Chang Kuo-t'ao moving westward to establish a separate base in what was then Sikang. These troops finally joined Mao's group in the winter of 1936 when Mao had been in north Shensi for about a year. Hsu Shih-yu remained with Chang's forces, only joining Mao with the remnant troops from Chang's army, which reached north Shensi after their disastrous defeats in the Kansu corridor ·as they marched north (see under Chang Kuo-t'ao). In 1937 Hsu was identified as a cadet at K'ang-ta

(Anti-Japanese Military and Political Academy), established in north Shensi, soon after the Communists reached the Northwest.

By at least 1939, he was reunited with his old commander Hsu Hsiang-ch'ien; Hsu Shih-yu was attached to the units of Liu Po-cheng's 129th Division (of the Communist Eighth Route Army), which Hsu Hsiang-ch'ien had led from east Shansi into southern Hopeh in August 1938. The troops subsequently entered Shantung where they were grouped into the First Column, again under Hsu Hsiang-ch'ien's command, in April 1939. Hsu Shih-yu spent the years of the Sino-Japanese War with these troops in Shantung, rising from the rank of commander of a brigade (1939) to commander of the Ch'ing-ho Military District by 1942, and finally as commander of the Po-hai Military District in 1944. Both areas lie north of the Yellow River in an area stretching almost to Tsinan, the capital. By 1944 Po-hai was one of five military districts into which the Communists had divided the territory they controlled in Shantung. At the end of the war, Hsu's troops moved eastward into the Shantung Peninsula; here he served as a commander of the coastal defense area for the ports of Chefoo and Wei-hai-wei (1946), a strategic area for the Communists because it was from here that many of their forces crossed over into Manchuria. For the next several years Hsu remained in Shantung with the Communist armies. In 1947 his troops were organized into the East Front Army Corps of the East China Field Army, commanded by the present foreign minister, Ch'en I. From September to December 1947, three columns of this army fought against the remnants of the Chiang Kai-shek armies in eastern Shantung, while forces under the command of Hsu, T'an Chen-lin, and others are credited by the Communists with recovering more than 10 hsien and wiping out more than 63,000 Nationalist troops.[1] During the time Hsu served as commander of the troops, T'an Chen-lin was their political commissar. In 1948 Hsu was identified as commander of the Chiao-tung Military District of Shantung, an area on the peninsula running north and east from Tsingtao. Tsinan, the capital, fell to the Communists in an attack led by Hsu on September 26, 1948.

Early in 1949 the East China Field Army, reorganized into the Third Field Army, began to move south from Shantung to take over the coastal provinces, finally establishing its headquarters in Shanghai. Although Hsu retained his Third Field Army commands at the army corps level, his services were retained in Shantung, where in 1949 he was identified as commander of both the Shantung Military District and the 11th Army of the Third Field Army. In his capacity as a top military leader for Shantung he now began to take part in the provincial, regional, and national civil administrations, which

the Communists were establishing in the wake of their conquering armies. However, Hsu's role as a civilian administrator has always been distinctly secondary to his position as a military commander. As a delegate from the East China Military District, he attended the First CPPCC of September 1949, the meeting that brought into being the central PRC government in October. During the course of the CPPCC meetings, Hsu served on the committee established to draft the Organic Law of the CPPCC, one of the key documents adopted at that time. Also, from 1950 to 1954 he served as a member of the East China Military and Administrative Committee (ECMAC), which was called the East China Administrative Committee (ECAC) after December 1952. From mid-1950 he served for a time as a member of the Shantung People's Government and briefly as deputy director of that government's Public Security Department. A report stating that between 1950 and 1953 he took part in the Korean War cannot be verified, though the fact that there was little mention of his activity during this time suggests that the report may be true.

By 1954 he was back at work in east China, identified as a member of the CCP Committee for the East China Military Region. As a deputy from the PLA in east China, he was elected to serve in the First NPC (1954–1959), but he was not re-elected to the Second NPC, which opened in April 1959. Also in 1954, Hsu was a deputy commander of the Third Field Army. In September 1954, with the inauguration of the constitutional government, the field armies were abolished and the military regions they had controlled were reorganized. Hence, between 1954 and 1955, the names of the military regions were changed from regional geographic designations and have been known since by the names of the principal cities wherein the headquarters are located. Hsu now became the commander of the Nanking Military Region, a command covering a much smaller territory than the East China Military Region. As commander of the Nanking Military Region he is in charge of the PLA forces in Kiangsu, Chekiang, and Anhwei. (The East China Military Region had included these three provinces plus Shantung and Fukien.)

With the inauguration of the constitutional government and the creation of the military advisory National Defense Council in 1954, Hsu was made a Council member. He received unspecified military honors in September 1955 at the time that national military awards were first given, and shortly thereafter he was identified with the rank of colonel-general, personal military ranks also being designated for the first time that year.

Hsu won high Party rank in September 1956 when the CCP held its Eighth National Congress and elected him an alternate member of the

Central Committee. Then in September 1959 he received his first ministerial post, becoming a vice-minister of National Defense at the time that Lin Piao became minister.

Though he holds a cabinet office in Peking, Hsu is principally concerned with the command of the Nanking Military Region and, since his appointment there in 1954, has made his headquarters in the city. Here he is seen at a certain number of the routine protocol functions that his position requires him to attend. He has twice been noted as taking part in the movement to give the officers a tour of duty in the ranks, once in September 1958 and again in 1961. In November–December 1964 Hsu was a member of a delegation led by Politburo member Li Hsien-nien to the celebrations marking the 20th anniversary of the "liberation" of Albania from Nazi Germany.

---

1. *Selected Works of Mao Tse-tung* (Peking, 1961), IV, 216.

Hsu Te-heng

(1895–   ; Kiukiang, Kiangsi). Intellectual leader; chairman, Chiu San Society; minister of Aquatic Products.

Hsu Te-heng was one of the more important student leaders during the May Fourth Movement, which began in 1919. A prominent professor of social sciences from the 1920's to the 1940's, he joined the Communist government in 1949 and has since served in a variety of administrative posts. He has been chairman of the Chiu San Society, one of the non-Communist political parties, since its creation in 1945.

Hsu was a student at Peking University when the May Fourth (1919) Movement erupted in opposition to the humiliating policies toward Japan then followed by the Chinese government. His activities in connection with the famous movement are treated extensively in Chow Tse-tsung's *The May Fourth Movement*.[1] Briefly, Hsu was among the most important of the students in Peking and was one of 32 students arrested on May 4 for participation in activities directed against the Chinese authorities. He was soon released and then went to Shanghai where, at a series of meetings, he advocated the continuation of the boycott of Japanese products and other measures designed to preserve Chinese independence. He belonged to several organizations that were created shortly before or after the May Fourth Incident, including the Young China Association (YCA), the Mass Education Speech Corps (established to propagate "progressive" ideas among the masses), and the Student Union of the Republic of China. His participation in these organizations brought him into close contact with such important figures as Li Ta-chao, Chang Kuo-t'ao, and Teng Chung-hsia (qq.v.),

all of whom became important Communist leaders following the establishment of the CCP in 1921.

After graduating from Peking University, Hsu studied sociology and economics at the universities of Paris and London. Following his return to China in the mid-twenties he taught at universities in Canton, Shanghai, and Peking, the most prominent among them being his alma mater, where he was a professor from 1931 to 1937. Hsu had also participated in the Northern Expedition in 1926, serving in the Political Bureau of the National Revolutionary Army. During the twenties and thirties he wrote extensively on historical and sociological problems and also translated important Western works into Chinese, including Emile Durkheim's *Principles of Sociology* and Marx's *The Poverty of Philosophy*.[2] (The latter was translated under the name of Hsu Ch'u-sheng.) Hsu was among the many professors in Peking who gave open support to the students active in the "December Ninth Movement" (1935), which, in many respects, was a historical offspring of the May Fourth Movement.[3] (For a discussion of the "December Ninth" events, see under Li Ch'ang.)

After the outbreak of the Sino-Japanese War in mid-1937, Hsu returned to his native Kiangsi where he participated in the training of propagandists. His fame as an intellectual won him a seat on the Nationalists' legislative body, the People's Political Council, during the war years and in the immediate postwar period. While he was in Chungking during the war he organized the Democracy and Science Discussion Group (also known as the Democracy and Science Society). Then, following V-J Day, the organization was renamed the Chiu San Society (i.e., the "September Third" Society, to commemorate the day the Japanese officially surrendered). Hsu has been the chairman of the society since its inception. In 1949, the Communists decided to permit the society to participate in the affairs of state as one of the so-called "democratic" political parties (see below). In the postwar years Hsu returned to Peking and taught at his alma mater.

Among the many intellectuals who remained in Peking when the Communists took over the city in January 1949, Hsu immediately began to participate in a wide variety of political and intellectual activities, one of the first of which was participation in the large delegation led by Kuo Mo-jo to the Communist-sponsored World Peace Congress held in April in Paris and Prague; the Chinese contingent went to Prague when the French government forbade their participation in the Paris congress. After his return to China he was appointed (June 1949) to Standing Committee membership on the Higher Education Committee under the North China People's Government. In June and July Hsu participated in founding conferences for two professional organizations, the China New Legal Research Society and the China New Philosophy Research Society. A useful indication of his prestige at this time is found in the fact that he was named to membership on the Preparatory Committee of the CPPCC, established in June 1949 under the chairmanship of Mao Tse-tung. Then, when the CPPCC met in September to inaugurate the new central government, Hsu attended as a representative of the Chiu San Society. During these meetings he served on the *ad hoc* committee to draft the "Common Program" (the equivalent of a constitution during the period from 1949 to 1954). At the close of the session he was named to membership on the First National Committee, and since that time has been among the more active participants in the work of the CPPCC. He has been a member of the Standing Committee since February 1953 and was elevated to a vice-chairmanship when the initial meeting of the Fourth National Committee closed in January 1965. In the weeks immediately after the new government was inaugurated (October 1, 1949), when most of the key political assignments were made, Hsu was named to membership on the Political and Legal Affairs Committee under the Government Administration Council (the cabinet). He was also appointed a vice-chairman of the Law Commission, a position that was to occupy much of his time over the next few years. The Law Commission chairman from 1949 to 1954 was Ch'en Shao-yü (Wang Ming, q.v.), but Ch'en's political life under the Maoist leadership had been precarious since the thirties and by the early fifties he had fallen to near political oblivion. As a consequence, from at least the summer of 1951 Hsu served as the acting chairman of the Law Commission. It was in this capacity that he delivered a major report in September 1951 before the Central People's Government Council on the "provisional regulations governing the organization of people's courts." He received two related assignments in 1953 when he was made a member of both the Committee to Draft the Election Law (under the provisions of which the elections to the NPC were held) and the National Council of the China Political Science and Law Association. He still retains his membership in the latter organization. When the First NPC was established in 1954, Hsu attended as a deputy from his native Kiangsi; he also served as a deputy to the Second NPC (1954–1959) and to the Third NPC, which opened in December 1954.

At the close of the initial session of the First NPC in September 1954, Hsu was appointed as a member of the NPC Standing Committee. However, he relinquished this legislative post in mid-1956 shortly after assuming a ministerial portfolio in the executive branch of government.

Hsu's new post was as minister of Aquatic Products (often translated "Marine Products"), an appointment received in May 1956 when the ministry, mainly concerned with the fishing industry, was established. In the middle and late fifties, he was frequently mentioned in the Chinese press in connection with the ministry, as in July 1957 when he reported on the marine products industry before a session of the NPC. He was also quite active in connection with the Western Pacific Fisheries Research Commission (WPFRC). The WPRFC had been formed in June 1956 in Peking at a meeting attended by delegates from China (led by Hsu), the Soviet Union, North Vietnam, and North Korea. The permanent Commission, of which Hsu is chairman, meets annually; Hsu led the Chinese delegations abroad to the second through the fourth meetings of the Commission held in Moscow (August 1957), Pyongyang (August 1958), and Hanoi (December 1959). He also headed the Chinese delegation to the meeting held in Peking in November 1960, but since that time one of his vice-ministers (Shih Min) has carried out most of the work of the Fisheries Commission (although Hsu remains as the nominal chairman).

In addition to his 1949 trip to the peace conference in Prague and his travels related to the Fishery Commission, Hsu has been abroad on two other occasions. In August 1950 he was a member of the Chinese delegation to North Korea to attend celebrations commemorating the fifth anniversary of the end of the war, and in November–December 1954 he was among the Chinese delegates to a meeting of the World Peace Council in Stockholm. He has also held the following positions on three of the more active "mass" organizations: member, Executive Board, Sino-Soviet Friendship Association, October 1949 to date; member, China Peace Committee, October 1949–July 1958; member, Asian Solidarity Committee of China, February 1956 to date (known since 1958 as the Afro-Asian Solidarity Committee).

Hsu has not been particularly active since the late fifties, although he continues to make appearances at events requiring the presence of prominent non-Communist Party leaders, particularly when the regime wishes to have a display of unity or to emphasize its ties with revolutionary events in 20th-century China. For example, in late 1961 he was among a number of political leaders in Peking who publicly condemned India for its "anti-China" campaign, and in September of that year he was named to membership on the preparatory committee to commemorate the 50th anniversary of the 1911 Revolution.

1. Chow Tse-tsung, *The May Fourth Movement* (Cambridge, Mass., 1960); Chow Tse-

tsung, *Research Guide to the May Fourth Movement* (Cambridge, Mass., 1963).

2. Chang Ching-lu, ed., *Chung-kuo ch'u-pan shih liao pu-pien* (Supplementary historical materials on Chinese publishing; Peking, 1957), p. 444.

3. Chiang Nan-hsiang et al., *The Roar of a Nation* (Peking, 1963), p. 169.

Hsu T'e-li

(1877–1968; Changsha, Hunan). Party "elder"; educator; member, CCP Central Committee.

Party "elder" Hsu T'e-li was a teacher of Mao Tse-tung and several other leading members of the Chinese Communist Movement. An educator in Hunan for many years and a participant in the 1911 Revolution, he did not join the CCP until he was over 50. Hsu took part in some of the landmark events in Communist history, including the Nanchang Uprising and the Long March. From the early 1930's to the late 1950's when he went into semi-retirement, he was one of the Party's most important officials in the educational field. Hsu is the oldest member of the CCP Central Committee, on which he has served since 1945. He and his colleagues Lin Po-ch'ü, Wu Yü-chang, Tung Pi-wu, and Hsieh Chueh-tsai are often described by the Chinese Communists as the "five elders" (*wu-lao*).

Born on February 1, 1877, Hsu was the second son in a family of four children, who lived a few miles east of Changsha, the Hunan capital. He described his illiterate father as "half-farmer, half-coolie."[1] After receiving a traditional Chinese education Hsu began his career as an educator in the mid-1890's. In 1905 he attended a normal school in Changsha for a brief period, and after a few more years of teaching he studied for four months in Shangshai under the auspices of the Kiangsu Provincial Government. In 1910 he spent two months in Japan investigating the educational system. Returning to Changsha Hsu joined Sun Yat-sen's T'ung-meng hui in 1911, and in the fall of that year he participated in the 1911 Revolution. By this time he had begun to teach at the Chou-nan Girls' School in Changsha. Among his pupils were Party founder Hsiang Ching-yü and her future sister-in-law, Ts'ai Ch'ang (qq.v.). Concurrently with his teaching duties at Chou-nan, Hsu was also an instructor at the Hunan First Normal School from 1913 to 1919.[2] By the late teens the normal school was one of China's leading centers of political agitation, and among its students were such famed latter-day Communists as Ts'ai Ho-sen (Ts'ai Ch'ang's brother) and Mao Tse-tung (qq.v.). Thus, although Hsu himself did not join the CCP until 1927 (see below), he was on close terms with some of its earliest and most important members. On one occasion while he taught at the Hunan school, Hsu is said to have been instrumental in helping Mao escape expulsion because of the latter's authorship of a "manifesto" which charged the headmaster with mismanagement.[3] Hsu was also known and admired by many of the students for his steadfast opposition to the attempts by Yuan Shih-k'ai to restore the monarchy in China.

Toward the end of 1919 Hsu arrived in France to take part in the work-and-study program. He first spent seven months studying French and gained a rudimentary knowledge of the language. The work-and-study scheme, described in the biography of Chao Shih-yen, was intended primarily for college-age students. Hsu, already in his forties, was an exception. Contrary to the standard picture painted by Communist historians, the participants in the program included persons of widely varying political views—ranging from nationalists to socialists to anarchists. According to the autobiography that Hsu gave Nym Wales many years later, he "first read Marx in Kautsky's version while in Europe and didn't like it, though I did not know then that Kautsky was a reformist." He also expressed to Miss Wales his dislike and distrust of parliamentary government. During his years in France, Hsu claims that he studied for a year in Lyons and for three years at the University of Paris. (In discussing the work-and-study program with Western journalists, a number of exaggerated claims were made about the educational aspects of the scheme. It is doubtful if Hsu received as much education as he suggested.) To earn money he was a metal worker and tutored other Chinese students.[4] In addition, he took part in various political activities. Most of his contacts in France seem to have been with Communists, particularly Chou En-lai and Wang Jo-fei (qq.v.), but he also participated in the affairs of the overseas Chinese association in France and was in contact with Tseng Ch'i, the founder of the Chinese Youth Party (Chung-kuo ch'ing-nien tang). After spending more than three years in France, Hsu went on "inspection" trips to Belgium for half a year and to Germany for four months, after which he returned to China in 1924.

Returning to Changsha, Hsu established and became the principal of a girls' normal school. It was during this period that he became a Marxist; he claims that his reading of Stalin's *Problems of Leninism* (first published in 1926) influenced him "decisively."[5] He continued to teach until 1927 when, not long after the Northern Expedition had reached Hunan, he left the school to take part in the work of the provincial peasants' association. In the same year he joined the left-KMT. His association with the KMT was short-lived, however, for when both its right and left wings broke with the Communists in the spring and summer of 1927, Hsu fled to Wuhan where, by his own testimony, he lived as a "fugitive." There he encountered Li Wei-han (q.v.), a top Communist, and upon Li's recommendation joined the CCP.[6] By this time Hsu was in his 51st year.

Immediately after joining the Party, Hsu went to Nanchang where he participated in the August First Uprising, which is celebrated as the birth of the Red Army (see under Yeh T'ing). Hsu was a member of the Revolutionary Committee which the Communists set up to control the city, and he was concurrently named as the CCP representative in the Third Division. The Third Division, commanded by Chou I-ch'ün, was one of the three divisions under Ho Lung's (qq.v.) 20th Army.[7] The Red forces were quickly driven from Nanchang; Hsu went southward to Kwangtung with the retreating Communist units and then made his way to Shanghai by ship. He was en route with Ho Lung (q.v.) to the Hunan-Hupeh border area to establish a guerrilla base when illness forced him to turn back to Shanghai for medical treatment. He had recuperated by the latter part of 1928 when he left for the Soviet Union.

In Moscow Hsu studied at Sun Yat-sen University (later known as the Communist University of the Toilers of China).[8] Among those in his class were Lin Po-ch'ü, Wu Yü-chang, and Ho Shu-heng (qq.v.), all of whom, like Hsu, were a generation older than most of their classmates. After two years in Moscow Hsu returned to China in 1930 and in 1931 went to the Kiangsi area, where Mao Tse-Tung and Chu Te had established their soviet base. In November 1931, at the First All-China Congress of Soviets, he was elected to the Central Executive Committee (CEC), the governing body of the Chinese Soviet Republic. Utilizing Hsu's extensive experience as an educator, he was appointed deputy people's commissar for Education (one of the cabinet posts subordinate to the CEC), and a few months later, in March 1932, he became acting commissar in place of Ch'ü Ch'iu-pai (q.v.), who did not arrive in Juichin, the Soviet capital, until the winter of 1933–34. Also in March 1932 Hsu was appointed president of the newly established Lenin Normal School,[9] which was apparently an alternate name for the Central (chung-yang) Normal School. He received a related assignment three months later when he was named supervisor of the editing committee, subordinate to the Commissariat for Education.[10] Moreover, by early 1934 Hsu was vice-president of Soviet University (Su-wei-ai ta-hsueh).[11] In brief, Hsu seems to have been the most important education official during the Kiangsi period.

At the Second Congress of Soviets, held in Juichin in January–February 1934, Hsu was re-elected to the CEC. In October of the same year the Long March began. Despite his advanced years, Hsu successfully weathered the rigors of the Long March of 1934–35 to north Shensi. Because Ch'ü Ch'iu-pai did not make the Long March (and was captured by the KMT in early 1935), Hsu succeeded him as commissar for Education. He retained this position two years later when the Communists established the Shensi-Kansu-Ninghsia (Shen-Kan-Ning) Border Region Government, continuing in this capacity throughout most of the war years. In 1936 Edgar Snow interviewed Hsu, who described the extreme difficulty of developing an educational system in the remote and culturally backward area of north Shensi.[12]

In the early stages of the Sino-Japanese War, the Nationalists and the Communists cooperated in various ways to further the war effort. To carry out the necessary political and military liaison work, the CCP had small missions in areas predominantly under Nationalist control. For example, Lo Ping-hui (q.v.) was director of the Eighth Route Army's Wuhan office, and from the latter part of 1937 Hsu worked as a CCP representative in Changsha; he apparently remained there until it fell to the Japanese a year later. Returning to Yenan, he established and became president of the Natural Sciences Institute (Tzu-jan k'o-hsueh yuan) in 1940, a position he retained until the late forties when, after the Communist conquest of the mainland, the school was reorganized into the Peking Institute of Technology. At the end of 1941, on the eve of the famous cheng-feng (rectification) movement that began in 1942, the various political and military academies underwent reorganizations. The Politburo directive which ordered the reorganization described the Natural Sciences Institute, as well as Yenan University and the Lu Hsun Art Academy, as schools for the training, at both higher and middle levels, of Communists and non-Communists who had special political, literary, scientific, or artistic talents. In order to strengthen the leadership of these three schools, the directive further ordered that they be placed directly under the Party Central Committee's Culture Committee.[13] Speaking to journalists many years later 1961, Hsu described the institute in more informal and human terms; he said that it had been set up to accommodate the many university students who had gone to north Shensi, an area notably lacking in higher education facilities. He commented that the "majority" of the students in the "university section" of the institute were "advanced intellectual youths" and that many of them were from "rather well-off families."[14]

By 1940 Hsu was identified as a deputy director of the Party Central Committee's Propaganda Department, a post he was to hold for about two decades. From late in the next year until 1946, he also served as a representative from Anting (now Tzu-ch'ang) hsien, located north of Yenan, in the Second Assembly of the Shensi-Kansu-Ninghsia Border Region Government. At the Seventh National Party Congress in Yenan (April–June 1945), he was one of the speakers and was elected a member of the Central Committee. In the postwar years Hsu remained in the Yenan area until it fell to the Nationalists in March 1947. He spent the next two years with Mao and the other key Party Center leaders moving from place to place in north China until, after the fall of Peking in January 1949, they moved there. Throughout the spring and summer of that year he was engaged in organizing "mass" and professional organizations, such as the Sino-Soviet Friendship Association (SSFA) and the China New Philosophy Research Society, in addition to serving on the Higher Education Committee under the North China People's Government, which was headed by Tung Pi-wu, another of the Party "elders."

When the Communists convened the CPPCC in September 1949 to establish the PRC, Hsu attended as a representative of the CCP and was elected a member of the Central People's Government Council, the highest governmental organ until its dissolution in 1954. Concurrently, from 1949 to 1954 he was a member of the Culture and Education Committee under Chou En-lai's Government Administration Council (the cabinet). In the "mass" organizations he was an Executive Board member of the SSFA (1949–1954) and a National Committee member of the China Peace Committee (1949–1950). Hsu was also appointed to the Standing Committee of the Association for the Reform of the Chinese Written Language when it was formed in October 1949. He had worked on the language reform problem in Juichin in the early thirties and in 1937 had expressed a strong interest in the subject to American journalist Nym Wales,[15] an interest shared by two of Hsu's elderly colleagues, Lin Po-ch'ü and Wu Yü-chang.

Hsu was already in his mid-seventies when the national government was formed under the Communists, but he continued to be surprisingly active during the early PRC years. He was among the few persons, for example, who attended most of the Central People's Government Council meetings held between 1949 and 1954. This important body (chaired by Mao) was vested with broad legislative, executive, and judicial powers, and at its 34 meetings it passed on virtually every key policy adopted in the formative years of the PRC. In August 1950 Hsu took part in establishing the All-China Educational Workers' Trade Union, and in January 1953 he was elected a council member of the China Geographic Society at its first congress. He was dropped from the council in 1956, but since that date he has been honorary chairman of the society.

Since the mid-1950's Hsu has been much less active, although he has nominally continued as an important member of government organiza-tions, most notably the NPC, which was convened in September 1954 to inaugurate the constitutional government. Serving in the Congress as a deputy from his native Hunan, he has been a member of its Standing Committee since 1954. When the CCP held its Eighth National Congress (September 1956), Hsu was again elected to the Central Committee. He was the oldest member elected. By 1958 he had been retired from the Propaganda Department, and even in his special field—education—he has done little since the mid-1950's. Since that time most of his appointments have been honorary in nature, as in 1961 when he was named to a special committee to commemorate the 50th anniversary of the 1911 Revolution.

Hsu was interviewed by reporters of *Chung-kuo ch'ing-nien* (China youth) on several occasions in the late fifties and early sixties. The theme of these pieces is that "old Hsu" has served the Party faithfully and that young Chinese should emulate his worthy example. Several of these interviews have yielded useful information about his career, as well as those of Mao Tse-tung and other top leaders. The authoritative *Peking Review* carried an unusual tribute to Hsu in 1962 in the form of a quotation from Mao Tse-tung. It stated that Mao had made the following "sincere and humble tribute" to Hsu on his 60th birthday in 1937: " 'Twenty years ago, you were my teacher. You are my teacher now and it is certain that in the future you will continue to be my teacher.' " The *Peking Review* editors commented that "This tradition of enduring respect and honour from pupils is very alive today and widespread."[16]

Although Hsu seldom wrote for the Party press after the establishment of the PRC, he was a contributor during the Yenan period. He contributed to a volume published in 1939, which attacked the Trotskyites in China, and toward the end of the war he wrote articles on educational affairs.[17]

Hsu's father had him married to a "slave girl," but as of 1937 he had not seen her for a decade. The Hsu's had four children; one son died and a daughter had been arrested in Shanghai for having put up a "revolutionary poster." The definitive biography of Hsu, *Wo-men te shih-piao* (Our model teacher), was published in Peking in 1958 by Chou Shih-chao, who was once a student of Hsu's in Hunan.

[Hsu died in Peking on November 28, 1968.]

---

1. Nym Wales, *Red Dust* (Stanford, Calif., 1952), p. 44.
2. *SCMP* 2891, p. 16.
3. Jerome Ch'en, *Mao and the Chinese Revolution* (London, 1965), p. 43.
4. Wales, p. 45.
5. *Ibid.*
6. *SCMM* 270, p. 36.

7. *Ti-erh-tz'u kuo-nei ko-ming chan-cheng shih-ch'i shih-shih lun-ts'ung* (Accounts of the second revolutionary civil war; Peking, 1956), p. 4.

8. *Chung-kuo ch'ing-nien* (China youth), no. 12:14 (June 16, 1960).

9. *Hung-se Chung-hua* (Red China; Juichin), March 2, 1932.

10. *Ibid.*, June 16, 1932.

11. *Hung-ch'i p'iao-p'iao* (Red flag fluttering; Peking, 1958), VIII, 53.

12. Edgar Snow, *Red Star over China* (New York, 1938), pp. 229–230.

13. *Cheng-feng wen-hsien* (Rectification documents; Hong Kong, 1949), p. 58.

14. *SCMM* 253, p. 22.

15. Nym Wales, *Inside Red China* (New York, 1940), pp. 144–146.

16. *Peking Review*, no. 17:19 (April 27, 1962).

17. Chün-tu Hsüeh, *The Chinese Communist Movement, 1937–1949* (Stanford, Calif., 1962), pp. 57, 109.

Hsu Ti-hsin

(c.1900–   ; Chieh-yang, Kwangtung). Specialist in economic affairs; vice-chairman, All-China Federation of Industry and Commerce; deputy director, CCP United Front Work Department.

Hsu Ti-hsin is one of Communist China's more important economic specialists and since the war years has worked closely with non-Communist industrial and commercial leaders. He is the key Party official in the All-China Federation of Industry and Commerce and he also heads the central government's Administrative Bureau of Industry and Commerce. Because of his extensive contacts with non-Communists, he has been placed in the Party's United Front Work Department, where he serves as a deputy director. Hsu is also the author of a number of books and articles dealing with economic affairs.

Hsu was born into an impoverished family in the town of Chieh-yang, a few miles west of Swatow, a major port in eastern Kwangtung. He joined the Communist Youth League in 1925, and from that same year until 1927 he studied in Canton at Chung-shan (Sun Yat-sen) University. Canton was then a major center of Communist activity in China, and during all or a portion of Hsu's time there such major Party figures as Mao Tse-tung, Chou En-lai, Lin Po-ch'ü, Teng Chung-hsia, and Su Chao-cheng (qq.v.) were in the city. At some time after the break between the CCP and the KMT in mid-1927, Hsu was expelled from Chung-shan, after which he went to Swatow where he taught in 1928 in an elementary school. In that same year he attended Amoy University for a brief time and then went to Shanghai, where he studied at

Futan University and the "Labor University" (probably a Communist-managed institute). He completed his education in 1933 when he graduated from the Shanghai College of Commerce.

From his graduation in 1933 until 1935 Hsu worked in the Communist underground in and around Shanghai, activities that may have put him in contact with such top Communist underground operatives as Li K'o-nung and K'o Ch'ing-shih (qq.v.). He was arrested by Nationalist authorities in the spring of 1935 and held in prison until war broke out with Japan in mid-1937. Hsu spent the war years in Hankow and Chungking as a staff member for various Communist publications, most notably the *Hsin-hua jih-pao* (New China daily) and the *Hsin-hua yueh-pao* (New China monthly). In addition to his own writings, in 1939 Hsu published a translation in Shanghai of Engels' writings on capitalism, a translation done in collaboration with Chang Han-fu (q.v.), a journalist and later a diplomat.[1] As part of his work writing on economic problems during and after the war, Hsu came into contact with industrial and commercial leaders, many of them non-Communists. Contacts such as Hsu was developing were regarded as one aspect of the Communists' "united front," and they were to serve him well in later years.

Hsu spent the year 1948 and the first part of 1949 in Hong Kong, a refuge for many Communist journalists and ideologues (e.g., Ch'iao Kuan-hua, Hu Sheng, Chin Chung-hua) in the latter stages of the civil war between the Communists and Nationalists. After about a year there, he went to Peking, arriving in May 1949. He remained there long enough to participate in two large conferences in July—one attended by social scientists of all types and the other attended only by economists. Out of the latter came the Preparatory Committee of the China New Economics Research Association, chaired by the leading ideologue Ch'en Po-ta (q.v.). Hsu was named to the Standing Committee of this organization, but it seems to have faded into inactivity after the early fifties.

By the end of the summer of 1949 Hsu was transferred to Shanghai where he was to remain as an important economic official for most of the time until 1954. His assignment to Shanghai was probably based upon his prior experience there, plus the fact that many of the industrialists and commercial figures he had been cultivating since the war years were working there. Hsu's initial post was as a vice-chairman of the East China Military Region's Finance and Economics Committee, where he served under Tseng Shan (q.v.). This was, in effect, an *ad hoc* body, but it became a permanent organization in February 1950 when it was transferred to the jurisdiction of the East China Military and Administrative Committee (ECMAC), the governmental organ that administered the provinces of Shantung, Kiangsu, Anhwei, Chekiang, and Fukien, as well as Shanghai and Nanking. Still working under Tseng Shan, Hsu continued as a vice-chairman until the regional governments were disbanded in 1954. Over the winter of 1949–50 he also assumed two additional posts in the financial-economic field, both subordinate to the Shanghai Government. The first of these was as vice-chairman of the Finance and Economics Committee and the other was as director of the Industry and Commerce Bureau; he held the former until 1952, the latter until 1954.

By the time Hsu had settled into his new assignments in east China his stature as an economic theoretician had been given national recognition in the Party's top journal, *Hsueh-hsi* (Study). The first, third, and fourth issues carried advertisements for three of his works, *Ching-chi Lun-heng* (Economic discussions), *Kuang-i cheng-chih ching-chi hsueh* (A general study of political economics), and *Tsui-chin ching-chi szu-hsiang te p'i-p'an* (Criticisms of recent economic thought). He received his first national post in March 1950 when he was named as a supervisor of the Bank of China, the overseas arm of the People's Bank of China (see under Nan Han-ch'en). He continues to serve in this capacity.

Hsu received two further assignments in the Shanghai Government in 1950–1951. From late 1950 until mid-1954 he was a member of the Shanghai Government Council, and from November 1951 to July 1952 he served as secretary-general of the Council. He was a prime mover in Shanghai for two major nationwide campaigns, the *san-fan* (three-anti) and *wu-fan* (five-anti) movements; the former was directed against corruption, waste, and bureaucratism within Party and state agencies, and the latter against the bourgeoisie for their alleged acts of bribery, tax evasion, fraud, theft of government property, and the theft of state economic secrets. Thus, as secretary-general of an *ad hoc* committee in Shanghai to increase production and practice economy, Hsu gave a report in May 1952 on the "disposition" of cases involving members of the bourgeoisie found guilty of offences against the state. In June 1952, just after the peak of the nationwide five-anti campaign, the Communists established the Preparatory Committee of the All-China Federation of Industry and Commerce (ACFIC) at a meeting attended by over 400 persons in Peking. Hsu led a 99-member delegation from east China (the largest to attend), and at the close of the preparatory conference he was elected one of the vice-chairmen. Composed mainly of industrialists and businessmen, like many Chinese Communist "mass" organizations the ACFIC is ostensibly led by a non-Communist, the industrialist and former publisher Ch'en Shu-t'ung.

It is evident, however, that Hsu and Nan Han-ch'en (q.v.), two of the vice-chairmen, were the key Party members within the organization, whose purpose is to "guide industrialists and businessmen in implementing the government's economic policies and plans." When the Federation was established on a permanent basis in November 1953, Hsu and Nan were again elected as vice-chairmen. However, at the Second Congress in December 1956, Nan was dropped as a vice-chairman, leaving Hsu as the only CCP member among the federation's vice-chairmen and presumably making him the *de facto* head of the organization.

Closely related to the ACFIC is the China Democratic National Construction Association (CDNCA), one of the eight non-Communist (or "democratic") political parties and an organization whose membership is also drawn principally from business circles. The two organizations have become virtually indistinguishable since the early sixties, because since that time most of their meetings have been held jointly. In addition to his vice-chairmanship in the ACFIC, Hsu has been a Standing Committee member of the CDNCA since July 1952. He received an appointment in the same field with the central government in August 1952 when he was appointed director of the Privately Operated Enterprises Control Bureau, replacing another leading economic specialist, Hsueh Mu-ch'iao (q.v.). By this time Hsu was dividing his time almost equally between Shanghai and Peking, a situation that prevailed until he transferred to Peking upon the establishment of the constitutional government in 1954.

Hsu was a deputy from Shantung to the First NPC (1954–1959). He was re-elected from Shantung to the Second NPC (1959–1964) but was transferred to represent his native Kwangtung in the Third NPC, which opened in December 1964. At the close of the inaugural session of the First NPC in September 1954, the central government was reorganized. In the following month Hsu (who by now had relinquished all his posts in east China) was named as a deputy director under Li Wei-han of the State Council's Eighth Staff Office, the organ that coordinated the work of government commissions, ministries, and bureaus involved in united front, overseas Chinese, and national minority affairs. He remained in this post until it was abolished in September 1959. A month after his assignment to the Eighth Office, he was appointed to a post he still holds, the directorship of the State Council's Central Administrative Bureau of Industry and Commerce. The Bureau is concerned with state enterprises, private firms, and what the Communists call "joint state-private enterprises." It was in this capacity that Hsu was among the most active officials in the nationwide campaign of late 1955 and early 1956 to "transform" the relatively few remaining private companies into socialist (i.e., state) enterprises. At this time, in February 1956, he was identified as a deputy director of the Party's United Front Work Department, his most important political post and one he still holds. He served again under Li Wei-han in this position until 1965, and thereafter under Hsu Ping (q.v.).

In the meantime, Hsu had received other new assignments. From 1954 to 1959 he represented the CCP on the Second and Third National Committees of the CPPCC, which, after the formation of the NPC, became largely a united front organization. He was also a vice-chairman of the CPPCC's Publications Editorial Committee from 1959 to 1964. From 1955 (presumably to date) Hsu has been a member of the Editorial Committee of *Ching-chi yen-chiu* (Economic research), one of China's most influential journals. And since the formation of the Academy of Sciences' Department of Philosophy and Social Sciences in May–June 1955, he has been a department member. Although he has concentrated mainly on domestic matters, Hsu has been involved to some degree in international affairs. From the formation of the China Committee for the Promotion of International Trade (CCPIT) in May 1952 he has been a member, and he has also held membership on the CCPIT's Foreign Trade Arbitration Committee since April 1956 (see under Nan Han-ch'en). The most unusual departure from his normal activities occurred in March–June 1958 when he led a cultural delegation to Italy, England, and Switzerland.

Since the mid-fifties Hsu has not made many public appearances, a situation that probably derives from the fact that by this time the task of organizing the "private" sector of the economy was largely completed. When he does appear it is usually in connection with his field of special competence, as in January 1961 when he spoke at a joint conference of the ACFIC and the CDNCA. Nonetheless, he has been very active, particularly as a writer on economic matters. He published a book in 1957 entitled (in translation) *An Analysis of the National Economy of China during the Transitional period (1949–1957)*. In a review of a revised edition in 1962, it was noted that Hsu was "concentrating his energies on his study of the national economy since the Great Leap Forward" (i.e., since 1958).[2] He has also been a prolific writer for such key Party journals and newspapers as *Hung-ch'i* (Red flag), *Ching-chi yen-chiu,* and the *JMJP*.[3]

1. Chang Ching-lu, ed., *Chung-kuo ch'u-pan shih liao pu-pien* (Supplementary historical materials on Chinese publishing; Peking, 1957), p. 449.
2. *SCMP* 2731, p. 9.

3. E.g., *Hung-ch'i,* August 1, 1959, February 1, 1961, August 10, 1961, June 1, 1962; *Ching-chi yen-chiu,* December 17, 1962; *JMJP,* October 28, 1959, December 27, 1961, August 28, 1962.

Hsu Tzu-jung

Vice-minister of Public Security; alternate member, CCP Central Committee.

Hsu became a member of the Communist Party in his youth but he did not come into prominence until after the end of the Sino-Japanese War. By the end of the war he was attached to Li Hsien-nien and Cheng Wei-san's Fifth Division of the New Fourth Army in central China. The Fifth Division fought in the region north of Hankow during the war with Japan, an area bordering on Hupeh, Honan, and Anhwei provinces. With the end of hostilities in 1945, portions of the New Fourth Army were redesignated the Central Plains Liberation Army. Hsu served with this army as political commissar of the First Brigade of the First Column, a unit under the Central Plains Military Area. This was in the Hupeh-Honan border area.[1]

Soon after the establishment of the government in the fall of 1949, Hsu received two appointments, being described at the time as a former PLA political commissar. In December 1949 he was named as director of the Personnel Affairs Bureau in the Ministry of Public Security. He held the personnel appointment until 1951. In January 1950 Hsu was made concurrently the director of the Staff Office of the same ministry, holding this post until at least mid-1952. Then, in April 1952, he was promoted to the position of vice-minister of Public Security, serving under Lo Jui-ch'ing until 1959 and under Hsieh Fu-chih thereafter. As of 1965, only Vice-minister Yang Ch'i-ch'ing (q.v.) had served as long as Hsu in this important ministry.

During the period from 1952 until the constitutional government was inaugurated in the fall of 1954, Hsu served on three special short-term committees under the jurisdiction of the Government Administration Council (the cabinet). In February 1952 he became one of the nine members of the Committee for the Management of Production of Government Offices, a group headed by Li Fu-ch'un; in July of the same year he was named to serve as a member of a committee charged with the task of dealing with problems of unemployment. And in January 1953 he was appointed a member of a newly established committee to implement the Marriage Law, a statute that had come into force in May 1950.

From the inauguration of the constitutional government in 1954, Hsu has served in the chief legislative body, the NPC. He was elected as a deputy from Honan to the First NPC (1954–

1959) and was re-elected to serve in the Second NPC (1959–1964). Under the Second NPC he was also a member of the permanent Bills Committee. He was once again elected to the Third NPC as a deputy from Honan, and when the First Session was held in December 1964–January 1965 he was not only reappointed to the Bills Committee but was also elevated to the NPC Standing Committee, the important body that manages the affairs of the Congress between the annual sessions. From 1959 to 1964 he also held a seat in the quasi-legislative CPPCC. When the Third National Committee of the CPPCC was formed in April 1959, Hsu served as a representative of the CCP and was selected for membership on the Standing Committee of the CPPCC. He was not, however, re-elected to the Fourth National Committee, which first met in late 1964.

Recognition for his work was given in September 1956 at the Eighth Party Congress when he was elected an alternate member of the Party Central Committee. He received another important post in August 1965 when he was named as a deputy director of the Internal Affairs Office of the State Council. This Office is presumed to coordinate the activities of all ministries, commissions, and bureaus of the central government engaged in security work. The importance of this office is suggested by the fact that it is headed by Public Security Minister Hsieh Fu-chih.

Probably because of the nature of his work, Hsu's activities have never received much attention from the national press. On occasion he has served on committees to mark some special holiday or event; for example, he was a member of the Preparatory Committee established in September 1959 to celebrate the 10th anniversary of the PRC. In addition, he is sometimes reported in the company of the most senior leaders of the regime. He was present in June 1964, for example, when Mao Tse-tung received delegates to a conference of public security specialists. However, the small number of public appearances is not a reliable guide to his importance. Apart from his membership on the Party Central Committee, he has also been the ranking vice-minister in the Ministry of Public Security since the major governmental reorganization in September 1959.

1. *Chieh-fang chan-cheng hui-i-lu* (Reminiscenses of the liberation war; Peking, 1961), pp. 55–83.

Hsu Yun-pei

(c.1910–   ; Hopeh). Minister, Second Ministry of Light Industry.

Hsu Yun-pei is a Party bureaucrat who rose to a cabinet-level post by the mid-1960's. Although his early background is obscure, he is known to have made the Long March in the mid-1930's from south China to Yenan.[1] He did not emerge again until the late 1940's and early 1950's when he was serving as a Party and government official in Kweichow Province and in the multi-provincial Southwest Military and Administrative Committee (SWMAC), which included Kweichow in its jurisdiction. The Communists captured Kweiyang, capital of Kweichow, in November 1949 and immediately formed a Military Control Commission to govern the city. Hsu was named as a member of this organization, serving under such important Party leaders as Su Chen-hua and Yang Yung (qq.v.). From his association with these two men at this time, it may be inferred that he entered Kweichow with the men of Liu Po-ch'eng's Second Field Army, which conquered the southwest after participating in the war against the Nationalists in central China in 1948–49.

The other posts Hsu held in the southwest include the following: 1950–1952: member, Kweichow Provincial People's Government Council and chairman of this government's Nationalities Affairs Committee; deputy secretary, Kweichow Party Committee; 1951–1952: member, Land Reform Committee, SWMAC. Although few details are available about his work in the southwest, it is evident that he attracted the attention of the central authorities, because in November 1952 he was relieved of all his posts in the southwest and transferred to Peking to become a vice-minister of Public Health, serving under Li Te-ch'üan, who at that time was not a Party member. In the spring of 1953 he was elected an Executive Committee member of the All-China Federation of Trade Unions but relinquished the post at the next congress in December 1957. Another position he held in the mid-1950's was with the State Council's Scientific Planning Commission; from its establishment in March 1956 until its reorganization in May 1957, Hsu served as one of the deputy secretaries-general.

Hsu's 12-year stint in the Ministry of Public Health was one of a steady climb in importance. One of his first important appearances occurred in May–June 1954 when he was a keynote speaker at a ministry-sponsored industrial health conference, at which he emphasized the relationship between sound safety practices and production. More interesting was a speech made in December 1955 at the inauguration of the ministry's Research Academy of Traditional Chinese Medicine. Hsu emphasized that more work was needed to promote the spread of Chinese medicine (in addition to, though not necessarily in opposition to, Western medicine). At this same time, another vice-minister of Public Health, Ho Ch'eng, was severely criticized for having "belittled" Party leadership in the ministry and for "despising the medical traditions of the fatherland." A person who worked in the ministry at this time claims that Ho Ch'eng's fall from power (he was removed at the senior vice-minister) contributed greatly to Hsu's rise within the ministry.[2] Because Minister Li Te-ch'üan was not politically important, the real power rested with the vice-ministers, and with the political demise of Ho, Hsu's stature rose, until in about 1958 he became the head of the Party Committee within the ministry (during the Great Leap Forward).[3] Other facts tend to support this claim. Hsu was among those who spoke at the important Eighth Party Congress in September 1956 (an honor not accorded to many vice-ministers), where he once again stressed the importance of traditional Chinese medicine. (His speech was given significant publicity by being published in the 1957 *Jen-min shou-ts'e* [People's handbook].) He claimed that failures by health departments to promote this form of medicine had "seriously set back the cause of public health." Other evidence of Hsu's rise is found in the annual issues of the *Jen-min shou-ts'e,* in which Hsu is listed first among the several vice-ministers after the Great Leap began in 1958. Also in 1958 he became deputy secretary of the special team to prevent and cure schistosomiasis, one of the more serious health burdens long endured by the Chinese peasantry.

Befitting his role as a ranking vice-minister, Hsu was often on hand to welcome and entertain visiting health delegations or to attend important conferences or ceremonies. He was, for example, a member of the presidium for the national conference of "advanced" cultural and educational workers in June 1960, one of the largest conferences ever held in China (attended by over 6,000 delegates), and in April 1964 he was the senior public health official at a ceremony honoring a military hospital in Peking for its work.

In 1958 Hsu was elected a deputy from Shantung to the Second NPC (1959–1964) but was transferred to the Kweichow constituency for the Third NPC, which held its first session in December 1964–January 1965. A month later, in February 1965, when the Handicraft Industry Administrative Bureau of the State Council was abolished, the Second Ministry of Light Industry was established, with Hsu as the minister. Other persons appointed to this ministry further suggest that its chief work will be involved with the handicraft industry, still a major source of production in China. Hsu has not apparently had any special training or experience in this field; his major qualification appears to be Party loyalty. His former colleague has described him as a very serious-minded person

and one completely dedicated to the Party. This same person also stated that as of the early 1960's Hsu's wife was working as a director of a bureau in the State Council.[4]

1. Interview with former employees of Ministry of Public Health, May 1965, Hong Kong.
2. *Ibid.*
3. *Ibid.*
4. *Ibid.*

Hsueh Mu-ch'iao

(c.1905–   ). Economist; statistical specialist; director, National Commodity Price Commission; vice-chairman, State Planning Commission.

Hsueh Mu-ch'iao is one of the PRC's leading economic officials and the father of the economic statistical network established in China during the fifties. He has been a major figure involved in both short- and long-range economic planning in the fifties and sixties, although he was eclipsed for a time during the Great Leap Forward, which began in 1958.

Little is known of Hsueh's early life, and the report that he graduated from Tsinghua University in Peking is not substantiated by a listing of graduates published by the university in 1937.[1] He has also been described as "probably" Soviet-trained,[2] but in any case it is clear that he received some higher education in economics. In the mid-thirties Hsueh was editing an irregular periodical entitled *Chung-kuo nung-ts'un* (Chinese peasant villages). By 1937 he was with the Communists in Yenan, where he taught at the Anti-Japanese Military and Political Academy, often known by its abbreviated name in China, K'ang-ta. Lectures delivered there by Hsueh in 1938 were published in Hong Kong in a revised edition (1948) under the title *Chung-kuo ko-ming chi-pen wen-t'i* (Fundamental problems of the Chinese revolution).[3] This is one of the better-known of his many works on political economics.

By 1943 Hsueh had been transferred from Yenan to east China, and from that year until 1947 he taught at Shantung University, located in Lin-i, an area under the control of Ch'en I's New Fourth Army forces. From 1946 to an uncertain date he served concurrently as director of the Industry Department and secretary-general of the Shantung Provincial Government then headed by Governor Li Yü (q.v.). Shantung was not then completely controlled by the Communists, and portions of the province were hotly contested during the latter stages of the civil war between the Communists and Nationalists (see under Ch'en I). Hsueh's activities in the late forties are not documented, but he was in Peking soon after it was surrendered to the Communists in January 1949. In July 1949 he chaired a meeting of economists who decided to establish the Preparatory Committee of the China New Economic Research Association. Hsueh was named as a Preparatory Committee vice-chairman under ideologue Ch'en Po-ta (q.v.), but nothing further was heard of the organization after 1953.

Hsueh's stature as a Party economist was clearly evident by 1949. In October of that year, when given an appointment in the new central government, he was identified as the former secretary-general of the Party Central Committee's Finance and Economics Department. Because there was no central government until October 1949, it is probable that the Party undertook direct responsibility for the Department until the new government was established. This supposition seems to be borne out by the fact that Hsueh was appointed in October as secretary-general (as well as member) of the Finance and Economics Committee (FEC), now under the Government Administration Council (the cabinet). The FEC, one of the four major committees under the Council, was chaired by Ch'en Yun, the top economic specialist during the first decade of the PRC.

Soon after the government was established Hsueh was also named to head the Privately Operated Enterprises Control Bureau, then subordinate to the FEC. Over the next three years much of his time was devoted to the work of this Bureau; thus, in December 1950 and January 1951, respectively, it fell to Hsueh to report before the cabinet on regulations governing private enterprises and on rules for the "liquidation" of public holdings and assets in industrial enterprises. Similarly, he took part in establishing a special office in October–November 1951, which led to the convocation of a large meeting of businessmen (most of them not Communists) in Peking in June 1952. This meeting, in turn, established the Preparatory Committee of the All-China Federation of Industry and Commerce (see under Hsu Ti-hsun). Hsueh was named to membership on the Federation's Preparatory Committee, holding the post until November 1953 by which time he was involved in other activities. On August 1, 1952, just a month after the Preparatory Committee was formed, Hsueh delivered a report before the cabinet on the Federation's draft rules. Hsueh held another economic post in the early fifties, serving from July 1950 to July 1954 on the Board of the All-China Federation of Cooperatives (see under Ch'eng Tzu-hua).

A number of organizational steps were taken in the latter half of 1952 in preparation for the launching of the First Five-Year Plan in January 1953. In August 1952 the State Statistical Bureau was established under the jurisdiction of the cabinet's FEC, and three months later the State Planning Commission was set up at a level parallel to the cabinet. Paving the way for new assignments, Hsueh relinquished to Sung Shao-wen (q.v.) in August the secretary-generalship of the FEC (although he remained a member until 1954), and in the same month he was also succeeded as director of the Privately Operated Enterprises Control Bureau by Hsu Ti-hsin. Relieved of these assignments, Hsueh was now appointed to head the Statistical Bureau (August) and to membership on the State Planning Commission (November).

Few officials in the history of the PRC have so completely dominated a field of endeavor as Hsueh did that of economic statistics. Aside from directing the Statistical Bureau, he was the keynote speaker at the annual national statistical conferences and his articles and speeches filled the pages of *T'ung-ch'i kung-tso t'ung-hsin* (Statistical work bulletin; known as *T'ung-chi kung-tso* after 1957) until the late fifties. Indeed, Professor Choh-ming Li's *The Statistical System of Communist China,* the definitive work on Communist statistics, is virtually a catalog of Hsueh's contributions to the establishment of a nationwide statistical system in the years from 1952 to the late fifties.

The task of setting up a statistical network throughout China was as monumental as it was necessary to the fulfillment of the ambitious goals set out in the five-year plan. Hsueh's numerous articles and speeches reflect a man fully committed to the development of an accurate statistical system and one who seldom indulged in the use of Marxian platitudes. He alternately cajoled his subordinates and pleaded with them for better performances, particularly at the grass-root level, and he was usually frank about the shortcomings of the system. Despite these shortcomings, the system had clearly made impressive gains by the end of the First Five-Year Plan (1957).

Hsueh's principal task in the fifties was the establishment of the statistical network, but during these same years he undertook other assignments as well. In 1954 he was elected a Kiangsu deputy to the First NPC; he was re-elected to the Second NPC (1959–1964) as well as to the Third NPC, which held its initial session in December 1964–January 1965. During the term of the First NPC he was a member of its Bills Committee, and since the establishment of the Second NPC he has been a vice-chairman of the Budget Committee. In October 1954 he was elevated to a vice-chairmanship on the State Planning Commission, which was now placed under the State Council; here Hsueh served under economic planner Li Fu-ch'un. He has been a member of the Academy of Sciences' Department of Philosophy and Social Sciences since its formation in May–June 1955, and from

1956 to 1958 he served first as a deputy secretary-general and then as a member of the State Council's Scientific Planning Commission.

Even after the inauguration of the Great Leap Forward in 1958, Hsueh continued to make numerous public appearances and to write for the nation's top political and economic journals. He received still another important post in October 1958 when he became a vice-chairman of the State Economic Commission. This commission is in charge of annual planning, as opposed to the long-range planning of the State Planning Commission. Thus, when Hsueh received this appointment he was head of the national statistical system, a vice-chairman on the commissions in charge of short-range and long-range economic planning, and still a member of the Scientific Planning Commission. Yet within a year he fell victim to the excesses of the Great Leap. In September 1959 a large number of changes were made in the State Council that resulted in the removal of many men, who, apparently, had opposed the Great Leap. The most important of these affecting Hsueh was his removal as head of the Statistical Bureau. According to Professor Li Choh-ming, Hsueh "was dismissed . . . at the height of the Great Leap Forward . . . for his staunch defence of the professional character of statistical and planning work."[4] His successor was Chia Ch'i-yun, a relatively unknown figure who had served as one of Hsueh's deputies during the previous five years.

At the same time that he lost his Statistical Bureau post, Hsueh was also removed as a vice-chairman of the State Planning Commission. He did, however, retain his vice-chairmanship on the Economic Commission (and was also made a member of the Commission). Paralleling these changes, Hsueh ceased making public appearances; in the four-year period from mid-1959 to mid-1963 he apparently did not appear at any public functions. In Hsueh's case, this meant that he no longer played a principal role in major economic meetings. Despite this absence from the public scene, Hsueh made a partial comeback in December 1960. At this time he relinquished his vice-chairmanship on the State Economic Commission, although he remained a member until June 1964. More important, however, he was reappointed a vice-chairman of the State Planning Commission, a position he continues to hold. It is noteworthy that Hsueh's partial return to political favor coincided with the nadir of the Chinese economy—the winter of 1960–61—thus suggesting that China's top leaders were anxious to utilize again the talents of a skilled administrator.

Hsueh published an article in the April 16, 1963, issue of the authoritative *Hung-ch'i* (Red flag) urging that better use be made of the so-called free market (in contrast to over-reliance on the planned market).[5] Coinciding almost exactly with the publication of this article, the State Council created the National Commodity Price Commission. Five months later, in September, Hsueh was appointed as Commission director, a post he still holds. Commenting on Hsueh's appointment, Choh-ming Li has written: "The establishment of the new machinery under his leadership seems to augur for a much more flexible state pricing policy than before, which would take into account the effects of prices in both the state trading channels and the uncontrolled rural markets on production and market supply."[6] It is doubtful that Hsueh has regained the prestige and authority he enjoyed in the mid-fifties, but in the relatively relaxed economic atmosphere that prevailed in the early sixties in the wake of the Great Leap failures, he seems to have again become one of the PRC's more important economic officials.

Hsueh's work has been principally concerned with domestic matters, but he has been involved to some degree in international economic relations. He has been a member of the China Committee for the Promotion of International Trade since its formation in May 1952 (see under Nan Han-ch'en). He also led a delegation to Moscow in December 1954 to take part in the first meeting of the Joint Commission for Sino-Soviet Scientific and Technical Cooperation, a body set up under the terms of an agreement reached the previous October when Soviet leaders Khrushchev and Bulganin had visited Peking. On December 28, after two weeks of negotiations, Hsueh signed a protocol defining the obligations of both sides in scientific-technical aid in various fields of the national economy, as well as the regulations governing the work of the Commission (which has subsequently met about twice a year). In August 1964 Hsueh was one of China's delegates to the so-called 1964 Peking Scientific Symposium, a gathering of 367 natural and social scientists, mainly from African, Asian, and Latin American nations (see under Chou P'ei-yuan).

---

1. Choh-ming Li, *The Statistical System of Communist China* (Berkeley, Calif., 1962), p. 13.

2. *Ibid.*

3. Chün-tu Hsüeh, *The Chinese Communist Movement, 1937–1949* (Stanford, Calif., 1962), pp. 8–9.

4. Choh-ming Li, "China's Industrial Development 1958–63," *The China Quarterly,* no. 17:36 (January–March 1964).

5. Franz Schurmann, "China's 'New Economic Policy'—Transition or Beginning?" *The China Quarterly,* no. 17:81 (January–March 1964).

6. Choh-ming Li, *The China Quarterly,* no. 17:36.

Hu Ch'i-li

(c.1924–   ). Youth and student leader.

Hu Ch'i-li has been a prominent youth and student leader since the mid-1950's. According to someone who knew him at that time, he was born about 1924 and had been active in youth affairs in Yenan sometime prior to the Communist conquest of the mainland in 1949. In the mid-fifties he was ostensibly a student at Peking University (Peita), China's foremost institute of higher learning, but those who knew him believed he was there principally as a representative of the New Democratic Youth League (NDYL).[1] He was, in fact, identified in July 1954 as the secretary of the Peita NDYL chapter.

Hu became more active at the national level early in 1956 when he replaced T'ien Te-min as chairman of the All-China Students' Federation (ACSF), a position he retained until January 1965. A great portion of Hu's time in this nine-year span was devoted to the affairs of the ACSF. Within two years of receiving his ACSF position, Hu was admitted to the higher councils of two related organizations, the Communist Youth League (CYL) and the All-China Youth Federation (ACYF). He was elected a CYL Central Committee alternate member in May 1957 at a League congress; at the next congress (June 1964), Hu was elected a member of the Standing Committee of the Central Committee, as well as an alternate secretary of the important League Secretariat. He has made comparable progress on the hierarchical ladder of the Youth Federation. At an ACYF Congress in April 1958 he was elected to the Standing Committee of the National Committee; he was renamed to this position in April 1962 and then in January 1965 was elevated to a vice-chairmanship.

As an elite member of the youth and student world in Communist China, Hu has frequently traveled abroad as a representative of one of the organizations described above. Usually a ranking member or a leader of the delegations, he has been in the following nations since 1954. 1954: North Korea, National Conference of Korean Youth Activists, July; 1956: Czechoslovakia, Fourth World Student Congress, August; 1958: United Arab Republic, at the invitation of the Cairo University Union, February–March; 1960: Morocco, Czechoslovakia, Tunisia, Fifth Conference of the National Union of Moroccan Students; Czechoslovakia (purpose unknown), July; Fourth Congress of the General Union of Algerian Muslim Students and the Congress of the National Union of Tunisian Students (both held in Tunisia), July–August; 1961: USSR, meetings of the Permanent Secretariat for the World Youth Forum, March; 1962: Cuba, First National Congress of the Association of Insurgent Youth of Cuba, March–April; celebrations for fourth anniversary of Cuban Revolution,

December; Czechoslovakia, purpose unknown, December; 1963: Brazil, a students' seminar on underdeveloped nations and the 26th Congress of the National Student's Union of Brazil, July.

As in the case of almost all Chinese Communist delegates of the 1960's, Hu came into open conflict with Soviet or Soviet-backed representatives on at least one occasion. At the meetings in Brazil in July 1963 (cited above), he advocated the necessity of "national liberation" movements in underdeveloped nations (then a much-employed slogan of Peking) and called for a resolution asserting that "imperialism for aggression and war will never change." During these same years many youth or student groups visited China from various parts of the world— signing with their Chinese counterparts joint communiqués, which inevitably denounced the United States. Hu was the signatory to five such statements with groups from Japan (October 1960 and June 1964), Cuba (December 1960), Ecuador (December 1960), and Palestine (September 1964). Aside from these groups he has been mentioned in the press in connection with scores of other youth and student delegations that have visited China.

Hu's increasingly active role in international affairs made him a logical candidate for membership in several quasi-official (or "mass") organizations devoted to foreign relations. He has received (and still retains) the following positions: member, National Committee, China Peace Committee, July 1958; council member, China-Latin America Friendship Association, March 1960; council member, China-Africa People's Friendship Association, April 1960. And, like so many other Chinese leaders, he has attended a host of rallies protesting one fact or another of U.S. foreign policy. A typical example was his presence at a rally of 400,000 before the Cuban embassy in Peking in November 1962 (during the peak of the U.S.-Soviet missile crisis). Similarly, he has written articles and served on *ad hoc* organizations related to foreign affairs. For instance, he co-authored an article for the August 10, 1956, issue of *Chung-kuo ch'ing-nien pao* (Chinese youth daily) supporting Egypt's "resistance to aggression over the Suez Canal"; and, following the Anglo-French-Israeli invasion of Egypt that fall, he served as a member of the "Chinese People's Committee in Support of Egypt's Resistance to Aggression" (November 1956).

Technically, Hu held no official position in the government until 1959. In April of that year he became a member of the Third National Committee of the CPPCC as a representative of the All-China Youth Federation. As such, he spoke at the first session of the Third CPPCC (April 1959), condemning the Indian "expansionists" for utilizing the Tibetan rebellion (of March 1959) to "interfere in China's internal affairs." Hu was not re-appointed to the CPPCC in 1964, but that same year he was elected as a Heilungkiang deputy to the more important NPC, which held its first session in December 1964–January 1965.

1. Interview with former Peking University student, Hong Kong, June 1964.

Hu Ch'iao-mu

(c.1911–   ; Yen-ch'eng, Kiangsu). Party historian and propagandist; alternate member, Central Secretariat, CCP; member, CCP Central Committee.

One of the most important Party propagandists, Hu Ch'iao-mu is the author of the official Maoist history of the CCP, written in 1951 to commemorate the 30th anniversary of the Chinese Communist Movement. He has been involved with virtually every important CCP news and propaganda organ since the mid-thirties, including the New China News Agency (NCNA), the *JMJP,* and the Party's Propaganda Department, and since 1956 he has been an alternate member of the highly important Central Secretariat.

Hu was born of a wealthy landowning family in Yen-ch'eng hsien, Kiangsu, also the home of Communist propagandist Ch'iao Kuan-hua (q.v.). His father, Hu Ch'i-tung, was a political leader of some prominence and once served as a member of the Peking Parliament. Hu Ch'iao-mu's original name was Hu Ting-hsin and he has also been widely known by the pen name Ch'iao Mu. At the outset of any discussion of Hu, it must be noted that both he and Ch'iao Kuan-hua used the *nom-de-plume* Ch'iao Mu for a number of years in the thirties and forties. Because both men were prolific writers and propagandists, the use of the same pseudonym led to considerable confusion and erroneous statements about their careers. The Communists have distinguished between them by nicknaming Hu Ch'iao-mu as Pei ("north") Ch'iao-mu and Ch'iao Kuan-hua as Nan ("south") Ch'iao-mu. Fortunately, the confusion ended after 1949 when both men dropped "Ch'iao Mu" as a pen name.

As a youth, Hu graduated from a middle school in Yang-chou (Kiangsu) and then studied in Peking from 1930 to 1932 in the physics department of Tsinghua University, one of China's leading schools. Contrary to numerous reports, however, he did not graduate. It was probably at Tsinghua, a missionary-run school, that Hu learned English. In the period from 1932 to the outbreak of war in 1937, Hu spent time in both Hangchow (Chekiang) and Shanghai. He attended Chekiang University in 1932, and for most of the period from 1933 to 1937 he was active as a specialist in propaganda and cultural

activities for the CCP in Shanghai. It was probably during these years that he joined the Party.

Hu apparently spent most of the mid-thirties in Shanghai, but he was known to have been in Hangchow in 1934 (and perhaps 1935–36). In a Communist account of 1961, he is credited with having led Chekiang University students in the "struggles" against "reactionaries" and against a "facist education." It appears that he was still in the Hangchow area in late 1935 when students at the university protested against KMT policies they regarded as a surrender to continuing Japanese aggression in north China.[1] The student activities in Hangchow were part of a nationwide protest known as the "December Ninth Movement," which began in Peking and quickly spread to the rest of the nation (see under Li Ch'ang).

When the war broke out in mid-1937 Hu went to the Communist headquarters in Yenan where, in association with youth leader Feng Wen-pin (q.v.), he directed a youth training class in north Shensi. During the war years he was also dean of school affairs at the Mao Tse-tung Youth Cadre School in Yenan and an editor of *Chung-kuo ch'ing-nien* (China youth), one of the most important journals published in Yenan. During the latter stages of the war Hu was a "political secretary" to Mao Tse-tung. It was apparently in this capacity that he accompanied Mao from Yenan to Chungking where Mao held talks with Chiang Kai-shek on KMT-CCP problems. These negotiations, held from late August to early October 1945 (immediately after the Japanese surrender), had been arranged in large part through the efforts of U.S. Ambassador Patrick Hurley. (See under Mao Tse-tung.) While in Chungking Hu served as one of the editors of *Hsin-hua jih-pao* (New China daily), the important organ of the CCP.

Hu's exact whereabouts in the late forties are not known in detail, but he was among those who left Yenan with Mao Tse-tung when the Communist capital was captured by the Nationalists in March 1947. He presumably remained with the Maoist leadership in northwest and later north China. He was in Peking soon after the "liberation" in January 1949, and that spring he was elected to posts in the two major Communist youth organizations, the New Democratic Youth League (NDYL) and the All-China Federation of Democratic Youth (ACFDY). In the former, Hu became a member of the Central Committee and in the latter a member of the National Committee, retaining these positions until mid-1953 when both organizations held their second congresses. In the summer and fall of 1949 he was also very active in the work leading to the establishment of the numerous "mass" organizations as well as the central government. In July he attended three important conferences; one of these was a gathering of over 800 literary and art "workers," and a second was a conference of social scientists. But most important was his participation in a conference of the Preparatory Committee of the All-China Journalists Association (ACJA). Hu presided over this conference, made the keynote speech, and was elected president of the Preparatory Committee; he held the post until succeeded by Teng T'o (q.v.) in 1954. Hu took part in the work of the CPPCC (the organization that brought the central government into existence on October 1) from the time the CPPCC Preparatory Committee was established under Mao Tse-tung's chairmanship in June 1949. When the CPPCC held its first session in September (which Hu attended as a representative of the ACJA), he served as a member of the presidium (steering committee), spoke about the work of the ACJA, and at the close of the meetings was elected to the CPPCC's First National Committee. In February 1953 he was elevated to membership on the Standing Committee, but he dropped his affiliation with the organization in late 1954 when the Second National Committee was established.

When the assignments to the new government administration were made in October 1949, Hu became a member and the secretary-general of the Cultural and Education Committee of the Government Administration Council (GAC). He retained his membership until 1954 but relinquished the secretary-generalship to Ch'ien Chün-jui (q.v.), another specialist in educational affairs, in November 1952. Another major assignment received in October 1949 was the directorship of the Press Administration, a post he held until its abolition in August 1952. The Press Administration, subordinate to the Culture and Education Committee, had a wide range of duties, including jurisdiction over the New China News Agency (NCNA) and Radio Peking. Among his subordinates in the Press Administration were some of Peking's top specialists in propaganda and journalism, including Ch'iao Kuan-hua, Fan Ch'ang-chiang, and Wu Leng-hsi (qq.v.).

By late 1949 Hu was also the managing director of the Party Central Committee's major organ, the *Jen-min jih-pao* (People's daily), but he relinquished this post to Fan Ch'ang-chiang in 1950. (There is some evidence that he was also the editor-in-chief of the *JMJP*.) In 1949 Hu had also headed the NCNA for a brief period, apparently succeeding Liao Ch'eng-chih. Hu, in turn, was replaced by Party journalist Ch'en K'o-han toward the end of the year. However, much the most important post held by Hu by 1949 was that of a deputy directorship of the Party's Propaganda Department, headed by Lu Ting-i. Hu was in the department until at least late 1954.

Rounding out his appointments in 1949, Hu became a member of the Executive Board of the Sino-Soviet Friendship Association (SSFA) when it was formed in October, after having served on the Association's Preparatory Committee established the previous July. He continued his affiliation with the SSFA until December 1954. He also became vice-chairman of the China Association for the Reform of the (Chinese) Written Language upon its establishment in October 1949. This was a prelude to a considerable amount of work in the field of language reform in later years (see below).

In view of Hu's prominence as one of China's top journalists, it was logical that he would represent Peking in the Communist-supported International Organization of Journalists (IOJ). At an IOJ meeting in Helsinki in September 1950, he was elected (apparently *in absentia*) as one of the IOJ vice-chairmen, a position he seems to have held until 1956 when Teng T'o was elected to the post. In October of 1950, Hu was added to the National Committee of the China Peace Committee (a post he held until the committee was reorganized in July 1958). Also by 1950 he must have been working on the book that has brought him lasting fame. Published in June 1951 on the eve of the Party's 30th anniversary (July 1), Hu's *Chung-kuo kung-ch'an-tang te san-shih-nien* (Thirty Years of the Communist Party of China) became an instant best seller; by the end of 1952 some 2.8 million copies had been sold.[2] Less than six months after publication, his short volume had already become "required reading"; for example, when the Party issued a list of documents in November 1951 that intellectuals were required to study, Hu's book was placed among the writings of such top Communists as Chou En-lai, P'eng Chen, and fellow propagandist-historian Ch'en Po-ta (qq.v.).[3] Hu's history of the Party is, of course, purely a Maoist interpretation. All past contenders for Party leadership, like Ch'en Tu-hsiu, Li Li-san, and Ch'en Shao-yü (qq.v.), are severely criticized for their "erroneous lines," whereas Mao's leadership is invariably described as "correct." Inconvenient chapters in Mao's life are either glossed over or completely ignored. Whatever its shortcomings for the historian, Hu's book will probably remain the standard interpretation as long as Mao lives.

In the early years of the PRC there were few events related to propaganda, publications, ideological campaigns, and language reform in which Hu was not involved. In March 1951, for example, he delivered a major address before a national secondary education conference on patriotism "as guided by Marxism, Leninism, and Mao Tse-tung's ideology." On August 10, he reported to the GAC on the work of his Press Administration, and at nationwide conferences of publications administration and translation work (held, respectively, in August–September and November 1951), he delivered major reports. During the period from late 1951 until 1955 he was also deeply involved in various movements to "re-mold" the intellectuals, most notably the campaigns against Yü P'ing-po, an authority on the novel *The Dream of the Red Chamber,* and writer Hu Feng (q.v.).[4] In additional, after Hu Ch'iao-mu had presented a report before the CPPCC (January 5, 1952), the decision was made to create a Study (hsueh-hsi) Committee subordinate to the CPPCC. When the Committee was established in February to study the works of Marx, Lenin, Mao, and others, Hu was named as a member, retaining the post until the CPPCC was reorganized in late 1954.

Hu's participation in language reform began, as already described, in late 1949 and continued at least through the 1950's. The complex problem of language reform had been a major concern of the CCP leadership (including Mao) for many years prior to the assumption of power in 1949 (see under Lin Po-ch'ü and Wu Yü-chang). As a consequence of this interest by the top leaders, a number of prominent persons (Hu among them) have devoted a considerable amount of time to the subject. Thus, in December 1951 Hu was named to membership on a research committee to reform the language, and in December 1954 he was named to a similar organization known as the Committee for the Reform of the Chinese Written Language. In the latter capacity, he spoke at a CPPCC meeting on March 15, 1955, on the problem of simplifying Chinese, and in October 1955 he addressed a national conference on the same subject; on this occasion the conference adopted a draft plan for the use of over 500 simplified characters and agreement was also reached to promote the "standard spoken language" (*p'u-t'ung-hua*) based on the Peking pronunciation. To advance the use of the standard language, the State Council established a committee in February 1956, with Hu as a member, and in the following month he was also named to membership on the National Association for the Elimination of Illiteracy. In October of the same year he was appointed a vice-chairman of still another committee related to language and literacy, this one the Committee for the Examination and Formulation of the Plan for the Phoneticization of the Han Language. Although Hu is clearly a major figure in the efforts to simplify, phoneticize, and standardize Chinese, his role has been less important than that of Wu Yü-chang (q.v.), the Party's leading specialist in this field.

In the meantime, Hu had taken part in the steps leading toward the establishment of a constitutional government in 1954. In 1953–54 he served as a member of the Committee to Draft the Constitution, which was headed by Mao Tse-tung, and when elections to the First NPC were held in 1954, Hu was elected a deputy from his native Kiangsu. At the close of the first session of the First NPC in September 1954, he was named to membership on the NPC Standing Committee. He was re-elected to the Second NPC (1959–1964) and to the Third NPC, which closed its first session in early January 1965. In each case he was again named to the NPC Standing Committee. When the Academy of Sciences formed four major academic departments in May–June 1955, Hu became a member of the Department of Philosophy and Social Sciences, another position he continues to hold.

Hu's long Party career was given official recognition at the Eighth National Congress in September 1956 when he was elected a member of the Central Committee. He was one of 33 men elected to full membership who had been neither full nor alternate members on the Seventh Central Committee elected in Yenan in 1945. Immediately after the Congress, Hu was appointed an alternate member of the Party's Central Secretariat. Headed by Teng Hsiao-p'ing, this important body is charged with the task of executing the policies decided upon by the Politburo. As originally constituted, the Secretariat had 10 members (seven full and three alternate members). Among this group Hu was the only one working in the field of propaganda and education; this situation was changed, however, in September 1962 when Propaganda Department Director Lu Ting-i was added as a member.

In the years since the 1956 Party Congress, Hu seems to have concentrated mainly on liaison activities with foreign Communist parties, although it is probable that together with ideologues Lu Ting-i and Ch'en Po-ta he has some voice at the policy level in matters involving culture, education, and propaganda. Hu's involvement in international Communist affairs is best illustrated by the fact that he was a member of two of the most important missions ever sent abroad by the Chinese Communists—the one led by Mao Tse-tung to Moscow in November 1957 and the other led by Liu Shao-ch'i to the same city in November–December 1960. The ostensible purpose of these two delegations was to attend celebrations marking the 40th and 43rd anniversaries, respectively, of the Russian Revolution. However, the importance lay in the fact that both occasions were used to hold "summit" meetings of international Communist leaders, meetings that left unresolved serious disputes between China and the Soviet Union (see under delegation leaders Mao and Liu).

In domestic affairs, Hu has made relatively few public appearances since the Eighth Congress in 1956. Nonetheless, the type of appearance he has made suggests that he works closely with the top leaders. He attended, for example, a session of the Supreme State Conference called by Mao in September 1958 at which time the communes were being launched, and the month before that he was among a select few who took part in the signing ceremony of the joint communiqué agreed upon by Mao and Khrushchev (shortly before the "off-shore islands" crisis of 1958). He was also a vice-chairman of the preparatory committee for a June 1960 conference of "advanced workers" in the fields of culture (one of the largest meetings ever held in China —see under Lin Feng, the keynote speaker). Hu's continuing involvement in domestic propaganda work was reaffirmed in August 1964 when he accompanied Mao to see a Peking opera with a "contemporary theme"; the staging of the opera was part of a campaign to substitute current (i.e., Communist and revolutionary) themes for the traditional or classical ones.

Hu's career is closely linked to that of Mao Tse-tung, especially in the sense that he first came to prominence at about the same time that Mao was consolidating his power in Yenan in the late thirties and early forties. He was then far outshadowed politically by such Maoist ideologues as Liu Shao-ch'i and Ch'en Po-ta, but in the ensuing years he became increasingly important—an importance that reached a peak with the publication of Hu's Maoist-oriented history of the CCP in 1951. Since that time he has concentrated less on the day-to-day problems of propaganda and more on domestic policy matters and international Communist liaison activities.

1. Li Ch'ang et al., *"I-erh-chiu" hui-i-lu* (Reminiscences of "December Ninth"; Peking, 1961), p. 127.
2. *People's China,* no. 24, December 16, 1952, p. 8.
3. *CB* 169, p. 16.
4. Yang I-fan, *The Case of Hu Feng* (Hong Kong, 1956), pp. 15, 83–84, 93, 152; C. T. Hsia, *A History of Modern Chinese Fiction, 1917– 1957* (New Haven, Conn., 1961), pp. 331–332.

Hu Feng

(1903–   ; I-tu hsien, Hupeh). Marxist literary critic and writer; purged, 1955.

Hu Feng, Marxist literary critic, essayist, and poet, allied himself for almost 30 years with the CCP and left-wing groups. Although he was politically active and highly respected in intellectual circles, he became the main focus of attack in the intensive campaign against intellectuals in 1955. Because of his independent approach to Marxism, he was singled out as an appropriate scapegoat in the Party's drive to impose a unified, orthodox ideology.

Hu was born in I-tu hsien in southern Hupeh, but his family later moved to Kichun (Ch'ich'un) hsien in the eastern part of the province. His original name was Chang Ku-fei. Although Hu's father was an unskilled laborer, the family finances improved during his youth, and he was sent to school in the city. He knew little about

Chinese culture, but he responded quickly to the Western ideas which were affecting China at the time. While at school in Nanking in 1923–1925, he joined the Communist Youth League, participated in the May 30 demonstrations of 1925, and joined the revolutionary movement developing in the south. It appears, however, that he never became a member of the Communist Party. During this period he wrote poetry in a pessimistic vein.

In 1928 he went to Japan where he began to write essays on political and social issues. He was expelled from Japan in 1933 for participating in leftist demonstrations. Returning to Shanghai in 1934, he began to work as a professional writer and editor and joined the League of Left-Wing Writers, nominally led by Lu Hsun but in fact dominated by CCP member Chou Yang (q.v.). Hu soon became one of Lu Hsun's leading disciples and was himself surrounded by a coterie of talented young writers.

In the atmosphere of relative freedom that prevailed in Communist literary circles during the 1930's, Hu articulated independent literary theories and debated his views freely. At this time he defined his political and aesthetic ideas more precisely. Although a Marxist in name, he did not conform to the Party line but attempted to fuse certain orthodox Marxist beliefs with his own ideas about literary creativity. His view deviated from the orthodox Communist theory that literature was a reflection of the class struggle. He believed that literature was the fusion of the writer's emotional intensity and spontaneity, which he called the "subjective struggling spirit," with objective reality, which he frequently equated with the demands of the people for a livelihood and a democratic government. In assimilating objective reality into his consciousness, he felt that a writer moves closer to Marxism.

Though Hu used his concept of the "subjective struggling spirit" to explain the individual personality and the creative process, he used Marxian dialectics to explain social and political trends. Nevertheless, his belief that a person acquires political ideology through his own experience and that Party discipline should direct a writer's political life but not his creativity were bound in time to conflict with a party intent on imposing ideological control.

Hu's sophisticated views plus the backing of Lu Hsun and a devoted coterie gradually gained him a leading position in left-wing literary circles. Even at this time, his group contended with more orthodox factions in a fierce struggle for pre-eminence which was motivated as much by personal antagonism as by aesthetic differences. Hu fought his most vehement battles with Chou Yang, a Party representative in the League of Left-Wing writers. Whereas to Chou politics and ideology were the foremost concern of literature, to Hu they were secondary to literary value. This basic conflict underlay all Hu's controversies with the Party's literary officials. In the factional squabbles of the 1930's, Hu was charged with unorthodoxy and subversion. The dispute subsided with the outbreak of the Sino-Japanese War when Chou and his associates followed Mao to the Communist areas in Yenan. Hu and his followers went into KMT territory (principally Chungking) where they helped prepare for the eventual triumph of the Communist Party. Nevertheless, their writings continued free and unorthodox.

Mao's "Talks on Art and Literature" of 1942, which formalized the doctrine that literature must be an instrument of political utility, aroused Hu and his group to a concerted campaign of opposition. Safe from direct Party pressure, they still were able to insist on independent aesthetic values and to criticize Party literary theory in public. In January 1945, Hu began to publish a magazine, *Hsi-wang* (Hope), in Chungking that was intended as a sounding board for his ideas and as a weapon against the doctrinairism prevailing in left-wing literary circles. A colleague's article, "On Subjectivism," in the first issue, aroused a literary controversy which raged for nine years. Hu was investigated by the Party, was forced to take part in ideological remolding sessions, and was obstructed in publishing his journal. Still, he was able to preserve a degree of independence in the period before the Party seized power in 1949. The advantages of his opposition to the KMT apparently outweighed the disadvantages of his heterodoxy.

Soon after the fall of Peking in early 1949 Hu was in Peking and in July of that year he attended the All-China Congress of Literary and Art Workers. While the congress was in session he served on two *ad hoc* committees, one to organize Chinese poets and the other to draft the regulations for the All-China Federation of Literary and Art Circles (ACFLAC), which was established at this time. He was elected to membership on the Federation's National Committee as well as to Standing Committee membership in the All-China Association of Literary Workers, the Federation's most important subordinate organization, which was known after 1953 as the Union of Chinese Writers. Hu then went to Shanghai where he was to spend most of his time over the next five years. In February 1950 he was made a member of the East China Military and Administrative Committee's Culture and Education Committee, retaining this post until the regional governments were disbanded in 1954.

While the Communist Party was consolidating its monolithic power structure from 1949 to 1951, Hu appears to have conformed. His expression of the proper political sentiment overbalanced his remarks on literature, and his

poetry praised Mao in superhuman terms. Soon, however, he began to bridle under the literary restrictions imposed by the Party. He did not condemn the political leadership whose authority he accepted, but he charged those responsible for literary policy with distorting the leadership's program. At the same time, he sought to gain Party sanction for his own literary ideas. He was no longer allowed to debate freely, nor was he equal to his opponents. Because of his stature in literary circles he was appointed to the above-mentioned positions in 1949–50 but was given no real authority. Doctrinal interpretation of literature was largely in the hands of his old rival, Chou Yang, then vice-chairman of the ACFLAC. Although Hu's posts were nominal, they indicated that the Party still wanted his cooperation and this gave him some leeway to maneuver. His strategy seems to have been to comply with Party directives at first in order to gain a position in the hierarchy from which he could influence these directives.

In the ideological remolding movement begun in 1951, Chou Yang engineered formal attacks against Hu and his colleagues by means of public criticism in literary magazines. The attempts to reform Hu's thinking failed, but he still was not condemned beyond reprieve. The primary aim of the Party in the early 1950's was to incorporate Hu into its thought reform drives. He was not yet made the focus of a specific campaign. As these campaigns subsided in 1953 and the first half of 1954, Hu's position in Party circles improved. He was made a deputy from Szechwan to the First National People's Congress (1954–1959) and was appointed to the editorial board of *Jen-min wen-hsueh* (People's literature), an important Party literary magazine.

With characteristic impulsiveness, he jumped to the conclusion that his own position had risen to the point where an open struggle could bring victory. In July 1954 he presented a report to the Central Committee in which he blamed China's intellectual sterility on the literary authorities. He hoped to break their control by his criticism of their policies: (1) He opposed the ideological remolding of writers. Instead he suggested that a writer would come closer to Communism if he applied his "subjective struggling spirit" to the problems of everyday life. He believed that thought reform diverted writers from reality. (2) He opposed the idea that a writer may draw his material solely from the lives of peasants, workers, and soldiers. Literature, he felt, should not merely portray certain classes, but should describe the daily struggles of all men. (3) He opposed the evaluation of literature according to its subject matter. He insisted that the value of a work should be judged not by the writer's choice of material, but by how he treats the material. (4) He objected to imposing the old literary folk styles of the past onto literary works of the present. In his view, new times and new subject matter required new styles. He also presented a program to eliminate rigid control over writers. Instead of one official writers' organization and official literary publications, he proposed the creation of several independent writers' groups who would edit their own publications free from inspection. This, he hoped, would lead to free competition in creative work.

Because no action was taken against him after the presentation of his report to the Central Committee, he believed the time had finally come to ask publicly for Party sanction for his theories. At a meeting in November 1954 he once again outlined his views of literature and then openly accused the literary authorities of the same charges he brought against them in his earlier report. The rapidity with which the emphasis of the meeting suddenly switched to an all-out assault on Hu seems to indicate that an attack on him had already been decided on and that he had been invited to participate so as to furnish a pretext to open the assault.

The intensity and the nationwide proportions of the subsequent campaign can be explained by the Party's internal policy at the end of 1954. As the Chinese Communists moved into the period of intensive collectivization and industrialization, it became imperative for them to eradicate all unorthodox tendencies. Hu provided an excellent symbol with which to attack heterodox views and independent thinking. One of the chief forces behind the drive for ideological purity was Hu's old enemy Chou Yang. The campaign was not free from personal vindictiveness, but it must be considered largely as another phase in the Party's over-all program of thought reform.

The 1955 campaign was different from the previous attacks on Hu. Whereas the previous aim had been to make him reform, the purpose now was to liquidate his unorthodoxy. He was no longer regarded as a deviationist guilty of "subjectivism, emotionalism, and aestheticism" in his thinking, but as a "counter-revolutionary" leader. The accusations brought against him were half-truths because, although the charge that he disagreed with the Party's literary rulings could be substantiated, there was no evidence to show that his ideas were anti-Marxist in principle or that he intended to subvert political authority.

The campaign reached its climax in May and June of 1955, when the *JMJP* published three batches of letters between Hu and his followers. They were accompanied by interpretations which distorted Hu's remarks about undermining the literary hierarchy into plans to overthrow the Party's political leaders. On May 13, 1955, Hu presented a self-criticism which the Party rejected as false. Although Hu had begged his followers to dissociate themselves from him, with few exceptions they resisted the campaign against their own master. He was officially stripped of all his posts and on July 18, 1955, he was arrested and imprisoned.[1]

The campaign did not end with his arrest and became greater in scope and more intense, proving that it had a function beyond mere destruction of a single disturbing influence. As the drive picked up steam, it developed a momentum of its own that went far beyond the scope the regime had intended. It evolved from an orderly instrument of the Party into a reign of terror, particularly among the intellectuals. Ironically, one of the results of this drive was to intensify the very problems Hu attempted to resolve—the increasing estrangement between the Party and the intellectual.

The inauguration of the Hundred Flowers movement in 1956 and the first half of 1957 was in part a response to the demoralization of the intellectuals in the previous period. Hu's views, which the Party had pronounced as heresy just a year earlier, were echoed by intellectuals criticizing Party bureaucrats. Hu's name became an example of protest against totalitarian control of intellectual and artistic activity. There were public pleas, especially from the youths, to re-examine the charges against him. The demand to try Hu in open court became a *cause célèbre*. The Hu Feng case was compared to the Dreyfus affair, and several pointed out that the Hundred Flowers campaign was the implementation of Hu's demands. His conflict with the Party apparently inspired many of the rebellious intellectuals during the Hundred Flowers period.

1. Merle Goldman, "Hu Feng's Conflict with the Literary Authorities," *The China Quarterly,* no. 12:102–137 (October–December 1962).

Hu K'o-shih

Secretary, Communist Youth League.

Hu K'o-shih, whose antecedents are unknown, rose from a position of obscure youth leader in 1949 to be the second-ranking man in this work by the mid-1960's. The organization in which he has been mainly active is the Communist Youth League, known prior to 1957 as the New Democratic Youth League (NDYL). The League has held four congresses—in 1949, 1953, 1957, and 1964. At the April 1949 Congress Hu was elected an alternate member of the League's Central Committee. In May 1949 Wuhan fell to the Communists, and in the following month the League established there the Central China Work Committee with Hu as the second deputy secretary. By the turn of the year 1949–50, when most of south China had been captured, the Central China Work Committee was renamed the Central-South Work Committee; from approximately this time he headed the Committee's Organization Department and by 1952 he was the Committee deputy secretary. His work must have come to the favorable attention of his superiors, because in September 1952 he was appointed as a deputy secretary of the League's management organ, the Secretariat, headquartered in Peking.

It was at this same time that Hu Yao-pang (q.v.) replaced Feng Wen-pin (then in political trouble) as the ranking secretary of the Youth League. From this period onward, Hu K'o-shih worked directly under Hu Yao-pang, a veteran youth leader and a Party Central Committee member after 1956. With this new promotion, Hu K'o-shih moved to Peking and has worked there since.

In the meantime, Hu had also been active in both Party and governmental work activities in central-south China. In the Party Central-South China Bureau, he was by early 1950 deputy secretary (under Secretary Chao I-min) of the Youth Work Committee, and in the governmental Central-South Military and Administrative Committee he was a member of both the People's Supervision Committee (from March 1950) and the Political and Legal Affairs Committee (from December 1951). He was officially removed from both positions in May 1953, not too long after his transfer to Peking.

Hu played a far more significant role at the Second Youth League Congress of June–July 1953 than he had at the 1949 meeting. He served on the Congress presidium (steering committee), was elected to the Central Committee and, immediately after the Congress, was named to the Standing Committee and reappointed to the Secretariat. He was re-elected to identical posts at the Third Congress in May 1957 and the Fourth Congress in June 1964. Between the Third and Fourth congresses, other senior Youth League leaders were transferred elsewhere, and thus by mid-1964 Hu was subordinate only to Hu Yao-pang in the League. This became apparent at the June 1964 congress when Hu spoke on revisions to the League's constitution, the second most important speech after the keynote address by First Secretary Hu Yao-pang.

Aside from participation in the youth congresses, Hu has been involved in a wide variety of other activities related to youth work. Some of the more significant include: member of the Board of Directors of the China Youth Publishing House, established in April 1953, to which he may still belong; speaker at a national conference of "young activists in building socialism," September 1955, and member of the presidium for a similar conference in November–December 1958; member of the preparatory committee for celebrating the 40th anniversary of the May Fourth Movement, April 1959; representative of the Youth League, signing a joint communiqué with a visiting Japanese Democratic Youth

League delegation, October 1960. Moreover, Hu led six youth delegations to bloc nations between 1954 and 1961. These delegations went to: North Korea, July 1954; USSR, April–May 1955, February–March 1957, and April 1958; East Germany, May 1959; North Vietnam, March–April 1961. Probably the most important of these was the April 1958 trip to Moscow when he led the Chinese delegation to the 13th Congress of the All-Union Young Communist League.

Although youth affairs have clearly been Hu's main concern, he has also had other assignments. In January 1953 he was named a deputy secretary-general of the Committee for the Implementation of the Marriage Law, and from 1954 to 1959 represented Hupeh on the First NPC. Representing youth circles, Hu replaced Feng Wen-pin as a member of the National Committee of the Chinese People's Committee in Defense of Children in about 1956, and in July 1958 became a National Committee member of the China Peace Committee (CPC); he continues to hold the former post but was dropped from the CPC in June 1965. From 1959 to 1964 he was a member of the Third CPPCC as a representative of "organizations for peaceful and friendly relations with foreign countries," but under the Fourth CPPCC Hu represented the Communist Youth League. When the Fourth CPPCC held its first session in December 1964–January 1965, Hu was named to the governing body, the Standing Committee. In the interim, when the Spare-time Education Committee was established under the State Council in January 1960, Hu was named as a member.

As a senior youth leader, he has authored a number of articles, including:

"To Nurture New People for Socialism," *People's China,* December 1, 1953 (based on a speech at the Second National Conference on Young Pioneers' Work held in November 1953).

"Dedicate Youth to Socialism," *JMJP,* September 13, 1955.

"A Discussion with Young Friends about the Questions of Mastering Science," *Chung-kuo ch'ing-nien pao* (China youth daily), June 1, 1956.

"New Men of Communism Are Growing," *JMJP,* November 21, 1958.

"Current Propaganda Work of the Communist Youth League," *Chung-kuo ch'ing-nien* (China youth), February 16, 1959.

"The New Stage in the Communist Education of Chinese Youth," *ibid.,* June 1, 1960.

"The New High Tide of Mass Study of Theory," *Hung-ch'i,* June 1, 1960 (translated in JPRS 3814).

"Problems of Fostering Communist Morals in Youth," *Chung-kuo ch'ing-nien pao,* March 17, 1962 (translated in SCMP 2712).

Hu Sheng

(1911–   ; Su-chou, Kiangsu). Deputy-director,
CCP Propaganda Department; deputy editor-in-
chief, *Hung-ch'i* (Red flag).

Hu Sheng is one of the more important propagandists in Communist China. A historian, Hu
has written extensively on the Taiping Rebellion
as well as on the history of Marxism-Leninism
and contemporary political problems. In addition to being a deputy director of the Party's
Propaganda Department he is also a deputy
editor of *Hung-Ch'i* (Red flag), the Party's
leading journal since its creation in 1958.

Hu was born in Su-chou (Soochow), Kiangsu,
not far west of Shanghai. He was trained at
Peking University, presumably in philosophy or
the social sciences. Hu began to write professionally in the mid-thirties and had a number
of essays on history and political science published in Shanghai magazines and newspapers.
After the war began in 1937 he went to Chungking where he continued to write on public
affairs. By this time he was probably already a
member of the CCP. In 1941 he went to Hong
Kong but left the city after it fell to the Japanese
in the wake of the attack on Pearl Harbor.
Returning to Chungking, Hu began to write for
the important Communist newspaper, the *Hsin-
hua jih-pao* (New China daily), and also edited
the paper's cultural column.

After the war Hu returned to Hong Kong
where he continued to write and engage in CCP-
sponsored cultural and literary work in association with such important Party intellectuals as
Ch'iao Kuan-hua (q.v.). In 1946 he published
his first full-length Marxian work, entitled (in
translation) *Systems of Thought and Study*.[1]
Two years later he was one of the Party pro-
moters of a "rectification" campaign conducted
in the city against deviants from then current
Party literary policies. Following the surrender
of Peking to the Communists in January 1949,
he moved to Peking. There he was assigned to
the North China People's Government (NCPG),
the government organ, headed by veteran Party
leader Tung Pi-wu, that administered Communist-held portions of north China until it was
absorbed by the new national government in
October 1949. Under the NCPG Hu served as
a vice-chairman of a committee to "compile
and examine" textbooks, an activity not dissimilar to his previous work in Hong Kong. In
the spring and summer of 1949, Hu was a major
participant in the detailed preparations to establish the central PRC government and various
"people's" and professional organizations. In
May he was elected to the National Committee
of the All-China Federation of Democratic
Youth and two months later he attended a nationwide conference of literary and art workers,
serving as a member of a committee to draft the
constitution and other important documents for
the All-China Federation of Literary and Art
Circles, which was formed at that time. It was
also in July that he became one of two secretaries for the Preparatory Committee of the
China New Philosophy Research Association,
and a few days later he was named as a deputy
secretary-general of the Preparatory Committee
for the All-China Social Science Workers' Conference. One outgrowth of this conference was
the establishment of a liaison office to organize
a number of social science associations, including the above-mentioned New Philosophy Research Association; Hu was made a deputy director of the liaison office. (Later, when the
Chinese Philosophy Association was established
as a permanent organization in March 1951, he
was named to the national council and still
retains the position.)

Hu's concentration on work with the Chinese
intelligentsia even before the inauguration of the
central government was a forerunner of his
work in the ensuing years. Because so many
of the important intellectuals in the early days
of the PRC were non-Communists, the Party
required the services of special cadre to deal
with this class. Thus, in the late forties and early
fifties, Hu directed most of his intellectual and
organizational efforts toward this end. Later,
however, as the regime began to rear its own
generation of intellectuals, his principal activities
were directed more toward the intelligentsia
within the Party.

Hu received his first assignments in the new
central government when it was inaugurated at
the first session of the CPPCC (the organization
that set up the national government in September
1949), meetings that he attended as an alternate
delegate from the Social Science Workers' Conference described above. In the following month
he was named to the Council of the newly established China Association for the Reform of the
Written Language. In December he received two
assignments in the Publications Administration,
which was headed by veteran publisher and
editor Hu Yü-chih (q.v.). The Administration
was directly subordinate to the Government
Administration Council (the cabinet) and had
charge of the publication of books and periodicals on a nationwide basis. Hu served as director
of the Staff Office as well as deputy director of
the Compilation and Examination Bureau, posts
he held until January 1951.

In the meantime, Hu had already begun contributing to *Hsueh-hsi* (Study), the major political and theoretical Party journal from its establishment in September 1949 until it was replaced
by *Hung-ch'i* (Red flag) in 1958. In his article
for the inaugural issue of *Hsueh-hsi,* he wrote
on the relations between the Taipings and the
West. Most of his later contributions, however,
dealt with the Chinese Communist Party and

Marxism-Leninism. Together with Yü Kuang-yuan (q.v.) and Wang Hui-te, he published in *Hsueh-hsi* one of the longest series of articles that has ever appeared in a Chinese Communist publication. Under the general title "Lectures on the Fundamental Knowledge of the Social Sciences," the series ran in 29 issues from October 1950 until March 1952, covering such topics as "class struggle," "the state and revolution," and "strategy and tactics of the Communist Party." Several of these articles dealt with the "five-anti" movement, directed against businessmen and industrialists over the winter of 1951–52. Apparently, however, Hu's superiors felt that his attack on the businessmen had been too strong, because in August 1952 he wrote a self-critical essay for *Hsueh-hsi* stating that the articles had been too dogmatic and one-sided and conceded that private enterprise still had an important role to play in the future. The Party, he argued, must "unite" with the bourgeoisie, but at the same time it had to "struggle" with this class to ward off its "reactionary" aspects.

Hu, in the interim, had become a deputy secretary-general of the Party's Propaganda Department by 1950; he presumably held this post until mid-1958 when he was identified as a deputy director, a post he still retains. Closely related to propaganda work was a position he received in February 1952 when a Study (hsueh-hsi) Committee was formed under the auspices of the CPPCC to encourage the study of Marxism-Leninism and the "thought of Mao Tsetung"; he served on this committee until it was disbanded in 1954. By the spring of 1953, he was affiliated with the Marxist-Leninist Institute in Peking, the CCP's most important school for training Party cadres and ideologues and known in later years as the Higher Party School. In August–September of that year he attended the Communist Fourth World Festival of Youth and Students in Bucharest, his only known trip abroad after 1949.

In the period from 1952 to 1954 Hu became an editorial board member of three important Party publications. He was identified in August 1952 in this capacity on the *Hsueh-hsi* board (although he may have been a member before this date), and then in 1953 and 1954 he joined the boards of *Li-shih yen-chiu* (Historical research) and *Hsin chien-she* (New construction), respectively. He presumably continues to hold the latter two posts. All these posts were, of course, closely related to his work in the Propaganda Department, the organization that directs the editorial policies of Chinese Communist publications.

Hu was elected as a deputy from Shantung to the First and Second NPC's (1954–1964), but was changed to the Shanghai constituency for the Third NPC, which opened in December 1964. Over the winter of 1954–55, he was deeply

involved in an important CCP campaign to discredit Hu Shih, one of the most important intellectuals of twentieth-century China. He participated in a number of forums that systematically criticized Hu Shih's personal life and his political and social thought. At this same time (December 1954), a decision was taken to establish a Research Institute of Philosophy under the Academy of Sciences; to effect this, a preparatory committee was set up, a committee that included Party theoreticians-propagandists Ai Szu-ch'i and Yang Hsien-chen (qq.v.) as well as Hu. In the initial discussions of the work of the Institute, which was established in 1955, it was decided that it would include divisions to study dialectical materialism, historical materialism, logic, and the history of Chinese philosophy. Also under the Academy, Hu was named to the Standing Committee of the Department of Philosophy and Social Sciences, which was formed in May–June 1955, and when the Academy set up a committee in October 1955 to award prizes for scholarly work he was named as a member. In 1956 Hu was appointed to two special committees dealing with the Chinese language, the first (February) was formed to popularize standard spoken Chinese (*p'u-t'ung-hua*) and the second (October) was established to work on a plan to phoneticize Chinese. From May 1957 to November 1958 he also served as a member of the State Council's Scientific Planning Commission, headed by science administrator Nieh Jung-chen, but Hu relinquished this position when the Commission was merged with another organization.

As already described, Hu had served in the Youth Federation from 1949 until 1953. Although he did not participate in the Second National Committee (1953–1958), he was elected as a vice-chairman of the All-China Youth Federation at its third congress in April 1958; but when the Fourth Committee was organized (April 1962) he was once again dropped. It was also in 1958 (July) that he was named to the Standing Committee of the China Peace Committee, a position he continues to hold. Already a deputy director of the Party's Propaganda Department (by June 1958), Hu was identified in September of that year as a deputy director of the Department's Political Research Office, a position he may still retain.

In June 1958 the Party began to publish *Hung-ch'i,* a journal under the direct supervision of the Party Central Committee and edited by one of the top Party theoreticians and propagandists, alternate Politburo member Ch'en Po-ta (q.v.). As already noted, *Hung-ch'i* replaced *Hsueh-hsi* (which suspended publication later in 1958) as the Party's most important journal. *Hung-ch'i* and the daily *JMJP,* also an organ of the Central Committee, are the two most authoritative publications in Communist China. Hu immediately began to contribute articles to *Hung-*

ch'i and was probably an editorial board member from its inception; in any case, by early 1961 he was specifically identified as a deputy editor-in-chief. In addition to his extensive writings for Party journals, Hu has often been reported in the Communist press as a lecturer at various institutes of higher learning. For example, in 1957 he lectured on history at Peking University and in 1958 he lectured on philosophy at the so-called Institute of Journalism for Training Red and Expert Personnel. Hu is probably most famous for a book entitled *Ti-kuo-chu-i yü Chung-kuo cheng-chih,* which was published in 1948 and translated into English in 1955 under the title *Imperialism and Chinese Politics.* The work deals with China's reactions to the Western powers during the period from 1840 to 1924. (The sources employed by Hu in this study suggest a working knowledge of the English language.) He was also a chief editor of a history of the Taipings published under the auspices of the China New History Research Society in 1952. Hu's work on the Taipings is part of a rather major historical effort in Communist historiography, one which views the rebellion "as a direct ancestor of the Chinese Communist revolutionary movement."[2] Under the Communists the Taiping Rebellion is interpreted "not only as a peasant revolution against the feudal Manchu regime, but also as a struggle of the people against the foreign aggressors who assisted the Manchu ruling class in suppressing the revolutionary movement."[3]

Although Hu Sheng does not frequently appear in public, the nature of his work must bring him into rather close contact with many of the Party's top figures. His earlier work for the Party put him in association with such veteran Party leaders as Ch'iao Kuan-hua, Tung Pi-wu, and Nieh Jung-chen. Presently, his assignments in the Propaganda Department and with *Hung-ch'i* place him directly under two alternate Politburo members, Lu Ting-i (the Propaganda Department director) and Ch'en Po-ta (the *Hung-ch'i* editor).

1. Hu Sheng, *Szu-hsiang fang-fa ho tu-shu fang-fa* (Systems of thought and study; Shanghai, 1946).
2. Albert Feuerwerker and S. Cheng, *Chinese Communist Studies of Modern Chinese History* (Cambridge, Mass., 1961), p. 77.
3. *Ibid.*

Hu Yao-pang

(c.1913–   ; Hunan). First secretary, Communist Youth League; member, CCP Central Committee.

One of the younger members of the Party Central Committee, Hu Yao-pang has had a long association with the Communist Youth League (or Corps) and is today the most important youth leader in China. He was born in Hunan province, but nothing is known of his early life. Hu was said to have been connected with the Communist Youth League's "Central Bureau" by 1933, presumably in the central Soviet area in Kiangsi. In 1935, at the end of the Long March (in which he probably participated), he was head of the League's Organization Department, and in mid-1936, when Edgar Snow interviewed youth leader Feng Wen-pin (q.v.), the latter listed Hu as among the 15 members of the League's Central Committee.[1] He reportedly attended the Anti-Japanese Military and Political Academy (K'ang-ta) in north Shensi, but by the early stages of the Sino-Japanese War there is little evidence to suggest that he was still active in youth affairs. He did, however, return to youth work on a full-time basis many years later (see below). Hu was a political officer during the war years and by the latter stages of the civil war against the Nationalists in the late forties, he was head of a political department at the regimental level in Liu Po-ch'eng's Second Field Army. Most of Liu's forces in early 1949 were poised north of the Yangtze River in central China and were to push into southwest China before the year ended. However, some of Liu's units remained in Shansi, and in late April 1949 they succeeded in capturing Taiyuan, the Shansi capital, under the command of Hsu Hsiang-ch'ien (q.v.). To manage the civil and military affairs of the city, the Communists immediately established the Taiyuan Military Control Commission under Hsu's direction. Lo Jui-ch'ing, Lai Jo-yü (qq.v.), and Hu were named as the three vice-chairmen of the Commission.

Just as Taiyuan was being captured by the PLA forces (April 1949), the New Democratic Youth League was holding its first Congress in Peking. Although Hu was later to become the head of the League, at this time he was only elected to Central Committee membership (presumably *in absentia*). He was also named to be one of the League's representatives at the inaugural session of the CPPCC, which established the new central government in the early fall of 1949. Immediately after the PRC was founded, the Sino-Soviet Friendship Association was formed (October); Hu was named to the Executive Board of the Association and retained this position until 1954.

After the new government was established, Hu rejoined Liu Po-ch'eng's Second Field Army as head of the Political Department of the 18th Corps, a unit led by Li Ching-ch'üan and Chou Shih-ti (qq.v.). Hu was thus a participant in the conquest of Szechwan in the closing days of 1949. From 1949 to 1952, Szechwan was unique among the Chinese provinces in that it was divided into four geographic sub-districts (north, east, south, and west Szechwan). The governmental organ for north Szechwan where Hu was stationed was known as the North Szechwan People's Administrative Office (NSPAO), with its capital at Nan-ch'ung, a city on the Chia-ling River, a Yangtze tributary. Hu was named in February 1950 as the director of the NSPAO and concurrently (in June 1950) as the head of the Office's Finance and Economics Committee. In early 1950 he also became political commissar of the North Szechwan Military District and, although specific information is lacking, it is probable that Hu also headed the Party organization in north Szechwan. In brief, Hu was the dominant figure in the area until the four sectors were merged to form Szechwan province in August 1952. He was also a participant in the regional government apparatus for southwest China, the Southwest Military and Administrative Committee (SWMAC), which was established in July 1950. He was a member of the SWMAC (chaired by Liu Po-ch'eng) and retained this post until his transfer to Peking in 1952.

The dissolution of the North Szechwan administration coincided by chance with the third plenum of the New Democratic Youth League, held in Peking in August and early September 1952. By then League Secretary Feng Wen-pin (q.v.) had run into political troubles, and to replace him Hu was transferred to Peking to assume Feng's role as head of the League. He was re-elected as NDYL secretary at the Second Congress in mid-1953 and again at the Third Congress in May 1957 when the senior secretarial post was redesignated "first secretary" and the NDYL itself was renamed the Communist Youth League (CLY). He was once more named as first secretary immediately following the Ninth Congress in June 1964. (The Ninth Congress was actually the fourth held since 1949, but the new numbering system was adopted to take cognizance of the first five congresses held by the League's predecessors in the period from 1922 to 1935). Hu's dominance over League affairs is probably unrivaled in any other important organization in China. For example, since assuming the secretaryship of the League, Hu has delivered the keynote address at each of the congresses, and he is usually the main figure at the plenums of the League's Central Committee or at specialized meetings held under League sponsorship. Hu's predominance in the League derives in part from his importance in the CCP hierarchy. Prior to the 1957 Youth Congress, a number of top Party leaders (e.g., Liao Ch'eng-chih) held important posts within the League, but since then Hu has been the only person in the League who is concurrently a member of the Party Central Committee.

In addition to his role in the Youth League, Hu also served from 1953 to 1958 as a member of the National Committee of the All-China Federation of Democratic Youth, the second most important youth organization (after the Youth League). His ties with these two youth groups took him abroad twice, in both cases as the leader of the delegation. In July–August 1953 he was in Bucharest for the Third World Youth Congress organized by the Communist-sponsored World Federation of Democratic Youth (WFDY); at the close of the Congress he was elected as a vice-chairman of the WFDY, a post he retained until 1959. When the Chinese served as host for a WFDY meeting in August 1954 in Peking (the first in Asia), Hu headed the Chinese delegation to the meetings. His other trip abroad in connection with youth affairs was in July–August 1957 for the Sixth World Youth Festival, held in Moscow under the sponsorship of the WFDY. The delegation consisted of over 1,200 members—probably the largest single delegation ever sent abroad by the Chinese. Immediately after the festival, Hu led a portion of his delegation to Kiev where he attended the Fourth World Youth Congress.

Although Youth League work has occupied much of Hu's time since his transfer to Peking in 1952, he has also been deeply involved in a variety of other activities in the CCP, the central government, and the "people's" organizations. Apart from his League posts, Hu received his first national position in January 1953 when he was named to a committee to implement the Marriage Law (originally passed in 1950). In the following month he became a member of the Central Election Committee, established as one of the first steps leading to the formation of the constitutional government in 1954. And when the elections were held in 1954, he was named as a deputy from Shantung to the First NPC (1954–1959). He was re-elected from Shantung for the Second NPC (1959–1964) but was changed to the Szechwan constituency for the Third NPC, which opened in December 1964. For all three Congresses he has also been a member of the NPC Standing Committee, the governing body between the annual congressional sessions. On occasions, as at the initial session of the Second NPC (April 1959), Hu has delivered reports concerning youth affairs.

Aside from his continuing youth work, Hu was given the following three additional assignments in the mid-fifties: member, Executive Committee, All-China Federation of Trade Unions (May 1953–December 1957); member, Central Work Committee for the Popularization of Standard Spoken Chinese (February 1956–?); vice-chairman, National Association for the Elimination of Illiteracy (March 1956–?). Far more important, however, was his advance in the CCP hierarchy at the Eighth Party Congress in September 1956. He was a member of the Congress presidium (steering committee) and also presented a lengthy report on youth affairs in which he claimed that the Youth League had a membership of 20 million, or "about 11 per cent of all youths" in China. At the close of the Congress he was elected to the Party Central Committee; then about 43 years old, Hu was one of the youngest elected. In another speech in May 1957, he revealed a rapid growth in the Youth League, claiming that membership has risen to 23 million (a gain of three million in eight months).

Since assuming the leadership of the Youth League in 1952, Hu's activities have been constantly reported in the national press, including the *Chung-kuo ch'ing-nien pao* (China youth newspaper), the organ of the League. He himself has been a regular contributor to the press, writing always on youth affairs. For example, to mark the 10th anniversary of the PRC, Hu wrote an article that appeared in the *JMJP* of October 1, 1959. Hu has also lent his name to numerous *ad hoc* bodies formed to celebrate major events in Chinese or Communist history. For example, he was a member of the presidium for a meeting held in September 1959 to celebrate the 10th anniversary of the PRC, and he served in a similar capacity in September 1961 in connection with commemorative ceremonies honoring the 80th birthday of Lu Hsun, China's foremost modern writer. He also made another trip abroad in September–October 1962 when he led a "friendship" delegation to Albania where he was received by the top Albanian leaders. In a move suggestive of Hu's increasing importance, he was scheduled to accompany Politburo member P'eng Chen (q.v.) to attend the Ninth Congress of the Japanese Communist Party in November 1964. However, because the Japanese Government refused to allow the group to enter Japan, the visit was cancelled.

Hu received still another position at the national level in December 1964 when he was named as a CCP representative to the Fourth National Committee of the quasi-legislative CPPCC. Soon after, however, the illness of Shensi First Party Secretary Chang Te-sheng (q.v.) brought about Hu's transfer for a brief time from Peking to the northwest. By February 1965 Hu was identified as the acting first secretary in Shensi as well as the third secretary of the important Northwest Party Bureau headed by Liu Lan-t'ao. Following the death of Chang Te-sheng on March 4, 1965, Hu remained in Shensi for a few more months, but by the end of 1965 Huo Shih-lien was named to the Shensi first secretary position and Hu returned to youth work in Peking (presumably also relinquishing his position in the Northwest Bureau).

Hu's role as the top youth leader in China is all the more noteworthy in view of the Youth League's intimate ties into the CCP structure. The League is specifically mentioned in the CCP constitution, being described as the "assistant of the Party," and it is also now the main source

from which the CCP recruits its members. With its estimated 30-odd million members (mid-sixties), the League is charged with the following task under article 56 of the CCP Constitution: "In all spheres of socialist construction Communist Youth League organizations should play an active role in publicizing and carrying out Party policy and decisions."

1. Edgar Snow, *Random Notes on Red China, 1936–1945* (Cambridge, Mass., 1957), p. 52.

Hu Yü-chih

(1896–   ; Shang-yü, Chekiang). Journalist; former director, Publications Administration; vice-chairman, China Democratic League.

Hu Yü-chih was a leading Shanghai journalist in the twenties and thirties. He spent most of the war and postwar years in Hong Kong and Southeast Asia, returning to mainland China just before the Communists came to power in 1949. For the first five years of the PRC he directed the national government's Publications Administration, but since then he has devoted most of his time to foreign affairs. One of the key members of the China Democratic League since the mid-1940's, he has been a vice-chairman of this political party since 1958.

Hu was born in August 1896 in Shang-yü, Chekiang, but he was reared in the nearby intellectual center at Shao-hsing. He received a classical Chinese education and then studied at the Shao-hsing Middle School when Lu Hsun taught there. He attended a foreign-language school in Hangchow, where he presumably developed his abiding interest in foreign languages, including Esperanto. After graduation he went to Shanghai and began his career in journalism. Hu worked as an editor in the famous Commercial Press and then in 1921 he became editor-in-chief of one of China's best-known and respected journals, *Tung-fang tsa-chih* (Eastern miscellany).[1] He continued as an editor and writer on political affairs throughout the 1920's and also translated a large number of literary works by European writers.[2] In 1930–31 he visted the United States and the Soviet Union as a spokesman for the Esperanto movement. One of his many books, *Mo-szu-k'o yin-hsiang-chi* (Impressions of Moscow), was published in 1931 after this trip. Hu is also said to have studied international law at the University of Paris, possibly during this trip.

Like many of Shanghai's intellectuals in the thirties, Hu was drawn into left-wing circles that were discontented with government policies they regarded as ineffectual in curbing the steady Japanese encroachments on Chinese sovereignty. He became associated with Tsou T'ao-fen, one of modern China's most famous journalists. In addition to working with Tsou in the National Salvation Association (see under Shih Liang),

Hu was associated with him in the mid-thirties in editing the left-wing *Sheng-huo chou-k'an* (Life weekly), and from its inauguration in September 1934 he was editor of *Shih-chieh chih-shih* (World knowledge), an influential journal that is still published on the mainland (in spite of many disruptions during the war years). A number of "anti-Japanese" and left-wing causes were espoused on the pages of these publications in the middle thirties.

When war broke out in mid-1937, Hu remained in Shanghai, using the pages of Tsou T'ao-fen's *Ti K'ang* (Resistance) to oppose the Japanese. But in 1938 he went to Wuhan to join the Nationalist Government, working under Kuo Mo-jo in the Third Section of the Political Training Department, which was subordinate to the National Military Council. He soon went to Changsha and then Kweilin where he took part in establishing *Kuo-chi hsin-wen she* (International news agency), an important news organization discussed in the biography of journalist Fan Ch'ang-chiang. He spent the years 1939 and 1940 in Hong Kong where he helped to organize the *Hua-shang pao* (Commercial daily). In 1940 Hu left for Southeast Asia where he was to spend most of the decade. With the support of Singapore millionaire Ch'en Chia-keng (Tan Kah-kee), Hu edited the *Nan-yang shang-pao* (South Seas commercial daily) until February 1942 when the city fell to the Japanese. He fled to Sumatra, spending the next three years moving from place to place to avoid arrest by the Japanese.

Soon after the war ended Hu returned to Singapore where he continued to work for the next two and a half years as an editor and publisher, again with the support of Tan Kah-kee. He was also chairman of the local branch of the China Democratic League from 1946 to 1948. In the spring of 1948 he returned to Hong Kong where for a few months he was an editorial board member of the pro-Communist newsletter *Far Eastern Bulletin*. In the fall he entered Communist-held areas of north China. After Peking was surrendered to the Communists in January 1949, Hu went there, and in June he became editor of the *Kuang-ming jih-pao* (Kwangming daily). This important newspaper was then the organ of the China Democratic League, but in later years it was placed under the joint direction of the eight "democratic" (i.e., non-Communist) political parties of which the League was one. Hu was given his first government post in June when the Communists, under the chairmanship of Mao Tse-tung, established the CPPCC Preparatory Committee. Hu served as a member of this body, and in the following month he received two other posts on preparatory committees of organizations whose tasks were closely connected with his career. The first of these was a vice-chairmanship of the Returned Overseas

Chinese Federation, a post he held until 1956. Second, he became a vice-chairman of the Preparatory Committee for the All-China Journalists' Association, holding this post until the organization was permanently established in 1954. In September 1949, representing the China Democratic League, Hu attended the inaugural meeting of the CPPCC, the organization that brought the new central government into existence on October 1. When the major government assignments were made later in October, Hu became a member of the Culture and Education Committee, one of the four major committees under Chou En-lai's Government Administration Council (the cabinet). His most important assignment, however, was as director of the Publications Administration, which was subordinate to the Culture and Education Committee.

Like most persons who held top posts in the government hierarchy, Hu also received other positions in the numerous "mass" and professional organizations established in the late months of 1949. He was made a member of the China Peace Committee's National Committee (to date), an Executive Board member of the Sino-Soviet Friendship Association (to date), and a member of the Standing Council of the Association for Reforming the Chinese Written Language (to 1954). In December 1949 he became a vice-chairman of the Chinese People's Institute of Foreign Affairs, a position he still holds (see under Chang Hsi-jo). In the same month the China Democratic League held its first major meeting after the conquest of the mainland by the Communists. Since that time Hu has been a member of the League's Standing Committee, and in the early fifties he held top posts in its Organization and Overseas Chinese Affairs Departments. He was the League's secretary-general from 1953 to 1958, and he has again held this post since December 1963. In addition, he has been a vice-chairman since December 1958.

During the PRC's first five years, Hu devoted most of his time to the Publications Administration, an organization that was clearly given high priority as the Communists attempted to organize the publishing industry to disseminate their educational, cultural, and propaganda materials. His reports before the First and Second National Publishing Conferences (September 1950 and October 1952) provide useful research materials for those periods. These materials were published by the Foreign Language Press in 1952 in a pamphlet entitled *Culture, Education and Health in New China,* the essence of which was also published in an article by Hu for *People's China* (no. 24, December 16, 1952). In 1951–1954 he received four new posts, all of which he still holds. He was made president of the China Esperanto Association when it was formed in March 1951, and in May 1952 he became a Standing

Committee member of the newly established China-India Friendship Association. Third, he was made a member of the Board of Directors of the China News Service (Chung-kuo hsin-wen-she). This news organization, not to be confused with the better known New China News Agency, was established on October 1, 1952, and is concerned mainly with news relating to overseas Chinese. Finally, he has been a Standing Committee member of the Chinese People's Association for Cultural Relations with Foreign Countries since its formation in May 1954.

When the First NPC met in September 1954 to inaugurate the constitutional government, Hu attended as a deputy from Shanghai. He represented Liaoning in the Second NPC (1959–1964) and also in the Third Congress, which opened in December 1964. Subordinate to the NPC, he has been a member of its Standing Committee since 1954 and one of the several deputy secretaries-general since 1959. Between 1954 and 1956 he received three posts in a field that has been one of his major concerns since his youth—language reform. In November 1954 he became the only vice-chairman under Chairman Wu Yü-chang of the State Council's Committee for Reforming the Chinese Written Language. And since early 1956 he has been a member of both the Central Work Committee for the Popularization of Standard Spoken Chinese (p'u-t'ung-hua) and the National Association for the Elimination of Illiteracy. Communist efforts in this field are discussed in the biography of Wu Yü-chang. In December 1954 Hu was elected as a China Democratic League delegate to the Second National Committee of the CPPCC, and he was re-elected to the Third and Fourth National Committees, which opened in 1959 and 1964, respectively.

Since the mid-fifties Hu has been fairly active in foreign affairs, and in this connection has made seven trips abroad, which can be briefly summarized: delegation member to a World Peace Council meeting, Stockholm, November–December 1954 (and in the following June he was elected a member of the World Peace Council); leader of a Sino-Soviet Friendship Association delegation to Moscow for May Day celebrations, April–May 1956; delegation member to the Conference on Disarmament and International Cooperation, Stockholm, July 1958; delegation member for an extraordinary session of the World Peace Council to celebrate the 10th anniversary of the "world peace movement," Stockholm, May 1959; NPC delegation member to Indonesia and Burma, August–September 1961; leader of a friendship delegation to Nepal, February 1964; and, leader of a cultural delegation to Rumania, June–July 1964. Hu also received the following posts in organizations dealing primarily in international affairs: vice-chairman, China-Indonesia Friendship Association,

May 1955; vice-chairman, China-Latin America Friendship Association, March 1960; and vice-president, Asia-Africa Society of China, April 1962. Because of his numerous positions in the field of foreign relations, Hu has spent considerable time since the mid-fifties serving as a host in Peking for foreign visitors, particularly visitors from underdeveloped nations in Asia. Within the central government, Hu has also been a vice-minister of Culture since September 1959, but there are few indications that he has devoted much time to this assignment, particularly in view of his various activities in foreign affairs.

As one of the earliest members and a senior official in the China Democratic League, Hu is presented to the Chinese public as a non-Communist intellectual who chose to work with the Communists. However, though no information is available to indicate that he has been concurrently a Party member, the outline of his career suggests that he may have been a covert member for many years—possibly as far back as the 1920's. His wife, journalist Shen Tzu-chiu, has been a CCP member since the mid-twenties. She and Hu were married in Singapore in 1941. A native of Hangchow, Chekiang, and trained in Japan, Shen has paralleled her husband's career in many ways. She too, for example, has served in the Sino-Soviet Friendship Association, the China Peace Committee, and the government's Culture and Education Committee. Shen has been a member of the National Women's Federation since 1949 and a deputy from Chekiang since 1954. Since the establishment of the PRC she has visited Korea (1952), Bulgaria (1958), the Soviet Union (1960), and Indonesia and Burma (with her husband in 1961).

1. Chow Tse-tsung, *Research Guide to the May Fourth Movement* (Cambridge, Mass., 1963), p. 124.
2. Chang Ching-lu, ed., *Chung-kuo hsien-tai ch'u-pan shih-liao* (Historical materials on contemporary Chinese publishing; Peking, 1954), *passim*.

Huang Chen

(1908–   ; T'ung-ch'eng hsien, Anhwei). Ambassador to France.

Huang Chen is one of Pekings most experienced diplomats. From early in the history of the PRC he has been in the Ministry of Foreign Affairs, serving as ambassador to Hungary, to Indonesia, and now to France. He was born into a peasant family in T'ung-ch'eng hsien in southwestern Anhwei, an area just east of the Hupeh-Honan-Anhwei (Oyüwan) Soviet in the early thirties. Huang went to school in An-ch'ing (Anking), Anhwei, a Yangtze River port city about 30 miles south of his native T'ung-ch'eng. Afterwards, he graduated from Hsin-hua ("New

China"?) Fine Arts Academy in Shanghai; he is one of the few Chinese Communists to have received training of this sort.

Huang became a Party member at the age of 23 (1931), and was a political commissar at the divisional level during the Kiangsi period from 1931 to 1934 when the Communist soviet capital was at Juichin in southeast Kiangsi. He fought with the army of Mao Tse-tung and Chu Te at this time. He is known to have participated in the fifth and last of the Annihilation Campaigns waged against the Communists in central China by the Nationalists. During the fifth campaign, which opened in October 1933, Huang commanded his own force, the 13th Regiment, which belonged to the Third Army Corps commanded by P'eng Te-huai and T'eng Tai-yuan (qq.v.).[1] During the Long March (1934–35) Huang served as a propaganda worker with the Fifth Red Army Corps, a unit of the First Front Army led by Chu Te and Mao Tse-tung.[2] While on the Long March, Huang wrote two plays that were staged for the soldiers during a rest period just after the Red armies had made the difficult crossing of the Upper Yangtze in the spring of 1935. This dramatic crossing of the Chin-sha (Golden Sand) River, which forms the boundary between Yunnan and Szechwan Provinces is now described as one of the milestones of the Long March. When Mao's forces reached Shensi at the end of the March, Huang served as a member of a small liaison group that made contact with the 15th Army Corps, which had already been operating in the province for several years before the Long Marchers arrived. Through the efforts of this small group, the two armies met and merged in late October 1935 (see under Hsu Hai-tung).

In Sino-Japanese War times Huang was attached to Liu Po-ch'eng's 129th Division, one of the three divisions that made up the Communist Eighth Route Army of north China. In 1938 he was among those studying conditions for beginning political work in the areas of south and central Hopeh, into which the 129th Division expanded during the course of the year.[3] Huang worked with Liu's division during the war and immediate postwar years and apparently spent the war period in the important border region territory controlled by the 129th Division, for by 1944 he had risen to the rank of deputy director of the Party Political Department for the Military Region of the Shansi-Hopeh-Shantung-Honan (Chin-Chi-Lu-Yü) Border Region Government (see under Liu Po-ch'eng). In 1945 he was a deputy director of the Political Department at the T'ai-hang Military Region base, the mountain base in southern Shansi, which belonged to the original T'ai-hang—T'ai-yueh Military Base of the 129th Division.

After the end of the Sino-Japanese War he served on the Communist delegation to the Peking Executive Headquarters created by the Cease-fire Agreement signed in January 1946 to implement the terms of the agreement. Holding the simulated rank of major-general, he was also a member of the Headquarters field team, which operated in the Hsin-hsiang area in Honan north of the Yellow River. He was taken prisoner there by the Nationalists at one point when the attempts for negotiation in his Hsin-hsiang area had broken down.[4] Then in 1947, with the resumption of civil war between the two parties, Huang went back to the Red Army and became political commissar of the Ninth Column of the PLA force stationed in the Chin-Chi-Lu-Yü area that he knew so well. The Ninth Column belonged to the military force commanded by Ch'en Keng (q.v.), an important contingent of Liu Po-ch'eng's army known as the Central Plains PLA. This army expanded into central China after 1947 and then moved on into the Southwest but Huang's connection with it seems to have ended about 1947.

When the central government was formed in the fall of 1949, Huang was working in the General Political Department of the People's Revolutionary Military Council, then the highest military organ of the PRC. It was to represent the Political Department that Huang was named as a member of the preparatory committee of the All-China Athletic Federation when it was formed in October 1949. However, he was reassigned to the Foreign Ministry in 1950 and in June of that year was named as Peking's first ambassador to Hungary; he presented his credentials in Budapest on August 24, 1950. Huang's tour of duty in Budapest was largely uneventful. Most of the Sino-Hungarian negotiations during his tenure as ambassador (1950–1954) took place in Peking—of the 12 agreements signed during this period, all but two were negotiated and signed in Peking. Most of the public appearances Huang made in Hungary were of a protocol nature—for example, attending exhibitions put on by the embassy in Budapest to illustrate the achievements of "new China." After negotiating and signing a trade agreement in April 1954, he returned to China. He was officially removed as ambassador in September 1954, being replaced by Hao Te-ch'ing.

Just a few days after his official removal as ambassador to Hungary, Huang was named as Peking's ambassador to Indonesia. He presented his credentials to President Sukarno on November 29, 1954, and remained in this post six and a half years, far longer than the average tour of duty for a Chinese Communist ambassador. His stay in Jakarta was marked by both high and low points. The most flourishing period, from Huang's viewpoint, occurred in April 1955 when he was a member of Chou En-lai's delegation to the famous Afro-Asian ("Bandung") Conference, meetings from which the Chinese emerged with a very positive image throughout much of

Asia. Riding the crest of the goodwill established at Bandung, the Chinese immediately invited Indonesian Prime Minister Ali Sastroamidjojo to China. Huang accompanied the prime minister to China and took part in the elaborate festivities arranged in his honor, including the formation (on June 1, 1955) of the Sino-Indonesian Friendship Association. On at least four other occasions Huang returned to China, two of them visits of consequence. In August 1956 he went back to Peking to prepare for the visit to China of President Sukarno (September–October 1956) and was frequently reported in the press during the time of Sukarno's visit. Huang's second important home visit took place in June 1958 when, together with several other PRC ambassadors, he returned briefly to Peking at the time of the Middle Eastern crisis in 1958 (when U.S. and British military forces were sent to Lebanon and Jordan).

The most difficult aspect of Huang's ambassadorship in Jakarta centered around the problem of overseas Chinese in Indonesia, a minority group of approximately three million people. The first serious negotiations to solve the problems of the overseas Chinese (mainly questions concerning citizenship) took place in Peking in late 1954 when Vice-minister of Foreign Affairs Chang Han-fu (q.v.) conducted preliminary talks with Indonesian officials for almost two months. These talks were formalized and shifted to Jakarta in March 1955, with Huang named as head of the Chinese side. Huang held talks for three weeks, and then on April 22 Chou En-lai (then in Bandung for the Afro-Asian Conference) signed the Dual Nationality Treaty. However, many years dragged on before the treaty was to come into effect, and it was not ratified by the two governments until the latter half of 1957. Two more years moved by, but still no action was taken to implement the treaty. Then, in the fall of 1959, the Indonesians promulgated a series of decrees that had the effect of banning most overseas Chinese in Indonesia from certain small and retail trade activities and forcing many Chinese to evacuate certain areas of Indonesia. As a consequence, serious "anti-Chinese" riots broke out, resulting in the death of some Chinese and large-scale destruction of their property. On several occasions in November 1959 Huang protested Indonesian actions. Apparently in an endeavor by both sides to calm the tense situation (which still continued through the first half of 1960), the Indonesians and Chinese exchanged the instruments of ratification in Peking in January 1960, and at the same time agreed to establish the Joint Committee for Implementing the Dual Nationality Treaty. With Huang as the head of the Chinese side, the negotiations were conducted throughout most of 1960, culminating on December 15, 1960, in Jakarta when he signed documents to arrange for the implementation of the treaty.

Though the outcome of the dual nationality question was fairly successful from Peking's viewpoint, Huang had also been faced with a related problem, namely the closure of Chinese schools in Indonesia. In April 1959 the Indonesian minister of Education announced that some 1,500 "foreign schools" (the majority of them Chinese) had been closed. Even though this left about 500 schools (mostly Chinese) still open, Huang lodged an unsuccessful protest. In rejecting the protest, the Indonesians wryly commented that the PRC would take a jaundiced view of so many "foreign schools" in China. There the matter rested.

On April 22, 1961, Huang Chen was named as a vice-minister of Foreign Affairs. Two weeks later he left Jakarta for Peking and was officially removed as ambassador to Indonesia on June 4, being replaced by Yao Chung-ming (q.v.) shortly thereafter. For the three years that Huang was a vice-minister he devoted most of his time to relations with the Afro-Asian world. His work in the Foreign Ministry was highlighted by four trips abroad. The first was a whirlwind tour of Burma, Indonesia, Ceylon, the U.A.R., Ghana, and Guinea in November–December 1962 to explain to premiers and heads of state in these nations the Chinese version of the Sino-Indian conflict, which had broken into open warfare. In the following April–May he accompanied Liu Shao-ch'i and Ch'en I on a quick friendship tour of Indonesia, Burma, Cambodia, and North Vietnam. More important, he accompanied Chou En-lai on his much publicized visit to 10 nations in Africa (the U.A.R., Algeria, Morocco, Tunisia, Ghana, Mali, Guinea, the Sudan, Ethiopia, and Somali), plus a quick side trip to Albania. After returning to south China for a brief respite, the same group (Huang included) made brief visits to Burma, Pakistan, and Ceylon. Finally, in April 1964 he accompanied Foreign Minister Ch'en I to Jakarta to attend preparatory meetings for the Second Afro-Asian Conference—the conference that ultimately collapsed in late 1965 owing to the combination of the overthrow of the president of Algeria (where the meetings were to have been held) and the continuing squabbles between Moscow and Peking as each side sought to influence the tone of the conference.

In April 1964 Huang was removed as a vice-minister and named as Peking's first ambassador to France, formal diplomatic relations having been agreed upon in January of that year. He presented his credentials to President de Gaulle on June 6, 1964. The embassy that Huang presides over is one of the most active of the Chinese diplomatic missions and also one of the largest. In addition to a staff estimated at 100, the mission is undoubtedly responsible for the guidance of approximately 100 young Chinese students who were sent to Paris in late 1964. He is assisted in his work by two highly experienced assistants: Cultural Counselor Szu-ma Wen-sen (who was with Huang in Indonesia) and Ch'en Ming, one of Peking's most talented trade negotiators and a man quite familiar to many Westerners because of the fact that he was one of the leading negotiators for the huge grain purchases made by China in the early 1960's from Australia and Canada.

Persons who have observed Huang in Paris claim that he has a relaxed and affable manner. In contrast to the rest of his staff (who appear in public in Western-style business suits), Huang usually wears the Lenin-style uniform. He does not know French (although he is reported to know German). However, his wife, Chu Lin, knows French and is quite active in making contacts with various French groups as well as the modest overseas Chinese community in France. According to Western news reports,[5] Huang was engaged in intensive negotiations in March 1965 with the largest manufacturer of heavy trucks in France. These took place in Lyons, where he also attended the Lyons International Fair in which the Chinese had a large exhibition.

As a general rule, the Chinese Communists do not name persons posted abroad to the NPC. However, an exception was made in Huang's case; in the fall of 1964, he was elected as a deputy from his native Anhwei to the Third NPC, which opened in December 1964.

As already noted, Huang studied at a fine arts academy in Shanghai. During the Long March he made sketches of the military action and the daily life of the troops, which were later published in a collection.[6] He is said to maintain an active interest in the arts. Huang's niece is Miss Huang Sung-k'ang, who is the author of a work on Lu Hsun, modern China's most famous writer, published in Amsterdam in 1957 under the title *Lu Hsun and the New Culture Movement of Modern China.*

1. *Hung-ch'i p'iao-p'iao* (Red flag fluttering; Peking, 1957), III, 97.
2. *JMJP,* July 1, 1962.
3. *SCMP* 2723, p. 9.
4. *Chung-kuo ch'ing-nien pao* (China youth newspaper), January 10, 1963.
5. *New York Times,* March 22, 1965.
6. *JMJP,* July 1, 1962.

Huang Ching

(1911–1958; Shao-hsing, Chekiang). Party worker with the 1935–36 student movement; government administrator; member, CCP Central Committee.

Huang Ching, a key figure in the CCP manipulation of the student movement in north China during the mid-1930's, held important posts in north China "liberated areas" during the war. After the Communists came to power in 1949 he was the top official in Tientsin, and then an important administrator in Peking. Huang was elected to the Party Central Committee in 1956, only a year and a half before his death.

Huang came from Shao-hsing, an important intellectual center in Chekiang. His real name was Yü Ch'i-wei, and he was also known as David Yui and David Huang. He is known in CCP histories as Huang Ching, a name he seems to have adopted about the time of the Sino-Japanese War. Huang had a number of prominent relatives. One uncle, Yü Ta-wei, held cabinet posts in the Nationalist government, and another uncle was an adviser to the Japanese-sponsored Hopeh-Chahar Political Council in the mid-1930's. Huang studied physics at Shantung University in Tsingtao, where he was enrolled when the Japanese marched into Manchuria in September 1931. Student demonstrations were immediately held throughout the nation to protest this event. Huang took part in demonstrations in Tsingtao, as well as Nanking, the national capital, where many students went from all over China to protest directly to the KMT government. In 1932, when Huang was back in Tsingtao, he joined the CCP and was made a member of the Party's committee there. At approximately this time, his activities as an agitator brought him to the attention of the authorities. He was arrested and imprisoned, but then he was put on probation through the influence of his prominent family. Afterwards, Huang went to Shanghai to join his sister (some say cousin), Yü Shan. She was then making a name for herself in dramatics and introduced Huang to some of her politically minded theatrical friends who were interested in modern drama. He worked with them in Shanghai for a time, but by 1933 he was back in Tsingtao where he was placed in charge of the Party Committee's Propaganda Department.

There are numerous rumors that while Huang was in Tsingtao he had an affair with an aspiring young actress whom he had met through Yü Shan. (Some sources assert that they were married for a short time.) This would be of passing importance, except for the fact that the young actress, known by the stage name of Lan P'ing, later went to Yenan where, using the name Chiang Ch'ing, she became the wife of Mao Tse-tung.

In the period from 1933 to 1935 Huang worked in the Party underground in Tsingtao, Tientsin, and Peking. His special responsibility seems to have been liaison work with students, a group particularly sensitive to the steady incursions by the Japanese upon Chinese sovereignty in north China. By the fall of 1935 Huang was permanently assigned to Peking where he took part in the activities of the Peking Students' Federation, which was formed in secret in late October.[1] Working with Huang at this time were

Yao I-lin, a Tsinghua University student and secretary of the Students' Federation, and P'eng T'ao (qq.v.), a student at Fu Jen (Catholic) University. Both later became alternate members of the CCP Central Committee. The Students' Federation, with its Party backers, played an important part in the student protests that first erupted on December 9, 1935; these were provoked in part by the prospect of the Japanese-sponsored Hopeh-Chahar Political Council, the Chinese puppet government for north China which was scheduled to be inaugurated on December 16. As the movement spread to student groups in other cities it came to be known as the December Ninth Movement, and the groups of students it aroused later provided a core of younger leaders for the ranks of the CCP.

At this time, Huang was nominally a student at Peking University.[2] However, it is reasonably clear from his intensive political activities over the next year and a half that his student status was principally a convenient means of maintaining contacts with Peking's important student groups. One such group was formally organized in February 1936 into the National Liberation Vanguards of China (NLVC, described in greater detail in the biography of Li Ch'ang). Most of the original NLVC members were not then Communists, but through intensive efforts on the part of the CCP (in which Huang apparently played a leading role), many of them had joined the Youth League or the Party by mid-1936. In the meantime, Huang was moving back and forth between Peking and Tientsin in his efforts to stimulate the development of the student movement. When the NLVC underwent a reorganization in August 1936, Huang was sent as a representative of the CCP Peking Committee to the NLVC headquarters; he had been sent, in the words of one of the NLVC leaders, in order "to lead us."[3] During this period, 1936–37, Huang was secretary of the CCP Peking Committee and also director of its Propaganda Department.

By the latter half of 1936 the CCP was rapidly moving toward a united-front policy—designed to rally all sectors of society to take a determined stand against Japan. In the year prior to the outbreak of war in Japan, this policy was supported by Chinese of many political persuasions. The National Salvation Association, for example (see under Shih Liang), received strong support from CCP propaganda organs, and Communist operatives like Huang were called upon to work closely with these groups. It was in this atmosphere that the NLVC met for its first congress in February 1937; if Huang did not actually attend, it can be presumed that he was working behind the scenes. The congress proclaimed, in the words of one authority on the student movement, that the NLVC "was more than a mere promoter of the united front; it was

itself a united-front organization, and would welcome to its ranks all who shared its anti-Japanese national salvation views."[4]

In the spring of 1937, presumably to strengthen relations with student groups in Peking, the Communists invited a number of the NLVC members to visit Yenan, the Communist capital.[5] Huang accompanied the NLVC leaders, including Li Ch'ang, and they arrived in time to take part in May Day celebrations. They heard a talk by Mao Tse-tung on the question of the role of young people in resisting Japan and also attended a CCP conference, at which Huang delivered a report on the student movement.[6] While Huang was in Yenan he saw American writer Nym Wales, whom he had previously known very well in Peking, and he claimed to her that he was the number two Party leader in north China. This may have been a slight exaggeration, but there is little doubt that Huang was one of the more important Party figures in north China where, at one time or another, he probably took his orders directly from such top men as Liu Shao-ch'i and P'eng Chen.

Huang returned to Peking on the eve of war with Japan in mid-1937. When hostilities began, most of the student leaders in north China fled from the cities or went underground. Members of the NLVC and officials from the CCP North China Bureau left Peking immediately. Huang went to Tientsin for a short time and then accompanied a number of his student colleagues to Taiyuan, the Shansi capital, which was still held by the Nationalist-allied general, Yen Hsi-shan. For a brief period rather strong anti-Japanese forces were assembled in Taiyuan, but when it fell to the Japanese in November 1937, they were dispersed. A bit earlier, as the Japanese pushed into the north China cities, the three divisions of the Communists' Eighth Route Army crossed the Yellow River from Shensi to Shansi to engage the enemy. Of these, the 115th Division under Lin Piao and Nieh Jung-chen advanced to the Wu-t'ai mountain area of northeast Shansi, and from his headquarters Nieh dispatched Party agents over the border into the Fou-p'ing area of Hopeh. Huang was one of those sent to Hopeh to build up resistance to the Japanese among the peasants of the countryside and the people of the towns. As a Party representative he attended and was one of the speakers at the conference held at Fou-p'ing in January 1938, which brought the Shansi-Chahar-Hopeh (Chin-Ch'a-Chi) Border Region Government into being. The development of this Communist base is described in the biographies of Sung Shao-wen, chairman of the Chin-Ch'a-Chi government, and of Lü Cheng-ts'ao. Lü was the military head of the central plains area of Hopeh, an integral part of the Chin-Ch'a-Chi Border Region, and the part of the region to which Huang was first sent.

U.S. Naval observer Evans Carlson was also in Fou-p'ing in early 1938 where he saw Huang. He met him again in mid-1938 at Huang's headquarters in An-kuo, not far southeast of Pao-ting. Huang had just been ordered to An-kuo (recently captured by the Communists) by the area military commander, Lü Cheng-ts'ao. When Carlson met Huang at Fou-p'ing he was directing political education at a military academy (perhaps a branch of the Communists' Anti-Japanese Military and Political Academy). Later, Huang was engaged in similar work at An-kuo for the "central Hopeh Government."[7] He remained in north China through most of the war. His obituary reveals that in the period from 1937 to 1944 he was initially secretary of the CCP Chin-Ch'a-Chi Committee, then secretary of the Central Hopeh Committee, and finally, secretary of the Hopeh-Shantung-Honan Committee. To judge from this impressive array of Party posts, Huang probably worked with Liu Shao-ch'i, P'eng Chen, Teng Hsiao-p'ing, and Po I-po (qq.v.), to mention only a few of the key leaders in those areas.

When the Japanese surrendered in the late summer of 1945, there were very few Nationalist troops in north China, and thus the Communists were able to occupy a number of cities. Communist troops moved into Kalgan (Chang-chia-k'ou), the capital of Chahar, a few weeks after the war ended. For a short period, until replaced by Chang Su (q.v.) in November, Huang served as the mayor of Kalgan. But for most of the postwar period his major post was deputy secretary of the Party's Chin-Ch'a-Chi Committee. In this period the Chin-Ch'a-Chi area was a vital corridor through which Communist troops were able to move from north China into Manchuria, and it also served as the base from which the Communist armies were able to disrupt the rail lines leading into Peking from the west and the south.

By mid-1948 the Communists had nearly completed their conquest of north China. Therefore, in August 1948 they created the North China People's Government (NCPG), which continued in existence until October 1949 when its functions were taken over by the newly created central government in Peking. During its brief existence, Huang was a member of the NCPG Council, a vice-chairman of the Finance and Economics Committee, and director of the State-operated Enterprises Department (the organization in charge of industry). His connection with this department was his first in the field of industrial development, to which he was to devote the final years of his career.

When Tientsin fell to the Communists in January 1949, the Municipal Military Control Commission was immediately established under Huang K'o-ch'eng, with T'an Cheng (qq.v.) and Huang Ching as his two deputies. However, both Huang K'o-ch'eng and T'an left the city very shortly afterwards to continue their military campaigns in central-south China. Thus, within a brief period, Huang Ching was the top official in Tientsin. In addition to his post with the Control Commission, Huang was also the ranking Party secretary, mayor of the Tientsin government, and (from March 1950) the head of the government's Finance and Economics Committee. At the regional level, he was a member of the Party's North China Bureau under Po I-po, and when the North China Administrative Committee (NCAC) was established at the end of 1951, Huang was made a member. The NCAC was, in effect, a latter-day version of the North China People's Government, and had jurisdiction over Hopeh, Shansi, Suiyuan, Chahar, and Ping-yuan.

Peking, like Tientsin, was taken by the Communists in January 1949, and over the next several months preparations were under way to establish the national government. This took place in Peking in September 1949 when the inaugural session of the CPPCC was held. Huang attended these meetings as a member of a joint group representing both Peking and Tientsin. He served on the CPPCC presidium (steering committee) and, though not elected to the permanent National Committee, he was a member representing the CCP on the Second National Committee, which was established in late 1954. From 1949 to 1954 Huang was also a member of the Executive Board of the Sino-Soviet Friendship Association. He received this position in October 1949, after which he returned to Tientsin to resume his duties as the senior Party official.

Huang nominally retained his Party and government posts in Tientsin and North China until 1953, but by the late summer of 1952 he had been transferred to Peking to assume a ministerial assignment. In August 1952, sections from the Ministry of Heavy Industry were split off and established as the First and Second Ministries of Machine Building. Huang was named to head the First Ministry. Four years later, in May 1956, he was made chairman of the newly established State Technological Commission. For the two remaining years of his life he held these two ministerial-level posts, an unusual but not completely unprecedented assignment. His stature as a leading government administrator was recognized when the Eighth Party Congress was held in September 1956. Huang served on the Congress presidium, spoke on the development of China's machine building industries, and at the close of the meetings was elected a member of the CCP Central Committee. The following May he received still another important post as a vice-chairman of the national government's Scientific Planning Commission. In this capacity, he presided over an expanded session of the commission in June 1957. Less than a year later, on February 10, 1958, he died in Canton.

Few Westerners knew Huang as well as Nym Wales, whose writings about Huang and others are a key source of information about the student movement in the mid-1930's. She had a high regard for his character and intelligence and was particularly struck by his detailed knowledge of events in north China. She described him as fairly tall and handsome, though a "little unkempt in his long Chinese gown." "Well-bred" and "tolerant," Huang spoke good English (a point also made by Evans Carlson) and had the "quality of leadership."[8] In addition to the relatives mentioned above, he had another uncle who was a grandson of the famous Ch'ing scholar-official, Tseng Kuo-fan. This uncle, Tseng Chao-lun, studied at the Massachusetts Institute of Technology in Cambridge, Massachusetts, and was a professor of chemistry at Peking University, where he befriended a number of the student radicals of the mid-1930's. Tseng remained on the mainland when the Communists came to power in 1949, and in the following years he was prominent in scientific and educational circles. Ironically, however, just at the time Huang was dying, his uncle was severely censured as a "rightist." He was later partially reinstated, but after he had been publicly criticized he was seldom mentioned in the press.

At the time of his death, Hang was married to Fan Chin, a prominent journalist and a member of the CCP. She was a vice-mayor of Peking and head of the *Pei-ching jih-pao* (Peking daily) until the late spring of 1966, when she became one of the earliest victims of the Great Proletarian Cultural Revolution.

---

1. Wang Lin, "In Memory of Comrade Huang Ching," *The Roar of a Nation* (Peking, 1963), pp. 130–145.

2. Nym Wales, *Notes on the Chinese Student Movement* (Madison, Conn., 1959), p. 36 (mimeographed).

3. *SCMM* 297, p. 30.

4. John Israel, *Student Nationalism in China, 1927–1937* (Stanford, Calif., 1966), pp. 176–177.

5. *SCMM* 297, p. 34.

6. Wales, p. 37.

7. Evans Fordyce Carlson, *Twin Stars of China* (New York, 1940), pp. 241, 244.

8. Wales, pp. 36–41.

Huang Hua

(c.1910–   ; Hopeh?). Former student-youth leader; diplomat; ambassador to the United Arab Republic.

One of the most senior members of the Chinese Communist diplomatic service, Huang Hua was a student leader in Peking in the mid-thirties and Edgar Snow's interpreter in the northwest in 1936 when Snow was collecting material for *Red Star over China*. Huang did not adopt his revolutionary alias until the mid-thirties, prior to which he was known by his real name, Wang Ju-mei. He appears to have been born in Hopeh, but Japanese sources claim he is native to Kiangsu, and journalist Nym Wales, who knew Huang quite well, has written that he is from the northeast (*tung-pei*).[1] Trained in a middle school, by 1935 Huang was a student at Yenching University in Peking, which was then under Dr. J. Leighton Stuart, who became American ambassador to China in 1946. As president of Yenching's student council, Huang played a leading role in the events that led to the dramatic December Ninth (1935) student demonstrations in Peking staged in protest against what the students regarded as inadequate national policies to resist the steady Japanese encroachments on Chinese sovereignty and territory.[2] He was jailed for his activities in December[3] but was apparently released after a short period.

During these stormy events (described in the biography of Li Ch'ang) Huang was in close touch with Edgar Snow and his wife, Nym Wales, who were then living in Peking and acquainted with a number of the leaders of the student movement.[4] On March 31, 1936, Huang was among about 50 students arrested for their participation in a demonstration held to commemorate the death of a middle school student who had died in prison.[5] His experiences during his two-week imprisonment have been recorded in detail by Nym Wales,[6] and after his release he took refuge in the Snow's apartment. In the meantime, Huang had become affiliated with the National Liberation Vanguard of China (NLVC), the most important of the several student organizations established in the wake of the December 9, 1935, demonstrations and one which, by the spring of 1936, was rapidly coming under the domination of the CCP. NLVC leader Li Ch'ang has written that after the March 31 arrests, the organization undertook a number of steps to strengthen itself, among them training classes in guerrilla tactics and political studies; Li has credited Huang with having "borrowed" the sitting room of a Yenching professor to conduct a one-day class. Li has also written that after the 1936 summer vacation Huang and another student were the first to go to the "Soviet zone."[7] What he failed to record was the fact that Huang's departure for the Communist base in the northwest was the work of Edgar Snow, who had arrived in the Communist zone earlier in the summer. Snow had sent word back to his wife to send Huang from Peking to act as his interpreter; this had been done "with the consent of Mao Tse-tung."[8] Aided by funds given to him by Mrs. Snow, Huang made his way to the northwest, where he remained with Snow throughout the latter part of 1936. Snow's wife saw Huang again in mid-1937 when she was in

Yenan; according to her, he was "regarded as a delegate from the Peking students"; she also noted that most of the students who arrived in Yenan "passed through his inspection, so I gathered he was responsible for 'guaranteeing' them." Describing Huang at this period in his life, Mrs. Snow called him proud, self-possessed, discreet, and much admired for his courage.[9]

By mid-1938 Huang was working in Wuhan as an official in the NLVC branch there, which was under the direction of the CCP's Yangtze Bureau. Among his youthful colleagues were such prominent latter-day Communists as Chiang Nan-hsiang and Yü Kuang-yuan (qq.v.). When Wuhan fell to the Japanese in October 1938 he returned to Yenan and a year later, when Edgar Snow returned to the Communist-held areas, Huang once again served as his interpreter.

Huang apparently remained in Yenan throughout the war, but little is known of his activities aside from the fact that by 1944 he was serving as a secretary to Chu Te, commander-in-chief of the Communists' Eighth Route Army. By now fluent in English (which he had not been during his days in Peking), he also became at about this time a liaison officer to the U.S. military mission stationed in Yenan. Toward the end of the war he spent some time in Chungking working with Chou En-lai's liaison mission to the Nationalist government, and in November 1945 he was the Party's representative dealing with Western correspondents (including Americans) then visiting Yenan. As a result of the mediation efforts of U.S. Special Envoy George C. Marshall, a Cease-fire Agreement was signed between the Nationalists and Communists in January 1946, and to implement the agreement the Peking Executive Headquarters was established in the same month. The Communist delegation in Peking was headed by General Yeh Chien-ying (q.v.), and from the establishment of the Headquarters in January 1946 until it was disbanded 13 months later, Huang served as Yeh's personal secretary and as head of the Communist press section. In Peking, as well as in his previous contacts with foreign journalists, Huang made a favorable impression upon the Americans with whom he worked.

In March 1949, following the Communist occupation of Tientsin two months earlier, Huang became director of the Tientsin Alien Affairs Office. He transferred to the same post in Nanking in May, and after the central government was inaugurated in October, the Nanking office became, in effect, a branch of the Foreign Ministry. The post in Nanking was of peculiar importance, for it was there, the former Nationalist capital, that a number of Western diplomats remained while they awaited the actions of their home governments, a number of which were debating whether or not to recognize the new Communist government. It was for this reason, for example, that Huang was the recipient on the last day of 1949 of the official notification from the Indian government that India had broken relations with the Nationalists. The unusual diplomatic situation that prevailed in Nanking is described at length in K. M. Panikkar's *In Two China's*. (Panikkar was India's last ambassador to the Nationalists and the first to the Communists.) Huang's assignment in Nanking also had an ironic twist, for the president of his alma mater, Dr. Stuart, was now ambassador to China—Nationalist China. Nonetheless, Huang paid an informal visit on Stuart and broached the subject of recognition, but the American parried this with the comment that no consideration could be given to the question until a central government existed (and Stuart himself left in August, two months before the PRC was formally established).[10]

By early 1950 Huang was heading the Shanghai Alien Affairs Office, a post he was to hold for three years. In the meantime, in the spring of 1949, he was given positions that related to his experiences of earlier years as a student and youth leader; he was elected both to Central Committee membership in the New Democratic Youth League and to National Committee membership in the All-China Federation of Democratic Youth, retaining his seat in these organizations until mid-1953. In January 1953 Huang was transferred to Peking where he became a counsellor of the Foreign Ministry, and in the fall of that year he received his first major assignment when he was appointed as the chief Chinese delegate to the talks held at Panmunjom from late October to mid-December 1953, negotiations designed to work out the arrangements for the convocation of a political conference to settle the outstanding problems in Korea, where the war had ended shortly before. Huang's opposite number on the American side was Arthur H. Dean. Both Dean and his chief interpreter, Robert B. Ekvall, had a high regard for Huang's abilities and his mastery of English, but both men have also suggested that Huang's persistent and vitriolic denunciations of the American side were at least a partial cause in breaking off the talks which, in effect, ended when Dean walked out of a session on December 14.[11] Huang remained in Panmunjom through January 1954 and during these weeks issued a number of statements urging a continuation of the talks, emphasizing that the American side would be held responsible if it did not return to the conference table.

Whatever Dean and Ekvall may have thought of Huang, it was clear that the latter's superiors approved of his handling of the Panmunjom talks, for when the negotiations moved to a higher level with the convocation of the Geneva Conference in April 1954, Huang accompanied Chou En-lai as an adviser, remaining in Switzerland (where he also served as an official Chinese spokesman to the press) until the negotiations ended in July. Not long after his return to Peking he became head of the Foreign Ministry's West European and African Affairs Department. In the late summer of 1956 the Department was shorn of its responsibilities for Africa, but Huang continued to head the West European Department until early 1959. In April 1955 he was abroad again, once more serving as an adviser to Chou En-lai when the Chinese attended the historic Afro-Asian ("Bandung") Conference. Two months later he assumed membership on the Board of Directors of the Chinese People's Institute of Foreign Affairs (see under Chang Hsi-jo) and at the same time he was also named to head the Institute's Research Department. He probably retains his Board membership, but in view of his later foreign assignments he presumably is no longer in charge of research.

Huang was frequently in the news throughout the late fifties, particularly when visitors from Western Europe were in Peking. And, appropriately, he was present to greet Edgar Snow when he arrived in the capital in June 1960. Shortly thereafter Huang left for his first diplomatic post following the agreement to establish diplomatic relations with Ghana in July 1960. He arrived in Accra in late August and presented his credentials as ambassador to President Kwame Nkrumah on September 5, 1960. Under Huang's direction, Accra became Peking's major diplomatic base in west Africa. On three occasions he was successful in efforts to gain diplomatic recognition of the PRC by other African nations. The first of these took him to Tanganyika where he attended independence ceremonies in December 1961 and won the agreement of the Tanganyikans to establish an embassy there. Similarly, in February 1964 he reached agreement with the Congo (Brazzaville) for the establishment of diplomatic relations, and in November 1964 he performed the same task in Dahomey.

Between Huang's arrival in Accra and early 1965, he signed at least six agreements or protocols (e.g., trade and technical cooperation agreements). He also returned to Peking on at least two occasions, the most important in August 1961 when he was present for the negotiations between Nkrumah and key Chinese leaders, which led to a treaty of friendship between the two nations. In the early sixties an unusually large number of Chinese delegations visited Ghana, a fact that brought Huang into the news on numerous occasions during these years. The most important of these visits took place in January 1964 when Chou En-lai and Foreign Minister Ch'en I spent six days in Accra. Huang remained as ambassador to Ghana until January 19, 1966, when he was appointed as ambassador to the United Arab Republic to replace Ch'en

Chia-k'ang (q.v.). He arrived in Cairo two months later and presented his credentials to President Nasser on March 28. He thus assumed the direction of the PRC's most important diplomatic post in the Middle East and Africa. In addition to the above-mentioned post in the Institute of Foreign Affairs, Huang's only other position in Peking is membership on the Council of the China-Cuba Friendship Association which he has held since it was formed in December 1962.

Huang is regarded by Western diplomats as a "tough" negotiator, but when the occasion is appropriate he has shown that he can be affable and an interesting conversationalist. Westerners who had an opportunity to deal with him socially in Ghana found him well-versed in a number of non-political topics; for example, he displayed a keen interest in American toys and games. Huang was married by at least the mid-forties to a woman described as the "daughter of an old revolutionist,"[12] but nothing more is known about her.

1. Nym Wales, *Notes on the Chinese Student Movement, 1935–1936* (Madison, Conn., 1959), p. 6.

2. John Israel, "The Chinese Student Movement, 1927–1937," Ph.D. diss. (Harvard University, 1963), p. 200; John Israel, *Student Nationalism in China, 1927–1937* (Stanford, Calif., 1966), p. 119.

3. Wales, p. 162.

4. Edgar Snow, *Journey to the Beginning* (London, 1960), pp. 139–143.

5. John Israel, *Student Nationalism*, p. 145.

6. Wales, pp. 112–117.

7. *SCMM* 297, p. 31.

8. Edgar Snow, *Random Notes on Red China, 1936–1945* (Cambridge, Mass., 1957), p. 47.

9. Wales, pp. 6, 112.

10. Tang Tsou, *America's Failure in China, 1941–50* (Chicago, 1963), pp. 513–514.

11. Robert B. Ekvall, *Faithful Echo* (New York, 1960), *passim;* Arthur H. Dean, "What It's Like to Negotiate with the Chinese," *New York Times Magazine,* October 30, 1966.

12. Wales, p. 115.

Huang Huo-ch'ing

(1900–   ; Hupeh). First secretary, Liaoning CCP Committee; secretary, Northeast CCP Bureau; alternate member, CCP Central Committee.

A veteran Party member and Red Army political officer, Huang Huo-ch'ing was an important Party official in Tientsin from 1949 to 1958. Since 1958 he has been the senior Party leader in Liaoning. Huang was born in 1900 in Hupeh province. He participated in the May Fourth Movement in 1919,[1] possibly while he was a student at Peking University. He joined the CCP in 1926 and in that same year headed a section of the Party's Central Social Affairs Department, suggesting that he was involved in intelligence work. In this same year he was also a section head of the Party's Labor Department. Because the Party headquarters were then in Shanghai, Huang presumably was working there when he held these positions.

By 1927 Huang was in the Soviet Union where he was a student at a Soviet military academy, a fact revealed in 1957 when he mentioned this in public when greeting Soviet leader K. E. Voroshilov, then on a state visit to China.[2] Huang remarked that he had participated "30 years ago" in a parade that had been reviewed by Voroshilov. Upon his return to China, Huang worked in the peasant movement. In about 1932 he probably belonged to Hsu Hsiang-ch'ien's Fourth Front Army, which was forced out of the Hupeh-Honan-Anhwei (Oyüwan) Border Region and sought refuge in north Szechwan that year (see under Chang Kuo-t'ao). Huang was a cadre with the 30th Army (a unit of the Fourth Front Army) during the Long March, when the Fourth Front Army and Mao Tse-tung's forces were united in far western Szechwan in the summer of 1935. That summer Mao moved on to northwest China, but the Fourth Front Army did not follow him, moving westward instead into Sikang province. This "West Route" Army began to move north a year later, but suffered severe losses while crossing the Kansu corridor when it encountered the armies of Moslem warlords Ma Pu-ch'ing and Ma Pu-fang, which almost annihilated its troops. In the fighting that ensued the 30th Army troops, which were part of Chang Kuo-t'ao's army, suffered especially heavy losses. Huang was among the survivors, said to number only about 1,000 men. He subsequently belonged to the "Left Column" of the "West Route" Army when this was reorganized in 1937 from the surviving marchers. At that time Chang Kuo-chien (q.v.) was heading the Political and Organization Departments of the 30th Army, and because Huang belonged to a "political work committee" in the "Left Column," he probably worked under Chang's supervision. This "Left Column" of Chang Kuo-t'ao's original army made another march westward after the serious defeat in the Kansu corridor. In the spring of 1937 a small group led by Li Hsien-nien (q.v.), Huang Huo-ch'ing and others reached Sinkiang where they made contact with Communists working there. These men later made their way to north Shensi to join forces with Mao Tse-tung. Presumably Huang spent the remainder of the war years in north China.

In the period after the end of hostilities in August 1945, Huang engaged in political work among the peasants and students. He emerged as an important official at the time the Communists captured Tientsin (January 15, 1949) when he became a member of the Tientsin Military Control Commission, which was chaired by Huang K'o-ch'eng (q.v.). For the next nine years Huang made Tientsin his base of operations. He was occupied there in several fields, including the activities of the Sino-Soviet Friendship Association (SSFA), the Tientsin Government, the Tientsin branch of the Communist labor organization, and in the municipal Party committee where he did his most important work. Huang became a member of the First Executive Board of the SSFA when it was formed on a nationwide basis in October 1949, and in the same year he was named as a vice-chairman of the Tientsin branch, holding this post until he was promoted to the chairmanship in 1953. In December 1954 Huang attended the Second National Conference of the SSFA, but he has not had any further connections with the association since that time.

While in Tientsin Huang devoted considerable time to the trade union movement. From 1950 to about 1955 he was head of the municipal branch of the All-China Federation of Trade Unions (ACFTU), and when the Federation established a North China Work Committee in April 1952, he became a member of its Standing Committee (a position he held until 1954 when the regional committees were abolished). Huang was also a member of the national ACFTU Executive Committee from 1953 to 1957. From 1950 to 1955 he was a member of the Tientsin Municipal People's Government Council, remaining on the Council until January 1955 when he replaced Wu Te (q.v.) as the mayor. However, Huang's major role in Tientsin was as a Party functionary. When Tientsin Party Secretary Huang Ching (q.v.) was transferred to Peking in August 1952, Huang Kuo-ch'ing became the acting secretary. In 1953 he became the ranking secretary (a position that was redesignated first secretary in 1956), thus making Huang the senior figure in both the Tientsin Government and the Party Committee until his transfer to Liaoning in 1958.

Huang did not belong to the national organization of the CPPCC during his years in Tientsin, but he did go to Peking to attend the important second and third sessions of the CPPCC National Committee, held in June 1950 and October–November 1951, respectively. Then, when the First Tientsin Committee of the CPPCC was established in March 1955, Huang became the chairman. As the Communists made preparations to establish a constitutional government in 1954, they organized election committees at the provincial and municipal levels throughout China in preparation for the First NPC, which opened in September 1954. In

Tientsin, an Election Committee was formed in May 1953 under the chairmanship of Huang. Then in 1954 he was elected as a Tientsin deputy to the First NPC, and at the first session in September 1954 he was named to the NPC Standing Committee, the governing body when the full congress is not in session. He was not, however, re-elected to the Second NPC, which opened in April 1959.

Huang attended the Party's Eighth National Congress in Peking in September 1956. He presented a written report to the Congress on the "reform" of the Tientsin "capitalists," and at the close of the sessions was elected as an alternate member of the CCP Central Committee. Until the Second Session of the English National Congress in May 1958, Huang was very active in Tientsin. Then, immediately after the Congress he was suddenly transferred to Liaoning, the important industrial province of southern Manchuria, where in June of 1958 he became the Party first secretary, replacing Huang Ou-tung (q.v.), who was made the second secretary. Since moving to Manchuria Huang Huo-ch'ing has assumed several other responsible positions; in November 1959 he replaced Huang Ou-tung as the chairman of the Liaoning Committee of the CPPCC, and by February 1960 he was identified as the political commissar of the Liaoning Military District. One year later, in February 1961, he was identified with the PLA rank of lieutenant-general when he attended a meeting at PLA headquarters in Peking to celebrate the 43rd anniversary of the founding of the Soviet Army.

The regional Party bureaus that had been abolished in 1954–55 were re-created in accordance with the Party Central Committee's Ninth Plenum in January 1961. By July 1961 Huang was identified as a secretary in the Northeast Bureau, placing him directly under First Secretary Sung Jen-ch'iung, Second Secretary Ouyang Ch'in, and Third Secretary Ma Ming-fang (qq.v.). In October–November 1963 Huang accompanied Sung Jen-ch'iung to North Korea. The purpose of the trip was not revealed, but while in the Korean capital the delegation was received by the top Korean Party leader, Kim Il-sung. Since Huang's transfer to Manchuria in 1958, his activities in Liaoning have been frequently reported in the Chinese press, often in connection with visits to the important industrial city of Shenyang (the Liaoning capital) by both senior Chinese leaders and foreign dignitaries.

Little is known of the personal life of Huang aside from the fact that he is married to Ma Hsin, whose antecedents are unknown.

────────

1. *Tientsin jih-pao* (Tientsin daily), January 1, 1953.
2. *SCMP* 1516, p. 26.

Huang K'o-ch'eng

(1902–   ; Yung-hsing, Hunan). Former PLA chief-of-staff; former member, CCP Central Secretariat; member, CCP Central Committee.

Huang K'o-ch'eng, who has occasionally used the alias Huang Chen-hsing, is a native of Yung-hsing, Hunan. Tseng Hsi-sheng, a colleague on the CCP Central Committee, also comes from Yung-hsing in southern Hunan, and as the two men are contemporaries in age and probably attended Whampoa Military Academy at about the same time, it is possible they were early associates. Huang graduated from the Third Normal School in Heng-yang, Hunan, before going to Canton to attend Whampoa. At the military academy he was in the first class, which began in June 1924, and graduated in February 1925. Two years later Huang joined the CCP. He is said to have become a Party member while he belonged to Mao Tse-tung's small insurrectionary army, which fought the Autumn Harvest Uprisings in Hunan in September 1927. When the insurrection ended in failure, Mao led the survivors, among them Huang K'o-ch'eng, to the retreat he established in the Chingkang Mountains on the Hunan-Kiangsi border. Huang thus belongs to the small group of the CCP elite who survived the difficult winter of 1927–28 at Chingkangshan and formed the nucleus of the Red Army. In the fall of 1928 Mao was joined by another group of founding members of the Red Army, the Fifth Army of P'eng Te-huai that came to Chingkangshan after being defeated at P'ing-chiang in northern Hunan (the area where Mao had also been during the Autumn Harvest Uprisings of September 1927). Huang joined P'eng's army when it returned to P'ing-chiang in the fall of 1929 and remained with the unit for the next six years, during which it was involved in much of the fighting that took place in the Communist-held areas of Kiangsi before these were evacuated in the fall of 1934, at the start of the Long March.

During the years from 1929 to 1935 when Huang served with P'eng's Army (known after 1930 as the Third Army Corps), he held several different posts. Although most of his work was that of a political officer, he also served as a military commander at the divisional level. In 1932 he was the political commissar of the Fourth Division of the Third Army Corps; a little later he became the director of the Corps' Political Department. In this post he came directly under the command of P'eng's principal political officer, T'eng Tai-yuan (q.v.). There are reports that at some time before the Communists embarked upon the Long March T'eng was forced to seek medical treatment in the USSR for a brief period, and if T'eng were absent some of his responsibilities as chief political officer of the Third

Army Corps would have fallen upon Huang. Huang made the Long March with P'eng's army as the officer in charge of procuring food supplies, but he also continued to do political work with the troops.

When the Communists reached north Shensi in the fall of 1935, Huang began to do important political work for the Party itself, serving for a time as the director of the CCP Organization Department. After the Sino-Japanese War broke out in the summer of 1937 and the CCP created its Eighth Route Army in north China, he entered the ranks of the new army. Official accounts indicate that he was for a time connected with Jen Pi-shih's Political Department of the Eighth Route Army. In 1938 Huang was in charge of rear services (logistics) and he appears to have been connected with the 115th Division commanded by Lin Piao and Nieh Jung-chen (qq.v.) and to have been briefly in the Wu-t'ai Mountains of eastern Shansi where the division made its headquarters.[1] There is also an account stating that as of 1940 he was connected with Tso Ch'üan, deputy chief-of-staff of the Eighth Route Army then stationed in the T'ai-hang Mountain area of southern Shansi, where Liu Po-ch'eng's 129th Division made its headquarters; he was also with Yang Te-chih, who was operating in the Hopeh-Shantung-Honan (Chi-Lu-Yü) Border Region in 1940.[2] This border area was one of the strategic regions controlled by the Communists during the war, an area facilitating a communications route between the military bases in Shansi and Shantung. Huang carried a letter from Tso to Yang in the spring of 1940 that may have laid the groundwork for the transference of some of the Second Column troops (then under Tso) to Chi-Lu-Yü, an event that also took place in the spring of 1940.

Huang and his own troops must have passed through Chi-Lu-Yü in the first half of 1940 on their way to Anhwei to aid Lo Ping-hui (q.v.) of the New Fourth Army. The first unit (numbering about 1,000 men) of Huang's Fifth or Eighth Column of Eighth Route Army troops passed through Shantung into Anhwei and joined forces with Lo Ping-hui on the Anhwei shores of Lake Kao-yu in January 1940. These were soon followed by the main body of Huang's force of 15,000 men, a force that proceeded via Hopeh and Shantung into northern Anhwei, where in August 1940 it joined forces with the Sixth Detachment of the New Fourth Army at Ko-yang, a small town in northern Anhwei (see under P'eng Hsueh-feng). In the following weeks Huang moved farther eastward into Kiangsu, and after crossing the Grand Canal he eventually made his headquarters at Fou-ning. By the fall of 1940 Huang's Column had officially become a part of the North Yangtze Command of the New Fourth Army troops commanded by Ch'en I (q.v.). Huang fought in east Kiangsu with his Eighth Route Army Column from the fall of 1940 until February 1941 when, following the New Fourth Army Incident of January (see under Yeh T'ing), the top echelons of the Army staff were reorganized. At this time Ch'en I became the Army's acting commander and Huang was made commander and political commissar of the newly created Third Division of the New Fourth Army.[3]

The Third Division was based in north Kiangsu in an area north of a line drawn between Huai-an and Fou-ning. This area east of the Grand Canal was known to the Communists as the North Kiangsu Military District. Huang operated here from 1940 to 1946, and from 1941 until 1946 was the military commander of the District. For at least part of this period he also headed the Party Committee in the District, but it is uncertain when he assumed the latter post, because in 1941 it was held by Liu Yen who was then also the political commissar of Su Yü's First Division of the New Fourth Army. Between the end of 1940 and early March 1941 the New Fourth Army set up about 10 units to train soldiers and civil administrators for the areas the Party controlled. The most important of these, known as the Fifth Branch of K'ang-ta (the Anti-Japanese Military and Political Academy), a branch of the well-known military school in north Shensi, was established in late 1940 at Yen-ch'eng, the site of Ch'en I's headquarters, not far south of Fou-ning in east Kiangsu. The Fifth K'ang-ta Branch was formed from two older army schools started by the New Fourth Army, plus a training unit that accompanied Huang's guerrilla column of the Eighth Route Army;[4] it may have been staffed with some personnel from the original K'ang-ta. Once Huang's training unit became part of the Fifth Branch of K'ang-ta there is no direct evidence that he continued connections with the training school. However, there are several reports that tell of his earlier connections with the Fifth Branch of K'ang-ta when his forces were still in north China and before the school was created in New Fourth Army territory. It is possible that these reports refer to his connections with the training unit he brought from north China, or they may refer to connections that he maintained with the military academy once it was established in Yen-ch'eng.

An important Party official in north Kiangsu by 1945 when the CCP held its Seventh National Congress (meeting in Yenan, April–June), Huang received recognition for his services when he was elected to the CCP Central Committee as an alternate member. At the end of the war he was separated from the New Fourth Army and given other important assignments with the army that Lin Piao took to Manchuria when hostilities with the Japanese concluded. Thus

Huang went to Manchuria in 1946 where he was in charge of some of the military operations in the Jehol-Liaoning Military District. He was commander of the Third Division of the West Manchurian force of Lin's army, known as the Northeast Democratic Allied Army from early 1946. In the next two years Huang took part in a number of the important battles of the Manchurian campaign, serving as commander of the Third Division and later as commander of field operations in the Jehol-Liaoning Military District. He participated in the campaigns of Lin's army through Manchuria and entered China proper with the army late in 1948. Early in 1949 (by which time Lin's army became the Fourth Field Army), Huang was political commissar of the 12th Army Corps, the unit commanded by Hsiao Ching-kuang (q.v.).

Immediately after the Communists captured Tientsin in mid-January 1949, Huang was named to chair the municipal Military Control Commission and to serve as the political commissar of the Tientsin Garrison Command. The Garrison commander was Hsiao Ching-kuang, Huang's colleague in the Fourth Field Army's 12th Army Corps. Huang did not, however, remain long in Tientsin but rather continued with the Fourth Field Army as it pushed southward. When Ch'eng Ch'ien, the Nationalist governor of Hunan, and Ch'en Ming-jen, the KMT garrison commander in the Hunan capital of Changsha, went over to the Communists in the late summer of 1949, the Fourth Field Army moved into the province with virtually no fighting. Huang immediately assumed key positions within the province, most notably as secretary of the Hunan Party Committee, a post he held until the latter part of 1952. He was also the political commissar of the Hunan Military District (HMD) from its formation in late August 1949 to 1950; here he was once again associated with Hsiao Ching-kuang, the HMD Commander. Hsiao relinquished his Hunan post in 1950 to assume command of the Chinese Navy and was apparently replaced by Huang K'o-ch'eng; in any event, Huang was the commander in Hunan at the time of his transfer to Peking in 1952. He was also made a member in August 1949 of the Changsha Military Control Commission (chaired by Hsiao Ching-kuang), presumably holding this post until 1952.

After the initial steps were taken to organize Hunan, Huang returned briefly to Peking to participate in the formation of the national PRC government at the first session of the CPPCC in September 1949. He attended the CPPCC sessions as a representative of the Central China Liberated Areas, and during the course of the meetings served on the *ad hoc* committee to draft the Organic Law of the new government, one of the key documents adopted at this time. He also spoke before the conference, briefly describing how central China was being organized as the main base for the Communist armies to push into south and southwest China. At the close of the meetings he was elected to membership on the CPPCC National Committee, continuing to hold this position until the Second National Committee was established in December 1954.

After the CPPCC meetings, Huang returned to central-south China where he soon assumed new positions in the Hunan provincial government and in the Central-South Military and Administrative Committee (CSMAC), the regional government that included Hunan within its jurisdiction, as well as Hupeh, Honan, Kiangsi, Kwangtung, and Kwangsi. Huang was a member of the CSMAC from its formation in February 1950 until his transfer to Peking in 1952. In the following month he was named as a member of the Hunan Provincial People's Government (HPPG), another post he held until 1952. Subordinate to the HPPG, he was also chairman of the Finance and Economics Committee from September 1950 to 1952. And, although Huang has never been particularly active in the mass organizations, from 1950 to 1952 he was a vice-chairman of the Hunan chapter of the China Peace Committee.

As already described, Huang had been elected an alternate member of the Party Central Committee in 1945. Then, as the top man on the alternate list, he was promoted to full Committee membership following the death of Central Committee member Jen Pi-shih (q.v.) in October 1950. As stated, Huang continued to work in Hunan until mid-1952, although he was seldom mentioned in the press in 1951 and early 1952. One of the relatively few times occurred in October 1951 when he spoke at a Hunan Provincial Party conference, urging that the Party weed out undesirable elements and enlist those with "clear political backgrounds and class consciousness," who had proved themselves in the struggles to carry out the land reform movement, one of the major national programs of the early fifties.

By August 1952 Huang had been transferred to Peking to become a deputy chief-of-staff of the People's Revolutionary Military Council (PRMC), the highest military organ within the central government. In this position Huang served under veteran military leader Nieh Jung-chen, the acting chief-of-staff until the PRMC was abolished at the time of the government reorganization in 1954. Not long after Huang's transfer to the capital, the State Planning Commission was established (November 1952) in preparation for the First Five-Year Plan launched in 1953. As originally constituted, the Commission had a chairman, one vice-chairman, and 15 members. Huang and P'eng Te-huai were the only two active military figures appointed to Commission membership.

Huang was elected as a deputy from the Central-South Military Region to the First NPC, which inaugurated the constitutional government in September 1954. At this time he relinquished his posts as a deputy chief-of-staff of the PRMC and as a State Planning Commission member. However, he received posts of equal if not greater importance. At the close of the NPC session he was named to membership on both the NPC Standing Committee and the National Defense Council, the latter being the successor to the PRMC. Within the next few weeks he was given even more important assignments when he was named (October 1954) as a vice-minister in the newly created National Defense Ministry (serving here under P'eng Te-huai) and as director of the PLA's Rear Services Department (November 1954). In September 1955 the PRC first awarded military decorations to its officer corps and also gave them personal military ranks. Huang was given the three highest military awards, the Orders of August First, Independence and Freedom, and Liberation. At the same time he was made a senior general of the PLA, the equivalent of a four-star general in the U.S. Army, a rank only below that of marshal.

Huang's importance among the CCP elite was reaffirmed at the Party's Eighth National Congress in September 1956. He served on both the Presidium (steering committee) and the Credentials Committee, and at the close of the meetings was re-elected to the Party Central Committee. More important, at the First Plenum of the new Central Committee (held the day after the Congress closed), he was elected as a member of the Party's Central Secretariat. Headed by Teng Hsiao-p'ing and charged with the task of executing the policies of the Politburo, the Secretariat then consisted of only seven full and three alternate members. Huang and T'en Cheng (q.v.) were the only members then on active duty with the PLA. Possibly because of this new assignment with the Secretariat, Huang was replaced in December 1956 as director of the PLA Rear Services Department by Hung Hsueh-chih (q.v.), a PLA officer who had served under Huang in the 1940's and who was to share Huang's political difficulties in 1959 (see below).

In October 1958, during the closing stages of the Quemoy (or "offshore islands") crisis, Huang was named to succeed Su Yü (q.v.) as PLA chief-of-staff, an assignment that has been described as a strengthening of Party control over the military establishment because of Huang's membership on the important CCP Central Secretariat.[5] In April 1959 he was reappointed to membership on the National Defense Council at the first session of the Second NPC. However, because he was not re-elected as a deputy to the NPC, he was dropped from NPC Standing Committee membership at this time. Then, without any evident forewarning, he was replaced in September 1959 by Lo Jui-ch'ing (q.v.) as PLA

chief-of-staff, a position Huang had held for only 11 months. The change occurred at the same time that Lin Piao succeeded P'eng Te-huai as China's Defense Minister. Further, Huang was also removed as a vice-minister of National Defense, thereby being stripped of both his active military posts. Then he dropped out of public sight and was not heard of again for six years.

Huang's political troubles were confirmed by the secret Chinese Communist military journal known as the *Kung-tso t'ung-hsun* (Bulletin of activities). Issues of this journal for the year 1961 (released by the U.S. Government in 1963) revealed that P'eng Te-huai and Huang had been accused of constituting an "anti-Party group." "Modern revisionism," the Chinese euphemism for Soviet policies, was also linked with the "erroneous" line of P'eng and Huang, which suggests that these two men had been willing to make political compromises with the Soviet Union in order to continue the flow of Soviet military assistance to China.[6] Several other charges against P'eng and Huang were revealed in the *Kung-tso t'ung-hsun*. These included the direct or indirect assertions that the two men had advocated or condoned a "simple military viewpoint" and "militarist" practices, that they had neglected Party organizations in the PLA, and had disregarded the military thought of Mao Tse-tung.[7] Hung Hsueh-chih, Huang's longtime colleague and the man who had replaced him in the Rear Services Department in 1956, was also involved in the charges revealed in the *Kung-tso t'ung-hsun*.

In view of these charges, it is not surprising that Huang was removed from the Party's Central Secretariat. Though it is virtually certain that he ceased to take an active part in Secretariat affairs after 1959, the circumstances surrounding his ultimate removal are somewhat unusual. The 1960 issue of the *Jen-min shou-ts'e* (People's handbook) did not list Huang's name on the Secretariat; it reappeared in the 1961 edition but was again omitted in the 1962 handbook. In any case, at the Party's 10th Plenum in September 1962, Huang was officially removed. The only mitigating factor was the reference at the 10th Plenum to "comrade" Huang, an appellation suggesting that although he was in serious political trouble he had not been stripped of his Party membership. Political officer T'an Cheng (q.v.) was also removed at the 10th Plenum from the Secretariat, but there does not appear to have been any political connection between the dismissals. The Plenum also appointed Lo Jui-ch'ing to the Secretariat, apparently as the military representative to take the place of Huang and T'an Cheng.

As described, Huang had been reappointed in 1959 (not long before his political difficulties were revealed) to membership on the National Defense Council (NDC). He continued to be officially listed in this capacity until the NDC officials were again reappointed at the close of the first session of the Third NPC in January 1965. Predictably, Huang was not among those reappointed. Huang was thus left with only his membership on the Party Central Committee, but in view of his political problems even this post seemed largely nominal. But then, after more than six years of political oblivion, in December 1965 he was elected as a vice-governor of Shansi, a position placing him subordinate to Wang Ch'ien, a man who is not even a member of the Party Central Committee. This pattern of accusation-purge-reappearance is not peculiar to Huang. Other persons of Central Committee rank (e.g., Shu T'ung, P'an Fu-sheng, Chao Chien-min) underwent a similar cycle of events. Nonetheless, Huang's place as a significant figure in the CCP elite appears to have ended in the late fifties.

Little is known of Huang's personal life aside from the fact that in May 1957 he was said to have written to a nephew in Hunan advising him to "take part in agricultural production" if he could not get into a military academy or university after completing senior middle school.

1. *Hung-ch'i p'iao-p'iao* (Red flag fluttering; Peking, 1957), I, 191.

2. *Hung-ch'i p'iao-p'iao* (Red flag fluttering; Peking, 1957), V, 136.

3. Chalmers A. Johnson, *Peasant Nationalism and Communist Power* (Stanford, Calif., 1962). Information on Huang's activities with the New Fourth Army is from chapter 5.

4. *Ibid.*, p. 153.

5. Alice Langley Hsieh, *Communist China's Strategy in the Nuclear Era* (Englewood Cliffs, N.J., 1962), p. 117.

6. Ellis Joffe, *Party and Army: Professionalism and Political Control in the Chinese Officer Corps, 1949–1964* (Cambridge, Mass., 1965), pp. 100–102.

7. *Ibid.*, 103.

Huang Kung-lueh

(1898–1931; Hsiang-t'an, Hunan). Early Communist military leader.

Huang Kung-lueh played an important role in the Communists' military operations in central-south China for a brief period from 1928 to 1931. He was born into a fairly well-to-do family in Hsiang-t'an hsien,[1] the birthplace of Mao Tse-tung and Huang's colleague, P'eng Te-huai. Huang attended a middle school and then graduated from the Whampoa Military Academy, which opened in the late spring of 1924 under the presidency of Chiang Kai-shek. During the course of the Northern Expedition, begun in mid-1926 to unify China under the KMT, Huang became close friends with P'eng Te-huai.

Huang and P'eng were then serving in the Fifth Independent Division under T'ang Sheng-chih's Eighth Army, one of the major components of the National Revolutionary Army. Through P'eng's assistance, Huang was placed in charge of a battalion-level cadet corps, but he was soon transferred to command the Second Battalion of the Second Regiment. P'eng Te-huai was then in command of the First Regiment.

P'eng and Huang participated in the many campaigns conducted in central China by T'ang Sheng-chih during the Northern Expedition in the latter part of 1926 and the year 1927. At some time in 1927, probably after the KMT-CCP split in mid-year, Huang joined the CCP. By the first part of 1928, P'eng (not yet a Party member) and Huang were serving in the First Division of Ho Chien's 35th Army, which was stationed just west of Tung-t'ing Lake in northern Hunan. In the second quarter of the year, their division was transferred to the area around P'ing-chiang and Liu-yang hsien in northeast Hunan, the region which had witnessed some of the Autumn Harvest Uprisings only a few months earlier. In late July 1928, allegedly in defiance of orders to suppress the local peasantry, the Communists within the division mutinied and staged the P'ing-chiang Uprising. Orthodox Communist accounts attribute the leadership of the uprising to P'eng and Huang, as well as T'eng Tai-yuan (q.v.), who had been sent to the P'ing-chiang area by the CCP to organize the peasantry. The rebels immediately established the Fifth Red Army; P'eng became the commander and T'eng Tai-yuan the Party representative (later redesignated political commissar). Huang was made the Party representative for the Second Regiment of the 14th Division. After some heavy fighting in the P'ing-chiang area, P'eng and T'eng withdrew and took most of the Fifth Army southward to Chingkangshan where in November 1928 they joined forces with Mao Tse-tung and Chu Te.

Huang was left behind in charge of some 1,000 men.[2] During the course of the next year he established the Hunan-Hupeh-Kiangsi base[3] and conducted guerrilla operations. This base, situated amid a triangle formed by Wuhan, Changsha, and Nanchang (all KMT strongholds), proved to be a far less viable area for Communist operations than other bases in central-south China. Nonetheless, it appears that Huang was able to strengthen his forces somewhat by recruiting local peasants and miners.[4] After operating in relative isolation for a year, Huang's units were reinforced in the fall of 1929 by the arrival of two units from P'eng Te-huai's Fifth Army; these were grouped together in a single command, and Huang was made deputy commander of the division (presumably still the 14th Division). By early 1930 Huang had moved southward to an area in Kiangsi not far east of Chingkangshan. After holding a meeting with Fifth Army commanders P'eng Te-huai and T'eng Tai-yuan, the scattered Communist units from southwest, central, and west Kiangsi were merged to form the Third Red Army under Huang's command. The units drawn from central Kiangsi were led by Lo Ping-hui (q.v.), who had recently defected from the Nationalists. Several years later, in response to a question by authoress Nym Wales about the quality of Red Army commanders, Lo rated Huang and P'eng Te-huai as the two ablest he had known.[5]

In the first half of 1930 the various Communist forces in central-south China began to prepare for military advances upon the main industrial cities of the central Yangtze Valley, a policy then espoused by Li Li-san (q.v.). As a part of a general reorganization, Huang's Third Army was placed under the First Army Corps, commanded by Chu Te and Mao; P'eng Te-huai's Fifth Army became the Third Army Corps. The Chu-Mao army marched north and advanced on Nanchang on August 1, 1930. But the Nationalist forces proved too strong, and after serious losses to the Red Army, the attack was called off within 24 hours (see under Chu Te). After participating in this action, as well as an equally abortive attempt to capture Changsha in September, Huang led his Third Army troops on a retreat to central Kiangsi. In coordination with troops led by Mao, Chu, P'eng Te-huai, and Lo Ping-hui, Huang took part in the capture of the important city of Chi-an (Kian) in early October.

Chi-an was quickly retaken by the Nationalists, by which time Li Li-san's ambitious plans to capture major cities had collapsed. However, remnants of the Li leadership still controlled many of the Party organs within the Kiangsi Provincial Committee, as well as the Southwest Kiangsi Special Action Committee, and these men became involved in a power struggle with Mao Tse-tung. There is little reported about Huang's activities at this critical juncture, but it is reasonably clear that he supported the Mao group in December 1930 at the time of the Fu-t'ien Incident.[6] This was touched off by a revolt of certain officers, among them Liu Ti in the 20th Army (under P'eng Te-huai's Third Army Corps) at Tung-ku, some 60 miles southeast of Chi-an. The rebels then attacked a Communist stronghold in the neighboring town of Fu-t'ien, where Mao had previously imprisoned Tuan Liang-pi and Li Wen-lin on grounds of belonging to the so-called A-B (Anti-Bolshevik) group in Kiangsi. This provoked retaliation from Mao who had some 70 members of the Kiangsi Provincial Soviet arrested on December 7, 1930.[7] Mao's action in turn brought forth more trouble within the Communist military ranks, until Mao's supporters, among them Chu Te, P'eng Te-

huai, and Huang, finally gained the ascendancy.

Even before the Fu-t'ien Incident was fully resolved, the Nationalists mounted the first of the Annihilation Campaigns against the Communists in the closing days of 1930. Huang fought in this brief campaign, as well as the second and third campaigns in 1931, commanding his Third Army in southeast and east-central Kiangsi. The Communists had proved a match for the Nationalists in the first two battles, but the Third Annihilation Campaign, under the personal command of Chiang Kai-shek, was going badly for the Red Army. However, the Japanese attack in Manchuria in September 1931 diverted Chiang's attention and brought the battle to an end. In response to the Japanese action in Manchuria, the Red Army immediately issued an open "letter" to the men of the KMT armies, urging them to revolt, overthrow the KMT, and join the ranks of the Communist armies. It is perhaps some measure of Huang's stature that this proclamation was signed by only five Red Army leaders: Mao, Chu Te, Ho Lung (q.v.), P'eng Te-huai, and Huang.[8] In the following month (October), as Huang was leading his troops to the Communist capital at Juichin, he was killed in an air raid near Tung-ku. To commemorate Huang, who died at the age of 33, the Communists established "Kung-lueh" hsien in central Kiangsi and named a military academy in the Juichin area the "Kung-lueh Infantry School" (*pu-ping hsueh-hsiao*). Mao Tse-tung himself commemorated Huang in a few lines of poetry written in connection with the 1930 attack on Nanchang:

On the far side of the Kan River
   a patch of ground has turned red,
Thanks to the wing
   under the command of Huang Kung-lueh.[9]

1. *Hu-nan ko-ming lieh-shih chuan* (Changsha, 1952), p. 54.

2. Agnes Smedley, *The Great Road* (New York, 1956), p. 235.

3. Wang Shih, et al., *Chung-kuo kung-ch'antang li-shih chien-pien* (A brief history of the Chinese Communist Party; Shanghai, 1958), JPRS translation no. 8756, August 16, 1961, p. 127.

4. Smedley, p. 288.

5. Nym Wales, *Inside Red China* (New York, 1939), p. 126.

6. Tso-liang Hsiao, *Power Relations within the Chinese Communist Movement, 1930–1934* (Seattle, Wash., 1961), pp. 98–102.

7. Benjamin I. Schwartz, *Chinese Communism and the Rise of Mao* (Cambridge, Mass., 1952), p. 176.

8. Stuart R. Schram, *The Political Thought of Mao Tse-tung* (New York, 1963), pp. 149–152.

9. Jerome Ch'en, *Mao and the Chinese Revolution* (New York, 1965), p. 329.

Huang Ou-tung

(c.1907–   ; Kiangsi). Governor of Liaoning; alternate member, CCP Central Committee.

Huang Ou-tung was born about 1907 in Kiangsi but has spent a major part of his life working in Manchuria. Nothing is known of his early career, but soon after the end of the Sino-Japanese War he was serving as governor of those portions of Liaoning held by the Communists. The province went out of existence in 1946, but was then re-created over the winter of 1948–49, only to be abolished once again in 1949. (Liaoning was once more re-created in 1954—see below.) Huang again served as the provincial governor in 1949. When he lost his post a second time owing to the administration reorganizations, he became (by the fall of 1949) the ranking Party secretary and vice-mayor of Shenyang (Mukden), a city then directly subordinate to the central government. In July 1952 he replaced Chu Ch'i-wen as the Shenyang mayor, but Huang was in turn replaced by mid-1953 by Chiao Jo-yü. By the end of 1954 Chiao had also replaced him as the first secretary of Shenyang. One other Shenyang post held by Huang was as an executive member of the Municipal Trade Union, a position he held from October 1949.

Huang's work in Shenyang, the most important city in Manchuria, was apparently viewed with favor by higher authorities. In mid-1954 he was promoted from the municipal to provincial level when he assumed the ranking secretaryship of Liaoning Province at the time Liaoning was re-created (from Liaotung and Liaohsi Provinces). On August 1, 1954, Huang was one of the principal speakers at the inaugural ceremonies in the provincial capital of Shenyang. (His position was redesignated as first secretary by September 1956.) Soon after assuming the ranking secretaryship, he was elected a deputy from Shenyang to the First NPC, which first met in September 1954 at which time the constitutional government was inaugurated. By the time of the elections to the Second NPC (1958), Shenyang had lost its status as a special municipality, having been incorporated into Liaoning Province. Huang, therefore, was elected as a Liaoning deputy to the Second NPC (1959–1964) and was again re-elected from this province for the Third NPC, which first met in December 1964–January 1965.

Already the ranking Liaoning Party official, Huang assumed three new positions in early 1955. After presiding over the preliminary meetings leading to the establishment of the Liaoning Committee of the CPPCC in February 1955, he was named as the chairman of the First Liaoning Committee in the following month. (In November 1959 he was succeeded as chairman by Huang Huo-ch'ing.) Also in February 1955 he was elected as a member of the Provincial People's Council at the time Manchuria-born Tu Che-heng became governor. Still another post he assumed in February 1955 was as head of the Preparatory Committee for the Liaoning chapter of the Sino-Soviet Friendship Association, and when the chapter was established in May 1956, he became the president. He probably still retains this position, but little has been heard of the organization since the open deterioration of Sino-Soviet relations in the early 1960's.

Huang attended the Eighth Party Congress in Peking in September 1956. He served on the Credentials Committee for the Congress, and at the close of the sessions was elected an alternate member of the Party Central Committee. Then, after having served as the ranking Party secretary in Liaoning for nearly four years, Huang Ou-tung was replaced there (June 1958) by the man who had been the principal Party secretary as well as the mayor of Tientsin, Huang Huo-ch'ing. The latter Huang is a few years older than Huang Ou-tung and presumably outranks him in the CCP, because on his arrival in Liaoning Huang Ou-tung was dropped back to the post of second secretary in the provincial Party Committee. However, the intensive pace of Huang Ou-tung's work (as reflected in the national press) gave no indication that he had suffered politically. In fact, when the Liaoning governor, Tu Che-heng, was charged with "anti-Party" activities (December 1958) and purged from his post, it was Huang Ou-tung who replaced him and who continues to hold his post.

In early 1961 the decision was made to re-establish the regional Party bureaus that had been abolished in 1954–55. By October 1962 Huang was identified as a secretary of the Northeast Bureau, a position in which he ranked fifth behind Sung Jen-ch'iung, Ouyang Ch'in, Ma Ming-fang, and his colleague Huang Huo-ch'ing (qq.v.). Huang Ou-tung has been reported in the press with great regularity since the mid-1950's in the performance of his duties in Liaoning. And because Shenyang is frequently visited by important foreign officials, as well as top CCP officials (e.g., Chou En-lai in June 1962), he has occasion to meet many of them in the normal course of his work. Huang has apparently not been a regular contributor to the Party press, although he did write an article dealing with agriculture in Liaoning for the February 1, 1960, issue of the *JMJP*.

Huang Yen

(c.1917–   ; Liu-an hsien, Anhwei). Former east China guerrilla leader; Anhwei governor.

Huang Yen was born in Liu-an hsien, the same hsien from which Ch'en Shao-yü (better known as Wang Ming) hails, but there is no known connection between Huang and Ch'en.

Moreover, Ch'en is about 10 years senior to Huang.

Huang became associated with revolutionary activities while still a teenager. He reportedly led a unit in a peasants' uprising in March 1931 in his native hsien and then participated in the formation of a "soviet" in that area. Liu-an hsien was in the important Oyüwan Soviet district (see under Chang Kuo-t'ao), and presumably the "soviet" which Huang helped develop was incorporated into Oyüwan.

Nothing was heard of Huang for a decade until Japanese sources report that as of April 1941 he had served as director of a "joint defense office" west of the Tientsin-Pukow Railway; three years later he was serving as a deputy secretary of a Party Committee in the same region. In addition to providing a direct rail link between Tientsin and Nanking (situated on the south shore of the Yangtze directly across from Pukow), the Tientsin-Pukow rail line connected the North China Plain and the lower Yangtze valley, both fertile and heavily populated areas. By the end of the war Huang was, according to Japanese sources, secretary of the Huai-nan (south of the Huai River) Border Region Party Committee under the Central China Party Bureau. As the Communists were operating mainly in military formations in these East China areas, Huang was presumably serving under the command of the Second Division of the New Fourth Army, the division that controlled this area.

In the late 1940's, as the Communists swept the mainland, Huang apparently devoted himself to the organization of the peasantry. He was serving as chairman of a preparatory committee for the North Anhwei Peasants' Association, and attended the First CPPCC as a representative of peasant organizations in the "liberated areas."

Until August 1952 Anhwei province was divided into northern and southern sections. Over the 1949–50 winter Huang assumed important assignments in the three major segments of the Communist power structure, the government, the Party, and the military. He became a deputy secretary of the North Anhwei Party Committee under Party Central Committee member Tseng Hsi-sheng, the ranking secretary, a post Huang held until August 1952. He also served with Tseng in the military structure; Tseng was the commander of the North Anhwei Military District, and Huang, for a brief time in early 1950, was a deputy political commissar. The third post, perhaps Huang's most significant during this period, was as director of the North Anhwei People's Administrative Office, the governmental organ.

In addition to these Anhwei posts, Huang held two other significant positions in the early 1950's. In February 1950 he was appointed as a member of the Land Reform Committee of the East China Military and Administrative Committee, renamed the East China Administrative Committee (ECAC) in early 1953. He held the post, under chairman T'an Chen-lin, a senior Party leader, until the ECAC was abolished in 1954. His other task was as a member of the Huai River Harnessing Commission, an organ established under the national Ministry of Water Conservancy in November 1950 and chaired by Tseng Shan, then a senior economic official in eastern China. Little is known of Huang's activity on this Commission aside from the fact that he attended its second conference held in April–May 1951 at Pang-fou, a city in Anhwei on the Huai River.

In August 1952, north and south Anhwei were merged to form Anhwei province. In the governmental structure, Huang was named as a vice-governor under Tseng Hsi-sheng, holding this post until March 1955 when he replaced Tseng as governor. Huang was subsequently re-elected as governor in November 1958 and in September 1964. In the military sphere Japanese sources identified him as a deputy commander of the Anhwei Military District in August 1952, but no later information is available about this activity. Although Huang was not identified as a secretary of the Anhwei Party Committee until January 1957 (serving, once again, under first secretary Tseng Hsi-sheng), it is likely that he held this post from the 1952 period.

Huang has been fairly active in the NPC since its formation in 1954. He was an Anhwei deputy to the first through the third congresses which opened, respectively, in September 1954, April 1959, and December 1964. At a June 1956 session of the first congress he spoke on the Anhwei harvest and in April 1959 on an industrial "leap forward" in Anhwei.

Throughout the middle and late 1950's, Huang was reported with regularity, and during this period assumed still two more posts, though both of apparently short duration. He was named in April 1958 as chairman of the Anhwei Provincial Election Committee, the body that directed the electoral work for the elections to the Second NPC late in 1958. Second, in December 1958 he was named as chairman of the Wuhu Committee for Building the Yangtze River Bridge, a committee inaugurated on December 9, 1958.

Beginning with the early stages of the Great Leap Forward (1958), he was often in the company of the regime's most senior leaders on inspection trips in Anhwei. Thus, he accompanied Chou En-lai on a visit to an agricultural producer cooperation in January 1958 and was with Mao Tse-tung in September 1958. He visited mines and factories in Anhwei with Teng Hsiao-p'ing in February 1960, accompanied Tung Pi-wu on another inspection in May 1960, and Ch'en Yun on still another in October–November 1960. It was during this period that

Huang wrote an article for the *JMJP* (August 2, 1960) entitled "The Development of the National Economy Must Be Based on Agriculture," one of the first articles stressing this theme, at a time when the Great Leap Forward was proving to be inadequate to the economic needs of China.

It is interesting that Huang was out of the news for over two years after being identified with Ch'en Yun in November 1960. This situation may have been due solely to the inadequate reports available, although two facts suggest difficulties in Anhwei during this period. First, Tseng Hsi-sheng, under whom Huang had served for many years, was transferred out of the province in late 1960. He returned to Anhwei in 1961, only to disappear completely from the news in 1962, at which time Party Central Committee Li Pao-hua was assigned to Anhwei as the first secretary, replacing Tseng. Second, even though Huang reappeared in the news in early 1963, he was demoted from secretary to deputy secretary of the Anhwei Party Committee at least by October 1963. Such a procedure is quite abnormal and suggests that Huang became entangled in political difficulties affecting the Anhwei political hierarchy.

Despite the possible political difficulties of the early 1960's, Huang was active again by early 1963 taking part in activities typical of a provincial leader of his stature. He was, to cite a few examples, on hand for May Day and National Day festivities in 1963 and attended the sessions of the Third Anhwei Congress of Women in May 1964.

Huang Yung-sheng

(c.1905–   ; Yung-feng, Kiangsi). Commander, Canton Military Region; alternate member, CCP Central Committee.

Huang Yung-sheng is a career army officer who has served in important military and political posts in central-south China since it was occupied by the Communist armies in 1949. He was born about 1905 in Yung-feng, a town in central Kiangsi east of the Kan River and slightly northeast of Kian (Chi-an). In the late 1920's and early 1930's there was considerable peasant unrest and guerrilla fighting in this area and Huang, who was a peasant, took part. At the time of the Autumn Harvest Uprisings in 1927 he was with a Nationalist unit which defected to the Communists. He subsequently made his way to Chingkangshan on the Hunan-Kiangsi border where Mao's forces met Chu Te's in the spring of 1928. By 1930 he was commander of the Guards Regiment of the Red Army Headquarters (Kiangsi). Two years later, in 1932, he was still with the Chu-Mao army (called the First Front Army in the early 1930's) as commander of the First Division's Third Regi-

ment. Later, Huang attended the Red Army Academy, which the Communists opened at Juichin in 1933. When the Communists arrived in north Shensi in the fall of 1935 after the Long March, the military academy was relocated there with Lin Piao as its head. Huang, who made the Long March, enrolled in the first class in 1936.

After the Sino-Japanese War began in 1937, Huang was a regimental commander in the Communist Eighth Route Army's 115th Division, which was led by Lin Piao and Nieh Jung-chen. He served throughout the war in guerrilla units under Nieh, which defended the Shansi-Chahar-Hopeh (Chin-Ch'a-Chi) Border Region, whose headquarters was in the Wu-t'ai Mountain area of Shansi. Most of Huang's time was spent in western Hopeh where, sometime before 1945, he was commander of the Shansi-Chahar-Hopeh Military Region's Third Sub-district. Although no specific post is mentioned, he was identified in the same area at the end of the war, when he was said to be a commander of Communist units operating in the vicinity of the Hopeh cities of Shih-chia-chuang and Paoting. After August 1945, when the war ended, Nieh's army moved north from the Shansi-Hopeh region into Jehol and Manchuria. In 1945 they occupied Kalgan, the capital of Chahar Province. Huang probably accompanied Nieh's forces, but in any case by 1947 he was in north China serving as commander of the 23rd Sub-district of the Hopeh-Jehol Military Region. Later he was commander of the Jehol-Liaoning Military Region.

By 1949 Huang had been transferred to Lin Piao's Fourth Field Army. After taking control of Manchuria, Lin's forces moved south to prepare for the attack on Tientsin and Peking in January 1949, capturing the former in mid-month and "peacefully liberating" the latter on January 31. Huang took part in some of these operations as a corps commander in the Fourth Field Army.[1] He apparently remained with the Army as it moved south, occupying Kwangsi and its principal cities, Kweilin and Nanning, in November–December 1949. In December Huang became a deputy commander of the newly established Kwangsi Military District under Commander Chang Yun-i (q.v.). In March 1950 Huang received two civil posts when he was named as a member of the Central-South Military and Administrative Committee (CSMAC), the regional administration governing the territory occupied by the Fourth Field Army, as well as of the Kwangsi Provincial People's Government. He was removed from the Kwangsi post in June 1952. However, these positions in the civilian administration never equalled his standing in the military establishment. As of 1950 Huang was a deputy commander of the Fourth Field Army's 13th Army Corps. The following year he was promoted from deputy commander to commander of the Kwangsi Military District.

However, he must have held this post only briefly because in 1951 he was also identified as deputy commander of the Kwangtung Military District (to 1953) and commander of the Kwangtung Air Defense Command.

In addition to his provincial military posts, Huang has been given responsibilities at the regional level. In 1951–52 he was a deputy commander of the South China Military Region (SCMR), being promoted to commander in 1953. The SCMR, controlling Kwangsi and Kwangtung, was a sub-district of the Central-South Military Region. From 1952 to 1954 Huang was chief-of-staff of both the Central-South Military Region and the Fourth Field Army, and in 1954 he became a deputy commander of both. In the 1954–55 period the Central-South Military Region was reorganized and the provinces subordinate to it were placed under three different regions, one of which was the Canton Military Region (responsible for Kwangtung, Kwangsi, and Hunan). Huang became the commander and has retained the post except for the years from 1958 to 1962 when Li T'ien-yu temporarily replaced him.

Although Huang's career has been centered in central-south China, he has received recognition at the national level. When the constitutional government was inaugurated in September 1954 he became a member of the newly created National Defense Council, a military advisory organ of little authority but considerable prestige. He was reappointed to the Council in April 1959 and January 1965. In September 1955 Huang was one of the recipients of the first national military awards, but the specific honors given him were not reported. (However, in June 1957 he received the Order of Independence and Freedom, the decoration denoting service during the Sino-Japanese War.) Personal military ranks in the PLA were also created in 1955, and by February 1956 Huang was identified as a colonel-general, the equivalent of a three-star general in the U.S. Army. Finally, in September 1956 at the Eighth Party Congress in Peking, he was elected an alternate member of the Central Committee.

Huang's active role in the military establishment has continued in the late 1950's and 1960's. In September 1958, in an effort to curtail the development of special privilege in the officer class, the PLA ordered all officers to do an annual tour of duty in the ranks. Huang is reported to have made such tours in 1958, 1962, and 1964. In December 1961 he made his first trip outside China as a member of Yeh Chien-ying's military delegation, which spent two weeks in North Vietnam. Moreover, the fact that his headquarters is in Canton has brought him into official contact with other foreign leaders. For instance, in April 1963 he welcomed the Indonesian Army commander-in-chief and in

February 1964 he was on hand to greet a leader of the Japanese Communist Party. On the latter occasion Huang was identified for the first time as a secretary of the Central-South Party Bureau. The regional Party bureaus had been re-created in January 1961, with the Central-South Bureau being headed by T'ao Chu (q.v.), another veteran of Lin Piao's Fourth Field Army,

1. *The Great Turning Point* (Peking, 1962), p. 209.

Hui Yü-yü

(c.1906–   ; Shensi). Governor of Kiangsu province.

Hui Yü-yü has worked for the Communists in Kiangsu since the Sino-Japanese War and has been the provincial governor since 1955. Nothing is known of Hui's early career, but by the middle years of the Sino-Japanese War he was working in Kiangsu in areas under the control of the Communists' New Fourth Army. He remained in this region in the postwar period and by 1946 he was in command of the Second Sub-district of the South Kiangsu Military District. Three years later, as the Communists were completing their conquest of east China, Hui was the director of the political department of an army unit under Ch'en I's Third Field Army. When Soochow fell to the advancing Communist armies in late April 1949, Hui became a member of the Soochow Military Control Commission, and in September he succeeded Wei Kuo-ch'ing (q.v.) as Commission chairman. Hui concurrently served as mayor of Soochow (April–August 1949) and secretary of the CCP Soochow Municipal Committee (1949–50).

From 1949 to November 1952 the Communists administered Kiangsu province as two separate units, designated the North and the South Kiangsu People's Administrative Offices. By at least the latter part of 1950 Hui was transferred from his Soochow posts to Yang-chou, the capital of the northern office, to become chairman of this body. In addition, from 1951 to 1952 he was chairman of the North Kiangsu Political and Legal Affairs Committee and a vice-chairman of its Finance and Economics Committee. Hui was concurrently a vice-chairman, under Tseng Shan (q.v.), of the important Huai River Harnessing Commission, which was set up in November 1950 under the auspices of the Ministry of Water Conservancy in Peking. Then in November 1952, when Kiangsu province was restored to its traditional boundaries, Hui became a member of the Kiangsu Provincial People's Government Council under Governor T'an Chen-lin (q.v.). With this change Hui transferred from Yang-chou to Nanking, the provincial capital. Within a brief time he became the leading Party and government figure in Nanking, serving as the mayor and ranking secretary of the municipal Party Committee. He relinquished these posts by approximately February 1955 when he replaced T'an Chen-lin as the Kiangsu governor, a post Hui still holds. While he was rising in the governmental structure, Hui was also advancing in the Party apparatus. By November 1954 he had become a deputy secretary of the Kiangsu Party Committee, and since mid-1956 he has been a secretary under Kiangsu First Secretary Chiang Wei-ch'ing (q.v.), a colleague of Hui's from the 1940's.

Hui was a Kiangsu deputy to the First (1954–1959) and Second (1959–1964) NPC's, and he was re-elected to the Third Congress, which held its first session in December 1964–January 1965. Other posts held by Hui from the mid-1950's include the chairmanship of the Kiangsu and Nanching branches of the Sino-Soviet Friendship Association and the chairmanship of the Nanking Yangtze River Bridge Construction Committee (set up in October 1958). Since becoming the Kiangsu governor in 1955 he has been reported in the press quite regularly in activities normally associated with provincial leaders of his stature, e.g., addressing provincial meetings, making inspection tours, and conferring with foreign dignitaries or top leaders from Peking on visits to Kiangsu.

Hui is married to Ku Ching, but nothing is known of her background.

Hung Hsueh-chih

(c.1908–   ; Kiangsi). Former military leader and Korean War veteran; alternate member, CCP Central Committee.

Reports that Hung Hsueh-chih is a native of Kiangsi conflict with others calling him a Honanese, but the best evidence suggests Kiangsi as his birthplace. Little is known of his career until the closing years of the Sino-Japanese War. By that time he had already served as a battalion and regimental commander, before being identified about 1945 as the chief-of-staff of the Third Division of the Communist New Fourth Army. (For the history of this division, see under Huang K'o-ch'eng.) In 1955 Hung was given the highest national military honors for his services since the late 1920's or early 1930's, a clear indication that his earlier career was more outstanding than the available record indicates.

From 1948 to 1949 Hung was identified as a deputy commander of the 15th Army Corps of Lin Piao's Fourth Field Army. It was Lin's army that took over Manchuria for the Communists before moving south to Peking in January 1949 and then again sweeping south to Kwangsi and Kwangtung to reach Hainan Island in April 1950. The best equipped and the elite of PLA armies, the Fourth Field Army had no sooner conquered its southernmost target than much of it was transferred to Korea where it bore the brunt of the fighting done by the "Chinese People's Volunteers" in Korea. In the years between 1948 and 1954 Hung's career is closely linked with this army. Once it had reached Kwangtung he became a deputy commander of the Kwangtung Military District (1949–50), ranking below only Yeh Chien-ying and Teng Hua, the top military commanders in the area. At the same time he was a member of Military Control Commission for Canton, headed by Yeh and Lai Ch'uan-chu. In January 1950 the Communists established their civil government in Kwangtung, known as the Kwangtung Provincial People's Government; Yeh Chien-ying was named as governor and Hung as one of the members. Hung nominally held a position there until June 1954, a few months prior to the inauguration of the constitutional government (September). But in fact he spent little time in Kwangtung because by 1951 he had been transferred to Korea.

By 1950 Hung was identified as political commissar of the 16th Corps of the Fourth Field Army, the corps commanded by Ch'en Tsai-tao, military commander in Wuhan after 1955. This corps went to the battlefields of Korea where Hung was also sent sometime in 1951. He was identified in 1952 as director of the Rear Services Department of the CPV. He probably remained in Korea until 1954, for there is no report of his activities elsewhere until September 1954 when he returned to China to attend the First NPC, sitting in the Congress as a deputy from the CPV. He served throughout the First NPC but was not re-elected to the Second Congress, which opened in April 1959. With the establishment of the constitutional government brought into being by the First NPC, Hung was also elected to the newly created National Defense Council. In April 1959 the membership of the National Defense Council was reappointed, with Hung continuing to serve there.

In the fall of 1954, Hung's wartime chief, Huang K'o-ch'eng, became director of the PLA General Rear Services Department. Hung was appointed simultaneously to serve under him as a deputy director, a post he held until he succeeded Huang in December 1956 as Department director. Hung was Rear Services director for three years.

The decade of the 1950's was an active time for Hung, whose services were frequently in demand at military meetings, especially those concerned with matters of logistics. In April 1957 and again in January 1958, he addressed important conferences on logistics. Also during the fifties he often attended Party functions held in Peking to honor important foreigners, especially visiting military delegations. In September 1955, when the first PRC national military

honors were awarded, Hung received the three
PRC top honors, the August First, the Independence and Freedom, and the Liberation
Orders, important military decorations given for
distinguished service in three periods of Communist history between 1927 and 1950. Personal
military ranks were designated by the PLA for
the first time that same year, with Hung being
given the rank of colonel-general. A year later,
at the Eighth Party Congress in September 1956,
he was elected an alternate member of the Central Committee.

In November–December 1957 Hung was a
member of P'eng Te-huai's military mission (an
important part of the Chinese delegation headed
by Mao Tse-tung), which visited the Soviet
Union for the 40th anniversary of the founding
of the USSR. The delegation returned home via
Khabarovsk and Vladivostok. Then in June
1959 Hung was in Tibet on what, in hindsight,
would seem to have been a trip to inspect conditions in the PLA in Tibet shortly after the Dalai
Lama escaped to India. The Tibetan papers
spoke only of Hung's being there to give an
important report at a logistics conference of the
Tibetan Military District.

Soon after his appearance in Tibet, he was
replaced as director of the PLA Rear Services
Department by Ch'iu Hui-tso, a relatively obscure officer. The reasons for Hung's disappearance after this time are clearly connected with
the dismissal of certain high-ranking military
leaders in 1959, most notably Defense Minister
P'eng Te-huai and PLA Chief-of-Staff Huang
K'o-ch'eng (qq.v.). Hung's dismissal from the
Rear Services Department (October 1959) occurred just one month after the removal of
Huang K'o-ch'eng, his former chief. Hung's
political troubles were confirmed by the secret
Chinese Communist military journal known as
the *Kung-tso t'ung-hsun* (Bulletin of activities).
Issues of this journal for the year 1960–61 were
released by the U.S. Government in 1963. They
specifically linked Hung with both P'eng Te-
huai and Huang K'o-ch'eng. It was claimed that
at a meeting of the Rear Services Department in
October–November 1960 the "harmful influence" of P'eng, Huang, and Hung had been
"further eliminated." It was also asserted that
an "anti-dogmatist" movement of 1958 was
thwarted as a result of Hung's "resistance." He
was further charged with "liquidationism" in
the handling of the logistics for the PLA, having
"blindly made big reductions and cancellations,
being destructive without being constructive."[1]
The one mitigating factor in these charges is
that the journal continued to refer to Hung by
the appelation "comrade," suggesting that although he is in serious political trouble, he retains his Party membership.

The final blow to Hung's career occurred in
January 1965 at the close of the first session of

the Third NPC. At this time the members of
the National Defense Council were reappointed.
All but a small handful—including Hung, as
well as P'eng Te-huai and Huang K'o-ch'eng—
were again named to membership. For all practical purposes, Hung's career as a senior PLA
officer appears to be closed.

<hr>

1. *Kung-tso t'ung-hsun* (Bulletin of activities), no. 2:17–18 (December 16, 1960).

Jao Shu-shih

(c.1901–   ; Lin-ch'uan, Kiangsi). New Fourth
Army political commissar; former first secretary,
East China Bureau, CCP; former director, Or-
ganization Department, CCP; former member,
CCP Central Committee; purged 1955.

Veteran Party member Jao Shu-shih was a top
political officer with the Communists' New
Fourth Army during the Sino-Japanese War.
During the early years of Communist rule after
1949 he was the senior Communist in east
China, transferring to Peking in 1952 to become
head of the Party's Organization Department.
A Party Central Committee member from 1945,
Jao fell from power in the major 1954–55
purge, which also witnessed the downfall of
Politburo member Kao Kang. An assessment of
Jao's career, particularly his earlier years, is
complicated by the fact that Maoist historians
have completely ignored his contributions to
the early development of Communism. Aside
from occasional pejorative comments linking him
with Kao Kang, for historical purposes he has
become an "unperson" in the true Orwellian
manner.

Jao was born in Lin-ch'uan hsien, located in
Kiangsi just south of P'o-yang Lake and not far
from the provincial capital at Nanchang, which
has also been cited as his birthplace. He graduated from a middle school in Nanchang, probably about 1920. Jao is reported to have studied
in the early twenties at Shanghai University, an
institute that produced a number of important
Communists and that had on its faculty such outstanding Party members as Ch'ü Ch'iu-pai,
Teng Chung-hsia, and Jen Pi-shih (qq.v.). Joining the CCP in 1925, Jao was active in the mid-
twenties as a labor organizer in Wuhan,[1] doing
work that may have placed him close to the
important Communists who participated in the
Northern Expedition (e.g., Liu Shao-ch'i). The
murkiest period of Jao's career falls in the decade
after the KMT-CCP split in 1927. Unauthenti-
cated reports place him in the Soviet Union,
East Europe, France, Canada, and the United
States, while yet another asserts that he was
imprisoned in Manchuria until the Japanese takeover there in 1931. In connection with the report
regarding the United States, one knowledgeable
former PRC official claims that it was widely

rumored in the early 1950's that Jao had studied at an American university.[2]

According to Japanese sources, Jao once worked with the newspaper *Chiu-kuo shih-pao* (Salvation news), established by Party veteran Wu Yü-chang (q.v.) in Paris in 1935 in response to the Comintern policy adopted that year to propagate an international united front. The possibility that Jao worked for this paper in Paris gains credence when it is noted that Miss Lu Ts'ui, who became his wife, went to Paris about 1936, where she helped establish a branch of the National Salvation Association (see under Shih Liang).[3] The Association was one of the most active Chinese organizations in propagating the united front theme in China—a theme frequently expressed in the term *chiu-kuo* ("salvation" or, literally, "save the nation").

By 1939 Jao was back in China and in that year was sent from Yenan to south Anhwei where he became deputy political commissar of the New Fourth Army, the major Communist military force operating in the lower Yangtze River Valley under the overall command of Yeh T'ing, whose biography contains a discussion of the New Fourth Army's operations. Following the New Fourth Army Incident in January 1941 (also described in Yeh's biography), the Communist units and the CCP committee in charge of the area were reorganized. Ch'en I became the Army's acting commander and Liu Shao-ch'i became the political commissar as well as the secretary of the Central China (Hua-chung) Bureau. Jao served directly under Liu in two capacities; he continued as deputy political commissar and by this same year (1941) he was also deputy secretary of the Party's Central China Bureau. Moreover, he also directed the Bureau's Propaganda Department.[4]

When Liu Shao-ch'i left the New Fourth Army area of operations in 1942, Jao assumed the senior Party post, becoming also the acting political commissar and rising to political commissar in the last year of the war. His place among the Party elite was confirmed when he was elected (possibly *in absentia*) to membership on the CCP Central Committee at the Party's Seventh National Congress held in Yenan from April to June 1945. Jao remained in east China until early 1946 when he was sent to Peking to be a senior political adviser to Yeh Chien-ying (q.v.), the head of the Communists' mission at the Peking Executive Headquarters, which had been established in accordance with the January 1946 cease fire agreement worked out between the CCP and the KMT under the auspices of the U.S. Special Envoy George C. Marshall. It may have been at this time (if not a decade earlier in Paris) that Jao married Lu Ts'ui, who was also a member of the Communist mission in Peking. Holding the simulated rank of lieutenant general, Jao remained in

Peking until the late spring when he was named as chief of the Communist mission at the Changchun (Manchuria) Advance Headquarters of the Peking Executive Headquarters. Robert B. Rigg, an American assistant military attaché in China at this time, has described the diminutive Jao as "shrewd" and "well liked by some Americans" who knew him in Peking and Changchun.[5] In mid-1946 warfare between the Communists and Nationalists intensified, and as a result the Communists began to withdraw some of their key officials from the Executive Headquarters, Jao among them. He returned to his former post as political commissar in east China where the Communist military forces were now known as the East China Field Army; the designation was later changed to East China PLA (1947–48), and then in early 1949 to the Third Field Army. In the late forties, working in conjunction with units in north-central China led by Liu Po-ch'eng (q.v.) and with others led by Lin Piao (q.v.) that had come south from Manchuria, the east China armies took part in the operations resulting in the Communist victories in portions of central China. Finally, in the early months of 1949, the Third Field Army bore the brunt of the fighting that led to the conquest of the coastal provinces, battles described in the biography of Ch'en I, with whom Jao had now been associated for a decade. Jao is seldom mentioned in Communist accounts of these battles, including those written before his political fall; the implication is that he devoted most of his time to political work behind the front lines in areas the Communists were trying to consolidate under their rule.

Jao was with the victorious Communist armies that marched into Shanghai in late May 1949, remaining there while elements from the Third Field Army pushed southward into Chekiang and Fukien. When the east China victories had been consolidated, the Communists established the East China Military Region (ECMR), with jurisdiction over the five provinces of Shantung, Kiangsu, Anhwei, Chekiang, and Fukien. Jao now assumed the concurrent post of political commissar of the ECMR, still working with Ch'en I, the commander of the ECMR and the Third Field Army. However, with the fighting completed, Jao turned principally to CCP and government affairs, a career pattern that is typical of many former PLA political officers. He immediately became the Party's chief official in the area, serving as head of the East China Bureau and concurrently as secretary of the Shanghai Party Committee. Over the winter of 1949–50 the Communists established governmental organizations with responsibility over areas that were identical with the boundaries under the jurisdiction of the military regions; Jao became chairman of the East China Military and Administrative Committee (known from 1953 to 1954 as the East China Administrative Committee). Such an array of regional posts meant that Jao controlled three of the four top positions in East China—heading the Party apparatus and the government hierarchy and serving as political commissar of the military region. He only failed to hold the command of the ECMR. Comparing Jao's role in east China with that of the leadership in the five other administrative regions of China, he was surpassed only by Kao Kang, who held all four top posts in Manchuria.

Like virtually all key regional leaders, Jao was also given important posts in the central government, established at Peking in the autumn of 1949. He was named to membership on the Central People's Government Council (CPGC), which was chaired by Mao Tse-tung and which was the most important organ of government until the constitutional government was established in 1954. In addition, he was appointed as a member of the People's Revolutionary Military Council (also chaired by Mao), and from 1949 to 1954 he served on the First Executive Board of the Sino-Soviet Friendship Association (concurrently heading the Association's East China branch when it was formed in November 1951). However, Jao worked principally in east China and did not attend many of the CPGC meetings until his transfer to Peking in 1952. His dominance in east China during the early fifties was demonstrated by his frequent public appearances and, more significantly, by the fact that he usually gave the keynote policy speeches before the ECMAC and the Party's East China Bureau. Similarly, the issues of *Hsin-hua yueh-pao* (New China monthly), the equivalent of a government gazette, carried a large number of Jao's speeches and reprints of his articles for the Shanghai *Chieh-fang jih-pao* (Liberation daily), the organ of the East China Bureau.

As the period of "reconstruction and rehabilitation" drew to a close in the latter half of 1952, a number of organizational and personnel changes were made in the central Party organs and the central government, principally to prepare for the inauguration of the First Five-Year Plan in 1953. By the late summer of 1952 Jao was identified as director of the Party Central Committee's powerful Organization Department, a position he assumed from P'eng Chen, a key member of the Politburo. With the assumption of this post in Peking, Jao's most important position in east China, the first secretaryship of the Party's East China Bureau, fell to T'an Chen-lin (q.v.). In October 1952 Jao received his next assignment, accompanying Liu Shao-ch'i to Moscow for the 19th Congress of the Soviet Communist Party, the last held before Stalin's death. Then in November, while Jao was still abroad, the State Planning Commission was created. As originally constituted, the Commission

had Kao Kang as its chairman, Teng Tzu-hui as its vice-chairman, and 15 members, a group composed of some of the most powerful figures in the Party hierarchy, including, Jao, Ch'en Yun, Lin Piao, P'eng Chen, P'eng Te-huai, and Teng Hsiao-p'ing (qq.v.). In a little over two years Kao and Jao were to be linked in an "anti-Party" plot and purged in what was probably the most important intra-Party struggle from the fall of Chang Kuo-t'ao (q.v.) in the late thirties through the mid-fifties.

But before the drama unfolded, Jao gave every appearance of being a rising star in the Party's inner elite. Already the head of the Organization Department, he was appointed in January 1953 to membership on a committee chaired by Mao Tse-tung, which was established to draft the PRC constitution, and in May of that year he was elected a member of the Seventh Executive Committee of the All-China Federation of Trade Unions. Similarly, Jao's public appearances had an aura of high-level authority, as when he spoke before the Second National Women's Congress in April 1953 "on behalf of the CCP Central Committee" or in November when he attended Mao Tse-tung's reception for North Korean leader Kim Il Sung. He continued to appear in public until New Year's Day of 1954, and then, with no advance warning, he dropped from sight. His disappearance coincided with the Party's Fourth Plenum (February 1954) when Liu Shao-ch'i, in a report on Party unity, noted that "certain high-ranking cadres . . . regard the region or department under their leadership as their personal property or independent kingdom." These key lines, in retrospect, obviously referred to Kao Kang and Jao Shu-shih and suggested that Kao regarded Manchuria as his "kingdom" and the State Planning Commission as his "personal property," and it appears that the same charges applied to Jao in regard to the east China region and the Party's Organization Department.

After the Fourth Plenum a year passed with no mention of either Kao or Jao. Then in March 1955 the Party convened a national conference, which featured a sensational speech by Teng Hsiao-p'ing denouncing the "conspiratorial activities" of Kao and Jao, which were aimed at "seizing leadership in the Party and the state." The Kao-Jao purge and its aftermath is dealt with in detail in the biography of Kao, but the importance of the case and of Jao himself requires some elaboration of the charges specifically directed against Jao. It was said that his attempts to "seize power" dated from 1943 (when he was with the New Fourth Army), and during "his tenure of office in east China" he had done his "utmost to adopt in the cities and countryside a rightist policy of surrender to the capitalists, landlords, and rich peasants." He was also accused of protecting "counterrevolutionaries" in east China, and after he was transferred to Peking he came to believe that "Kao Kang was on the point of success in his activities aimed at seizing power." Therefore, according to the official resolution, Jao had "used his office as director of the Organization Department" to oppose leading Party members and to "split the Party." Both men had allegedly been warned at the 1954 Plenum, but neither would "admit his guilt" nor show any sign of "repentance." It was claimed that Kao Kang committed suicide, but no explanation has been offered for Jao's fate beyond the enigmatic comment that he "still persists in an attitude of attacking the Party." He was, of course, stripped of all his posts and nothing has been heard of him since.

As already mentioned, Jao is married to Lu Ts'ui, one of the more prominent women leaders in China until the political fall of her husband. A native of Chekiang, she entered Tsinghua University in 1934 and was one of the most active participants in the December Ninth Movement (see under Li Ch'ang), a name taken from the date of student demonstrations held in Peking on December 9, 1935, in opposition to KMT policies regarded as inadequate in the face of steady Japanese encroachments on Chinese sovereignty.[6] Lu's presence in Paris in the mid-thirties and her participation in the Peking Executive Headquarters have been described above. In the spring of 1949, when the All-China Federation of Democratic Women (ACFDW) was established, Lu was named to the Standing Committee and she was re-elected in April 1953 at the next women's congress. From 1949 she was also the deputy director of the Federation's International (liaison) Department and then succeeded to the directorship in late 1952, at the same time as her husband's transfer to Peking. Representing the ACFDW, Lu had attended the first session of the CPPCC in September 1949 when the new national PRC government was brought into existence. In the next month she was named to the National Committee and Executive Board, respectively, of the China Peace Committee and the Sino-Soviet Friendship Association. Between 1953 and 1954 she made three trips abroad, the first to the Communist-sponsored World Congress of Women in Copenhagen in June 1953. Both her other trips were to attend meetings of the Communist World Peace Council, one in Vienna in November 1953 and the other in Berlin in May 1954.

In May 1954 she was named to the Standing Committee of the Chinese People's Association for Cultural Relations with Foreign Countries, and in December of the same year she attended the Second National Conference of the Sino-Soviet Friendship Association and was also named to membership on the Second National Committee of the CPPCC (representing the ACFDW). All these appointments in 1954, as well as her trip to Berlin in the same year, are of particular interest because they post-date the Party Central Committee's Fourth Plenum (February 1954) and the disappearance of her husband. The two appointments in December 1954 —less than three months before her husband was openly accused of plotting against the regime—suggest that the CCP hierarchy was still in the process of building its case against Jao and did not want to reveal its hand. For example, Lu's prominence in the Women's Federation made her a logical choice to serve as one of its representatives in the CPPCC, and thus the Party may have felt that it would be more conspicuous to omit than to include her. Also of interest is the fact that the annual issues through 1957 of the *Jen-min Shou-ts'e* (People's handbook) continued to list Lu in her various official positions. However, she dropped from sight at the end of 1954, and since that date nothing further has been heard of her.

1. Eugene Z. Hanrahan, "The Birth of the Chinese Red Army," M.A. thesis (Columbia University, 1953), p. 39.

2. Interview, Hong Kong, September 1964.

3. John Israel, *Student Nationalism in China, 1927–1937* (Stanford, Calif., 1966), p. 158.

4. *Sohoku kyōsan chiku jitsujō chōsa hōkokusho* (Investigation report on the current situation in the North Kiangsu Communist region; Shanghai, 1941), chart following p. 222.

5. Robert B. Rigg, *Red China's Fighting Hordes* (Harrisburg, Penn., 1951), p. 88.

6. Israel, p. 127.

Jen Pi-shih

(1904–1950; Hsiang-yin hsien, Hunan). Early Youth League and Party leader; member, CCP Politburo and Secretariat.

Jen Pi-shih was one of the major political figures during the first three decades of the Chinese Communist Movement. Trained in the Soviet Union, he returned to China to become one of the most important leaders of the Youth League in its formative years. A Party Central Committee member from 1927, he was one of the few leaders able to ride out the political storms which rent the Communist leadership in the twenties and thirties. Jen became a Politburo member in 1931, and from 1933 to 1938 he was a key political officer in the Red Army. He worked in close association with Mao Tse-tung during the 1940's and continued to be one of the Party's chief policy-level officials until his death in 1950.

Jen was born on April 30, 1904, in Hsiang-yin hsien, which is near Tung-t'ing Lake in northern Hunan and not far from Changsha, the provincial capital. Communist sources describe his family as impoverished teachers, but other sources refer to them as rich peasants. The information about Jen's cousin (see below), suggests that his family was reasonably well-to-do. After attending elementary school, Jen entered the First Middle School in Changsha. Mao Tsetung had studied there briefly a few years earlier, before attending the better known Hunan Provincial Normal School. Among Jen's middle school classmates was Hsiao Ching-kuang (q.v.), who later became a top Red Army commander. Jen was in Changsha when the May Fourth Movement erupted in 1919, and like many other students there he was influenced by the new and revolutionary ideas which the movement spread. Graduating in 1920, he and Hsiao went to Shanghai where they studied Russian at a foreign language school headed by Yang Mingchai (q.v.). Jen and Hsiao also joined the Socialist Youth League, which was founded in Shanghai in August 1920. Comintern representative Gregory Voitinsky was instrumental in the establishment of the foreign language school and the Youth League, both of which were designed to unearth young talent for further training in the Soviet Union. Thus, during the winter of 1920–21 Hsiao and Jen left for Moscow, traveling via Vladivostok, which was still occupied by the Japanese. The two young men enrolled in the Communist University of the Toilers of the East,[1] which was established in the spring of 1921, and both of them studied there until 1924 together with several hundred other Asian students. In early 1922, when Jen was just 18, he joined the CCP in Moscow. Aside from his friend Hsiao Ching-kuang, other young Communists then in the Soviet capital included Liu Shaoch'i and Lo I-nung (qq.v.).

Returning to Shanghai in 1924, Jen joined the staff of Shanghai University where he taught Russian. This school, the training ground for a number of young Communists, had on its staff such top Communists as Ch'ü Ch'iu-pai, Teng Chung-hsia, and Chang T'ai-lei (qq.v.). The university was closed for its radical activities in June 1925, but by that time Jen was more deeply involved in the affairs of the Communist Youth League (as the Socialist Youth League was now known). In January 1925, at the League's Third Congress in Shanghai, Jen had been elected a member of the Central Committee, and from the same year to 1927 he served as director of the League's Organization Department. In 1926, in the absence of Chang T'ai-lei, Jen was acting secretary of the League, and when the youth organization met for its Fourth Congress in May 1927, he was elected secretary, continuing in this post until mid-1928 when he was succeeded by Kuan Hsiang-ying (q.v.).

In connection with Jen's senior posts in the Youth League, it should be noted that the League was then an organization which in some respects rivaled the authority of the Communist Party. As one writer has noted, the League "often took a tack somewhat to the left" of the Party, "its youthful spirit disposing it to take [Party] programs too literally. It could afford such deviations because it managed to retain some autonomy . . . until the late 1920's."[2] There is considerable documentation from the twenties to indicate rather serious differences between the two organizations; however, none of these materials specifically links Jen with such differences, and, in fact, Party scribes writing after Jen's death claim that he led the way in 1927 in opposing tendencies within the Youth League to pursue radical policies described as "vanguardism" (hsien-feng chu-i).

Only a few days before Jen had become the top Youth League official, he was elected a member of the Party Central Committee at the Fifth CCP Congress (Wuhan, April–May 1927). Then only 23 years old, Jen was probably the youngest Central Committee member (and perhaps the youngest person to achieve this rank in the history of the Communist movement). The Fifth Congress was convened at a time of mounting crises for the Communists; the "Right" KMT under Chiang Kai-shek had all but shattered the CCP apparatus in Shanghai, and the "Left" KMT in Wuhan was growing restive in its relations with the Communists. Quite naturally, then, the Congress sought to find new policies to cope with the difficult situation, and it also witnessed considerable opposition to the leadership of Party chief Ch'en Tu-hsiu (q.v.). Mao Tse-tung and Ch'ü Ch'iu-pai were among those known to have differed seriously with Ch'en (whom they regarded as a vacillating leader), and Maoist historians have in later years claimed that Jen also opposed Ch'en Tu-hsiu.[3] In view of the then rapidly shifting alliances within the Party leadership, this may be true, but it must be judged in light of the fact that a few weeks later (when the CCP was in even more dire straits) Jen lent his support to Ch'en.[4]

The crisis situation reached a climax on August 1, 1927, when the Communists staged their famed uprising at Nanchang (see under Yeh T'ing). At this juncture the Party leadership was turned over to Ch'ü Ch'iu-pai who convened the so-called Emergency Conference on August 7 (probably in Hankow). Jen reportedly attended this meeting,[5] but little is known about his work or whereabouts for the next year. As noted above, Jen relinquished the direction of the Youth League in mid-1928, and at that time he was transferred to the Party Center (and presumably worked in the Party underground in Shanghai). Soon afterwards, he was sent to work in the underground in Anhwei where, in Nan-ling hsien (south of Wu-hu in southeast Anhwei) he was arrested. After his release in March of 1929 he became a member of the Standing Committee of the Kiangsu Provincial Party Committee, then headed by Lo Teng-hsien (q.v.). Still operating in the underground, Jen was again arrested in September 1929 and imprisoned in Shanghai for two months. In the meantime, while Jen had been in the underground, the Party was forced to hold its Sixth Congress (June–July 1928) in Moscow. He was re-elected *in absentia* to the Central Committee, and in the following year, after being released from prison a second time (November 1929), he was sent to Wuhan where he became a member of the Yangtze Bureau and secretary of both the Wuhan Municipal Committee and the Hupeh Provincial Committee. Jen remained there for about a year, and was thus in the central Yangtze Valley in mid-1930 when the Li Li-san leadership made its bold but abortive efforts to capture and hold key cities in that area (see under Li Li-san and P'eng Te-huai). Jen was back in Shanghai by about the end of 1930, and Wang Shou-tao (q.v.) has written that he attended a "secret training class" there at which Jen lectured on Party organizational methods.[6] Well entrenched in the inner-Party circles by 1930, Jen weathered the political storm which finally deposed Li Li-san by the end of the year, and he was again re-elected to the Central Committee at the Fourth Plenum in January 1931 when a new group of leaders took control of the Party. It was a sign of Jen's accommodation to the new leaders, the Russian-returned students (see under Ch'en Shao-yü), that he was also elected a member of the Politburo. A week later the Central Bureau for the Soviet Areas (Su-ch'ü chung-yang chü) was established, and among its nine members were Mao, Chu Te, Chou En-lai, Jen, and Hsiang Ying, the secretary.[7] Apparently the Bureau's major assignment was the supervision of Party activity in the guerrilla bases where the Communists had been working for a few years to build up peasant armies and establish viable Party organizations. In March 1931, as head of the Bureau's Organization Department, Jen proceeded to Juichin, Kiangsi, where he worked in Party organizational affairs for most of the next two years, excepting only a period in 1932 when he was in T'ing-chou (Ch'ang-t'ing) in west Fukien. At the First All-China Congress of Soviets, which met in Juichin in November 1931 and established the Chinese Soviet Republic, Jen was among those elected a member of the Republic's leading political body, the Central Executive Committee.

In early 1933 the Party press opened a strong attack on the so-called Lo Ming line, which derived its name from the acting secretary of the Party Committee in Fukien. Lo, it was alleged, had fostered policies in the face of Nationalist attacks that were defensive in nature, in contrast to the prevailing line of the period, which was described as being "forward and offensive" in nature. The Lo Ming line, it was argued by

its opponents, had damaged the Communist efforts in military, political, and economic affairs. The Russian-returned student leadership led the way in these attacks, and they were joined by such key leaders as Chou En-lai and Jen Pi-shih.[8] The attacks on the Lo Ming line lasted into 1934, and in terms of personalities, one of the major results was that many supporters of Mao Tse-tung were removed from important posts (see under Lo Ming). One such person was Hsiao Ching-kuang, Jen's close friend and schoolmate. Many years later (1945), in a resolution adopted by the Central Committee when Mao was firmly in control of the Party, Lo was cast in a rather favorable light and the Returned-student leadership was denounced for its actions against Lo and others. The 1945 resolution conveniently ignored the fact that many others—like Chou En-lai and Jen—had lent their support to the Returned-student leadership in the attacks on the Lo Ming line.

In May 1933 the Party sent Jen to be secretary of the Hunan-Kiangsi Border Region Committee and political commissar of the Military Region. The military unit there, commanded by Hsiao K'o (q.v.), was known as the Sixth Army; it operated in and around the area which several years earlier had formed part of Mao Tse-tung's famous Chingkangshan base. In addition, the Hunan-Kiangsi base maintained close connections with the Hunan-Kiangsi-Hupeh base to the north. When the Nationalists began their Fifth Annihilation Campaign in the fall of 1933, the Sixth Army was driven northward from its base; because of rather severe losses in personnel, the army was reorganized and redesignated the 17th Division. (By the next year it had increased in strength and was then designated the Sixth Army Corps.) Not long after the Nationalist 1933 campaign began, Jen left the fighting front and returned to Juichin. According to an eyewitness account,[9] this took place in January 1934, and because this date coincides with the convocation of the Second All-China Congress of Soviets, it is presumed that he went to Juichin to attend these meetings (as well, perhaps, as the Party's Fifth Plenum, which was also held at that time in Juichin). In any event, he was again elected a member of the Chinese Soviet Republic's Central Executive Committee.

Jen was back in the Hunan-Kiangsi border region by the summer of 1934, and in August of that year orders were received to retreat westward across Hunan to join Ho Lung's Second Army Corps. Even if it was not realized at the time, this move, in effect, was the beginning of the Long March for the Sixth Army Corps. The normal command structure for Red Army units in that period consisted of the commander and the political commissar. In the case of the Sixth Army Corps, however, in July 1934 (just before the retreat) Jen was appointed chairman of the Corps' Political Committee, and Hsiao K'o and Wang Chen (q.v.) continued to be the commander and political commissar, respectively. By October 1934 the Sixth Corps had moved to northeast Kweichow where they met Ho Lung's Second Army Corps. After spending the winter there, the combined force, now called the Second Front Army, moved to Ho's former base in west Hunan (April 1935) and then expanded into an area on the borders of Szechwan, Hunan, Hupeh, and Kweichow provinces. They proceeded to establish a base area named for the four provinces (see under Ho Lung). The formation of the Second Front Army brought about a new command structure; Ho Lung was the commander, Jen was the political commissar, and Kuan Hsiang-ying (q.v.), who had been Ho's chief political officer, was the deputy political commissar. In addition, and probably more important, Jen was also secretary of the Party Sub-bureau for the Hunan-Hupeh-Szechwan-Kweichow base.

In November 1935, by which time the forces led by Mao Tse-tung had already arrived in north Shensi, the Second Front Army began the next leg of its Long March. Moving out of west Hunan, it followed a route roughly similar to that taken by Mao the year before and arrived in Sikang province in June 1936 where it joined yet another formation of Red Army troops—the Fourth Front Army commanded by Chang Kuo-t'ao, Hsu Hsiang-ch'ien, Chu Te, and Liu Po-ch'eng. The Fourth Front Army was in Sikang because of serious rifts in the Communist leadership a year earlier; because of these differences Mao had moved north to Shensi with his troops in 1935, but Chang Kuo-t'ao had separated himself from Mao's Long March troops and then moved into Sikang. Thus, when Jen and the Second Front Army joined Chang Kuo-t'ao in Sikang, it was necessary to arrive at a decision regarding the ultimate destination of their troops. The decision was soon made to move north to join Mao in Shensi but (according to orthodox Maoist accounts) only after a "resolute struggle" against Chang Kuo-t'ao. Jen is credited with a major role in forcing Chang to take this course of action. Chang, on the other hand, claims that Jen took a rather conciliatory attitude toward him.[10] In any event, the two armies started north in July 1936; in October they were met in Kansu by some of Mao's units, and soon afterwards Jen and most of his colleagues joined Mao in north Shensi.

In mid-1937, slightly more than half a year after Jen arrived in Shensi, the Sino-Japanese War broke out. The Communists immediately organized their forces into the Eighth Route Army. Chu Te was the commander-in-chief, P'eng Te-huai was his deputy, and Jen was made director of the Political Department, the top political post. The Communist troops moved eastward into Shansi in September to engage the Japanese. Agnes Smedley, who was with the Eighth Route Army during the first few months of the war, has provided several glimpses of Jen at or near the frontlines during this period. She first saw Jen in the Wu-t'ai area of northeast Shansi in October, and over the next several weeks she had a number of conversations with him as the Eighth Route Army Headquarters was moved southward toward Lin-fen in the face of the advancing Japanese forces.[11] U.S. Naval Observer Evans Carlson also saw Jen in late 1937 and described him as one of the "brains" of the Eighth Route Army.[12] Jen was still in Shansi in early 1938, and for the January 28, 1938, issue of the Yenan Party organ Chieh-fang (Liberation) he wrote an account of the fighting in Shansi.

At some time in 1938 Jen relinquished the Political Department post to Wang Chia-hsiang, and then went to Moscow. The reasons for this trip are not clear; he may have gone for medical treatment, because he was known to have been in poor health since at least the mid-1930's. En route to and from the Soviet Union he passed through Sinkiang, where he conferred with Sheng Shih-ts'ai, the semi-independent warlord who controlled the province and who was then cooperating with the Chinese Communists (see under Teng Fa and Ch'en T'an-ch'iu).[13] By 1940 Jen was back in Yenan, where he was assigned to work in the Party Secretariat, then the most important organ in the CCP political structure. There is relatively little detailed information on Jen's activities during the next few years, but an account by Wang Shou-tao, in spite of its ebullient tone, provides a general picture of the work in which Jen was engaged.[14] From Wang's account, it appears that Jen worked mainly on economic problems, which, from the early forties, were particularly pressing in Shensi because of the blockade by the Nationalists as well as the continuing struggle against Japan. He is credited with having personally directed programs to increase production and to urge upon the populace measures designed to conserve the scanty resources of the Communists' Shensi-Kansu-Ninghsia Border Region. On one occasion, according to Wang, he set a personal example by going to an area near Yenan where he set up a special brigade to grow cotton. It is evident that Jen was well established in the inner councils of the Mao Tse-tung leadership by the time the Party met for its Seventh Congress (April–June 1945). As one of the 15 members of the Congress presidium, as well as its secretary-general, Jen was given the honor of opening the meetings. He was subsequently re-elected a member of the Central Committee, and although Central Committee rankings are not always the best guide to actual political authority, it is noteworthy that Jen was placed fourth on the Seventh Central Committee (after Mao, Chu Te, and Liu Shao-ch'i). More important, at the First Plenum, held immediately after the Congress, Jen was re-elected to the Politburo and elected for the first time as a secretary of the Secretariat. The last-named post, in effect, placed him among the half dozen top leaders of the CCP.

In the immediate postwar period, as the Communist armies began to engage the Nationalists in the civil war, Jen remained with Mao in Yenan. But they were forced to evacuate their capital to the Nationalists in March 1947. Presumably with a view to possible emergency situations, the Secretariat was divided into two groups. Mao, Chou En-lai, and Jen remained in the Shensi-Kansu-Ninghsia Border Region, and a "working committee" of the Secretariat headed by Liu Shao-ch'i and Chu Te moved into the Shansi-Chahar-Hopeh area to set up a headquarters in P'ing-shan hsien, not far from Shih-chia-chuang in west Hopeh.[15] They were joined there by Mao and his group 14 months later, in May 1948. In the interim, Jen devoted himself principally to basic policy questions which were arising as the Communist armies conquered more and more territory. (From Wang Shou-tao's account, it appears that Jen was then head of the Party's Research Office.) Among the more pressing problems was the need to formulate policies to handle agrarian questions, and still other policies were required to deal with industrial and business interests in the large cities which the Communist armies were beginning to capture. On the land question, in particular, Communist policies fluctuated rather quickly from "radical" to "conservative" from the end of 1946 to the early part of 1948. Like several top leaders, Jen's positions underwent quite notable changes; in the latter part of 1947 he called for "radical" actions by the "masses," but by the turn of the year 1947–48 he was among those articulating a new, more "conservative" policy—both in terms of the landed elements in the rural areas and of the business interests in the cities.[16] It is noteworthy that Mao Tse-tung frequently addressed himself to these questions in a series of speeches and directives from the end of 1947 to the spring of 1948.[17]

Jen was almost certainly among those who attended the Party Central Committee's Second Plenum near Shih-chia-chuang in March 1949, immediately after which the Central Committee and the PLA Headquarters were transferred to Peking. In the following month Jen made his last major speech when he addressed the First Congress of the New Democratic Youth League. His talk dealt with the main theme enunciated at the Second Plenum, namely, the shift in work from the countryside to the cities which the

Communists were then capturing in rapid succession. The choice of Jen to deliver this address was fitting, because he was one of the few surviving youth leaders from the 1920's. At the close of the Congress, he was elected honorary chairman of the Youth League.

Jen's health had been failing since the end of 1947, and it took a turn for the worse in 1949. When the PRC was inaugurated in October, he was the only top Party leader who did not receive a post in the new government. He went to Moscow in early 1950 for medical treatment and returned home in the summer. Jen made one of his rare public appearances on October 18, 1950, but nine days later, on October 27, he died of a cerebral hemorrhage in Peking. His death and funeral were given wide coverage in the press, and he was described in that particular phrase reserved for the select few: "a close comrade-in-arms of Mao Tse-tung."

Jen was a frequent contributor to Party publications during his long career, especially the youth journals to which he first contributed in the twenties when he was actively engaged in youth work. In 1924 his translation of a work by Lenin dealing with China was published in Shanghai by the *Tung-fang tsa-chih* (Eastern magazine).[18] In later years Jen wrote on a number of subjects, including the above-mentioned problems the Party was having in postwar times with land reform. Many of his writings are cited in the bibliographies of Chün-tu Hsüeh.[19]

Jen's wife, Ch'en Tsung-ying, was with him in Shanghai in the mid-twenties, as well as on the Long March a decade later. She has been a member of the Executive Committee of the National Women's Federation since 1957. They apparently had five children, four of whom were identified in mid-1951 (their given names being Yuan-chih, Yuan-cheng, Yuan-fang, and Yuan-yuan), but nothing further is known about them. In 1962 a nephew named Jen Hsiang was lecturing at the Peking Geological Institute.[20] In political terms, Jen Pi-shih's most important relative was a cousin named Jen Tso-min. He also came from Hsiang-yin hsien in Hunan (1899) and, in the words of his obituary,[21] he was from a petty bourgeois family. His father graduated from a Japanese university and was later a law professor and lawyer in Hunan. Jen Tso-min graduated from an agricultural school in Hunan, and then in 1921 he went to Moscow (possibly with his cousin) where he too studied at the Communist University of the Toilers of the East. In January 1922, on the recommendation of Liu Shao-ch'i and Lo I-nung, he joined the CCP. Jen Tso-min returned to China in 1925, and by 1927 he was in covert communications work in Shanghai.[22] He was captured by the authorities about 1927 and was imprisoned for seven years. After the Sino-Japanese War began in 1937, Jen was assigned to Party work in Changsha where he probably worked under Hsu T'e-li (q.v.). He was called back to Yenan in 1939, and after a period of study in 1940 at the Marx-Lenin Institute he became deputy secretary-general of the Party's Northwest Bureau. He was holding this post at the time of his death in February 1942.

Because Jen Pi-shih is regarded as one of the greatest Youth League and CCP leaders, his career has been rather extensively documented in Communist publications. The most valuable of these is a small book published in Canton in 1950 under the title *Hsueh-hsi Jen Pi-shih T'ung-chih* (Learn from Comrade Jen Pi-shih). This contains his official obituary, as well as essays on Jen by his friends, colleagues, and relatives.

---

1. *Hung-ch'i p'iao-p'iao* (Red flag fluttering; Peking, 1957), IV, 23.
2. Conrad Brandt, *Stalin's Failure in China, 1924–1927* (Cambridge, Mass., 1958), p. 47.
3. *CB* 410, p. 35.
4. Brandt, p. 129.
5. Conrad Brandt, Benjamin Schwartz, and John K. Fairbank, *A Documentary History of Chinese Communism* (Cambridge, Mass., 1952), p. 33.
6. *JMJP,* Oct. 27, 1951.
7. Tso-liang Hsiao, *Power Relations within the Chinese Communist Movement, 1930–1934* (Seattle, Wash., 1961), p. 150.
8. *Ibid.,* pp. 237–238.
9. Teng Hung, *Ti-i-ko feng-lang* (The first storm; Hong Kong, 1962), pp. 48–49.
10. Modern China Project, Columbia University, New York, Howard L. Boorman, director.
11. Agnes Smedley, *China Fights Back* (London, 1938), pp. 85, 124, 228–232, 256, and 268–269.
12. Evans Fordyce Carlson, *Twin Stars of China* (New York, 1940), photo opposite p. 64.
13. Allen S. Whiting and Sheng Shih-ts'ai, *Sinkiang: Pawn or Pivot?* (East Lansing, Mich., 1958), pp. 55, 187.
14. *JMJP,* October 27, 1951.
15. *Selected Works of Mao Tse-tung* (Peking, 1961), IV, 132.
16. Jerome Ch'en, *Mao and the Chinese Revolution* (London, 1965), pp. 297–298; Chao Kuo-chun, *Agrarian Policy of the Chinese Communist Party, 1921–1959* (Bombay, 1960), p. 75.
17. *Selected Works of Mao Tse-tung* (Peking, 1961), IV, 157–210, 219–259.
18. Chang Ching-lu, ed., *Chung-kuo ch'u-pan shih-liao pu-pien* (Supplementary historical materials on Chinese publishing; Peking, 1957), p. 455.
19. Chün-tu Hsüeh, *The Chinese Communist Movement, 1921–1937* (Stanford, Calif., 1960) and *The Chinese Communist Movement, 1937–1949* (Stanford, Calif., 1962).
20. *SCMP* 2644, p. 9.
21. Yenan, *Chieh-fang jih-pao* (Liberation daily), February 23, 1942.
22. Liu Chien-hua, et al., *Wu-ling feng-yun* (The gathering clouds on the Wuling Mountains; Hong Kong, 1961), p. 47.

Jung Kao-t'ang

(c.1910–　　; Shensi?). Vice-chairman, All-China Sports Federation; vice-chairman, Physical Culture and Sports Commission.

Sports leader Jung Kao-t'ang was probably born about 1910 to judge from the date he was in college. His original name was Jung Ch'ien-hsiang, and he was also known as Kao T'ang as late as the early 1950's. A 1958 article in the Communist press noted that Jung had entertained his colleagues by singing Shensi folk songs, thereby suggesting his place of nativity, although he may simply have become familiar with the Shensi dialect and folklore during wartime days in Yenan.

Jung's first apparent contact with the Chinese left-wing occurred in the winter of 1935–36 when he was a participant in the December Ninth Movement, which derives its name from student demonstrations that began on December 9, 1935, in opposition to Japanese incursions into north China. One outgrowth of the movement was the formation of the National Liberation Vanguard of China (NLVC), an organization originally motivated by nationalism but soon captured by the Communist apparatus in north China (see under Li Ch'ang). The NLVC carried out a variety of activities aimed at arousing the general populace to the dangers of Japanese imperialism. For example, NLVC members journeyed into the countryside around Peking to explain world events to simple peasants and also organized groups to visit and entertain Chinese armies stationed in north China. One favorite tactic of the NLVC was to present a play with a patriotic theme, after which more politically oriented speeches would be made to the gathered assembly. A ranking Communist, writing in 1961, stated that Jung wrote one such play which was particularly popular and that it helped the NLVC recruit new members.[1]

A large number of the NLVC students came from the best schools in Peking, especially Peking and Tsinghua Universities. Jung is known to have studied engineering at the latter, but there are no indications that he utilized this training in his later career. It is probable that Jung joined the Communist Youth League in 1936 or soon thereafter. In any event, a number of his colleagues of that period (such as Li Ch'ang) were known to have joined, and after the war against Japan broke out in mid-1937 many of them fled to the northwest areas controlled by the Communists. Jung must have been among them, because during the war he was a member of the Communist-backed "Liberated Areas Youth Federation," an organization centered in Yenan, which included Communist as well as non-Communist youths.

No record is available of Jung's wartime activities, but he must have impressed some of the more senior Communists in the northwest with his loyalty or capabilities, or both. This became evident in 1946 when he was given responsible positions under the Peking Executive Headquarters, the organization established under the cease-fire agreement by the Nationalists, Communists, and Americans in January 1946. Holding the rank of colonel, Jung served as head of the Personnel Section and concurrently as director of the Administrative Section of the Communist delegation.

When the truce broke down in early 1947 the Communist delegation in Peking returned to the Communist capital of Yenan. Once more, Jung fades from the record, but then he reappears in Peking in 1949 to assume a number of key positions within the New Democratic Youth League (NDYL). At the first League congress in April 1949 he was elected to the Central Committee, as well as to the Standing Committee, then consisting of only nine members. Moreover, before the year was out, he assumed four additional posts within the League: director, Students Department (1949–c.1950); director, Staff Office (1949–c.1953); director, Social Services Department (1949–c.1953); and secretary-general (1949–1951). The last post was clearly the most important because several of the other top youth leaders of that period (e.g., Feng Wen-pin, Liao Ch'eng-chih, Chiang Nan-hsiang, qq.v.) all had important collateral duties, which of necessity lessened the amount of time they could devote to the League. In brief, it appears that in the early years of the League Jung was one of the most important of its leaders in terms of the day-to-day management of the organization. In October 1951 the League underwent a slight reorganization, during which a Secretariat was created. Jung was named to this Secretariat, and following the second congress of the League in June–July 1953, he was re-elected to it (as well as to the Standing Committee of the Central Committee at the Congress). However, by 1953 Jung had become more deeply involved in other activities, and his role in the Youth League was nominal after this time. He was dropped from the Secretariat and the Standing Committee at the 1957 Youth League congress (when the organization was renamed as the Communist Youth League), and then at the next congress (1964) he was dropped from the Central Committee, thus bringing to a close his career as a youth leader. Paralleling his work in the Youth League, Jung also served from 1949 to 1953 as a National Committee member of the other important youth organi-

zation, the All-China Federation of Democratic Youth.

The central government was organized at the initial session of the CPPCC in September 1949, a meeting Jung attended as a representative of the Youth League. During this session he served on the ad hoc committee to draft the Common Program of the CPPCC, a committee headed by Chou En-lai. The Common Program was one of the principal documents ratified at the CPPCC session and served as the precursor of the Constitution adopted in September 1954. Jung received no job under the central government, but in the following month (October 1949) he took part in the organization of the All-China Athletic Federation (sometimes called the China Olympic Committee and officially renamed the All-China Sports Federation in July 1964). He was named secretary-general of the Preparatory Committee as well as one of the vice-chairmen under Chairman Feng Wen-pin, a prominent youth leader of the period and also Jung's superior in the Youth League. He was also selected as a vice-chairman and secretary-general when the organization was formally established in June 1952 and was then re-elected to the vice-chairmanship during a reorganization of October 1956. Following the 1956 reorganization, the Athletic Federation was placed under the titular leadership of the elderly Ma Yueh-han (John Ma), the father of modern sports in China and a long-time professor of physical education at Tsinghua University. Because American-educated Ma (d. October 1966) was not a Party member, it has been evident that from about the mid-1950's Jung Kao-t'ang has been, in fact, the single most important figure in Chinese sports, a situation that can be illustrated in a number of ways. As in all Communist countries, the Chinese Communists have placed a premium on the organization of sports, making heavy investments in such things as new gymnasiums and stadiums of impressive size. Paralleling this, the government established at the cabinet level the Physical Culture and Sports Commission in November 1952 under the veteran PLA leader Ho Lung, later to be a PLA marshal and a Party Politburo member. Ho, of course, has had only a limited amount of time to devote to the Commission, and thus it has probably been Jung, the Commission secretary-general by 1953, who has played the most significant role in the daily operations of this body. Following the reorganization of the government in the fall of 1954, Jung was elevated to his present position as a vice-chairman of the Commission. As such he is often the man who reports before governmental bodies on the development of sports in China. To cite but two examples, he gave reports before the 64th and 94th NPC Standing Committee meetings held, respectively, on October 5, 1962 and April 27, 1963. Or, to mention other examples, he served on the preparatory committee for the first national sports meet (1958–59), and when the meet was held in September 1959 Jung was the master of ceremonies. Similarly, in January 1965 he was again named to the preparatory committee for the second national meet scheduled for later in the year.

One of the obvious by-products of a large investment in sports has been a much increased participation in international athletic events. The Chinese Communists have become increasingly active in this field and have, in many respects, been quite successful, especially in competition with other Asians. Jung has played a singularly important role in these activities. He has been a member—or more frequently a leader—of sports delegations or teams which have been abroad nine times from 1952 to early 1965. Briefly, these trips include visits to: Finland, July–August 1952, for the 15th Olympic Games (in which the Chinese Communists only partially participated); the USSR, July 1954, for a Soviet sports festival; France, June 1955, for a meeting of the International Olympics Committee; Japan, March–April 1956, for the 23rd World Table Tennis Championship matches and for a meeting of the International Table Tennis Federation; Japan, October 1962, for table tennis matches; Indonesia, October–November 1963, for the first Games of the New Emerging Forces (GANEFO); Cuba and Albania, February–March 1964, for meetings with Cuban and Albanian sportsmen and sports officials; and Yugoslavia, April 1965, for the 28th World Table Tennis Championship matches.

Additional comments are necessary regarding the Olympic Games and the GANEFO. As already noted, Jung had led a group to the 1952 Olympic Games in Helsinki. While there, the International Olympics Committee took a decision (by a 105 to 83 vote) to postpone the decision of Peking's entry into the international organization, even though this same body had invited the Chinese Communists to the Helsinki games. While still in Helsinki Jung bitterly protested the postponement in a letter of August 3. Furthermore, in 1956 the Chinese team was just on the eve of departure for the 16th Games in Australia (with Jung to serve as a deputy leader of the Chinese delegation) when a top-level decision was made in Peking not to participate owing to the participation of a team from Taiwan. Thus, Peking was immediately responsive when Indonesian President Sukarno, angered by alleged mistreatment from the International Olympics Committee, decided to hold the GANEFO in 1963. The Chinese attended a preparatory conference in Jakarta and then formed a Preparatory Committee for Participation in the GANEFO in June 1963. Ho Lung was named as chairman and Jung as one of the vice-chairmen. In October of that year Jung led a huge delegation to Indonesia for the games held in November, which

were won by the Chinese. (Ho Lung led the official government delegation.) During the following spring (1964) the Indonesian minister of Sports visited Peking and at the close of this visit signed a joint communiqué with Jung, in which the Chinese pledged future cooperation. This was given organizational expression in August 1964 when a permanent National Committee of the PRC for the GANEFO was established with Jung as chairman.

Although Jung's time has been devoted chiefly to athletic endeavors, he has held several other official and semi-official posts over the years and has served on various *ad hoc* committees. From October 1950 to July 1958 he was a National Committee member of the China Peace Committee. In May 1954 he was named to the Standing Committee of the newly organized Chinese People's Association for Cultural Relations with Foreign Countries, a position he still holds. Four years later a parallel body was formed under the government known as the Commission for Cultural Relations with Foreign Countries; Jung was named as a member in March 1958 and still retains the post. Also in 1954 he was elected a Hopeh deputy to the First NPC; he was re-elected for the Second NPC (1959–1964) and again for the Third NPC, which held its first session in December 1964–January 1965. In September 1955 he chaired the presidium (steering committee) of a huge nationwide conference of "Young Activists in Socialist Construction" and in the fall of 1959 served as a presidium member for a national conference of "advanced" (or "progressive") workers. In September 1958 the China–(East) Germany Friendship Association was established with Jung as one of the vice-chairmen, another position he continues to hold. His only known writing of importance is an article entitled "Let Physical Culture Better Serve Socialist Construction" that he wrote for *Hung-ch'i* (Red flag), June 1, 1960, in which he asserted that 100 million Chinese were taking part in organized athletic programs.

1. *Chung-kuo ch'ing-nien* (China youth), November 16, 1961, translated in *SCMM* 297.

Jung Tzu-ho

(c.1907–   ; Ling-ch'iu hsien, Shansi). Director, Finance Committee, Northwest Bureau, CCP.

Jung Tzu-ho is a specialist in finance, who, until around 1949, was known by the name of Jung Wu-sheng. Together with such well-known Communist figures as Po I-po and Lei Jen-min (qq.v.), Jung attended the Kuo-min Normal School in Taiyuan, the Shansi capital, and while attending this school joined the Communist Party in 1928. Later he attended and graduated from Shansi University. Like many of his Shansi compatriots, Jung was caught up in the wave of anti-

Japanese sentiment which swept the nation—and especially north China—in the mid-1930's, as the outbreak of war approached. In Shansi this took the organizational form of the "Shansi Sacrifice and Save-the-Nation League," an organization founded in September 1936 on the fifth anniversary of the 1931 Manchurian Incident, Japan's first major thrust into China. Jung joined this league and served on its Standing Committee.

After the war against Japan broke out in mid-1937, Po I-po and others formed "Dare-to-Die" units, which fought against the Japanese in southeastern Shansi. These were originally subordinated to the "New Army" of Shansi Governor Yen Hsi-shan, but in late 1939 the bulk of the New Army forces defected to the Communists. In this same period, Jung was working with Po I-po and other important Party leaders (such as Li Hsueh-feng) in the formation of the T'ai-yueh Anti-Japanese Base in southeastern Shansi, of which the military unit was known as the T'ai-yueh District Column, a subordinate unit of Liu Po-ch'eng's 129th Division.[1] Jung served as the commander of this column, apparently for the remainder of the war against Japan.

In 1940 and 1941 the Communists began to reorganize the T'ai-yueh, T'ai-hang (northern and eastern Shansi), South Hopeh, and the Hopeh-Shantung-Honan districts to form, in July 1941, the Shansi-Hopeh-Shantung-Honan Border Region Government. For the balace of the Sino-Japanese War this stood on a par with the Shensi-Kansu-Ninghsia and the Shansi-Chahar-Hopeh Border Region governments as one of the three most important administrative units in north and northwest China. Yang Hsiu-feng (q.v.), a Peking university professor who had turned to guerrilla warfare and joined the Communists, was the chairman of this new government. Po I-po and Jung were named as the two vice-chairmen.[2] At some point over the next few years Jung was also named to head the government Finance Department, and from this time onward his career was strongly oriented toward financial work. This was evident from an interview which Jung gave American journalist Anna Louise Strong at Han-tan (southwest Hopeh) in 1946; Jung's comment to Miss Strong dealt with the attempts of the border region government to balance the budget in the face of attacks upon the region by Nationalist forces.[3]

As the Communists were winning victories in north China in 1947, they were able to link together the Shansi-Chahar-Hopeh (Chin-Ch'a-Chi) and the Shansi-Hopeh-Shantung-Honan border regions. To formalize this merger, the North China People's Government was brought into being by a conference held in August 1948, at which Jung gave one of the reports. At the close of the congress top Party leader Tung Pi-wu was named as chairman, and Jung as one of the members of the government; in the following month (September 1948) he was named to head

the Finance Department and to membership on the Finance and Economics Committee (which Tung Pi-wu concurrently headed).

Peking was peacefully surrendered to the Communist forces in January 1949, and because a number of senior officials of the North China People's Government were in this area, they were called upon to assume posts in Peking to take over the municipal administrative posts vacated by the Kuomintang. As the Communist military forces were moving into the city in late January and early February 1949, the Communist authorities formed a "joint administrative office" for Peking, which operated under the jurisdiction of General Lin Piao's Peking-Tientsin Front Command. The administrative office was composed of seven members, headed by Party veteran Yeh Chien-ying. The other six members —half Communists and half from the Kuomintang—were placed on one of three committees: military; political and cultural; or financial. On the Communist side, T'ao Chu (q.v.) was placed on the military committee, Hsu Ping (q.v.) was named to the political and cultural committee, and Jung to the financial committee.[4] Jung was thus the first head of finance in the Communist capital-to-be. Less than a month after these events transpired, the North China People's Government moved into Peking (February 1949), but then in October 1949 this government was dissolved when the central government was established. Jung received appointments under the central government comparable to those he had held in the North China Government. He was named to membership on the important Finance and Economics Committee, under the chairmanship of the senior economic specialist of that period, Ch'en Yun. He was also named as a vice-minister of Finance, a post he was to hold for the next 12 years, serving under three of the top members of the Party elite, Po I-po (Jung's long-time colleague), Teng Hsiao-p'ing, and Li Hsien-nien.

During Jung's long term as vice-minister of Finance, it was evident that he was one of the senior men in the ministry, serving, for example, as acting minister in 1953 for Po I-po. His importance was also emphasized by the frequency with which he gave official ministry reports before sessions of the Government Administration Council (1949–1954) and the State Council (1954 to date). When special organizations involving financial or economic work were set up, Jung was often a member, especially in the early years of the PRC. For example, in 1950 he was a member of the National Material Inventory and Appropriation Board and in late 1951 was named to membership on the Central Austerity Examination Committee. He received appointments of apparently longer duration when he was named in December 1954 as chairman of the Board of Directors of the Bank of Communications and in July 1957 when he received an appointment on the newly formed Central Relief Administration (an organization dealing with emergency measures such as floods and droughts.)

Although never a deputy to the NPC, Jung has given several reports before this legislative organization, most notably in April 1959 and April 1960. Unlike many high-ranking Party leaders in Peking, he has not been engaged in the time-consuming processes of entertaining foreign visitors. The overwhelming majority of the times that Jung has been mentioned in the press has been in connection with specific affairs of state—such as budgetary matters—thus suggesting that the authorities have attempted to utilize his fiscal talents to the maximum. For reasons which are not clear, Jung fell from public attention in 1960 and was subsequently removed as a vice-minister of Finance in July 1961. Nothing was heard about him for three years until July–August 1964 when he was a member of a delegation to Cuba led by Central Committee alternate Li Ch'ang for the 11th anniversary of the founding of Fidel Castro's resistance movement. In March 1965 Jung was further identified, being mentioned as a "responsible member" of the Northwest Bureau of the Party Central Committee. This was clarified in June 1965 when he was identified as director of Bureau's Finance Committee. The regional Party bureaus, abolished in 1954–55, had been re-created in 1961 and in the years following a number of senior specialists were sent from Peking to staff them. It is therefore possible that Jung was working in the northwest from about 1961. It is also probable that he relinquished his post as head of the Bank of Communications sometime about 1961.

Although a long-time financial and economics official, Jung is not known to have published much in this field. However, he did write two articles on financial matters for *Ts'ai-cheng* (Finance), no. 1 (1958) and no. 18 (1959).

1. *K'ang-Jih chan-cheng shih-ch'i chieh-fang-ch'ü kai-k'uang* (A sketch of the liberated areas during the Anti-Japanese War; Peking, 1953), p. 44.
2. *Ibid.*, p. 64.
3. Anna Louise Strong, *Tomorrow's China* (New York, 1948), pp. 77–79.
4. A. Doak Barnett, *China on the Eve of Communist Takeover* (New York, 1963), pp. 336–337.

K'ai Feng

(1907–1955; Hunan). Youth leader; Party ideologue.

Moscow-trained K'ai Feng was a prominent youth leader in the early thirties and an important propagandist-ideologue in the late thirties and early forties when he headed the Party's Propaganda Department. He faded into obscurity during the latter years of the Sino-Japanese War, then re-emerged to hold only minor posts in the early years of the PRC. He was known at various times throughout his career as Ho K'o-ch'üan and Ho K'ai-feng.

K'ai was born in 1907 in Hunan and studied in Moscow,[1] probably in the late 1920's. He attended the CCP's Sixth Congress, which was held in Moscow in mid-1928,[2] and because he was then only 21 it is likely that he attended while he was a student. He studied at the revolutionary Sun Yat-sen University in Moscow and came to be associated with the group known as the "28 Bolsheviks" who were protégés of University Chancellor and Comintern representative Pavel Mif. The activities of this group upon their return to China are described in the biographies of Ch'en Shao-yü and Ch'in Pang-hsien. K'ai's political fortunes in the ensuing years seem to have coincided with the rise and fall of the "28 Bolsheviks."

K'ai's activities are unreported at the time the "28 Bolsheviks" returned to China in 1930 and took over the leadership of the CCP at the Fourth Plenum in January 1931. However, an article he wrote in 1932 suggests that he may already have been active in the student movement; written for the Party journal *Hung-ch'i chou-pao* (Red flag weekly) of January 15, 1932, it dealt with the current state of student activities. By 1933 the CCP had been forced to close its headquarters in Shanghai and move the seat of Party authority to Kiangsi where Mao Tse-tung, Chu Te, and others had established the Chinese Soviet Republic (November 1931) to administer the scattered rural Communist bases. K'ai was in Kiangsi in 1933, the year he became secretary of the Communist Youth League, a position he held for three years.

The principal leadership of the Party was congregated in Kiangsi in early 1934 for two important meetings, the Fifth Party Plenum, which was in session on January 18, and the Second All-China Congress of Soviets, which opened in Juichin, Kiangsi, in late January. Ch'in Pang-hsien, one of the most prominent of the "28 Bolsheviks," presided over the Party meeting, and Mao chaired the Soviet Congress. At the close of the Congress K'ai was elected to membership on the Soviet Republic's Second Central Executive Committee (CEC), the governing body for the soviet government. Thus by early 1934 he had become one of the leaders responsible for the affairs of the Chinese Soviet Republic. Other members of the "28 Bolshevik" group on the CEC with K'ai were Chang Wen-t'ien, Ch'in Pang-hsien, Ch'en Shao-yü, and Wang Chia-hsiang (qq.v.).

The Fifth Plenum and the Second Soviet Congress both dealt with the Communists' relations with the revolt of dissident KMT leaders in

Fukien against Chiang Kai-shek's government. The Fukien rebels, led by Ch'en Ming-shu and others and supported by Ts'ai T'ing-k'ai's famous 19th Route Army, proclaimed a "people's government" in November 1933. However, Chiang Kai-shek's forces quelled the rebellion just as the Fifth Plenum was held. The Communists' relations with the Fukien rebels have become obscured partially because of latter-day Maoist interpretations blaming the "28 Bolsheviks" for the fact that the Communists did not give sufficient help to the rebels. The writings of K'ai, published shortly after the rebellion was crushed, provide some insight into the situation and indicate that he was one of the Party polemicists entrusted with "re-examining the rebellion and reappraising Communist policy toward it."[3] Writing for *Tou-cheng* (Struggle), the Party's official journal in Kiangsi, K'ai declared that a small group within the Party had opposed assistance to the rebels, even to the extent of mere encouragement. Prior to the rebellion, the Communists had signed a preliminary agreement with the rebels; it was apparently to justify this involvement that K'ai wrote his second long tract for *Tou-cheng* on February 23, 1934.[4]

It is evident that there were differences between the Maoist faction and the "28 Bolsheviks" (K'ai among them) regarding the Fukien rebels. And it is equally evident that disagreements existed within the "28 Bolsheviks" group. This complex situation, including a discussion of Comintern attitudes at the time, is outlined succinctly in Stuart Schram's biography of Mao. Schram concludes that the "problem of the policy of the Chinese Soviet Republic toward the Fukien rebels . . . remains one of the most obscure ones in the whole history of the Chinese Communist Party."[5]

It is probable, though undocumented, that K'ai made the Long March (1934–35) as a member of the forces led by Chu Te and Mao. The peak of his career seems to have been during the years after the Communists reached north Shensi at the end of the March. He relinquished the secretaryship of the Youth League to Feng Wen-pin (q.v.) in 1936, although he continued to serve on the League's Central Committee.[6] According to a Japanese source, K'ai became a Politburo member in 1937 as well as director of the Party's Propaganda Department.[7] The latter position seems to follow logically from K'ai's previous writings as a Party ideologue, but the report of his Politburo membership must be treated with caution in view of the number of unreliable reports in the mid-thirties about such membership. However, there are other indications that K'ai was at this time among the top CCP leaders. For example, although American author Edgar Snow has little to say about him, from the context of the brief comments he made about K'ai in 1936 it is evident that he associated closely

with key Party leaders.[8] Moreover, K'ai was a regular contributor to several leading CCP publications during the early years of the war.[9] For *Ch'ün-chung* (The masses), *Chieh-fang* (Liberation), and other publications he wrote a number of articles on the war and the united front in the years between 1937 and 1941, a period when others of the "28 Bolshevik" group like Ch'en Shao-yü, Ch'in Pang-hsien, and Wang Chia-hsiang were similarly prolific.

K'ai apparently played a key role in the Party's *cheng-feng* ("rectification") movement, which began in early 1942. Mao Tse-tung opened his famous speech on Party "formalism" (February 8) with the words: "Comrade K'ai Feng has just spoken on the purpose of today's meeting."[10] One writer has commented that "propaganda chief K'ai Feng [had] elaborated on the evils of formalism in Party literature and propaganda to an audience of 800."[11] K'ai's stature within the Party elite at this time is also illustrated in an article by novelist Chou Li-po on the 20th anniversary of Mao's May 1942 talks on literature at Yenan. Describing the meeting, Chou wrote: "Leading comrades from the Party center, including Liu Shao-ch'i, Chu Te, Jen Pi-shih, Ch'en Yun, Ch'en Po-ta, Hu Ch'iao-mu, K'ang Sheng, Po Ku [qq.v.; for Po Ku see Ch'in Pang-hsien] and K'ai Feng had all taken their seats."[12] However, after the early stages of the *cheng-feng* movement K'ai faded from the scene and nearly a decade passed before he appeared again.

During the latter stages of the war he was clearly supplanted as a top propagandist and idealogue by such men as Lu Ting-i (q.v.), Ch'en Po-ta, and Hu Ch'iao-mu. Any doubts about his political decline were dispelled when the Party held its Seventh National Congress from April to June 1945. K'ai apparently took no part in the meetings, nor was he elected to membership on the Central Committee.

K'ai re-emerged, but only inconspicuously, in February 1951 when he was appointed to membership in the Northeast People's Government (NEPG), then headed by Kao Kang (q.v.). He was identified then as a member of the Party's Northeast Bureau, also headed by Kao. A year later (January 1952), K'ai was further identified as a deputy secretary of the Mukden CCP Committee, serving here under Huang Ou-tung (q.v.). And later in 1952 the Communist press reported him among a number of Party officials in Manchuria who were participating in an intensive study of Mao Tse-tung's essay, "On Contradiction." He then faded from the news again, and when the NEPG was reorganized into the Northeast Administrative Committee in January 1953, K'ai was among the few not reappointed to membership.

Nothing further was heard of K'ai Feng until his death in Peking on March 23, 1955, when he was identified as a deputy director of the Party's Propaganda Department. The Chinese Communists have a highly formalistic style of announcing the deaths of their members—the most senior leaders receiving page one coverage in the *JMJP,* with elaborate reportage in subsequent issues on funeral and memorial services. The death of somewhat lesser leaders is normally reported on page two, while all others are mentioned on the last page in small type and without comment. The announcement of K'ai's death fell into the last category, and thus the passing of one who had been an important Party leader in earlier years was presented to the Chinese public of the mid-fifties as a minor happening.

1. *Hsin ming-tz'u tz'u-tien* (New terminology dictionary; Shanghai, 1949), biographic section, p. 17.

2. Conrad Brandt, Benjamin Schwartz, and John K. Fairbank, *A Documentary History of Chinese Communism* (Cambridge, Mass., 1952), p. 124.

3. William F. Dorrill, unpublished manuscript, "Mao Tse-tung and the Chinese Communist Movement: 1927–35," chap. 6, p. 11.

4. *Ibid.;* Tso-liang Hsiao, *Power Relations within the Chinese Communist Movement, 1930–1934* (Seattle, Wash., 1961), pp. 256–258.

5. Stuart Schram, *Mao Tse-tung* (New York, 1966), pp. 158–161.

6. Nym Wales, *Inside Red China* (New York, 1939), p. 99; Edgar Snow, *Random Notes on Red China, 1936–1945* (Cambridge, Mass., 1957), p. 52.

7. Hatano Kenichi, *Mo Taku Tō to Chu-goku no kō-sei* (Mao Tse-tung and China's Red stars; Tokyo, 1946), p. 107.

8. Edgar Snow, *Red Star over China* (New York, 1938), p. 366.

9. Chün-tu Hsüeh, *The Chinese Communist Movement, 1937–1949* (Stanford, Calif.), pp. 5, 24, 33, 38.

10. *Selected Works of Mao Tse-tung* (Peking, 1965), III, 53.

11. Boyd Compton, *Mao's China: Party Reform Documents, 1942–44* (Seattle, Wash., 1952), p. xxxiv.

12. *CB* 685, p. 18.

Kan Szu-ch'i

(1904–1964; Hunan). Korean War officer; former deputy director, PLA General Political Department; alternate member, CCP Central Committee.

Kan Szu-ch'i, a Red Army political officer for more than three decades, was trained in the Soviet Union and took part in many of the landmark events of Chinese Communist history. A veteran of the Korean War, he was elected an alternate member of the Party Central Committee in 1956. Kan was born into a poor peasant family in Hunan. It is probable that he grew up in or near Ning-hsiang, located some 50 miles west of Changsha, because during his teenage years he was active in Ning-hsiang in the widely supported movement to rid Hunan of the hated and rapacious governor-general, Chang Ching-yao. Mao Tse-tung himself was very active in the anti-Chang campaign, and his activities forced him to flee from Changsha in late 1919 (a half a year before Chang was finally overthrown). Kan, a middle school graduate (probably from a Changsha school), received his next taste of political life in the period immediately following the May 30 (1925) Incident. This had begun in Shanghai as a result of broadly backed demonstrations to protest foreign encroachments upon Chinese sovereignty, but when a number of demonstrators were killed, the "incident" quickly mushroomed into a "movement" that spread to most major Chinese cities, including Changshà. Kan, then in Changsha, helped organize students to support the May 30 Movement and also worked in the nearby rural areas to organize the peasantry for the same goals. Work of this kind apparently drew him to the Communist movement, for in 1925 he joined the Communist Youth League, and at approximately the same time he left for Moscow where in 1926 he joined the CCP.

During his four or five years in the Soviet Union, Kan attended Sun Yat-sen University, the name of which was changed to the Communist University of the Toilers of China in the late 1920's. After finishing his course work there, he remained with the school as a translator. In 1930 Kan returned to China; he was assigned as a political officer to the Hunan-Kiangsi base where Hsiao K'o (q.v.) commanded the Sixth Army Corps. The territory under the control of Hsiao's forces included the original stronghold of Mao Tse-tung and Chu Te at Chingkangshan. In the years before the Long March, Kan served as director of the Propaganda Department of the CCP Hunan-Kiangsi Provincial Committee and as political commissar of the Hunan-Kiangsi Military Region. In the spring of 1933 Jen Pi-shih (q.v.) was sent from Juichin to assume the political commissar post, presumably replacing Kan. In addition to these political and military assignments, Kan also held two posts in the Hunan-Kiangsi Provincial Soviet Government: director of the Finance Department and director of the National Economic Department (Kuo-min ching-chi pu). These two departments were local counterparts to the "ministries" of the same titles subordinate to the Chinese Soviet Republic, which was established in Juichin, southeast Kiangsi, in November 1931.

Sometime after the arrival of Jen Pi-shih in 1933, Kan became political commissar of the 18th Division of the Sixth Army Corps. He was holding this post in mid-1934 when the Corps retreated from its Hunan-Kiangsi base and moved west into northeast Kweichow (see under Hsiao K'o) to join the Second Army Corps led by Ho Lung. When the two units met in October 1934, Kan became director of the Political Departments for both corps, and still later, he held the same position for the Second Front Army (the name given to the overall command for the two army corps after their rendezvous and merger). In this post Kan worked under the Second Front Army's two top political officers, Jen Pi-shih, the political commissar, and Kuan Hsiang-ying, the deputy political commissar (who had been Ho Lung's chief political officer before the merger). Kan continued to head the front army's Political Department throughout the Long March (see under Ho Lung).

The Second Front Army arrived in north Shensi in the latter part of 1936. Half a year later, when war with Japan began in mid-1937, Kan remained with Ho Lung's unit, now known as the 120th Division of the newly established Eighth Route Army. Kan continued in his role as political officer, serving as head of the division's Political Department, a post which placed him under division political commissar Kuan Hsiang-ying. In the earliest days of the war Ho led his division into northwest Shansi where it began to take part in the battles against the Japanese. Kan apparently remained in northwest Shansi throughout the war years. In 1938 he assumed two concurrent posts, one as a member of the Party's Northwest Shansi District Committee and the other as director of the Political Department of the newly formed Shansi-Suiyuan Military Region.

There is rather little information on Kan's wartime activities, but it is fairly clear that he was more deeply involved in political than in purely military affairs. For example, in the early years of the war the Communist troops in Shansi fought in relatively close coordination with units under the jurisdiction of Yen Hsi-shan, the Shansi warlord. The Communists, anxious to maintain these relations with Yen, often called upon their political and military figures to write articles supporting the united front with the Shansi governor. Kan was among those who contributed to this effort,[1] but after relations with Yen were severely strained in the middle years of the war (see under P'eng Shao-hui), the Communist military leaders in north China were forced to turn their attention to the severe economic shortages which beset the military regions under their control. The extensive efforts to gain economic self-sufficiency (*tzu-li keng-sheng*) in northwest Shansi were described by Kan in an article for the Yenan *Chieh-fang jih-pao* (Liberation daily) of February 24, 1942.

In the postwar years Kan was assigned to the units led by P'eng Te-huai, Ho Lung, and Hsi Chung-hsun (qq.v.), known as the Northwest PLA until the winter of 1948–49 when it was redesignated the First Field Army. Kan con-

tinued in his familiar post as director of the army's Political Department. After defeating Nationalist forces in Shensi, Ninghsia, Kansu, Tsinghai, and Sinkiang during the late forties, the Northwest Military Region was established; Kan was now given the concurrent assignment of director of the Region's Political Department. During the course of these campaigns, Sian, the Shensi capital, fell to the Communists in May 1949. The Sian Military Control Commission was immediately established under the chairmanship of Ho Lung, and Kan was named as one of the three vice-chairmen. Fighting continued for several more months, but when the vast northwest region was under almost complete Communist control by the turn of the year 1949–50, the Northwest Military and Administrative Committee (NWMAC) was set up to administer the area. In early 1950 Kan was made a member of the NWMAC, as well as a member of its Land Reform Committee and director of its Public Security Department.

In October 1950 the Chinese entered the Korean War. Soon afterwards, Kan was relieved of his duties in Sian, the capital of the NWMAC, and transferred to Korea to become a deputy political commissar in P'eng Te-huai's Chinese People's Volunteers (CPV). Kan was concurrently director of the CPV's Political Department until the winter of 1952–53 when he was replaced by Li Chih-min (q.v). In October 1952 he returned to Peking for a brief period to lead a CPV delegation which took part in celebrations marking Chinese National Day (October 1). In February 1953 he was awarded the National Flag Medal, the highest award of the North Korean government, and then in July (the month the war ended), he returned to Peking where he was made a deputy director of the General Political Department, at that time under the top military body, the People's Revolutionary Military Council (PRMC). When the constitutional government was established in September 1954 and the PRMC abolished, the department was transferred to the PLA Headquarters, with Kan continuing to hold this post in the Political Department until his death in 1964. He was elected to the First NPC (1954–1959) as a representative of the Northwest Military Region and he also sat on the NPC Bills Committee. However, he was not re-elected to the Second NPC which opened in April 1959.

In September 1955 Kan was among a group of military leaders to receive the first military honors given by the PRC; he was awarded the three top PRC honors—the August First, the Independence and Freedom, and the Liberation Orders. With the creation of personal military ranks in the same year, he was made a colonel-general. He won high Party recognition in September 1956 when the Eighth National Party Congress elected him an alternate member of the Central Committee. Kan returned to Korea from September to October 1958 as the deputy leader of the Chinese delegation led by Kuo Mo-jo, which went to celebrate "Korea-China Friendship Month."

After attaining high national ranks in Party and government, as well as in the army, Kan was very active in Peking; from 1953 until his death his activities were constantly reported in the press. Examples of this include his address to the Third Session of the NPC (June 1956) on military expenditures and to the Fifth Session (February 1958) on the PLA and its share of work for the socialization program; there was also frequent mention of the conferences he attended that ranged from high-level technical meetings on military logistics to less important conferences to promote morale among military dependents. In his last years Kan attended an average of one social function a week given for important visitors to Peking whom he often saw in the company of high-ranking members of the Party. By the end of his 40-year career in the Chinese Communist Movement, he ranked high on its list of political generals. Kan remained active until his death in Peking on February 5, 1964. His funeral committee was headed by his long-time colleague, Marshal Ho Lung.

Kan's wife, Li Chen, the only woman general officer in the PLA, has been a member of the party since 1927. Born in Liu-yang hsien, Hunan, about 1908, she too has spent a lifetime in political work for the army. Li is one of the relatively small group of women who made the Long March and was awarded the Order of Liberation in 1955 for her military services in the postwar period. Since 1957 she has been a deputy chief procurator of the Military Procuratorate. Like her husband, she was a deputy to the First NPC (1954–1959), representing her native Hunan, and in the same capacity she was re-elected to the Second NPC (1959–1964) and to the Third NPC, which opened in December 1964. Li Chen spent at least part of the Korean War period in Korea where in 1953 she was secretary-general of the CPV's Political Department, which her husband had headed until early that year. She is easily one of the most important among the few prominent women in the present Chinese Communist elite.

1. Lyman P. Van Slyke, *Enemies and Friends* (Stanford, Calif., 1967), p. 139.

K'ang Sheng

(1899–   ; Chu-ch'eng, Shantung). Intelligence and security official; specialist in liaison with foreign Communist parties; member, CCP Politburo.

An early member of the CCP, K'ang Sheng ranks with Teng Fa, Li K'o-nung, and Lo Jui-ch'ing as one of the most important Party specialists in intelligence and security. Since the mid-fifties he has specialized in liaison with foreign Communist parties and in this capacity has been one of the most active CCP leaders in the Sino-Soviet dispute.

K'ang was born in Chu-ch'eng, located some 40 miles west of the Shantung port city of Tsingtao. His father was a well-to-do landlord. K'ang's original name was Chao Yun; he later changed this to Chao Jung and then to K'ang Sheng. He received a primary school education in Shantung and later he attended the middle school attached to Shanghai University. The university had been founded in the latter half of 1923 by Yü Yu-jen, a KMT official, but it soon came under the domination of such prominent Communists as Ch'ü Ch'iu-pai, Teng Chung-hsia, Yun Tai-ying, Chang T'ai-lei, and Jen Pi-shih. During the school's rather brief history (it was closed in June 1925), it served as a training ground for scores of Youth League and young CCP members. K'ang later attended the university itself, and while there he joined the Communist Youth League.

K'ang joined the CCP in 1924, and by early 1925 he was working as a labor organizer in Shanghai together with Teng Chung-hsia, Li Li-san (qq.v.), and others.[1] From the time K'ang entered the CCP until his assignment to the Comintern in Moscow in the thirties, his life in Shanghai was shrouded in the secrecy which might be expected of an underground organizer. During the years 1925–1927 he remained in the labor field when it was particularly active in Shanghai (see under Li Li-san), and during approximately this same period K'ang was also director of the Organization Department of the CCP Shanghai District Committee. He stayed in Shanghai after Chiang Kai-shek's anti-Communist coup in April 1927, and it was probably at that time that he first became directly associated with Party's intelligence and security organs. K'ang's colleagues in this work included Li K'o-nung and K'o Ch'ing-shih (qq.v.); his knowledge of the inner-workings of the Party apparatus in Shanghai in the late twenties and early thirties was revealed in a Moscow-published collection of essays (1936) on CCP "martyrs" to which K'ang contributed short biographies on Ch'en Yen-nien and Lo Teng-hsien (qq.v.).[2]

K'ang was arrested in Shanghai in 1930, and according to one account he quickly gained his release through the intervention of Ting Wei-fen, a prominent KMT leader from Shantung, whose nephew had also been apprehended by the authorities.[3] In any event, he appears to have taken part in the Party's Fourth Plenum in Shanghai in January 1931. It was at this plenum that the so-called Russian-returned student faction (see under Ch'en Shao-yü and Ch'in Pang-hsien) gained control of the Party apparatus and took over most of the leading Party posts. Although

K'ang is not known to have had any particular ties with this group, he was made director of the Party's Organization Department. Moreover, some reports assert that K'ang was placed on the Politburo in 1931 (presumably at the Fourth Plenum). However, it should be noted that there is no other high-ranking Party official about whom there are such widely conflicting reports concerning Politburo membership. K'ang remained in the Shanghai underground after the Fourth Plenum, and toward the end of 1932 or early 1933 he was living in the French Concession in Shanghai. It was at this time that his "secret house" was used as a shelter by Ch'en Keng (q.v.) when the latter came to Shanghai for medical treatment during the winter of 1932–33.[4]

K'ang was relieved of his Shanghai assignments in 1933 and sent to Moscow where he studied Soviet security and intelligence techniques and also acted as a CCP representative to the Comintern. Writing in September 1933 for a Comintern publication, K'ang claimed there were two million trade union members in the Soviet areas of China, and that the CCP had 300,000 members, of whom 20 per cent were industrial workers.[5] Three months later he attended the 13th Plenum of the Executive Committee of the Comintern (ECCI), as did Ch'en Shao-yü (Wang Ming), one of the Russian-returned student faction leaders. Both men gave lengthy speeches at the meeting, and their addresses were published in several languages and countries in the following months; one such edition was published in New York in April 1934 by the Workers Library Publishers (their names being romanized "Wan Ming" and "Kang Sin"). K'ang's speech, though shorter and less important than the one given by his colleague, is a useful (though obviously exaggerated) account of the Chinese revolutionary movement outside Communist-controlled areas (or, in K'ang's phrase, in "non-Soviet China"). In particular, it contains a considerable amount of information about the resistance movement in Japanese-controlled Manchuria and the growth of Party and trade union work in other "non-Soviet" areas. One of the main themes of the speech was the necessity to "mobilize" the entire nation against Japan, and in this regard he pledged the support of the CCP in the event of a "military attack by Japanese imperialism upon the Soviet Union."

In January–February 1934 the Chinese Soviet Republic convened the Second All-China Congress of Soviets in Juichin, southeast Kiangsi. K'ang was still in Moscow, but he was elected a member of the Central Executive Committee, the leading political organ of the Republic. In that same year he also wrote a preface for the copy of Mao Tse-tung's speech at the congress, which was published in Moscow for a Comintern audience.[6] In July–August 1935 K'ang was a delegate to the Seventh Comintern Congress in Moscow. He was again among the speakers, and he was also elected an alternate member of both the ECCI and the ECCI Presidium. Ch'en Shao-yü, Mao Tse-tung, Chou En-lai, and Chang Kuo-t'ao were elected full ECCI members, and Ch'in Pang-hsien (qq.v.), like K'ang, was elected an alternate.[7] K'ang was thus on hand for the important meeting which set the course for the Comintern's "united front against fascism"—a policy developed in the wake of the rise of Hitler (and one that was equally relevant to Chinese of many political persuasions because of the increasing encroachments upon China's sovereignty by the Japanese militarists). In the period after the 1935 Comintern Congress, K'ang was called upon to take up his pen in defense of the "united front" against Japan. For example, he and Ch'en Shao-yü, in a joint article, denounced as specious comparisons between Lenin's acceptance of the famous 1918 Brest-Litovsk Treaty with Germany (buying time by sacrificing space) and the situation in China vis-à-vis Japan. Their argument, in brief, was that all Chinese must stand and fight. This article appeared in the *Chiu-kuo shih-pao* (Salvation times), published in Paris by Wu Yü-chang (q.v.), and was quoted in a Comintern journal in early 1936.[8]

K'ang learned Russian during his stay in Moscow, and he is also said to have a limited knowledge of English and German. In 1937 he was called back to the Communist capital at Yenan in north Shensi. En route home he passed through Tihwa (now Urumchi) where he and Ch'en Shao-yü allegedly negotiated with Sheng Shih-ts'ai, the semi-independent Sinkiang warlord, in an attempt to work out closer political relations between the Communists at Yenan and Sheng, a mission that was only partially successful (see under Teng Fa and Ch'en T'an-ch'iu).[9]

Back in Yenan, K'ang was attached to the Party Organization Department where he may have worked at various times under such Party stalwarts as Li Fu-ch'un, Ch'in Pang-hsien, Liu Shao-ch'i, and Ch'en Yun (qq.v.). Once again there are reports that he assumed (or reassumed) a seat as a member (or alternate member) of the Politburo, and still others that he also became a member of the Party Secretariat. But perhaps most important is the fact that he returned to his special field of security and intelligence work. For reasons of security the Communists have published very little about the chief security organ, the Social Affairs Department (She-hui pu), but it is probable that K'ang headed this important organ from the late 1930's until about 1946 when he was replaced by Li K'o-nung (q.v.). Although there is further uncertainty and ambiguity of data, K'ang was also known to have held a high position in one of the leading Party schools in Yenan. Communist leader Ch'in Pang-hsien, in an interview with Edgar Snow in

July 1938, stated that the "Communist Party School" was under K'ang Sheng and Ch'en Shao-yü and had about 500 students enrolled.[10] Other reports state that K'ang was vice-president of the "Central Party School" during the Sino-Japanese War period. K'ang apparently retained some connections with the labor movement in the Communist-held areas of the northwest. He was described in a Party newspaper as a "labor leader" when he spoke in Yenan on February 7, 1942, on the 19th anniversary of the February Seventh (1923) Incident.[11] (In this incident, described in the biography of Teng Chung-hsia, a number of Communist labor officials lost their lives when warlord Wu P'ei-fu suppressed the activities of the Peking-Hankow Railway Workers' Trade Union.)

K'ang attended the important Seventh National Party Congress in Yenan, held from April to June 1945. Some indication of his stature within the Party is suggested by the fact that he was one of only 15 members of the Congress presidium (steering committee). He was one of the speakers, and at the close of the congress he was elected a member of the Seventh Central Committee. The Communists did not publish a list of the new Politburo, and once again, conflicting reports arose about his seat (or lack of it) on this all-important body. In any case, there do not appear to be any official identifications of K'ang as a Politburo member until December 1954. In the decade after the Seventh Congress, remarkably little was heard of K'ang, particularly for a man of his stature. Perhaps the most plausible explanation is that his involvement in security work shielded him from the publicity normally accorded to senior leaders. However, he is known to have been in Yenan in the spring and summer of 1946, and he is mentioned twice in Mao Tse-tung's *Selected Works*. In an April 1, 1948, speech given by Mao at a cadre conference in the Shansi-Suiyuan Liberated Area, he referred to the work that K'ang had done in the spring and summer of 1947 in Lin-hsien (west Shansi, near the Yellow River). Certain "deviations" in the work of land reform and "Party consolidation," according to Mao, had been corrected. On balance, Mao praised K'ang's work, but he seemed also to direct some unfavorable comments toward him, criticizing the policy (apparently espoused by K'ang) of doing "everything as the masses want it done." Mao contended that it was the duty of the Party to lead and educate the masses.[12]

Mao mentioned K'ang a second time in connection with the Red Army drive southward in early 1949 as the Communist forces stood poised north of the Yangtze River after the successful Huai-Hai campaign (see under Liu Po-ch'eng). In a directive of February 8 entitled "Turn the Army into a Working Force," Mao's instructions dealt mainly with the pending takeover of the cities and the uses to which the army should be put as a civil force. He continued: "We have talked at length with Comrade K'ang Sheng and asked him to hurry to [the headquarters of the Second and Third Field Armies] . . . to confer with you . . . Turn all your rear-area work over to the Shantung Sub-bureau."[13] After carrying out this assignment, K'ang apparently proceeded directly to Shantung where, by March 1949, he was identified as the Shantung governor; before the year ended he had also become the political commissar of the Shantung Military District and secretary of the CCP Shantung Sub-bureau, thus becoming the dominant figure in his native province.

When the new central government was formed in the fall of 1949, K'ang became a member of the Central People's Government Council, the most important organ of government until 1954. He was also named to the First Executive Board of the Sino-Soviet Friendship Association (1949–1954). As the Communists consolidated their position in east China, the East China Military and Administrative Committee (ECMAC) was established (January 1950). K'ang was named as a member of the ECMAC (with jurisdiction over Shantung) and when the ECMAC was reorganized into the East China Administrative Committee (ECAC) in December 1952, he was reappointed. Despite all these important appointments at the central, regional, and provincial levels, K'ang made no public appearances from 1949 to the end of 1954. Illness or further involvement in security work may explain this prolonged absence from the limelight. It may also be noteworthy that K'ang's reappearance in late 1954 coincided with the purge of Kao Kang and Jao Shu-shih (qq.v.), the latter being the chairman of the ECMAC–ECAC, to which K'ang was assigned. One of the major figures purged with Kao and Jao was Hsiang Ming, the Shantung CCP Sub-bureau second secretary, who on occasion served as the acting secretary for K'ang. (For a discussion of Hsiang Ming, see under Kao Kang.)

After Kang's long absence, he reappeared in December 1954 when he attended the first session of the CPPCC's Second National Committee as a representative of the CCP. (He was promoted to a vice-chairmanship of the Third National Committee, which existed from 1959 to 1964, but with the formation of the Fourth National Committee in December 1964 he relinquished his vice-chairmanship but continues to serve as a CCP representative on the CPPCC National Committee.) By this time (the end of 1954) K'ang was working in Peking, if indeed he had not already been there for some time, and it was also at this time, as previously noted, that he was officially identified as a Politburo member. He was formally replaced by January 1955 as the Shantung Party first secretary by Shu T'ung and as the provincial governor in March 1955 by Chao Chien-min (qq.v.). Then, in March 1955, K'ang participated in the Party's National Conference (not to be confused with a Party Congress), at which time Kao Kang and Jao Shu-shih were formally purged. Together with the most important leaders of the Party, K'ang delivered an "important" (but unpublished) speech.

Since his re-emergence over the winter of 1954–55, K'ang's activities have been prominently featured in the Chinese press. His work has been devoted to two different types of activities—a somewhat unusual combination of duties in the field of higher education and liaison with foreign Communist parties. In the former category, for example, in February 1956 he became a vice-chairman of a newly organized committee to promote the usage of the "common national language" (*p'u-t'ung-hua*) and from time to time (especially in the late fifties) he appeared at educational conferences. More important, however, has been his work as a senior liaison official with foreign Communist parties and as a major figure in the Sino-Soviet dispute. His first assignment in this field was in March 1956 when he led a delegation to East Germany to attend the Third Congress of the Socialist Unity Party (i.e., the East German Communist Party). In January–February 1959 he was in Moscow as a member of Chou En-lai's delegation to the 21st Congress of the CPSU. K'ang was back in Moscow in February 1960 leading the Chinese "observer" delegation to the Warsaw Treaty Political Consultative Committee. His speech at the meetings was a milestone in the Sino-Soviet dispute; prior to this time Chinese commentary on Soviet policies had been couched in highly veiled language. Now, however, although the Soviets were not specifically mentioned by name, K'ang made it plain that Peking strongly disagreed with Soviet policies *vis-à-vis* the West (particularly regarding disarmament) and intended to follow a more independent policy, which would ultimately become a major factor in the Sino-Soviet rift of the sixties. In particular, he stated that any disarmament agreement reached without Peking's participation would not have any "binding force on China." In sharp contrast, the declaration issued by the conference stated that the situation was now "more favorable than ever before" for reaching fruitful disarmament talks. The clash in Sino-Soviet views became far more evident in June 1960 at the Third Congress of the Rumanian Workers' (Communist) Party in Bucharest; K'ang also attended this congress (see under P'eng Chen, the leader of the Chinese delegation).

Between these visits to Moscow and Bucharest in 1960 and the end of 1964, K'ang was a member of five other highly important delegations—each of which was deeply involved in the continuing Sino-Soviet rift. He was a member of the following delegations (see under the delegation leader for details): USSR, November 1960, to attend the 43rd anniversary of the Russian Revolution, led by Liu Shao-ch'i; North Korea, September 1961, to attend the Fourth National Congress of the Korean Workers' (Communist) Party, led by Teng Hsiao-p'ing; USSR, October 1961, to attend the 22nd Congress of the CPSU, led by Chou En-lai; USSR, July 1963, to hold bi-lateral talks with CPSU officials, led by Teng Hsiao-p'ing; USSR, November 1964, to attend the 47th anniversary of the Russian Revolution, led by Chou En-lai. In the interim, K'ang frequently took part in Peking in talks with visiting foreign Communist leaders as the Chinese attempted to present their case to these men. As a result of his extremely active participation in the Sino-Soviet polemics, K'ang has gained the reputation (whether deserved or not) of being an advocate of a very "tough" foreign policy, particularly *vis-à-vis* the United States. His involvement in international Communist liaison work has also put him in close contact with other top specialists in this field, such as Wu Hsiu-ch'üan, Yang Shang-k'un, and Liu Ning-i (qq.v.), in addition to the leaders of the delegations mentioned above.

In the meantime, K'ang's positions within the Party hierarchy had undergone some rather unusual changes. At the Eighth Party Congress in September 1956 he was re-elected to the Party Central Committee. However, at the First Plenum of the new Central Committee (held the day after the Congress closed), he was dropped from full to alternate membership on the Party Politburo. Chang Wen-t'ien (q.v.) was also lowered to alternate membership at the Plenum. Initially, it appeared that K'ang had run into political troubles, but such a suggestion seems to be contradicted by his very active role in later years (as described above).

K'ang has not been a frequent contributor to the press in the post-1949 period, but he wrote an important article for the Party's leading journal, *Hung-ch'i* (Red flag, October 1, 1959) entitled "A Communist Should Be a Marxist-Leninist, Not a Fellow-traveler of the Party." This was subsequently reprinted in a collection of major articles commemorating the 10th anniversary of the PRC.[14] The timing of K'ang's piece was noteworthy; it was published immediately after the removal of Defense Minister P'eng Te-huai (q.v.), who has since fallen into political disgrace. K'ang did not mention P'eng and his colleagues by name, but he discussed at some length the Party's Eighth Plenum (August 1959), the meeting which almost certainly took the decision to purge P'eng. K'ang attacked the "slanders" of the "right opportunists" who had opposed domestic policies, particularly the Great Leap Forward and the "people's communes"—programs which P'eng had apparently resisted.

Kang's political fortunes rose sharply at the 10th Party Plenum, held in September 1962. At that time two military figures were removed from the Party's Central Secretariat, T'an Cheng and Huang K'o-ch'eng. It may be significant that Huang had been a close colleague of P'eng Te-haui. Three new members were added to the Secretariat: Lu Ting-i, Lo Jui-ch'ing (qq.v.), and K'ang. The highly important Secretariat, headed by Teng Hsiao-p'ing (q.v.), is responsible for the daily execution of policies laid down by the Politburo. K'ang received his first post in the national legislature in 1958 when he was elected a deputy from his native Shantung to the Second NPC (1959–1964). He was re-elected in 1964, and when the Third NPC closed its first session in January 1965, K'ang was elevated to a vice-chairmanship of the NPC Standing Committee. A year and a half later, in the early stages of the Great Proletarian Cultural Revolution, K'ang was identified as the "adviser" to the Cultural Revolution Group under the CCP Central Committee (July 1966), and within a few weeks he was also identified as a member of the Politburo's Standing Committee. These new posts placed K'ang among the half-dozen top leaders in China.

In the mid-fifties K'ang was known to have married and to have had at least two children. He suffers from extreme myopia and has been described by a former Communist as a dogmatic and tenaciously stubborn man.[15]

---

1. *Hung-ch'i p'iao p'iao* (Red flag fluttering; Peking, 1958), VIII, 34.

2. *Lieh-shih chuan* (Biographies of martyrs; USSR [Moscow?], 1936), pp. 50–54, 154–161.

3. Modern China Project, Columbia University, New York, Howard L. Boorman, director.

4. *SCMM* 281, p. 5.

5. Jane Degras, ed., *The Communist International, 1919–1943, Documents,* 3 vols. (London, 1965), III, 312.

6. Chün-tu Hsüeh, *The Chinese Communist Movement, 1921–1937* (Stanford, Calif., 1960), pp. 75–76.

7. Charles B. McLane, *Soviet Policy and the Chinese Communists, 1931–1946* (New York, 1958), p. 61.

8. *The Communist International,* New York, special number, 13:151 (February 1936).

9. Allen S. Whiting and Sheng Shih-ts'ai, *Sinkiang: Pawn or Pivot?* (East Lansing, Mich., 1958), pp. 55, 187.

10. Edgar Snow, *Random Notes on Red China, 1936–1945* (Cambridge, Mass., 1957), p. 24.

11. Yenan, *Chieh-fang jih-pao* (Liberation daily), February 9, 1942.

12. *Selected Works of Mao Tse-tung* (Peking, 1961), IV, 231–232.

13. *Ibid.,* p. 339.

14. *Ten Glorious Years* (Peking, 1960), pp. 245–254.

15. Modern China Project.

K'ang Yung-ho

(1915–   ; Shansi?). Representative to the international Communist trade union movement.

K'ang Yung-ho was probably born in Shansi. He has risen in the Chinese Communist movement to be one of the most important officials in the Communist-sponsored World Federation of Trade Unions. He was a trade unionist in Shansi when the Sino-Japanese War broke out in 1937. As head of a Communist-backed trade union in Shansi, he organized guerrilla units which were incorporated into the Eighth Route Army in 1938. He presumably operated mainly in Shansi during the war, because a decade later he was officially identified as the former chairman of the Shansi General Trade Union. This identification occurred in August 1948 at the Sixth Labor Congress held in Harbin. At that congress K'ang was elected to the Executive Committee and to alternate membership on the Standing Committee (which was re-entitled the Presidium at the 1953 labor congress) of the All-China Federation of Labor (ACFL). He was re-elected to the Executive Committee and promoted to full membership on the Presidium at the 1953 congress (after which the ACFL became known as the All-China Federation of Trade Unions). Finally, and most important, at the congress held in December 1957 he was elevated to membership on the Federation's Secretariat, thus being placed among the most important of the trade union leaders in China. In the early years of the PRC the All-China Federation of Labor had regional branches. K'ang headed the "North China Work Committee" of the federation from its formation in April 1952 until he was transferred to Peking toward the latter part of 1953.

Aside from his work in establishing the trade union organization in China, K'ang also participated both in the organization of the central government and the provincial government of his native Shansi in 1949. When Taiyuan, the Shansi capital, fell to Communist forces in April 1949, K'ang was named to membership on the Taiyuan Military Control Commission, then headed by General Hsu Hsiang-ch'ien (q.v.). When the provincial government was formed later in 1949, K'ang was appointed as a member of the Shansi Government Council, and in August 1950 he was also appointed to membership on the Shansi Finance and Economics Committee. Furthermore, at the semi-official level, he was elected as chairman of the Shansi Provincial Trade Union Council, a position which, in effect, amounted to a reappointment because he had held this post in earlier years. K'ang went to

Peking as a Federation of Labor delegate in September 1949 to attend the initial session of the CPPCC, the organization that brought the central government into existence on October 1.

He was relieved of all his positions in Shansi in 1953 and transferred to Peking. There, in September 1953, he assumed the chairmanship of the Preparatory Committee of the First Machine Building Workers' Trade Union, and when this union held its first congress in August 1955, he was named as the chairman. In February 1958 the "First" and "Second" Machine Building Unions were merged (to coincide with the merger of the government's First and Second Ministries of Machine Building). K'ang was once again named as chairman, holding the post until the summer of 1959.

In the meantime K'ang had begun to take part in the international Communist labor union movement, an activity that was to occupy most of his time in the years ahead. In January 1950 he was elected chairman of the Agricultural and Forestry Workers' Trade Unions International, one of the member unions of the Communist-dominated World Federation of Trade Unions (WFTU). This took place in Warsaw at the constituent conference which formed the union, but K'ang was apparently not a member of the Chinese delegation. In October 1953 he was a member of the delegation led by trade union leader Liu Ning-i (q.v.) to the Third Congress of the WFTU in Vienna, then the WFTU headquarters. At that congress he was elected to the WFTU General Council, a position he probably still holds. In succeeding years he received more significant posts within the WFTU; in 1957 he became an alternate member of the Executive Committee and a full member in 1960. Finally, in June 1962 he was named to the Secretariat, being placed as the second-ranking Chinese official below WFTU Vice-Chairman Liu Ch'ang-sheng. K'ang's trip to Vienna in 1953 was a harbinger of things to come. Between that time and the end of 1964 he went abroad 18 times to 11 different nations. Of these 18 trips, 11 concerned trade union work, whereas the others were occasioned by meetings to promote activities such as disarmament or the Communist-backed peace movement. His travels have taken him to the USSR, East Germany, Hungary, Bulgaria, Mongolia, Cuba, Austria, Japan, the United Arab Republic, Indonesia, and North Vietnam. A few of these trips require some elucidation. In addition to the above-mentioned third WFTU Congress in 1953, K'ang attended the fourth and fifth congresses held, respectively, in Leipzig, East Germany, in October 1957 and in Moscow in December 1961, both times under leader Liu Ch'ang-sheng. In August 1956 and August 1962 he attended the second and eighth World Conferences against Nuclear Weapons in Japan. He led a group to Cairo in September 1958 to a conference to "support the Algerian workers and people" and to a conference of an almost identical title in Cuba in October–November 1960. But perhaps his most important journey abroad took place in November 1962 when he accompanied Central Committee member Wu Hsiu-ch'üan to Bulgaria for the Eighth National Congress of the Bulgarian Communist Party. This was the first of four Party congresses which Wu attended in East Europe in the fall and winter of 1962–63. It marked a turning point in Sino-Soviet relations in that the long-simmering ideological dispute broke into open verbal warfare between Peking and Moscow. It is not known what role K'ang may have played at the Bulgarian congress, but his mere presence was probably sufficient to label him in the eyes of Russians and East Europeans as an implacable advocate of an extremely harsh and tough foreign policy vis-à-vis the West. K'ang's involvement in foreign affairs is further suggested by his membership on a delegation to a meeting in Hanoi in November–December 1964 with the cumbersome but revealing title, "International Conference for Solidarity with the People of Vietnam, against United States Imperialist Aggression and for the Defense of Peace."

Although his career has been clearly oriented toward foreign affairs, he has also had a hand in various domestic endeavors. Within the government he has served as a Shansi deputy in the First through the Third NPC's, which opened their initial sessions in September 1954, April 1959, and December 1964, respectively. Further, he was named to the Bills Committee for the Second and Third Congresses. Within semi-official organizations he was named to membership on the councils (board of directors) of the China-Iraq Friendship Association (FA) and the China-Africa People's FA from their formation (September 1958 and April 1960); he retains membership in both organizations. K'ang also makes appearances at the numerous conferences held in China, as, for example, in October 1959 when he served as a deputy secretary-general of a conference of "outstanding workers" in Peking.

As might be expected from his work in international labor relations from the early 1950's, K'ang is often cited in the press in connection with visiting trade union delegations. On five different occasions between 1956 and 1962 he signed joint statements with visiting trade union groups, three of them with Japanese labor delegations. It appears, in fact, that K'ang has specialized to some degree in Japanese labor matters. In addition to signing these three statements (calling for closer ties), he has been on hand on scores of occasions to entertain and negotiate with visiting Japanese trade union groups. In this connection it is noteworthy that in August 1962 K'ang led a trade union group to the 19th

Congress of the General Council of Trade Unions of Japan (SOHYO) where he was one of the speakers.

Apart from his organizational work in the Federation of Trade Unions, he is the author of articles on labor affairs. The most important of these appeared in the Party Central Committee's principal organ, *Hung-ch'i* (Red flag) of August 16, 1959, entitled "Conscientiously Develop Socialist Labor Emulation."

Kao Feng

(Tsinghai). Former Tsinghai First Party Secretary.

Born in Tsinghai, Kao has spent his entire career in his native northwest as a Party and government official. He was first reported in 1946 as a delegate from Yen-ch'ih hsien to the Third Assembly of the Shensi-Kansu-Ninghsia (Shen-Kan-Ning) Border Region, the first session of which was held in April 1946. He presumably remained a delegate until the dissolution of the Border Region in early 1949. Yen-ch'ih hsien is located in present-day Ninghsia, just south of the Great Wall where Ninghsia merges with Inner Mongolia and Shensi. By 1947 Kao was the ranking Party secretary of the San-pien District Committee, San-pien being one of the five districts into which the Shen-Kan-Ning Border Region was divided (and the district controlling Yen-ch'ih hsien). In this same year he attended a conference of high-level cadres of the Northwest Party Bureau, which was also attended by such senior Party leaders as Lin Po-ch'ü and Ho Lung. At this conference Kao and others admitted shortcomings in their work and promised to improve. Such "self-confessions" are not uncommon among the Chinese Communists and are usually thought of in the sense of self-reform rather than as a preliminary to a purge.[1]

Although there is no record of Kao's activities in the late forties and early fifties, he must have been rather important in the northwest because he suddenly emerged in 1954 as the ranking Party secretary for Tsinghai province. By August 1954 Kao had replaced Chang Chung-liang as the ranking Tsinghai Party secretary, a post redesignated as first secretary by 1956. In the closing days of 1954, Kao was elected a member of the Tsinghai Provincial People's Council under Governor Sun Tso-pin (q.v.), later purged in the 1957–58 Rectification Campaign. Kao was re-elected to the Tsinghai Council in mid-1958, and in the interim was elected as chairman of the first Tsinghai CPPCC Committee in May–June 1955 and then elected to the second committee in January–February 1959.

Kao's stature was such by 1956 that he attended the historic Eighth Party Congress and spoke on the execution of the Party's policies toward the national minorities in Tsinghai. During the next two years he was reported rather frequently in the press, often in connection with the 1957–58 Rectification Campaign. Part of this campaign involved the performance of manual labor as a means of getting "closer to the masses," and Kao was among the first to participate. In May 1957 he was named to head the Tsinghai "rectification movement leadership team." Kao attended the second session of the Eighth Party Congress (May 1958) and immediately afterward joined Mao Tse-tung and other top leaders in performing manual labor at the Ming Tombs Reservoir north of Peking. It was not long after that the New China News Agency (July 1, 1958) reported that Kao had contributed an article entitled "Liberate Your Thinking to Build Up Tsinghai" for the leading organ of the Tsinghai Party Committee, a local counterpart of *Hung-ch'i* (Red Flag), the organ of the Party Central Committee.

Kao's activity in Tsinghai in the performance of inspections and attendance at a host of meetings of the provincial Party Committee and government organs was reported with regularity during the period from 1958 through 1960. In 1960 he assumed two more positions in Tsinghai. The first was related to a nationwide program to promote spare-time education. Coinciding with the establishment in January 1960 of a Spare-time Education Committee under the State Council in Peking, Tsinghai province inaugurated in the same month a university for persons working in government organs at the provincial level. Kao was named to head this school. The second position, assumed by July 1960, was as director of the Office of Capital Construction under the Party Committee. During this same period he authored articles dealing with agriculture in Tsinghai which appeared in the *JMJP* of March 17, 1959, January 9, 1960, and July 11, 1960.

Then, rather suddenly, Kao disappeared at the end of 1960, and by the next October another man (Wang Chao) was serving as acting first secretary of the Tsinghai Party Committee. The time that Kao fell from the public limelight coincided with the period generally considered the worst point in the wake of the failure of the Great Leap Forward, but there is no specific evidence relating his disappearance to those troubled days. Kao technically remained as head of the Tsinghai CPPCC, but in December 1963 he lost even this rather unimportant post when Yang Chih-lin was elected chairman.

(Kao should not be confused with a person of the same name who is a Party official in Kiangsu.)

---

1. *Wei ch'un-chieh tang-te tsu-chih erh tou-cheng* (Struggle to purify the Party organization; Hong Kong, 1948), p. 65.

Kao Kang

(c.1902–c.1954; Heng-shan, Shensi). Early Shensi Soviet leader; Assembly chairman, Shensi-Kansu-Ninghsia Border Region; former State Planning Commission chairman and Politburo member; purge announced, 1955.

One of the earliest members of the CCP in Shensi Province, Kao Kang and his colleague Liu Chih-tan played key roles in the development of a Communist base there that served as a haven for Mao Tse-tung and his troops at the end of the Long March in 1935. During the Sino-Japanese War Kao was one of the principal officials in the Communists' Shensi-Kansu-Ninghsia Border Region Government, and in the late forties and early fifties he was the senior official in Manchuria. By 1952 he was a Politburo member and late in that year he became the first chairman of the State Planning Commission. The ouster of Kao and his "accomplice" Jao Shu-shih in 1954–55 was the most celebrated purge in the Chinese Communist Movement from the late thirties to the mid-sixties. It is claimed that Kao committed suicide sometime prior to the public announcement of his purge in April 1955.

Kao was born in Heng-shan, just south of the Great Wall in northern Shensi, into a small landlord family. He studied at the Yü-lin Middle School not far from Heng-shan. He was a student there during approximately the same years as Liu Chih-tan (1921–1924), a man whose career was closely linked with Kao's in the twenties and thirties. The Yü-lin school was strongly influenced in the early twenties by several Communist instructors, the most prominent of whom was Wei Yeh-ch'ou, an early Communist and protégé of Li Ta-chao (q.v.). In 1926 Kao joined the CCP, one year after his friend Liu Chih-tan. In the fall of that year warlord Feng Yü-hsiang, who was then cooperating with both the Nationalists and the Communists, established the Chung-shan Military and Political Academy at Sian to train poltical workers for his armed forces. Liu Chih-tan and Teng Hsiao-p'ing (q.v.) were among the many Communist instructors, and Kao and Hsi Chung-hsun (q.v.), another important Shensi Communist, were students.

In mid-1927 Feng broke with the Communists and proceeded to suppress the Communist movement throughout the province. In the spring of the next year Liu led an insurrection in Wei-nan and Hua-yin hsien to the east of Sian. It is unlikely that Kao participated in this endeavor, but in any event, after the revolt was suppressed, Liu and Kao were together in the Pao-an hsien area of northwest Shensi where Liu was an official in the CCP's North Shensi Special Committee. According to Communist accounts, Committee Secretary Yang Kuo-tung was resisting all attempts to foster armed peasant uprisings. As a consequence, Liu Chih-tan overthrew the Yang leadership with the assistance of Kao Kang and others. Little is known of Kao's activities during the next few years, but by 1931 he was a leader of the Communists' 26th Red Army, which was operating on the Shensi-Kansu border. Over the next few years Kao remained one of the key military and political officers in the Red guerrilla units as the Communists attempted to establish a viable, peasant-based movement in Shensi. These developments are briefly summarized in the biography of Liu Chih-tan and are comprehensively covered in Mark Selden's "The Guerrilla Movement in Northwest China," *The China Quarterly* (nos. 28–29, October–December 1966 and January–March 1967).

Throughout the early 1930's Kao had had serious differences with several CCP leaders sent to Shensi by the Party Center over the "correct" guerrilla strategy. These disputes persisted into the fall of 1935 after the arrival of the 25th Red Army from the Communists' former Oyüwan Soviet area. The 25th Army, led by Hsu Hai-tung, was merged with the Shensi units led by Liu and Kao to form the 15th Army Corps. Hsu was made the commander and Liu the deputy commander; Ch'eng Tzu-hua (q.v.), who had come with Hsu, became the political commissar and Kao Kang was made head of the Corps' Political Department. Soon afterward, under circumstances that are unclear, the entire local guerrilla leadership, including both Kao and Liu, was arrested—either by Central Committee representatives who had arrived in mid-1935 or by political officers who had come with Hsu Hai-tung's 25th Army. But within a brief time both men were released and restored to their posts following the arrival in north Shensi of elements of the First Army Corps led by Mao Tse-tung, Chou En-lai, and P'eng Te-huai.

In the early months of 1936 Kao participated in a military thrust into Shansi, which the Communists mounted in an effort to dramatize their demands for action against the Japanese and to get food, supplies, and recruits for the badly depleted Red armies. Liu Chih-tan was killed during this operation, and thus Kao Kang emerged as the most significant of the "local" Shensi Communist leaders. When war with Japan broke out in mid-1937, a number of key Communist military and political leaders moved eastward to engage the Japanese, but Kao remained in the Yenan area of Shensi where he quickly became a key figure. He served throughout the war years in a quasi-military post as commander of the Shensi-Kansu-Ninghsia (Shen-Kan-Ning) Border Region's Peace Preservation Corps, but his primary duties were in connection with the Party apparatus and the Shen-Kan-Ning Border Region Government. Within the Party structure he was secretary of the CCP Committee for the Shen-Kan-Ning Border Region from 1938 to 1940, and then from 1940 to the end of the war he was secretary of the Party's Northwest Bureau. The Shen-Kan-Ning Government had been established in 1937, but its initial meeting was not held until the convocation of the First Assembly in January–February 1939. At this time Kao was elected Assembly chairman, and in November 1941 he was re-elected chairman of the Second Assembly, retaining this post until his departure for Manchuria in 1945. It appears that within the Border Region Government Kao was second only in importance to Lin Po-ch'ü (q.v.), the chief executive officer, until the *cheng-feng* (rectification) movement began in 1942. After that time Kao probably surpassed Lin in importance as the Communists paid less attention to the united front and began to stress the necessity of the "mass line" to implement their programs.

Kao was a frequent contributor to the Party press during the war years and he also spoke at Party-sponsored meetings on numerous occasions. Many of these articles and speeches are cited in Chün-tu Hsüeh's bibliography of Communist materials for the years 1937–1949.[1] In terms of Communist historiography, the most important of Kao's talks was delivered in November 1942 at a meeting of Party cadres in the Shen-Kan-Ning Border Region. Entitled "An Examination of Questions Concerning Party History in the Border Region," it describes the history of the Shensi guerrilla movement prior to the arrival of Mao Tse-tung in 1935. Earlier in 1942, at the outset of the famous *cheng-feng* movement, Mao Tse-tung spoke of Kao in the most flattering terms. "The 'outside' cadres," according to Mao, "must certainly be somewhat inferior [to] the local cadres in their detailed knowledge of the (local) conditions and their relations with the masses. Take my case as an example. I came to northern Shensi five or six years ago, yet I cannot compare with comrades like Kao Kang in my knowledge of conditions here or in my relations with people of this region." Mao concluded that "No matter what progress I make in investigation and research, I shall always be somewhat inferior to the northern Shensi cadres."[2] Predictably, after Kao's purge in the 1950's these lines were altered; the key passage involving Kao now reads: "Although I have been in northern Shensi five or six years, I am far behind the local comrades in understanding local conditions."[3]

When the Party held its Seventh National Congress from April to June 1945, Kao served on the 15-member Congress presidium and was one of the speakers. He was elected a member of the Party Central Committee—the only one of the Shensi Soviet leaders to gain this distinction (although Hsi Chung-hsun and Ma Ming-

fang were elected alternates). According to some sources, Kao was also elected a Politburo member at this time, but it seems more likely that he did not rise to this post until 1952. He remained in Yenan until the fall of 1945, after which he was sent to Manchuria at about the same time that the Party dispatched such prominent military and political leaders as Ch'en Yun, P'eng Chen, Lin Piao, Li Fu-ch'un, and Lin Feng (qq.v.). By 1946 and until 1947 he commanded the Communists' Kirin-Heilungkiang Military Region. In 1947 Kao was elevated to become deputy commander and deputy political commissar of the Northeast Military Region, serving in these posts under Lin Piao, the commander.

Kao's rise to great prominence in Manchuria coincided with the conquest of this critical region over the winter of 1948–49 and the departure from the area of virtually all other top leaders, who went south with Lin Piao's military forces or transferred to Peking to assume political posts. Li Fu-ch'un and Chang Wen-t'ien (q.v.) remained for a brief time, but then they too left to assume new duties elsewhere. Only Central Committee member Lin Feng remained, serving in positions subordinate to Kao. In the first half of 1949 Kao became secretary of the Party's Northeast Bureau, and commander and political commissar of the Northeast Military Region. Then, when the Northeast People's Government was established in August 1949, he became its chairman. Of the six regional areas of China, only Kao Kang held all four of these key posts—not even such prominent leaders as Lin Piao in central-south China or P'eng Te-huai in the northwest were vested with such broad powers.

In July 1949 Kao went to Moscow where he negotiated a one-year barter agreement providing that the Manchurian government would send soy beans, vegetable oils, and grains to Russia in return for industrial equipment, petroleum, automobiles, textiles, paper, and medicines. The agreement was significant in a number of ways. First, it was concluded while the Soviet still maintained diplomatic relations with the Nationalists (an action which the Nationalists formally protested) and it was also the first agreement between the Russians and a formally organized Chinese Communist governmental organ. It was also negotiated, of course, before the PRC was officially inaugurated in October 1949, a fact which gave rise to the interpretation that Kao had acted independently of Mao Tse-tung and his colleagues in Peking. Though this interpretation is tempting in view of Kao's later political fall (see below), there is little to indicate that the Maoist elements in the CCP regarded it as anything more than a simple trade agreement concluded with the first region of China under complete Communist control.

Shortly after Kao returned from Moscow he

went to Peking to take part in the inaugural session of the CPPCC, the organization that brought the new central government into existence. He attended and spoke at the session, held in late September 1949, as the ranking delegate representing the Northeast Liberated Area. Kao served on the Standing Committee of the CPPCC's Presidium (steering committee) and also headed the *ad hoc* Credentials Committee. He emerged from the meetings as one of the most powerful national leaders when he was appointed under Chairman Mao Tse-tung as a vice-chairman of the Central People's Government Council. Three of the other five vice-chairmanships were given to non-Communists Chang Lan, Li Chi-shen, and Mme. Sun Yat-sen in an obvious gesture of bi-partisanship that bore little relationship to actual political power. Liu Shao-ch'i and Chu Te (qq.v.) were the other two vice-chairmen, and thus Kao was the only regional leader to become a vice-chairman of the most important governmental organ from 1949 to 1954.

Immediately after the central government was established on October 1, 1949, Kao was made a member of the central government's People's Revolutionary Military Council (PRMC), and two years later (November 1951) he was elevated to a vice-chairmanship. Still another position he received in October 1949 was membership on the Executive Board of the Sino-Soviet Friendship Association, one of the most active "mass" organizations in the early years of the PRC. Kao concurrently served from 1949 as the chairman of the Association's Northeast branch. After participating in these preliminary steps to organize the central government, Kao returned to Mukden, the capital of the Manchurian administration, where he spent most of the next three years. During these years Kao completely dominated the political scene in Manchuria. It was a rare occasion when he was not the keynote speaker at the innumerable conferences held by the Northeast Bureau or the Northeast People's Government—on subjects ranging from land reform to industrial management to afforestation. Many of his speeches were published in the *JMJP* and the *Tung-pei jih-pao* (Northeast daily), the Party organ for Manchuria. A number of these were also reprinted in the authoritative government gazette *Hsin-hua yueh-pao* (New China monthly) or the English-language journal *People's China.* Several of Kao's more important reports are conveniently assembled in *Current Background, no.* 163 (March 5, 1952).

The manner in which Kao performed his numerous tasks in Manchuria was of particular importance to the Chinese Communists. As China's first "liberated" area, for example, many of the key Party policies were first tested and implemented there (e.g., the land reform pro-

gram). Although the Russians had stripped Manchuria of much of its industrial plant in the immediate postwar period, it still remained the most highly industrialized area of China. While Kao was in Manchuria Chinese relations with the Soviet Union were more complex there than in any other region, because the Russians and the Chinese jointly administered the important Chinese Changchun Railway as well as the strategic naval facilities at Port Arthur-Dairen. Finally, Manchuria served as the logistical base and the staging area for Chinese troops when they entered the Korean War in the fall of 1950.

In November 1952, in anticipation of the First Five-Year Plan, which began in 1953, the State Planning Commission was established. Kao was brought to Peking to become its first chairman. The significance of the Commission was underscored by the fact that it was placed directly subordinate to the Central People's Government Council, that is, on a par with Chou En-lai's Government Administration Council (the cabinet). Kao, by now definitely identified as a Politburo member, retained his positions in Manchuria, and in January 1953, when the Northeast People's Government was reorganized and redesignated the Northeast Administrative Committee, he was again named as chairman. In fact, however, he spent virtually all his time in Peking after the early part of 1953. By March he was described as one of Mao's "close comrades-in-arms," an accolade accorded only to the select few. He made his last major report in September 1953 at the 26th meeting of the CPGC, stressing the need to concentrate resources on the development of heavy industry. He continued to appear in public until January 20, 1954, when he attended a meeting to commemorate the 30th anniversary of Lenin's death. Only two weeks later he was attacked (though not by name) at a Party Plenum and within a year he had died by his own hand.

The famous purge of Kao Kang and his alleged accomplice Jao Shu-shih (q.v.) was by far the most important one in the first decade and a half of the PRC. Numerous writers have commented on the affair, but the most persuasive case has been presented by Franz Schurmann in his *Ideology and Organization in Communist China.*[4] Schurmann argues that the struggle against Kao involved many issues: "a personal struggle between Mao Tse-tung and Kao . . . , disagreement over basic economic strategy, over methods of administration, over allocation of resources, over control of the Party apparatus." In particular, he points to Kao as the arch advocate of the so-called "one-man management" system in industry—as opposed to a collective leadership involving Party committees and the managerial class. In this regard it is noteworthy that as early as March 1950 Kao, in a speech in

Mukden on the role of factory managers, had emphasized that the managers should be in charge and dismissed as "absurd" the idea that Party secretaries should be supreme.[5]

Basic decisions regarding Kao and his "incorrect" policies were initially adopted at a Politburo meeting in December 1953 when Mao spoke on Party unity. The first major step to implement these decisions was taken two months later (February 1954) at the Party's Fourth Plenum when Liu Shao-ch'i called for a return to collective leadership by the CCP. Liu also castigated "certain high-ranking" but unnamed cadres who regarded the "region or department under their leadership as their personal property or independent kingdom." Schurmann points to a number of highly suggestive articles that indirectly attacked Kao (the first of them on February 16, 1954), but Kao's actual denunciation did not take place within the CCP until the National Party Conference of March 21–31, 1955, and he was not publicly denounced until the Fifth Plenum a few days later. This year-long gap between the basic decisions and the public announcement of Kao's purge has not been entirely explained. However, there is evidence to suggest that the extent of Kao's "anti-Party plot" was not fully apparent to the Party Center until mid-1954. Kao and Jao were allegedly given a "serious warning" at the February 1954 Plenum, yet it is noteworthy that one of Jao's followers who was later purged, Shantung Party Second Secretary Hsiang Ming (see below), gave a report about a month *after* the Fourth Plenum at a meeting called to "transmit the resolutions" of the Plenum—thereby suggesting that all the "accomplices in the plot" had still not been uncovered even after the Plenum in February. Moreover, Jao's wife, Lu Ts'ui (see under Jao), continued to receive attention in the Chinese press through the end of 1954. Perhaps the best evidence comes from the transfer of Ouyang Ch'in (q.v.) in mid-1954 from Port Arthur-Dairen to Heilungkiang. Ouyang had been the Party's first secretary in Port Arthur-Dairen where he had Ch'en Po-ts'un (one of the Kao "clique") as his second secretary. Then, in what appears to have been a sudden move, Ouyang was transferred to replace Chao Te-tsun, another of the "conspirators," who had been the Party secretary in Heilungkiang. It seems possible that Ouyang had gotten wind of the "plot," a suggestion that gains credence from the fact that Ouyang's stature advanced notably after the Kao-Jao purge.

In any case, by the Fifth Plenum in April 1955, the "plot" was in the open and steps were being taken to rid the Party of the "conspirators." The Fifth Plenum's resolution on the Kao-Jao "anti-Party bloc" was based on a report made by Party Secretary-General Teng Hsiao-p'ing who, significantly, was elevated to the Politburo at that time. In the elaborate charges against Kao it was claimed that his "conspiratorial activities" to seize power dated back to 1949; he had regarded Manchuria as his "independent kingdom" and had "even tried to instigate Party members in the army to support his conspiracy." To this end he had "invented the utterly absurd 'theory' that the Party consisted of two parties—one, the so-called 'Party of the revolutionary bases and the army,' the other, the so-called 'Party of the white areas.' " Kao, it was asserted, claimed to represent the "Party of the revolutionary bases and the army." The "white areas" was a reference to KMT- and Japanese-occupied areas where the Communists did not have bases. Liu Shao-ch'i had spent considerable time during the Sino-Japanese War in these areas as the leading Party operative. On the other hand the "revolutionary bases" referred to the rear areas, such as the Shen-Kan-Ning base, where the Communists exercised uncontested control, and to the guerrilla bases that were completely or partially behind Japanese lines, such as the Shansi-Chahar-Hopeh base. Kao Kang, of course, had been a senior leader in the "revolutionary bases."

The resolution also claimed that Kao was attempting to become the Party general secretary (*tsung shu-chi*) or vice-chairman and State Council premier, that is, that he was trying to usurp the authority of Teng Hsiao-p'ing, Liu Shao-ch'i, and Chou En-lai. It was asserted that Kao, when given the "serious warning" at the February 1954 Plenum, "not only did not admit his guilt . . . , but committed suicide as an ultimate expression of his betrayal of the Party." (The separate charges against Jao Shu-shih are reviewed in his biography.) The resolution concluded with a renewed call for Party unity.

When Kao and Jao were purged, seven other men were also swept out of the Party for their part in the "anti-Party bloc." Even if Kao and Jao had not been involved, these seven were so significant themselves that their purge alone would have constituted a major debacle within the CCP ranks. As it is, the fame of Kao and Jao has tended to overshadow the importance of the seven "co-conspirators." In examining their careers, two major facts stand out: six of the seven were clearly Kao's men and these six worked closely together in Manchuria. A brief sketch of each man follows.

Chang Hsiu-shan came from the same town as Kao, suggesting an association covering many years. He graduated from a Party school in Yenan and was with Kao in Manchuria as a deputy political commissar of the Northeast Military Region and a deputy secretary-general of the Party's Northeast Bureau. He was a member of the Northeast People's Government (NEPG) and the Northeast Administrative Committee (NEAC) and concurrently chairman of the

NEPG–NEAC People's Supervision Committee from 1950 to 1954. From 1950 to about 1953 Chang also headed the Northeast Party Bureau's Organization Department. He was second deputy secretary of the Northeast Bureau (1952–1954), a position subordinate only to Secretary Kao and First Deputy Secretary Lin Feng. Moreover, he was secretary of the Bureau's Discipline Inspection Committee in the early fifties.

Chang Ming-yuan, a native of Hopeh, served as a deputy to Chang Hsiu-shan in the NEPG People's Supervision Committee from 1950 to 1952. From 1952 to 1954 he was secretary-general of the NEPG–NEAC, and in 1953–54 he was a NEAC vice-chairman. In the Northeast Party Bureau he was the secretary-general from 1952 to 1954, as well as third deputy secretary of the Bureau—placed fourth in line under Kao Kang, Lin Feng, and Chang Hsiu-shan.

Chao Te-tsun was the ranking Heilungkiang Party secretary from 1950 to 1954 and governor of the province from 1952 to 1953. Within the Northeast Party Bureau he was a deputy director in 1951 of the Organization Department (serving under Chang Hsiu-shan), and when purged in 1954 he was heading the Bureau's Rural Work Department.

Ma Hung served under Chang Ming-yuan as a deputy secretary-general of the Northeast Party Bureau. In November 1952 Ma was transferred to Peking to become a member of the State Planning Commission under Kao Kang, and by late 1953 he was concurrently Commission secretary-general. Ma appears to have been the only one of Kao's men who transferred to Peking with him in 1952.

Kuo Feng, a native of Kirin, accompanied Kao Kang to Manchuria after the war and then served in the Northeast Democratic Allied Army. From 1950 to 1954 he was the ranking Party secretary in Liaohsi Province, and in 1951 he was also head of the provincial Economic Planning Committee. In mid-1952 he replaced Ch'en Po-ts'un as head of the NEPG's Personnel Department. In 1952–53 he served under Chang Hsiu-shan in the Northeast Party Bureau's Organization Department, and then replaced Chang as director in 1953. Kuo was also under Chang Hsiu-shan as a deputy secretary of the Bureau's Discipline Inspection Committee.

Ch'en Po-ts'un was head of the NEPG's Personnel Department until replaced by Kuo Feng in mid-1952. He was deputy director under Chang Hsiu-shan in the Northeast Party Bureau's Organization Department in 1950 and in the next year became a member of the Northeast Branch of the Procurator General's Office. In 1952–53 he was also the second secretary of the Port Arthur-Dairen Party Committee under Ouyang Ch'in (q.v.). In addition, Ch'en served under Chang Hsiu-shan as a deputy secretary

of the Northeast Bureau's Discipline Inspection Committee.

Hsiang Ming, a native of Shantung, was the only one of the seven who was associated (at least indirectly) with Jao Shu-shih. In 1952 he became a member of the East China Military and Administrative Committee, which was chaired by Jao. Hsiang's principal place of work was in Shantung province where from 1950 to 1954 he was second secretary of the Party's Shantung Sub-bureau; on occasion he served as the acting secretary in the absence of Secretary K'ang Sheng (q.v.). From 1951 to at least 1953 he was also a Shantung vice-governor. In the charges against Hsiang it was asserted that he "not only impudently restricted" the work of the Shantung Sub-bureau's Discipline Inspection Committee, but he also "drove out of Shantung" personnel sent by the Central Discipline Inspection Committee. Of interest is the fact that, when Shantung Governor Chao Chien-min (q.v.) was purged in late 1958, it was claimed that he had attempted to exonerate Hsiang—one of the rare instances in which any of the Kao-Jao clique was mentioned in the years after the 1955 purge.

As these seven brief case histories indicate, the Kao-Jao accomplices held a large number of key positions in organizations that wield great power—discipline inspection committees, supervision committees, and organization and personnel departments. There were no apparent reverberations in east China (except, of course, for the removal of Jao Shu-shih and Hsiang Ming), but the northeast was badly hit. With the important exception of First Deputy Secretary Lin Feng, the Northeast Party Bureau was virtually swept clean of its key personnel (although this became an academic point when the Bureau itself was dissolved in May 1955). There is also excellent evidence that the suspicion cast upon personnel working in Manchuria lingered on at least until the convocation of the Party's Eighth National Congress in September 1956. An examination of those appointed in January 1953 (just 13 months before the Fourth Plenum) to the six large Administrative Committees shows that of the 345 chairmen, vice-chairmen, and members of the Committee, an average of nearly 25 per cent were elected from each region to the Party Central Committee. The important exception, however, was in Kao's Northeast Administrative Committee where only 11 per cent were elected. Similarly, in the new Politburo elected immediately after the Party Congress, each of the six regions had one representative on the Politburo—excepting only the northeast, which had none.

A more concrete result of the purge was the establishment of a new Party control apparatus. From 1949 the Party had had central and local Discipline Inspection (*chi-lu chien-ch'a*) Committees. These, however, were found to be inadequate and were replaced at the time of the purge by central and local Party Control (*chien-ch'a*) Commissions, which were "given much wider powers" than the predecessor organizations. The purpose was to strengthen Party discipline and the "struggle against all kinds of violations by Party members of law and discipline, and particularly to prevent a recurrence of so serious a case as that of the anti-Party bloc of Kao Kang and Jao Shu-shih, which gravely imperiled Party interests." Tung Pi-wu (q.v.), one of the Party's most senior leaders, was named to head the new Central Control Commission.

1. Chün-tu Hsüeh, *The Chinese Communist Movement, 1937–1949* (Stanford, Calif., 1962), *passim.*
2. Conrad Brandt, Benjamin Schwartz, and John K. Fairbank, *A Documentary History of Chinese Communism* (Cambridge, Mass., 1952), p. 387.
3. *Selected Works of Mao Tse-tung* (Peking, 1965), III, 45.
4. Franz Schurmann, *Ideology and Organization in Communist China* (Berkeley, Calif., 1966), pp. 267ff.
5. *CB* 6, pp. 2–22.

Kao K'o-lin

(Shensi). Secretary, CCP Northwest Bureau; member, CCP Control Commission; alternate member, CCP Central Committee.

Kao K'o-lin was not identified until 1941 when he was connected with the newly founded Nationalities Institute in Yenan. The Institute, which opened in September 1941 in Yenan, was a training school for national minorities' cadres. It was headed by the then secretary of the CCP's Northwest Bureau (though the secretary's name was not given it was probably Kao Kang) and numbered on its staff the veteran Party leader of Mongol origin, Ulanfu, who headed the education department. Kao K'o-lin was vice-president of the Institute.

Kao's activities received no further attention until early 1949 when the Communists were rapidly expanding throughout China. He was then identified as the political commissar of the Suiyuan–Mongolia Military District, retaining this position when the District was reorganized in mid-1949 into the Suiyuan Military District. In December 1949 the Military District underwent a change of top personnel, with Kao being replaced as political commissar by Po I-po, a man of greater political importance. Kao, in turn, was made a deputy political commissar. In addition to these military assignments in Suiyuan, he was also a prominent figure in the Party and governmental structures for the province. He was the ranking Party secretary for the province from

mid-1949 until July 1952 when the Suiyuan Party Committee was changed into the Suiyuan–Inner Mongolia Sub-bureau. The civil and quasi-military government structure in Suiyuan was different from that of other provinces, which simply had "provincial people's governments." In Suiyuan there was a Military and Administrative Committee as well as the provincial people's government, both established in December 1949. In the former Kao served as a vice-chairman under Fu Tso-i, the Nationalist general and a long-time leader in the Suiyuan area, who had peacefully surrendered Peking. Kao was not immediately given any post under the Suiyuan Provincial People's Government, but in September 1950 he was named to head the provincial Finance and Economics Committee.

Although Kao's main contributions in the early days of the PRC were made in Suiyuan, he also took part in the fall of 1949 in the establishment of the central government in Peking. He attended the inaugural meeting of the CPPCC in September 1949 as a delegate from the north China "liberated areas," which suggests that the north had been his main base of operations from wartime days until 1949.

In the latter part of 1952 Kao was transferred to Shansi, thereby relinquishing his Suiyuan posts. In Shansi he became the ranking Party secretary, and when the North China Administrative Committee was reorganized in January 1953, he was named to membership, a post he held until this multi-provincial body was dissolved in 1954. Kao's tenure in Shansi lasted only about a year; in September 1953 he was called to Peking where he was named as a deputy procurator-general in the Supreme People's Procuratorate, a judicial office roughly analogous to the Attorney General's Office in the United States. In the fall of 1954 the initial session of the First NPC brought the constitutional government into existence. Kao attended as a deputy from Kweichow and at the close of the sessions was named to the Bills Committee, one of the two permanent organs under this legislative body. In the general reorganization of the central government that followed the NPC sessions, he was transferred from the Procuratorate (November 1954) to a vice-presidency on the Supreme People's Court, serving under Politburo member Tung Pi-wu, the president of the Court. Four years later he was again elected as a Kweichow deputy to the Second NPC and during its term (1959–1964) again served on the Bills Committee.

In September 1956, when the CCP met for its Eighth National Congress, Kao was elected an alternate member of the Central Committee. When the First Plenum of the new Central Committee met, immediately after the Congress, he was elected a member of the powerful Party Control Commission, here again serving under Tung Pi-wu. Rather little was heard about Kao in the late 1950's, but he did make a report on the work of the Supreme Court since 1955 before a session of the NPC in April 1959.[1] Then, in January 1961, the Party reactivated the regional Party bureaus, which had gone out of existence in 1954–55. Soon after, in July 1961, he was identified as an official in the Northwest Bureau based in Sian, Shensi. His position there was not clarified until October 1963 when he was identified as a secretary of the Bureau, serving under First Secretary Liu Lan-t'ao and Second Secretary Chang Te-sheng (qq.v.). With this transfer back to Party channels, Kao was removed from the Supreme People's Court; an exact date is not available, but it was approximately in mid-1961. With this loss of office, his only known legal ties are through his connections with the Political Science and Law Association of China. He was named to the Third National Council of the Association in August 1958 and then was re-elected to the Fourth Council in October 1964. The organization was headed by Tung Pi-wu until 1964 and thereafter by Wu Te-feng (q.v.).

In 1964 Kao was once more re-elected to the NPC, only on this occasion he was elected from Shensi. When the first session of the Third NPC met in December–January 1965, he was selected for membership on the Credentials Committee. (In the First and Second NPC's he had served on the Bills Committee.) Kao's only known trip abroad occurred in September–October 1959 when he led a delegation to East Germany for celebrations marking the 10th anniversary of the German Democratic Republic. During this trip he was identified as a vice-president of the China-Germany Friendship Association, which had been established a year earlier. It is evident, however, that he has devoted little time to this organization.

---

1. *CB* 569.

Kao Yang

(Liaoning). Government bureaucrat and minister, Chemical Industry.

Kao Yang, a native of Liaoning in Manchuria, may have begun his career in trade union work, as is suggested by the fact that when he first became known in 1950 he was serving in the Liaotung Provincial Labor Department and also by the fact that he was a member of the funeral committee for Lai Jo-yü, head of the All-China Federation of Trade Unions, who died in 1958.

Kao's career is first documented in the spring of 1950 when he was identified as a deputy secretary of the Shenyang (Mukden) CCP Committee, as well as head of the Organization Department of the same committee. He was holding both positions in May 1950 when he was named governor of Liaotung, a post he held until July 1952. Concurrent with this post he was from

October 1950 director of the Liaotung Labor Department.

To judge from these important positions that Kao was given in both the government and Party in Liaotung, one of the most important of China's industrial provinces, it would appear that he had already gained considerable recognition before 1950.

From September 1951 until its reorganization in January 1953, Kao served as a member of the Northeast People's Government, the Manchurian administration then headed by Kao Kang, who was officially purged in 1955. Kao Yang attended the third session of the First CPPCC in October–November 1951, one of the few reported events of his career at this stage.

In the spring of 1953 Kao replaced Chang Ch'i-lung as the ranking Party secretary in Liaotung, but when Liaotung was merged with Liaohsi Province in mid-1954 to form Liaoning, he was dropped as CCP secretary. He was, however, elected to the First NPC in 1954 as a deputy from Liaoning; he also served in the Second NPC (1959–1964) and was again re-elected to the Third NPC, which began its first session in December 1964.

In the wake of the 1955 purge of Politburo member Kao Kang, the Party established a central Control Commission to tighten discipline and insure loyalty. At the time, only the name of the commission chairman, Politburo member Tung Pi-wu, was known. However, at the first plenum of the eighth Party Central Committee, held in September 1956 immediately after the historic Eighth Party Congress, Kao was named to the Commission. The Control Commission has members representing various fields of work, and thus it may be inferred from Kao's career that his role was in connection with Party supervision of industrial enterprises, perhaps specializing in those located in Manchuria.

In January 1957 Kao was appointed as a vice-president of the Shenyang College of Physical Education, and in the fall of 1958 he was identified as one of the deputy directors of the Industrial Work Department of the Party's Central Committee, a department that is one of the key CCP organs in controlling the economic sector.

For reasons that are not clear, Kao's name was dropped from the official roster of the Control Commission in 1960. At first this seemed to be associated with the failures of the Great Leap Forward occurring that year. In the following year his membership on the commission was restored, but it was again dropped in 1962. However, the latter happening is more easily explained, because Kao was given an important ministerial appointment at this time. The former minister of Chemical Industry, P'eng T'ao, had died in November 1961, and in July 1962 Kao was named to succeed him, an appointment roughly coinciding with an increased attention to the importance of chemical fertilizers, which were especially necessary to support the greatly accelerated program to boost agricultural production.

Kao's activities have never received much attention from the Chinese press, but he received somewhat better coverage in 1963 and 1964. His most significant appearances occurred in early 1963 when he attended a national agricultural science and technology conference and in December 1964 when he spoke before the first session of the Third NPC on the performance of the chemical industry in 1964, claiming that it had overfulfilled the State plan.

Keng Piao

(1909– ; Li-ling hsien, Hunan). Veteran PLA officer; diplomat.

From the mid-twenties to the end of the civil war with the Nationalists in the late forties, Keng Piao was a Red Army commander. Aside from three and a half years as a vice-minister in the Ministry of Foreign Affairs during the early sixties, Keng has been abroad almost the entire time since the establishment of the PRC in 1949, serving as Peking's first ambassador to Sweden and as its first minister to both Denmark and Finland. From 1956 to 1959 he was the ambassador to Pakistan, and he has also been ambassador to Burma since 1963. His service in these five nations has given him more experience abroad than any other Chinese diplomat.

Keng was born in Li-ling hsien, which lies in east-central Hunan near the Kiangsi border and is the home of a number of important Communists, among them Li Li-san, Chang Chi-ch'un, Yang Te-chih, and Liao Han-sheng (qq.v.). Although Li and Chang are several years older than Keng, Yang and Liao are almost exact contemporaries. In the mid-twenties, while still a teenager, Keng was already participating in the Communist Party underground and engaging in guerrilla activities, presumably in his native Hunan. By 1930 he had joined the Chinese Workers' and Peasants' Red Army, the force led by Chu Te and Mao Tse-tung, which was headquartered in Juichin in southeastern Kiangsi. Keng made the Long March in 1934–35 as commander of the Fourth Regiment of the Second Division commanded by Liu Ya-lou (q.v.). The Second Division was one of the major components of the First Army Corps led by Lin Piao and Nieh Jung-chen (qq.v.). During the Long March, Keng is credited with a major role in the crossing of the Wu River in Kweichow in January 1935, an episode described in the biography of Liu Ya-lou.[1]

After arriving in northern Shensi at the end of the Long March, Keng was sent to the Red Army Academy at Wa-yao-pao, a small town a little to the east of Pao-an, then the Communist capital. After graduating in 1936, he remained as an instructor; he was thus probably still with the academy after it moved to Yenan in early 1937, when it was renamed the Anti-Japanese Military and Political Academy, more familiarly known by its abbreviated Chinese name, K'ang-ta. Keng's activities during the early and middle stages of the Sino-Japanese War are not documented, except for the fact that he worked in Yenan at the Eighth Route Army Headquarters. In 1944 he was serving as director of the Liaison Bureau of the Shansi-Chahar-Hopeh (Chin-Ch'a-Chi) Border Region Government (see under Sung Shao-wen), and from the same year to 1946 he was deputy chief-of-staff of the Chin-Ch'a-Chi Military Region. This important military command was headed by Nieh Jung-chen, under whom Keng had served during the Long March.

In accordance with the Cease-fire Agreement worked out in January 1946 between the CCP and the KMT by U.S. Envoy George C. Marshall, the Peking Executive Headquarters was established to monitor the agreement. Holding the simulated rank of major-general, Keng was assigned to head the Communist unit in the Railway Control Section, but later that year was assigned to Szu-p'ing-k'ai (Szeping, located on the rail line between Mukden and Changchun) where he headed the Communist side on the 28th Field Team, which was under the jurisdiction of the Peking Headquarters. In 1947, following the collapse of the truce, Keng returned to active duty with the armed forces and in the later part of the year took part in the attack on Shih-chia-chuang in western Hopeh, the city that served temporarily as the Communist capital until the surrender of Peking in early 1949.

Keng's exploits in the latter stages of the civil war with the Nationalists are cited in the writings of Mao Tse-tung.[2] Serving as deputy commander of the Communists' 19th Corps, which was operating to the west of Peking, he took part in the battles of December 1948 that led to the defeat of the strong armies led by KMT General Fu Tso-i. The Communist successes in these battles led directly to the fall of Tientsin and Peking in January 1949. Keng was serving at this time with Lo Jui-ch'ing (q.v.) and Yang Te-chih, his fellow native from Li-ling. Keng's activities after the end of 1948 are not recorded, but it is probable that he moved westward to Ninghsia province with Yang Te-chih in 1949.

Apart from his brief association with Americans while a member of the Peking Executive Headquarters, Keng had had no contact with foreigners prior to the establishment of the PRC in the fall of 1949. However, he was to spend most of the next decade and a half abroad as a foreign service officer. Sweden, Denmark, and Finland were three of the earliest non-Communist governments to recognize the PRC, and by the time the new Communist government was a year old, Keng had been named as Peking's first envoy to each of them. On May 9, 1950, he was appointed as ambassador to Sweden, and two days later as minister to Denmark. He presented his credentials in Stockholm on September 19 and in Copenhagen on November 8. In the interim, in late October, he was also appointed as minister to Finland, presenting his credentials in Helsinki on March 31, 1951. He resided in Stockholm and apparently spent little time in either Denmark or Finland. However, he did go to these nations from time to time to take part in protocol functions. It should be noted that during Keng's early years abroad the Korean War was still being fought, a fact that tended to inhibit Chinese relations with non-Communist nations—particularly in the field of trade, then subject to a rigorous embargo by the West. This situation is best illustrated by the fact that during Keng's tour in Sweden, Denmark, and Finland, only one government-to-government agreement was signed—a trade agreement that Keng signed with the Finns in Helsinki in June 1954. Nonetheless, a Western diplomat familiar with Keng's work in Stockholm asserts that he was regarded as a competent official.[3]

After the Korean War ended in mid-1953, the Communists made greater efforts to expand their contacts abroad. As a consequence, resident envoys were assigned to Finland in the fall of 1954 and to Denmark in the spring of 1955, Keng thus being relieved of two of his posts. Then, after more than five years in Stockholm, he was replaced in February 1956 by Han Nien-lung (q.v.) and was himself appointed ambassador to Pakistan. He returned home from Stockholm for a brief visit and then in March accompanied Vice-premier Ho Lung to Karachi to take part in the ceremonies inaugurating the Pakistan Islamic Republic. A few days later, on April 10, he presented his credentials. Of interest is the fact that Keng was still identified as a major-general. During his three and a half years in Karachi, Sino-Pakistani relations were probably best described as cool and correct. Pakistan was formally allied to the West under the SEATO arrangement; more important, in the mid-fifties the Chinese were making a major effort to curry the favor of the Indians. Notwithstanding these facts, steps were taken by the Chinese to increase diplomatic contacts and to foster increased trade. The first of these moves was an invitation to the Pakistani prime minister to make a state visit to China. In preparation for this, Keng returned to Peking in June 1956. The visit was temporarily postponed, however, and he returned to Pakistan where on July 13, 1956, he signed a contract for the sale of rice to the Pakistanis and announced Chinese intentions to donate rice to alleviate famine conditions in East Pakistan. Keng was back in China in August, remaining there through

October, the month when the Pakistani prime minister made his state visit. Except for two further trips back to Peking, in mid-1957 and mid-1958, Keng remained at his post for the balance of his tour. On a number of occasions he took part in talks with Pakistani leaders when important Chinese visitors were in Karachi. The most notable of these occasions was in December 1956 when Chou En-lai traveled to Pakistan as part of a goodwill mission to several south and southeast Asian nations.

Keng was replaced in December 1959 as Peking's ambassador in Karachi by Ting Kuo-yü, who had formerly been ambassador to Afghanistan. Keng returned home with over nine years' experience abroad and was thus one of China's most seasoned diplomats. Immediately thereafter, in January 1960, he was assigned to the Foreign Ministry as a vice-minister, a post he was to hold for three and a half years. During this period he was reported with great regularity in the Chinese press; he dealt with foreign envoys and visitors from virtually all nations having diplomatic relations with Peking, but he was particularly active in the handling of relations with south and southeast Asian countries. In several instances he signed protocols on behalf of the Chinese government, as in November 1961 when he signed the protocol on the exchange of the instruments of ratification of the Sino-Nepalese Treaty of Peace and Friendship. On three occasions he accompanied top Chinese officials abroad, the first of which occurred in August 1960 when he went to Afghanistan with Foreign Minister Ch'en I to attend Afghan independence celebrations. In January 1961 he was in Burma as a member of the huge 400-member delegation led by Chou En-lai and Ch'en I to attend the celebrations commemorating the 13th anniversary of Burmese independence and to exchange the instruments of ratification of the Sino-Burmese Boundary Treaty. He was again with Ch'en I in March–April 1961 on a friendship visit to Indonesia, and back in Peking on June 19 he signed the instruments of ratification of the Treaty of Friendship, which had been negotiated by Ch'en in Jakarta on April 1. Keng's most dramatic moment came in the early hours of the morning of October 21, 1962, when he summoned the Indian chargé d'affaires to deliver a note of protest against the alleged "massive general attacks launched by the Indians" on the Sino-Indian border. In fact, of course, Chinese military forces had just moved into Indian territory in the prelude to the brief Sino-Indian border war. In June 1963 he was named to membership on the Preparatory Committee for Participation in the Games of the New Emerging Forces, better known by its abbreviated name "GANEFO" (see under Jung Kao-t'ang).

In September 1963 Keng was removed as a vice-minister and named to succeed Li I-mang (q.v.) as ambassador to Burma. He arrived in Rangoon soon after and presented his credentials on September 20. Because of the relatively close relations between China and Burma, Keng is frequently mentioned in the press in connection with visits of Chinese leaders to Rangoon. As of 1965 he had spent 12 years abroad, a record unmatched by any other Chinese diplomat.

1. *Stories of the Long March* (Peking, 1958), p. 14.
2. *Selected Works of Mao Tse-tung* (Peking, 1961), IV, 289–291.
3. Interview with Western diplomat, New York, November 1962.

K'o Ch'ing-shih

(1902–1965; Anhwei). Former underground operative; former mayor of Shanghai and member, CCP Politburo.

K'o Ch'ing-shih was one of the earliest members of the CCP and spent most of the twenties and thirties (until the war broke out) engaged in underground work in east and north China. He was an important official in the Party's United Front Department in Yenan during the war, and in the early years of the PRC he was the top Communist official in Nanking and then Kiangsu. He was elected to the Party Central Committee in 1956 and to the Politburo two years later. During the decade before his death in 1965, K'o was the dominant Party official in Shanghai, serving there as mayor and Party first secretary.

K'o was born into a "middle-class landowning family" in "Huangshan," Anhwei (presumably a reference to the Huang-shan mountain range in southern Anhwei).[1] In the early twenties or just before, K'o spent some time in Wu-hu, then a rather important center for revolutionary activities (see under Li K'o-nung). At about this time he was associated with Li K'o-nung, a young Anhwei revolutionary who also spent his youth in Wu-hu and who in the late twenties became an important Party intelligence operative in Shanghai. According to K'o's obituary, he joined the Socialist Youth League in 1920, the year it was founded in Shanghai by Ch'en Tu-hsiu and others. In September of the following year, K'o was arrested in Shanghai and held for a few days; the incident is described in the biography of Ch'en Tu-hsiu, who was also arrested. K'o, not yet 20, was probably then affiliated with *Hsin ch'ing-nien* (New youth), the organ of the Youth League. In 1922 he joined the CCP, and then, it appears, he returned to school. K'o has been reported as a graduate of the South Anhwei Normal School; however, in a 1960 interview with journalist Edgar Snow, he stated that "I was a student in normal college in Nanking in the twenties, when I left to join the Nationalist revolution. I was the only student in my class who

became a Communist." He is also reported to have taught school in his native Anhwei, probably during the twenties.

The details of K'o's career in the twenties and thirties are not available, but a broad picture can be painted on the basis of his obituary, his 1960 interview with Snow, and an article written by Li K'o-nung's son. K'o's obituary states that during the "long period from 1920 to 1936, he engaged in Party work and led the working class movement, the peasant movement, and the soldiers' movement [*ping-yun*] in Shanghai, Nanking, Wuhan, Anhwei, and other places. He was the secretary of the Anhwei CCP Committee, director of the Political Department of the Eighth Army of the Chinese Workers' and Peasants' Red Army, secretary-general of the CCP Central Committee, secretary of the Front Committee and concurrently director of the Front Committee's Organization Department under the Hopeh CCP Committee."

The period from the late twenties to the early thirties was apparently spent mainly in Shanghai where K'o worked with Party underground agents Li K'o-nung and Ch'en Keng (q.v.).[2] However, his obituary makes it clear that he spent at least brief intervals in the rural hinterlands, when he directed the Eighth Army's Political Department. Because there were two separate Red "Eighth Armies" in the 1930 period, one operating in Kwangsi and the other in Kiangsi (see under Chang Yun-i and T'ang Liang), it is not possible to know with which K'o was associated.

From the sequence of posts listed in K'o's obituary, it appears that he was secretary-general (*pi-shu-chang*) of the CCP Central Committee in the early thirties. This position, not to be confused with the Party's top post in that period—general secretary (*tsung shu-chi*)—was probably occupied in Shanghai at approximately the time when the key leaders of the Party Center were in the process of transferring the CCP headquarters to the Central Soviet area in Kiangsi. The Party underground operatives were then operating under extremely difficult conditions, and many of them were apprehended by the KMT. Thus, by 1933 (the year some accounts state that the CCP headquarters in Shanghai was closed) most of the important Party officials had fled from the city. In about that year K'o was apparently sent to north China where he is reported to have continued his underground work in Tientsin with Ch'en Po-ta and Nan Han-ch'en (qq.v.). According to Snow, he was associated with Liu Shao-ch'i in running the north China underground and was a key figure in arranging Snow's visit to the Communist headquarters in Shensi in 1936. K'o told Snow that before the latter went to Shensi, "It was I who wrote that invisible-ink letter to Mao Tse-tung . . . I wrote the letter for Professor [Hsu Ping, q.v., a friend of Snow's in Peking] to give to you."[3]

Snow records that when the Sino-Japanese War broke out in mid-1937, Liu Shao-ch'i and K'o "went into the villages together to organize guerrillas."[4] This assignment was apparently of brief duration, for by the latter part of 1937 K'o was in Hankow where the Communists maintained a liaison office. In 1938 he must have been associated with Ch'en Shao-yü (q.v.), who came to Hankow that year as a CCP representative to the first People's Political Council. Both men were in Yenan by 1938, at which time Ch'en had assumed the directorship of the Party's United Front Department, a post he held throughout most of the war period. K'o spent most of the war in Yenan as Ch'en's deputy in the United Front Department, and in 1944 was serving as its acting director. In the postwar period he was assigned to the Chin-Ch'a-Chi (Shansi-Chahar-Hopeh) Border Region Government (see under Sung Shao-wen), where he served as deputy director of the Finance Committee and director of the Civil Affairs Office.

In November 1947 Shih-chia-chuang fell to the Communist forces. An important rail junction in western Hopeh, it was the first important city in north China captured by the Communists. Possibly because of his familiarity with the north China area, K'o was named as the mayor. He held this post until he was replaced by Liu Hsiu-feng (q.v.) in April 1949.[5] The reason for K'o's transfer became apparent in the following month when the onrushing Communist armies captured Nanking. Liu Po-ch'eng, one of the military conquerors of Nanking, became the mayor and K'o one of his vice-mayors. In the latter part of 1949 Liu left Nanking to lead his forces into the southwest, and thus K'o became the acting head of the Nanking government, a post that was formalized in May 1950 when he was appointed as mayor. (From 1951 to 1952 he was also a member of the Nanking government's Finance and Economics Committee.) In October 1949 he had also become a member of the Nanking Military Control Commission, then headed by Su Yü (q.v.). In 1949 he additionally assumed the vice-chairmanship of the Nanking chapter of the Sino-Soviet Friendship Association, and by 1952 the chairmanship. Finally, by early 1950 he was the ranking secretary of the Nanking CCP Committee. In brief, from 1950 to the end of 1952, K'o was the top Communist official in Nanking.

Like most important east China officials, K'o was affiliated with the regional East China Military and Administrative Committee (ECMAC), established in Shanghai in January 1950. In the following month he was appointed to membership on the ECMAC's Finance and Economics Committee, and in September 1952 he was named as a member of the ECMAC, retaining his membership when the ECMAC was reorganized into the East China Administrative Committee (1953–54). In November 1952 the Communists merged the northern and southern sectors of Kiangsu (which they had established in 1949 as separate administrative districts) into the traditional provincial boundaries. T'an Chen-lin became the governor and K'o one of the vice-governors. However, T'an was principally occupied with his duties with the Party's East China Bureau (headquartered in Shanghai) and thus K'o was probably the de facto governor. His pre-eminence in Kiangsu is best illustrated by the fact that he was the first secretary of the provincial Party committee from the end of 1952 until succeeded by Chiang Wei-ch'ing in early 1955. Moreover, he served during this same period as political commissar of the Kiangsu Military District.

K'o received his first post in the national government in 1954 when elections were held for the First NPC, the organ that brought the constitutional government into existence at its initial session in September. He was a deputy to the First NPC from Kiangsu, but owing to his later transfer to Shanghai (see below), he represented that city in the Second NPC (1959–1964) and the Third NPC, which opened in December 1964. By January 1955 K'o had been transferred from Nanking to Shanghai where he became the ranking secretary of the Shanghai Bureau of the Party's Central Committee and first secretary of the Shanghai Municipal CCP Committee. The jurisdiction of the Shanghai Bureau has never been revealed; in fact, virtually nothing was heard about its activities and it apparently went out of existence by the early sixties. K'o continued to head the Municipal Party Committee until his death in 1965. From February 1955 to 1958 he was also a member of the Shanghai Government Council under Mayor Ch'en I. The latter, however, was mainly occupied (after September 1954) with his duties in Peking as a vice-premier and consequently spent little time in Shanghai. For this reason K'o succeeded him as the mayor in November 1958 and held the post until his death. He also held other positions in Shanghai that were largely ceremonial; these included the chairmanship of the Shanghai Committee of the CPPCC (1955–1958) and the presidency of the municipal chapter of the Sino-Soviet Friendship Association (1955–1959).

For a figure who was not yet a Party Central Committee member, K'o had a significant role in the proceedings of the Party's Eighth National Congress in September 1956. He served on both the Congress Presidium (steering committee) and the Credentials Committee and addressed the gathering on the "reform" of "capitalistic commerce." (Most of China's few remaining private businesses had, in effect, been nationalized during the previous winter; many of these were located in Shanghai where K'o was working.) At the close of the congress K'o was elected a member of the Party Central Committee; on the official list he was placed 36th—the highest rank of any member who had been neither a full nor an alternate member of the Seventh Central Committee elected in 1945. This indication of K'o's rising stature in the CCP received an emphatic endorsement at the Central Committee's Fifth Plenum, held immediately after the Second Session of the Eighth Party Congress in May 1958, when he was elevated (together with T'an Chen-lin and Li Ching-ch'üan) to Politburo membership. (The addition of K'o, T'an, and Li raised the number of full Politburo members to 20.)

Between the two Party Congress sessions, K'o had apparently proved himself to the Party's most senior leaders. He was prominent in the promotion of the "rectification" movement of 1957–58 directed against the "rightists," who had allegedly taken advantage of the relatively "liberal" (or Hundred Flowers) period in the spring of 1957. For example, a speech by K'o on this subject given in August 1957 was published in the *JMJP* of August 27, 1957. There may also have been significance in the fact that just prior to the May 1958 Congress K'o toured various Yangtze Valley cities (including Chungking and Wuhan) with Mao who, presumably, was making first-hand investigations in the provinces to witness for himself the progress of the Great Leap Forward inaugurated in early 1958. The May 1958 Fifth Plenum had also provided for the establishment of a new Party journal, the now famous *Hung-ch'i* (Red flag). K'o had the distinction of writing an article ("The Laboring People Must Make Themselves Masters of Culture") for the initial issue (June 1, 1958).

Because of Shanghai's great importance and size, its affairs receive more attention in the national press than any other city except Peking. And for these same reasons it is frequently visited by China's top leaders and foreign visitors. As a consequence, K'o was reported with great regularity in the decade before his death in 1965. His election to the Politburo in 1958 confirmed what was already apparent: he had become the top CCP leader in east China. This was given organizational expression following the re-establishment of the regional Party bureaus by the CCP's Ninth Plenum, held in January 1961. K'o presumably assumed the first secretaryship of the East China Bureau upon its formation in early 1961, but it was not until the spring of 1962 that he was specifically identified in the post. At the time of his death it was also revealed that he was the first political commissar of the Nanking Military Region with jurisdiction over Kiangsu, Chekiang, Anhwei, and (presumably) Shanghai itself.

In the last years of his life, K'o was a rather prolific contributor to the Party press. In addition to the *Hung-ch'i* article already cited, he contributed four more articles dealing with either economic or ideological questions (issues of February 16, 1959, May 1, 1959, November 1, 1959, and August 15, 1964). He seems to have taken a special interest in the Chinese drama. In a speech given before the East China Drama Festival in December 1963 he attacked traditional Chinese dramas and insisted that drama companies present works reflecting "real life and struggle," a theme that was repeated by K'o in his *Hung-ch'i* article of August 15, 1964.

K'o remained very active until his death on April 9, 1965. In fact, only three months earlier he had been appointed a vice-premier of the State Council, an appointment that might have been a prelude to a permanent transfer to Peking where he spent most of the last year of his life. At the time of his death he was in Chengtu, Szechwan—apparently on an inspection tour with such top leaders as Chu Te, Tung Pi-wu, and Ho Lung. Predictably, K'o's death received elaborate attention in the Chinese press. His funeral committee was chaired by Liu Shao-ch'i (who had probably been K'o's mentor since the thirties) and he was described as a "close comrade-in-arms" of Mao Tse-tung, an accolade reserved for the most select few. Virtually nothing is known of K'o's personal life apart from the fact that at the time of his death he had at least two sons and a daughter.[6] Edgar Snow has provided a brief description: "A big man, powerfully built, with a shock of black hair and wide, searching eyes, he looked fortyish but was in his late fifties. He is direct and forceful in his speech."[7]

---

1. Edgar Snow, *The Other Side of the River* (London, 1963), p. 544.
2. *SCMP* 2695, p. 6.
3. Snow, p. 544.
4. Snow, p. 544.
5. *JMJP* April 12, 1949.
6. *SCMP* 2464, pp. 9–11.
7. Snow, p. 544.

K'o Pai-nien

(c.1904–   ). Diplomat.

K'o Pai-nien has spent most of his career specializing in international relations and has served as an ambassador of the PRC to Rumania and Denmark. He was born about 1904, probably in central or south China. He is said to have graduated from one of the missionary-run schools in China—possibly Yenching University in Peking or St. John's University in Shanghai. To judge from his later career, he apparently studied the social sciences, possibly law, political science, or economics. It was probably during those years that K'o gained a good knowledge of English, and possibly also of Russian and French. Using the pseudonym Li Ch'un-fan, in the mid-1920's K'o began to translate works by and about Lenin for Chinese journals.[1] He joined the CCP in 1927, the year the Communists and the KMT broke their uneasy alliance following anti-Communist coups carried out by the KMT. K'o's brother was killed in these purges, an act said to have left him with a "burning hatred" for the KMT.[2]

Little is known of K'o's career over the next decade, but apparently he worked in Shanghai. It was there in 1930 that he published a work entitled *Tsen-yang yen-chiu hsin-hsing she-hui k'o-hsueh* (How to study the new social sciences), a work containing a list of some 140 books in the social sciences that had been translated into Chinese.[3] Three years later, also in Shanghai, he edited *Ching-chi hsueh tz'u-tien* (Economics dictionary). By no later than 1938 K'o had gone to the Communist headquarters in Yenan where he worked as an international relations researcher and as a translator of basic Marxist-Leninist works. Between 1939 and 1942 he translated at least six works by Marx, Engels, or Lenin, each of them published under the auspices of the Liberation Society in Yenan; in translating two of these works, he collaborated with other specialists in Marxism-Leninism, the most notable among them being Ai Szu-ch'i (q.v.).[4] In the latter stages of the Sino-Japanese War he was an interpreter and liaison official for foreign correspondents and for a U.S. military observers' team that was briefly posted in Yenan. Among the journalists for whom he interpreted was Harrison Forman, who visited Communist-held areas in 1944 and afterwards published *Report from Red China.*

As one of the relatively few veteran Communists who had a good command of English, K'o was assigned to head the Translating and Interpreting Section of the Communist delegation to the Peking Executive Headquarters, the organization established after U.S. Special Envoy George C. Marshall had worked out a temporary truce between the Communists and the KMT in January 1946. When full-scale war broke out in the latter part of the same year, K'o returned to Yenan, and for the next three years headed the Foreign Affairs Research Office, an office directly subordinate to the Party Central Committee.

In mid-1949, as the Communists prepared to establish the new regime, K'o was among those engaged in organizing Marxist-oriented professional organizations. In July he was one of the conveners of a nationwide social sciences conference out of which grew such important organizations as the Political Science and Law Association of China, a society with which he was later affiliated (see below). He received a similar assignment in mid-December 1949 when he was named to the Board of Directors of the newly established Chinese People's Institute of Foreign Affairs (CPIFA); the CPIFA purports to engage in research on foreign affairs, but it has also been utilized as a quasi-official organization to maintain contacts with nations not having formal diplomatic relations with the PRC. By 1952 he was the deputy director of the Institute's Research Committee and two years later he was the director, a position he held until he was named as ambassador to Rumania in 1954. On the day after K'o was appointed to the CPIFA, he was named as head of the American and Australasian Affairs Department of the Foreign Ministry. However, because of the absence of diplomatic relations with countries in the Americas or Australasia, K'o seldom made public appearances in this capacity. Rather, he appears to have spent much of this time writing for various Communist magazines, including *Hsueh-hsi* (Study), the most important Party journal until it ceased publication in 1958. A typical article appeared in the second issue of *Hsueh-hsi* (October 1949) under the title (in translation), "The Foreign Policy of New Democracy."

It was also in the early years of the PRC that K'o became active in the Communist-dominated International Association of Democratic Lawyers (IADL). He was a Council member of the IADL from 1951 to at least 1961 and in this capacity was a member of Chinese delegations to IADL meetings held in East Berlin (September 1951), Vienna (April 1952 and January 1954), and Prague (April 1953). The April 1952 trip to Vienna was made in connection with the charges by the IADL (and other Communist-front organizations) that the United States was using "germ warfare" in the Korean War. In March 1952 K'o had gone to North Korea to "investigate" the charges as a member of a special IADL commission. He then proceeded to Vienna where he delivered his report before the IADL Council. The Chinese affiliate to the IADL is known as the Political Science and Law Association of China (PSLAC). K'o took part in the preparatory work that led to the establishment of the PSLAC in April 1953, at which time he was named as one of the vice-chairmen under Party veteran Tung Pi-wu. K'o was also named to head the Association's International Liaison Department. He was, in effect, dropped from these posts when he went to Rumania in 1954 as ambassador, but in 1958 (not long before he returned from Rumania) he was elected to the National Council, a position he still holds.

K'o's last important assignment before being sent to Rumania was as an adviser to Chou En-lai's delegation to the famous Geneva Conference (April–July 1954) where a temporary settlement of the Indochinese War was worked out. In November 1954 he was named to replace Wang Yu-p'ing (q.v.) as ambassador to Rumania; K'o formally assumed the post in February and remained there for slightly over four years, when he was replaced by Hsu Chien-kuo (q.v.). Insofar as the published record is concerned, K'o's tour in Bucharest was largely uneventful. He did, however, participate in negotiations that led to the signing of various agreements and protocols, such as the 1955 plan for Sino-Rumanian cultural cooperation, which he signed in Bucharest in March 1955. He also returned to China on at least two occasions, the more important of which occurred in March–April 1958 when he accompanied Chivu Stoica, chairman of the Rumanian Council of Ministers, on a state visit to China.

K'o was replaced as ambassador to Rumania in April 1959, after which he resumed the sort of work in which he had previously been engaged in China. In April 1960 he was named to the Council of the newly formed China-Africa People's Friendship Association; this appointment is perhaps the reason he was sent as a deputy leader of the Chinese delegation to the preparatory meeting of the Asian-African Lawyer's Conference in Tokyo in March–April 1961. Shortly before this, in October 1960, K'o had been a deputy leader of the Chinese delegation to the Seventh Congress of the IADL held in Sofia.

In August 1961 K'o was identified in a post for which his past experience made him a logical choice, namely, as a deputy director of the International Relations Research Institute of the Academy of Sciences. Here he worked under Director Meng Yung-ch'ien (q.v.), another specialist in international relations. He presumably relinquished this position when he was appointed in October 1963 as Peking's ambassador to Denmark. K'o presented his credentials in Copenhagen in December 1963 and has been there since. Because Sino-Danish relations are relatively inactive, he is seldom mentioned in the Chinese press. However, his tour in Denmark coincides with concerted Chinese efforts to increase their technical and trade contacts with non-bloc nations; it is therefore possible that his assignment in Copenhagen will become increasingly important.

1. Chang Ching-lu, ed., *Chung-kuo hsien-tai ch'u-pan shih-liao* (Historical materials on contemporary Chinese publishing; Peking, 1954), p. 12 of photographs and p. 66.

2. Harrison Forman, *Report from Red China* (New York, 1945), p. 192.

3. T. A. Hsia, *Enigma of the Five Martyrs* (Berkeley, Calif., 1962), p. 107.

4. Chang Ching-lu, ed., *Chung-kuo ch'u-pan shih liao pu-pien* (Supplementary historical materials on Chinese publishing; Peking, 1957), pp. 449, 450, 461.

Ko Pao-ch'üan

(c.1912–   ; Tung-t'ai hsien, Kiangsu). Writer and translator of Russian literature.

Since being stationed in Moscow in the thirties as a reporter, Ko Pao-ch'üan has been closely linked to the promotion of Sino-Soviet relations and is well known for his translations of Russian and Soviet literature into Chinese. He remained a prominent figure in China until the early sixties when, as a result of the Sino-Soviet rift, he faded into relative obscurity. Ko was born about 1912 in Tung-t'ai hsien in central Kiangsu into a family that includes two well-known professional men, journalist Ko Kung-chen and Ko Shao-lung, a medical doctor.

Ko reportedly received some of his education in the Soviet Union. If true, this might explain why he was sent in 1935 to the USSR as a correspondent for the Tientsin *Ta-kung pao*, one of China's most important newspapers. Initially, Ko went to cover a tour of Russia by China's foremost Peking opera star, Mei Lan-fang, but he remained in Moscow for three years, returning home in 1938 after the Sino-Japanese War had broken out. He spent the remainder of the war in Chungking, the wartime capital of the Nationalists, working as an editor-translator (from Russian and English into Chinese) for the important Communist newspaper, the *Hsin-hua jih-pao* (New China daily). Concurrently, he edited a literary monthly put out by the left-wing Sino-Soviet Cultural Association (SSCA). His association with the SSCA may have brought him into contact with Ch'ien Chün-jui (q.v.), one of the founders of the SSCA and a man with whom Ko was to be closely associated in later years.

After the war Ko went to Shanghai where he continued to promote Sino-Soviet relations. In the period from 1946 to 1947 he was a translator for the Russian-sponsored weekly *Shih-tai* (Epoch), chief of the Translation Department of the Shanghai branch of *Sheng-huo shu-tien* (Life bookstore; one of the largest left-wing publishing companies in China) and head of the Shanghai branch of the Sino-Soviet Cultural Association. Following the collapse of KMT-CCP cooperation in 1946–47, almost all Communist Party members were evacuated from Nationalist-held areas. Ko apparently left Shanghai for the Communist-held areas at this time; in any event, he was with the Communists in the spring of 1949 when he accompanied Kuo Mo-jo (q.v.) to Prague for the World Peace Congress. Following his return to China he attended the All-China Congress of Literary and Art Workers held in Peking in July 1949. At the close of the meetings the All-China Federation of Literary and Art Circles was established, as well as several subordinate organizations, including the All-China Association of Literary Workers (ACALW; known as the Union of Chinese Writers after 1953). Ko was named to membership on the ACALW's National Committee. Although he was abroad when the next congress was held in September–October 1953, he was reappointed to the Executive Committee (the new name of the National Committee) of the Writers' Union.

As one of the more knowledgeable Chinese in regard to Soviet affairs, Ko was a logical choice for membership in the Sino-Soviet Friendship Association (SSFA), which, in effect, was the successor organization of the Sino-Soviet Cultural Association, in which Ko had played a leading role. He served on the SSFA Preparatory Committee when it was set up in July 1949, and when the organization was permanently established in October 1949 (just a few days after the inauguration of the PRC), he was named to the SSFA's First Executive Board. However, because of an appointment abroad (see below), he played no role in the activities of the organization until his return to China in 1954. Ko's assignment abroad was as counselor and concurrently chargé d'affaires of the Chinese embassy in Moscow; he has the distinction of being the first diplomat appointed in the history of the PRC—his appointment coming a few days before that of Wang Chia-hsiang, Peking's first ambassador to Moscow.

On three occasions during his tour in Moscow, Ko went on missions outside the Soviet Union. The first of these trips took him to Montreux, Switzerland, in May 1950 when he served as an adviser to the Chinese delegate at meetings of the Universal Postal Union (UPU), described by the Chinese press as the first United Nations agency to seat a representative of the PRC. Less than a year later, in January 1951, he was again the adviser to the Chinese delegate to UPU meetings in Cairo. In the interim, in November 1950, Ko had visited Poland as a guest of a Polish writers' association. During his stay in Moscow, where Ko often served as the chargé d'affaires in the absence of the ambassador, he also took part in one of the most important rounds of negotiations between China and the Soviet Union in the early fifties. These took place in August–September 1952 when Chou En-lai negotiated the return to China of the Chinese Changchun Railway, as well as the continued joint use by China and the USSR of the naval facilities at Port Arthur. As already described, at a congress of writers, which closed in Peking in October 1953, Ko was elected *in absentia* to the Executive Committee of the Union of Chinese Writers (UCW), a position he continues to hold. At about this same time he was also named as a vice-chairman of the UCW's Foreign Literature Committee (although official Chinese sources after 1956 list him only as a member). In the latter part of 1953, presumably in anticipation of his return to China, Ko was also named as a deputy secretary-general of the Sino-Soviet Friendship Association (SSFA), a post that placed him directly under Ch'ien Chün-jui, the most important Party leader in the SSFA at that time. Not long after receiving these appointments, Ko returned to Peking (early 1954) where he resumed his past work as a leading figure in the Chinese literary world, especially in connection with the promotion of Soviet cultural ties. From 1954 to 1960, most frequently in his capacity as a deputy secretary-general of the SSFA, Ko was constantly in the news—writing articles or giving lectures about leading Soviet cultural figures (like Gorky or Pushkin) or escorting the numerous delegations from Moscow that visited China so frequently in the 1950's. Moreover, on three occasions he returned to the Soviet Union. The first of these trips was in April 1956 when he was a deputy leader of a SSFA delegation sent to Moscow for the May Day celebrations; Ko remained in Moscow to confer with Soviet literary figures, returning to China in June. He was back in Moscow in mid-1958 to take part in preparations for the convocation of the First Afro-Asian Writers' Conference, and when this was held in Tashkent in October of the same year, Ko was a member of the Chinese delegation led by writer Shen Yen-ping (q.v.). In accordance with a decision taken at the Tashkent meetings, a permanent bureau for the writers was established; when the Chinese established the China Committee for Liaison with the Permanent Bureau of Afro-Asian Writers in April 1959, Ko was named as a member (see under Yang Shuo, the secretary-general of the Chinese Committee).

Like most Chinese officials who have close connections with international affairs, Ko has been appointed to some of the mass organizations devoted to foreign relations. From 1958 to 1965 he was a Standing Committee member of the China Peace Committee, and since the formation of the China-Albania Friendship Association in September 1958 Ko has been a member of the Association's national Council. As might be expected from his background, he has been associated with Chinese journals dealing with foreign literature. Since at least 1956 he has been a member of the editorial committee of *I-wen* (Translated literature), an organ of the Union of Chinese Writers. (*I-wen* was changed to *Shih-chieh wen-hsueh* [World literature] in January 1959.) Another journal with which he has been associated (since at least 1961) is *Wen-hsueh p'ing-lun* (Literary review), where he also serves on the editorial committee. A typical example of Ko's writings in recent years is found in this publication (issue no. 3, June 24, 1961), an article commemmorating the 25th anniversary of Gorky's death. Also in the literary field, Ko has been head of a research unit for Soviet literature in the Academy of Sciences' Literary Research Institute since its formation in October 1957, a date when the propagation of Soviet literature in China was still very much in vogue. However, since the Sino-Soviet split of the early sixties, Soviet literature has received much less attention, as is reflected by the change in Ko's writings since that time. For example, in what is a departure from his usual writings, for the June

1963 issue of the English-language *China Reconstructs* he wrote a survey article entitled "Asian and African Literature in China."

Ko has not appeared in public very often since mid-1960—after years of making frequent appearances in connection with Sino-Soviet relations. This abrupt change in his work is almost certainly a result of worsening Sino-Soviet affairs and is reflected by the fact that sometime in 1960 or 1961 he was removed as a deputy secretary-general of the SSFA. It is noteworthy that his superior, SSFA Secretary-general Ch'ien Chün-jui (q.v.), an alternate member of the Party's Central Committee, was also removed from the SSFA at the same time and has since suffered a serious decline in his career. But Ko's public appearances and published writings since 1960 have been sufficient in number to suggest that he has not been purged; rather, it seems that he has been relegated to the background because of his long and intimate association with the Soviet Union.

Ku Cho-hsin

(c.1909–   ; I-hsien, Liaoning). Economic official; secretary, Northeast Bureau, CCP.

The major portion of Ku Cho-hsin's career has been spent in his native Manchuria as an official specializing in economic affairs. He also served for nine years as a vice-chairman of the important PRC State Planning Commission. Ku was born in I-hsien in western Liaoning. In 1925, while still a teenager, he became involved in revolutionary underground work and sometime between this date and 1932 joined the CCP. Apparently he was assigned to work in Shanghai, because he was arrested there by the KMT authorities in 1932. Like many Party members, Ku was released upon the outbreak of the Sino-Japanese War in 1937, after which he made his way to Communist-held areas in north China. He spent most of the war engaged in Party work, with a particular emphasis on financial-economic work in the Shansi-Hopeh-Shantung-Honan Border Region (see under Yang Hsiu-feng, the regional chairman).

At the close of hostilities in 1945, when thousands of Chinese Communist soldiers and cadres were sent to Manchuria under the leadership of such prominent Party members as Kao Kang, Lin Piao, Ch'en Yun, and Li Fu-ch'un, Ku was among those who administered the portions of Liaopei and Nunkiang provinces (in central Manchuria) which the Communists occupied. There he apparently continued to specialize in economic affairs. At this time Manchuria was divided into nine provinces (the administrative demarcations having been made by the Nationalists). In 1946 the Communists established the Northeast Administrative Committee (NEAC) to govern their territory in Manchuria;

Ku served as chairman of the NEAC Finance Department from May to August 1949, replacing commerce and trade specialist Yeh Chi-chuang (q.v.). In August 1949, just prior to the establishment of the central PRC government in Peking, the NEAC was reorganized into the Northeast People's Government (NEPG) under the chairmanship of Kao Kang. Ku was then named to membership on the NEPG Council while at the same time he continued to head the Finance Department for the new government until July 1952.

Ku's stature as an economic specialist in Manchuria was further enhanced when, in August 1950, he was named as a vice-chairman of the NEPG's People's Economic Planning Committee. He also served on occasions as the acting chairman in the absence of Committee Chairman Kao Kang and then, in 1953, was promoted to the chairmanship; the name of the committee was changed to the Finance and Economics Committee. This change took place following the reorganization of the NEPG into the (new) Northeast Administrative Committee (NEAC) in January 1953. In addition to holding the key economic portfolio in the NEAC from 1953 to 1954, Ku was also one of the NEAC vice-chairmen. Also, when the NEAC formed an *ad hoc* committee in 1954 to discuss the new draft national constitution, he was appointed as a vice-chairman. Although Ku's work was concentrated on economic affairs, he was also identified in early 1954 as a member of the Northeast Party Bureau.

The caliber of Ku's work in Manchuria must have been known to such top economic specialists as Ch'en Yun and Li Fu-ch'un, both of whom had also served there. This might account for Ku's transfer to Peking in 1954 at the time the new constitutional government was inaugurated (September). He was named (October) as a vice-chairman of the State Planning Commission under Chairman Li Fu-ch'un, a post Ku held for nearly nine years. His primary responsibilities appear to have been centered around international economic problems and negotiations. In December 1958 he led an economic delegation to Budapest and from there apparently went directly to the USSR; in any case, he was present in Moscow in early February 1959 when Chou En-lai signed an important agreement on the "further expansion" of Sino-Soviet economic cooperation, the terms of which provided for large-scale credits to the Chinese. Ku returned to Moscow in April 1961 as the head of a scientific and technical delegation. After extended negotiations, he signed an agreement covering economic, scientific, and technical cooperation. Ku's activities abroad were reflected in Peking where he frequently took part in talks with delegations visiting China to negotiate economic agreements, as illustrated in December 1960 when he was among those officially participating in the talks with a delegation led to Peking by Prince Sihanouk of Cambodia. He has also written on occasion for the Party press or specialized economic journals; for example, in July 1959 for the important magazine *Chi-hua yü t'ung-chi* (Planning and statistics) he wrote a survey of industrial development covering the first decade of the PRC.

In January 1961 the CCP re-created regional Party bureaus. Gradually, over the next two years, a large number of senior leaders in Peking (many of them economic experts) were transferred to these bureaus. By May 1963 Ku had been reassigned to Manchuria (at Shenyang, the bureau headquarters), and by October he was specifically identified as a Bureau secretary, a post that makes him subordinate to First Secretary Sung Jen-ch'iung (q.v.). It was therefore logical that Ku would relinquish his vice-chairmanship of the State Planning Commission, a step formally taken in September 1963. Ku continues to hold only one post in the national government. He is a member of the quasi-legislative CPPCC, but the position has become largely nominal since the inauguration of the constitutional government in 1954 when the importance of the CPPCC declined. He was named to the CPPCC's Third National Committee in April 1959 as a "specially-invited personage" and was again named in this capacity to the Fourth Committee, which first met in December 1964–January 1965. Unlike the majority of Communist officials, Ku has not been called upon to engage in the innumerable political activities of the "mass" organizations (such as the China Peace Committee). Rather, he has been permitted to devote himself almost exclusively to economic affairs, and presumably continues to fulfill such a role in Manchuria, China's industrial heartland.

Ku Mu

Economic administrator; chairman, State Capital Construction Commission.

Ku Mu, an east China Party official in the early years of the PRC, has been one of the more prominent economic administrators in Peking since 1954. He first came to prominence in 1950 as the mayor of Tsinan, the Shantung capital. In the next year he became the ranking secretary of the Tsinan Party Committee as well as a member of the Shantung Provincial People's Government Council.

Although Ku formally held these posts in Shantung until November 1952, he was transferred to Shanghai in mid-1952 where he served for about half a year as director of the Shanghai Party Propaganda Department. Toward the end of 1952 he became a deputy secretary of the Shanghai Party Committee and by February 1953 was promoted to second deputy secretary. In

both posts he served under Ch'en I. Little information is available on Ku during these early years, although he was occasionally mentioned as attending celebrations marking important events in Chinese Communist history (e.g., National Day on October 1, 1952) or in connection with such organizations of minor importance as the Shanghai branch of the Sino-Soviet Friendship Association.

In 1954 Ku was transferred to Peking and assigned to work on economic policy. Although his background provides no hint of special competence in the field, he has remained in economic work at a very high level since then.

Ku's first appointment in the national capital came in December 1954 when he was named a vice-chairman of the State Construction Commission, then headed by economic specialist Po I-po. Within the next two years Ku was to be appointed to two more posts directly under Po: in September 1955 as a deputy director of the State Council's Third Staff Office and in November 1956 as a vice-chairman of the State Economic Commission. The Third Staff Office was responsible for guiding the work of governmental organs dealing with heavy industry and construction, and the State Economic Commission is responsible for planning on an annual basis (as opposed to the State Planning Commission, which handles longer-range plans). Ku held the Construction Commission post until November 1956 and the Third Staff Office position until September 1959; he continued to work in the State Economic Commission until 1965.

In March 1956 a Scientific Planning Commission was formed under the State Council, headed by Ch'en I, under whom Ku had previously served in Shanghai. Ku was named one of the deputy secretaries-general. Fourteen months later, when the Commission was reorganized, he was removed as a deputy secretary-general but was named as a member, holding the post until November 1958 when the Commission was merged with another State Council commission. Ku was a Shantung deputy to the Second NPC (1959–1964) and at each of the four sessions of the Congress served as a member of the Motions Examination Committee. During this same period he also was a member of the Third CPPCC. Ku was re-elected to the Third NPC, which first met in December 1964–January 1965, when he was elected chairman of the important NPC Budget Committee; he replaced Tseng Shan, who held the post in the Second NPC. During the same session he also served on the Motions Examination Committee, a committee post he had held under the Second NPC.

One of the few times Ku was reported in the national press was in November 1958 when he spoke on industrial questions before the "second national conference of young activists in building socialism." Yet the paucity of information is clearly no measure of his stature. This was illustrated in early 1964 when political departments were established in at least 15 ministries engaged in industrial or communications work. Paralleling this government structure, the Party formed the "Industrial and Communications Political Department" under the Central Committee with Ku as director. This new structure was apparently designed to enhance the role of politics within ministries in which political matters tended to be neglected in favor of technical competence. Some idea of Ku's thinking at this time can be gained from two articles written by him. The first appeared in *Peking Review* no. 21, May 22, 1964, and was entitled "New Stage in China's Mass Movement in Industry" and the other in the Peking *Kung-jen jih-pao* (Daily worker), July 22, 1964, translated in *SCMP* 3280 under the title "Consciously Transform Your Thought and Become a Staunch and Reliable Successor to the Revolution."

In March 1965 the State Capital Construction Commission was re-established. (It had previously existed from 1958 to 1961—see under Ch'en Yun.) Ku was appointed chairman, and a month later he was officially removed as vice-chairman of the State Economic Commission, a post in which he had served for over eight years.

Ku Ta-ts'un

(1897–1966; Wu-hua hsien, Kwangtung). Former Kwangtung guerrilla leader; vice-governor, Kwangtung; alternate member, CCP Central Committee.

A local guerrilla leader in Kwangtung for some 20 years, Ku Ta-ts'un was an alternate member of the Party Central Committee from 1945 until his death 21 years later. He was one of the major victims of the 1957–58 "Rectification" campaigns against "rightists," and although he later re-emerged, his last years were spent under a political cloud. Born into a peasant family, Ku came from the small town of An-liu in the rural interior of Kwangtung, a region where the Communists have long been active. Located in Wu-hua hsien, An-liu lies some 50 miles north of Lu-feng, a coastal city in eastern Kwangtung, which was one of the two centers where in 1922 the early Communist leader P'eng P'ai (q.v.) started to organize the peasants. Several years later P'eng was instrumental in establishing the Hailufeng (Hai-lu-feng) Soviet situated in Hai-feng and Lu-feng hsien, the earliest though short-lived of the CCP rural soviet governments. The Hailufeng region belonged to the larger East River (Tung-chiang) Region where the Chinese Communists maintained a small but important guerrilla base during the Sino-Japanese War. Ku apparently received little or no formal education and made his living as a farmer. Then in 1924, when he was about 27 years old, he joined the CCP,

possibly as a result of contacts with the peasant associations that P'eng P'ai and his followers were organizing in the early and mid-twenties. Ku himself is known to have been among the organizers of a peasant association in his native Wu-hua hsien in 1924.

According to Ku's obituary, he was a "war area propagandist" for the National Revolutionary Army (NRA); this might indicate that he participated in the Northern Expedition, which began in mid-1926, but given Ku's working locale in east Kwangtung, it seems more likely that this refers to one of the two so-called "Eastern Expeditions" of 1925, in which the NRA carried out punitive expeditions against Kwangtung leader Ch'en Chiung-ming. Ku subsequently served as the secretary of a CCP hsien committee and, in the words of his obituary, as the secretary of the "Seven-hsien Combined CCP Committee," presumably in reference to seven hsien in Ku's native East River area. In 1927 Ku became a member of the Standing Committee of the East River Special Committee, which was the secret CCP organ that actually controlled the affairs of the Hailufeng Soviet when it came into existence in the fall of 1927.[1] He also served at approximately this same time as "military director" of the East River Soviet Government and was probably in contact with the important Communist military units that passed back and forth through the Hailufeng district following the Communist military disasters in 1927 at Nanchang, Swatow, and Canton (see under Chu Te and Yeh T'ing). Further details on Ku's political and military activities at this time are found in the biography of Miss Li Chien-chen, one of his subordinates.

Following the destruction of the Hailufeng Soviet, Ku organized his remnant guerrilla units into the 11th Army, a fighting force that by 1930 had some 5,000 men and 3,500 rifles[2] and was nominally under the command of the Chu-Mao armies in Kiangsi. Ku was the commander of the 11th Army and concurrently served as its acting political commissar. His guerrilla units operated in the Kwangtung-Fukien border area where he reportedly maintained contact with the West Fukien Soviet, which included such prominent Communists as Chang Yun-i and T'an Chen-lin (qq.v.).

In November 1931 Ku attended the First All-China Congress of Soviets at Juichin, which established the Chinese Soviet Republic. He was elected to membership on the Soviet government's Central Executive Committee (CEC) and a little over two years later, at the Second Congress (January–February 1934), he was re-elected to the CEC. When the main Red armies led by Chu Te and Mao Tse-tung set out on the Long March in the fall of 1934, Ku was among those who remained behind to conduct guerrilla warfare. For the next few years he led guerrilla units against the Nationalists and continued to do so when the Japanese war broke out in mid-1937. He seems to have operated mainly in the Ch'ao-chou and Mei-hsien areas of the Kwangtung East River district, somewhat to the north and east of Hailufeng on the coast. It is stated in Ku's obituary that he was at one time the commander-in-chief of the Red Army guerrilla forces in the East River District. In various secondary sources Ku has been credited with commanding the East River Column (Tung-chiang tsung-tui), but no mention is made of him in a highly authoritative Party history of wartime "liberated areas"[3] (nor is this mentioned in Ku's obituary). In any event, Tseng Sheng (q.v.) was the East River Column commander by at least 1943 and·probably earlier.

Sometime toward the end of the war Ku went to the Communist headquarters in Yenan and was among the speakers at the Party's Seventh National Congress, held from April to June 1945.[4] Although no specific dates are indicated, according to Ku's obituary he once served (presumably at the end of the war) as director of the "First Section" of the Central Committee's Party School. As the war was drawing to a close in the summer of 1945, the Party sent a number of high-level military commanders and Party leaders to Manchuria, among them Lin Piao, Ch'en Yun, P'eng Chen, and Kao Kang. Ku probably accompanied these men, because subsequently, in the late forties, he was a Standing Committee member of the Party's West Manchurian Committee, a deputy director of the Northeast Bureau's Organization Department (then headed by P'eng Chen), and a deputy director of the Communications Department of the Northeast Administrative Committee, a governmental organization headed by Lin Feng (q.v.), which existed from 1946 to 1949.

Ku was in Peking in September 1949 to attend the first meeting of the CPPCC, the organization that brought the central government into existence. Attending as a delegate of the South China PLA, while the sessions were in progress he served on the *ad hoc* committee to draft the Organic Law of the CPPCC, one of the basic documents adopted at this time. Immediately after the meetings, he proceeded to his native Kwangtung, where he was appointed a vice-governor, serving then under fellow Kwangtungese Yeh Chien-ying (q.v.). Soon afterward (January 1950), he was appointed as director of the important Civil Affairs Department, holding this post in the Kwangtung Government until about 1954. Under the chairmanship of Lin Piao, the Communists established the Central-South Military and Administrative Committee (CSMAC) in February 1950 to govern the provinces of Kwangtung, Kwangsi, Kiangsi, Honan, Hunan, and Hupeh. Ku was appointed as a CSMAC member and continued as such when the CSMAC was reorganized into the Central-South Administrative Committee in January

1953, retaining this post until the latter committee was dissolved in 1954 with the advent of the constitutional government.

In the early years of the PRC the Party organization that paralleled the geographic boundaries of the CSMAC was known as the Central-South China Bureau. However, this bureau was distinct from other regional bureaus in that it had a special sub-bureau: the South China Sub-bureau, headquartered in Canton and responsible for Party affairs in Kwangtung and Kwangsi. (The headquarters of both the CSMAC and the Central-South China Bureau were located in Wuhan, the Hupeh capital.) By 1950 Ku was a member of the South China Sub-bureau; he rose to fourth deputy secretary and then to first deputy secretary by the time the Sub-bureau was abolished in July 1955. Among his superiors during these years were such key Party leaders as Yeh Chien-ying, T'an Cheng, and T'ao Chu (qq.v.). However, during the early fifties Ku's primary tasks were with the Kwangtung Government, in which he held the following posts: member, Land Reform Committee, 1951–c.1954; chairman, (*ad hoc*) Kwangtung-Canton Opium and Narcotics Suppression Committee, May 1952; chairman, Kwangtung Labor Employment, 1952–1954; member, Kwangtung Election Committee, 1953–54.

Ku was elected from Kwangtung as a deputy to the First NPC in 1954, and when the NPC held its initial session in September to bring the constitutional government into existence, he was elected to the NPC Standing Committee. Not long after, in February 1955, Ku was elected to a vice-chairmanship on the Kwangtung Committee of the CPPCC, and by mid-1955 he was identified as a deputy secretary of the Kwangtung CCP Committee; by November 1956 Ku had advanced to a secretaryship on the Kwangtung Party Committee, but he was still subordinate to First Secretary T'ao Chu (q.v.). On the eve of the Party's Eighth National Congress in September 1956 there were over 60 full and alternate members of the Central Committee who had been elected at the 1945 Congress. In retrospect, it is apparent that Ku's political troubles had already begun by the time of the Eighth Congress, for even though the size of the Central Committee was tripled, he was one of only four alternates not promoted to full membership. Of the foursome, Tseng Ching-ping (q.v.) was dropped altogether, and Wan I, Chang Tsung-hsun, and Ku were only re-elected as alternates. Ku's political difficulties were confirmed in a dramatic fashion in May 1958 at the Second Session of the Eighth Party Congress when a number of "rightists," the victims of the 1957–58 "Rectification" campaign, were denounced. These "rightists" fell into two groups; men like Chekiang Governor Sha Wen-han (q.v.) were accused of "crimes" and were summarily expelled from the CCP, but a second group, for example, Central Committee alternates Ku and Feng Pai-chü (q.v.), were merely "exposed" and were treated more leniently in that they were allowed to retain their seats on the Central Committee.

In the final communiqué issued at the close of the May 1958 Congress, the charges against Ku and Feng were limited to the brief statement that they had carried out "localist activities," the CCP euphemism for policies that emphasized local (usually provincial) as opposed to national interests. Soon thereafter, however, a major article appeared in a Kwangtung Party journal, which was subsequently reprinted in the authoritative *Hsin-hua pan-yueh-k'an* (New China semimonthly).[5] The article, written by the then head of the Kwangtung CCP Organization Department, Miss Ou Meng-chueh (q.v.), elaborated on the charges against Ku and Feng Pai-chü (who had been a local guerrilla leader on Hainan Island and also a Party member since the mid-twenties). Ku's "anti-Party" activities were said to have dated from the early fifties; both men were accused of "parochialism," but Ku had also been an "extreme individualist" and a "rightist opportunist." Long dissatisfied with the Party, from about 1956 Ku had allegedly thrown his support to Feng and together they led an "anti-Party" faction. Like Feng, Ku was accused of having impeded the land reform campaign of the early fifties, which was so important a part of the CCP program. Considering the land reform movement "too radical," Ku was charged with colluding with the much-vilified landlord class and of attempting to find jobs for "renegades, enemy agents, and counterrevolutionaries." He was further accused of creating antagonisms between the many northern cadres sent to Kwangtung and the local Kwangtungese; it was asserted that the northerners were "coming to Kwangtung to scramble for spheres of influence."

However, after cataloging these and numerous other charges, Ou Meng-chueh took note of Ku and Feng's 30-year-long revolutionary history and the Maoist principle of "curing the disease to save the man" and stated that the Party had decided that the two men could retain their Party membership as well as part of their duties but that they would be relieved "of their more important posts." In view of the seriousness of the charges, Ku's eclipse did not last long—less than a year later, in February 1959, he was elected a vice-chairman of the Kwangtung Committee of the CPPCC. He continued to hold this post until November 1961 when he was removed, but at the same time he was reinstated to his previous and more important post as a Kwangtung vice-governor. In general, after 1958 Ku appeared in public rather infrequently, although he was elected a Kwangtung deputy to the Third NPC, and when the initial session of the Third NPC

closed in January 1965 he was elected to the permanent NPC Standing Committee. At the end of 1965 he resigned his Kwangtung vice-governorship for reasons of health, but he was still an alternate member of the Party Central Committee and a member of the NPC Standing Committee on November 4, 1966, when he died of illness in Canton at the age of 69. In his official obituary, Ku's long Party career was reviewed in some detail, but no mention was made of his alleged anti-Party activities of the 1950's.

1. Shinkichi Eto, "Hai-lu-feng—The First Chinese Soviet Government," *The China Quarterly*, no. 9:165–166 (January–March 1962).
2. *Ibid.*, p. 180.
3. *K'ang-Jih chan-cheng shih-ch'i chieh-fang-ch'ü kai-k'uang* (A sketch of the liberated areas during the Anti-Japanese War; Peking, 1953).
4. Conrad Brandt, Benjamin Schwartz, and John K. Fairbank, *A Documentary History of Chinese Communism* (Cambridge, Mass., 1952), p. 293.
5. *SCMP* 1899, pp. 16–23.

Kuan Hsiang-ying

(1902–1946; Liaoning). Youth Leader; Red Army political officer; member, CCP Central Committee.

One of the early CCP and Communist Youth League leaders, Moscow-trained Kuan Hsiang-ying worked in the Party headquarters in Shanghai in the late twenties and early thirties and then served as political commissar in Ho Lung's forces in central China prior to the Long March. He continued as Ho's chief political officer during the early years of the Sino-Japanese War, but ill health forced him into semi-retirement. Kuan was a Party Central Committee member from 1928 until intra-Party disputes forced him off the Committee in 1931. He was then re-elected to membership in 1945, just one year before he died of tuberculosis. In his early revolutionary career Kuan was sometimes known by the alias Hsiao Kuan.[1]

A native of Liaoning province in Manchuria, Kuan was born in 1902 into a worker's family of Manchu origins, and during his youth he was a factory hand in a printing shop. His family was apparently quite poor, for he is said to have been self-educated.[2] Moving to Shanghai, probably in his late teens, Kuan joined the Socialist Youth League about 1922. Two years later the League sent him to the Soviet Union where he enrolled at the Communist University of the Toilers of the East, and in 1925, probably while still in Moscow, he joined the CCP.[3]

Returning to China in the summer of 1925, Kuan worked for a time in the Communist underground in Shanghai before going to Honan as secretary of the provincial Party Committee (possibly to replace Wang Jo-fei, q.v.). However, by 1927 he had been called back to Shanghai to take over the direction of the Communist Youth League's Organization Department from Jen Pi-shih (q.v.), who was being given a more important position in the League. In the next year he went again to the USSR to attend the Sixth National CCP Congress, held in Moscow in the summer of 1928 to escape the vigilance of the Nationalist police, and perhaps also to seek closer guidance from the Comintern, whose Sixth Congress opened a week after the CCP closed its Congress on July 11. The CCP Congress elected Kuan to the Central Committee, and at the Fifth Youth League Congress held immediately afterwards (also in Moscow) he succeeded Jen Pi-shih as League secretary, a post he apparently retained until replaced by Ch'in Pang-hsien (q.v.) in the spring of 1931, shortly after Kuan had been deprived of his seat on the Party Central Committee (see below).

Returning to China, Kuan was working by 1930 on the Military Committee of the Chinese Workers' and Peasants' Red Army and serving in the CCP Yangtze Bureau, although his whereabouts during that year are not known. During this period, when the CCP was dominated by Li Li-san (q.v.), Kuan may well have been involved in the power struggle that eventually caught up with Li and caused his dismissal from the Party Politburo in the fall of 1930. Li's place was taken by leaders of a group of Chinese students who had attended Sun Yet-sen University in Moscow and had become close followers of the Stalinist chancellor of the university, Pavel Mif (see under Ch'en Shao-yü). In the spring of 1930 Mif went to China at the behest of the Comintern, bringing with him a number of his former protégés and students. He and his group, the so-called "28 Bolsheviks," proceeded to take over the CCP's governing bodies and to oust Li Li-san and his supporters. The final accomplishment of the change-over in leadership came when the Party met in January 1931 for its Fourth Plenum, at which time a new Central Committee was elected. Among the Central Committee members removed were Li Wei-han and Kuan Hsiang-ying.[4]

By approximately the time of the Fourth Plenum, Kuan had returned to Shanghai where he was secretary-general of the Shanghai Federation of Labor Unions, which the Communists were attempting to reactivate under extremely difficult circumstances in view of the Nationalists' control of the city. Like many leading Communists still operating in Shanghai, Kuan was arrested in 1931 and apparently remained in jail throughout most of the year. About the time of his release, the Communists who had been working and fighting in the hinterlands convened the First All-China Congress of Soviets in Juichin

(November 1931). Although Kuan may not have been present, he was elected to the Central Executive Committee (CEC), the governing body for the newly established Chinese Soviet Republic. Moreover, immediately afterwards the CEC appointed him as a member of the Central Revolutionary Military Council, of which Chu Te was the chairman.[5] At this juncture Kuan was assigned to Ho Lung's area, the territory in west Hunan-Hupeh where Ho had been building a guerrilla base since the abortive attempts to capture Nanchang and Swatow in 1927. At the time when Kuan went to the Hunan-Hupeh Soviet, there was considerable dissension within the CCP leadership over the political program to be followed and the military strategy to be employed. Two of the political officers who had preceded Kuan to Ho's area have come under attack from one faction or another of the CCP leadership. In this connection, Teng Chung-hsia had been recalled from Hunan, and Hsia Hsi (qq.v.), once an associate of Mao Tse-tung, has been criticized by Mao's military leadership.[6] Because Kuan had already been dropped from the Central Committee it is not clear why he was sent to Ho's area. Ho had not known Kuan before the latter came to him as a political officer, but the team they established proved successful enough to remain intact until the end of the Sino-Japanese War and they remained close colleagues until Kuan's death in 1946. Kuan's functions upon his arrival at the Hunan-Hupeh base are not known, but by the latter half of 1932 he had replaced Hsia Hsi as political commissar of Ho's forces.

At the Second All-China Congress of Soviets in January–February 1934, Kuan was elected to the Second CEC (almost certainly in absentia). In the meantime he had taken part in the developments of the Hunan-Hupeh Soviet, the campaigns fought against Nationalist forces, and the establishment of the Szechwan-Hupeh-Hunan-Kweichow Soviet in late 1934. At this juncture Ho's forces were merged with the Sixth Army Corps, led by Hsiao K'o and Jen Pi-shih (qq.v.), and known thereafter as the Second Front Army. Ho Lung was the commander and Jen Pi-shih, senior to Kuan, became the political commissar, with Kuan serving as his deputy. The Second Front Army later embarked on its own Long March, moving along much of the route traveled earlier by Mao's Long Marchers until coming to Sikang province, where they followed a less hazardous and more westerly course to reach the encampment of Chang Kuo-t'ao's Fourth Front Army in Sikang in the late spring of 1936. From Sikang Ho's units made the next lap of the journey into north Shensi, where they joined forces with Mao Tse-tung's in the latter part of 1936. Kuan's part in these endeavors has been singled out for praise by two important Maoist historians, Ho Kan-chih and Hu Ch'iao-mu (q.v.).[7] Kuan is linked with Chu Te, Jen Pi-shih, and Ho Lung for having displayed "persistent efforts . . . in the face of Chang Kuo-t'ao's opposition," which enabled them to bring their units northward to join Mao's forces.

Once in Shensi, Kuan continued his close association with Ho Lung. Ho's Second Front Army was now posted in the area of Fu-p'ing (some 30 miles northeast of Sian), and Kuan replaced Jen Pi-shih (q.v.) as political commissar when the latter moved on to more important assignments. American authoress Nym Wales identified Kuan in this capacity when she visited Shensi in 1937, and a group of young Communists from Peking visited Ho's and Kuan's units in Fu-p'ing in the late spring of the same year.[8] Kuan remained as Ho's chief political officer when their forces were transformed into the 120th Division of the Eighth Route Army after the outbreak of the Sino-Japanese War. He moved with Ho's Division into northwest Shansi in September 1937 and established a base headquarters near the border of Suiyuan. In 1938 Ho led the main force of his division across Shansi into Hopeh to assist Nieh Jung-chen's 115th Division (of the Eighth Route Army) as well as the local Hopeh resistance led by Lü Cheng-ts'ao (q.v.). The efforts of the two to organize the peasants of the countryside had been under attack from both the Japanese and the Nationalists. Ho and Kuan remained in Hopeh for about two years, but in 1940 they moved back to the Shansi-Suiyuan border, where Ho was the commander and Kuan the political commissar of the border area's Military Region (see under Ho Lung).

The hardships of civil war and of fighting the Japanese were beginning to tell on Kuan, who had contracted tuberculosis, and he had to be recalled to Yenan in the first half of 1940 for rest and recuperation. He remained there only briefly and then returned to northwest Shansi. However, by October of that year his illness had become so serious that he was forced to return again to Yenan, where he remained as a hospital case for the balance of his life. When the Party met in Yenan for its Seventh Congress in April–June 1945, Kuan was elected to the Seventh Central Committee, but in view of his poor health the position was essentially honorary. His health continued to deteriorate and he finally died in Yenan on July 21, 1946, at the age of 44. In addition to the already-cited favorable judgments of Kuan's career by Maoist historians, his life is extolled in the fifth volume of the important collection of revolutionary reminiscences entitled *Hung-ch'i p'iao-p'iao* (Red flag fluttering; Peking, 1957). This account provides one of the major sources on Kuan's life as a revolutionist, Party official, and political officer. Another important source on Kuan's career is Hua Ying-shen's *Chung-kuo kung-ch'an tang lieh-shih chuan* (Biographies of Chinese Communist martyrs; Hong Kong, 1949).

1. Tso-liang Hsiao, *Power Relations within the Chinese Communist Movement, 1930–1934* (Seattle, Wash., 1961), p. 122.
2. Nym Wales, *Inside Red China* (New York, 1939), p. 334.
3. Modern China Project, Columbia University, Howard L. Boorman, director; *Ch'ün-chung chou-k'an* (Masses weekly; Shanghai, September 14, 1946), 12.8:20-21.
4. Hsiao, p. 115.
5. *Hung-se Chung-hua*, December 18, 1931.
6. *JMJP*, February 1, 1962.
7. Hu Ch'iao-mu, *Thirty Years of the Communist Party of China* (Peking, 1952), pp. 36–37; Ho Kan-chih, *A History of the Modern Chinese Revolution* (Peking, 1960), pp. 272–273.
8. Nym Wales, *Red Dust* (Stanford, Calif., 1952), p. 19; *SCMM* 297, p. 35.

K'uei Pi

(1903–   ; Tumet Banner, Inner Mongolia). Vice-chairman, Inner Mongolia Autonomous Region; alternate member, CCP Central Committee.

K'uei Pi is the second-ranking Mongol in the CCP and one of the few members of the Party's top elite who is not a Han Chinese. Like Ulanfu (q.v.), the top Mongol in the Party, he belonged originally to the Tumet Banner of the Bayan Tala League, a minor sinicized Mongol group living in the area west of Kweisui (Huhehot). This city, the capital of the Inner-Mongolia Autonomous Region (IMAR), was formerly the capital of Suiyuan province, created by the Nationalists in 1928 and absorbed into the IMAR in 1954. In the postwar period there were only some 12,000 Mongols in the Tumet Banner; a sedentary, agricultural people, they speak mostly Chinese and many have long forgotten their Mongol language. A number of their leaders preserve their Mongol names, although these too have become partially sinicized by Chinese pronunciation.

K'uei apparently had some secondary schooling, because when he went to Peking from Inner Mongolia at the age of 20 he was able to enroll in a leading Chinese institution for the training of his fellow Mongols as well as for Tibetans. A former Chinese ambassador to Mongolia, Chi Ya-t'ai (q.v.), also a Tumet Banner Mongol, has written about K'uei's education from mid-1923 when he arrived in Peking with a group from his native banner, including Ulanfu, Chi (the author of the account), To-sung-nien, and Li Yü-chih.[1] To-sung-nien has been described by the Communists as a "prominent Inner Mongolian revolutionary." Li, whose Mongol name was Batochir, commanded the People's Revolutionary Army of Inner Mongolia in 1926. All of them were slated to play a part in Sino-Mongolian relations. The last two were killed between 1926 and 1927, but Ulanfu, Chi, and K'uei have been active in the Communist Revolution from its beginning. In 1923 the Mongol newcomers enrolled at the Mongolian and Tibetan Institute, which had been established not long before by a Chinese government intent on educating and training future leaders of the two minorities. The CCP, then in existence only two years, had a very active branch in Peking led by Li Ta-chao, one of the Party founders and a Peking University professor. Quick to search out those who had become disenchanted with the existing Chinese society, the Party made the national minorities one of the principal targets for its work. Already in the winter of 1923–24, Li Ta-chao made overtures to the Tumet Banner Mongols at the Peking Institute, and Chi reports that they joined the CCP at this time, becoming the first Mongols to enter the ranks of the Party.

The rising generation of Mongols in the 1920's found themselves involved in the struggles of national and international politics whether they remained at home for their education or journeyed to Moscow or Peking. Rivalry between China and the Soviet Union over the fate of Outer Mongolia inevitably affected the fate of the Mongols. Within China there was the struggle between left and right wings of the KMT, and between the KMT and the Communists, each group playing upon Mongol aspirations. Within the domains of Chinese Mongolia, these aspirations were affected also by fortunes of the local warlord, Feng Yü-hsiang. Feng had his own political ambitions to satisfy by siding with the KMT, the Chinese Communists, other local warlords, or with the Russians. There were, in addition, the Mongols themselves, compounding the difficulties because they differed among themselves on the solutions for their future. When the government of the Mongolian People's Republic was inaugurated in November 1924, its opening meeting was attended by one group of Chinese Mongols who supported a union of Mongols from Inner and Outer Mongolia, that is, pan-Mongolism (even if under Soviet influence) and independence from China. Several other approaches to pan-Mongolism also attracted Chinese Mongols who did not attend the meeting, but there were many others whose aim was a larger degree of self-government for the Mongols within a federative framework of China. K'uei and his colleagues supported the latter view.[2]

In Peking, elements of the political scene affected K'uei and the others from early 1925. Hoping to bring China together under one central government, Sun Yat-sen traveled to Peking to negotiate with the northern leaders and died there in March 1925 without accomplishing his purpose. According to the Chi account, the Tumet Banner group at the Peking institute was organized to support Sun when he came to Peking. To arouse support for the cause of uniting China, the Party had sent K'uei back to his native area early in 1925 to organize a "Suiyuan Association for Promoting the National Assembly"; the National Assembly, which had been suspended a few years earlier, was the national parliament which Sun was hoping to reopen. In the fall of 1925 the Tumet Banner group from the school in Peking was instrumental in founding the Inner Mongolian People's Party (IMPP), inaugurated at a congress of Mongols held in Kalgan in October 1925. Ulanfu and his associates immediately became active in the new party, which, at its opening meeting, had received congratulations from Feng Yü-hsiang, the left-KMT, and representatives of the Outer Mongolian Government. Among the aims enunciated at the 1925 congress were full self-determination for nationality groups within China. The new party was soon embroiled in Chinese politics. In April 1926 Feng Yü-hsiang was defeated by the combined forces of rival warlords and fled to Outer Mongolia and then to the Soviet Union. Somewhat earlier, Ulanfu had also gone to Moscow by way of Outer Mongolia. No longer under the protective influence of Feng's troops in western Inner Mongolia, the remnants of the IMPP and its military forces probably went underground. When Feng returned to China in September 1926 and resumed command of his forces in northwest China, he may for a short time have continued to support the IMPP with its inner core of Communists, but when by June 1927 he decided to join forces with the KMT, there was the need to weed out former more radical supporters. When the Communists and KMT split in August 1927, Feng must have been obliged to purge from the Inner Mongolian People's Party the Mongol Communists who were not willing to follow his line of cooperation with the KMT. It was probably at this time that Tumet Banner Mongols To-sung-nien and Li Yü-chih were killed.[3]

After 1925 little is known of K'uei's career, but he was in Outer Mongolia as a student at the "Higher Party School of Mongolia," graduating about 1929. Because his career has always been closely connected with that of Ulanfu, it is reasonable to suppose that K'uei went to Outer Mongolia with Ulanfu about 1925. However, he was back in China after the start of the Sino-Japanese War, when he was a political officer with Pai Hai-feng's forces. Pai, a Mongol, was the commander of the Peace Preservation Corps for Suiyuan, a military group probably belonging to the Suiyuan-Mongolian Local Autonomous Political Council and organized during the war with CCP support to offer resistance to the

Japanese, whose troops nominally controlled Suiyuan. In 1937 Ulanfu was a political commissar with the same Suiyuan Preservation Corps, and K'uei may have been attached to the Corps at this time.

In 1941 K'uei was serving under Ulanfu at the Communists' headquarters in Yenan. Ulanfu then held several posts, among them the directorship of the Nationalities Affairs Commission under the Shensi-Kansu-Ninghsia Border Region Government. If K'uei was in fact serving with Ulanfu on the Commission, this was the beginning of a career in minority affairs, which has since become one of his principal occupations. Since at least 1945 he has been active in Inner Mongolia and has participated in every development of the CCP program to integrate his people into "New China."

With the entry of the Russians into Manchuria at the close of the Sino-Japanese War, the Chinese Mongols were left in a chaotic situation. Several groups soon established semi-independent governments throughout the Mongol territory stretching from western Manchuria through the provinces of Jehol, Chahar, and Suiyuan. Some of the groups, especially those in Manchuria, were led by Mongols who had formerly received recognition from the Japanese. The Mongols still differed in the aims they sought; some groups held differing views even among themselves. At varying times they made overtures to the stronger forces of the Nationalist Chinese, to the Chinese Communists, the Russians, and even to the Outer Mongolians. Soon after the cessation of hostilities, the Chinese Communists moved their forces from Jehol into Chahar (portions of both provinces were later absorbed by Inner Mongolia), and for a time they occupied Kalgan, the capital of Chahar. In November 1945 they inaugurated the Inner Mongolia Autonomous Movement Association, with Ulanfu as chairman. From this moment the Party worked steadily to enlarge the areas under its control and to absorb into the new association the most important of the other Mongol groups. In March–April 1946, delegates from Ulanfu's group and delegates from an important Mongol group in western Manchuria met in Ch'eng-te, Jehol. The meeting resulted in a merger of the two groups and the dissolution of the non-Communist one which had existed in western Manchuria at Ulanhot (Wang-yeh-miao). Later, another group from Hailar in northwest Manchuria was absorbed by the Ulanfu group. In October 1946 the Nationalists took Kalgan, and the next spring they occupied Jehol, forcing Ulanfu to transfer his capital to Ulanhot whose separate government he had already eliminated. On May 1, 1947 at a meeting at Ulanhot, the People's Government of the Inner Mongolian Autonomous Region was proclaimed.[4] Prior to 1949 its territory included the Hulanbuir, Nawenmujen, Hsingan, Silingol, and

Chahar leagues, located in the predominantly Mongol areas of western Manchuria and the northern portions of Jehol and Chahar. Territory from Suiyuan was added after the Communists took over there in 1949. In early 1950 the capital of the IMAR moved back to Kalgan, and in July 1952 it was relocated in its present site, Huhehot.

K'uei was in Inner Mongolia from at least 1945. From November 1945 to May 1947 he was a member of the Standing Committee of the Inner Mongolia Autonomous Movement Association, headed by Ulanfu. At the same time he was director of the Association's Organization Department, and from about 1947 until 1952, director of the IMAR government's Civil Affairs Department.

In June 1949 K'uei was in Peking to attend the meetings of the Preparatory Committee chaired by Mao Tse-tung in preparation for the convocation of CPPCC, the organization that brought the PRC into existence that fall. K'uei was not an official member of the Preparatory Committee but rather attended as a substitute for Ulanfu, who was occupied elsewhere. When the CPPCC first met in September, he attended as a representative of the national minorities and was elected a member of the CPPCC's First National Committee. However, he was not re-elected to the Second CPPCC, which opened in December 1954, by which time he had been transferred to the more important NPC. He also held a seat on the Nationalities Affairs Commission of the Government Administration Council (the cabinet) from 1949 to 1954. At the time K'uei was a Commission member, Ulanfu was one of its vice-chairmen.

Although K'uei has held various posts in the national government and Party bureaucracies, most of his time since 1949 has been spent in Inner Mongolia. From 1949 to 1954 he was a member of the IMAR Government Council, and from the latter year to the present he has been a vice-chairman; during all these years he has served under Chairman Ulanfu. In a rather unusual arrangement, K'uei also held positions of authority in Suiyuan province from 1949 until it was absorbed by the IMAR in 1954. He was a Suiyuan vice-governor during these years, and from early 1950 he also headed the Suiyuan government's Nationalities Affairs Committee. Within the CCP, K'uei was a member of the Inner Mongolia Sub-bureau from 1949 until July 1952, when the Party organizations in Inner Mongolia and Suiyuan were merged to form the Inner Mongolia–Suiyuan Sub-bureau. At the time of the merger he was promoted to be second deputy secretary, and a year later he was advanced to the post of deputy secretary. In the year 1953–54 K'uei concurrently headed the Sub-bureau's Organization Department and its Discipline Inspection Committee. Following the dissolution of Suiyuan Province in 1954, the name of the Party organization reverted to the Inner Mongolia Sub-bureau, but then in 1955 it was renamed the Inner Mongolia Autonomous Region Committee. K'uei's title was changed from deputy secretary to secretary in 1956, but he still remains subordinate to First Secretary Ulanfu. He attended the Party's Eighth National Congress in September 1956, submitting a written report to the Congress entitled "The Victory of the Party's Nationalities Policy in Inner Mongolia." At the close of the meetings he was elected an alternate member of the Party Central Committee; Ulanfu and K'uei are the only two Mongols on the Central Committee.

In 1953–54 K'uei was a member of the IMAR Election Committee, established in preparation for the nationwide elections to the NPC. He was then elected an IMAR deputy to the First NPC, which opened in September 1954. He was re-elected to the Second NPC (1959–1964), as well as the Third NPC, which held its initial session in December 1964–January 1965. Representing the Mongols, K'uei has also been a member of the NPC Nationalities Committee since 1954, and since 1955 he has also served as a vice-chairman of the committee. Among the more active members of the NPC, K'uei was a member of the presidium (steering committee) for eight of the 10 NPC sessions held between 1954 and 1965. He has made two trips abroad since the PRC was established, one of them in connection with Mongolian affairs. In August–September 1959 he was a member of Politburo member Lin Po-ch'ü's NPC delegation to Outer Mongolia. While in Ulan Bator K'uei received an honorary degree from the Advanced Party School of Mongolia, from which he had graduated 30 years before. He also made an earlier trip abroad as a member of a delegation led by Mme. Sun Yat-sen (q.v.) to the Communist-sponsored World Peace Congress in Vienna in December 1952. He was identified at this time as a member of the North China Bureau of the China Peace Committee (CPC). From 1950 to 1954 K'uei served as a vice-chairman of the Suiyuan branch of the CPC, and since mid-1958 he has been a member of the CPC's National Committee.

There are few men in the Chinese Communist elite whose careers are so closely intertwined as Ulanfu and K'uei Pi. K'uei continues to serve as Ulanfu's alter ego in the IMAR, but because Ulanfu is so important in the national bureaucracy, he is often called to Peking to meet with his Politburo colleagues. During his frequent absences from Huhehot, his lifelong colleague K'uei normally presides over the administration of the Party and governmental organs in the IMAR, where he is the number two man.

1. *SCMM* 281, pp. 21–24.
2. Human Relations Area Files, (HRAF), *A*

Regional Handbook on the Inner Mongolia Autonomous Region (New Haven, Conn., 1956), pp. 49–50.
3. *Ibid.,* pp. 52–53.
4. *Ibid.,* pp. 65–67.

Kung Tzu-jung

First secretary, CCP Central State Organs Committee; member, Control Commission, CCP.

A specialist in Party organization and control, Kung Tzu-jung first emerged in 1953 during a Party campaign to train personnel in the study of key Communist Party documents. Kung was placed in charge of a two-month class to "provide personnel to guide intermediate study groups in the study of the *History of the Communist Party of the Soviet Union (Bolsheviks),"* one of the most important documents in the history of modern Communism. After the appropriate cadres were trained in this preparatory class, a nationwide campaign began in July 1953 to study this guide book to Communist Party theory and organization. The class was organized by two important but little-publicized organs of the Party Central Committee: the Committee for Organs Directly under the Party Central Committee and the Committee for Organs Directly under the Central People's Government (the latter is also known as the Central State Organs Committee). Kung's exact position at this time is not known, but it was probably associated with the Central State Organs Committee, the body charged with the supervision of Party members working in the central government. In any event, he was serving as the first secretary of this committee by 1957 (see below).

Kung's involvement with central government personnel made him a logical person for assignment to the State Council following the reorganization of the central government organs in the fall of 1954. He was named as one of the deputy secretaries-general of the State Council, a post that placed him under Secretary-General Hsi Chung-hsun, another specialist in Party organizational work. Presumably, one of his major tasks has been as a liaison man between the State Council and the Party Central Committee. Little was heard of Kung until the Party's Eighth National Congress in September 1956, when he served on the important 29-member Credentials Committee under the chairmanship of Party veteran Tung Pi-wu. Although he was the only one of the 29 not elected to the Party Central Committee at the close of the Congress, he received an appointment of considerable significance at the First Plenum, immediately after the Congress. The new post was as an alternate member of the Party's Central Control Commission, a body also headed by Tung Pi-wu. The Commission had been established in 1955 in the wake of the alleged plot by the Kao Kang group to usurp Party leadership. When the Control Commission was reorganized and approximately tripled in size in September 1962 (at the 10th Plenum of the Central Committee), Kung was raised from alternate to full membership.

As already noted, Kung became first secretary of the Party's Central State Organs Committee by 1957. This identification occurred in December 1957 during the peak of the 1957–58 "rectification" campaign designed to eliminate "rightist" thinking from Chinese society. In this post Kung is presumably the person in charge of the day-to-day training, guidance, and discipline of Party members working for the central government. It was in this capacity that he reported to a meeting of the Central State Organs Committee on December 5, 1957, on the progress of the "rectification" campaign among Party workers in the government. He spoke in a similar vein and in the same capacity to another meeting of the Committee held in mid-January 1958, as well as before a conference of Communist Youth League members employed by the central government (March 1958) and still another conference of "youth activists in socialists construction working for the national government" (October 1958). Kung also took part, in June 1958, in one of the Party campaigns to promote the egalitarian image of a leadership willing to work side by side with the masses in manual labor. Along with some of the most senior members of the Party elite, he participated in the work on the Ming Tombs Reservoir near Peking, serving as the "political commissar of a sub-division of workers" during this brief stint at toiling among the masses.

In October 1958 Kung was first identified in still another significant Party post, that of deputy director of the Staff Office of the Central Committee, an office that might be described as the headquarters of the Party's Central Secretariat. In this position he serves under Yang Shangk'un, who also heads the Committee for Organs Directly under the Party Central Committee, thus being placed in work that is very similar to that engaged in by Kung. In September 1959, Kung was reappointed as a deputy secretary-general of the State Council. Although he was relieved from this post in March 1965, the fact that he continues to hold three important Party posts suggests that this removal had no political significance. Furthermore, Kung had received another new post not long before; he was named in late 1964 to membership on the Fourth National Committee of the CPPCC as a representative of the CCP, and when the National Committee ended its initial session in January 1965, he was elected to membership on the Standing Committee of the CPPCC.

The type of work that Kung is engaged in precludes the press attention normally accorded to someone of his stature. Nor has he written often for the Party press. He is, however, the author of two rather lengthy articles, both appearing in 1961. One, written for the January 5, 1961, issue of the *JMJP,* dealt with the importance of "rectification" campaigns to the CCP. Another, appearing in the *Chung-kuo ch'ing-nien pao* (China youth news) of June 29, 1961, discussed the qualifications for membership in the CCP.

K'ung Yuan

(c.1910–   ; P'ing-hsiang hsien, Kiangsi). Foreign trade specialist; alternate member, CCP Central Committee.

K'ung Yuan has been one of the most important foreign trade specialists since the establishment of the PRC. K'ung, whose original name was Ch'en T'ieh-cheng, was born in P'ing-hsiang hsien, west Kiangsi, the locale of one of China's largest coal mine areas. Under the direct guidance of Mao Tse-tung, Liu Shao-ch'i, and Li Li-san, the CCP had been active in P'ing-hsiang and neighboring An-yuan from the early 1920's, and in the late 1920's the newly formed Red Army drew many of its recruits from the same region (see under Huang Kung-lueh). At sometime in the late twenties or early thirties, K'ung left middle school in P'ing-hsiang to join the Red Army, and at approximately this same time he also joined the CCP. Little is known about his activities over the next decade, but he was a contributor to a volume of essays entitled *Lieh-shih chuan* (Biographies of martyrs), which was published in the Soviet Union in 1936. Although K'ung may not have been in Moscow in 1936, it is noteworthy that he has a command of Russian and that he studied in the Soviet Union from 1939 to 1940.

K'ung went to Yenan from the Soviet Union, and at the end of the war in 1945 he was among the thousands of administrators who accompanied the Communist military units into Manchuria. By 1946 he was head of the CCP Committee in Fushun, the important iron and coal center near Mukden. In October 1949, when the Communists established the central government, he received two important posts: membership on the Finance and Economics Committee of the Government Administration Council (GAC) and the directorship of the Customs Administration, a position which until 1952 came under the direct jurisdiction of the GAC. In December 1952 the Customs Administration was absorbed by the Ministry of Foreign Trade, which had been created in August. K'ung held both posts until 1954. (He was replaced in the Customs Administration by Lin Hai-yun [q.v.].) Especially in the early 1950's he was active in customs work, attending conferences, and frequently addressing government meetings of cadres in customs administration. His speeches stressed the need to eliminate corruption and waste, to simplify customs procedures, and to avoid bureaucracy.

In January 1953 K'ung was named a vice-minister of Foreign Trade under Yeh Chi-chuang, a position he held until September 1957. In his four and a half years with the Foreign Trade Ministry he was very actively engaged in negotiations with Communist and non-Communist countries and made a number of trips abroad for this purpose. From June to August 1954 he headed a trade delegation to Indonesia, which negotiated a Sino-Indonesian trade protocol and a payments agreement, signed by K'ung on September 1. From Indonesia he went to India to work out final terms for the first trade agreement of its kind between China and India, signing it on October 14, 1954. In Peking, on December 31, 1954, he signed the Sino-Korean protocol on the exchange of goods for 1955, and another on the granting of aid to Korea. In June 1955, when the China-Indonesia Friendship Association was formed, K'ung became a member of the council.

From 1955 to 1957 K'ung was active in trade negotiations with the Soviet satellites in Europe. In November 1955 he led a trade delegation to Yugoslavia. In early 1956 he was in Hungary for the signing on January 27 of the Sino-Hungarian goods exchange and payments agreement for 1956. He returned to Yugoslavia to sign a trade and payments agreement on February 17. K'ung was in Prague five months later, where on July 4, 1956, he signed a protocol with Czechoslovakia covering essential goods to be exchanged by the two countries from 1958 to 1962. Back in Peking, on January 4, 1957, K'ung signed a trade protocol for 1957 with Yugoslavia, an extension of the payments agreement he had concluded in Belgrade the previous February. Later that month he again went to Prague, where he negotiated the Sino-Czech Agreement on the Exchange of Goods and Payments for 1957, signed on March 6.

On September 9, 1957, K'ung was relieved of his position as a vice-minister of Foreign Trade, but in February 1958 a new Foreign Affairs Office was added to the seven functional offices of the State Council. The new office was headed by Ch'en I, the foreign minister, and K'ung was made a deputy director (March 1958), along with important Party members Liao Ch'eng-chih, Liu Ning-i, and Chang Yen.

In May 1958 K'ung was elected an alternate member of the Party Central Committee at the second session of the Eighth Party Congress. This was followed by appointments to legislative and quasi-legislative branches of the PRC. In October 1958 the Kiangsu Provincial Congress elected him a deputy to the Second NPC, which first met in April 1959. Five years later he was re-elected to the Third NPC (this time as a deputy from Kweichow), and when the first session of the Third NPC met in December 1964–January 1965, he was elevated to the Standing Committee, the important body that runs the NPC between the annual sessions. K'ung's assignment in the quasi-legislative CPPCC came in 1959 when the Third National Committee was formed. K'ung was named as a representative of the CCP and when the Committee held its first session in April 1959, he was named to the Standing Committee. He was not, however, re-elected to the Fourth National Committee, which first met in late 1964.

When the China-Africa People's Friendship Association was formed in April 1960, K'ung became a member of the Council, whose chairman is Liu Ch'ang-sheng, an important Party member and veteran trade union leader. In August 1960 Foreign Minister Ch'en I led a delegation to Afghanistan, where on August 26 the China-Afghanistan Treaty of Friendship and Non-Aggression was signed. K'ung was present as a member of the Chinese delegation. He was abroad again in 1963–64 accompanying Premier Chou En-lai and Ch'en I on their historic tour of 10 African nations and Albania. From mid-December 1963 to early February 1964, the delegation visited the United Arab Republic, Algeria, Morocco, Tunisia, Ghana, Mali, Guinea, the Sudan, Ethiopia, and Somalia in a major bid to enhance the prestige of Communist China in Africa. After a brief rest in south China, Chou took his entourage to Burma, Pakistan, and Ceylon for short goodwill visits during February 1964.

In the interim, in mid-1963, K'ung was identified as a "responsible member" of a department of the Party Central Committee. In view of his background, the department in question may be the Finance and Trade Work Department, or perhaps some department concerned with foreign affairs. Most of his numerous public appearances, however, continue to be in his capacity as a deputy director of the governmental Foreign Affairs Office. In this post he is frequently present to entertain or negotiate with the many foreign visitors to Peking. His only noted article, appearing in the April 25, 1955, issue of the *JMJP,* was entitled "The Development of Normal Trade and Economic Cooperation Is the Common Desire of the Asian-African Peoples."

K'ung's second wife, Hsu Ming, was with her husband in the late forties in Fushun, where she was secretary-general of the municipal Party Committee and concurrently headed its Women's Work Committee. Then, when her husband headed the Customs Administration in the early fifties, Hsu was in charge of the Administration's Personnel Office. In her capacity as chairman of the Tientsin Women's Federation, Hsu spoke on the "reform of capitalists" at the Party's Eighth Congress in September 1956, and one year later she was elected to the Executive Committee of the National Women's Federation, a post she still holds. In February 1960 Hsu became a deputy director of the Staff Office of the Premier (i.e., Chou En-lai), and five years later she assumed the concurrent post of deputy secretary-general of the State Council. She has also served as a deputy from Hopeh to the Third NPC, which opened in late 1964. The couple had two children as of 1950.

Kuo Mo-jo

(1892–   ; Chia-ting, Szechwan). Literary figure; Creation Society founder; propagandist; chairman, All-China Federation of Literary and Art Circles; chairman, China Peace Committee; president, Academy of Sciences.

Kuo Mo-jo is one of the most versatile of China's twentieth-century revolutionists. Although trained in Japan as a medical doctor, he never practiced his profession; rather he became a prolific poet, translator, novelist, dramatist, essayist, and propagandist. Kuo took part in the Northern Expedition, but after siding with the Communists at the time of the KMT–CCP split in 1927, he was forced into a decade-long exile in Japan. He returned to China when war broke out in 1937 to participate in the war effort against Japan. Kuo joined the Communist administration in 1949 as a "non-Party democratic personage." Since that time he has headed the most important literary and art organization, the Academy of Sciences, and the China Peace Committee. As one of Peking's best known spokesmen for the "peace" movement, he traveled abroad on numerous occasions during the first 15 years of the PRC.

Kuo was born in November 1892 in a small market town in southwest Szechwan not far from Chia-ting. Kuo was originally named Kuo K'ai-chen and he was the fifth child of a merchant-landlord family. As a youngster he received training from a private tutor in the classics, and in 1906–07 he studied at a higher-level primary school in Chia-ting. In the fall of 1907 he enrolled in a new middle school in Chia-ting, and in the next year he took up the study of English and Japanese. The study of Japanese in that period was in proportion to the large number of Chinese who were then going to Japan for their higher education (see under Wu Yü-chang), and there was an added impetus in Kuo's case because two elder brothers were then students in Japan. Kuo earned something of a reputation as a playboy during these school years, and it was also in this period that an illness left him with a bad back and seriously impaired hearing. In 1909 he was expelled for leading a strike to protest the inaction of school authorities in regard to a fight between the students and soldiers posted nearby. However, early in the next year he entered a preparatory institution under the Chengtu Higher School, but again he was more attracted to the good life than scholarly pursuits.

Kuo's first serious commitment to political activism took place during the winter of 1910–11 when, in an attempt to force the government to adopt a constitution, the students staged a strike. Kuo was expelled, and it was only through the intervention of an older brother, now returned from Japan, that he was readmitted. In June 1911 he was present at the meeting which established the Railway Protection Club of Szechwan, an organization that played an important role in sparking the Revolution of 1911 which overthrew the Manchus. Kuo himself, however, apparently took no active part in the Revolution. In the next year, when he was just 19, he was married by his family to an unattractive and uneducated woman, but he abandoned her within a week and returned to Chengtu to continue his studies. Because the preparatory school where he had studied had been abolished, he enrolled in the Chengtu Prefectural Middle School. Despite further dissipation he graduated in 1913 and entered the Chengtu Higher School. Kuo found this unsatisfactory, and in June 1913 he passed an entrance exam for a military medical school in Tientsin, where he arrived that fall. Kuo never entered the school, but rather in late 1913 he left for Japan where, in September 1914, he entered a preparatory class at the First Higher School in Tokyo to study medicine. Among his classmates were Yü Ta-fu (1895–1945) and Chang Tzu-p'ing (1895–1947), both of whom were associated with him in establishing the famous Creation Society in 1921.

Like all his countrymen, Kuo was outraged by Japan's Twenty-One Demands in early 1915, and in protest he left for home with other students in the spring. However, he returned to Japan a few days later, and in the summer he was admitted to the Sixth Higher School in Okayama where he was to study for three years. Only a few years earlier Wu Yü-chang (q.v.), also a Szechwanese, had graduated from the Okayama school. One of Kuo's schoolmates was Ch'eng Fang-wu, another co-founder of the Creation Society, who became an important educational official in the Communist government after 1949. During these years Kuo continued his study of English, and he also began to learn Latin and German. In 1916 he met Satō Tomiko, a nurse at St. Luke's Hospital, an American mission institution in Tokyo. Kuo persuaded her to come to Okayama to enroll in a women's medical school, and for the next two decades they lived together as man and wife. Apart from his medical studies, Kuo became keenly interested in a variety of other pursuits. These included the works of the Ming idealist Wang Yang-ming, the Indian poet Rabindranath Tagore, and several German writers. Kuo began his extraordinarily prolific writing career in 1917 when he translated some of Tagore's poetry, and in the next year he wrote his first story. It was also during this period that he changed his name to Mo-jo. In 1918 he graduated from the Okayama school. That fall he entered the Kyushu Imperial University medical school in Fukuoka; Kuo graduated in March 1923, but he never practiced medicine.

About 1919 Kuo became acquainted with the works of Walt Whitman. In the judgment of one of Kuo's biographers, there is little evidence that he was "much perturbed over the terrible chaos in China before he encountered Whitman," who "may have been as influential as the May Fourth Movement in opening Kuo Mo-jo's eyes to the terrible realities of the Chinese situation." [1] In 1920 he became acquainted with T'ien Han, a latter-day dramatist of considerable fame. This was done through Tsung Pai-hua, the editor of a popular literary supplement of a Shanghai newspaper. T'ien, then a student in Tokyo, began a lively correspondence with Kuo on literature and aesthetics. These letters, together with others written by Tsung, were published in the spring of 1920 under the title San-yeh-chi (Cloverleaf). This was Kuo's first appearance in book form, and it was well received by the Chinese literary world.

In the fall of 1920, Kuo, Ch'eng Fang-wu, T'ien Han, and others, began to discuss the establishment of a literary periodical. In the following spring Kuo returned to Shanghai where he took an informal position with the T'ai-tung Book Company. Not long afterwards he edited a collection of his poetry entitled Nü-shen (The goddesses); this work, which quickly brought him real recognition, was published under the newly organized Creation Society. Kuo then decided to return to his medical studies in Japan, and because of this the publication which he and his colleagues had been planning, Ch'uang-tsao chi-k'an (Creation quarterly), was turned over to the editorship of Kuo's friend Yü Ta-fa. The journal first appeared in May 1922, with the announced intention of counterbalancing the influence of the Literary Research Society in which Cheng Chen-to and Shen Yen-ping (q.v.) were major figures. This declaration laid the foundation for the antagonism between the Literary Research Society and Kuo's Creation Society, "which came to depend more on their rivalry than on any fundamental difference in their basic outlooks." [2] Both organizations were among the most important of their kind in China during these years of intellectual ferment.

Kuo returned to Shanghai during the summer vacation of 1922, and it was then that he first began to pay serious attention to political issues. He had displayed a limited interest in Marxism as early as 1919, but a few more years were still to pass before he acquired any real knowledge of Marxism-Leninism. Kuo went back to Japan for his final school year, and then returned to Shanghai in the spring of 1923. He, Yü Ta-fu, and

Ch'eng Fang-wu immediately laid plans for a second periodical, Ch'uang-tsao chou-pao (Creation weekly), which first appeared in May 1923. Two months later they brought out still another one, Ch'uang-tsao jih (Creation daily), which was published as a supplement to Chung-hua hsin-pao (China news).

In the fall of 1923, when the Creation Society was at the height of its influence, it began to "collapse from within." [3] It appears that Kuo's high-handed manner in dealing with his colleagues was largely responsible for this. Yü Ta-fu, for example, left to take up a post at Peking University. The daily came to an end a few days later, and the quarterly was stopped in January 1924. Kuo's family, who could not speak Chinese, was unhappy in Shanghai and left for Japan in early February 1924. Kuo himself left for Japan several weeks later, and in a gloomy mood swore that he would never return to China. A month later, the third and last of the Creation Society's publications was terminated, and it was not until a year later that the organization was revived.

In the two-year existence of the Creation Society publications, Kuo had displayed a growing alienation with the West and an increasing attraction to Marxism. One piece, published in May 1923, has been described as historically significant "because it was one of the first calls for proletarian-oriented literature issued in the Chinese literary world." [4] His conversion to Marxism continued in Japan where he began to translate some essays by Kawakami Hajime, one of the earliest Japanese Marxists. In a letter of August 1924 he described this as a "turning point" in his life and declared that he had "now become a thoroughgoing believer in Marxism." [5] In November Kuo returned to Shanghai where he earned his living as a freelance writer and a part-time lecturer on literature at Ta-hsia University. Even before he left for home, Kuo had already begun to question some aspects of Marxism, and in the period from his self-pronounced conversion in August 1924 until July 1925, there was no indication in the works he produced that he was a Marxist-Leninist.[6] By the latter date, the Chinese political scene had been shaken to its foundations by the May 30th Incident in Shanghai (see under Li Li-san), and like many intellectuals he took up his pen to join in the nationwide protest movement. It was during this same period that the Creation Society was rejuvenated. A new fortnightly, Hung-shui (The flood), was brought out in August 1925. Kuo contributed several Marxist-oriented articles, but he was less active in editorial work, which was carried out by younger members of the society, than he had been in the earlier Creation Society publications. It was also in the post-May 30th period that Kuo began to develop a number of personal contacts with members of the CCP in Shanghai, and during the same year he joined the KMT, which then stood at the forefront of the revolutionary movement against the Peking government and the northern warlords. He remained in Shanghai through 1925, but in March 1926 he went to Canton, then the revolutionary center of China, to assume the post of dean of the Faculty of Literature at Chung-shan (Sun Yat-sen) University.

Kuo's arrival in Canton coincided with the final stages in the preparations for the Northern Expedition. It also coincided approximately with the date when Mao Tse-tung assumed the directorship of the Peasant Movement Training Institute (see under P'eng P'ai). Kuo was among those who lectured at the institute, but his teaching in Canton was terminated by the inauguration of the Northern Expedition in July 1926. Prior to this time Kuo's contribution to the revolution had been principally as a polemicist, but during the next year he found himself in the midst of a complex and treacherous political milieu which ruined the careers of many revolutionists and took the lives of still more. He began the northward march in July as chief of the Propaganda Section of Teng Yen-ta's General Political Department. In November, not long after the capture of the Wuhan cities, he was promoted to deputy director of the Political Department, and at the same time he was sent to the field headquarters of Chiang Kai-shek in Nanchang to set up an office of the Political Department. Over the next few months there was a sharp rise in the tensions between Chiang Kai-shek and the left-wing of the KMT in Wuhan, the group which Kuo supported. For a brief period in March 1927 Kuo was at the military front in Anhwei as head of the Political Department in Chiang's field headquarters, but when the generalissimo staged his famous anti-Communist coup in April, Kuo (by then back in Nanchang) departed for Wuhan. Soon afterwards he became director of the Political Department in the army of Chang Fa-k'uei, which in theory was the mainstay of the Left-KMT elements in Wuhan.

Relations between the Left-KMT and the CCP rapidly deteriorated in the spring and summer of 1927, and when the Communists were expelled from the Wuhan government, they responded by touching off the Nanchang Uprising on August 1 (see under Yeh T'ing). Kuo did not participate in the uprising, but he arrived in Nanchang a few days later. In the meantime, led by Chou En-lai, Chang Kuo-t'ao, Chu Te (qq.v.) and a host of other top-level Communists, the rebels established a 25-member Revolutionary Committee, which in turn had a seven-member Standing Committee. Kuo was made a member of both committees, as well as director of the subordinate Political Department. He was also the chief of the Propaganda Committee, but until his arrival on the scene Yun Tai-ying (q.v.) acted in his place. The rebels were quickly driven from Nanchang, and from there they moved their military forces,

numbering about 20,000, on a southward march. En route to Kwangtung Kuo joined the CCP.[7] The debacle at Nanchang was repeated on a grander scale in a totally abortive effort to attack and hold Swatow. The battered Communist military units withdrew into the Kwangtung countryside, and many of the top Party leaders fled abroad. Kuo made his way to Hong Kong and then to the International Settlement in Shanghai. He remained there for four months, half the time recuperating from an illness, and then in February 1928 he left for Japan. Kuo had already spent 10 years in Japan, and now, in his 35th year, he was about to embark upon another decade there.

In terms of literary output, Kuo's years in Japan were among the most productive during his life. He wrote novels, plays, essays, autobiographies, and a history of the Creation Society, and he translated works ranging from Marx to Upton Sinclair. He also immersed himself in the study of history and archaeology. Though Kuo was removed from the mainstream of Chinese political life in one sense, he maintained close contacts with the Chinese publishing world, particularly in Shanghai, and he also kept in touch with many of the literary luminaries of the day. A number of them banded together in 1930 to form the important League of Left-Wing Writers (see under Chou Yang), an organization which had a considerable impact during the years immediately prior to the Sino-Japanese War. Kuo was a regular contributor to the organs of the league and to books published under the league's auspices.

Immediately after the outbreak of war in July 1937, Kuo returned to Shanghai, leaving his family in Japan. His name having been removed from the list of political enemies of the Nationalist government, he was free to pursue his work, and like most Chinese writers of that period, he took up his pen as an anti-Japanese polemicist. Shanghai fell to the Japanese in November; Kuo went into hiding in the French Concession and a few days later sailed for Hong Kong. From there in January 1938 he went to Hankow, the temporary national capital and also the focal point of a wide variety of activities designed to mobilize the nation for the war against Japan. In March he joined with Shen Yen-ping and some 40 other literary figures in establishing the All-China Resistance Association of Art and Literary Workers, which published anti-Japanese periodicals and sent writers to the front lines to report on the war. At the same time, in response to an invitation from the Nationalists, he became chief of the Third (Propaganda) Section of the National Military Council's Political Training Department. The department was headed by the important Nationalist general Ch'en Ch'eng, and Chou En-lai was one of Ch'en's deputies. Shortly afterwards, Kuo was readmitted to the KMT.

When Hankow was captured in the fall of 1938, Kuo went to Changsha where the Political Training Department had been transferred, and then at the end of the year he went to Chungking, the new wartime capital. The early war period had been characterized by relatively close cooperation between the Nationalists on the one hand and Communists and left-wing elements on the other. But by the 1938–1940 period, relations had cooled and steps were taken by the KMT to reduce the participation and influence of the leftist elements. As a consequence, Kuo was removed from the Third Section in 1940 and given a less important post as chief of the Cultural Work Committee under the Political Training Department, an undemanding position which gave him ample opportunity to pursue his many other interests.

Like his earlier years of exile in Japan, the last five years of the war were another period of great literary productivity. Kuo turned out several historical dramas, as well as works on intellectual history and archaeology. He was also a frequent contributor to the press and the many journals which flourished in the wartime capital. One of his essays, first published in the Communists' *Hsin-hua jih-pao* (New China daily) in Chungking, attracted the attention of Mao Tse-tung. Kuo's essay, which dealt with the career of the famed late Ming dynasty rebel leader Li Tzu-ch'eng, was cited by Mao in 1944 as a useful reminder to his subordinates that they should "not repeat the error of becoming conceited at the moment of success." [8] During these same years Kuo continued to head the Cultural Work Committee, but then in March 1945 the committee was dissolved by the Nationalists; the Communists claim that this action was taken in response to a declaration signed a month earlier by Kuo and others which called for a "democratic coalition government."

Kuo left Asia for the first time in June 1945 when he went to Moscow to attend celebrations marking the 220th anniversary of the Russian Academy of Sciences. In addition to Moscow, Kuo visited Leningrad, Stalingrad, and Uzbekistan before returning to Chungking in August, shortly after the Japanese surrender. Negotiations between Chiang Kai-shek and Mao Tse-tung paved the way for the convocation in January 1946 of the Political Consultative Conference (PCC). The PCC was attended by delegates from the KMT, the CCP, the China Democratic League, the China Youth Party, as well as nine persons not affiliated with any political party. Kuo attended as a representative of the last-mentioned category, and during the three-week session he served on a committee to draft a national constitution and another committee to formulate policies in a reorganized government. In fact, however, little came of these endeavors, and the KMT–CCP military truce which had taken effect when the PCC began was soon violated by both sides. On February 10, at a public meeting in Chungking to celebrate the conclusion of the PCC, Kuo and two other speakers were injured when rioting broke out. The Communists and Nationalists exchanged accusations concerning the responsibility for this incident.

Kuo went to Shanghai in the spring of 1946, and for the next year he divided his time between scholarly writings and the abortive efforts which a number of non-partisans made to bring about a truce between the KMT and the CCP. During 1947, as civil war raged throughout the land, the Nationalists grew increasingly impatient with the ever-mounting criticisms from non-partisan intellectuals and leaders of the minor parties. A major turning point was reached in late October 1947 when the China Democratic League was dissolved by the Nationalists. Fearing arrest, a number of Democratic Leaguers and others, Kuo among them, left for Hong Kong in November and December. During the next year Kuo continued his research and polemical writing, and finally, in November 1948, when the Communists controlled most of Manchuria, Kuo left for there.

In late February 1949, just three weeks after the Communists marched into Peking, Kuo and 34 other "democratic personages" arrived there from Manchuria. They were greeted and feted in the style of a new administration seeking the approval of well-known public figures. A month later Kuo left Peking as the leader of a 44-member delegation to the First World Peace Congress. This was scheduled to be held in Paris in late April, but because the French government would not allow all the 2,000-odd delegates to enter France, 360 of them (including Kuo's group) went to Prague where they convened separately. Kuo's participation in this congress was a forerunner of many similar trips abroad during the ensuing years.

Throughout the summer and fall of 1949 Kuo was busily engaged in the preparations which led to the establishment of the central government and many "mass" and professional organizations. In early June he was made a member of the Higher Education Committee; this was subordinate to the North China People's Government (see under Tung Pi-wu), which served in effect as the substitute for a national government until one was inaugurated on October 1. In mid-June, at a meeting presided over by Mao Tse-tung, Kuo was elected a vice-chairman of the CPPCC Preparatory Committee. But his most important role in mid-1949 was in connection with the Congress of Literary and Art Workers (July 2–19), which was attended by over 800 persons. The convocation of the congress had been proposed by Kuo in March, and he had served as chairman of the Preparatory Committee. He headed the congress presidium, and delivered the keynote address on the "struggle" to achieve a "new people's literature and art," as well as a summation report on the last day of the congress. The delegates established the All-China Federation of Literary and Art Circles (ACFLAC) under Kuo's chairmanship. He continues in this post, having been re-elected at congresses in September–October 1953 and July–August 1960. In the days immediately following the 1949 congress, six subordinate national associations were set up for writers, dramatists, cinema workers, musicians, artists, and dancers, as well as preparatory committees for drama reform and ballad singing and story telling. The most important of these, the All-China Association of Literary Workers, elected Shen Yen-ping as its chairman and Kuo as a member of the National Committee. Kuo was re-elected to this post at the congress in September–October 1953 when the name of the organization was changed to the Union of Chinese Writers (and when the National Committee was renamed the Executive Committee). In 1950 the ACFLAC set up still another subordinate body, the Chinese Folklore Research Society, and by about 1957 Kuo became its chairman.[9]

On July 1, 1949 Kuo became chairman of the Preparatory Committee for the China New Historical Research Society; he has continued as chairman since the Chinese Historical Society was established on a permanent basis in July 1951. At still another conference in July 1949, which set up the Preparatory Committee for the Sino-Soviet Friendship Association, Kuo gave the keynote address and was elected to the Preparatory Committee. And six weeks later, in early September, he was elected chairman of the Preparatory Committee of the China Peace Committee.

By the time the CPPCC was convened on September 21, 1949, it was clear that the CCP hierarchy had chosen a select few to symbolize its cooperation with non-Communists in the formation of the new national government. With the possible exception of the widow of Sun Yat-sen (Sung Ch'ing-ling, q.v.), Kuo was the most important of these persons. In the new national administration he was made a vice-chairman of the CPPCC and the Central People's Government Council, both of which were chaired by Mao. In the Government Administration Council (the cabinet), Kuo was made one of the four vice-premiers under Premier Chou En-lai. In addition, Kuo was appointed chairman of the cabinet's Culture and Education Committee. This committee, in turn, was in charge of the Culture, Education, and Public Health ministries, the Press Administration (abolished in 1952), and the Academy of Sciences. Kuo himself was appointed president of the academy, a post he still holds. Soon after assuming this position he went to Moscow to hold talks with leading Soviet science administrators.[10]

Kuo added to this impressive cluster of posts in the days and weeks following the establishment of the PRC. In early October he was elected chairman of the China Peace Committee and a vice-chairman of the Sino-Soviet Friendship Association; he continues to hold these posts. He was also named in October to the Standing Committee of the newly formed Association for the Reform of the Chinese Written Language. Kuo appears to have spent most of the first half of 1950 in connection with the organization of cultural and educational activities. He reported on this subject on March 17, 1950, to a meeting of the Government Administration Council, and in June, at the second session of the CPPCC National Committee, he delivered a major report on the same topic. The last-mentioned address, a particularly useful source of information on culture and education, was reproduced in a condensed version in the August 16, 1950, issue of *People's China*. An equally useful report was made at the next CPPCC session (October–November 1951); this too was published in *People's China* (December 1, 1951), as well as in a pamphlet entitled *New China Forges Ahead* (Peking, 1952).

In mid-August 1950, during the early weeks of the Korean War, Kuo was sent to Pyongyang as head of a delegation to participate in the celebrations marking the fifth anniversary of the "liberation" of Korea from the Japanese. At the end of October he left Peking as head of a 65-member delegation slated to attend the Second World Peace Congress in Sheffield. However, when the British banned the meeting, it was held in Warsaw in mid-November. By this juncture the Chinese had entered the Korean War, and thus at this and subsequent meetings of the World Peace Council (WPC), the theme of American "imperialism" was stressed by Chinese delegates. Kuo was elected a WPC vice-chairman at the Warsaw meeting. From there he led a portion of his group to Budapest for the 125th anniversary of the Hungarian Academy of Sciences; the delegation then spent a few days in Moscow before returning to China on December 21.

In 1951 Kuo led two more delegations to WPC meetings, one to East Berlin in February and the other to Vienna in November. In April of the same year he went to Moscow in his capacity as a vice-chairman of the International Stalin Peace Prize Committee. Sung Ch'ing-ling was selected as the recipient for the year 1950. In March 1952 Kuo attended a WPC meeting in Oslo, after which he went to Moscow where on April 10 he himself received the Stalin Peace Prize (which had been awarded in December 1951). The Oslo WPC meeting had focused on a new set of charges against the United States, namely, that germ warfare was being conducted by American forces in Korea. This theme dominated the world "peace" movement throughout 1952, and it was the major agenda item at the WPC-sponsored Asian and Pacific Regions Peace

Conference held in Peking in October (see under Liu Ning-i). Kuo attended this meeting and was elected a vice-chairman of the Peace Liaison Committee for Asian and Pacific Regions. In the meantime, in July 1952, he led the Chinese delegation to another WPC meeting in East Berlin, and in mid-December he was a deputy leader under Sung Ch'ing-ling of the delegation sent to Vienna for the Congress of Peoples for Peace. Kuo remained in Europe, and on January 13, 1953, he was received by Stalin in Moscow. Then, when the Soviet leader died in early March, Kuo accompanied Chou En-lai from Peking to Moscow for the funeral. A few days later he went with Chou to Prague for the funeral of Czech leader Klement Gottwald.

Kuo, by now over 60, continued his heavy pace of foreign travel in 1953. In May, June, and November, respectively, he led delegations to WPC meetings in Stockholm, Budapest, and Vienna. Early in the same year the Chinese formed a committee to draft a national constitution and another to arrange for elections; these were the first of several organizational steps which led to the convocation of the NPC. Kuo was a member of both committees, and in 1954 he was elected a deputy from his native Szechwan to the First NPC, which convened in September 1954 and reorganized the central government. Kuo was elected a vice-chairman of the NPC Standing Committee. He also attended the Second and Third NPC's as a Szechwan deputy, and on each occasion (April 1959 and January 1965) he was again named a Standing Committee vice-chairman. In December 1954 and April 1959, respectively, Kuo was re-elected a vice-chairman of the Second and Third National Committees of the CPPCC, but in January 1965, when the inaugural session of the Fourth National Committee ended, he was only elected a member of the CPPCC Standing Committee.

The year 1954 also saw Kuo at four more WPC-sponsored meetings in East Berlin (May), Budapest (June), and Stockholm (June and November), and in May of the same year he was made a member of the Board of Directors of the newly established Chinese People's Association for Cultural Relations with Foreign Countries. In January 1955 Kuo was a member of the delegation sent to a WPC meeting in Vienna, and in June he attended the World Assembly for Peace in Helsinki. However, this was the last year in which he attended more than one WPC meeting. In retrospect, it appears that this was a result of a gradual reorientation by the Chinese toward a more active role in regional "peace" and "solidarity" movements, and a concomitantly less active role in the Soviet-dominated WPC. Thus, in March 1955, Kuo was named chairman of the preparatory committee for Chinese participation in the Asian Countries Conference, and in the next month he led a large delegation to New Delhi for this meeting. Many Asian nations were then displaying an impatience with what they felt was a near total domination of the world political scene by Moscow and Washington. The New Delhi conference, which was attended by 16 nongovernmental delegations, might have been of considerable political significance in Asia; however, its impact was soon overwhelmed in the Asian press a few weeks later by the Bandung Conference, which was attended by such famous government leaders as Chou En-lai, Nehru, and Nasser. Nonetheless, the Asian Countries Conference served as a forerunner of the Afro-Asian Solidarity Conferences held in later years (see below).

Kuo's work during the formative years of the PRC was not, of course, confined to his many travels abroad. These same years witnessed a considerable expansion of the Chinese scientific establishment, including the Academy of Sciences, which Kuo headed. For example, the number of institutes under the Academy grew from 14 in 1949 to 41 in 1954, and the sums spent for science in 1954 were over four times as large as those for 1951. In an effort to consolidate the expanding facilities of the Academy, four departments were set up in a preparatory status in April 1954. Kuo was selected to head the Department of Philosophy and Social Sciences, and he continued in this post when the departments were placed on a permanent footing in June 1955. In October of the same year he was made chairman of the Academy's Scientific Awards Committee. Then, following the adoption of a 12-year scientific plan early in 1956, Kuo served (March 1956–November 1958) as a vice-chairman of the newly established Scientific Planning Commission, a body subordinate to the State Council. Not long before this, in December 1955, Kuo led a group of top-level scientists to Japan to confer with their counterparts there for three weeks. This was Kuo's first visit to Japan in nearly two decades.

In the post-1949 period Kuo, as head of the Federation of Literary and Art Circles, was involved to one degree or another in virtually all of the numerous Party-directed assaults on the Chinese cultural world. In none of these attacks, however, did Kuo lead the way—that task was assumed by such Party stalwarts in the federation as Chou Yang (q.v.). These campaigns in the name of Party orthodoxy ruined the careers of some of China's most able literary figures (for example, Hu Feng and Ting Ling, qq.v.). Like most men of letters in post-1949 China, Kuo has made more than one "confession" in which he condemned himself for such shortcomings as "petty-bourgeois sentiments." But the most striking fact in Kuo's case has been his ability to shift with the changing prescriptions for the "correct" literary posture of the moment.

In the latter part of 1953 the first steps were taken to publish the important journal *Li-shih yen-chiu* (Historical studies). Since its inaugural issue in February 1954 Kuo has been the convenor of the journal's editorial committee. *Li-shih yen-chiu* is published by the Institute of History of the Academy Sciences. An institute for modern history had been set up in 1950 under Fan Wen-lan (q.v.), but then two parallel institutes were added in 1954. Kuo headed the First Institute of History, which in 1960 was merged with the Second Institute to form the above-mentioned Institute of History (with Kuo continuing as the director). The mid-fifties also witnessed a concerted effort to reform the Chinese language (see under Wu Yü-chang), and thus in February 1956 Kuo was named a vice-chairman of a committee to popularize standard spoken Chinese (*p'u-t'ung-hua*), and in October he became chairman of another committee to examine a plan to phoneticize the language.

At the above-mentioned Asian Countries Conference in 1955, it was decided that the participating delegations would set up "solidarity" committees. This was carried out in Peking in February 1956 with the formation of the Asian Solidarity Committee of China. Kuo was elected chairman, but he relinquished this post to Liao Ch'eng-chih (q.v.) in July 1958, by which time the organization, reflecting its expanded horizons, had been renamed the Afro-Asian Solidarity Committee. (Kuo gave up the chairmanship, but he continues to be a member of the National Committee.) When the committee was formed in 1956, Peking had diplomatic relations with several Asian nations, but none in the Middle East. However, owing to vigorous diplomatic and commercial efforts, relations were established before the end of the year with Egypt, Syria, and Yemen. This year also witnessed the Suez crisis and the resulting orientation of several Middle East nations away from the West. Capitalizing on this situation, the Chinese offered financial aid to Egypt and in November 1956 they formed an ad hoc organization chaired by Kuo with an unwieldy but descriptive title: the Chinese People's Committee to Support Egypt's Resistance to Aggression.

The year 1956 was the first since 1949 in which Kuo had not been abroad, but he was on the foreign circuit again in June 1957 when, with Burhan (q.v.), he was co-leader of a delegation to a WPC meeting in Ceylon. In November Kuo went to Moscow as a member of a delegation led by Mao Tse-tung. The ostensible purpose of the trip was to take part in the celebrations commemorating the 40th anniversary of the Russian Revolution. Far more important, however, were Mao's political negotiations with Khrushchev and other heads of Communist parties, and the talks held by the various sub-delegations which had accompanied Mao. In addition to his membership on Mao's official delegation, Kuo headed a 77-member group of scientists—by far the largest group of high-level scientific talent the Chinese have ever sent abroad at one time. Mao returned to Peking in November, but Kuo and his scientists remained in Moscow for extended negotiations, and there, on December 11, he signed a protocol on cooperation between Academies of Sciences for 1958–1962, as well as a 1958 plan for cooperation. Kuo then returned home, but shortly afterwards, in late December, he led a delegation to the first Afro-Asian Solidarity Conference in Cairo (see under Chu Tzu-ch'i and Yang Shuo). In early January 1958, just as Kuo was about to leave Cairo, Rumanian Presidium President Petru Groza died. Kuo led the Chinese delegation to Bucharest for the funeral, and then, on January 13, he returned to Moscow where his scientific delegation was still negotiating with the Russians. Five days later Kuo signed an agreement on joint research in science and technology and assistance in these fields to China. In subsequent years Kuo signed agreements for cooperation between the Chinese Academy of Sciences and counterpart academies in the USSR, June 1, 1959; Poland, October 9, 1960; Czechoslovakia, September 30, 1962; and Cuba, June 25, 1963; and on March 25, 1964, he signed a similar agreement between the Chinese Academy and the State University of Tirana in Albania.

In July 1958 Kuo led the Chinese delegation to Stockholm for the WPC-backed Congress on Disarmament and International Cooperation, and in September–October he headed another group to North Korea to attend Korean-Chinese Friendship Month celebrations. The latter trip was occasioned by the withdrawal of the last of the Chinese military units, which had remained there five years after the Korean War ended. In June of the same year Kuo was placed in charge of the preparatory work for a new University of Science and Technology in Peking, and when the school was formally established in September under the joint control of the Academy of Sciences and the Ministry of Education, he became its first president (a post he still holds). In the final days of 1958 Peking announced that Kuo and a number of other intellectuals had been admitted during the year to the CCP. Kuo, as already noted, had joined the Party in 1927, but his membership had apparently lapsed during his long interlude in Japan.

In April 1959 Kuo was again in Moscow in his capacity as a vice-chairman of the committee to award Moscow's peace prize, which, in the Khrushchev era, had been transformed from the Stalin to the Lenin Peace Prize. He returned to Sweden once again in the following month for an extraordinary session of the WPC, which was convened to celebrate the 10th anniversary of the "world peace movement." Shortly before that, in April, he had been put in charge of organizing the Asian-African Society of China which, unlike the Afro-Asian Solidarity Committee, purported to be essentially a research organization. Three years later (April 1962), when the society was inaugurated, Kuo was elected to its Council.

In the closing days of 1960 Kuo arrived in Cuba heading a delegation sent there to participate in the second anniversary of the Castro government (January 1). He was one of the first high-level PRC officials to visit Havana where he remained for almost two weeks. In August–September 1961 he spent three weeks in Indonesia and Burma as the leader of an NPC delegation on a friendship visit. In both nations he held talks with high government officials, including Sukarno and U Nu. Shortly after his return home he was made a vice-chairman of a committee to commemorate the 1911 Revolution; though there was nothing exceptional about this appointment, it was typical of many similar ad hoc bodies on which he served in the years after 1949. A month later Kuo received an honorary doctorate from Humboldt University in East Germany. In the decade prior to this Kuo had been made an honorary academician of Academies of Sciences in at least seven other Communist countries, a figure probably unmatched by any other Chinese Communist intellectual.

In July 1964 Kuo spent 10 days in North Vietnam as head of a combined delegation drawn from the China Peace Committee and the Afro-Asian Solidarity Committee. The group had been sent there to take part in ceremonies marking the 10th anniversary of the signing of the Geneva accords, which ended French control in Indochina. Then in his 72nd year, Kuo had visited (through 1964) no less than 19 different nations as a participant in 39 delegations. Only a handful of other leaders surpassed this record during the first decade and a half of the PRC. Moreover, this vigorous record of foreign travel is more than matched by his extraordinarily active pace in Peking where he has received a countless number of visitors. In this regard, because he is one of the very few state leaders fluent in Japanese, he has met with hundreds of Japanese and was thus a logical choice to become honorary chairman of the China-Japan Friendship Association when it was established in October 1963. In addition to these activities related to foreign affairs, Kuo has attended scores of national meetings dealing with a wide range of topics. To cite only one example, he has regularly participated in the sessions of the NPC, and his reports before this body (particularly in the 1950's) provide an important source of material in the fields of culture, education, and science. Kuo has also found the time to be a prolific contributor to many popular and specialized publications—ranging from the national press to journals dealing with history, literature, and archaeology. Western students of Chinese literature have frequently derided the quality of Kuo's creative writing, but few men throughout history can match the volume or versatility of a writing career which spans half a century. Kuo's name

and works crop up in all serious studies of Chinese intellectual life in the twentieth century. He may well be, in short, the closest thing to a Renaissance man that China has produced in this century.

When Kuo returned to China in 1937 he abandoned his Japanese wife and soon afterwards set up house with Yü Li-ch'ün. Yü was the granddaughter of Yü Shih-mei, secretary to the famed Ch'ing statesman Li Hung-chang and later an important official in the last years of the Ch'ing dynasty. Yü has received scant attention in the Communist press, although she has been an executive committee member of the National Woman's Federation since 1957. Kuo has five children by his Japanese wife and four by Yü Li-ch'ün. His Japanese wife went to China in 1948; all five of her children also live on the mainland, and this is presumably true for the children by his Chinese wife. One son, Kuo Po, a graduate of Tokyo University, was described in 1962 as a "returned overseas Chinese from Japan" who was living in Shanghai where he worked as an architectural engineer.

It would require scores of pages for a detailed bibliography of works on Kuo's writings and a description of the various literary and political controversies in which he has been involved. Many of these works and controversies can be found in: David Roy, *Kuo Mo-jo: The Early Years* (Cambridge, Mass., 1970); Milena Dolezelova-Velingerova, "Kuo Mo-jo's Autobiographical Works," in Jaroslav Prušek, ed., *Studies in Modern Chinese Literature* (Berlin, 1964), pp. 45–75; Tsi-an Hsia, *The Gate of Darkness* (Seattle, Wash., 1968); C. T. Hsia, *A History of Modern Chinese Fiction, 1917–1957* (New Haven, Conn., 1961); Chün-tu Hsüeh, *The Chinese Communist Movement, 1937–1949* (Stanford, Calif., 1962); Clarence Moy, "Kuo Mo-jo and the Creation Society," *Papers on China,* Regional Studies Seminars, Harvard University, East Asian Research Center (Cambridge, Mass., 1950), IV, 131–159; and Merle Goldman, *Literary Dissent in Communist China* (Cambridge, Mass., 1967).

1. David Roy, *Kuo Mo-jo: The Early Years,* (Cambridge, Mass., 1970), p. 82.

2. *Ibid.,* p. 120.

3. *Ibid.,* p. 127.

4. *Ibid.,* p. 150.

5. *Ibid.,* p. 161.

6. *Ibid.,* p. 172.

7. C. Martin Wilbur, "The Ashes of Defeat," *The China Quarterly,* no. 18:24–31 (April–June 1964).

8. *Selected Works of Mao Tse-tung* (Peking, 1965), III, 174, 176.

9. *1958 Jen-min shou-ts'e* (People's handbook; Peking, 1958), p. 313.

10. *CB* 257, p. 5.

Lai Chi-fa

(Szechwan). Specialist in heavy industry; minister, Ministry of Building Materials Industry.

Lai Chi-fa has been one of the more prominent administrators in the fields of heavy industry and building materials since the Communists came to power in 1949. A native of Szechwan, he first came to prominence in 1948 with the establishment of the North China People's Government (NCPG). This government existed from August 1948 to October 1949, when its activities were taken over by the national government (see under Tung Pi-wi). Subordinate to the NCPG was the State-operated Enterprises Department, which controlled industry in north China. Lai served as a deputy director of this department under Huang Ching.

From 1950 to 1956, Lai's attention was devoted mainly to the important Ministry of Heavy Industry. From March 1950 to August 1952 he was head of the ministry's Staff Office, serving under Minister Li Fu-ch'un, a top economic specialist. When Wang Ho-shou replaced Li in August 1952, Lai was promoted to vice-minister. In this capacity he took part in the transfer of the Soviet shares to China of the Sino-Soviet Joint Stock Non-ferrous and Rare Metals Company. This company had operated mainly in Sinkiang from 1950; the decision to transfer it to sole Chinese jurisdiction came during the Khrushchev-Bulganin visit to China in September–October 1954. On December 30, 1954, Lai officiated at a meeting in Urumchi, the Sinkiang capital, in celebration of the transfer, at which time he presented medals to Soviet experts who had worked for the company.

In the interim, Lai was elected as a Chungking deputy to the First NPC (1954–1959), being re-elected from Szechwan to serve in the Second (1959–1964). He was not, however, elected to the Third NPC, which opened in late 1964. In May 1955 Lai made his only known trip abroad when he accompanied the then Defense Minister P'eng Te-huai to celebrations marking the "liberation" of Germany. P'eng went on to Poland for a Warsaw Pact meeting and then stopped over briefly in Moscow, but apparently Lai did not make this portion of the trip.

In May 1956 the Ministry of Heavy Industry was abolished, with its various departments being placed under other and sometimes new ministries. One of the new ministries was the Ministry of Building Materials Industry, and Lai was given the portfolio. The ministry and, by implication, Lai came under serious criticism on November 30, 1957, when the JMJP reported shortcomings at Kuan-chuang, a small industrial town a few miles east of Peking. Almost all the 15,000 people at Kuan-chuang were working in enterprises (e.g., a cement research institute) directly subordinate to Lai's ministry. In re-

sponse to these criticisms the State Council dispatched an investigation team to Kuan-chuang in early December. Several weeks went by, and then the January 14 to 16, 1958, issues of the JMJP carried a series of articles on the "state of anarchy" which prevailed at Kuan-chuang. The ministry (but not Lai personally) was criticized for "bourgeois" and "rightist" thinking and conservatism, and a demand was made for strengthening ideological work, claiming that the neglect of such work was at the root of the anarchy. Lai himself wrote a piece for the JMJP on January 15; the criticisms were phrased in the collective "we," but he took his own ministry seriously to task. On the following day, at a mass meeting held in Kuan-chuang, it was announced that 29 "counterrevolutionaries and criminals" were arrested.[1] At about the end of April, Lai spoke at a meeting at Kuan-chuang celebrating the "victory" in the struggle. Most of these events, of course, transpired during the peak of the 1957–58 rectification movement, and the difficulties at Kuan-chuang may have been somewhat exaggerated in order to set an example.

In the interim, in the midst of these investigations and charges, there was a partial reorganization of the State Council. On February 11, 1958, Lai's ministry was merged with two others (the ministries of Building and of Urban Construction) to form a new Ministry of Building. Lai was not given any post after the reorganization. In the summer of 1958 he was re-elected to the NPC, and the following spring he represented the CCP on the Third CPPCC, and was subsequently elected to the CPPCC Standing Committee (1959–1964). Then in September 1959, during still another State Council reorganization, Lai was named as a vice-minister of the Ministry of Building (under Minister Liu Hsiu-feng), the ministry which had taken over Lai's Ministry of Building Materials Industry a year and a half earlier. In sum, it appears that the Kuan-chuang incident did not inflict any major damage on Lai's career.

Lai's public appearances after 1959 are rather few, yet they do not suggest a pattern of activities for a man in political trouble. He has occasionally served as a host for visiting groups (such as a Cuban building delegation in April–May 1961) and participated in negotiations leading to the signing of a protocol by the Sino-Polish Joint Standing Commission on Scientific and Technical Cooperation in September 1961. For the Peking Kung-jen jih-pao (Daily worker), January 22, 1963, he wrote "Building Departments Must Provide More Vigorous Aid for Agriculture," and Chien-chu (Building), no. 8, April 23, 1963, carried a report entitled "Penetratingly Unfold the Movement for Production Increase and Economy, Comprehensively Step Up Enterprise Management Work," which Lai delivered at a conference of heads of building engineering departments and bureaus on March 25, 1963.[2]

In late 1964 Lai was named to the Fourth National Committee of the CPPCC. Previously he had served as a CCP representative to the CPPCC, but on this occasion he was named to represent the China Scientific and Technical Association. Although Lai is not known to have any previous ties with this association, his technically oriented career would make him a suitable person to serve as its representative. At the close of the first session of the Fourth CPPCC in January 1965, he was again named to the Standing Committee. Two months later the Ministry of Building was divided into a new Ministry of Building and the Ministry of Building Materials Industry. Lai, who had been a vice-minister of Building, was now transferred to head the Ministry of Building Materials Industry and thus returned to the same post he had lost eight years earlier.

---

1. *SCMP* 1702.
2. *SCMP* 2917; *SCMM* 375.

Lai Ch'uan-chu

(1910–1965; Kiangsi). Chief-of-staff, New Fourth Army; former deputy director, General Cadres Department, PLA.

Lai Ch'uan-chu devoted his career to political work with the Red Army, coming to hold important positions with the New Fourth Army during the Sino-Japanese War and serving under Lin Piao in the Fourth Field Army in the immediate postwar period. After serving in Peking from 1950 to 1959 with the headquarters of the PLA, Lai transferred to Manchuria, where he was a political commissar with the PLA forces in Shenyang (Mudken) at the time of his death.

Lai joined the CCP in 1927 and entered the Red Army in the following year. He probably began his military career by becoming a political officer; the first reference to his work in the Red Army identifies him as a Party representative returning from Kwangtung with a unit of the Fourth Red Army, which was moving into west Fukien (November 1929). He was present there at the noted Ninth Conference of the Party organization in the Fourth Army, which met in Ku-t'ien in December 1929.[1] The Fourth Red Army (then commanded by Chu Te, with Mao Tse-tung as the principal political officer) adopted Mao's report "On the Rectification of Incorrect Ideas in the Party," which was used as the signal to remove certain dissident Party leaders from the Fourth Army. Lai must have been an insignificant figure at this time, but not long afterwards he began to receive recognition. In mid-1930 the Fourth Red Army became a part of the newly organized First Army Corps, and the Fourth Red Army column in which Lai

was serving became the 11th Division. By the end of the year he was the political commissar of one of the 11th Division's regiments. Before the Long March Lai rose in rank, serving with the First Army Corps as chief-of-staff and then as political commissar at the divisional level. During the Long March he was an officer with the First Army Corps headed by Commander Lin Piao and Political Commissar Nieh Jung-chen; the Corps belonged to the Chu-Mao First Front Army. During the march Lai served as political commissar both with the First Division and with the Fifth Regiment of the Second Division of the First Army Corps. After the Communists arrived in north Shensi he was assigned to the headquarters there, and when the government for the Shensi-Kansu-Ninghsia Border Region was established in March 1937, he became acting director of its Military Affairs Department.

Nothing further was heard about Lai until 1939 when he met the American author Agnes Smedley, who visited his detachment in Anhwei in the fall of that year. When Miss Smedley met Lai he was the chief-of-staff of the Fourth Detachment, a unit of the New Fourth Army, the Communist army in east-central China.[2] The history of the Fourth Detachment, which had been sent from Hankow with some 1,000 men in March of 1938 not long after the New Fourth Army was activated, is described in the biography of Chang Yun-i. Chang, the detachment commander, had made the Long March, as did Lai, and had been sent from Shensi to join the New Fourth Army in the latter part of 1938. In November 1939, not long after Smedley visited his headquarters, Chang was made the head of the North Yangtze Command and put in charge of all the New Fourth Army units fighting north of the Yangtze River. At this time Lai became the chief-of-staff of Chang's North Yangtze Command, as well as the head of the "Staff Office" under the New Fourth Army's chief-of-staff, Chang Yun-i. In November 1940 the Communists created a Fifth Branch of their military academy K'ang-ta. Headed by Ch'en I, with Lai as his deputy, the new institution was located at Ch'en's headquarters, Yen-ch'eng, in east Kiangsu. It combined three training schools, two of them former training units attached to the New Fourth Army (Ch'en's own unit, and one from the former North Yangtze command under Chang Yun-i, which had been located at Hsu-i on the south shore of Lake Hung-tse), plus a special training squad that had been dispatched from the Eighth Route Army (see under Huang K'o-ch'eng).[3]

Early in 1941 there was a complete reorganization of the top command in the New Fourth Army. This was necessitated by the new Fourth Army Incident of January 1941 when New Fourth Army Commander Yeh T'ing was captured and Deputy Commander Hsiang Ying was killed as they were trying to lead their forces across the Yangtze to join the rest of the army, which had already made the crossing and was fighting north of the river (see under Yeh T'ing). Following the incident the Revolutionary Military Council, the top military committee in the CCP at Yenan, issued an order naming the Army's new top echelon staff.[4] Chang Yun-i, who had been chief-of-staff, was appointed army deputy commander, and Lai, Chang's subordinate, was moved up to the post of chief-of-staff. Lai held the post with the New Fourth Army until 1946 when he was transferred to Manchuria to join the army of Lin Piao.

With the end of the Sino-Japanese War, Lin Piao began to maneuver Red military forces into Manchuria. He transferred to the northeast most of his former 115th Division from the Eighth Route Army and also added officers and men from the Communist forces that had fought in east-central China during the war. Thus Lai took part in the Manchurian campaign, which lasted from 1946 to late in 1948, serving as a political commissar with Lin's army and as the deputy commander of the East Manchuria Military Region. By early 1949, when Lin's army (now named the Fourth Field Army) had moved south into China proper and was ready to take over Peking, Lai was identified as the political commissar of the Fourth Field Army's 15th Army Corps (commanded by military veteran Teng Hua). After assisting in the takeover of Peking, Lin's army turned south to move through central China and capture Canton in October 1949, and Kweilin and Nanning in Kwangsi by the end of November and early December. The army's conquests were completed in April 1950 when Teng Hua lead a force from the Fourth Field Army to take over Hainan, an operation in which Lai participated.

As Lin Piao's Fourth Field Army pushed southward in 1949, some of the operations (especially in central China) were conducted in close coordination with Liu Po-ch'eng's Second Field Army and Ch'en I's Third Field Army. It appears that Lai was briefly working with Liu Po-ch'eng's forces, because following the conquest by the Second Field Army of the Kiangsi capital of Nanchang in May 1949, Lai was named to membership on the municipal military control commission. However, by the latter part of 1949 he was back in Lin's command and was given new military and civil assignments. With the fall of Canton to the Communists in October 1949, Lin was named as vice-chairman of the Canton Military Control Commission under Chairman Yeh Chien-ying (q.v.). At about this same time he also became deputy commander and political commissar of the Canton Garrison Command, as well as first deputy political commissar of the Kwangtung Military District. In the civil administration, he was named in December 1949 to the Kwangtung Provincial People's Government Council and as a member of the Central-South Military and Administrative Committee (CSMAC). With its headquarters in Wuhan, the CSMAC had jurisdiction over four central China provinces as well as the southern provinces of Kwangtung (including Hainan) and Kwangsi.

As already noted, Li took part in the capture of Hainan Island in April 1950, the last major Communist military operation in the conquest of the mainland (excluding Tibet in 1951). He nominally retained his posts in the CSMAC and the Kwangtung government until 1951 and 1954, respectively. However, by sometime in 1950 (according to his obituary) he was assigned to Peking where he became a deputy director of the General Cadres' (Personnel) Department under the People's Revolutionary Military Council (PRMC) and political commissar of troops stationed in Peking. It is not clear how long he retained the latter position, but he continued to serve in the Cadres' Department until his transfer to Shenyang in 1959 (see below). Lai's position in the Cadres' Department placed him directly under Lo Jung-huan until 1956 and thereafter under Hsiao Hua (qq.v.), two of the most important political officers in the PLA.

Lai's activities in Peking during the early fifties were seldom mentioned by the Communist press. It is known, however, that he attended the third session of the First National Committee of the CPPCC in October–November 1951, at which time decisions were taken to intensify the "anti-U.S." campaign and to promote a nationwide austerity campaign. In August of the following year he was a member of the presidium (steering committee) for the All-PLA Sports Meet in Peking and in January 1953 he presented a report before the Government Administration Council (the cabinet) regarding decorations to be awarded soldiers in the PLA. In 1954 Lai was elected as a deputy from the Central-South Military Region to the First NPC, the legislative body that brought the constitutional government into existence at its first session in September 1954. He was re-elected to the Second NPC (1959–1964), only on this occasion as a deputy from the Shenyang Military Region. He was once again elected from the Shenyang Region to the Third NPC, which opened in late 1964. Although Lai was apparently not very active in the First NPC, he was more deeply involved in the Second and Third NPC's, serving as a member of the presidium (steering committee) for the last three sessions (1960, 1962, and 1963), as well as for the initial session of the Third NPC, held in December 1964–January 1965.

Lai's long service in the Red armies was given official recognition in September 1955 when he was given all three of the top military awards, the August First, the Independence and Freedom, and the Liberation Orders, awards granted for service from the founding of the Red Army in 1927 to 1950. It was also in 1955 that the Communists created personal military ranks; Lai was made a colonel-general, the equivalent of a three-star general in the U.S. Army. In October 1958 he made his only known trip abroad when he was a member of a military delegation to Poland led by Marshal Yeh Chien-ying, Lai's former superior in Kwangtung. At the first session of the Second NPC in April 1959, Lai was named to membership on the National Defense Council, an organization with very limited power and authority, but one with considerable prestige. (He was reappointed to the Council in January 1965.) Later in 1959 he was transferred to the headquarters of the Shenyang Military Region (SMR), the headquarters responsible for military affairs in all of Manchuria. There he became the SMR political commissar, replacing Chou Huan (q.v.). However, Central Committee member Sung Jen-ch'iung, a more senior political leader than Lai, was sent to Manchuria in 1961 to become the first secretary of the Party's Northeast Bureau. By at least 1964 Sung had become the first political commissar of the SMR; as a consequence, Lai was lowered to the subordinate position of second political commissar, his major post at the time of his death. Owing to the paucity of source materials from Manchuria in the 1960's, little is known about the last years of Lai's life. He was occasionally mentioned in the national press when, for example, he was on hand to welcome foreign visitors in Shenyang. And, as already noted, he returned to Peking for the sessions of the NPC held in 1960, 1962, 1963, and 1964. One of the last times Lai was mentioned in the press occurred in 1964 when he wrote an article for the *JMJP* (May 23) entitled "Revolution Calls for a Careful Study of the Works of Chairman Mao."

Lai Ch'uan-chu died at the age of 55 in Shenyang on December 24, 1965, of an illness. Defense Minister Lin Piao was named to head the funeral committee for Lai, and the funeral service held on the following day was prominently featured in the *JMJP*. His 38-year record of service to the Communist movement was described in his obituary, which noted that he had been a "good student of Comrade Mao Tse-tung."

---

1. Lai Ch'uan-chu, "Before and after the Ku-t'ien Conference," *JMJP,* June 23, 1961.

2. Agnes Smedley, *Battle Hymn of China* (New York, 1945), p. 317.

3. Chalmers A. Johnson, *Peasant Nationalism and Communist Power* (Stanford, Calif., 1962), p. 153.

4. Mao Tse-tung, *Selected Works* (New York, 1954), III, 225.

Lai Jo-yü

(1910–1958; Wu-t'ai hsien, Shansi). Former chairman, All-China Federation of Trade Unions; member, CCP Central Committee.

Lai Jo-yü began his career as a Party official in north China where he worked from the late twenties until 1952, when he became secretary-general of the All-China Federation of Labor. From then until his death in 1958 he led the PRC trade union movement. Lai was born on January 1, 1910, in Wu-t'ai hsien in eastern Shansi, the hsien where the sacred Buddhist Wu-t'ai Mountain is located and also the headquarters during the Sino-Japanese War of the Communists' Shansi-Chahar-Hopeh (Chin-Ch'a-Chi) base. Communist military leader Hsu Hsiang-ch'ien (q.v.), with whom Lai was associated, was also a native of Wu-t'ai. In 1929, when Lai was 19, he joined the CCP and began his revolutionary activities as an underground operative. He was arrested in Peking in 1930, and after his release in 1932 he continued his revolutionary work, presumably in north China.

According to Lai's obituary and a memorial address by Li Hsueh-feng, the two major sources for Lai's career before 1949, he spent most of the years of the Sino-Japanese War and the civil war that followed in his native Shansi.[1] After the war began in mid-1937, he served in the T'ai-hang mountain area, a district that was a major sub-division of the Communists' Shansi-Hopeh Military Region, where Liu Po-ch'eng and Teng Hsiao-p'ing's 129th Division (of the Eighth Route Army) was stationed. In 1941, following the expansion of the Communist bases, the Shansi-Hopeh base was enlarged into the Shansi-Hopeh-Shantung-Honan (Chin-Chi-Lu-Yü) Border Region (see under Yang Hsiu-feng). Lai was assigned to Party organizations in the T'ai-hang area, located in eastern Shansi and western Hopeh, serving successively as a hsien Party secretary, as a local (*ti-wei*) Party committee secretary, and finally as director of the T'ai-hang's Organization Department. In Li Hsueh-feng's memorial address, Lai was praised for the excellence of his work in strengthening Party bases behind Japanese lines during the years from 1940 to 1943. During a portion of this time he was said to have worked directly under Teng Hsiao-p'ing, then the 129th Division's Political Commissar and now the Party Central Committee's General Secretary. Lai remained in the T'ai-hang area during the civil war against the Nationalists, rising to the post of secretary of the T'ai-hang Party Committee.

Lai was with the forces led by Hsu Hsiang-ch'ien that captured Taiyuan, the Shansi capital, in late April 1949. The Communists immediately established the Taiyuan Military Control Commission under the chairmanship of Hsu, with Lai, Lo Jui-ch'ing, and Hu Yao-pang (qq.v.) as his deputies. Hsu, Lo, and Hu were soon reassigned elsewhere, but Lai remained in Shansi until late 1951. Before the end of 1949 he was holding three additional positions of importance: deputy political commissar of the Shansi Military District, secretary of the Taiyuan Party Committee, and deputy secretary of the Shansi Provincial Party Committee. In the meantime, however, he went to Peking in September as a representative from the "North China Liberated Area" to the first session of the CPPCC, the organization that brought the new central government into existence on October 1, 1949. While the CPPCC was in session, Lai served on the *ad hoc* committee charged with the task of preparing public statements on the work of the CPPCC.

Returning to Shansi in the fall of 1949, Lai became one of the most active and important Party officials there through 1951, although he was politically outranked by Ch'eng Tzu-hua (q.v.), who was the provincial Party secretary, the governor, and the commander and political commissar of the Shansi Military District (as well as an alternate member of the Party Central Committee from 1945). However, by mid-1950 Ch'eng was mainly occupied with responsibilities in Peking, and it is probable that Lai was regarded as the senior leader in the province. In April 1950 he became a member of the Shansi Provincial People's Government Council (serving under Governor Ch'eng Tzu-hua), and four months later he was named as chairman of the government's Finance and Economics Committee. In February 1951 Lai succeeded Ch'eng as the provincial governor, and at approximately this same time he also became the ranking secretary of the Shansi Party Committee.

In December 1951 Lai was named to membership on the newly established North China Administrative Committee (NCAC), the governmental organ responsible for the provinces of Hopeh, Chahar, Shansi, Pingyuan, and Suiyuan. He remained on the NCAC, chaired by Liu Lan-t'ao (q.v.), until it was reorganized in February 1953. More important, however, was Lai's transfer to Peking over the winter of 1951–52, relinquishing the Shansi governorship to P'ei Li-sheng (q.v.) in December 1951. Lai's first national assignment came in December 1951 when he was appointed a member of the Central Austerity Examination Committee, an appointment probably made on the basis of the experience he had gained as chairman of the Shansi Finance and Economics Committee. Headed by Po I-po (q.v.), one of the top economic specialists of the PRC, the Examination Committee was given the task of implementing the nationwide drive to uncover such abuses as graft, corruption, and waste. From February 1952 to 1954 Lai was also a member of the CPPCC's Study Committee, established to promote the dissemination of the works of Marx, Engels, and Mao Tse-tung.

In the spring of 1952 Lai assumed an important post with the All-China Federation of Labor (ACFL), and until his death six years later he led the Federation, one of the most important of the many "mass" organizations. Lai's initial post in the ACFL was as secretary-general, replacing Hsu Chih-chen (q.v.) who, unlike Lai, had had a long career in the labor movement. Lai's appointment to the ACFL may have resulted from the serious "errors" of leadership that were "exposed" during a meeting of the Federation's Party Committee in December 1951.[2] At first glance it appeared that the "errors" were attributable to Hsu Chih-chen, but Hsu's later career suggests that another person was involved—most probably Li Li-san (q.v.), the former *de facto* head of the CCP and a labor leader from the early twenties. When Lai assumed the Federation secretary-generalship in 1952, he was theoretically outranked by Chairman Ch'en Yun and vice-chairmen Liu Ning-i (q.v.), Li Li-san, and Chu Hsueh-fan. However, Ch'en was then fully occupied at the policy level in Party and PRC Government affairs, Liu was heavily engaged in liaison work with the World Federation of Trade Unions (and therefore often abroad), Li was probably in political difficulties, and Chu Hsueh-fan was (and remains) mainly a figurehead, retaining his post as a demonstration of the Party's willingness to cooperate with non-Communists.

Lai's pre-eminence in the labor field was soon illustrated in 1952; he began to write the major articles on the subject (e.g., *JMJP,* April 26, 1952) and to give the major public speeches, as on May Day of 1952 when he delivered a general review of trade union work in China. His position within the ACFL was further consolidated by August 1952, when he was identified as head of the Federation's Policy Research Office. A month earlier he was given a new post closely related to the labor field, becoming a member of the PRC Labor Employment Committee, which was formed to deal with unemployment problems and was headed by Li Wei-han (q.v.).

In the early months of 1953 Lai was mainly occupied with preparations for the convocation of the ACFL's Seventh Congress, the first to be held since the 1948 congress in Harbin. Preparations for the congress began at a plenum of the Federation's Executive Committee in January 1953. At this time Lai was added to membership on the Executive Committee, and he, Vice-chairman Liu Ning-i, and Organization Department Director Hsu Chih-chen were highly critical of the "erroneous" leadership the ACFL had been following; the object of their attacks became apparent when the Seventh Congress met in May and dropped Li Li-san, who had been the Federation's first vice-chairman. Lai completely dominated the congress; he was secretary-general for the congress and delivered the keynote report, a lengthy address entitled "Struggle for the Task of Accomplishing the Industrial Construction of the Nation." At the close of the meetings the leadership organs were reshuffled and the Federation was renamed (in the official English translation, but not in Chinese) the All-China Federation of Trade Unions (ACFTU). Under the new structure the Executive Committee remained as the leading organ between congresses, but the post of secretary-general was abolished and in place of the previous Standing Committee, two new organs were created: the Presidium, charged with carrying out the decisions of the Executive Committee, and the Secretariat, responsible for routine work. Lai was elected to the Executive Committee, the Presidium, and the Secretariat and replaced Ch'en Yun as the ACFTU Chairman, thereby being reconfirmed in his leadership of the Federation.

Earlier in 1953 Lai had been named to two other posts under the administration of the central government. In January he became a member of a committee to "thoroughly implement" the Marriage Law, which had been promulgated in 1950, and in the next month he was named as a member of the Central Election Committee. Chaired by Liu Shao-ch'i, the Election Committee was responsible for the conduct of nationwide elections to the forthcoming NPC. When the elections were held in 1954, Lai was named as a deputy from Honan, and at the close of the initial session of the First NPC in September 1954, he was appointed as a member of the NPC Standing Committee. At each of the five annual sessions of the First NPC (1954–1958) Lai served as a member of the Congress Presidium (steering committee). In December 1954 he attended the meetings of the CPPCC as a representative of the Trade Union Federation and was elected to the Second National Committee, a post he held until his death in 1958. Because the ACFTU plays a major role in the education of workers (see under Li Chieh-po), Lai was a logical nominee for membership on two special organizations formed in 1956 to advance literacy in China. In February of that year a committee to popularize standard spoken Chinese (p'u-t'ung-hua) was created, and in the next month the National Association for the Elimination of Illiteracy was established. Lai served as a member of both organizations until his death. Similarly, he was named to chair a special committee established in July 1956 to "disseminate scientific and technical knowledge" among workers and employees. In this connection, it appears that Lai took a special interest in the application of

technology to Chinese industry. He was cited for his efforts in these endeavors in Li Hsueh-feng's memorial address and also by labor leader Liu Tzu-chiu (q.v.) in a brief article in the JMJP of May 23, 1958.

In the mid-fifties Lai was particularly active. He presided over most of the ACFTU meetings and usually participated in national conferences where trade union interests were involved, as in May 1956 when he addressed a national conference of "outstanding workers" on the need to fulfill the First Five-Year Plan ahead of schedule. He also spoke before the annual sessions of the NPC and presented reports before the State Council on trade union work. In addition, Lai was a frequent contributor to the press, including the JMJP, the Kung-jen jih-pao (Workers' daily, the organ of the ACFTU), and Hsueh-hsi (Study). For the last-mentioned publication, then the most important CCP journal, Lai wrote an article on leadership in the trade unions for the second issue of 1958 (January 18).

At the Party's Eighth National Congress in September 1956, Lai delivered the major report on trade union work and at the close of the meetings was elected to membership on the Party Central Committee. Then 46 years old, he was one of the youngest men elected to full membership. His election was also notable in that he was one of only 33 men elected a Central Committee member who had been neither a full nor an alternate member of the Seventh Central Committee elected in 1945. Two of Lai's colleagues in the ACFTU, Liu Ning-i and Liu Ch'ang-sheng (q.v.), also became full Central Committee members at this time. In contrast to the two Liu's, both of whom have been extremely active in the international activities of the Trade Union Federation, Lai's contributions were mainly in domestic affairs. He did, however, make two trips abroad on behalf of the Federation, in both cases to the Soviet Union. In May 1954 he led a delegation to Moscow to attend the 11th All-Soviet Trade Union Congress (remaining there until August), and in July 1957 he led a group to a meeting of the World Federation of Trade Unions.

Lai's last major activity, quite fittingly, was in connection with the Eighth All-China Congress of Trade Unions in December 1957. He completely dominated the proceedings of the congress, just as he had at the 1953 meetings. He delivered the keynote address and at the close of the meetings was re-elected to all his positions within the Federation. Lai last appeared in public in February 1958 at a session of the NPC. Three months later he died of liver cancer (May 20). He was given the full honors normally accorded to a leader of his stature; his funeral committee was headed by Liu Shao-ch'i, the dean of the Chinese Communist labor movement (in the Maoist version of history), and at a memorial service on May 23, veteran north China Party leader Li Hsueh-feng delivered a eulogy.

During Lai's six-year period of leadership of the Trade Union Federation, membership had climbed from 10 million in 1952 to over 16 million in late 1957, an expansion that approximately coincided with the First Five-Year Plan (1953–1957). His death, of course, necessitated a reshuffling of the ACFTU leadership. At a special meeting of the Federation in August 1958, Liu Ning-i succeeded to the ACFTU chairmanship.

1. *JMJP,* May 21 and 24, 1958.
2. *SCMP* 513, p. 5.

Lei Jen-min

(c.1912–   ; Shansi). Vice-minister of Foreign Trade.

Lei Jen-min, a foreign trade specialist, was a student in Taiyuan, the Shansi capital, in the late 1920's. Prior to the mid-1920's, Shansi had been virtually the private domain of Shansi governor Yen Hsi-shan. However, under the impact of the May 30th Movement (1925) and the Northern Expedition, which began in mid-1926, the province was increasingly opened up to the political activities of both the KMT and the CCP. Lei was apparently influenced by these events, because in 1928, while still in his teens, he joined a CCP cell at the Kuo-min Normal School. Other prominent present-day Communists who attended the school include Po I-po and Jung Tzu-ho (qq.v.). After graduation about 1930, Lei went to the Peking-Tientsin area where he engaged in Party activities for two years. He returned to Shansi in 1932 and, because of his political work among the students in Taiyuan, he was imprisoned by the Yen Hsi-shan government.

After ostensibly renouncing Communism, Lei was released from prison in 1935. In the following year, Yen Hsi-shan, who was increasingly apprehensive about Japanese incursions into north China, created the so-called Sacrifice League and in 1937 a paramilitary organization known as the Dare-to-Die Corps. Both organizations were heavily infiltrated with Communists and other leftist elements. About the time war broke out in 1937, Lei was a brigade commander in Yen Hsi-shan's Shansi Army, but by 1939 he was commanding the Fourth Column of the Dare-to-Die Corps in northwest Shansi near the Shensi border.[1] Lei's column was subordinate to the "New Shansi Army," which, though nominally under Yen's control, was cooperating with Communist units in waging guerrilla warfare against the Japanese. In the last days of 1939, under a set of complex circumstances described in the biography of P'eng Shao-hui, Lei took his men over to the Communist side. He presumably remained

for the balance of the war in northwest Shansi, where the principal Communist unit was the 358th Brigade under P'eng Shao-hui's command.

Under the terms of the truce worked out in early 1946 by U.S. Envoy George C. Marshall, special field teams were assigned to various cities to keep the peace between opposing Communist and Nationalist military forces. With the simulated rank of colonel, Lei was assigned for a brief period in 1946 to the truce field team at Anyang, a city in northern Honan, astride the important Peking-Hankow (Pinghan) Railway. When the truce arrangements broke down completely over the winter of 1946–47, Lei was ordered back to his native Shansi. Little is known of his activities in the latter stages of the civil war aside from the fact that in 1948 he was serving as a deputy commander of a military subdistrict in northwestern Shansi, a command headed by Wang Shang-jung (q.v.), a veteran Communist military commander.

In August 1948 the Communists established the North China People's Government (NCPG) to govern those portions of north China then under their control. When the NCPG was staffed in the following month, Lei was named as a deputy director of the Civil Affairs Department. In February 1949 the NCPG moved from Shih-chia-chuang to Peking, and from that date until October 1949 when the Communists established their central government and absorbed the NCPG, the NCPG was an approximation of a central government. In December 1949, just two months after the inauguration of the central government, Lei was named to head the Staff Office of the Ministry of Internal Affairs as well as the Cadres Office in the same ministry. He held these two posts until September 1951 when he became a vice-minister in the Ministry of Trade, then responsible for both foreign trade and domestic commerce. It soon became evident that Lei's responsibilities involved foreign trade. The first concrete evidence of his new responsibility occurred in April 1952 when he was named as a member of the delegation sent by the PRC to the "International Economic Conference" in Moscow (see under Nan Han-ch'en), one of Peking's first major efforts to break out of the trade embargo imposed upon the Communist bloc by the Western allies as a result of the Korean War. Immediately upon the return of the delegation from Moscow, the Chinese formed the China Council for the Promotion of International Trade (May 1952). Lei, named as a member of the Council, had by 1954 been promoted to a vice-chairmanship (and since that date has served on occasion as the acting chairman in the absence of Chairman Nan Han-ch'en). This council in subsequent years has been the principal channel for the PRC to conduct trade negotiations with nations with which it does not have formal diplomatic relations.

In August 1952 the Ministry of Trade was divided into the ministries of Commerce and Foreign Trade. Logically, Lei was assigned as a vice-minister to the latter ministry; as of the mid-1960's he shares the distinction with Li Ch'iang (q.v.) of being the only men to have served continuously as vice-ministers in this important ministry. In addition, Lei has served from time to time as the acting minister in place of Minister Yeh Chi-chuang. In the 13-year period between 1952 and 1965, he has been extremely active as one of China's top international trade negotiators. In general, he has tended to deal more with the non-bloc nations than with the Communist bloc; he is known to have negotiated and signed trade agreements on at least 24 occasions with non-Communist countries in Europe, Africa, and Asia, as opposed to only five such agreements with Communist countries. Such negotiations have taken Lei abroad on several occasions, some of these trips being quite noteworthy. From April to July 1954 he was an adviser to Premier Chou En-lai at the Geneva Conference, which brought about a peace settlement in Indochina. While in Geneva Lei held a press conference for the large number of foreign correspondents attending this important conference; the press conference placed great stress upon the "bright prospect" for increased trade with "new China."

From March to May 1955 Lei was in Japan leading a trade delegation, and while there he signed a trade agreement with the Japanese. Though delegations to and from Japan became commonplace in the ensuing years, as of 1955 extremely few Chinese groups had been in Tokyo. In September 1958, during a visit to Tunisia, he signed the first Sino-Tunisian trade agreement—an agreement signed five years prior to the establishment of diplomatic ties between the two nations. From Tunis he proceeded to Morocco, another nation then lacking formal diplomatic ties with Peking. Not only did Lei negotiate a trade agreement, but before he left Rabat the Moroccans had agreed to the establishment of formal diplomatic relations. Several years later he was involved in similar negotiations when he accompanied Liao Ch'eng-chih to Italy, ostensibly at the invitation of the Italian Peace Committee. However, in his capacity as a vice-chairman of the China Council for the Promotion of International Trade, Lei negotiated an agreement whereby "non-official" commercial representative bureaus of each country were to be established in each other's country. (The bureaus were in fact opened in 1965 in Rome and Peking.)

Unlike the majority of Chinese leaders Lei has not had to devote much time to relatively peripheral activities (such as "peace" or "friendship" organizations). Even his few extracurricular duties have been rather closely related to his main function as a foreign trade specialist. For example,

from 1953 to 1956 he was a member of the Executive Committee of the All-China Federation of Industry and Commerce; from July 1955 to the present he has served on the Board of Directors of the Chinese People's Institute of Foreign Affairs; and since March 1957 he has been a member of the State Council's Overseas Chinese Affairs Commission. In short, Lei has apparently been categorized as a specialist and allowed to devote his time almost exclusively to his main activity, foreign trade.

1. *Kuang-ming jih-pao,* December 25, 1958.

Li Ch'ang

(c.1915–   ). Former youth leader; alternate member, CCP Central Committee.

Li Ch'ang was a leader of the December Ninth Movement, which began in 1935 as a student response to Japanese incursions into north China. In the formative years of the PRC he was the top youth leader in Shanghai and east China, and from 1954 to 1965 he was president of Harbin Industrial University. Li was elected an alternate member of the Party Central Committee in 1956.

Nothing is known of Li's career until 1935 when he was a student at Tsinghua University in Peking. North China in general and Peking in particular were in a constant state of agitation throughout 1935 as Japanese pressures on the Chiang Kai-shek government mounted. The situation was further aggravated in the final weeks of the year when the Japanese announced their intention to form an "autonomous" government in north China, which, as was apparent to all concerned, would have been a puppet regime under Japanese domination. Chinese of virtually all political persuasions were opposed to the steady Japanese incursions, but none were more incensed than the students in Peking. Student agitation reached the first in a series of climaxes on December 9, 1935, when thousands of youths demonstrated in Peking. These demonstrations, which came to be known in Chinese Communist history as the beginning of the December Ninth Movement, led to further demonstrations in the ensuing days and weeks in Peking and other north China cities. Li Ch'ang took part in these, and in later years he became one of the CCP's major chroniclers of these events. He and other Communist writers have attempted to portray the December Ninth events as Communist-inspired from the very outset,[1] but from other studies on the subject it is clear that simple patriotism and nationalism were initially the major motivations for the students.[2] On the other hand, there is little doubt that the CCP moved quickly to capitalize on the situation and there is also small room for doubt that the Party was playing an important behind-the-scenes role by the spring of 1936.

In the early days of 1936 the students organized four "propaganda corps" to disseminate patriotic themes to peasants in the countryside around Peking and Tientsin. Li was a member of the so-called Third Corps, whch consisted mainly of students at Tsinghua. This endeavor lasted only a few weeks, and then on February 1 several youth and student organizations met in Peking and decided to merge into the National Liberation Vanguard of China (NLVC). Li's account indicates that the NLVC was initially beset with a number of problems, including serious factional disputes and suppression by the "reactionary" authorities in Peking. Li's colleagues at this time included Chiang Nan-hsiang and Yao I-lin (qq.v.), both of whom were to become important members of the CCP. In February 1936 the NLVC headquarters at Tsinghua was reorganized under the direction of five students, among them Li. Two months later he joined the Communist Youth League, and in the League's branch at Tsinghua he was in charge of organization. Only a month later (May 1936), Li joined the CCP, and according to his account it was "during this period that many NLVC members in Tsinghua and other universities and middle schools joined the Party."

Although Li does not elaborate on the point, he has recorded that as of the spring of 1936 the NLVC members were in touch with Liu Shao-ch'i, who was then in Tientsin. Liu "transmitted" to the NLVC the CCP policy on the "national united front of resistance against Japan." Throughout the rest of 1936 and early 1937 the NLVC and other youth and student organizations engaged in varied activities designed to arouse the general populace against the Japanese. For example, anti-Japanese demonstrations and rallies were held, and attempts were made to befriend members of the KMT 29th Army (stationed in the Peking area), which was known to harbor men who felt that the Nationalist government had not done enough to resist Japanese encroachments. The NLVC also organized a reading society, a choir, and mess halls for the poor, but the "principal thing," in Li's words, was to conduct "training in guerrilla tactics and political studies." The NLVC members received lectures from a CCP member who was a guerrilla warfare expert, and in late April 1936 they organized two "battalions" from Tsinghua and Yenching universities to practice guerrilla operations.

In the summer of 1936 the NLVC set up a "military department," and in the months that followed there was an increase in paramilitary training. In this connection, in the autumn the students received military instructions from Chu Ming and Yuan Yeh-lieh, who were given this assignment by the CCP Peking Committee. (After the establishment of the PRC, Chu became political commissar of the PLA Signal Corps and Yuan became a vice-minister of Aquatic Products.) In the meantime, in the summer of 1936 Li was assigned to the general headquarters of the NLVC, and when it was reorganized in August he was placed in charge. At this same time, the CCP Peking Committee sent Huang Ching (q.v.) to be the Party man to exercise overall control.

In the latter part of 1936 the Peking students became more militant, and on December 12, 1936, they staged another large anti-Japanese demonstration. Li, still a student at Tsinghua, took part in this and, according to his own account, personally commanded the "procession," although Huang Ching was in charge of the entire demonstration. In this same month the NLVC general headquarters was placed in direct contact with P'eng Chen (q.v.), one of the Party's top underground operatives in north China. It was under P'eng's direction that the NLVC held its first congress in early February 1937. This was attended by 24 delegates representing 6,000 members from 18 different cities in China. (There were even NLVC members in Japan and Europe, but none of them attended the congress.) The delegates resolved to step up the pace of their work among all strata of society, to expand the NLVC, and to continue with their military and paramilitary activities. Li was elected as head (tsung-tui chang) of the NLVC, whose Executive Committee numbered 39. An impressive percentage of the 39 went on to have significant careers. In addition to Li, Lu P'ing, Wu Heng, and Chiang Ming (qq.v.), the following held posts of importance in the post-1949 period: Ch'ien Ying-lin, vice-minister of Railways: Hsieh Pang-chih, ambassador to Bulgaria; Chang Chen-huan, a member of the Party Committee of the Scientific and Technological Commission for National Defense; Chao Te-tsun, governor of Heilungkiang, purged with Kao Kang (q.v.) in 1955; Ku Ta-ch'uan, vice-minister of agriculture; Li Lien-pi, counselor of the embassy in Poland; Ting Hao-ch'uan, acting president of Kirin University; and Miss Yang K'o-ping, secretary of the CCP Anshan Municipal Committee.

In the spring of 1937 the CCP instructed Li to go to Yenan. Huang Ching and Yang Hsueh-ch'eng went with him; the latter, who was then working with the CCP branch at Tsinghua, was a Party official in a Communist guerrilla base in Hupeh until his death toward the end of the Sino-Japanese War. They arrived in time for May Day celebrations and then took part as delegates to the CCP National Conference, at which Mao Tse-tung spoke. After the conference Li and the others attended another conference devoted to work in "white areas," that is, underground work in KMT-controlled areas. Liu Shao-ch'i, the featured speaker at this meeting, instructed them to legalize their "hitherto illegal activities" and, in view of the imminence of war with Japan, to prepare to "take off their robes and bear weapons and join guerrilla bands." En route to and from Yenan, Li and his colleagues met and conferred with a number of top CCP political and military leaders, including Chu Te, Lin Piao, Wang Chen, Ho Lung, and Kuan Hsiang-ying (qq.v.).

Li and others arrived back in Peking only a few weeks before war erupted on July 7, 1937. The NLVC immediately joined with other patriotic organizations to form an *ad hoc* association to assist Sung Che-yuan's 29th Army, the only viable Chinese force in the area, in resisting the Japanese. However, within two weeks Sung was forced to evacuate Peking and Tientsin. Being marked men, the NLVC members left these cities—some went to frontline areas to join Chinese regular or guerrilla units, and others went to Communist districts which had not yet been attacked. Li and Chiang Nan-hsiang went to Tientsin. Soon afterwards, Li made his way to Taiyuan, the Shansi capital, which in the early weeks of the war was a major center for Communist activity in north China and also the temporary seat for the NLVC headquarters. When Taiyuan fell to the Japanese in November 1937, the NLVC headquarters were transferred to Lin-fen in southwest Shansi where Li and his colleagues, including Lu P'ing, engaged in various activities to gain popular support for the war effort.

When Lin-fen was captured in February 1938, both the NLVC and the Party's North China Bureau were transferred to Sian in Shensi. Li claims that his efforts there to make the NLVC an "open and legal organization" were suppressed by the KMT and that in the late spring of 1938, fearing arrest, he was forced into hiding. He was assisted at this time by Lin Po-ch'ü (q.v.), then in charge of the Communists' Eighth Route Army liaison office in Sian. In the early summer, disguised as an Eighth Route Army officer, Li went to Wuhan where, with his NLVC colleagues Chiang Nan-hsiang, Yang Hsueh-ch'eng, and Yü Kuang-yuan (q.v.), he engaged in youth work under the direction of the Party's Yangtze Bureau. A short time later, in August 1938, the KMT ordered the dissolution of the NLVC, and in the same month Li, once again in the disguise of an Eighth Route Army officer, accompanied Chou En-lai back to Yenan. In November, at a youth conference in Yenan, the NLVC was absorbed by the Association of Youths for National Salvation, and this organization, in turn, was placed under the control of the Joint Office of China Youth Organizations for National Salvation (see under Feng Wen-pin).

There are no reports about Li's activities for the next decade, but it seems safe to assume that he, like other members of the December Ninth group (e.g., Chiang Nan-hsiang, q.v.), continued to engage in youth work. In any case, in April 1949, soon after the Communist armies marched into Peking, he was elected a member of the Central Committee and the Standing Committee of the New Democratic Youth League (later renamed the Communist Youth League). It is noteworthy that five of the nine Standing Committee members had been participants in the December Ninth Movement, the others being Chiang Nan-hsiang, Lu P'ing, Jung Kao-t'ang (qq.v.), and Sung I-p'ing. In the following month he was elected a member of the First National Committee of the All-China Federation of Democratic Youth, the second most important youth organization. When Shanghai fell to the PLA in late May, Li was assigned there, and he immediately became chairman of the preparatory committee for the East China branches of both of the above-mentioned youth organizations, as well as a member of the preparatory committee of the Shanghai Democratic Youth Federation and the secretary of the Shanghai Work Committee of the Youth League. In brief, during the formative period of Communist rule, Li was the top youth leader for both east China and Shanghai.

In addition to his work with youth organizations, Li also held other posts at the national, regional, and municipal levels. In May 1949 he was made a member of the Culture and Education Control Committee of the Shanghai Military Control Commission. In October the Communists established the All-China Athletic Federation under the chairmanship of Feng Wen-pin; Li was a member of the Federation's Preparatory Committee from then until mid-1952. During the winter of 1949–50 the East China Military and Administrative Committee (ECMAC) was established; Li served as a member of both the ECMAC and its subordinate Land Reform Committee. In late 1950 and early 1951 he was a member of a youth delegation led by Feng Wen-pin, then head of the Youth League, which visited the Soviet Union. His stock within the League rose notably in November 1951 when he was promoted to membership on the League's Secretariat (the highest organ within the League), which then consisted of only six men. Li was listed fourth on the Secretariat, after Feng Wen-pin, Liao Ch'eng-chih, and Chiang Nan-hsiang (qq.v.). In the same month he was named to the National Committee of a welfare organization known as the Chinese People's Committee for the Protection of Children.

In September 1952 Li was appointed director of the Young Workers' Department of the All-China Federation of Labor (a post he held only until the next May), and at the same time he was removed from the ECMAC and transferred to Peking. Two months later, in November, he was appointed a vice-chairman of the newly established Commission for the Elimination of

Illiteracy. The commission, chaired by Ch'u T'u-nan (q.v.), was subordinate to the Government Administration Council (the cabinet) until the constitutional government was inaugurated in September 1954. In January 1953 he received another appointment in a Government Administration Council organ when he became a member of the newly formed Committee for the Implementation of the Marriage Law. In the meantime, Li continued his work in the Youth League; he gave the main report, which was devoted to the development of the organization and cadre work, at a League work conference held in late November and early December 1952. In June–July 1953, at the Youth League's Second National Congress, Li spoke on amendments to the League's regulations. This talk, however, represented his farewell to an active role in youth work. He was re-elected to the League's Central Committee and its Standing Committee, but most significant was the fact that he was not reappointed to the Secretariat. Similarly, at this same time (June 1953), Li was not re-elected to any post within the All-China Federation of Democratic Youth. Li continued to hold his Youth League posts until the Third Congress in May 1957, but at that time he was removed from that organization.

In June 1954 Li was transferred to Harbin where he succeeded Ch'en K'ang-pai as president of Harbin Industrial (*kung-yeh*) University, one of China's more important institutes of higher learning. He held this post for nearly 11 years (until February 1965) and served concurrently as secretary of the CCP Committee within the school. Very little was reported during that period about his work at the university, but other evidence suggests that he performed to the satisfaction of his superiors in Peking. From 1954 to 1958 Li served as a deputy from Harbin to the First NPC. In September 1956, at the Eighth National Congress of the CCP, he was elected an alternate member of the Party Central Committee. Four years later, in March 1960, he was elected a member of the CCP Heilungkiang Committee, then headed by Ouyang Ch'in (q.v.).

For a month in July–August 1964 Li was in Cuba as head of an eight-member delegation sent to Havana to take part in the celebrations marking the 11th anniversary of Fidel Castro's revolutionary movement. This apparently signaled a new assignment for Li, because in October he was made a vice-chairman of the State Council's Commission for Cultural Relations with Foreign Countries. Six weeks later, as a representative of "organizations for peaceful and friendly relations with foreign countries," he was named to the Fourth National Committee of the CPPCC. Moreover, at the close of the inaugural session of the Fourth Committee in early January 1965, he was made a member of the CPPCC Standing Committee. A few weeks later, as already noted, he was formally removed

from the presidency of the Harbin Industrial University, and in April 1965 he was appointed president of the Second Institute of Foreign Languages, located in Peking. A few days later, in early May, he went to Moscow as a member of the delegation led by Lin Feng (q.v.) to attend the celebrations commemorating the 20th anniversary of the victory over Nazi Germany. Lin's delegation returned home a week later, but Li proceeded to Rumania as head of a cultural delegation where he signed a cultural cooperation agreement. He continued to be active until mid-1966, but a year later, during the course of the Great Proletarian Cultural Revolution, he was denounced as a "revisionist."

1. *SCMM* 296, pp. 27–36; *SCMM* 297, pp. 28–43; Li Ch'ang, et al., *"I-erh-chiu" hui-i-lu* (Reminiscences of "December Ninth"; Peking, 1961); Shih Li-te, et al., *The Roar of a Nation* (Peking, 1963).

2. John Israel, *Student Nationalism in China, 1927–1937* (Stanford, Calif., 1966), pp. 111–156; John Israel, "The December 9th Movement: A Case Study in Chinese Communist Historiography," *The China Quarterly*, no. 23:140–169 (July–September 1965); Jessie G. Lutz, "December 9, 1935: Student Nationalism and the China Christian Colleges," *The Journal of Asian Studies*, 26.4:627–648 (August 1967); Edgar Snow, *Journey to the Beginning* (London, 1960), pp. 139–146; Nym Wales, *Notes on the Chinese Student Movement, 1935–1936* (Madison, Conn., 1959), pp. 26–34, *passim*.

Li Che-jen

(c.1910–   ). Foreign trade specialist; Vice-minister, Ministry for the Allocation of Materials.

Li Che-jen was probably born about 1910 to judge from the period when he was a college student. He was one of the more active participants in the December Ninth Movement, which took its name from a series of demonstrations which started among students in Peking on December 9, 1935, in opposition to Japanese incursions into North China. One outgrowth of the movement was the formation, early in 1936, of the National Liberation Vanguard of China (NLVC), initially composed mainly of students from north China colleges (see under Li Ch'ang). Li Che-jen was then a student at one of the schools in Tientsin and took part in the formation of the NLVC branch in Tientsin early in 1936. He was, in fact, probably the head of the Tientsin group. One of the first efforts of these students was to send teams into the countryside around Peking to explain to simple peasants the need for unity to oppose the Japanese. Li was among those who took part in such activities in early 1936. A year later, in February 1937, the NLVC held its first Congress in Peking—

a congress of 24 delegates representing a reported 6,000 youths. By this time the Communist Party was deeply involved, as suggested by the fact that P'eng Ch'en (then a senior Party official in north China) attended the congress. Li was among those elected as "responsible persons" in the headquarters of the NLVC in Peking.[1]

When the Japanese struck in force in mid-1937, the vast majority of students at institutes of higher learning in Peking fled the city. Li, almost certainly already a Communist Youth League member (and very possibly also a Party member), fled to the Communist-held areas. Eventually he was assigned to south Shansi and by the close of the war against Japan was working in the T'ai-yueh region (southern Shansi), which came under the military control of Liu Po-ch'eng's 129th Division of the Eighth Route Army. It may also have put Li in contact with such important Party leaders as Po I-po and Li Hsueh-feng (qq.v.), then working in this same area.

When the Communists came to power in 1949, Li remained in north China, assuming (by at least July 1950) the post of head of the Research Section of the Party's North China Bureau, the bureau then headed by Po I-po. Also, by April 1951, Li was concurrently a deputy director of the Finance and Economics Work Committee of the same bureau, a committee directed by Liu Lan-t'ao. In the latter capacity, Li delivered a major report at a conference in Peking in March 1951, devoted to the promotion of the sale of native products. It is not known how long he held these North China Bureau posts; perhaps it was until mid-1954 when the Bureau was abolished.

Li assumed two new posts in 1950, one semiofficial and the other under the central government. In July 1950 he was elected a member of the provisional Board of Directors of the important mass organization known as the All-China Federation of Cooperatives, whose task it was to stimulate economic relations between the countryside and the cities. He attended the first conference of the provisional Board in November 1950 and was selected as one of the seven members of the Standing Committee; he was also re-elected to the Board and its Standing Committee when the organization was formally inaugurated in July 1952. However, when the Federation was transformed into the All-China Federation of Supply and Marketing Cooperatives in mid-1954, Li was removed from both posts. The other post he assumed in 1950 was as head of the Agriculture Department of the Ministry of North China Affairs. The ministry was established in September 1950 under Minister Liu Lan-t'ao; Li was appointed in November 1950 and held the post until December 1951 when the ministry was transformed into the North China Administrative Committee (NCAC),

thereby being placed on an organizational basis closer to the other large administrative areas of China. Under the NCAC, which had jurisdiction over the five provinces of Hopeh, Shansi, Chahar, Pingyuan, and Suiyuan, Li was appointed to NCAC membership (December 1951), as director of the Trade Bureau (January 1952), and as a vice-chairman of the Finance and Economics Planning Committee (March 1952).

When the NCAC was reorganized in January 1953, he was transferred to the central government, being assigned to the Ministry of Foreign Trade where he was selected as a vice-minister, a post he was to hold until September 1959. At approximately this same period, he also took part in the establishment of the All-China Federation of Industry and Commerce, the organization designed to gain maximum cooperation from leading industrialists and businessmen, the majority of them non-Communists. Li served on the preparatory committee (from June 1952) and when the Federation was formally established at a nationwide meeting in October–November 1953, he was named to membership on the first Executive Committee, retaining this position until the next conference in December 1956.

As a vice-minister of Foreign Trade, Li's responsibilities were confined almost exclusively to trade with the Communist bloc, and with the USSR in particular. On four different occasions he led trade delegations to Moscow where he signed trade agreements or protocols in February 1955, December 1955, April 1957 and February 1959. He also headed trade groups abroad which led to the signing of agreements in Mongolia in April 1954 and in Poland in April 1957. Li also signed other trade pacts in Peking, each with a Communist nation excepting only an August 1956 accord with India, by which China agreed to the sale of rice. His concentration on trade with bloc countries was also illustrated in two articles he wrote; one was in the Tientsin *Ta-kung pao* (October 6, 1954) and the other in the English-language monthly *China Reconstructs* (August 1955). On at least two occasions during the period when he was a vice-minister of Foreign Trade, Li served as the acting minister in place of Yeh Chi-chuang. Also during this period he served as a Hunan deputy to the First NPC (1954–1959) but was not re-elected to the Second NPC, which opened in April 1959.

When the central government underwent a reorganization in September 1959 Li was transferred from the Ministry of Foreign Trade to a vice-ministership in the Ministry of Commerce. He served briefly (until February 1960) under Ch'eng Tzu-hua but thereafter was under Minister Yao I-lin who, like Li, was an active participant in the December Ninth Movement in 1935. Virtually nothing was heard of Li during his year and a half in the Ministry of Commerce, and then in April 1961 he was again transferred, this time to the State Council's Bureau for Economic Relations with Foreign Countries. The Bureau, headed by alternate Central Committee member Fang I, was in charge of China's foreign aid program. When it was elevated to the commission (or ministerial) level in June 1964, Li was not reappointed. In the meantime, however, he had assumed other positions. In May 1963 the State Administrative Bureau of Supplies was established under the State Council to oversee the allocation of strategic materials in industry and agriculture. When a North Vietnamese technical delegation was in Peking in August 1963 to study supply work, Li was identified as an official in this Bureau (but without an exact title). Then in September he was officially appointed as a deputy director. In October 1964 the Bureau was elevated to the ministerial level and named the Ministry for the Allocation of Materials. In December Li was appointed as a vice-minister, a position he continues to hold. Another post of importance that he held in the 1963–64 period was membership on the State Economic Commission (September 1963 to December 1964), the organization charged with annual planning under the chairmanship of Po I-po, who was probably an associate of Li during the Sino-Japanese War period.

Li's normal working life seems relatively unencumbered with the many protocol functions (e.g., banquets, airport farewells) that consume so much of the time of many Chinese leaders. Rather, he appears to be one of a growing corps of "technocrats" whose talents are mainly utilized in the governmental organizations requiring a fairly high degree of technical knowledge and ability.

1. *Chung-kuo ch'ing-nien* (China youth), November 16, 1961, translated in *SCMM* 297.

Li Ch'iang

Telecommunications specialist; vice-minister of Foreign Trade.

Li Ch'iang is known to have been a Party member as early as 1929. In that year the Party was searching for two persons to undergo training in telecommunications work. The only requirements were that they be Party members and college graduates. One of the two was to study the mechanical aspects of radio work and the other the operational side. Li, who must have been a college graduate, was selected to study the mechanical side of radio work. From the context of the Communist-published article on which this information is based, it is clear that Li had not received his college training in a technical field and therefore had to begin anew in this field.

His telecommunications training took place in the French concession in Shanghai. Because Party members were fugitives from Kuomintang authority in 1929, Li joined together with a few radio supply merchants and opened a small store which served as a cover while he learned his trade. In 1930 a small radio station was secretly established in Shanghai to keep in contact with Party organizations in south and north China and in the Yangtze River area; in the same year a class was set up in Shanghai to train radio personnel for the Central Soviet district in Kiangsi and for the Red Army. Li probably participated in these activities in 1930, but specific information is lacking.[1]

Nothing was heard of Li for almost two decades although his technical specialization would suggest that he was employed in covert communications work or, perhaps, in work at Radio Yenan during the Sino-Japanese War. In any event he maintained his specialization because in August 1948, when elected to the Sixth Executive Committee of the All-China Federation of Labor (a post he held until 1953), he was identified as a "radio specialist." Furthermore, in late 1949 he was noted as having served as an engineer at the Research Institute of the "People's Posts and Telecommunications Committee" in Moscow; presumably he was in Moscow in the 1948–49 period.

When the Communists were forming the central administration in 1949, Li took part in those phases requiring a technical background. For example, in July 1949 he was a member of the preparatory committee for the First All-China Natural Scientific Workers' Conference. And in May 1949 he was serving as one of the four deputy-directors (under Wang Cheng, another telecommunications specialist) of the Telecommunications Bureau of the People's Revolutionary Military Council (PRMC). When this bureau was transferred (with a slight alteration in the bureau title) from the PRMC to the Ministry of Posts and Telecommunications (December 1949), Li was named as director. In the same month he was appointed as director of the Broadcasting Affairs Bureau under the Government Administration Council's Press Administration. Among other activities, this bureau had control over Radio Peking. Li directed this bureau until the Press Administration was abolished in August 1952.

Shortly after receiving these appointments, Li was reported in Moscow (presumably in the entourage of the delegation taken there by Mao Tse-tung and Chou En-lai). On February 7, 1950, he signed two pacts, the Sino-Soviet Agreement on the Establishment of Telecommunications and the Sino-Soviet Agreement on the Exchange of Mail and Parcels, of historic significance if only because they were the first two official agreements signed between Soviet Russia and Communist China.

Already established as one of China's senior

communications specialists, it was natural that Li should have been designated in 1950 as Peking's delegate to the International Telecommunications Union (ITU) and to the International High Frequency Broadcasting Conference held in Florence, Italy. However, political complications prevented the attendance of Chinese Communist delegations at the conferences.

In 1950 a Radio Bureau was established in the Ministry of Posts and Telecommunications and apparently absorbed the Telecommunications Bureau, which Li had headed since December 1949. In any event, Li was appointed director of the Radio Bureau in July 1950 and retained the post until 1952.

By mid-1952 Li had given up all his posts in telecommunications work and was transferred to the field of foreign trade. Such a change was not fortuitous. The growing complexities of the Chinese economy required an increased number of specialists to deal with foreign trade and aid problems, especially vis-à-vis the Soviet Union. It was in August 1952 that Li was appointed as a vice-minister of Foreign Trade, a post he still retains. In the same month, he took up the position of Commercial Counselor of the Chinese Embassy in Moscow. He was thus present in Moscow to serve as an adviser to a delegation led by Chou En-lai in August–September 1952 and was also on hand for the lengthy negotiations in Moscow conducted by Li Fu-ch'un (q.v.), one of Peking's leading economic specialists. These important talks culminated in agreements by which Moscow granted assistance for China's First Five-Year Plan (1953–1957).

Li remained in Moscow until 1955. Not long after his return to Peking he was selected to be a member of the Department of Technical Sciences, one of four departments established under the Academy of Sciences in June 1955. In June of the following year he became a member of the Chinese side on the Joint Committee for Sino-Soviet Scientific and Technical Cooperation (which meets once or twice a year in Moscow or Peking). In his capacity as acting chairman of the Joint Committee, Li signed protocols on cooperation at the fifth, sixth, and eighth sessions of the Committee; he took a nine-member delegation to Moscow for the fifth meeting in December 1956, whereas the sixth and eighth sessions were held in Peking in July 1957 and January 1959. In the meantime, in October 1956 he was identified among a group of persons engaged in the work preparatory to the formation of the Institute of Electronics, under the Academy's Department of Technical Sciences. Li was subsequently named to head this Institute but was replaced by early 1959. A related appointment was made in May 1957 when the State Council's Scientific Planning Commission was reorganized. Li was named as a member and a deputy secretary-general, holding these positions

until the Commission was merged with another organization in November 1958. He received still another post in this line of work in about 1959 when he was named a vice-chairman of the Preparatory Committee of the China Electronics Society, an organization under the China Scientific and Technical Association; Li held this post until about 1961.

Beginning in 1958 Li became particularly active in foreign trade negotiations, both in Peking and abroad. He was obviously assigned to conduct trade relations with Communist nations; of the many agreements and protocols he signed through 1964, every one was with a bloc nation. Li has visited the following countries to negotiate trade or aid agreements: Poland (1959), Czechoslovakia (1959), North Korea (1960, 1963), Mongolia (1960), the USSR (1961, 1962, 1963), and North Vietnam (1963). On all but two occasions he led the Chinese delegations. Perhaps the most difficult negotiations were with the USSR in view of the growing strains in the alliance during Li's three visits to Moscow in the 1961–1963 period. In addition to these visits, he made two more trips to East Europe in 1964. In August he accompanied Vice-premier Li Hsien-nien to Rumania as a member of the delegation to the 20th anniversary celebration of the Rumanian "liberation"; the group utilized this visit to inspect a number of petroleum installations. And in October 1964 he accompanied another vice-premier, Ulanfu, on a visit to East Germany to celebrate the 15th anniversary of the founding of the East German regime.

In January 1960 the General Bureau for Economic Relations with Foreign Countries was established under the State Council, presumably to manage the Chinese foreign aid programs. No appointments were made to the bureau until April 1961, when Fang I was named as the director and Li as one of the deputy directors. In June 1964 this bureau was raised to the commission (or ministerial) level, but Li was not appointed as a vice-chairman until March 1965. In late 1964 he was elected as a deputy from Anhwei to the Third NPC, which held its first session at the end of the year and early 1965.

1. *Wu-ling feng-yun* (The gathering clouds on the Wuling Mountains; Hong Kong, 1961), pp. 54–58.

Li Chieh-po

(c.1910–   ; Feng-jun hsien, Hopeh). Labor leader; alternate member, CCP Central Committee.

Li Chieh-po (whose name is sometimes transliterated Li Hsieh-po or Li Chi-po) has been in the Communist labor movement since the late twenties. From the late forties to the sixties he was abroad on numerous occasions, usually in connection with trade union activities. He has been an alternate member of the CCP Central Committee since 1958.

Li was born about 1910 in Feng-jun hsien, Hopeh, midway between Peking and the coastal city of Chinwangtao (Ch'in-huang-tao). Described by the Communists as an "intellectual,"[1] he joined the CCP at an early age, possibly while still a student. After the KMT-CCP split in 1927, Li worked as a laborer on the railways and in the coal mines in the Peking–Tientsin–T'angshan area and later became a labor organizer in these enterprises. Sometime between the Japanese takeover in Manchuria (1931) and the outbreak of the Sino-Japanese War (1937), he worked in the Party underground in Manchuria where he was reportedly imprisoned for a time by the Japanese.

When war broke out in 1937 Li went to Shansi where he worked for the League of Self-Sacrifice for National Salvation, an organization established by Shansi warlord Yen Hsi-shan, but strongly influenced by the Communists (see under Po I-po). Later he was transferred to Yenan, probably about 1940. American journalist Edgar Snow, interviewing Li in 1960, reported that he was a "veteran of Yenan Academy," presumably a reference to Yenan University, which was established in 1941 through a merger of several schools in the Yenan area. Snow also reported that Li had been a "protégé" of Politburo member Liu Shao-ch'i for 20 years (i.e., from about 1940).[2] After studying at the Yenan school Li became a member of the Party Central Committee's Industrial Workers' Committee (Chih-kung wei-yuan-hui), then headed by top labor leader Teng Fa (q.v.) In this capacity he had close connections with the Shensi-Kansu-Ninghsia Border Region Labor Federation, which had been created in 1940. The federation claimed a membership of 55,000, of whom 63 per cent were farm laborers, 22 per cent handicraft workers, and only 15 per cent industrial workers.[3] In the spring of 1945 the federation joined with other labor organizations in Communist-held bases in north China to establish the Liberated Areas Trade Union Federation Preparatory Committee. Teng Fa was named chairman of the Preparatory Committee, with Li serving as its secretary-general.

By 1948 Li had returned to Manchuria, then almost wholly under Communist control, where he played an important role in Party efforts to reactivate the labor movement. After several months of preparation these efforts resulted in the convocation of the Sixth National Labor Congress, which purported to be a continuation of the congresses supported by both the Communists and Nationalists in the 1920's. The Fifth Congress had been held secretly in Shanghai in 1929, whereas the Sixth Congress met in Communist-held Harbin in August 1948. Li, who by now had 20 years' experience in the labor movement, was a dominant figure at the meetings. In his capacity as a member of the Northeast Trade Union Council and as secretary-general of the Liberated Areas Trade Union he served on the preparatory committee for the Sixth Congress. He also served on the Congress presidium (steering committee) and gave the report on the work of the Credentials Committee, which had selected the 500 delegates to the Congress. Li was elected to the Executive Committee and to the smaller and more important Standing Committee of the All-China Federation of Labor (ACFL). He also served as the ACFL secretary-general until the spring of 1949 when he relinquished the post to Hsu Chih-chen.

In addition to the national organization, the ACFL has a number of constituent trade unions. Li has centered his activity on the transportation workers, whom he represented at a number of meetings of the Communist-dominated World Federation of Trade Unions (WFTU), held in Europe (see below). From 1949 to 1950 he was chairman of the preparatory committee of the China Railway Workers' Trade Union and, when the union was formally established in February 1950, became its first chairman. He continued in this post until 1956 when he was succeeded by Wang Chih-chieh, another labor leader.

In late 1949, Li entered a new phase of his career as a specialist in international liaison with the world Communist labor movement—a phase that occupied much of his time over the next eight years. This began in December 1949 when he was a member of the Chinese delegation to the WFTU-sponsored Trade Unions' International of Land and Air Transport Workers, which met in Bucharest. He was made a member of the Executive Committee of the Land and Air Transport Workers' International at this time and was promoted to a vice-chairmanship by June 1952. More important, from the spring of 1950 until 1957, he served on the WFTU Executive Committee.

In September 1950, Li led an 11-member delegation of the China Railway Union to Warsaw for an executive committee session of the Trade Unions' International of Land and Air Transport Workers. He ended his affiliation with this organization about 1953 but continued connections with the WFTU Executive Committee until 1957. In October 1953, Li was re-elected to the Committee at the Third WFTU Congress in Vienna, which he attended as secretary-general of the Chinese delegation headed by Liu Ning-i. The Fourth WFTU Congress was held in Leipzig in October 1957, at which time Li was dropped from the Executive Committee.

When the Seventh National Congress of the ACFL met in Peking in May 1953, its name was changed to the All-China Federation of Trade Unions (ACFTU). It was attended by over 800 delegates and 73 foreign observers, including Louis Saillant, the secretary-general of the WFTU. As in the case of the 1948 labor congress, Li played an active role in the 1953 meetings. He served as a member of the presidium (steering committee) for the Congress and also presented a report on Chinese railway workers. At the close of the meetings he assumed more important posts than he had previously held. He was re-elected to both the Executive Committee and the permanent Presidium (the new designation for the Standing Committee). In addition, he was elected to the permanent Secretariat. The Presidium is responsible for carrying out the decisions of the Executive Committee when the latter is not in session, and the Secretariat is charged with the task of attending to the routine work under the direction of the Presidium.

Reflecting Li's active role in the international relations of the ACFTU, he succeeded Liu Ning-i by mid-1955 as head of its International Liaison Department. He was replaced in this position by Ch'en Yü (q.v.) in 1957. It was also in 1957 that Li began to be phased out of the higher echelons of the trade union movement, although the death of a colleague brought about a reversal of this situation in 1958 (see below). Li attended the Eighth National Congress of the ACFTU in December 1957 where he served as a member of the Congress presidium (steering committee). Although he was re-elected to the Executive Committee, he was neither re-elected to the permanent Presidium nor to the Secretariat, the two key organs of the ACFTU. Another indication of a change in career emphasis was his identification in February 1958 as a deputy director under Yang Shang-k'un (q.v.) of the Party Central Committee's important Staff Office. Not long afterward, in May 1958, he was elected an alternate member of the Central Committee at the second session of the Eighth Party Congress. However, the death of ACFTU Chairman Lai Jo-yü (q.v.) in the same month necessitated a major shift in the Federation's leadership. Liu Ning-i was named to replace Lai Jo-yü, and Li Chieh-po was made one of the vice-chairmen. He was also returned to membership on the Federation's Presidium and Secretariat. The effect of these changes was to make Li one of the two or three most important labor leaders in China. Owing to his transfer back to a top executive post in the ACFTU it is likely that Li was removed from his position in the Party Staff Office. In any event, he has apparently not been active in the department since the single identification in 1958.

Because of his extensive connections with the international labor movement, particularly in the early and mid-1950's, Li has frequently traveled abroad. In addition to the already described visits to Bucharest, Warsaw, and Vienna (1949–1953), he participated in the following delegations. 1951: secretary-general, Chinese people's "comfort" delegation to North Korea, May; member, Chinese delegation to the fifth session of the General Council of the WFTU, East Berlin, November; 1953: leader, WFTU delegation to the ninth session of the United Nations' Economic Commission for Asia and the Far East (ECAFE) in Bandung, Indonesia, February; 1954: chief, WFTU delegation to the 10th session of ECAFE in Kandy, Ceylon, February; chief, Chinese trade union delegation to India to study labor problems, February–March; 1955: chief, WFTU delegation of "observers" to an ECAFE meeting in Japan, March–April; 1960: deputy-chief (under Li Te-ch'üan), Chinese delegation to 15th anniversary of "liberation of Korea"; 1961: leader, 10-member Chinese trade union delegation to Japan at the invitation of the General Confederation of Trade Unions (SOHYO), January–February (he attended the 29th Congress of the Japan Mine Workers' Union, an affiliate of SOHYO, speaking before the Congress on February 6); 1963: leader, Chinese trade union delegation to Colombo, Ceylon, to attend the 16th annual meeting of the Ceylon Trade Union Federation, December.

Although Li's activities have been overwhelmingly concentrated in the labor field, he has also held posts in both the executive and legislative branches of government. Representing the labor federation he attended the first session of the CPPCC in September 1949 when the central government was brought into existence. He did not participate in the Second CPPCC (1954–1959), but when the Third National Committee of the CPPCC was established in April 1959, he was named to both the National and Standing Committees. He was again named to the National Committee (but not the Standing Committee) for the Fourth National Committee, which first met in December 1964–January 1965. In 1954 he was elected to the First NPC as a deputy from Tientsin and attended the first session in September 1954, which inaugurated the constitutional government. He was also in the Second NPC (1959–1964) as a deputy from Hopeh (which had absorbed the Tientsin constituency in the interim). In the executive branch of government he has served as vice-chairman of the Spare-time Education Commission, which was established in February 1960 under the State Council. When interviewed by Edgar Snow in 1960, Li made it clear that he devoted a great deal of time to the problem of spare-time education. He claimed, for example, that the ACFTU operated "almost as many schools as the Ministry of Education. In fact, you might call the Trade Union Federation a ministry of part-time education."[4]

Although less important than his role in

either the trade union movement or the government, the affairs of the "people's" organizations have taken some of Li's time. He was a member of the First Executive Board of the Sino-Soviet Friendship Association from 1949 to 1954, and from 1950 to 1954 he served on the Supervisory Committee of the All-China Federation of Co-operatives. From 1954 to at least 1959 he was a member of the Chinese People's Association for Cultural Relations with Foreign Countries, and he has been a Council member of the China-Korea Friendship Association since 1960.

Edgar Snow describes Li as a "ruggedly built man," who is "obviously an executive of great energy" with a "detailed grasp of his work." He told Snow that he often worked 16 hours a day.[5] If true, these energies and abilities may help to explain Li's rise to the higher echelons of the trade union movement.

1. Li Kuang, ed., *Ti-liu-tz'u ch'üan-kuo lao-tung ta-hui* (The Sixth All-China Labor Congress; Hong Kong, 1948), p. 55.
2. Edgar Snow, *The Other Side of the River* (London, 1963), p. 234.
3. Nym Wales, *The Chinese Labor Movement* (New York, 1945), p. 91.
4. Snow, p. 235.
5. *Ibid.*, pp. 234, 236.

Li Chien-chen

(1907–　　　　; Feng-shun hsien, Kwangtung). Secretary, Kwangtung CCP Committee; alternate member, CCP Control Commission; alternate member, CCP Central Committee.

One of the early women members of the CCP, Miss Li Chien-chen has spent most of her life in her native Kwangtung. A veteran of the Long March, she is now one of the Kwangtung Party secretaries and is also a member of the Party's Central Control Commission. When American authoress Nym Wales visited Yenen in mid-1937, Li gave her a short autobiographic statement, an account that provides most of the information for this biography through the mid-thirties.[1]

Li was born in Feng-shun hsien, about 50 miles northwest of Swatow in Kwangtung province. Her parents were coolies who worked as hod carriers for house builders. One of 12 children (10 sons and two girls), Li was adopted in infancy by a family that lived in the East River area of Kwangtung near Hai-lu-feng, later to become famous as an important early Communist soviet (see under P'eng P'ai). At the age of 17 Li was married to a son of her adopted family (petty merchants who also owned about half an acre of land). The husband liked her, but Li stated that she "did not love him because he was ten years older than I." When a peasant uprising occurred in the mid-twenties, Li was chosen to

engage in "revolutionary work." She explained that the "revolutionary slogans then demanded equality of men and women and individual choice in marriage instead of the old family contract, and this was the main slogan which attracted me." Li's husband joined the CCP in 1926 and Li joined herself in the following year.

In April 1927, as a local repercussion of the fighting between the KMT and the CCP, a peasant uprising took place in the East River (Tung-chiang) area, allegedly in opposition to oppressive landlords. Li took part in the revolt as head of the propaganda team, and her brother-in-law, who led the uprising, was executed by KMT troops. Four members of her adopted family were killed in early revolutionary struggles, including her husband who fell in battle in 1930. Following the abortive 1927 uprising in the East River District, about 140 of the insurgent peasants fled the area to join the forces of Ku Ta-ts'un (q.v.), one of the most important of the early Kwangtung CCP guerrilla leaders. In Li's autobiographical account, she states that she remained with Ku's troops for over a year; they fought, redistributed the land, and "made propaganda," mainly in eastern Kwangtung near the Fukien border. Li also helped to organize coolies and workers and in 1928 was engaged in political work for Ku's forces. In the following year, still under Ku's jurisdiction, Li was in charge of women's work in the small city of Ta-p'u, Kwangtung, about 80 miles north of Swatow.

The areas where Li had been working in Kwangtung were quite close to sections of western Fukien that were under partial Communist control and where the Fukien Soviet had been established under the leadership of Chang Ting-ch'eng, Teng Tzu-hui, and T'an Chen-lin (qq.v.). Li was sent there by the Party in 1930 to work in a branch of the Communist government. In 1933 she was sent to the central Soviet capital in Juichin, Kiangsi, where at the Second All-China Congress of Soviets, held in January–February 1934, she was elected a member of the Central Executive Committee, the governing body of the Chinese Soviet Republic. She remained in Juichin until the Long March began in the fall of 1934.

During the Long March Li led the women's squad of the First Cadre Company, a company that included such prominent Communists as Lu Ting-i, Hsieh Chueh-tsai, and Hsu T'e-li (qq.v.).[2] In her own account, Li states that she was a "political director" during the course of the year-long trek, most of which she made on foot.

When Nym Wales interviewed Li in mid-1937, the latter was said to be "Chief of the Soviet Women's Department," a post presumably subordinate to the Party Central Committee. Li said that she was then married to Teng Chün-hsiung (whose antecedents are otherwise unknown) and had a 12-year old child. Nym Wales has described Li as among the Party elite who were self-educated and who received training at the "Chinese Red Academy," training she may have received at Juichin prior to the Long March or in north Shensi where the Red Army Academy was re-created at the end of the March. Li's activities during the Sino-Japanese War are not documented, but by the end of the war she was the secretary of the Party Committee in Ch'ang-t'ing hsien in Fukien, an area that in the early thirties had come under the control of the Chinese Soviet Republic, whose capital was at Juichin, Kiangsi.

Li apparently remained in east China throughout the civil war with the Nationalists in the late forties. In February 1949, the First East China Women's Conference (held at an undisclosed location) elected her as a delegate to the First National Women's Congress, convened in Peking in March–April. At this meeting she was elected to the Executive Committee of the All-China Federation of Democratic Women (ACFDW), a post she held until the convocation of the next congress in April 1953. As a delegate of the East China Liberated Areas, Li also attended the first session of the CPPCC (September 1949), at which time the new national government was inaugurated. After the CPPCC sessions, Li returned to her native Kwangtung where she assumed several new positions, the first of which was as secretary of the Women's Work Committee of the Party's South China Sub-bureau (responsible for both Kwangtung and Kwangsi provinces), a post she probably retained until the Sub-bureau was dissolved in mid-1955. She also became, in December 1949, a member of the South China Branch of the Sino-Soviet Friendship Association (SSFA), then one of the most active of the "people's" organizations. Three years later (November 1952) she became a member of the Kwangtung Branch of the SSFA.

From 1949 to 1954 the PRC had large government organizations with jurisdiction over the six regions of China. The organization that governed Kwangtung (as well as Hupeh, Hunan, Honan, Kiangsi, and Kwangsi) was known as the Central-South Military and Administrative Committee (CSMAC). When the CSMAC was inaugurated in February 1950, Li was named as a member, holding this post until the Committee was reorganized into the Central-South Administrative Committee in early 1953. She was also a member (from March 1950 to May 1953) of the Land Reform Committee, one of the most important of the CSMAC's subordinate organs and one headed by important Party leader Li Hsueh-feng (q.v.). Paralleling this position at the regional level, Li was appointed in November 1950 as a vice-chairman of the Kwangtung

Provincial Land Reform Committee. Li's participation on the land reform committees, the organs largely responsible for the land reform "movements" of the early fifties, was probably made on the basis of her experiences in the countryside as a youth. Other positions held by Li in the early fifties included the chairmanship of the Preparatory Committee of the Kwangtung Democratic Women's Federation (by April 1951–?) and membership on the joint Kwangtung Province–Canton Municipal Opium and Narcotics Suppression Committee (May 1952–?). In the latter post she served under the chairmanship of her former superior from the twenties, Ku Ta-ts'un. But Li's most important tasks in the early fifties were probably her Party assignments in both central and eastern Kwangtung; in the period from 1950 to 1956 she served as first and second secretaries for the Party's East Kwangtung District Committee as well as its counterpart for central Kwangtung.

Li was working in central Kwangtung in mid-1954 when she chaired a special committee established to discuss the draft national constitution. Soon after, she was named as a deputy from this area to the Kwangtung Provincial People's Congress (KPPC), and when the Congress held its first meeting in August 1954, she was elected to the First NPC, her first national post. She was subsequently re-elected to the Second NPC (1959–1964), as well as to the Third NPC, which opened in December 1964. At the next session of the KPPC (February 1955), she was elected to the Kwangtung Provincial People's Council, the executive arm of the Kwangtung Government. Li presumably continues to hold her seat on both the KPPC and the Government Council; at most of the numerous sessions of the KPPC held since 1954 she has served on the *ad hoc* presidium (steering committee).

In the wake of the Kao Kang (q.v.) purge, the national Party authorities decided to replace the former national and provincial Discipline Inspection Committees with more powerful Control Commissions. The Kwangtung Control Commission was set up in September 1955; serving initially as a deputy secretary, Li has been the senior secretary since at least August 1957, a position she continues to hold. As a consequence of this assignment, she was a logical candidate for membership on the national CCP Central Control Commission following the decision taken at the Party Central Committee 10th Plenum (September 1962) to expand and strengthen the Control Commission. Within the Kwangtung Party structure Li was also a deputy secretary by 1956 and a secretary by 1960, positions that placed her directly under T'ao Chu, the senior Kwangtung secretary from 1955 to 1965 and one of the most powerful men in the entire central-south China region.

At the Party's historic Eighth National Congress, held in Peking in September 1956, Li was elected an alternate member of the Party Central Committee. Although she had then been a Party member for nearly three decades, her importance seemed considerably less than many persons who failed to be elected to the powerful Central Committee. Her election, therefore, may have been largely a gesture, signifying the CCP elite's willingness to include women within the top ranks of the Party. Nonetheless, only eight women were elected to the Central Committee—four as full members and four as alternates.

Since the mid-fifties Li's activities, confined almost exclusively to her native Kwangtung, have been regularly reported in the press, particularly the *Nan-fang jih-pao* (South China daily), the important Party newspaper published in Canton. She has made numerous inspection trips into the Kwangtung countryside to inspect agricultural production, and she is a frequent speaker at meetings of the Kwangtung Party Committee. Also, because Canton is often an entrance and exit point for visiting dignitaries, Li has frequently been cited in the press in connection with foreign visitors, especially foreign Communist Party leaders (e.g., Japanese Communist Party General Secretary Kenji Miyamoto in September 1964). It should be noted, however, that Li tends to be overshadowed in Kwangtung owing to the fact that the province has an unusually high proportion of the Party Central Committee members working there (e.g., T'ao Chu, Ch'en Yü, Wang Shou-tao).

---

1. Nym Wales, *Inside Red China* (New York, 1939), pp. 178–182, 334.
2. *Hsing-huo liao-yuan* (A single spark can start a prairie fire; Hong Kong, 1960), pp. 209–211.

Li Chih-min

(c.1908–   ; Hunan). Military leader in Korea; alternate member, CCP Central Committee.

Li Chih-min, born in Hunan about 1908, was associated with the Communists by 1930 when he was a regimental commander in the Third Army Corps of P'eng Te-huai. In the civil war period of the early and middle 1930's, Li is reported to have worked with the First Army Corps of the Red Army. The First Army Corps was the designation for the units brought together by Chu Te and Mao Tse-tung in June 1930. The nucleus of this force made the Long March, with those under Mao's direction reaching north Shensi in the fall of 1935.

Li's record until the 1940's is obscure. By 1949 he was serving as the political commissar of the 19th Corps, which was fighting in the northwest as a part of P'eng Te-huai's First Field Army. The 19th Corps was commanded by Yang Te-chih, a fellow Hunanese who, like Li, had fought with P'eng Te-huai from the early 1930's. Also, from 1949 he was a member of the Shensi Provincial People's Government, relinquishing the post about 1953. From 1950 to 1953 Li was a member of the regional administration for northwest China, the Northwest Military and Administrative Committee (NWMAC). He received this appointment in June 1950 but it is unlikely that he devoted much time to it, for about that time he was sent to Korea where he served as a political commissar with the 19th Corps, commanded by Yang Te-chih. The Corps entered the Korean War in early 1951. By February 1953 he had succeeded Kan Szu-ch'i (q.v.), also an alternate Central Committee member, as director of the Political Department of the Chinese People's Volunteers (CPV), the Chinese forces in Korea; while he held this position he was awarded the Korean National Flag Medal in February 1953. In September 1953, after the truce in Korea had been signed, Li was deputy chief of a delegation sent from CPV to Peking for the celebration of National Day on October 1. By August 1954 he was further identified as a deputy political commissar of the CPV; he was promoted to political commissar by October 1955. From 1954 Li also began to represent the CPV in various organizations of the national government. He was chairman of the CPV committee appointed to discuss the draft constitution before it was promulgated at the First NPC in September 1954, and he represented the CPV at the Congress for the term of the First NPC from 1954 to 1959.

In the meantime, Li was also active in Korea as a top representative of the CPV. In May 1956, for example, he led a CPV delegation to Pyongyang for May Day celebrations, and in that same month he spoke before the first congress of the CCP organization of the CPV. In September of 1956, at the Eighth National Party Congress in Peking, Li was elected (possibly *in absentia*) as an alternate member of the Party Central Committee. In view of the fact that his pre-1949 record is rather unnoteworthy, it may be that Li's election to the Central Committee was based principally upon his Korean War service. His tour of duty in Korea—approximately six years—was one of the longest of any Chinese officer of his rank. He returned to China to speak before the Fourth Session of the First NPC (June–July 1957) on "rightists." This came at the time of the Party's drive against the "rightists," which followed in the wake of the "blooming" period of the Hundred Flowers Movement. Li presumably did not return to Korea, because not long after (October 1957), Wang P'ing (q.v.) was identified as the new political commissar of the Chinese forces in Korea. Moreover, the fact that Li was not re-elected as a deputy from the CPV to the Second NPC (opening in April 1959) provided another indication that he had been transferred permanently away from Korea.

After returning from Korea to Peking in 1957, Li was apparently assigned to the Ministry of National Defense. Although he was identified in late 1958 as a "representative" of the ministry, the exact nature of his work was not revealed in the press. It was also in 1958 that he was first identified as a colonel-general (the equivalent to a three-star general in the U.S. Army), although it is possible that he held this rank from 1955 when the Chinese Communists first created personal military ranks.

Since his return from Korea in 1957, Li has been reported in the press with regularity. He has usually been cited by his military rank and on occasion as the "former political commissar" of the CPV. As a consequence of his lengthy tour in Korea, he was apparently assigned the task of conferring with and entertaining many of the visitors from North Korea to China. Though he was obviously engaged in tasks more important than merely serving as host to foreign guests, the nature of his work remained unclear until October–November 1963 when he led a military delegation to Algeria for 20 days for the celebration of Algerian National Day. At this time he was identified as the political commissar of the PLA Military Academy (Chün-shih hsueh-yuan) in Peking.

Li has written for the national Party press with some frequency, often in relation to Korea (*e.g.*, *Kuang-ming jih-pao,* June 25, 1954; *JMJP,* June 25, 1960). A more important article, published in *Hung-ch'i* (Red flag, December 1, 1960) dealt with the problem of being "red and expert" in the army, and another article of significance (appearing in the *JMJP,* May 6, 1964) dealt with the political training of senior military officers.

Li Ching-ch'üan

(c.1906–   ; Hui-ch'ang hsien, Kiangsi). First secretary, CCP Southwest Bureau; member, CCP Politburo.

Li Ching-ch'üan was not particularly prominent when the Communists came to power in 1949, but within a decade he was a Politburo member and the chief Communist leader in southwest China. A veteran of the Kiangsi Soviet and the Long March, he served in the Shansi-Suiyuan area during the Sino-Japanese War and took part in the conquest of Szechwan in 1949. Li was born in Hui-ch'ang hsien, Kiangsi, a rural district about 25 miles southwest of Juichin. In the mid-twenties he studied at the Peasant Movement Training Institute. Although nominally under KMT jurisdiction, the Institute, which was located in Canton, was dominated by the Communists. Li was a student there about 1926 when Mao Tse-tung headed the school.

Nothing further is known of Li's career until 1931 when he was back in his native Kiangsi as a political commissar of a guards regiment in the First Front Army led by Chu Te and Mao Tse-tung. Three years later he was head of the Political Department of the Fouth Division in P'eng Te-huai's (q.v.) Third Army Corps, one of the main components of the First Front Army. In the fall of 1934 Li embarked on the Long March, but when the Chu-Mao forces met those of Chang Kuo-t'ao (q.v.) in Szechwan in mid-1935, Li left Mao, as did Chu Te, Liu Po-ch'eng, and others, to follow Chang Kuo-t'ao into Sikang. In mid-1936 Chang's forces were joined in Sikang by units led by Ho Lung (q.v.). Chang recalls that Li was assigned to Ho's Second Front Army as a political commissar and that he was an intelligent, energetic, and versatile officer.[1] The forces led by Chang and Ho did not join Mao in north Shensi until the latter part of 1936.

Soon after the Communists reached north Shensi, Li graduated from the Communists' Anti-Japanese Military and Political Academy (K'ang-ta). With the outbreak of the Sino-Japanese War in 1937 he was sent to the Shansi-Suiyuan border where Ho Lung's 120th Division of the Eighth Route Army was stationed. Ho's original base was expanded during the war to cover large areas in northwest Shansi, the Ta-ch'ing mountain district in Suiyuan, and western Chahar. The history of the 120th Division, with which Li remained throughout the war, is contained in Ho Lung's biography. From 1937 Li was the political commissar of the Suiyuan-Mongolian Military Region as well as a member of the Suiyuan Party Committee. Early in 1938 Ho's forces cooperated with the KMT 35th Army against the Japanese, but when the latter withdrew in the spring, the Communists joined forces with the local resistance groups known as Battle Mobilization Committees and continued to fight against the Japanese. Li was in charge of a detachment in Ho's 120th Division, which was sent north into the Ta-ch'ing Mountain area in August 1938.[2] He apparently remained in this region throughout most of the war, although journalist Harrison Forman met him in Sui-te, Shensi (north of Yenan), in 1944. Li was then political commissar of the Sui-te branch of K'ang-ta. Forman described him as an "old battle-scarred veteran."[3] Li was back in the Shansi-Suiyuan area in the 1946–47 period as political commissar and secretary of the CCP Committee. In 1947 he was also reported serving as secretary-general of the headquarters in Ho Lung's Joint Defense Command for the Shansi-Suiyuan and Shensi-Kansu-Ninghsia area. This special command had been created during the war (see under Ho Lung) and was head-quartered in Yenan until the Nationalists captured the city in March 1947 during the civil war.

Li remained in the northwest until the fall of 1949 when the Red armies began to move into the southwest, territory not yet under their control when the central government was established in October 1949. The thrust into Szechwan was led by the Second Field Army under Liu Po-ch'eng and Teng Hsiao-p'ing, who moved in from the east, while a portion of the Northwest PLA under Ho Lung came in from the north. Li took part in Ho Lung's operations[4] as political commissar of the 18th Corps, a unit commanded by Chou Shih-ti (q.v.). On December 27 the Communist armies led by Chou and Li occupied Chengtu, the Szechwan capital.

Immediately after these successes the Communists established civil and military organs to administer the newly conquered territory. On the first day of 1950 Li became chairman of the Chengtu Military Control Commission, and at approximately this same time he also became a deputy political commissar of the Southwest Military Region (SWMR) under Political Commissar Teng Hsiao-p'ing. The SWMR was in charge of military affairs in Szechwan, Yunnan, Kweichow, and Sikang provinces, and when the PLA began to push into Tibet in the latter part of 1950 the military operations there were carried out under its jurisdiction. Szechwan was unique in the first three years of the PRC in that it was divided into four sectors for administrative purposes. During the first half of 1950 Li became the dominant figure in west Szechwan; by February 1950 he was identified as the political commissar of the West Szechwan Military District, and in the following month he became chairman of the West Szechwan People's Administrative Office (WSPAO), the civil administration for the area until 1952. Soon after, in June 1950, he was named as chairman of the Finance and Economics Committee, one of the most important subordinate organs of the WSPAO. On the regional administrative level, paralleling the Southwest Military Region, the Communists established (July 1950) the Southwest Military and Administrative Committee (SWMAC) under Chairman Liu Po-ch'eng. Li was named to membership on the SWMAC, and when it was reorganized into the Southwest Administrative Committee in February 1953, he was reappointed. He held this position until the regional administrations were abolished in 1954.

Although Li received little national press attention in the early years of the PRC, his later career indicates that his superiors approved of his work. This was illustrated in the latter half of 1952 following the abolition of the four sectors of Szechwan and the restoration of the province as a single administrative unit. Within less than a year Li held the key positions of power in China's most heavily populated province, beginning in August 1952 when he became the Szechwan governor. Two months later, when the Szechwan Military District was established, he was named as the political commissar (which, in normal Chinese Communist practice, is a more important post than that of the commander). Most important, he became the ranking Party secretary of the Szechwan CCP Committee, a position he was to hold for the next 13 years.

Already the top Szechwan leader by 1952, within two years Li was to be the key figure for the entire southwest region. This rise to regional supremacy resulted from the permanent transfer to Peking from the southwest of a number of the Party's most significant leaders, particularly Teng Hsiao-p'ing, Liu Po-ch'eng, and Ho Lung. Li's importance has been demonstrated in a number of ways, especially by the fact that he appears to have attended virtually every significant meeting of the Party and other organizations in the southwest since 1954. Similarly, he has usually headed the regional and provincial inspection teams that the Communists so often establish to investigate the state of industry or agriculture.

Following the abolition of the greater administrative areas in 1954, parallel changes were made in the military regions. As described above, Li had been a deputy political commissar of the Southwest Military Region and political commissar of the Szechwan Military District. After the 1954 reorganization the SWMR was abolished and the Szechwan Military District became known as the Chengtu Military Region, with its jurisdiction limited to the province of Szechwan. It is not clear whether Li continued to serve as political commissar of the Chengtu region in the middle and late fifties, and by the early sixties another man held this post. However, in 1964 Li was identified as the first political commissar for the region. His primacy in the southwest was given formal expression following the Party's decision in January 1961 to re-create the regional Party bureaus. By the summer of that year Li was identified as first secretary of the Southwest Bureau, responsible for Party affairs in Szechwan, Kweichow, Yunnan, and (presumably) Tibet.

Although Li's major work since 1949 has been in the southwest, he has also been involved in the national bureaucracy. He received his first national post in December 1954 when he was named as a Party representative to the Second National Committee of the quasi-legislative CPPCC. He was re-elected to the Third National Committee (1959–64) but has not served with this organization since the Fourth Committee was formed in late 1964 (see below).

His stature within the national Party hierarchy was confirmed at the historic Eighth Party Congress in September 1956. Li was named to the 63-member Congress Presidium (steering committee), and, more important, to the Congress Credentials Committee. Li spoke before the Congress about industry and agriculture in Szechwan and the need to work out a careful balance between production by the peasants of basic agricultural crops and subsidiary products. At the close of the Congress he was elected a member of the Central Committee. Li was one of the 33 persons elected to full membership who had been neither a full nor an alternate member of the Seventh Central Committee elected in 1945. He reached a new peak in his career at the fifth plenum of the Central Committee in May 1958 when he was elevated to Politburo membership together with K'o Ch'ing-shih and T'an Chen-lin. An interesting aspect of their election is that they bypassed six alternate Politburo members, including such veteran leaders as Ulanfu, Lu Ting-i, and Ch'en Po-ta (qq.v.).

In the decade from the mid-fifties to the mid-sixties, Li assumed new posts and relinquished others. In January 1955 he became the chairman of the Szechwan CPPCC Committee and in the same month stepped down as the provincial governor, being replaced by Li Ta-chang (q.v.), another important Szechwan political figure. He was, however, elected at this same time to membership on the Szechwan Provincial People's Government Council, a position he probably still holds. A decade later other changes took place concerning his affiliation with the CPPCC and the NPC. As already described, Li had served on the National Committee of the CPPCC from 1954 to 1964. In December 1964–January 1965, when both the CPPCC and the NPC held national meetings, Li was transferred, in effect, from the CPPCC to the more important NPC. He attended the Third NPC as a deputy from Szechwan, and at the close of the meetings in January 1965 was elected a vice-chairman of the NPC Standing Committee, the body that exercises the powers of the Congress between the annual sessions. Paralleling this shift, at the provincial level he was replaced in late 1965 as the chairman of the Szechwan CPPCC Committee by Liao Chih-kao (q.v.). Liao also replaced Li in the spring of 1965 as Szechwan Party first secretary.

Li's relinquishment of these provincial posts was apparently due to the fact that by the 1960's he had new and more important responsibilities at the national and regional levels, as exemplified by his Politburo membership and his primacy in both the Party and military hierarchies in the southwest. Li's position as a national leader of prime importance is illustrated in still another way. Since the establishment of the regional Party bureaus in 1961, he has regularly visited Peking, where he is usually mentioned in the press in connection with Mao Tse-tung, Liu Shao-ch'i, and the other most senior CCP leaders. His visits to the capital, often coinciding with those of other top regional leaders (such as T'ao Chu from the Central-South Bureau), suggest that these men are regularly called to Peking to help formulate regional policies.

Although Li's involvement in foreign affairs has been minimal, he did participate in one of the most important international conferences in the history of the PRC. This occurred in November–December 1960 when he accompanied Liu Shao-ch'i to Moscow. Ostensibly, the delegation went to attend the 43rd anniversary celebrations of the Russian Revolution. Far more important, however, was their presence at the "Moscow Meeting of Representatives of Communist and Workers' Parties," attended by delegates from 81 parties. The conference was held in an atmosphere of rising tensions in the Sino-Soviet dispute and was described by one authority (writing in late 1961) as "probably the most important gathering of its kind in the entire history of Communism."[5] Briefly stated, the Chinese urged an aggressive bloc posture vis-à-vis the West, characterized by a determination to foment "wars of national liberation." The importance the Chinese attached to the meeetings can be gauged from the composition of their delegation. In addition to Liu Shao-ch'i and Li, the group included Teng Hsiao-p'ing, P'eng Chen, Lu Ting-i, and K'ang Sheng, all members or alternates of the Politburo.

1. Modern China Project, Columbia University, New York, Howard L. Boorman, director.
2. *K'ang-Jih chan-cheng shih-ch'i chieh-fang-ch'ü kai-k'uang* (A sketch of the liberated areas during the Anti-Japanese War; Peking, 1953), p. 96.
3. Harrison Forman, *Report from Red China* (New York, 1945), p. 196.
4. *Selected Works of Mao Tse-tung* (Peking, 1961), IV, 389.
5. Donald S. Zagoria, *The Sino-Soviet Conflict, 1956–1961* (Princeton, N.J., 1962), p. 343.

Li Ch'iu-shih

(1903–1931; Chin-k'ou, Hupeh). Early Youth League leader.

Li Ch'iu-shih was among the most important Youth League leaders in the 1920's and was closely associated with Yun Tai-ying. After serving in various district and provincial League posts, he was elected to its Central Committee and as its propaganda chief in 1927. Li participated in the Canton Commune and by 1929 he was head of the CCP's Propaganda Department. In his last years he was associated with the Li Li-san leadership.

Born in 1903, Li spent his early childhood in Chin-k'ou, south of Wuhan. He was one of nine children and his father's income as a teacher and petty official was scarcely sufficient to support the family. To better their financial situation the family moved to Wuchang when Li was still very young. At 14 he entered the Wuchang Commercial High School (Wu-ch'ang kao-teng shang-yeh hsueh-hsiao) and is reported to have done well.

Although he is said to have been influenced by the "new thought" before 1919, Li's first real revolutionary experience came after the May Fourth Incident when he was 16. At this time he became active in the Wuhan "student patriotic movement" led by Yun Tai-ying (q.v.). This was apparently the first of Li's many associations with Yun. With Lin Yü-nan, Yun and Li founded the Social Benefit Book Store in the fall of 1919 to provide revolutionary literature for young people in the area (see under Yun Tai-ying). They also wrote and sold a newspaper to inspire the youth. It is reported that Li's revolutionary determination was further encouraged in the early summer of 1920 when one of his three older brothers was killed by warlord Wang Chan-yuan's troops and a second was forced to commit suicide. His third brother fled, leaving Li responsible for the family. It is probable that Li's first contact with the Socialist Youth League came in the late fall of 1920 when a branch was organized in Wuchang. At approximately this same time he left home and went north to Huang-p'i hsien where he taught in a village primary school. Communist sources assert that he took the post to participate in the revolution without endangering his family and that while there he awakened the consciousness of poor peasants and began to organize them. However, considering his family's financial position, one reason was probably his need for an income.

When the Communist Party was established in July 1921 several activists from the Social Benefit Book Store, including Li and Yun, joined it. Soon after, Li accompanied Yun to Lu-chou in Szechwan where they set up the Lu-chou Associated Normal School. This was a training center for young cadres, which was attended by students from Szechwan, Yunnan, and Kweichow (see under Yun Tai-ying). Yun and Li also established branches of the Party and Youth League at the school. When the school was closed by a Szechwan warlord in 1922, Li was forced to return to Wuhan. He registered at Wuhan University, but this was a cover for his Party activities. As editor of the Wuhan Jih-jih hsin-wen (Daily news) he propagandized Party proposals. He also collaborated with Ouyang Yü-ch'ien, who later became a noted playwright, in editing a play condemning feudalism and imperialism.

In Wuhan, Li had worked with laborers as well as students, but by 1923 he was primarily involved in the workers' movement. He helped organize the Peking-Hankow Railroad Workers' Union in the early part of the year and then spent the rest of it in the mining areas of Hunan and Hupeh. In late 1923 or early 1924 the Youth League sent Li to study at the Communist University of the Toilers of the East in Moscow. He also served as a representative of the League in Moscow.

After the May 30th Incident in 1925, Li returned home to become a district secretary in Honan. Early the next year he was transferred to Canton to become propaganda chief of the League's Kwangtung Committee and editor of Shao-nien hsien-feng (Youth vanguard). Because the League branch at Sun Yat-sen University was directly subordinate to the League's Provincial Committee, Li regularly took part in its meetings. He also lectured at the University and was particularly active there after the Chung-shan Incident of March 20, 1926, when Chiang Kaishek took control of Canton and arrested many Communist political workers among his forces (see under Chou En-lai).

Li was transferred again in late 1926 when the armies of the Northern Expedition occupied Hunan and Hupeh. This time the League sent him to Changsha to be secretary of its Hunan Provincial Committee. He lived with Shih Hsunch'uan, the Committee's propaganda chief, and T'ien Po-yang, a youth leader who apparently succeeded Li as secretary in 1927.[1] The Committee set up a cadre training class for which Li organized lectures. Having gone to Wuhan in April 1927, he participated in the League's Fourth Congress in May and was elected a member and propaganda chief of the Central Committee. This trip probably saved his life because Shih and T'ien were both killed in the wake of Hsu K'o-hsiang's May 21 coup against the Communists in Changsha. In the late summer or fall of 1927 Li went to Shanghai with the rest of the League Central Committee where they made plans to continue their struggle clandestinely. He then returned to Canton, becoming secretary of the League's Provincial Committee. He was active in the preparations for the Canton Commune in December (see under Chang T'ai-lei) in which his long-time colleague Yun Tai-ying played a major role.

After the failure at Canton, Li began to work in factories to reorganize the rank and file, which had been severely shaken by the Communist defeat. In the process he became ill and went to Shanghai to recuperate. It was during his illness that Li had the opportunity to write. He also translated some Russian literature into Chinese. Among his pen names were Li Kuo-wei, Li Pei-p'ing, and Li Wei-sen. At the Fifth Youth League Congress in 1928 Li was re-elected as a member of the Central Committee and as its propaganda head. He also became chief editor of the League's organ, *Chung-kuo ch'ing-nien* (China youth).[2] By 1929 he had become the propaganda chief of the Party's Central Committee, apparently his first CCP post. In this capacity he is credited with having started the *Shang-hai pao* (Shanghai news), a Party organ later renamed *Hung-ch'i pao* (Red flag news). The Shanghai General Labor Union's *Kung-jen jih-pao* (Worker's daily) was also published under his direction.

The League of Left-wing Writers (see under Ch'ü Ch'iu-pai and Chou Yang) was established in Shanghai in March 1930. Li participated in its work and was especially active in trying to involve the membership in political activity among workers and peasants. During these months Li also had primary responsibility for the preparations for the Conference of Delegates from Soviet Areas held in Shanghai in May 1930. The conference was designed to reaffirm the leadership of the cities over the countryside and to prepare for urban insurrections (see under Li Li-san). Li's leading role in this conference, which was initiated by the Li Li-san leadership, suggests that despite Communist allusions to the contrary, Li Ch'iu-shih was one of Li Li-san's supporters. Li Ch'iu-shih's role at the Fourth Plenum in January 1931 when Li Li-san was deposed is ambiguous. His biographer condemns the Ch'en Tu-hsiu and Li Li-san lines as deviations and mentions that Li Ch'iu-shih opposed Ch'en. Nothing is said about Li's attitude toward Li Li-san. It is merely noted that Li Ch'iu-shih was considered unreliable by the "28 Bolshevik" group (see under Ch'en Shao-yü) because he differed with them when the Fourth Plenum's resolution was discussed.[3] These suggestions of Li Ch'iu-shih's relationship to Li Li-san are supported by Shen Tse-min's (q.v.) assertion that the Li Li-sanists included Li Wei-han (q.v.), Ho Ch'ang, Wang K'o-ch'üan, and Li Ch'iu-shih.[4]

Li's career came to an abrupt end in early 1931 shortly after the Fourth Plenum when he and 35 others were arrested in a Shanghai hotel by the British police on January 17. This occurred at a meeting of the Preparatory Committee of the All-China Congress of Soviets (see under Ho Meng-hsiung). The British turned them over to the KMT and they were put in the Lung-hua prison. After a summary trial most of them, including Li, Ho Meng-hsiung, Lin Yü-nan, and Hu Yeh-p'in (the husband of Ting Ling, q.v.) were executed on February 7, the anniversary of the strike on the Peking-Hankow Railroad in which many of them had participated. Li died when he was only 28.

In the Maoist version of CCP history, Li was cleared of any association with former "deviationist" lines by the "Resolution on Some Questions in the History of Our Party" adopted in

1945 at the Seventh Party Plenum. This stated: "But as to the twenty-odd important cadres of the Party, including Lin Yü-nan, Li Ch'iu-shih, and Ho Meng-hsiung, they did much useful work for the Party and the people, maintained excellent connection with the masses and, when arrested shortly afterwards, stood up firm to the enemy and became noble martyrs."[5]

1. *Hu-nan ko-ming lieh-shih chuan* (Biographies of Hunan revolutionary martyrs; Changsha, 1952), p. 91.
2. *Selected Works of Mao Tse-tung* (London, 1956), IV, 340.
3. *Kung-ch'ing-t'uan, wo-te mu-ch'in* (The Communist youth league, my mother; Peking, 1958), p. 287.
4. Tso-liang Hsiao, *Power Relations within the Chinese Communist Movement, 1930–1934* (Seattle, Wash., 1961), pp. 139–140.
5. *Selected Works*, p. 183.

Li Chu-ch'en

(1881–   ; Yung-shun, Hunan). Non-Communist industrialist; minister of Light Industry.

Li Chu-ch'en, a leading industrialist before 1949, is one of the more important non-Communists who has worked in technical and administrative posts since the PRC was established. He was born in August 1881 in Yung-shun hsien in northwest Hunan. After graduating in 1908 from a normal college in Ch'ang-te where he studied physics and chemistry, he taught at a technical middle school in Changsha, the provincial capital. Winning a government scholarship, Li continued his study of physics and chemistry at the Asakusa Higher Technical Institute (later known as the Tokyo Industrial College). He returned home after his graduation in 1918 and for the next two decades he worked in technical and managerial positions in two important companies in present-day Hopeh —the Chiu-ta Salt Company and the Yung-li Alkali Manufacturing Corporation. Like so many coastal industrialists, Li went to Szechwan when war with Japan broke out in 1937. He is credited with major contributions in the restoration of the important salt industry in the southwest and the development of industry in free China. In the closing years of the war he was a member of the National Federation of Industries and chairman of its Chungking branch.

Dissatisfied with the Nationalist government, Li joined with other businessmen and industrialists in Chungking to establish the China Democratic National Construction Association (CDNCA) in 1945. When the Communists came to power four years later, the Association was recognized as one of the several non-Communist "democratic" political parties. After V-J Day in 1945 Li returned to Tientsin to resume his career as an industrialist with the two companies mentioned above. During the immediate postwar years he also served in various executive and legislative posts in the Nationalist Government, and as late as 1949 he was still nominally a member of the Legislative Yuan. Immediately after the fall of Tientsin in January 1949, Li began to cooperate with the Communists, who were then particularly eager to enlist the skills of the managerial class.

In June 1949 Li participated in the meetings presided over by Mao Tse-tung to prepare for the establishment of the Communists' national government. Representing industrial and commercial circles, he attended in September 1949 the inaugural session of the CPPCC, the organization that formally brought the new government into existence. With the formation of the central government in October he was appointed to membership on its most important body, the Central People's Government Council, which was chaired by Mao. Although he regularly attended the Council meetings in Peking until it was abolished in 1954, he spent most of the early PRC years in Tientsin where he managed the Yung-li Chemical Works. He also continued as an active member of the CDNCA and has served since at least 1953 as one of its vice-chairmen. In addition, in the early fifties he was chairman of the Association's Tientsin branch.

The Communists took their first steps toward organizing managerial talent in the fall of 1951 when they established a special office to create a nationwide organization of industrialists and businessmen (see under Hsu Ti-hsin). Li played a major role in the various meetings that led to the formation in November 1953 of the All-China Federation of Industry and Commerce (ACFIC). He has served since that time as the ranking vice-chairman of this organization, which, since the late 1950's, has worked in close cooperation with the Democratic National Construction Association. In 1954 he was elected to represent Tientsin at the First NPC when the constitutional government was inaugurated. (Since the Second NPC was convened in 1959 he has represented Hopeh province.) At the close of the inaugural meetings of the First NPC in September 1954, he was elected to its permanent Standing Committee, but he relinquished this legislative post after being appointed to head the Ministry of Food Industry in May 1956. Two years later (February 1958), his ministry was merged with the Ministry of Light Industry. Li has continued as the minister of the combined ministries, known as the Ministry of Light Industry. The name of his ministry was changed once again in February 1965 to the First Ministry of Light Industry. (The new Second Ministry is headed by Hsu Yun-pei, q.v.) As of the mid-sixties Li was one of the oldest

members of the central government. Moreover, he was one of the very few non-Communists to hold a ministerial portfolio—most of the "democratic" leaders having been replaced by CCP members in the late fifties or early sixties.

Li's principal functions have been related to domestic industry and commerce, but he has also been a fairly active participant in the international relations of the PRC. This began in the spring of 1952 when the Communists, in an effort to circumvent American efforts to curtail Chinese trade, established the China Committee for the Promotion of International Trade (see under Nan Han-ch'en). Li was named as a Committee member, and since at least 1955 he has been a vice-chairman. His various trips abroad are outlined below. 1952: member, delegation led by Nan Han-ch'en to the International Economic Conference, Moscow, April; member, delegation led by Mme. Sun Yat-sen to a world peace congress, Vienna, December; 1954: member, delegation led by Kuo Mo-jo to the International Conference on the Relaxation of World Tension, Stockholm, June; 1955: deputy leader, trade delegation led by Lei Jen-min to Japan, March–May; 1959: member, delegation led by Nieh Jung-chen for 10th anniversary of German Democratic Republic, East Germany, October; 1960: deputy leader, delegation led by Liu Ch'ang-sheng to celebrations marking the 10th anniversary of Sino-Soviet Treaty of Alliance, Moscow, February (in the same month he went to East Germany to attend the opening of the Leipzig Trade Fair); 1961: member, delegation led by Chou En-lai to attend the 13th anniversary celebrations of Burma's independence and to exchange the instruments of ratification of the Sino-Burmese Boundary Treaty, January (while in Rangoon, Li took part in economic talks with the Burmese); deputy leader, NPC delegation led by Kuo Mo-jo to Burma and Indonesia, August–September; 1962: member, NPC delegation led by P'eng Chen to North Korea on a goodwill visit, April–May.

As late as January 1965 Li was reappointed to his ministerial post and also elevated to a vice-chairmanship of the CPPCC. But by this time he was approaching his 85th year and his lack of regular public appearances after the early sixties suggests that he was in fact semi-retired.

Li Chü-k'uei

(c.1906–   ; Hunan). Red Army veteran; Political Commissar, General Rear Services Department, PLA.

Japanese sources credit Li Chü-k'uei with having graduated from Moscow University, but the other known facts of his career suggest that this may be in error. Li participated in the P'ing-chiang (Pingkiang) Uprising of July 1928 led by P'eng Te-huai, who was to become one of the most senior Red Army leaders.[1] At the time of the uprising (see under T'eng Tai-yuan), Li was a section leader in the Ninth Company under the First Regiment of the 35th Army led by T'ang Sheng-chih, a military leader in the Nationalist Army. The revolting forces were then organized into the Fifth Army of the Chinese Workers' and Peasants' Red Army, which left the P'ing-chiang area for the Communist stronghold at Chingkangshan in August 1928, arriving there in November. Presumably Li was associated with this force, which went to Chingkangshan to join forces with Chu Te and Mao Tse-tung.

The activities of Li from the 1928 uprising until 1935 are unknown, but in the latter year he was heading the First Division of the First Red Army Corps during the Long March, which ended in Shensi in 1935. This corps was the main force which began the Long March in October 1934 from the Kiangsi Soviet under the command of Mao Tse-tung and Chu Te.

Immediately after the outbreak of the Sino-Japanese War in mid-1937, the Communists organized their forces in northwest China into three units under the Eighth Route Army: the 115th, the 120th, and the 129th Divisions. Li was assigned to the last-mentioned division and by January 1939 was leading an "advanced" or "vanguard" column in northwestern Shantung, an area under the jurisdiction of the Communists' Shansi-Hopeh-Shantung-Honan Border Region.[2] The thrust into Shantung was made in response to a request from guerrilla units operating there, most notably those which had been under the command of Fan Chu-hsien, a guerrilla leader killed in action in 1938. In March 1939, Hopeh and Shantung units which had originally served under Liu Po-ch'eng's 129th Division were transferred to Lin Piao's 115th Division.

After Li's work in 1939 in Shantung, there is no further information about his career until a decade later when he was named to the Tientsin (Hopeh) Military Control Commission following the capture of Tientsin on January 15, 1949 by the armies moving south from Manchuria under the leadership of Lin Piao. These armies, known as the Fourth Field Army by early 1949, thrust southward from Tientsin and eventually occupied the central-south portions of the mainland. Li's position in Tientsin was obviously of brief duration, because later in 1949 he was serving as a deputy chief-of-staff of the Fourth Field Army and the Central-South Military Region, both under the command of Lin Piao. He held these posts until at least the spring of 1950 and probably throughout that year. By no later than February 1951 Li was transferred to Manchuria, because by that date he was identified as director of the Rear Services (logistics) Department of the Northeast Military Region of the PLA, a position in which he was identified in February 1951 when appointed a member of the Northeast People's Government, the civil administration in charge of the Manchurian provinces.

Apparently Li was transferred out of Manchuria by 1953, because he was not named in early 1953 to the Northeast Administrative Committee, the successor organization to the Northeast People's Government. He was next mentioned in the press (but without title) in early 1954 at a Peking rally in support of the PLA. Then in July 1955, when the Ministry of Fuel Industry was split into three ministries, Li was given one of the three, the Ministry of Petroleum. He headed this ministry for the next two and a half years.

On several occasions in 1956, Li's activity in the Petroleum Industry Ministry was reported in the press. For example, he reported on oil prospecting work during 1955 at an oil exploration conference in January 1956; in the next month he spoke before the first national congress of the newly formed China Petroleum Workers' Trade Union; and in May 1956 he delivered an address at a conference of "outstanding" petroleum workers. In that same year, at the Eighth National Party Congress in September, Li submitted a written speech on the responsibilities of the petroleum industry. He continued to head this important ministry until a governmental reorganization in February 1958, at which time he was replaced by Yü Ch'iu-li (q.v.). Then, less than a month later, Li in turn replaced Yü Ch'iu-li as Political Commissar of the PLA General Rear Services. By the early fall of 1958 Li was identified with the rank of colonel general, equivalent to a three-star general in the U.S. Army.

In April 1959, at the first session of the Second NPC, Li was named to membership on the National Defense Council, an organization with very limited power and authority but one with considerable prestige. He was reappointed to membership in January 1965. Since receiving his military appointments in 1958–59, Li has often appeared at functions in Peking marking military anniversaries (such as Army Day on August 1) or has taken part in festivities honoring foreign visitors to China.

In 1964 he was elected to the Third NPC (which first met in December 1964–January 1965). Although Li appeared regularly in Peking up to this election in October 1964, the New China News Agency dispatch reporting this election grouped Li among those elected from PLA units in Nanking, Inner Mongolia, Sinkiang, or Tibet. Though not necessarily an indication that Li has been transferred away from Peking permanently, this suggests that he may be spending time in Nanking, the center for several important PLA training academies.

1. *Kuang-ming jih-pao,* July 23, 1957.

2. *K'ang-Jih chan-cheng shih-ch'i chieh-fang-ch'ü kai-k'uang* (A sketch of the liberated areas during the Sino-Japanese War; Peking, 1953), p. 49.

Li Ch'u-li

Former Red Army political officer; member, CCP Central Control Commission.

Li Ch'u-li, a former Red Army political officer, served in the Ministry of Personnel from 1951 to 1954 and has been a member of the Party's Central Control Commission since 1956. He was a political officer in the Shansi-Chahar-Hopeh and the Hopeh-Jehol Military Regions during the Sino-Japanese War. Toward the end of the conflict he must have been transferred to the Communist guerrilla base in east Hopeh, for he was in An-p'ing, a small town on the Peking-Tientsin Railroad, in August 1945. The Communists had maintained small guerrilla forces and conducted sporadic raids on the Japanese in east Hopeh all during the years of conflict, attempting to neutralize the strategic area covering the approaches to Peking and the railroad and highways leading to Manchuria. The area, known as the East Hopeh District, was located east of Peking, running from the eastern suburbs to the coast. Soon after hostilities ceased, the Communists came into conflict in east Hopeh with American and Nationalist forces intent on taking over north China. One incident involved a conflict at An-p'ing, which the Communists claim they had taken on August 23, 1945, and which they were holding when American and Nationalist troops passed through on their way to Peking in July 1946.[1] The ensuing fight brought forth an investigating team sent in 1946 from the Peking Executive Headquarters, which was attempting to implement the terms of the Cease-Fire Agreement of January 10, 1946. Li was involved in the on-the-spot negotiations held in nearby Hsiang-ho with members of the Peking team. He was then identified as a political commissar of the East Hopeh Military District, responsible to his commander, Nieh Jung-chen (q.v.), whose troops were in central and eastern Hopeh at the end of the war.

Nothing more was heard of Li until March 1950, by which time he was a deputy secretary of the Kwangsi Party Committee and a member of the Kwangsi Provincial People's Government. It is not known how long he held the Party post, but he was removed from the Kwangsi government in December 1951. Prior to this, in May 1951, he became chairman of the Kwangsi government's People's Supervision Committee, a body having responsibility over government agencies and personnel in their performance of duty. He held the latter post only until December when he left the Kwangsi government.

Although Li was not removed from his posts in Kwangsi until December 1951, he was probably already in Peking by that time, for he was made a vice-minister of the Ministry of Personnel in September, and as a government official he attended the third session of the First CPPCC, held from October 23 to November 1, 1951. In May of 1952 he was given an additional office in the Ministry of Personnel, the directorship of the Ministry's First Office. Li dropped his Personnel Ministry positions when the ministry was abolished with the inauguration of the constitutional government in September 1954.

In December 1954 he became one of the Party representatives on the Second National Committee of the CPPCC, which opened that month. He was reappointed as a Party delegate to the Third National Committee, which convened its initial session in April 1959 and was also named to membership on the Standing Committee, the governing body of the CPPCC. He was named again to both posts when the Fourth CPPCC held its first session in December 1964–January 1965.

Li received his first high-ranking Party post, membership on the Central Control Commission, at the First Plenary Session of the Eighth Central Committee, held the day after the Eighth Party Congress closed on September 27, 1956. In 1960 he became a deputy director of the CCP Organization Department, a post that places him under Organization Department Director An Tzu-wen (q.v.), who was also Li's superior in the Personnel Ministry in the early fifties. Li continues to hold both posts in the control and organization organs, positions that make him one of the more important men in Party discipline and security work.

1. *SCMP* 2818, pp. 1–9.

Li Fan-wu

(Mu-ling hsien, Heilungkiang) Early Communist leader in Manchuria; Heilungkiang governor.

Li Fan-wu is a native of Mu-ling hsien in eastern Heilungkiang about 100 miles from the Soviet Maritime Province. He is one of the few Manchurians to rise to prominence in the Chinese Communist Party. Li studied in Harbin and at a university in Peking, probably in the 1920's. Shortly after the Mukden Incident precipitated by the Japanese in September 1931, he joined the CCP.[1]

Toward the end of 1932 Li returned to Manchuria and took part in the work of the "Anti-Japanese Self-Defense Army," one of the several guerrilla forces formed at this time in Manchuria. In early 1933 this "army" was badly damaged by Japanese forces and Li apparently went into hiding. He reportedly taught primary school during the 1932–1935 period in his native hsien while at the same time engaging in the resistance movement against the Japanese.[2]

It was probably not difficult for Li to remain in contact with Communists and guerrilla forces because the heart of the resistance movement in Manchuria centered in the region close to Li's native area. In 1935 several guerrilla forces in Manchuria were merged to form the Northeast Allied, or the Allied Anti-Japanese Army (AAJA), led by Yang Ching-yü, Chao Shang-chih, and Chou Pao-chung (q.v.). Li's career was closely linked with that of Chou, who ultimately became a Central Committee alternate member. With the formation of the AAJA, Chou became commander of the Fifth Army, with Li as the political commissar.[3]

In addition to his military activities, Li was also reported to have been chairman of the "Eastern Kirin Anti-Japanese Association" in about 1935, apparently an offshoot of the Northeast People's Anti-Japanese Salvation Association, an organization formed in June 1934. After the outbreak of the war in 1937, he made his way westward and by 1938 became associated with the newly formed Shansi-Chahar-Hopeh (Chin-Ch'a-Chi) Border Region, one of the several such Communist regions established in the early stages of the Sino-Japanese War. This Border Region served as the contact point between interior China and Manchuria during the war years, and it was under the auspices of this governmental body that Li engaged in underground activities in the Manchurian areas closest to the Border Region.

At the war's end, Li returned eastward to his native Mu-ling to organize local forces against the Nationalist Government's troops. At this critical juncture of modern Chinese history, both the Communists and Nationalists were engaged in a race for the control of Manchuria. Although details are lacking, Li must have gone to Mu-ling at about the time General Lin Piao was leading cadre of the Eighth Route Army into Manchuria to organize troops for the coming struggle against the Nationalists. At the close of the war the Nationalists had reorganized the governmental divisions of Manchuria. One of these provinces was Hokiang (Ho-chiang); Li served as a vice-governor of those portions held by the Communists from February 1946 until October 1948 when the Communists, then in almost complete control of Manchuria, abolished it. Li was then transferred to a comparable post in Sungkiang province, serving there in 1948–49 as vice-governor.

Li was evidently scheduled to remain as a governmental official in Manchuria as the Com-

munists were making their initial plans for staffing the government there in 1949. In August 1949, the Northeast People's Government was formed, and Li was named as one of the members of the Government Council. However, when these appointments were being confirmed in December 1949, it was officially announced that Li's name had been withdrawn because of a transfer in assignments. The transfer had taken place, in effect, in October 1949 when Li was appointed as a vice-minister of the Ministry of Forestry and Land Reclamation (known as the Ministry of Forestry after November 1951). The original minister (Liang Hsi) and the other vice-minister were both non-Party members who had been named because of their technical competence. This meant that Li was the senior Party member and therefore the most powerful official in the ministry at the time of the formation of the PRC in 1949. He was to remain in the ministry for over eight years.

He was only occasionally mentioned in the press in the early 1950's. The more significant reports stated that he was: a deputy secretary-general for the National Conference of Labor Models in September–October 1950; reporting on forestry work for 1950 and plans for the 1951 before a GAC meeting on April 13, 1951; a member of the GAC's Labor Employment Committee from its formation in July 1952, holding this post to the dissolution of the committee in the fall of 1954; a member of the National Committee of the newly established (July 1954) All-China Federation of Supply and Marketing Cooperatives, a post he still holds.

Li has been a rather active NPC member. He was elected to all three Congresses from Heilungkiang (1954–1959; 1959–1964; 1964 to date); he was a member of the Budget Committee for each, and served on the Presidium for all four sessions of the Second NPC. At the April 1959 session he spoke on agriculture and industry in Heilungkiang, and at the session which closed in January 1965 he spoke on agricultural production in Heilungkiang.

In February 1958 there was a partial reorganization of the State Council; Li was then transferred from the Ministry of Forestry to Heilungkiang, becoming a Secretary on the provincial Party committee; by February 1961 he was promoted to the post of Second Secretary. In both instances he served under Central Committee member Ouyang Ch'in, a long-time senior Party official in Manchuria. When Ouyang relinquished the Heilungkiang gubernatorial post in September 1958, it was Li who succeeded him; he continues to hold this post.

From 1958 Li has been reported performing the tasks which are normal for a provincial official of his rank. Random examples include: deputy leader of a rural work inspection delegation in March 1961; speaker at a Harbin meeting in October 1961 marking the 50th anniversary of the 1911 Revolution; speaker at a Heilungkiang Young Communist League Congress in July–August 1963; speaker at a January 1964 rally in Harbin protesting American "aggression" in Panama. Residing in Harbin, Li is also obliged to spend some of his time hosting the many foreign visitors who come to that important city.

1. Chou Erh-fu, *Tung-pei heng-tuan-mien* (Northeastern cross section; Hong Kong, 1946), p. 118.
2. *Ibid.*
3. *Ibid.*

Li Fu-ch'un

(1899–   ; Hunan). Economic administrator; chairman, State Planning Commission; member, CCP Central Secretariat and Politburo Standing Committee.

Li Fu-ch'un, one of the earliest members of the CCP, has been Communist China's leading economic administrator since the late 1950's. Trained in both France and the Soviet Union, Li was a participant in many of the landmark events of modern Chinese revolutionary history, including the Northern Expedition and the Long March. He was one of the Party's top officials in Manchuria in the late forties, and throughout the 1950's he took part in most of the negotiations with the USSR, particularly those pertaining to economics. Li has been a Party Central Committee member since 1934 and a Politburo member since 1956.

Li was born near Changsha, the Hunan capital, in 1899.[1] He and his three brothers were reared in a family in which the father was a teacher in a boys' school. American authoress Nym Wales has written that Li was among those Chinese Communists who had been "produced by the old Confucian scholars . . . whose aristocratic families were bankrupt."[2] He studied in a normal school in Changsha in the mid-teens during the same years that Mao Tse-tung, Li Wei-han, and Ts'ai Ho-sen (his future brother-in-law) were there. As a member of the important Hsin-min hsueh-hui (New people's study society; see under Li's wife, Ts'ai Ch'ang), whose original members in Hunan produced a large number of leading Communists, Li was enlisted in the "work-and-study" program to go to France. In preparation, he and a number of others, including Liu Shao-ch'i, went to Peking in 1918, and from there to Paoting to take a French language course. Then in 1919 he left for France, going to the Collège de Montargis south of Paris where Ts'ai Ho-sen headed the branch of the Hsin-min hsueh-hui. However, in the five-odd years that Li was in France it appears that he,

like most of the worker-students, was more deeply involved in earning a living and in political affairs than in formal study. In the summer of 1920 a split occurred within the ranks of the Hsin-min hsueh-hui members in France. One group, headed by Ts'ai Ho-sen, led the more radical elements in establishing the Young China Communist Party and a Socialist Youth League in 1921–1922. The latter was, in fact, reorganized from the Kung-hsueh hu-chu she (Work-and-study cooperative society), whose membership included Li, Li Wei-han, Ts'ai Ch'ang, and Hsiang Ching-yü (Ts'ai Ho-sen's wife).[3] Thus, by 1922 Li was a member of what proved to be the equivalent of the French branch of the CCP, formed in China the previous year, and in this sense he can be described as one of the founding members of the CCP. Edgar Snow, in accordance with interviews he recorded in 1936 in Kansu, has written that in 1921 Li joined the French Communist Party, but there is little to suggest that he was active in it.

Snow has also written that Li and a fellow student, Nieh Jung-chen (q.v.), were tutored in both French and Marxism by the same teacher and that in 1923 he spent some time with Nieh in Berlin. Apparently, the visit was brief, because he married Ts'ai Ch'ang in 1923 in France, and in the next year he and Chou En-lai both became members of the KMT Executive Committee in France.[4] Membership at this time in both the KMT and the CCP was a common thing among Communists. Sometime in 1924 Li left for Moscow where he spent half a year studying at the Communist University of the Toilers of the East, returning to China by late 1924 or early 1925. Going to Canton, then the revolutionary center of China, he quickly took up important posts in the KMT. He is said to have been an instructor in the Whampoa Military Academy's Political Department where Chou En-lai was a key official. Li Jui, Mao Tse-tung's biographer, has written that Li Fu-ch'un headed a KMT political training class (*cheng-chih chiang-hsi pan*), at which Mao lectured on at least one occasion on the "peasant question." Li Jui also claimed that the most of the graduates of this class later took part in the Northern Expedition as political workers.[5]

In 1926 Li became director of the Political Department of T'an Yen-k'ai's Second Army, a force consisting of Hunanese troops and one of the major units of the National Revolutionary Army. In this capacity Li made the Northern Expedition, which began in mid-1926. In broad terms, the Northern Expeditionary forces followed three northward routes: one of these took the coastal route to Shanghai; another marched due north from Canton to Wuhan (the army which included the troops led by the important Communist Yeh T'ing, q.v.). A third route was taken by the Second Army, which went through

Nanchang and then marched through Anhwei before arriving in Nanking in March 1927. The Sixth Army, in which Lin Po-ch'ü (q.v.) headed the Political Department, also took the route leading to Nanking. Within a few weeks of the arrival of the Second Army in Nanking, Chiang Kai-shek staged his anti-Communist coup; like many of the surviving Communists working in KMT armies in Shanghai or Nanking, Li fled to Hupeh where the CCP was still maintaining its uneasy alliance with the "Left" KMT in Wuhan, the Hupeh capital. He reportedly continued to work as a political officer in the Wuhan armies, but then all relations with the "Left" KMT were broken when the Communists engineered the Nanchang Uprising on August 1, 1927. One source suggests that Li may have been scheduled for some role in this famous revolt,[6] but from other evidence it appears that he remained in Hupeh. In any case, within a few weeks after the Nanchang Uprising Li was in north Hupeh where, it appears, he was making preparations in one of the areas in which the Communists were planning to stage peasant uprisings.[7] However, these did not materialize in north Hupeh, and Li soon made his way to Shanghai where for most of the next four years he worked in the Party underground. According to Edgar Snow's 1936 interview with Li, he was forced to flee to Hong Kong in 1931, but then he returned to Shanghai.[8] In 1932, presumably because of the ever increasing suppression of the Communists by the KMT, Li went to Kiangsi where the rural base established by Mao Tse-tung and Chu Te had grown to sizable proportions. In Kiangsi Li served in the Red Army's Political Department and by the fall of 1933 he was secretary of the CCP Kiangsi Provincial Committee.[9] In December 1933 he was elected to Executive Committee membership in the Kiangsi Provincial Soviet (see under Tseng Shan and Ch'en Cheng-jen), one of the member soviets of the Chinese Soviet Republic established in Juichin in November 1931. When the Second Congress of the Republic was held in January–February 1934, Li and his wife were elected as members of the Republic's Central Executive Committee, the governing body of the Juichin government until the Long March began in the fall of 1934.

In January 1934, just prior to the above-mentioned Juichin Congress, Li was elected to membership on the Party's Sixth Central Committee; of interest is the fact that Li's wife had been elected to the Central Committee nearly six years earlier. Li made the Long March as a political officer in Mao Tse-tung's First Front Army. After the completion of the March Li worked in the Yü-wang area (then in Kansu, but now in Ninghsia) where Edgar Snow interviewed him in the late summer of 1936. Snow identified him at the time as "chairman of the Central Committee of the Shensi-Kansu-Ninghsia Communist party,"

and a year later Snow's wife (Nym Wales) described him as "acting Chairman of the Kansu Provincial Soviet." Perhaps more important was his role in the Party headquarters, which was at Pao-an in northern Shensi until the end of 1936 and thereafter at Yenan. There Li reportedly headed the Central Committee's Organization Department from 1935 until he relinquished the post to Ch'in Pang-hsien (q.v.) in 1937. From then to at least 1948 Li served as a deputy to Ch'in, Liu Shao-ch'i, Ch'en Yun, and P'eng Chen (qq.v.).

By the early 1940's Li moved into financial and economic work, a field in which he seems to have been without experience, but one in which he has sinced worked. From 1940 to about the end of the war he again served under Ch'en Yun as deputy director of the Party's Finance and Economics Department, and as part of this work he was in charge of a major campaign in the Shensi-Kansu-Ninghsia area to boost production in the fact of an economic blockade enforced by the Nationalists, which worked severe hardships on the Communists' main base. The necessities of the situation required that virtually all organizations take part in productive enterprises, and thus it is probable that Li was in constant contact with Party leaders, heads of cooperatives, and even with elements of the Red Army (see under Wang Chen) who were called upon to increase food and material supplies needed to sustain the military forces and the local population. Like most important leaders in Yenan during the war, Li contributed articles from time to time to the journals and newspapers published in Communist-held areas or to the few journals that were allowed to publish in the Nationalist capital.[10]

From April to June 1945 Li served as deputy secretary-general under Secretary-general Jen Pi-shih of the Party's Seventh National Congress in Yenan. He was among the speakers at the Congress, and when it closed he was elected to the Seventh Central Committee, as was his wife. After the Japanese surrender in the late summer of 1945, Li was among the top Communists sent to Manchuria, a group that included Ch'en Yun, Kao Kang, P'eng Chen, and Lin Piao (qq.v.). When Communist journalist Liu Pai-yü (q.v.) visited Tsitsihar, then the capital of Nunkiang province, in 1946, he identified Li as a general and as political commissar of the West Manchurian Military Region.[11] Within a year or so he was serving as deputy political commissar of the Northeast Military Region (covering all of Manchuria) where he worked under P'eng Chen and Lo Jung-huan. Within the Party organization in Manchuria, the Northeast Bureau, he was first a Bureau member and by 1948 a deputy secretary. Here too he worked under P'eng Chen and afterwards under Lin Piao and Kao Kang.

The Communists' governmental organization in Manchuria from 1946 to 1949 was known as the Northeast Administrative Committee (NEAC), and then from 1949 as the Northeast People's Government (NEPG). From 1948 Li was vice-chairman of the Finance and Economics Committee where he was subordinate to Chairman Ch'en Yun, with whom he had worked so closely in past years; and when the NEAC was reorganized in August 1949 he became a NEPG vice-chairman under Kao Kang. Kao and Li were the senior Communists in Manchuria when the central government was established in Peking, by which time most of the other key leaders in Manchuria had been transferred to the capital. When the new government was formed in October Li was named to membership on the Finance and Economics Committee (FEC), the most important economic body in the early years of the PRC. This was his only assignment in the central government, and the fact that he was the number two man in Manchuria suggests that the Party intended to keep him there for the time being. However, by early 1950 Li was called to Peking and thereafter his positions in Manchuria were largely nominal. In mid-January he left Peking as the ranking member of a group led by Chou En-lai, who was going to Moscow to join Mao Tse-tung in the critical negotiations with the Soviet Union, which led to a series of agreements. On February 16, just two days after the conclusion of the Sino-Soviet Treaty of Friendship, Alliance, and Mutual Assistance, Li was present when Stalin received the Chinese delegation. On the following day Mao and Chou left for home, but Li and Trade Minister Yeh Chi-chuang (q.v.) remained to carry out further negotiations with Soviet leaders. Coinciding with Li's return to Peking in mid-April he received two important posts in the central government. He was promoted to a vice-chairmanship on the government's FEC and he was concurrently named to replace Ch'en Yun as head of the Ministry of Heavy Industry, clearly one of the most important ministries in the central government. Speaking in both capacities, Li made a major report on industry at the third session of the CPPCC in October 1951, a meeting that stressed the importance of increasing production and practicing economy. Thus, when the Central Austerity Committee was formed a few weeks later as an *ad hoc* body, Li was named as one of the vice-chairmen, and not long after, in February 1952, he was made the chairman of another *ad hoc* committee established to improve the efficiency of central government offices.

In August 1952 Li left Peking for Moscow on what proved to be one of the most important missions ever undertaken by a PRC leader and one that was to keep him abroad for nine months. The group was led by Chou En-lai and included such key figures as Ch'en Yun, PLA

deputy chief-of-staff Su Yü, Air Force chief Liu Ya-lou, and Minister of Heavy Industry Wang Ho-shou (who had replaced Li in this post just prior to the delegation's departure). Over the next month this team of specialists negotiated the return to China of the Chinese Changchun Railway and an extension for the joint use of the naval facilities at Port Arthur. Chou and the rest of the group returned to Peking, but Li Fu-ch'un remained in Moscow and a few weeks later, in October, he was a member of Liu Shao-chi's delegation to the 19th CPSU Congress. Li remained in Moscow after this delegation returned home, and then in March 1953 he was a member of Chou En-lai's delegation to Stalin's funeral; two months later Li went to Prague from Moscow for the eighth anniversary of the end of World War II. In the interim, Foreign Trade Minister Yeh Chi-chuang (q.v.) had arrived in Moscow, and together with Li Fu-ch'un he negotiated and signed on March 21, 1953, a trade protocol for 1953, a protocol to the February 1950 agreement on credits to the PRC, and an agreement for Soviet assistance to China for the construction of new power stations. As already indicated, Li remained in Moscow for several weeks after the signing of these agreements, but the importance of his delayed departure did not become public knowledge until four months after his return to Peking (May) when, speaking before a meeting of the Central People's Government Council on September 16, he revealed that the Soviets had agreed to assist the Chinese in the construction and renovation of 141 large-scale projects, most of them related to heavy industry. It was revealed in the Chinese press at this time that the 141 projects were to be in addition to the 50 already under construction with Soviet assistance.

In November 1952, while Li was in Moscow, the PRC established the State Planning Commission in preparation for the launching of the First Five Year Plan (1953–1957). As originally constituted, the commission had Kao Kang as its chairman, Teng Tzu-hui as vice-chairman, and 15 members, one of whom was Li Fu-ch'un. Then in September 1953, Li and Chia T'o-fu (q.v.) were made vice-chairmen. Soon after Li received this promotion, Planning Commission Chairman Kao Kang fell from power, and so it is probable that Li became de facto chairman until the commission was reorganized at the first session of the First NPC in September 1954. The reorganized commission was placed directly under Chou En-lai's State Council (a somewhat lower status than it had previously held) and Li was made the commission chairman, also assuming at this time a vice-premiership under Chou. Li has continued to hold these key posts since that time. The day after the First NPC session closed in late September 1954, an important Soviet delegation led by Khrushchev and Bulganin arrived in Peking to conduct top-level negotiations regarding many facets of Sino-Soviet relations. Li was one of only nine official Chinese negotiators, and on October 12 he signed the Sino-Soviet Scientific and Technical Cooperation Agreement, one of several negotiated during the visit.

With the assumption of the Planning Commission chairmanship in 1954, Li moved into the number two spot in the PRC's economic hierarchy, ranking behind Politburo member Ch'en Yun. Although a precise delineation cannot be made between their functions in the mid-fifties, it appears that Ch'en worked principally at policy levels, whereas Li (although obviously involved in policy decisions) was primarily responsible for the day-to-day functioning of the economy through his chairmanship of the State Planning Commission. The relationship between the two men is perhaps best illustrated by events in 1955, the year that the First Five-Year Plan was officially adopted (even though it had theoretically been in operation since 1953). It was Ch'en who spoke on the Plan before the Party Conference in March 1955, but it fell to Li to present it to the government before the second session of the First NPC in July 1955. His extremely long speech is one of the most important made in the history of the PRC and, together with the Plan itself, provides a wealth of data on China's economy.

In March 1956 Li became a vice-chairman of the newly established Scientific Planning Commission under the State Council, but he relinquished the post 14 months later when the commission was reorganized. At the Party's Eighth Congress in September 1956 Li was one of the featured speakers, his address dealing with the strengthening of state planning work. When the meetings closed he was elected to membership on the Eighth Central Committee, and, on the following day, when the new committee held its first plenum, he was elected for the first time to the Politburo. A year and a half later, at the Fifth Plenum (May 1958), he was added as a new member of the Party's Central Secretariat, the organ responsible for implementing Politburo policies. While the Plenum was in session, Li was once again in Moscow, this time as the ranking deputy to Ch'en Yun, who had gone there to attend (as an observer) a meeting of the Council for Mutual Economic Assistance, the economic arm of the Warsaw Pact nations. Both Ch'en and Li were received by Khrushchev during this visit, and Ch'en attended a one-day session of the Warsaw Pact, a meeting that Li may also have attended.

During the first decade of the PRC, Li's prime responsibilities had been within the CCP and government, but he also belonged to two "mass" organizations. From 1949 to 1954 he was a member of the Executive Board of the Sino-Soviet Friendship Association, and from 1953 to 1957 he was an Executive Committee member of the All-China Federation of Trade Unions (ACFTU). He was not re-elected to the new ACFTU Executive Committee when the Federation held its Seventh Congress in December 1957, but he did make a major address to the Congress that summarized the state of the economy as the First Five-Year Plan drew to a close. As an official of the executive branch of government Li had taken part in the annual sessions of the First NPC, although he himself was not a deputy. But he was a deputy from his native Hunan to the Second NPC (1959–1964) and was again elected to the Third NPC, which opened in late 1964. In September 1959, when the State Council was partially reorganized, he received a new post as director of the Office of Industry and Communications, an office that coordinates the work of several subordinate ministries and bureaus within the State Council. However, after holding the post for a year and a half, he relinquished it to one of his deputies, Po I-po (April 1961).

Although no precise date can be established, it is evident that by about 1959 Li had replaced Ch'en Yun as the PRC's top economic official, Ch'en presumably having fallen into political disfavor during the early stages of the Great Leap Forward, which began in 1958. Suggestive of this change was the publication of a collection of articles written in commemoration of the 10th anniversary of the PRC.[12] Because the volume contained articles by the nation's most prominent officials (e.g., Liu Shao-ch'i, Chou En-lai, Lin Piao), Ch'en Yun, as the key economic official during the first decade of the PRC, might have been expected to write the leading article on economics, but instead the task fell to Li. Similarly, at the Party's important Ninth Plenum in January 1961, Li delivered the only report on economics, a role that Ch'en Yun had normally played at previous plenums. Li's ability to shift with the changing political tides seems to account in part for his passing through the difficult years of the Great Leap Forward and its rather disastrous aftermath without falling into political disfavor.

Since the mid-fifties Li has taken part in talks with visiting delegations, particularly economic groups from Communist nations. He has, in addition, participated on occasion in negotiations with visiting Communist delegations, especially in the early sixties when the Sino-Soviet ideological dispute sharply intensified. In this connection, Li led a delegation to Hanoi in August–September 1960 for the 15th anniversary of the North Vietnamese government and to attend the Third Congress of the Vietnamese Workers' (Communist) Party. But principally his role has been in the domestic economic field, and there have been few occasions (particularly since he

eclipsed Ch'en Yun) that he has not been a featured speaker at one of the innumerable economic conferences held in China. Li rose to
new heights during the early stages of the "great
proletarian cultural revolution" launched in 1966.
In the fall of that year he was identified as a
member of the Politburo's Standing Committee,
the most powerful single organization in China,
a position to which he was probably elected at
the Party's 11th Plenum in August 1966.

1. Edgar Snow, *Random Notes on Red China,
1936–1945* (Cambridge, Mass., 1957), p. 132.
2. Nym Wales, *Inside Red China* (New York,
1939), p. 337.
3. Chow Tse-tsung, *The May Fourth Movement* (Cambridge, Mass., 1960), p. 249; *ECMM*
77, p. 10.
4. Information supplied by Dr. Conrad Brandt.
5. Li Jui, *Mao Tse-tung t'ung-chih te ch'u-ch'i
ko-ming huo-tung* (Comrade Mao Tse-tung's
early revolutionary activities; Peking, 1957), p.
249.
6. Jerome Ch'en, *Mao and the Chinese Revolution* (London, 1965), p. 129.
7. Roy Hofheinz, Jr., "The Autumn Harvest
Insurrection," *The China Quarterly,* no. 32:47
(October–December 1967).
8. Snow, p. 133.
9. Ch'en Ch'ang-feng, *On the Long March
with Chairman Mao* (Peking, 1959), pp. 14–15.
10. Chün-tu Hsüeh, *The Chinese Communist
Movement, 1937–1949* (Stanford, Calif., 1962).
11. Liu Pai-yü, *Huan-hsing tung pei* (Traveling in the northeast; Shanghai, 1946), p. 146.
12. *Ten Glorious Years* (Peking, 1960), pp.
129–150.

Li Han-chün

(?–1927; Hupeh). Early Chinese Marxist; a CCP
founder.

Li Han-chün was among the small group that
founded the CCP. He was only a Party member
for a very brief time, but he had a strong influence in turning veteran Communist leader
Tung Pi-wu to Marxism. Li's exact birthplace is
unknown; he may have been born in Ch'ien-
chiang where the Li family originated or in the
town of Ching-shan where his parents later
moved. He grew up in an intellectual revolutionary environment; his older brother Li Shu-
ch'eng was a T'ung-meng hui member who took
part in the overthrow of the Manchu Dynasty
and became a secretary to Sun Yat-sen in 1912.
Probably influenced by his brother who had
studied in Japan, Li also went there about 1913
to finish his secondary schooling. During his
six years in Japan Li studied in the engineering
department of Tokyo Imperial University, but
more important for his later career, he became
acquainted with Marxian ideas. He returned to

China in 1919, the year of the opening of the
May Fourth Movement, which made such an
impact on the young intellectuals of Li's generation. He went to Shanghai where he shared a
large house in the French Concession with a
number of relatives. Because the family had
means, Li was not pressed to find work and was
able to devote himself to the translation of
Marxist literature and the exchange of ideas with
other young students also interested in Marxism. Being fluent in Japanese he was able to
translate radical Japanese works. He also served
as an editor in the important Commercial Press
in Shanghai. Among his particular friends were
Li Ta, Ch'en Tu-hsiu, Shao Li-tzu, and Tai
Chi-t'ao, the last two soon to leave the Marxists
and become important members of the KMT.
The group frequently met in secret at Tai's residence in Shanghai where they made plans to
organize a Communist party in China. Ch'en
Tu-hsiu (q.v.), who was one of the prime
movers, introduced the group to Comintern
representative Gregory Voitinsky when the
latter visited Shanghai in early 1920. It was
through the efforts of Voitinsky Ch'en, Li, and
their friends that a small nucleus of a communist party came into being in Shanghai in May
1920.[1] A year later this nucleus, plus small cells
of Marxists from other cities, founded the CCP.

As part of a program to develop other cells in
China, Li went to Wuhan in the latter part of
1920 to discuss the matter with Tung Pi-wu and
Ch'en T'an-ch'iu (q.v.). Returning to Shanghai
he and a colleague established a "committee of
the workers' movement" in January 1921, which
distributed large quantities of socialist literature.[2] In the meantime, Li had taken part in the
publication of Shanghai weekly entitled *Lao-
tung chieh* (The world of labor), probably as the
chief editor.[3] The views he expressed in this and
other publications illustrated his preference for
a legalistic approach to Marxism, an approach
that would be rejected when the Party was
founded in Shanghai in July 1921.

The first sessions of the founding congress of
the CCP were held in Li's home. He and Li Ta
represented the Marxists from Shanghai. The
meetings were interrupted by a police raid on
Li's home; everyone fled but Li Han-chün and
Ch'en Kung-po (q.v.), who had to face a police
search and interrogation.[4] They were therefore
unable to attend the final meeting of the congress, which took place on a houseboat on a
lake near Chia-hsing, Chekiang. According to
Ch'en T'an-ch'iu, a delegate from Wuhan, the
Party established a provisional central bureau
with Li Han-chün as one of its three alternate
members.[5] Tung Pi-wu remembered Li as one of
those elected to the first Central Committee.[6]

By the early part of 1922 Li was in Wuhan,
where he was deeply involved in the labor
movement, working in cooperation with Ch'en

T'an-ch'iu and Hsiang Ying (qq.v.). In March of that year he participated in the inaugural meeting of a "club" (chi-lo pu) for workers on the important Peking-Hankow Railway.[7] The "club," in turn, took an active part in the preparations for the inauguration of a union of the Peking-Hankow railroad workers. However, these endeavors were forceably suppressed by northern warlord Wu P'ei-fu in February 1923; events are described in the biography of Teng Chung-hsia.

Li's participation in the Peking-Hankow Railway labor movement seems to have been his last important association with the CCP. At sometime in the early twenties he left or was expelled from the Party.[8]

He did, however, continue his interest in politics and also taught economics at a university in Wuhan. He participated in the left-KMT government established in Wuhan in late 1926, becoming minister of Education in the Hupeh Provincial Government at about this time. Li remained in Wuhan after the mid-1927 break between the CCP and the KMT, and toward the end of the year he and his friend Tung Pi-wu went into hiding in the Japanese concession. The KMT generals in charge of Wuhan sent a unit to surround the concession. Tung managed to escape, but Li was captured and immediately executed (December 17), allegedly in connection with the Communists' attempt to capture Canton (the "Canton Commune"). This would seem to contradict the generally accepted supposition that Li had given up his CCP membership in the early twenties. It is possible, of course, that he had rejoined the Party—as suggested in Tung Pi-wu's interview with Nym Wales a decade later.[9]

Li's *Ma-k'o-szu tzu-pen ju-men* (How to study Marx's *Das Kapital*) was a popular reference for some of the early Marxist study groups. He also wrote for a number of the literary publications of the May Fourth period, which were oriented toward Marxism. These writings are amply referenced in Chow Tse-tsung's *Research Guide to the May Fourth Movement* (1963). Li was concerned with theoretical Marxism but his intellectual approach to the subject has been scorned by the surviving leadership of the CCP. At the First Congress he voiced his objections to an active organizational program before further study had been undertaken, and he felt that anyone accepting Marxist principles should be admitted to the Party without having to take part as an activist. In the words of one writer, Li made the "remarkable suggestion that delegates be sent to Germany and Russia to examine the relative merits of the German and Russian revolutions. In this he was supported by Ch'en Kung-po [q.v.] and others."[10] This view, however, was rejected. Li's position has been called "Menshevist legalism" by the impor-

tant CCP leader Ch'en Yun (q.v.). This derogatory term appeared in Ch'en's essay "How to be a Communist Party Member," which belongs to the official handbook of essays propagating the thought of Mao Tse-tung and which was used during the ideological movement launched in 1942.

Li's older brother, Li Shu-ch'eng (1877–1965), was also arrested in 1927 but later released. When the Communists took over the mainland in 1949 he became the first PRC minister of Agriculture, holding the post until September 1954.

1. Chow Tse-tsung, *The May Fourth Movement* (Cambridge, Mass., 1960), p. 248.

2. Jean Chesneaux, *Le Mouvement ouvrier chinois de 1919 à 1927* (Paris, 1962), p. 248.

3. *Ibid.,* p. 250.

4. C. Martin Wibur, ed., *The Communist Movement in China: An Essay Written in 1924 by Ch'en Kung-po* (New York, 1960), pp. 23–24.

5. C. Martin Wilbur and Julie Lien-ying How, eds., *Documents on Communism, Nationalism, and Soviet Advisers in China, 1918–1927* (New York, 1956), p. 80.

6. Nym Wales, *Red Dust* (Stanford, Calif., 1952), p. 40.

7. Hsi-wu lao-jen [Elder Hsi-wu], *"Erh-ch'i" hui-i-lu* (Reminiscences of "February Seventh"; Peking, 1957), pp. 59, 67–68.

8. Wilbur and How, pp. 48, 491–492.

9. Wales, p. 43.

10. Benjamin I. Schwartz, *Chinese Communism and the Rise of Mao* (Cambridge, Mass., 1951), p. 34.

Li Hsien-nien

(c. 1907–   ; Huang-an hsien, Hupeh). Minister of Finance; vice-premier; member, CCP Politburo and Secretariat.

Li Hsien-nien, one of Peking's leading specialists in economic affairs, led guerrilla units in the Oyüwan Soviet in the late 1920's and early 1930's. After completing the Long March he was a top commander with the New Fourth Army in Hupeh during the Sino-Japanese War. He was elected to the Party Central Committee in 1945, and during the formative years of the PRC he was the senior Party official in Hupeh. The minister of Finance since 1954, Li was elected to the Politburo in 1956 and to the Central Secretariat in 1958.

Li comes from a poor peasant family in Huang-an (now Hung-an) hsien in east Hupeh not far from the Honan border and about 100 miles northeast of Wuhan. Other prominent Communists native to Huang-an include Tung Pi-wu and Cheng Wei-san (qq.v.). Li worked as a carpenter in his youth and, according to a colleague, he "did not study in a university or receive any kind of higher education."[1] After the Northern Expeditional forces reached Hupeh in 1926, Li spent a brief period in the army as a soldier, but when the KMT and the CCP split in mid-1927 he returned to his native hsien. By now a CCP member, Li began organizing the peasantry in and around Huang-an; similar activities were being conducted in this same region by Wang Shu-sheng, Cheng Wei-san, Hsu Hai-tung (qq.v.), and a number of other young Communists. Over the next few years they developed armed guerrilla bands that, in the late 1920's and early 1930's, provided an important part of the military strength for the Oyüwan (Hupeh-Honan-Anhwei) Soviet, which was second only in importance to the Kiangsi Soviet where Mao Tse-tung and Chu Te were in command.

Military leader Hsu Hsiang-ch'ien had been working in the Oyüwan area from about the same time as Li, and then in 1931 the political leadership of the base was strengthened by the arrival of such top Communist leaders as Chang Kuo-t'ao, Shen Tse-min, and Ch'en Ch'ang-hao (qq.v.). In this same year the Party and government organs were reorganized, and in November the various military units were combined into the Fourth Front Army under Hsu Hsiang-ch'ien's command. By approximately that time Li was secretary of the Party Committee in Huang-an hsien, chairman of the small "soviet government" in the same hsien, and commander of the Huang-an Detachment. The Nationalist government, apprehensive of the growing strength of the Oyüwan base, conducted a series of strong attacks against the Communists. The Red Army was able to withstand the first of these, but a campaign begun in mid-1932 led to the evacuation of most of the units in the fall of 1932. (Information on the Communists who remained behind in Oyüwan is contained in the biography of Hsu Hai-tung.)

In late 1932 and early 1933 the Fourth Front Army moved in a generally westward direction and, after fighting a number of engagements with Nationalist forces, settled down in northern Szechwan. There they established the T'ung-Nan-Pa Soviet (see under Wang Hung-k'un) and reorganized their military forces. At approximately this time Li was made political commissar of the 30th Army, one of the five armies under the Fourth Front Army.[2] Chang Kuo-t'ao, Hsu Hsiang-ch'ien, and their men remained in this area for nearly two years. Then, in the early summer of 1935, the Chang-Hsu forces met the Long Marchers led by Mao and Chu Te in west Szechwan. The conflict that developed between Mao and Chang Kuo-t'ao at this time is described in Chang's biography. In brief, the two leaders separated and went toward different destinations, each taking under his command some of his own units and some from his opponent.

Much of Li's 30th Army went north to Shensi with Mao Tse-tung, but Li remained with Chang and Hsu Hsiang-ch'ien, who were now joined by Chu Te and Liu Po-ch'eng.

Not long after separating from Mao, Chang Kuo-t'ao led his troops into the Kan-tzu area of west Sikang where in the summer of 1936 they were joined by still another major element of the Long March—the Second Front Army led by Jen Pi-shih, Ho Lung, and Hsiao K'o (q.v.), which had come from west Hunan. These Long Marchers then proceeded northward, and in the fall of 1936 they rendezvoused in east Kansu with elements from Mao's armies which had been sent to help them make the last lap of the Long March to join Mao in north Shensi (see under Tso Ch'üan). However, still another dispute broke out, and as a result, the Fifth, Ninth, and 30th Armies were ordered to march westwards toward far-off Sinkiang. Maoist scribes claim that this was ordered personally by Chang Kuo-t'ao, and that it involved more than 10,000 men.[3] In late December 1936, under the command of Hsu Hsiang-ch'ien, the three armies crossed the Yellow River at Ching-yuan (northeast of Lanchow) and began their ill-fated march up the Kansu Corridor. By the time they reached the vicinity of Chiu-ch'üan, some 400 miles northwest of Lanchow, Hsu and his men were a badly mauled and demoralized force of less than 2,000. At this juncture, Hsu Hsiang-ch'ien and a handful of others were ordered to turn back and proceed directly to north Shensi, and thus the command in Kansu was turned over to Li, who was still political commissar of the 30th Army. Prior to this the Fifth Army had been virtually wiped out in encounters fought by the Communists with Nationalist General Hu Tsung-nan and northwest warlords Ma Pu-fang. Among those already dead were Tung Chen-t'ang, the Fifth Army commander, Yang K'o-ming, the director of the Fifth Army's Political Department, and Ch'en Hai-sung, the political commissar of the Ninth Army.

With Li now in command, the remnant forces were divided into Right and Left Detachments. Li's Oyüwan colleague Wang Shu-sheng took charge of the 500-man Right Detachment, and Li became head of the Left Detachment of under 1,500 men. Both units then moved into the Ch'i-lien mountains on the Kansu-Tsinghai border and proceeded a few hundred miles westward. Plagued by endless difficulties, including desertions, they now received orders from Mao to conserve their strength and to move to either Sinkiang or Mongolia. Soon after this they arrived at the westernmost edge of Kansu, and from there they moved northward where in the spring of 1937 they reached Hsing-hsing-hsia on the Kansu-Sinkiang border. Li's men, now down to 700, were met by Ch'en Yün (q.v.), who had been sent by Mao and who also arranged to have

Li and his men trucked to Tihwa, the Sinkiang capital. From there they were transported to north Shensi, having suffered through what may have been the most difficult part of the Long March. The disastrous Kansu trek is presented by its major chronicler, Li T'ien-huan (the director of Li's Political Department), as an example of Chang Kuo-t'ao's duplicity and poor leadership.[4] In taking part in this extraordinary event, Li and his colleagues traveled some 2,000 more miles than their fellow Long Marchers who had proceeded directly to north Shensi. Aside from those mentioned above, other men who made this march and who went on to have careers of significance after 1949 include Huang Huo-ch'ing (q.v.), Chu Liang-ts'ai, Li Cho-jan, Ch'eng Shih-ts'ai, Tseng Ch'uan-liu, and Kuo T'ien-min.

After going to Yenan, Li enrolled in the Anti-Japanese Military and Political Academy (K'ang-ta) in late 1937. Then, at approximately the time that Wuhan fell to the Japanese (October 1938), Li was sent back to the old Oyüwan area to organize and lead resistance units which were ultimately incorporated into the New Fourth Army, the Communists' chief force in east-central China. According to one account, Li had arrived in the Oyüwan region with only 37 men.[5] A unit known as the Fourth Detachment had been operating around Li's native Huang-an hsien from early in the war, but in early 1939 it moved to north Anhwei. Therefore, from 1939 Li's Hupeh-Honan Assault Column (t'ing-chin tsung-tui) became the Communists' most important unit operating north of Wuhan; its major area of operations was a fairly wide region on both sides of the important Peking-Hankow Railway between Hsin-yang, Honan, and Ying-shan, Hupeh, as well as sectors in the Ta-pieh Mountains on the Hupeh-Honan-Anhwei border.

In addition to directing his guerrilla bands, Li was also fighting in cooperation with KMT armies in the early war years. However, KMT–CCP relations rapidly worsened, particularly in the 1939–40 period, which was marked by an ever increasing number of "incidents" between Communist and KMT troops. Mao Tse-tung took note of these in a directive of May 1940, which praised Li for having "repulsed" KMT attacks in central and eastern Hupeh.[6] These episodes reached a grand climax at the time of the New Fourth Army Incident of January 1941 (see under Yeh T'ing), when important elements of the New Fourth Army (but not Li's) were badly mauled by the Nationalists. The Communists immediately reorganized their forces, at which time Li's troops were designated the Fifth Division. Li became the commander and political commissar, positions he held throughout the war.

In the latter war years (especially 1942–43), guerrilla units under Li's command were operating throughout much of the rural areas of cen-

tral and east Hupeh, and in small portions of Honan, Anhwei, Hunan, and Kiangsi.[7] In this regard, the Fifth Division operated a great distance away from the other six divisions of the New Fourth Army, the major strength of which was concentrated in the regions north of Shanghai. According to a 1944 U.S. Army estimate, Li then had 22,000 men under his command who were armed with 14,000 weapons.[8]

At the Party's Seventh National Congress, held in Yenan from April to June 1945, Li was elected, probably in absentia, a member of the CCP Central Committee. Not long afterwards, when the Japanese surrendered in August 1945, Chu Te, commander of the Communist armies, sent a series of instructions to the commander-in-chief of the Japanese armies in China. Among these was an order to send "your representative" in Wuhan to General Li's headquarters in the Ta-pieh Mountain region to arrange for the surrender of Japanese troops in Hupeh and Honan.[9] Predictably, this order was not obeyed, because the Japanese surrendered to representatives of Chiang Kai-shek's national government. In the immediate postwar period, as the Communists and Nationalists jockeyed for strategic positions, a series of skirmishes took place in many parts of China. Li's forces were badly mauled by the Nationalists in October 1945, and this was noted by Mao Tse-tung a few days later in a bitterly worded statement.[10] Li's men were forced to retreat to the mountainous regions of north-central Hupeh. The difficulties for the Communists abated considerably in early 1946 following the signing of the cease-fire agreement worked out between the Communists and Nationalists by U.S. Special Envoy George C. Marshall. However, in June 1946, Li's men were again under heavy attack; known by this time as the Central Plains Liberation Army (commanding the Central Plains Liberated Area), they shifted eastward across the Peking-Hankow Railway and settled around the town of Hsuan-hua-tien, not far north of Li's native Huang-an hsien. But continuing KMT assaults were so severe that Li was ordered to evacuate most of his troops westward where, over the next few months, he established bases in south Shensi, southwest Honan, and northwest Hupeh. Some of his troops remained in central and eastern Hupeh to conduct guerrilla warfare, and others moved northeast to Anhwei to join other units of the New Fourth Army.[11]

Li was back in the Oyüwan region by mid-1947, and over the course of the next year and a half his troops played a significant role in the conquest of the area. Many of his battles were fought in coordination with Liu Po-ch'eng's troops, which, in the period from 1947 to 1949, made a number of thrusts into the Central Plains region. By 1948 Li was serving under Liu as a deputy commander of the Central Plains PLA, which was redesignated the Second Field Army during the winter of 1948–49. By the spring of 1949 the Second Field Army was preparing to assault the major Yangtze River cities in cooperation with Lin Piao's Fourth Field Army. The Wuhan area fell to the Communists in April–May 1949; Liu Po-ch'eng's army soon moved into the southwest, but Lin Piao's men remained in Wuhan, and thus in 1949 Li served for a time as a deputy commander of Lin's Fourth Field Army.

With the Communist conquest of Hupeh, Li quickly emerged as the dominant official there. In May 1949 he became the first Communist governor, as well as commander and political commissar of the Hupeh Military District. At this same time, or soon thereafter, he also became the ranking secretary of the CCP Hupeh Committee. He relinquished the post of commander to Wang Shu-sheng in 1950, but he retained the other three until 1954. Li was also a member of the Central Plains Provisional People's Government, which was established in March 1949 (see under Teng Tzu-hui); this temporary, multi-provincial government organ was abolished in February 1950, when it was replaced, in effect, by the larger Central-South Military and Administrative Committee (CSMAC), which had jurisdiction over Honan, Hupeh, Hunan, Kiangsi, Kwangtung, and Kwangsi provinces. Li was a member of the CSMAC, which was headquartered in Wuhan under Lin Piao's chairmanship, and from March 1950 he was also a member of the CSMAC's Land Reform Committee. Six months later, in September, Li was appointed chairman of the Hupeh government's Finance and Economics Committee.

In the meantime, like most major regional and provincial leaders, Li was given an assignment in the national government when it was established in October 1949. From then until the reorganization of the central government in 1954, he was a member of the People's Revolutionary Military Council. However, Li spent little time in Peking during the first five years of the PRC; rather, he worked in Wuhan where he was one of the top administrators and where, in the course of these years, he began to specialize more and more in economic affairs. In the latter part of 1951 and early 1952, a number of key officials in Wuhan were occupied with the so-called Sung Ying case (see under Chang P'ing-hua). This major instance of corruption within the Party reached a climax in February 1952 when the hierarchy in Wuhan was reshuffled. Among the many dismissals, demotions, and even imprisonments, two directly affected Li. Both the Wuhan mayor, Wu Te-feng (q.v.), and the Wuhan Party secretary, Chang P'ing-hua, were removed, and Li was named to succeed both men. However, because Wang Jen-chung (q.v.) became both acting mayor and acting secretary by early 1953, it appears that Li had been given, in effect, a short-term, trouble-shooting task.

In October 1952 Li was promoted from member to vice-chairman (one of several) of the CSMAC, a post to which he was reappointed in January 1953 when the CSMAC was reorganized into the Central-South Administrative Committee (CSAC). In May he relinquished his post on the regional Land Reform Committee, but at the same time he succeeded Lin Piao as chairman of the CSAC's Finance and Economics Committee. Not long before this, in March 1953, Li was identified as third deputy secretary of the Party's Central-South Bureau. These posts, taken together with those already mentioned, suggest that until his transfer to Peking in mid-1954, Li was among the half-dozen top leaders in central-south China. He was clearly outranked by Lin Piao and Lo Jung-huan, but Lin was ill for much of this period and Lo spent most of his time in Peking. Other central-south China regional leaders of approximately equal stature to Li included Teng Tzu-hui, Yeh Chien-ying, T'an Cheng, Chang Yun-i, T'ao Chu, and Li Hsueh-feng, but none of these six had reached the Politburo in 1956, the year Li Hsien-nien was elected.

Like most top regional leaders, Li held nominal posts in the "mass" organizations, serving as chairman of the Hupeh chapter of the China Peace Committee from 1950 and as a vice-chairman of the central-south China branch of the Sino-Soviet Friendship Association from the same year. He relinquished these, and his numerous other posts, in June 1954 when he was transferred to Peking. Li replaced Teng Hsiao-p'ing as minister of Finance, and he also became a vice-chairman under Ch'en Yun of the Government Administration Council's Finance and Economics Committee. A short time later Li was elected a deputy from Hupeh to the First NPC which, at its first session in September 1954, inaugurated the constitutional government and partially reorganized the central government. Li was reappointed minister of Finance, and he was also appointed a vice-premier of the State Council and a member of the National Defense Council, the successor organ to the People's Revolutionary Military Council to which he had previously belonged. In the following month he became director of the newly established Fifth Staff Office under Chou En-lai's State Council. This office was charged with coordinating the work of the various State Council ministries and bureaus involved in financial and trade affairs. An employee in the ministry of Finance throughout most of the 1950's has stated that Li was seldom present at the ministry, but rather spent most of his time at the more important Fifth Staff Office.[12] Li continues to head this important body which, since September 1959, has been known as the Finance and Trade Staff Office. Three years later, in October 1962, he was given further responsibilities in the economic sector when he was appointed as an additional vice-chairman of the State Planning Commission, which is engaged in long-range planning.

In September 1956, at the Party's Eighth National Congress, Li delivered a major speech on price policy, and at the close of the meetings he was re-elected a member of the CCP Central Committee. Immediately afterwards, at the First Plenum of the new Central Committee, he was elected for the first time to the Politburo. Of the 17 Politburo members elected at that time, only three specialized in economic affairs: Ch'en Yun, Li Fu-ch'un, and Li Hsien-nien. (Another economic specialist, Po I-po, was elected an alternate Politburo member.) A year and a half later, at the Fifth Plenum (May 25, 1958), Li and his colleague Li Fu-ch'un were made additional secretaries of the Party's Central Secretariat, the organ charged with implementing the decisions of the Politburo. This appointment was made immediately after the second session of the Eighth Party Congress, which had given a strong endorsement to the Great Leap Forward launched a short time before. It is not clear if Li's appointment was related to this important program, but from an organizational viewpoint he was then one of only five men to hold membership on both the Politburo and the Secretariat, and one of three vice-premiers (out of a total of 12) who was concurrently on the Secretariat.

Prior to Li's transfer to the capital in 1954, he had worked almost exclusively in domestic affairs. Since then, however, he has become increasingly involved in foreign affairs, and in the decade between 1954 and 1964 he was abroad on six occasions. Three of these trips took him to Albania; he led a group to Tirana in November–December 1954 to attend celebrations marking the 10th anniversary of the "liberation" of Albania from Nazi Germany and to sign credit and trade agreements. He was there again in February 1961 as leader of the CCP delegation to the Fourth Congress of the Albanian Communist Party, and in November–December 1964 he led the Chinese delegation to the 20th anniversary of the "liberation" from the Germans. In July 1956 Li headed the Chinese delegation to Ulan Bator on the occasion of the 35th anniversary of the Mongolian People's Republic, and in November 1957 he was a member of Mao Tse-tung's important group which went to Moscow to take part in the 40th anniversary of the Bolshevik Revolution. When Czech President Zapotocky died while the Chinese were in Moscow, Li was dispatched to Prague to head Peking's delegation to the funeral. Finally, in August 1964 Li led a group to Bucharest to attend ceremonies commemorating the 20th anniversary of Rumania's "liberation."

In addition to these trips abroad, Li has taken part in negotiations with scores of delegations visiting China. Apart from the above-mentioned agreements signed in Albania in December 1954, Li was the signatory for China to at least 18 treaties, agreements, protocols, or joint communiqués dealing with commercial matters in the period from January 1959 to November 1962. These were signed with representatives from Albania (January 1959, February 1961, April 1961, and January 1962), East Germany (January 1960), North Korea (October 1960 and November 1962), Cuba (November 1960), and Ghana (August 1961).

From the mid-1950's Li has appeared in public on countless occasions. Many of these have been purely ceremonial, but the most important have been in connection with financial matters. He continues to serve as a deputy from Hupeh to the NPC (the Second, from 1959 to 1964, and the Third, which opened in December 1964). Li has seldom written for the professional economic journals, but he is widely known for his major reports on the national budget delivered to the NPC sessions (or to meetings of the NPC Standing Committee when the full Congress is not in session). Collectively, these reports represent a major source of information on the financial system, a fact well reflected in Western texts on China's economy. In addition to these reports, and the important, above-mentioned speech to the Eighth Party Congress, Li is also the author of three economic articles for the Party's leading journal, *Hung-ch'i* (Red flag, no. 10, 1958; no. 2, 1959; no. 1, 1960). Another useful article appeared in the *JMJP* (September 29, 1959) to mark the 10th anniversary of the PRC, and this was reprinted in Peking in 1960 in a series of articles entitled *Ten Glorious Years*.

Li is married to Lin Chia-mei, a minor official in the Public Health Ministry in the mid-1950's, and an employee in her husband's Finance and Trade Staff Office since 1958. Li has at least one son who, in 1965, was studying English in Peking at the Number Two Foreign Languages Institute.[13]

1. *SCMP* 2362, p. 11.
2. Norman Hanwell, "The Chinese Red Army," *Asia*, no. 5:317–322 (May 1936).
3. *Selected Works of Mao Tse-tung* (Peking, 1964), I, 252.
4. *Hung-ch'i p'iao-p'iao* (Red flag fluttering; Peking, 1957), III, 206–210; *Ibid.*, X, 73–111.
5. Anna Louise Strong, *Tomorrow's China* (New York, 1948), p. 53.
6. *Selected Works of Mao Tse-tung* (Peking, 1965), II, 431–436.
7. *K'ang-Jih chan-cheng shih-ch'i chieh-fang-ch'ü kai-k'uang* (A sketch of the liberated areas during the Anti-Japanese War; Peking, 1953), p. 114; *Chung-kuo kung-ch'an tang tsai chung-nan-ti-ch'ü ling-tao ko-ming tou-cheng te li-shih*

tzu-liao (Historical materials on the revolutionary struggles led by the CCP in central-south China; Wuhan, 1951), I, 20.

8. Lyman P. Van Slyke, ed., *The Chinese Communist Movement: A Report of the United States War Department, July 1945* (Stanford, Calif., 1968), pp. 180–181.

9. *Selected Works of Mao Tse-tung* (Peking, 1961), IV, 39.

10. *Ibid.*, pp. 65–69.

11. *Ibid.*, pp. 91, 113–118; Strong, pp. 58–59.

12. Interview, Hong Kong, July 1964.

13. Interview with a former teacher at the Foreign Languages Institute, New York, August 1967.

Li Hsueh-feng

(c.1906–   ; Yung-chi, Shansi). First secretary, North China Bureau, CCP; member, Central Secretariat, CCP; member, CCP Central Committee.

A Party organizational specialist, Li Hsueh-feng is a veteran north China Party leader who has risen to a secretaryship on the powerful Party Central Secretariat. The course of his career since the mid-fifties suggests that he ranks just below the Politburo members.

Li was born in Yung-chi, in southwest Shansi near the Yellow River. Nothing is known of his early career, but by the winter of 1937–38 he was one of the top leaders in Party organizational work in southeast Shansi.[1] Little is known of Li's wartime record, but judging from his participation in a memorial service (1965) for Chang Yu-ch'ing, a leading north China official and one-time secretary of the Shansi CCP Committee until his death in 1942, it appears that Li remained in the Shansi area throughout the war. It is also probable that he was affiliated with the Shansi-Hopeh-Shantung-Honan (Chin-Chi-Lu-Yü) Border Region (see under Yang Hsiu-feng and Liu Po-ch'eng), because in March 1946 Li was a member of the presidium for a session of the Chin-Chi-Lu-Yü Assembly. In the next month Li was identified as secretary of the T'ai-hang CCP Committee.[2] T'ai-hang was one of the major sub-divisions of the Chin-Chi-Lu-Yü Border Region, and its eastern border roughly paralleled the important rail line from Shih-chia-chuang in Hopeh to Hsin-hsiang in north Honan. In the late forties, during the civil war against the Nationalists, the armies led by Liu Po-ch'eng moved from the Chin-Chi-Lu-Yü area to central China, and in 1948 Li was serving as a member of the Party's Central China Bureau. In the following year he was head of the bureau's Organizational Department; he was identified in this capacity in March 1949 when, in the wake of the southward-advancing Communist armies, the Communists formed the Central Plains Provisional People's Government, whose capital was at Kai-

feng in north Honan. Li was named to the government council when it was established in March 1949, serving under important Party leader Teng Tzu-hui, a man with whom he would be directly associated for the next five years. It was also in 1949 that he was the political commissar for the Honan Military District. Apparently this army post was one of his few formal associations with the Communist military forces, a fact which tends to set him apart from the top Chinese Communist leaders, the vast majority of whom have had extensive military backgrounds.

In accordance with the steady southward progress of the PLA in 1949, the Central China Bureau of the Party was redesignated as the Central-South Bureau; Li retained his post as head of the Organization Department and held it until mid-1952. Along with the change of the Party title, the governmental apparatus underwent changes; the capital of the Central Plains Provisional Government was shifted southward from Kaifeng to Wuhan in June 1949. Then, on February 5, 1950, the Central Plains Government was dissolved in favor of the Central-South Military and Administrative Committee (CSMAC), which had jurisdiction over Honan, Hupeh, Hunan, Kiangsi, Kwangtung, and Kwangsi.

During the period from 1950 to 1954, Li was one of the most important officials in the CSMAC (known after January 1953 as the Central-South Administrative Committee). In addition to membership on the CSMAC, he was also named in March 1950 to head one of the most important subordinate organs, the Land Reform Committee. It was not long afterward (June 1950) that the national land Reform Law was adopted by the central government, following explanatory remarks by top Party leader Liu Shao-ch'i at a session of the CPPCC. From that point on, the program was put into high gear. As the senior official dealing with this topic in central-south China, Li was called upon to give a major address on the subject before the second plenary meeting of the CSMAC in September 1950. Among other things, Li warned against tendencies to carry out the "reform" too quickly. Some idea of the magnitude of the program can be gained from the December 1950 Communist claim that land reform during the winter of 1950 and the spring of 1951 would encompass 247 hsien in central-south China, which had an agrarian population of over 63,000,000.

Li's position within the CSMAC was notably enhanced in December 1951 when he was named to chair still another of its key subordinate organs, the Political and Legal Affairs Committee. Shortly thereafter, a major bureaucratic scandal in the Central-South area was exposed. It was known as the Sung Ying case (see under Chang P'ing-hua) and involved serious mismanagement in a hospital in Wuhan, a situation that led to a false arrest, theft, and serious breaches of Party discipline. Among the significant Party officials demoted was Wu Te-feng (q.v.), then the Wuhan mayor, who later made an impressive comeback. Although Li was not the most important Party personality involved in the final settlement of this case (playing a lesser role than such top men as Teng Tzu-hui), he did address a meeting called to discuss the Sung Ying (February 1952), at which time he called for stern punishment of the guilty.

It was at the meeting to discuss the Sung Ying case that Li was first identified as second deputy secretary of the Central-South Party Bureau, the Party organ having parallel responsibilities with the governmental CSMAC over Honan, Hupeh, Hunan, Kiangsi, Kwangtung, and Kwangsi. This post placed Li in the fourth-ranking position in the bureau, below Secretary Lin Piao, Second Secretary Teng Tzu-hui, and First Deputy Secretary T'an Cheng (qq.v.). Along with this post, Li received a promotion to a vice-chairmanship of the CSMAC in October 1952 (retaining the position following the reorganization of the CSMAC into the Central-South Administrative Committee in January 1953). A month later (November 1952), he was named to chair a CSMAC committee to eliminate illiteracy, paralleling a national committee formed at the same time. It was also at this time (October–December 1952) that Li first traveled abroad, serving as a deputy leader to military veteran Ho Lung, who led a delegation to North Korea to inspect and "comfort" the large Chinese army stationed there (known as the "Chinese People's Volunteers"). In May 1953 Li relinquished the chairmanship of both the Land Reform Committee and the Political and Legal Affairs Committee, but he remained as a vice-chairman of the CSMAC and as second deputy secretary of the regional Party Bureau until both were abolished in 1954.

In 1954 Li was transferred to Peking. His initial post in the national government was as a deputy from Honan to the First NPC (1954–1959), the organization that brought the constitutional government into existence at its first session in September 1954. Since that date, Li has been among the key leaders of the PRC's principal legislative body, serving on the NPC Standing Committee for the duration of the First and Second NPC's (1954–1964), after which he was promoted to a vice-chairmanship when the Third NPC closed its first session in January 1965. Li served as a deputy from Honan to the First and Second NPC's but was transferred to the Hopeh constituency for the Third NPC. During the First NPC (1954–1959), Li was especially active in congressional affairs, serving as a member of the presidium (steering committee) for the second through the fifth sessions (1955–1958), as well as chairman of the *ad*

hoc Motions Examination Committee for these same sessions. However, probably because of his other duties (see below), he has been less active in the affairs of the NPC since the Second Congress opened in 1959.

Even more important than his work in the NPC was his assignment for the first time to a position directly subordinate to the Party Central Committee. In 1955 he was identified simply as a "leading member of one of the departments of the Central Committee." This position was clarified by September 1956 when he was identified as the head of the Party's Industrial and Communications Work Department, a post which apparently gave him a powerful voice in the decisions taken by those organizations in China related to industry and communications. By mid-1957 the communications portion of the department was separated from Li's jurisdiction, but he continued to head the "Industrial Work Department" until at least late 1958.

Li made a significant stride in his career at the historic Eighth National Party Congress held in September 1956. He served as a member of the Congress Presidium (steering committee) and was one of the featured speakers. His very important speech dealt with a problem that had troubled Chinese management from the inauguration of the First Five-Year Plan in 1953. Using the Soviet model, the Chinese had employed the "single-director" system of industrial management, which, in Li's words, had "wrongly emphasized that the man responsible for the management of the enterprise had full authority, that the duties of the Party organization were only to guarantee production and give general supervision, and that the director or manager [did not need to] carry out the resolutions of the Party organization regarding the management of production if he disagreed with them." As one writer put it, the "single-director" system had produced "little despots" and had brought about a situation (anathema to the CCP) in which the factory director had become the "most powerful individual in the enterprise, far overshadowing the Party secretary."[3] Li informed the delegates to the Congress that the Central Committee had already decided to replace the "single-director" system with one in which the factory managers would assume the responsibility of the enterprises—but he made it completely clear that such responsibilities would be "under the leadership of the Party committee."

In the broadest sense, Li's speech at the Eighth Congress represented a rejection of the Soviet model for industrial management. More narrowly, it has been argued that his speech was a repudiation of Kao Kang (q.v.), a major spokesman for the "single-director" system.[4] Kao had not only been the top Party leader in Manchuria, but during the first two years of the First Five-

Year Plan he had also been chairman of the national State Planning Commission. A continuing debate, it appears, had gone on in 1953–54; the first turning point occurred in February 1954 at the Party Central Committee's Fourth Plenum, which stressed the principle of collective leadership by the Party. The problem was emphatically resolved in March 1955 when Kao Kang was purged as an "anti-Party" leader.

At the close of the Eighth Congress, Li was elected a full member of the Party Central Committee, one of the 33 elected to full membership who had been neither a full nor an alternate member of the Seventh Central Committee elected in 1945. Even more important is the fact that on the day following the Congress (at the First Plenum of the new Central Committee) Li was named as a secretary of the Central Secretariat, the powerful organ of the Party, which is headed by Teng Hsiao-p'ing and charged with the task of carrying out the policies of the Politburo. At the time Li was named to the Secretariat, there were only seven full members and three alternates.

The major stress in Li's career since the mid-1950's has been on Party organizational work. Until about 1959 his tasks were mainly involved with domestic problems, but since then he has also had an increasingly important role in relations with foreign Communist parties. This was illustrated in January–February 1959 when he was one of the few members of the delegation led by Chou En-lai to Moscow for the 21st CPCU Congress. Li was also abroad again in August 1965 when he led a delegation to Indonesia; ostensibly, he went on a "goodwill" visit to attend ceremonies marking the 20th anniversary of the proclamation of Indonesian independence, but it is noteworthy that while there he conferred with Indonesian Communist Party Chairman D. N. Aidit. Moreover, from the late 1950's Li has also made a large number of appearances in the company of visiting foreign Communist visitors, a role that has brought him into constant association with such top Party leaders as Mao Tse-tung, Liu Shao-ch'i, Teng Hsiao-p'ing, and P'eng Chen.

Li received a very significant new appointment by June 1963 when he was identified as the first secretary of the North China Party Bureau. It may be that he held the post from the time of the Ninth Party Plenum in January 1961 when the decision was taken to re-create the six regional bureaus to "act for the Central Committee in strengthening leadership over the Party committees in the . . . provinces, municipalities, and autonomous regions." This post places Li on the same level as such important regional leaders as Politburo member Li Ching-ch'üan (of the Southwest Bureau) and Central Committee member T'ao Chu (of the Central-South Bureau).

The jurisdiction of the bureau covers the provinces of Hopeh and Shansi, as well as the Inner Mongolia Autonomous Region. Although Li serves as the senior member of the North China Bureau, he continues to make numerous appearances in Peking in his capacity as a member of the Party Secretariat.

Despite his stature as a Party leader, Li has not been a frequent contributor to the Party press. He did, however, write an article for *Chung-kuo ch'ing-nien* (China youth, issue number 10, May 16, 1964) in which he described the life of a production brigade leader in Shansi as a model to be followed by Chinese youths. This was subsequently reprinted in the *JMJP* of May 28, 1964, and still later (in the *JMJP* of June 24, 1964) it was singled out as a pertinent article for Party members to read and study.

The pattern of Li's career suggests close ties with such top Party organizational leaders as Liu Shao-ch'i and P'eng Chen. It is probable that he was associated with both of them in north China from as early as the late 1930's, and he has definitely worked closely with them in the fifties and sixties in connection with both the NPC and the Party. When these personal ties are considered in the light of his important political positions (head of the North China Party Bureau, member of the Party Secretariat, and a vice-chairman of the NPC Standing Committee), it is apparent that Li belongs to that small group of men who rank just below the members of the Party Politburo.

1. *K'ang-jih chan-cheng shih-ch'i chieh-fang-ch'ü kai-k'uang* (A sketch of the liberated areas during the anti-Japanese war; Peking, 1953), p. 44.

2. *Chui-tao "szu-pa" yü-nan lieh-shih chi-nien-ts'e* (In memory of the martyrs who died in the accident of "April 8"; Kalgan, 1946), p. 276.

3. H. F. Schurmann, "Organizational Contrasts between Communist China and the Soviet Union," in Kurt London, ed., *Unity and Contradiction* (New York, 1962), pp. 71–72.

4. *Ibid.*, p. 74.

Li I-mang

(1904–   ; Chia-ting, Szechwan). Writer; diplomat; deputy director, Foreign Affairs Office, State Council.

Li I-mang is a writer and early member of the CCP, who worked in the areas controlled by the New Fourth Army during the Sino-Japanese War. After the establishment of the PRC in 1949 he was active in the Communist-sponsored international peace movement and was then ambassador in Burma for five years. Born in October 1904 in Chia-ting (now Lo-shan hsien), Szechwan, Li was trained as an economist. He changed his name from Li Min-chih to Li I-mang in 1927.

Li was in Shanghai in the early twenties, where he was associated with the Creation Society (see under Kuo Mo-jo), one of the many literary organizations established in the wake of the May Fourth Movement (1919). He studied at the radical Shanghai University, which, though nominally headed by KMT member Yü Yu-jen, was dominated by such important Communists as Ch'ü Ch'iu-pai, Teng Chung-hsia, and Yun Tai-ying (qq.v.). The school existed from 1923 until June 1925, when it was closed down by the authorities in the aftermath of the May 30th demonstrations. By this time Li had already joined the CCP.

In the spring of 1926 Li went to Canton, then the revolutionary center of China. When the Northern Expedition was launched by Chiang Kai-shek in mid-1926, Li participated as an official in the Propaganda Section, which was subordinate to the National Revolutionary Army's Political Department. During this period he worked directly under fellow Szechwanese Kuo Mo-jo, a senior official in the Political Department. He remained with Kuo as the latter's assistant in Nanchang when the Revolutionary Army captured the city. But after Chiang Kai-shek began to expel Communists and leftists from his army in early 1927, Kuo and Li fled to Shanghai and then to Wuhan, the headquarters of the left-KMT which opposed Chiang. Kuo and Li were in Kiukiang (Chiu-chiang) at the time of the Communists' Nanchang Uprising on August 1 (see under Yeh T'ing). They went to Nanchang but were forced to leave almost immediately when the Communists were driven from the city. Still working under Kuo, Li took part in the march led by Yeh T'ing and Ho Lung (q.v.) from Nanchang to Swatow, but after their defeat there he made his way to Shanghai.[1]

Like most Communists in Shanghai after the 1927 split with the KMT, Li was under constant threat of arrest, which probably accounts for the fact that he changed his name to Li I-mang. Apart from his work in clandestine activities for the CCP, he also published a translation of Marx's *The Poverty of Philosophy* under the name of Tu Chu-chün. The work was published in Shanghai in 1929 and re-issued in the same city in 1946.[2] In 1930 a research society in Shanghai brought out his translation of the first volume of Marx's selected works.[3]

By 1933 Li had gone to the Communist-held areas in Kiangsi, where Chu Te and Mao Tse-tung had their headquarters. In that year he was serving in the Chu-Mao First Front Army as head of the Political Department's Staff Office. At the Second All-China Congress of Soviets, held in Juichin in January–February 1934, Li was elected an alternate member of the Central Executive Committee, the governing body of the Chinese Soviet Republic. Later that year he embarked on the Long March, arriving in Shensi in the fall of 1935. He engaged in Party activities there until 1938, when he was assigned to the newly activated New Fourth Army, which operated in the lower reaches of the Yangtze Valley throughout the Sino-Japanese War.

Li's work with the New Fourth Army was largely confined to political and administrative duties. When he first joined it in 1938 he worked in the Political Department, and by 1941 he was secretary-general of the Army headquarters. In addition to its military and political responsibilities, the New Fourth Army also sponsored a wide variety of "people's" (or "mass") organizations. Apart from his duties with the Army headquarters, Li was also a vice-president in 1941 of the "Resist-the-Enemy Dramatic Society." (Many popular organizations during the war had "anti-Japanese" or "resist-the-enemy" prefixes in an attempt by the CCP to arouse support by this appeal to nationalism.) By 1943 Li was working in the Huai-hai area, which was under the control of Huang K'o-ch'eng's (q.v.) Third Division. With its rich agricultural resources, the Huai-hai district was a focal point of Japanese attention. In early 1944 they established a "Model Peace Zone" there, making part of the area into a new province called Huai-hai. It consisted of 21 hsien taken from Kiangsu, Anhwei, and Shantung. But the Japanese were never successful in this endeavor, in part because of the Communists' ability to infiltrate the area. Late in 1944 New Fourth Army units penetrated deep into the area around Tung-hsien, Kiangsu, recruiting many inhabitants into their forces. By 1945 most of the rural areas in Huai-hai were controlled by the Communists.[4] From 1943 to an uncertain date Li was director of the Huai-hai Administrative (government) Office, and from the same year to about 1947 he was also chairman of the Kiangsu-Anhwei Border Region Government.

Following the conquest of Manchuria and much of north China in 1948–49, Li was assigned to Port Arthur-Dairen, then under joint Chinese-Soviet control. By the spring of 1949 he was the first vice-chairman of the Port Arthur-Dairen District Administrative Committee, the governmental organ in charge of these important twin cities. In 1950 he was also reported to be the president of Dairen University. Over the winter of 1949–50, and again in mid-1950, the newly established PRC government attempted to have its representatives accepted by the United Nations. Foreign affairs specialist Chang Wen-t'ien (q.v.) was designated chief delegate to the U.N. Security Council, with Li appointed as his deputy as well as a delegate to the General

Assembly. These attempts failed, of course, and by early 1951 Li was in Peking where he embarked on a new, although related, career as a leading spokesman in Communist-sponsored international "peace" organizations.

Li's first assignment took him to East Berlin in February 1951 for a session of the World Peace Council (WPC). In April of the same year he led a group bound for a meeting of the British-Chinese Friendship Association; however, upon reaching Prague the group turned back following a refusal by the British to grant visas. From September to December 1951 Li was a deputy leader of one of the first major cultural delegations sent abroad by the PRC. The visit of this group to India and Burma was described by Li in the May 1, 1952, issue of the English-language journal *People's China*. In mid-1952 he was again in Europe to attend another WPC meeting in East Berlin. At this time Li was elected to the WPC Executive Committee and the Secretariat; for the next four years he devoted most of his time to WPC affairs and for a portion of this period was stationed in Vienna, then the WPC headquarters. In addition to those WPC sessions already mentioned, between 1952 and 1956 he attended WPC-sponsored meetings in the following places and times: Vienna (December 1952, November 1953, November 1954, January 1955); Budapest (January 1953, June 1953); Stockholm (June 1953, June 1954, November 1954, April 1956); East Germany (July 1952, July 1953, May 1954); and Helsinki (June 1955). These meetings were uniformly devoted to campaigns directed against the United States (such as the alleged use of "germ warfare" in the Korean War). Apart from the activities directly sponsored by the WPC, Li was also a participant in delegations to other countries, as in July 1952 when he was a member of a cultural delegation to Bulgaria, and in January 1953 when he attended a congress of the Czech Peace Defenders in Prague. In April 1953 he was in Paris for a memorial meeting for the late president of the French National Peace Committee, and in May 1953 he attended the leftist "American Continental Cultural Conference" in Santiago, Chile. (As of that date Li was one of the very few Chinese Communists who had been in Latin America.) He was also a participant in one of Peking's first major efforts in the Afro-Asian world, namely the Asian Countries' Conference in New Delhi in April 1955, a conference intended to influence the tone of the more famous Afro-Asian ("Bandung") Conference held later that month in Indonesia. Subsequently, a series of "Afro-Asian Solidarity Conferences" were held (the first of them in Cairo in late 1957—see under Yang Shuo), although Li himself did not participate in these.

In the meantime, Li had received new assignments in China. In 1954 he was elected a deputy from his native Szechwan to the First NPC (1954–1959). He was not, however, re-elected to the Second NPC (1959–1964), presumably because of a new overseas appointment (see below). More closely related to his work abroad was his appointment in March 1955 to the Board of Directors of the Chinese People's Association for Cultural Relations with Foreign Countries; he probably retained his seat on the Board in April 1959 when the Association was reorganized, but complete information is not available. In mid-1955 the Chinese set up a special committee to gain entry into the (non-Communist) International Parliamentary Union (IPU). Li was named to the delegation to attend the 44th conference of the IPU in Helsinki and led the advance group there. However, when the Chinese delegation was refused admission, Li returned to China where he was assigned the task of writing Peking's official denunciation of the IPU for failing to admit the PRC.

From 1958 to 1963 Li was Peking's ambassador to Burma. Replacing Yao Chung-ming (q.v.), Li presented his credentials in Rangoon on April 30, 1958. During his tenure in Rangoon, the Burmese gradually shifted their political alignment toward more intimate relations with the PRC, a shift for which Li presumably must be given some credit. Two important agreements between Burma and China were signed in these years: the Treaty of Friendship and Mutual Non-aggression and the Sino-Burmese Boundary Agreement. Li accompanied Prime Minister Ne Win to Peking in January 1960 for the formal signing of the former. At this same time a preliminary agreement covering the boundary question was also signed, under the terms of which a joint Sino-Burmese committee was formed to work out the details (see under Yao Chung-ming, the chairman of the Chinese side of the joint committee). Li was back in Peking again in October 1960 when Prime Minister U Nu signed the boundary treaty. Over the turn of the year 1960–61 the Chinese sent a 400-member delegation to Burma, one of the largest ever sent abroad by the Chinese. Led by Chou En-lai, the Chinese group went to Burma to participate in the celebrations marking the 13th anniversary of Burmese independence and to exchange the instruments of ratification for the boundary treaty. For his part in fostering Sino-Burmese relations, Li was given the Burmese governments' "heroic honor" medal at this time. He was again back in China in the fall of 1961 when both U Nu and Ne Win were on a state visit to China.

Apart from these major events in connection with the treaties and state visits to China by Burmese leaders, Li was frequently in the news during his five-year tour in Burma. He was often mentioned in connection with the numerous

Chinese delegations that visited Rangoon or the protocol activities associated with Burmese groups departing for Peking or returning from China. Li left Rangoon for home on August 31, 1963, and was formally replaced in Burma a few days later by Keng Piao (q.v.). Since returning to Peking he has continued to work in the field of foreign relations. In April 1962, prior to his return, he had been named to the Council of the Asia-Africa Society of China, an organization ostensibly devoted to research on Asia and Africa. And by November 1963 Li had become a deputy director of the State Council's Foreign Affairs Office (FAO). Headed by Ch'en I, the FAO coordinates the activities of the many Chinese government and quasi-government agencies that operate abroad. Although relatively little is known about the Office, its significance can be judged in part from the political importance of Ch'en I himself as well as Li's fellow deputy directors (e.g., Liao Ch'eng-chih, Liu Ning-i, both Central Committee members). Li assumed two further positions related to foreign affairs in 1964 and 1965; in December 1964 he was named a vice-president of the Chinese People's Institute of Foreign Affairs (one of Peking's chief instruments for dealing with nations not having formal diplomatic relations with China), and in June 1965 he was named to the Standing Committee of the China Peace Committee.

Li is married to Wang I, who in the late fifties was secretary-general of the China-Poland Friendship Association. Since 1964 she has been a deputy director of the Second Department (in charge of Asian affairs) of the Commission for Cultural Relations with Foreign Countries.

1. *She-hui hsin-wen* (Social news; Shanghai), January 21, 1935.
2. Chang Ching-lu, ed., *Chung-kuo ch'u-pan shih-liao pu-pien* (Supplementary historical materials on Chinese publishing; Peking, 1957), p. 444.
3. *Ibid.,* p. 445.
4. Chalmers A. Johnson, *Peasant Nationalism and Communist Power* (Stanford, Calif., 1962), pp. 65–66.

Li K'o-nung

(1898–1962; Ch'ao-hsien, Anhwei). Intelligence and security official; member, CCP Central Committee.

Li K'o-nung was one of the most important Party intelligence and security specialists in the history of the Communist movement, ranking with such other specialists as Teng Fa, K'ang Sheng, and Lo Jui-ch'ing (qq.v.). A Party member from the twenties, Li was a senior intelligence figure in the Shanghai underground and later held important posts as a liaison official with the KMT during the Sino-Japanese War. In general, there was little known about his early life until the Communists published an official obituary and reminiscences after his death.

Li was born in Ch'ao-hsien on the eastern shore of Lake Ch'ao in Anhwei province but spent his youth in Wu-hu, a major Yangtze River port some 40 miles to the southeast of Ch'ao-hsien. He attended primary and middle schools in Wu-hu together with Ch'ien Hsing-ts'un (Ah Ying), a prominent Communist literary figure, who in 1962 wrote a commemorative article on Li's career.[1] At the middle school, whose principals included early KMT leader Chao Po-hsien and revolutionary poet Su Man-ju (a colleague of Ch'en Tu-hsiu), Li was said to have learned of China's revolutionary heritage. It is also claimed that he was engaged in "progressive activities" during the May Fourth Movement, which began in 1919 partially in opposition to the Chinese government's humiliating policy toward Japan. Li was a reader of journals associated with the May Fourth Movement, including *Hsin ch'ing-nien* (New youth), *New Tide* (Hsin ch'ao), and Mao Tse-tung's Hunan journal, the *Hsiang-chiang p'ing-lun* (Hsiang River review). It may also be presumed that Li read the publications in Wu-hu, which were begun in the early twenties to propagate the spirit of the May Fourth Movement.[2] He also became acquainted with prominent writers of the period, such as Chiang Kuang-tz'u (also known as Chiang Hsia-seng and Chiang Kuang-ch'ih), a left-wing writer who contributed to the *Hsin Ch'ing-nien*. Ch'ien Hsing-ts'un has written that K'o Ch'ing-shih (q.v.), a CCP member by 1922 and later a Politburo member, was a frequent visitor to Li's home.

Following the May 30th Movement of 1925 (which instigated a series of demonstrations and strikes throughout China), Li, his former schoolmate Ch'ien Hsing-ts'un, and others established the Min-sheng Middle School in Wuhu, a school that spread revolutionary ideas and served as a training ground for future revolutionists. In 1926 Li joined the CCP and thereafter his home was used as a rendezvous point for revolutionists. The school was soon closed by the KMT authorities, after which he helped organize CCP-sponsored uprisings in the Anhwei countryside.

Li remained in Anhwei until after the spring of 1927 when Chiang Kai-shek turned on the Communists in a series of coups (most notably in Shanghai) that cost the CCP thousands of lives. According to Li's son's account,[3] his father barely escaped arrest by the authorities, after which the Party sent him to Shanghai where he went into training in the CCP intelligence apparatus then being established under Chou En-lai and Ku Shun-chang (q.v.). From 1928 to 1931 Li is credited with having played a major role in Communist intelligence, "safeguarding the central leading organs" (i.e., the CCP headquarters), and penetrating the "most dangerous places." According to a non-Communist account, Li was even able to penetrate the Nationalist intelligence apparatus. Among his colleagues in the underground were K'ang Sheng, Ch'en Keng, and K'o Ch'ing-shih (qq.v.), later to become Party Central Committee members.[4]

In 1931 the Communist position in Shanghai was seriously compromised by the treachery of Ku Shun-chang. Li was presumably among those compromised by Ku's action; in any event, he was sent to the Kiangsi Soviet district that same year. In Kiangsi Li continued to specialize in intelligence work, including cryptography. In November 1931, at the First All-China Congress of Soviets, which established the Chinese Soviet Republic, the National Political Security Bureau (Kuo-chia cheng-chih pao-wei chü) was set up under the direction of Teng Fa. Li, who probably ranked second only to Teng in the intelligence-security network in Kiangsi, became director of the Security Bureau's Administrative Department (Chih-hsing pu). It is not known how long Li retained this post, but it is clear that he remained in the intelligence field. By no later than the fall of 1933 he was identified in Chien-ning hsien (west Fukien) serving as head of the Political Security Bureau under the First Front Army.[5] Chou En-lai was then the political commissar of the First Front Army. Not long after this, when the Soviet Republic convened its Second Congress (January–February 1934), Li was elected an alternate member of the Republic's Central Executive Committee. In October 1934 Li set out on the Long March with the First Front Army (led by Chu Te and Mao Tse-tung), presumably taking his orders from Teng Fa, who continued to be the over-all security chief.

After arriving in Shensi in late 1935, Li became head of the Party Central Committee's Liaison Bureau (Lien-lo chü), an organization that probably had intelligence functions. When Edgar Snow visited Shensi several months later he described Li as chief of the "communications department of the Foreign Office."[6] It seems certain that this department and the Liaison Bureau were in some way related—if in fact they were not one and the same. When Chiang Kai-shek was kidnapped in December 1936 by dissident Nationalist generals Yang Hu-Ch'eng and Chang Hsueh-liang (the "Sian Incident"; see under Chou En-lai), the Communists sent a group of top men to negotiate with Chiang in hopes of reaching a temporary united front to fight the constantly threatening Japanese. The delegation sent to Sian was headed by Chou En-lai, and included Yeh Chien-ying (q.v.). Li was present as secretary-general of the delegation, and it appears that security chief Teng Fa was also involved behind the scenes. The Sian talks were a prelude to further negotiations (which included Chou and Li) held in Hankow in 1937,

where the Nationalist government had retreated following the invasion of China by Japan in mid-1937. Out of these talks came a series of agreements to cooperate in the common effort against the Japanese, agreements that included KMT recognition of the Communist Eighth Route Army and the establishment of Eighth Route Army liaison offices in Nationalist-held areas.

In the period between the outbreak of war and the New Fourth Army Incident of early 1941 (see under Yeh T'ing, the New Fourth Army commander), Li was a major figure in liaison activities between the Nationalists and the Communists. In 1937 he was director of the Eighth Route Army's Offices in Shanghai and Nanking (which were evacuated before the onrushing Japanese in November and December 1937, respectively). In the summer of 1937, while working in Shanghai, Li was also in contact with the CCP's Shanghai Committee, then working "semi-secretly." Aside from his liaison and (presumably) intelligence activities, Li was also given the task of gaining the release by the Nationalist Government of CCP "political prisoners."[7]

After the fall of Nanking, Li was assigned to Kweilin (in Kwangsi) where from 1938 he headed the Office of both the Eighth Route and the New Fourth Armies, the latter force having been activated and officially recognized by the KMT in early 1938. In the early years of the war Kweilin became a major center for Communist and Communist-front organizations, particularly after the fall of Canton and Wuhan in October 1938. In addition to Li's liaison office, Kweilin was the locale of the *Chiu-wang jih-pao* (Salvation daily), the *Kuo-chi hsin-wen she* (International news agency), and the Kweilin office of the *Hsin-hua jih-pao* (New China daily), the important Communist newspaper published in Chungking. In the words of a Communist writer, Kweilin was "a center of communications for our Party with east and south China and even with Hong Kong and places overseas, and a frontline command post for directing revolutionary cultural work and united front work in southwest China. Comrade [Li] K'o-nung was commander-in-chief of this center."[8]

One of the repercussions of the New Fourth Army Incident of January 1941 was the closure of the liaison office in Kweilin. As a consequence, Li was reassigned to Yenan where he assumed important new jobs. He first became secretary-general of the Eighth Route Army Headquarters and later served as secretary-general of the Party's Yangtze Bureau. The latter assignment presumably took him away from Yenan occasionally to work with Chou En-lai and Tung Pi-wu in Chungking. But Li's most important wartime post was probably with the Party's Social Affairs Department (She-hui pu), the Communist euphemism for an intelligence bureau. During the latter part of the war he was the deputy director of the Social Affairs Department, a post that probably placed him under K'ang Sheng, one of the Communists' top intelligence operatives. He advanced to the directorship of the department by about 1946, the same year in which he became secretary-general of the Communist delegation to the Peking Executive Headquarters, established in early 1946 pursuant to the Cease-Fire Agreement negotiated between the Communists and the KMT by U.S. General George C. Marshall. Li's intelligence background was presumably a major factor in his selection for this assignment; among other things, the Executive Headquarters served the Communists as a repository of information about the Nationalists' forces, as well as a useful listening post regarding American attitudes toward the civil war.

When the Executive Headquarters was disbanded in early 1947, Li returned to Communist-held areas in the northwest, where he presumably continued his work in intelligence. Lo Jui-ch'ing, another security specialist, eulogized Li's activities during the Sino-Japanese War and the civil war with the Nationalists in the following words: "He . . . did great work . . . in gathering enemy intelligence, in safeguarding the CCP, and in suppressing counter-revolutionaries."

By mid-1949 Li was in Peking serving on a preparatory committee for the China New Legal Research Society, but nothing further is known of his work in this connection. In September 1949, as a representative of the CCP, he attended the first session of the CPPCC, at which time the PRC was inaugurated. When the new government was staffed in October, Li was named as a vice-minister of Foreign Affairs, serving under Chou En-lai, his colleague from the late twenties. It can be presumed that within the ministry Li had major responsibilities involving security and intelligence work. His most notable public work in the ministry occurred in the spring and summer of 1954, when he accompanied Chou En-lai to Geneva for the famous conference that brought a temporary halt to the fighting in Indochina. When the conference was briefly adjourned in June, Chou left for visits to India and Burma. During this time Li was left in charge of the delegation, and when the conference closed in July he returned home separately, visiting the Czech foreign minister in Prague on behalf of Chou and also stopping over briefly in Moscow.

Like so many of the elite, Li was named in October 1949 to the Executive Board of the Sino-Soviet Friendship Association, a post he held until 1954. Relatively little was recorded about his career in the early fifties, but Lo Jui-ch'ing's funeral oration provides useful clues about his work. Lo noted that after 1949 Li was a department director within both the Party's

Central Committee and the Central Committee's Military Affairs Committee. Given Li's background and the natural reluctance of the Chinese to discuss publicly security work, it is probable that both posts were related to intelligence and security work. This seems to be confirmed in part by Lo's further comment that in the post-1949 period Li had performed outstanding work in "safeguarding socialist construction." According to his obituary, he was still serving as a department director under the Central Committee at the time of his death. It would seem that the department in question was the Social Affairs Department, the one that Li had headed since about 1946 (as described above). However, when appointed to the Foreign Ministry in 1949 he was described as the "former" director, possibly as a security precaution. In any event, according to an authoritative source, the Social Affairs Department was not mentioned in the Chinese press after 1950.[9]

In 1954 Li was named as a deputy from his native Anhwei to the First NPC (1954–1959); he was re-elected to the Second NPC (which opened in April 1959) and was holding this post at the time of death in 1962. At the close of the first session of the First NPC (September 1954), he was dropped as a vice-minister of Foreign Affairs. However, by June of 1955 he was identified as a deputy chief-of-staff of the PLA, another post he was holding at his death. In 1955 the PRC first awarded military decorations and personal military ranks. Li was given the three highest awards for his services in the periods from 1927 to 1950 (the Orders of August First, Independence and Freedom, and Liberation), and he was also made a PLA colonel-general, the equivalent of a three-star general in the U.S. Army. A year later, at the Party's Eighth Party Congress (September 1956), he was elected a member of the Party Central Committee. The last official post Li received was in April 1959 when he was named as a Party deputy to the CPPCC's Third National Committee, as well as a member of the CPPCC Standing Committee. However, by this time Li was already seriously ill. Li's son has written that his father, already a victim of coughing and asthma spells, fainted and seriously injured his brain in a fall (October 1957), an injury from which he never fully recovered. He was chronically ill for the remaining four years of his life. He made one of his last public appearances in April 1960 when he attended a national conference of the militia, but after this his name appeared in the press only in connection with ceremonial functions (as in March 1961 when he was listed as a member of the funeral committee for Ch'en Keng, his colleague from the Shanghai underground days). Li died in Peking on February 9, 1962. His death and funeral were given elaborate coverage in the press, including commemorative pieces by such Party stalwarts as Tung Pi-wu and condolence messages from abroad.

Li was married by the early twenties to a woman named Chao Ying, who died just 13 months before her husband. He had at least three sons; one of them (Li Ning) is known to have survived him. After Li went to Kiangsi in 1931 he was completely separated from his family, and during this period his wife earned a living as a primary school teacher in Wuhu, Anhwei. Chao was reunited with her husband in the late thirties and was with him both in Kweilin and (after 1941) in Yenan. One or more of his sons (including Li Ning) are known to have gone to Yenan in 1938 to study.

1. *JMJP,* February 14, 1962.
2. Chow Tse-tsung, *Research Guide to the May Fourth Movement* (Cambridge, Mass., 1963), pp. 95–96.
3. *SCMP* 2695, pp. 6–9.
4. *Ibid.*
5. *Kuang-ming jih-pao* (Kwangming daily), January 23, 1959.
6. Edgar Snow, *Red Star over China* (New York, 1938), p. 336.
7. *SCMP* 2813, p. 8.
8. *Ibid.,* p. 9.
9. *Directory of Party and Government Officials of Communist China,* no. 271, U.S. State Department, July 20, 1960, p. 5.

Li Li-san

(c.1899–   ; Li-ling hsien, Hunan). Early labor leader; Party leader and "deviationist"; former member, CCP Politburo; member, CCP Central Committee.

One of the earliest members of the CCP, Li Li-san was very active in the labor movement in the twenties and again for a brief time in the late forties and early fifties. However, his place in Chinese Communist history rests mainly upon his role as the chief protagonist in one of the Party's major controversies. Li's policies, known as the "Li Li-san line," dominated the Party from mid-1928 until his downfall in late 1930. He then went to Moscow for questioning before the Comintern and did not return to China until he accompanied the Russian Army into Manchuria in 1945. Li was again prominent in the labor movement for a few years, but since the mid-fifties he has held only secondary positions. Mao and his ideologues have taken Li to account for committing the "second leftist deviation" (see Ch'ü Ch'iu-pai for the first and Ch'in Pang-hsien for the third). His history is especially noteworthy as a case study of the Party's handling of important "deviationists" in both past and present times.

Li was born in Li-ling hsien, Hunan. The rural hsien is located in eastern Hunan, south of Changsha. As a young student Mao Tse-tung roamed the countryside of Li-ling, and it was one of the five hsien he visited in early 1927 before writing his important "Report on an Investigation of the Peasant Movement in Hunan." The area was a focal point of peasant organization and also the birthplace of other important Communists (e.g., Li Wei-han and Tso Ch'üan). Li's courtesy name is Li Lung-chih and he has also been known by the aliases Pai Shan and Li Min-jan. His father was an impoverished rural school teacher.

Li Li-san has written that as a youngster he was deeply impressed by the revolutionary exploits of Miss Ch'iu Chin and Hsu Hsi-lin, revolutionists at the turn of the century, who were executed in 1907 for their anti-Manchu activities. He learned of their exploits in the period just prior to the 1911 Revolution from Sun Hsiao-shan, an older schoolmate. Sun was a member of Sun Yat-sen's T'ung-meng hui, and he explained its programs and policies to Li. Sun Hsiao-shan later joined the CCP, and when Mao wrote his 1927 report on the Hunan peasantry he praised him for his work as chairman of the peasants' association in Li-ling.[1]

Between 1911 and 1914 Li attended middle schools in Li-ling as well as the Ch'ang-chün Middle School in Changsha. When in 1917 Mao Tse-tung was organizing his study group for young Hunanese intellectuals, the Hsin-min hsueh-hui (New people's study society), he advertised in a Changsha paper for interested young students. He received "three and a half" replies, the half reply coming from a "noncommittal youth named Li Li-san"; he listened to all Mao had to say but then went away and their "friendship never developed."[2] The story may be apocryphal, because when Mao related it to Edgar Snow in 1936 he was openly opposed to Li Li-san, who had been banished to Moscow six years earlier. However, it suggests a way in which Li may have become associated with the Hunanese student group organized by Mao and Ts'ai Ho-sen, which played a major role in preparing students to go to France on the work-and-study program (see under Ts'ai).

In August 1918 Li joined one of the classes organized in Peking for students preparing to study in France, and in the following year he left China with a number of others. In France he was employed in a metal-working factory and attended the Collège de Montargis, south of Paris, where Ts'ai Ho-sen established his Changsha study group. Li also studied at St. Charmond, a suburb of St. Etienne near Lyons, where he helped organize a socialist study group with Chao Shih-yen (q.v.). While in France Li worked closely with Ts'ai Ho-sen, Chou En-lai, and the two sons of Ch'en Tu-hsiu, the first CCP general secretary (see under Ch'en Yen-nien). In 1921 a university was established at Lyons for Chinese students in France, and thinking they would be admitted, Li, Ts'ao Ho-sen, Ch'en I, and others went to Lyons to enter the school. However, when they were refused admission, they occupied the school buildings by force on September 21. The French police immediately ejected them, and after being jailed for a few weeks Li and the others were deported.

Returning to China in late 1921, Li was immediately assigned as a labor organizer at the An-yuan coal mines on the Hunan-Kiangsi border east of Changsha. The mines supplied most of the fuel for the famous Han-yeh-p'ing iron and steel works in the Wuhan area. Working under the auspices of the Labor Secretariat (the forerunner of the All-China Federation of Labor, see under Teng Chung-hsia), Li established an evening school for miners in January 1922. He selected a number of the more able students to organize units within the various sections of the mines. Then in May 1922, they established the An-yuan Mine and Railroad Workers' Club[3] (a euphemism for a labor union), with Li as the director. He was also associated in these organizational endeavours with Mao Tse-tung, who was working in nearby Changsha as chairman of the Hunan branch of the Labor Secretariat. The workers' organization had grown strong enough by September 1922 to enable Li Li-san and Liu Shao-ch'i to lead a successful strike (regarding wages, working conditions, etc.).

Ts'ai Shu-fan (q.v.), then an apprentice for the Han-yeh-p'ing company, told American authoress Nym Wales in 1937 that Li Li-san "had a great influence among the workers. He was a student but a good labor leader and an unusually convincing agitator, influencing nearly everyone who heard him speak."[4] His organizational abilities were also praised by a Hunanese miner interviewed by Anna Louise Strong in 1927 at the Fourth Labor Congress.[5] In the two or so years that Li spent in the An-yuan area he gained a wide following among the laborers, and Liu Shao-ch'i has written that on one occasion the foremen and contractors at the mine, who opposed the unionization of workers, contemplated the assassination of Li.[6]

In June 1923 the CCP held its Third Congress in Canton. It is not certain whether Li attended, but he is known to have opposed the decision adopted then to cooperate with the KMT (which is discussed in the biographies of Ch'en Tu-hsiu and Li Ta-chao).[7] He particularly opposed a policy he felt would place the labor unions under KMT jurisdiction. In 1924 Li went to Shanghai, where he quickly rose in prominence as a Party and labor leader. He gained his greatest fame in the labor movement during the midtwenties in connection with the events surrounding the May 30th Movement (1925). Shortly before this date, in the early days of the month, the Second All-China Labor Congress was held

in Canton. It decided to establish the All-China Federation of Labor (with Li as a member of its Executive Committee), to affiliate with the Russian-based Red International of Trade Unions (the Profintern), and to step up the already quickening pace of labor activities throughout China. Then, in the middle of the month a Chinese laborer was killed during a strike in Shanghai. This led to a series of protests, culminating in a large demonstration on May 30. Several demonstrators were killed by the British-officered police, thereby ushering in a nationwide series of strikes and protests that dwarfed all previous anti-foreign demonstrations. The Communists were quick to capitalize on the situation and on the next day established the Shanghai General Labor Union under purely Communist leadership. The new union, established largely through the efforts of Li Li-san, Ts'ai Ho-sen, and Ch'ü Ch'iu-pai (qq.v.), played a major role in a series of strikes over the ensuing weeks and months. Li became chairman of the Shanghai Union, which claimed a membership of over 200,000 within three weeks of its inauguration.[8] According to one writer, who described Li as the Party's "best public speaker," he "gained more stature" in the May 30th Movement than "any of its other leaders, and henceforth acted in party councils as chief spokesman for the workers. In fact, it was through the . . . Movement, and thanks to Li Li-san's energy" that the CCP "acquired its first real taste of leading a workers' struggle."[9]

Li spent much of the summer of 1925 negotiating on behalf of the Shanghai laborers with representatives of the Shanghai government, the influential Chamber of Commerce, and even with representatives of foreign governments that had strong interests in Shanghai (e.g., the British and Japanese).[10] Following a conversation with Li, the Japanese consul general in Shanghai correctly concluded that he was an "authentic" Red,[11] and before the summer ended the Shanghai authorities agreed: Li's Shanghai Union was outlawed in September 1925 and a warrant was issued for his arrest. Li then fled to Canton where the All-China Federation of Labor headquarters was located.

Li was one of the first representatives from the ACFL to attend Profintern meetings in Moscow. There is conflicting information, but apparently he attended such meetings in Moscow in late 1925 or early 1926. Within the ACFL he was advanced to a vice-chairmanship at the Third Labor Congress, which was held in Canton in May 1926 when the important Party leader Su Chao-cheng (q.v.) became the chairman. At this same time Li assumed the directorship of the Federation's Organization Department, and he lectured on the workers' movement at the Peasant Movement Training Institute (see under P'eng P'ai) during its sixth class (May–October

1926) when Mao Tse-tung was the principal.[12] In mid-1926, at approximately the time when the Northern Expedition was launched, Li was sent to Hupeh to carry on his labor activities. With Liu Shao-ch'i and others he was among the participants in late 1926 in demonstrations held to protest the existence of the British concession in Hankow, a section of Wuhan where the left-KMT had just established its seat of government. The protests were successful and in early 1927 the British relinquished their control of the concession to the KMT government, with which the Communists were still cooperating.[13] In May 1927 the Profintern-sponsored Pan-Pacific Trade Union Congress was held in Hankow; a permanent Secretariat of the Pan-Pacific Trade Union was created with Li as a member. A month later, in June, he gave the keynote speech before the Fourth All-China Labor Congress (also held in Hankow) and was elected ACFL secretary-general. (It is worth noting that Maoist historians have neglected Li's major role in the Communist-led labor movement of the early and middle twenties, often in favor of Liu Shao-ch'i who, though certainly a key labor agitator and organizer, was clearly less important than Li at that time.)

Concurrently with his rise in the labor movement, Li was rapidly advancing in the CCP hierarchy. He was elected to the Politburo at the Fifth CCP Congress, held in Wuhan in April–May 1927. The stormy meeting witnessed considerable dissension between those who supported Party General Secretary Ch'en Tu-hsiu (with his Comintern backing) and those who opposed Ch'en's attempt to continue cooperation with the KMT (see under Ch'ü Ch'iu-pai and Ch'en Tu-hsiu). After the July 1927 split between the Communists and the left-wing KMT government in Wuhan, Li made his way to Chiu-chiang (Kiukiang), arriving July 19 with Teng Chung-hsia (q.v.). Li was one of the principal organizers of the Communist-led Nanchang Uprising on August 1 (see under Yeh T'ing). Together with Communist military leader Ch'en Keng (q.v.), Li was given the task of arresting "counterrevolutionaries" and dealing with the Provincial Bank of Kiangsi once the rebels had taken the city. Moreover, when the city fell on August 1, he was named to the 25-member Revolutionary Committee and headed its Political Security Office.[14] However, he was not able to exercise his authority for long, because the Communists were driven from Nanchang only five days after it fell into their hands.

Li's report on the failure at Nanchang, entitled "The Experience and Lessons of the August First Revolution," has been translated and briefly commented upon by C. Martin Wilbur.[15] Li indicates that he played an important role in the execution of the uprising, and he also describes the experiences of the Red military forces after they were driven from Nanchang and made their way south to Swatow for the attack there in September. Analyzing the organization of the CCP at the time of the Nanchang revolt and the reasons for its failure, Li stated: "On the surface it appeared that the August First Revolution was entirely under the leadership of the Party, but in reality it was no more than under individual leadership of many CP members." (In the end, the official view placed the major blame for the failure upon T'an P'ing-shan.) Because Li was with the forces that fled from Nanchang, he was unable to attend the Emergency Conference of August 7, 1927, held in the wake of the Nanchang defeat to form a new CCP leadership and to oust Ch'en Tu-hsiu as general secretary. Although not enough Central Committee members were present to select a "legal" Central Committee and Politburo, provisional organs were established under the leadership of Ch'ü Ch'iu-pai. Li was elected to the "revised" Central Committee and, apparently, to the provisional Politburo. Then, following the defeat of the Communists at Swatow in September 1927, he escaped to Hong Kong and after working to bring about the coup at Canton in December, he replaced Chang T'ai-lei (q.v.) as chairman of the Kwangtung Provincial Committee after Chang's death during the Canton Commune. Subsequently, Li was transferred to Party headquarters at Shanghai.

Ch'ü Ch'iu-pai led the CCP in the difficult year from August 1927 until the Party met for its Sixth Congress in mid-1928. This was held in Moscow and was attended by over 100 delegates, Li among them. The Congress removed Ch'ü as head of the CCP, replacing him with Hsiang Chung-fa (q.v.), a rather colorless individual with so little dynamism that all factions could agree on him. Ch'ü's demotion worked to Li's advantage, because as head of the Propaganda Department he was in a strong position to influence Party opinion and soon became the dominant leader. Chou En-lai, at first director of the Organization Department (a post later assumed by Li Wei-han), subsequently became head of the Military Affairs Department. Chou was referred to as the "right hand of Li," and Ch'ü Ch'iu-pai and Ho Ch'ang were among Li Li-san's influential supporters. Li Wei-han (q.v.) and Ho Ch'ang, who continued to back him, were severely reprimanded and removed from their high Party posts at the Fourth Plenum in 1931 by the leaders who replaced Li (see under Ch'in Pang-hsien). Ho Ch'ang became deputy director of the First Front Army's Political Department on the eve of the Long March and was killed soon after the marchers left Juichin, Kiangsi, in 1934.

Returning to Shanghai in late 1928, Li sought to strengthen Party organizational work, especially in the urban labor field. He made little progress, however, in contrast to the growing successes of the various Red Army units in 1929 and early 1930. By April 1930 the Party claimed some 50,000 armed troops scattered in the rural hinterlands of central-south China, which were moving into regions from which they could seriously threaten the important industrial complex at Wuhan and the provincial capitals of Hunan and Kiangsi. A vital component of the Red forces was the First Army Corps led by Chu Te and Mao Tse-tung. This was concentrated along the Kiangsi-Fukien border with about 20,000 troops, of which 9,000 were armed. P'eng Te-huai's (q.v.) units protected the important Hunan-Hupeh-Kiangsi base with some 10,000 troops, of which perhaps 7,000 were armed. There were also Ho Lung's (q.v.) 6,000 men on the Hunan-Hupeh border. In all, about 14 separate detachments claimed control of all or parts of 150 hsien in central-south China. At the same time the CCP organization, variously estimated at 65,000 to 120,000 members, listed only about 2,000 who could in any sense be considered "proletarian."[16]

Benjamin I. Schwartz and Tso-liang Hsiao have written in detail about this important phase of Li Li-san's career,[17] a period characterized by a complex triangular relationship between the Comintern, the CCP headquarters in Shanghai, and the Red military forces in the hinterlands. From a series of Party directives issued in 1929–30, it is apparent that Li began to turn his attention more and more toward the rural military bases, which he visualized as fertile grounds for recruiting and building up strong Red military forces with which to surround and gain control of the industrial centers. However, these rural soviet areas were to follow the urban leadership (where Li must have realized that the Party was weak in numbers). Consequently, it was natural to think of using the Red armies organized by Mao, Chu, Ho Lung, and the others to come to the aid of the lagging workers' movement. Li's timing of this decision was determined by a combination of Comintern pressures to take advantage of the new "revolutionary wave" proclaimed after the outbreak of the world economic depression in 1929 and of domestic opportunities emerging from renewed fighting by warlords Yen Hsi-shan and Feng Yü-hsiang against the national government in the spring and summer of 1930.

However, as late as March 1930 Li denounced any suggestion of undue reliance on the Red Army, and in any case Central Committee control over the partisan units was minimal. (A member of P'eng Te-huai's army stated: "1930 was the first year the Fifth Red Army established direct" connections with the Central Committee.) The Party Center attempted to tighten its control over the partisan groups, especially at the May 1930 congress of delegates from the Soviet areas. By June, despite continuing opposition, Li felt secure enough within the Party to lay plans for attacks on Changsha, Nanchang, and Wuhan, attacks he hoped would lead to uprisings in all key cities throughout the nation. "Committees of action" were established to guide revolutionary events and the revolutionary program was unfolded in the June 11 resolution of the Central Committee, "The New Revolutionary Rising Tide and Preliminary Successes in One or More Provinces."[18] This document, which contained Li's credo, attempted to justify and elaborate its exhortation: "Actively prepare from now on for armed insurrection." It notes the "basic economic and political crisis in China" and the world and then presents its main theme: the necessity to fuse all available power, "peasant uprisings, soldiers' mutinies, powerful assaults of the Red Army, and a (whole) combination of various revolutionary forces" to seize the revolutionary victory. A "stubborn adherence to the military concept of guerrilla warfare, in opposition to the expansion of the Red Army" was, the report stated, one of the weaknesses of Communist bases in the hinterlands, which must discard "the guerrilla tactics of the part" and "undergo a fundamental change."

Battle plans for the Red Army units called for a convergence on Wuhan, which was to be the center of the revolution. Li's optimism that the masses would rise (the June 11 Resolution had boldly stated "The masses said long ago, 'Whenever the insurrection comes, notify us, [and] we will come.'") is difficult to understand, but presumably he looked back on the great days of the May 30th Movement and was beguiled by Comintern pressures. In any case no significant Red Army units ever reached Wuhan, where there were only about 200 Party members in 1930. In fact, the capture of Changsha by P'eng Te-huai on July 27 and the organization of a Soviet government there on August 1 was the first and only real success of the Li Li-san line. Even in Changsha the masses failed to respond, and despite Party boasts perhaps only 3,000 turned out for the August 1 celebrations. By August 3 P'eng had withdrawn to the east, presumably to join Chu Te and Mao Tse-tung for the march on Wuhan. The latter two had probed the defenses of Nanchang but failed to press the attack despite Li's urgings. Now the combined armies were ordered to retake Changsha and attacks were renewed in early September. Li Li-san probably decided to make Changsha rather than Wuhan the capital of the new Soviet government. The Comintern had hailed the first victory and perhaps believed Changsha could be recaptured. However, Chu Te, Mao, and possibly P'eng Te-huai were by now increasingly skeptical of the possibility or desirability of the "Li Li-san line." Accordingly, on September 13, they decided to call off the second attack on

Changsha in open definace of the Party Center.

As the failures became obvious, the Comintern moved to sacrifice Li as it had Ch'en Tu-hsiu in 1927 and (to a lesser extent) Ch'ü Ch'iu-pai in 1928. It dispatched Chou En-lai and Ch'ü Ch'iu-pai back to China in mid-1930, allegedly to rebuke Li Li-san, although the attitudes of the Comintern toward Li were quite ambiguous prior to the autumn of 1930. When the Third Party Plenum opened in late September both Ch'ü and Chou made some effort to represent the Comintern view, but in the end both compromised, maintaining that Li had erred not in following the Comintern "line" but only in his timing. The Comintern had spoken of taking "industrial centers" but "only in the future" in an eleventh-hour telegram to the CCP (dated July 23 according to Chinese sources, but June in some Comintern sources). The Plenum was further complicated for Li by the presence of a domestic opposition represented by labor leaders Ho Meng-hsiung and Lo Chang-lung (qq.v.), who had a considerable following of their own and who objected to Li because his aggressive approach had had devastating effects on the labor movement. Li's labor policies, they felt, had only resulted in reprisals by the KMT and caused the pro-Communist union membership to decline. Thus, while the Plenum heard much criticism of Li, no one faction got control of the meeting, probably largely because of the compromise attitude taken by Chou and Ch'ü. In the end Li retained his leading post in the Party hierarchy.

Later in the autumn Moscow increased its pressure on Li, notably in a letter dated October by the Comintern (but November 16 in Chinese sources), which pointedly outlined his mistakes. It was made clear that he had definitely not followed the Comintern line: "The problem is not one of disagreement or of a relatively unimportant difference . . . concerning an estimate or timing or an understanding of tactics and tasks." Rather, the Comintern and Li were following "mutually antagonistic" lines which could not be "coexistent."[19] Finally, at an urgent meeting of the CCP Central Committee (November 23–28), Comintern agent Pavel Mif and his returned-student group from Sun Yat-sen University in Moscow (see under Ch'in Pang-hsien), who had also been dispatched to China in the late spring of 1930 presumably to checkmate Li, were able to get control of the situation. Li was expelled from the Politburo (though not from the Party itself) on November 25 and exiled to Moscow. Simultaneously, his influence was destroyed within the partisan units that had survived the failures of the summer. In December 1930, during a rebellion at the small town of Fu-t'ien, Kiangsi, Mao Tse-tung decisively purged a great number of his own opposition, many of whom were supporters of Li Li-san.

Known as the Fu-t'ien Incident (see under P'eng Te-huai), Mao was able to arrest many Kiangsi Communists who opposed him and supported Li. This was done on the pretext that all were members of a group attempting to subvert the CCP in Kiangsi, a group Mao calls the "anti-Bolshevik Corps." Finally, at the Fourth Party Plenum held in Shanghai in January 1931, Mif's Russian-returned students gained virtually complete control of the Party apparatus and were able to oust the last of Li Li-san's supporters on the Central Committee from their positions of authority (see under Li Wei-han and Jen Pi-shih).

In December 1930, coinciding with the Fu-t'ien Incident, Li was in Moscow where he was being interrogated by Comintern officials, most notably Dimitri Manuilsky, a key member of the Comintern Presidium, and Otto Kuusinen, the chief of the Comintern's Far Eastern Bureau. In essence, Li was on trial and confessed to the basic charges brought against him, admitting that he had exaggerated the Party's strength and the revolutionary situation existing in China in 1930. Though he admitted that these errors of judgment had led him into a policy of putschism, he also charged that the Comintern "did not understand conditions in China" and that "comrades in Moscow did not trust the comrades doing practical work in China."[20]

Manuilsky gave Li credit for coming to Moscow to meet the Comintern. (Ch'en Tu-hsiu, when offered a similar opportunity, had refused.) But he was not willing to accept Li's easy confession without some measure of atonement. He wanted Li to "understand the substance of his mistakes" and thought that he should not return at once to China; therefore, regarding Li's punishment, "We want him to attend the Bolshevik school here."[21] Li's stay in Russia was to last 15 years. In his first years he is reported to have attended the Lenin School (run by the Comintern's International Relations Section) and to have been associated with the Profintern. One source states that he was imprisoned from 1936 to 1938 as a Trotskyite,[22] but this cannot be confirmed. Prior to 1936 he had headed the Eastern Section of the Foreign Languages Publishing House, and from 1938 to 1945 he was director of a translating department for the same publishing house. According to Chang Kuo-t'ao, Li held only very insignificant positions and had a difficult time in his years in Moscow.[23] Li's difficulties were mentioned again in his speech before the Eighth Party Congress in 1956 (see below); he picturesquely described the seven years he worked directly under Ch'en Shao-yü, the Chinese representative to the Comintern, as being like years "endured by an unwelcome daughter-in-law under the rule of overbearing 'in-laws." Moreover, in keeping with the spirit of his 1956 speech, he chided himself for his irresolute spirit and his failure to defend the Party's interests against Ch'en's "mistaken views and acts."

After nearly 15 years of what amounted to exile, Li returned to China in the closing days of World War II, entering Manchuria with Soviet forces. Using the alias Li Min-jan, he initially took up residence in Harbin and served as an adviser and political commissar under Lin Piao. In the late spring of 1946 he traveled to Yenan where, in a meeting that must have been laden with irony, he met Mao Tse-tung for the first time since the late twenties. Li remained in Yenan only briefly, returning via Nanking and Peking to Harbin in June. Back in Manchuria he served for a short time as a CCP representative to the Changchun Advance Headquarters, which had been set up under the terms of the Cease-Fire Agreement worked out by U.S. General George C. Marshall in early 1946. At about this same time he was also in charge of negotiations regarding the distribution of UNRRA supplies in Manchuria. (For a discussion of UNRRA activities in China, see under Wu Yun-fu.)

According to one author, "sometime in 1947" Li went to North Korea where he concluded a mutual assistance agreement that provided for Manchurian foodstuffs in return for Korean military aid to Lin Piao's military forces in Manchuria, which were then hard-pressed by a Chinese Nationalist offensive. The agreement "resulted in the entry [into Lin's forces] of some 100,000 youths chosen mainly from among the two million Korean minority in Manchuria and partly from North Korea."[24]

During the period from 1946 to 1949, Li's most important position in Manchuria was as a member of the CCP's Northeast Bureau, then under the leadership of Lin Piao (q.v.). But most of his time during those years seems to have been devoted to the labor movement, in which he had been deeply involved since the early twenties. As described above, the Chinese Communists' influence on the labor movement had been very weak after 1930, and thus their ties with organized labor were marginal until the late 1940's. Now, however, with nationwide victory not far off, the CCP set about reorganizing their dormant labor movement. The first major effort was the convocation of the Sixth National Labor Congress in Harbin in August 1948. For two months before the Congress Li was engaged in preparatory work, and when the meetings opened he was named to the Presidium (steering committee). A featured speaker, at the close of the Congress he was elected first vice-chairman of the All-China Federation of Labor (ACFL) under Chairman Ch'en Yun (q.v.). The two other vice-chairmen were Liu Ning-i (q.v.) and the well-known non-Communist labor leader Chu Hsueh-fan. Within a year Chairman Ch'en Yun was occupied with more important work in Peking, and it is evident that Chu Hsueh-fan had little effective power within the ACFL. Liu Ning-i, the only other vice-chairman of consequence, was rather fully occupied with overseas assignments in the late forties and early fifties. Therefore, although Li probably operated under the watchful eye of the Maoist leadership, he was one of the most active labor leaders in the early days of the PRC. Apart from his ACFL vice-chairmanship, in 1949 Li assumed the presidency of the Federation's school to train trade union cadres, as well as the directorship of the ACFL's Department of Wages.

In June 1949 the Communists established a committee to prepare for the convocation of the CPPCC, the organization that was to bring the new Communist government into existence. Representing the ACFL, Li served on this committee, which was chaired by Mao Tse-tung, and when the CPPCC held its first session in September he was named to the *ad hoc* Credentials Committee. Then, when the PRC Government was formed in October 1949, Li received four key assignments. The first was membership on the Central People's Government Council (CPGC). Chaired by Mao, the CPGC had six vice-chairmen and 56 members; endowed with broad executive, legislative, and judicial powers, the CPGC passed on virtually all important matters of state from 1949 until it went out of existence in 1954. Second, Li was made one of the 15 members of Chou En-lai's Government Administration Council (GAC), the equivalent of the cabinet. Third, he was given the portfolio for the Ministry of Labor and finally he was made a member of the GAC's Finance and Economics Committee, a highly important body headed by Ch'en Yun, Peking's top economic specialist during the first decade of the PRC. Concurrently, Li served with two of the more important "mass" organizations, the Sino-Soviet Friendship Association (SSFA) and the China Peace Committee. He was an SSFA Executive Board member from 1949 to 1954 and a Standing Committee member of the Peace Committee from 1950 to 1958, but in neither instance was he particularly active.

Although Li was never to recapture his importance in the Chinese Communist movement of two decades earlier, he was quite active in the early years of the PRC. He received an additional assignment in October 1949 when he was named to a small group to study the problems of translating the names of Chinese government organizations into foreign languages—presumably Li's contributions concerned the Russian language (although he also has some knowledge of French and English). But most of his work was carried out in his dual capacity as minister of Labor and vice-chairman of the ACFL. When, for example, the Chinese convened the important Asian-Australasian Trade Union Conference in November 1949 (see under Liu Shao-ch'i), Li presented a historical summary of the Chinese labor movement, and in January 1950 he presided over an ACFL meeting that provided for the establishment of several new trade unions subordinate to the national Federation and also formed a special committee to draft national labor laws. In addition to such conferences, typical of those in which he participated in the early fifties, Li made frequent reports before the Government Administration Council (GAC) on trade union activities and, more particularly, on labor insurance regulations. For example, in October 1950 he spoke before the GAC on the draft labor insurance law, and four months later he again addressed the GAC when the law was adopted. Activities of this sort continued to engage Li through the summer of 1954. In the meantime, he made one trip abroad and received further assignments in the government and "mass" organizations. He went abroad in August 1950 as deputy leader of a "people's" delegation led by Kuo Mo-jo, which was sent to North Korea to take part in celebrations marking the fifth anniversary of Korea's "liberation" from the Japanese. The timing of the trip is of interest, coming just a month after the outbreak of the Korean War. During the visit Kuo and Li reportedly presented the Koreans with 100,000 blankets and "enormous quantities of medicine."[25] Li's new assignments were: director, Wages Office, Ministry of Labor (1950–?); member, Board of Directors, All-China Federation of Cooperatives (1950–1954); member, Cinema Guidance Committee, Ministry of Culture (1950–?); member, Labor Employment Committee, Government Administration Council (1952–1954); instructor, Party cadres' special training class, Marxist-Leninist Institute (1952–?).

Li continued to appear in public with considerable regularity through the spring of 1953. However, at a January 1953 meeting of the ACFL, it was revealed that "errors of the leadership" within the organization had been "exposed" at an earlier meeting held in late 1951. No names were mentioned at the 1953 meeting, but it soon became apparent that Li Li-san was once again in political trouble with the Maoist leadership. Li's second fall was presaged in early 1952 when Lai Jo-yü (q.v.) was brought into the ACFL as the secretary-general. Then, at the Seventh Congress of the ACFL in May 1953, Lai succeeded to the ACFL chairmanship. Technically, Lai succeded Ch'en Yun as chairman, but in view of the fact that Li Li-san was the most active ACFL leader, it would seem more accurate to assume that Lai Jo-yü was brought in to replace Li. Moreover, he failed to be re-elected as an ACFL vice-chairman, and he was not even selected for a seat on the Executive Committee. Li mentioned his downfall in the ACFL in his 1956 speech to the Eighth Party Congress, tersely commenting that in 1950 he had "again committed serious mistakes of a subjectivist nature."

After the 1953 labor congress Li continued to make a few public appearances, but in September 1954 his career received another severe blow when the constitutional government was established by the First NPC. Unlike most high-ranking leaders he was not elected to the NPC. More important, at the close of the First NPC session he was replaced in the Labor Ministry by Ma Wen-jui (q.v.). Almost a year passed before Li was again mentioned in the press—and then only at a minor protocol function. Still another year went by before he came into prominence again, this time at the CCP's Eighth Congress in September 1956. Significantly, Li was one of only four Central Committee members elected in 1945 not named to the Congress Presidium (steering committee). Presidium membership was for the most part honorary—but it soon became evident that Li was not to be honored. Rather, he delivered a remarkable speech, or more correctly a confession of past "errors," which was a comprehensive recantation supplemented by profuse expressions of gratitude to the Party for its leniency and patience in dealing with him.

At the close of the Congress Li was re-elected as a full member of the Central Committee. He was placed 89th on the list of 97 members, and although this cannot be taken as an accurate indicator of Party stature, in this instance Li was clearly being dealt a calculated blow by the Maoist leadership. However, during the course of the Congress it was revealed that he had been made a deputy director (under Director Li Hsueh-feng, q.v.) of the Central Committee's Industrial and Communications Work Department. For a younger leader rising within the hierarchy such an assignment would have been regarded as important, but in Li's case, given his long service in the CCP, it was a comedown. By mid-1957 the department had been divided into two sections; Li continued as deputy director of the new Industrial Work Department, still serving under Li Hsueh-feng. But he has not appeared in this post since late 1959, so he has probably relinquished even this assignment.

Since the 1956 Party Congress Li has made only infrequent appearances, and as the years pass it becomes increasingly evident that the Maoist leadership has relegated him to the most minor tasks. For example, as a representative of the CCP he was named to membership on the Third National Committee of the relatively unimportant CPPCC, which opened in April 1959. He was also appointed as a CPPCC Standing Committee member and was then re-elected to both posts in the Fourth National Committee, which held its first session from December 1964 to January 1965. By April 1962 Li had received a more important assignment when he was identified as a secretary of the Party's North China Bureau, a post that again placed him under Li Hsueh-feng, the first secretary. Notwithstanding this new assignment, his public appearances continue to be mainly ceremonial, as in October 1964 when he was among those reviewing a parade to commemorate China's National Day.

In the early history of the Chinese Communist Movement Li Li-san had a brief moment of great importance, but he has never recovered from his fall from grace in 1930, and even his minor "comeback" after the mid-forties must be viewed as a symbol of tolerance rather than an act of trust on the part of the Maoist leadership. This is well reflected in Li's occasional writings of the PRC era. For instance, in 1963 he recorded his reflections for the *JMJP* (August 4) after seeing a movie that dealt with labor unrest in the twenties. He denigrated his own important contribution to the labor movement and exaggerated the roles of Mao Tse-tung and Liu Shao-ch'i. Apart from his self-denigration, he is the butt of even the most humble propagandists, who seem to have free rein to castigate him when the occasion is fitting; thus all students of contemporary China have become familiar with the pejorative "Li Li-san line."

Li has been married three times. One of his wives, Moscow-trained Li Han-fu, was allegedly killed by the KMT. Another wife, Wang Hsiu-chen, was reportedly arrested by the KMT in 1932. During his long stay in Moscow Li married a Russian woman to whom he is still wed. By one of his earlier marriages he had a son (born about 1930), and by his present marriage he has two daughters, one born about 1938 and the other about 1944. In 1959 the older girl, reared in the Soviet Union, was in the Foreign Students' Department of Peking University where she was taking a two-year course to learn Chinese.[26]

---

1. *SCMP* 2727, pp. 12–14.
2. Edgar Snow, *Red Star over China* (New York, 1938), p. 130.
3. Anna Louise Strong, *China's Millions* (Peking, 1965), p. 93; Jean Chesneaux, *Le Mouvement ouvrier chinois de 1919 à 1927* (Paris, 1962), p. 272; *Chung-kuo kung-ch'an-tang tsai chung-nan-ti-ch'ü ling-tao ko-ming tou-cheng te li-shih tzu-liao* (Historical materials on the revolutionary struggles led by the CCP in central-south China; Wuhan, 1951), I, 57–60.
4. Nym Wales, *Red Dust* (Stanford, Calif., 1952), p. 85.
5. Strong, p. 93.
6. Chesneaux, p. 273.
7. Conrad Brandt, *Stalin's Failure in China* (New York, 1958), p. 37.

8. Liu Li-k'ai and Wang Chen, *I-chiu i-chiu chih i-chiu erh-ch'i te Chung-kuo kung-jen yun-tung* (The Chinese workers' movement from 1919 to 1927; Peking, 1954), p. 39.
9. Brandt, p. 52.
10. Chesneaux, pp. 523, 549, 553.
11. Akira Iriye, *After Imperialism* (Cambridge, Mass., 1965), p. 66.
12. Chesneaux, p. 553; Chang Ching-lu, ed., *Chung-kuo hsien-tai ch'u-pan shih-liao* (Historical materials on contemporary Chinese publishing; Peking, 1954), p. 77.
13. *Ti-i-tz'u kuo-nei ko-ming chan-cheng shih-ch'i te kung-jen yun-tung* (The workers' movement during the period of the first revolutionary civil war; Peking, 1963), pp. 383–384.
14. Wei Hung-yun, ed., *"Pa-i" ch'i-i* (The "August First" uprising; Wuhan, 1957), p. 12; *Ti-erh-tz'u kuo-nei ko-ming chan-cheng shih-ch'i shih-shih lun-ts'ung* (Accounts of the second revolutionary civil war; Peking, 1956), p. 3.
15. C. Martin Wilbur, "The Ashes of Defeat," *The China Quarterly*, no. 18:3–24 (April–June 1964).
16. James P. Harrison, "The Li Li-san Line and the CCP in 1930," pts. I and II, *The China Quarterly*, no. 14:178–194 (April–June 1963) and no. 15:140–159 (July–September 1963).
17. Benjamin I. Schwartz, *Chinese Communism and the Rise of Mao* (Cambridge, Mass., 1952), chap. 10, pp. 144–163; Tso-liang Hsiao, *Power Relations within the Chinese Communist Movement, 1930–1934* (Seattle, Wash., 1961), chaps. 3 and 4, pp. 14–38.
18. Conrad Brandt, Benjamin Schwartz, and John K. Fairbank, *A Documentary History of Chinese Communism* (Cambridge, Mass., 1952), pp. 184–200.
19. Robert C. North, *Moscow and Chinese Communists* (Stanford, Calif., 1953), p. 142.
20. *Pu-erh-sai-wei-k'o* (Bolshevik), 4.3:11, 56.
21. North, p. 145.
22. Union Research Institute, *Who's Who in Communist China* (Hong Kong, 1966), p. 352.
23. Modern China Project, Columbia University, New York, Howard L. Boorman, director.
24. Kiwon Chung, "The North Korean People's Army and the Party," *The China Quarterly*, no. 14:109 (April–June 1963).
25. *Ibid.*
26. Interview with a former student at Peking University, Cambridge, Mass., June 1966.

Li Pao-hua

(1908–   ; Lo-t'ing hsien, Hopeh). First secretary, Anhwei CCP Committee; member, CCP Central Committee.

Li Pao-hua was born in Lo-t'ing hsien, about 100 miles east of Tientsin in Hopeh province near the Gulf of Chihli (Po Hai). There are reports from non-Communist sources that he is the son of Li Ta-chao (q.v.), one of the Party founders, but these cannot be confirmed. Li Ta-chao married in his teens and was known to have had two sons, and if Li Pao-hua were his son he would have been born when the father was only 19. Li Pao-hua was known by his revolutionary alias, Chao Chen-sheng, until the late 1940's; he was using this name in 1945 when elected an alternate member of the Party Central Committee.

For Li to have reached the level of the Party Central Committee by 1945, it is evident that he must have been a CCP leader of considerable significance at least by the time of the Sino-Japanese War. However, very little is known about his early career. He joined the CCP in 1928, when he was 20, just one year after Li Ta-chao was executed by the gendarmes of Manchurian warlord Chang Tso-lin. In war times Li Pao-hua is said to have been a member of the Party Committee for the Shansi-Chahar-Hopeh (Chin-Ch'a-Chi) Border Region (see under Sung Shao-wen), formed in early 1938. The Chin-Ch'a-Chi area, one of the most important regions controlled by the Communists during the war, had among its leaders such important persons as Nieh Jung-chen and Huang Ching (qq.v.). Like many of the Chin-Ch'a-Chi leaders, Li was also active in the Party's North China Bureau and at some time during the latter stages of the war reportedly headed the Bureau's Organization Department.

As noted above, he was elected an alternate member of the Party Central Committee at the Seventh Party Congress held in Yenan from April to June 1945. At that time the Central Committee was a relatively small body, consisting of only 44 full and 33 alternate members. During the civil war with the Nationalists in the late 1940's Li evidently remained in north China. Following the surrender of Peking to the Communists in January 1949, he became a deputy secretary of the municipal Party Committee, then headed by P'eng Chen (q.v.), another veteran north China operative and a man with whom Li may well have been associated for a number of years.

Li participated in the formation of the PRC Government when it was established at the first session of the CPPCC in September 1949. He attended the CPPCC meetings as a representative of the Peking-Tientsin municipalities and served on the *ad hoc* committee that drafted the organic laws of the CPPCC, the major legislative body of the new government until it was superceded by the NPC in 1954. In October, when the major assignments to the government were made, Li was named a vice-minister of the Ministry of Water Conservancy (at which time he relinquished his Peking CCP post). He remained in this ministry for the next 13 years (the ministry becoming known as the Ministry of Water Conservancy and Electric Power in

February 1958 when it absorbed the Ministry of Electric Power Industry). During his long term of office Li Pao-hua was probably the most important figure in the ministry, particularly because Minister Fu Tso-i, the KMT general who peacefully surrendered Peking, does not belong to the Party. Moreover, until Central Committee alternate Liu Lan-po (q.v.) joined the ministry in 1958, Li was the only official there of Central Committee rank. Li's primacy within the government body was given further confirmation both in 1957, when he was identified as secretary of the ministry's Party Committee, and in 1958, when he served briefly as the acting minister. While serving as a vice-minister of Water Conservancy, Li was often a participant in the many PRC conferences dealing with the pressing problems of water conservancy and flood prevention. Similarly, he was called upon from time to time to deliver reports on these subjects, as he did on August 29, 1956, before a session of the NPC Standing Committee.

Unlike most senior Party leaders who frequently held several concurrent posts in the early years of the PRC, Li apparently centered his activities almost exclusively around the work of the Water Conservancy Ministry. The one exception—and probably a rather minor one—was his selection for membership on the Executive Board of the Sino-Soviet Friendship Association (SSFA) in 1950. He retained this post until the second national conference of the SSFA in December 1954 (which he attended as a representative of the CCP), but since then he has had no further association with this organization.

When the Second National Committee of the CPPCC was formed in December 1954, Li was named to the National Committee (as a representative of the CCP), as well as to the Standing Committee that manages the affairs of the CPPCC when the National Committee is not in session. He was reappointed to both posts under the Third CPPCC when it was established in April 1959. However, probably because of his transfer to east China in 1961 (see below), he was not named to the Fourth CPPCC, which first met at the end of 1964. Li's work for the CCP was given recognition when, at the Eighth Party Congress in September 1956, he was promoted to full membership on the CCP Central Committee. Li made his only known trip abroad in May 1960, accompanying economic planner Po I-po to Poland for a three-week visit, made at the invitation of the Polish United Workers' (Communist) Party to discuss economic cooperation between the two nations.

In January 1961, at the Party Central Committee's Ninth Plenum, six regional bureaus were created to strengthen the work of the CCP throughout the nation. To staff the new bureaus, a number of top-level Party leaders in Peking (many of them from the various PRC ministries)

were dispatched to one of the new regional bureaus. Almost immediately after the Plenum closed, Li was transferred to east China. Although his new assignment was not clarified, indirect evidence suggested that he was assigned to the Party's new East China Bureau, headquartered in Shanghai. Initially, Li worked in Shanghai, but then in the early fall of 1962 he was identified as the Party first secretary in Anhwei, one of the provinces under the jurisdiction of the East China Bureau. In becoming the Anhwei first secretary, Li replaced Central Committee member Tseng Hsi-sheng (q.v.), who apparently suffered a political decline at this time. Not long after receiving the assignment in Anhwei, Li was officially removed as a vice-minister of Water Conservancy and Electric Power (April 1963).

Since his transfer to Anhwei, Li has assumed virtually all the key positions within the province—excepting only the governorship, a post held by Huang Yen (q.v.), who, although a Party member, does not belong to the Party Central Committee. By February 1964 Li was identified as the chairman of the Anhwei Committee of the CPPCC and, more important, by September 1965 he was identified as the first political commissar of the Anhwei Military District. In both instances, Li succeeded Tseng Hsi-sheng.

Li's activities in Anhwei are typical of key provincial leaders throughout China, who attend festivities commemorating national holidays, address major conferences devoted to questions of industrial and agricultural production, and make inspections throughout the province. For example, at the Anhwei Congress of Poor and Lower-middle Peasants held in February 1965, Li was a featured speaker, and at the close of the congress he was elected as chairman of the provincial Preparatory Committee of the Poor and Lower-middle Peasants Association. A year later (January 1966), when the Association was established on a permanent basis, he was elected as the chairman.

Li Shih-ying

(Honan). Specialist in Party security work; member, CCP Control Commission; a secretary, the Kiangsu CCP Committee.

Li Shih-ying, a native of Honan, is a specialist in security work. He may have had some security training in Vladivostok in the mid-1930's. During the Sino-Japanese War he was active in the Communist-held areas of Shantung. Presumably, this was after 1939 when elements of the 115th Division of the Eighth Route Army went to Shantung to establish a guerrilla base there. Little is known about his career until 1948, when he was identified as the director of the Public Security Department in Tsinan, the Shantung capital.

As Communist forces pushed into Shanghai in the late spring of 1949, Li accompanied them, thus temporarily giving up his work in Shantung. After the fall of Shanghai, the Communists immediately formed a Military Control Commission as well as the Municipal People's Government. Under both organizations Li was named to head the Public Security Department, which, given the Communist view of Shanghai as a stronghold of business and a target for socialization, stands as a testimony to his stature within Party circles. During Li's stay in Shanghai regional governments were formed, with the eastern coastal provinces placed under the jurisdiction of the East China Military and Administrative Committee (ECMAC), and with its formal establishment in January 1950, Li was named as a member. In the following month he was also appointed as director of the ECMAC Public Security Department. Not long afterward, he gave up his posts in the Shanghai public security network, probably because of the much heavier responsibilities of security work for the ECMAC. Perhaps because of the secrecy involved in this work, little was heard of Li over the next year and a half, although in March and November 1951 he delivered reports in Shanghai on "bandit activities" and the "suppression of counterrevolutionaries" in East China.

In November 1951 Li was transferred back to Shantung. At this time he was demoted to deputy director of the ECMAC Public Security Department (being replaced by Hsu Chien-kuo, q.v.); the demotion probably resulted from the need to have the public security chief present at the ECMAC headquarters in Shanghai. With his transfer he assumed three important posts in the Shantung Government: director, Public Security Department, November 1951–c.1955; chairman, Political and Legal Affairs Committee, October 1952–1954; vice-governor, December 1953–March 1955. Within the ECMAC he was appointed in September 1952 as a member of the Political and Legal Affairs Committee, which was chaired by Chang Ting-ch'eng (q.v.). And, when the ECMAC was reorganized into the East China Administrative Committee in December 1952, he was named as a member of the newly organized Committee.

In the meantime, like many other regional and provincial officials, Li held posts directly subordinate to the national government in Peking. When the central government was formed in the fall of 1949, he was named a member of the Supreme People's Procuratorate (with powers broadly akin to the U.S. Attorney General's Office) under Chief Procurator Lo Jung-huan, later to become a Politburo member. He held this post until the governmental reorganization in September 1954.

Little was heard of Li after his transfer from Shanghai to Shantung in November 1951. He served, however, in February 1954 as a deputy leader of a "comfort" delegation, a group sent to entertain and inspect PLA troops stationed in East China. And in early 1955 he was reported as a deputy secretary of the Shantung Party Committee, his first known Party post. Then, after almost four years in Shantung, Li was transferred to Peking where he resumed work in the Supreme People's Procuratorate. Formerly only a member of the Procuratorate (1949–1954), Li was now appointed (August 1955) as a deputy procurator-general under Chang Ting-ch'eng, his former superior in east China. Thirteen months later, on the day following the Eighth Party Congress, the first plenum of the newly elected Party Central Committee elected Li a member of the Party Central Control Commission under Politburo member Tung Pi-wu. The Control Commission has duties involving discipline and inspection similar to those of the governmental Procuratorate, and it is thus logical that Li should hold these broadly parallel posts. In about 1961 a Standing Committee was created in the Control Commission, and Li was named as one of the alternate members. However, after the 10th Party Plenum in September 1962, the Control Commission was reorganized; Li remained as a Commission member but was removed as a Standing Committee alternate. The reason for his removal is almost certainly because Standing Committee members, who actually manage the Commission, reside in Peking, and by 1962 Li had been transferred to Kiangsu.

Li was suddenly transferred in 1962 from Peking back to east China, this time to Kiangsu where in April he was identified as a secretary of the Kiangsu Party Committee headed by Chiang Wei-ch'ing, an alternate member of the CCP Central Committee. At about the same time he became a provincial vice-governor under Kiangsu Governor Hui Yü-yü (q.v.). As a consequence of his transfer, Li was removed as a deputy procurator-general; although his name was deleted from the 1961 Jen-min shou-ts'e (People's handbook), he was not officially removed until September 1962.

After his arrival in Kiangsu, Li was elected for the first time to the national legislature. At the first session of the Third Kiangsu Provincial People's Congress (September 1964) he was elected one of Kiangsu's deputies to the Third NPC, which opened in Peking in December 1964. At the same session of the Kiangsu Congress, Li gave the keynote report on the work of the provincial government and at the close of the session was re-elected a vice-governor.

Since 1958 Li has been involved in activities outside the field of security work. In June 1958 he was among a group of political and legal experts invited to lecture at the Peking University Law Department. In August of that year he was elected a member of the national council of the Political Science and Law Association of China, the mass organization in the legal field. More important, he was elected a secretary of the small secretariat that runs the association on a day-to-day basis. The organization was then headed by Tung Pi-wu (Li's superior on the Control Commission) and Wu Te-feng, another public security expert. Until his transfer to Kiangsu in 1962, Li occasionally appeared in this capacity at social functions given for visiting foreign jurists and legal experts. In October 1964 the Political Science and Law Association held a congress and elected new officials; Li was dropped as a secretary (once again because of his 1962 transfer out of Peking), but he was re-elected to the national council.

Li Szu-kuang

(1889–   ; Huang-kang hsien, Hupeh). Minister of Geology; Vice-president, Academy of Sciences.

Li Szu-kuang, a geologist, is one of the most outstanding scientists in the PRC. He joined the Communist government in its earliest days and since that time has been a major participant in the efforts to modernize science in China. He is often known in Western circles as J. S. Lee or Jonguei Su-kuang Lee (the "Jonguei" deriving from his courtesy name, Chung-k'uei). In his youth Li received a classical education and then studied at a cadets' school in Hupeh founded by Chang Chih-tung, the famed Ch'ing reformer. Because of his good record, Li was sent to Japan to study shipbuilding and engineering. As in the case of so many young Chinese students in Japan in the early 1900's, Li joined Sun Yat-sen's T'ung-meng hui (c.1908). After his return to China he taught at a technical school in Wuchang and took part in the 1911 Revolution, which overthrew the Ch'ing Dynasty.

Following the establishment of the Chinese Republic, Li went to England where he studied geology. He earned his bachelor's and master's degrees from the University of Birmingham (1917 and 1918), and after his return to China was awarded his doctorate (1926) from that university. As a result of his education, Li is known to be proficient in English, German, and French, and presumably has some command of Japanese. Returning to China in 1920, Li took up a professorship of geology at Peking University (Peita) and for the next two decades was among the most active Chinese scientists in the promotion of science in China. He was, for example, a charter member of the Geological Society of China in 1922 and later the president of the organization; from 1930 to 1933 and again from 1943 to 1949 he headed the Geology Research Institute under the Academia Sinica; and from 1933 to 1943 he chaired the Geology Department at Peita. During these same years

Li maintained his contacts with the international scientific community through his writings and other activities. In this connection, he spent part of 1935 in England lecturing on geology and he also served as a member of the Sino-British Cultural Association, which had been formed in Nanking in 1933.

In 1948 Li was in England again to attend the 18th session of the International Geological Congress. Probably because of the unsettled political situation in China, he did not return home when the congress adjourned. But when the PRC was inaugurated in 1949, Li was given a number of appointments, and the implication is that the Communist authorities were confident of his return to the mainland. When he did return to Peking (May 1950), he had already been named (October 1949) a vice-president of the Academy of Sciences and a member of the Culture and Education Committee of the PRC's Government Administration Council (the cabinet). Then in August 1950 he was given two positions more specifically related to his profession: the directorship of the Palaeontology Institute under the Academy (a post he held until 1954) and the chairmanship of the Geological Work Planning and Guidance Committee. The latter was the precursor of the Ministry of Geology; thus, just a few days before the Committee was abolished (September 1952), the ministry was established with Li as the first minister, a post he continues to hold. As of January 1965, when all cabinet ministers were appointed or reappointed, Li was one of the very few who had held a ministerial-level post for so many continuous years.

In the same month that Li received the two above-described positions (August 1950), the PRC held a large conference of scientific personnel. Out of this conference came two permanent nationwide scientific organizations, the All-China Federation of Scientific Societies (ACFSS) and the All-China Association for the Dissemination of Scientific and Technical Knowledge. Attesting to Li's stature as a man of science, he was named to head the former (and more important) organization. Furthermore, when the two bodies were merged in September 1958 to form the China Scientific and Technical Association (CSTA), Li was named to head the combined organization—another position that he retains. One of the scientific organizations under the jurisdiction of the ACFSS (and later the CSTA) is the Geological Society of China, the organization that Li had helped to found in 1922. Like all such societies, it was reorganized in the early 1950's after the Communists had come to power. Following this reorganization, Li was named to the chairmanship and continues in this post. Although the major portion of Li's time has been devoted to scientific activities, he has also been a nominal participant in the legislative bodies of the PRC. Li was a member of the First National Committee (1949–1954) of the CPPCC and was then elevated in 1954 to a vice-chairmanship, holding this post on the Second, Third, and Fourth National Committees, the first sessions of which were held, respectively, in December 1954, April 1959, and December 1964–January 1965. Similarly, he has been a deputy from his native Hupeh to the First, Second, and Third NPC's (which opened in 1954, 1959, and 1964).

Unlike many present-day Chinese scientists and scholars of note, Li has apparently not been heavily burdened with political responsibilities by the Communists. Although he has nominally served on the National Committee of the China Peace Committee since 1949, he does not seem to have been required to take part in the political self-criticism sessions that have been the lot of so many of the non-Party intellectuals. An important exception to this lack of participation in political affairs took place in 1952 in connection with the Asian and Pacific Regions Peace Conference (see under Liu Ning-i). Li was active in the preparations for the conference and was an official Chinese delegate when it was held in Peking in October 1952. One of the principal themes expressed at the conference was the alleged use of bacteriological warfare by the United States in the Korean War, a propaganda theme constantly stressed by the PRC throughout 1952. After the meetings closed, a declaration was issued in the name of the conference condemning the United States for its alleged use of bacteriological warfare and atomic weapons; Li was one of the signers for the Chinese.

In the fifties and sixties, Li received a series of new appointments, some of importance and others that were largely nominal or symbolic. When the Academy of Sciences created four departments in May–June 1955, he was named to the Department of Biology, Geography and Geology, and in October of the same year he was named to the Academy's Committee on Scientific Awards. In March 1956, when the State Council established the Scientific Planning Commission, Li was named as one of the vice-chairmen, holding the post until the Commission was merged with another in November 1958. From 1953 to 1954 he served as a member of the Central Election Committee (established to prepare for the NPC elections), and from 1954 to the present he has been a vice-president of the Sino-Soviet Friendship Association. He has also served on ad hoc committees created to honor special occasions or persons, for example, the 40th anniversary of the May Fourth Movement (April 1959), the 50th anniversary of the 1911 Revolution (September 1961), and the 80th anniversary of the birth of writer Lu Hsun (September 1961).

Until 1958 the Communist press often described Li as a "non-partisan," a term used by the Communists to apply to persons who belong neither to the CCP nor to any of the eight so-called democratic political parties. The term is used to symbolize the cooperation, or united front, between virtually all other elements of Chinese society and the CCP. Up to and through the year 1958 Li's importance as a "non-partisan" leader was probably only exceeded by Mme. Sun Yat-sen and the cultural leader Kuo Mo-jo. Then, late in 1958, it was announced that Kuo, Li, and a few other prominent "non-partisans" had been admitted to the CCP. Though this action must have somewhat weakened the image of the united front, the Party apparently felt it more useful to claim the support of such prominent scientists as Li as Party members.

Understandably, Li's far-ranging international scientific contacts have been utilized by the PRC. He attended the second congress of the Communist-dominated World Federation of Scientific Workers (WFSW) in Prague in the spring of 1951, and at this congress was elected a vice-president of the WFSW, a post he held for the next 11 years. For his work and writings, Li has also been honored by foreign countries, particularly the Soviet Union. In 1958, for example, he was elected as an "academician" of the Department of Geology and Geography of the Soviet Academy of Sciences and in the same year received the 1958 A. P. Karpinsky gold medal (named for a prominent Soviet scientist) for his "outstanding work" in geology, paleontology, petrography, and mineralogy. Years earlier, in 1945, he had been given an honorary doctorate by the University of Oslo. Li's international contacts are regularly illustrated by his numerous appearances in Peking as a host for visiting scientific groups. Thus, as a scientist of international reputation, Li was called upon in August 1964 to deliver the closing address before the Peking Scientific Symposium, a gathering that brought together 367 delegates from 44 countries (mainly from Asian, African, and Latin American nations).

It is difficult to assess the importance of any scientist in China, particularly when, as in Li's case, admission to the CCP came so late in life. Li was 69 when he became a Party member. However, at least one important Western study of science in Communist China suggests that his contribution to the Chinese Communists has been a significant one.[1] His significance may follow from the importance placed upon geology in a nation seeking to exploit its natural resources, and when taken together with the apparent ease with which Li has escaped political problems, implies that his talents have been utilized to a greater degree than those of many scientists now working in China.

Little is known of Li's private life aside from the fact that he is married to Hsu Shu-pin. Nothing further, however, is known about her background.

---

1. E. C. T. Chao, "Progress and Outlook of Geology," in Sidney H. Gould, ed., *Sciences in Communist China* (Washington, D.C., 1961), pp. 497–522.

Li Ta

(1905–   ; Shensi). PLA officer; vice-chairman, Physical Culture and Sports Commission; chairman, National Defense Sports Association.

Li Ta, a Red Army officer since the late 1920's, participated in the Long March and was chief-of-staff of the 129th Division throughout the Sino-Japanese War and the civil war with the Nationalists in the late forties. He spent the early years of the PRC in the southwest, and after a brief tour of duty in Korea, he was a vice-minister of National Defense from 1954 to 1959. Since the late 1950's Li has devoted most of his time to the promotion of athletics, particularly the martial sports.

Li Ta (not to be confused with a Party founder of the same name) was trained at the Red Army Academy in the Soviet Union during the late twenties or early thirties. He is said to have been a Party member and a veteran of the Red Army from the latter part of 1927, when he was with Mao Tse-tung's forces in the Chingkang Mountains on the Hunan-Kiangsi border. Little is known of his work over the next few years, but he made the Long March from 1934 to 1936 as a staff officer with the Sixth Red Army Corps and later the Second Front Army (see under Jen Pi-shih and Ho Lung).

When war with Japan broke out in mid-1937, Li became chief-of-staff of the 129th Division, one of the three divisions in the Communists' Eighth Route Army. The wartime record of the 129th Division is reviewed in the biography of its commander, Liu Po-ch'eng, a man with whom Li was associated for many years. Li continued as a staff officer throughout the war, and in the immediate postwar period (1945–46) he was concurrently commander of the T'ai-hang Military District in southeast Shansi. Over the next two years Liu Po-ch'eng's forces moved to the east and then southward into central China. Accordingly, the 129th Division was first redesignated the Shansi-Hopeh-Shantung-Honan PLA and then the Central Plains Liberation Army; in both units Li Ta continued as Liu's chief-of-staff. In the spring of 1949 Li participated in the capture of Nanking with Liu Po-ch'eng's forces, which were by now known as the Second Field Army. After a brief pause in the spring and summer of 1949, the Second Field Army pushed into southwest China, which it captured by the end of the year.

In its conquest of the southwest, the Second Field Army had been assisted by armies led by Ho Lung, which had moved into the area from northwest China. The military hierarchy for the southwest was established in early 1950. Liu Po-ch'eng continued to command the Second Field Army, which operated under the jurisdiction of the Southwest Military Region commanded by Ho Lung. Ch'en Keng, Chou Shih-ti, both seasoned Red Army officers, and Li Ta were appointed deputy commanders under Ho, an assignment that Li continued to hold for most of the next four years. Concurrently, he served as chief-of-staff of the Second Field Army. Like most of the key military officers in the area, when the Communists established their organization for civil rule in July 1950—the Southwest Military and Administrative Committee—Li was appointed as a member. He retained his membership when the Committee was reorganized and redesignated the Southwest Administrative Committee in February 1953.

Li remained in Chungking, the headquarters for Communist civil and military authority in the southwest, during the early 1950's, although on occasion he was reported in Peking. In mid-1953, just as the Korean War was drawing to a close, Li replaced Yang Te-chih (q.v.) as chief-of-staff of the "Chinese People's Volunteers." However, he remained in Korea for less than a year and by the following spring had resumed his post as deputy commander of the Southwest Military Region in Chungking. He remained there through the summer of 1954, but in October, a month after the First NPC had established the constitutional government, he was transferred to Peking to become a vice-minister under P'eng Te-huai in the newly established Ministry of National Defense. In September 1955 Li was among the recipients of the newly created military orders and personal ranks. He was made a colonel general (a three-star rank) and was given the Orders of August First, Independence and Freedom, and Liberation, awards for military service from the birth of the Red Army in 1927 to the final conquest of the mainland in 1950.

For a brief time in the first half of 1958 Li served under Hsiao K'o (q.v.) as a deputy director of the PLA's General Training Department. Probably as a result of this assignment he soon became a top administrator of the PRC's quite extensive program to promote military-related athletic activities (e.g., marksmanship). In April of that year he headed a special committee to prepare for a sports meet in East Germany, which brought together athletes from the armed forces of the various Communist nations. Then, immediately after Ts'ai Shu-fan (q.v.) was killed in an air crash in October 1958, Li succeeded him as chairman of the National Defense Sports Association, a post he still holds. A year later (September 1959) he received a collateral assignment in the national government when he was appointed a vice-chairman under Ho Lung of the Physical Culture and Sports Commission. As a consequence he relinquished his post as a vice-minister of National Defense. From 1960 to 1964 Li represented the Sports Association or the Commission abroad on four occasions. The first of these trips took him to Czechoslovakia in June 1960 for an athletic meet. In July–August 1961 he was in the USSR at the invitation of the Soviet Voluntary Sports Society for the Promotion of the Army, Navy and Air Force, and while in Moscow he also attended Soviet Army Day celebrations. In November–December 1963 Li was in Albania as a guest of an association similar to the one in the Soviet Union, and in October 1964 he led a sports delegation to North Vietnam.

Li's work on behalf of defense-related athletics is illustrated in still other ways. He is almost always present for the many sports events sponsored by the Chinese armed forces, and since February 1964 he has been a vice-chairman of the All-China Athletic Federation. In 1963 Li was named to the Preparatory Committee for Participation in the Games of the New Emerging Forces, better known as "GANEFO," and when the Chinese established a permanent organization to take part in GANEFO in August 1964, Li was named to its national committee. The GANEFO scheme had been sponsored by Indonesian President Sukarno as a means of circumventing the International Olympics Committee (IOC), and because the Chinese had been excluded from the IOC, they were willing participants in GANEFO until Sukarno's political fall in 1965. In August 1964 Li attended a meeting that decided to establish the Chinese People's Aviation Sports Federation, and three months later he presided over the Amateur Gliding Conference. He wrote an article for the journal Hsin t'i-yü (New sports), which stressed the Maoist dictum that sports competition and physical fitness were useful in developing a "revolutionary spirit" and a willingness to "struggle." Li's article was reprinted in the 1962 edition of the authoritative Jen-min shou-ts'e (People's handbook).

Li has been a member of the NPC since 1959. He served in the Second NPC (1959–1964) as a deputy from the Tibet Military Region. He has had no known direct connection with Tibetan affairs, although it should be noted that Tibet was conquered in 1950–51 by troops under the jurisdiction of the Southwest Military Region in which Li was then a senior officer. However, when the Third NPC held its initial session in December 1964–January 1965, Li attended as a deputy from his native Shensi. He has also been a member of the central government's National Defense Council since April 1959. On numerous occasions he has served as a host for visiting dignitaries. In 1957, for example, he escorted the East German Defense Minister on a tour of Chinese military installations, and in 1960 and again in 1961 he accompanied U.K. Field Marshal Montgomery on the latter's visits to China.

Li Ta-chang

(1910–   ; Szechwan). Governor of Szechwan; secretary CCP Southwest Bureau; alternate member, CCP Central Committee.

Li Ta-chang is a PLA veteran who fought in north China and Manchuria prior to the Communist conquest of China in 1949. He has been a senior official in the southwest since 1950 and for the most of the period since 1955 has been the governor of Szechwan. Li's first known position of prominence in the Red Army was in the Shansi-Chahar-Hopeh (Chin-Ch'a-Chi) area, where he was chief-of-staff of the Chin-Ch'a-Chi Military Region during the Sino-Japanese War (see under Nieh Jung-chen, the commander of the region). Toward the end of the war and shortly thereafter, Li headed the Propaganda Department of the T'ai-hang Sub-bureau, which was subordinate to the Party's North China Bureau, and by 1946 he was director of the North China Bureau's Propaganda Department.

Following the cessation of hostilities in 1945, the Communists began to infiltrate troops and cadres into Manchuria, many of them from the north China areas where Li had been working. Early in 1946 Li was head of the Industry Office in Antung province and by the middle of the year he was working in Suining, a short-lived province created by the Communists in eastern Manchuria, with its capital at Mu-tan-chiang (Mutankiang), about 100 miles west of Vladivostok.[1] There Li served as the political commissar of the Suining Military District and as speaker of the Suining Provincial People's Congress. In the period from 1946 to 1949, he was also deputy director of the Northeast Party Bureau's Propaganda Department where he served under important Party leader Lin Feng (q.v.).

By early 1950 Li was transferred to his native Szechwan where he soon became one of the more important leaders. From 1949 to 1952, Szechwan was unique among the Chinese provinces in that it was divided into four geographic sub-districts (north, east, south, and west Szechwan). The governmental organ for south Szechwan where Li was stationed was known as the South Szechwan People's Administrative Office (SSPAO), with its capital at Lu-chou (Lu-hsien), a city on the Min River. In early 1950 Li became director of the SSPAO as well as political commissar of the South Szechwan Military District, and although specific information is lacking, it is probable that he also headed

the Party organization in south Szechwan. In brief, Li was the dominant figure in the area until the four sectors were merged to form Szechwan province in August 1952. He was also a participant in the regional government apparatus for southwest China, the Southwest Military and Administrative Committee (SWMAC), established in July 1950. Li was a member of the SWMAC (chaired by Liu Po-ch'eng); he was reappointed to membership when the SWMAC was reorganized into the Southwest Administrative Committee (SWAC) in February 1953, retaining this post until the SWAC was abolished in late 1954.

When Szechwan province was re-established in its traditional boundaries in August 1952, Li was named as a vice-governor under Governor Li Ching-ch'üan (q.v.), who later became a Politburo member. Li Ta-chang remained in this post until January 1955 when he succeeded Li Ching-ch'üan as the governor. Li Ta-chang also served under Li Ching-ch'üan in the Szechwan Party structure; by late 1952 he was a deputy secretary of the Szechwan CCP Committee, a position whose designation was changed to secretary by 1957 but that was still subordinate to First Secretary Li Ching-ch'üan.

Li received his first national post in 1954 when he was elected from his native Szechwan as a deputy to the First NPC (1954–1959). He was re-elected to the Second NPC (1959–1964) as well as to the Third NPC, which held its first session in December 1964–January 1965. Li has been a fairly active participant in the NPC, especially since the Second NPC opened in 1959; he served on the Presidium (steering committee) for each of the four annual sessions of the Second NPC and twice (in April 1959 and April 1960) delivered major speeches before the Congress. He has also gone to Peking on occasion to deliver reports before the NPC Standing Committee (the governing organ of the NPC between the annual sessions), as in April 1955 when he gave a report on agricultural work in Szechwan.

At the historic Eighth National Congress in September 1956, Li was elected an alternate member of the Party Central Committee. Since that time he has been reported very regularly in Szechwan, especially in matters related to agriculture, but also in relation to the development of the communes and the youth movement. Within Szechwan, a rich rice-surplus area and China's most heavily populated province, Li ranks after Politburo member Li Ching-ch'üan and approximately on par with Party First Secretary Liao Chih-kao (q.v.), also a Central Committee alternate member.

As described above, Li was first elected to the Szechwan governorship in January 1955. He was re-elected to the position in July 1958 and September 1963. Then, quite suddenly, he was transferred in February 1965 for a brief period to neighboring Kweichow. The circumstances were not clear, but apparently the Kweichow governor and first secretary, Chou Lin (q.v.), was either ailing or in political difficulties. In early 1965, several new men were brought into Kweichow, Li being the most prominent among them. He became the Kweichow Party first secretary and at this same time was also identified as a secretary of the Party's Southwest Bureau, serving once again under Li Ching-ch'üan, the first secretary. Li Ta-chang's work in Kweichow, possibly a trouble-shooting mission, was short-lived. By June 1965 he was back in Szechwan, once again as the provincial governor. During his brief absence from Szechwan in the first half of 1965, Liao Chih-kao succeeded Li Ching-ch'üan as the Szechwan Party first secretary. Thus, although Li Ta-chang is the provincial governor and a secretary of the Southwest Party Bureau, he is subordinate to Liao Chih-kao in the provincial Party hierarchy.

1. Chou Erh-fu, *Tung-pei heng-tuan-mien* (Northeastern cross section; Hong Kong, 1946), p. 129; Liu Pai-yü, *Huan-hsing tung-pei* (Traveling in the Northeast; Shanghai, 1946), p. 33.

Li Ta-chao

(1888–1927; Lo-t'ing, Hopeh). A founding member of the CCP; Marxist theoretician; member, CCP Central Committee.

Chinese Communism owes its inception largely to two men, Ch'en Tu-hsiu (q.v.) and Li Ta-chao, who, prior to their conversion to Marxism-Leninism, were among the foremost leaders of the Westernized Chinese intelligentsia. A man with a passionate concern for the salvation of China, Li's activist temperament left a permanent stamp on his re-interpretation of Marxism to Chinese reality. Some ten years younger than Ch'en Tu-hsiu, who emerged as the patriarch of the Communist movement, Li was associated with Peking University during most of his career as a Communist. In his professorial position, he occupied the key role as the preceptor of a host of youths who avidly turned to Marxism-Leninism as a solution to China's problems. With Ch'en Tu-hsiu's fall in 1927, Li's posthumous stature has steadily risen in official history. Significantly, however, latter-day Maoist historians view his writings on Marxism as not entirely orthodox, because they have discovered in certain areas "traces of non-Marxian thought" and even some manifestations of "the bourgeois scholar's view of Marxism."

Li Ta-chao was born on October 6, 1888, into a poor peasant family in Lo-t'ing, northeastern Hopeh. Orphaned when still an infant, he was brought up by his grandparents. In his youth he studied the Chinese classics in a village school and began his Western education from 1905 when he entered the Yung-p'ing-fu Middle School. Two years later he enrolled at the Peiyang College of Law and Political Science at Tientsin where he spent the next six years studying political economy. Reportedly in response to the current radical nationalism of the time, he joined Sun Yat-sen's T'ung-meng-hui and carried on anti-Manchu activities in Hopeh. He graduated from the Peiyang College in 1913 and went to Peking for a few months to help some classmates edit *Yen-chih tsa-chih* (Statesmen's magazine). In the fall of 1913 he went to Japan for further studies with the financial patronage of T'ang Hua-lung, a leader of the Progressive Party. For the next two and a half years he was a student at the Department of Political Economy at Waseda University in Tokyo where he acquired some knowledge of historical materialism. Disillusionment with Yuan Shih-k'ai's regime led him to found the Shen-chou hsueh-hui (The China Study Society), which carried on secret anti-Yuan activities and worked closely with Sun Yat-sen's Chung-hua ko-ming tang (Chinese Revolutionary Party), a clandestine organization based in Japan. News of the Twenty-one Demands served by the Japanese government on Yuan Shih-k'ai (January 1915) made him interrupt his studies to embark on an effort to enlist the opposition of Chinese students throughout Japan. He edited a volume of essays called *Kuo-ch'ih chi-nien lü* (In commemoration of national shame) and also wrote on behalf of these students "An Open Letter to Our Countrymen," urging the Chinese public to resist Japanese encroachments. Failing to keep up with his studies he was expelled in February 1916 from Waseda.

In the spring of 1916 he returned to China, and for the next six months, first in Shanghai and then in Peking, he was closely associated with T'ang Hua-lung's faction in the Progressive Party. He served as T'ang's secretary and edited the Party's organ *Ch'en-chung pao* (Morning bell) which was later renamed *Ch'en-pao* (Morning post). He became a member of the Yen-chiu hsi (Research Clique), the parliamentary grouping which succeeded the Progressive Party with its reunited factions, but he soon terminated his connection with the clique when it gave support to Tuan Ch'i-jui, leader of the powerful Peiyang warlord faction. In January 1917 he accepted the invitation of Chang Shih-chao, a leading advocate of constitutionalism, to edit *Chia-yin jih-k'an* (Tiger daily) but it was suppressed after four months, and Li fled to Shanghai where he remained to the end of the year. Meantime, he was involving himself in the new culture movement, centered around Ch'en Tu-hsiu's *Hsin ch'ing-nien* (New youth), and he became one of its editors in January 1918. A month later he accepted the appointment of librarian of Peking

University where later in the year he had as an assistant Mao Tse-tung, who was then immersing himself in the tide of "new thought." In September 1920 Li was given the additional appointment of professor of history, political science, economics, and law, and subsequently became concurrently secretary to the University chancellor. Thus, within a brief period, Li emerged as one of the most revered leaders of the Westernized Chinese intelligentsia. After Ch'en Tu-hsiu's resignation from Peking University in March 1919 and departure for Shanghai toward the end of the year, Li was to provide the leadership and guidance for a group of radical students at the intellectual storm center of the nation who were to emerge as leaders of the Chinese Communist Movement.

Before Li became interested in Marxism-Leninism in late 1918 he had evolved his own philosophy, which synthesized ancient Chinese philosophy with Western theories of progressive evolution (especially those of Emerson and Hegel), as outlined in two essays, "Youth" (which was his first essay for *New Youth* on October 1, 1916) and "Now" (also for *New Youth,* of April 15, 1918). Li espoused an optimistic faith in China's capacity for self-renewal, which he thought could be brought about by discarding certain elements of her dead past and relying on her new youth to inaugurate a revitalized China. Within the framework of his passionate nationalistic concerns, he grappled with the problem of reconciling tradition with modernity, and politically he reposed his faith in constitutional democracy. However, his rapidly growing pessimism over the prospect of constitutionalism in China made him look elsewhere for solutions. On June 30, 1918, he helped found the Shao-nien Chung-kuo hsueh-hui (Young China Association), one of many student organizations he helped to establish. Within that organization in the winter of 1918 he attracted a group of students to engage in the study of Marxism, and from this group emerged such prominent CCP leaders as Mao Tse-tung, Chang Kuo-t'ao, Ch'ü Ch'iu-pai, Teng Chung-hsia, Yun Tai-ying, Chang Wen-t'ien, Chao Shih-yen, and Shen Tse-min (qq.v.). In December he helped Ch'en Tu-hsiu to launch *Mei-chou p'ing-lun* (Weekly critic), which immediately became a forum for the famous debate on "Problems and Isms" between Li Ta-chao and Hu Shih, representing the two emerging wings of the intelligentsia; one stood for radical political activism within the framework of an all-embracing ideology, whereas the other inclined toward pragmatism and cultural activism and eschewed politics.

Li was always ready to provide material or other support to organized student groups. Among those to which he lent his sponsorship were Hsin-ch'ao she (New Tide Society, founded

in November 1918), Ch'üan-kuo hsueh-sheng chiu-kuo hui (All-China Student Society for National Salvation), whose journal, *Min-kuo* (The Republic), first appeared in January 1919, and Chueh-wu she (Awakening Society, founded in Tientsin in September 1919).

As the May Fourth Movement expanded, Li himself was making rapid strides in his intellectual evolution toward Marxism. The most important impetus was the news about the Russian Revolution. In July 1918, in *New Youth,* he compared the significance of the Russian and French revolutions, and in November 1918 expressed his enthusiasm for the Russian events in two articles in the same journal, "The Victory of Bolshevism" and "The Victory of the Masses." Having accepted the messianic message of the Russian Revolution in an emotional way, from late 1918 he proceeded to investigate its doctrinal base, and by late 1919 he had been converted to Marxism-Leninism. Approaching Marxism-Leninism from his activist nationalistic temperament, he adapted it to Chinese conditions and produced a unique synthesis of militant nationalism and voluntaristic Marxism-Leninism. The deterministic premise of the necessary social economic base and the doctrine of proletarian class struggle in Marxism-Leninism were either disregarded or toned down. The Communist revolution, in Li's conception, became a populist revolution involving the whole nation exploited and oppressed by foreign imperialism and a voluntaristic effort aimed at the remolding of Chinese reality, with an overwhelming emphasis on the central role of the peasantry. In a country blistering with national resentment against foreign aggression, chafing at its backwardness, and predominantly peasant in population, this conception had decisive relevance and is strikingly similar to the core of the thinking of Mao Tse-tung.

In December 1919 the She-hui-chu-i yen-chiu hui (Society for the Study of Socialism) was formed at Peking University with the chancellor's blessings and under Li's guidance. Its membership included Ch'en Tu-hsiu, Ch'ü Ch'iu-pai, Teng Chung-hsia, Mao Tse-tung, and Chou En-lai. But this group broke up in a short time, after which Li formed another in March 1920 known as the Ma-k'o-szu hsueh-shuo yen-chiu hui (Society for the Study of Marxism), which included some of the above members, as well as Lo Chang-lung (q.v.) and Liu Jen-ching. It became a formal organization after October 1921 with a library of Marxist literature, and it also sponsored lectures and discussion groups; in short, it was a center of theoretical study for the early Chinese Communists.

In March 1920, through his Russian colleague Sergei A. Polevoy, Li met Comintern official Gregory Voitinsky who led a mission to investigate the May Fourth Movement. Li Ta-chao seems to have felt that Ch'en Tu-hsiu, then publishing *New Youth* in Shanghai, was in a better position to benefit from Voitinsky's preferred assistance and skill in organizing a Bolshevik party. He therefore directed Voitinsky and his group to Ch'en Tu-hsiu. Ch'en's receptivity to the idea of organizational activity is shown by the fact that scarcely a month had passed when in May the first Communist nucleus was organized in Shanghai. In August the Socialist Youth League was also formed. Li Ta-chao was responsible for forming corresponding units in Peking in September, with the help of Chang Kuo-t'ao, Lo Chang-lung, Teng Chung-hsia, and others. The Peking Communists next embarked on organizing labor. With Chang Kuo-t'ao and Teng Chung-hsia, Li established a night school for the workers and their children at Ch'ang-hsin-tien, a terminal of the Peking-Hankow Railroad 40 miles outside of Peking where a concentration of railroad workers was to be found. The Peking branch also published a workers' tabloid, *Lao-tung yin* (Voice of labor). When Ch'en Tu-hsiu left Shanghai for Canton to be Ch'en Chiung-ming's provincial educational Commissioner, Li Ta-chao became the senior leader of the Communist movement in north China.

In May 1921 Li went to Shanghai to participate in a conference preliminary to the formal inauguration of the CCP, which took place two months later. However, he was unable to attend the First Congress, spending the summer with Teng Chung-hsia in a lecture tour in Szechwan on Yun Tai-ying's invitation. Nonetheless, at the First CCP Congress he was elected regional secretary for north China.

Li was largely instrumental in securing for the Communists a foothold among the workers of the northern railroad network, which fell within the domain of Wu P'ei-fu. In April–May 1922 the latter had defeated Manchurian warlord Chang Tso-lin in the Fengtien-Chihli War and announced the "protection of labor" as one of his policies, by which he hoped to court mass support. Through personal connections with Wu P'ei-fu's retinue Li succeeded in working out an agreement with Wu whereby Communists would be employed as secret inspectors on the railroads of north China. Their function would be to help Wu eliminate whatever influence Chang Tso-lin's ally, the Communications Clique, still exerted over the railway workers. In return, the Communists would have the opportunity to organize and influence the workers. Among the Communists whom Li Ta-chao recommended were An T'i-ch'eng, Ch'en Wei-jen, Ho Meng-hsiung, and Pao Hui-seng.

At the Second CCP Congress, held in July 1922 in Shanghai, Li was elected to the Central Committee; among other members were Ch'en Tu-hsiu, Chang Kuo-t'ao, Kao Chün-yü, Ts'ai Ho-sen, and Hsiang Ching-yü. The Congress re-

solved to lend support to Sun Yat-sen's KMT in the form of a two-party alliance, but under Comintern pressure this was changed to mean Communists joining the KMT as individuals, a policy that was resisted by the Chinese Communists. Li Ta-chao appears to have been somewhat more amenable and he played a key role in persuading his colleagues to accept the policy. His earlier association with the T'ung-meng-hui and personal friendship with Sun Yat-sen placed him in a unique position in the KMT-CCP collaboration. Therefore, after the Second CCP Congress, Li represented the Communist Party in discussions with Sun Yat-sen in Shanghai of plans for the KMT-CCP collaboration. Together with Ch'en Tu-hsiu, Ts'ai Ho-sen, and Chang T'ai-lei, Li was among the first Communists admitted into the KMT (August 1922), being admitted on the recommendation of his personal friend Chang Chi, a KMT veteran. In June 1923 the Third CCP Congress opened in Canton, for the first time under legal conditions. A sharp debate ensued over the question of Communist entry into the KMT; supported by Teng Chung-hsia, Ch'ü Ch'iu-pai, and others, Li opposed Chang Kuo-t'ao, who led the opposition to the united front, and in the end the Congress endorsed the policy of entering the KMT.

In the meantime, in 1922 Li had been elected secretary of the North China branch of the Chinese Labor Unions' Secretariat and with Teng Chung-hsia he played a leading role in the February 7 (1923) strike of the Peking-Hankow Railway workers. Li was present as a delegate from Hopeh at the First Congress of the reorganized KMT held in Canton in January 1924 with Communist participation. On behalf of the Communists he issued a circular letter among the delegates to allay the deep current of fears and suspicions held by some KMT members concerning the motives of the CCP in entering the KMT. At the Congress he was one of three Communists (the other two being T'an P'ing-shan, the most active Communist member in working out the reorganization, and Yü Shu-te) to be elected as regular members of the Central Executive Committee. (In Peking he was to play a prominent role in the KMT branch, and he was re-elected to the Central Executive Committee at the Second Congress held in January 1926).

In May 1924 Li had led a CCP delegation to attend the Fifth Comintern Congress, held in June–July 1924. Li delivered a speech which indicated the "mounting pressure of imperialism on China" and the satisfactory progress of the collaboration of the Communists within the KMT, assisted by Sun Yat-sen's cooperative attitude, and announced that the aim of the CCP within the KMT was to obtain the leadership of both the labor movement and the nationalist movement by developing into a truly revolutionary mass movement. After the Congress, he lectured briefly at the Communist University of the Toilers of the East and then made a trip through Russia to observe conditions. He returned home in the winter of 1924.

The next major highlight in Li's career was his role in the tragic mass student demonstrations in Peking on March 18, 1926. Early that year Feng Yü-hsiang, in a maneuver against the coalition of Chang Tso-lin and Wu P'ei-fu, which had been formed against himself, sent his army, the Kuominchün, to blockade the Taku fort near Tientsin, thus violating the Boxer protocol of 1901. Chang's ally, Japan, immediately sent naval forces to the scene, and eight foreign governments presented the Tuan Ch'i-jui government in Peking with an ultimatum, demanding the removal of the blockade within 48 hours. This was seized upon as another instance of foreign encroachment, and the students in Peking, organized and led by Li Ta-chao and other young radicals, staged a mass demonstration on March 18, 1926, at T'ien-an-men. The police responded by firing into the crowd, and Li himself was wounded in the head. The national university proved to be enough of a sanctuary for Li; much as they wanted to seize Li, the authorities had to reckon with hostile public opinion, which was bound to follow from an encroachment upon the principal educational institution of the country. Furthermore, as long as Feng Yü-hsiang's forces were in the vicinity, Li felt safe to continue his activities in Peking. However, in December 1926 Feng's army was forced out of Tientsin and Peking, and Chang Tso-lin seized the authority of the central government; a warrant of arrest for Li and many others was promptly issued. Li was forced to take refuge in the Soviet Embassy and continued his leadership of Communist activities in north China for another three months, until April 6, 1927, when he was arrested on the embassy compound following a raid by Chang Tso-lin's gendarmes. Notwithstanding the intercessions of more than 300 prominent men of the country for his release, Li was executed (by strangulation) in prison on April 28, 1927, along with 19 other Communists.

When Li was only 11 years old, his grandfather had him married to Chao Chi-lan, the daughter of a neighboring peasant. They had two sons and four daughters. One of the sons spent some time in Japan and then joined the Communists at Yenan, their wartime capital. It is reported in non-Communist sources that Li Pao-hua (q.v.), also a native of Lo-t'ing hsien, is a son of Li Ta-chao. Li Pao-hua emerged as an important Communist during the Sino-Japanese War, and after 1949 he was a vice-minister of Water Conservancy.

The major study of Li Ta-chao is Maurice Meisner's *Li Ta-chao and the Origins of Chinese Marxism* (Cambridge, Mass., 1967). The lengthy bibliography in this volume contains many of the works by and about Li. A valuable biographic sketch of Li is contained in *Li Ta-chao hsuan-chi* (Selected works of Li Ta-chao; Peking, 1962), and some of his early writings are translated in Huang Sung-k'ang's *Li Ta-chao and the Impact of Marxism on Modern Chinese Thinking* (Paris, 1965).

Li T'ao

(1906– ; I-chang hsien, Hunan). Colonel-General, PLA; alternate member, CCP Central Committee.

Li T'ao, not to be confused with the Liaoning vice-governor of the same name who was purged in 1958, has also been known by the name of Li Hsiang-ling. A veteran of the Red Army since the 1920's, he has spent most of his career as a military officer and has been an alternate member of the Party Central Committee since 1956. He comes from I-chang hsien, a coal-producing region in southeast Hunan. I-chang was an area in which the Communists early found supporters; Chu Te's small military force retreated into southern Hunan after its defeat near Swatow in the fall of 1927, and in January 1928 he established a short-lived local soviet at I-chang. A middle school graduate, Li took part in the establishment of a "peasant self-defense corps" in 1925 in areas nearby his native hsien. Then, when Chu Te was in this region during the winter of 1927–28, Li and a colleague led a contingent of the self-defense corps to join Chu's troops at Ch'en-hsien, not far north of I-chang.[1] Not long after this, Chu's units were merged with those led by Mao Tse-tung to form the Fourth Red Army, based at Chingkangshan on the Hunan-Kiangsi border.

By 1930, when Li was presumably already a CCP member, he was serving as a political commissar in P'eng Te-huai's Third Army Corps in Kiangsi. In 1932 he was an officer in the Political Department of the First Front Army, formed from Chu Te's First Army Corps and P'eng Te-huai's Third Army Corps following a reorganization of Red Army forces in mid-1930. The First Front Army was led by Chu and P'eng and in these years did most of its fighting in the Kiangsi-Fukien border area. Li was given a logistics assignment in 1933, probably in the same army, and then made the Long March from Kiangsi to Shensi in 1934–35.

In north Shensi Li studied in 1936 at the Red Army Academy. In December 1936 he was among the group that accompanied Chou En-lai to Sian to negotiate the release of Chiang Kai-shek, who had been captured by the forces of Manchurian warlord Chang Hsueh-liang. The latter had sent his private plane to Pao-an, then Chou's headquarters, to bring the Communists to Sian. Among this group were such leading Communists as Ch'in Pang-hsien, Yeh Chien-ying, and Li K'o-nung (qq.v.). In 1937–38 Li served successively as director of the Sian and then the Hankow Office of the Communists' Eighth Route Army. Then, after the fall of Hankow to the Japanese in October 1938, he accompanied Yeh Chien-ying to Hunan to work in a KMT-sponsored guerrilla training class in Heng-shan, located about 100 miles south of Changsha, the Hunan capital.

Li returned to the Communist capital at Yenan sometime during the Sino-Japanese War, serving as head of the Third Office of the Central Intelligence Department, then as chief of the Second Bureau of the Army's General Staff, and finally as director of the Operations Department. From 1941 to 1946 he was a deputy to the Second Assembly of the Shensi-Kansu-Ninghsia (Shen-Kan-Ning) Border Region, serving as a representative of "those working for the Border Region Government." He attended both the first and second sessions of the Second Assembly, held in November 1941 and December 1944, respectively.

In the postwar period Li is reported to have served on Lin Piao's staff in the Northeast Democratic Allied Army, the force that conquered Manchuria by the winter of 1948–49. He was in Peking after the surrender of that city in January 1949, and in April of that year was identified as a spokesman for the PLA Headquarters. In June he participated in the meetings of the Preparatory Committee for the first session of the CPPCC, which was to bring the PRC Government into existence on October 1, 1949. Li was not an official member of the Committee but rather served as a substitute for Ch'en I pending the latter's arrival from east China where his troops were locked in battle. When the First Session of the CPPCC met in September 1949, Li attended as a representative of the PLA Headquarters, and since that time he seems to have been principally occupied with military staff work. Immediately after the central government was established, he was identified as director of the Operations Department of the People's Revolutionary Military Council (PRMC), the highest military organ in the government, chaired by Mao Tse-tung. It is not known how long Li retained the Operations post, but another man was holding this position by early 1953. From 1949 to 1954 Li also served in the PRMC's National Defense Research Council; the PRMC and its subordinate bodies were abolished in 1954.

Li has made extremely few public appearances in the years since the establishment of the PRC in 1949, and when he does appear it is usually in connection with the PLA. From June 1950 to at least 1951 he was a deputy director of the Central Flood Prevention Headquarters; he was presumably given this assignment because of the important role of the PLA in flood prevention work. In September–October 1950 he participated in a large conference of "fighting heroes" from the PLA, and in October–November 1951 he took part in the Third Session of the CPPCC's First National Committee, attending as a representative of the PRMC. He made a few more appearances of minor importance between 1952 and 1954 and then in 1954 was elected as a deputy from his native Hunan to the First NPC. However, he was not re-elected to the Second NPC, which opened in 1959. In September 1955, when national military awards were made for the first time, Li was given the three top honors, the Orders of August First, Independence and Freedom, and Liberation, covering military service from 1927 to 1950. Although military ranks were also first created in 1955, Li was not identified until mid-1963 by his present rank, colonel-general, the equivalent of a three-star general in the U.S. Army.

At the Party's Eighth National Congress in September 1956, Li was elected an alternate member of the Central Committee. He was not again mentioned in the press until February 1962 when he served on the funeral committee for Li K'o-nung, a colleague since at least 1936. Li T'ao received another assignment in the military establishment at the close of the initial session of the Third NPC in January 1965 when he was named to membership on the National Defense Council, an organization with very limited power and authority, but one with considerable prestige.

1. *Chung-kuo Kung-ch'an tang tsai chung-nan-ti-ch'ü ling-tao ko-ming tou-cheng te li-shih tzu-liao* (Historical materials on the revolutionary struggles led by the Chinese Communist Party in central and south China; Wuhan, 1951), I, 127–132.

Li Te-ch'üan

(1896–   ; T'ung-hsien, Hopeh). Women's movement leader; former Minister of Public Health; former President, Red Cross Society of China; widow of General Feng Yü-hsiang.

Li Te-ch'üan, the widow of Feng Yü-hsiang, was one of the most important women leaders in the first decade and a half of the PRC, serving as minister of Public Health and as president of the Red Cross Society. Combining her pre-1949 trips to the Soviet Union and the United States with visits to 24 nations since the establishment of the PRC, she is the most widely-traveled woman in China today. Li was born on July 1, 1896, in T'ung-hsien in Hopeh province, near Peking. Her family had been Christians for three generations; one of Li's Christian uncles had been killed during the Boxer Rebellion[1] and her father was a Protestant minister. She was reared a Christian and educated as a girl in schools run by American missionaries (a fact that presumably accounts for her mastery of English). Li went to Peking for further education, graduating from the Bridgeman Girls' Middle School and a women's college that later became part of Yenching University. After completing her schooling, Miss Li taught at the Bridgeman School, worked as a pastor's assistant in a Congregational church in Peking, and worked in the Peking YWCA.[2] Then in February 1924 she married the powerful north China warlord Feng Yü-hsiang, widely known as the "Christian General" and a man 14 years her senior. Working closely with Feng in his various endeavors, Li was a first-hand witness to the stormy and chaotic events that characterized Feng's life in north and northwest China in the twenties and early thirties.[3] Li made her first trip abroad at age 30 when she accompanied her husband on his trip to Mongolia and the Soviet Union from March to September 1926. It may have been at this time that she first acquired some knowledge of Russian; writing about 30 years later, former French Premier Edgar Faure noted (on the basis of his 1956 trip to Peking) that she spoke both English and Russian.[4]

From the latter part of 1935 the Fengs lived in Nanking, the Nationalist capital, and then spent the war years in Chungking when the capital was transferred there after the fall of Nanking to the Japanese in 1937. During these years Li was engaged in a variety of quasi-political and charitable activities, working for the National Women's Association for War Relief, and serving as president of both the Chinese Women's Association and the Chinese Women's Christian Temperance Union and as a board member of the National Refugee Children's Association and of the Sino-Soviet Cultural Association. The last-named organization had a strong leftist orientation (see under Ch'ien Chün-jui) and was a forerunner of the Sino-Soviet Friendship Association established by the Communists in 1949.

In April 1946 Li was elected a delegate to the KMT National Assembly, but she did not attend any sessions, possibly because by this time she and her husband were preparing to go abroad again. Highly dissatisfied with the course of political events in China, Feng Yü-hsiang wanted to leave the country, and to do so he asked the Nationalist Government to send him to the United States to investigate irrigation and water conservancy facilities. The request was granted and in September 1946 the Fengs sailed from Shanghai. They lived for a brief time in Berkeley, California, toured conservation sites, and then settled in New York City where they remained until mid-1948. At this time relations between Feng and his wife were reported to have been so strained that Mme. Feng was considering a divorce.[5] In the United States Feng quickly became an active spokesman for anti-Chiang Kai-shek sentiment, urging the U.S. Government to maintain a strict neutrality between the Communists and the Nationalists,[6] a position with which his wife presumably agreed.

After spending nearly two years in the United States, the Fengs sailed from New York in July 1948 on a Russian ship. In early September, just before docking at a Black Sea port, Feng died in a fire aboard the ship; this gave rise to rumors of foul play, but Feng's biographer, James E. Sheridan, believes it was simply an accident.[7] Li proceeded to Manchuria and then arrived in Peking in February 1949, the month after the city was surrendered to the Communists. Even before her arrival in Peking it was evident that she had already decided to throw in her lot with the Communists, for in December 1948 she had been elected a member of the Communist-dominated Women's International Democratic Federation (WIDF) at a meeting in Budapest (although it is not clear if she attended). Moreover, in January 1949 she had been made a vice-chairman of the Preparatory Committee of the All-China Federation of Democratic Women (ACFDW), an affiliate of the WIDF, and when the first national women's congress was held that spring, she was elected an ACFDW vice-chairman, a post she still retains.

In June 1949 Li attended the meetings chaired by Mao Tse-tung of the Preparatory Committee for the CPPCC, and when the CPPCC held its first session in September to bring the new central government into existence, she attended as a delegate of the Kuomintang Revolutionary Committee (KMTRC), one of the "democratic" political parties that ostensibly shares political power with the CCP. Li has continued to hold a seat in the CPPCC since her election to the First National Committee in 1949, but since 1954 she has represented "social relief and welfare organizations" (rather than the KMTRC). She was elevated to the CPPCC Standing Committee in 1953 and to a vice-chairmanship in early 1965. When the assignments in the new government were made in October 1949, Li became a member (until 1954) of the Culture and Education Committee under the Government Administration Council (the cabinet). But her most important assignment was to head the Ministry of Public Health, a post she was to hold for over 15 years. Although not a medical doctor by training, Li brought to the ministry much experience in charity and relief work. Moreover, unlike many non-Communists who have held nominal posts in the cabinet, it appears that Li was given genuine powers within the ministry. She was, at any rate, extremely active in the first decade of the PRC, as evidenced by the many reports on public health she presented before governmental bodies, by the tours she made throughout the nation, and by the fact that she was sent abroad on several occasions (see below) to attend meetings related to public health. It should also be noted that the Public Health Ministry had particularly burdensome responsibilities as a consequence of years of warfare, with the resulting deterioration of public health facilities. For example, one of the first measures taken by the new government was the formation (October 1949) of a Central Epidemic Prevention Committee, a body to which Li was appointed as a member. Writing of Miss Li at this time, the Indian ambassador in Peking commented that she was a "picture of quiet efficiency" and "obviously full of energy and competence."[8]

At the same time that the new government was formed, several "mass" organizations were established. Li was named to two of the most active of these, the Sino-Soviet Friendship Association (SSFA) and the China Peace Committee. In the SSFA she was named to the First Executive Board, rising to a vice-chairmanship in December 1954, a post she still holds. Moreover, from 1949 to 1954 she was also one of the SSFA deputy secretaries-general and a deputy director of the Liaison Department. In the Peace Committee she has served since 1949 as a National Committee member (and as a Standing Committee member from 1958 to 1965). In 1950, as conditions on the mainland became more stabilized, steps were taken to reorganize a number of relief and social welfare organizations into a single organization. Li took an active part in these endeavors and in April 1950 was made a vice-chairman of the Chinese People's Relief Administration (see under Wu Yun-fu), a post she still retains. In the late summer of the same year the Chinese Red Cross Society was reorganized, with Li assuming the presidency, a position to which she was to devote much time until she was replaced in 1965.

In the early years of the PRC Li assumed still other posts in the government and "mass" organizations. Toward the end of 1951 she was named to the central government's *ad hoc* Central Austerity Committee to examine the state of the nation's economy, and a few days later she was appointed to membership on the North China Administrative Committee, retaining this post until the regional governments were dissolved in 1954. From 1952 to 1956 she was a vice-chairman of the All-China Athletic Association, and from 1952 to 1954 she served on the national government's Labor Employment Committee, which was established to deal with chronic unemployment problems. Li was also named to the Board of Directors of the Chinese People's Association for Cultural Relations with Foreign Countries upon its formation in May 1954, a post she may still hold.

One of the most outstanding features of Li's career has been the frequency with which she has traveled abroad on behalf of the PRC or one of the "mass" organizations to which she is affiliated. Forty-two separate trips abroad have taken her to 24 nations; she had visited every country in the Communist bloc except North Vietnam, seven in West Europe, three in Asia, one in the Middle East, and Canada. Her trips can be divided into four principal categories: Red Cross work, public health, women's liaison, and the "peace" movement. Traveling either to meetings of the International Red Cross (IRC) or paying visits at the invitation of Red Cross chapters in other nations, Li was in the following nations: Monaco, 1950; Switzerland, 1951 (twice), 1953; Canada, 1952; Norway, 1954; Japan, 1954, 1957; England, 1955; India, 1957; and the Soviet Union, 1959. Among these trips the most notable was that to Toronto in July–August 1952 when she led the Chinese Red Cross delegation to the 18th International Conference of the IRC, thus becoming one of the extremely small number of PRC officials to have visited North America since 1949. Li's efforts at the Toronto meetings were devoted primarily to opposing Chinese Nationalist participation in the IRC and to castigating the United States for its alleged use of "germ warfare" in the Korean War. Her foreign travels on behalf of the Public Health Ministry have taken her to India (1953), the Soviet Union (1954), the Mongolian People's Republic (1960), and Cuba (1962), in addition to a five-nation tour in 1958 of Poland, Czechoslovakia, Rumania, Bulgaria, and Albania. The purpose of most of these trips was to inspect public health facilities.

Li's journeys in connection with women's affairs have been either to attend WIDF-sponsored meetings or to visit various nations in her capacity as a vice-chairman of the Chinese Women's Federation. In one or the other of these capacities she has traveled to Bulgaria, 1951; Denmark, 1953, 1960; Switzerland, 1955; Pakistan, 1955; Italy, 1956; Yugoslavia, 1956; England, 1956; and East Germany, 1957. The fourth major category, the world "peace" movement, has taken Li to Czechoslovakia, 1949; Poland, 1950; Denmark, 1951; Hungary, 1953; Sweden, 1954 (twice), 1959, in each instance to attend meetings of the Communist-backed World Peace Council (WPC). She has served as a member of the WPC since her election at the Second World Peace Congress in Poland in November 1950.

In addition to the major categories described above, Li has made still other trips. In the fall of 1950 she was in England at the invitation of the Britain-China Friendship Association (see under Liu Ning-i), and in March 1952 she led a 70-member group to North Korea to "investigate the germ warfare crimes committed by the American imperialists." During and after this visit to Korea, Li's group received a tremendous amount of publicity in the Chinese press, as the alleged findings of her group formed the backbone of Peking's major "germ warfare" campaign against the United States. She returned to North Korea in August 1960 to take part in celebrations marking the 15th anniversary of the "liberation" of Korea from Japan. In March 1953 Li accompanied Chou En-lai to Moscow for Stalin's funeral, and she returned to Moscow for undisclosed purposes in July of that year. Finally, in July 1959 she was in Baghdad for the first anniversary celebrations of the Iraqi revolution.

Interspersed with her already numerous administrative responsibilities and her foreign travels, Li was fully occupied in the late fifties and early sixties with still other duties. She has served since 1954 as a deputy from her native Hopeh in the NPC, and from its establishment in February 1956 she was a vice-chairman of the Asian (later Afro-Asian) Solidarity Committee of China; Li was dropped from her vice-chairmanship in June 1965, but she remains a member. From 1956 to 1958 she was a member of the State Council's Scientific Planning Commission and she has served for a number of years on the editorial board of the English-language monthly *China Reconstructs*. Presumably in recognition of her advancing years (she was 70 in 1966), Li's active official life began to taper off in the early sixties, as suggested by the fact that she made her last trip abroad in 1962 after having been abroad at least once each year since 1946 (excepting only 1961). Finally, in January 1965, she was replaced in the Public Health Ministry by Ch'ien Hsin-chung (q.v.), and three months later Ch'ien also replaced her as president of the Red Cross Society (although Li remains a member of the Society's Standing Committee). She continues to make public appearances, but most of them are of a ceremonial nature. Among the foremost accomplishments of the PRC are the elimination of some of the major diseases that have plagued China for centuries and the establishment of a nationwide public health network reaching into virtually every village. As the Public Health minister for more than 15 years, Li Te-ch'üan would seem to deserve some of the credit for these accomplishments. The Public Health Ministry was not devoid of political struggles during Li's term of office, particularly in regard to the controversy of traditional Chinese versus Western medicine. It appears, however, that the politically more important Hsu Yun-pei (q.v.), a former vice-minister, served as the chief spokesman for Chinese medicine in this battle. Regarding another important and sensitive issue—birth control—Li reportedly expressed Chinese eagerness to cooperate with the Family Planning Fed-

eration of Japan to a Japanese family planning expert when he visited Peking in 1964.[9] At the end of 1958 it was announced that Li had been admitted to the CCP together with a number of prominent intellectuals (e.g., Li Szu-kuang, q.v.). However, this action by the Party can probably be regarded more as a reward for long service than as an indication that Li Te-ch'üan and the others had advanced to a new level of political importance.

Between 1925 and 1930, Li bore Feng Yü-hsiang five children, two boys and three girls. Li is also the stepmother of at least three other children by Feng's first marriage. Eight of these children were in the United States with the Fengs in the late forties; one of the sons was then a student at the University of California (Berkeley) and a daughter was at the College of the Pacific. While the Fengs were in New York, this daughter married a Chinese student who (as of 1954) was a research fellow in the Political Science and Economics Department at Leningrad University. Two of Feng's sons were with Li in October 1953 when her husband's remains were buried at T'ai Shan, a mountain retreat in Shantung where he had spent much time in the early thirties.

1. James E. Sheridan, *Chinese Warlord, The Career of Feng Yü-hsiang* (Stanford, Calif., 1966), p. 130.

2. *Ibid.*

3. *Ibid.*, pp. 130, 175.

4. Edgar Faure, *The Serpent and the Tortoise* (New York, 1956), p. 8.

5. Sheridan, p. 277.

6. *Ibid.*, pp. 278–280.

7. *Ibid.*, p. 281.

8. K. M. Panikkar, *In Two Chinas* (London, 1955), p. 86.

9. *International Planned Parenthood News* (London), no. 141, November 1965.

Li Wei-han

(1897–   ; Li-ling hsien, Hunan). Early CCP member; specialist in united front work; member, CCP Central Committee.

Li Wei-han, one of the earliest CCP members, comes from the region of Hunan that produced such top Communist leaders as Ts'ai Ho-sen and Mao Tse-tung. He was deeply involved in some of the most bitter political feuds that divided the Party in the twenties and early thirties. Li made the Long March and spent most of the war years as a top operative in organs directly subordinate to the Central Committee, including the United Front Work Department, which he headed from the end of the war until 1965. The political controversies in which he was involved may account for the fact that he reached the apex of his career in the twenties but has since never been among the inner elite of the CCP. And they may also explain his political fall in the mid-sixties.

Li Wei-han's birthplace has been variously reported as Changsha, Hsiang-hsiang, Hsiang-t'an, and Li-ling. The best evidence points to Li-ling, a small town southeast of Changsha, the Hunan capital, but all are in the same region, with Li-ling and Hsiang-hsiang forming the east and west base angles of a triangle under the apex of Changsha. Hsiang-t'an is located on the western side between Changsha and Hsiang-hsiang. All four places have revolutionary significance to the Communists; they were the locales of peasant insurgency in the early 1920's and were visited by Mao Tse-tung in early 1927 when he collected data for his famous "Report of an Investigation into the Peasant Movement in Hunan." A significant number of the CCP's elite come from this revolutionary triangle, including Mao himself who is from Hsiang-t'an hsien. From Li-ling came Li Li-san and Chang Chi-ch'un (qq.v.), who are about contemporary in age with Li Wei-han. The education given to Li and to his brother Li Chün-lung (see below) strongly suggests that he comes from the intellectual class, although there is very little information about his origins and early upbringing. He received his education at the Hunan First Normal School in Changsha.

When Li's political career opened he was a member of the radical student group who were friends and early associates of Mao Tse-tung in Changsha, many of them students at the Hunan First Normal School, as was Mao also between the years 1913 and 1918. Thirteen of the group under the direction of Mao and of his close friend Ts'ai Ho-sen (q.v.) organized the Hsin-min hsueh-hui (New people's study society); preliminary meetings were held at the Ts'ai family home, and the organization came formally into being in April 1918. Also among the founding members were Ho Shu-heng, Miss Hsiang Ching-yü, Hsia Hsi (qq.v.), Hsiao San, and his brother Hsiao Yü, who did not join the CCP but like Hsiao San wrote a biography of Mao Tse-tung. Ts'ai Ho-sen and his sister Ts'ai Ch'ang (q.v.) were other founders and both were associates of Li Wei-han in this and the next phase of his career.[1] The Society met regularly and formed a recruiting center for many Hunanese students who wished to take advantage of the project for working while studying in France. In order to prepare himself, Li attended French language classes in Pao-ting with Liu Shao-ch'i, Li Fu-ch'un, and others, before leaving for France from Shanghai with Ts'ai Ho-sen in November 1919. The Hunanese student group, led by Ts'ai, took up residence at Montargis, south of Paris and attended the Collège de Montargis for most of the time they were in France. Of

course, they engaged in political activity and formed a branch of the Hsin-min Hsueh-hui at the Collège as soon as they arrived. Active in their group were Hsiang Ching-yü, who soon became the wife of Ts'ai Ho-sen, and Li Fu-ch'un, who later married Ts'ai Ch'ang (qq.v.). The former Changsha students kept in constant communication by letter with Mao and other members of their Society who had remained at home.[2] While in France, Li Wei-han was said to have worked part-time in factories and to have participated in the labor movement. Further details of the Hunanese group and of the actual founding of a small CCP unit in France in mid-1922 are given in the biographies of Ts'ai Ho-sen and Chao Shih-yen.

Li Wei-han returned to China at an uncertain date, probably during the year 1922; he is said to have gone directly to Hunan to stay at the home of Mao Tse-tung at Ch'ing-shui-t'ang village in Changsha, then a headquarters for the Provincial Party Committee in Hunan.[3] Two other reports at this period place Li among the young Communists working closely with Mao Tse-tung in Hunan. In the years between 1922 and 1924 he contributed to the *Hu-nan hsueh-sheng lien-ho-hui chou-k'an* (Hunan Student Union weekly) published in Changsha. Mao's friend Hsia Hsi was one of the early editors of this small paper for the student union membership, among whom Mao's brother, Mao Tse-min (q.v.), was a leader.[4] The student union headquarters were located in the same building in Changsha that housed the Self-Education College founded in August 1921 by Mao Tse-tung and Ho Shu-heng (q.v.) upon their return to Changsha after they had attended the founding congress of the CCP. Li Wei-han taught at the college (see under Mao Tse-min) and contributed to its short-lived publication, the *Hsin shih-tai* (The new age), established in April 1923. The Self-Education College was closed by the Hunan governor in November 1923, but later in the same month, in cooperation with Hsieh Chueh-tsai (q.v.) and others, Li took part in re-establishing the school under the name Hsiang-chiang Middle School.

By 1926 Li had gone to Shanghai and in the middle part of that year he was said to have conducted current events study meetings together with Hsiang Ying and Wang Jo-fei (qq.v.). In the next period of his career Li played an important role in Party affairs, but his activities are somewhat obscured because he became involved in some of the major controversies of Chinese Communist history from the late twenties to the mid-1930's. He became a member of the CCP Politburo at the Fifth Party Congress in April–May 1927 and was thus placed at the center of the controversy then dividing the leadership over such vital questions as land distribution and how or whether to continue to work with the KMT. Mao Tse-tung, who had just given his report on the peasant situation in Hunan before the KMT Land Committee, was promoting a somewhat drastic division of landholdings; this proposal was opposed both by the Nationalist Government at Wuhan and, because he wanted continued cooperation with the KMT, by Ch'en Tu-hsiu (q.v.), the CCP general secretary. The matter that especially involved Li Wei-han, the question of what to do about dividing the land, became a sore issue. In early May T'ang Sheng-chih, the military supporter of the Wuhan government, ordered Mao's arrest. Mao was then one of the leading officials in the Hunan Provincial Party Committee and was largely responsible for instigating peasant insurgency in the rural areas around Changsha. He and his companions Hsia Hsi and T'eng Tai-yuan (qq.v.), among others, were in Changsha in early May, when they got wind of T'ang's orders just in time to escape to safety in the Liu-yang countryside of Kiangsi across the provincial border. Then on May 21, 1927, T'ang's subordinate Hsu K'o-hsiang, whose troops were garrisoning Changsha, attacked the workers and leftist supporters within the city and destroyed the headquarters of the peasant union. Following this outbreak, Hsu's troops went into the countryside and attacked local peasant groups, thus calling forth a mobilization for a counterattack by the peasant self-defense corps. According to Ts'ai Ho-sen, who supported Mao at this time, the Hunan Provincial Committee had actually begun to mobilize some 300,000 peasants for an attack upon Hsu K'o-hsiang and Changsha. But the Fifth CCP Congress had not voted to support peasant insurrection (see under Ch'en Tu-hsiu), and such actions on the part of the peasantry in the Changsha vicinity provoked an angry statement from Li Wei-han. Li, who at about this time became head of the Hunan Provincial Committee, found the undertaking of the CCP at Changsha "mere child's play." His thinking followed the line that if Changsha were captured by the CCP-organized peasants, T'ang Sheng-chih would march on Wuhan and overthrow the Nationalist government. "In that way," he said, "we shall lose Wuhan." As long as the Wuhan government existed, Li felt that "We [Communists] must ask it to end insurrection by lawful means."[5] Thus Li gave the orders to call off the insurrection in the face of the large troop movements that had already started to advance toward Changsha. His orders came too late to stop some of the peasant troops that were nearing the city, and these could not turn and retreat in time to escape the savage attacks from Hsu K'o-hsiang's troops.

Li was among those who planned the Communist insurrection at Nanchang on August 1, 1927, the coup that completely severed all relations between the CCP and the KMT (see under Yeh T'ing). According to a report from Chang Kuo-t'ao (q.v.), Li was one of the members of the Party Politburo and Secretariat who were hastily summoned for a special emergency planning session, where some of the CCP's top leaders and their Russian advisers discussed final plans for the coup. Among others attending this meeting in addition to Li and Chang were Chang T'ai-lei, Chou En-lai, Ch'ü Ch'iu-pai, and Li Li-san (qq.v.). After the Communists' failure at Nanchang an emergency meeting was held on August 7, 1927. This meeting, which was not attended by a sufficient number of the Politburo and Central Committee members to constitute a quorum, established a "rump" Politburo which ousted Ch'en Tu-hsiu as general secretary and put Ch'ü Ch'iu-pai in his place. The prime movers besides the above-mentioned leaders included Hsiang Chung-fa, Jen Pi-shih, and Su Chao-cheng (qq.v.). At this time Li Wei-han was apparently not given a place on the Politburo, although he must have retained his seat on the General Committee.

A new and legal set of Party officers were elected when the Party held its Sixth Congress in Moscow in 1928. Ch'ü and Li now came in for some frank criticism, Li being accused of having fled the scene of disaster during the abortive peasant uprisings in Hunan (the Autumn Harvest Uprisings that began in September 1927) and of saving himself in a cowardly fashion. He did not attend the Congress, but Chang Kuo-t'ao, who did, reported that the attacks on Li were the only ones that were personal and were extremely vituperative; Li was openly called a coward and said not to be "qualified to be a revolutionary."[6] Chang felt that he was only re-instated to the Central Committee through the influence of Ch'ü Ch'iu-pai. (Li, previously a full member, was elected only to alternate membership.) However, it should be noted that at sometime after the Congress closed, Li took over the role of Party Organization chief, which had initially been given to Chou En-lai, and thus must have regained his status in the top ranks of the CCP. Moreover, it is possible that some of the treatment he had received may have been magnified as it was seen through the eyes of Chang Kuo-t'ao. For the next two years Li worked in the Shanghai Party underground, reportedly in association with K'ang Sheng (q.v.).

The years 1928 to 1931 while Li was in Shanghai were chaotic ones for the CCP leadership. The Sixth Congress had chosen Hsiang Chung-fa as a compromise candidate for the post of Party general secretary to replace Ch'ü Ch'iu-pai. Hsiang was not particularly influential and Li Li-san, who had been given charge of Party propaganda, now became the dominant leader. His was one of the stormiest periods of leadership that the CCP has seen, so it is not surprising that Li Wei-han again became involved in political in-fighting among the Party elite. In the next round Li Wei-han came out on the side of Li Li-san. The problems of Li Li-san's headstrong leadership and the faults found in his policies by both the Comintern and many CCP members are treated in his biography. The account of his chief protagonists, the "28 Bolshevik" clique that arrived in China fresh from training at Sun Yat-sen University in Moscow in the late spring of 1930, is included in the biographies of this new leadership (see under Ch'in Pang-hsien). With the returned-student group came Pavel Mif, Comintern agent and former head of Sun Yat-sen University, who directed some of the activities of his former students. Then in the summer of 1930 the Comintern also returned Chou En-lai and Ch'ü Ch'iu-pai to China, again to attempt to check the headstrong Li Li-san. In the latter part of September the Third CCP Plenum was called, at which all the above factions played a part. Also present at the Plenum was yet another dissenting faction, this one from the home front led by Ho Menghsiung and Lo Chang-lung (qq.v.), powerful labor leaders who were finding Li Li-san's labor policies devastating to the Party interests in the labor movement. In the course of the Plenum (about which reporting is rather confusing) Chou and Ch'ü somewhat compromised their stand on Li Li-san and made a stronger attack upon Ho and Lo with the result that Li Li-san managed to keep the upper hand. Three of his supporters were elected or re-elected to the Politburo, Li Wei-han, Hsiang Chung-fa, and Ho Ch'ang, who had been a firm Li Li-san supporter in the CCP North China Bureau and the Party Provincial Committee for Hopeh.

Following the Plenum Li Wei-han carried on in support of Li Li-san. A speech he made in September 1930 attacked the labor group of Li's opponents and was addressed to combating the "opportunistic line represented by Ho Menghsiung."[7] But Li Li-san was ousted from the Party's top leadership in November and sent to the Soviet Union. In January 1931 the CCP held its Fourth Plenum in Shanghai, and Mif and the "28 Bolsheviks" took control of the Party hierarchy (see under Ch'in Pang-hsien), dealing a "crushing blow" to those who had played a major role in shaping or following the Li Li-san line.[8] At this time Li Wei-han, Ho Ch'ang, and Kuan Hsiang-ying (q.v.) were removed from the Central Committee. In February an official Party journal published a "Statement by Comrade Lo Mai." Lo Mai was the pseudonym by which Li Wei-han was often known and under which he quite frequently wrote. The statement was Li's public confession for having "mistakenly" supported the Li Li-san policies. When he wrote he had just been removed from both the Polit-

buro and from the Kiangsu Provincial Party Committee. The editors of the journal found Li's statement unsatisfactory and wanted him to make another public confession.[9] The same issue of the journal called upon both Ch'ü Ch'iu-pai and Li Wei-han to make their attitude known not only toward the Li Li-san line but also toward the "rightists," by which the "28 Bolshevik" leadership that sponsored the journal meant Ho Menghsiung and Lo Chang-lung. They did not feel that he had been sufficiently clear in his previous attacks on Ho. Despite these criticisms Li Wei-han probably continued to engage in Party underground work in Shanghai for a time. It is not known when he left the city, but he had escaped by April 1931 when his underground address was given to the police by a former colleague, Ku Shun-chang, who had been arrested. Under "police surveillance" Ku turned traitor and gave away the addresses of Li, Ch'ü Ch'iu-pai, Chou En-lai, and Hsiang Chung-fa; the first three had escaped before the police could find them. Like Chou and Ch'ü, Li escaped to the hinterlands of southeast Kiangsi to join the headquarters of Mao Tse-tung and Chu Te at Juichin.

At Juichin Li Wei-han does not seem to have entirely sided with Mao Tse-tung. There is little reporting about his activity there but in 1933 he wrote attacks on the "Lo Ming Line" (see under Lo Ming). This is one of the controversial issues of the Kiangsi period treated in the biographies of Ch'in Pang-hsien and Chang Went'ien, leaders of the "28 Bolshevik" clique who led the anti-Lo Ming attack. The Lo Ming line was also attacked at this time by Chou En-lai, but in later times it has been given official sanction because Lo Ming has been supported by Mao Tse-tung, who has made the attack upon his policies a basis for his own criticism of the Ch'in Pang-hsien leadership. In 1933 Li Wei-han wrote his views on the Lo Ming line for the official Party journal Tou-cheng (Struggle).[10] While in Kiangsi Li was said to have headed a Party training school. At the time of the Second All-China Congress of Soviets held in Juichin in January–February 1934, Li became a member of the 17-member Presidium of the Chinese Soviet Republic, as well as its governing Central Executive Committee, both of which were chaired by Mao. Similarly, his associates Chang Wen-t'ien, Ch'in Pang-hsien, Chou En-lai, and Ch'ü Ch'iu-pai were named to the same two organizations.

Li and his wife made the Long March from Kiangsi to north Shensi with Mao's army. In Shensi before and during the Sino-Japanese War his political role was important if not outstanding. When Edgar Snow interviewed Mao in 1936 Li was identified as the "secretary" of the Party's Organization Department, and the title, from the context, suggests that he was the organizational chief, a post he had held after the Sixth Congress in 1928.[11] However, other reports indicate that Li Fu-ch'un (q.v.) had assumed the directorship of the Organization Department by 1935. In any event, when Nym Wales visited Shensi in 1937, she identified Li Wei-han as head of the Communist Party School;[12] he continued in this capacity until about 1940 when he was succeeded by Teng Fa (q.v.). In addition to his purely political assignments, Li also participated in an activity that had long interested a number of Party intellectuals—the reform of the written Chinese language. Thus, when the Sin Wen (*Hsin wen-tzu;* "New Writing") Society was established in Yenan in November 1940, Li was a member of the presidium that brought the organization into existence.[13]

Toward the end of the war Li became secretary-general of the Shensi-Kansu-Ninghsia Border Region Government, which had its capital in Yenan; he held the post for about a year. At approximately the time that he assumed this post (c.1944) he also became director of the Party's United Front Work Department, which was to be his major assignment for the next two decades. The wide-ranging activities of this department are concerned primarily with gaining the allegiance of non-Communists (e.g., business and industrial leaders, overseas Chinese) and in working with the many non-Han national minority groups. At the war's end Li was named to the Communist delegation to the Political Consultative Conference to negotiate the vast political differences between the CCP and the KMT. Serving in this capacity with Chou En-lai and Tung Pi-wu he attended meetings in Chungking and Nanking between April and November 1946 and then returned to Yenan when negotiations became impossible.

Li was among the first Communist leaders to arrive in Peking after the fall of the city in late January 1949. Soon afterward, when the Nationalist Government sent a "peace" negotiation mission to Peking for talks that began on April 1, the high-level Communist delegation was composed of Chou En-lai, Lin Po-ch'ü, Lin Piao, Yeh Chien-ying, Nieh Jung-chen (qq.v.), and Li. In fact, however, because the Communists had already conquered most of north China and were advancing rapidly southward, the talks quickly collapsed when it became apparent that the Communists were interested only in terms that were tantamount to surrender. Growing ever more confident in their ultimate success, the Communists convened a meeting in Peking in June to prepare for the convocation of the CPPCC later in the year. The meetings, chaired by Mao, established a Preparatory Committee as well as the more important Standing Committee. Li was named secretary-general of the Standing Committee, serving also as head of a subordinate body whose task it was to select the delegates to the First CPPCC, which opened in

Peking in September. And, when the permanent First National Committee was appointed at the close of the September meetings, Li was selected as the CPPCC secretary-general.

With the establishment of the new central government, Li received three important posts in the cabinet, which was known from 1949 to 1954 as the Government Administration Council (GAC) and was headed by Premier Chou En-lai. Li became secretary-general of the GAC, a post he retained until September 1953 when it was assumed by Hsi Chung-hsun (q.v.), and a member of the GAC's Political and Legal Affairs Committee, one of the more powerful organs of the central government. Moreover, he was appointed to chair the GAC's ministerial-level Nationalities Affairs Commission, a task that was to occupy much of his time over the next five years and one closely linked to his work in the Party's United Front Department. Like many top Party leaders, he was also named in October 1949 to serve on the Executive Board of the Sino-Soviet Friendship Association, continuing in this post until the Second Board was elected in December 1954.

As already indicated, Li devoted much of his time in the early PRC years to the affairs of China's numerous non-Han national minority groups in his capacity as chairman of the Nationalities Affairs Commission (NAC). He was often mentioned in the press, for example, in connection with the frequent visits to Peking made by minority delegations. Speaking before a session of the NAC in December 1951, Li extolled the "unprecedented unity" already achieved among the minority nationalities in China and asserted that over 100 "autonomous" government administrations had been established throughout the nation. His over-all direction of national minority affairs probably accounts for the fact that he was the chief Chinese negotiator in the talks with local Tibetan leaders in the spring of 1951. The negotiations, climaxing in an agreement for the "peaceful liberation" of Tibet signed by Li on May 23, resulted directly from the invasion of Tibet, which began in late 1950 and are discussed in greater detail in the biography of Chang Ching-wu.

Apart from his work with minority groups, Li was also one of the prime movers in the campaign to "reform" China's industrialists and businessmen and, ultimately, to transform their enterprises into government-controlled businesses. The "five-anti" campaign, the name given to the movement, was held on a nationwide scale during the first few months of 1952; more specifically, it was intended to wipe out bribery, tax evasion, fraud, theft of government property, and the theft of state economic secrets by the business community. Organizationally, the movement seems to have begun in the fall of 1951 when a special body was established to prepare for the convocation of a national association of business and industrial leaders. This small "Preparatory Office" was under Li's direction, ostensibly assisted by Ch'en Shu-t'ung and Chang Nai-ch'i, both prominent but non-Communist business leaders. Then, immediately following the "victory" of the "five-anti" campaign, the Preparatory Committee of the All-China Federation of Industry and Commerce (ACFIC) was established at a meeting in June 1952, which was attended by Li. He was not given any formal position in the new organization, but when the First National Congress of the ACFIC was held in October–November 1953, he was the keynote speaker, addressing the delegates on the tasks of the bourgeois class during the "transitional period leading to socialist industrialization." (A further discussion of the CCP's control over the ACFIC is contained in the biography of Hsu Ti-hsin.) Li's knowledge of the Chinese business community probably accounts for his appointment in mid-1952 as chairman of the central government's Labor Employment Committee (which dealt with the problem of unemployment), as well as his selection for membership in September 1953 on the GAC's Finance and Economics Committee.

In 1953–54 Li served on three committees whose work paved the way for the establishment of the constitutional government in the latter year. First, in January–February 1953 he served on the body that drafted the Election Law, and then in February (when the law was formally adopted) he was named to the Central Election Committee, which was responsible for supervising the electoral processes throughout the nation. Finally, from its establishment in January 1953 under the chairmanship of Mao Tse-tung, Li served on the Committee to Draft the Constitution, which continued to meet until the document was formally promulgated at the First NPC in September 1954. Li attended the First NPC as a deputy from his native Hunan, as he did also during the term of the Second NPC (1959–1964). He was secretary-general of the inaugural session in September 1954 and at the close of the meetings was elected as a vice-chairman of the NPC Standing Committee, which controls the affairs of the national legislative body between the annual sessions of the full Congress.

In the changes made in the executive branch of the national government at and immediately after the inaugural NPC sessions, Li relinquished his chairmanship of the Nationalities Affairs Commission to Ulanfu (q.v.), but he assumed the directorship of the newly established Eighth Staff Office of the State Council. This office, in effect, was the governmental counterpart of the Party United Front Work Department and was in charge of directing and coordinating the activities of central government bodies that dealt in "united front" affairs (e.g., the Overseas Chinese Affairs Commission). With the establishment of the NPC, the CPPCC became a much less important organization. And thus, when the Second CPPCC was opened in December 1954, Li relinquished the secretary-generalship to Hsu Ping (q.v.), although he was named as one of the vice-chairmen, a position that was now largely honorary. He was named again as a vice-chairman when the Third CPPCC was formed in April 1959.

When the Party held its Eighth Congress in September 1956, Li delivered a major speech on the "united front" and was elected to the CCP's Eighth Central Committee. In the next two years, during the Party-directed *cheng-feng* ("rectification") movement, he was particularly active and was reported in the press on scores of occasions speaking before meetings of China's eight "democratic" (non-Communist) political parties or such professional organizations as the above-mentioned ACFIC. His talks generally concentrated on the alleged wrong-doings of the "rightists" and demanded greater conformity to the wishes and policies of the CCP. Ironically, his own brother (see below) was one of the victims of this massive nationwide campaign.

Li was once again named as a vice-chairman of the NPC when the Second Congress opened in April 1959. Five months later, however, his Eighth Staff Office was abolished during a partial reorganization of the State Council. Like most CCP leaders of prominence, Li made innumerable public appearances in the late fifties and early sixties at protocol functions, and he continued to speak with frequency before various forums and meetings in connection with "united front" work. Dealing with the same subject, he wrote a long, three-part article for the Party's top Journal, *Hung-ch'i* (Red flag, issues 11 and 12 in 1961 and joint issue 3–4 in 1962). When this was published as an English-language pamphlet in 1962, the official New China News Agency commented that the question of the leadership of the "revolutionary united front" was "one of the three key weapons of the Chinese revolution," the other two being the CCP and the "armed struggle."

Li continued to appear regularly in public until the fall of 1964. Then, in what seemed to be a rather unusual move, he was elected to represent the Sinkiang-Uighur Autonomous Region (rather than Hunan) in the Third NPC, which first met in December 1964–January 1965. Moreover, when the NPC meetings ended, he was not re-elected to his NPC vice-chairmanship. Similarly, when the CPPCC convened its Fourth National Committee (simultaneously with the holding of the NPC session), Li was not re-elected to his vice-chairmanship, although he was named to the National Committee as a CCP representative. Most important, however, was the fact that Hsu Ping succeeded to the directorship of the Party's United Front Work Department by March 1965. Thus, within a brief time, Li was stripped of an important Party position and two other posts of lesser but symbolic importance, and he no longer made even the most insignificant protocol appearances that virtually all top CCP leaders make with regularity. His apparent political fall was indirectly suggested in an article appearing in the *JMJP* (December 20, 1964) on the eve of the NPC session; this piece, which was a blistering attack on Central Committee member and former Higher Party School President Yang Hsien-chen (q.v.), linked Yang's name with Li in a guilt-by-association manner. More important, when Premier Chou En-lai spoke before the NPC on the day after the above-mentioned *JMJP* article appeared, he stated that "quite a number of people" had "actively advocated . . . capitulationism in united front work." In view of Li's removal from the Party's United Front Work Department at this time, Chou's remarks were almost certainly directed against Li Wei-han.

Not much is known of his personal life, characteristics, or abilities, aside from the fact that he speaks French and English. His wife, who made the Long March with him, is named A Chin; authoress Nym Wales transliterates the name as "Ah (Ch'ing) Hsiang."[14] Wales described her as a native of Kwangtung. Nothing further is known about her aside from the fact that she was in charge of a women's unit at the Anti-Japanese Military and Political Academy (K'ang-ta) in Yenan in the late 1930's. Li's brother, Li Chün-lung, a graduate of Columbia University, was formerly prominent in the San-min chu-i Youth Corps and a vice-minister of the Nationalists' Ministry of Information in 1947. He stayed on the mainland after the Communist victory in 1949 and became a Central Committee member of the Kuomintang Revolutionary Committee (KMTRC), one of the most important of the "democratic" parties. He had risen to the KMTRC Standing Committee and was also deputy director of its Organization Department when he fell victim to the 1957–58 *Cheng-feng* campaign. In the early years of the PRC he had served as a member of the Councillor's Office of the GAC, of which his brother was the secretary-general. Li Chün-lung has represented the KMTRC on the National Committee of the CPPCC since 1954. Although the designation of "rightist" was formally removed by the CCP Central Committee in November 1960, little has been heard of his activities.

1. Jerome Ch'en, *Mao and the Chinese Revolution* (London, 1965), p. 50.

2. Conrad Brandt, *The French-Returned Elite in the Chinese Communist Party*, reprint no. 13, Institute of International Studies, University of California, Berkeley, Calif., 1961.

3. Union Research Institute, *Who's Who in Communist China* (Hong Kong, 1966), p. 366.

4. Chow Tse-tsung, *Research Guide to the May Fourth Movement* (Cambridge, Mass., 1963), p. 111.

5. Robert C. North and Xenia J. Eudin, *M. N. Roy's Mission to China* (Berkeley, Calif., 1963), p. 106.

6. Modern China Project, Columbia University, New York, Howard L. Boorman, director.

7. Tso-liang Hsiao, *Power Relations within the Chinese Communist Movement, 1930–1934* (Seattle, Wash., 1961), p. 53.

8. *Ibid.*, p. 115.

9. *Ibid.*, pp. 130–131.

10. *Ibid.*, p. 243.

11. Edgar Snow, *Red Star over China* (New York, 1938), p. 131.

12. Nym Wales, *Inside Red China* (New York, 1939), p. 328.

13. John De Francis, *Nationalism and Language Reform in China* (Princeton, N.J., 1950), p. 130.

14. Wales, p. 175.

Li Yü

(c.1905–   ; Shansi?). Former alternate member, CCP Central Committee; vice-minister, Eighth Ministry of Machine Building.

Li Yü is one of the very few persons dropped from the Party Central Committee who later made a comeback of moderate proportions. Sources vary on both Li's date of birth and his native province; apparently he was born about 1905 in Shansi, though some sources assert that it was in Shantung and use dates from 1903 to 1907. He joined the Party in 1929 and then engaged in covert Party work among students at Cheloo University in Tsinan, Shantung. Japanese sources state that at the outbreak of the Sino-Japanese War in mid-1937 Li was an official of the Communist Kiangsu-Shantung-Honan-Anhwei Military Region. His main activity there was in leading a small guerrilla force, and when Hsu Hsiang-ch'ien's (q.v.) troops moved into southern Hopeh in 1938, Li joined his forces to Hsu's and became political commissar of the First Column. By early 1940 he was identified as political commissar of the Shantung Corps, a unit commanded by Chang Ching-wu (q.v.),[1] and by 1944 he was deputy political commissar of the Shantung Military District.[2] In the latter position he was serving under the important military leader Lo Jung-huan (q.v.) who was both commander and political commissar of the military district. Toward the end of the war Li was with the New Fourth Army (then commanded by Ch'en I), but the exact circumstances are not clear from the available record.

By the spring of 1945 Li had obviously attracted the attention of senior Party leaders, for at the close of the Seventh Party Congress (April–June 1945) he was elected an alternate member of the Central Committee. Only 44 full and 33 alternate members were elected, and thus Li became a member of a very exclusive group. It is not known if he went to Yenan for the Congress, but if so he had already returned to Shantung by June 1945 where he delivered a report on provincial economic conditions before the Shantung Industrial and Commercial Conference.[3] However, he was in Yenan in April 1946, where he participated in funeral services for four top Party leaders killed in an air crash in that month (see under Yeh T'ing).[4] Aside from this trip to Yenan, he seems to have spent most of the postwar period in Shantung where he was a member of the Shantung Party Committee and governor of the Communist-held portions of the province from 1945 to 1949, and by 1947 he was also serving as head of the Shantung Government's Justice Department. However, when the Communists gained full control of Shantung in the spring of 1949, he was replaced as governor by K'ang Sheng (q.v.), a senior Party leader and later a Politburo member. In late 1949 and early 1950 he participated in the establishment of the multi-provincial East China Military and Administrative Committee (ECMAC). He was named to membership on the ECMAC in December 1949 and in the following March was appointed a member of an *ad hoc* committee responsible for organizing the various governmental departments and bureaus under the jurisdiction of the ECMAC.

For reasons that are not clear, Li apparently got into political difficulties in 1950. The semi-official handbooks published by the Communists in 1950 list him as an alternate member of the Party Central Committee, but another such handbook of early 1951 does not (nor does it list another alternate, Liu Tzu-chiu, q.v.). In the interim, in June 1950, the Party Central Committee had held its Third Plenum. Apparently it was at this meeting that Li was removed, but no charges were made public and later (in December) in the same year he was appointed as a member of the Shanghai Municipal People's Government. In fact, in 1951 he assumed three more posts in Shanghai of moderate importance (secretary-general of the Shanghai Party Committee, secretary-general of an *ad hoc* Shanghai government committee to check up on the austerity program, and chairman of the Shanghai government's Civil Construction Committee). Then in early 1952 Li became involved in serious trouble, but this time he was publicly denounced. He was charged with a "patriarchal style of work," "arrogance and the abuse of his positions," and a "slovenly attitude towards the demands of . . . the masses." For these and similar charges, he was stripped of all his positions in the Party and government. This case occurred during the peak of the *san-fan* (three-anti) movement against the three "evils" of corruption, waste, and bureaucracy. Several other Party leaders in China were severely criticized at this time, yet many of them went on to significant careers (e.g., Wu Te-feng, q.v.). Li was ordered to reflect upon his "mistakes in thinking and action" and was admonished that the ultimate settlement of his case would be based upon the extent of his "repentance." He dropped completely out of sight for over two years, but in the meantime he had been transferred to Peking and quietly given the rather modest post as head of the Finance Section of the Finance and Economics Committee in the Government Administration Council (the cabinet).

By June 1954 Li had made a comeback of sufficient strength to win an appointment as a vice-minister of the First Ministry of Machine Building, and six months later (December 1954) he was named to membership on the Board of Directors of the Bank of Communications, a specialized bank subordinate to the Ministry of Finance, which handles the state's investments in the joint state-private enterprises. Through the 1950's Li was reported in the press rather regularly in the performance of his duties, mainly those concerning the First Ministry. For example, he spoke at a gathering in Port Arthur in December 1954 marking the transfer of the Soviet shares of the Sino-Soviet Joint Shipbuilding Company to China and in the next month spoke at the opening of the Harbin Measuring Instruments and Cutting Tool Plant. In January 1959 Li was added as a member of the China Committee for the Promotion of International Trade, the semi-official organization which attempts to promote Chinese trade with nations not having diplomatic relations with Peking; however, he does not appear to have been very active in this body. In September 1959, during a general reshuffle of government personnel, Li was transferred from his vice-ministership in the First Ministry of Machine Building to the same post under the Ministry of Agricultural Machinery. In the following month Li went to Loyang where he inspected the Number One Tractor Plant and, on November 1, 1959, spoke at the official inauguration. Four years passed before Li made another appearance; in October 1963 he attended a meeting marking the opening of a Japanese industrial exhibition. During these years of apparent inactivity, Li continued to be listed in the official directories as a vice-minister of Agricultural Machinery, remaining in this capacity after it was renamed the Eighth Ministry of Machine Building in January 1965. Li's career began to wane by 1950, and by the 1960's was of interest mainly from the historic viewpoint of a man who once held membership on the Party Central Committee.

1. Ko Han, *The Shansi-Hopei-Shantung Border Region, Report I, 1937–38* (Chungking, New China Information Committee, bulletin no. 13, 1940; printed in Manila).

2. Chün-tu Hsüeh, *The Chinese Communist Movement, 1937–1949* (Stanford, Calif., 1962), p. 124.

3. *Ibid.*, p. 242.

4. *Chui-tao "szu-pa" yü-nan lieh-shih chi-nien-ts'e* (In memory of the martyrs who died in the accident of "April Eighth"; Kalgan, 1946), p. 26.

Li Yu-wen

(c.1901–   ; Liao-yang hsien, Liaoning). Governor of Kirin.

A former associate of Manchurian warlord Chang Hsueh-liang, Li Yu-wen has spent the major part of his career as a Party-government official in his native Manchuria and has been the Kirin governor since 1952. Li was born in Liao-yang hsien, which lies between the important cities of Anshan and Mukden in Liaoning province. He graduated from Peking University and, according to Japanese sources, also studied at Moscow University. In his younger days, Li was a teacher in Manchuria, but after the Japanese occupation of Manchuria in 1931 he went to China proper where for the next several years he engaged in anti-Japanese activities. Prior to the Sino-Japanese War his activities centered around his work for Chang Hsueh-liang, often known as the "Young Marshal." Chang and his troops were driven out of Manchuria in 1931, after which they operated in north and northwest China, with their headquarters in Sian. Writing in 1946, Communist journalist Liu Pai-yü (q.v.) described Li as a "secret assistant" to Chang.[1] Another "secret assistant" to Chang at this time was Tsou Ta-p'eng (q.v.), a long-time specialist in intelligence work.

Li was also an important figure in the Northeast branch of the National Salvation Association, which, in effect, was an organization-in-exile that sought to arouse the Chinese people against the Japanese during the mid-thirties. After the war broke out in 1937, Li joined the Communists and served during the war as secretary-general of the Yenan Garrison Command and after 1940 as head of the Liaison Bureau, subordinate to the Political Department of the Joint Defense Headquarters, which had jurisdiction over the military forces in the Shensi-Kansu-Ninghsia and the Shansi-Suiyuan Border Regions. (See under Ho Lung, the commander of the Joint Headquarters.)

At the close of the Sino-Japanese War in 1945, the Communists sent a large number of their top leaders to Manchuria in an attempt to gain control there; among them were such key figures as Kao Kang, Ch'en Yun, Lin Piao, and Lin Feng (qq.v.). Similarly, Li Yu-wen was sent to his native Manchuria and was named as governor of Liaopei, one of the nine provinces in Manchuria created by the Nationalists at the end of the war, with its capital at Liao-yuan (Shuang-liao). Li relinquished his gubernatorial post within a year, probably because he had received more important assignments with the Communists' government administration for Manchuria, known as the Northeast Administrative Committee (NEAC). Created in the spring of 1946 in Harbin, the NEAC was headed by Lin Feng, a member of the CCP Central Committee and then the director of the Organization Department of the Party's Northeast Bureau. Li was named as a member of the NEAC as well as secretary-general. By 1948 he was also serving as head of the Justice Department, one of the eight departments of the NEAC as it was originally constituted in 1946.

In August 1949, on the eve of the establishment of the Chinese Communist central government, the NEAC was reorganized into the Northeast People's Government (NEPG) with the capital now in Shenyang (Mukden). Under the new administration Kao Kang replaced Lin Feng as the chairman, and Li, in effect, was reappointed to two of the positions he had held under the NEAC, being named to the NEPG Council and to the post of secretary-general. According to Japanese sources, he was also a deputy secretary of the Party's Northeast Bureau from 1949 to 1953, another position which placed Li under Kao Kang, the ranking secretary.

Under circumstances that have never been clarified, Kirin Governor Chou Ch'ih-heng was removed in April 1952 for "violations of the law." To replace Chou, Li was relieved of his duties with the NEPG in July 1952 and made the new Kirin governor. He continues to hold this post, having been re-elected in February 1955, July 1958, and December 1963. Because Changchun, the Kirin capital, is frequently visited by both top Chinese leaders and many foreign visitors, Li has often been in the news since becoming the Kirin governor. Changchun's attraction to visitors has been all the more significant since the opening in 1956 of the Changchun First Automobile Factory, one of the major industrial "showpieces" of the PRC. To judge by the speeches he makes at the frequent sessions of the provincial government council and by the types of inspection missions in which he has been engaged, it appears that Li concentrates on industrial affairs, a logical outgrowth of the fact that Kirin is one of China's most industrialized provinces.

For a period of four years from 1952, when

he first became the Kirin governor, Li Yu-wen was apparently the top Party leader in the province. However, with the transfer in 1956 to Kirin of Wu Te (q.v.), an alternate member of the Party Central Committee, it appears that Li has been politically outranked. In 1956 Li also became a secretary of the Kirin Party Committee, a post that places him under First Secretary Wu Te. In addition, Li has served in the national administration as a deputy to the NPC from Kirin. He was elected to all three NPC's, the initial sessions of which met in September 1954, April 1959, and December 1964–January 1965.

1. Liu Pai-yü, *Huan-hsing tung-pei* (Traveling in the Northeast; Shanghai, 1946), p. 197.

Liang Hsi

(1883–1958; Wu-hsing, Chekiang). Non-Communist; scientist; former minister of Forestry.

Liang Hsi was a well-known academician who joined the Communist government in 1949 and headed the Ministry of Forestry until his death nine years later. He was born in Wu-hsing, Chekiang, located just south of Lake T'ai, some 50 miles north of Hangchow, the provincial capital. In the latter years of the Ch'ing Dynasty he won a government scholarship and went to Japan for naval training, but he later transferred to Tokyo Imperial University where he received his bachelor's degree in science in 1916. He studied forestry at the Forstliche Hochschule in Saxony, Germany (1923–1928), and for the next two decades taught at Chekiang University and National Central University (Nanking), heading the forestry departments in both institutes. After the fall of Nanking in 1937 Liang spent the war years in Chungking where National Central University was relocated, and while there he was a board member of the China Forestry Association and a vice-president of the China Agriculture Association.

Liang returned to Nanking after the war and continued to teach until early 1949 when he went to Peking to join the Communists, a decision that was warmly welcomed by the CCP because Liang was by then one of the best-known and most highly regarded academicians in China. He received his first post with the Communists in June when he was named as a member of the Higher Education Committee of the North China People's Government, the administration that approximated a national government until it was disbanded when the PRC was brought into existence in October 1949. In mid-1949 the Communists took their first step toward the mobilization of scientific talent by establishing a preparatory committee for the First All-China Scientific Workers' Conference, a committee to which Liang was named, and in this capacity he attended in September the First CPPCC, the body that brought the new central government into existence. While the CPPCC was in session, he served on the Credentials Committee (the only scientist to do so), and when the meetings closed he was elected to the Standing Committee of the First CPPCC, as he was again in 1954 when the Second CPPCC was formed.

When the cabinet was formed in October 1949 Liang was named to head the Ministry of Forestry and Land Reclamation and to serve as a member of the Finance and Economics Committee (FEC). He returned briefly to Nanking to wind up his affairs at Nanking University (the new name for National Central University), which he had headed since the city fell to Communist armies in April of that year. Liang returned to Peking in November and remained there until his death nine years later, continuing to serve on the FEC until it was abolished in 1954. He retained his ministerial portfolio until his death, but in November 1951 his responsibilities for land reclamation were turned over to the Ministry of Agriculture after which his ministry was redesignated as the Ministry of Forestry. In February 1958, less than a year before he died, Liang's ministry absorbed the Ministry of Timber Industry (coinciding with the purge of former Timber Minister Lo Lung-chi), but in this instance the ministry was not renamed.

Like many prominent national administrators, Liang was also given extracurricular assignments in non-governmental organizations in the fall of 1949. Serving first on the Preparatory Committee of the Sino-Soviet Friendship Association (SSFA) from July, Liang was named to membership on the national Executive Board when the SSFA was established in October, and in the same month he was also appointed a member of the China Peace Committee's National Committee, retaining both posts until 1958. But these assignments were essentially nominal, particularly after 1950 when the Communists took their next major step toward organizing China's scientists, efforts in which Liang was to play a major role. A conference of scientists was held in August 1950, resulting in the establishment of two new organizations, the All-China Federation of Scientific Societies (ACFSS) and the All-China Association for the Dissemination of Scientific and Technical Knowledge (ACADSTK). The former was a federation of professional associations (e.g., chemistry, physics), whereas the latter, though headed by trained scientists, was more akin to a "mass" or "people's" organization in that its principal function was to spread rather rudimentary technological information on a wide scale. Liang chaired the ACADSTK from its formation, and writing of its activities in late 1953 he claimed that it had well over 100 branches and sub-branches with over 23,000 members; nearly 17 million people, he continued, had heard some 26,000 lectures or had seen various types of scientific exhibits.[1] Within the more professional ACFSS, Liang was named to membership on its National Committee in 1950, and when the China Society of Forestry was established in February 1951 he became its chairman, remaining so until his death. Finally, in September 1958 (less than three months before Liang's death), the two large organizations were merged to form the China Scientific and Technical Association, with Liang as the ranking vice-chairman under his colleague Li Szu-kuang (q.v.), a prominent geologist.

From the closing stages of World War II, Liang had been associated in Chungking with a small organization of scientists and educators, which from 1945 was known as the Chiu San Society (see under Hsu Te-heng, the chairman). From December 1950 until his death Liang was the vice-chairman of the Society, which by this time had been designated by the Communists as one of the eight "democratic" political parties. In 1954 he was elected to represent Anhwei in the First NPC and was re-elected to the Second NPC in 1958 just a few days before his death. Liang received further scientific posts in 1955–56, the first of these in May–June 1955 when he became a member of the newly established Department of Biology, Geology, and Geography of the Academy of Sciences, and that fall he became vice-chairman of a special committee under the Academy to award prizes for outstanding scientific achievements. From March 1956 to shortly before his death, Liang also served on the State Council's Scientific Planning Commission. In April 1956, when the Communist-dominated World Federation of Scientific Workers (WFSW) held a meeting in Peking, Liang represented the Chinese and served on the presidium (steering committee).

In the post-1949 period Liang was abroad on two occasions, the first of which was in April 1951 when he led the Chinese delegation to the Second Congress of the WFSW in Prague. His second trip was as a member of a delegation that visited the Soviet Union, Rumania, Czechoslovakia, Bulgaria, Albania, and Yugoslavia from November 1956 to January 1957 under the leadership of Politburo member P'eng Chen. Liang was active until shortly before his death from lung cancer in Peking at the age of 76 on December 10, 1958. The Communists gave prominent press coverage to his passing and held a memorial service in his honor that was attended by several hundred persons, including some of the leading CCP officials.

---

1. Liang Hsi, "Popularising Scientific and Technical Knowledge," *People's China*, no. 24: 23–25 (December 16, 1953).

Liao Ch'eng-chih

(1908–   ; Tokyo, Japan). Veteran youth leader; specialist in international "peace" movement; chairman, Overseas Chinese Affairs Commission; member, CCP Central Committee.

Liao Ch'eng-chih has had a long and extremely varied career in the Chinese Communist movement, work that has involved him in the Party underground, youth affairs, propaganda, international liaison activities, and overseas Chinese affairs. The son of the famous KMT leader Liao Chung-k'ai, Liao Ch'eng-chih has been a CCP member since 1927. He was a CCP liaison official in Hong Kong during the early years of the Sino-Japanese War, but he spent the latter years in a KMT prison. He was elected an alternate member of the Party Central Committee in 1945 and was later elevated to full membership. Since the formation of the PRC he has devoted the major portion of his time to the promotion of China's international relations, including its ties with Japan, the international "peace" and "Afro-Asian solidarity" movements, and overseas Chinese.

Liao was born in September 1908 in Tokyo where his parents were students and active members of Sun Yat-sen's T'ung-meng hui, the predecessor of the KMT. His American-born and reared father, Liao Chung-k'ai, was one of the leading heirs-apparent to KMT leadership after the death of Sun Yat-sen in March 1925, but five months later he was assassinated in Canton, allegedly by the right-wing KMT. Liao Ch'eng-chih is the only important member of the CCP born abroad, although he regards his ancestral home as Hui-chou (now Hui-yang), located in Kwangtung some 50 miles north of Hong Kong. He received his primary education at a Catholic school in Tokyo where he studied both Chinese and Japanese and was also tutored in English and French. In 1937 he described his early life to American authoress Nym Wales, whose biographic sketch of Liao serves as the basis for much of the information about him through the mid-thirties.[1] In 1918 he was taken to Shanghai where for the next 15 months his father gave him daily English lessons and friends instructed him in mathematics. He next went to Canton where he attended a Baptist middle school as well as one attached to Lingnan University. While a student in Canton he joined the KMT (c.1924) and participated in various demonstrations against the constituted authorities, thus initiating his revolutionary career while still a teenager.

Liao returned to Japan and studied at Waseda University in Tokyo during the 1927–28 school year. In the former year he joined the CCP and in the spring of 1928 he took part in anti-Japanese student demonstrations following the Tsinan Incident of May 3, when Japanese forces in Shantung took hostile actions against Chinese

Northern Expeditionary forces, ostensibly to protect Japanese nationals. Deported for these activities, Liao went to Shanghai where he continued briefly to engage in anti-Japanese agitation. Later in 1928 he sailed as a seaman for Europe where he attempted to organize Chinese seamen and foment strikes in several of Europe's major ports, including Marseilles, Antwerp, Rotterdam, and Hamburg. He was imprisoned for two weeks in Rotterdam and then deported; he was again arrested in Hamburg and once more, about the year 1932, he was deported. Liao then proceeded to Moscow where he remained for a brief time, returning to Shanghai in 1932 where he engaged in underground activities under the name Ho Liu-hua. Shanghai was then a perilous place for CCP members; most of the key Party leaders had left the city for the rural soviet areas and continuous KMT surveillance was driving the remaining Communists deeper underground in Shanghai. Among Liao's associates in the Shanghai underground were K'ang Sheng, Lo Teng-hsien, and Ch'en Keng (qq.v.). He was arrested in March 1933 with the latter two in the International Settlement but was soon transferred to the Chinese authorities. He obtained his release a few months later, largely through the efforts of Mme. Sun Yat-sen and his mother, Ho Hsiang-ning, a well-known figure because of her marriage to Liao's famous father.[2]

After his release, Liao left for the rural hinterlands, arriving about 1934 in Szechwan where he began to work in the Political Department of the Communists' Fourth Front Army (see under Chang Kuo-t'ao). In the following year, when the main Long March forces from Kiangsi led by Chu Te and Mao Tse-tung passed through Szechwan, Liao joined them and proceeded to north Shensi, where from 1935 to 1937 he worked for the *Chieh-fang she* (Liberation news agency) and for a brief time edited the *Chieh-fang chou-k'an* (Liberation weekly). Throughout the early stages of the Sino-Japanese War Liao continued to contribute to and edit Communist publications,[3] serving also as chief of the Communists' "Press Relations Bureau." Not long after the war broke out in mid-1937, he was assigned to Hong Kong as the CCP representative and as purchasing agent for the Communists' Eighth Route Army. The assignment probably fell to Liao because of his familiarity with underground work and the Hong Kong–Canton region, as well as his family connections in south China, which would be useful to the Communist cause.

Liao remained in Hong Kong until shortly after its fall to the Japanese in late December 1941. Smuggled out of the city, he made his way to Communist guerrilla areas in nearby Kwangtung but within a year (May 1943) was arrested by the KMT, whose relations with the CCP by this time were extremely hostile in spite of their ostensible agreement to collaborate in resisting the Japanese. Liao languished in KMT jails for nearly three years, completing his sentence in a Chungking prison. The Communists made frequent but futile efforts to secure his release[4] but were not successful until January 1946, a few days after the Communists and Nationalists signed the cease-fire agreement, which was worked out through mediation efforts of U.S. Special Envoy George C. Marshall. Meanwhile, at the CCP's Seventh National Congress held in Yenan from April to June 1945, Liao had been elected as the ranking alternate member of the Party Central Committee. Sources differ on the date of Liao's elevation to full membership on the Central Committee; some claim that this occurred following the death of Kuan Hsiang-ying in July 1946, and others place the date in early 1949 when the Party held its Second Plenum.

After Liao's release, he was assigned as a Communist member of the truce team seeking a settlement in the Kwangtung East River area, a team established under the terms of the above-mentioned cease-fire agreement. He also worked a portion of the year 1946 in Shanghai as an assistant to Chou En-lai, then the Communists' chief representative on the so-called Committee of Three (i.e., the representatives of the Communists, Nationalists, and Americans).[5] Liao spent the years from 1947 to 1949 as secretary of the Party's South China Bureau, presumably spending most of this time in Hong Kong where most of the CCP's activities for south China were centered during the latter stages of the civil war.

Soon after Peking was occupied by the Communists in January 1949, Liao was there, serving briefly as director of the New China News Agency. Then only 40, Liao played a major role in establishing China's two leading youth organizations, the New Democratic Youth League (NDYL) and the All-China Federation of Democratic Youth (ACFDY), both of which held their inaugural congresses in the spring. He was elected a member of the League's Central and Standing Committees, as well as ranking deputy secretary under Feng Wen-pin (q.v.), the top youth official in the early years of the PRC. His position as deputy secretary was redesignated simply as secretary in 1951, although he remained subordinate to Feng Wen-pin and then Hu Yao-pang, who replaced the purged Feng in 1952. Liao was also the League's International Liaison Department director from 1949 to about 1950, as well as president of the NDYL-sponsored Youth Art Theater from 1949 to about 1951. In the ACFDY, Liao was chairman from 1949 until he was succeeded by Liu Hsi-yuan (q.v.) in the spring of 1958. By the latter year Liao was also being phased out of the Youth League, having by then assumed far more important posts in the CCP and the central government. A nominal member of the League's Central Committee until the summer of 1964, his days as an important youth leader had by then long since passed. Even in the early years of the PRC, Liao's numerous other responsibilities precluded a very active role in youth affairs despite the apparent importance of his positions. Other youth leaders, particularly Feng Wen-pin, Hu Yao-pang, Chiang Nan-hsiang, and Li Ch'ang (qq.v.), were clearly more deeply involved in domestic youth questions, whereas Liao's major contributions were made in connection with the international relations of China's youth organizations. Thus, in the summer of 1949 he led a 123-member delegation to Hungary to attend the second congress of the World Federation of Democratic Youth (WFDY), the Communist-dominated organization to which the ACFDW is affiliated. Liao was elected in Budapest as one of the WFDY vice-chairmen, but it is not known how long he retained this position. He was abroad again in mid-1950, traveling to Prague to attend a congress of the International Union of Students, another Communist-dominated organization. In November of 1950 he was in Vienna for a WFDY meeting, and in the spring of 1951 he returned to Budapest for still another WFDY meeting. Already well-traveled in his youth, these trips between 1949 and 1951 were merely a prelude to Liao's peregrinations in the fifties and sixties.

Apart from his work with the youth organizations, Liao was also deeply involved in the creation of various "mass" organizations and the new central government in 1949. He became one of the vice-presidents of the Preparatory Committee established in July 1949 to bring the All-China Journalists' Association into existence; he did not remain with the organization, however, when it was permanently established in 1954. Also in July 1949 he was named to the Preparatory Committee of the Sino-Soviet Friendship Association, and when the Association was established three months later he became an Executive Board member; he was advanced to a vice-presidency in late 1954, a position he still retains. Liao's role in the establishment of the new government began in June 1949 when he was appointed to the Preparatory Committee headed by Mao Tse-tung for the convocation of the First CPPCC, an organization that first met in September. Attending the September meetings as an ACFDY representative, Liao spoke before the delegates on youth affairs and was elected a member of the CPPCC's First National Committee. Then in February 1953 he was added as a member of the Standing Committee, holding this post until the term of the First CPPCC ended in late 1954.

When the central government was formed in October 1949, Liao was named as a member of the Political and Legal Affairs Committee, one of the four major committees under the Government Administration Council (GAC; the cabinet). At the same time he was appointed a vice-chairman of the GAC's Overseas Chinese Affairs Commission, one of his principal assignments in the new government. Liao remained as a vice-chairman under his mother, Ho Hsiang-ning, until 1959, but as Ho was already over 70 in 1949 and not a CCP member, it is probable that her son was de facto head of the Commission. In the early and mid-fifties, Ho frequently appeared in public on ceremonial occasions, as when overseas Chinese visited the capital, but her son made most of the major policy statements involving overseas Chinese affairs. Finally, in April 1959, Liao succeeded his mother as the Commission chairman and continues to hold this cabinet post in the State Council. Because of Liao's many other duties, Commission Vice-chairman Fang Fang has assumed most of the day-to-day responsibilities involving overseas Chinese affairs, but it is probable that Liao remains the Party's top policy maker on overseas Chinese affairs.

Liao received still other assignments in the "mass" organizations in 1949. In December he was appointed to Board membership of the Chinese People's Institute of Foreign Affairs (see under Chang Hsi-jo, the chairman), a position he continues to hold. More important, in October he was appointed to Standing and National Committee membership, as well as a vice-chairmanship on the China Peace Committee; when the Committee was reorganized one year later, he was dropped from the latter post but retained the former two. Then, in May 1954, he reassumed his role as a vice-chairman (a post he still retains) and was also named to succeed Liu Ning-i (q.v.) as secretary-general, holding this post until mid-1958. The Peace Committee, particularly in the early years of the PRC, was among the most active of the "mass" organizations, and Liao has appeared at countless Committee-sponsored meetings and mass rallies, most of which have been directed against American "imperialism." However, as with the youth organizations, his major contributions have been as one of China's key spokesmen abroad. The China Peace Committee is affiliated with the World Peace Council (WPC), which, until the early sixties, was principally an arm of Moscow's Foreign Ministry, and as a consequence most of the WPC meetings of the forties and fifties were pervaded by an atmosphere of unanimity. Since about 1960, however, WPC meetings have usually deteriorated into forums in which Chinese and Soviet delegates denounce one another's policies. Liao has been a leading Chinese participant in both phases of the WPC's existence. In the "pro-Soviet" phase, he led or was among the leaders of Chinese delegations to WPC meetings in the following nations: Czechoslovakia, April 1949; Poland, November 1950; Austria, December 1952 and November–December 1953; East Germany, May 1954 and March–April 1957; Sweden, June and November 1954, July 1958, and May 1959; Finland, June 1955; Ceylon, June 1957; and the Soviet Union, February 1959. Liao was elected to WPC membership at the Warsaw meeting in 1950 and still retains this affiliation.

The predictably harmonious nature of pre-1960 WPC meetings stands in contrast to the stormy sessions held since then. Liao has participated in four such meetings, leading the Chinese delegation on each occasion to: Sweden, July 1960 and December 1961; India, March 1961; and Poland, November–December 1963. At all these meetings he engaged in verbal duels with his Soviet or Indian counterparts, both sides employing the strongest language. Typical was the 1963 meeting in Warsaw where Liao accused the Soviets of distorting the world "peace" movement and castigated them for their "intolerable utterance of cursing the national independence movement as a 'movement of corpses.'"

Prior to the breakdown of cordial Sino-Soviet relations, Liao was active in a wide variety of other foreign missions, many of them undertaken in close coordination with Soviet officialdom. From March to May 1951 he was in North Korea leading a 575-man delegation sent there to "comfort" the Chinese and Korean troops then locked in battle with South Korean and United Nations forces. In early 1952 the Communist bloc mounted a major propaganda campaign to convince the world the United States was employing bacteriological warfare in Korea. One part of this multi-faceted program was the dispatch to North Korea of a Chinese "investigation group on germ warfare crimes committed by United States imperialists," a group working in close coordination with a number of scientists, most of them from Communist nations. Liao was a deputy leader of this group sent to Korea in March–April 1952. In October of the same year, he was a delegate at the Asian and Pacific Regions Peace Conference held in Peking, a conference that devoted much time to the "germ warfare" charges (see under Liu Ning-i).

While these events were transpiring, Liao was adding to his already impressive list of positions in the various Party, government, and "mass" organizations. In early 1951 he was identified as a deputy director of the Party Central Committee's United Front Work Department, which, among its many other responsibilities, is in charge of overseas Chinese affairs for the CCP. Liao may still hold this important post, although he has not been so identified since early 1956. From 1952 to 1956 he was a Standing Committee member of the All-China Athletic Federation, and from 1952 to 1954 a member of the central

government's Labor Employment Committee, established to deal with problems of unemployment. In May 1954 he became a Standing Committee member of the Chinese People's Association for Cultural Relations with Foreign Countries, a position he still retains. One of the earliest steps leading to the establishment of the constitutional government was the formation in early 1953 of a committee to draft the new election law. After serving on this committee headed by Chou En-lai, Liao was elected an overseas Chinese deputy in 1954 to the First NPC. NPC representation is by provinces and cities, except for the armed forces and the overseas Chinese, special groups that are allowed to have their own delegates. At the inaugural session of the First NPC, held in September 1954, Liao was elected to the NPC Standing Committee. However, when he assumed his cabinet post as chairman of the Overseas Chinese Affairs Commission in 1959, he was dropped from the NPC Standing Committee in deference to the concept of the separation of powers that the PRC ostensibly follows. He continues, however, to be an overseas Chinese representative in the NPC, serving in the Second NPC (1959–1964) and again in the Third NPC, which opened in December 1964.

Liao's most important single contribution to the Chinese Communists probably lies in his work as Peking's principal liaison official vis-à-vis the Japanese, a role for which he is singularly suited by virtue of his fluency in Japanese and his many years in Japan as a student. Sino-Japanese relations were inhibited in the early years of the PRC, mainly because of the Allied occupation of Japan, which did not end until the spring of 1952, but also because of the fact that Japan maintains diplomatic relations with Taiwan. However, since the occupation ended the Chinese Communists have devoted much time and energy to influencing developments in Japan —efforts that have not been altogether successful from the Peking viewpoint. In virtually all these endeavors Liao has played a key role, a fact that is acknowledged by the many Japanese who have dealt with the Chinese since the early fifties. One of the principal unsettled postwar issues in Peking-Tokyo relations was the question of the thousands of Japanese nationals detained in China; many of these persons were regarded by the Chinese as "war criminals," but the majority of them were technicians pressed into service or simply persons caught on the mainland by the vicissitudes of war (particularly in Manchuria). The first major effort to settle this problem began in early 1953 when a Japanese group arrived in Peking to discuss the repatriation of their nationals. Liao led the Chinese side in these talks (mid-February to early March), which resulted in the repatriation of over 20,000 Japanese within the next six months and many more thousands during the next few years. Because of the lack of formal diplomatic ties between the two nations, Liao conducted the negotiations on behalf of the Chinese Red Cross Society to which he was an "adviser." In this capacity he visited Japan in October–November 1954, his first visit there since he had been deported 26 years earlier, accompanying a Red Cross delegation, ostensibly as an adviser, although from his stature in the CCP it was clear that he was the *de facto* leader. He was once more in Japan in December 1957–January 1958 with another Red Cross group, of which he was the deputy leader, although once again it was apparent that he was the actual leader. He has continued to maintain his close ties with Japanese public and private figures, and it is a rare occasion when an important visiting Japanese delegation in Peking does not come into contact with Liao, who, aside from acting as host for scores of Japanese groups, frequently serves as the interpreter when these delegations are received by such top Communists as Mao Tsetung or Chou En-lai.

Liao's role as Peking's leading "Japan expert" was well illustrated in the latter part of 1962 when he signed a memorandum with the late Takasaki Tatsunosuke, a very prominent Japanese political figure and a member of the Japanese Diet. The purpose of the Liao-Takasaki negotiations was to increase the level of Sino-Japanese trade, and in order to place this trade on a more formal basis, a "Liao Ch'eng-chih Office" and a counterpart Takasaki office were established. Still later, in 1964, both sides exchanged missions, the Chinese delegate in Tokyo being known as the "representative to the Tokyo Liaison Office of the Liao Ch'eng-chih Office." This had had the effect of giving each nation a diplomatic representative in the other's country. Both sides, however, scrupulously hold to the theory that these representatives are not formal government diplomats, the Japanese wanting to minimize the damage to their relations with Taiwan, and the Chinese Communists trying to avoid any appearance of accepting what they term the "two Chinas plot." In October 1963, less than a year after the signing of the Liao-Takasaki agreement, the Chinese established the China-Japan Friendship Association. Predictably, Liao was named as chairman.

The energies Liao has devoted to Sino-Japanese relations have been closely paralleled since the mid-fifties by the amount of time he has given to what might be termed the "Afro-Asian solidarity" movement. This began in April 1955 when he attended the Asian Countries Conference in New Delhi (see under Chu Tzu-ch'i). In response to decisions taken at this meeting, the participating countries formed Asian "solidarity" organizations, the Asian Solidarity Committee of China being formed in February 1956.

Liao became a vice-chairman and then in July 1958, shortly after the name was changed to the Afro-Asian Solidarity Committee, he was elected chairman, a position he still retains. Liao returned to India in April 1959 for a conference of the Afro-Asian Solidarity Committee of India, and exactly one year later he led the Chinese delegation to the Second Afro-Asian Solidarity Conference held in Conakry, Guinea. He was in the United Arab Republic in December 1961 to attend a meeting of the permanent organization of the "solidarity" movement, known as the Afro-Asian People's Solidarity Organization, and in May 1965 he led Peking's delegation to the Fourth Afro-Asian Solidarity Conference in Accra, Ghana. In general, the remarks above concerning the periodization of the World Peace Council meetings also apply to the Afro-Asian Solidarity Conferences, that is, prior to 1960 the meetings were essentially harmonious gatherings, but afterwards they tended to be forums for airing China's disputes with both the Soviet Union and India.

In addition to the numerous trips abroad already discussed, Liao has served on several other delegations of considerable importance. He attended Stalin's funeral in March 1953, and just over two years later he attended the historic Afro-Asian ("Bandung") Conference in Indonesia, in each case accompanying Chou En-lai. During the Bandung Conference Liao was present for the signing, and presumably took part in the negotiations, of the dual nationality treaty with Indonesia signed by Chou. The treaty, which spelled out the terms of citizenship for Chinese living in Indonesia, is discussed in the biography of Huang Chen, then Peking's ambassador in Jakarta. Liao returned to Southeast Asia over the winter of 1955–56 when he accompanied Mme. Sun Yat-sen on a goodwill tour of India, Burma, and Pakistan. In August–September 1960 he accompanied Li Fu-ch'un (q.v.) to Hanoi for the 15th anniversary celebrations of the North Vietnam Government and to attend the Third Vietnam Workers' (Communist) Party Congress. Shortly thereafter, in November–December, he was a member of Liu Shaoch'i's delegation to the 43rd anniversary celebrations of the Russian Revolution, and while in Moscow probably took part in the "summit" meeting of Communist parties from all over the world, a meeting that stands as a landmark in the deterioration of Sino-Soviet relations. Liao was in Italy in November–December 1964 leading a China Peace Committee delegation; his group succeeded in gaining permission for the opening in Rome of a quasi-official Chinese trade office (see under Lei Jen-min). Liao's impressive record of travels abroad since the establishment of the PRC is matched by few other leading Party officials. His travels in the period from 1949 to 1965 have taken him on 38 missions to 20 different nations in Asia, Africa, and Europe.

In the late fifties and early sixties Liao continued to add new positions to the large number he already holds. Perhaps the most important of these is a deputy directorship of the State Council's Office of Foreign Affairs, established in March 1958 under Foreign Minister Ch'en I. The Office is charged with the responsibility for coordinating the work of the various government commissions, ministries, and bureaus involved in international relations, and doubtless also coordinates its work with the many "mass" organizations concerned with foreign affairs. Liao's extremely varied background makes him peculiarly suited for this assignment. In 1960 and 1963 he received two *ad hoc* assignments that also reflect his background and experience in overseas Chinese affairs. In February 1960 the Chinese established a special committee to "receive and resettle" overseas Chinese who were then returning from Indonesia in large numbers because of practices by the Indonesian authorities regarded as discriminatory; and in April 1963, under very similar circumstances, another committee was set up to handle Chinese returning from India as a result of the Sino-Indian border war in late 1962. In both cases Liao was named as the committee chairman. He received a related post in January 1961 when he was appointed president of the Overseas Chinese University. The university, established in 1960, is located in Ch'üan-chou, Fukien, an area heavily populated by overseas Chinese families; because Liao is almost always in Peking (if not abroad), it is doubtful that he devotes much time to this position. Finally, upon the establishment of the China-Africa People's Friendship Association in April 1960, he was named to Standing Committee membership. In addition to these formal positions, Liao has also been among the more active participants in negotiations with visiting Communists from abroad, work that brings him into regular contact with such Party leaders as Liu Shao-ch'i, Teng Hsiao-p'ing, Liu Ning-i, and Wu Hsiu-ch'üan. He presumably brings to these talks a wide knowledge of leftist organizations throughout the Afro-Asian world, where he has had extensive contacts.

The extraordinary range of Liao's activities places him before the Chinese public and newspaper readers with a frequency equaled by few others. Although impossible to document, it is probable that he has conferred with more important visitors in China than any other single CCP leader—including Chou En-lai and Ch'en I, the two men most noted for their wide contacts with foreigners. Liao has probably not reached the highest policy levels, but he is clearly among the most important persons just below this echelon. As suggested by his career, he is probably most closely linked with Chou and Ch'en among China's top leaders.

Liao's value to the Chinese Communists is enhanced by the stature of his family in modern Chinese history. His famed father is considered a martyr to leftist causes, and continuity to the PRC is provided by Liao's mother, who married Liao Chung-k'ai in 1897. Like her husband, Ho Hsiang-ning was extremely close to Sun Yat-sen and was among the first women to join Sun's T'ung-meng hui. She even has early links with Mao Tse-tung, having taught at the Peasant Movement Training Institute in Canton when Mao was the director in 1926. A native of Kwangtung where she was born in 1877, she runs a close second to Mme. Sun Yat-sen as the most respected and honored woman in Communist China. And even more than Mme. Sun, she personifies the links to China's immediate revolutionary past, a fact well illustrated by noting that she has shared with Mme. Sun the honorary chairmanship of the National Women's Federation since its establishment in 1949. Ho's ties with the past are also demonstrated by her association with the Kuomintang Revolutionary Committee (KMTRC), of which she was one of the founders in 1948. Since 1960 she has been chairman of the KMTRC, one of the eight non-Communist political parties in China. She has held numerous positions in the PRC government and "mass" organizations, but because of her advanced age it is doubtful whether she has been very active in other than protocol functions. Probably her most important post was as chairman of the central government's Overseas Chinese Affairs Commission (1949–1959), but as explained above, her son has undertaken the major burdens of this office.

Liao's sister, Meng-hsing, has had in many respects a career paralleling her mother's, although she is not nearly so well known. Five years older than her brother, she was well known to Westerners during the thirties and forties, when she was known by the name Cynthia Liao. Her contacts with Westerners were made mainly through Mme. Sun Yat-sen, for whom she was a personal secretary for many years. She too was born and partially educated in Japan, and she also has a claim to martyrdom, her husband having been executed by the Nationalists in Chungking in October 1945. Liao Meng-hsing has been a member of the Executive Committee of the Women's Federation since its establishment in 1949, and since 1954 she has served as a Kwangtung deputy to the NPC.

In private life Liao is married to Ching P'u-ch'un, the daughter of Ching Heng-i, an educator of some prominence during the May Fourth Movement (1919) and a member of the KMT Central Executive Committee in the twenties and thirties. The Liaos had three children by 1947, a nine-year old girl, a six-year old boy, and an infant daughter. Except for an occasional public appearance with her husband, Ching P'u-ch'un is not politically active.

1. Nym Wales, *Red Dust* (Stanford, Calif., 1952), pp. 25–34.
2. *SCMM* 281, p. 6; Edgar Snow, *Random Notes on Red China, 1936–1945* (Cambridge, Mass., 1957), p. 93.
3. Chün-tu Hsüeh, *The Chinese Communist Movement, 1937–1949* (Stanford, Calif., 1962), pp. 24, 78, 80, 146.
4. *China Handbook, 1937–1945* (New York, 1947), p. 92.
5. U.S. Department of State, *United States Relations with China* (Washington, D.C., 1949), p. 657.

Liao Chih-kao

(c.1908–   ; Ch'ien-ning hsien, Szechwan).
First secretary, Szechwan CCP Committee;
alternate member, CCP Central Committee.

Liao Chih-kao was probably born about 1908, although Japanese sources use approximately 1915 as a date of birth. He hails from Ch'ien-ning hsien in present-day Szechwan. Ch'ien-ning was under the jurisdiction of Sikang, the defunct province that existed from 1928 to 1955. It lies about 60 miles southwest of Mao-kung where in June 1935 the Long March forces led by Mao Tse-tung and Chu Te joined with the Fourth Front Army led by Chang Kuo-t'ao and Hsu Hsiang-ch'ien. It is possible (though speculative) that Liao's first contact with the Communists occurred at this time. Nothing further is known of his younger days apart from a Japanese report that he graduated from Tsinghua University in Peking.

Liao apparently spent the period of the Sino-Japanese War in the northwest. In any event, he was in Yenan in March 1947 when Nationalist forces began their successful assault on the Communist capital. In evacuating Yenan, the top Communist leadership divided into two groups, one led by Liu Shao-ch'i and Chu Te and the other by Mao Tse-tung and Chou En-lai. Liao joined the latter, serving as head of the Political Department of a small detachment.[1] By about 1949 he presumably joined the Second Field Army of Liu Po-ch'eng, the force that conquered southwest China in the latter half of that year. In the closing days of 1949 and early 1950, Sikang fell with little resistance to the Communist troops. The PLA marched into Ya-an, the provincial capital, on February 1, 1950. Liao was named as chairman of the Ya-an Military Control Commission, and when the provincial government was formed in the next month, he was named as the governor. At the same time he assumed the other two posts of significance within the province when he became the ranking secretary of the provincial Party Committee and political commissar of the Sikang Military District. Liao continued to hold all three posts during the five years that the province existed under the Communists, thereby remaining the dominant figure there for that period. The other post of significance that he held was as chairman (from October 1950) of the provincial government's Finance and Economics Committee.

Liao was also a participant in the multi-provincial Southwest Military and Administrative Committee (SWMAC), established in Chungking in July 1950 under the chairmanship of veteran military leader Liu Po-ch'eng. Liao was named to membership on the SWMAC; he retained his membership in February 1953 when the SWMAC was reorganized into the Southwest Administrative Committee and continued to hold this position until the Committee was abolished in November 1954.

In 1954 he was elected as a Sikang deputy to the First NPC, which brought the constitutional government into existence at its first session in September 1954. At the close of this session he was also named to the permanent Nationalities Committee of the NPC, the committee with legislative responsibilities in connection with China's millions of national minorities (many of whom live in and around Liao's native area). By the time the Second NPC was formed in 1959, Sikang had been absorbed by Szechwan, and Liao was therefore a deputy to the Second NPC (1959–1964) from Szechwan, serving once again on the Nationalities Committee. When the Third NPC was formed in late 1964, he again was selected as a deputy from Szechwan, and at the first session of the Third NPC (December 1964–January 1965) he served on the *ad hoc* Credentials Committee. However, possibly owing to heavier responsibilities in Szechwan (see below), he was not reappointed to the permanent Nationalities Committee.

In July 1955 the central government decided to abolish Sikang. This was formally carried out on October 1, 1955, with the eastern portion of the province (including Liao's native area) incorporated into Szechwan. Almost immediately afterward (December 1955), Liao was elected a member of the Szechwan Provincial People's Council, a position that placed him under Governor Li Ta-chang (q.v.). And within a year (November 1956), he was identified as a secretary of the provincial Party Committee, serving here under First Secretary Li Ching-ch'üan, who became a Politburo member in 1958. From October 1956 Liao has also been a vice-chairman of the Szechwan committee of the quasi-legislative CPPCC. Thus, from the mid-1950's, the two Li's and Liao have been the dominant figures in Szechwan, China's most populous province. With the abolition of Sikang, Liao moved to Chengtu, the Szechwan capital and has been a very active figure there since that time.

At the second session of the Eighth Party Congress in May 1958 Liao was elected an alternate member of the Party Central Committee. In 1958–59 he apparently played an active role in the early stages of the Great Leap Forward and the commune movement. He served, for example, as a deputy leader of a special delegation organized in August 1958 to inspect industrial and agricultural production in Szechwan. Similarly, in January 1959, he led a Party group that conducted a province-wide inspection of the communes. In January 1961, the Ninth Party Plenum re-established the regional Party bureaus. By February 1965 Liao had reached a new plateau in his career when he was identified as a secretary of the Southwest Party Bureau, serving under First Secretary Li Ching-ch'üan. Three months later Liao replaced Li as the Szechwan first secretary (presumably to allow Li more time to devote to the multi-provincial regional bureau).

1. *Hung-ch'i p'iao-p'iao* (Red flag fluttering; Peking, 1957), I, 348.

Liao Han-sheng

(1910–   ; Li-ling hsien, Hunan). Vice-minister of National Defense; alternate member, CCP Central Committee.

Liao Han-sheng is a career Red Army officer. He was a political officer during the Long March, the Sino-Japanese War, and the conquest of the northwest in the late 1940's. In the early years of the PRC he was a senior military-political figure in Tsinghai province, and since 1954 he has been a vice-minister of National Defense. Liao was elected an alternate member of the Party Central Committee in 1956.

Liao was born in Li-ling hsien, also the native hsien of such prominent Communists as Li Li-san and Tso Ch'üan (qq.v.). In 1929, when he was only 19, Liao joined Ho Lung's (q.v.) Red guerrillas in northwest Hunan on the Hupeh border, and for the next 20 years served under Ho's command. Ho's army made its Long March to the northwest in 1935–36, a year later than the main Communist forces commanded by Mao Tse-tung, which reached north Shensi in the fall of 1935. From at least the summer of 1934 through the Long March Liao served as a divisional political commissar in Ho's forces.

When the Sino-Japanese War broke out in mid-1937, Liao was made political commissar of the 716th Regiment in Ho Lung's 120th Division, one of the three divisions in the Communists' Eighth Route Army. In the early fall of 1937 the 120th Division moved into north-west Shansi to the west of the rail line running between Ta-t'ung and Taiyuan. In an attempt to stop the advancing Japanese armies, Liao's regiment fought a delaying action at the important Yen-men Pass in north Shansi, a battle that has been described by Ho Ping-yen, the commander of the 716th Regiment.[1] Little is known about Liao's activities during the remaining war years, but he apparently remained in the Shansi-Suiyuan border area.

In the postwar years Liao continued to serve as a political officer. He was political commissar of the Northwest PLA's First Column in 1947 and he held the same post in the Second Army Group in 1949. In the latter part of 1949 Ho Lung led some of his forces into the southwest. However, Liao remained with P'eng Te-huai's First Field Army, which controlled the northwest (and which had absorbed many of the units formerly under Ho Lung's command). In the early fall of 1949 Liao was with the forces that captured Tsinghai province. In late September the Communists established the short-lived body known as the Tsinghai People's Military and Administrative Committee, with Liao as the chairman. The Committee was apparently dissolved when the Tsinghai Provincial People's Government was established on January 1, 1950, at which time Liao became a vice-governor, ostensibly subordinate to Governor Chao Shou-shan, a former KMT general. Also at the time of the takeover, the Tsinghai Military District was established (October 1, 1949); Liao was appointed as the political commissar (although he was replaced by Chang Chung-liang in 1950). These assignments gave Liao a degree of authority in the province that was probably equaled only by Chang Chung-liang (q.v.), the Party secretary for the province from 1949 to 1954. In addition, Liao was chairman of the People's Supervision Committee in the Tsinghai government from 1950.

Liao also served in the regional administration to which Tsinghai belonged, the Northwest Military and Administrative Committee (NWMAC, called the Northwest Administrative Committee [NWAC] after early 1953). He was a member of the NWMAC from 1950 to 1953 and was reappointed in 1953 to the NWAC, serving there until regional administrations were abolished in 1954. From 1953 to 1954 he was concurrently director of the Political Departments for the Northwest Military Region and the First Field Army. In the spring of 1954 he was promoted to the post of deputy political commissar of the Northwest Military Region.

Liao was a PLA deputy to the First NPC (1954–1959), and although not elected to the Second Congress (1959–1964) he was returned to the Third NPC, which opened in December 1964 as a deputy from the PLA Headquarters in Peking. At the first session of the First NPC in September 1954, when the constitutional government was inaugurated, he was appointed a member of the newly established National Defense Council, a post he still holds. Far more important was his appointment in the following month as a vice-minister of the National Defense Ministry. He was then only 44 and the youngest of the seven vice-ministers. Moreover, since the establishment of the Defense Ministry at that time 12 men have been vice-ministers, but only three of them have served continuously from then until the mid-1960's: Hsiao Ching-kuang, Wang Shu-sheng (qq.v.), and Liao. In September 1955, when personal military titles were created for the first time, Liao was made a lieutenant-general, the equivalent of major-general in the U.S. Army. He was ranked below his fellow vice-ministers of National Defense, four of whom were made senior generals and two others colonel generals. At the same time Liao was among the recipients of the first national military decorations, but the awards he received were not specified.

When the CCP met for its Eighth National Congress in September 1956, Liao was elected an alternate member of the Central Committee. In 1957 he succeeded military veteran Liu Po-ch'eng (q.v.) as head of the Nanking Military Academy, Peking's equivalent to a Western command and staff college. While holding this post he represented Defense Minister P'eng Te-huai at a ceremony in Nanking in February 1958 to confer PLA titles upon 159 former Nationalist officers who had surrendered the city to the Communists nine years before.

By the spring of 1960 Liao had been transferred to Peking, suggesting that he had relinquished his Academy post in Nanking. As of 1962 he was identified only as "head of army units stationed in Peking." In July 1963 he was "political commissar of the PLA units in Peking." Thus, he is apparently an important military commander in the Peking area, though his exact role there is not certain. In February 1965 Liao was identified as a secretary of the North China Party Bureau, which is headed by Li Hsueh-feng (q.v.).

1. *CB* 777, pp. 1–5.

Liao Lu-yen

(c.1908–   ; Kiangsu). Minister of Agriculture; alternate member, CCP Central Committee.

Liao Lu-yen, the minister of Agriculture since 1954, was elected an alternate member of the Party Central Committee in 1956. He was probably born about 1908, but some sources date his birthyear a decade earlier. Although Liao was holding very important positions by the mid-1950's, there is very little information available on his career prior to the establishment of the

PRC in 1949. He is known to have been in a KMT jail in Peking in the mid-thirties, and afterwards he worked for the Party's North China Bureau. Nothing further is known about Liao until the formation of the central government in the fall of 1949 at which time he was serving as secretary-general of the Party's Policy Research Office. Within less than a year (by August 1950) he was the deputy director of the Research Office, but he apparently relinquished the post in the early 1950's in favor of more important positions. Liao's initial assignment in the government came in December 1949 when he was appointed as the only deputy director of the Councillors' Office, an advisory body subordinate to the Government Administration Council (the cabinet). When non-Communist Kuo Ch'un-t'ao, the titular Office director, died in June 1950, Liao was named to replace him (September 1950). He remained in this post until August 1952, at which time he was transferred to become a deputy secretary-general of the Government Administration Council (GAC), serving under Li Wei-han until September 1953 and thereafter under Hsi Chung-hsun. Concurrently, Liao served as secretary-general of the Labor Employment Committee of the GAC from its establishment in July 1952, another position in which he served under Li Wei-han. Liao held both these government posts until the constitutional government came into being in September 1954.

By the summer of 1950 there was already evidence that Liao was specializing in agricultural affairs. In August of that year he spoke on land reform questions before a rural youth conference sponsored by the New Democratic Youth League. Not long afterward he wrote an article entitled "Rural Class Status and Land Reform," which appeared as a supplement to the October 16, 1950, issue of the English-language *People's China*. The article dealt with the Land Reform Law, which had been adopted in June 1950, and with the decisions taken to implement the law. Liao discussed earlier decisions that had been adopted by the Chinese Soviet Republic in Juichin in 1933 and re-issued in May 1948 by the Party Central Committee. According to Liao, they "played an important role in correcting 'leftist' deviations and in successfully concluding the land reform in the old liberated areas in the spring of 1948." By October 1953 Liao was serving as a deputy director of the highly important CCP Rural Work Department, clearly an indication of his rising importance in the field of agricultural policy. This department, charged with implementing Party policy in the field of agriculture, has been headed by Party veteran Teng Tzu-hui from 1953.

In 1954 Liao was elected as a deputy from Kiangsu to the First NPC (1954–1959), although he was not re-elected four years later.

When the first session of the NPC was held in September 1954, at which time the constitutional government was inaugurated, Liao was named as the minister of Agriculture, a position he still retains. He replaced the elderly Li Shu-ch'eng, a non-Communist who had participated in the 1911 Revolution and who died in 1965. Among the numerous changes made in the government structure in the fall of 1954 was the creation of eight staff offices under the State Council, offices charged with the task of coordinating the work of several governmental ministries and bureaus. A year later, in November 1955, Liao was named as a deputy director of the Seventh Staff Office (redesignated the Agriculture and Forestry Office in September 1959). Liao initially served in this position under Teng Tzu-hui, and under Politburo member T'an Chen-lin after November 1962. Thus, by 1955, Liao held three critical posts in the government and Party related to agricultural affairs.

Between 1955 and 1960 Liao received several new appointments, the most important occurring in September 1956 when he was elected an alternate member of the Party Central Committee at the Eighth National Congress. The other posts include: member of an *ad hoc* committee to collect signatures against the use of atomic weapons, February 1955; member of the National Association for the Elimination of Illiteracy, March 1956—presumably to date; member of the State Council's Scientific Planning Commission, May 1957 to November 1958; member of the Central Relief Committee of the State Council, July 1957—possibly to date; vice-chairman of the State Council's Spare-Time Education Committee, January 1960 to date. In addition, when the Third National Committee of the CPPCC was formed in April 1959, Liao was named as a representative of the "peasants," a position to which he was again elected when the Fourth National Committee was formed at the end of 1964.

Since becoming minister of Agriculture in 1954, Liao has been abroad on four occasions (three of them related to agricultural affairs) and has signed three agreements with Communist bloc nations dealing with technology and agriculture. In November 1954 he accompanied Ulanfu to Mongolia for the 12th Congress of the Mongolian People's Revolutionary (Communist) Party. He spent almost two months in Yugoslavia, Bulgaria, and the USSR in mid-1957 as head of a seven-member agricultural delegation; he also led agricultural delegations to Korea for two weeks in January 1959 and to Mongolia in December 1959, in both cases attending congresses dealing with agricultural affairs. The three agreements Liao signed were with the Albanians, the Hungarians, and the East Germans, signed in Peking on October 14, 1954, December 28, 1954, and December 25, 1955, respectively. Also since the mid-1950's, Liao has been frequently in attendance to receive visitors to Peking, particularly those having some connection with agriculture.

With his many responsibilities in a field of great concern to the present government, Liao has often been reported in the national press. In the mid-1950's in particular he delivered a number of key agricultural reports, probably the most important being a speech before a Party Central Committee-sponsored conference of intelligentsia in January 1956, which dealt with the Draft 1956–1967 National Program for Agricultural Development. The frequency and importance of Liao's reporting before official and semi-official conferences in the mid-1950's suggested that he was not only a Party spokesman, but also an important person in the formulation of agricultural policy. However, with the inauguration of the Great Leap Forward and the communes in 1958, Liao seems to have played a somewhat less important role. Since that time, other men (particularly Politburo member T'an Chen-lin) have played a more important role than Liao.

Liao has written frequently for technical and Party journals, always on the subject of agriculture. In addition to the 1950 article mentioned above, he has written for the following publications: *Sen-lin kung-yeh t'ung-hsun* (Forestry industry bulletin), August 18, 1955; *Hsueh-hsi* (Study), February 3, 1958; *Hung-ch'i* (Red flag), January 1, 1959 September 1, 1960, and February 1, 1961; and the *JMJP,* September 26, 1959. One of his most interesting articles was written for the October 1963 issue of the Havana publication *Cuba Socialista* and reprinted in *Peking Review* (November 1, 1963). In this he made the rather startling revelation that there were over 70,000 communes, a figure nearly three times the past "official" figures.

Lin Feng

(1906–   ; Wang-k'uei hsien, Heilungkiang). Vice-chairman, NPC Standing Committee; president, Higher Party School; member, CCP Central Committee.

Lin Feng is one of the most important leaders of the Party elite, whose work has brought him into extremely close contact with the top members of the Politburo. A veteran of the Party organization in north China in the thirties and forties, Lin has been a member of the Party Central Committee since 1945. He was formerly a senior leader in Manchuria (1945–1954) where he came into conflict with Soviet officials and probably also Kao Kang, the Politburo member who was purged in 1955. Since Lin's transfer to Peking in 1954 he has specialized in cultural and education affairs and is today head of the important Higher Party School.

Lin was born in Wang-k'uei hsien, about 70 miles north of Harbin in Heilungkiang province. Although he joined the CCP in 1927, relatively little is known of his younger days. He is said to have studied political economy at Peking University and to have been a student at Waseda University in in Tokyo (although a usually reliable Japanese Who's Who does not indicate that he studied in Japan). Another source claims that he was educated at Nankai University in Tientsin. Lin is also said to have studied in Moscow at the Far Eastern University.[1] He apparently spent most of the thirties in north China where he held at various times the following CCP positions: secretary, Peking Committee; secretary, Tientsin Committee; deputy secretary, Shansi Committee; director, Organization Department, North China Bureau; and secretary, Southwest Shansi Committee. From these fragmentary details, it is probable that during these years he became acquainted with such top Communist leaders as Liu Shao-ch'i, P'eng Chen, Po I-po, and Huang Ching (qq.v.). And, like most prominent north China leaders, much of his work for the Party must have been as an underground operative. It is also probable that he was in contact with the participants in the December Ninth Movement, which began in Peking on December 9, 1935, among middle school and university students in protest against Japanese incursions into north China (see under Li Ch'ang). This assumption is based on the fact that Lin's wife, Kuo Ming-ch'iu (see below), was one of the December Ninth leaders. Many students involved in the movement later joined the CCP.

Most of Lin's early work was with the Party apparatus, but in the early years of the Sino-Japanese War he served as a political officer in Ho Lung's 120th Division which moved into northwest Shansi in the fall of 1937. For at least a brief time in late 1939 and early 1940, he was political commissar of a detachment which fought against units of Shansi warlord Yen Hsi-shan.[2] This situation of Chinese opposing Chinese arose because of a revolt within Yen's army led by KMT member Hsu Fan-t'ing, who, with the cooperation of Communists within his units, had led his men over to the Communist side (see under Lo Kuei-po). This defection to the Communists coincided with the formation of the Shansi-Suiyuan Liberated Region. In early 1940, prior to the creation of the Region, the CCP convened the All-Northwest Military-Political-People's Representative Congress at Hsing-hsien, Shansi, near the Yellow River. The Congress established an executive organ of government, known at first as the Northwest Shansi Administrative Office and later as the Shansi-Suiyuan Border Region Administrative Office. At a meeting held in October 1941, Lin attended as a deputy from the West Shansi CCP Commit-

tee (of which he was the secretary). His proposal to establish a provisional assembly was adopted, and to effect this a preparatory committee was established, with Lin as one of the members. One year later (October 1942), the Northwest Shansi Provisional Assembly met and elected officials to both the executive organ (the Northwest Shansi Administrative Office) and to the Provisional Assembly. At this time, because the Communists were still ostensibly carrying out the policies of a united front, a number of non-Communists were elected to nominally high posts. Thus, Hsu Fan-t'ing became the head of the Administrative Office. In the legislative assembly, however, Lin was named as the chairman and was clearly the dominant figure in that body.[3] By this same time (1942) and until the war ended in 1945, Lin was also secretary of the Shansi-Suiyuan Sub-bureau of the CCP as well as political commissar for the Shansi-Suiyuan Military Region, which was commanded by Lü Cheng-ts'ao (q.v.).

In 1944 Lin gave a lengthy statement on Party work in the Shansi-Suiyuan area to correspondent Israel Epstein, then reporting on China for American newspapers and magazines.[4] Lin, characterized by Epstein as the "dour, thick-set Manchurian," emphasized the role of the Party in the war against Japan. He described the three basic tasks of resisting Japan as "military struggle, war production and cultural advance." According to Lin, the "last two are as important as the first because their success makes it impossible for the Japanese to smash us economically or to poison our minds."

Lin's work in north China received recognition at the Party's Seventh National Congress held in Yenan from April to June 1945 when he was elected a member of the Party Central Committee. His election was especially noteworthy because he was one of the few among the 44 full members elected who had not participated in the central Kiangsi Soviet nor the Long March. When the war against Japan ended in the summer of 1945, the Communists dispatched to Manchuria large numbers of troops and cadres, as well as such top leaders as Lin Piao, Kao Kang, Ch'en Yun, and P'eng Chen. Lin accompanied this group and soon assumed a number of important positions in the military, governmental, and Party hierarchies that controlled those portions of Manchuria under Communist control (mainly in the countryside). From 1945 until his transfer to Peking in 1954 (see below), Lin was a member of the Northeast Party Bureau's Standing Committee, serving under Secretaries P'eng Chen, Lin Piao, and Kao Kang. By 1946 he concurrently headed the Bureau's Propaganda Department (until about 1949), and for a brief period in 1946 he was also director of the Bureau's Organization Department; P'eng Chen replaced Lin in the latter post in

1946. At approximately this same period he was also political commissar of the Liaoning-Kirin Military Region, an assignment that put him in association with Chou Pao-chung (q.v.), who had been in Manchuria fighting in the resistance movement against the Japanese since 1931. In 1946 the Communists also established their governmental apparatus for Manchuria, known as the Northeast Administrative Committee. Lin was the chairman of this body and held the post until the Committee was reorganized into the Northeast People's Government in 1949 (see below).

In the immediate postwar period there were also Soviet armies and administrators in Manchuria. Within less than a year of his arrival in Manchuria, Lin apparently came into conflict with Soviet officials. In a rare revelation of the personal factors involved in the Sino-Soviet disagreements about the area, the Russians have subsequently charged that a group led by P'eng Chen and Lin "intentionally distorted the role of the Soviet Army [in Manchuria] and disseminated slander against the USSR." The Russians further claimed that instances of "anti-Soviet statements" in the "higher echelons" of the CCP became "so open" that the CCP Central Committee (apparently as a result of Soviet pressure) "was forced to condemn the 'mistakes'" of P'eng's and Lin's group. "But this decision," the Russian charges continued, "was not made known to Party organs. It was only in 1949, when similar cases occurred," that the CCP's Northeast Bureau reviewed the situation. The Soviets complained that even then only a "formal condemnation" was made against the nationalistic and "anti-Soviet tendencies espoused by the [P'eng-Lin] group." These Soviet charges, made in 1964 as part of the Sino-Soviet polemics, concluded: "Now [1964] there is no longer any doubt that nationalist and great-power ideas had long ago crept into the minds of the leadership of the CCP, and the bearers of those ideas were simply waiting for the proper (in their opinion) time for stating them openly."[5] Viewed from the vantage point of the mid-sixties, both P'eng and Lin could (in the Chinese view) take pride in their apparent early hostility to the Soviet Union; if anything, it may have elevated them in the eyes of the Maoist leadership. Even considering their careers up to the late forties, there is little to suggest that either P'eng or Lin suffered politically as a result of the Russian criticisms. Both men were already key leaders and both rose steadily through the forties and fifties —in periods prior to the open Sino-Soviet polemics of the sixties. Inferentially, these strong statements by the Soviets add credence to the widely held notion that Kao Kang (q.v.), the Northeast Bureau Party secretary from 1949 until his purge in 1954–55, might have sided with the USSR against the P'eng-Lin "group."

(See under Kao Kang for his allegedly "pro-Soviet" views during this period.)

In the late forties Lin also participated in the programs to push land reform. In late 1947, in his capacity as chairman of the Northeast Administrative Committee, he delivered a report on the "land law" and as late as December 1949 he and Kao Kang presided over a meeting of hsien officials to discuss rural work problems.[6] He also participated in united front work as the CCP attempted to gain support of non-Communists working in the Manchurian cities. For example, when a large group of Chinese "democratic persons" (i.e., non-Communists) visited Manchuria in mid-1949, Lin held talks with the group and described to them the developments in Manchuria under the Communists. By early 1951 he was identified as director of the Northeast Party Bureau's United Front Work Department.

When the major city of Mukden (Shenyang) was captured from the Nationalists in November 1948, Lin was named to membership on the Municipal Military Control Commission. In the same year he also became an Executive Committee member of the Northeast Sino-Soviet Friendship Association (SSFA)—an ironic assignment in view of the Soviet complaints about Lin described above. (By 1952 he was vice-chairman of the Northeast SSFA Branch.) In August 1949 the Northeast Administrative Committee (NEAC), which Lin had headed, was reorganized into the Northeast People's Government (NEPG). Kao Kang was named as the new chairman, in effect replacing Lin, who was lowered to a vice-chairmanship. Kao also assumed the chairmanship of the NEPG's Finance and Economics Committee, with Lin serving as one of his vice-chairmen (a post he held until 1952). In light of later developments, an even more significant assignment for Lin was his chairmanship in 1949–50 of the NEPG's People's Supervision Committee, the watchdog organization within the governmental apparatus. Lin was removed from this post in May 1950, at which time three men were named to leadership posts on the Supervision Committee: Chairman Chang Hsiu-shan and Vice-chairmen Chang Ming-yuan and Ch'en Po-ts'un. The dénouement did not come until 1955 when, during the purge of Kao Kang and Jao Shu-shih, all three of these men were implicated and purged as protégés of Kao Kang. (See under Kao Kang for brief sketches of his "accomplices.") Thus, although documentation is not available, it appears that Kao Kang was able to remove Lin from a critical post and replace him with his own men.

The year 1949 also witnessed Lin's entrance into the field of education, an activity in which he was to be heavily engaged in the fifties and sixties (see below). The 1949 assignment was the chairmanship of the Northeast Higher Education Committee, an organ presumably subordinate to the NEPG and one charged with setting basic policy in higher education. Although he did not attend the first session of the CPPCC in September 1949 when the new national government was established, he was elected to the CPPCC's First National Committee (1949–1954). More important, Lin was named to membership on the Central People's Government Council (CPGC), the most important organ of the national government (chaired by Mao Tse-tung). Many of the 56 CPGC members worked in the provinces and did not regularly attend the 34 CPGC meetings held between 1949 and 1954; Lin, however, frequently came from Mukden to Peking for these meetings. For example, at the 17th meeting held in August 1952, he delivered a report on the situation in the northeast.

One of Lin's first assignments in Manchuria after the establishment of the PRC was to manage the takeover of properties that Soviet economic agencies had acquired from the Japanese at the end of World War II. The provisions for the Chinese takeover were made in February 1950 when Mao Tse-tung and Chou En-lai negotiated several key agreements with the Russians, including the Sino-Soviet Treaty of Friendship, Alliance, and Mutual Assistance. Thus, when the Sino-Soviet Properties Transfer Commission was established in July 1950, Lin was named as the ranking Chinese member; the two other Chinese were Wang Ho-shou (q.v.) and Chu Ch'i-wen (then the Mukden mayor). The Transfer Commission held three meetings between July 8 and August 7, 1950, after which concrete measures were established to transfer the properties. A final agreement was signed on August 28 that spelled out the actions taken; a total of 302 items of property were transferred (including 47 factories and 33 warehouses), mostly in Manchuria, but some of them also in Peking.[7]

In the period from the end of 1948 to the first part of 1950, a number of the top CCP leaders working in Manchuria had been transferred to China proper—either as leaders of the PLA (for example, Lin Piao) or as Party leaders who were transferred to Peking to assume jobs there (for example, Ch'en Yun). The last of these transfers of major personnel was in April 1950 when Li Fu-ch'un moved to Peking to head the Ministry of Heavy Industry. (Li nominally continued to hold positions in the northeast until 1952, but his work in Peking and his extended negotiations with the Russians in Moscow removed him from active work in Manchuria). These transfers had the effect of making Lin the second ranking CCP leader in the northeast, although he was far overshadowed by Kao Kang. Not only was Kao a Politburo member, but he was also the ranking Party secretary, the head of the NEPG, and the commander and political commissar of the

Northeast Military Region. This situation prevailed until the winter of 1952–53 when Kao was transferred to Peking, but by that time (from at least November 1952) Lin had become the First Deputy Secretary of the Northeast Bureau (the second-ranking post in the Bureau). It was also in January 1953 that the NEPG was reorganized into the Northeast Administrative Committee (not to be confused with the earlier NEAC, which had existed from 1946 to 1949). Lin was appointed as a vice-chairman, but because Chairman Kao Kang was by then working in Peking, Lin was effectively in charge of both the government and Party apparatus in Manchuria, remaining there until his transfer to Peking in mid-1954. If the charges against Kao Kang are to be believed, Lin was practically the only leader of significance in Manchuria who was not in league with Kao. When the charges against Kao were made public in 1955, it was revealed that the following posts in the Northeast Bureau were held by Kao's colleagues: the second and third deputy secretaries; the secretary-general and deputy secretaries-general; the director and deputy director of the Organization Department; and the head of the Rural Work Department. The fact that Lin rose so fast in the national bureaucracy from the mid-fifties may well derive from his loyalty to the Maoist leadership in opposition to Kao. (See under Kao Kang for the complete details.)

One of the earliest steps leading toward the establishment of the constitutional government was the formation in January 1953 of a committee to draft the constitution. Chaired by Mao Tse-tung, most of the members were working in Peking, but a few (e.g., Lin) were from the outlying regions. In the following year Lin was elected as a deputy from Mukden to the First NPC (1954–1959). At the close of the first session of the First NPC in September 1954 he was named to the NPC Standing Committee, the governing body for the legislature when the full NPC is not in session. When the Second NPC was formed in April 1959, he was elevated to a vice-chairmanship of the NPC Standing Committee and was re-elected a vice-chairman of the Third NPC, which held its first session in December 1964–January 1965. He was a deputy from Mukden to the First NPC and was elected from Heilungkiang province to the Second and Third NPC's. Unlike many senior leaders who have only *pro forma* associations with the NPC, Lin has been an active participant, as evidenced by the fact that he has served on the presidium (steering committee) for all but one of the 10 annual NPC sessions held between 1954 and 1965.

At the close of and immediately after the inaugural meeting of the First NPC in September 1954, the central government was reorganized and restaffed; many of the new appointees, such as Lin, had just come to Peking from the provinces. In addition to his legislative post in the NPC described above, Lin also received an important new position in the executive arm of the government when he was appointed (October 1954) as director of the State Council's Second Staff Office, the office in charge of co-ordinating the activities of the State Council's ministries and commissions in the fields of culture, education, and science. In addition to speaking before a number of national conferences concerned with these activities, Lin received three closely parallel assignments in 1956–57 in organs subordinate to the State Council: vice-chairman, Committee for the Popularization of Standard Spoken Chinese (*p'u-t'ung-hua*), February 1956 to date?; vice-chairman, Association for the Elimination of Illiteracy, March 1956 to date?; and, vice-chairman, Scientific Planning Commission, May 1957–November 1958. Although Lin was re-placed in September 1959 as the director of the Second Staff Office by Chang Chi-ch'un (q.v.), another Party specialist in cultural and edu-cational affairs, he continued to be deeply in-volved in these fields in later years (see below).

In the meantime, Lin had advanced further in the Party hierarchy, a fact well illustrated at the Party's Eighth National Party Congress. To manage the affairs of the Congress, three major *ad hoc* bodies were formed: a 63-member Presid-ium, a 13-member Secretariat, and a 29-mem-ber Credentials Committee. Although many Party leaders sat on two of these bodies, only Lin and six others (Li Hsueh-feng, Liu Lan-t'ao, Ma Ming-fang, Sung Jen-ch'iung, T'an Chen-lin, and T'an Cheng) were members of all three. He was also one of the executive chairmen for two of the daily Congress sessions and delivered an address entitled "On the Ques-tion of Nourishing and Building Up the Na-tion's [Human] Talent." At the close of the Congress he was re-elected to the Party Central Committee. Within the Party hierarchy Lin be-gan to assume a more active role in the late fifties in negotiations with visiting Communist Party leaders, an activity that became more pro-nounced in the sixties as the CCP conducted an increasing number of talks with foreign Com-munists in an attempt to win them over to their side in the dispute with the USSR. An illustra-tion of this work occurred in September 1963 when Lin was the number two member of a delegation led by Liu Shao-ch'i to North Korea for the obvious purpose of wooing the Koreans to the Chinese viewpoint in the Sino-Soviet dispute. Soon after returning to Peking, Lin presented a report on the trip before the 15th session of the NPC Standing Committee (No-vember 8, 1963).

In January 1960 Lin received a new appoint-ment in educational affairs when he was named to head the State Council's newly established Spare-time Education Committee. In fact, how-ever, one of his deputies (Li Chieh-po, q.v.) has been more active in the conduct of the Committee's work. In the following month Lin became vice-chairman of a committee to pre-pare for the convocation of a national confer-ence on culture and education. The conference, held in June 1960, had the self-descriptive title of the "national conference of outstanding groups and individuals in socialist construction in education, culture, health, physical culture, and journalism." Attended by over 6,000 dele-gates (one of the largest meetings ever held in China), the conference heard Lin's lengthy key-note speech, which reviewed cultural and edu-cational endeavors under the Communists. The breadth of the Chinese endeavors in these fields was revealed by Lin's assertion that "China has already established a professional cultural and educational army of more than seven million people and a non-professional one of some 30 million."

Lin received a new and significant assign-ment in the spring of 1963 when he became president of the Higher Party School, replacing Wang Ts'ung-wu (q.v.). Directly subordinate to the Party Central Committee, this institute, the most important of its kind, directs the training of the younger Party elite. It is also in charge of research involving philosophic matters pertain-ing to the CCP history and theory. As president, Lin is placed in a pivotal position in the develop-ment of both Party cadres and Communist theory.

Since becoming a vice-chairman of the NPC Standing Committee in 1959, Lin has become increasingly prominent. He attends most of the numerous national conferences held in Peking and is very often present when the most senior leaders (e.g., Mao Tse-tung or Chou En-lai) receive domestic or foreign delegations. Chinese press releases usually list him immediatly after the Politburo members on such occasions, thus placing him among a handful of men who will probably be future Politburo members—a group that includes T'ao Chu, Li Hsueh-feng, and Liu Lan-t'ao (qq.v.). It was in his capacity as a vice-chairman of the NPC that Lin led a delega-tion to Moscow in May 1965 to take part in the celebrations marking the 20th anniversary of the victory over Nazi Germany.

Lin continued to have an active political life until the late summer of 1966 when, during the early phase of the Great Proletarian Cultural Revolution, he was denounced and presumably removed from all positions of authority.

In private life Lin is married to Kuo Ming-ch'iu, whom he may have known since the thirties. A native of Hopeh, Kuo was born in 1917. While still a teenager she became active in revolutionary work as a student at the First

Girls' High School of Peking and as a leading figure in the Peking Students' Federation. Her participation in the December Ninth Movement of 1935 brought her into close contact with such important leaders as Huang Ching, Yao I-lin, and P'eng T'ao (qq.v.).[8] She was with Lin in Manchuria in the early fifties where, as well as holding other positions, she was a member of the Culture and Education Committee and the People's Supervision Committee of the Northeast People's Government (and later the Northeast Administrative Committee). She was also the second vice-chairman and then chairman of the Northeast Women's Federation. Since 1953 Kuo has been a member of the national Executive Committee of the Federation and has belonged since 1957 to the Federation's Presidium, the organ in charge of much of the work of the Federation between congresses. She was a deputy from Hopeh to the First NPC (1954–1959) and represented the women's federation on the Third National Committee of the CPPCC (1959–1964). In September 1961 Kuo visited the USSR as a member of a Sino-Soviet Friendship Association delegation.

1. Biographical Service no. 22, Union Research Institute, Hong Kong, September 14, 1956.

2. *Hung-ch'i p'iao-p'iao* (Red flag fluttering; Peking, 1957), V, 249–251.

3. Mu Hsin, *Chin-sui chieh-fang ch'ü niao-k'an* (A bird's-eye view of the Shansi-Suiyuan Liberated Region; Hsing-hsien, Shansi, 1946), pp. 19–21.

4. Israel Epstein, *The Unfinished Revolution in China* (Boston, Mass., 1947), pp. 282–285.

5. *Kommunist* (Communist), no. 7, Moscow, May 1964; translated in "Translation on International Communist Developments," no. 605, *JPRS* 24,801, May 27, 1964.

6. *Wei ch'un-chieh tang-te tzu-chih erh tou-cheng* (Struggle to purify the Party organization; Hong Kong, 1948), pp. 43–46.

7. *CB* 62, p. 16.

8. Chiang Nan-hsiang *et al., The Roar of a Nation* (Peking, 1963), pp. 135, 139.

Lin Hai-yun

(c.1915–   ). Vice-minister of Foreign Trade.

Lin Hai-yun first emerged in 1948 with the formation of the North China People's Government and from this time has been concerned almost exclusively with trade, and in particular, foreign trade. The North China government was established in August 1948 when the Communists had already captured large areas in north China; when it was abolished in October 1949 its activities were taken over by the central government. Lin served in this temporary government as the deputy director of the Industry and Commerce Department, as well as head of the Foreign Enterprises Affairs Office. After the central government was established, Lin assumed two important positions in the Ministry of Trade; in December 1949 he was named head of the Ministry's Staff Office (a post he relinquished in June 1950) and in March 1950 he became head of the Foreign Trade Department.

In August 1952 the Ministry of Trade was divided into the ministries of Commerce and Foreign Trade. Predictably, Lin joined the latter and has remained in it since that date as a senior official under Minister Yeh Chi-chuang. Not long after the creation of the new ministry Lin was named (October 1952) to head the Staff Office, an administrative post he had also briefly held under the Ministry of Trade in 1949–50. He held this position to about 1954. In December 1954 he succeeded K'ung Yuan, a foreign trade specialist and later a Central Committee alternate, as director of the Customs Administration (subordinate to the Foreign Trade Ministry), a post Lin held until replaced by Chiang Ming (q.v.) in 1964. The following year (June 1955) he was promoted to assistant minister of Foreign Trade and in October 1956 to vice-minister, a position he still retains.

In the interim, Lin was busily engaged in the negotiations of trade agreements with foreign countries. The pattern of his work has been clear: until late 1962 he worked almost exclusively with Communist bloc nations; after 1962 he has also been concerned with relations with Afro-Asian countries. Either in Peking or abroad, Lin has signed trade or aid agreements with the following 10 Communist nations: Czechoslovakia (June 1950), East Germany (October 1950, April 1958, and February 1959); Mongolia (December 1956); North Vietnam (July 1957); Bulgaria (March 1958, December 1958, and March 1961); Rumania (March 1958, March 1959, and March 1960); Albania (January 1959); Poland (February 1960); Hungary (February 1960); and Cuba (January 1964). The one agreement signed before 1962 with a non-Communist nation was signed in Helsinki in July 1956 with Finland. These negotiations often took Lin abroad; either as leader or deputy leader of delegations, he has been to all the nations that are listed above with the exception of Mongolia, Albania, and Hungary.

As already noted, after 1962 Lin also negotiated trade agreements with nations outside the Communist bloc. Such accords were signed in Burma in December 1962 and in Pakistan in January 1963. Back in Peking, he signed still another trade pact with Morocco in March 1963.

Though the above facts have dealt only with agreements that Lin himself signed, he has also taken part in many negotiations resulting in agreements signed by another vice-minister of Foreign Trade or by Minister Yeh Chi-chuang. Moreover, Lin has made a huge number of appearances in Peking since the mid-1950's in welcoming or entertaining the members of foreign government or business delegations who have come to China in great numbers. He is also frequently reported in the press making reports to government organs or to meetings of customs workers. For example, in December 1956 he spoke at the first nationwide conference of "advanced customs workers" as well as the second such conference in May 1960. In July 1958 he made explanations to the NPC Standing Committee about the Sino-Soviet Treaty of Commerce and Navigation (which had been concluded in April 1958) and in December 1962 made two reports before the same organization on the progress of China's foreign trade. Lin has also written articles on the state of foreign trade. He summarized Peking's trade with Communist nations in a piece marking the 10th anniversary of the PRC, which was published by the China News Service on September 3, 1959. For the Peking *Ta-kung pao* of September 29, 1964, he wrote on the expanding foreign trade of China, claiming that Peking had held 25 economic exhibitions and had taken part in 67 international trade fairs in more than 40 nations since 1949. Finally, in an article of January 1965 entitled "China's Growing Foreign Trade," Lin claimed trade relations with 125 nations.[1] In September 1964 he was elected a deputy to the Third NPC, which held its first session in December 1964–January 1965. He was elected from Fukien, the only clue to his native province. Some indication of Lin's stature in the Ministry of Foreign Trade was revealed in February 1965, when he was identified as the acting minister of Foreign Trade.

---

1. These three articles appear, respectively, in *CB* 606, *SCMP* 3310, and *Peking Review*, January 22, 1965.

Lin Piao

(1907–   ; Huang-kang hsien, Hupeh). Veteran military leader; vice-chairman, Central Committee, CCP.

Lin Piao, one of modern China's greatest military commanders, has been with the Red Army since its formation in 1927. He was one of the youngest and most able commanders during the Kiangsi Soviet period, the Long March, and the early stages of the Sino-Japanese War. Lin was the senior military commander in Manchuria during the civil war, and his Fourth Field Army played a major role in conquering the mainland in 1949. Lin's chronic illness forced him into temporary retirement during the early 1950's, but he re-emerged in the mid-1950's to take an increasingly active part in the military establishment. Elected to the Politburo in 1955, Lin replaced P'eng Te-huai as National Defense minister in 1959, and since that time he has been the top military figure in China. In 1966 he succeeded Liu Shao-ch'i as heir apparent to Mao Tse-tung.

Lin, whose original name was Lin Yü-yung, was born on December 5, 1907, in a village in Huang-kang hsien, located on the north bank of the Yangtze River east of Wuhan. He was the second of four boys. His father was a petty landowner and proprietor of a small handicraft factory, but when this went bankrupt he became a purser on a Yangtze river boat. Lin received his primary school education in Huang-kang, and then attended a middle school in Wuchang (one of the Wuhan cities). Wuhan was the center of activities for a group of men who were becoming increasingly involved in radical ideas and causes in the years before and after the May Fourth (1919) Movement. The group, which included Yun Tai-ying, Tung Pi-wu, Ch'en T'an-ch'iu, and Li Ch'iu-shih (qq.v.), was one of the most important nuclei around which the CCP was established in 1921, the year Lin arrived in Wuchang to enroll in middle school. Lin may have been drawn to Wuchang by two elder cousins, Lin Yü-nan and Lin Yü-ying (qq.v.), who were associated with Yun and the others. The Wuhan group had already established various organizations, including study societies, schools, and bookstores, to disseminate their ideas. Lin was a member of at least one of these, the Social Welfare Society, the details of which are contained in the biography of Yun Tai-ying. It was probably during Lin's years in the middle school, where he was a student activist, that he joined the KMT.

After completing middle school in 1925, Lin went to Shanghai where, in July, he attended the seventh national congress of the National Student Association. Meeting only a few weeks after the May 30th Incident (see under Li Li-san), the congress resolved to further the struggle against imperialism and adopted a strongly worded anti-Christian resolution. Remaining in Shanghai, Lin soon joined the Communist Youth League, in which Yun Tai-ying was a senior figure and editor of its journal, the influential *Chung-kuo ch'ing-nien* (China youth). According to Lin's comments to American journalist Edgar Snow a decade later, membership in the Youth League helped him gain admission to the Whampoa Military Academy in Canton.[1] Lin was admitted to the fourth class and specialized in infantry training. Chiang Kai-shek was the academy commandant, and because this was a period of close KMT–CCP collaboration there were several important Communists on the Whampoa staff, among them Chou En-lai, Yun Tai-ying, Hsiao Ch'u-nü, Nieh Jung-chen, and

Yeh Chien-ying (qq.v.). The academy also trained a number of cadets who later became prominent CCP members; among those in Lin's class was Ouyang Ch'in (q.v.).

Lin told Snow that in 1925 Chiang Kai-shek ordered Whampoa cadets holding dual membership in the KMT and the CCP to renounce one or the other. Accordingly, Lin "left" the KMT and joined the CCP. Lin's fourth class officially matriculated from October 1925 to October 1926, but many members of his class (which numbered over 2,600) were given their commissions as lieutenants earlier in order to take part in the Northern Expedition. Lin was assigned to Yeh T'ing's Independent Regiment in the famous Fourth ("Ironsides") Army. As described in the biography of Yeh, who was also a Communist, the Independent Regiment moved northward into Hunan several weeks before the main elements of the National Revolutionary Army left Kwangtung in July. Lin, who is regarded by even the most hostile sources as an outstanding military commander, rose quickly during the next year from deputy platoon leader to platoon leader, to company commander, and then to battalion commander.

Lin was not yet 20 and still a junior officer on August 1, 1927, when elements of the National Revolutionary Army staged the Nanchang Uprising under the leadership of Yeh T'ing, Ho Lung, and Chou En-lai. This event is celebrated as the birth of the Red Army, although at the time the rebels maintained that they were still fighting under the banner of the KMT. Driven from Nanchang a few days later, they marched south to Kwangtung where the two main columns, led by Yeh T'ing and Ho Lung, assaulted Swatow in late September. The Yeh–Ho troops were quickly defeated and almost totally destroyed, but a small detachment, stationed to the north as a rear-guard force, fared better. Lin was apparently with the rear-guard troops who, led by Chu Te and Ch'en I, escaped to the Kiangsi-Kwangtung-Hunan border area in the latter part of 1927. The biographies of Chu Te and Ch'en I contain further details about this westward march, the establishment of a small "soviet" in south Hunan, and the merger of Chu's troops in the spring of 1928 with those led by Mao Tse-tung to form the Fourth Red Army.

In the Fourth Red Army, then located in the Chingkang Mountains on the Hunan-Kiangsi border, Lin was initially a battalion commander, but he was promoted to command the 28th Regiment following the death in August 1928 of regimental commander Wang Erh-cho. For the remainder of the year the army fought against KMT and provincial troops on the Hunan-Kiangsi border and on the Kwangtung border to the south of the Chingkang Mountains. Because of the relentless attacks, the Fourth Army abandoned the Chingkangshan base during the winter of 1928–29 and moved eastward. In February 1929, Lin participated in the battle of Ta-po-ti (in the vicinity of Juichin and Ning-tu in Kiangsi); the Communists suffered heavy losses, but they won the battle and thereby laid the basis for what is commonly called the Kiangsi Soviet. In the spring, Chu Te and Lin led two elements of the Red Army, which scored victories in and around Lung-yen, Yung-ting, and Shang-hang in southwest Fukien.[2] These successes enabled them to develop the West Fukien Soviet District (which became the seat of the West Fukien Soviet Government established in March 1930). In addition, drawing upon Communist guerrillas already in the area (see under Chang Ting-ch'eng), they set up the Fourth Column (*tsung-tui*) under the Fourth Red Army. Lin had begun the year 1929 as a regimental commander, but he was soon promoted to commander of the First Column. By the second half of 1929 the Fourth Army consisted of four columns; each numbered about 1,600 men, half of whom were armed. In December 1929 Lin attended the Ku-t'ien Conference, in Shang-hang hsien, where Mao sharply criticized the "purely military viewpoint" and stressed the acute need for political training to bolster discipline and bring the Red Army into closer contact with the populace.

In January 1930 Mao wrote a letter to Lin to dispel a spirit of pessimism which apparently pervaded certain units of the Fourth Army. Mao argued that China's semi-colonial status contained inherent "contradictions" (for example, warlords fighting other warlords) beneficial to the Communists, and that if the Red Army carefully built base areas there would be a "revolutionary upsurge" which, he predicted, "will arise . . . very speedily." Possibly to save Lin embarrassment, this "Letter to Comrade Lin Piao," as it was known in earlier editions of Mao's *Selected Works,* is now entitled "A Single Spark Can Start a Prairie Fire."[3] Mao's letter coincides approximately with the period when the Li Li-san leadership in Shanghai began to put pressure on the Chu–Mao forces to prepare for assaults on the major cities in the Yangtze Valley. As described in the biography of Chu Te, both Mao and Chu resisted Li's entreaties, but finally, in the early summer of 1930 they reorganized their troops and prepared to move toward the Yangtze. In the new order of battle (June 1930), several armies were joined together to form the First Army Corps. Chu Te assumed command of the Corps, and he in turn placed Lin in command of the Fourth Army.[4] The Fourth Army political commissar was Lo Jung-huan (q.v.), a man with whom Lin would be closely associated for the next quarter of a century.

While P'eng Te-huai's Third Army Corps

took and held Changsha for a few days in late July and early August 1930, the Chu–Mao forces (Lin's Fourth Army among them) made an abortive thrust against Nanchang, the Kiangsi capital. Immediately afterwards the P'eng and Chu–Mao forces rendezvoused and merged their troops into the First Front Army. Chu became the commander of the new force and continued also to command the First Army Corps. After a second and equally abortive attack on Changsha, they retreated in a southeast direction. In the early fall Lin's Fourth Army took part in the capture of Chi-an (Kian), but a few weeks later the Red Army units moved back to their base in southeast Kiangsi. At this juncture Chiang Kai-shek was positioning his troops for the first of the famous Annihilation Campaigns against the Communist bases. In collaboration with units led by Huang Kung-lueh (q.v.), Lin played a significant part in defeating the initial campaign in the closing days of 1930 and the early days of 1931. He was equally active in defeating the Second and Third Campaigns in the spring and summer of 1931.

Earlier, in January 1931, the Party high command in Shanghai established the Central Bureau of the Soviet Areas, apparently to coordinate the activities of the various Red Army units in central-south China (see under Hsiang Ying). Sources differ on the composition of the bureau, but some accounts claim that Lin was a member.[5] In November of the same year, at Juichin, the Communists convened the First All-China Congress of Soviets. Lin was elected a member of the Central Executive Committee (CEC), the highest political body in the newly established Chinese Soviet Republic. He was also made one of the 15 members of the republic's important Central Revolutionary Military Council. The council was then chaired by Chu Te, and Wang Chia-hsiang and P'eng Te-huai were the two vice-chairmen. A few weeks later, in January 1932, Chu Te turned over to Lin the command of the First Army Corps, a post he would hold for the next few years. Lin's political commissar and colleague for many years was Nieh Jung-chen (q.v.).

In the spring of 1932 Lin and Nieh took part in what was probably the most eastward advance of the Red Army prior to the Long March. Crossing the mountains in Fukien, they pushed to the coastal plains in areas around Chang-chou, only 25 miles west of the port of Amoy. This effort to expand the perimeter of Communist-held areas was part of a broader plan to capitalize on Chiang Kai-shek's preoccupation with the Japanese who provoked the Mukden Incident in September 1931 and attacked Shanghai in January 1932. Chiang acquiesced in the Japanese occupation of Manchuria, and in the spring of 1932 he reached a settlement with Japan regarding the hostilities in Shanghai. Chiang, who felt he had been stabbed in the back by the Communists, determined anew to crush the Red Army before attempting to deal with Japanese aggression. Accordingly, the Fourth Annihilation was begun in mid-1932. Lin, once again deeply involved, fought a series of battles in east Kiangsi; they were successfully concluded in March 1933. In January–February 1934, at the Second All-China Congress of Soviets, Lin was re-elected to the CEC. By then the Red Army was hard-pressed by the Fifth Annihilation Campaign, which had begun in the fall of 1933. (In 1936, in an interview with Edgar Snow, Lin described the Fifth Campaign and spoke frankly of errors committed by the Red Army, which, in his view, might have been prevented by different tactics.)[6]

When the Long March troops set out from Kiangsi in October 1934, Lin was still in command of the First Army Corps, one of the major units on the year-long trek. His troops were involved in many of the key battles throughout the march (see, for example, under Yang Ch'eng-wu), and like all his fellow commanders he lost a large proportion of his troop strength and equipment. Midway through the march some of the important units and commanders separated from the First Front Army and remained in the Szechwan-Sikang border until 1936 (see under Chu Te), but Lin went straight to north Shensi with Mao, Chou En-lai, and P'eng Te-huai. By the time Mao's element of the Long Marchers arrived in Shensi (October 1935), Lin was already something of a legendary figure. This picture of him has been greatly embellished in the post-1949 period, but even before the Long March was completed Lin's name was familiar to readers of Comintern journals.[7] Accounts of the Long March also indicate that Lin was already chronically ill.

In December 1935 Lin attended a Politburo meeting at Wa-yao-pao in north Shensi, which apparently decided upon an "eastern expedition" into neighboring Shansi province, the stronghold of Governor Yen Hsi-shan. Lin and P'eng Te-huai were two of the most important commanders on this foray (February–April 1936); the Red Army was driven back across the Yellow River into Shensi, but the expedition enabled the army to gain recruits for its depleted ranks and a large amount of captured supplies (see under Liu Chih-tan). In the late spring of 1936, the Communists re-established the Red Army Academy (Hung-chün ta-hsueh), which had been set up in Kiangsi before the Long March. Lin temporarily turned over command of the First Army Corps to his chief-of-staff Tso Ch'üan (q.v.) and became the academy president and political commissar.

Over the ensuing years, the Communists' Red Army Academy came to be what Whampoa has been for the Nationalists. The first class of the school, located at Pao-an (now Chih-tan), numbered about 2–300, all of them drawn directly from the ranks of the Red Army. In early 1937, when the Communist capital was moved from Pao-an to Yenan, the school was moved there too and renamed the Anti-Japanese Military and Political Academy (K'ang-Jih chün-cheng ta-hsueh). K'ang-ta, the abbreviated and widely used name, set up several branches in other Communist-held bases in northwest, north, and east China during the Sino-Japanese War. In the early war years enrollment was about 5,000 students in the parent school in Yenan, and because this was a period of relatively close cooperation with the Nationalists, some of the students were KMT members. (For further details, see under Lo Jui-ch'ing, who became acting head of the academy after the war began.)

Soon after war broke out in July 1937, the Red Army was reorganized into the Eighth Route Army under Commander Chu Te and Deputy Commander P'eng Te-huai. The three major components were the 115th, the 120th, and the 129th Divisions. Lin commanded the 115th Division, with his colleague Nieh Jung-chen as the political commissar. The 15,000-man division drew its men from Lin's old First Army Corps, troops that had been in Shensi before the Long Marchers arrived (see under Liu Chih-tan), and others that had been in the Hupeh-Honan-Anhwei base before the Long March (see under Hsu Hai-tung). In September Lin's division moved across the Yellow River and late in the month scored a notable victory against a crack Japanese division at the P'ing-hsing Pass, near the Great Wall in northeast Shansi. The victory only momentarily delayed the Japanese thrust into Shansi, but it was a great psychological boost for Chinese of all political persuasions. The Chinese Communists have enshrined the battle, and uniformly neglected the fact that Yen Hsi-shan's Shansi troops made a significant contribution. Among the numerous accounts of the victory is one Lin gave to journalist Haldore Hanson a year after the battle.[8] Lin himself wrote about the battle in an article published in the leading Yenan journal, Chieh-fang (Liberation; no. 28, January 11, 1938). Perhaps the most useful account is one by a Chinese military historian, who presents a balanced picture and also describes Lin's skills as a tactician.[9]

Lin's 115th Division was clearly no match for sustained action against the invading Japanese armies, and therefore the Communists turned to guerrilla warfare tactics immediately after the P'ing-hsing Pass battle. Nieh Jung-chen was left in northeast Shansi to establish a guerrilla base

in the Wu-t'ai area, while Lin withdrew the rest of the division southward. The strategy during the ensuing weeks was to thwart Japanese advances by harassing their supply lines, especially along the T'ung-pu Railway, which runs the length of Shansi in a north-south direction, and the Cheng-tai Railway, which connects Taiyuan (the Shansi capital) with the rail junction of Shih-chia-chuang to the east in Hopeh. Lin's division fought in conjunction with Liu Po-ch'eng's 129th Division in southeast Shansi and Ho Lung's 120th Division in northwest Shansi. Despite the efforts of the Red Army, as well as regular KMT troops and provincial units under Yen Hsi-shan's jurisdiction, Taiyuan fell in November 1937 and Lin-fen (in southwest Shansi) in February 1938. Lin's fast-moving troops are brought to life in a vivid account by author-journalist Agnes Smedley, who was an eye-witness to these turbulent months in late 1937.[10]

In the spring of 1938 Lin was wounded in west Shansi, after which he retired to Yenan where he re-assumed the presidency of K'ang-ta. On July 1 he published in Chieh-fang an article on the development of guerrilla warfare in north China, and a month later the same journal carried under Lin's name regulations for recruiting students into K'ang-ta. He was interviewed in September 1938 by journalist Haldore Hanson, who reported that Lin had fully recovered from his wound.[11] Nevertheless, in late 1938 or early 1939 he left for Moscow for medical treatment. Little is known about Lin's stay in Moscow. In July 1940 he wrote an article on the war in China,[12] and secondary sources frequently assert that he took part in the defense of Leningrad, which began in September 1941. However, this is not mentioned in a 1954 biographic sketch of Lin prepared for a Russian encyclopedia.[13] Nor is it mentioned in Chinese Communist sources, including the brief news item in the February 14, 1942, issue of Chieh-fang jih-pao (Liberation daily), which reported Lin's return to Yenan, via Sian, on February 8. This news story simply reported that he had spent three years in the USSR where he had been hospitalized and "resting."

Following Lin's return to Yenan he became a vice-president of the Central Party School. However, he was soon removed and sent to Sian in October 1942 to confer with Chiang Kai-shek. The Chinese Communists have apparently left no record of these talks, but they are mentioned in some detail in a book by Chiang. The Generalissimo claimed that Lin assured him of a "sincere desire" to cooperate in the central government's policies to resist Japan.[14] Later in the same month, Lin left for Chungking, the wartime capital, reportedly at Chiang's invitation. Communist and Nationalist troops had had a number of clashes, and both sides were apparently anxious to work out arrangements to curtail these incidents. Lin's visit may also have been the result of informal pressures on the Nationalists by American diplomatic and military personnel who felt that a unified military effort was necessary to the success of the war.

During the next few months Lin and Chou En-lai, the Communists' permanent representative in Chungking, held numerous conversations with American diplomats who gained the impression that they were counting on American influence as the "only force that may be able to improve" KMT–CCP relations. In December 1942 Lin expressed concern to an American over clashes between the government and the Communists' New Fourth Army and Chungking's "insistence on that Army's *actual* as well as *theoretical* elimination." (KMT attitudes and actions toward the New Fourth Army are described in the biography of Yeh T'ing, the commander of this army until January 1941, when he was captured by the Nationalists.) The same diplomat observed that Lin was "obviously gloomy and discouraged" and that Lin felt negotiations were "impossible because of the uncompromising attitude of Chungking military leaders."[15] In March 1943 Chou and Lin held talks with Ho Ying-ch'in, the chief-of-staff of the National Army, but they made no headway in gaining official approval for their proposal to expand Communist forces to four armies consisting of 12 divisions.[16] Lin remained in Chungking for nine months, but he was able to see Chiang Kai-shek only three times, the last of which was in early June 1943. Lin indicated again to American diplomats that he was not optimistic about achieving a settlement, and then in late June he and Chou departed for Yenan. At a plenary session of the KMT Central Executive Committee in September, Chiang Kai-shek delivered a speech which was widely interpreted as conciliatory in tone. Soon afterwards, Lin returned to Chungking for further negotiations on the reorganization of Communist forces. However, his renewed suggestion that Communist troops be expanded to four armies was rejected,[17] and it was not until the following spring that another top Communist, Lin Po-ch'ü (q.v.), continued talks with the KMT.

After returning to Yenan, Lin once again assumed the presidency of K'ang-ta, and for the last two years of the war he was also in charge of training garrison troops in the Shensi-Kansu-Ninghsia Border Region. Some secondary accounts claim that he spent a portion of this period in Moscow. However, he was definitely in Yenan in mid-1944, when, in conversations with an American diplomat, he asserted that Communist units in north China had been successful against Japanese forces but could do even better with more and better arms.[18] In November, Lin delivered a report to senior

Communist cadres on troop training, and in the next month another American diplomat visiting Yenan reported that he was "impressed anew by the younger military commanders: Nieh Jung-chen, Ch'en I, and Lin Piao."[19]

At the Party's Seventh National Congress, held from April to June 1945, Lin was one of the speakers (although the speech was not published). He was also elected a member of the Party Central Committee for the first time. Then only 37 years old, Lin was already a military veteran of two decades, but his greatest exploits lay ahead. At the time of the Japanese surrender in August 1945, the Communists immediately began to move troops and cadres into Manchuria. The troops led by Lin reportedly numbered about 30,000, to which were added thousands more from Hopeh and Shantung. In addition, under the leadership of Chou Pao-chung (q.v.), the Communists had been able to build up a small guerrilla network since the Japanese occupation of Manchuria in 1931. In total, Lin had about 100,000 troops under his command by the fall of 1945. The newly organized force was known as the Northeast Democratic Allied Army (NEDAA). His three deputy commanders were Chou Pao-chung, Hsiao Ching-kuang, and Lü Cheng-ts'ao (qq.v.). Because military events overshadowed all others in Manchuria, Lin is often portrayed as the top Communist there during the civil war period. In fact, several officials were senior to him in Party rank (though less experienced in military affairs), among them Ch'en Yun, P'eng Chen, and Kao Kang (qq.v.). P'eng Chen was NEDAA political commissar and secretary of the Party's Northeast Bureau.

By the spring of 1946, Lin's troops numbered about a quarter of a million, and their firepower was augmented by captured Japanese weapons. (The point is much disputed, but it appears that the NEDAA also received a considerable store of weapons and supplies from Russian occupation forces—particularly Japanese arms which the Russians had taken in the closing days of World War II.) After an initial organizational phase, Lin's forces began to occupy the major Manchurian cities immediately after the Russians withdrew from them. But these same cities were being contested for by crack KMT armies sent to Manchuria at Chiang Kai-shek's insistence (against the advice of some of his best generals, as well as American military advisers). Lin fought some losing battles, most notably in April–May at Szu-p'ing-k'ai (midway between Shenyang and Changchun). But by mid-1946, when the ineffective KMT–CCP truce gave way to nationwide civil war, Lin evolved a policy of "strategic withdrawal and mobile warfare," abandoning the towns for the country." He concentrated his forces north of the Sungari River, where they spent "as much of their time . . . promoting land reform as in fighting the Nationalist army."[20]

In early 1947 Lin began his counteroffensive with probes into the vast areas south of the Sungari. These attacks gathered momentum by mid-year, and in the winter of 1947–48 he mounted a three-month offensive against the increasingly overcommitted KMT armies. In a five-week period from early February to mid-March 1948 the Communists captured Liaoyang, An-shan, Chi-lin (Kirin), and Szu-p'ing-k'ai, which further isolated the KMT garrisons in Shenyang and Changchun. The stage was now set for the Liaohsi–Shenyang campaign, described as one of the three greatest campaigns of the civil war.[21] After a series of battles lasting nearly two months, Shenyang fell on November 2, 1948, and within weeks all Manchuria was in Communist hands. Lin's forces were then known as the Northeast PLA, but over the turn of the year they were redesignated the Fourth Field Army. Earlier, in mid-1946, P'eng Chen had turned over the secretaryship of the Party's Northeast Bureau to Lin. But now, as Lin prepared to move south, this post was assumed by Kao Kang.

In the closing weeks of 1948 forces led by Lin and Lo Jung-huan passed beyond the Great Wall and, in combination with troops commanded by Nieh Jung-chen, began to close the net around Kalgan, Tientsin, and Peking. Kalgan fell in late December, Tientsin in mid-January 1949, and on the last day of the month Lin's troops, now numbering some 800,000, marched into Peking—the city having been surrendered without a fight by General Fu Tso-i. Shortly before this, Chiang Kai-shek's temporary "retirement" as president opened the way for Acting President Li Tsung-jen to begin "peace" talks with the Communists. Li sent an unofficial team to Peking in mid-February, but because the Communists terms were tantamount to surrender, the group returned to Nanking. Lin took part in these talks, and again in early April he was part of the six-man Communist group led by Chou En-lai, which held further talks, this time with an official group. The Communists were now even less willing to make concessions, and when the talks collapsed in mid-April Lin returned to his troops, then poised north of the Yangtze.

In the last part of April 1949 three huge PLA field armies, led by Ch'en I, Liu Po-ch'eng, and Lin, crossed the Yangtze. Wuhan fell in mid-May, after which Lin's units conducted mopping-up operations in Hupeh and prepared for the next thrust southward. On June 8 the Communists established the Central China Bureau (Hua-chung chü) and the Central China Military Region. Lin was appointed secretary of the bureau and commander of the region; subordinate to him Lo Jung-huan was second secretary

and first political commissar, and Teng Tzu-hui (q.v.) was third secretary and second political commissar. Within a few weeks Lin's troops were advancing southward. Their path was eased considerably when the two leading KMT officials in Hunan, Ch'eng Ch'ien and Ch'en Ming-jen, went over to the Communists in early August. Canton fell in mid-October and in December the major cities in Kwangsi were captured. Only Hainan Island remained to be captured, and that was done in a quick operation in the spring of 1950.

Reports of the advances of the Fourth Army in the last half of 1949 often refer to "Lin Piao's troops," but it appears that by mid-year he had turned over the field command of his forces to subordinates and planned the grand strategy from Wuhan. In early August, for example, he was still in Wuhan where he addressed a mass meeting on the need for simplifying administration and economizing on state expenditures, and a week later he took charge of a committee to implement these suggestions. Lin did not return to Peking in September to attend the inaugural session of the CPPCC, the body which brought the PRC into existence (October 1). However, he was elected a member of the Central People's Government Council, the People's Revolutionary Military Council, and the Standing Committee of the CPPCC; all three organizations were chaired by Mao. Moreover, he was elected a member of the First Executive Board of the Sino-Soviet Friendship Association (October 1949–December 1954).

The conquest of south China in late 1949 necessitated a reorganization of the Communists' administrative structure. The Central China Party Bureau and the parallel military region were redesignated "Central-South" (bureau and military region). Lin retained the top post in both cases. The provinces in the area were Honan, Hupeh, Hunan, Kiangsi, Kwangtung, and Kwangsi. Of the six multi-provincial regions throughout China, this was the largest in terms of population (about 175,000,000). In addition to the regional Party and military organs, the governmental body—the Central-South Military and Administrative Committee (CSMAC)— was formally established in February 1950. Lin was appointed chairman, and when the CSMAC was reorganized into the Central-South Administrative Committee in January 1953, he was reappointed. (All three regional organizations were abolished in the mid-1950's.) The headquarters for the bureau, military region, and the CSMAC were located in Wuhan, but because of the importance of Canton in Kwangtung, there were special "south China" organs established there during this period (see under Yeh Chien-ying, the key figure in Canton). Finally, with the establishment in early 1950 of the PLA's Central-South Military and Political Academy in Wuhan, Lin was appointed president. However, because of his protracted illness (see below), other officials, most notably Teng Tzu-hui and Yeh Chien-ying, assumed most of the major functions in central-south China during the formative years of the PRC.

At an April 11, 1950, meeting of the Central People's Government Council, Lin delivered a report on conditions in south China. In June the national government adopted a decision on the partial demobilization of the PLA, and on August 20 Lin was placed in charge of the Demobilization Committee for central-south China. In the meantime, however, the Korean War had begun (June 25), and major components of Lin's crack Fourth Field Army had been or were in the process of being transferred to Manchuria. In October, when the North Korean Army was on the brink of total disaster, the Chinese entered the Korean war—their troops designated the Chinese People's Volunteers (CPV). Large numbers of Lin's Fourth Field Army troops unquestionably went into Korea, but there is little to sustain the claim found in so many secondary sources that Lin himself commanded the CPV. On the contrary, only seven weeks after the CPV crossed the Yalu into Korea, the official New China News Agency, in a dispatch from Peking, reported that Lin sent a message of congratulations to CPV troops for the capture of Pyongyang, and from the context of the news report it was clear that he was not then in Korea. Two weeks later (December 26), Lin received a new assignment, scarcely compatible with wartime command responsibilities, as chairman of the Finance and Economics Committee of the Central–South Military and Administrative Committee (a post held until May 1953). Finally, when official biographies of top military figures were published in September 1955, P'eng Te-huai was explicitly described as the CPV commander from 1950, but there was no mention of any sort about Korea in Lin's biography.

The March 11, 1951, issue of the *Ch'ang-chiang jih-pao* (Yangtze daily), Wuhan's leading paper, carried an article by Lin on the importance of spring plowing. But many months passed before he was mentioned again. He missed the third meeting of the CPPCC (October 23–November 1, 1951), and two weeks later he was reported on "temporary leave" in regard to an important meeting in Wuhan. Between these dates, however, he made one of his extremely infrequent public appearances when, on November 5, he attended a meeting of the Central People's Government Council in Peking. At that time he was promoted from member to vice-chairman of the central government's People's Revolutionary Military Council, a post he held until the council was dissolved in 1954. Lin's prolonged absence from public affairs,

widely rumored to be the result of tuberculosis, received a partial explanation in September 1952 when an organization in Wuhan sent him a "get well" message. Lin's illness apparently lasted for several years.

In November 1952, on the eve of the First Five-Year Plan (1953–1957), Lin was appointed a member of the newly created State Planning Commission. Like his other posts, however, this was apparently nominal, and he was not re-appointed to the commission when the central government was reorganized in September 1954 at the inaugural session of the First NPC. He was elected a PLA deputy to the NPC, and at the first session he was elected one of the 10 State Council vice-premiers under Chou En-lai and one of the 15 vice-chairmen of the newly established National Defense Council. In December he was elected a vice-chairman of the Sino-Soviet Friendship Association (a post to which he was re-elected in May 1959). Despite his infirmity, Lin reached new political heights in April 1955 at the Fifth Plenum of the Central Committee when he was elevated to Politburo membership. At that juncture he was listed next to last among the 13 Politburo members. He received further honors in September 1955 when the PRC created personal military ranks and awarded decorations to its military veterans. Lin was listed third (after Chu Te and P'eng Te-huai) among the 10 men who were made marshals (the highest rank), and he was also given the three top decorations—the Orders of August First, Independence and Freedom, and Liberation.

At the Eighth Party Congress in September 1956 Lin made his first public appearance in five years. However, he was one of the few top-level men who did not address the congress. He was re-elected to the Central Committee, and at the First Plenum of the new Central Committee (held the day after the congress closed), he was re-elected to the Politburo. Significantly, of the 17 Politburo members, Lin was listed seventh—after Mao, Liu Shao-ch'i, Chou En-lai, Chu Te, Ch'en Yun, and Teng Hsiao-p'ing—and thus moved ahead of P'eng Te-huai, who for many years was second only to Chu Te in the military establishment. At that time, however, this ranking seemed to be of little consequence. Not only was Lin absent from public life, but P'eng was extremely active in military affairs and he had just delivered a major report on military affairs at the Eighth Congress. Moreover, P'eng was then de facto head of the Party's important Military Affairs Committee and minister of National Defense.

In the year and a half between the Eighth Congress and May 1958, Lin appeared in public only twice—both were protocol appearances in Shanghai in connection with the visit of Soviet military leader K. E. Voroshilov in April 1957. Whatever the nature of Lin's ailment, it apparently took a turn for the better by the spring of 1958, and from that time he began to appear in public with some regularity. In late May, at the Fifth Plenum (held immediately after the second session of the Eighth Party Congress), he was elected a vice-chairman of the Central Committee and a member of the Politburo Standing Committee. The Standing Committee then consisted of only seven men: Chairman Mao, Vice-Chairmen Liu Shao-ch'i, Chou En-lai, Chu Te, Ch'en Yun, Lin, and General Secretary Teng Hsiao-p'ing.

In mid-1958 Lin was elected a PLA deputy to the Second NPC, and when the congress held its first session in April 1959, he was re-elected a vice-premier and a vice-chairman of the National Defense Council. At the same time P'eng Te-huai was re-appointed minister of National Defense. By then there were signs that the Great Leap Forward, launched in 1958, was seriously faltering. The Great Leap policies had been discussed at the Sixth Plenum in Wuhan in November–December 1958 (which Lin attended), and they were again reviewed at the Eighth Plenum, held in Lushan, Kiangsi, in August 1959. Serious charges were made at Lushan against P'eng (see under P'eng and his colleague Huang K'o-ch'eng), and a month later, in mid-September, Lin was named to replace him as minister of National Defense. Although not announced publicly, it was subsequently revealed that Lin also took over P'eng's post as de facto head of the Party's Military Affairs Committee. Two weeks later Lin published an article which, ostensibly, was only one of many pieces written to commemorate the 10th anniversary of the PRC. However, this article ("March Ahead under the Red Flag of the Party's General Line and Mao Tse-tung's Military Thinking") provided a preliminary explanation for Lin's assumption of his new posts. It revealed serious tensions between the CCP and professional soldiers regarding military affairs and made clear that the PLA would henceforth give greater attention to ideological training. While conceding that military equipment is vital and must not be neglected as an element in warfare, Lin stressed that the "human factor" is even more important. His article was widely circulated, including publication in the October 1 issue of *Hung-ch'i* (Red flag).

Over the next few years Lin devoted most of his energies to strengthening political control over the PLA. His campaign moved into high gear in 1960, a period of particular concern to the Party leadership because of the severe economic crisis and the recent withdrawal of Soviet aid. At an important military conference in September–October, Lin charged that insufficient attention had been paid to ideological questions, but he also noted that the situation was improving because 120,000 PLA function-aries had gone to work in companies and at grass-roots levels where they had closer contact with the lowest echelon soldiers. At the same time he initiated the first in a series of campaigns to emphasize political work. He outlined four basic principles, known as the "four firsts," which have been paraphrased by one authority in the following terms: the "human factor" comes first in the relationship between weapons and men; politics comes first in the relationship between political work and other kinds of military work; ideology comes first in the relationship between routine and ideological political education; and, "living thought" comes first in the relationship between "book learning and its practical application."[22]

Lin also initiated a series of national political work conferences which were held about once a year through the mid-1960's (March 1961, October–November 1961, February 1963, December 1963–January 1964, and December 1965–January 1966). The primacy of politics was always stressed, but in a context "acceptable to the professional [military] mind."[23] For example, one of Lin's subordinates (in transmitting directives from Lin in December 1960) noted that even though "politics is first and most important," the complexities of modern weaponry require that more time be devoted to normal military training than to political training.[24]

Lin's importance in the military and political hierarchy might not have been fully appreciated had it not been for the release in 1963 by the United States Department of State of the hitherto secret *Kung-tso t'ung-hsun* (Bulletin of activities.)[25] These invaluable documents, which have been a prime source for many books and articles about the PLA, revealed that Lin was clearly the major figure in the PLA. Lin remained something of a behind-the-scenes man during the early and mid-1960's, but his stature was reinforced again at the inaugural session of the Third NPC, held in December 1964–January 1965. Lin attended the session as a PLA deputy, and was re-appointed minister of National Defense, a vice-premier, and a vice-chairman of the National Defense Council. He had previously been the second vice-premier (after Ch'en Yun), but now he became the senior vice-premier. Similarly, he had been the second vice-chairman of the National Defense Council, but now he became the ranking vice-chairman in place of the long-since disgraced P'eng Te-huai. In September 1965, on the occasion of the 20th anniversary of the defeat of Japan, Lin published an article entitled "Long Live the Victory of the People's War." This piece, which received world-wide attention, likened North America and Europe to the "cities of the world" and Asia, Africa, and Latin America to the "rural areas of the world."

Lin's theme was that all true revolutionists, drawing primarily upon their own resources and not upon foreign aid, should devote themselves to developing "people's armies" in order to surround and crush the "cities," that is, American imperialism. Less than a year later, in the early stages of the Great Proletarian Cultural Revolution, Lin emerged the heir apparent to Mao Tse-tung, and thus replaced Liu Shao-ch'i as the number two political figure in China.

Despite Lin's fame, relatively little is known about his personal life and family. In 1937 he married Liu Hsi-ming (also known as Chang Mei), one of his students at K'ang-ta, and by 1941 they had a son and daughter. Nothing further is known about this woman. Yeh Ch'ün, apparently Lin's second wife, quickly emerged during the Cultural Revolution as a prominent political figure, although prior to this the Chinese press had not mentioned her name. Like so many of the senior Party leaders, Lin has been the subject of numerous sketches by former colleagues which typically picture him as a man of simple habits. Perhaps the best of these was published in the leading youth journal in 1960 by a former officer who served in Manchuria under Lin.[26] Many broader assessments of Lin as a military leader have been published, particularly by Western journalists who met him during the war years. Nym Wales' commentary is probably as valid in the 1960's as it was in the 1930's when she wrote, "The Communists consider that Lin . . . ranks with the half-dozen military geniuses of recent Chinese history . . . When I first talked with him, he was regarded as the most expert and original tactician among all the military men." A clue to Lin's military and political success may be found in the following repartee with Miss Wales. "Lin . . . told me . . . that he was a veteran of a hundred battles and had never once been defeated when he led the First Army Corps. When I asked how he could be infallible, he smiled and raised his heavy black brows. 'We never engage the enemy,' he answered, 'unless we are certain of victory.'"[27]

1. Edgar Snow, *Random Notes on Red China, 1936–1945* (Cambridge, Mass., 1957), p. 26.

2. Wu Min and Hsiao Feng, *Ts'ung "Wu-Szu" tao Chung-hua jen-min kung-ho-kuo te tan-sheng* (From "May Fourth" to the birth of the PRC; Peking, 1951), p. 93.

3. *Selected Works of Mao Tse-tung* (Peking, 1964), I, 117–128.

4. Nym Wales, *Inside Red China* (New York, 1939), p. 250.

5. Shanti Swarup, *A Study of the Chinese Communist Movement* (London, 1966), p. 247; O. Edmund Clubb, *Communism in China: As Reported from Hankow in 1932* (New York, 1968), p. 91.

6. Snow, pp. 27–31.

7. *The Communist International*, London, XII, 549–557 (June 20, 1935).

8. Haldore Hanson, *"Humane Endeavour"* (New York, 1939), pp. 101–106.

9. Sydney Liu, "The Battle of Pinghsingkuan: A Significant Event in Lin Piao's Career," *The China Mainland Review* (Hong Kong), 2.3:161–173 (December 1966).

10. Agnes Smedley, *China Fights Back* (London, 1938).

11. Hanson, p. 263.

12. *Kommunisticheskii Internatsional* (Communist International), no. 7:52–64 (July 1940).

13. *Bol'shaya Sovetskaya Entsiklopedya* (Large Soviet Encyclopedia), XXV, 177–178.

14. Chiang Kai-shek, *Soviet Russia in China* (New York, 1957), pp. 96–97.

15. *Foreign Relations of the United States: 1943, China* (Washington, D.C., 1957), pp. 192, 197, 200, 202, 230, and 257–258.

16. Chiang Kai-shek, pp. 107–108.

17. *United States Relations with China: With Special Reference to the Period 1944–1949* (Washington, D.C., 1949), pp. 54, 532, and 542.

18. *Foreign Relations of the United States: 1944, China* (Washington, D.C., 1967), p. 541.

19. *Ibid.*, p. 753.

20. John Gittings, *The Role of the Chinese Army* (London, 1967), p. 6.

21. *Selected Works of Mao Tse-tung* (Peking, 1961), IV, 261–264.

22. Gittings, p. 245.

23. *Ibid.*, p. 243.

24. Ellis Joffe, *Party and Army: Professionalism and Political Control in the Chinese Officer Corps, 1949–1964* (Cambridge, Mass., 1965), p. 7; J. Chester Cheng, ed., *The Politics of the Chinese Red Army* (Stanford, Calif., 1966), pp. 8–11.

25. Cheng, *The Politics of the Chinese Red Army*.

26. *SCMM* 217, pp. 25–37.

27. Nym Wales, *Red Dust* (Stanford, Calif., 1962), p. 163.

Lin Po-ch'ü

(1886–1960; Ling-ling, Hunan). Early T'ung-meng hui and KMT member; chairman, Shensi-Kansu-Ninghsia Border Region Government; member, CCP Politburo.

Party "elder" Lin Po-ch'ü, usually known by the name Lin Tsu-han in his early days, began his revolutionary career shortly after the turn of the century. An early member of the T'ung-meng hui and the KMT, he worked for both the KMT and the CCP in the early and middle 1920's. After the KMT–CCP split in 1927 he studied in Moscow and taught in Vladivostok. Returning to China he joined the Communist administration in Kiangsi, and after making the Long March he became chairman of the Shensi-Kansu-Ninghsia Border Region Government. During the war years he frequently served as a negotiator with the KMT. Lin's major post after 1949 was as secretary-general of the Central People's Government Council. He was a member of the Party Central Committee from 1938 and of the Politburo from 1945. Lin and his colleagues Tung Pi-wu, Wu Yü-chang, Hsu T'e-li, and Hsieh Chueh-tsai are often referred to as the "five elders" (*wu-lao*).

Lin was born in Ling-ling (Yung-chou) in south Hunan. His father has been described as an elementary school teacher who was a moderately wealthy landlord, but journalist Nym Wales, who met Lin in 1937, has written that he was among the revolutionary leaders "produced by the old Confucian scholars of the dynasty whose aristocratic families were bankrupt." [1] From 1900 to 1904 Lin studied at the Ch'ang-te Normal School in northern Hunan, and then in 1904 he went to Japan on a government scholarship where he attended the Tokyo Normal School and Chuō University. During this period he met Sun Yat-sen and joined Sun's Hsing-Chung hui (Revive China society), which Sun had set up in the 1890's. Lin's later close ties with Liao Chung-k'ai, who became one of Sun's chief lieutenants, suggest that he may have also met Liao in Tokyo. Liao also attended Chuō University and graduated in 1909. When Sun and Huang Hsing established the T'ung-meng hui in 1905, Lin was among the earliest members. Of the 863 persons who joined within the first two years, the largest contingent (157) consisted of natives of Hunan, the birth place of Huang Hsing and Lin.[2]

Under orders from the T'ung-meng hui, Lin went back to China in 1906, and for the next five years he engaged in revolutionary work against the Manchus, first in Kirin where he taught school, and then in his native Hunan where he attempted to subvert Manchu-sponsored militia units. In 1912, after the overthrow of the Manchus, Lin served briefly in the Hunan provincial government, and in the same year he became a charter member of the KMT. In the latter part of 1913, after the failure of the "second revolution" against Yuan Shih-k'ai, the "father of the warlords," Lin fled to Japan where he assisted Sun Yat-sen in raising funds for his revolutionary cause. In 1915 Lin returned to China, and for the next year or so he was an aide to Ch'eng Ch'ien, one of Sun's colleagues who was then attempting to wrest control of Hunan for the anti-Yuan Shih-k'ai forces. The struggle against Yuan ended in the spring of 1916, and soon afterwards he died, but warlordism continued to be the order of the day.

Little is known of Lin's activities for the next few years. According to a biographic sketch of Lin by his long-time colleague Wu Yü-chang, Lin was among those influenced by the October Revolution in Russia.[3] This, of course, is a conventional CCP formulation to describe Chinese revolutionists of this period. In Lin's case it has an added ring of truth, because (again according to Wu) from 1918 Lin regularly corresponded with Li Ta-chao (q.v.), the famous radical professor at Peking University who was then moving toward an acceptance of the Marxist creed. Edgar Snow, who met Lin in Shensi in the 1930's, also learned that he had been "much influenced" by the other co-founder of Chinese Communism, Ch'en Tu-hsiu (q.v.).[4]

In 1921 Comintern representative Maring (whose real name was Sneevliet) arrived in China. Li Ta-chao arranged for Maring to see other important Communists, as well as Sun Yat-sen. Because of Lin's close ties with Sun, Li Ta-chao purportedly used Lin to arrange for Maring's meeting with Sun in Kweilin the late summer of 1921.[5] The Sun-Maring meeting was one of the first steps toward the informal entente between the Russians and Sun, which in turn led to the reorganization of the KMT. Shortly before the Sun-Maring talks, the CCP held its inaugural congress in Shanghai. Lin did not attend, but he secretly joined the CCP shortly afterwards.

In conversations with Edgar Snow in 1936, Mao credited Lin and P'eng P'ai (q.v.) with major roles in establishing the CCP branch in Canton in the period after the first congress.[6] Mao clearly exaggerated Lin's contributions, if only in contrast to P'eng. Similarly, a CCP historian ascribes to Lin an importance equal to Mao and Hsia Hsi (q.v.) in the development of the KMT branch in Hunan during the early period of KMT-CCP cooperation (c. 1923).[7] This too appears to be an exaggeration. In fact, Lin's importance in the revolutionary movement between 1921 and 1924 seems to have been his continuing effort to convince Sun Yat-sen to ally with the Soviet Union and cooperate with the CCP. In this regard another CCP historian singles out the "useful work" done by Li Ta-chao and Lin in influencing Sun to accept a "united front" between the two revolutionary parties,[8] and Sun's wife has written that Li and Lin held talks to this effect with Sun (presumably in Shanghai).[9] These talks apparently took place early in 1923 at the time of the famous declaration between Sun and Soviet ambassador Adolph Joffe, which became the cornerstone of the KMT-Soviet entente. At this juncture, January 1923, Sun announced the personnel in his newly reorganized hierarchy, which included the appointment of Lin as deputy director of the General Affairs Department of the KMT, then headquartered in Shanghai. In the months which followed, he was able to arrange for a number of CCP members to join the KMT.[10]

The informal KMT-CCP alliance became a reality, in effect, at the First KMT Congress, held in Canton in January 1924. Lin attended as a delegate from Hunan where a joint KMT-CCP branch had only recently been organized. Significantly, five of the nine delegates from Hunan were Communists, and incuded Lin, Li Wei-han, Hsia Hsi, and Mao Tse-tung. The KMT Congress elected a Central Executive Committee (CEC) of 24 full and 17 alternate members. Three Communists—T'an P'ing-shan, Li Ta-chao, and Yü Shu-te—were elected full members, and seven—Ch'ü Ch'iu-pai, Mao Tse-tung, Lin, Chang Kuo-t'ao, Han Lin-fu, Yü Fang-chou, and Shen Ting-i— were elected alternates. The CEC also established several departments in which the CCP was able to gain key appointments. T'an P'ing-shan, who headed the Organization Department, was a Communist, as was the department secretary, Yang P'ao-an. The Workers' Department was headed by left-KMT leader Liao Chung-k'ai, but the secretary was the Communist Feng Chü-p'o. Lin Po-ch'ü was made head of the important Peasants' Department, and under him P'eng P'ai (q.v.) was made department secretary. In the politically fluid days ahead, these posts were shuffled on several occasions. Lin, for example, headed the Peasants' Department from January to April 1924, and then over the next year and a half it was assumed by. other men. Lin returned to the post again from January to May 1926. However, as one writer has observed, "Regardless of the kaleidoscopic change of Heads, the Communist core of the Department remained the same." [11]

In addition to the functional departments, the CEC also provided for the creation of regional KMT headquarters for Canton, Peking, Szechwan, Shanghai, Hankow, and Harbin. Concurrent with his directorship of the Peasants' Department, Lin was made an alternate member of the Canton Executive Committee. However, he was only in these posts a few weeks when, about March 1, 1924, he went to Hankow to take charge of the headquarters there (in effect, to replace T'an Chen who was the original appointee to this post). The Hankow headquarters, which was an underground operation, was responsible for KMT affairs in Hupeh, Hunan, and Shensi. Several Communists were already working in Hankow, including the important labor leader Hsiang Ying (q.v.). Lin quickly formed an organization dominated by Communists, with himself as one of the Standing Committee members and director of the Organization Department. However, the apparatus quickly fell apart when several of Lin's Communist colleagues were arrested, and shortly afterwards the KMT Headquarters in Canton placed the Hankow operation under the Shanghai Headquarters. In the wake of the arrests, Lin fled from Hankow back to Kwangtung.[12]

Lin was in Peking in early 1925, and was there in March when Sun Yat-sen died, but he was back in Canton by the late spring. By the time the Sec-

ond KMT Congress was convened in January 1926 in Canton, the left-wing elements of the KMT, including the Communists, were in a majority position. This is reflected in the important role the Communists played during the congress. Wu Yü-chang, Lin's close colleague, was the congress secretary-general, and Lin, Mao Tse-tung, and T'an P'ing-shan gave the Communists a majority on the five-men Credentials Committee. (At least 90 of the 256 delegates to the congress were CCP members.) Several Communists, including Mao, made key speeches. When the new 36-member Second CEC was elected, it included many left-wing KMT members, as well as eight Communists: Lin Po-ch'ü, Li Ta-chao, Yü Shu-te, Wu Yü-chang, Yang P'ao-an, Yun Tai-ying, T'an P'ing-shan, and Chu Chi-hsun. (Some scholars dispute Chu Chi-hsun's membership in the CCP.) Similarly, of the 24 alternates, six were Communists: Mao Tse-tung, Hsu Su-hun, Hsia Hsi, Han Lin-fu, Tung Pi-wu, and Teng Ying-ch'ao (Mme. Chou En-lai). Of the nine members of the Standing Committee elected by the new CEC at its first session on January 22, 1926, three men were Communists: T'an P'ing-shan, Lin Po-ch'ü, and Yang P'ao-an. At the same meeting, the directors and secretaries of eight departments under the CEC were appointed, and of the 15 posts filled at that time, eight were held by Communists, including Lin, who resumed the directorship of the Peasants' Department, T'an P'ing-shan (director of the Organization Department), and Teng Ying-ch'ao (secretary of the Women's Department). Lin also became chairman of the Finance Examination Committee, and in the Central Party Headquarters' Secretariat, Communist Liu Fen was the chief secretary, and T'an P'ing-shan and Lin were two of the three secretaries.

In still other ways the Communists made their influence felt during the early part of 1926. For example, three out of the five men in charge of the KMT's Political Training Class were Communists (Lin, Mao, and Li Fu-ch'un), and Communist control of the Peasant Movement Training Institute (see under P'eng P'ai) was even more pronounced. Lin was among the many Communists who gave occasional lectures at the institute. Chiang Kai-shek, of course, was not unaware of these developments, and in the first half of 1926 he was deeply involved in maneuvers to curb Communist influence—not only the Chinese Communists, but also the many Russians who were then advisers to the KMT (for example, in the important Whampoa Military Academy). In brief, the famous Chung-shan anti-Communist maneuver of March 20 (see under Chou En-lai) dealt a serious blow to the CCP apparatus in Kwangtung. Capitalizing on this situation, Chiang was able to bring about a reorganization of the KMT in mid-May 1926, a maneuver which had Russian approval and CCP acquiescence. Presumably in an effort to give the CCP at least a nominal voice in the forthcoming changes, Lin was the one and only Communist in the nine-member group which drafted the reorganization proposals.[13] As a consequence, a few days later Lin was removed as head of the Peasants' Department, and his Communist colleagues T'an P'ing-shan and Mao Tse-tung relinquished parallel posts in the Organization and Propaganda Departments.

But if the Communists had been temporarily outmaneuvered, they were by no means totally stripped of power. The KMT was then in the final stages of planning the Northern Expedition, and Communist assistance was needed. When the Expedition began in mid-1926, CCP members held several top political posts; Chou En-lai was with the First Army, Li Fu-ch'un with the Second Army, and Huang Jih-k'uei, later a participant in the Nanchang Uprising, was with the Seventh. Lin was assigned to head the Political Department in the Hunanese Sixth Army, commanded by his erstwhile colleague Ch'eng Ch'ien. Another Communist, Chou Pao-chung (q.v.), was a staff officer in this force. The Northern Expeditionary forces moved north along three different routes. Lin's Sixth Army and Li Fu-ch'un's Second Army took the middle course, which led through central Kiangsi to Kiukiang, then in a northeast direction along the Yangtze, culminating in the capture of Nanking on March 24, 1927. On the day these armies entered Nanking, Chinese troops looted the British, American, and Japanese consulates; many foreigners were robbed and several killed. American and British ships countered with a bombardment to help foreigners escape. The details of the Nanking Incident, as this came to be called, are much disputed. Chiang Kai-shek placed the blame upon Lin and Li, asserting the incident was designed to embarrass him. Whatever the Communist involvement may have been, Lin was not then in Nanking. In fact, according to Wu Yü-chang's account, Lin had been in Canton with Wu as far back as the early fall of 1926 (that is, a half a year before the Nanking Incident). Moreover, toward the end of the year Lin is known to have been in Wuhan where many of the left-wing KMT and CCP members were then located, and where plans were being formulated to move the national capital from Canton to Wuhan. To prepare for the arrival of still more left-wing KMT and CCP members, a Joint Council was established on December 13 to serve as a temporary organ. Lin and Wu Yü-chang were among the organizers, as well as Soviet representative Borodin.[14]

Over the next few months Lin continued to work in Wuhan, principally in financial and political affairs. During this period the divisions deepened between Chiang Kai-shek and his opponents in Wuhan. An important test of strength took place at the Third Plenum of the KMT Central Executive Committee. This was held in Wuhan in mid-March 1927, and in the words of an authoritative work on this period, it "marked the height" of KMT-CCP collaboration.[15] Lin was dropped from the KMT Standing Committee, but he was named to the reorganized and highly important Political Council.[16] Moreover, according to Wu Yü-chang, Lin was also made the secretary-general of the KMT's Military Council, a body which had been abolished in mid-1926, but which was now "re-established as the highest organ for administering military affairs . . ."[17] Lin's new posts became academic in short order. Soon after the Third Plenum, Chiang engineered his anti-Communist coup in Shanghai (April 12) and quickly gained the upper hand against the left-KMT. Moreover, the alliance between the left-KMT and the CCP deteriorated sharply as the spring wore on. In particular, the goals of the revolution (for example, the degree to which land reform would be extended) came to be a major issue between the left-KMT and the CCP. Finally, in mid-summer, the left-KMT decided to expel the Communists from its ranks, and this in turn triggered the Communist-led Nanchang Uprising on August 1, 1927 (see under Yeh T'ing). At some time after mid-July Lin fled from Wuhan to Nanchang where he took part in the revolt. The Communists immediately established a Revolutionary Committee, ostensibly under the banner of the KMT. Lin was named to the 25-member Committee, as well as chairman of its Finance Committee.

The Communists success at Nanchang was short-lived. Driven from the city in a few days, the rebel army pushed south to the Kwangtung coast where they took Swatow in late September. Their success there was equally short-lived, and the shattered remnants fled to the countryside. Lin made his way to the Communist-held Hai-lu-feng area (see under P'eng P'ai) and then with Ho Lung and Liu Po-ch'eng to Hong Kong. From Hong Kong Lin went to Japan, and by the summer of 1928 he had reached Moscow, where he attended the CCP's Sixth Congress. Lin and his colleagues Wu Yü-chang enrolled in Sun Yat-sen University (later renamed the Communist University of the Toilers of China). Both graduated in 1930, and then went to Vladivostok to begin a new chapter in their many-faceted careers.

In Vladivostok Lin and Wu taught at the Far Eastern Industrial University, which was later renamed the Far Eastern Normal University.[18] (Another source calls this the Far Eastern Workers' School of Leninism.[19]) The institute had a Russian president, and Chinese and Korean vice-presidents. Lin taught politics and Wu languages. Both men had had prior interests in simplified versions of the Chinese language, based in part on research which Ch'ü Ch'iu-pai (q.v.) had done, and both attempted to develop their system when they taught Chinese students there, many of whom had no knowledge of Russian. In September 1931 both men attended the First Conference on the

Latinization of Chinese in Vladivostok, and Lin (but probably not Wu) also was at the second conference in October 1932. (Further details on the large number of Chinese then living in the Soviet Far East, as well as the language reform program, are contained in the biographies of Liu Ch'ang-sheng and Hsu Chih-chen.)

In late 1932 Lin returned to China, going to Juichin, the capital of the Chinese Soviet Republic in Kiangsi. In August 1933, Teng Tzu-hui (q.v.), accused of following the "Lo Ming (q.v.) line," was removed as People's Commissar for Finance and for National Economy (the equivalent of cabinet posts). Lin succeeded Teng in both posts. At the Second All-China Congress of Soviets, held in January–February 1934, Lin was one of the featured speakers (on the economic situation). In the reorganized Council of People's Commissars, he retained the portfolio for Finance, but he was replaced by Wu Liang-p'ing as the commissar for National Economy. At the same time, he was elected a member of the Republic's Central Executive Committee, as well as a member of the smaller and more important Presidium which served as the supreme political organ when the CEC was not in session. The Presidium, consisting of only 17 members, was headed by Mao Tse-tung. Thus, in the closing phase of the Kiangsi period, Lin was one of the key CCP figures.

Lin left the Juichin area in October 1934 on the Long March, and during the year-long trek to north Shensi he was in charge of the Red Army Supply Department. Then almost 50, he was among the oldest of the Long Marchers. After arriving in Shensi in late 1935, Lin continued to be in charge of financial affairs for the transplanted Communist government apparatus which was known then as the Northwest Office (of the Chinese Soviet Republic). He was working in this capacity in mid-1936 when Edgar Snow met him in Pao-an, then the Communist capital. A year later, in December 1936, he was among the several key assistants to Chou En-lai when Chou carried out the negotiations with Chiang Kai-shek at the time of the Sian Incident (see under Chou). This was one of the first major steps toward a new period of cooperation with the KMT, which reached a peak in the early days of the Sino-Japanese War. In the meantime, the Communists began to establish the famed Shensi-Kansu-Ninghsia (Shen-Kan-Ning) Border Region Government in Yenan, their new capital. In Lin's various pronouncements of this period he stressed the need for sound administrative policies. He also pressed for a shift from an emphasis on class struggle to a policy which stressed national unity in order to prepare for the coming struggle with Japan.[20]

Within a few days of the outbreak of war on July 7, 1937, Chou En-lai, Ch'in Pang-hsien, and Lin went to central China where they worked out a new "united front" with the Nationalists. This,

in effect, was the final step in gaining formal recognition of the Shen-Kan-Ning Border Region Government, and from then until 1948 Lin continued as the chairman. As part of the overall agreement the Communists placed their Eighth Route Army under the ostensible leadership of the national government, and the CCP pledged its cooperation with the KMT in the fight against Japan. Concurrent with this assignment, Lin also served in the early days of the war as chief of the Eighth Route Army's Office (pan-shih-ch'u) in Sian, where the KMT garrisoned large numbers of troops. He was in Sian for most of the latter half of 1937 and first half of 1938, but then in mid-1938 the Communists were invited to participate in the newly formed People's Political Council, a consultative organ set up by the national government in Wuhan (which became the capital after the fall of Nanking in the latter part of 1937). The seven-member Chinese Communist delegation was comprised of Mao Tse-tung (never more than a nominal member), Lin, Wu Yü-chang, Tung Pi-wu, Ch'en Shao-yü, Ch'in Pang-hsien, and Teng Ying-ch'ao. The first Council session met in Wuhan in July 1938, but when Wuhan fell to the Japanese the meetings were held in Chungking (from the second session in October–November 1938). From this time until 1941, Lin divided his time between Chungking, where he worked under Chou En-lai as a member of the CCP liaison mission to the KMT government, and Yenan, where he continued to head the Shan-Kan-Ning Border Region Government. At the CCP's Sixth Plenum, held in Yenan in October–November 1938, Lin was elected a member of the CCP Central Committee. (Some secondary sources assert that Lin was elected an alternate member in 1928 and a full member in 1934, but both a Soviet source[21] and Lin's obituary mention only his election in 1938).

Although the Shen-Kan-Ning Border Region had been in existence since 1937, it was not until January–February 1939 that the First Assembly was held. Lin was again elected chairman, as he was in November 1941 at the Second Assembly when he delivered a lengthy report on the work of the government for the intervening period. Lin was once more reelected to head the government at the Third Assembly in April 1946. After the capture of Yenan by the Nationalists a year later, the Border Region government became, in fact, a government-in-exile. It continued to exist until February 1949 when it was merged with the neighboring Shansi-Suiyuan Border Region. Mark Selden's exhaustive study of the Shen-Kan-Ning Border Region concludes that Lin was the dominant figure in the region from its inception to about 1942, after which he was overshadowed by Kao Kang (q.v.).[22] Kao himself was a senior figure in the Border Region government as head of the assembly, but his influence derived mainly from his top positions within the Party's Northwest Bureau. Elaborating on this point, Selden writes that Lin was the "spokesman . . . for the values of new democracy—primarily [the] United Front, rationalized administration along bureaucratic lines, universal elections and the three-thirds system [in which, in the spirit of the united front, Communists would hold no more than a third of key posts in various levels of administration]. With the rectification movement [beginning in 1942]," Selden continues, "one again hears echoes of a more down-to-earth and elemental tone, increasingly attuned to the peasantry rather than the bourgeoisie, and suitable to the independent stand of the Communist Party within the United Front." Continuing this theme, Selden also notes that the "bureaucracy was the stronghold of the 'intellectual cadres,' primarily students from outside the border region, and other elite elements who joined the Party after 1937 primarily because of its united front stance against Japan. On the other hand, the Northwest Bureau and lower echelons of the Party (and public security forces) were bastions of strength of local partisans many of whom fought in the land revolution, had little education and were attracted to Communism by its promise of social revolution and justice for the poor. Lin . . . by temperament and career was closely associated with the interests of the former and Kao Kang with the latter."[23]

In 1940 Lin was among the original sponsors for the establishment of the Border Region's Sin Wenz ("New Writing") Society. Speaking at the inaugural ceremonies in November, he noted that the government had already given it legal standing, that is, it had equal validity with the ideographic script in reports, documents, and so forth.[24] Like most senior leaders in Yenan, Lin was involved in the rectification (*cheng-feng*) movement, which began in 1942. In accordance with an April 1942 directive of the CCP Central Committee, he assumed the chairmanship of a special "study committee" to carry out a "thorough examination of work" in the region. Lin delivered a major speech on this theme at the two-month-long conference of "senior cadres" held in Yenan from October 1942 to January 1943. A year later, in January 1944 at a meeting of the Border Region Assembly, he presented a fact-laden report on the government, which was later published in Stuart Gelder's *The Chinese Communists*.[25]

Beginning in the spring of 1944 Lin found himself again cast in the role of a major negotiator with the KMT. Spurred on by renewed Japanese military offensives, as well as behind-the-scenes persuasion by the United States, many segments of Chinese political life were eager for a settlement of outstanding issues between the KMT and the CCP. To this end Lin was sent to

Sian in early May for preliminary talks with two senior KMT officials, Chang Chih-chung and Wang Shih-chieh. After a few days the talks were shifted to Chungking where the negotiations continued, without notable success, until November. During this period Lin conferred with Chiang Kai-shek and American diplomats, as well as General Patrick J. Hurley (then President Roosevelt's personal representative in China, and later the ambassador there). Lin also presented the Communist case before a session of the People's Political Council in September. Finally, in early November Lin accompanied Hurley to Yenan for two days of conferences. Chou En-lai returned to Chungking with Hurley for still more talks, but Lin remained in Yenan. Chou's discussions were equally fruitless, as were still further talks in late January 1945 when Chou once more went to Chungking. No significant progress was made, in fact, until after the war when Mao flew to Chungking for discussions with Chiang Kai-shek.

In April–June 1945 Lin attended the Party's Seventh National Congress; he was a member of the 15-member presidium (steering committee) and one of the speakers. He was reelected to the Central Committee and promoted to membership on the Politburo. He remained in Yenan until, during the civil war, the city was evacuated in March 1947. Lin left Yenan with Mao, Chou En-lai, and other key members of the elite, who for much of the next year shifted from place to place in north Shensi before proceeding to west Hopeh in the spring of 1948. Lin, however, appears to have remained in north Shensi, because he was back in Yenan not long after it was recaptured in April 1948.

In early 1949, Lin was among the first of the Communist leaders to arrive in Peking, a city he had not visited for a quarter of a century. In March he was named to the Communist delegation, which included Chou En-lai (the chief), Lin Piao, Yeh Chien-ying, Li Wei-han, and Nieh Jung-chen, to hold peace talks with the Nationalists. With the Communists controlling most of north China, and with their armies poised on the north bank of the Yangtze, these talks, held in April, were scarcely more than an eleventh-hour gesture by the Nationalists, who rejected the Communist terms which were tantamount to surrender terms. For the next few months, Lin was heavily engaged in the preparatory work which culminated in the establishment of the central government and various "mass" organizations in the fall.

In the middle and late summer of 1949 Lin became a member of the Preparatory Committees of both the New Legal Research Society and the Sino-Soviet Friendship Association, and chairman of the Preparatory Committee of the New Political Science Research Society. He also chaired the Social Sciences Workers' Conference held in July. Earlier, in June, Lin was made a Standing Committee member of the CPPCC Preparatory Committee, which was chaired by Mao. When the inaugural CPPCC session was convened in September to establish the PRC, Lin attended as a CCP delegate and delivered a report on the work of the Preparatory Committee. At the close of the meetings he was elected a member of the CPPCC's First National Committee (and in February 1953 he was elevated to the Standing Committee). On October 1, Lin was at Mao's side at the festivities inaugurating the People's Republic.

As Lin embarked on the last decade of his life, he could be described as a revolutionist with nearly half a century's experience. But within that span he had spent a decade as chief administrator of the Communists' most important border region government. Presumably for this reason, in the new central government he was made secretary-general (as well as a member) of the Central People's Government Council (CPGC), the supreme government organ invested with broad legislative, executive, and judicial functions. Chaired by Mao, the 34 meetings of the CPGC passed on most of the major measures adopted by the PRC in the formative years from 1949 to 1954. Immediately after the central government was formed, Lin received two additional appointments, one as a member of the First Executive Board of the Sino-Soviet Friendship Association (SSFA), and the other as a Council member of the Association for the Reform of the Chinese Written Language (chaired by his colleague Wu Yü-chang). From 1954 to his death he was one of the SSFA vice-chairmen.

Wu Yü-chang, in his brief sketch of Lin's life, notes that in the post-1949 period Lin was frequently in ill health. Yet he was relatively active during the next decade. In the spring of 1951 he led an SSFA delegation to Moscow for May Day celebrations which stayed there for a month, and in February 1952 he was appointed chairman of a newly formed Study (hsueh-hsi) Committee under the CPPCC, which was set up to encourage a more detailed study of the works of Mao, as well as other writings dealing with cultural, educational, and economic policies. Early in the next year he was named to a committee to draft a national constitution. This was adopted in September 1954 when the inaugural session of the First NPC was held. Lin attended as a deputy from his native Hunan, and he was elected one of the NPC Standing Committee vice-chairmen. In the subsequent years he attended each of the four NPC sessions, and in every case was a member of the Congress presidium. Returned again from Hunan, Lin was re-elected a vice-chairman of the Second NPC in April 1959. In the meantime, at the Party's Eighth Congress in September 1956, he was re-elected to the Central Committee. He delivered a brief, orthodox speech on the "historical lessons" of the Chinese Revolution. Immediately afterwards, at the First Plenum of the new Central Committee, he was once more named to the Politburo.

In October 1958 Lin was the representative of the CCP and the central government at the inauguration of the Ninghsia-Hui Autonomous Region, and in August–September 1959 he was in the Mongolian People's Republic as head of an NPC goodwill delegation. During the ensuing months he appeared at several public functions, the last on May 4, 1960. A few weeks later, on May 29, Lin died of a heart disease in Peking in his 75th year. Lin's funeral committee included most of China's major political figures, and at his funeral Teng Hsiao-p'ing described him as one of Mao's "closest comrades-in-arms," an accolade reserved for the select few.

Lin's elder brother, Lin Yu-mei, served as a military commander in the post-1911 period under Hunan Governor T'an Yen-k'ai; his younger brother, Lin Tsu-lieh, was a CCP member and political instructor at the Whampoa Military Academy in the mid-1920's.[26] Lin Po-ch'ü was married at least twice, and he is known to have had two sons and a daughter. One of the sons was a student at Peking Normal University in the late 1950's.

---

1. Nym Wales, *Inside Red China* (New York, 1939), pp. 336–337.

2. Chün-tu Hsüeh, *Huang Hsing and the Chinese Revolution* (Stanford, Calif., 1961), p. 44.

3. *Chung-kuo ch'ing-nien* (China youth), no. 12:13–15 (June 16, 1960).

4. Edgar Snow, *Red Star over China* (New York, 1938), pp. 224–225.

5. *Chung-kuo ch'ing-nien*.

6. Snow, p. 141.

7. Hu Hua, ed., *Chung-kuo hsin min-chu-chu-i ko-ming shih* (A history of China's new democratic revolution; Hong Kong, 1950), p. 44.

8. Ho Kan-chih, *A History of the Modern Chinese Revolution* (Peking, 1960), p. 81.

9. *SCMP* 2867, pp. 1–7.

10. Li Yun-han, *Tsung jung kung tao ch'ing tang* (From the admission of the Communists to the purification of the [Nationalist] Party; Taipei, 1966), pp. 138, 159.

11. Shinkichi Eto, "Hai-lu-feng—The First Chinese Soviet Government," *The China Quarterly*, no. 8:179 (October–December, 1961).

12. Li Yun-han, pp. 275–286.

13. *Ibid.*, p. 505.

14. C. Martin Wilbur and Julie Lien-ying How, *Documents on Communism, Nationalism, and Soviet Advisers in China, 1918–1927* (New York, 1956), p. 381.

15. *Ibid.*, p. 399.

16. Li Yun-han, p. 550.

17. *Chung-kuo ch'ing-nien;* Wilbur and How, p. 398.

18. *Hung-ch'i p'iao-p'iao* (Red flag fluttering; Peking, 1957), IV, 164–170.

19. Ho Ch'i-fang, *Wu Yü-chang T'ung-chih ko-ming ku-shih* (The revolutionary story of Comrade Wu Yü-chang; Hong Kong, 1949), p. 33.

20. Mark Selden, "Yenan Communism: Revolution in the Shensi-Kansu-Ninghsia Border Region, 1927–1945," Ph.D. diss., Yale University, 1967, pp. 124, 149.

21. *Bol'shaya Sovetskaya Entsiklopedya* (Large Soviet Encyclopedia; Moscow, 1954), XXV, 177.

22. Selden, p. 152.

23. *Ibid.,* pp. 230–232.

24. John De Francis, *Nationalism and Language Reform in China* (Princeton, N.J., 1950), pp. 130–131.

25. Stuart Gelder, *The Chinese Communists* (London, 1946), pp. 111–139.

26. Li Yun-han, p. 461.

Lin T'ieh

(c.1905–   ; Szechwan). First secretary, Hopeh Party Committee; member, CCP Central Committee.

Lin T'ieh is a graduate of the Kwangtung Agricultural Institute. Assuming a birthdate of 1905, he would probably have graduated in the middle to late 1920's.

No information is available on Lin until 1945 when he was serving as chief of a political committee (CCP) of the Red Army forces in "the central Hopeh liberated area." The area had been a base of Communist operations all during the Sino-Japanese War and politically was a part of the larger Shansi-Chahar-Hopeh (Chin-Ch'a-Chi) Border Region Government, established under CCP auspices at the conference at Fou-p'ing, west Hopeh, in January 1938. Headed on the political side by Sung Shao-wen (q.v.), the Chin-Ch'a-Chi's military commander was Nieh Jung-chen of the 115th Division of the Eighth Route Army. A year later, in 1946, Lin was identified as the political commissar of the Third Column of the Chin-Ch'a-Chi Military Region, the name for the military command in the territory of the border region government. And in late 1947 he was also identified as the secretary of the Central Hopeh CCP Committee. These postwar positions held by Lin suggest that during the war he may also have been connected with the Chin-Ch'a-Chi Border Region Government. The flatness of the central Hopeh terrain, where Lin operated, made it impossible for the Communists to maintain long-term military bases there, and the frequency of Japanese attacks made it difficult to organize the area politically. Nonetheless, the Communists continued to conduct guerrilla skirmishes in the area throughout the war and were thus in position to take it over after the Sino-Japanese War.

In the immediate postwar period of Communist expansion throughout the mainland, the boundaries of the Chin-Ch'a-Chi Border Region were greatly extended and by November 1947 were linked with the boundaries of the border government to the south, the Shansi-Hopeh-Shantung-Honan (Chin-Chi-Lu-Yü) Government. Yang Hsiu-feng was the political head of this government, and Hsu Hsiang-ch'ien (q.v.) the military commander. In May of 1948 the two border regions were officially merged, and in August they became the major portions of the territory controlled by the newly established North China People's Government. As a representative of the North China Liberated Areas, Lin attended the inaugural sessions of the First CPPCC in September 1949, at which time the PRC was officially brought into existence. However, his principal assignment was in Hopeh province where he has been the ranking Party secretary since August 1949 (a position redesignated as first secretary in 1956). He also served from 1949 to the mid-fifties as political commissar of the Hopeh Military District.

In Hopeh Lin has had a number of tasks to perform both in the provincial Party Committee and in the provincial government administration. From 1949 to 1952 he was a member of the Hopeh Provincial People's Government. In November 1952 he was promoted to the provincial governorship, succeeding Yang Hsiu-feng, who was called to Peking that month to serve in the Ministry of Higher Education. In February 1951 Lin had been made chairman of the Finance and Economics Committee of the Hopeh government, but it is not known how long he held the post. At the regional level, Hopeh was under the jurisdiction of the multiprovincial government organ known as the North China Administrative Committee (NCAC). When this body was reorganized in February 1953, Lin was named as a member, holding the post until the NCAC was abolished in 1954. Since 1954 he has been a Hopeh deputy to the NPC, serving in the First NPC (1954–1959), in the Second NPC (1959–1964), and being re-elected to the Third NPC, which opened in December 1964.

Lin played a rather important role at the historic Eighth National Party Congress in September 1956. He served on the Presidium (steering committee) for the Congress, as well as on the Credentials Committee. On September 18 he addressed the Congress on the higher stage cooperatives in Hopeh province. Finally, at the close of the meetings, he was elected a full member of the Eighth Central Committee, one of only 33 men elected to full membership who had not served on the Seventh Central Committee elected in 1945.

In May of 1957, the State Council established the Hai River Harnessing Committee to control the river that flows through Tientsin, Hopeh's major city. Lin was named as chairman, but it is not known how long he held this position. Less than a year later, at a session of the Hopeh Provincial People's Congress in April 1958, Lin requested and was granted permission to resign from the governorship of the province "in order to concentrate his efforts on his post as provincial Party first secretary." He was succeeded by Liu Tzu-hou (q.v.).

From the early 1950's, Lin has been quite active in Hopeh government and Party affairs. In 1957 and 1958, for example, he was a leading provincial figure in the "rectification" campaign that swept China. He has also been frequently reported in the company of senior Chinese leaders who were making inspection tours of Hopeh; examples include Mao Tse-tung (April 1959), Chou En-lai (June and November 1959), and Liu Shao-ch'i (March 1960). Also, partly owing to the fact that Tientsin is one of north China's major cities, Lin has frequently entertained visiting foreign dignitaries, like the president of the North Korean Assembly in June 1963. In April 1960 he made his only trip abroad, leading a CCP delegation to the 13th Congress of the Belgian Communist Party. He has been a rather frequent contributor to the Chinese press, including articles on economies and politics for the *JMJP* (e.g., issues of May 13, 1958, June 29, 1959, July 13, 1960, and November 26, 1963) and *Hung-ch'i* (Red flag) issues of October 1, 1958, and August 1, 1960.

In March 1965, Lin was identified as the third secretary of the North China Party Bureau. The regional Party bureaus had been re-created in January 1961 in accordance with a decision of the Ninth Plenum of the Party Central Committee. Lin's position in the Bureau placed him under First Secretary Li Hsueh-feng and Second Secretary Ulanfu (qq.v.). In addition, he continues to retain his post as the Hopeh first secretary. As of 1965 Lin had served continuously from the Communist takeover of the mainland as the senior Party official in Hopeh. The only other provincial-level official to parallel this record of continuity is Ulanfu who has been the ranking Party official in Inner Mongolia from the late 1940's.

Lin Tsu-han, see **Lin Po-ch'ü**

Lin Yü-nan

(?–1931; Hupeh). Early student and labor leader.)

Lin Yü-nan, an early Communist leader, was particularly influential in the student movement at the beginning of the 1920's. He was also active in the labor movement then, as was his brother Lin Yü-ying (q.v.). Lin Yü-nan opposed the Russian-returned student clique at the Fourth

CCP Plenum in January 1931 and lost his life when a group with whom he was meeting was apprehended, turned over to the Nationalists, and executed in February 1931.

Presumably born about the turn of the century, Lin was a student in Wuhan at the time of the May Fourth Movement (1919). Like so many of the young intellectuals of this period, he was influenced by anarchist thought.[1] He was one of the founders in 1919 of the Social Benefit Book Store (Li-ch'ün shu-she), which dealt in anarchist literature and, at a later date, Marxian materials. The Book Store was affiliated with the Communal Society (Kung-ts'un she) founded by Yun Tai-ying (q.v.), a colleague of Lin's in Wuhan.[2] (The Communal Society may have been another or alternate name for Yun's Social Welfare Society [She-hui fu-li hui]—see under Yun Tai-ying.)

In 1920 Lin belonged to a little-known student association in Wuchang, the Society of Mutual Assistance (Hu-chu she). He was a contributor to the only issue of the Society's journal, *Hu-chu* (Mutual Assistance), a publication that expressed the anarchist and socialist leanings of its student audience.[3] During this period he also contributed to a similar publication entitled *Wu-han hsing-ch'i p'ing-lun* (Wuhan weekly review), published in Hankow from 1921 to 1923. Initially attempting to imitate the influential KMT Shanghai weekly *Hsing-ch'i p'ing-lun,* the Wuhan journal opposed warlords and capitalists, whom it charged with being enemies of Chinese society. It soon became a Communist publication and numbered among its contributors such prominent Communists as Li Han-chün, Tung Pi-wu, and Ch'en T'an-ch'iu (qq.v.), all CCP founders, as well as Hsiao Ch'u-nü (q.v.),[4] a young student leader from Hupeh and an important Party propagandist who lost his life in 1927.

As a member of the Communal Society Lin went with Yun Tai-ying, Hsiao Ch'u-nü, and others to rural Szechwan in the summer of 1921 to teach the peasantry.[5] Back in Wuhan by the following spring, Lin attended the CCP-sponsored Far Eastern Oppressed People's Conference as a representative of the Wuhan students. This seems to have been his last major involvement with the youth movement. A somewhat refined and fastidious man, he was especially effective in working with students (much more so than with labor leaders, with whom he worked at a later period). Among the students he is said to have influenced through personal contacts or through his writings were Cheng Wei-san (q.v.), now a Central Committee member, and Tai Chi-ying, an early Party member from Hupeh and later a member of the Communists' New Fourth Army.[6] Lin may have also played a role in attracting his cousin Lin Piao into the Communist movement.

Soon after the above-mentioned conference of Oppressed Peoples in the spring of 1922, the

Communal Society was disbanded and most of its key members, including Lin, joined the newly founded CCP. Concurrent with the establishment of the Party in mid-1921, the Secretariat of the Chinese Labor Unions was established in Shanghai (see under Teng Chung-hsia). Lin was named to head the Secretariat's Wuhan branch, sometimes known as the Yangtze branch.[7] (Mao Tse-tung headed another branch in neighboring Hunan.) The highlight of Lin's career as a labor organizer in the twenties took place in early 1923 when he was one of the principals in the famous February Seventh incidents along the Peking-Hankow Railway, which cost the lives of more than 40 Communists and labor leaders. (The "February Seventh Massacre," as the Communists describe it, is discussed at greater length in the biography of Teng Chung-hsia.) During these events Lin Yü-nan was director of the Secretariat of the Hupeh Labor Federation.[8]

Lin's primary responsibilities were with the Wuhan labor movement, but he also served for a brief time in the early twenties as secretary of the Hupeh branch of the Socialist (later Communist) Youth League. By early 1925 he was a member of the CCP's Special Labor Committee; this was headed by Chang Kuo-t'ao (q.v.), who, like Lin, was a key official in the Labor Secretariat. The latter organ was superseded in the spring of that year with the formation of the All-China Federation of Labor (ACFL). Lin was a member of the ACFL Executive Committee and secretary-general of the organization,[9] but the dates he held these posts are not known.

By 1927 Lin was director of the Propaganda Department of the CCP Hupeh Committee. He was holding this post in Wuhan (the Hupeh capital) in mid-1927 after the final break between the CCP and the KMT, and thus, in effect, was operating in the Party underground. Any post in Wuhan at that period was particularly dangerous because, among other things, the Party headquarters was also in the city, a fact which brought about unceasing efforts by the KMT to ferret out the Communist operatives. In his capacity as Hupeh propaganda chief, Lin was associated with the Party journal *Ch'ang-chiang* (Yangtze River), then being edited by Hsiang Ching-yü (q.v.). At some time in the late twenties, Lin left Hupeh for Shanghai where he appears to have remained for the rest of his life. He was a key figure in the expanding labor movement at a time when it was becoming a battleground, not only between the Communists and Nationalists but also among the differing factions within the CCP. These inner-Party struggles affected Lin, who opposed Li Li-san's attempts to consolidate his control of the Party in the two years after the Sixth CCP Congress in 1928. Li Li-san, also a top labor leader, had employed aggressive tactics in his attempts to build up a strong trade union movement. And these

tactics, according to his critics, had antagonized the KMT, causing it to be more vigilant against Communist activity within the unions. As the struggle sharpened, rank-and-file membership declined. This continued to cause opposition within the CCP, where Li Li-san had several groups of opponents, one of which was led by Ho Meng-hsiung, a former railway union organizer, and supported by Lin Yü-nan.

Communist historians do not describe Lin's role in the ensuing feud, which ended in the ouster of Li Li-san in late 1930, but it is possible to indicate the pattern of his activities from subsequent events and from Mao Tse-tung's 1945 "Resolution on Some Questions in the History of Our Party." Ho Meng-hsiung and his labor colleagues vociferously opposed Li Li-san at the Third CCP Plenum in September 1930. This opposition was undoubtedly felt soon afterward when Li was ousted at a Politburo meeting in November (see under Li Li-san). But the faction that succeeded Li was no more sympathetic to Ho Meng-hsiung's supporters, nor they to it, than Li Li-san's followers had been. This became apparent at the Fourth Plenum in January 1931 when the "28 Bolsheviks," headed by Ch'en Shao-yü (q.v.), gained control of the Party apparatus in Shanghai. Refusing to accept Ch'en's authority any more than they had Li's, Ho and his followers withdrew from the Plenum (see under Ho Meng-hsiung and Lo Chang-lung) and were subsequently expelled from the Party by the Ch'en Shao-yü leadership. On the night of January 17, 1931, a number of them, including Ho and Lin, were holding a secret meeting at a Shanghai hotel when they were arrested by the British police, who had apparently been tipped off about the meeting place. They were handed over to the KMT and about 20 of them were taken to Lung-hua outside the city where they were executed on February 7, 1931.[10]

The circumstances surrounding Lin's arrest have never been clarified, and he, like many of his colleagues, died under the cloud of having been expelled from the Party. Later, however, the mark against them was partially erased. At a Party plenum held in April 1945 (just prior to the Seventh Congress), the above-mentioned resolution on Party history was adopted, having presumably been drafted by Mao himself. Mao accounted for his own successes and took note of the major "mistakes" of previous leaders. He was, of course, critical of Li Li-san and equally so of Ch'en Shao-yü. It was Ch'en's leadership that had expelled Ho Meng-hsiung and his group as "rightists," and thus, as Mao criticized Ch'en, he at the same time "rehabilitated" Ho and Lin Yü-nan. Though his remarks did not entirely absolve them, it was clear that extenuating circumstances were involved. Mao concluded: "But as to the twenty-odd important cadres of the

Party, including Lin Yü-nan, Li Ch'iu-shih, and Ho Meng-hsiung, they did much useful work for the Party and the people, maintained excellent connection with the masses and, when arrested . . . stood up firm to the enemy and became noble martyrs."[11]

Lin's "rehabilitation" may derive in part from family ties. As noted above, his brother, Lin Yü-ying, was an early labor leader, and he went on to have an active career until his death in 1942. Perhaps more important, the Lin brothers were first cousins of Lin Piao (q.v.), one of the most outstanding military commanders in Chinese Communist history and a man whose career has been closely associated with Mao's since the late 1920's.

1. Jean Chesneaux, *Le Mouvement ouvrier chinois de 1919 à 1927* (Paris, 1962), p. 284.

2. Hsi-wu lao-jen [Elder Hsi-wu], *"Erh-ch'i" hui-i-lu* (Reminiscences of "February Seventh"; Peking, 1957), pp. 8–9.

3. Chow Tse-tsung, *Research Guide to the May Fourth Movement* (Cambridge, Mass., 1963), p. 84.

4. *Ibid.*, p. 97.

5. Hsi-wu lao-jen, p. 9.

6. Modern China Project, Columbia University, New York, Howard L. Boorman, director.

7. Chesneaux, p. 284; Hu Hua, ed., *Chung-kuo hsin min-chu-chu-i ko-ming shih* (A history of China's new democratic revolution; Hong Kong, 1950), p. 25.

8. Hsi-wu lao-jen, p. 85.

9. *Selected Works of Mao Tse-tung* (London, 1956), IV, 340.

10. Benjamin I. Schwartz, *Chinese Communism and the Rise of Mao* (Cambridge, Mass., 1951), p. 166.

11. *Selected Works*, p. 183.

Lin Yü-ying

(1896–1942; Hupeh). Early CCP labor leader; member, CCP Central Committee.

Lin Yü-ying was also known by his Party name Chang Hao. His real name was Lin Chung-tan (according to his obituary),[1] but apparently he seldom used it during his adult life. He was a student in Hupeh (probably Wuhan) at approximately the time of the May Fourth Incident in 1919 and, according to Mao Tse-tung, was one of the early members of the Social Welfare Society.[2] (The importance of this organization in the development of Marxism in China is discussed at length in the biography of Yün Tai-ying.) Lin's brother, Lin Yü-nan, and his first cousin on his father's side, Lin Piao (qq.v.), were also members of the society. Following a political awakening during his student days, Lin joined the CCP about 1922 (the year ·his brother joined). Chang Kuo-t'ao, who knew

them both, regarded Yü-ying as less able and intelligent than his brother.[3]

Like his brother, Lin was in the Communist labor movement during the 1920's. In the course of this work, he traveled widely throughout China; his obituary revealed that he had worked in Harbin, Tientsin, Shanghai, Wuhan, Changsha, and Canton. In the last four cities in particular, the CCP was very active in the 1920's. In addition, he also spent some time in Hong Kong. During the course of his work Lin was twice jailed, and during one prison term he was seriously injured.

In the latter half of 1931 Lin became director of the Propaganda Department of the Communists' All-China Federation of Labor.[4] However, he was not in this post for long, because about 1932 he was dispatched to Moscow as a Chinese representative to the Red Trade Union International (Profintern), which was subordinate to the Comintern. He was said to have little or no knowledge of Russian but was apparently regarded by the Soviets as politically trustworthy.[5] Details on Lin's work in Moscow are lacking, but it appears that he attended the Seventh Comintern Congress in mid-1935, which resolved to foster the famed international "united front against fascism." At the time of the Comintern meeting, Mao Tse-tung's Long Marchers were in west China where they became involved in a bitter dispute with the Communist troops led by Chang Kuo-t'ao. At this juncture, or soon thereafter, Lin was reportedly sent back to China (via Outer Mongolia). One of his missions was to bring back a detailed report on the Comintern Congress. The second task was to attempt to mediate (or at least present Soviet views) on the ultimate destination of the Long Marchers, one of the key points in the Mao-Chang dispute. Chang Kuo-t'ao asserts that the Russians favored his plan to settle in Sinkiang.[6]

A year later, in mid-1936, Mao commented briefly about Lin (referring to him as Chang Hao) in an interview with Edgar Snow. Mao said that Lin was "now in charge of work among White troops"; another source asserts that in the previous January Lin had already become deputy secretary under Chou En-lai of the newly established CCP Committee for Work among White Troops.[7] The task of the committee was to woo Nationalist troops to the Communist cause or, at a minimum, to arouse within KMT ranks the growing sentiment that Chinese of all political shades should devote their energies toward resisting the steady Japanese encroachments against Chinese sovereignty. At the very time that Snow was interviewing Mao, the Communists were already active in nearby Sian in a concerted attempt to induce key KMT generals and officers toward the acceptance of the "united front" policies espoused by the CCP (see under Teng Fa and Wang Ping-nan). Teng

Fa, with whom Lin was later closely associated, was then in Sian, and it seems possible that Lin may have been working with him there.

Lin was back in the Yenan area by 1937, and in that year he delivered a series of lectures on the "tactical line of the CCP." These were later published in a small book which, though its authenticity has been disputed, has been frequently used by the KMT to "prove" the duplicity and perfidy of the Communists' united front policies and to demonstrate that the CCP was the willing tool of the Russians.[8] As late as October 1950 it was cited in detail by the influential Hu Shih in an article for *Foreign Affairs* entitled "China in Stalin's Grand Strategy." Dr. Hu, quoting passages from Lin, asserted that it was CCP obedience to the teachings of Lenin and Stalin on the strategy of retreat that had led to the decision to abandon Kiangsi and to make the Long March (although Hu does not suggest that Lin played any role in that decision).

Lin remained in Yenan where he worked closely with Teng Fa, who was also a labor leader as well as a top figure in the Communists' intelligence apparatus. In 1940 Lin and Teng participated in publishing *Chung-kuo kung-jen* (Chinese workers).[9] During this same period Lin was also head of a school for workers in Yenan and deputy secretary under Teng Fa of the Party Central Committee's Industrial Workers' Committee (Chih-kung wei-yuan-hui). In the spring of 1941 Lin suffered a brain hemorrhage and spent the last year of his life partially paralyzed. He died in Yenan on March 6, 1942. His funeral committee was headed by the important Party veteran Li Fu-ch'un and included among its members Teng Fa and Lin Piao. Lin Yü-ying's obituary revealed that he was a member of the Party Central Committee at the time of his death. There is extremely little information on the composition of the Central Committee during the war years, but it is known that some changes were made at the Party's Sixth Plenum in the fall of 1938. Lin may have been among those added at that time.

Lin was survived by his wife, Hsu Sung-lan, and three sons. At the time of Lin's death, his wife was working in the bank subordinate to the Shensi-Kansu-Ninghsia Border Region Government, and his second and third sons were students at Yenan University.

1. *Chieh-fang jih-pao* (Liberation daily), March 7, 1942.
2. Edgar Snow, *Red Star over China* (New York, 1938), p. 46.
3. Modern China Project, Columbia University, New York, Howard L. Boorman, director.
4. *Issues and Studies* (Taipei), October 1966, p. 46.
5. Modern China Project.

6. Robert C. North, *Moscow and Chinese Communists* (Stanford, Calif., 1953), p. 175; Charles B. McLane, *Soviet Policy and the Chinese Communists, 1931–1946* (New York, 1958), p. 58.
7. Snow, p. 132; *Issues and Studies* (Taipei), August 1968, p. 38.
8. McLane, p. 88; Lyman P. Van Slyke, *Enemies and Friends, The United Front in Chinese Communist History* (Stanford, Calif., 1967), p. 157; Chün-tu Hsüeh, *The Chinese Communist Movement, 1937–1949* (Stanford, Calif., 1962), p. 51.
9. Hua Ying-shen, ed., *Chung-kuo kung-ch'an tang lieh-shih* (Biographies of Chinese Communist Party martyrs; Hong Kong, 1949), p. 273.

Liu Ch'ang-sheng

(1904–1967; Hai-yang, Shantung). Vice-chairman, All-China Federation of Trade Unions; vice-president, World Federation of Trade Unions; member, Standing Committee, NPC; member, CCP Central Committee.

One of China's leading trade union officials, Liu Ch'ang-sheng spent many of his younger years in Vladivostok and then worked in the Shanghai underground during most of the Sino-Japanese War and the civil war against the Nationalists. He worked as a leading official in Shanghai in the early years of the PRC and after 1953 had close ties with the international Communist trade union movement. Liu was one of the most widely traveled members of the CCP hierarchy; his travels ranged from Australia to Africa to Chile, in addition to frequent trips to the Communist bloc nations.

Liu was born into a poor peasant family in 1904 in Hai-yang (Chiu-hai-yang) hsien, located on the southern shore of the Shantung peninsula 100 miles northeast of Tsingtao. He received three years of schooling in the years from 1913 to 1917, after which he went to Dairen where he worked in a tea shop. From Dairen, he went to Vladivostok in 1920. This move to the USSR may have been related to the fact that a rather large number of Chinese—mainly from Shantung—migrated to Russia via Manchuria in the early part of the 20th century.[1] By the time Liu arrived in Vladivostok there were about 20,000 Chinese living there. He spent the next decade and a half in the Soviet Union, most of it apparently in and around the port of Vladivostok where he worked as a cobbler, log-roller, and longshoreman.

In the early twenties Liu furthered his education by attending a night school for wharf workers and was eventually employed in both a gold miners' labor union and a union of forestry workers. His first association with Communism may have been during these formative years. In any case, in 1924 he is said to have joined the

Youth League, although it is not clear whether this was the Chinese Communist Youth League or the Soviet Komsomol. Four years later, in 1928, Liu joined the CCP.

During Liu's long stay in Vladivostok he apparently took a fairly active part in a movement sponsored by the Soviet government from the late twenties to devise a system of teaching Chinese to assist in training the approximately 100,000 Chinese living within Soviet borders, most of whom were poorly educated. A version of Latinized Chinese, which was largely the work of Ch'ü Ch'iu-pai (q.v.), was published in 1930. Ch'ü's pamphlet served as a catalyst for a discussion of the subject in a Chinese paper published in Vladivostok, *The Worker's Way*. Later, in 1931, another script was adopted for general use and efforts were made to provide courses for instructors, including men in "workers' faculties." It was possibly in this capacity that Liu was among the 87 persons who attended the First Conference on the Latinization of Chinese in a Chinese theater in Vladivostok in September 1931. A second conference was held in Vladivostok in October 1932, but it is not known if Liu was among those attending.[2] It is probable that Liu was in contact with Wu Yü-chang and Lin Po-ch'ü (qq.v.), both of whom were involved in the problem of latinizing Chinese and both of whom spent some time in the Soviet Far East during the period that Liu was there. Another possible colleague was Hsu Chih-chen (q.v.), who was in the Soviet Far East after 1927 and who, like Liu, later became an important Chinese Communist trade union official.

In the mid-thirties Liu returned to China. With some notable exceptions, like Li Li-san and Ch'en Shao-yü (qq.v.), few Chinese Communist leaders have spent so many years in the Soviet Union. On his return Liu went to the Communist capital at Yenan where, probably because of his background in labor unions, he became an official of the Northwest Executive Bureau of the All-China Federation of Labor (1936–37). With the outbreak of the war in 1937, Liu was assigned to Shanghai as an underground operative. He appears to have divided his time throughout the war years between the Shanghai underground and the Party apparatus in that city and nearby areas under the control of the Communist New Fourth Army, which operated in east-central China. Liu is reported to have been a member of the Kiangsu Party Committee by 1938 and head of the Policy Research Office of the Party's East China Bureau by 1942. In addition, at sometime during the war he was director of the Political Department of the New Fourth Army's Sixth Division, which was commanded by T'an Chen-lin.

Although Liu was a relatively unknown figure by the time the Party's Seventh Congress was

held in Yenan in April–June 1945, he was elected to alternate membership on the Party Central Committee. At the time only 44 full and 33 alternate members were elected; in view of Liu's work in Shanghai, it is possible that he was elected *in absentia*. In the postwar period he apparently spent most of his time in and around Shanghai, continuing his work there as a Party official on the Shanghai Party Committee and as a labor organizer. Shanghai was an area of relatively open CCP operations during the period of the Marshall Mission (early 1946 to early 1947) when the KMT and CCP were ostensibly attempting to work out a nationwide truce. But from early 1947 to the conquest of the city by the Communists in May 1949, the Communists had to operate underground. Consequently, relatively little is known of Liu's work in this period. In August 1948 the Communists held the Sixth Labor Congress in the Manchurian city of Harbin. Liu was elected a member of the Standing Committee of the Executive Committee under the All-China Federation of Labor (known after 1953 as the All-China Federation of Trade Unions—ACFTU). In later years he was to assume far more important posts in this organization (see below).

From the time the Communists marched into Shanghai in May 1949 until his transfer abroad in 1953 (see below), Liu was one of the most active and important CCP officials there, although he was overshadowed by such top Party leaders as Jao Shu-shih, Ch'en I, Tseng Shan, and Liu Hsiao (qq.v.). He was an Executive Committee member of the Shanghai Party Committee from 1949 to 1952, and in 1952–53 he was the third secretary (subordinate to Secretary Ch'en I and Second Secretary Liu Hsiao). Within the Shanghai Municipal People's Government, Liu Ch'ang-sheng was a Government Council member from 1950 to 1955 and a member of the Government's Finance and Economics Committee from 1951 to 1954. He also served in the regional government organ known as the East China Military and Administrative Committee (ECMAC) from 1950 to 1952 and as the East China Administrative Committee (ECAC) from 1952 to 1954. He was a member of both the ECMAC and ECAC, headed the ECMAC's Labor Department, and served as a member of the ECMAC's Finance and Economics Committee.

Like most important Party-government leaders in the early years of the PRC, Liu held posts in the "mass" organizations. He headed the Shanghai chapter of the China Peace Committee from 1950 and from the following year he was vice-chairman of the Sino-Soviet Friendship Association's Shanghai branch. During his four years in Shanghai after 1949, his most significant contributions were probably in the field of labor and trade union activities. As already mentioned, he headed the Labor Department for the five-province ECMAC. In addition, from 1949 he directed both the East China and Shanghai Offices of the All-China Federation of Labor. He was also identified in 1952 as president of the Federation's East China Trade Union Cadres' School. In addition, Liu served on various *ad hoc* bodies connected with labor affairs, as in 1950 when he was a vice-chairman of a special committee to provide relief for unemployed workers. Similarly, it often fell to Liu to deliver major reports dealing with labor matters in east China; an example of this occurred in October 1950 when he spoke on the problem of unemployment before a Shanghai legislative body.

Although Liu spent almost all the early years of the PRC in Shanghai, he received two national posts when the government and many of the important "mass" organizations were formed in the fall of 1949. He was a member of the CPPCC's First National Committee from 1949 to 1954 (and was promoted to the Standing Committee in February 1953), and for the same years he was also a member of the Sino-Soviet Friendship Association's Executive Board.

In October 1952 Liu was a member of the CCP delegation to the 19th CPSU Congress in Moscow (the last held before the death of Stalin), accompanying such key Party leaders as Liu Shao-ch'i, Jao Shu-shih, Ch'en I, Li Fu-ch'un, and Wang Chia-hsiang (qq.v.). After that time Liu spent a large portion of his time abroad, mainly in connection with labor activities. In the month after the 19th Congress in Moscow, he headed a Chinese trade union delegation to the 35th anniversary of the Russian Revolution, and in March 1953 he was again in Moscow for Stalin's funeral. A month later he attended a session of the World Federation of Trade Unions (WFTU) in Vienna where the WFTU headquarters were located. At this meeting Liu was elected as a secretary of the WFTU, the international Communist-dominated organization to which the ACFTU is affiliated. (A month later, in May 1953, he was promoted to a vice-chairmanship of the ACFTU.) Two months later, in June 1953, he left Peking to become a full-time staff member at the WFTU headquarters in Vienna. From that time until his recall to China in 1957 he was in charge of regional liaison bureaus and "colonial questions." Significantly, Liu was the first important Chinese Communist to be assigned on a long-term basis to the WFTU in Vienna where, incidentally, the Chinese Communists have no diplomatic representation. In the years that followed, Liu was constantly traveling, usually to attend some event sponsored by the WFTU. And logically, when WFTU meetings were held in Vienna, he usually led the Chinese delegation, as in October 1953 when the WFTU held its third congress there.

In June 1954 he represented the CCP at the 10th Congress of the Czech Communist Party and in February 1955 he led the Chinese delegation to the Fourth Congress of the Albanian Trade Unions in Tirana. In these same years of the middle fifties, Liu was also active in the World Peace Council (WPC), which, like the WFTU, was headquartered in Vienna. Although it is not certain whether he attended the meeting, he was elected to membership on the WPC in Budapest in June 1953. He was a member of the Chinese delegation to a WPC meeting in Vienna in November 1953 and to the World Peace Congress in Helsinki in June 1955. In 1955 he also traveled to Paris twice, first as China's representative to the 30th National Congress of the Confédération Général de Travail (CGT) in June, and again in September when he attended ceremonies commemorating the 10th anniversary of the WFTU and the 60th anniversary of the CGT.

Liu was officially recalled from his WFTU post in early 1957, but he had already returned to Peking just prior to that date. His travels on behalf of the PRC after that time continued at an intensive pace. In November 1956 Liu joined a delegation to Europe headed by Politburo member P'eng Chen. Officially, the group went abroad as a joint NPC-Peking Municipal Government delegation, but in fact it appeared to be part of a major effort by the Chinese to mediate the disputes that had broken out between Moscow and its satellites in East Europe in the period before and after the famous Hungarian Revolution in the fall of 1956. In the period from mid-November 1956 to the end of January 1957, the group visited the USSR, Czechoslovakia, Rumania, Bulgaria, Albania, and Yugoslavia. Also, while most the delegation members were in Czechoslovakia in December, P'eng and Liu left the group briefly to attend the Eighth Congress of the Italian Communist Party, thus becoming the first important Chinese Communists to visit that nation.

In the meantime, during his years abroad, Liu had received new assignments in the PRC government and the CCP. He was elected in 1954 as a deputy from his native Shantung to the First NPC (1954–1959); he was re-elected to the Second NPC (1959–1964) and to the Third NPC, which first met in December 1964–January 1965. In all three congresses Liu was a member of the governing Standing Committee. More important, at the Party's Eighth National Congress in September 1956, he was promoted from alternate to full membership on the Central Committee.

In the period from 1957 to 1963, Liu made numerous trips abroad; most, but not all, were in some way connected with trade union activities. The more important of Liu's trips are discussed in the paragraphs below, followed by a chronological list of his less important journeys. In October 1957 he led the Chinese delegation to the Fourth World Trade Union Congress in Leipzig, East Germany. As described above, Liu had been recalled from the WFTU Headquarters in early 1957, at which time he relinquished his post as a secretary on the WFTU Secretariat. At the Leipzig Congress, however, he was promoted to a vice-presidency in the WFTU, a post to which he was re-elected as late as October 1965. In the month after the congress at Leipzig, Liu was a member of a "working people's" delegation sent to Moscow to participate in the celebrations marking the 40th anniversary of the Russian Revolution. A large number of top Chinese leaders were in Moscow for this occasion, including Mao Tse-tung, who led the principal Chinese delegation. Liu's next trip of note occurred in November–December 1959 when he led a delegation to Chile to attend the Second Congress of the United Confederation of Labor of Chile. His trip to Santiago stands out because extremely few Chinese Communists have visited South America. In fact, Liu was the first member of the CCP Central Committee to visit that continent. Another "first" for Liu occurred in October 1960 when he led a trade union group to Australia—once again, he was the first Central Committee member to visit that country. Of interest is the fact that Liu's appearance in Brisbane caused a riot when he visited that city in mid-October, an event that naturally received much attention in the Australian press.[3]

The year 1960 witnessed the emergence of a large number of new African nations, most of them former French colonies. In preparation for this, the Chinese created the China-Africa People's Friendship Association (CAPFA) in April 1960 and named Liu as the chairman. Although he was already one of the most widely traveled Chinese leaders, Liu had not yet visited Africa. However, less than a year later he left Peking for Africa on one of the longest trips abroad ever taken by a top Chinese Communist leader. From early March to mid-June 1961 he toured and held talks with top government officials in the following nations: Guinea, Mali, Ghana, Niger, Upper Volta, Senegal, Togo, and Dahomey. As of that time the Chinese had diplomatic relations only with the first three countries mentioned.

Liu's less significant travels are listed in chronological order below; unless otherwise indicated, he led the delegation.

1957: First Congress of Workers' Councils of Yugoslavia, June; member, Chinese delegation to WFTU Executive Committee meeting, Moscow, July; 1958: 19th Congress of National Federation of Free Hungarian Unions, February; 1959: 12th Congress of the All-Soviet Union of Trade Unions, March; WFTU Executive Committee meeting, Warsaw, April; trade union delegation to Iraq for first anniversary of Iraqi Revolution, July; Third National Congress of the General Federation of Trade Unions of (North) Korea, October–November; 1960: Ninth Congress of Italian Communist Party, January–February; delegation to celebrations marking 10th anniversary of Sino-Soviet Treaty of Friendship, Alliance, and Mutual Assistance, Moscow, February; trade union delegation to Belgium, March; trade union delegation to Burma, November; 1961: WFTU Executive Committee meeting, East Berlin, February; member, NPC friendship delegation to Indonesia and Burma, August–September; Fifth Congress, WFTU, Moscow, December; 1962: WFTU Executive Committee meeting, Budapest, May–June; 1963: WFTU Executive Committee meeting, Prague, January; meeting of the International Trade Union Committee for Solidarity with the Workers and People of South Vietnam, Hanoi, October.

Liu's intimate ties with the WFTU, one of the most important of the many Communist front organizations, naturally involved him in the Sino-Soviet dispute as both of these major powers vied for control of the WFTU. As explained in the biography of alternate Politburo member K'ang Sheng (q.v.), the Chinese had seriously challenged certain aspects of Soviet foreign policy (notably disarmament) in early 1960. Not long after, Liu was given the task of elaborating on K'ang's criticisms. This occurred at a WFTU meeting held in Peking in June 1960. Liu, who headed the Chinese delegation, sharply criticized Soviet disarmament policies and described as an "illusion" Khrushchev's position that war could be eliminated while "imperialism" still existed. He also dwelt on the inevitability of wars, especially "wars of national liberation." Writing in 1962, one authority has described this meeting as the "beginning of the most acute phase of the Sino-Soviet conflict."[4] At the many WFTU meetings attended by Liu after mid-1960 (listed above), he time and again attacked Soviet policies, directly and indirectly. Such a role had the inevitable affect of placing Liu among the Peking leaders who allegedly favor a very "tough" foreign policy, but such a judgment about Liu ignores the likelihood that he was merely carrying out CCP policies decided upon at a higher level. Even the Russians (in a Radio Moscow commentary of April 27, 1964) took note of Liu's many charges, sarcastically commenting that he had stated that "all proposals on disarmament now being put forward are but illusions which bear no relation to reality."

As already mentioned, Liu was elected a vice-chairman of the All-China Federation of Trade Unions (ACFTU) at the Seventh Congress in May 1953. At this time he ranked third in this organization behind Chairman Lai Jo-yü and

Vice-chairman Liu Ning-i (qq.v.). At the next congress, held in December 1957, Liu Ning-i stepped down as a vice-chairman and Liu Ch'ang-sheng replaced him as the senior vice-chairman. However, following the death of Lai Jo-yü in May 1958, the highest echelons of the ACFTU were reorganized (August 1958). Liu Ning-i, who had previously seemed to be phasing out of trade union work, was brought back to become ACFTU chairman. Liu Ch'ang-sheng continued as the senior vice-chairman, and is thus the second most important man in Federation. The careers of the two Liu's were in many ways quite similar after the PRC was established. Liu Ning-i's travels to WFTU in the early fifties were strikingly similar to Liu Ch'ang-sheng's in more recent years. The latter, in fact, replaced the former as a WFTU vice-president in 1957.

In the late fifties and sixties Liu received further posts, each closely related to his work in international relations. After mid-1958 he was a Standing Committee member of the China Peace Committee, and in April 1959 he was given a similar post on the Chinese People's Association for Cultural Relations with Foreign Countries, an organization often used to contact persons and groups in nations not having diplomatic relations with Peking. As already noted, it was in 1960 that Liu became chairman of the China-Africa People's Friendship Association. Five years later, in mid-1965, he was named to the Standing Committee of the Afro-Asian Solidarity Committee of China, one of the most active of the "people's" organizations in the sixties. When not abroad, Liu occasionally took part in trade union activities in Peking, as in late 1959 when he attended a conference of "advanced" workers. But even in Peking most of his time was devoted to liaison with visiting trade union delegations from abroad. Because visiting trade unionists are usually given priority treatment, Liu was often reported in Peking in the company of China's top leaders (e.g., Mao Tse-tung) when they received the visitors.

Other men in the PRC who have traveled almost as much as Liu, like Kuo Mo-jo and Shen Yen-ping, ranked far below Liu politically. The only other important political leaders equally well-traveled are Chou En-lai, Ch'en I, Liao Ch'eng-chih, and Liu's immediate superior in the ACFTU, Liu Ning-i. Among China's top leaders, Liu Ch'eng-sheng was probably most closely linked with Liu Shao-ch'i, who is characterized by the Communists as the spiritual father of the Trade Union Federation and who was the honorary chairman of this organization from 1948 to 1957. Both men had long ties with organized labor, both were connected with the New Fourth Army, and both had prominent roles in international liaison work with foreign Communist parties.

A Yugoslav news source reported that Liu

missed a meeting of the WFTU in Bulgaria in March 1964. Rather little was heard of his activities after that date, and then on January 20, 1967, he died.

1. John De Francis, *Nationalism and Language Reform in China* (Princeton, N.J., 1950), p. 88.
2. *Ibid.,* pp. 89–100.
3. *New York Times,* October 16, 1960; Melbourne, *Sun News Pictorial,* October 17, 1960.
4. Donald S. Zagoria, *The Sino-Soviet Conflict, 1956–1961* (Princeton, N.J., 1962), p. 320.

Liu Chen

(1909–   ; Hupeh). Air Force deputy commander; alternate member, CCP Central Committee.

A career military officer since the 1930's, Liu Chen is one of the top officers in the PLA Air Force. He spent the Sino-Japanese War years in north China and Kiangsu as a brigade commander and then participated in the conquest of Manchuria in the late forties. Liu directed Communist air operations during the Korean War and was elected an alternate member of the Party Central Committee in 1958. A colonel-general, he has been a deputy commander of the Air Force since 1959.

Nothing is known of Liu Chen's career until the late spring of 1935 when he was serving as a battalion political officer in the Communists' 25th Army, units of which were fighting in southeastern Shensi near the borders of Hupeh and Honan. The 25th Army was initially recruited in the Hupeh-Honan-Anhwei (Oyüwan) Soviet and had begun an independent long march to Shensi about a year before the main force of Long Marchers had left Kiangsi in October 1934 led by Chu Te and Mao Tse-tung. Led by Hsu Hai-tung (q.v.), the 25th Army had arrived in southern Shensi by the fall of 1934; in early 1935 Hsu proceeded on his march to northern Shensi by way of Kansu, but left some of his forces under Cheng Wei-san (q.v.) in southeastern Shensi. Apparently, Liu Chen was among the men under the over-all control of Cheng. According to an account by Liu, he was fighting in southeast Shensi near the Hupeh-Honan border when he was wounded in a battle that took place there in May–June 1935.[1]

By the latter part of 1936 Liu was in north Shensi with the main Communist units, but reports on his activities at this time are somewhat conflicting. According to one report he studied at the Red Army Military Academy located near Yenan, the military institution that Mao's Long Marchers re-established in north Shensi in mid-1936. Some reports state that Liu was sent from Shensi to the Soviet Union for military training;

according to one of these, however, he went there during the year 1939–40. In any event, Liu was in north Shensi by mid-1937 when the Sino-Japanese War began. At this time the Communists regrouped their forces in north China into the Eighth Route Army, which was composed of three divisions, one of them the 115th Division led by Lin Piao. Liu was given command of the 690th Regiment, a post that placed him under his old commander, Hsu Hai-tung, who led the 344th Brigade, one of the major components of the 115th Division.

Liu's activities in the late 1930's are not recorded, but according to another wartime account written by Liu, in the year 1940–41 he was commanding a unit known as the 10th Brigade fighting in "north China."[2] Then, following the New Fourth Army Incident of early 1941 (see under Yeh T'ing), his brigade was sent southward to operate in an area north of the Huai River and west of the important rail line linking Tientsin and Nanking. With this change of locale, the brigade was placed under the Fourth Division of the New Fourth Army, the major Communist force in east-central China, which was commanded from 1941 by Ch'en I. In July 1941 Liu's unit was ordered to move eastward to the Huai-Hai area, located in north Kiangsu in a region bounded on the north by the important Lunghai Railway and on the west by the Grand Canal. The task of the brigade, as explained to Liu Chen by Liu Shao-ch'i, then political commissar of the New Fourth Army, was to build a solid base in north Kiangsu that would provide a link between the New Fourth Army and other Communist units fighting in north China. According to Liu Chen's account, he and some of his 10th Brigade comrades preferred mobile warfare to the more mundane tasks of building a Communist base area. But after being "sternly criticized" by Liu Shao-ch'i, he was allegedly persuaded to see the "correctness" of the latter's view. In cooperation with Chin Ming (q.v.), who was secretary of the Party Committee for the Huai-Hai area as well as political commissar of the military district, Liu Chen remained in this important region until the end of the war, taking part in numerous battles with Japanese forces during this period.[3]

After the Japanese surrender in August 1945, Liu's 10th Brigade was ordered to Manchuria; Liu was once again placed under the command of Lin Piao, who was then establishing the Northeast Democratic Allied Army (NEDAA), the force that conquered the Nationalists in Manchuria by the end of 1948. Liu fought in various battles in Manchuria and remained with the NEDAA after it was redesignated the Fourth Field Army in early 1949. In January 1949, as a troop commander, Liu took part in the capture of Tientsin and then moved southward with Lin Piao's field army, whose conquests were completed in April 1950 with the capture of Hainan Island. Liu's exact position in the Fourth Field Army is not known, but when receiving an official appointment in 1951 he was identified as a "former" deputy commander of a PLA corps, presumably in reference to his stint with Lin Piao's forces.

Soon after the outbreak of the Korean War in June 1950, major components of the Fourth Field Army—then regarded as the PLA's best fighting unit—were transferred from central-south China to Manchuria. U.S. intelligence reports of early November 1950 (just a few days after the Chinese entered the Korean War) placed Liu in command of the Fourth Field Army's 39th Army, a 30,000-man force located in the Yalu River area opposite Korea.[4] At this juncture, Liu's forces moved across the Yalu to engage American and South Korean units. However, it is not certain if Liu himself led his troops, although it is probable that he at least made periodic visits to the front in the early stages of the fighting. Rather, it appears that he operated mainly in Manchuria. This supposition is suggested by the fact he was appointed to membership on the Northeast People's Government Council in March 1951, only a few months after the entry of the Chinese into the Korean War. (Other Chinese commanders were usually not given such civilian-oriented tasks once they had arrived in Korea.) Furthermore, by December 1952 Liu was also identified as commander of the PLA Air Force of the Northeast Military Region, headquartered in Mukden. When the war began, the PLA Air Force was virtually non-existent, but massive Soviet aid quickly transformed it into one of the world's largest. The Chinese Air Force did not operate from airfields in Korea but from fields in the Manchurian "sanctuary." Consequently, as head of the Northeast Air Force, Liu was effectively in charge of Chinese air operations during most or all of the Korean War.

Rather surprisingly, after the end of 1952 nothing was heard of Liu until mid-1957. For example, when the Northeast People's Government was reorganized into the Northeast Administrative Committee in January 1953, he was not reappointed to membership. He did not reappear in public again until mid-1957 when he attended a PLA art exhibit in Peking; he was identified then as a PLA colonel-general, equivalent to a three-star general in the U.S. Air Force. Liu was a member of the military delegation led by P'eng Te-huai to Moscow for the 40th anniversary of the Russian Revolution in November 1957. The main Chinese delegation was led by Mao Tse-tung. P'eng's military group returned to China in early December via Vladivostok and Khabarovsk. In the following May, at the second session of the Party's Eighth National Congress, Liu was elected an alternate member of the Central Committee. Exactly a year later he was identified as a deputy commander of the PLA Air Force where he served under Liu Ya-lou until the latter's death in May 1965. Because the two Liu's were the only Air Force officers of Central Committee rank, it would have been logical for Liu Chen to assume command of the Air Force following Liu Ya-lou's death. However, the assignment went to Wu Fa-hsien, who had previously been the Air Force political commissar. It is possible that Liu was not given the post because of poor health, a supposition that is suggested by his rather unusual pattern of public appearances since 1949, most of which have been confined to two periods—1957–1959 and 1963–64. Nothing is known of Liu's personal life aside from the fact that he is married to Li Ling, whose antecedents are unknown.

1. *Hsing-huo liao-yuan* (A single spark can start a prairie fire; Hong Kong 1960), pp. 239–245.
2. *CB* 777, p. 18.
3. *Ibid.*, pp. 17–25.
4. Charles A. Willoughby and John Chamberlain, *MacArthur, 1941–1951* (New York, 1954), p. 394.

Liu Chien-hsun

(c.1908–   ; Hopeh). First secretary, Honan Party Committee; alternate member, CCP Central Committee.

Liu Chien-hsun joined the Communist Party in the middle thirties at about the time of the Long March. Subsequently, he was active in Shansi where he served with the guerrilla forces commanded by Po I-po, whose headquarters in the early years of the Sino-Japanese War were in the T'ai-hang mountain area, which formed the border between southeast Shansi and north Honan. Po's forces were part of the guerrilla army of the Shansi-Hopeh-Shantung-Honan (Chin-Chi-Lu-Yü) Border Region.

When the war ended, Liu took part in the work of the Peking Executive Headquarters, which was charged with implementing the cease-fire agreement, brought about through the efforts of U.S. Special Envoy George C. Marshall (January 1946). Liu served for a period as the head of the Communist side on the truce team stationed at Taiyuan, the Shansi capital, and also as a section chief of the military sub-committee of the headquarters in Peking. Chinese Communist officers were given no personal ranks before 1955, but during the period he worked under the Executive Headquarters (1946–47) he held the simulated rank of colonel.

From the establishment of the Communist regime in 1949 until the mid-1950's, Liu's activities were centered in Hupeh where the senior Party official was Li Hsien-nien, a leading government administrator and a Politburo member after 1956. Liu held significant posts in the Party, government, and military administrations, his principal posts being: deputy secretary, Hupeh Party Committee, 1950–1952; second secretary, Hupeh Party Committee, 1952–1954; secretary, Hupeh Party Committee, 1954–1955 (under the ranking secretary, Liu Tzu-hou, q.v.); member, Hupeh Provincial People's Government, 1950–1954; chairman Land Reform Committee, Hupeh Provincial People's Government, 1950 to at least 1951; political commissar, Hupeh Military District, 1952; deputy from Hupeh to the First NPC, 1954–1959.

In addition to these provincial posts, Liu also held assignments under the regional Party and government administrations, both of which had their headquarters in Wuhan, the capital of Hupeh, where Liu was stationed. From mid-1951 until 1953 he was a member of the Central-South Military and Administrative Committee (CSMAC), which had jurisdiction over Honan, Hupeh, Hunan, Kiangsi, Kwangtung, and Kwangsi. The CSMAC was reorganized into the Central-South Administrative Committee in January 1953 at which time Liu was reappointed to membership, a position he held until the CSAC was abolished in 1954. Within the regional CCP structure, having jurisdiction over the same provinces as the governmental CSMAC, Liu served in 1953–54 as the secretary-general of the Party's Central-South Bureau, a position that placed him under such significant Party figures as Yeh Chien-ying, Teng Tzu-hui, and Li Hsueh-feng, as well as his immediate superior in Hupeh, Li Hsien-nien.

By January 1956, Liu was relieved of all his posts in Hupeh and transferred to a position in the higher echelons of the national Party structure when he was made a deputy director of the Central Committee's Rural Work Department under Director Teng Tzu-hui, a former superior in the central-south area. However, it was not long after this that there was trouble in the Party Committee in Kwangsi, and in June 1957 Party First Secretary Ch'en Man-yuan (q.v.) and 10 other important Kwangsi officials were removed from office on charges of malfeasance. Soon after, in September 1957, Liu was sent to Kwangsi to replace Ch'en as first secretary. Presumably Liu had gained a familiarity with the problems of Kwangsi from his experience as an official of the Central-South Party Bureau in the early 1950's. In addition, he also became a member of the Kwangsi Provincial People's Government (September 1957). At this time the first steps were being taken to transform Kwangsi from a provincial administration to that of an autonomous region for the Chuang ethnic minority, a Thai group living in the province since ancient times and forming the largest ethnic minority in China. Kwangsi was reorganized into the Kwangsi-Chuang Autonomous Region in March 1958. Some 500 persons, including delegates from other autonomous regions, attended the inaugural meeting, which was addressed by veteran Communist Ho Lung, a member of the Politburo and a vice-premier of the State Council. Liu retained his post as first secretary of the Party Committee for the region and at this same time (March 1958) was also re-elected to membership on the region's government council. He was, moreover, elected to the chairmanship of the First Kwangsi Committee of the CPPCC, a post previously held by Ch'en Man-yuan. His Party colleague in Kwangsi was Wei Kuo-ch'ing (q.v.), a Chuang nationality member, who was elected as chairman of the newly formed Kwangsi-Chuang Autonomous Region. At the time that this reorganization in Kwangsi was taking place (March 1958), Wei Kuo-ch'ing outranked Liu in the national Party hierarchy, Wei having been elected an alternate member of the Party Central Committee at the Eighth National Party Congress in September 1956. However, when the Eighth Congress held its second session in May 1958, Liu was also elevated to alternate membership on the Party Central Committee.

Late in November 1958, Liu was reported in Wuhan, presumably to attend the important Sixth Party Plenum, at which time some of the more radical aspects of the movement to establish the famous people's communes were curtailed. In February 1960 he was named as one of the vice-chairmen of a special committee set up by the State Council in Peking to "receive and resettle" returned overseas Chinese, a committee chaired by Liao Ch'eng-chih, Peking's top specialist in overseas Chinese affairs. The organization had been formed in the wake of serious differences in Sino-Indonesian relations, which centered around the alleged ill-treatment of Chinese in Indonesia. As suggested by the appointment of Liu, many thousands of the Chinese who returned to China at this time settled in Kwangsi.

Liu remained as one of the key officials in Kwangsi until mid-1961 when he was transferred to Honan. (He was replaced as first secretary in Kwangsi by Wei Kuo-ch'ing, his colleague there for over five years.) In Honan Liu replaced Wu Chih-p'u (q.v.) as first Party secretary by July 1961. Wu in turn was demoted to second secretary. As in the case of his relations in Kwangsi, Liu was once again placed above a man who ranked above him in the national Party hierarchy. When he assumed the senior Party post in Honan, he was only an alternate member of the Central Committee, in contrast to Wu's stature as a full member.

Already the senior Honan Party official, Liu assumed two new posts in Honan in 1964 and another in 1965. In September 1964 he was elected a member of the Honan Provincial People's Council at the same time that Wen Min-sheng was re-elected as governor. In the same month Liu was elected to chair the Third Honan Committee of the CPPCC, thereby replacing Wu Chih-p'u, who had headed the Second Honan Committee. In May of 1965 Liu was elected chairman of the preparatory committee of the Honan Association of Poor and Lower-Middle Peasants; this association was formed at a time when the importance of class background was being stressed in all parts of China. Soon after, in mid-1965, he was further identified as a secretary of the Central-South Party Bureau, a bureau headed by T'ao Chu. The Central-South Bureau that Liu had served in during the early fifties was abolished in 1954, but it was re-created in accordance with a directive of the Ninth Party Plenum in January 1961.

Liu Chih-tan

(1902–1936; Pao-an hsien, Shensi). Early Shensi Soviet leader.

Liu Chih-tan was one of the founders and key leaders of the Communist guerrilla movement in north Shensi in the twenties and thirties. After receiving his training at the Whampoa Military Academy he worked for the military forces of warlord Feng Yü-hsiang and then returned in 1928 to Shensi, where over the next seven years he fought in a series of engagements against local Shensi military-political leaders and KMT troops. The soviet area that Liu developed was the haven into which Mao Tse-tung brought his Long Marchers in 1935. In the next year, while taking part in a Communist military thrust in Shansi, Liu was mortally wounded.

Liu Chih-tan, whose name is frequently romanized Liu Tzu-tan, was born in Pao-an hsien, northwest Shensi. He came from a family of middle class peasants. Liu attended Yü-lin Middle School in northern Shensi from 1921 to 1924. Kao Kang (q.v.), who was closely associated with Liu in the late twenties and early thirties, was one of Liu's schoolmates. The school was one of the major channels through which young Shensi intellectuals were recruited into the Youth League and the CCP. In large part this was the work of Wei Yeh-ch'ou, one of the earliest members of the CCP and a former colleague of Li Ta-chao (q.v.) in Peking.[1] In the latter part of 1921 Wei became a teacher at Yü-lin. He organized a student group and in 1922 Liu Chih-tan became its chairman. In the next year Liu led two student boycotts, one of which was directed against a classmate who was the son of Ching Yueh-hsiu, the most powerful warlord in north Shensi. The student organization was sufficiently influential to have the younger Ching transferred to a middle school in Sian. Liu joined the Socialist Youth League in late 1924 and the CCP in early 1925. He thus became one of the earliest members in northwest China of both the League and the CCP, which did not have branches in Shensi until 1924.

In the fall of 1925 Liu went to Canton where he enrolled in the Whampoa Military Academy's fifth class,[2] which began in February 1926. Many members of this class, Liu among them, took part in the Northern Expedition, which began in mid-1926. In September of that year warlord Feng Yü-hsiang returned to China from the Soviet Union. He immediately entered into an agreement with the KMT to utilize his Kuominchün (Nationalist Army) to defeat the alliance of warlords in north and northwest China who were opposing the Northern Expedition. As part of his reorganization of the Kuominchün, Feng used some Soviet advisers as well as political officers from the CCP and the left-KMT. It was under these circumstances that in the fall of 1926 Liu became chief of the Political Section of the Kuominchün's Fourth Route Army. Concurrently, he was an instructor at the Chung-shan Military and Political Academy, which Feng had just established at Sian to train political workers. Most of the other instructors were Communists, among them Teng Hsiao-p'ing (q.v.), and the student body included Kao Kang and Hsi Chung-hsun (q.v.). According to a Communist account, Liu was with the Kuominchün in the spring of 1927 when it moved eastward from Sian into Honan, where it defeated elements of the Peiyang warlords.[3]

In mid-1927 Feng agreed to cooperate with the wing of the KMT led by Chiang Kai-shek. As a consequence he broke off relations with the left-KMT in Wuhan and expelled Liu and 30 to 40 other Communists from the Kuominchün. Moreover, in the latter half of 1927 Feng dealt the CCP organization in Shensi a series of "devastating blows," going to great lengths to weed out all Communists from the provincial labor, peasant, and student movements. While these developments were taking place, Liu had been active in the Anhwei-Hopeh border area where he attempted in vain to organize peasant uprisings. In April 1928 he returned to Shensi, where in Wei-nan and Hua-yin hsien, located along the Wei River east of Sian, he organized the so-called Wei-Hua Uprising. Liu's 500 troops were drawn in part from defectors from the Kuominchün and included a number of cadets from the Chung-shan Academy. However, within less than a month his forces were crushed by Feng Yü-hsiang's troops. Although the Wei-Hua Uprising was not the first Communist-led armed revolt in Shensi, it is characterized in orthodox Communist histories as the origin of Communist power in the northwest.

After the Wei-Hua failure Liu returned to his native Pao-an hsien where he became secretary of the Military Committee, which was subordinate to the CCP's North Shensi Special Committee. Within a brief time Special Committee Secretary Yang Kuo-tung, described in Maoist histories as a rich peasant who wanted the Party to operate underground and who opposed armed peasant uprisings, was overthrown by Liu. Among those supporting Liu's call for peasant uprisings were Kao Kang, Liu Lan-t'ao, and Chia T'o-fu (qq.v.). Liu's actions over the next few years were in the main thwarted by a number of factors, one of the most important being the fact that the Party organization in Shensi was very small in contrast to various areas in east and central-south China. In 1928, for example, nationwide CCP membership was about 40,000, but fewer than 1,000 of these members were in Shensi. Moreover, Party organizations in other parts of China were being vigorously suppressed by the KMT and were therefore in no position to assist their colleagues in Shensi. In Shanghai, Canton, and Wuhan the Communists had gained considerable experience in organizing urban workers, but a proletarian class scarcely existed in Shensi. As a consequence the task facing Liu Chih-tan and his associates after 1928 was much the same as that faced by Mao Tse-tung in the Kiangsi area, namely, the development of Communist power based almost exclusively on the peasantry.

In 1929, in an attempt to gain military support for the Shensi Communists, Liu managed to become commander of the militia in Pao-an through his local connections. However, because of his aggressive policies (e.g., arresting landlords), he was driven from the post. Later in the same year, using an alias, he became a regimental and then brigade commander in Kuominchün forces stationed on the Shensi-Kansu border. He was arrested when his identity was revealed, but he quickly gained his release, again on the strength of his numerous contacts in the area. In addition to his connections with the Kuominchün, Liu's ability to maneuver in the complex political milieu in Shensi seems to have derived in part from his membership in the Ko-lao-hui, the secret society that was one of the principal political forces in Shensi for over two decades after the 1911 Revolution. Writing in 1936 Mao Tse-tung appealed to the Ko-lao-hui to join in the struggle against the Japanese, noting that the "revolution in northern Shensi has also benefited from the considerable aid, support and active participation of comrades from the Ko-lao-hui." He went on to praise Liu Chih-tan as an "exemplary" member of the Ko-lao-hui.[4] It is noteworthy that Liu is one of the few members of the CCP elite who is known to have been an active member of a secret society.

In 1931 Liu was leading guerrilla operations in the Huang-lung Mountains in Shensi near the Shansi border. In the fall of that year, soon after the Japanese invasion of Manchuria, Liu's forces, augmented by defectors from a Nationalist unit in Shansi, were reorganized into the Northwest Anti-Imperialist Allied Army. The army was composed of 600 men armed with 300 weapons; Liu served as its deputy commander and chief-of-staff. The guerrilla forces then moved westward to the area around Hsun-i hsien in Shensi not far from the Kansu border. In 1932 these units were designated as the Shensi-Kansu Guerrilla Detachment of the 26th Red Army and the first steps were taken toward the formation of the Shensi-Kansu Border Soviet.

Although some progress was made in 1932–33 in developing the Communist movement in Shensi, a crack guerrilla unit was routed by the KMT in July 1933 in the Wei-Hua area, where the Communists had been defeated several years earlier. This Communist force, the Second Regiment of the 26th Red Army's 42nd Division, was commanded by Wang Shih-t'ai (q.v.) and Liu Chih-tan was its chief-of-staff. Wang and Liu then took the remnants of their military force northward to the Shensi-Kansu border. There they were merged with other units, and the "guerrilla movement enjoyed a resurgence on the Shensi-Kansu border, taking firm root in north Shensi for the first time."[5] In February 1934 the Shensi-Kansu Border Region Revolutionary Committee was formed under the chairmanship of Hsi Chung-hsun (q.v.), with Liu serving as chairman of its Military Committee.

Liu and his colleagues enjoyed further successes in 1934. One writer attributes this to two basic factors. First, the Communists abandoned their mobilization efforts in the Wei River Valley area in favor of a concentration of their energies in north Shensi and on the Shensi-Kansu border, where "logistical, political and economic factors were more favourable." Second, they began to develop a more effective "guerrilla style."[6] In June 1934 elements of the 42nd Division joined with other units to form the North Shensi Revolutionary Area. Liu Chih-tan was at that time serving as chief-of-staff of the 42nd Division. By mid-1934 the north Shensi Communist guerrillas numbered over 3,000 men armed with 1,000 weapons. To combat this force Nationalist troops were brought in from outside Shensi for the first time, but they were successfully repulsed by the Communists in late 1934. In the wake of this victory the First North Shensi Soviet Congress was held in January 1935 in An-ting hsien in north-central Shensi. The Shensi-Kansu Provisional Soviet Government was established, as well as two subordinate bodies to coordinate work in the major guerrilla regions—the Northwest Work Committee (a Party organ) and the Revolutionary Military Committee. Ma Ming-fang became chairman of the Soviet Government, and Liu and Kao Kang were made vice-chairmen of the Military Committee.

During the course of 1935 Liu's forces withstood another KMT attack. At this juncture he commanded the 26th and 27th Red Armies with a total of about 5,000 men. The Communist military strength was considerably augmented in September 1935 with the arrival of the 25th Red Army, led by Hsu Hai-tung (q.v.). Hsu's forces, which had been a part of the Fourth Front Army in the Oyüwan area, are normally characterized as the first units of the Long Marchers that arrived in north Shensi. The Hsu-Liu forces were immediately reorganized into the 15th Army Corps with Hsu in command. Liu became deputy commander and chief-of-staff. Ch'eng Tzu-hua (q.v.), who had come with Hsu, was made political commissar, and Kao Kang headed the Political Department. The 15th Corps successfully resisted still another Nationalist attack. Immediately afterwards under circumstances that have never been adequately explained, Liu and some of his closest north Shensi colleagues were arrested and stripped of their posts either by Central Committee representatives who had arrived earlier in 1935 or by political officers who had come with Hsu Hai-tung's 25th Red Army. In any event, within a matter of days the remnants of the First Army Corps led by Mao Tse-tung, Chou En-lai, P'eng Te-huai, and Lin Piao arrived in north Shensi (October 25) and immediately released Liu and returned him to his military posts.

In early 1936, as commander of the 28th and Northern Route Armies, Liu was one of the key military leaders in an eastward thrust across the Yellow River in Shansi. The campaign is described in Maoist histories as an "anti-Japanese expedition," but in fact it was launched to get food, supplies, and recruits for the Communist armies. More than 30,000 men (constituting most of the troops available to the Communists in Shensi) took part in this campaign, which resulted in the occupation of about a third of Shansi within a month. Mao Tse-tung, Lin Piao, and Hsu Hai-tung were among the participants. Chiang Kai-shek sent central government troops to aid Yen Hsi-shan, the Shansi warlord, and by April the Communists were driven back into Shensi. Although defeated in this sense, the Communists were able to capture significant quantities of supplies and weapons and to augment the Red Armies by several thousand troops.[7]

When Liu was badly wounded in the Shansi campaign, his political commissar, Sung Jen-ch'iung (q.v.), assumed command of the 28th Army. Liu was carried back to Shensi where in April 1936 he died of battle wounds.

After Liu's death the Communists renamed Pao-an (Liu's native hsien) Chih-tan hsien. A number of brief biographies have been written about Liu, all of which portray him as the founder and major figure in the development of Communism in Shensi. His importance as a military leader cannot be doubted, but it seems significant that aside from his brief tenure in the late twenties as secretary of the North Shensi Special Committee he never held a significant Party position. Like almost all the Communist guerrilla areas, the Shensi base was affected by the attempts of the Party Center to impose its policies during the stormy Party history of the late twenties and early thirties (e.g., the Li Li-san "line"). However, it appears that Liu played only a minor role in these events and was in fact bypassed by the Party Center when it sent representatives to Shensi. This was strongly suggested in an article written in 1951 by one of Liu's colleagues, Hsi Chung-hsun (q.v.), who claimed that "leftist opportunists" had "several times grasped the leading positions" in the Shensi Party apparatus, thereby causing "great harm" to the revolutionary movement in Shensi.[8] It is also worth noting that many of the Communist accounts of the Shensi developments have been written since the purge of Kao Kang in 1954–55. As a consequence Kao's contributions have been virtually erased from the official records, with the result that Liu's role has been somewhat artificially enhanced. The standard Communist account of Liu's life appears in *Chung-kuo kung-ch'an-tang lieh-shih chuan* (Biographies of Chinese Communist martyrs), edited by Hua Ying-shen and published in Hong Kong in 1949. The most comprehensive treatment of the origins and development of the Communist movement in Shensi is Mark Selden's "The Guerrilla Movement in Northwest China," *The China Quarterly,* nos. 28 and 29, October–December 1966 and January–March 1967.

Liu was survived by his wife and a daughter whom Edgar Snow met in 1936 in Shensi, and eight years later journalist Harrison Forman saw Liu's father, Liu P'ei-chi, who was then active in the Shensi-Kansu-Ninghsia (Shen-Kan-Ning) Border Region Government.[9] Liu Chih-tan was also survived by a younger brother, Liu Ching-fan, who fought alongside his brother in the thirties. Born about 1910 in Pao-an, he also graduated from the Yü-lin Normal School. He was one of the most prominent officials in the Shen-Kan-Ning Border Region during and after the Sino-Japanese War. By 1941 he was the deputy secretary-general of the Region's Assem-

bly as well as a member of the executive organ, known as the Government Council. In 1946 he was promoted to the secretary-generalship of the Assembly and to a vice-chairmanship of the Government Council, and in 1949 he served briefly as the acting chairman of the Council. When the national government was established in the fall of 1949, Liu Ching-fan was transferred to Peking. From 1949 to 1954 he was a vice-chairman of the People's Supervision Committee, one of the major committees under the Government Administration Council (the cabinet). When the People's Supervision Committee was reorganized into the Ministry of Supervision in 1954, he became a vice-minister, holding this position until 1955 when he was transferred to the Ministry of Geology, where he also served as a vice-minister (until April 1965). In addition, he was a Honan deputy to the First NPC (1954–1959) and a CCP representative on the Third National Committee of the CPPCC (1959–1964).

1. *Hung-ch'i p'iao-p'iao* (Red flag fluttering; Peking, 1957), V, 20, 108.
2. *Hsing-huo liao-yüan* (A single spark can start a prairie fire; Hong Kong, 1960), p. 229.
3. *Hung-ch'i p'iao-p'iao,* p. 111.
4. Stuart R. Schram, "Mao Tse-tung and Secret Societies," *The China Quarterly,* no. 27:1–11 (July–September 1966).
5. Mark Selden, "The Guerrilla Movement in Northwest China," *The China Quarterly,* no. 29:67 (January–March 1967).
6. *Ibid.,* pp. 68–69.
7. Donald S. Gillin, *Warlord Yen Hsi-shan in Shansi Province, 1911–1949* (Princeton, N.J., 1967), pp. 220–222.
8. *CB* 100, p. 28.
9. Harrison Forman, *Report from Red China* (New York, 1945), p. 101.

Liu Hsi-wu

Member, Control Commission, CCP.

Liu Hsi-wu is a little-known member of the Party hierarchy, who has risen to membership on the important Control Commission, the organ of the Party charged with discipline and inspection responsibilities. Imprisoned in Peking in the mid-1930's, he was next reported in early 1950 when he was serving as the senior Party secretary in Kirin province in Manchuria. In May of that year Liu was named as a member of the Kirin governmental organization, known as the Kirin Provincial People's Council. He was replaced in his Kirin Party post by September 1952 but remained in the government position until September 1954.

Nothing further was heard about Liu until early 1956 when he replaced a deceased member of the Second National Committee of the

CPPCC. Membership on the CPPCC is by occupational groups (e.g., educators or trade unionists) or by political parties; Liu was named to serve on this quasi-legislative body as a representative of the CCP. In April 1959, when the Third National Committee was formed, Liu was again named as a Party delegate, only on this occasion he was elevated to the Standing Committee, the body in charge of the CPPCC when the National Committee is not in session. He was once more named to both the National and Standing Committees when the Fourth CPPCC was formed at a meeting held in December 1964–January 1965.

Until the fall of 1956, Liu's career seemed barely noteworthy. Then at the first plenum of the Party Central Committee, held the day after the Eighth Party Congress (September 1956), he was given a position of considerable significance. He was named to membership on the Control Commission headed by Party veteran Tung Pi-wu. Moreover, he was selected as one of the deputy secretaries under Tung, of whom there are only five. In 1961 a Standing Committee was created within the Control Commission, and Liu was named to this committee too; presumably this new organ, more limited in number, meets more often than the full Control Commission and serves as the governing body when the full commission is not in session.

Control Commission personnel, being involved in internal Party security work, receive extremely little attention in the press. This has been especially true of Liu. Aside from being reported at the Peking airport to bid farewell to important Party leaders en route abroad, the only other published report of Liu's activity was in connection with Central Committee alternate Chang Hsi. When Chang died in January 1959, Liu was one of the members of the funeral committee.

Liu Hsi-yuan

Youth leader.

Liu Hsi-yuan first came to prominence as the political commissar of a column in Lin Piao's Northeast People's Liberation Army when this army was fighting in the Lin-chiang area in south Manchuria in early 1947. Eight years later, when national military honors were first awarded, Liu was given the Order of Liberation, the award presented for service in the 1945–1950 period. There is no further information about him until 1953 when he was a deputy director of the Youth Department of the People's Revolutionary Military Council (PRMC), a position he held to about 1955 or 1956 (under the PLA Headquarters after the PRMC was abolished in September 1954).

From the mid-1950's to the mid-1960's, Liu was probably the most important youth leader in China except for Youth League First Secretary Hu Yao-pang. He began his rise on the hierarchical ladder of the two key youth organizations in mid-1953 when both the New Democratic Youth League (NDYL, renamed the Communist Youth League in 1957) and the All-China Federation of Democratic Youth (ACFDY, renamed All-China Youth Federation in 1958) held national congresses. Within the ACFDY Liu was named to both the Standing Committee and the National Committee, and with the more important Youth League he was also named to the Standing Committee. Then, in late 1955 and early 1956, Liu rose from moderate to top importance in both youth organizations; in each instance he succeeded the former youth leader Liu Tao-sheng, who transferred to the science field. Liu Hsi-yuan was elected a member of the ruling Secretariat of the Youth League in October 1955 and in February 1956 became a vice-chairman of the ACFDY. He remained a Secretariat member until the June 1964 Youth League Congress, serving always under League First Secretary Hu Yao-pang, and within the ACFDY he replaced Liao Ch'eng-chih (q.v.) as the chairman in April 1958, holding this post until January 1965 when he was in turn replaced by Wang Wei.

Aside from these posts, so suggestive of his authority in both organizations, Liu's importance in youth work was illustrated in numerous other ways. At many sessions of the national or central committee (or at the more important national congresses), Liu was a frequent speaker. At one of the congresses of the Youth League (May 1957), he chaired the important credentials committee. He often participated in national congresses which emphasized youth work, or had a prominent place in celebrations marking significant dates in the history of the Chinese youth movement. For example, he was on the presidium for national conferences of "youth activists in building socialism" in September 1955 and November–December 1958, and in April 1959 he served as a vice-chairman for the preparatory committtee for celebrating the 40th anniversary of the famous May Fourth Movement of 1919, the great intellectual watershed for China's youths. Moreover, in the late 1950's, Liu went to several important youth gatherings abroad, in each instance leading the Chinese delegation. His travels are summarized as follows:

1956: East Germany, meeting commemorating the 10th anniversary of the Free German Youth Association, March; Albania, Congress of Unions of Albanian Working Youth, October–November; 1957: Japan, Youth friendship visit, March–May; India, Burma, Second All-Indian Convention of the Youth Congress, October–November (stopping in Burma en route home); 1959: United Arab Republic, Afro-Asian Youth

Conference, January–February; Austria, Czechoslovakia, Seventh International Youth Festival attended by over 400 Chinese, Vienna, July–August; Executive Committee meeting of the World Federation of Democratic Youth, Prague, August.

At the above-mentioned World Federation of Democratic Youth (WFDY) meeting in Vienna in August 1959, Liu was elected a vice-president of this Communist-backed international organization. No further information is available about this position, and the fact that he surrendered his youth organization positions in China in 1964–65 strongly suggests that he is no longer active in the international organization.

Aside from his youth work, Liu began to assume other duties in official and semi-official organizations in the 1956–1960 period. In March 1956 he was named to the Study (*hsueh-hsi*) Committee of the CPPCC National Committee, an organ designed to stimulate the study of Marxism-Leninism throughout China, especially among the non-Party intellectuals. Three years later, in April 1959, Liu was named to the Third National CPPCC Committee as a representative of the All-China Youth Federation, as well as to the governing body of the CPPCC, the Standing Committee. (Under the fourth committee, formed in 1964, Liu represented the Party; see below.) In mid-1956, to replace a deceased deputy, he was elected a deputy from Hupeh to the First NPC; he was re-elected to the Second NPC (1959–1964) but not to the Third, which opened its first session in late 1964. During the term of the Second NPC (1959–1964), he served on the important Bills Committee.

Five of the positions Liu assumed in the 1956–1960 period relate to foreign affairs: council member, China-Nepal Friendship Association, September 1956; Standing Committee member, Chinese People's Committee in Support of Egypt's Resistance to Aggression, November 1956; Standing Committee member, China Peace Committee, July 1958; Standing Committee member, Chinese People's Association for Cultural Relations with Foreign Countries, April 1959; vice-chairman, China-Africa People's Friendship Association, April 1960. Liu continues to hold all these positions, except that related to Egypt (an *ad hoc* organization) and the China Peace Committee, from which he was removed in June 1965.

Liu continued to be mentioned in the national press in connection with visiting youth organizations with great regularity through 1964. As late as September 1964, in his capacity as a youth leader, he signed a joint statement with a visiting youth delegation from Zanzibar denouncing American "imperialism." Then, although still Chairman of the All-China Youth Federation, Liu was not reappointed as a Federation representative on the Fourth CPPCC, which first met in December 1964–January 1965. Rather, he was elected as a Party representative. The situation was clarified in January 1965 when he was removed as the Youth Federation chairman. Like so many other youth leaders before him, it appears that by 1965 Liu was in the process of shifting from youth affairs to the higher levels of Communist Party activity.

Liu Hsiao

(1907–   ; Hunan). Veteran Party official; diplomat; member, CCP Central Committee.

Liu Hsiao spent much of the period from the twenties to the forties as a Communist underground operative in east China, and he remained as a Party leader there following the Communist conquest of the mainland in 1949. He was elected an alternate member of the Central Committee in 1945, and 11 years later was promoted to full membership. Liu was the ambassador in Moscow from 1955 to 1962, a period that coincided with the deterioration of Sino-Soviet relations.

In a 1936 interview with Edgar Snow (the major source for Liu's early career),[1] Liu stated that he was born into a family of "middle landlords" in "Shenking," Hunan. His father spent two years studying in Japan, and then returned to teach school. Liu described his father as somewhat "modernized" but still "backward" in point of view. At five Liu entered his father's school. He described his childhood as an unhappy one, mainly because of a "cruel" second wife that his father took when Liu was six. Liu emphasized that he had studied only in "technical, or so-called Westernized" schools; after four years in primary school he entered a higher primary school where he claimed he was introduced to revolutionary ideas. A friendly teacher interested him in joining a "Save China Society" (Chiu-kuo hui) when he was only 10 and took the young boy with him into the countryside where the teacher was working to reform some "bandits." After graduating from the higher primary school in 1922, Liu was sent for further study to the Chao Yang (Eastview?) Mission School run by the American Christian Reformed Church. The school, Liu stated, was located at "Shengchoufu," Hunan. (This is probably Shen-chou [Ch'en-chou], an alternate name for Yuan-ling, a small city on the Yuan River.)

Liu spent the next two years learning English at the insistence of the principal, J. Frank Booker. He also studied the Bible, became a Christian, joined the YMCA, and even went out to preach in the streets on Saturdays and Sundays. But more lasting than the Christian training was the impression made upon young Liu by a politically minded Chinese preacher from Nanking named Li, who visited the school in 1923 and told Liu about the blossoming Chinese student movement. The next year the school was visited by a friend of Liu's from the Hunan Normal School (probably Mao Tse-tung's alma mater). It was this friend who finally awakened Liu to the possibilities of aggressive student participation in political action and turned his mind against his missionary training and the presence of foreigners in China. The immediate result was Liu's dismissal from the mission school and a partial estrangement from his family. However, at the persuasion of an uncle, Liu's father agreed to provide funds for his son's education. Liu then left for more schooling in Nanking, where he was to have further contacts with the Reverend Li. In Nanking, under the combined influence of Reverend Li and an uncle who was also a teacher and a revolutionary, Liu was introduced to two influential publications of the day, the *Hsin ch'ing-nien* (New youth) and the CCP organ *Hsiang-tao chou-pao* (Guide weekly). These influences soon had their effect. After a half-year in Nanking Liu went to Shanghai and entered the Political Science Institute at Wusung (Woosung), but he lasted there only six months before he was dismissed as a suspected Communist. He was next forced to seek refuge in Shanghai's French Concession, where he stayed briefly before becoming a Party member in 1926. He was then in his nineteenth year.

Working in the Communist underground for the first years of his Party career gave Liu considerable experience in the dangerous life of a revolutionary. He participated in the Communist-led opposition to the warlord control of Shanghai, opposition that mutinied to the side of Chiang Kai-shek when the latter's forces entered the city in March–April 1927 only to be put down by Chiang once he got control of the city. Escaping from Shanghai, Liu joined some other young Communist teachers who found refuge working in a middle school north of the Yangtze. From there he went to work among salt workers at P'u-tung (Pootung), outside Shanghai, and organized a Party cell among the workers with the result that he had to return to hiding in Shanghai. In June 1928 he was found by the French police from the International Concession and jailed for a year. He was not free for long before he was again apprehended and returned to prison. This time Liu did a term in the dreaded Lunghua prison on the outskirts of Shanghai where a number of political prisoners were then confined.

When released from prison in 1931, Liu was again forced into hiding. At that period Communist operations in Shanghai were becoming steadily more precarious, and one by one the Party leaders escaped to the rural hinterlands where the Communists had built up a sizable base for their guerrilla operations. Liu went to the Communist-held areas on the Kiangsi-Fukien border and was assigned to work in the Party apparatus in Fukien. In early 1933 the Fukien Party Committee underwent a major reorganization as a result of a serious political struggle between the followers and opponents of the so-called Lo Ming line (see under Lo Ming). In his 1936 interview with Edgar Snow, Liu claimed that he had been made the secretary of the Party Committee in Fukien. In fact, he was only one of three men appointed to an interim committee to take over the duties of Lo Ming, who had been the acting Fukien secretary.[2] Later in 1933 or 1934, Liu was transferred to southern Kiangsi where the Communists had established the capital of the Chinese Soviet Republic in November 1931. At the Second Congress of the Republic, held in Juichin in January–February 1934, Liu was elected a member of the Central Executive Committee, the governing body of the Republic.

Liu made the Long March in 1934–35 as a member of the Political Department of the First Army Corps, led by Lin Piao and Nieh Jung-chen. He continued to serve as a political officer after the Red Army reached the Shensi-Ninghsia area, and it was at a military headquarters in Ninghsia that Edgar Snow interviewed Liu in mid-1936. At some time roughly coinciding with the outbreak of the Sino-Japanese War in mid-1937, Liu was sent to Kiangsu to work in the underground. Party work there was important not only because it centered in the major cities of Shanghai and Nanking, but also because Red guerrilla forces were soon able to gain a foothold in the countryside near these cities and to harass Japanese troops along the railroads leading into them. The Communists' army in east-central China, the New Fourth Army, went into operation in the spring of 1938, and by mid-1940 Ch'en I (q.v.), one of its principal commanders, had established his headquarters at Yen-ch'eng in east-central Kiangsu. By at least 1942 and probably earlier, Liu was the secretary of the Kiangsu Provincial Party Committee. Although he presumably held this position for the remainder of the war, he apparently held no post in the New Fourth Army as did most other top Party officials in the area. Perhaps this is another indication that Liu's work in Kiangsu was essentially concerned with the Party underground. He may have been returned to Yenan sometime before the spring of 1945 when the Party opened its Seventh National Congress. At the close of the Congress in June, Liu was elected an alternate member of the Party Central Committee.

In the period from 1945 to 1949 Liu worked in Shanghai for the CCP. During the existence of the Marshall Mission from early 1946 to early 1947, the Communists were able to operate in Shanghai with relative safety. But in late February 1947 the Nationalist government ordered all Communist liaison missions in Shanghai (and other cities) to return their personnel to Yenan. Liu, however, remained in the Shanghai underground, and by some time in 1947 he was serving as secretary of the CCP Shanghai Committee. He was thus in Shanghai when the forces led by Ch'en I and Jao Shu-shih (qq.v.) marched into the city in May 1949.

From 1949 until his transfer abroad in 1955 (see below), Liu was one of the most important officials in Shanghai and east China, although he was overshadowed by such top leaders as Jao Shu-shih, Ch'en I, and T'an Chen-lin. One of Liu's top posts was as second secretary of the Shanghai Party Committee where he served under Jao until 1952 and thereafter under Ch'en. He was also head of the committee's Organization Department from 1949 to 1951. In the Shanghai Municipal People's Government he was a government council member from 1950 until 1955, another position that placed him subordinate to Mayor Ch'en I. To administer Shanghai and Nanking, as well as the five provinces of Shantung, Kiangsu, Anhwei, Chekiang, and Fukien, the Communists established the East China Military and Administrative Committee (ECMAC) in January 1950 under the chairmanship of Jao Shu-shih. Liu was named to membership on the ECMAC and one month later (February 1950) he was given the concurrent assignment of directing the ECMAC's People's Supervision Committee, an important body charged with the task of ensuring compliance with directives issued by the ECMAC. When the ECMAC was reorganized into the East China Administrative Committee in January 1953, Liu was reappointed to both of his positions, retaining them until the regional governments were abolished in 1954. He also held an important post in the Party's East China Bureau in which Jao Shu-shih was the senior secretary; from 1952 to 1954 Liu headed the bureau's Organization Department.

Although Liu's major responsibilities were in east China, he also took part in the formation of the central government in the fall of 1949. In September he attended the first session of the CPPCC (the organ that brought the PRC into existence in October) as the head of a nine-man delegation from "various people's organizations in Shanghai." In this capacity he gave a brief talk extolling the past struggles in Shanghai that led to the final Communist victory. During the course of the CPPCC sessions he was also a member of the *ad hoc* presidium (steering committee), and at the closing session was named to membership on the First National Committee of the CPPCC, ostensibly the most important legislative body in China until the inauguration of the NPC in 1954. In December 1954 Liu was again named to the CPPCC (the Second National Committee), although on this occasion he served as a representative of the All-China Federation of Trade Unions (ACFTU). He is not known to have had any other affiliation with the ACFTU, but the heavy concentration of trade unionists in Shanghai might explain why he represented the Federation. Liu was also named to the CPPCC's Standing Committee, although his membership was largely nominal because he was abroad from 1955 to 1962.

Relatively little was heard of Liu's activities in east China in 1953 and 1954, a fact that was noted by the American consulate general in Hong Kong when Liu (unlike most Central Committee members) was not elected to the First NPC.[3] In retrospect, however, it appears that he may have been preparing for his new assignment in Peking's most important diplomatic post —the embassy in Moscow. Possibly in preparation for his new post (if only symbolically), Liu attended the Second National Conference of the Sino-Soviet Friendship Association (SSFA) in December 1954 and was named to the SSFA Council. (He had also been a member of the association's branch in Shanghai from 1950.) Soon after, on January 13, 1955, he was appointed as ambassador to the Soviet Union where he replaced Chang Wen-t'ien (q.v.). Liu presented his credentials in Moscow on February 7 and remained there until late 1962; his service in Moscow—almost eight years—is one of the longest tours abroad by an ambassador in the history of the PRC.

Liu's ambassadorship in Moscow was, if nothing else, an eventful one. When he arrived in the Soviet Union relations were probably at their peak between the two Communist giants. His arrival had coincided with the return to China of joint stock companies and the gradual removal of Soviet troops from Port Arthur—steps taken as a result of agreements that Soviet leaders Khrushchev and Bulganin had signed in Peking in October 1954. In addition, of course, there was a growing air of partnership between Peking and Moscow that stood in contrast to the subservient Chinese position prior to Stalin's death in 1953. Nonetheless, within a relatively short period, Sino-Soviet relations had deteriorated to an icy cordiality and, finally, to the open exchange of mutual recriminations and denunciations of the 1960's. There is little reason to think, however, that Liu had much to do with these events; to a large degree he was simply the man caught in the middle of the cross-fire.

Because Moscow was so frequently visited by Chinese leaders in the middle and late fifties, Liu was frequently mentioned in the Chinese press in connection with these visits. In addition to such protocol activities as giving banquets to mark the PRC's National Day (October 1), he was an official member of CCP delegations to Moscow for important meetings. For example, he was a member of the delegations to the 20th, 21st, and 22nd CPSU Congresses held in Moscow in February 1956, January–February 1959, and October 1961, which were led by Chu Te (the 20th) and Chou En-lai (the 21st and 22nd). Similarly, he was a member of Mao Tse-tung's delegation to Moscow in November 1957 to take part in the celebrations marking the 40th anniversary of the Russian Revolution. As a consequence of Liu's participation in these important events, it is obvious (in retrospect) that he witnessed at close hand the steady deterioration of the Sino-Soviet alliance.

Liu returned to Peking on at least two occasions, the first in April 1957 when he accompanied Soviet leader V. K. Voroshilov on a state visit to China. His second known trip to Peking occurred in June 1958 when he and at least eight other Chinese ambassadors were temporarily called home, possibly in connection with a major crisis in the Middle East (during which American and British troops were briefly stationed in Lebanon and Jordan). It is also probable that Liu was in Peking for the Eighth Party Congress held in September 1956. At this time he was elevated from alternate to full membership on the Party Central Committee.

On three occasions Liu traveled from Moscow to other European countries. The first of these trips took him to Warsaw in March 1956 when he accompanied Chu Te to the funeral of Polish leader Boleslaw Bierut. He made a similar trip in late November 1958 as leader of the Chinese delegation to the funeral of G. Damyanov, a Bulgarian Party Politburo member. More important was his trip to Geneva in May 1961, where he apparently served as an adviser to Ch'en I at the Geneva Conference on Laos. He took part in talks held between Ch'en and Soviet Foreign Minister Gromyko, and later, when Ch'en was returning home via Moscow in July, Liu participated in the round of talks that Ch'en held with Khrushchev and others.

After nearly eight years in Moscow, Liu left for home in October 1962. He was replaced in November by P'an Tzu-li (q.v.). The following May he was appointed a vice-minister of Foreign Affairs under Ch'en I. To judge from the ranking in semi-official Chinese handbooks, Liu became the senior vice-minister. (He was the only vice-minister who was a full member of the Party Central Committee; one other vice-minister, Chang Han-fu, is an alternate member.) After his recall from Moscow, Liu returned then on one occasion when he accompanied Chou En-lai in November 1964 to attend celebrations marking the 47th anniversary of the Russian Revolution. Unlike some of the other vice-ministers who seem to specialize in one area (e.g., Southeast Asian affairs), there did not seem to be any notable pattern in Liu's contacts with foreign visitors which might suggest an area specialization.

During his years abroad, Liu had received appointments (or reappointments) in the Party, the central government, and the "people's" organizations. As already noted, he was elected to the Party Central Committee in 1956. In April 1959 he was named to the Third National Committee (representing the CCP) and the Standing Committee of the CPPCC; he was appointed to both committees for the Fourth CPPCC, which first met in December 1964–January 1965. Finally, in May 1959 he was named to the Third National Council of the Sino-Soviet Friendship Association, a position he still retains. Liu's writings for the Chinese press have apparently been quite limited; one of the few is an article on the Soviet Union's seven-year economic plan, which appeared in *Hung-ch'i* (Red flag, issue of August 1, 1959).

Liu remained in Peking until early 1967 when he was appointed ambassador to Albania, then China's staunchest ally in East Europe. He presented his credentials in Tirana on April 7.

1. Edgar Snow, *Random Notes on Red China, 1936–1945* (Cambridge, Mass., 1957), pp. 64–68.
2. Warren Kuo, "The Struggle against the Lo Ming Line in the CCP," *Issues and Studies* (Taipei), August 1967, pp. 31–43.
3. *CB* 290, p. 14.

Liu Hsiu-feng

(Wan-hsien, Hopeh). Former minister of Building; government administrator.

Liu Hsiu-feng comes from Wan-hsien in Hopeh, which lies midway between Paoting and Fou-p'ing, the latter being the original headquarters of the Shansi-Chahar-Hopeh Border Region Government, with which he was later associated. While still quite young, Liu joined the Socialist Youth League (1924), after which he was an active participant in student activities. For work of this sort he was briefly imprisoned in 1926. Following his release in the same year, he became the secretary of the Party Committee in his native Wan-hsien. Liu apparently remained in Wan-hsien for only a short time, after which he was transferred to Tientsin and, while engaged in the work of the Party underground in that city, he was again arrested and imprisoned. On this occasion, however, he spent several years in jail, not being released until 1935.

After being released, Liu immediately went back to Party work, serving as the head of the Organization Department of the Hopeh Party Committee. It is probable that he worked with such important Party figures in North China at that time as Huang Ching, a suggestion that gains credence from the fact that Liu served on the funeral committee for Huang when he died in 1958. When the Sino-Japanese War broke out in mid-1937, Liu remained in Hopeh, organizing guerrilla activities in the Paoting area, the region in and around his native birthplace. He went to Yenan in 1939 to deliver a report to the Party Center, but rather than return to Hopeh he remained in Yenan as a student at the Marx-Lenin

Institute.[1] Liu and Wang Ts'ung-wu (q.v.) were later assigned to assist the important Communist leader Wang Jo-fei in an investigation of land policies. Their investigation finally led to the adoption by the Politburo in January 1942 of a land policy for "anti-Japanese base areas," which has been described as the "mildest" agrarian program that the CCP had ever attempted to apply as of that date. It was pointedly based on the "anti-Japanese united front" and was designed to gain maximum support from all sectors of society, including the much-maligned landlord class.[2] By this time Liu had joined the staff of the Party's Research Office, where for four years (until early 1944) he worked under Wang, the Office director.

Sometime toward the end of the war, or soon thereafter, Liu was sent to work in the Shansi-Chahar-Hopeh (Chin-Ch'a-Chi) Border Region (see under Sung Shao-wen). By 1945 he was Party secretary for Kalgan (Chang-chia-k'ou), the capital of now defunct Chahar province. Kalgan fell to the Nationalist military forces in October 1946 and was not recaptured by the Communists until December 1948. Liu's activities in these two years are undocumented, but he presumably remained in the Chin-Ch'a-Chi area. In any event, in April 1949 Liu was named to succeed K'o Ch'ing-shih as the mayor of Shih-chia-chuang, an important city in western Hopeh. It was in Shih-chia-chuang and nearby villages that the Party Central Committee and the North China People's Government had made their headquarters until just a few weeks before Liu assumed his post there. By the fall of 1949 Liu was transferred to Tientsin where he was to remain for the next two years. There he assumed the vice-mayoralty under his probable comrade from earlier years, Mayor Huang Ching. Liu also served in Tientsin as vice-chairman of the municipal Finance and Economics Committee in 1950–51, and during these same years he was also a vice-chairman of the Tientsin branch of the China Peace Committee, one of the more active of the "people's" organizations in the early 1950's.

By mid-1951 Liu was transferred to Peking to work in the North China Party Bureau headed by Po I-po (q.v.), a member of the Party Central Committee. In the latter half of 1951 Liu headed the bureau's Organization Department, but his former Yenan colleague Wang Ts'ung-wu replaced him by December 1951. By March 1953 Liu was identified as the third deputy secretary of the bureau, a position he held until the bureau was dissolved in August 1954. The March 1953 identification was made when he gave a speech before a meeting of the North China Bureau on the details of the Fourth Party Plenum, the important meeting at which Liu Shao-ch'i spoke on the need for strengthening Party unity, which provided the first hints of the purge a year later

of Kao Kang and Jao Shu-shih (see under Kao Kang).

With his transfer from Tientsin to Peking in 1951, Liu also assumed important positions in the North China Administrative Committee (NCAC), which was created out of the Ministry of North China Affairs in late December 1951. Liu was named as a vice-chairman of the NCAC; a few days later (early January 1952) he was appointed as head of the NCAC's Industry Department and still later (March 1952) as chairman of the Finance and Economics Committee. It is uncertain how long he held the latter two posts, but he retained the vice-chairmanship until the NCAC was abolished in August 1954. During its existence the NCAC had jurisdiction over Hopeh, Shansi, and Suiyuan, in addition to Chahar and Pingyuan until the latter two provinces were abolished in late 1952. During the period he served with the NCAC, he also took part in the work of various *ad hoc* bodies that were related to financial and economic matters. For example, he was named in June 1952 as a vice-chairman of a special committee to increase production and promote austerity measures; at the inaugural meeting of this organization Liu spoke on industrial production in north China.

With the abolition of both the North China Party Bureau and the NCAC in the late summer of 1954, Liu naturally lost his posts in these organizations. However, at the same time (early September 1954) he was made a vice-minister of Building in the central government, his first post in the national government bureaucracy. Almost immediately afterward, when the government underwent a complete reorganization at the first session of the First NPC, which closed in late September, he was named to succeed Ch'en Cheng-jen as minister of Building, a post that Liu was to hold for slightly more than a decade. The Ministry of Building (sometimes translated as the Ministry of Construction and Engineering) was mainly concerned with problems related to design engineering, the uses of cement products, and the production of machine tools, in addition to supervising the work of a construction institute that carried out research and training. In December 1954 he was also named as a CCP representative to the Second National Committee of the quasi-legislative CPPCC; he was not, however, re-elected to the Third CPPCC, which was formed in the spring of 1959.

In the span of years between 1954 and 1961, Liu was reported with regularity in the Party press. On a number of occasions he made inspection trips to various places in China in connection with building construction work, an example of which occurred in June 1958 when he was in Shanghai. He was also a frequent speaker at the numerous conferences in Peking dealing with construction work. For instance, in

February 1955 he spoke before a "planning and construction work conference," and more important, in September 1956 he addressed the Eighth Party Congress on various problems related to industrial construction. Like so many specialists in industrial affairs, he was among the many leaders taking part in the frequently held national conferences of "advanced workers," attending two of the largest of these conferences (held in April–May 1956 and October–November 1959). In a similar vein, Liu has been abroad on two occasions, both related to economic matters. He led a group to the USSR in August–November 1955 to inspect building construction work, and in May 1960 he accompanied State Economic Commission Chairman Po I-po to Poland to discuss economic issues with the Poles.

In February 1958, during another reorganization of the central government, Liu assumed added responsibilities. This occurred at a session of the NPC, when the ministries of Building Materials and of Urban Construction were amalgamated into Liu's Ministry of Building. Until 1961 he was a frequent contributor to the Party press. Important examples of his articles appeared in the *JMJP* (June 11, 1958, and September 26, 1959) and the Party journal *Hung-ch'i* (Red flag, September 1, 1960). However, since 1961 he has made few appearances, most of which have been perfunctory. Although he had served as a deputy from his native Hopeh in the Second NPC (1959–1964), he was not elected to the Third NPC when the Hopeh provincial elections were held in October 1964. Moreover, in the next month Li Jen-chün was named to succeed Liu in the Ministry of Building. Thus, within the space of a month, Liu lost his only posts in both the executive and legislative branches of the central government. There are no apparent political reasons for his loss of these important positions, suggesting that failing health may be the cause.

1. Hua Ying-shen, ed., *Chung-kuo Kung-ch'an Tang lieh-shih chuan* (Biographies of Chinese Communist Party martyrs; Hong Kong, 1949), pp. 217–220.

2. Conrad Brandt, Benjamin Schwartz, and John K. Fairbank, *A Documentary History of Chinese Communism* (Cambridge, Mass., 1952), pp. 275–285.

Liu Jen

(c.1909–   ; Szechwan). Former second secretary, Peking CCP Committee; alternate member, CCP Central Committee.

Liu Jen was born about 1909. He is said to have graduated from the University of Moscow, probably in the 1930's. During the Sino-Japanese War Liu directed the Organization Department belonging to the Northern Sub-bureau of the CCP North China Bureau. In 1945 he was a Party representative in Peking, and in the period prior to January 1949 when the Communist forces entered the city, he was a leader in the Communist underground there. As of 1949 he became director of the Organization Department of the CCP Municipal Committee for Peking. After the Communists took over the historic capital, Liu was one of the most important Party officials in the city, serving as a top aide to P'eng Chen, the leader of the municipal Party apparatus. Liu's ties with P'eng appear to be particularly close, and their association probably reaches back to the mid-1930's when both men worked underground in north China. Liu was a deputy secretary of the Peking Party Committee from 1950 and was then promoted to second secretary by April 1955, a position he held for over a decade and the one which occupied most of his time. He has been very active in and about Peking since the Communists' arrival there in 1949. Liu has served on a number of committees concerned with different phases of the program to socialize Chinese society and has spoken before important conferences as part of the normal tasks of a Party bureaucrat. The peace and labor movements have also claimed his attention, as well as the local committee of the CPPCC, which he has chaired for a number of years.

From 1949 to 1955 Liu was a vice-chairman of the Peking Consultative Committee, a forerunner to the CPPCC. He became chairman of the Peking Committee of the CPPCC in April 1955; he was re-elected chairman of the Second Peking CPPCC in February 1961, and has headed the Third municipal CPPCC since its first meeting in December 1962. A brief list of the principal committees and organizations with which Liu has served since 1949 indicates the wide range of his activities. 1949: vice-president, Peking branch of the Sino-Soviet Friendship Association, November; 1950: vice-chairman, Peking branch of the China Peace Committee, November; vice-chairman, Peking Municipal Government's Finance and Economic Committee, November; vice-chairman, Peking General Labor Council, December; 1951: member, Peking Municipal People's Government, February; member, Peking-Tientsin General Study Committee for Teachers of Higher Educational Institutions, October.

The length of his service in the above positions is not known except for the Peking Municipal Government position to which he was re-elected as late as September 1964. He has also served in the following posts in the mid-1950's — 1953–1957: member, Seventh Executive Committee, All-China Federation of Trade Unions (May 1953–December 1957); 1953–1954: chairman, Peking Municipal Election Committee; 1955:

vice-chairman, Peking committee to collect signatures for the prohibition of atomic weapons, February; 1956: member, the presidium, National Conference of Representatives of Advanced Producers, April.

In September 1956, when the Eighth National Party Congress was held, Liu was elected as an alternate member of the Central Committee. While attending the Congress he addressed the delegates on "the question of socialistic reform and construction in the capital city." In May 1957 he took part in a demonstration of physical labor sponsored by the CCP as part of an attempt to have white collar workers set an example to the masses by performing manual labor. It was noted in the press at this time that he had only recently recovered from a serious illness. Despite the illness he has continued to be very active, especially since the mid-1950's, entertaining many foreign visitors to China. The huge number of foreign guests in Peking each year presents the mayor and First Party Secretary P'eng Chen with an impossibly burdensome protocol load, particularly because P'eng must deal with many policy-level problems in his capacity as one of the key Politburo officials. From the frequency with which Liu is cited in the press, it is evident that one of his main tasks is to relieve P'eng of many of these burdens.

In July 1960 Liu was identified as the political commissar of the Peking Garrison Command. He was again mentioned in this capacity in 1961, but the lack of later identifications suggests that he may no longer hold the position. The most recently assumed post is with the North China Bureau of the Central Committee. The regional bureaus were re-created in January 1961 and by October 1964 Liu was identified as one of the Bureau secretaries, a position that placed him under First Secretary Li Hsueh-feng, a veteran Party official whose career in north China also reaches back to the underground days of the 1930's.

Liu continued to be a prominent figure until the late spring of 1966 when he became one of the first victims of the Great Proletarian Cultural Revolution. He was replaced by Wu Te (q.v.) in early June in his most important post, the second secretaryship of the Peking Party Committee, and over the ensuing months he was attacked on countless occasions in "official" and Red Guard publications, very often in connection with P'eng Chen, his long-time colleague.

Liu has apparently not been a regular contributor to the Party press. However, he did write an article that was excerpted in the December 1, 1958, issue of *Hung-ch'i* (Red flag), the most important Party journal since its creation in 1958. The article dealt with various problems in the management of the "people's communes," particularly in the suburbs of Peking.

Liu Ko-p'ing

(c.1912–   ; Hopeh). National minorities specialist; member, CCP Central Committee.

Liu Ko-p'ing, a Hui (Moslem) from Hopeh, is one of the extremely few non-Han Chinese to have risen to the level of the Party Central Committee. It is evident from the high positions he held in the early 1950's that he must have had a rather outstanding Party record prior to the Communist conquest in 1949. However, the only established fact is that he became a Party member in about 1931. Possibly he joined other Huis in his native Hopeh in participating in guerrilla warfare against the Japanese in the 1930's (see under Ma Yü-huai). The first known position held by Liu was in 1949 when he served as vice-president, under Shu T'ung (q.v.), of the East China People's Revolutionary University, located at Soochow (Su-chou) near Shanghai. Later in that year he was in Peking for the first session of the CPPCC, the organization that inaugurated the central government in October 1949. Liu attended the session as a representative of the national minorities; he served as a member of the Standing Committee of the Presidium (steering committee) and also on the *ad hoc* committee that drafted the Organic Law of the Central People's Government, one of the key documents adopted at the first CPPCC session.

As already mentioned, Liu received positions of considerable importance for an almost completely obscure man at the time of the Communist takeover. The most surprising of these was his appointment to membership on the 63-member Central People's Government Council (CPGC), the highest organ of state until 1954 and one vested with executive, legislative, and judicial functions. To create a façade of cooperation with non-Communists, the CPGC had given membership to a number of non-Communists (e.g., Ch'en Ming-shu, Ts'ai T'ing-k'ai). However, among the 33 Communist members, only two were not Central Committee members: Liu and Saifudin, a Uighur from Sinkiang. At the same time, he received two other appointments of significance. He was named as a vice-chairman of the Nationalities Affairs Commission and as a member of the Political and Legal Affairs Committee, both bodies subordinate to the Government Administration Council (the cabinet). He held all these posts until the governmental reorganization in the fall of 1954.

During the early 1950's Liu was stationed in Peking and devoted most of his time to national minorities' affairs. In May 1950 he was appointed as vice-president of the newly established Central Nationalities Institute in Peking, a school headed by China's foremost national minority leader, Ulanfu. In March 1955 he replaced Ulanfu as president, but then Liu was in turn replaced in July 1961. Twice he made lengthy tours of national minority areas. The first of these was an eight-month tour (July 1950–March 1951) of minority regions in the southwest, where Liu led a 120-man team. He led another group to Sinkiang in mid-1952 to inspect work among minority groups, and while there attended the Second Sinkiang Party Congress (August 1952). Upon his return from the visit to south-west China (March 1951), he was named as a vice-chairman of a special committee to direct the study of national minority languages. In 1952–53 he was involved in the establishment of two organizations related to Moslems. He was one of the conveners of a meeting in Peking in July 1952 that began the preparations for the establishment of the China Islamic Association; however, when this association was established in the spring of 1953 he was not named to any leadership post. The other organization for Moslem affairs was the Chinese Association for the Promotion of Hui People's Culture. It was formed in May 1953, with Liu serving as its first and only chairman. Little was heard about the work of this association and in October 1958 it was formally disbanded. On three occasions (May 1951, September 1953, and May 1954) he presented major reports to the Government Administration Council on national minority affairs. Liu's work in minority affairs was re-warded by August 1952 with an appointment as a deputy director of the Central Committee's United Front Work Department, then headed by Li Wei-han (q.v.). One of the major tasks of this department is to win and hold the allegiance of the non-Han peoples of China, who number some 50 million. Liu held this post until at least 1958 when he was transferred to the northwest (see below).

In 1953–54, Liu served on two of the major committees in preparation for the inauguration of the constitutional government. One of these, headed by Premier Chou En-lai, was charged with the task of drafting the election law (January 1953) and the other was responsible for the actual holding of the elections, a committee established in February 1953 under the chairman-ship of Liu Shao-ch'i. When the elections were held in 1954, Liu Ko-p'ing was elected as a deputy from Tientsin. During the term of the First and Second NPC's (1954–1964), Liu was one of the most active officials within the NPC. He served as a member of the Standing Committee and also chaired the Nationalities Committee, and on all but one of the nine annual sessions of the NPC he served as a member of the Presidium (steering committee). Because of his transfer to the Northwest in 1958, he served as a deputy from Ninghsia to the Second NPC (1959–1964).

In the wake of the Bandung Conference in 1955, the Chinese Communists began to develop their international contacts on a very active basis. Although he never left the country, Liu played a limited role in the efforts to improve ties with the Afro-Asian world. He was named as one of the vice-chairmen of the Asian Soli-darity Committee of China upon its formation in February 1956. (The name was changed to "Afro-Asian Solidarity Committee" in May 1958.) When this body was reorganized in July 1958, Liu relinquished his vice-chairmanship (once again because of his transfer away from Peking), but he remained as a member, a posi-tion he still retains. In preparation for the visit of the Pakistani prime minister, the Chinese founded the China-Pakistan Friendship Associa-tion in May 1956; Liu was named as chairman, another position he still retains. He was given membership in still another mass organization in December 1956, when he was named to the Standing Committee of the Chinese People's Association for Cultural Relations with Foreign Countries; he was re-appointed in April 1959. Soon after the governmental counterpart was organized (under the title of the Commission for Cultural Relations with Foreign Countries), Liu was named as a member (March 1958), but he relinquished this post in September 1959 during a general government reorganization.

Liu emerged from the Eighth Party Congress in September 1956 as a more important figure within the CCP. He served on the Congress Presidium (steering committee) and was elected to full membership on the Central Committee—one of only 33 persons who had not previously served on the Seventh Central Committee, elected in 1945. Moreover, on the day after the Congress closed, he was named to the Control Commission, the powerful organ in charge of Party discipline and control. Not long after, in November–De-cember 1956, Liu was in Szechwan serving as a deputy leader of a "comfort" delegation to visit areas inhabited by Tibetan minority groups. There was a degree of irony connected with this visit—in August 1956 Liu had granted an in-terview to an Italian correspondent that gained world-wide press attention. Liu conceded that there had been a rebellion in Tibetan-inhabited areas of Szechwan in February 1956.[1]

In 1958, a decision was taken to re-establish Ninghsia province. However, instead of creating it as a provincial unit, it was established as the Ninghsia-Hui Autonomous Region, similar to existing "regions" in Sinkiang and Kwangsi. In June 1958 Liu was named to chair the prepara-tory committee, and when the region formally came into existence in October 1958, Liu (him-self a Hui) was named as the first chairman of the Ninghsia-Hui Autonomous Region (NHAR). Within the Party structure in the region he served as a secretary but was subordinate to First Secretary Wang Feng (q.v.), a Han Chinese who specializes in minority affairs. There did not seem to be anything noteworthy about Liu's work in Ninghsia, but then in mid-1960 he became involved in political difficulties. He was apparently accused of what the Party termed "local nationalism," that is, placing the interests of the local inhabitants above national interests.[2] He was replaced in September 1960 as NHAR Chairman by Yang Ching-jen (q.v.), another Hui. It was not until the spring of 1962 that there was any further reporting on Liu's activities, and for the next few years the press coverage about him was sparing and perfunctory. The most noteworthy events concerned the NPC; Liu served as a member of the Presidium for both the third and fourth sessions of the Second NPC (in 1962 and 1963, respectively). However, rather solid (though somewhat confusing) evidence was already in hand that indicated a serious decline in his political career. The annual *Jen-min shou-ts'e* (People's handbook) for 1960, prepared at about the time he was removed in Ninghsia, did not list him in his post on the important Party Control Commission. Rather oddly (and perhaps owing to editorial oversight), he was listed in the 1961 edition, but subsequent editions omitted his name. It was also in 1961, as already noted, that he was removed from the presidency of the Central Nationalities Institute in Peking. Further and convincing evidence of his political misfortunes became available in late 1964 when the Third NPC was organized. He was re-elected as a deputy (from Hopeh rather than Ninghsia), but when the Third NPC held its first session in December 1964–January 1965 he was not re-elected to the NPC Standing Committee nor to the chairmanship of the important Nationalities Committee. He was, however, elected a member of the Nationalities Committee, and in December 1965 he was elected a vice-governor of Shansi. Nonetheless, in view of his past positions both of these assignments were peculiarly anticlimactic.

Among Liu's writings is a useful survey of nationalities work that appeared in *People's China*, no. 20, October 16, 1952. He is also the author of articles, all on nationalities questions, which appeared in the *JMJP* on January 11, 1958, April 12, 1959, October 27, 1959, and March 30, 1960.

1. *CB* 409, p. 7.
2. *New York Times,* September 21, 1960.

Liu Lan-po

(c.1906–   ; Feng-ch'eng, Liaoning). Vice-minister, Ministry of Water Conservancy and Electric Power; alternate member, CCP Central Committee.

Manchurian-born Liu Lan-po comes from Feng-ch'eng, a few miles north of the industrial city of Antung in Liaoning.[1] Something of his family background may be surmised from the fact that he is reported to be a younger brother of Liu To-ch'üan, a former Nationalist governor of Jehol province. Born in Liaoning in 1896, Liu To-ch'üan was a graduate of the Paoting Military Academy. During and shortly after the Sino-Japanese War he served as the nominal governor of Jehol. He later joined the Communists for whom he has served in the CPPCC and, from 1962, as director of the Communications Department in his native Liaoning.

While Liu To-ch'üan was serving with the Nationalists, his younger brother joined the CCP, and is reported at sometime in the 1930's to have been the secretary of a Party committee among certain of the military forces in Manchuria. Later he was a member of the Standing Committee of the Yenan branch of the "Northeast General National Salvation Association," whose name suggests that it was part of the Communist student association that came into existence when the Northwest China Association of Youths for National Salvation convened a congress in Yenan in November 1938 and set up an office of Chinese Youth Associations for National Salvation with headquarters in Yenan.

There is no further reporting of Liu's activities until the CCP held its Seventh National Congress in Yenan (April–June 1945), where he was one of the speakers.[2] By the following year he had returned to his native Antung region and became a vice-governor of Antung, secretary of the Antung Provincial Party Committee, deputy political commissar of a "Fourth Detachment" of military forces there, and a member of the Manchurian regional administration known as the Northeast Administrative Committee, established by the Communists in 1946 to govern the Northeast. He held all the above posts from 1946 to 1949. In 1946, Communist journalist Chou Erh-fu visited Manchuria, where he interviewed Liu, describing him as one of the busiest officials in Antung. Chou also met Liu's wife, a woman surnamed Yang.[3]

Antung province, which was abolished by the Communists in the winter of 1948–49 was one of the nine Manchurian provinces created by the Nationalists immediately after the end of hostilities in 1945, but which they were never able to control. In 1949 it was merged into Liaotung province under a Communist government, and by late that year Liu was identified as the governor. At this time he also became a deputy secretary of the Liaotung Provincial Party Committee. Early in 1950 he served for a brief period as the ranking Party secretary in Liaotung. In addition to these responsibilities, he was a member of the regional administration for Manchuria, the Northeast People's Government, established in August 1949 as the successor to the Northeast Administrative Committee. From 1948 to 1949 he was also a member of the executive committee of the Northeast branch of the Sino-Soviet Friendship Association.

During the year 1950 Liu was transferred to Peking where his work centered in the national government rather than the Party and in the programs for developing power for industry. In mid-1950 he was replaced as governor of Liao-tung by Kao Yang, a Manchurian Party leader. About this time Liu was named deputy director of the Industrial Department of the national Ministry of Fuel Industry; he held the post from 1950 to 1952. He was named to a higher post in the same ministry in September 1950, becoming a vice-minister under Minister Ch'en Yü. Liu was not often reported in the national press in the early 1950's, although he did present a major report in Peking before a national conference on the supply of electricity convened by his ministry in November–December 1952, and on January 7, 1954, he presented an official report before the Government Administration Council on the current situation in the fuel industry.

In the summer of 1954 he was sent abroad for the first time, traveling to Prague in July to negotiate an agreement on scientific and technical cooperation. The Chinese and the Czechs have a permanent joint committee for scientific and technical cooperation, a committee that meets once or twice a year. On September 2, 1954, he signed the protocol to the second meeting of the joint committee. Fifteen months later in Peking he was again the chief Chinese negotiator for the third meeting of the joint committee, signing another protocol on December 9, 1955.

In September 1954 Liu attended the first meeting of the First NPC as a deputy from Penki (Pen-ch'i), the iron-producing, railroad center near Mukden, which had special administrative status in 1954. Liu continued to represent Penki for the term of the First NPC (1954–1959), but when the Second NPC opened in April 1959 he was a delegate from Liaoning province, which had absorbed Penki in the interim. He was once again elected as a Liaoning deputy to the Third NPC, and at the close of its first session in January 1965 he was named to membership on the NPC Standing Committee, the body in charge of NPC affairs when the congress is not in full session. He made his second trip abroad in February 1955 as head of a delegation visiting the USSR on behalf of the Chinese electrical industry. In July 1955 the Ministry of Fuel Industry was reorganized into three separate ministries concerned with developing industrial power: Coal Industry, Petroleum Industry, and Electric Power Industry. Liu was given the portfolio for the Ministry of Electric Power. He retained the post from July 1955 to February 1958. On February 8, 1958, the *JMJP* carried an article criticizing the ministry for its neglect in the renovation of a certain power

plant. On February 16 Liu spoke at a public forum concerning this criticism. Just three days after the newspaper article, there was a partial reorganization of the State Council during which the Electric Power Ministry was merged with the Ministry of Water Conservancy, which had been headed by the former KMT general Fu Tso-i. Fu was made the minister of the newly created Ministry of Water Conservancy and Electric Power. No vice-ministers were appointed, but by June 1958 Liu was identified in this position. From the date of the merger until April 1963, the ranking Party member in the ministry was Li Pao-hua (q.v.), another vice-minister and also a full member of the Party Central Committee. Li was transferred from the ministry in April 1963, after which Liu became the senior Party official in the ministry. Fu Tso-i, the minister, has never belonged to the Party.

Coinciding with his work in power development for the government, Liu played a major role in the organization of a learned society in the same field. In June 1956 he became chairman of a Preparatory Committee to organize a society for electrical engineering. The Committee carried on its preparatory work until the Chinese Society of Electrical Engineering was established in the years between 1958 and 1960. Liu served on the society's Standing Committee until at least 1963, but it is not certain if he remained as an official after that date. Also in 1956 Liu was for the first time elected to the national Party bureaucracy. The Eighth National Congress elected him an alternate member of the Central Committee in September 1956.

In May 1957 he became a member of the Scientific Planning Commission of the State Council but was dropped from this post when the Commission was reorganized into the Scientific and Technical Commission in November 1958. In addition to serving in the legislative branch of the PRC, Liu was also active in the legislative advisory body, the CPPCC, where non-Party elements of the Chinese society are nominally represented. He was a CCP representative to the Third National Committee of the CPPCC (1959–1964) and also sat on the Standing Committee. He was not, however, elected to the Fourth Committee, which first met in late 1964. Liu made a third trip outside China in April–May 1962 as one of 10 NPC members led by Politburo member P'eng Chen to North Korea for a "goodwill" visit.

Apart from his purely governmental duties, Liu has made appearances at national conferences of a technical nature. For example, he attended the National Agricultural Science and Technology Conference held in February 1963 in Peking. He has also been a rather prolific writer for important Party publications. Articles by Liu, all dealing with some aspect of power generation, have appeared in the *JMJP* (October 11, 1956, June 21, 1958, and November 15, 1959), the Hong Kong *Ta-kung pao* (October 1, 1958), and *Hung-ch'i* (Red flag; issues of December 16, 1958, and July 1, 1960).

1. Chou Erh-fu, *Tung-pei heng-tuan-mien* (Northeastern cross section; Hong Kong, 1946), p. 58.

2. Conrad Brandt, Benjamin Schwartz, and John K. Fairbank, *A Documentary History of Chinese Communism* (Cambridge, Mass., 1952), p. 293.

3. Chou Erh-fu, p. 59.

Liu Lan-t'ao

(1904–   ; Mi-chih, Shensi). First secretary, Northwest Bureau, CCP; member, Central Control Commission, CCP; alternate member, Central Secretariat, CCP; member, CCP Central Committee.

One of the early Communist leaders in Shensi in the twenties, Liu Lan-t'ao was an important Party leader and political officer in north China during the Sino-Japanese War and the civil war that followed. In the early years of the PRC he was among the key officials in the government and Party administrations for north China, and in the mid-fifties he assumed critical positions within the Party central apparatus—most notably on the Party's Central Secretariat and the Central Control Commission. Following the re-creation of the regional Party bureaus in 1961, Liu was assigned to the northwest as the senior Party official.

Liu was born in Mi-chih, Shensi, a small town about 80 miles north of Yenan, and was educated at the San-min Number Two Middle School in Mi-chih and later at Peking University. He presumably returned to his native area in the mid-twenties. Although geographically rather isolated, northern Shensi had been deeply influenced by the May Fourth Movement, which erupted in Peking in 1919; many of the unsettling ideas of the movement had been brought back to Shensi by students who had been in Peking (possibly including Liu). (For a discussion of these influences, see under Chia T'o-fu.) Liu belonged to the Party by at least 1928, and in the summer of that year he took part in a Party-led peasant uprising organized by Liu Chih-tan and Kao Kang (qq.v.; see under Chia T'o-fu) in and around the towns of Wei-nan and Hua-yin in southern Shensi (the Wei-Hua Uprising). After this uprising, Liu Chih-tan became secretary of the North Shensi CCP Special Committee, a committee on which Liu and Chia T'o-fu also served.[1]

Liu was imprisoned in Peking by the KMT during the mid-1930's, but by 1938 he was the Party secretary of the District Committee in Pei-yueh, an area south of the P'ing-sui (Peking-Suiyuan) Railway and to the west of the P'ing-han (Peking-Hankow) Railway. Pei-yueh was one of the major sub-divisions of the Shansi-Chahar-Hopeh (Chin-Ch'a-Chi) Border Region (see under Sung Shao-wen). By 1940 Liu was a deputy secretary of the Chin-Ch'a-Chi Border Region's Party Committee, as well as deputy political commissar of the military region for the same area. In the latter post he served under Political Commissar and Commander Nieh Jung-chen (q.v.), until at least 1946 and possibly later.[2] Despite the paucity of information about Liu's early Party career, it is evident that he was a figure of some prominence by the time the CCP held its Seventh National Congress in April–June 1945 at Yenan. The Congress elected 44 full and 33 alternate members to the new Central Committee. Liu was placed last on the list of alternates, but within a decade he was to pass many of the men placed ahead of him. Shortly after the war ended (August 1945), the Communists moved into Chang-chia-k'ou (Kalgan), the capital of Chahar province. In order to establish a provincial government, a congress was held at Chang-chia-k'ou in November 1945, which Liu attended as a deputy from the Party's Chin-Ch'a-Chi Central Bureau (see under Chang Su, elected at that time to head the Chahar Provincial Government Council).[3]

Nothing further was heard of Liu's activities until early 1949 by which time he was the third secretary of the Party's North China Bureau, a post he held under First Secretary Po I-po. When the Communists conquered the various parts of China in the late forties, they immediately established "revolutionary" institutes to offer short-term training courses for cadres. Thus, when the North China Bureau established the North China People's Revolutionary University in Peking in early 1949, Liu was named to the presidency, a post he held until the school was closed in January 1953. The school, offering four-month courses, trained Communist and non-Communist personnel in military, political, economic, cultural, and "mass work" affairs, as well as Marxism-Leninism and the thought of Mao Tse-tung. In September 1949, as a representative of the CCP, Liu attended the inaugural session of the CPPCC, the legislative body that brought the new central government into existence (October 1). Liu did not receive any appointments in the central government at this time, but in April 1950 he was added as a member of the Political and Legal Affairs Committee (PLAC). Headed by veteran Tung Pi-wu, the PLAC was one of the four key committees subordinate to the Government Administration Council (the cabinet); Liu remained on the committee until it was abolished at the time of the inauguration of the constitutional government in the fall of 1954.

In the period from the 1949–50 takeover until 1954, China was divided for administrative purposes into six regions. Four of the regions had "military and administrative committees" (or, in the case of Manchuria, a "people's government"), but no such organizations existed in north China following the dissolution of the North China People's Government (see under Tung Pi-wu) in October 1949. Then, in September 1950, a decision was reached to create a Ministry of North China Affairs directly under Chou En-lai's Government Administration Council. Liu was named as minister, thereby being placed at the head of provincial affairs in Hopeh, Shansi, Chahar, Pingyuan, and Suiyuan. He continued to head this governmental body when it was reorganized into the North China Administrative Committee (NCAC) in December 1951, remaining in this post until the NCAC was abolished in 1954. Because the NCAC was headquartered in Peking (and thus under close control of the central authorities), it was probably a less significant organization than the five in the outlying regions. Nonetheless, by directing a regional governmental apparatus, Liu was placed on par with such prominent CCP leaders as Kao Kang (in Manchuria), Lin Piao (in central-south China), and Liu Po-ch'eng (in the southwest).

During the years from 1950 to 1954, Liu was outranked in the North China Party organization by Po I-po and (for most of the period) by Nieh Jung-chen. However, Po and Nieh were very much occupied with their duties in the central government and the PLA, respectively, thereby leaving much of the work in north China to Liu. It was usually Liu, for example, who made the official reports before central government bodies on north China affairs, as in October 1951 when he spoke before the third session of the CPPCC. Similarly, when *ad hoc* committees were formed in north China, Liu was usually the senior figure; for example, he was named in December 1951 to the Central Austerity Examination Committee and was also appointed to head the examination (or inspection) committee responsible for north China. He devoted much of his time in the first half of 1952 to this committee as the Communists mounted a major effort to curtail bureaucracy, corruption, waste, and similar abuses. Although he was apparently mainly concerned with the government apparatus in north China during the early fifties, Liu also held posts in the North China Bureau and in at least one of the "mass" organizations. As noted above, he was the North China Bureau third secretary from 1949, a position he held until the Bureau was abolished in 1954. In addition, he was identified in March 1951 as chairman of the Bureau's Finance and Economics Work Committee when he spoke at a conference held to promote the sale of native products throughout north China. The "mass" or "people's" organization to which Liu belonged was the All-China Federation of Co-operatives. Headed by Po I-po, it was one of the most important "mass" organizations in the early years of the PRC. Liu sat on the Federation's Standing Committee from November 1950 until it was reorganized in mid-1952.

Liu's rather active involvement in economic affairs probably accounts for his appointment to the State Planning Commission when it was established in November 1952 on the eve of the First Five-Year Plan (1953–1957). He remained on the commission until it was reorganized with the inauguration of the constitutional government in September 1954. In preparation for the convocation of the First NPC, the legislative body that brought the constitutional government into existence, the PRC established the Central Election Committee in February 1953 under the chairmanship of Liu Shao-ch'i. Liu Lan-t'ao was named to this committee, and when provincial elections were held in the following year, he was elected as a deputy from Hopeh to the First NPC, which initially met in September 1954 (by which time he had relinquished all his north China posts). At the close of the First NPC session he was elected to membership on the NPC Standing Committee, as well as to the chairmanship of the NPC Budget Committee. He relinquished the Budget Committee assignment when the Second NPC opened (April 1959) but continued as a Standing Committee member. However, although re-elected as a deputy to the Third NPC, at the close of the first session in January 1965, he was dropped from membership on the Standing Committee. Whereas Liu had been a Hopeh deputy to the First and Second NPC's, he was changed to the Shensi constituency for the Third NPC, a reflection of a transfer in assignments in about 1961 (see below).

Far more important than his participation in NPC affairs, however, was Liu's entry in the mid-fifties into the inner circles of the Party elite. For a brief period in the middle 1950's the Party Central Committee had a secretary-general (*pi-shu-chang,* not to be confused with the post of general secretary, *tsung shu-chi,* created at the Eighth Party Congress). From 1954 to 1956 Teng Hsiao-p'ing, then rising to the supreme elite of the CCP, was the secretary-general, and by late 1955 Liu was serving as one of his deputies. Liu's growing stature was also illustrated in November 1955 when he wrote an important article (*JMJP,* November 20, 1955) on the Party's "rural class policy," an interpretation of events following in the wake of Mao Tse-tung's famous July 31, 1955, speech calling for a great "upsurge" in the establishment of agricultural producers cooperatives. Further indications of Liu's increasing importance were revealed at the Party's Eighth Congress in September 1956. To manage the affairs of the congress, three *ad hoc* bodies were formed: a 63-member Presidium, a 13-member Secretariat, and a 29-member Credentials Committee. Although many Party leaders sat on two of these bodies, only Liu and six others (Li Hsueh-feng, Lin Feng, Ma Ming-fang, Sung Jen-ch'iung, T'an Chen-lin, and T'an Cheng) served on all three. (Liu was a vice-chairman of the Credentials Committee and a member of the other two.) At the close of the meetings he was elected to Central Committee membership and at the new Central Committee's First Plenum (held a day after the Congress closed), he was appointed as an alternate member of the Central Secretariat (thereby continuing to serve under Teng Hsiao-p'ing) and as a member and deputy secretary of the Central Control Commission. Significantly, Liu is the only man who has ever served in both the Secretariat and Control Commission, a fact that provides further affirmation of his position among the Party's elite. (He was also a member of the Control Commission's Standing Committee after its creation in about 1961.)

The Central Control Commission had been created in March 1955 in the wake of the purge of Politburo member Kao Kang and Organization Department Director Jao Shu-shih (qq.v.). At the time of its creation, only Tung Pi-wu, the secretary of the Commission, was identified among the leadership personnel of this important organization. However, the internal evidence drawn from the speeches delivered at the Eighth Party Congress strongly suggests that Liu held a senior position on the commission prior to the Eighth Congress. Whereas Secretary Tung Pi-wu spoke on legal work, Liu's speech was devoted exclusively to control work; significantly, his speech was entitled "Enforce Party Discipline Correctly, Strengthen Party Control Work." Of the five deputy secretaries elected in 1956, Liu was the only one who had advanced to the level of the Central Committee as early as 1945. Also, in view of Tung Pi-wu's advanced age (he was over 70 when the Eighth Congress was held), it is probable that Liu was the *de facto* head of the Control Commission until his transfer to the northwest in the early sixties.

It was also in the mid-fifties that Liu began to take part in the Party's international liaison activities. In December 1955 he accompanied Chu Te to Bucharest for the Second Congress of the Rumanian Workers' (Communist) Party. In January 1956 they went to East Germany to attend the 80th birthday celebrations of President Wilhelm Pieck, after which they visited Hungary, Czechoslovakia, and Poland. In early February the group went to Moscow where the CPSU was about to convene the famous 20th Party Congress. Chu remained as China's delegate, but Liu left for home on February 15, 1956, the day after the Congress began. He was back in Europe again in November 1958 when he led the Chinese delegation to the 20th Congress of the Danish Communist Party in Copenhagen. Immediately afterwards, he went to Moscow as head of the Chinese delegation to the 41st anniversary celebrations of the Russian Revolution, and while there held talks with Party First Secretary N. S. Khrushchev. From approximately this time until his transfer to the northwest in the early sixties, Liu was very often present in Peking for talks held with visiting Communist Party leaders—negotiations usually involving the highest CCP leaders (e.g., Liu Shao-ch'i and Teng Hsiao-p'ing).

In the fall of 1959, by which time he could be regarded as a top specialist in Party organizational affairs, Liu wrote another important article for the *JMJP* (September 28). Ostensibly written to commemorate the 10th anniversary of the PRC (under the title "The CCP is the Supreme Commander of the Chinese People in Building Socialism"), the article was in fact a strong affirmation of Party supremacy. It was written only a few weeks after the Central Committee's Eighth Plenum (when the CCP mounted its "counterattack" on the "rightists" who had opposed the Great Leap Forward), and it appeared in print only a few days after P'eng Te-huai (presumably a leading "rightist") had been replaced by Lin Piao as National Defense minister. The article was subsequently reprinted in an important collection of essays commemorating the 10th PRC anniversary.[4]

Liu appeared regularly in Peking until the latter part of 1960, after which he made no further appearances in the capital for nearly three years. His disappearance from the public scene in Peking was almost certainly related to the re-creation of the regional Party bureaus at the Party Central Committee's Ninth Plenum held in January 1961 (not long after Liu last appeared in Peking). Although he was not specifically identified as the Party First Secretary of the Northwest Bureau until October 1963, it seems likely that Liu assumed this position soon after the January 1961 Plenum was held. Moreover, at the next Plenum (the 10th, in September 1962), he was dropped as deputy secretary and Standing Committee member of the Party's Control Commission, although he retained his position as a member, a change which can be explained by the fact that the Control Commission secretaries and Standing Committee members all work in the national capital. Thus, Liu's transfer to Sian probably took place in 1961 or, at the latest, in 1962.

Since transferring to the northwest, Liu has

attended a number of Party meetings in the provinces and autonomous regions under the jurisdiction of the Northwest Bureau—Kansu, Ninghsia, Tsinghai, and Sinkiang, as well as Shensi where the Bureau headquarters are located (Sian). Few details of such meetings have been released by the Chinese press beyond the terse statement that Liu had issued "important instructions." Like most of the other regional Party Bureau secretaries, he returns to Peking rather frequently, presumably to report on the affairs within his Bureau. When back in Peking he is usually reported as associating with the top leaders, as in June 1964 when he was with Mao Tse-tung as the latter received delegates to the Ninth Congress of the Communist Youth League. He was again in Peking in December 1964–January 1965 when the NPC and the CPPCC held simultaneous sessions. Liu attended the NPC as a deputy from Shensi, but, as noted above, he was not re-elected at this time to the NPC Standing Committee. However, at this same time he was named to the Fourth National Committee of the CPPCC as a representative of the CCP, and when the session closed in January 1965 he was elected to a CPPCC vice-chairmanship.

Liu's position in the northwest was further consolidated in October 1965 when he was identified as political commissar of the Lanchow Military Region, the region responsible for Shensi, Ninghsia, Kansu, Tsinghai, and possibly Sinkiang. His role as the senior Party-PLA official in one of China's six regions placed him on par with some of the Party's most important leaders—Politburo member Li Ching-ch'üan in the southwest, Politburo member (until his death) Ko Ch'ing-shih in east China, and veteran Party leaders T'ao Chu, Sung Jen-ch'iung, and Li Hsueh-feng, who are the top Party officials in central-south China, Manchuria, and north China, respectively.

---

1. *Hung-ch'i p'iao-p'iao* (Red flag fluttering; Peking, 1957), V, 112.

2. *Chin-Ch'a-Chi hua-pao* (Shansi-Chahar-Hopeh pictorial; n.p.; March 1944), no. 5, no pages; *Chin-Ch'a-Chi jih-pao* (Shansi-Chahar-Hopeh daily), March 1, 1946; published in Chang-chia-k'ou (Kalgan).

3. *Chin-Ch'a-Chi hua-pao* (December 1945), Nos. 9–10.

4. *Ten Glorious Years* (Peking, 1960), pp. 283–297.

Liu Ming-fu

Vice-chairman, State Planning Commission.

Liu Ming-fu, a senior economic planner, was a Chinese delegate to the Young Communist International (YCI) in Moscow in the late 1920's. The Chinese Communist Youth League was then affiliated to the YCI, but extremely little information is available on their relations. In any case, it appears that Liu was in Moscow in the period after mid-1928 when both Ch'ü Ch'iu-pai and Chang Kuo-t'ao (qq.v.) were members of the Chinese delegation to the Comintern, the parent body of the YCI. In the second half of 1930, in the wake of the disasters brought about by the Li Li-san (q.v.) policies, various factions were contending for supreme power within the CCP. The struggle was fought out at top-level meetings in the fall and winter of 1930 and culminated in January 1931 at the Party's Fourth Plenum. Although full details are lacking, it appears that Liu acted as a spokesman for Ch'ü Ch'iu-pai, one of the major actors in the struggle for power, at the Third Plenum, held in September 1930. Liu denounced Chang Kuo-t'ao along lines similar to those expressed by Ch'ü, namely, that Chang had distorted CCP and Comintern policies (see under Ch'ü Ch'iu-pai). Ultimately, however, Liu's attack on Chang Kuo-t'ao was rejected by the CCP Politburo in December 1930, and Liu, rather than Chang, was condemned by the Politburo.[1]

Ch'ü Ch'iu-pai never recovered his effective political power after the events of late 1930. If, in fact, Liu was one of Ch'ü's protégés, it is perhaps for that reason that Liu seemingly disappeared from the Communist political scene for such a long period. He did not emerge again until the early 1950's when he was serving as a deputy secretary-general of the People's Economic Planning Commission under the Manchurian government administration, known as the Northeast People's Government (NEPG). He was removed from this post in July 1952 but at the same time was appointed to a closely related position as deputy director of the NEPG's Trade Department. However, he only held this post for a short period, because by the end of the year he was transferred to Peking to become deputy director of the Commercial Planning Bureau of the State Planning Commission. The Planning Commission was formed in November 1952, just prior to the inauguration of the First Five-Year Plan in 1953, and was headed by Politburo member Kao Kang (who was formally purged from the Party in early 1955).

When the central government was reorganized in the fall of 1954, Liu was named as a member of the Planning Commission, and then in January 1957 he was promoted to a vice-chairmanship. Among the many vice-chairmen on this important commission, Liu was junior in seniority only to Wang Kuang-wei (q.v.) as of the mid-1960's (although both men were politically outranked by such top Party members as Vice-Chairman Li Hsien-nien and Chairman Li Fu-ch'un, who has headed the commission since 1954). By 1955 Liu had been promoted to the directorship of the Commercial Planning Bureau of the Planning Commission, but he apparently did not continue in this post after 1956 (probably relinquishing it when he became a commission vice-chairman in January 1957).

In July 1954 Liu Ming-fu was elected to the National Committee of the All-China Federation of Supply and Marketing Cooperatives at the first congress of this important "mass" organization, which attempts to promote trade between the rural areas and the cities; Liu still holds this position. In 1956 he published a book dealing with commerce in the First Five-Year plan (1953–1957).[2]

By 1958 Liu was taking a larger role in foreign economic relations and may in fact be in charge of some aspects of foreign trade and aid for the State Planning Commission. In August–September 1958 he took part in talks with visiting North Koreans on economic cooperation, negotiations which led to the signing of four agreements and protocols on trade and Chinese economic aid to Korea. Two years later, in May–June 1960, Liu accompanied Premier Chou En-lai to Mongolia; the negotiations in Ulan Bator led to various agreements, including one under which China pledged a 200 million-ruble long-term loan, as well as assistance in industrial enterprises, water conservancy projects and public utilities. Then in January–February 1961 he took part in extended negotiations with an Albanian government economic delegation; on February 2 the Chinese and Albanians signed six economic agreements, including a treaty of commerce and navigation. With this background in international economic negotiations, Liu was a logical choice for a deputy directorship on the General Bureau for Economic Relations with Foreign Countries. This bureau, directly subordinate to the State Council, was formed in January 1960, but no appointments were made until April 1961 when Central Committee alternate member Fang I was named as director and Liu as one of the deputy directors. In June 1964 the bureau was elevated from the bureau to the commission (or ministerial) level; Fang I was reappointed to head the commission, but by 1965 Liu had not been reappointed. Through mid-1964 Liu was regularly reported in the press, usually in connection with visiting foreign economic delegations from Communist nations.

1. Warren Kuo, "Chu Chiu-pai's Policy of Conciliation," *Issues and Studies* (Taipei), July 1966, pp. 25–35 and August 1966, pp. 49–64.

2. *Ti-i-ko Wu-nien chi-hua chung-te shang-yeh* (Commerce in the first five-year plan; Peking, 1956).

Liu Ning-i

(1906–   ; Man-ch'eng hsien, Hopeh). Chairman, All-China Federation of Trade Unions; liaison specialist with international "peace" and labor movements; member, CCP Central Committee; member, CCP Central Secretariat.

The most widely traveled of all Chinese Communist leaders, Liu Ning-i came into the Party movement as a labor leader in the twenties, finally rising to the chairmanship of the All-China Federation of Trade Unions in 1958. He has spent a large amount of time since the mid-forties traveling abroad on behalf of the CCP, most frequently in connection with the international trade union and the "peace" movements. He holds or has held a host of positions, particularly in the "mass" organizations related to international affairs. He has been a CCP Central Committee member since 1956 and a member of the Party's Central Secretariat since 1966.

Liu was born in December 1906 in Man-ch'eng hsien, located in Hopeh midway between Peking and Shih-chia-chuang. He graduated from Hopeh Provincial Normal School and in 1925, presumably while still a student, participated in the May 30th Movement. The movement was ignited by the killing of Chinese demonstrators by British police in Shanghai and immediately led to nationwide demonstrations, strikes, and boycotts aimed at foreigners with special privileges in China. Liu's revolutionary career dates from this period, and it is probable that he joined the CCP about this time. He went to work at the famous Kailan mines, located in the T'ang-shan vicinity in northeast Hopeh. In the period from about 1927 to 1932 he was a labor organizer and agitator in the coal mining regions, spending about four years of this period in jail. He was arrested again in 1932 for leading a strike in the T'ang-shan area and once more imprisoned.

Like many left-wing and Communist elements, Liu was released from prison upon the outbreak of the Sino-Japanese War in July 1937. In the words of a 1950 Communist account, he was then "assigned the task of guiding the labor movement in Shanghai and . . . worked at this post until 1943."[1] Details about Liu's work during this period are not available, but these years must have been difficult and dangerous, particularly after the refuge provided by Shanghai's International Settlement was closed following Pearl Harbor in 1941. In 1943 Liu was called to Yenan where he studied and, according to Japanese sources, he became a leader of the Shensi-Kansu-Ninghsia Border Region Labor League. By the following year he had become associated with the Liberated Areas Labor Federation, working under Teng Fa (q.v.), then the Communists' top labor official.

Over the winter of 1945–46 Liu was a member of Chou En-lai's delegation in Chungking, which was conducting top-level negotiations with senior KMT officials (see under Chou), and then in early 1946 he surveyed labor conditions in Shanghai, which was then open to Communist operations under the terms of the cease-fire agreement signed by the Communists and the Nationalists in early 1946.

Already an important labor leader, Liu rose to greater prominence in the Communists' trade union movement after the death in April 1946 of Teng Fa in an air crash. In that year he became chairman of the Preparatory Committee of the Liberated Areas Trade Union Federation, a post he retained until the All-China Federation of Labor (ACFL) was inaugurated in 1948 (see below). The Communists had apparently intended to use Teng as their principal liaison official with the Communist-dominated World Federation of Trade Unions (WFTU); he had attended the Federation's inaugural congress in Paris in 1945, but after his death the assignment with the WFTU fell to Liu. He spent much of the late forties attending WFTU meetings in Europe and conferring with trade union leaders in the Communist nations of East Europe, trips that took him to Moscow (1946), Prague (1947 and 1949), Belgrade (1947), Paris (1947 and 1949), Budapest (1948 and 1949), Rome (1948), Bucharest (1949), and Warsaw (1949). While in Belgrade in mid-1947 he was received by Marshal Tito, and thus he is one of the few Chinese Communists to deal with the Yugoslav leader prior to his expulsion from the bloc in 1948.

Liu reached a new level of importance in the Chinese labor movement in August 1948 at the Sixth National Labor Congress held in Harbin. A member of the committee that arranged for the convocation of the Congress, he was elected one of the vice-chairmen of the All-China Federation of Labor under Chairman Ch'en Yun (q.v.). Concurrent with this position, Liu was identified in November 1948 as director of the Federation's International Liaison Department, although he was not formally appointed to the post until May 1949. He continued in the latter post until late 1955 when he was succeeded by Ma Ch'un-ku, another specialist in international liaison work. Liu was later to play a more prominent role in the domestic affairs of the Labor Federation, but especially in the late forties and early fifties he spent a great deal of time abroad as a labor liaison official. Excluding the travels described above, Liu's trips abroad as a Chinese delegate to WFTU meetings or as head of ACFL delegations took him to the following 13 nations: The Soviet Union, 1950; Hungary, 1950; Rumania, 1950, 1954; Burma, 1951; Pakistan, 1951; Austria, 1951, 1952;

1953, 1954; Poland, 1954; Yugoslavia, 1955; Finland, 1955; India, 1956; Italy, 1956; Japan, 1960; and Czechoslovakia, 1962. He was also scheduled to lead a Chinese delegation to the Second WFTU Congress in Milan in June 1949, but the Italian government forbade the entry of his group. For much of this period he was a senior official in the WFTU, serving as an alternate member of the Executive Committee from 1949 to 1951 and as a WFTU vice-president from 1949 until succeeded by his trade union colleague Liu Ch'ang-sheng (q.v.) in October 1957. In short, until the mid-fifties, Liu Ning-i was China's leading liaison official within the framework of the international Communist trade union network.

The inaugural meetings of the CPPCC were held in Peking in September 1949. This was the organization that brought the new central government into existence on October 1. Liu attended these meetings as a representative of the Labor Federation and was named to membership on both the First National Committee and its Standing Committee, retaining these posts until the Second CPPCC was established at the end of 1954. On October 2, 1949, just one day after the new government was inaugurated, the Chinese established the China Peace Committee, one of the most important of the "mass" organizations, particularly in the 1950's. He became a vice-chairman at this time, but when the Peace Committee was reorganized a year later he lost this post. However, he became a Standing Committee member and, more important, assumed the role of secretary-general—probably the most important post within the organization in terms of actual authority, because Kuo Mo-jo, the chairman of the Peace Committee since 1949, is regarded as essentially a figurehead. Liu remained as secretary-general until May 1954 when, because of "heavy duties," he asked to be relieved, the post then passing to Liao Ch'eng-chih (q.v.). Liu continued as a Standing Committee member, and then in July 1958 he was elevated to a vice-chairmanship. Nonetheless, his major contributions to the "peace" movement took place in the period from the late forties to the mid-fifties. Internationally, the China Peace Committee is an affiliate of the World Peace Council (WPC), an organization that was under Soviet domination until the rift in the Sino-Soviet bloc dating from about 1960. Paralleling his work in the international trade union movement, Liu has been almost equally active in the international "peace" movement. His trips to WPC meetings or related peace conferences have taken him to nine nations: Czechoslovakia, 1949; England, 1950; Poland, 1950, 1963; Austria, 1952; East Germany, 1952; Hungary, 1953; Sweden, 1954 (twice), 1956, 1961; Finland, 1955 (twice); Ceylon, 1957; and

India, 1961. At the meetings held prior to 1960, Liu's speeches merely repeated the current Soviet-imposed policies, but at the post-1960 meetings he was often engaged in bitter conflict with Soviet delegates. A typical example of the acrimonious nature of the meetings took place at a WPC session in November–December 1963 in Warsaw. According to the Chinese version of the proceedings, when Liu took the floor to make a speech, "Soviet delegates took the lead in pounding the table and letting out cat-calls," actions that the Chinese press described as "hooliganism."[2] Closely related to his attendance at WPC functions, is his participation in four of the annual conferences in Japan to "prohibit atomic and hydrogen bombs," leading groups there in 1955, 1960, 1964, and 1965. In terms of Sino-Soviet relations, these too were initially harmonious gatherings, but the conferences in the sixties witnessed acid exchanges between Liu and his Soviet counterparts, a typical example of which occurred at the 1964 meeting when the Chinese press reported that Liu had "exposed the criminal attempts of the Soviet revisionists to sabotage and split the Japanese movement" against nuclear weapons. Liu served as a member of the WPC from 1950 to 1955, and in 1955 he became a member of the WPC Executive Committee; it is not known, however, if he retains this post, but because of the deterioration of relations between the WPC and the China Peace Committee, the assignment is no longer important.

In addition to the positions previously mentioned, Liu holds or has held numerous others. Since the inauguration of the Chinese People's Institute of Foreign Affairs in December 1949 (see under Chang Hsi-jo), he has been a member of its Board of Directors, and he has similarly held membership on the China Committee for the Promotion of International Trade from its formation in May 1952. He was a vice-chairman of the All-China Athletic Federation from 1952 to 1956, and in 1952 he was heavily engaged in the management of one of the largest "peace" conferences ever held in Communist China. This meeting, known as the Asian and Pacific Regions Peace Conference, was held in October 1952 after several months of preparation. Liu served as secretary-general of the Preparatory Committee and dominated the proceedings in October, most of which were devoted to denunciations of the United States for its alleged use of bacteriological warfare in the Korean War (then still being waged). At the close of the conference he was elected to the key post, the secretary-generalship, in the permanent Peace Liaison Committee of Asian and Pacific Regions, but relatively little was heard of the organization after the mid-fifties. At the Seventh Labor Congress in May 1953, Liu's position within the Labor Federation was reaffirmed. He made the

opening speech at the Congress and was subsequently re-elected to a vice-chairmanship; in addition, he was elected to membership on both the Presidium and the Secretariat, the two organs that run the organization between meetings of the Executive Committee. (The English translation of the All-China Federation of Labor was changed at this time to the All-China Federation of Trade Unions.) Liu has also been a Standing Committee member of the Chinese People's Association for Cultural Relations with Foreign Countries since its inauguration in May 1954.

Besides his numerous other responsibilities, Liu has played a significant role in the NPC. His activities in this connection began in 1953 when he served on the national committee to draft the constitution. In the following year he was elected as a Shantung deputy to the First NPC, and at the close of the initial session in September 1954 he was elected a member of the NPC Standing Committee. He served again as a Shantung deputy to the Second NPC (1959–1964), once again serving on the Standing Committee. He was transferred to the Hopeh constituency (his native province) for the Third NPC, which held its first session in December 1964–January 1965. At this time he advanced to a vice-chairmanship on the Standing Committee and, more important, he succeeded P'eng Chen as the NPC secretary-general. During P'eng's 10-year tenure as secretary-general, it became evident that this was the critical post within the organization. Thus, if the precedent established during P'eng's term continues, Liu can probably be regarded as the key CCP official within the government's highest legislative body.

In the closing days of 1954 Liu was named to a vice-chairmanship in the Sino-Soviet Friendship Association (SSFA), a post to which he was re-elected in May 1959. His affiliation with the SSFA is laden with irony in view of his frequent and bitter clashes with Soviet officials during the 1960's. In early 1955 he was named secretary-general of a committee to prepare for participation in the "Asian Countries' Conference" in New Delhi. Liu attended the New Delhi meeting in April, which was originally intended to influence the developments at the far more famous Bandung Conference held in Indonesia later in the same month. One of the major results of the meeting in India was a decision by the participating nations to establish national "Asian Solidarity Committees," and when the Asian Solidarity Committee of China (ASCC) was formed in February 1956, Liu became a vice-chairman and secretary-general. In the spring of 1958 the ASCC was renamed the Afro-Asian Solidarity Committee of China, and in July of that year Liu relinquished the secretary-generalship to Chu Tzu-ch'i (q.v.), although he retained his vice-chairmanship. In its formative period the committee seemed to be principally a regional offshoot of the World Peace Council, but like all international organizations involving the Communists, it became a battleground for the Sino-Soviet polemics in the sixties. As secretary-general of the Chinese delegation, Liu attended the First Afro-Asian Solidarity Conference in Cairo in December 1957–January 1958. These meetings were pervaded by a spirit of unanimity (e.g., denouncing American "imperialism"); however, by the time the Second Conference was held in Guinea in April 1960, Sino-Soviet tensions had grown considerably, though they were still muted. Liu attended the meetings in Guinea as deputy leader of the Chinese delegation. Three years later he led the Chinese group to the Third Conference, held in Moshi, Tanganyika (February 1963). By this time the Sino-Soviet dispute was completely in the open, and as head of the Chinese delegation Liu was called upon to attack both the Indians (with whom the Chinese had just fought a border war) and the Russians. Later in the year the Russians accused the Chinese delegation of having introduced racial considerations into the conference, which was attended by 400 persons. Although the Russian report must be viewed with caution, they claim that Liu said: "We regret that you [Russians] have come here at all. What need is there for you here? The whites have nothing to do in Moshi. Do as you please. We shall be against you."[3] The Chinese officially denied that Liu made these statements, but it is clear that the CCP has gone to great lengths to keep the Soviet Union out of the Afro-Asian People's Solidarity Organization (AAPSO), as the permanent organ located in Cairo is known. In addition to the AAPSO meetings already described, Liu attended other conferences sponsored by the organization in Indonesia (April 1961) and the United Arab Republic (December 1961).

Beginning about 1957 Liu began to take an active role in CCP relations with foreign Communist parties. His first specific role in these endeavors occurred in April 1957 when he was the CCP delegate to the 12th Congress of the Belgian Communist Party in Ghent. Since that time he has conferred on innumerable occasions in Peking with top-ranking foreign Communist leaders visiting Peking, activities that have also characterized the careers of such top Chinese Communists as Liu Shao-ch'i, Teng Hsiao-p'ing, P'eng Chen, Yang Shang-k'un, and Wu Hsiu-ch'üan (qq.v.). Liu's assignment to this sort of work obviously derived from his etxensive contacts with foreign Communists in the course of his duties within the international trade union and "peace" movements. As such, he has participated in some of the most important international conferences within the Communist world since 1957. In November of that year he was in Moscow leading a "Chinese working people's delegation" to the 40th anniversary celebrations of the Russian Revolution, and it is probable that he also participated in the Communist "summit" conference held in Moscow at that time, talks that were led on behalf of the Chinese by Mao Tse-tung. Sino-Soviet differences were then glossed over, as they were again in January–February 1959 when Liu accompanied Chou En-lai to the 21st CPSU Congress. However, the dispute became more apparent in November–December 1960 when Liu was again in Moscow, this time as a member of a delegation led by Liu Shao-ch'i. Once again a Communist "summit" meeting was held—and once more the results were inconclusive in terms of the points of view of the Chinese and Soviet Communist Parties.

Probably the most dramatic and far-reaching encounter between Chinese and Soviet leaders took place in July 1963 when Teng Hsiao-p'ing led a small delegation to Moscow. Five of the seven members of Teng's group had previously been in open conflict with Soviet leaders at various international conferences, for example, Liu Ning-i at the meeting in Tanganyika described above. From the outset, therefore, the 1963 meetings in Moscow were clearly foredoomed. Whether or not Liu actually opposes any cooperation with the Soviet Union must remain a moot point, but from the Soviet viewpoint he is probably regarded as one of the leading "anti-Soviet elements" in the CCP hierarchy. The Russians probably felt confirmed in this view in December 1964 when they read Liu's speech at a session of the NPC. Liu's talk was devoted to a refutation of what the Chinese Communists call the "three reconciliations and one reduction," that is, the idea that the "revisionists" (the Chinese term of opprobrium for the Soviet Union) favor reconciliation with "imperialism, the reactionaries, and modern revisionism, and the reduction of aid and support to the revolutionary struggles waged by the oppressed peoples and nations throughout the world." Liu's one other trip to a foreign Communist party meeting took place in April 1963, when he led the CCP delegation to a national conference of the Communist Party of New Zealand in Auckland, thereby becoming one of the extremely few Chinese Communists to have visited that nation.

By 1957 Liu's activities suggested that he would play a less important role in the All-China Federation of Trade Unions (ACFTU). This became evident in December of that year when the ACFTU convened its Eighth Congress. He was re-elected to the Executive Committee, but he was dropped as a vice-chairman and from membership on both the Presidium and Secretariat. The relinquishment of these responsibilities seemed to be a logical result of his increasingly important role in CCP affairs. However, the situation was altered in May 1958 with the death of Lai Jo-yü, then the top man in the ACFTU. The Party apparently felt that it needed a top man to be in charge of the ACFTU, one of the two or three most important of the many "mass" organizations. Consequently, in August 1958, Liu was brought back to the ACFTU to serve as the chairman, a post he still retains.

Liu's long Party experience was given official recognition at the Eighth National Party Congress in September 1956 when he was elected to membership on the Party Central Committee. During the Congress itself he served on the small Secretariat headed by Teng Hsiao-p'ing that was in charge of the conduct of the sessions. A decade later he rose to new heights when he was identified as a member of the Party's Central Secretariat. The new assignment was of special significance because it came amid the "great proletarian cultural revolution" of 1966 when several of the CCP's top leaders were ousted from power. Politically, the three most important figures to fall were P'eng Chen, Propaganda Department Director Lu Ting-i, and PLA Chief-of-Staff Lo Jui-ch'ing, each of whom had also been members of the Central Secretariat. In addition to the elevation of Liu, T'ao Chu and Yeh Chien-ying (q.v.) also became Secretariat members in mid-1966. Consequently, it is evident that Liu, T'ao, and Yeh had not merely become additional members of the Secretariat but rather were named to this crucial organization to replace purged officials.

Few Chinese Communist officials of importance hold so many and such varied positions as Liu. In addition to the large number already described, he has been a deputy director of the State's Council Office of Foreign Affairs since its creation in early 1958. Headed by Foreign Minister Ch'en I, the office is responsible for coordinating the activities of the various government commissions, ministries, and bureaus concerned with international relations. He has also been a leading official in the following "friendship associations" since their establishment: Chairman, China-Iraq Friendship Association (FA), September 1958; member, Executive Council, China-Africa People's FA, April 1960; and member, Standing Committee, China-Cuba FA, December 1962. In addition, he has frequently lent his name to ceremonial occasions, as in 1959 when he was named to membership on the presidium (steering committee) to celebrate the 10th anniversary of the PRC, or in September 1961 when he was a member of the Preparatory Committee for Commemorating the 50th Anniversary of the 1911 Revolution.

Probably the most striking aspect of Liu's career is the amount of traveling he has done on behalf of the Chinese Communists. From 1946 through 1965 he was abroad on at least one occasion in each year. In addition to the impressive travel record already described, he has made still other important trips. In May 1950 he was in Prague to celebrate the fifth anniversary of the victory over the Nazis, and in October of the same year he led a group to London at the invitation of the Britain-China Friendship Association. A vivid description of the unfriendly nature of this "friendship" visit has been provided by Michael Lindsay, who was intimately familiar with many top Communists from his experience with them in the Chinese northwest during the Sino-Japanese War. According to Lindsay's account, the delegation "refused almost every invitation through which they could have met people in a position to explain or influence British policy, often with gross rudeness."[4] In November–December 1964 Liu was in North Vietnam leading a Chinese delegation to meetings with the cumbersome but descriptive title of the "International Conference for Solidarity with the People of Vietnam, against United States Imperialist Aggression, and for the Defense of Peace," a conference held at a time when the war in South Vietnam was rapidly intensifying. Finally, from March to April 1965 he led a "friendship" delegation of the NPC to Guinea, Mali, the Central African Republic, the Congo (Brazzaville), and Ghana, conferring in each of these nations with important local leaders (e.g., Ghanian President Kwame Nkrumah).

Liu's extraordinary amount of time abroad is unmatched by any other Chinese Communist leader of comparable stature. Summarizing the record, one finds that he has visited at least 30 different nations in Asia, Africa, the Middle East, and Eastern and Western Europe on 66 different occasions. The majority of these travels have been in connection with four major endeavors: trade union activities, the "peace" movement, Afro-Asian "solidarity," and liaison (or sometimes "confrontation") with foreign Communist parties. In view of all these activities, it is not surprising that he has been a relatively infrequent contributor to the Chinese press since the inauguration of the PRC in 1949. In contrast, prior to the Communist takeover he was a rather frequent contributor in the period from 1946 to 1949 to *Ch'ün-chung* (The masses), a leading Communist journal published in Shanghai and then Hong Kong.[5] Since then, however, most of his articles have been confined to prosaic descriptions of his trips abroad (e.g., the *JMJP*, April 21, 1950, regarding the world "peace" movement). Perhaps his most important article since 1949 was the one appearing in the Party's top journal, *Hung-ch'i* (Red flag, issue of November 16, 1959), in which he discussed the role of "advanced workers" (i.e., "model workers") in mass movements.

In private life Liu is married to Li Shu-ying who is also a trade unionist. She has been an alternate member of the Federation of Trade Union's Executive Committee since 1953 and in 1957 she was elected to membership on its Auditing Committee. Li has also been a vice-chairman of the Light Industry Workers' Trade Union since August 1957. She serves in the CPPCC as an ACFTU representative, and since January 1965 she has been a member of the CPPCC's Standing Committee. Li has also served with her husband on the Council of the China-Cuba Friendship Association since its formation in 1962.

1. Shanghai, *Chieh-fang jih-pao* (Liberation daily), January 20, 1950.

2. *Peking Review,* no. 50:12 (December 13, 1963).

3. Hong Kong, *South China Morning Post,* September 14, 1963, quoting Reuters, Moscow, September 13, 1963.

4. Michael Lindsay, *China and the Cold War* (London, 1955), pp. 12–16, 275.

5. Chün-tu Hsüeh, *The Chinese Communist Movement, 1937–1949* (Stanford, Calif., 1962), pp. 5, 8.

Liu Pai-yü

(1915–   ; Peking). Vice-chairman, Union of Chinese Writers; vice-minister, Ministry of Culture.

Although he has less literary talent than many contemporary Chinese writers, war correspondent-turned-writer Liu Pai-yü is one of the most politically important writers in the Chinese Communist regime. Born in Peking in 1915,[1] Liu received his higher education at Min-kuo University in his native city. When the Sino-Japanese War broke out in 1937, Liu was only 22. Like so many young intellectuals, he made his way to the Communist wartime capital in Yenan where he spent most of the war as a New China News Agency (NCNA) reporter. He became well acquainted with U.S. Naval observer Evans Carlson, who visited the Communist areas in 1938. Liu and four other young intellectuals accompanied Carlson on an extensive tour of Communist guerrilla areas in Shensi, Shansi, and Hopeh in the spring and summer of 1938. Carlson presents an extremely flattering description of Liu who acted as the leader of the five-man team accompanying the American: "He was tall, slender and graceful, and he carried himself with a quiet dignity that was natural and unaffected. It was probably his remarkable self-discipline which caused him to be selected as leader, for during the five months we were together I never saw him lose his self-control. When called upon to make a decision he calmly examined all sides of the question, and then made up his mind. Any action which involved the group as a whole was considered by them jointly. At the end of each day's journey Liu would lead them aside, at some convenient time, and they would hold a meeting in which each discussed his observations and criticized himself.

They were seeking to perfect their conduct and their self-possession, and to add to their knowledge and broaden their understanding of life. The leader of such a group had to be a man of spiritual serenity and exceptional patience."[2]

An account written in 1963 described Liu's writings of the Sino-Japanese War period as reflective of "the heroic struggle of the Chinese people against Japanese aggression and for liberation."[3] Apart from his reporting for the NCNA, during the war years in Yenan he was also associated with *Ta-chung wen-i* (Literature of the masses), a popular journal of the period. Chou Yang (q.v.), who was later to become China's "literary czar," was an editor of this periodical. A close working relationship between Chou and Liu began during these years together in Yenan.

In 1944 Liu was transferred to the Nationalist capital at Chungking where with ideologue Hu Sheng (q.v.) he was co-editor of the literary section of the Communists' *Hsin-hua jih-pao* (New China daily).[4] He spent most of the time from 1946 to 1949 in Manchuria covering the exploits of Lin Piao's Northeast Democratic Allied Army and working in the publishing and literary fields. When the Northeast Literary and Art Work Committee was formed in March 1948, he became one of its leading members, and he also edited a journal known as the *Tung-pei wen-i yueh-k'an* (Northeast literature and arts monthly). Two of his more important books were published at this time, *Huan-hsing tung-pei* (Traveling in the northeast; Shanghai, 1946) and *Shih-tai te yin-hsiang* (Impressions of the time; Harbin, 1948), both of which deal with his days in Manchuria. When Lin Piao's forces pushed southward into China proper at the end of 1948, Liu reported on their conquest of the Nationalists in central-south China.

In July 1949 Liu returned to Peking for the large congress that inaugurated the All-China Federation of Literary and Art Circles (ACFLAC), the chief vehicle for organizing the literary and artistic talents of China. Representation to the congress, attended by over 800, was by geographic areas, except for a military delegation. Liu attended as a member of this military delegation, led by Chang Chih-hsiang (q.v.), a leading political figure in the PLA. During the congress he served on a special committee which evaluated the political and literary merits of novels (presumably for publication and dissemination throughout the nation). At the close of the conference, he was elected to the ACFLAC National Committee. Several subordinate organizations were formed under the ACFLAC at the same time, one of them being the All-China Association of Literary Workers, to which Liu was named to National Committee membership.

In September 1949, Liu attended the session of the CPPCC (which inaugurated the PRC on October 1) as a representative of the Fourth

Field Army, whose exploits he had reported earlier that year. By this time Liu's usefulness as a journalist, novelist, and short story writer was recognized by the Party. This was evident from the fact that his works were advertised in the earliest issues of *Hsueh-hsi* (Study), the Party's most important journal from 1949 to 1958. He also participated in the filming of "The Victory of the Chinese People" in 1949, for which he was awarded a Stalin Prize in 1950 (the award being given in 1951). In 1950 he visited Moscow, resulting in the publication of a series of articles based on this trip where he met such important Soviet literary figures as Ilya Ehrenburg.

Prior to the end of the Korean War in 1953, extremely few Chinese Communists traveled beyond the Communist bloc. An early and important exception to this general practice occurred from September 1951 to January 1952 when playwright Ting Hsi-lin led a large cultural delegation to India and Burma. Liu served as the secretary-general of this delegation. Not long after his return to China, he was elected to the China-India Friendship Association, which was formed in May 1952. Very soon after this Liu was assigned as a war correspondent to North Korea where the "Chinese People's Volunteers" had been fighting since October 1950. He remained there until the end of the war in July 1953 and then returned to Peking; an English-language account of the war by Liu appears in *People's China* of September 1, 1953. In September–October 1953 the second congress of the ACFLAC was held simultaneously with a congress of the Union of Chinese Writers, one of the constituent organizations of the ACFLAC. Liu was again elected to membership on the National Committee of the ACFLAC and on the Executive Committee of the Union of Chinese Writers (the new name for the All-China Association of Literary Workers).

In May 1954 he was selected for membership on the Board of Directors of the Chinese People's Association for Cultural Relations with Foreign Countries, a position he probably still retains. In the same year he was elected a Hopeh deputy to the First NPC (1954–1959); he was re-elected from Hopeh to the Second NPC (1959–1964), but he then became a deputy from his native Peking to the Third NPC, which first met in December 1964–January 1965. In December of 1954 he attended the second national conference of the Sino-Soviet Friendship Association (SSFA), at which time he was elected to the new SSFA Council; he was re-elected at the third conference in May 1959. Liu's power and authority within the Union of Chinese Writers rose sharply after 1955. In January of that year he became a member of the Editorial Committee of *Wen-i pao* (Literary gazette), the organ of

the Union, and in the following month he became chairman of the Union's Creative Work Committee (*ch'uang-tso wei-yuan-hui*), a committee apparently charged with the task of outlining Party policies for the guidance of Chinese writers. It is not certain if Liu continues to hold this post. When the Union established a Secretariat in December 1956, he was named as one of the secretaries, and by May 1957 he was identified as a deputy secretary of the Party Committee within the Union. The Union is ostensibly headed by Shen Yen-ping (Mao Tun), the non-Communist chairman, but until the "great proletarian cultural revolution" that began in 1966 it was evident that the actual head was Chou Yang, assisted by his two long-time confidants, Liu Pai-yü and Shao Ch'üan-lin. Then in the early sixties Shao, another member of the Union Secretariat, got into political difficulties for his continual promotion of writings with a greater diversity of style and theme, and in mid-1966 Chou Yang was savagely attacked by the Party press and fell from power. Thus, by the mid-sixties, it is probable that Liu had become the single most important CCP figure in the Writers' Union. Paralleling his rise in the Union's Secretariat, Liu became a vice-chairman of the organization in August 1960.

During the years when Liu was steadily climbing the hierarchical ladder of China's literary and cultural world, he was also deeply involved in the wide-scale campaign against writer Hu Feng in 1955. In this instance he served as a right-hand man for Chou Yang, echoing Chou's criticism of Hu Feng, his long-time enemy. He was equally active in the nationwide 1957–58 rectification campaign directed against the "rightists." Liu was among those who outlined a series of harsh measures announced at a meeting of the Union of Chinese Writers in October–November 1957. For example, it was decided then that many writers would be sent to rural areas and to factories "to mingle with the masses," that about half of all the cadres working in the subordinate organizations of the Union would be sent to the countryside, and that Union-sponsored literary study classes would be discontinued in order to discourage the practice of training only in the classrooms. Among those whom Liu attacked during this extensive campaign was authoress Ting Ling, a former colleague on the *Ta-chung wen-i* in Yenan and one of the chief targets of attack during the rectification movement.

In the meantime, he was becoming more active in the growing international contacts of the Union of Chinese Writers. He led a writers' delegation in December 1956 to Yugoslavia, where he was received by President Tito. In August 1958 he attended in Tashkent, Russia, a preparatory meeting of the Afro-Asian Writers'

Conference; two months later he was a member of the delegation (led by the then Minister of Culture Shen Yen-ping) to the first Afro-Asian Writers' Conference. One outgrowth of this conference was the formation of a Permanent Bureau of Afro-Asian Writers in Ceylon. The Chinese responded to this in April 1959 with the formation of the "China Committee for Liaison with the Permanent Bureau." Shen Yen-ping was named as chairman and Liu as one of the two vice-chairmen. In January 1961 he led a Chinese delegation to a meeting of this bureau in Colombo, Ceylon, and two months later he was a deputy leader of a delegation to an "emergency meeting" of the Afro-Asian Writers' Conference in Tokyo. He was abroad once again in April–May 1962 when he served as a member of a cultural delegation to North Korea.

Like so many other literary figures, Liu has been called upon to lend his name and prestige to the multifarious "people's" organizations of the PRC. In July 1958 he was added to the National Committee of the China Peace Committee, and two months later was named as a vice-chairman of the newly established China-Albania Friendship Association. In April 1960 he was also selected for Standing Committee membership within the newly formed China-Africa People's Friendship Association, and by August 1960 he was identified as a Council member of the China–Korea Friendship Association (an organization formed in September 1958). Finally, in June 1965, he was named as a vice-chairman of the reorganized Afro-Asian Solidarity Committee of China.

Although Liu has been a deputy to the NPC since 1954, he held no other post in the central government until April 1965 when he was appointed as a vice-minister of Culture. This appointment, made not long after Shen Yen-ping was removed as the minister, was apparently laden with political significance. Moreover, at the same time that Liu was appointed to the ministry, two other vice-ministers were removed. One of the two was Hsia Yen who lost his post at a time when he was under attack in the Party press for a scenario he had written for a film based on one of Shen Yen-ping's novels written many years earlier. Thus, Liu received this new appointment at a time when two important cultural figures fell under a political cloud.

In addition to his several journeys abroad, Liu has also traveled rather extensively within China in recent years in search of literary material. As he explained in an article published in 1964 under the title "Some Thoughts on Reportage," he had returned to journalistic reporting "in this new age of socialist construction."[5] Another writer, in a foreword to a collection of prose works published from 1959 to 1961, singled out Liu for praise when he commented that he had been among the "most active" of the professional writers.[6] His writings of these years have varied from reportage on Manchuria to the building of industrial cities along the Yangtze.

---

1. *Chinese Literature,* no. 8:96–101 (August 1964).
2. Evans Fordyce Carlson, *Twin Stars of China* (New York, 1940), pp. 178–179.
3. *SCMP* 2947, p. 16.
4. Chün-tu Hsüeh, *The Chinese Communist Movement, 1937–1949* (Stanford, Calif., 1962), p. 158.
5. *Chinese Literature,* no. 8:96–101 (August 1964).
6. *SCMM* 340, p. 30.

Liu Po-ch'eng

(1892–   ; K'ai-hsien, Szechwan). Veteran military leader; PLA marshal; CCP Politburo member.

Liu Po-ch'eng, one of the most able and battle-tested Red Army veterans, participated in many landmark events in Chinese Communist history, including the Nanchang Uprising and the Long March. He received military training in both China and the Soviet Union, and during the Sino-Japanese War and the ensuing civil war with the Nationalists he was among the most active and successful Red Army commanders. Liu's units captured southwest China in 1949–50, and in the early period of nationwide Communist rule he was a key political-military figure in that region. From 1951 to 1957 he headed one of the PLA's top military institutes (in Nanking) and concurrently, from 1954 to 1957, he was director of the PLA General Training Department. A CCP member since 1926, Liu was elected to the Central Committee in 1945 and the Politburo in 1956. He has been a senior member of the Party's Military Affairs Commission since at least 1961.

Liu Po-ch'eng was born in 1892 in or near K'ai-hsien in eastern Szechwan. Liu's father was a traveling musician and was able to give his son some traditional Chinese schooling. Liu prepared for the imperial *Hsiu-ts'ai* examination but never passed it. Just before the outbreak of the 1911 Revolution he graduated from a military school in Chengtu, the provincial capital, and became a junior officer in the army of Szechwan military leader Hsiung K'o-wu. Liu served with Hsiung for several years; in one campaign he lost an eye and was later nicknamed the "one-eyed dragon." Through Hsiung he met two men who later became prominent Communists, Wu Yü-chang and Chu Te (qq.v.). Hsiung was a revolutionary who supported the overthrow of the Manchus and led the resistance in Szechwan against Yuan Shih-k'ai's attempted imperial restoration. As a result, Hsiung had considerable contact with Wu Yü-chang, who was about his age and was as important in Szechwan academic circles as Hsiung was in military ones. For instance, in late 1917 after Hsiung had taken control of most of the province, he asked Wu to visit Sun Yat-sen in Canton and request Szechwan's representation in the Military Government. Since Liu was also sympathetic to the revolutionary cause he probably became acquainted with Wu during these years. At about the same time that Hsiung asked Wu to see Sun, he also sent Liu, who was then a brigade commander, to Yunnan to negotiate with Chu Te, who was the commander of a Yunnan army.[1]

There are reports that after Yuan Shih-k'ai died in 1916 Liu left Hsiung's army to travel through China, but it is not known what period this covered or whether he returned to Hsiung's army afterwards. However, it seems likely that by the early 1920's he was back in Chengtu, which Hsiung had recovered late in 1920 after it had been taken briefly by other warlords. In that year Wu Yü-chang had returned to the city to direct the Chengtu Normal Middle School and had set up his own Communist Party organization. By 1924 his agitation among the students, workers, and peasants had grown so irritating to the warlords then in power that he was forced to flee to Shanghai after sponsoring a May First anniversary demonstration. Wu has written that Liu Po-ch'eng accompanied him,[2] and the implication is that they had been previously associated in the movement. Influenced by Wu, Liu joined the CCP in 1926 and, according to an account Chu Te gave Agnes Smedley, he was sent to southern Szechwan to command a revolutionary army that was pitted against Szechwan warlord Liu Hsiang. Two of Chu Te's nephews are said to have served under Liu Po-ch'eng at this time, but both were killed when Liu Hsiang's forces defeated Liu Po-ch'eng's in early 1927.[3] Liu Po-ch'eng escaped to Wuhan where the Nationalist government had been transferred in late 1926 and then became a KMT representative in the army of another Szechwan general, Yang Sen. At about the same time Chu Te was also assigned to Yang's army as head of the political department. However, Yang was becoming increasingly disenchanted with the Nationalists, so Chu and Liu soon left his army, Liu returning to Wuhan and Chu going to Nanchang, the Kiangsi capital. Liu became a KMT representative to the troops in western Hupeh, and the CCP subsequently made him its special representative in the area.[4]

Liu was in Wuhan in mid-July 1927 when the final break occurred between the left-KMT government and the CCP. He immediately went to Nanchang, the Kiangsi capital, where he assisted Ho Lung and others in planning the Nanchang Uprising on August 1 (see under Yeh

T'ing), the date celebrated as the birth of the Red Army. Liu took part in the planning as a member of the Party's Front-line Committee, and then, when the city was captured by the Communists, he became chief-of-staff of the Revolutionary Committee, which was established to run the city.[5] Liu at this time served under Ho Lung, who headed the military command, and Yeh T'ing, Ho's deputy. However, Nanchang was only held for five days before the Communists were driven out. Moving south to attack Swatow, Liu is reported to have sided with Ho Lung and his Russian adviser in important decisions concerning the route to be followed (see under Ho Lung).[6] Ho's troops took Swatow on September 25, holding it for about a week. When the Communists were forced out of the city a number of the leaders fled to nearby Lu-feng, where the Party had already established a local organization (see under P'eng P'ai). Liu was among the escapees, along with Chang Kuo-t'ao (q.v.), Ho Lung, and Wu Yü-chang. Arriving in Lu-feng on October 7, they soon made their way to Hong Kong where they both Ho Lung and Liu asked to be sent to the Soviet Union. Ho Lung was given another assignment, but Liu and Wu proceeded to Shanghai and from there to Moscow at the end of the year.[7]

Liu spent two and a half years in the Soviet Union where he received military training and probably also some formal Communist indoctrination. After attending an advanced infantry academy, he studied at the Frunze (Red Army) Military Academy. While in Moscow Liu apparently attended the Sixth CCP Congress (June–July 1928).[8] In the summer of 1930 he returned to China to become a staff officer of the CCP Military Affairs Council, an organ of the Party Central Committee, whose headquarters were in Shanghai and which was then dominated by Li Li-san. Liu immediately became involved in Li's plans for seizing major industrial cities, and he himself participated in the attempt to take Changsha. When this failed he fled to eastern Hunan and began organizing partisan units. In the spring of 1931 he joined the forces of Chu Te and Mao Tse-tung in south Kiangsi, remaining there until the start of the Long March (October 1934). His principal role during these years was in connection with military staff work and military institutes established in the Juichin area. In 1931 he was president of the Red Army School (Hung-chün hsueh-hsiao; not to be confused with the more important Red Army Academy, Hung-chün ta-hsueh), and in late 1933 he lectured at the Red Army Academy.[9] Liu later relinquished the presidency of the Red Army School to Yeh Chien-ying (q.v.), probably in 1932 when he became chief-of-staff of the Central Revolutionary Military Council. (Some sources suggest that Liu and Yeh alternated as chief-of-staff from this time until 1937.) At the

Second All-China Congress of Soviets, held in Juichin in January–February 1934, Liu was elected a member of the Central Executive Committee, the governing body of the Chinese Soviet Republic. Then, on the Long March from Kiangsi to the northwest, he led a brigade of Red Army cadets,[10] concurrently serving as chief-of-staff of the Chu-Mao First Front Army (as well as chief-of-staff of the Central Revolutionary Military Council). Liu's importance on the Long March has been described in numerous accounts.[11] He played a major role in the capture of Tsun-i, Kweichow, in January 1935; in negotiations with minority tribesmen in Szechwan, which enabled the Red Army to proceed unmolested; and in diversionary actions that permitted the marchers to make their dramatic crossing of the Ta-tu River on the Szechwan-Sikang border.

Liu seems to have been an integral part of Mao Tse-tung's military leadership until Mao's army separated from Chang Kuo-tao's in August 1935 after a major dispute over the eventual destination of the Communists and the tactics to be followed during the march (see under Chang Kuo-t'ao). Mao continued north, taking with him the First and Third Army Corps from his own First Front Army, which had come from Kiangsi, and also two armies from the Fourth Front Army (the Fourth and the 20th), which had come to western Szechwan with Chang Kuo-t'ao. Chang, on the other hand, remained for a time in the region of the Tibetan center at A-pa with his own Ninth and 31st Armies, as well as the Fifth and Ninth Army Corps, which had previously been under Mao. Hsu Hsiang-ch'ien, assisted by Li Hsien-nien (qq.v.) and others, was Chang's principal military commander; Liu Po-ch'eng now joined this force. Orthodox Maoist histories maintain that Chu Te and Liu were both "detained" by Chang Kuo-t'ao and forced to accompany his troops.[12]

The activities of the Fourth Front Army during the next two years are described in the biographies of its principal leaders, Chang Kuo-t'ao, Hsu Hsiang-ch'ien, and Li Hsien-nien. The Fourth Front Army was joined in June 1936 by the Second Front Army, led by Ho Lung and others, from the Hupeh-Hunan-Szechwan-Kweichow border area. It appears that the leaders of the Second Front Army persuaded Chang Kuo-t'ao to give up fighting in Sikang and reunite with Mao (see under Ho Lung and Jen Pi-shih). The decision was evidently made with the help of Chu Te, who seemingly remained loyal to Mao. Official Communist sources state that Liu Po-ch'eng supported his former commander-in-chief in a "resolute struggle against the runaway policy advocated by Chang Kuo-t'ao."[13] The Communist armies in west Sikang began their trip to reunite with Mao's forces in July 1936, traveling through Tung-ku, A-pa (where they

had turned south the year before), and Pao-tso in Sikang on their way east. As they passed through the Kansu corridor they were attacked by the cavalry troops of Moslem militarist Ma Pu-fang and suffered serious losses, some of the troops fleeing toward Sinkiang. Chu Te and Liu Po-ch'eng both escaped and were with the forces which had survived the attack when they finally rendezvoused with those from the First Front Army at Hui-ning, not far southeast of Lanchow, the Kansu capital, in October 1936.

With the outbreak of the Sino-Japanese War in July 1937, the Communists reorganized their troops in north China, forming the Eighth Route Army. Liu Po-ch'eng commanded one of the Army's three divisions, the 129th, with fellow Szechwanese Teng Hsiao-p'ing (q.v.) as his political commissar. Liu's 129th Division absorbed most of Chang Kuo-t'ao's Fourth Front Army, and Hsu Hsiang-ch'ien, the Fourth Front Army's former commander, became the division's deputy commander. Also on the staff were Ch'en Keng, commander of the 386th Brigade, and Sung Jen-ch'iung (qq.v.), director of the Political Department. The Eighth Route Army advanced into Shansi province (September 1937) in a three-pronged drive by the Army's three divisions. Liu's 129th Division took the southernmost route, penetrating southeast Shansi in the mountainous area north of Ch'ang-chih, including Ho-shun, Yü-she, and Liao-hsien. After Taiyuan, the Shansi capital, had fallen to the Japanese (November 1937), the division established its headquarters in the T'ai-hang Mountains, creating the T'ai-hang–T'ai-yueh Military Base. Liu's troops, which were particularly adept at organizing local guerrilla forces, soon expanded into central and south Hopeh to set up the South Hopeh Military District in the summer of 1938. Sung Jen-ch'iung was made the military commander in this area, which was strategically significant because it provided the Communists with access to Shantung. From Hopeh Liu's forces crossed into Honan and Shantung, going as far as the Grand Canal. This became the eastern boundary for the Shansi-Hopeh-Shantung-Honan (Chin-Chi-Lu-Yü) Border Region Government established in July 1941.[14] Liu headed the military operations in the territory with Teng Hsiao-p'ing as his chief political officer, while the head of the Chin-Chi-Lu-Yü Government was Yang Hsiu-feng (q.v.). Liu remained in the field with his troops throughout most of the war, although he returned to Yenan for the Seventh Party Congress held from April to June 1945. He was one of the 44 persons elected a full member of the Seventh Central Committee.

On V-J Day Liu's army was based at Han-tan in southern Hopeh. Strategically placed astride an important segment of the rail line from Peking to Hankow, this army's operations were coordinated with elements of Ch'en I's New Fourth Army to the east, which were concentrated along portions of the rail line connecting Tientsin with Nanking. The two armies threatened to keep north-south rail communications broken and prevent the consolidation of Nationalist armies in the Yangtze Plain with those in north China. Making one of his lightning thrusts in the late summer of 1946, Liu crossed the Yellow River and fought several successful battles in southwest Shantung along the strategic Lunghai Railroad between Kaifeng and Hsuchou. Before the Nationalists could mount a counterattack Liu withdrew north of the Yellow River. Liu repeated this operation in early 1947, by which time full-scale civil war was being waged. On this occasion he crossed the Lunghai Railroad and threatened Hsu-chou. When this maneuver had the desired effect of relieving the pressure on Ch'en I's forces to the east, Liu again withdrew to the north.

These operations were minor in contrast to the major offensive mounted by Liu in mid-1947 when his units, now known as the Shansi-Hopeh-Shantung-Honan PLA, again crossed the Yellow River and the Lunghai Railroad and pushed southward. Ch'en I moved elements from his forces into southern Hopeh to "fill the gap left by Liu,"[15] thereby allowing Liu to cross the central plain of China. Penetrating to the boundaries of the old Oyüwan Soviet in the Ta-pieh Mountains, Liu was able to drive a wedge between the Nationalist forces, stretched from Wuhan to Nanking. This extended campaign, which lasted more than half a year, had the effect of isolating Nationalist-held cities and seriously disrupting the Nationalists' supply system in this vital area, which the Communists now called the Central Plains Liberated Region. (At the time of these events, Liu's forces were renamed the Central Plains Liberation Army.) These actions were coordinated with a second southern drive begun in mid-1947 by another unit of Liu's army, which moved from southern Shansi into western Honan. This threatened T'ung-kuan on the Lunghai Railroad and eventually isolated the Nationalist force at Loyang from the force farther east (see under Ch'en Keng).

Liu's and Ch'en I's armies were still cooperating in June 1948 when a drive was launched in the Chengchow-Kaifeng sector of Honan, during which the Communists captured Kaifeng on June 19 and held it for about a week. Afterwards they continued to take over more and more territory in the area. Early in November the two armies began the great Huai-Hai campaign. Deploying great numbers of troops along the eastern part of the Lunghai line, the Communists succeeded in cutting the communication lines in the large area extending from the railroad south to the Huai River.[16] When the fighting ended on January 12, 1949, a fatal blow had been dealt to the Nationalist armies in central China. By this time Liu's forces were known as the Second Field Army.

The Communist armies in east-central China regrouped their forces in the early months of 1949, but then in April–May elements from Lin Piao's Fourth Field Army, Ch'en I's Third Field Army, and Liu's Second Field Army fought their way across the Yangtze River. Liu's and Ch'en's units took Nanking, the Nationalists' capital, in April. Liu became chairman of the Nanking Military Control Commission and a few days later, in early May, he was named mayor. At approximately this time he also became president and political commissar of the Central Plains People's Military and Political Academy, a school modeled on the wartime Anti-Japanese Academy in Yenan. Moreover, although he was primarily involved in military affairs, Liu was given a seat on the Central Plains Provisional People's Government Council, which was established in Kaifeng (Honan) and then moved to Wuhan as the Communist armies advanced southward (see under Teng Tzu-hui).

During the Sino-Japanese War and particularly in the ensuing civil war, Liu became known as one of the best field commanders in the Red Army. U.S. Naval observer Evans Carlson, who met Liu in 1938, wrote that he was "rated as one of the best tacticians and students of military history" in the Red Army.[17] A decade later Robert B. Rigg, once a U.S. assistant military attaché in China, observed: "If the term 'field soldier' were applied to one general in the PLA, this man would rate the title."[18] With a special flair for mobile warfare, Liu set the pattern for Communist tactics during the civil war with the Nationalists. He refused to engage in positional warfare or defend captured cities, because he led mobile units which had no armor.[19] Among his best known tactics were quick strikes and equally quick withdrawals, as well as ceaseless disruption of enemy communication lines. Liu's campaigns illustrated the strategy and tactics advocated by Mao Tse-tung, a fact demonstrated by Mao's praise for Liu's methods in the former's wartime directives to the Red Army.[20]

In June 1949 Liu was named to the Standing Committee of the CPPCC Preparatory Committee, chaired by Mao Tse-tung in Peking. Because he was still campaigning in the Yangtze area, Liu did not attend these meetings, but he was in Peking in September for the first session of the CPPCC, which formally inaugurated the central government on October 1. Attending as the ranking delegate from the Second Field Army, Liu served on both the Standing Committee of the CPPCC Presidium and the *ad hoc* committee to draft the Organic Law of the new government, and he also delivered a brief address. He was made a member of both the Central People's Government Council (the top governmental organ) and the People's Revolutionary Military Council, in addition to becoming an Executive Board member of the Sino-Soviet Friendship Association. At this juncture he returned to the command of his troops, which were poised for their final push into the southwest. During the ensuing months in the fall and winter of 1949–50, and now operating in conjunction with forces from the First Field Army led by Ho Lung, the Second Field Army pushed into Szechwan, Kweichow, Sikang, and Yunnan. These four provinces provided the new territorial base for the Second Field Army (and the Southwest Military Region), the Party's Southwest Bureau, and the Southwest Military and Administrative Committee. Military and political authority was divided roughly between three key leaders in this area—Liu, Teng Hsiao-p'ing, and Ho Lung—all of whom were stationed in Chungking. Teng headed the Party apparatus and was the regional political commissar, while Ho Lung commanded the Military Region. Liu held the other key posts; in addition to retaining command of the Second Field Army, he was second secretary of the CCP Southwest Bureau from late 1949 and assumed the chairmanship of the regional governmental apparatus—the Southwest Military and Administrative Committee (SWMAC)—when it was inaugurated in July 1950. In May 1950 the Southwest People's Revolutionary University was established in Chungking with seven branches throughout the southwest; Liu was the first president, but it is not known how long he held this post. In the fall of 1950, units of Liu's Second Field Army advanced into Tibet, an operation that was substantially completed by the spring of 1951. Liu is credited with directing this campaign, but the actual operations were carried out under the command of Chang Kuo-hua (q.v.).

Liu, Teng, and Ho nominally retained their key posts in the southwest until the constitutional government was inaugurated in 1954, but all three spent much of their time elsewhere after 1951–52. Liu, for example, did not attend the second, third, and fourth plenary sessions of the SWMAC (January and November 1951 and December 1952), even though he was its chairman. In the early and mid-fifties he was frequently in Peking for Central People's Government Council meetings, but the basic reason for his long absences from Chungking was apparently that he became president of the PLA Military Academy in 1951. Located in Nanking, this institute is China's equivalent to a Western command and staff college. For a brief time in 1954 (June–September), Liu served as a vice-chairman of the People's Revolutionary Military Council (PRMC). After this he appeared more frequently in Peking and ultimately relinquished the Academy presidency to Liao Han-sheng (q.v.) in 1957. Liu represented the East China Military Region in the First NPC, and at its first session in September 1954 he was elected a member of the NPC Standing Committee and a vice-chairman of the National Defense Council (which replaced the PRMC as a military advisory organ).

In November 1954, when the military hierarchy was reorganized, Liu became director of the PLA General Training Department. In the following July he delivered a major address at the second session of the First NPC. Largely because of this speech and Liu's October 1957 article commemorating the 40th anniversary of the Russian Revolution, one writer has argued that he was an important figure in an intra-Party policy debate concerning Chinese military strategy—with Liu standing on the side of the "professionals" within the PLA. The "professionals," according to this view, were more interested in the "regularization" of the PLA and its technological advancement than in its "political basis." They advocated the necessity of maintaining a strong air force and adequate air defense, a viewpoint which led them to envisage the "purchase of modern weapons from abroad" (i.e., from the Soviet Union).[21]

When the Communists created personal military ranks and awarded decorations in September 1955, Liu was named as one of China's 10 marshals (the highest rank) and was given the Orders of August First, Independence and Freedom, and Liberation, which covered the period from 1927 to 1950. Exactly a year later, at the Eighth Party Congress, he was re-elected to the Central Committee, and the day following the Congress he was elected for the first time to the Politburo. In November 1957 Liu relinquished the directorship of the PLA's General Training Department to Hsiao K'o (q.v.). However, it soon became evident that Liu continued to have an active voice in the military hierarchy. He was one of the speakers at a May–July 1958 conference of the Party's Military Affairs Commission, an organ hitherto seldom mentioned in the Chinese press. Subsequent events have shown that it is the most important military organ in China, and by the spring of 1961 it was revealed in the secret *Kung-tso t'ung-hsun* (Bulletin of activities) that Liu was one of the few members of the Commission's Standing Committee. In the meantime he had been elected a deputy from the Nanking Military Region to the Second NPC (1959–1964) and was elevated from membership to a vice-chairmanship of the NPC Standing Committee. When the Third NPC held its first session (December 1964–January 1965), Liu attended as a delegate from the Shenyang Military Region and was once again elected an NPC vice-chairman. In addition, he continues to serve as a vice-chairman of the National Defense Council, having been re-elected at the first sessions of both the Second and Third NPC's.

Among Chinese military leaders, Liu has been one of the more prolific writers and translators (from Russian). He is the author of a number of articles and essays on guerrilla warfare, tactics, and Russian military practices and has translated Soviet military articles and manuals into Chinese. He wrote a lengthy account of the Long March, which was published in a collection of articles entitled *Hsing-huo liao-yuan* (A single spark can start a prairie fire; Hong Kong, 1960). This was translated and published in 1963 in a book entitled *The Long March: Eyewitness Accounts.* The *JMJP* (June 21, 1962, and April 10, 1963) carried long articles by Liu dealing with Red Army exploits during the Sino-Japanese War and the civil war with the Nationalists in the late 1940's.

Liu has been married twice. His first wife and children remained in Szechwan when he went off to join the Communists. In 1936 he married Wang Yueh-hua, about whom nothing is known. Liu and his second wife had two sons and a daughter by 1947.

1. Agnes Smedley, *The Great Road* (New York, 1956), pp. 125, 188.

2. *ECMM* 173, pp. 12–13.

3. Smedley, p. 187.

4. Robert S. Elegant, *China's Red Masters* (New York, 1951), p. 86.

5. J. Guillermaz, "The Nanchang Uprising," *The China Quarterly,* no. 11:165 (July–September 1962); Wei Hung-yun, ed., *"Pa-i" ch'i-i* (The "August First" uprising; Wuhan, 1957), p. 14; *SCMP* 1139, p. 12.

6. C. Martin Wilbur, "The Ashes of Defeat," *The China Quarterly,* no. 18:14 (April–June 1964).

7. *Ibid.,* pp. 31, 34; *Chung-kuo ch'ing-nien* (China youth), no. 12:14 (June 16, 1960).

8. Conrad Brandt, Benjamin Schwartz, and John K. Fairbank, *A Documentary History of Chinese Communism* (Cambridge, Mass., 1952), p. 128.

9. *Hung-ch'i p'iao-p'iao* (Red flag fluttering; Peking, 1957), X, 46; *Ibid.,* VIII, 96–97.

10. Nym Wales, *Red Dust* (Stanford, Calif., 1952), p. 69.

11. *Ibid.,* pp. 67, 71–72; *Hsing-huo liao-yuan* (A single spark can start a prairie fire; Hong Kong, 1960), pp. 140ff; Ch'en Ch'ang-feng, *On the Long March with Chairman Mao* (Peking, 1959), p. 44.

12. *Stories of the Long March* (Peking, 1958), pp. vii–viii.

13. Ch'en Ch'ang-feng, p. 93.

14. Chalmers A. Johnson, *Peasant Nationalism and Communist Power* (Stanford, Calif., 1962), pp. 106–108.

15. O. Edmund Clubb, *Twentieth Century China* (New York, 1964) p. 282.

16. *Ibid.,* pp. 290–291.

17. Evans Fordyce Carlson, *Twin Stars of China* (New York, 1940), p. 91.

18. Robert B. Rigg, *Red China's Fighting Hordes* (Harrisburg, Pa., 1951), p. 32.

19. *Ibid.,* p. 33.

20. *Selected Works of Mao Tse-tung* (Peking, 1961), IV, 103–105.

21. Alice Langley Hsieh, *Communist China's Strategy in the Nuclear Era* (Englewood Cliffs, N.J., 1962), pp. 39–40 and *passim.*

Liu Shao-ch'i

(1898–   ; Ning-hsiang hsien, Hunan). Early labor leader; theoretician and specialist on Party organization; vice-chairman, CCP Central Committee.

Liu Shao-ch'i, among the first Chinese Communists to study in Moscow, began his political career as a CCP labor leader. After the KMT–CCP break in 1927 he spent many years in the underground in north China, Manchuria, and Shanghai. During the Sino-Japanese War he emerged as a principal theoretician and specialist in Party organization, and by the middle or late 1940's he was second only to Mao in the hierarchy. In the post-1949 period he held numerous top positions in the government, including the chairmanship of the PRC. Elected to the Party Central Committee in 1927, Liu has been a Politburo member since the early 1930's. Several of his essays and books are regarded as among the most important works in the history of the Chinese Communist movement.

Liu was born in Ning-hsiang hsien, not far west of Changsha, the Hunan capital, and only a short distance from Mao Tse-tung's birthplace. He comes from a rich peasant family, and his father was a primary-school teacher. According to Edgar Snow, Liu was a "radical student" by 1914;[1] during his later teenage years he studied in Changsha at the Hunan First Normal School, where Mao and Ts'ai Ho-sen established the *Hsin-min hsueh-hui* (New people's study society) in 1917–18. Liu joined the society, which sponsored a "work-and-study" program to enable students to continue their education in France (see under Ts'ai Ho-sen). For about a year in 1918–19 Liu was in Pao-ting at a special school designed to prepare students for their stay in France. Li Fu-ch'un and Li Wei-han (qq.v.) were among the other Hunanese students at Pao-ting. Liu apparently abandoned his plans to study in France, and by 1920 he was in Shanghai where, in August, the Socialist Youth League was established. He was among the first to join.

For a period in 1920 Liu worked as a labor organizer in Shanghai, after which he was among the handful of Youth League members enrolled in a foreign language school established under Comintern auspices to prepare for further studies in Moscow (see under Yang Ming-chai). Others who studied there at this period included Lo I-nung and Jen Pi-shih (qq.v.). In early 1921 Liu left for Moscow. Reminiscing four decades later, Liu commented that he "only knew that socialism was good"; he had "heard about" Marx, Lenin, the October Revolution, and the Bolshevik Party, but he was "not clear" about the nature of socialism, nor the means to implement it.[2] Traveling via Vladivostok (still occupied by Japanese troops in the aftermath of World War I), the trip consumed three months because of the unsettled conditions. In Moscow Liu spent about half a year at the newly opened Communist University of the Toilers of the East which trained many would-be Asian revolutionists during the next few years. In 1921, while still in Moscow, he joined the CCP.

Liu returned home in the spring of 1922 and was assigned to work with Chang Kuo-t'ao (whom he had met in Moscow) in the Secretariat of the Chinese Labor Unions, then headquartered in Shanghai. The Secretariat was one of the most active Party organizations, and its leaders included such important early Communists as Teng Chung-hsia, Hsiang Ying, Mao Tse-tung, and Lin Yü-nan (qq.v.). According to Liu, it consisted "mostly of students" recently returned from Moscow or France, plus some from Peking colleges.[3] The Secretariat sponsored the First National Labor Congress in May 1922 in Canton, after which its activities were expanded (see under Teng Chung-hsia). Liu helped organize the congress,[4] but it is not certain if he attended. He was soon given his first major assignment as an assistant to Mao Tse-tung, then head of the Hunan Secretariat branch and secretary of the CCP Committee in Hunan. Mao and Liu were from the same section of Hunan and had gone to the same school, but according to Edgar Snow they did not meet until 1921.[5] Thus the active association of Mao and Liu, which was to last for over four decades, apparently began in 1922.

In the late summer of 1922 Liu was assigned to the An-yuan mining area in P'ing-hsiang hsien. (P'ing-hsiang is in western Kiangsi, but it was under the jurisdiction of Mao's Hunan CCP Committee, of which Liu was a member.) The An-yuan mines were part of the Han-yeh-p'ing complex, one of the largest industrial and mining enterprises in China, and the CCP had already begun its initial organizational work there many months earlier. In later years Maoist historians gave Liu and Mao the lion's share of the credit for Party activities in An-yuan, but the dominant figure in 1922 was Li Li-san, whose biography contains further information about An-yuan. Li had chaired the An-yuan Mine and Railroad Workers' Club (a euphe-

mism for a labor union) from its establishment in May 1922, and in September Li, Liu, and others led a largely successful strike for better working conditions. Immediately after the strike, the club was reorganized, still under Li Li-san's direction. Communist sources differ on Liu's post then; one describes him as a "special representative" (*t'e-p'ai yuan*)[6] and another as head of the section of miners working inside the mines (as opposed to another group working outside the mines).[7] Mao Tse-min (q.v.), one of Mao Tse-tung's younger brothers, was also a club official. By early 1923 Liu had assumed the direction of the An-yuan labor organization. His first writings, describing the activities at An-yuan, date from this period, and in 1958 they were republished in the Changsha journal *Hunan li-shih tzu-liao* (Materials on the history of Hunan; nos. 1–2).

Liu continued to run the An-yuan organization until early 1925,[8] but from 1923 the scope and variety of his responsibilities extended beyond An-yuan. This situation arose as a consequence of the developing cooperation between the KMT and the CCP. From the latter half of 1922, Communist Party members began to join the KMT under an agreement worked out between top CCP leaders and Sun Yat-sen (see under Li Ta-chao). Moreover, the two revolutionary parties cooperated in endeavors to counter the influence of the northern government and various warlords. Thus, in the spring of 1923 Liu and fellow Communist Hsia Hsi were directed to establish a joint KMT–CCP headquarters to step up the pace of underground work in Changsha, Ning-hsiang (to the west of Changsha), and P'ing-hsiang (the locale of the An-yuan mines).[9] At this time, or soon thereafter, Liu joined the KMT.[10] Further details on the work in Hunan are contained in the biography of Hsia Hsi who, like Liu, had attended the First Normal School in Changsha.

In early 1925 Liu was assigned to Shanghai where the labor movement was gaining considerable momentum. There he worked again with Chang Kuo-t'ao, this time on a labor committee subordinate to the CCP Central Committee. In the spring he went to Canton to take part in preparatory work for the convocation of the Second National Labor Congress which was held in May. Liu was among the speakers and he was elected one of the two vice-chairmen of the newly established All-China Federation of Labor (ACFL). The ACFL, in effect, replaced the Labor Secretariat, and although the federation had some non-Communist officials, it was dominated by the CCP. Other Communists elected to key posts included Teng Chung-hsia, the ACFL secretary-general and Propaganda Department director.

Soon after the Canton labor congress a series of events led to the May 30th Incident in Shanghai, and this in turn blossomed into a nationwide protest and strike movement directed largely against foreign interests in China (see under Li Li-san). The CCP, deeply involved in these events, immediately established the Shanghai General Labor Union, with Li Li-san as chairman and Liu as head of the union's administrative affairs. The major Communist figures in Shanghai at this time were Li Li-san, Ts'ai Ho-sen, and Ch'ü Ch'iu-pai, but as in the case of the An-yuan union, Maoist historians often suggest that Liu's role was greater than Li's. In any event he worked closely with Li Li-san in organizational work undertaken by the union. Liu remained in Shanghai through the summer of 1925, but when the union was outlawed in September the leadership was forced to flee. Li went to Canton and Liu fled to Hunan. He was arrested and detained for a brief period, and then in late 1925 he too went to Canton. The city was the nerve center for the Canton–Hong Kong strike (1925–26), in which large numbers of left-wing and Communist labor leaders were involved (see under Su Chao-cheng, the head of the Strike Committee). Labor union membership was increasing rapidly and a number of new unions came into existence at this period; in this connection Liu was in Hong Kong for a brief time in March 1926 to attend the inaugural meeting of the Federation of Transport Workers' Unions.[11]

At the Third Labor Congress, held in May 1926 in Canton, Liu presented a report on the work of the ACFL after its establishment a year earlier. He was re-elected a vice-chairman and also put in charge of the Administration Department. A few weeks later the main elements of the National Revolutionary Army moved out of Kwangtung to begin the Northern Expedition. Like many of his CCP and Labor Federation colleagues, like Chang Kuo-t'ao, Li Li-san, and Lin Yü-nan, Liu was in Wuhan immediately after it fell to the advancing armies in October 1926. On the 10th of that month the Hupeh Provincial General Trade Union Federation was established; in this organization Liu was made secretary for "economic demands."[12] Over the next half year there were scores of strikes, many of them directed against the numerous foreign-owned enterprises in the key Yangtze Valley cities. The labor movement was particularly turbulent in Wuhan. A decade later, in conversations with American journalist Nym Wales, Liu commented that the strikes were initially "very Leftist in tendency and later more right-ist . . . The Labor movement was a high point but the experience of the leaders was inadequate," and, as an example, he said that "labor leaders did not know that farm employees are also workers, so they did not permit farm laborers to join unions."[13] Despite these problems there was rapid growth; according to a Communist historian, within two months of the fall

of Wuhan union membership there expanded to 300,000 and the number of unions to more than 200.[14]

The period of greatest labor tension and triumph in Wuhan took place in early 1927. On January 1, Liu gave an organizational report at the first congress of the Hupeh Trade Union Federation.[15] A few days later, in compliance with demands of the foreign minister of the left-KMT government in Wuhan, the British withdrew the marine contingent from their concession in Hankow. Emboldened by these events and the growing strength of the labor movement, Liu, Li Li-san, and other Communist labor leaders encouraged large numbers of citizens and unionists to occupy the concession. Soon afterwards the British relinquished the concession to the Chinese, a development then characterized as a great victory for the Wuhan government and its allies, the CCP.

The growing strength of the left-KMT and the CCP in Wuhan was not unnoticed by Chiang Kai-shek's right-KMT faction. As a consequence, a few days after Northern Expedition troops captured Shanghai, Chiang engineered his famous anti-Communist coup in April 1927. In this atmosphere the CCP held its Fifth Congress in Wuhan in late April and early May. The congress was marked by serious controversies, among them the question of the effectiveness of Ch'en Tu-hsiu (q.v.), then head of the Party. His critics claimed he was too conservative (that is, guilty of "right opportunism"). Orthodox histories assert that Liu joined Mao, Ch'ü Ch'iu-pai, and Jen Pi-shih in the forefront of the opposition to Ch'en. Nonetheless, Liu, Ch'ü, and Jen were elected members of the Central Committee, whereas Mao was demoted to alternate member. A month later, in the second half of June, the Fourth Labor Congress was held in Wuhan in the wake of a serious deterioration of relations between the Communists and the left-KMT. Liu spoke on organizational questions, stressing the difficulties local labor leaders were having in light of the rapidly changing relationship with the KMT. Such questions became academic a few days later when the split with the left-KMT became final. The Communists in Wuhan either fled or went underground, and on August 1 the CCP staged the abortive Nanchang Uprising (see under Yeh T'ing). The first phase of Liu's career, as one of the Party's more important labor leaders, had come to an end.

After the climactic events of mid-1927, Liu worked a few months in the Party underground in and around Wuhan, presumably in coordination with Lin Yü-nan, Hsiang Ying, and Hsiang Ching-yü (qq.v.). Late in the year he went to Shanghai, and then in early 1928, as the Party began to rebuild, he was assigned to the Hopeh Provincial Committee. There, according to a Russian biography of Liu, he became a leader in the "workers' movement in north China."[16] In the summer he was in Moscow for the CCP's Sixth Congress (June–July 1928). Definitive lists of the Sixth Central Committee members are not available, but it appears that Liu was re-elected. Moreover, the Russian biography of Liu states that he was made a member of the Party's Central Control Committee. Little is known about this body, but according to the 1928 Constitution it was responsible for controlling financial and accounting procedures within the Party. Liu was also made director of the CCP Workers' Department (*chih-kung pu*) at or soon after the congress.

By early 1929 Liu was back in China, where he worked in the Party headquarters in Shanghai. The dominant Party figure at that time was Li Li-san, Liu's erstwhile colleague in the labor movement. In the summer he was assigned to be secretary of the Manchurian Provincial Committee (*Man-chou sheng-wei*). There is only scanty information about this chapter of CCP history, but it is clear that Liu arrived at a difficult moment. In July the Chinese Eastern Railway, jointly managed by Chinese, Manchurians, and Russians, was seized by Manchurian warlord Chang Hsueh-liang, who was working in close collaboration with Chiang Kai-shek in Nanking. Chiang and Chang expected Moscow to acquiesce in this bold move, but instead the Russians responded after futile negotiations by an invasion of Manchuria in November, which completely crushed the resisting Chinese troops. Concurrently with these events, the Comintern ordered the CCP to come to the defense of Moscow; Red Army units in Kiangsi and elsewhere were expected to tie down Chiang Kai-shek's troops, and in urban areas unrest was to be fomented. The Russian biography of Liu claims he led a workers' movement "in defense of the Soviet Union" during the crisis, but contemporary sources do not indicate that the minuscule CCP apparatus in Manchuria played any significant role at that time.

The Fifth International Labor Congress (that is, the fifth congress of the Profintern, the labor arm of the Comintern) was held in Moscow in August 1930. Ts'ai Shu-fan (q.v.), another labor leader, claims that 20 Chinese attended the meetings, but it is not known if Liu was among them. In any case, he was elected a member of the Profintern's Executive Bureau. Liu was removed from his Manchurian post in early 1931, after which he went to Shanghai, perhaps in time for the Party's Fourth Plenum. This important meeting witnessed the assumption of Party leadership by the Russian-returned student faction, led by Ch'en Shao-yü and Ch'in Pang-hsien (qq.v.). The Russian biography claims that Liu was elected to the Politburo at the plenum, although a Chinese biography states that this happened in 1932.[17] The Party headquarters was still in Shanghai in 1931, but the

constant dangers led to the exodus of many top leaders, who went to the Juichin stronghold in Kiangsi where Chu Te and Mao had built a formidable military force. With the gradual dissolution of the key organs in Shanghai and their transfer to Kiangsi, the Party established a Central Bureau to handle affairs in Shanghai.[18] Liu was in charge of this organization, and for about a year more he remained in Shanghai in the underground. He reportedly took part in anti-Japanese activities among workers and students in the period after the Japanese seizure of Manchuria in September 1931. During this period Liu was a regular contributor to underground Party and labor journals published in Shanghai.

In the autumn of 1932 Liu went to Juichin where he soon became chairman of the All-China Federation of Labor. For much of the next two years he tried to increase the efficiency of the relatively small industrial base, whose output was essential to the Red Army. In addition to his Federation and CCP positions, Liu was also a senior official in the Chinese Soviet Republic. This had been set up at the First All-China Congress of Soviets, held in Juichin in November 1931. Liu was elected *in absentia* a member of the Central Executive Committee (CEC), the highest political organ of the Republic. In April 1933 he was appointed vice-commissar for Labor in the Council of People's Commissars,[19] the executive arm of the CEC, a post which placed him under Commissar for Labor Hsiang Ying. In January–February 1934, at the Second All-China Congress of Soviets, Liu served on the congress presidium (steering committee), gave a report on the labor movement in the Kiangsi Soviet during the previous two years, and at the close of the meetings he was re-elected to the CEC. Moreover, he was one of only 17 men elected to the permanent Presidium, the organ in charge of affairs of state when the CEC was not in session. It is not known, however, if he continued as vice-commissar for Labor. According to one source, Liu also served as secretary of the CCP Fukien Committee,[20] apparently replacing Ch'en T'anch'iu (q.v.), who had been censured and removed from this post in late 1933. Ch'en's removal resulted from an alleged failure to recruit sufficient manpower for the Red Army, which was particularly hard-pressed as KMT armies began the Fifth Annihilation Campaign against the Kiangsi Soviet. Working in Fukien in the spring of 1934, Liu was reportedly more successful in getting Red Army recruits.[21]

Liu was with the Long Marchers when they set out in October 1934. He was initially the Central Committee's representative to the Eighth and then to the Fifth Army Corps, and still later he headed the Political Department in P'eng Te-huai's Third Army Corps.[22] He apparently continued the march until early 1935, but most accounts assert that he left his colleagues to take up an underground post in north China. However, one Communist source claims he was with Mao and Chou En-lai in Shensi at the end of the Long March in the fall of 1935.[23] In any event, in early 1936 Liu was made secretary of the Party's North China Bureau (*pei-fang chü*). The CCP apparatus in north China was then very small, but some underground work was being conducted, principally in Peking and Tientsin, by P'eng Chen, K'o Ch'ing-shih, Ch'en Po-ta, Nan Han-ch'en, and Huang Ching (qq.v.).

When Liu assumed his north China post, the CCP was beginning to promote a united front policy directed against Japan. In this regard it found fertile recruiting grounds in the major north China cities where middle school and university students were vehement in demanding vigorous government action to resist Japanese incursions upon Chinese sovereignty. The political importance of the students had already been demonstrated by the December Ninth (1935) Movement, which had begun only a short time before Liu assumed his new post. The initial impetus for the movement did not come from the CCP (see under Li Ch'ang), but the Communists were quick to capitalize on the situation. Consequently, Liu and his principal aide P'eng Chen made contact with the students, and within a year were able to recruit many of them into the Youth League or the CCP. Edgar Snow added an interesting footnote many years later when he wrote that it was Liu who had "authorized the 'invisible ink letter' of introduction" which enabled Snow to reach the Communist base in north Shensi in 1936.[24]

In April 1937, Liu and P'eng Chen, accompanied by student leaders from Peking, went to Yenan for a conference of the CCP held in May. One student, writing many years later, noted that only then did they learn that Liu had been writing for a covert journal of the North China Bureau under the initials "K.V."[25] This same student also stated that after the Party meeting, Liu spoke to the students at a conference dealing with work in KMT-controlled areas. Liu said the moment had come to "legalize our hitherto illegal activities and to make the mass movement widespread." Moreover, because war with Japan was "imminent, the comrades in north China should get ready to take off their robes and bear weapons and join guerrilla bands."

At the above-mentioned May 1937 Party meeting or soon thereafter, Liu replaced Ch'in Pang-hsien as head of the Party's Organization Department. Liu remained in Yenan during the summer and early fall of 1937, and it was then that he was interviewed by Nym Wales. She described him as "Commissioner of Labor," apparently a reference to his post in Kiangsi a few years earlier. In July war with Japan began, and

in September the major units of the Communists' Eighth Route Army, as well as many of the senior Party leaders, crossed the Yellow River into Shansi. Liu was then in Taiyuan, the Shansi capital and temporary headquarters of the North China Bureau.[26] In October, using the pseudonym T'ao Shang-hsing, he published a detailed article on the problems of waging guerrilla warfare behind Japanese lines. When Taiyuan fell to the Japanese in November, Liu and the bureau moved to Lin-fen (southwest Shansi), and when Lin-fen was captured in February 1938, the bureau transferred to Sian, the Shensi capital. Details are lacking, but Liu apparently spent most of the period after Lin-fen fell in Sian and Yenan; he is known to have been in Yenan for much of the latter half of 1938 where he lectured at the Marx–Lenin Institute.

In October–November 1938 Liu attended the Party's Sixth Plenum in Yenan. At this same time (October), he was appointed to head the CCP's newly established Central Plains Bureau (*chung-yuan chü*), and by the end of the year he was replaced as director of the Organization Department by Ch'en Yun. The Central Plains Bureau was headquartered in Ch'ueh-shan hsien, astride the Peking-Hankow Railway in southern Honan. The purposes in establishing the bureau are not clear. In terms of timing it was set up the same month that the Japanese captured Hsin-yang (only 50 miles south of Ch'ueh-shan) and then the vital Wuhan cities. Perhaps the Party hoped to set up a guerrilla base to link the Shensi-Kansu-Ninghsia (Shen-Kan-Ning) Border Region and the New Fourth Army, which was then operating in areas not far east and south of Ch'ueh-shan. No important base was developed in the Ch'ueh-shan area, and in any case Liu was only there from late 1938 to the early part of 1939 when he returned to Yenan once again. During the following months he worked on lectures delivered at the Marx-Lenin Institute in mid-1939. These have been issued in various editions and under different titles; perhaps the best known title is *How to Be a Good Communist*. This oft-cited work, Liu's first major effort in the field of ideology and organizational work, dealt with the need to maintain absolute loyalty to the Party and to overcome individualistic and bureaucratic tendencies. Its importance as a major restatement of Leninist principles is discussed in the biography of Ch'en Yun, whose broadly similar essay was published a few weeks earlier.

As Central Plains Bureau chief Liu spent the latter part of 1939 and most of 1940 with various New Fourth Army units in Honan, Anhwei, and Kiangsu. From scattered evidence, he seems, to have concentrated on ways to develop bases behind Japanese lines, including the organization of the peasantry to support Communist troops.[27] By this period the early wartime KMT–CCP cooperation had deteriorated markedly, and thus, according to one account, Liu emphasized in talks with New Fourth Army commanders and cadres that they were cooperating too closely with KMT units and must henceforth operate more independently.[28] He then used the pseudonym Hu Fu. Liu was in the New Fourth Army operational area at the time of the famous New Fourth Army Incident of January 1941, the details of which are in the biography of Yeh T'ing, the New Fourth Army commander. Yeh was captured by the Nationalists, Political Commissar Hsiang Ying was killed, and several other top leaders were slain or captured. As a consequence, the army and Party structure were immediately reorganized. Ch'en I became acting commander, and Liu was named political commissar and secretary of the Party's Central China Bureau (Hua-chung chü). Other top appointments were: Chang Yun-i, deputy commander; Teng Tzu-hui, director, Political Department; and Lai Ch'uan-chu (qq.v.), chief-of-staff.

Prior to the New Fourth Army Incident, KMT–CCP relations had been severely strained. Afterwards, of course, the split was virtually total, and in this spirit Liu reemphasized the necessity to mobilize mass support. He instructed Party cadres and New Fourth Army officers to paint KMT forces as identical to the Chinese puppet troops who fought for the Japanese.[29] In July 1941 Liu delivered a speech at the Central China Party School (in Kiangsu), which was later published under the title On the Intra-Party Struggle. This tract, which came to be a key text in the cheng-feng movement (see below), emphasized the need for "struggle" as a positive means to achieve a truly independent and pure Leninist party. It also stressed moderation in dealing with "unorthodox" tendencies among Party members, and thus there are detailed comments on various forms of proper and improper struggle.

Liu was back in Yenan in the first part of 1942, when Mao was beginning the famous cheng-feng (ideological remolding) campaign. This campaign, which lasted to 1944, is generally regarded as the period when Mao gained virtually undisputed authority over the CCP. Liu's stature in the Maoist camp by this time is suggested by the fact that his writings formed an important part of the collection of materials usually known as the cheng-feng documents. The basic theme of the reform movement, in the words of one authority, was the "union of 'the universal truths of Marxism–Leninism with the concrete reality of the Chinese Revolution.' "[30]

Liu was again in the field in the latter half of 1942, this time inspecting units in Shantung and Hopeh. He made the slow and dangerous trip back to Yenan in late 1942 by way of the Shansi-Suiyuan region. Thereafter Liu's Central China

Bureau and New Fourth Army posts were assumed by Jao Shu-shih (q.v.). From 1943 through the end of the war Liu remained in Yenan. Many accounts of his wartime activities suggest that he spent almost the entire eight-year period separated from Mao and the Party headquarters. In reality, he was away from Yenan about half the time. Nevertheless, more than any other senior leader, he gained a first-hand knowledge of many of the top and second echelon men who emerged during the war years in Communist bases in north and east China.

In 1943 Liu received two appointments which placed him among the half-dozen most important men in the CCP. He was made a secretary of the Central Secretariat and a vice-chairman of the People's Revolutionary Military Council. The Communists have not published lists for either of these bodies (both headed by Mao), but the numbers of secretaries and vice-chairmen at that time probably did not exceed six or seven. In July 1943, Liu published a piece entitled "Liquidation of Menshevik Thought in the Party" (another of the cheng-feng documents) to commemorate the 22nd anniversary of the CCP. One analyst of Chinese ideology argues that this article, together with Mao's "In Opposition to Party Formalism" (dated February 1942), seemed to have been a direct attack on Ch'en Shao-yü, the leader of the Russian-returned student faction, which controlled the Party in the early 1930's. The same analyst, commenting on the broader period of the rise of Mao, writes that after 1937 "leading policy statements" came "more and more from Mao, Chou En-lai, and rising theoreticians Liu Shao-ch'i, Ch'en Po-ta, and Ch'en Yun" and that after the cheng-feng movement Ch'en Shao-yü, Chang Wen-t'ien, and Ch'in Pang-hsien "lost their voice."[31]

In April 1945, immediately before the convocation of the Party's Seventh Congress, the CCP adopted the "Resolution on Certain Questions in the History of Our Party." This resolution, which is contained in Mao's Selected Works, was in effect a revision of CCP history designed to prove the correctness of Maoist policies during the previous two decades. In this same resolution, Liu received singularly high praise for the policies he had espoused for Communist operations in "white areas" (that is, areas controlled by the enemy—either the KMT or the Japanese). In this connection, the resolution quotes at some length from two pieces written by Liu in April 1936 and March 1937, when he was head of the north China underground.[32]

At the Seventh Congress, held in Yenan from April to June 1945, three major speeches were delivered: Mao's general political report, Chu Te's report on military affairs, and Liu's speech on the revised Party constitution (best known under the title "On the Party"). This wide-ranging speech dealt with many aspects of organization, leadership, and discipline and has long been regarded as one of the key documents in the history of the CCP. Liu was re-elected to the Central Committee, and at its First Plenum (held immediately after the congress) he was re-elected to the Politburo and the Secretariat. By then he was probably second only to Mao in the hierarchy. In fact, later that year Liu was acting chairman of the Party when Mao went to Chungking for talks with Chiang Kai-shek.

In the immediate postwar period, Mao and Liu remained in Yenan until it was captured by the Nationalists in March 1947. In what appears to have been an effort to provide for the most drastic emergency, the Party Secretariat was divided into two groups. One, which included Mao, Chou En-lai, and Jen Pi-shih, stayed in the Shen-Kan-Ning Border Region, and the other, known as the Working Committee, included Liu (the head) and Chu Te. The Liu–Chu team went to the Shansi-Suiyuan Liberated Area, and then to P'ing-shan hsien, located in west Hopeh in the Communists' Shansi-Chahar-Hopeh Border Region. There, in September, Liu chaired the national land conference which adopted a draft land law. Communist land reform policies, as described in the biography of Jen Pi-shih, were then in a state of flux. The difficulties being encountered stemmed in part from the need to employ varying policies in different areas; as Mao explained in a February 1948 message to Liu, "different tactics" were necessary for old liberated areas, "semi-old" liberated areas (that is, those consolidated from September 1945 to August 1947), and newly liberated areas.[33]

Liu's Working Committee continued to function in P'ing-shan until Mao's arrival in May 1948. In the next month Tito's feud with Stalin culminated in the expulsion of the Yugoslavs from the Cominform. In the fall, Liu responded in a commentary ("Internationalism and Nationalism") generally regarded as the official Chinese viewpoint. He supported Stalin and castigated what he called Tito's bourgeois nationalism. By this time Communist armies were advancing from one victory to another; Manchuria was in PLA hands by the end of the year, and in January 1949 both Tientsin and Peking were taken. In March the Central Committee moved to Peking, and during the ensuing months the top leaders made preparations to establish the national government. Earlier, in 1948, Liu had been elected honorary chairman of the reconstituted All-China Federation of Labor, and then in June 1949 he was elected a vice-chairman of the Communist-dominated World Federation of Trade Unions (WFTU) at the Second WFTU Congress, held in Milan (see under Liu Ning-i). Both elections were *in absentia*. He was honorary chairman of the Chinese

federation until 1957 and a WFTU vice-chairman until 1953.

In September 1949, as a delegate from the CCP, Liu attended the inaugural session of the CPPCC, the organization which brought the PRC into existence on October 1. During the session he served on the standing committee of the presidium (steering committee), and he delivered a brief speech which emphasized the eagerness of the CCP to cooperate with the many non-Communists who were to hold a number of posts in the new government. Liu was appointed one of the six vice-chairmen of the Central People's Government Council (CPGC), which was chaired by Mao. The CPGC, the leading organ in the central government, was invested with broad legislative, executive, and judicial functions, and at its 34 meetings held from 1949 to 1954 it passed on virtually every major program adopted during the formative years of the PRC. Unlike many of his colleagues, Liu regularly attended the council meetings. He was also selected in 1949 as a vice-chairman of the People's Revolutionary Military Council and as a member of the Standing Committee of the CPPCC's First National Committee. These two organs were also chaired by Mao. Liu held these positions until the governmental reorganization in 1954, and during the same years he chaired the Sino-Soviet Friendship Association.

The PRC was only a few weeks old when, in November 1949, the Asian and Australasian Trade Union Conference met in Peking. Liu delivered the keynote address. The background to this speech can be traced to Liu's address in 1945 at the Seventh Party Congress when, "for the first time" he put "forward the idea . . . that China was not merely the pioneer but the leader and ideological mentor of anti-imperialist revolutions throughout Asia and Africa."[34] A year and a half later he elaborated on this theme in the course of an interview given to American author Anna Louise Strong. Interpreting the "thought of Mao Tse-tung," Liu claimed that Mao was the "first" man to link Marxist–Leninist principles to the "practical problems of China." Mao had given Marxism a "new development" —he had "created a Chinese or Asiatic form of Marxism." Liu confined his remarks mainly to China, but he commented to Miss Strong that there "are similar conditions in other lands of southeast Asia. The courses chosen by China will influence them all."[35] These remarks, in effect, were extended at the 1949 conference, held in the wake of the Communist triumph throughout China. In colonial and semi-colonial areas of China, Liu called for "national liberation movements" in which "armed struggle can and should become the main form" of "people's liberation" wars. Wherever possible a "people's liberation army" led by the Communist Party should be established. "This is the path of Mao Tse-tung. It can also become the main path of the peoples of other colonial and semi-colonial countries." Liu left no doubt as to the nations he had in mind, specifically citing Vietnam, Burma, Indonesia, Malaya, the Philippines, Korea, Thailand, and even Australia. His speech, of course, was widely disseminated in China, and it was also published in the December 30, 1949, issue of the Cominform journal *For a Lasting Peace, For a People's Democracy.* Moreover, a month later the same journal quoted Liu's speech in an article on revolution in Asia.[36] However, the Russians apparently had second thoughts regarding the suggestion that the Chinese, rather than the Russian, Revolution was the prime model for Asia to follow. Accordingly, during the next two years, Russian ideologues asserted that the correct path had already been worked out by Marx, Lenin, and Stalin.[37] Nevertheless, as described in the biography of Lu Ting-i, Peking continued to press the issue until 1951.

From December 1949 to March 1950 Mao was in the Soviet Union where, with Chou En-lai, he negotiated the Sino-Soviet Treaty of Friendship, Alliance, and Mutual Assistance (February 14, 1950). During this period Liu was in charge of Party and state affairs in China. In June the Communists took up the matter of the new land reform law at the Party's Third Plenum and, a few days later, at the second session of the CPPCC. Both Mao and Liu spoke, and both stressed a rather gradual and cautious approach, particularly in regard to the "rich peasants." According to Liu, the basic aim of the program, aside from "relieving the impoverished peasants," was to "set free the rural productive forces" in order to develop agricultural production and thus "pave the way for New China's industrialization."

Like a number of the senior Party Leaders, Liu often spoke at national conferences held in the 1949–1951 period as the Communists moved forward to mobilize virtually all strata of society. For example, within a one-month period in July–August 1950 he addressed the First National Cooperative Workers' Congress, the National Work Conference of Young Workers, and the First National Judicial Conference. Because the Sino-Soviet Friendship Association was particularly active during the formative years of the PRC, Liu made many public appearances in his capacity as association chairman—a fact which may account for the widespread rumors that he represented a "pro-Moscow" faction in the CCP. In reality most of the important work of the association was shouldered by its general secretary, Ch'ien Chün-jui (q.v.).

There had been a tremendous growth in CCP membership in the late 1940's and during the takeover period. From the Communist view-point, this situation was to be applauded, but it also raised problems. For example, as Liu noted in a May Day speech in 1950, nearly half of the four million Party members had joined within the previous two and a half years. Several weeks later the Central Committee announced a new ideological remodeling campaign to consolidate the ranks of the Party and to "strengthen its links with the broad masses of the people." Speaking a year later (June 30, 1951), by which time membership had grown to 5,800,000, Liu stated that further ideological struggles lay ahead, and in November he spoke on Party membership qualifications. The latter speech was not published, but from the context of the news release that announced it, it was apparently related to the "three-anti" campaign, which was just beginning, against corruption, waste, and bureaucracy (see under Po I-po).

In October 1952 Liu led the Chinese delegation to Moscow for the 19th CPSU Congress, the last held in Stalin's lifetime. This was the first important foreign Communist congress in which China participated, and accordingly Liu's delegation consisted of top Party leaders: Jao Shu-shih, Ch'en I, Li Fu-ch'un, Wang Chia-hsiang, and Liu Ch'ang-sheng (qq.v.). Rather little is known about Liu's activities in Moscow, but the fact that he did not return to Peking until January 11, 1953 (almost three months after the congress closed), suggests that he held extended talks with Soviet leaders. He might, for example, have discussed the Korean War or the economic negotiations which Li Fu-ch'un was then conducting with Soviet officialdom.

In early 1953 the first major steps were taken toward the adoption of a national constitution. In January, Liu was made a member of the Committee to Draft the Constitution, and in the next month he became chairman of the Central Election Committee. These procedures (see under Teng Hsiao-p'ing) led to the 1954 elections to the First NPC. Liu was elected a deputy from Peking, and he was returned from Peking to the Second and Third NPC's (initially convened in 1959 and 1964, respectively). At the inaugural session of the First NPC, held in September 1954, Liu presented a detailed report on the new constitution. At the close of the session the central government was reorganized. Liu was elected chairman of the Standing Committee of the NPC which, constitutionally, is the "highest organ of state authority." During the course of the First NPC (1954–1959) the Standing Committee was regularly convened, but the available evidence suggests that NPC Secretary-General P'eng Chen, rather than Liu, handled most of the work.

In the meantime, the Party was in the process of completing its first major purge of the post-1949 period. In December 1953 Mao advanced a proposal for "strengthening Party unity" at a

Politburo meeting. This was taken up at the Party's Fourth Plenum in February 1954. Liu, in effect, was in charge of the plenum in place of Mao who "was away on holiday." The resolution on Party unity, which was drawn from Liu's speech to the plenum, contained the well-known assertion that "certain high-ranking cadres" were attempting to create "independent kingdoms." The details were revealed a year later when Politburo member Kao Kang and Organization Department Director Jao Shu-shih were purged. This celebrated case is described more fully in the biographies of Kao, Jao, and Teng Hsiao-p'ing.

Liu's position as Mao's heir apparent was re-inforced at the Eighth Party Congress in September 1956. Mao delivered only a perfunctory speech and left to Liu the task of presenting the keynote political report. In an address exuding the confident air which then characterized the CCP, he reviewed the socialization of agriculture, industry, and commerce and the implementation of the First Five-Year Plan. The "dictatorship of the proletariat," he said, required strong leadership over all state organs, but further progress required energetic steps to insure greater participation by all sympathetic elements of society, and this in turn depended upon curtailing "intra-Party bureaucracy." As one means of curbing bureaucratic tendencies, Liu proposed visits by responsible personnel to subordinate levels. This "may be considered the beginning of the *hsia-fang* (lit.: to go to the lower levels) movement,"[38] which, after further directives were issued in 1957, resulted in the transfer of thousands of Party, government, and military officials to subordinate levels during the next few years.

At the close of the Eighth Congress Liu was re-elected to the Central Committee. On the next day, at the First Plenum of the new Central Committee, he was re-elected to the Politburo; he was also elected a vice-chairman of the Central Committee (and ex officio vice-chairman of the Politburo) and a member of the Politburo's Standing Committee. The post of vice-chairman and the Standing Committee had been created in accordance with the revised constitution. The Standing Committee, a kind of inner-Politburo, then consisted of only six men: Mao, Liu, Chou En-lai, Chu Te, Ch'en Yun, and Teng Hsiao-p'ing. (In 1958 Lin Piao was added.) The Central Secretariat, to which Mao and Liu no longer belonged, was completely revised and, in effect, replaced by the Standing Committee as the key political body in the CCP.

In the latter part of 1957 the Party began to reorient some of its basic economic and social policies. One observer has written that in October a "radical group headed by Mao . . . and Liu . . . finally succeeded in imposing [its]

policy of social mobilization on the Politburo, in opposition to the more cautious advocates of gradual economic development."[39] A month later, speaking on the 40th anniversary of the Russian Revolution, Liu further advanced this line of thought; the Party, he argued, must rely on the "initiative of the masses" to achieve "quantity, speed, quality, and economy." These remarks were a prelude to the Great Leap Forward launched in early 1958 (approximately concurrent with the Second Five-Year Plan). In delivering the keynote address at the second session of the Eighth Party Congress in May 1958, Liu gave strong endorsement to the Great Leap. He asserted that it resulted from the successful "anti-rightist" campaign (1957–58), and he charged that none of the many criticisms (which he enumerated) against the accelerated pace of construction and production could "hold water." To get a first-hand view of the rapidly changing situation, Liu and other top leaders went on extensive tours throughout the country. During this same period, with the strong personal backing of Mao, the famous people's communes were established at breakneck speed. Many of the Great Leap programs, including the communes, were sharply curtailed later in 1958 and in 1959. Nonetheless, Liu celebrated the Great Leap in September 1959 in an article commemorating the 10th anniversary of Communist rule.[40]

At the Party's Sixth Plenum in November–December 1958, which marked the first major retreat from the more extreme measures of the Great Leap, the announcement was made that Mao would not succeed himself as PRC chairman. This would enable Mao "to concentrate his energies on dealing with questions of the direction, policy, and line of the Party and the state." No successor was mentioned, but in April 1959, at the first session of the Second NPC, Liu was elected to replace Mao. (Chu Te, in turn, succeeded Liu as NPC chairman.) During Mao's tenure as PRC chairman, there was only one vice-chairman: Chu Te. Under Liu, however, there are two: Tung Pi-wu and Sung Ch'ing-ling (Mme. Sun Yat-sen). Liu, Tung, and Sung were all re-elected in January 1965 at the close of the first session of the Third NPC. The PRC chairmanship, according to the 1954 constitution, is considerably less important than the NPC or the NPC Standing Committee. The constitution provides that the chairman "commands the armed forces" and heads the National Defense Council (NDC). The chairman is also authorized to convene the Supreme State Conference (SSC), the views of which are submitted to the NPC, the State Council, or other bodies concerned for "their consideration and decision." There is little to indicate that the NDC and the SSC have played a significant part in PRC affairs—under Mao or Liu.

As chairman of the NPC and then of the PRC, Liu received scores of foreign visitors in the middle and late 1950's. He was not yet identified as a principal spokesman in foreign affairs, but he became increasingly active in this field as Sino-Soviet relations deteriorated (see under Teng Hsiao-p'ing and K'ang Sheng). Taking with him a top-flight delegation, which included Teng Hsiao-p'ing and P'eng Chen, Liu was in Moscow for a month in November–December 1960. The ostensible purpose was to attend celebrations marking the 43rd anniversary of the Russian Revolution. But far more significant was his participation in the Moscow conference of 81 Communist parties, which has been described by one authority (writing in 1961) as "probably the most important gathering of its kind in the entire history of Communism."[41] Despite the tone of unity in the "Moscow Statement," it was clear that the Chinese opposed what they regarded as Soviet appeasement of the Western powers and that they espoused a doctrine of revolutionary struggle. The statement also failed to resolve the question of authority within the Communist world. During the next few years Liu was frequently present in Peking when foreign Communists visited China to confer with senior CCP figures. Few details are available about these talks, but as the years passed it became clear that Liu and his colleagues were attempting to assume for China the leadership of the Communist bloc.

By the winter of 1960–61 the economy was faltering to a serious degree. Many Western analysts attributed this to Great Leap Forward policies, but Peking laid the blame on a series of natural calamities (and later, when the Sino-Soviet rift was more openly discussed, on the withdrawal of thousands of Russian technicians in 1960). Responding to this situation, the Party moved to tighten controls at the Ninth Plenum in January 1961. Among other things, the plenum communiqué noted that a rectification movement then under way was to be expanded to help functionaries "raise their ideological and political level" and weed out the "bad elements" who had "sneaked" into the Party and government. Liu elaborated on these points in an important address delivered in mid-1961 marking the 40th anniversary of the Party. His speech, which was replete with praise for Mao, revealed that CCP membership had risen to 17,000,000 (a gain of some three million over the previous year and a half). Noting that 80 percent of the members had joined since 1949 and 70 percent since 1953, Liu called for still further ideological training, which (repeating his theme of 1957) would yield "more, faster, better, and more economical results." Further emphasis was given to ideology in mid-1962 when Liu's *How to Be a Good Communist* was

re-issued in revised form. This was accompanied by considerable fanfare; it occupied six pages of the *JMJP* on August 1 (the anniversary of the Party), and on the same day it appeared in a joint issue (nos. 15–16) of the Party's leading journal, *Hung-ch'i* (Red flag). The New China News Agency pointedly commented that during the 1942 *cheng-feng* campaign it was a document which "all functionaries of the Party were required to read."

In addition to his dealings with foreign Communist Parties, Liu also became more active in state relations with foreign countries after assuming the PRC chairmanship in 1959. In the early and middle 1960's he signed several friendship or boundary treaties, as well as joint communiqués with numerous Asian and African heads of state who visited China (e.g., Sekou Touré, Sihanouk, Nkrumah). On three occasions (through 1964) he made state visits abroad. In April 1963, accompanied by Foreign Minister Ch'en I, Liu visited Indonesia and Burma, and after returning to China briefly, he went to Cambodia and North Vietnam in May. The visits to Burma and Cambodia were unexceptional goodwill trips, but in Indonesia and Vietnam Liu strove, with little apparent success, to gain support for Chinese foreign policy in terms of the then deeply exacerbated Sino-Soviet dispute. In the aftermath of the abortive attempt to settle Sino-Soviet differences in mid-1963 (see under Teng Hsiao-p'ing), Liu visited North Korea for a week in September 1963. To judge from the communiqué issued at the close of the talks, Liu had greater success in gaining Korean adherence to Chinese views on the international Communist movement than he had in Vietnam and Indonesia.

Liu was very active in Party and state affairs through the mid-1960's, and he also continued to be the widely accepted heir apparent. Then, during the Great Proletarian Cultural Revolution in 1966, he became one of its earliest—and the most important—victims. Politburo members Teng Hsiao-p'ing and P'eng Chen were just two among scores of men closely associated with Liu who fell from power at this time. It quickly became apparent that Defense Minister Lin Piao had replaced Liu as Mao's designated successor.

Liu Shao-ch'i was already a towering figure among Communist Party members by the end of the Sino-Japanese War. But unlike Mao, the charismatic leader, or Chou En-lai, the suave and widely known diplomat, or Chu Te, the "soldiers' soldier," Liu was seen as the *éminence grise*—the man who implemented what Mao decreed. The somewhat shadowy figure he cast derived in part from the simple fact that relatively few Chinese or Westerners outside the Party have seen and interviewed Liu. Those who have known Liu often describe him as dour, unemotional, and colorless in manner but an intelligent man who is practical, thorough, and assiduous in his work. Little is known of Liu's first four wives, but his fifth wife, Wang Kuang-mei, is an attractive and well-educated woman. She remained in the background until the 1960's when she began to appear rather regularly with her husband, especially when he received guests from non-Communist countries. Wang accompanied Liu on his trip to southeast Asia in 1963, and in the next year she was elected a deputy from Hopeh to the Third NPC. Like her husband, she became a major target during the early phase of the Cultural Revolution. Liu has had at least eight children. None has been politically prominent, but one of them was trained as a physicist in the Soviet Union and later worked in the Institute of Physics of the Chinese Academy of Sciences.[42]

1. Edgar Snow, *The Other Side of the River* (London, 1963), p. 338.
2. *SCMP* 2398, p. 31.
3. Nym Wales, *The Chinese Labor Movement* (New York, 1945), p. 29.
4. *Ibid.*
5. Snow.
6. Li Jui, *Mao Tse-tung t'ung-chih te ch'u-ch'i ko-ming huo-tung* (Comrade Mao Tse-tung's early revolutionary activities; Peking, 1957), p. 186.
7. *Chung-kuo Kung-ch'an-tang tsai chung-nan-ti-ch'ü ling-tao ko-ming tou-cheng te li-shih tzu-liao* (Historical materials on the revolutionary struggles led by the CCP in central and south China; Wuhan, 1951), I, 59.
8. Li Jui, p. 181.
9. Roy Hofheinz, Jr. "The Peasant Movement and Rural Revolution: Chinese Communists in the Countryside (1923–7)," Ph.D. diss., Harvard University, 1966, pp. 226–227.
10. Li Yun-han, *Tsung jung kung tao ch'ing tang* (From the admission of the Communists to the purification of the [Nationalist] Party; Taipei, 1966), p. 159.
11. Jean Chesneaux, *The Chinese Labor Movement, 1919–1927* (Stanford, Calif., 1968), p. 298.
12. *Ibid.*, p. 522.
13. Wales, pp. 48–49.
14. Hu Hua, ed., *Chung-kuo hsin min-chu-chu-i ko-ming shih* (A history of China's new democratic revolution; Hong Kong, 1950), p. 78.
15. *Ti-i-tz'u kuo-nei ko-ming chan-cheng shih-ch'i te kung-jen yun-tung* (The workers' movement during the period of the first revolutionary civil war; Peking, 1963), p. 407.
16. *Bol'shaya Sovetskaya Entsiklopedya* (Large Soviet encyclopedia; Moscow; 1954), XXV, 574–575.
17. *JMJP*, June 2, 1949.
18. Tso-liang Hsiao, *Power Relations within the Chinese Communist Movement, 1930–1934* (Seattle, Wash., 1961), p. 162.
19. *Hung-se Chung-hua* (Red China), Jui-chin, April 17, 1933.
20. *Bol'shaya Sovetskaya Entsiklopedya.*
21. Warren Kuo, *Analytical History of [the] Chinese Communist Party* (Taipei, 1968), II, 615.
22. *Bol'shaya Sovetskaya Entsiklopedya.*
23. Ch'en Ch'ang-feng, *On the Long March with Chairman Mao* (Peking, 1959), p. 70.
24. Snow, p. 337.
25. *SCMM* 297, p. 35.
26. *Ibid.*, p. 38.
27. *Hsing-huo liao-yuan* (A single spark can start a prairie fire; Peking, 1961), VI, 376.
28. *CB* 777, pp. 10–17.
29. Chalmers A. Johnson, *Peasant Nationalism and Communist Power* (Stanford, Calif., 1962), pp. 140–141.
30. Boyd Compton, *Mao's China* (Seattle, Wash., 1966), p. xxxix.
31. *Ibid.* p. xxxviii.
32. *Selected Works of Mao Tse-tung* (Peking, 1965), III, 198–203.
33. *Ibid.*, IV, 193–195.
34. Stuart Schram, *Mao Tse-tung* (New York, 1966), p. 217.
35. Anna Louise Strong, "The Thought of Mao Tse-tung," *Amerasia* (June 1947), 11.6:161–174.
36. Robert Carver North, "Introduction" in Nym Wales, *Red Dust* (Stanford, Calif., 1952), p. 22.
37. Donald S. Zagoria, "Some Comparisons Between the Russian and Chinese Models," in A. Doak Barnett, ed., *Communist Strategies in Asia* (New York, 1963), pp. 11–33.
38. John Wilson Lewis, *Leadership in Communist China* (Ithaca, N.Y., 1963), pp. 220–221.
39. Franz Schurmann, *Ideology and Organization in Communist China* (Berkeley, Calif., 1966), p. 360.
40. *Ten Glorious Years* (Peking, 1960), pp. 1–34.
41. Donald S. Zagoria, *The Sino-Soviet Conflict, 1956–1961* (Princeton, N.J., 1962), p. 343.
42. Mikhail A. Klochko, *Soviet Scientist in Red China* (New York, 1964), pp. 24–25.

Liu Tao-sheng

(c.1916–   ). Deputy Commander, Chinese Navy.

Liu Tao-sheng has been associated with the Red Army since he was a teenage soldier in the Hunan-Kiangsi border area in the early thirties, and he has been a high-ranking officer in the Chinese Navy since the early fifties. Liu was born about 1916, very probably in central-south China. In 1933 he was working in the

Political Department of the Eighth Red Army, then garrisoned in the Hunan-Kiangsi Soviet (see under Wang Chen). The soviet included Mao's old base in the Chingkang Mountains but was separated from the Communists' headquarters at Juichin in southeast Kiangsi by an area held by Nationalist forces. In an autobiographical account dealing with his youth, Liu told of receiving orders in the spring of 1933 directing him to go to the Juichin area to enroll in the Red Army Academy (Hung-chün ta-hsueh).[1] Then only 17 and, in his words, "very inexperienced," he had to pass through KMT-held areas to reach Juichin where he entered the Academy, which had six to seven hundred students in its first class. The Academy had three sections for its students: command, staff, and political. Liu studied in the last-named. Among his classmates was Ch'iu Ch'uang-ch'eng (q.v.), who became political commissar of the PLA Artillery Force in the 1950's. Among the subjects Liu studied were civil engineering, the history of the CCP and socialism, Red Army political work, military regulations, and the basic arts of warfare from squad to regimental level. His teachers included such important Communists as Teng Hsiao-p'ing, Liu Po-ch'eng, and Wang Chia-hsiang (qq.v.). In 1934, after eight months at the school, Liu graduated and was assigned to the Kwangtung-Kiangsi Military Region where he directed the 22nd Division's Political Department. This division, formerly a part of the Eighth Army (1932), was badly decimated in the fighting during the Nationalists' Annihilation Campaigns against the Communists prior to the Long March. It would appear that the 22nd Division had come south from the Hunan-Kiangsi Soviet during or following the Annihilation Campaigns. Li T'ien-chü, the commander of the Eighth Army as of 1932, was killed on the Kwangtung-Kiangsi border in 1936,[2] and it is possible that Liu was with his troops.

Nothing further is recorded of Liu's activities for the next decade, but it is clear that he was active in the Red Army in those years, because in 1955 he was given the three military decorations (the Orders of August First, Independence and Freedom, and Liberation) signifying military service from 1927 to 1950. It is equally clear that in this same decade he had made significant advances in the CCP hierarchy; in November 1945, representing the Party's Shansi-Chahar-Hopeh (Chin-Ch'a-Chi) Administrative Committee, he attended the Chahar People's Congress in Kalgan (Chang-chia-k'ou), the important rail junction that was occupied by the Communists immediately after the Japanese surrender.[3] Liu at that time was only about 30 years old, and a few months later, in the spring of 1946, he was identified as the Party secretary for Chahar.[4]

Following the Communist takeover of Peking, Liu was elected to the First Central Committee of the New Democratic Youth League in the spring of 1949, retaining his seat until mid-1953. In the early years of the PRC his activities were primarily in connection with athletics, a field in which a number of younger PLA officers were involved. In the early fall of 1951 he led a military delegation to Prague to take part in athletic events held in connection with Czech Army Day, and in the following summer he was elected to the National Committee membership in the All-China Athletic Federation, a post he retained for over four years. In August 1952 Liu served on the presidium (steering committee) for an All-PLA Sports Meet in Peking, and one year he spoke at an athletic meet in Tsingtao, where he stressed the importance of athletics and the need to popularize sports within the armed forces.

In the late summer of 1952 Liu was identified as deputy political commissar of the PLA's Navy, which, in contrast to the Army and Air Force, is a relatively modest force. He remained in this political post until at least August 1957, when he was identified as being in Tsingtao reviewing naval units stationed there. Then, a year later, he was identified as one of the Navy's deputy commanders, a post he still retains under Navy Commander Hsiao Ching-kuang (q.v.). In the interim, in the fall of 1955, he received the rank of vice-admiral (equivalent to a three-star U.S. admiral) in addition to the above-mentioned decorations for his past services. Since assuming his duties with the Navy Liu has attended a number of military conferences, a random but typical example being the First Congress of Heroes and Models of the People's Navy in March 1953. Since the mid-fifties he has also been reported in the national press with considerable frequency in connection with the visits of foreign military delegations to China.

Although Liu works in Peking, he has been reported from time to time in China's coastal cities, presumably on inspection tours. He received his first post in the national government when he was elected as a deputy from the Navy to the Third NPC, which held its initial session in December 1964–January 1965. Fittingly, in view of his past connections with athletics and his role in naval affairs, when the China Naval Sports Federation was established (c.1964), Liu became the chairman. Presumably this association promotes naval sports that have military overtones and is probably linked closely with the National Defense Sports Association headed by General Li Ta (q.v.).

1. *Hung-ch'i p'iao-p'iao* (Red flag fluttering; Peking, 1957), III, 45–50.
2. Nym Wales, *Red Dust* (Stanford, Calif., 1952), p. 99.

3. *Chin-Ch'a-Chi hua-pao* (Shensi-Chahar-Hopeh pictorial; n.p., December 1945), nos. 9–10, unpaginated.

4. *Chiu-tao "szu-pa" yü-nan lieh-shih chi-nien-ts'e* (In memory of the martyrs who died in the accident of "April Eighth"; Kalgan, 1946), p. 59.

Liu Ting

(c.1910–   ). Vice-minister, Third Ministry of Machine Building.

Liu Ting, an important cabinet official since the establishment of the PRC, is a specialist in heavy industry. Two Western accounts (neither of which give Chinese characters) mention a "Liu Ting" as far back as the mid-1930's. One, by Edgar Snow, has described how Liu came to know Dr. George Hatem, an American physician who has worked with the Chinese Communist since the 1930's. In about 1936 Hatem wrote a pamphlet on health conditions in Shanghai which attracted the attention of Agnes Smedley, then a correspondent for the *Frankfurter Zeitung* and a woman who had extensive connections with the Communist underground in Shanghai. Smedley introduced Hatem to Liu, a "young Red engineer" who "awakened" Hatem to conditions in Communist-held areas of China.[1] Not long after, in mid-1937, author Nym Wales referred to a "Liu Ting" as head of the Motor School of the Anti-Japanese Military and Political Academy in Yenan and commented that she knew him.[2] Liu Ting's later work, which strongly suggests that he had had technical training and experience, makes it seem plausible that he is the same person known to both Smedley and Wales.

There is still another Western source (which does supply the Chinese characters) that refers to Liu as a Communist liaison officer in Sian, the Shensi capital, in mid-1936.[3] Liu was then attached to the headquarters of General Chang Hsueh-liang, who, with General Yang Hu-ch'eng, was rapidly becoming disenchanted with the policies of Chiang Kai-shek. The Communists, who were based not far north of Sian, were at that time making concerted efforts to woo Generals Chang and Yang toward the policy of uniting with the CCP to resist the steady encroachments of the Japanese in north China. It seems probable that Liu was working directly under Teng Fa (q.v.), a top Communist intelligence operative, who was also in Sian. These complex circumstances, which culminated in the famed Sian Incident of December 1936, are described in the biographies of Wang Ping-nan and Chou En-lai.

Nothing further is known of Liu during the Sino-Japanese War or its immediate aftermath, but presumably he worked with the Red armies, then desperately short of technically trained persons. A year prior to the formation of the central government in 1949, the Communists had conquered sufficient portions of north China to merit the establishment of a government in the area. Therefore, in August–September 1948 the North China People's Government (NCPG) was formed and remained in operation until the central government was formed in October 1949. Liu served in the NCPG as a deputy director under Huang Ching (q.v.) of the State-operated Enterprises Department, which controlled industry in north China. In mid-1949, as part of the general preparations for the establishment of the government and public organizations, plans were laid for a nationwide conference of natural scientists; Liu was named as one of the standing committee members of the preparatory committee. He attended this preparatory conference in July 1949, and then 13 months later at the first All-China Natural Science Workers Conference he presented a major report (on heavy industry) and was then elected to the National and Standing Committees of the newly formed All-China Federation of Scientific Societies. During the interim, in the fall of 1949, he had taken part in the formation of the central government as a representative of the preparatory committee of science workers to the first CPPCC, which met in September 1949. When appointments to the government bureaucracy were made in October 1949, he was named as one of the vice-ministers of Heavy Industry under China's most important economic specialist, Politburo member Ch'en Yun. Concurrently, he was named to head the ministry's General Arsenal Bureau. Liu held these two positions within this important ministry until certain departments of the ministry were split off in August 1952 to form two new ministries, the First and Second Ministries of Machine Building. Liu joined the latter as a vice-minister; inferential evidence suggests that this ministry was engaged in the manufacture of munitions. Liu held this post until the constitutional government was formed in September 1954. Unlike most of his fellow vice-ministers, he was not reappointed to his post as a vice-minister. Then a few months later, in January 1955, he was appointed as an assistant minister, a position one rank lower than a vice-ministership. Two years later, in March 1957, he was promoted to his old position as a vice-minister of the Second Ministry of Machine Building. In still another reorganization in February 1958, the First and Second Ministries of Machine Building were merged, adopting the title of the First Ministry. Liu continued in this ministry, serving under Minister Chao Erh-lu, his superior since 1952 and a Central Committee member after 1956. Though the First Ministry is known to engage in munitions production, it also has a variety of other activities, one of which was suggested in May 1958 when Liu witnessed a demonstration in Peking of a new internal combustion pump for irrigation purposes.

In September 1960, the Third Ministry of Machine Building was established, and Liu was transferred to this ministry, again as a vice-minister. In view of the fact that three of the men appointed as vice-ministers together with Liu were on active military service (two Air Force generals and an admiral), it is probable that this ministry also engages in some phase of military production. In April 1961 he received another position under the State Council when he was named as a deputy director of the General Bureau of Economic Relations with Foreign Countries. This bureau had been established in early 1960 to manage Chinese Communist aid programs. From time to time in the early 1960's Liu was mentioned in the press in connection with visiting foreign economic delegations, though the frequency of these appearances did not suggest that he was particularly active in this field of work. When the bureau was elevated to the commission (or ministerial) level in mid-1964, Liu was not reappointed, and thus within the State Council he only retains his vice-ministership in the Third Ministry of Machine Building.

As already mentioned, Liu had played a prominent role in the formation of the All-China Federation of Scientific Societies (ACFSS) in 1949 and 1950. The ACFSS has a large number of member organizations, including the China Mechanical Engineering Society, which was formed in September 1951. Liu served on the board of directors of this society, and in 1960 succeeded to the chairmanship of the board; then, for reasons which are not clear, he stepped down to a vice-chairmanship in 1962 in favor of Wang Tao-han (q.v.), an important government administrator.

In celebration of the 10th anniversary of the PRC, Liu wrote an article entitled "More Things Done in Ten Years Than in a Hundred Years" for the China News Service (September 5, 1959), the news agency which directs its dispatches mainly to the overseas Chinese audience.

1. *The Other Side of the River* (London, 1963), pp. 263–264.

2. *Inside Red China* (New York, 1939), p. 107.

3. Lyman P. Van Slyke, *Enemies and Friends, The United Front in Chinese Communist History* (Stanford, Calif., 1967), p. 72.

Liu Tzu-chiu

(c.1901–   ; Shantung?). Former alternate member, Central Committee, CCP; trade union official.

Liu Tzu-chiu is one of the few persons who was removed from the Party Central Commit-

tee, but who continued afterwards to have a career of moderate significance. Communist sources conflict on Liu's birthplace and date; one account uses Kuang-jao, Shantung, in 1901, and another Kaifeng, Honan, in 1905. He joined the Communist Party in 1928 but was then jailed for several years (although the circumstances surrounding his imprisonment are unknown). Apparently he was released (along with a number of Communists) at the outset of the Sino-Japanese War, because in 1937 Liu re-emerged in Honan as head of the Honan Party Organization Department. Later in the war he was secretary of the West Honan District Party Committee, and in approximately the last two years of the war he was secretary of the Huai-pei (North of the Huai River) District Party Committee; this was the area which, after 1941, was the headquarters of the Fourth Division of the New Fourth Army (see under P'eng Hsueh-feng).

In the first half of 1944 Liu was apparently ordered to Yenan for study at the Central Party School. In an article by him of July 5, 1944, he mentions this period with the comment that this was his first "study" (*hsueh-hsi*) since joining the Party.[1] In Communist terminology this normally refers to the study of Marxism-Leninism and related problems rather than to a regular education. (His later career, in fact, suggests that he had a fairly good education.) Liu's importance at this stage in his career is suggested by the fact that this article appeared in a Communist-published pamphlet which contained contributions only from Mao Tse-tung, Ch'en Yun, and a few others. An even better gauge to his stature was his election to alternate membership on the Central Committee at the Seventh Party Congress, held in Yenan (April–June 1945).

Liu spent the period of the civil war against the Nationalists (1946–1949) in central China, serving as head of the Political Department of the North Hupeh-Honan Military Sub-District. The area was probably under jurisdiction of the Honan-Hupeh Volunteer Column, a unit of the New Fourth Army commanded by Li Hsien-nien (q.v.). The sub-district was located in the T'ung-pai Mountains north of Hankow, extending between Ying-shan in northern Hupeh and Hsin-yang in southeastern Honan. By 1949 he was heading the Propaganda Department of the Central Plains Bureau of the CCP. He was identified in this post when he was named as a member of the Central Plains Provisional People's Government (and concurrently the head of the Education Department) in March 1949 when this government was established with its capital at Kaifeng. However, the provisional administration never reached regular status and was abolished in February 1950.

Although technically assigned to the Central Plains Government, Liu spent most of his time from mid-1949 in Peking deeply involved in both trade union affairs and the work of the newly established CPPCC. He was a delegate from the Central Plains Liberated Area to the First CPPCC, and when it held its first session in September 1949 to form the central government, Liu served on the committee to draft the organic law of the CPPCC. At the close of this session he was named a member of the First National Committee, holding this post through the term of the committee, which ended in December 1954. When appointments to the central government were made in October 1949, Liu was selected for membership on the important Government Administration Council's Finance and Economics Committee, headed by top economic specialist Ch'en Yun; this committee was one of the four coordinating committees in charge of a number of subordinate ministries and bureaus.

Liu's entry into trade union work in mid-1949 was the beginning of his most significant work in the decade of the 1950's. At one time or another in the early 1950's he held the following positions under the All-China Federation of Labor (ACFL): director, Culture and Education Committee (1949–c.1953); director, Policy Research Department (c.1949); chairman, Committee to Draft the Trade Union Law (1950); deputy director, Staff Office (c.1950–1951); director, Workers' Publishing House (1952–1955). When the seventh trade union congress was held in May 1953, he was named to the Executive Committee, the Presidium, and the Secretariat of the All-China Federation of Trade Unions (as the ACFL's new name appeared in English translation from this time onward). Four years later, at the eighth congress (December 1957), Liu was elected to the Executive Committee and the Presidium, but was dropped from the exclusive and important Secretariat. In addition to belonging to the national organization, he was a senior official in one of the constituent unions, the All-China Educational Trade Union. He helped organize the union in August 1950 and was then elected a vice-chairman, holding this post until the second congress in August 1956. Liu also gave major reports before meetings of the union in August–September 1951 and in October 1952; at the former meeting he claimed a membership for the union of nearly 500,000. With such an emphasis on education among workers, Liu was a logical choice to be named a vice-chairman in January 1951 of the newly formed All-China Workers Spare-time Education Committee, although little was heard about this committee afterwards. In similar fashion, he was a natural selection for membership on an *ad hoc* "study committee" of teachers at university-level institutes in Peking and Tientsin, formed under the Ministry of Education in October 1951 as part of an ideological campaign "aimed at reforming their own thoughts and reforming higher education."

Having performed at this level of activity in both trade union and educational work, it is surprising that Liu was dropped from the Party Central Committee. He was listed as an alternate Central Committee member in semi-official handbooks of early 1950, but not in early 1951, and so was probably dropped at the Third Plenum of the Central Committee in June 1950. No charges were brought against Liu at the time, nor afterwards. Another man (Li Yü, q.v.) was also removed at this same period, and the circumstances were also unexplained in his case. But whereas Li Yü was subsequently criticized for wrongdoing during one of the Party's major "remolding" campaigns, Liu has never been publicly denounced and his dismissal remains the more puzzling. The one known similarity in their careers is that both Liu and Li served in the New Fourth Army.

As part of a campaign to break out of the economic blockade imposed on China by the Western powers during the Korean War, a major international conference was held in Moscow in April 1952. The Chinese formed a preparatory committee, with Liu as one of the members; he then attended the conference in Moscow as a member of the delegation led by international economic specialist Nan Han-ch'en and upon his return to China was named to the newly formed (May 1952) Chinese Council for the Promotion of International Trade, an organization dealing mainly with nations not having diplomatic relations with Peking. In the meantime, in April–May 1952 Liu returned to Moscow leading a Chinese delegation to May Day celebrations in Moscow. He led trade union delegations abroad on two other occasions; in January–February 1955 he was in Burma on a goodwill mission, and in May 1955 he traveled to Prague for the Third Congress of Czech Trade Unions.

In 1954 Liu was elected from Shantung to the First NPC and at the first session in September 1954 was named to the NPC Bills Committee. He was not, however, re-elected to the Second NPC, which first met in April 1959. He was appointed in April 1955 as a vice-minister of Labor and in September 1956 spoke before the Eighth Party Congress on wage reforms.

Aside from the numerous voting positions held by Liu in the early and mid-1950's, a few more of minor importance are worth brief tabulation: member, Executive Committee, Sino-Soviet Friendship Association, 1951–1954; member, National Committee, All-China Athletic Federation, 1952–1956; and member, National Committee, China Peace Committee, 1954–1958. Of perhaps greater importance are articles he wrote on labor questions during these same years: "Our Task Is to Organize Emulation," *JMJP*, January 20, 1954; "On Problems of Party Leadership over Labor Union Organs," *Hsueh-*

hsi (Study), October 2, 1955; "A Short Discussion on the Problem of Wages," *ibid.*, December 2, 1956; "Labor Education and Labor Practice," *JMJP,* November 26, 1957; "Everyone Is a Common Laborer in the Service of Society," *Chung-kuo ch'ing-nien pao* (China youth news), December 29, 1958; "On Raising Labor Productivity," *Hsin-hua pan-yueh-k'an* (New China semi-monthly), April 25, 1959.

In the late 1950's, Liu made fewer and fewer public appearances. He was, however, named to the Third National Committee of the CPPCC in April 1959 as a representative of the Federation of Trade Unions and in September 1959 was reappointed as a vice-minister of Labor. But after that appointment, nothing was heard of Liu until he was named to the Fourth National Committee of the CPPCC (again as a trade union representative), which held its first session in December 1964–January 1965. Clearly Liu had lost considerable influence by the late 1950's, a fact which became obvious when he was quietly dropped from his vice-ministership in the Ministry of Labor. Normally, officials at this level are officially removed. In Liu's case, however, he was simply dropped from the annual handbooks (failing to appear in the 1962 edition).

----

1. This article was first published in a pamphlet entitled *Fan tang pa-ku* (Oppose Party formalism), probably published in Yenan in 1944, pp. 58–73. It was reprinted in *Cheng-feng wen-hsien* (Rectification documents; Hong Kong, 1949), pp. 299–318.

Liu Tzu-hou

(c.1910–   ; Hopeh). Hopeh governor; second secretary, Hopeh CCP Committee; alternate member, CCP Central Committee.

Liu Tzu-hou, a native of Hopeh, was born about 1910. He was a student in Peking when the Japanese attacked Mukden in 1931, but because of his anti-Japanese activities he was soon expelled from school. He then made his way to Manchuria where he took part in guerrilla activities against the Japanese, an endeavor that may have put him in touch with Communist resistance fighters, such as Chou Pao-chung (q.v.). At some time prior to the outbreak of war with Japan in 1937, Liu joined the CCP. After the Japanese attack in 1937, he went to Honan where he became a secretary to the magistrate of Hsin-yang, a city in southeastern Honan. When Hsin-yang fell to the onrushing Japanese forces (October 1938), Liu fled to the countryside east of the city to engage in guerrilla warfare in the rural area between Hsin-yang and Lo-shan, a town some 30 miles east of Hsin-yang.

The Communists had established themselves in Shang-ch'eng, southeast of Hsin-yang, as early as 1929 and from this area had joined forces with guerrilla groups in the bordering regions of Hupeh and Anhwei provinces where the remoteness of the Ta-pieh Mountains give them protection from government forces. These guerrilla forces united to form the Hupeh-Honan-Anhwei (Oyüwan) Soviet after 1929 (see under Chang Kuo-t'ao). Although only pockets of resistance were left in the area after the Long March began in 1934, it is possible (though undocumented) that Liu took refuge in these areas during the Sino-Japanese War period. Apparently he remained in this general area, because at some time prior to 1948 he was serving as the director of the Finance Department of the Honan-Hupeh Border Region Administrative Office.

Liu remained in central China after the formation of the central government in Peking in the fall of 1949, assuming several important posts in Hupeh province. By early 1950 he was heading the Organization Department for the Hupeh Party Committee, and in March 1950 was named to membership on the Hupeh Provincial People's Government. Also in 1950 he assumed two posts with discipline and inspection functions; he became a member of the People's Supervision Committee of the Central-South Military and Administrative Committee (a post he held until May 1953), the multi-provincial government organization to which Hupeh was subordinate. The second such post was as chairman of the People's Supervision Committee for the Hupeh provincial government. He was removed from the latter position and made a vice-governor of Hupeh in February 1952 as part of a number of personnel changes that came in the wake of a major scandal, known as the Sung Ying case (see under Chang P'ing-hua). At almost the same time, Liu was identified in a new and important Hupeh Party position; by January 1952 he had become second deputy secretary. By October 1952 he had advanced to deputy secretary and was again promoted in August 1953 to second secretary. Both as Hupeh vice-governor and in his Hupeh Party positions, Liu served under Li Hsien-nien, then a senior Party figure in central China and a Politburo member since 1956. In 1953–54 Liu also served as a member of the Central-South Administrative Committee following its reorganization in January 1953.

In the summer of 1954 Hupeh Governor Li Hsien-nien was transferred to Peking to become minister of Finance. Liu was immediately appointed as the new governor, retaining the post until January 1956 when he in turn was replaced by Chang T'i-hsueh (q.v.). A new assignment took Liu north to the Honan-Shansi border where in 1956 he was identified as the director of the Sanmen Gorge Project, one of the most extensive and important projects undertaken by the Chinese Communists. The gorge is located on the Yellow River on the Honan-Shansi border due west of Loyang. The project is a multi-purpose scheme involving flood control, power generation, and irrigation. Liu had had some experience in this type of work during his tenure in Hupeh; in March 1952 he had been named to a "flood-harnessing" committee to tame the Ching River, a tributary of the Yangtze in southern Hupeh. Liu apparently developed something of a specialty in this line of work, for in mid-1958 (after being transferred to Hopeh—see below), he was identified as the political commissar of the Hopeh Provincial "Command Post for the Prevention of Floods."

In April 1958 Liu was again transferred, becoming governor of his native Hopeh. He replaced Lin T'ieh (q.v.), who resigned so that he might "concentrate his efforts on his post as first secretary" of the province. Soon after assuming the gubernatorial post, he also became (by July 1958) a secretary of the Party Committee under Lin T'ieh. In October 1964 he was identified as the second secretary of the Hopeh Party Committee. He continues to hold both these important government and Party posts in Hopeh. In the month following his transfer to Hopeh, Liu was elected as an alternate member of the Party Central Committee at the second session of the Eighth Party Congress (May 1958). A few months later he was elected a deputy from Hopeh to the Second NPC (1959–1964); he was re-elected to the Third NPC, which held its first session in December 1964–January 1965.

In the years since he has been in Hopeh, Liu has been reported in the national press with great frequency. In part this is owing to the fact that the province envelops (but does not administratively control) Peking, making Hopeh a convenient locale for inspections by top Party leaders. For example, Liu was reported in the company of Chou En-lai in November 1959, Liu Shao-ch'i in March 1960, and Mao Tse-tung in May 1960. Also, because Tientsin (the provincial capital) is a major city and is astride a major communications route, a large number of foreign guests are in the city, a situation that inevitably brings Liu into the news. A typical instance of this occurred in June 1963 when Liu was on hand to entertain the visiting president of the People's Supreme Assembly of North Korea.

In January 1961 the Party Central Committee decided to re-create the regional Party bureaus. By July 1963 Liu was identified as one of the secretaries of the North China Bureau, a bureau headed by First Secretary Li Hsueh-feng, a veteran north China Party official. Liu Tzu-hou continues to hold this post, in addition to his Party and government posts in Hopeh.

Liu Ya-lou

(1910–1965; Wu-p'ing hsien, Fukien). Former commander, PLA Air Force; member, CCP Central Committee.

A veteran of the Communist armies from the late twenties, Liu Ya-lou was commander of the PLA Air Force from 1949 to his death in 1965. He was born in Wu-p'ing hsien in southeast Fukien. A graduate of a middle school, Liu joined the Red Army and the CCP in 1929 when Chu Te's troops came through his native hsien during the Red military campaigns in Fukien, soon after Chu and Mao Tse-tung had been driven from Chingkangshan. From 1928 to the early summer of 1930 the Chu-Mao forces were known as the Fourth Workers' and Peasants' Red Army. Lin Piao was with this army and Liu was probably attached to his unit soon after he joined the Fourth Army. Liu served successively as a squad, platoon, company, and battalion commander until he was wounded and transferred to political work. He then served as a detachment officer and later as a regimental political officer. His long career in political work and his association with Lin Piao, which continued to the end of Liu's life, date from this period.

Liu participated in all five of the Annihilation Campaigns that Chiang Kai-shek mounted against the Communists in central-south China between 1930 and 1934. In 1932 he became political commissar of the Fourth Army's 11th Division (not to be confused with the earlier Fourth Army commanded by Chu Te). Earlier, in the summer of 1930 the Chu-Mao army had been reorganized and designated the First Army Corps. The Fourth Army to which Liu belonged was subordinate to the First Army Corps commanded by Lin Piao and had Nieh Jung-chen (q.v.) as its political commissar. At some later date prior to the Long March Liu was transferred to the Second Division, which was also under Lin Piao's First Army Corps. In the Second Division Liu served successively as director of its Political Department and then as political commissar and commander.

When the Long March began in the fall of 1934 Liu remained with the Second Division as its political commissar. During the course of the epic march he led his troops across the Wu River in Kweichow in a dramatic battle that led to the capture of Tsun-i, where the Communists held an important conference in January 1935 to decide on future strategy.[1] He was still with the Second Division in May of that year when his troops took part in one of the most celebrated events on the Long March—the capture of the bridge spanning the Ta-tu River at Lu-ting in eastern Sikang (see under Yang Ch'eng-wu).[2]

At approximately the time that Mao's Long

Marchers arrived in north Shensi in the fall of 1935 Liu Ya-lou assumed command of the First Division and was then deputy commander of the Second Column of the Shensi-Kansu Detachment; both units were under Lin Piao's First Army Corps. In early 1936 Liu took part in the thrust across the Yellow River into Shansi province, where the Communists hoped to replenish their supplies and to find recruits for the Red Army. (This brief but important campaign is described in the biography of Liu Chih-tan.) Later in 1936 Liu attended the first class of the Red Army Academy (Hung-chün ta-hsueh), then headed by Lin Piao. Liu remained at the Academy, which was moved to Yenan in early 1937 and renamed the Anti-Japanese Military and Political Academy (K'ang-ta). He served as head of its Training Department and later as dean of education (chiao-yü chang).[3] In 1938 Liu was sent to the Soviet Union where he received military training at the Frunze Military Academy. He alluded briefly to his days in Moscow (in 1939) in an article written for the Chieh-fang-chün pao (Liberation Army daily) of February 3, 1958. It appears that his stay in the Soviet Union coincided closely with the period when Lin Piao was there. In any event, Liu Ya-lou was back in Yenan by 1942, and from then until the end of the war he was director of a motorized army school in the Communists' wartime capital.

With the cessation of hostilities in August 1945 Lin Piao was placed in charge of Communist military operations in Manchuria. Early in 1946, when the Communist-controlled forces there were organized into the Northeast Democratic Allied Army, Liu became Lin's chief-of-staff. (The principal battles fought by this army in the three years before it conquered all of Manchuria are described in the biography of Lin Piao.) Early in the fighting the Communists fell heir to a few battered Japanese aircraft which became the nucleus of the Chinese Communist Air Force. This was said to have been at Kiamuze, near the Heilungkiang-Kirin border, where the Red forces were remote from the danger of a Nationalist attack. The small air force was reportedly placed under the command of Liu Ya-lou, who was said at the same time to have been the president of the newly created Air Force Academy.

As Lin's chief-of-staff, Liu probably took part in the direction of the battle for Mukden in the fall of 1948. This was the last Nationalist stronghold in Manchuria and after its fall the Communists turned south to conquer China proper. By the end of the year Lin's troops had joined those of Nieh Jung-chen to surround three major cities of north China—Kalgan, Tientsin, and Peking. Liu was in direct charge of the troops that captured Tientsin on January 15, 1949,[4] a battle he recounted in the October

28, 1960, issue of the JMJP. By this time Lin Piao's army had been redesignated the Fourth Field Army, and as such it moved through central and south China in the following months. Liu served briefly as chief-of-staff of this field army, but by March 1949 the post had been assumed by Hsiao K'o (q.v.). It is probable, in fact, that Liu did not go south with Lin Piao's forces, but rather remained in Peking. In any event, he was named as commander of the Air Force in August 1949. Four months later he became a member of the Board of Directors of the Central Aviation Company, which was taken over from the Nationalist Government.

From 1949 until his death in 1965 Liu's principal work was directing the development of the Chinese Communist Air Force. He was, of course, in charge of Chinese air power in the critical years of the Korean War and during the fighting over Quemoy and Matsu in 1958. The Chinese entered the Korean War the year after Liu received his appointment. The Chinese air arm was initially so weak that it suffered terrific punishment at the hands of the far better equipped and developed U.S. Air Force, but by the end of the war it had become one of the major air forces of the world, an improvement which cannot be separated from Liu's leadership. In the late 1950's and the early 1960's the Chinese Air Force suffered from obsolescence to such a degree that it lost much of its importance, but this was well beyond the control of Liu Ya-lou.

Beginning in 1949 with his appointment as Air Force chief, Liu's name continued to be frequently in the news until shortly before his death. During this time he took part in many of the activities designed to promote the development of Chinese air power and also represented his country abroad on several important military missions. In this connection he accompanied Premier Chou En-lai on the important mission to Moscow of August–September 1952 when the Chinese negotiated the transfer of the Chinese Changchun Railway from the Russians, as well as the extension of the term of joint use of the Chinese naval base at Port Arthur, the latter legalizing the Russian stay at the naval base for three more years. In February 1953 Liu was a member of the Chinese delegation that visited the Soviet troops at Port Arthur. He was there twice more in 1955. The first visit in February was made preparatory to the Soviet withdrawal from the naval base. On the second visit, in May, he served as a member of the military delegation to the Joint Sino-Soviet Military Commission, which was created to handle the takeover from the Russians. Possibly because of his work with Russians he served from 1954 until his death as an Executive Board member of the Sino-Soviet Friendship Association.

Liu was a deputy from the PLA to the First

NPC (1954–1959), which at its inaugural session in September 1954 established the constitutional government. At this time he was made a member of the government's new military advisory body, the National Defense Council; he was reappointed to this post in April 1959 and January 1965. In 1955, when military ranks and honors were created, Liu became a colonel general, the equivalent of a three-star general in the U.S. Army. He also won all three top honors, the Orders of August First, Independence and Freedom, and Liberation, covering military service from the birth of the Red Army in 1927 to 1950. The number of public appearances made by Liu increased greatly in the decade from 1954 to 1964. These occurred mainly in relation to the Air Force, and in this connection he saw members of virtually every military delegation visiting China that was interested in air power. He attended a number of functions for Party activists within the Air Force and he also wrote articles and spoke frequently before important conferences and meetings to expound official views on military matters. Then, when the CCP met for its Eighth Congress in September 1956, Liu was elected to the Central Committee.

Throughout his life Liu's career continued to be associated with Lin Piao. It may not have been coincidental that Liu was made a vice-minister of National Defense in September 1959 when Lin Piao succeeded the discredited P'eng Te-huai as minister. Liu received his last post in August 1964 when the Chinese People's Aviation Sports Federation was created in Peking and he was named the honorary chairman.

Apart from his 1952 trip to Moscow, Liu made several other visits abroad, mainly in connection with his work in the Air Force. In June–July 1956 he led a delegation that visited Moscow to attend Aviation Day celebrations there. He was a member of P'eng Te-huai's 12-member military delegation, which joined the entourage of Mao Tse-tung for the 40th anniversary celebrations of the Russian Revolution in November 1957. Three years later, when Sino-Soviet relations had seriously deteriorated and the Chinese were anxious to find support among Asian Communist parties, Liu spent three weeks in North Korea with the Chinese goodwill mission led by military veteran Ho Lung (October–November 1960). In December 1961 Liu took part in the important Chinese military mission to North Vietnam; he was one of two deputy chiefs of the delegation led by military leader Yeh Chien-ying. Then in mid-July 1963 Liu headed a military delegation to Cuba, ostensibly to celebrate the 10th anniversary of the storming of Camp Moncada, the date of the Cuban Revolution led by Castro. The delegation stayed there from July 13 to August 3 in Cuba; its members are among the very few Chinese military leaders to have visited Latin America. Liu's last foreign visit was in August 1964 when he accompanied Vice-

premier Li Hsien-nien to the celebrations marking the 20th anniversary of the "liberation" of Rumania from Nazi Germany. After visiting Rumanian petroleum installations, they departed for home. Liu, however, left the group and spent a few days in late August and early September visiting Pakistan where he called on the secretary of the Pakistan Defense Ministry and the Army commander-in-chief.

Liu died in Shanghai on May 7, 1965, after a serious but apparently short illness. Soon after his death Wu Fa-hsien, a veteran PLA political officer, became the new Air Force Commander. Among the many tributes written about Liu at the time of his death was one by a son of Lin Piao stating that Liu and his father had worked together for "a very long period." During Liu's illness, according to this account, Lin had flown to Shanghai several times especially to visit his old comrade.

Liu was married at least three times. His second wife, whom he married while he was in the USSR between 1938 and 1942, was the daughter of Su Chao-cheng (q.v.), an early Communist labor leader. As of September 1964 Liu's wife was Chai Yun-ying whose antecedents are unknown.

1. *Stories of the Long March* (Peking, 1958), pp. 11–22; *Hsing-huo liao-yuan* (A single spark can start a prairie fire; Hong Kong, 1960), pp. 29–37.

2. *Hung-ch'i p'iao-p'iao* (Red flag fluttering; Peking, 1957), III, 139–146; *SCMP* 3463, pp. 12–14.

3. Kusano Fumio, *Shina henku no kenkyu* (Research on China's border regions; Tokyo, 1944), pp. 79–83; *JMJP*, April 17, 1952.

4. *The Great Turning Point* (Peking, 1962), pp. 187–210.

Liu Yü-min

Minister of Building; vice-chairman, State Capital Construction Commission.

Although nothing is known of the early career of Liu Yü-min, he had risen to a cabinet post by 1965. He first received national attention in the fall of 1949 when he became director of the Industry Department of the Fukien Provincial Government soon after that province was captured by Communist forces. From that time onward virtually all of Liu's work has had some connection with industry or building construction work. In October of 1950 he received another post subordinate to the Fukien government when he was named as a vice-chairman of the provincial Finance and Economics Committee, and then in 1952 he became a member of the newly formed provincial Labor Employment Committee, one of numerous committees established at that time throughout China in an effort to solve problems of unemployment.

By early 1955 Liu had been transferred to Peking where he became the manager of an engineering company directly subordinate to the Ministry of Building, a ministry he would one day head. In May 1956 he was made an assistant minister of this ministry and was then promoted to a vice-ministership by June 1958. From its inception in 1952, the Ministry of Building underwent a number of reorganizations, divisions, and mergers. The latest occurred in March 1965 when it was divided into two ministries; one was named the Ministry of Building Materials and the other retained the old title of Ministry of Building. The original minister of Building, Li Jen-chün, was replaced by Liu when this split took place; Liu continues to hold the portfolio. Then, just one month later (April 1965), he received another prominent governmental appointment when he was named as a vice-chairman of the State Capital Construction Commission. The Commission had existed from 1958 to 1961 under the chairmanship of Ch'en Yun and was then re-created under Ku Mu (qq.v.) in March 1965. When it was dissolved in 1961 its functions were taken over by the State Planning Commission. Apparently, therefore, the re-created State Capital Construction Commission was formed from sections of the Planning Commission.

Representing the Ministry of Building, Liu has made two trips abroad. In the fall of 1958 he led a five-member group to Norway, Sweden, and Denmark where he inspected building construction facilities and was received by various cabinet-level officials in these nations. And in June 1963 he led a similar delegation to North Korea. Liu does not make many public appearances, and his writings seem to be confined to one article mentioned in a Mandarin broadcast from Peking on June 27, 1958, which stated that he had written an article on the need for China to improve itself in science and technology.

Lo Chang-lung

(1901–1949?; Liu-yang, Hunan). Early CCP labor leader; member, CCP Central Committee.

Lo Chang-lung, also known by the alias Wen Hu, was a renegade from Chinese Communism. He is important in CCP history because of his part in the intra-Party power struggle against both the leadership of Li Li-san and the Russian-returned Student faction led by Ch'en Shao-yü. The struggle culminated in January 1931 when Lo and his colleague Ho Meng-hsiung, both top labor leaders, were defeated in their bid for supremacy within the CCP.

Lo came from a wealthy Hunanese landlord family in Liu-yang hsien, a rural area of about 40 miles east of Changsha, which is also the home of such prominent Communists as Sung Jen-ch'iung, Wang Chen, and Wang Shou-tao

(qq.v.). Lo evinced an early interest in politics when, as a teenager, he answered an advertisement Mao Tse-tung had placed in a Changsha newspaper. Mao sought to make contact with "youths who were hardened and determined, and ready to make sacrifices for their country." In recounting this to Edgar Snow, Mao said that among those who responded was Lo, "who later was to join the Communist Party and afterwards to betray it."[1] After studying at Changsha Lo went to Peking for further education. This may have been at about the same time that Mao went there (fall 1918). At any rate, Lo was at Peking University (Peita) at the time of the May Fourth Incident (1919). He was then in the German Department where his study of Kant and Hegel led him to read Marx and Engels, who were becoming increasingly popular among students influenced by the May Fourth Movement. Both Li Ta-chao and Ch'en Tu-hsiu, early Chinese Marxists and founders of the CCP, were at Peita while Lo was there. They had considerable influence on Lo, as did another early Chinese Marxist, Chang Kuo-t'ao. Lo was one of the earliest and more active members of the University's Society for the Study of Marxism, which was formed in March 1920 under Li Ta-chao's guidance (see under Li Ta-chao). Lo was thus among the Peita group of Marxists who played a major role in founding the CCP in July 1921, a point acknowledged many years later by Mao in his conversations with Edgar Snow.[2]

Even before the formal inauguration of the CCP in mid-1921, Lo and his colleagues were becoming increasingly active in the north China labor movement, especially among the railway workers in areas near Peking (see under Teng Chung-hsia). As part of these endeavors they established the *Kung-jen chou-k'an* (Workers' weekly) in the spring of 1921. Lo was the editor of this publication, the purpose of which was to disseminate news about both the foreign and domestic labor movements.[3]

Lo did not attend the Party's First Congress held in Shanghai in July 1921, but rather he remained at Peita. Immediately after the Congress, the Secretariat of the Chinese Labor Unions was established in Shanghai, with Lo's friend Chang Kuo-t'ao in charge. Teng Chung-hsia became the director of the Secretariat's North China Branch at Peking, where he was assisted by Lo. Toward the end of 1921 Teng returned to Peking to become secretary of the Party's Municipal Committee, of which Lo was also a member. In May 1922, the Labor Secretariat convened the First National Congress of Labor in Canton. The delegates decided to move the Secretariat to Peking, whereupon Lo's *Kung-jen chou-k'an* was made the organ of the Secretariat.

In mid-1922, at the Party's Second Congress, Lo, Chang Kuo-t'ao, and Ho Meng-hsiung opposed those who advocated cooperation with the KMT (see under Ho Meng-hsiung), but soon afterwards, at a special meeting of the Party, the policy was adopted under strong Comintern pressures. The debate persisted among the Peking Communists; in late 1922, according to one account, the Peking group split in "radical" and "gradualist" factions. Lo was joined by Chang Kuo-t'ao and Ho Meng-hsiung in arguing for a labor-oriented Party and against Communist participation in the KMT. Teng Chung-hsia, who spoke for the "gradualists," contended that the time was not ripe for a proletarian class struggle and that cooperation with the KMT was the best way to carry out the necessary "national revolution."[4] Insofar as north China was concerned, the debate was soon settled by events; those elements of the north China labor movement controlled by the Communists were badly crippled by warlord Wu P'ei-fu's suppression of strikers on the Peking-Hankow Railway in February 1923, an event known in Communist annals as the "February Seventh Massacre." It is not known if Lo played a direct role in this disaster, but a month later he published a piece in Peking on the February massacre.[5] As a consequence of these events, Teng Chung-hsia fled to Shanghai. Lo may have replaced Teng as secretary of the Peking Party Committee, and it appears that he also took over Teng's function in the faltering trade union movement in north China.

Despite the fact that Lo was principally associated with the labor movement, he was one of the earliest Communists to write on the peasantry. In September–October 1923 the Communist journal *Hsiang-tao chou-pao* (Guide weekly) published three short articles by Lo on land problems and peasant rebellion in Shantung, Kiangsi, and Kwangtung.[6] There is a paucity of information about Lo during the next few years. Chang Kuo-t'ao asserts that in 1925 Lo was engaged in propaganda work under Ts'ai Ho-sen.[7] Ts'ai was then deeply involved in the labor movement in Shanghai, but it is not clear if Lo was also in Shanghai or still in Peking. Lo was in some way involved in the Autumn Harvest Uprisings in Hunan and Hupeh (September 1927). This was revealed in the charges brought against him in 1931 (see below), but nothing was mentioned aside from the rather standard generic accusation that he had been guilty of "opportunism."[8] Whatever the truth of these charges, Lo survived the intra-Party turmoil of 1927–28, and at the Party's Sixth Congress, which he attended in Moscow in mid-1928, he was elected a member of the CCP Central Committee. Later in 1928, speaking at a meeting in Shanghai of the All-China Federation of Labor, Lo presented a candid report on the severe setbacks suffered by the Communist-led labor movement in the period after the break with the KMT in 1927.[9]

By 1930 Lo had emerged as a top leader (possibly the chairman) of the All-China Federation of Labor and as an influential member of the Kiangsu Party Committee. His career reached its zenith in the months prior to the Fourth CCP Plenum in January 1931 when he was deeply involved in the controversy over Li Li-san, who had been the predominant Party figure after the Sixth Congress in 1928. Li's leadership was bitterly contested by various factions within the CCP, one of which was a labor group led by Ho Meng-hsiung (Lo's former colleague at Peita) and supported by Lo. Li Li-san's uncompromising policies were especially resented by the labor group because Li's aggressive tactics were evoking stern KMT countermeasures and the rank-and-file workers were becoming afraid to join the unions. Those opposing Li felt that this had helped to weaken the Party in China, as well as to alarm the Comintern. Various aspects of this inner-Party struggle are described in the biographies of Li Li-san, Chou En-lai, Ch'ü Ch'iu-pai, and Ho Meng-hsiung. Ho's biography contains a discussion of the Third CCP Plenum of September 1930 when an unsuccessful attempt was made to unseat Li. Soon afterwards, however, the continuing opposition to Li (in which Ho Meng-hsiung's group played an important part), combined with assistance from the Comintern (see under Li Li-san), was successful in "exiling" Li to Moscow.

Once Li was out of the way, other forces continued the quest for power. Earlier, alarmed by the trend of events, the Comintern had sent the chancellor of Sun Yat-sen University in Moscow, Pavel Mif, to China (spring 1930) as its agent to settle the inner-Party feud. Mif was accompanied by some of his former University students, the "28 Bolsheviks." The group was led by Ch'en Shao-yü (q.v.) who was soon to play a very active role. The Comintern-directed Ch'en group had been present at the Third Plenum in September 1930, but they were not then sufficiently strong to gain control of the Party. A very different situation existed by January 1931 when the CCP held its Fourth Plenum, called in Shanghai by Mif and his associates.

At the Fourth Plenum there was again intensive fighting, this time between Ch'en Shao-yü's supporters and other groups who contested their bid for power. Of these, the remnants of the Li Li-san clique were rather easily defeated. The more powerful group was that composed of the followers of Ho Meng-hsiung and Lo Chang-lung, who now presented a unified opposition to the "28 Bolsheviks." This Plenum is discussed by Hsiao Tso-liang in a work that summarizes a number of the Plenum documents.[10] It appears that the Lo-Ho group had questioned the desirability of holding a plenum on the grounds that the Party leadership shared the blame for Li Li-san's mistakes and was not able to bring about the needed reform. Hence, new leadership was necessary. To find it they advocated the convocation of an emergency conference like the one held on August 7, 1927, after the failure of the Communist coup at Nanchang (see under Ch'ü Ch'iu-pai). The Ch'en Shao-yü group did not accept their proposal and the Plenum was held in January 1931. The most outspoken of Li Li-san's supporters were removed from the Party Central Committee (see under Li Wei-han) and replaced by Ch'en's own men. Ho and Lo countered by withdrawing from the meeting, setting up an emergency committee, and advancing a slate of their own candidates for the Central Committee. This opposition cost Ho and Lo their important positions in the CCP.

A document entitled a "Resolution Concerning the Removal of Lo Chang-lung as a Member of the Central Committee and of the Party," adopted by the CCP Politburo on January 27, 1931, elaborated on Lo's expulsion. He was charged with having issued a resolution from the All-China Federation of Labor that opposed convening the Fourth Plenum and with obstructing the Party by refusing to comply with its policy. The victorious Ch'en Shao-yü leadership strenuously objected to a pamphlet issued by Lo for general circulation, which described the Fourth Plenum as dictatorial and "undemocratic" and which called for the recall of the Comintern delegate to Russia. The Politburo decision to expel Lo from the Party was referred to the Comintern for approval, and this was given six months later.[11]

Others expelled at this time included Politburo member Wang K'o-ch'üan, who was responsible for setting up a rival Kiangsu Provincial Committee after being expelled from the Party; Central Committee member Wang Feng-fei, who was responsible for setting up a rival Cha-pei District Party Committee in Shanghai; Central Committee member Hsu Hsi-ken, who had acted as the secretary of the emergency committee established by Lo and Ho; Lin Yü-nan (q.v.); and Li Ch'iu-shih (q.v.).

After his expulsion, Lo played a leading role in an attempt to establish a Party leadership independent of the returned-student clique. The emergency committee which he and Ho set up after the Plenum, the rival Kiangsu Provincial Party Committee of Wang K'o-ch'üan, and the rival District Party Committee of Wang Feng-fei were part of this effort. Probably more important in terms of mass support for the opposition was the strength of Lo's support from labor as a top leader in the All-China Federation of Labor. He had been accused at the Fourth Plenum of controlling the Party fraction within the Federation. This charge probably had some foundation because such important groups as the Railway Union, the Maritime Union, and the League of Left-wing Writers had passed resolutions denouncing the Fourth Plenum and the Comintern representative who had opposed the emergency conference.[12] The effectiveness of the Lo-Ho opposition was considerably diminished when Ho

and 35 others (including Lin Yü-nan and Li Ch'iu-shih) were arrested by the British police at a secret meeting in Shanghai on January 17, 1931 (see under Ho Meng-hsiung). The group was turned over to the KMT authorities and most of them were executed on February 7, 1931.

It is evident that Lo and his followers continued to trouble the CCP leadership. Speaking in Moscow at a meeting of the Comintern's Executive Committee in late 1933, Ch'en Shao-yü stated that in the fall of 1932 the "Right opportunists and the remnants of the counter-revolutionary followers of Lo Chang-lung, who had temporarily concealed themselves within the party, were shouting that the Chinese Communist Party and the Red Army were not in a position" to repulse one of Chiang Kai-shek's Annihilation Campaigns. Later in the same speech he charged that many of Lo's men were "openly" working for the "secret police in Nanking, Shanghai," and north China.[13] Lo was, in fact, politically active for a short time after his fall from the Party in early 1931. However, he was arrested in April 1933 by the Nationalists. After his release he taught at various schools and apparently retained some ties with the rather feeble Trotskyite group in China. An American Trotskyite journal claims that a "Liu Chia-lien" fled to Hong Kong in 1948, and from there to Macao and finally to North Vietnam where, in 1949, he died "in Ho Chi Minh's prison."[14] Given Lo's Trotskyist connections and the frequent mistransliterations of Chinese names in Western journals, this appears to be the same man.

Unlike his "co-conspirator" Ho Meng-hsiung, Lo has not been rehabilitated by the Maoist historians. In the well-known "Resolution on Questions in Party History," adopted in 1945, Lo was characterized as the head of a "handful of splitters" who "later became real Rightists, degenerated into counter-revolutionaries and were permanently expelled from the Party, and who, beyond any doubt, had to be resolutely combated."[15] The annotations to Mao's *Selected Works* carry the charges even further: Lo had "supported the counter-revolutionary stand of the Trotskyist Ch'en Tu-hsiu clique in opposition to the line of the Sixth National Congress . . . , vilified the Red Army and the Red base areas, and distributed leaflets in which he betrayed the names of Communist cadres to Chiang Kai-shek's gang."[16]

1. Edgar Snow, *Red Star over China* (New York, 1938), p. 130.

2. *Ibid.*, p. 141.

3. Teng Chung-hsia, *Chung-kuo chih-kung yun-tung chien-shih* (A short history of the Chinese labor movement; n.p., 1949), p. 16.

4. Maurice Meisner, *Li Ta-chao and the Origins of Chinese Marxism* (Cambridge, Mass., 1967), p. 219.

5. Harold R. Isaacs, *The Tragedy of the Chinese Revolution* (Stanford, Calif., 2nd rev. ed., 1961), p. 379.

6. Shinkichi Eto, "Hai-lu-feng—the first Chinese Soviet Government," *The China Quarterly*, no. 8:175 (October–December 1961).

7. Modern China Project, Columbia University, New York, Howard L. Boorman, director.

8. Tso-liang Hsiao, comp., *Power Relations within the Chinese Communist Movement, 1930–1934* (Seattle, Wash., 1967), II, 318.

9. Nym Wales, *The Chinese Labor Movement* (New York, 1945), pp. 72, 177–178.

10. Tso-liang Hsiao, *Power Relations within the Chinese Communist Movement, 1930–1934* (Seattle, Wash., 1961), pp. 114–119.

11. *Ibid.*, p. 135.

12. T. A. Hsia, *Enigma of the Five Martyrs* (Berkeley, Calif., 1962), p. 86.

13. *Revolutionary China Today* (New York, 1934), pp. 6, 29.

14. Ross Dawson, "Chinese Revolutionists in Exile," *International Socialist Review*, 3:80 (Summer 1963).

15. *Selected Works of Mao Tse-tung* (Peking, 1965), III, 188.

16. *Ibid.*, p. 221.

Lo Ch'iung

First secretary, Secretariat, National Women's Federation of China.

Although Lo Ch'iung is one of China's most important women leaders, little is known of her early career. By at least 1944 she was engaged in women's work in the Shansi-Kansu-Ninghsia (Shen-Kan-Ning) Border Region; in June of that year she apparently participated in a meeting of cooperative organizations in Yenan and, drawing from the reports and materials presented to the meeting, she published a small book in 1946 entitled *Shen-Kan-Ning pien-ch'ü min-chien fang-chih yeh* (The popular weaving industry in the Shensi-Kansu-Ninghsia Border Region). The book describes the measures taken by the Border Region to solve the clothing problem after the KMT blockade began in 1939.[1] Lo also edited a book entitled *Fu-nü yun-tung wen-hsien* (Documents on the women's movement), which was published about 1946 (the date of the preface). This work includes writings by a number of leading Communists, including Ts'ai Ch'ang (q.v.), China's top woman leader.[2]

Early in 1949, soon after the Communists had captured Peking, Lo was in a small group serving on the Standing Committee of the Preparatory Committee for the first nationwide women's congress, held in March–April 1949. At the close of the meetings she was elected to membership on the First Executive Committee and the Standing Committee of the All-China Federation of Democratic Women (ACFDW). As the various organs of the ACFDW were established in 1949–50, she concurrently served as a deputy director of the Propaganda Department (1949) and as a deputy secretary-general (by 1950 to 1953). In the fall of 1949, Lo represented the Women's Federation at the First Session of the CPPCC, the organization that brought the new central government into existence (October 1). In mid-1950 she took part in the establishment of one of the more important "mass" organizations, the All-China Federation of Cooperatives, an assignment presumably made on the basis of her wartime experience with cooperatives in the Shen-Kan-Ning area. She served on the Federation's provisional Board of Directors from July 1950 to July 1952, and thereafter to mid-1954 on the permanently established Board.

In December 1952 Lo made her first trip abroad when she was a member of the large delegation led by Mme. Sun Yat-sen (Sung Ch'ing-ling) to the World Peace Congress in Vienna. Her only other known trip outside China occurred in July 1955 when she accompanied Minister of Public Health Li Te-ch'üan as a deputy leader of the delegation to the Communist-backed World Mothers' Congress in Lausanne, Switzerland. In the interim, Lo was moving into higher positions in the Women's Federation. She served on the presidium (steering committee) for the National Women's Congress in April 1953 and was subsequently re-elected to both the Executive Committee and the Standing Committee. Exactly two years later (April 1955) the ACFDW established a Secretariat as the controlling organ of the Women's Federation between congresses, with Lo as one of the few members. Finally, two years later, at the Women's Congress in September 1957, Lo was again elected to the Executive Committee and the Presidium (the newly adopted name for the Standing Committee). Most important, however, was the fact that she was named to the newly created post of first secretary of the Secretariat. While it is evident that Lo is far outranked in political status by such Party stalwarts as Ts'ai Ch'ang (Mme. Li Fu-ch'un), Teng Ying-ch'ao (Mme. Chou En-lai), Ch'en Shao-min, Ch'ien Ying, and a few others of Party Central Committee rank, most of the women in the PRC who are technically high in Party rank are also elderly and, in some cases, in indifferent health. Thus it appears that by 1957 the effective reins of the day-to-day leadership of the women's movement in China had been handed over to Lo.

In 1954 Lo was elected as a Kiangsu deputy to the First NPC, which held its first session in September 1954. She was subsequently re-elected from Kiangsu to the Second and Third NPC's, which hold their initial meetings in April

1959 and December 1964–January 1965, respectively. At the last-mentioned session, Lo was elected as a member of the Standing Committee for the Third NPC. She spoke at a meeting of the NPC in April 1960 on the role of women in "socialist construction," but in general she does not seem to have been particularly active in the affairs of the Congress. However, her elevation in early 1965 to the Standing Committee suggests that she may play a more active role there in the future. Most of her time is devoted to the National Women's Federation (as it has been known since the name was changed from the ACFDW in 1957). On behalf of the Federation she has often attended meetings throughout China, entertained the many women who visit China from abroad, or served in organizations that draw from many walks of life (e.g., trade unionists, students, youths, women) in order to present a facade of broad representation. In the latter capacity she was named in November 1951 as a Women's Federation delegate to membership on a child-care organization known as the Chinese People's Committee in Defense of Children, and in February 1955 she was elected to serve on the *ad hoc* National Anti-atomic Weapons Signature Campaign Committee.

Aside from the books mentioned above, Lo's only other known writing appeared in the February 1953 issue of *China Reconstructs* under the title "Women Are Equals," an article that describes the advances made by women in "new China."

---

1. Chün-tu Hsüeh, *The Chinese Communist Movement, 1937–1949* (Stanford, Calif., 1962), p. 99.
2. *Ibid.*, p. 239.

Lo Fu, see **Chang Wen-t'ien**

Lo I-nung

(1901–1928; Hsiang-t'an, Hunan). Early CCP leader; member, CCP Politburo.

Lo I-nung, also known as Lo Chueh, was among the earliest leaders of the CCP. Trained in the Soviet Union, Lo later played a major role in the insurrectionary strikes in Shanghai which preceded the entry of Chiang Kai-shek's Northern Expeditionary Forces into that city in March 1927. After the break in the CCP–KMT alliance in mid-1927, he was among the Party's top leaders in Wuhan and then in Shanghai until his death in 1928.

Lo was the son of a rich peasant–small merchant family in Hsiang-t'an, the seat of the rural community in Hunan, which is also the home of Mao Tse-tung. In his 17th year, against his parents' wishes, he left home for Shanghai where he hoped to continue his education. He was there in 1919 when the May Fourth Movement erupted in Peking, and like many students of his generation, he was deeply affected by these events. In association with early Chinese Marxists Ch'en Tu-hsiu and Chang T'ai-lei (qq.v.), he helped found the Socialist Youth League in Shanghai in the late summer of 1920, and when the CCP was founded in mid-1921, he became one of its first members. In the early part of that year Lo attended Russian language classes at the Foreign Languages School, which had been set up in Shanghai under Yang Ming-chai (q.v.) to train Youth League members for further study in Moscow. Liu Shao-ch'i was one of Lo's classmates.[1] Immediately afterwards, Lo, Liu, and others went to the Soviet Union where Lo enrolled in the Communist University of the Toilers of the East, which had just opened under the jurisdiction of the People's Commissariat of Nationalities. The institution had a two-fold purpose: to train the eastern nationalities of the Soviet Union and to provide guidance in revolutionary activity to students from "colonial" countries. During his four years in Moscow Lo participated in the basic three-year program which the university initiated in the fall of 1922. Courses were offered in Leninism and the history of the Soviet Communist Party, history, historical materialism, mathematics, the natural sciences, and philology. Instruction for foreign students was initially in English, and it is uncertain how much the Chinese were able to understand. In addition to their language difficulties they apparently knew so little of Marxism that they regarded some of its most elementary principles as the "greatest discovery."[2] By 1923 the Chinese students had become so numerous that it was necessary to organize a special section for training them. Lo was the secretary of the new Chinese section, and because he had acquired a good knowledge of Russian, he also acted as an interpreter for some of his fellow students. In addition, he himself offered them a course in historical materialism. But hard work and the rigors of the Russian winters took their toll on Lo's health, and as a result he contracted tuberculosis.

Lo returned to China in early 1925 as a delegate from the Krestintern (the Peasant International, founded by the Comintern in October 1923). He went directly to Canton, then China's revolutionary center, where he participated in two important congresses in May. Lo attended and spoke at the Second All-China Labor Congress (May 1–7), and in his capacity as Krestintern delegate he opened the inaugural meeting of the Kwangtung Peasants' Association (May 3), proposing in his opening speech that the Association join the Krestintern.[3] Immediately afterwards, as an alternate member of the Kwangtung Regional Committee, he participated in the famous Canton–Hong Kong strike, which began in June 1925 (see under Su Chao-cheng).

Meanwhile, in KMT circles over the next few months a conflict arose between the right-wing group led by Tai Chi-t'ao, who was strongly opposed to the Communists, and the more extreme left-wing KMT elements. Recognizing the conflict, in October 1925 the CCP held an enlarged plenum in Peking to re-examine its relations with the KMT. The Kwangtung Committee, which Lo represented at the plenum, was harshly criticized on the grounds that it had not built up a sufficiently strong Party structure in Kwangtung. The plenum also took note of the weakness of the Party's development in north China, and resolved to open more Party schools at "various places" to train CCP cadres and overcome these weaknesses.[4] Lo, who had so recently received theoretical training in Moscow, was kept in Peking for a few weeks to direct a short, intensive program offered at one of the new Party training schools.

In January 1926 Lo was appointed secretary of the CCP Kiangsu-Chekiang Regional Committee, whose headquarters were in Shanghai. He spent most of that year organizing factory workers. In the meantime, in mid-1926, the Northern Expedition began from Canton with its various armies moving north into central and eastern China. As the campaign proceeded, it became apparent that there was a sharp cleavage between the right and left wings of the KMT. While the left-wing KMT forces advanced on Wuhan, Chiang Kai-shek's troops moved toward Shanghai. In this situation the role of the CCP was somewhat ambivalent, principally because it did not want to be entirely cut off from either side. Therefore, the Communists in Shanghai continued to cooperate with Chiang's plans, and thus in October 1926 Lo was involved in an abortive attempt to overthrow Sun Ch'uan-fang, the Shanghai militarist; this was the first of three "uprisings," as they are characterized in orthodox Communist accounts.

At this critical juncture the CCP was torn with dissension over the question of its relations with the KMT, especially Chiang Kai-shek's faction. Lo, with major assistance from Chao Shih-yen (q.v.) and others, organized a second and equally abortive insurrectionary strike in February 1927. Immediately afterward, the CCP Central Committee and the Kiangsu-Chekiang Committee held a joint meeting to reassess the situation. According to later testimony from Ch'en Tu-hsiu (q.v.), a group in Shanghai which included Ch'en himself (then head of the CCP), Lo, and P'eng Shu-chih, was dubious about further cooperation with the KMT and urged that the CCP "seize leadership of the Chinese Revolution."[5] They were overruled, however, by a Party faction led by Ch'ü Ch'iu-pai, which had the backing of Comintern representative Voitinsky, and thus the decision was taken to prolong the alliance. Ch'ü Ch'iu-pai's wife, in a description of these same events, mentions Ch'ü's op-

position to Ch'en Tu-hsiu and P'eng Shu-chih, both regarded in Maoist history as renegades, but Lo's part in the controversy is ignored.[6]

Working closely with Chou En-lai (q.v.) and Chao Shih-yen, Lo organized a third—and this time successful—insurrectionary strike on March 21, 1927. Chiang Kai-shek's troops, already in the outskirts of Shanghai, marched into the city immediately afterwards. Standard Communist histories normally give exclusive credit to Lo and his colleagues for "clearing the way" for the "ceremonial" entrance into the city by the Northern Expeditionary Forces. In fact, however, there was considerable non-Communist support within the city for a KMT takeover (for example, the Chamber of Commerce). Lo and his colleagues had been in contact with these groups, and the day before the March 21 strike Lo had been named to a provisional committee which transformed itself into the provisional city government immediately after the successful insurrection. Moreover, when the provisional government was established, Lo was one of 19 government members, the majority of whom came from the Shanghai bourgeoisie.[7] But Chiang Kai-shek, fearing the strength of the Communists (see also under Chao Shih-yen), engineered his famous coup of April 12, which virtually wiped out all opposition within the city. Lo and his colleague Chao Shih-yen went underground. But after a few days Lo left Chao in Shanghai and went to Wuhan to attend the Fifth CCP Congress, which opened on April 27 and lasted until early May.[8] Both men were elected to the Party Central Committee. Lo's work in Shanghai was taken over by Ch'en Yen-nien (q.v.) and Chao, and the congress further decided that Lo would become secretary of the CCP Kiangsi Committee.

Following the Fifth Congress Lo went to Nanchang, the capital of Kiangsi province. The city was held by the troops of General Chang Fa-k'uei, whose Second Army had been a proving ground for a number of young Communist officers (some of them recently trained at the Whampoa Military Academy). Although the atmosphere in Nanchang, then under the aegis of the left-KMT, was more favorable to the Communists than Shanghai under Chiang Kai-shek, here too the situation was growing difficult. Throughout China the uneasy alliance between the KMT and the CCP was fast coming to an end, and by mid-June 1927 the Left-KMT government at Wuhan decided to force all Communists to give up their government posts and to dismiss Borodin and other Soviet advisers. Communist Party members were formally expelled from the KMT in mid-July, and on August 1 the Communists' famous Nanchang Uprising took place (see under Yeh T'ing), and thus the CCP-KMT alliance was completely broken. Immediately before the Nanchang Uprising, Lo had been transferred to Hankow to become secretary of the important CCP Hupeh Provincial Committee.

The Communist insurrectionists in Nanchang were quickly routed from the city after their August 1 uprising, and their defeat caused serious disruptions within the Party. Therefore, on August 7, a new group of leaders headed by Ch'ü Ch'iu-pai held an "emergency conference" to repudiate the Ch'en Tu-hsiu leadership, which was held responsible for the Nanchang failure. Meeting secretly in Hankow, Ch'ü assembled a sufficient number of supporters to create an organization which could function as a "rump" Central Committee. The new organization then expelled its former chief, Ch'en Tu-hsiu. The "emergency conference" resolved to organize a series of peasant insurrections in central China—insurrections best known as the Autumn Harvest Uprisings. Lo was given primary responsibility for organizing and staging these uprisings in south Hupeh in an area strategically located within reach of Wuhan and Changsha.

Lo was on the scene in south Hupeh for the organizational phase of the planned uprisings, but just before they began in early September 1927 he returned to Wuhan, apparently turning over the actual leadership of the insurrections to his subordinates. The insurrectionists had a few initial successes and even managed to set up a short-lived revolutionary government in T'ung-shan hsien. However, faulty planning (in which Lo played a principal role) and the lack of effective Communist military and political strength doomed the uprisings, which, by the end of September, had failed ignominiously. While these abortive efforts were taking place in Hupeh, Mao Tse-tung and others were leading another part of the Autumn Harvest campaign in Hunan. Although these insurrections were somewhat more successful than the campaigns in Hupeh, they also soon failed. Therefore, in November 1927 the Ch'ü Ch'iu-pai leadership met to reassess the situation. Mao, who had directed some of the insurrections in Hunan, was held responsible for the failures, and it was at that time that he fell into disfavor with the CCP Central Committee. Lo, however, though his efforts in south Hupeh had been even less successful than Mao's, was not directly implicated in the failures. Indeed, he received important promotions, becoming a member of both the Politburo and the Central Committee's Standing Committee, as well as head of the Party's Organization Bureau.

These important new positions are cited in the "official" biography of Lo, but they tend to obscure the fact that in the latter half of 1927 and early 1928 Lo was involved in a series of intra-Party disputes as the Communists reeled from one disaster to another. Shortly before the November Party meeting Lo relinquished his post as secretary of the Hupeh Committee in favor of the more important assignment as secretary of the eight-province Yangtze Bureau. In this capacity he was a central figure in Wuhan as the Communists tried to work out new policies in the wake of their losses during the Autumn Harvest Uprisings. The situation grew more complex when in late October 1927 KMT General T'ang Sheng-chih rebelled against Chiang Kaishek's government in Nanking. Some of Lo's subordinates, especially the Youth League leaders, saw this as an opportunity to gain control of Wuhan. Lo, however, took a more cautious view, and this in turn led to a number of charges and countercharges against and by him. As the events turned out, T'ang was quickly crushed by Chiang's forces, and it seems unlikely that another Communist insurrection would have been successful. In any case, he was finally exonerated by early January 1928. By that time, apparently, Lo had been reassigned to the Party headquarters in Shanghai. In early April 1928 he was sent to Hunan and Hupeh to inspect conditions there. He then returned to Shanghai where on April 15, 1928, he was arrested in the International Settlement and immediately turned over to the Chinese authorities. His meteoric career came to an abrupt close six days later when he was executed, then only 27 years old.

The major source for Lo's career is a brief biographic sketch published in the Soviet Union (in Chinese) in 1936.[9] This account provides only a sketchy outline for the final year of Lo's life, but his major role in Party affairs during the last half of 1927 has been treated in great detail in articles by Roy Hofheinz and Hsiao Tso-liang.[10]

1. *Hsin kuan-ch'a* (New observer), no. 13:16 (July 1, 1957).

2. Xenia J. Eudin and Robert C. North, *Soviet Russia and the East, 1920–1927* (Stanford, Calif., 1957), pp. 85–86.

3. Roy Hofheinz, "The Peasant Movement and Rural Revolution: Chinese Communists in the Countryside (1923–1927)," Ph.D. diss. (Harvard University, 1966), pp. 66–67.

4. C. Martin Wilbur and Julie Lien-ying How, *Documents on Communism, Nationalism, and Soviet Advisers in China, 1918–1927* (New York, 1956), p. 124.

5. Wilbur and How, pp. 401–402.

6. *Hung-ch'i p'iao-p'iao* (Red flag fluttering; Peking, 1958), VIII, 39.

7. Harold R. Isaacs, *The Tragedy of the Chinese Revolution* (Stanford, Calif., 2nd rev. ed., 1961), p. 166; Jean Chesneaux, *Le Mouvement ouvrier chinois de 1919 à 1927* (Paris, 1962), pp. 497–499.

8. *Hung-ch'i p'iao-p'iao* (Peking, 1957), V, 9–11.

9. *Lieh-shih chuan* (Biographies of martyrs; USSR [Moscow?], 1936), pp. 80–88.

10. Roy Hofheinz, Jr., "The Autumn Harvest Insurrection," *The China Quarterly*, no. 32:37–87 (October–December 1967); Hsiao Tso-liang, "The Dispute over a Wuhan Insurrection in 1927," *ibid.*, no. 33:108–122 (January–March 1968).

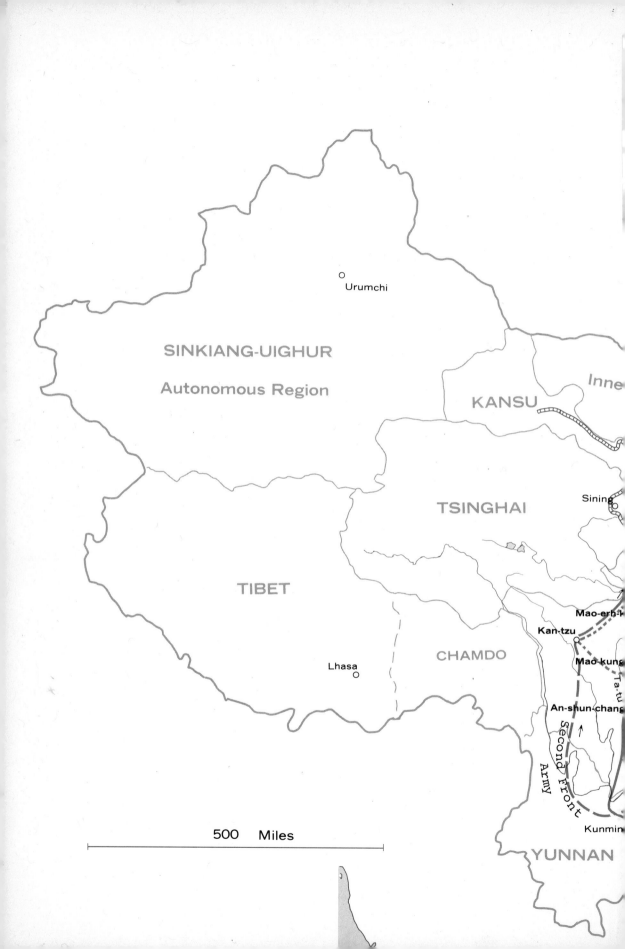